Dear West Customer:

West Academic Publishing has changed the look of its American Casebook Series®.

In keeping with our efforts to promote sustainability, we have replaced our former covers with book covers that are more environmentally friendly. Our casebooks will now be covered in a 100% renewable natural fiber. In addition, we have migrated to an ink supplier that favors vegetable-based materials, such as soy.

Using soy inks and natural fibers to print our textbooks reduces VOC emissions. Moreover, our primary paper supplier is certified by the Forest Stewardship Council, which is testament to our commitment to conservation and responsible business management.

The new cover design has migrated from the long-standing brown cover to a contemporary charcoal fabric cover with silver-stamped lettering and black accents. Please know that inside the cover, our books continue to provide the same trusted content that you've come to expect from West.

We've retained the ample margins that you have told us you appreciate in our texts while moving to a new, larger font, improving readability. We hope that you will find these books a pleasing addition to your bookshelf.

Another visible change is that you will no longer see the brand name Thomson West on our print products. With the recent merger of Thomson and Reuters, I am pleased to announce that books published under the West Academic Publishing imprint will once again display the West brand.

It will likely be several years before all of our casebooks are published with the new cover and interior design. We ask for your patience as the new covers are rolled out on new and revised books knowing that behind both the new and old covers, you will find the finest in legal education materials for teaching and learning.

Thank you for your continued patronage of the West brand, which is both rooted in history and forward looking towards future innovations in legal education. We invite you to be a part of our next evolution.

Best regards,

Heidi M. Hellekson
Publisher, West Academic Publishing

INTERNATIONAL HUMAN RIGHTS LAWYERING

CASES AND MATERIALS

■ ■ ■

By

Ralph G. Steinhardt
Arthur Selwyn Miller Research Professor of Law
The George Washington University Law School

Paul L. Hoffman
Schonbrun, De Simone, Seplow, Harris and Hoffman LLP

Christopher N. Camponovo
United States Department of State

AMERICAN CASEBOOK SERIES®

WEST®

Mat #18468255

American Casebook Series and West Group are trademarks registered in the U.S. Patent and Trademark Office.

© 2009 Thomson/Reuters
610 Opperman Drive
St. Paul, MN 55123
1–800–313–9378

Printed in the United States of America

ISBN: 978–0–314–26020–8

 TEXT IS PRINTED ON 10% POST CONSUMER RECYCLED PAPER

To Louis B. Sohn (1914-2006) and Thomas Buergenthal

"Let your life speak, let your light shine, that your works may be seen."

—Attributed to George Fox (1624-1691)

*

PREFACE

This casebook is motivated and structured by the principle that lawyering skills are critical in the articulation and enforcement of contemporary international human rights law. It is to our knowledge the first human rights casebook to reflect the differing perspectives of a government lawyer, a private practitioner, and an academic lawyer. In introducing students to the philosophy, doctrine, and history of human rights law, as well as the means of its enforcement, we have adopted an expansive conception of human rights law to include not only traditionally affiliated fields (like labor law, refugee law, and the law of war) but also traditionally unrelated fields (like corporate law, family law, criminal law, environmental law, international economic law). Pedagogically, the text enables students to develop their professional skills by reviewing and analyzing both the established and the emerging body of international human rights law from the perspective of a practicing lawyer—as a litigator or investigator or lobbyist, and as counsel to private clients, corporations, intergovernmental institutions, non-governmental organizations, and governments. Each module includes an optional practicum, consisting of exercises and simulations that require students to draft a variety of documents, strategize in small groups about the representation of a client's interest, investigate facts, negotiate a text (treaties, declarations of principles, domestic legislation), assess alternative means of redress, and argue in a moot court setting. The animating perspective throughout the text is that we can now speak meaningfully of human rights practitioners, just as previous generations have spoken meaningfully of tax lawyers or real estate lawyers.

The text also demonstrates that human rights law cannot stand in isolation from the structural changes in international law generally over the last twenty-five years, including the demise of orthodox distinctions that have given structure to that specialization for generations: *e.g.*, international law versus domestic law, public versus private international law, binding obligations versus aspiration, treaty versus custom, civil law versus common law systems, and the disciplinary separation between international law and comparative law. These distinctions are not entirely dysfunctional, but, especially for human rights lawyers, they have become simplistic and counterproductive.

This is also West Publishing's successor volume to the first casebook in the field of international human rights law—the path-breaking INTERNATIONAL PROTECTION OF HUMAN RIGHTS, written by Louis B. Sohn and Thomas Buergenthal and published in 1973. It is a mark of their vision and their inspiration that human rights law should have emerged as a discipline in the first place.

R.S.

P.H.

C.C.

November 2008

DOCUMENTS

The authors have compiled a collection of documents under the title "Human Rights Lawyering: Selected Documents," also published by West Publishing, for use in connection with this book. In most cases, when the casebook refers to an instrument, such as a treaty or a United Nations resolution, the text of the instrument may be found in "Selected Documents."

*

ACKNOWLEDGEMENTS

So many people—clients, colleagues, teachers, friends, associates, students, research assistants, partners, family members—have supported this project that it is impossible to pay each one of them a proper tribute. Sometimes they performed months of essential work, and sometimes they offered a single insight that altered the shape of the book. Sometimes they "consumed" these materials as students, and sometimes they were co-authors in all but name. Sometimes their encouragement and their patience were even more valuable than their substantive comments. To all of them, the three of us express our thanks and—in a few instances (and you know who you are!)—our apologies: William Aceves, Diane Amann, Michael Bazyler, Tom Buergenthal, Patty Blum, Joe Brand, Alex Canizares, Arturo Carillo, Heather Carney, Erwin Chemerinsky, Judith Chomsky, Sam Cleaver, Sarah Cleveland, Joseph Cohn, Sandra Coliver, Terry Collingsworth, Radhika Coomaraswamy, Rhonda Copelon, Nancy Craig, Cori Crider, Melissa Crow, Matt Eisenbrandt, Nate Ela, Noah Falk, Joan Fitzpartick, Felice Gaer, Julia German, Richard Goldstone, Jennifer Green, Liz Griffin, Elisabeth Hanratty, Christof Heyns, Bill Hoffman, Sinan Kalayoglu, Pegah Kamrava, Amanda Kaplan, Kunthea Ker, Harold Koh, Jen Kwon, Kathy Le, Suzy Lee, David Lin, Beth Lyon, Juan Mendez, Jonathan Miller, Bonnie Miluso, Sean Murphy, Joe Oloka-Onyango, Cindy Owens, Sri Panchalam, David Petrasek, Drue Preissman, Nicole Rentz, Abby Reyes, Naomi Roht-Ariaza, Robyn Rone, Colin Sampson, Beth Van Schaack, Patty Sellers, Andrew Shacknove, Lynn Sicade, Michael Soutar, Shana Stanton, Ruth Steinhardt, Beth Stephens, Steven Swerdlow, Alisa Valderrama, Connie de la Vega, Stephen Walls, David Weissbrodt, Rick Wilson, Daniel Zaheer. The fact that these people gave so generously of their time and their talents (thereby saving us from even more egregious errors) doesn't mean that no errors remain, and for those that do we are solely responsible.

The views expressed in this book are those of the authors and do not necessarily represent the views of the U.S. Department of State or the U.S. government.

Particular thanks to Helen Zeldes, Rachel Jensen, and Melanie Partrow for their assistance with the materials on international criminal justice. And to the "Mod Squad"—Christen Boeckner, Jessica Chen, Menaka Fernando, Carol Igoe, Ilene Leventhal, Nicole Murray Nicole Ochi, Ann Strimov, Cathy Sweetser—our continuing gratitude.

Professor Steinhardt wishes to thank Michael Young and Fred Lawrence, the former and the current dean of George Washington University Law School, for generously supporting this work and the GW-Oxford Programme in International Human Rights Law, where many parts of this book made their first classroom appearance.

Adrienne Quarry and Denise Williamson brought such good spirit and constant industry to this project that they deserve their own particular shout-out and in three-part harmony. Adrienne's contributions in particular can be found on every page.

Our wives—Donna Scarboro, Maggie Heim, and Maria Remedios Moya Gimenez—have lived with this project for years, and it would never have seen the light of day without them. For their support, and in ways only they can really understand, we are forever grateful.

Ralph Steinhardt
Paul Hoffman
Chris Camponovo

PERMISSIONS

The authors gratefully acknowledge the permission granted by the authors, publishers, and organizations to reprint portions of the following copyrighted materials.

Chapter 1

Louis B. Sohn, *The New International Law: Protection of the Rights of Individuals Rather Than States*, 32 AM. U. L. REV. 1 (1982). Reprinted by permission.

Ralph G. Steinhardt, INTERNATIONAL CIVIL LITIGATION: CASES AND MATERIALS ON THE RISE OF INTERMESTIC LAW 5-21 (2002).

Chapter 2

Princeton University Program in Law and Public Affairs, The Princeton Principles on Universal Jurisdiction, *available at* http://www1.umn.edu/humanrts/instree/princeton.html. The Princeton Principles in their entirety may be found in the Document Supplement.

Henry Kissinger, *The Pitfalls of Universal Jurisdiction: Risking Judicial Tyranny*, FOREIGN AFFAIRS (July/August 2001).

Kenneth Roth, *The Case for Universal Jurisdiction*, FOREIGN AFFAIRS (September 2001).

Chapter 3

Helfer and Slaughter, Reprinted by permission of The Yale Law Journal Company, Inc. and The William S. Hein Company, Volume 107, pages 273–391.

Initial Report of the United States to the Human Rights Committee, U.N. Doc. CCPR/C/81/Add.4 (Aug. 24, 1994).

Human Rights Watch, American Civil Liberties Union, *Human Rights Violations in the United States: A Report on U.S. Compliance with the International Covenant on Civil and Political Rights* (1993).

Concluding Observations of the Human Rights Committee: United States of America, U.N. Doc. CCPR/C/79/Add.50; A/50/40 (Oct. 3, 1995).

Third Periodic Report of the United States to the Human Rights Committee, U.N. Doc. CCPR/C/USA/3 (Nov. 28, 2005).

Human Rights Watch, Darfur in Flames: Atrocities in Western Sudan (Apr. 4, 2004), *available at* http://www.hrw.org/reports/2004/sudan 0404.

The United Nations Secretary-General's Address to the Commission on Human Rights (Apr. 7, 2004), *available at* http://www.un.org/apps/sg/printsgstats.asp?nid=862.

Situation of human rights in the Sudan, Commission on Human Rights, 2004/128, U.N. Doc. No. E/CN.4/2004/L.11/Add.8 (Apr. 23, 2004).

Accusation for Violation of Human Rights: A communication against the United States of America under ECOSOC Resolution 1503 (XLVI-II).

Response of the United States to Communications from Five Cuban Nationals under ECOSOC Resolution 1503 (May 1993).

Report of the Special Rapporteur on Violence against Women, Its Causes and Consequences, Ms. Radhika Coomaraswamy, *Integration of the Human Rights of Women and the Gender Perspective: Violence Against Women*, U.N. Doc. E/CN.4/1999/68/Add.1 (11 January 1999).

Report of the Special Rapporteur on Violence against Women, Its Causes and Consequences, Ms. Radhika Coomaraswamy, *Integration of the Human Rights of Women and the Gender Perspective: Violence Against Women*, U.N. Doc. No. E/CN.4/2000/68/Add.1 (27 January 2000).

Report of the Special Rapporteur on Violence against Women, Its Causes and Consequences, Ms. Radhika Coomaraswamy, *Integration of the Human Rights of Women and the Gender Perspective: Violence Against Women*, U.N. Doc. E/CN.4/2001/73/Add.1 (13 February 2001).

Report of the Special Rapporteur on Violence against Women, Its Causes and Consequences, Ms. Radhika Coomaraswamy, *Integration of the Human Rights of Women and the Gender Perspective: Violence Against Women—Report of the Mission to the United States of Violence Against Women in State and Federal Prisons*, U.N. Doc. E/CN.4/1999/68/Add.2 (4 January 1999).

Report of the Special Rapporteur on Violence Against Women, Its Causes and Consequences, Ms. Radhika Coomaraswamy, *Cultural Practices in the Family that are Violent Towards Women*, U.N. Doc. E/CN.4/2002/83 (31 January 2002).

Report of the Special Rapporteur on Violence Against Women, Its Causes and Consequences, Ms. Radhika Coomaraswamy, *Further Promotion and Encouragement of Human Rights and Fundamental Freedoms, Including the Question of the Programme and Methods of Work of the Commission Alternative Approaches and Ways & Means Within the United Nations System for Improving the Effective Enjoyment of Human*

Rights and Fundamental Freedoms, U.N. Doc. E/CN.4/1996/53 (6 February 1996).

Report of the Special Rapporteur on Violence Against Women, Its Causes and Consequences, Ms. Radhika Coomaraswamy, *Economic and Social Policy and Its Impact on Violence Against Women*, U.N. Doc. E/CN.4/2000/68/Add.5 (24 February 2000).

Report of the Secretary General Pursuant to Paragraph 5 of Security Council Resolution 955, U.N. Doc. S/1995/134 (1995).

Monroe Leigh, *The Yugoslav Tribunal: Use of Unnamed Witnesses Against Accused*, 90 Am. J. Int'l L. 235 (1996).

Christine M. Chinkin, *Due Process and Witness Anonymity*, 91 Am. J. Int'l L. 75 (1997).

Patricia Viseur Sellers, *Sexual Violence and Peremptory Norms: The Legal Value of Rape*, 34 Case W. Res. J. Int'l L. 287 (2002).

Kenneth Roth, *Yes A World Court*, WASHINGTON POST (June 26, 2000).

Dinah Shelton, *The Boundaries of Human Rights Jurisdiction in Europe*, 13 DUKE J. COMP. & INT'L L. 95 (2003).

Laurence R. Helfer & Anne-Marie Slaughter, *Toward a Theory of Effective Supranational Adjudication*, 107 YALE L.J. 273 (1997).

Report of the Secretary-General and the Chairperson of the African Union Commission on the Hybrid Operation in Darfur, S/2007/307/Rev.1 (5 June 2007).

Mary Kimani, *Community Frees Four Genocide Suspects During Pilot Gacaca Justice Process*, INTERNEWS NETWORK (May 30, 2001).

Penal Reform International, *Integrated Report on* Gacaca *Research and Monitoring (Pilot Phase) January 2002–December 2004*, (December 2005).

Amnesty International, *Rwanda: Gacaca: A Question of Justice* (2002).

Cairo Declaration on Human Rights in Islam, U.N. Doc. A/CONF.157/PC/62/Add.18 (1993).

Statement by the UN High Commissioner for Human Rights on the Entry into Force of the Arab Charter on Human Rights (30 January 2008).

Abdullahi A. An-Na'im, *Islam and Human Rights: Beyond the Universality Debate*, 94 AM. SOC'Y INT'L L. PROC. 95 (2000).

Chapter 4

Sarfaty, Reprinted by permission of the Yale Law Journal Company, Inc. and The William S. Hein Company, Volume 114, pages 1791–1818.

HESS CORPORATION, CORPORATE POLICIES, Hess Corporation, Corporate Policies, *available at* http://www.hess.com/ehs/policies.htm. © Hess Corporation 2008, reprinted with permission.

U.N. High Commissioner for Human Rights, Business and Human Rights: A Progress Report (2000), *available at* http://www.unhchr.ch/business.htm.

Fair Labor Association, Workplace Code of Conduct.

U.N. Sub-Commission on the Promotion and Protection of Human Rights: *Norms on the Responsibilities of Transnational Corporations and Other Business Enterprises with Regard to Human Rights*, U.N. Doc. E/CN.4/Sub.2/2003/12/Rev.2 (2003)

Organization for Economic Cooperation and Development, Declaration on International Investment and Multinational Enterprises (21 June 1976).

John Ruggie, Special Representative of the United Nations Secretary-General on the Issue of Human Rights and Transnational Corporations and Other Business Enterprises: *Protect, Respect and Remedy: a Framework for Business and Human Rights*, delivered to the Human Rights Council, U.N. Doc. A/HRC/8/5 (April 7, 2008).

World Bank Group, Articles of Agreement of the International Bank of Reconstruction and Development, December 27, 1945, 60 Stat. 1440, 2 U.N.T.S. 134.

Ibrahim Shihata, *Environment, Economic Development, and Human Rights: A Triangular Relationship?*, 82 AM. SOC'Y INT'L L. PROC. 40 (1988).

The World Bank Operation Manual: Operational Policies OP 4.12, Involuntary Resettlement (December 2001).

Galit A. Sarfaty, Note, *The World Bank and the Internalization of Indigenous Rights Norms*, 114 Yale L.J. 1791 (2005).

International Bank for Reconstruction and Development and the International Development Association, Resolution No. 93-10, Resolution No. IDA 93-6 (Sept. 22, 1993).

Daniel D. Bradlow, *Private Complainants and International Organizations: A Comparative Study of the Independent Inspection Mechanisms in International Financial Institutions*, 36 GEO. J. INT'L L. 403 (2005). Reprinted with permission of the publisher, Georgetown Journal of International Law © 2005.

World Bank Group, Investigation Panel Report, CAMEROON: Petroleum Development and Pipeline Project (2 May 2003).

Amnesty International, *Contracting Out of Human Rights: The Chad-Cameroon Pipeline Project*, September 2005.

Report of the U.N. High Commissioner for Human Rights, *Liberalization of Trade in Services and Human Rights*, U.N. Doc. E/CN.4/Sub.2/2002/9 (25 June 2002).

Andrew Guzman, *Global Governance and the WTO*, 45 HARV. INT'L L.J. 303 (2004).

Chapter 5

nized Human Rights and Fundamental Freedoms, G.A. Res. 53/144 (1998).

Human Rights First, *Protecting Human Rights Defenders: Analysis of the Newly Adopted Declaration on Human Rights Defenders*, available at http://www.humanrightsfirst.org/defenders/hrd_un_declarehrd_declare_1.htm.

Article 19, *Defining Defamation: Principles of Freedom of Expression and Protection of Reputation* (July 2000).

Kenneth Anderson, *The Limits of Pragmatism in American Foreign Policy: Unsolicited Advice to the Bush Administration on Relations With International Nongovernmental Organizations*, 2 CHI. J. INT'L L. 371 (2001).

Paul Wapner, *The Democratic Accountability of Non-Governmental Organizations: Defending Accountability in NGOs*, 3 CHI. J. INT'L L. 197 (2002).

Chapter 6

Dana Priest and Barton Gellman, *Stress and Duress' Tactics Used on Terrorism Suspects Held in Secret Overseas Facilities*, WASH. POST (Dec. 26, 2002).

Declaration on the Protection of All Persons From Enforced Disappearances, G.A. Res. 47/133, U.N. Doc. A/47678/Add.2 (Dec. 18, 1992).

1998 Draft Convention on the Protection of All Persons From Forced Disappearance, U.N. Doc. E/CN.4/Sub.2/1998/19, available at http://www.icrc.org/themissi.nsf/32db2800384e72adc12569dd00505ac6/68beca6e69f6546dc1256b0300290e38!OpenDocument.

International Convention for the Protection of All Persons from Enforced Disappearance, G.A. Res. A/RES/61/177, U.N. Doc. A/61/488, *adopted* Dec. 20, 2006.

Declaration on the Protection of All Persons From Enforced Disappearances, G.A. Res. 47/133, U.N. Doc. A/47678/Add.2 (Dec. 18, 1992).

1998 Draft Convention on the Protection of All Persons From Forced Disappearance, U.N. Doc. E/CN.4/Sub.2/1998/19 (1998).

Vienna Declaration and Programme of Action, U.N. Doc. A/CONF. 157/23 (12 July 1993).

Tom Lantos, *The Durban Debacle: An Insider's View of the UN World Conference Against Racism.* 26 Fletcher F. World Aff. 31 (2002).

Martha Minow, *The Hope for Healing: What Can Truth Commissions Do?*, *in* TRUTH V. JUSTICE (Robert I. Rotberg and Dennis Thompson eds.) (2000).

Thomas Burgenthal, *The United Nations Truth Commission for El Salvador*, 27 VAND. J. TRANSNAT'L L. 497 (1994).

Report of the Secretary General on the Rule of Law and Transitional Justice in Conflict and Post-Conflict Societies, U.N. Doc. S/2004/16 (August 23, 2004).

U.N. Security Council Resolution1272, U.N. Doc. S/RES/1272 (25 October 1999).

Regulation No. 1999/1 on the Authority of the Transitional Administration in East Timor, UNTAET/REG/1991/127 (27 November 1999).

Regulation No. 2000/11 on the Organization of Courts in East Timor, UNTAET/REG/2000/11 (6 March 2000).

Regulation No. 2000/14 Amending Regulation No. 2000/14, UNTAET/REG/2000/14 (10 May 2000).

Suzannah Linton, 'Rising from the Ashes: The Creation of a Viable Justice System in East Timor' (2001) 25 *Melbourne University Law Review* 122.

Office of the United Nations High Commissioner for Human Rights, *Rule-of-Law Tools for Post-Conflict States Vetting: an operational framework* (2006).

International Center for Transitional Justice, *Transitional Justice in Iraq: An ICTJ Policy Paper* (May 2003).

International Center for Transitional Justice, *Briefing Paper: Iraq's New "Accountability and Justice" Law* (January 22, 2008).

Chapter 7

Oscar Schachter, INTERNATIONAL LAW IN THEORY AND PRACTICE 126 (Martinus Nijhoff Publishers 1991).

Fernando R. Teson, *Collective Humanitarian Intervention*, 17 MICH. J. INT'L L. 323 (1996).

Bruno Simma, *NATO, the UN and the Use of Force: Legal Aspects*, 10 EUR. J. INT'L L. 1 (1999).

Christine M. Chinkin, *Editorial Comment: NATO's Kosovo Intervention: Kosovo: A "Good" or "Bad" War?*, 93 AM. J. INT'L L. 841 (1999).

Security Council Resolution, U.N. Doc. S/RES/1244 (10 June 1999).

INDEPENDENT INTERNATIONAL COMMISSION ON KOSOVO, THE KOSOVO REPORT (Oct. 23, 2000). By permission of Oxford University Press, Inc.

Gareth Evans and Mohamed Sahnoun, *The Responsibility to Protect*, FOREIGN AFFAIRS (2002).

Security Council Resolution 660, U.N. Doc. S/RES/660 (2 August 1990).

Security Council Resolution 678, U.N. Doc. S/RES/678 (29 November 1990).

Security Council Resolution 687, U.N. Doc. S/RES/687 (3 April 1991).

Security Council Resolution 1441, U.N. Doc. S/RES/687 (8 November 2002).

Human Rights First, *Statement of Avidan Cover* (August 2004).

Chapter 8

Michael J. Bazyler, *The Gray Zones of Holocaust Restitution: American Justice and Holocaust Morality*, in GRAY ZONES: AMBIGUITY AND COMPROMISE IN THE HOLOCAUST AND ITS AFTERMATH (Jonathan Petropoulos & John K. Roth, eds., 2005).

Beth Van Schaack, *Unfulfilled Promise: The Human Rights Class Action*, 2003 U. CHI. LEGAL F. 279 (2003).

Mary C. Daly, *The Dichotomy Between Standards and Rules: A New Way of Understanding the Differences in Perceptions of Lawyer Codes of Conduct by U.S. and Foreign Lawyers*, 32 VAND. J. TRANSNAT'L L. 1117 (1999).

David Weissbrodt, *Ethical Problems of an International Human Rights Law Practice*, 7 MICH. Y.B. LEGAL STUD. 219 (1985).

Melissa E. Crow, *From Dyad to Triad: Reconceptualizing the Lawyer-Client Relationship for Litigation in Regional Human Rights Commissions*, 26 MICH. J. INT'L. L. 1097 (2005).

ABA *Model Rules of Professional Conduct*, 2008 Edition. Copyright © 2008 by the American Bar Association. Reprinted with permission. Copies of ABA *Model Rules of Professional Conduct*, 2008 Edition are available from Service Center, American Bar Association, 321 North Clark Street, Chicago, IL 60654, 1-800-285-2221.

Jeffrey K. Shapiro, *Legal Ethics and Other Perspectives, in* THE TORTURE DEBATE IN AMERICA (Karen J. Greenberg ed. 2006). Reprinted with the permission of Cambridge University Press.

Stephen Gillers, *Legal Ethics: A Debate in The Torture Debate in America*, 238 (Karen J. Greenberg ed. 2006). Reprinted with the permission of Cambridge University Press.

Jane Mayer, *The Memo: How an Internal Effort to Ban the Abuse and Torture of Detainees was Thwarted*, THE NEW YORKER (Feb. 27, 2006).

Chapter 9

Philip Alston, *Conjuring Up New Human Rights: A Proposal for Quality Control*, 78 AM. J. INT'L L. 607 (1984).

Rio Declaration on Environment and Development, U.N. Doc. A/CONF. 151/5/Rev.1 (1992).

Declaration on the Right to Development, G.A. Res. 41/128 (4 December 1986).

United Nations Millennium Declaration, G.A. Res. 55/2 (8 September 2000).

*

Summary of Contents

TABLE OF CONTENTS

―――――――

TABLE OF CASES

The principal cases are in bold type. Cases cited or discussed in the text
are roman type. References are to pages. Cases cited in principal
cases and within other quoted materials are not included.

―――――――

*

INTERNATIONAL HUMAN RIGHTS LAWYERING

CASES AND MATERIALS

*

CHAPTER 1

THE IDEA OF INTERNATIONAL HUMAN RIGHTS LAW

■ ■ ■

"ALL HUMAN BEINGS ARE BORN FREE AND EQUAL
IN DIGNITY AND RIGHTS."
THE UNIVERSAL DECLARATION OF HUMAN RIGHTS,
ARTICLE 1
(1948)

"Where, after all, do universal human rights begin? In small places, close to home—so close and so small that they cannot be seen on any maps of the world. Yet they are the world of the individual person; the neighborhood he lives in; the school or college he attends; the factory, farm, or office where he works. Such are the places where every man, woman, and child seeks equal justice, equal opportunity, equal dignity without discrimation. Unless these rights have meaning there, they have little meaning anywhere. Without concerted citizen action to uphold them close to home, we shall look in vain for progress in the larger world."

Eleanor Roosevelt

A. ORIENTATION

The focus and the inspiration of this course is a single, radical, and complicated idea: human beings have rights simply by virtue of being human. They have these rights not as a matter of grace from governments or generosity or public relations or luck. To be human is to be assured a certain minimum level of respect and dignity that limits what governments can do, or allow others to do, to people. The trick for lawyers—and the purpose of this casebook—is finding effective techniques for enforcing what law exists, developing law when it is needed, and maintaining a sense of engagement and hope in the face of human rights violations around the world.

The idea that human beings have rights simply by virtue of being human is an idea with considerable power, although high-profile ac-

1

counts of continuing human rights abuses give it a utopian reputation. Certainly profound issues of compliance and enforcement remain on every continent, but the human rights idea has proven over the decades to be capable of overcoming the strongest bases for discrimination, like race, gender, and class. It is an idea that has proven on occasion to be stronger than tyrants, sometimes even fatal to tyrants. The nascent corporate responsibility movement suggests that the human rights idea can be stronger than the *laissez faire* marketplace and offers companies a new way to compete with one another. The human rights idea has sometimes proven to be stronger than some of the strongest armies on the planet and the empires they serve: whatever else contributed to the demise of the Soviet Union, for example, the Helsinki Accords of 1976 planted certain human rights ideals that gave rise to the Solidarity Movement in Poland, Vaclav Havel in Czechoslovakia, and Mikhail Gorbachev's restructuring ideals of *glasnost* and *perestroika*.

The idea that human beings have rights simply by virtue of being human is in some ways an ancient idea, although the notion that it has a *legal* dimension—and especially an *international legal* dimension—is of considerably more recent vintage. For most of human history, one state's treatment of its own citizens was its own business, a matter of legitimate political diversity and beyond the scrutiny of other nations. Human rights issues were said to lie within each state's exclusive domestic jurisdiction, and considerations of sovereignty would have prevented the government of France for example from complaining about the treatment of Japanese citizens by the Japanese government and *vice versa*. With very limited exceptions, human rights issues were matters of domestic affairs, in which no other state had the right to interfere. International law protected those domestic prerogatives, and thereby preserved more state power than it constrained.

But something fundamental changed at the end of World War II—a "constitutional moment"—when the preservation of international peace and security became intrinsically and pragmatically linked to the protection of human rights. The generation that survived World War II understood in the most immediate way that international peace and security are linked to the protection of human rights. They had seen that genocide could be both the cause and the consequence of war. They realized that civil and revolutionary wars are common symptoms of a human rights crisis in its late stages. They had seen that human rights abuses tend to escalate if they are tolerated by the world community. In our own time, we can think of Rwanda and Iraq as examples of human rights crises at an early stage that later devolved into international military and political crises. Similarly, the failure of the United States to assure that detainees at Abu Ghraib and Guantanamo Bay were well-treated has provided al Qaeda a wealth of recruitment material. In short, we should avoid thinking of human rights protection as only some soft-headed, more or less altruistic utopianism, but also see it as a kind of long-term pragmatic self-interest.

The Role of the United Nations and the International Bill of Rights

The framers of the United Nations Charter explicitly linked respect for and observance of human rights with the "stability and well-being which are necessary for peaceful and friendly relations among nations." U.N. Charter, art. 55. Article 1(3) of the Charter proclaims that one of the organization's central purposes is "to the achieve international co-operation* * * in promoting and encouraging respect for human rights and for fundamental freedoms for all without distinction as to race, sex, language, or religion." A lawyer might consider that language—"promote and encourage respect"—and conclude that it is remarkably soft and unambitious, especially when the framers of the United Nations might have used language like "enforce human rights" or "compel compliance with human rights norms." The human rights language of the Charter fell far short of the Allies' rhetoric during the war, and the "promote and encourage respect" phrasing lacked the crystalline clarity of Franklin Roosevelt's Four Freedoms speech of 1941, in which he envisioned a world founded upon four essential human freedoms: freedom of speech and expression, freedom of every person to worship God in his own way, freedom from want, and freedom from fear.

Of course, a fully-formed and autonomous system for the compulsory protection of these human rights was not a realistic possibility in 1945, because—among other things—each of the dominant victorious powers had profound human rights problems of its own. The Soviet Union had its gulag, the United States its *de jure* and *de facto* racial discrimination, France and Great Britain had colonial empires. But the framers of the Charter were first and foremost master politicians, acutely conscious of what was possible and how to achieve it, and they knew on the basis of their experience with the League of Nations that aggressive assertions of international power—without some sensitivity to political realities and the continuing power of sovereignty—were doomed to failure. They understood that a power grab by the United Nations was neither realistic nor in the end necessary: empowering the United Nations to take cognizance of human rights issues, even if only "to promote and encourage respect" for human rights, would make those issues a proper matter of international concern. It would be a chink in the armor of state sovereignty and potentially lead to the emergence of an entire body of articulated human rights standards with various means of enforcement.

Whether intended or not, that is what happened. The United Nations offered an institutional framework and a conceptual foundation for a variety of subsequent instruments that defined human rights and offered a partial system of enforcement. In fact, the 1948 Universal Declaration of Human Rights ("UDHR" or "Universal Declaration") in the Documents Supplement, was the first comprehensive catalogue of human rights by a global international organization. Human rights and fundamental freedoms had never before been articulated in such detail, and there was broad-based international support for the Universal

Declaration when it was adopted. Of course, at the time, the UN had only 58 members, compared to nearly 200 today, and many countries now recognized as independent sovereigns in Africa, the Middle East, and Asia were then territories within colonial empires. As a consequence, some governments have asserted that the Universal Declaration adopted a western version of rights and have called for its renegotiation.

But to dismiss the Universal Declaration as a western construct requires a certain revisionism: the declaration was supported by Asian and south Asian states like Pakistan, India, China, Japan, Thailand, and the Philippines; Middle Eastern states like Egypt, Syria, Morocco, Turkey, Iran, Iraq, Lebanon, and Afghanistan; African states like Ethiopia and Liberia. As Michael Ignatieff has observed,

> Many traditions, not just Western ones, were represented at the drafting of the Universal Declaration of Human Rights—for example, the Chinese, Middle Eastern, Christian, Marxist, Hindu, Latin American, and Islamic. The members of the drafting committee saw their task not as a simple ratification of Western convictions but as an attempt to delimit a range of moral universals from within their very different religious, political, ethnic, and philosophical backgrounds. This fact helps to explain why the document makes no reference to God in its preamble. The communist delegations would have vetoed any such reference, and the competing religious traditions could not have agreed on words that would make human rights derive from human beings' common existence as God's creatures. Hence the secular ground of the document is not a sign of European cultural domination so much as a pragmatic common denominator designed to make agreement possible across the range of divergent cultural and political viewpoints.

Michael Ignatieff, *The Attack on Human Rights*, 80 FOREIGN AFFAIRS (Nov.-Dec. 2001) at 102. The states that abstained but did not vote against the declaration were the Soviet Union and its client states, Poland and Czechoslovakia, as well as South Africa and Saudi Arabia. This is not a particularly monolithic group in ideology, or political system, or religious and cultural composition, or socio-economic development, or geographic location. And after 1948, the Universal Declaration was generally considered a common statement of goals and aspirations—a vision of the world as the international community would want it to become. In fact, at the World Conference on Human Rights held in Vienna in 1993, 171 countries reiterated the universality, indivisibility, and interdependence of human rights, and reaffirmed their commitment to the UDHR.

The principles in the Universal Declaration have also been incorporated into national legislation and the constitutions of many newly independent states. References to the UDHR have been made in charters and resolutions of regional intergovernmental organizations, as well as in treaties and resolutions adopted by the United Nations system. To some extent, the Universal Declaration echoes the U.S. Declaration of Independence and the French Declaration of the Rights of Man and of the Citizen, and consists of thirty articles grounded in the bedrock provision of Article 1 that "all human beings are born free and equal in dignity and rights." There follow provisions on the right to life, liberty and security of person; the right to an adequate standard of living; the right to seek and to enjoy asylum from persecution; the right to own property; the right to freedom of opinion and expression; the right to education, freedom of thought, conscience and religion; and the right to freedom from torture and degrading treatment, among many others. Many of these provisions became the basis of the two international covenants on human rights, *infra*, as well as the more specialized treaties like a refugee convention in 1951, a convention on the elimination of all forms of racial discrimination in 1969, a convention on the elimination of all forms of discrimination against women in 1981, and a convention prohibiting torture in 1984.

The Universal Declaration was understood to be non-binding at the time of its adoption, which may account for why no state voted against it. In a sense, the stakes couldn't have been lower, because voting "yes" cost the states nothing as a matter of law, and voting "yes" looked good in the hometown newspapers. But the Universal Declaration has had a remarkable trajectory towards normativity: it may have begun life as a purely aspirational or voluntary document, but it has gradually ratcheted towards something considerably more law-like, to the point now that governments, courts, advocates, and international bodies routinely consider the Universal Declaration an authoritative articulation of the human rights provisions of the UN Charter. In the words of Professor Sohn,

> The Declaration * * * is now considered to be an authoritative interpretation of the U.N. Charter, spelling out in considerable detail the meaning of the phrase "human rights and fundamental freedoms," which Member States agreed in the Charter to promote and observe. The Universal Declaration has joined the Charter of the United Nations as part of the constitutional structure of the world community. The Declaration, as an authoritative listing of human rights, has become a basic component of international customary law, binding on all states, not only on members of the United Nations.

Louis B. Sohn, *The New International Law: Protection of the Rights of Individuals Rather than States*, 32 Am. U. L. Rev. 16–17 (1982).

What this means for human rights lawyers is that they must break out of the traditional distinction between binding law and irrelevant aspiration. They need some third category between the obligatory and the aspirational. Even before some provisions of the Universal Declaration were incorporated into treaties or domestic law or UN resolutions, those provisions laid out non-binding norms that were nonetheless authoritative. International lawyers refer to this as "soft law." It isn't binding but it isn't irrelevant either, especially to the extent that it defines an issue of international importance and exerts a gravitational force on the evolution of law.

Linked to the Universal Declaration are the two international human rights covenants of 1966, namely the International Covenant on Economic, Social, and Cultural Rights ("ICESCR") and the International Covenant on Civil and Political Rights ("ICCPR"). Together, the Universal Declaration and these two covenants make up what is generally called the *International Bill of Rights*. The ideological and political conflict of the Cold War caused the treaties to be split between civil and political rights, on the one hand, and economic, social and cultural rights, on the other, when the UDHR itself made no such distinction. There is however one important textual difference between these two covenants, going to the immediacy with which these rights must be respected or implemented. Consider article 2(1) of the ICCPR:

> Each State Party to the present Covenant undertakes to respect and to ensure to all individuals within its territory and subject to its jurisdiction the rights recognized in the present Covenant, without distinction of any kind, such as race, colour, sex, language, religion, political or other opinion, national or social origin, property, birth, or other status.

Compare that with article 2(1) of the ICESCR:

> Each state party to the present Covenant undertakes to take steps, individually and through international assistance and co-operation, especially economic and technical, to the maximum of its available resources, with a view to achieving progressively the full realisation of the rights recognized in the present Covenant by all appropriate means, including particularly the adoption of legislative measures.

Whatever other substantive differences there may be between these two covenants, at a minimum one seems to require immediate implementation and the other refers to taking steps to the maximum of a state's available resources, with an eye towards progressive realization using all appropriate means. Many observers have suggested that this textual difference has undermined the effort to enforce economic, social and cultural rights and required the international community to develop a jurisprudence for considering all rights interdependent.

LOUIS B. SOHN, THE NEW INTERNATIONAL LAW: PROTECTION OF THE RIGHTS OF INDIVIDUALS RATHER THAN STATES
32 AM. U. L. REV. 1–62 (1982)

The modern rules of international law concerning human rights are the result of a silent revolution of the 1940's, a revolution that was almost unnoticed at the time. Its effects have now spread around the world, destroying idols to which humanity paid obeisance for centuries. Just as the French Revolution ended the divine rights of kings, the human rights revolution that began at the 1945 San Francisco Conference of the United Nations has deprived the sovereign states of the lordly privilege of being the sole possessors of rights under international law. States have had to concede to ordinary human beings the status of subjects of international law, to concede that individuals are no longer mere objects, mere pawns in the hands of states. * * *

[In the aftermath of World War II,] individuals gained rights under international law and, to some extent, means for vindication of those rights on the international plane. This development entailed four different law-building stages: assertion of international concern about human rights in the U.N. Charter;[1] listing of those rights in the Universal Declaration of Human Rights;[2] elaboration of the rights in the International Covenant on Civil and Political Rights[3] and in the International Covenant on Economic, Social and Cultural Rights;[4] and the adoption of some fifty additional declarations and conventions concerning issues of special importance, such as discrimination against women, racial discrimination and religious intolerance. The pyramid of documents, with the Charter at its apex, has become a veritable internationalization and codification of human rights law, an international bill of human rights much more detailed than its French and American counterparts. * * *

Even if governments and scholars were originally in disagreement regarding the importance, status, and effect of the Universal Declaration, practice in the United Nations soon confounded the doubters. Several of the governments that originally were skeptical about the value of the Declaration did not hesitate to invoke it against other countries. Thus, the United States invoked it in the so-called *Russian Wives Case*, and the General Assembly declared that Soviet measures preventing Russian wives from leaving the Soviet Union in order to join their foreign husbands were "not in conformity with the Charter," citing articles 13 and 16 of the Declaration in support of its conclusion.[5] The Soviet Union, which originally claimed that the Declaration violated the

---

1. *See, e.g.,* U.N. CHARTER art. 1, para. 3; *id.* art. 55. The U.N. Charter gives to the Economic and Social Council the responsibility for making "recommendations for the purpose of promoting respect for, and observance of, human rights and fundamental freedoms for all." *Id.* art. 62, para. 2. *See also id.* art. 13, para. 1(b).

2. *Approved* Dec. 10, 1948, G.A. Res. 217A, U.N. Doc. A/810 at 56 (1948) [hereinafter cited as Universal Declaration]. Among the rights included in the Universal Declaration are the following: the right to life, liberty, and security of person (art. 3); the right to be free from arbitrary arrest, detention, or exile (art. 9); the right to marry and found a family (art. 16); the right to freedom of thought, conscience, and religion (art. 18); and the right to education (art. 26).

3. *Entered into force* Mar. 23, 1976, G.A. Res. 2200A, 21, U.N. GAOR Supp. (No. 16) at 52, U.N. Doc. A/6316 (1966) [hereinafter cited as Covenant on Civil and Political Rights].

4. *Entered into force* Jan. 3, 1976, G.A. Res. 2200A, 21 U.N. GAOR Supp. (No. 16) at 49, U.N. Doc.A/6316 (1966) [hereinafter cited as Covenant on Economic, Social and Cultural Rights].

5. G.A. Res. 285(III), U.N. Doc. A/900 (1949).

Charter's prohibition against interference in a state's internal affairs, later voted for many resolutions charging South Africa with violations of the Universal Declaration.[6] * * *

When the Commission on Human Rights finished the Universal Declaration, it began preparing the other part of the International Bill of Rights, a convention containing precise obligations that would be binding on the States Parties. There were initial fears that the various rights would drown in a sea of limitations and exceptions, but this danger was avoided by careful delineation of the conditions under which rights could be limited, and identification of those rights that could not be limited under any circumstances. Another difficulty did, however, arise. It proved impossible to formulate in a parallel manner all the rights listed in the Universal Declaration; it became necessary to divide the materials into two categories: civil and political rights; and economic, social, and cultural rights. These two categories were embodied in two separate Covenants—a name that was preferred to the less solemn "convention"—each differing from the other in several respects. The main difference was in their treatment after coming into force. States Parties were to give the Covenant on Civil and Political Rights immediate effect through appropriate legislative or other measures and by making available an effective remedy to any person whose rights have been violated. In contrast, each State Party to the Covenant on Economic, Social and Cultural Rights agreed only to take steps, to the maximum of its available resources, toward a progressive realization of the rights recognized in that Covenant. The Covenant thus contained a loophole: because a state's obligation was limited to the resources available to it, a poor state could proceed slowly, progressing only as fast as its resources permitted. If its resources should diminish, for example, during an economic crisis, its progress could wane. In contrast, the Covenant on Civil and Political Rights permits no such excuses; a state must guarantee civil and political rights fully on ratification, subject only to [certain] limitations* * *[7]

---

6. *See, e.g.,* S.C. Res. 182, 18 U.N. SCOR Supp. (Oct.-Dec. 1963) at 103, U.N. Doc. S/5471 (1963).

7. [Editors' Note: Professor Sohn here references his prior discussion of limitations on rights, which includes this analysis: * * * There are two other categories of rights: first, those which a state can limit in times of emergency, such as freedom from compulsory labor, right to liberty and security of person, right to humane treatment in prison, right to certain minimum guarantees in criminal proceedings, and freedom from interference with privacy, family, home, or correspondence, and, second, those which the state can limit in order to protect national security, public order (*ordre public*), and public health or morals. The second category includes the following rights listed in the Covenant on Civil and Political Rights: the right to liberty of movement; the freedom to choose one's residence; the right to a public hearing; freedom to manifest one's religion or beliefs in public; freedom of expression and to seek, receive, and impart information and ideas, orally or in print; right of peaceful assembly; and freedom of association. *Id.*, at arts. 12, 14, 17, 18(33), 19, 21, 22. Of the rights listed in the International Covenant on Economic, Social and Cultural Rights, only the rights relating to trade unions are subject to similar restrictions. [*Id.*, at art. 8(1).] Other rights arising under that Covenant can be limited solely "for the purpose of promoting the general welfare in a democratic society." [*Id.*, art. 4.]]

[II. THE FIRST GENERATION OF RIGHTS: CIVIL AND POLITICAL RIGHTS]

C.   The International Covenant on Civil and Political Rights

1.   Implementation of the Covenant on Civil and Political Rights

The Covenant on Civil and Political Rights is to be implemented through a combination of international and domestic law. Its enforcement relies in the first place on national institutions, as each State Party has the duty to ensure that any person whose rights under the Covenant have been violated has an effective remedy against the violator and the access for that purpose to appropriate judicial, administrative, or legislative authorities.[8]

The Covenant on Civil and Political Rights also provides for international implementation measures. The Covenant not only requires States Parties to present periodic reports on the progress made in enjoyment of the rights recognized in the Covenant,[9] but also provides for a Human Rights Committee with jurisdiction over complaints by one state that another state has not fulfilled its obligations under the Covenant.[10] This jurisdiction can, however, be exercised only if both states previously have accepted the competence of the Committee to receive such complaints.[11] [As of 2008, 48] countries have accepted this jurisdiction * * * [As of 2008, over 120] states * * * have accepted another implementation measure, an optional protocol allowing individuals claiming to be victims of a violation of the Covenant to present to the Human Rights Committee communications against the state responsible.[12] Both of these new international remedies are subject to one of the oldest rules in the area of state responsibility: a complaint or communication can be presented only when all available domestic remedies have been exhausted and redress has not been obtained.

The guarantees in the Covenant on Civil and Political Rights are designed primarily to protect individuals against arbitrary government action and to ensure individuals the opportunity to participate in government and other common activities. Promotion and protection of human rights not only leads to good government, but is "the foundation of freedom, justice and peace in the world."[13] To ensure these common ideals, the Covenant was designed to help states improve their domestic laws and institutions so that human rights would be protected throughout the world. Although the Covenant relies primarily on domestic remedies, it also recognizes the new international status of individuals and gives them access to an international committee, at least against those states that have accepted the optional protocol. As noted earlier,

---

8. Covenant on Civil and Political Rights, *supra*, art. 2(3).

9. Covenant on Civil and Political Rights, *supra*, art. 40.

10. *Id.* art. 41(1).

11. *Id.*

12. Optional Protocol to the International Covenant on Civil and Political Rights, entered into force Mar. 23, 1976, G.A. Res. 2200A, 21 U.N. GAOR Supp. (No. 16) at 59, U.N. Doc. A/6316 (1966) [hereinafter cited as Optional Protocol].

13. Covenant on Civil and Political Rights, *supra*, preamble.

[over half] of all the states in the world have accepted this direct method of international vindication of individual rights. In addition, almost half of the members of the world community have, by becoming parties to the Covenant, accepted the new international rule that individuals are not mere objects of the provisions of the Covenant but have direct rights under that instrument and ultimately may be able to enforce these rights.* * *

3.   The first generation of human rights: conclusions.

The Covenant on Civil and Political Rights is the least novel of human rights instruments. It reflects human rights values that have been developing in many countries of the world since the signing of the Magna Carta. Both old and new national constitutions contain similar principles. * * * The law of human rights as embodied in the international instruments is not merely treaty law, but rather has become a part of international customary law of general application, except in areas in which important reservations have been made. These documents do not create new rights; they recognize them. Although the line between codification and development of international law is a thin one, the consensus on virtually all provisions of the Covenant on Civil and Political Rights is so widespread that they can be considered part of the law of mankind, a *jus cogens*[14] for all. Thus, an important step has been taken in enlarging the scope of international law and in providing international protection to many important individual rights. * * *

III.   THE SECOND GENERATION OF RIGHTS: ECONOMIC, SOCIAL, AND CULTURAL RIGHTS

A.   Development of the Concept of Economic, Social, and Cultural Rights

Civil and political rights are usually traced to the pronouncements of the American and French Revolutions; the concept of economic and social rights, in comparison, is generally assumed to have originated in the Russian Revolution of 1917. * * *[I]t was in response to the Nazi tyranny * * * that President Roosevelt conceived the idea of an instrument dealing with economic and social rights. In his "Four Freedoms" message to the U.S. Congress in 1941,[15] President Roosevelt mentioned not only freedom of speech and expression, freedom of religion, and freedom from fear (including freedom from wars of aggression), but also "freedom from want." The latter requires "economic understandings which will secure to every nation a healthy peacetime life for its inhabitants-everywhere in the world."[16] In his 1944 Message to Congress,[17] President Roosevelt spelled out in more detail the rights that were embraced in his concept of "freedom from want." He pointed out

---

14. [Editors' note: The concept of *jus cogens* is described and analyzed at p. 22, *infra*.]

15. Eighth Annual Message to Congress, Jan. 6, 1941 reprinted in 3 THE STATE OF THE UNION MESSAGES OF THE PRESIDENTS, 1790–1966, at 2855 (1966).

16. *Id*. at 2860.

17. Eleventh Annual Message to Congress, Jan. 11, 1944, reprinted in 3 THE STATE OF THE UNION MESSAGES OF THE PRESIDENTS 1790–1966, at 2875 (1966).

that "true individual freedom cannot exist without economic security and independence"; that "[p]eople who are hungry and out of a job are the stuff of which dictatorships are made"; and that "[i]n our day these economic truths have become accepted as self-evident."[18] He knew well that in the United States in the 1930's it was the New Deal, with its economic, social, and labor reforms, that prevented economic and social chaos. He felt that, similarly, global chaos and totalitarianism could be stopped only by drastic economic and social reforms throughout the world. Although his two messages were directed primarily to a domestic audience, his words had a worldwide impact, and were not forgotten when the United Nations began to address human rights issues.

In the Four Freedoms speech, President Roosevelt had emphasized "the social and economic problems which are the root cause of the social revolution which is today a supreme factor in the world."[19] He noted that there is nothing mysterious about the foundations of a healthy and strong democracy, and listed expressly "the simple and basic things that must never be lost sight of in the turmoil and unbelievable complexity of our modern world." They were:

> Equality of opportunity for youth and for others.
> Jobs for those who can work.
> Security for those who need it.
> The ending of special privilege for the few.
> The preservation of civil liberties for all.
> The enjoyment of the fruits of scientific progress in a wider and constantly rising standard of living.

* * * President Roosevelt's idea of freedom from want, announced to the world in 1941, was reflected in an international bill of rights drafted by the United States in 1942.* * *

B. The International Covenant on Economic, Social, and Cultural Rights

* * * Some states announced that they were unwilling to become parties to a binding instrument such as the Covenant if they would thereby have to commit themselves to clauses concerning economic, social, and cultural rights. * * * The basic civil and political rights were described by some as traditional, subjective, and negative; the economic, social, and cultural rights were characterized as new, objective, and positive. Others considered these latter rights to be indefinite, pro-motional, and programmatic. * * *

1. Implementation of the Covenant on Economic, Social and Cultural Rights

i. The progressive nature of the Covenant's implementation

The drafters had to solve several other general problems in connec-tion with the introductory clauses to the Covenant on Economic, Social

---

18. *Id.* at 2881.

19. Eighth Annual Message to Congress, *supra*, at 2859.

and Cultural Rights. It was agreed first that each State Party should undertake "to take steps, individually and through international assistance and co-operation, especially economic and technical, to the maximum of its available resources, with a view to achieving progressively the full realization of the rights recognized in the present Covenant by all appropriate means, including particularly the adoption of legislative measures."[20] This was an "umbrella" provision covering all the rights in the Covenant, replacing an unsuccessful attempt to incorporate detailed restrictions and exceptions into each article. Traces of the abandoned approach to exceptions still may be found in some articles of the Covenant, especially in the fine print of articles 13 and 14, which deal with the right to education.[21]

The main emphasis in the text of article 2 is on the "progressive" nature of the obligation to achieve economic, social, and cultural rights.[22] The drafters recognized in particular that many countries do not yet have the necessary resources, and that time would be needed to develop them. To speed up this development, the text included a gentle hint that states endowed with better resources and technological knowhow should help their less fortunate brethren. This should be accomplished "through international assistance and co-operation, especially economic and technical."[23] Although the Covenant allows states some latitude regarding the "appropriate means" required for the full realization of economic, social, and cultural rights, the drafters felt that "legislative measures" should not be neglected, because such measures could help establish the policies to be pursued and could provide the necessary legal and administrative framework for the implementation of these policies. * * *

ii.   *Guarantees against discriminatory implementation*

A general provision imposes on States Parties the obligation "to guarantee that the rights enunciated in the ... Covenant will be exercised without discrimination of any kind as to race, colour, sex, language, religion, political or other opinion, national or social origin, property, birth or other status."[24] Thus, whatever level a country reaches in the realization of economic, social, and cultural rights at any given time, the benefits thereof would have to be accorded equally to all persons. This anti-discrimination provision was adopted despite some opposition, which was based to a certain extent on the ground that some countries might be unable to provide immediately for equality of pay

---

20.   Covenant on Economic, Social and Cultural Rights, *supra*, art. 2, para. 1.

21.   *See id*. arts. 13, 14. Article 14, for example, provides that each State Party, which was not able to provide free, compulsory education when it became a Party, "undertakes, within two years, to work out and adopt a detailed plan of action for the progressive implementation, within a reasonable number of years, to be fixed in the plan, of the principle of [free] compulsory education." *See also id*. arts. 6(2), 12(2), 15(2).

22.   "Each State Party ... undertakes to take steps ... with a view to achieving progressively the full realization of the rights recognized in the present Covenant...." *Id*. art. 2(1).

23.   *Id*.

24.   [Covenant on Economic, Social and Cultural Rights, *supra*,] art. 2(2).

between the sexes. Unlike most of the other provisions of the Covenant, the anti-discrimination provision is not "progressive"; it applies as soon as a state ratifies the Covenant.[25] * * *

2. Substantive provisions of the Covenant on Economic, Social and Cultural Rights

Among the rights listed in the Covenant on Economic, Social and Cultural Rights, the right to work has been considered basic. Effective implementation of this right would presumably eliminate unemployment, thereby banishing poverty and its attendant evils. This in turn would create an atmosphere in which other rights, particularly civil and political rights, could be enjoyed by all. In addition, useful work would benefit both society, through the production of needed goods and services, and the individual, through the feeling of satisfaction that accompanies the use of one's talents and the opportunity to contribute both to individual well-being and the common good.

The Covenant specifies that the right to work means primarily that everyone should have an "opportunity to gain his living by work."[26] The idea that a person has an obligation to work was clearly rejected; such a duty might have led to forced labor, reminiscent of the Nazis' and certain countries' abuse of such labor. The right to work includes the concept of free choice of an occupation; the work must be one that a person "freely chooses or accepts."[27] The scope of this choice is not clear; no determination has been made about how long an individual can refuse offers of employment and still claim the opportunity to work. * * *

The Covenant's provision on social security[28] is the most succinct of all the provisions. * * * It speaks of social security in the broadest terms, to embrace not only social insurance but also other methods of social and economic assistance for the benefit of insecure members of the community. It provides social security to "everyone," not just workers. Attempts to narrow the application of the principle to workers only were unsuccessful. Similarly rejected were special financing schemes restricted to contributions by workers, or by workers and employers. Instead, each state was allowed to select any financing method it deemed appropriate.

To offer another example of the Covenant's breadth and flexibility, the Covenant recognizes the right to education and carefully sets out obligations relating to different stages of education: primary, secondary,

---

25. *Compare* Covenant on Economic, Social and Cultural Rights, *supra*, art. 2(1) (states may achieve progressively the rights recognized in the Covenant) with *id.* art. 2(2) (states undertake to guarantee that the rights recognized in the Covenant will be exercised without discrimination).

26. *Id.* [art. 6(1)].

27. *Id.*

28. Article 9 of the Covenant of Economic, Social and Cultural Rights, *supra*, provides in full: "The States Parties to the present Covenant recognize the right of everyone to social security including social insurance."

higher, and fundamental.[29] To avoid rigidity, the Covenant does not define these categories of education, thus allowing States Parties flexibility in implementing the provisions. It provides expressly for prompt implementation of "the principle of compulsory primary education free of charge for all," and for progressive achievement of free education at higher levels.[30] * * *

IV.   THE THIRD GENERATION OF RIGHTS: COLLECTIVE RIGHTS

* * *[I]nternational law not only recognizes inalienable rights of individuals, but also recognizes certain collective rights that are exercised jointly by individuals grouped into larger communities, including peoples and nations. These rights are still human rights; the effective exercise of collective rights is a precondition to the exercise of other rights, political or economic or both. If a community is not free, most of its members are also deprived of many important rights.

A.   Recognized Third–Generation Rights

1.   The right of self-determination.

International law has long been concerned with one of the most basic of collective rights: the right of self-determination.* * *

The Covenants clearly endorse not only the right of external self-determination [decolonization/independence], but also the right of internal self-determination: the right of a people to establish its own political institutions, to develop its own economic resources, and to direct its own social and cultural evolution. A people that cannot freely determine its political status can hardly determine its economic, social, and cultural status. A people should be free both from interference by other peoples or states and from deprivation of its right to self-determination by a tyrant or dictator. The right of self-determination could be construed to assure the right to exercise freely all other rights, particularly the Covenants' political and economic rights. * * *

This special problem aside, the principle or right of self-determination clearly has been one of the most influential legal and political doctrines of this century and had led to a revolutionary transformation of political relationships throughout the world, including the emergence of more than a hundred new states.

* * *

4.   Other third-generation rights.

* * *

One may also note that the Universal Declaration of Human Rights, in a similar spirit, but without express mention of the environment, proclaimed that everyone "has the right to a standard of living adequate for the health and well-being of himself and of his family, including

---

29. International Covenant on Economic, Social and Cultural Rights, *supra*, arts. 13, 14.

30. *Id.*

food, clothing [and] housing." There is a similar provision in the Covenant on Economic, Social and Cultural Rights* * *

B. Issues Raised by the Recognition of Collective Rights

Taken together, the third generation of human rights raises difficult issues. In the 1950's, the concept of and need for economic, social, and cultural rights were heatedly debated; today, the opponents of the new rights contend in a similar manner that the third-generation rights are not really legal rights but are either political or social principles, or, at best, "moral" rights, without any legal force. * * *

[T]he author of the phrase "third generation of human rights," Karel Vasak of UNESCO, views these rights as "infusing the human dimension into areas where it has all too often been missing having been left to the State or States." Such rights can be realized only "through the concerted efforts of all the actors on the social scene: the individual, the State, public and private bodies, and the international community." Vasak also has pointed out that the first two generations of human rights were designed to achieve the first two of the three guiding principles of the French Revolution—*liberté* and *égalité*—while the third generation is predicated on brotherhood—*fraternité*. According to Vasak, the new rights, even more than the rights belonging to the first two categories, are based on the sense of solidarity, without which the chief concerns of the world community, such as peace, development and environment, cannot be realized* * *.

Precursors to Contemporary Human Rights Law

As Professor Sohn suggests, international human rights law had its critical "constitutional moment" in the aftermath of World War II, but it requires a revisionist (and somewhat narcissistic) view of the world to suggest that human rights law is a product of the late 20th century, only now moving out of its infancy. To the contrary: contemporary human rights doctrine has evolved from historical "pockets" of discrete concerns that we can in retrospect classify as early human rights law:

The law of war/international humanitarian law. The proposition that some conduct even in wartime is unacceptable goes back to the ancients, notably Lao Tzu and Thucydides. Medieval notions of chivalry suggested that certain conduct in war, certain targets, certain weaponry, were unacceptable, at least in principle. In the middle of the 19th century, these standards began to be codified, which culminated in major treaties governing the conduct of hostilities in 1899, 1907, and 1929, and ultimately in the Geneva Conventions of 1949 and their subsequent Protocols. Today, literally scores of treaties and military codes of conduct have been adopted protecting certain non-combatant populations at risk in armed conflict, like the sick and wounded in the battlefield, or medical personnel, or civilians caught in the cross-fire, or prisoners of war who are no longer capable of fighting. It is no accident that the modern law of war emerged as the international community became conscious of the enormous destructive potential of modern warfare: the people who survived thought it morally imperative and deeply pragmatic to articulate standards which might protect innocents even if those standards were obviously imperfect in conception and enforcement. But it is not just people on the periphery of the conflict who have been protected. A number of treaties concluded before World War II prohibited certain weapons altogether, banning poison gas or other biological and chemical agents and most recently cluster bombs, which protect combatants and non-combatants alike.

Nuremberg and the emergence of international criminal responsibility. In the aftermath of World War II, the disconnect between the humanitarian goals of the law of war and the reality on the ground led to the development of a new conception of international humanitarian law, grounded in individual rights and responsibilities, and enforced through the instrument of international criminal law. The Nuremberg Tribunal, and its counterpart in Tokyo, refined and applied the laws of war, but new crimes were also recognized, specifically crimes against the peace and crimes against humanity. The innovative leap, with consequences to this day in the Rome Statute that established the International Criminal Court, was the notion of individual criminal responsibility under international law. The war crimes tribunals reasoned that violations are committed by people, not by abstractions like the state, and it is therefore proper to impose individualized punishment on people for violations of international standards. That approach was not only morally better, because criminals could not then hide behind abstractions, but it was also politically better for the process of reconciliation. Why? Because individualizing criminal responsibility can reduce (without eliminating) the kind of revenge group-think that can sustain cycles of ethnic or sectarian violence for generations.

There is the well-worn charge that Nuremberg was "victor's justice," that it was law in the service of vengeance, that it imposed *ex post facto* laws. The genetic marker of its inadequacy is the post-war conduct of the Allies themselves: Great Britain in Northern Ireland, the Soviet Union in Afghanistan, France in Algeria, the United States in Vietnam. Critics argue that the Allies were not willing to bind themselves to the Nuremberg principles in their own post-Nuremberg conflicts. There is also the irony of August 8, 1945, which arises out of the fact that on that date, the Allies were proclaiming the London Charter establishing the Nuremberg Tribunal, with its commitment to humanitarian law. At virtually the same hour, the United States was preparing to drop the atomic bomb on Nagasaki. And that raises this question: if the Axis powers had developed the atomic bomb and used it on New York but had still gone on to lose the war, is there any doubt that the indiscriminate destruction of New York would have been included as a war crime or worse? The concern is that because nuclear weapons were used by the winners, they have been exempt from serious legal scrutiny for decades, at least until the ICJ's advisory opinion on the use of nuclear weapons, *infra*.

Ritualized as the critique of Nuremberg has become, the reality is that the *ad hoc* tribunals for Yugoslavia and Rwanda and similar courts have built on the Nuremberg principle and avoided the victor's justice taint. If anything, the *ad hoc* tribunals have also enhanced their own credibility and the legitimacy of the enterprise by protecting the rights of defendants, even as they vindicate the rights of victims by prosecuting the guilty.

State responsibility to aliens. Traditionally, a state is answerable in international law for the treatment of aliens and their investments within that state's territory. For example, if the Guatemalan government abused a visiting Mexican citizen, Mexico would have the right to call the Guatemalan government to account, to exercise the right of *diplomatic protection*, and to seek remedies for the injury to its citizen. Typically, the state responsibility doctrine was enforced through bilateral diplomatic relations or arbitrations between the states; indeed, although the individual was the actual victim, the law effectively made him or her the representative of the home state, as though his or her government were the rights-bearer and had the presumptive right to compensation. Individuals had no standing in the traditional conception of international law, and the obligations collected under the rubric of state responsibility to aliens ran state-to-state. It was only the victim's nationality and alienage that triggered international standards. One success of the contemporary human rights movement over the last fifty years is the steady erosion of that nationality fixation and an understanding that people have rights by virtue of being human, not by virtue of their alienage. A government that tortures its own citizens is as much in breach of international law as a government that tortures an alien, and the individual survivor is the rights-bearer, not his or her state of nationality.

Labor rights and the development of the International Labour Organisation ("ILO"). The ILO was founded in 1919 and became the first specialized agency of the UN in 1946. The ILO formulates international labor standards in the form of Conventions and Recommendations setting minimum standards of basic workers' rights, like freedom of association, the right to organize, collective bargaining, abolition of forced labor, equality of opportunity and treatment, and other standards regulating conditions across the spectrum of work-related issues. The organization was created in a moment of reciprocal self-interest when governments and labor unions and employers realized that a completely unregulated international labor market would give every state an economic incentive to impoverish its own workers. As the power of international capital took hold, the economic incentives seemed irresistible to suppress wage rates, spend nothing on occupational health and safety standards, and do nothing in short that might cost employers money and therefore scare investment away. So, fearful of the race to the bottom but thinking themselves unable to act unilaterally, states along with employers and labor unions, created the ILO, with a unique tripartite governing structure that empowered each of these three stake-holders. The relative success of that structure, combined with the fact that labor law often overlaps other major human rights concerns—like employment discrimination or the exploitation of women or indigenous peoples—has meant that the ILO has been able to expand its agenda steadily, to the point that it is now one of the leading sources of standards for defining and protecting indigenous peoples or defining slavery and slave-like practices, including forced labor.

The minority rights treaty regime under the League of Nations. "Minority treaties" were drawn up primarily in Europe after World War I, when national borders were redrawn, inevitably breaking up national and ethnic groups and subjecting discrete minorities to repression. These minorities were not necessarily aliens, so the traditional doctrine of state responsibility could not apply, but, because of their minority status and their history of isolation or abuse, they were the object of concern by other states and to some extent by the international community at large. Essentially, the minority treaties allowed certain named states to invoke the jurisdiction of the Permanent Court of International Justice, the precursor of the International Court of Justice, in the interest of these special groups, even if there were no direct or tangible damage to that state and even if the victims were not nationals of that state. The practical and analytical significance of that move is not to be minimized. It marked the beginning of the end of a legal system tied to nationality and alienage and began the move toward a contemporary system of human rights protections, which has largely dispensed with such notions, recognizing rights simply by virtue of being human and not by virtue of being an alien, or a citizen, or a prisoner of war or even an "unlawful combatant." These 20th–century provisions had their own precursors, notably the protection of religious minorities in the Treaty of Westphalia (1648).

The anti-slavery campaigns. In the 19th century, in a demonstration of bottom-up, values-driven reform, a critical shift occurred in which governments and corporations not only gave up a lucrative economic practice, but even began to view the practice as criminal. Eventually, just as the pirate had been considered the enemy of all mankind in the 18th century, subject to prosecution wherever he or she could be found, the slave trader eventually came to be viewed in the same light, and today slavery and its correlatives are considered universally criminal.

The protection of refugees. The 1951 Convention relating to the Status of Refugees and the creation of the UN High Commissioner for Refugees reflected an awareness of the radical vulnerability of people displaced from their homelands by a well-founded fear of persecution. Although there were important limits on the scope of the Convention, at a minimum, it clearly protected certain free speech values and non-discrimination norms by assuring that those who fled persecution on those grounds would not be returned forcibly to any place where the persecution might occur. There had been earlier treaties that recognized the plight of refugees—also based on bitter experience—and they began the creation of an international regime to solve an international political problem, as well as a profound human problem.

Regional integration. Contemporary human rights law builds on a number of regional platforms created many decades ago. In the middle of the 20th century, countries in the Americas and in Europe became aware of the practical advantages of integration, and so emerged the Organization of American States, or in Europe the Council of Europe and the European Union, or ultimately in Africa, the African Union. With the exception of the Council of Europe, none of these organizations started out concerned primarily with human rights. Typically they came into being as economic or security or political institutions, but at some point they morphed into vehicles for the promotion of human rights institutions. The European Union is a decent example. As noted in Module 7A, *infra*, the EU began as the European Coal and Steel Community, which then began to find continent-wide common ground on a range of economic issues, to the point now that the EU's Court of Justice routinely turns to the human rights conventions to inform the interpretation of European administrative law. And admission to the EU is conditioned on a state's accession to—and compliance with—human rights treaties. Ultimately, human rights law offered the only ideology of continental unification to survive the violence and hostility of the 20th century.

The Problem of Enforcement

If international human rights law has a utopian reputation, it is presumably because the norms apparently exist on paper but are routinely violated. Cases of impunity—violations without accountability—seem notorious and routine. Lawyers and law students tend to suffer from "Langdell's Disease," which suggests that something is not really law unless some court says it is or someone goes to jail or pays damages. This course requires an expanded notion of enforcement—one that includes the payment of damages, as in *Filartiga, infra,* and incarceration, but which also includes "softer" forms of compelling compliance.

It is certainly true that violations of international human rights law are an everyday occurrence. Of course, murder, domestic violence, and antitrust violations occur daily as well, but we do not assume that these violations prove that criminal law or antitrust law are not really law after all. No law can prevent its own violation. We assume that this conduct is wrongful and that in principle whoever commits these wrongs will be liable for damages or will face some legitimate sanction. And if the murderer were caught, he wouldn't be released on the ground that other murderers remained at large. The law may be lumpy in the way it gets enforced, but we don't generally treat the underlying body of law as not really law.

In many respects, the most important way that international human rights law gets enforced is the least understood and appreciated: *internalization*. It is possible to identify a *culture of compliance* in which public and private actors routinely conform their behavior to international standards, as for example when human rights norms are incorporated into the training and disciplinary regimes of government officers, agents, the military, police officers, and the like. In Chapter 6, *infra*, you will encounter several examples of enforcement through internalization by governments themselves, completely outside of the Langdellian courtroom. In recent years, the role of *national human rights institutions* ("NHRI")—like human rights ombudsmen—has been especially prominent.

At the other end of the enforcement spectrum lies *internationalization*. As Professor Sohn suggested in his analysis of the two human rights Covenants, *supra*, there are many international institutions with various human rights mandates and powers. The two Covenants establish separate Committees, which review the periodic reports of governments and which can on occasion receive state-to-state or individual complaints. These institutions offer advocates clear pressure points in the enforcement of human rights standards, sometimes for the advancement of an individual case and sometimes for the mobilization of political will to address and resolve a global human rights issue. But the Covenants' Committees are just the tip of the iceberg: as shown in Chapter 3, *infra*, the international mechanisms for enforcing human rights standards against governments and individuals have proliferated over the last two decades, both inside and outside the United Nations and now include a range of international tribunals, human rights commissions, treaty-specific committees, and special offices and mechanisms.

Lying intermediate between internalization and internationalization is *judicial domestication*, *i.e.*, the use of domestic courts to enforce international human rights law locally when the culture of compliance fails. As shown in Chapter 2, *infra*, the domestic courts—civil and criminal, military and civilian, in common law and civil law jurisdictions—can be the workhorses of this particular legal order, even if the doctrinal and logistical obstacles to litigation can be daunting. The human rights project depends on continuing judicial oversight at the domestic level: no international institution has the resources (or the authority) to identify and redress human rights violations around the world.

At each of these levels will be found human rights *non-governmental organizations* (NGO's), whose legal work has had a demonstrable effect on the development and enforcement of human rights norms. As shown in Chapter 5, *infra*, human rights lawyers within these organizations can play multiple enforcement roles, from *mobilizing shame* about particular cases to commenting on the periodic reports of governments under the human rights treaties, to advocating legislative and cultural strategies for bringing international standards home. They demonstrate that these three levels of enforcement are not hermetically separate from one another and that developments in one setting tend to affect developments in another.

Finally on the issue of enforcement, it is important to avoid pathological thinking, to conclude on the basis of high-profile violations that there is something congenitally anti-law about international human rights norms or international law generally. Virtually every international border remained stable last night, and yet there are no headlines about it. Somehow, for yet another day, international organizations did their work within a framework of law for the protection of the people's health or the delivery of international mail or economic development. By historical standards, human rights received unprecedented protection yesterday, but the headlines focus on what violations there were, suggesting just how much we have come to expect in our dealings with governments. In short, you might look at the inkblot of state practices with respect to human rights and say with the skeptic that it only confirms your worst suspicions. Or you might consider the dog that didn't bark, and find it remarkable that human rights law received as much respect as it did yesterday. As Professor Louis Henkin famously observed, most states obey most international law most of the time,[1] suggesting that there is something naïve and somewhat distracting about our skeptic's hip dismissal of international law.

The Layered Critique of the Human Rights Project

We close this initial orientation recognizing the contemporary critique of the human rights project, because every advocate has to contend with certain recurrent forms of resistance to the argument that human rights law provides the rule of decision in a case or justifies activism in some other forum. These are arguments you will encounter many times and in many versions in this course, and it is important to acknowledge them early, even if only in outline form.

There is the argument for example that the strongest states ignore human rights routinely. Whether it's labeled *American exceptionalism or unilateralism*, the fact is that there are persistent human rights problems in the United States (the death penalty, police brutality, gender and race discrimination, violations of the laws of war and human rights in Afghanistan, Iraq, and Guantanamo Bay). From this perspective, enforcement is either too random or too hypocritical to qualify as law. At a minimum, runs this critique, the human rights movement has been better at articulating standards than it has been at enforcing them.

Second, there is the critique of *cultural relativism*. In this view, the human rights project rests on intrinsically western values and therefore reflects a kind of cultural imperialism. The relativist challenge also rests

---

1. LOUIS HENKIN, HOW NATIONS BEHAVE 320–21 (2d ed. 1979).

on the perceived tensions or contradictions within human rights law itself, like the rights of women versus the rights of religious practice.

There is also the argument that the rhetoric of law and rights is simply too blunt an instrument to handle the delicacy of most serious political conflict. From that perspective, rights talk impoverishes political talk. To frame something as a right is generally to try to remove an entire class of questions from the ordeal of politics. Rights talk is first and foremost about the community's most serious commitments, and it trumps the normal range of choices available to the government and to the people. To use the language of rights is to acknowledge that it won't really matter if the costs of compliance exceed the economic benefits. Rights-talk inevitably leads to adversarial rather than negotiated solutions to daily problems, and that effects a massive transfer of power to the courts. Rights by their very nature are typically enforced by the judiciary. According to this line of argument, that leads inexorably to government by injunction of the sort that has torn at the social fabric of the United States and threatens the credibility and legitimacy of the courts.

Or consider this objection: the expression of some rights may be perceived as the exclusion of others. The most trenchant objection to the American Bill of Rights came not from the Tories (or their post-revolutionary equivalent), but from the democrats and libertarians, who were concerned about being limited to the ten rights in the Bill of Rights.

None of these objections is trivial, but none of them necessarily derails the human rights project either, and the trick is understanding what that project needs now: it might be new or improved enforcement techniques (including using market forces or the internet to improve human rights protections or opening more of the enforcement institutions to individual petitions); it might mean raising new issues or generating new attention to old issues through a human rights lens (e.g. corruption, environmental protection, terrorism, AIDS); or it might mean bringing new actors into the human rights project (*e.g.* multinational corporations, public-private partnerships).

B. A SURVIVAL GUIDE TO INTERNATIONAL LAW

Contemporary human rights law blurs the received distinction between domestic and international law, but in order to understand the source, the content, and the status of human rights law—as well as the means of its enforcement—we must begin with the recognition that it is a species of international law. We cannot assess the legal consequences of a human rights treaty without a more general understanding of the international law governing treaties and their interpretation. To the extent that there is an unwritten or customary component to international human rights law, we must understand how custom emerges, how it is proven, and how it is enforced. What follows in this subsection is no substitute for a basic course in international law, but it may orient those who have never completed such a course, or who did but long ago.

RALPH G. STEINHARDT, INTERNATIONAL CIVIL LITIGATION: CASES AND MATERIALS ON THE RISE OF INTERMESTIC LAW 5–21

(2002)

The basic premise and its consequences

The basic premise of traditional international law is that the international community consists of numerous, independent, and co-equal states as actors. There is no supranational legislature or police force or court with universal and compulsory powers, and international law consists in the rules governing the legal relationships among states. It is commonly called a "horizontal legal order" because, in contrast to domestic law, there is no authoritative or coercive institution to hand down the law to anyone and enforce it by imprisoning or fining those who violate it. Traditionally, this has meant that a state could not be bound to any international norm to which it had not given its consent, though "consent" could take a variety of forms. It has also meant that the international legal system has been more successful at articulating expectations and incentives than it has been in administering punishments or awarding compensation.

The sources of international law

One particularly important consequence of the "horizontality" of international law is the multiplicity of sources that define a state's legal obligations. Article 38(1) of the Statute of the International Court of Justice articulates the traditional categories of authority in these terms:

> The Court, whose function is to decide in accordance with international law such disputes as are submitted to it, shall apply:
>
> a.   international conventions, whether general or particular, establishing rules expressly recognized by the contesting states;
>
> b.   international custom, as evidence of a general practice accepted as law;
>
> c.   the general principles of law recognized by civilized nations;
>
> d.   * * * judicial decisions and the teachings of the most highly qualified publicists of the various nations, as subsidiary means for the determination of rules of law.

These categories are not hermetically separate from one another, and there is some question whether the list accurately captures the range of relevant authorities in the contemporary world, but the general outlines of these four traditional sources are clear.

In its orthodox conception, international law comprises both contractual and behavioral forms of obligation, corresponding to treaties and customary international law. At first blush, these traditional forms of law seem to derive from two quite separate processes: a dynamic of *ad hoc* consent leading to obligations binding upon the parties to the agreement *versus* a dynamic of habitual usage observed by nations as law and binding upon each of them. As suggested below however, contemporary international law has witnessed—and survived—the proliferation of normative types that do not fit into the either/or world of treaties and custom and which blur any simple-minded distinction between them.

Treaties. Treaties are international agreements that create reciprocal legal obligations among or between the parties, "with corresponding duties of compliance and remedies, including rights of retaliation, in the event of a breach."[2] States have found common ground in an almost bewildering range of areas and declared their mutual self-interest through treaties covering for example: private investment abroad; intellectual and cultural property; the rights of workers and prisoners; international crimes; the environment; arms control and the use of force; borders; gender and race discrimination. Treaties set the conditions for international trade and telecommunications, establish uniform rules for wills and trusts and bankruptcy proceedings, limit the testing of nuclear weapons, and even provide for the delivery of mail or the service of process. There is virtually no area of law that remains untouched by treaties.

It is well-established that the word "treaty" need not be used to convey the existence of a binding international agreement. "The terminology used for international agreements is varied. Among the terms used are: treaty, convention, agreement, protocol, covenant, charter, statute, act, declaration, *concordat*, exchange of notes, agreed minute, memorandum of agreement, memorandum of understanding, and *modus vivendi*. Whatever their designation, all agreements have the same legal status, except as their provisions or the circumstances of their conclusion indicate otherwise."[3]

The international law governing treaties is largely contained in the *Vienna Convention on the Law of Treaties* (1969) ("VCLT"),[4] which articulates the fundamental norm that promises must be honored in good faith: "Every treaty in force is binding upon the parties to it and must be performed by them in good faith." This basic idea, *pacta sunt servanda*, brings with it a number of subsidiary principles which also appear in the VCLT. For example, the obligation to respect promises is so powerful that a state's domestic law can be no defense against a charge that it had breached an international treaty. In the words of the VCLT, "A party may not invoke the provisions of its internal law as justification for its

---

2. BARRY CARTER & PHILLIP TRIMBLE, INTERNATIONAL LAW 109 (2d ed., 1995).

3. American Law Institute, RESTATEMENT (THIRD) OF THE FOREIGN RELATIONS LAW OF THE UNITED STATES § 301 (comment).

4. The Vienna Convention on the Law of Treaties is reproduced in the Document Supplement.

failure to perform a treaty." And the basic rules of treaty interpretation require that a "treaty shall be interpreted in good faith in accordance with the ordinary meaning to be given to the terms of the treaty in their context and in the light of its object and purpose." Recourse may be had to the legislative history of the treaty, or *travaux preparatoires*, only as a supplementary means of interpretation and only in limited circumstances. States-party may attempt to modify their international obligations under a treaty through *reservations, understandings,* and *declarations,* though in no case may these unilateral modifications violate the object and purpose of the treaty.

Unobjectionable as these contractarian notions are, there are provisions of the VCLT that are controversial precisely because they qualify or undermine the *pure consent theory of international law,* that is, the view that a state's international obligations are strictly a function of its formal and on-going consent. To the extent that the VCLT contemplates international obligation even in the absence of such consent, controversy is inevitable. Article 18 of the VCLT, for example, provides that a state is obliged not to defeat the object and purpose of a treaty it has signed, even if the treaty is not yet in force and even before the state actually ratifies it. Article 38 contemplates the possibility that a treaty can become binding as customary law even on parties that have not signed it, and other provisions recognize the existence of peremptory norms of international law, *jus cogens,* which no treaty can contravene. These norms in effect represent communitarian limits on the power of consent, and they are in principle as applicable to states in treaty relations as they are to private citizens in contractual relations.

Finally with respect to treaties, it is important to note the paradox that a global order increasingly dominated by international treaty law is also increasingly dependent on each state's domestic law, especially "the domestic normative rank treaty provisions enjoy in the States parties to them."[5] In other words, even as treaties come to address an unprecedented range of subjects, at base their effectiveness is a direct function of how each state gives domestic legal effect to its treaty obligations.

Custom. States recognize the existence of customary international law, arising not out of an explicit agreement to some authoritative text but out of a "general practice accepted as law." The formulation in Article 38(1) suggests two criteria for custom: (i) a general practice among states, meaning that states conform in fact to a standard of behavior or that their conduct follows a consistent, empirical pattern, and (ii) a sense of legal obligation or *opinio juris,* meaning that states behave in these patterned ways not out of ideology or public relations but out of the conviction that the behavior is required by law.

In attempting to give content to this sometimes elusive body of law, international actors (like inter-governmental or non-governmental or-

---

5. Thomas Buergenthal, *Self-Executing and Non-Self-Executing Treaties in National and International Law,* 235 Recueil des Cours 304–400 (1992–IV), at 313.

ganizations, arbitrators, tribunals, and advocates) consider evidence in a variety of forms, including diplomatic exchanges, in which states define their legal expectations of one another; treaties in consistent form; the laws, constitutions, and high court decisions in the various countries; the writings of publicists; resolutions and declarations in consistent form in intergovernmental organizations like the UN; decisions of international tribunals and arbitral panels; and compendia or restatements of customary law, like the American Law Institute's RESTATEMENT OF THE FOREIGN RELATIONS LAW OF THE UNITED STATES.

Although the distinctions between treaty and custom are clear, the relationship between them can be quite complex. Treaties may be used as *evidence* of custom, especially where the treaty enjoys near universal support and the parties understand that the treaty is declaratory of customary law or where the same substantive obligation appears in numerous treaties signed by a variety of states. In this sense, treaties may serve a legislative function for the community at large and not merely a contractual function among the parties. Treaties may in principle also contribute to the demise of custom, as for example in the definition of the territorial sea, the customary breadth of which has moved over time from three miles to six miles to twelve miles in part as the result of international codification. *Jus cogens* also arises at the intersection of treaty law and customary law, consisting in those elite norms of custom from which no derogation by treaty is permitted.

General principles. Article 38(1) also lists "the general principles of law recognized by civilized nations" as a potential source of international law norms. The core of this category is that some principles of law seem valid across virtually all human societies or seem basic to the very idea of a legal system generally. International law can arise out of the comparative exercise of finding general principles in the various municipal systems of law in the world and applying them at the international plane. For example, virtually all domestic legal systems have some principle like "a party cannot take advantage of its own wrong" or "every violation of a promise or a duty triggers an obligation to make reparation." Although there is nothing distinctly international about these principles by their terms, states have reasoned that these principles—in spite of their domestic pedigree—may operate at the international plane. There can in short be a *comparative* element to *international* obligations.

Judicial decisions and writings of publicists. Article 38(1)(d) of the ICJ Statute identifies "as subsidiary means for the determination of rules of law," judicial decisions and the teachings of the most highly qualified publicists of the various nations. Though international law includes no formal notion of precedent or *stare decisis*, the decisions of national courts may nonetheless be relevant in giving content to international law, and the International Court of Justice routinely refers to its own prior decisions on the obvious principle that similar cases should be resolved similarly. The ICJ's determination in one case that a norm had become customary law would be considered virtually conclusive evidence in other settings. Scholarly writing—"the teachings of the most highly qualified publicists of the various nations"—may also exert considerable influence, not because scholars have or claim some authority to make law but because the collection and evaluation of state practice plays a critical *evidentiary* role in determining what the law is.

New sources of authority and the problem of normative variety. Article 38, though long considered the authoritative list of sources of international law, distorts the contemporary practice of international law. The ICJ and other international tribunals, not to mention international lawyers and states in their dealings *inter se*, routinely articulate international obligations on the basis of authorities that are not mentioned in Article 38. Most notable among these are: (i) the resolutions and declarations of intergovernmental organizations, like the United Nations, and their subsidiary agencies, especially when addressing legal issues, adopted by consensus, and consistent with the actual practice of states; (ii) decisions of international courts and arbitral tribunals on issues of general international law; and (iii) the expert submissions of non-governmental organizations on legal issues. The point is not that the work product from these sources is binding *per se*. Rather it is that they offer relevant evidence of what the law in its contemporary forms requires.

The softening of the distinction between treaty and custom and the proliferation of new sources of international law may be seen as part of a larger trend towards the emergence of "soft" forms of law—a range of normativity which complicates the task of defining a state's entitlements and obligations; indeed, the "blurring of the normativity threshold"[6] has been criticized precisely because it seems to expand international law beyond its consensualist base, making it incomprehensible and illegitimate in the process. But this difficulty is hardly new:. The difficulty of distinguishing between *lex lata*, the established law, and *lex ferenda*, the emerging law, has long undermined any simple dichotomy between binding law and irrelevant aspiration. Soft law instruments are best conceived as guideposts of greater or lesser persuasive value in discerning the law's trajectory.

Dramatis Personae

States. To qualify as a state, an entity must satisfy certain traditional criteria: territory, population, government, and the capacity to maintain diplomatic relations with other states. These criteria convey the sense that a state must comprise a physically and politically stable community,

---

6. Prosper Weil, *Towards Relative Normativity in International Law?*, 77 AM. J. INT'L L. 413, 415 (1983). Professor Weil continues:

While prenormative acts do not create rights or obligations on which reliance may be placed before an international court of justice or of arbitration, and failure to live up to them does not give rise to international responsibility, they do create expectations and exert on the conduct of states an influence that in certain cases may be greater than that of rules of treaty or customary law. Conversely the sanction visited upon the breach of a legal obligation is sometimes less real than that imposed for failure to honor a purely moral or political obligation. *Id.*

though history offers ample evidence that these standards are not applied mechanically or apolitically. Some states seem to emerge prematurely and other apparent states are not allowed to emerge at all. There is no centralized process for determining when and if an entity satisfies the statehood criteria, and the judgment that the somewhat formalistic criteria for statehood necessarily rests with every other government.

Traditionally, only states could be the subjects of international law, *i.e.,* only states could have rights and obligations cognizable at international law. Only states could enter into treaty relations. Only states' behavior could give rise to customary international law, and to the extent that individuals might bear rights or obligations, it was by virtue of their relationship to, or dependency upon, a state. Statehood connoted independence, the presumptive right to be left alone, to pursue the national interest without interference by other states or the international community at large, and international law was dominated by norms that preserved independence. As noted by the Permanent Court of International Justice—predecessor to the ICJ—in The Lotus Case:[7]

> International law governs relations between independent States. The rules of law binding upon States therefore emanate from their own free will as expressed in conventions or by usages generally accepted as expressing principles of law and established in order to regulate the relations between these co-existing independent communities or with a view to the achievement of common aims. Restrictions upon the independence of States cannot therefore be presumed.

The state, having served for centuries as the fulcrum of the international order, is now under sustained attack. As shown below, one counter-force is the regional integration of states and the related rise of intergovernmental organizations, which can enter into treaty relations themselves, provide a framework for the negotiation and adoption of treaties among states, and contribute to the creation of customary law and general principles. The traditional conception of the state is also under attack (somewhat more literally) from the opposite direction, namely the proliferation of internal separatist movements by indigenous peoples and ethnic minorities, who are themselves the bearers of international rights. In addition, to a limited extent, non-state actors have come to play a quasi-legislative role in the development of international standards: multinational corporations, the International Chamber of Commerce, along with hundreds of other non-governmental organizations, have contributed to the evolution of law in such fields as international trade, transportation, and commercial transactions, even as they have been made subject to it. States, though still at the center of international law, can no longer claim to be the exclusive subject of international law.

---

7. *The Lotus Case* (Fr. v. Turkey), 1927 P.C.I.J., Ser. A, No. 10.

Intergovernmental organizations. Intergovernmental organizations now routinely address substantive issues of law that a prior generation of lawyers would have considered entirely within the domestic realm: environmental protection, communications, human rights, labor standards, commercial law, family law, wills and trusts. Quite apart from the political advantages of such organizations, they provide a ready arena for the negotiation of international instruments and the formal approval of standards, as well as a forum for the authoritative expression of *opinio juris*. They increasingly have a measure of investigative or supervisory authority, and thus contribute to the enforceability of international standards.

There is no suggestion that the United Nations or any other organization operates as an international legislature: under the terms of the U.N. Charter itself, the resolutions of the General Assembly are not binding. But the U.N. and other intergovernmental organizations clearly do provide a forum for the progressive development and codification of international law. Regional groupings of states like the Organization of American States or the Organization of African Unity [now the African Union] or the European Union contribute to the creation or articulation of international norms, by developing regional treaties and directives or by attempting to harmonize the domestic laws of their member-states around an international standard. Specialized or functional organizations like the World Bank, the International Telecommunications Union, the International Civil Aviation Organization, or the U.N. Committee on Peaceful Uses of Outer Space similarly contribute to the emergence of international law, through their deliberations and their development of treaties and formal principles.

Intergovernmental organizations have also contributed to the blurring of the received distinction between treaty and custom. The World Trade Organization and the Organization for Security and Cooperation in Europe for example have evolved from legal foundations that were neither strictly conventional nor strictly customary, and their legal work-product must be deliberately distorted to fit into only one of those two analytical boxes.[8] An equally salient example in the contemporary evolution of international commercial law (*lex mercatoria*) is provided by the United Nations Commission on International Trade Law (UNCITRAL), which was established to promote "the progressive harmonization and unification of the laws of international trade." UNCITRAL has been

---

8. With respect to GATT/WTO for example, Professor Stephen Zamora has shown that "relatively 'hard' rules, such as interdictions against export subsidies or against the use of quantitative restrictions, are vitiated by a system of enforcement that is 'soft.'" He continues:

> Some international economic "soft law" exists in the form of international instruments that are not intended to be binding, such as codes of conduct, declarations, resolutions, and other non-binding texts. Though not binding on states, the principles set forth in such instruments do influence the economic practices of states; they may also become enforceable rules when adopted by national legislation. One example of this phenomenon can be found in the adoption of UN resolutions on permanent sovereignty over natural resources. These resolutions have influenced national laws, treaties, and judicial case law.

Stephen Zamora, *Economic Relations and Development*, THE UNITED NATIONS AND INTERNATIONAL LAW 232, 258 (Christopher C. Joyner, ed., 1997).

largely successful in this effort, operating through multiple types of law, including the promulgation of model laws, the negotiation of conventions, the articulation of standard contracts, and the like. Given the effectiveness of these standards, lawyers who dismiss or minimize this work product on the ground that it qualifies as neither treaty nor custom (nor any other traditional mode of law) do so at their peril.

Individuals. Prior to the expansion of international human rights law after World War II, individual human beings could be a matter of concern only by virtue of their relationship with a state. The law of *state responsibility* for example protected individuals against violations of their rights but only if their nationality were not that of the offending state and turned on the fiction that an injury to an alien was an injury to the state of her nationality. That state could advance a claim for compensation only if it could demonstrate the existence of *real and effective links* to the individual victim.[9] Groups of individuals were also protected by *minority treaties* under the League of Nations on the ground that their collective treatment was a matter of concern to states with ethnic or cultural ties to the protected class. And even the emergence of individual responsibilities and obligations was a function of the relationship between the person and the state. Where conduct like piracy or attacks on diplomats represented a threat to the community of nations, individual responsibility would be imposed. As shown below, the contemporary law of human rights does not depend on the link of nationality or identity group, nor does it indulge the fiction that a government's injury to an alien is an injury to the alien's home state. Rather individuals have rights simply by virtue of being human, including, but not limited to, a right to non-discrimination; due process and other measures of fair treatment in all interactions with the government; freedom of expression, belief, movement, and association; freedom from forced assimilation and *refoulement* (*i.e.* return to a territory where they have a well-founded fear of persecution); freedom from torture and cruel, inhuman, or degrading treatment; economic, social, and cultural rights; the protections of humanitarian law in times of armed conflict. * * *

Equally important, international law has come to recognize the possibility of *individual responsibility* for violations of international law. The Nuremberg Tribunal and the contemporary tribunals for war crimes committed in Rwanda and the former Yugoslavia reaffirm that violations of international law are committed by individuals and not by some abstraction called the state. Individual accountability is not limited to human rights and is increasingly common in environmental protection and international criminal law.

Finally, the received distinction between state and non-state actors has come to obscure not only the substance of contemporary international law but its enforcement as well. Private parties—meaning individ-

---

9. *Nottebohm Case* (Liech. v. Guat.), 1955 I.C.J. REP. 4. *Cf. re* the required links between the claimant state and a corporation, Case *concerning the Barcelona Traction, Light and Power Co.* (Belg. v. Spain), 1970 I.C.J. 3.

uals in both human and corporate form—now routinely use the domestic courts to enforce international rules governing investment, trade, civil aviation, pre-trial discovery, banking, commercial transactions, and refugee status.[10] In each of these and similar cases, individuals are the bearers of rights and obligations in ways that would have been anomalous under the traditional conception of international law.

Non-governmental organizations ("NGOs"). In virtually every field of international law, non-governmental organizations have played a profound role in the process by which international norms are created and enforced. In international commercial law for example, the International Chamber of Commerce has articulated the governing rules for documentary credits and trade and the conduct of arbitration. In international environmental law, NGOs are perhaps best known for the direct action they take in bringing environmental concerns to public consciousness, but they have also been involved in the development of legal principles that ultimately command the assent of states, like the Stockholm and Rio Declarations.[11] In international human rights, NGOs like Amnesty International and Article 19 often provide critical triangulation on a government's version of facts and can be effective voices in the adoption of treaties and the use of international standards in domestic proceedings.

Some inter-governmental institutions have formalized the role of NGOs, offering them a consultative status or relying upon them *de facto* for reliable information and analysis. But the variety of these organizations and their internal mandates makes it difficult to generalize about their role in contemporary international law other than to observe their contribution to civil society and the rule of law at the international level.

Dispute resolution

Article 33(1) of the U.N. Charter catalogues a range of methods that are typically used to resolve international disputes:

> The parties to any dispute, the continuance of which is likely to endanger the maintenance of international peace and security, shall, first of all, seek a solution by negotiation, enquiry, mediation, conciliation, arbitration, judicial settlement, resort to regional agencies or arrangements or other peaceful means of their own choice.

Non-judicial methods, like negotiation, mediation or good offices, and conciliation tend to be the least formal means of resolving disputes, preserving maximum flexibility and confidentiality for the parties. Quasi-judicial methods, like arbitration, tend to follow more formal procedures and result in a judgment or award that is typically binding upon

---

10. *Chan v. Korean Airlines*, 109 S.Ct. 1676 (1989) (aviation); *Société Nationale Industrielle Aérospatiale v. District Court*, 482 U.S. 522 (1987) (pre-trial discovery); *Cardoza-Fonseca v. Immigration and Naturalization Service*, 480 U.S. 421 (1987) (refugee status).

11. REPORT OF THE UNITED NATIONS CONFERENCE ON THE HUMAN ENVIRONMENT, U.N. Doc. A/CONF.48/14/Rev. 1 (1973) ("The Stockholm Declaration"); United Nations Conference on Environment and Development, UNCED Doc. A/CONF.151/5/Rev.1 (1992) ("The Rio Declaration").

the parties. Arbitrations may proceed under treaty, by *ad hoc* agreement (or *compromis*), or by contract between the parties, any one of which may specify the procedures to be followed in the proceeding, including the appointment of the arbitrator(s), the jurisdiction of the panel, the burden of proof, the means of enforcement, *etc.* Though arbitral awards technically bind only the parties to the proceeding, the principles on which the award rests may provide authoritative evidence of what the law is. See, e.g., *The Texaco/Libya Arbitration*,[12] addressing the constraints on a state's power to nationalize the property of aliens, and *The Trail Smelter Case* (United States v. Canada),[13] establishing principles governing the liability of states for transborder pollution.

The judicial methods of dispute settlement include the International Court of Justice, which is the principal judicial organ of the United Nations, and numerous regional and specialized courts, including the European Court of Justice within the European Union, the European Court of Human Rights, the Inter—American Court of Human Rights, the African Court of Human Rights, the Law of the Sea Tribunal, the war crimes tribunals for the former Yugoslavia and Rwanda, and the International Criminal Court. Although states' record of compliance with international judicial decisions is mixed, the proliferation of international courts suggests the extent to which states are willing to submit to a regime of law, enforced through judicial means. It also suggests that the process by which international norms emerge and are implemented will continue to be profoundly decentralized.

C. CASE STUDY

DOLLY AND JOEL FILÁRTIGA v. PEÑA–IRALA

630 F.2d 876 (2d Cir. 1980)

Upon ratification of the Constitution, the thirteen former colonies were fused into a single nation, one which, in its relations with foreign states, is bound both to observe and construe the accepted norms of international law, formerly known as the law of nations. Under the Articles of Confederation, the several states had interpreted and applied this body of doctrine as a part of their common law, but with the founding of the "more perfect Union" of 1789, the law of nations became preeminently a federal concern.

Implementing the constitutional mandate for national control over foreign relations, the First Congress established original district court jurisdiction over "all causes where an alien sues for a tort only [committed] in violation of the law of nations." Judiciary Act of 1789, * * *

---

12. Award of 19 January 1977, 17 INT'L LEGAL MATS. 1 (1978).

13. 3 U.N. REP. INT'L ARB. AWARDS 1905 (1949).

codified at 28 U.S.C. § 1350. Construing this rarely-invoked provision, we hold that deliberate torture perpetrated under color of official authority violates universally accepted norms of the international law of human rights, regardless of the nationality of the parties. Thus, whenever an alleged torturer is found and served with process by an alien within our borders, § 1350 provides federal jurisdiction. Accordingly, we reverse the judgment of the district court dismissing the complaint for want of federal jurisdiction.

I

The appellants, plaintiffs below, are citizens of the Republic of Paraguay. Dr. Joel Filártiga, a physician, describes himself as a long-standing opponent of the government of President Alfredo Stroessner, which has held power in Paraguay since 1954. His daughter, Dolly Filártiga, arrived in the United States in 1978 under a visitor's visa, and has since applied for permanent political asylum. The Filártigas brought this action in the Eastern District of New York against Americo Norberto Pena–Irala (Pena), also a citizen of Paraguay, for wrongfully causing the death of Dr. Filártiga's seventeen-year old son, Joelito. Because the district court dismissed the action for want of subject matter jurisdiction, we must accept as true the allegations contained in the Filártigas' complaint and affidavits for purposes of this appeal.

The appellants contend that on March 29, 1976, Joelito Filártiga was kidnapped and tortured to death by Pena, who was then Inspector General of Police in Asuncion, Paraguay. Later that day, the police brought Dolly Filártiga to Pena's home where she was confronted with the body of her brother, which evidenced marks of severe torture. As she fled, horrified, from the house, Pena followed after her shouting, "Here you have what you have been looking for for so long and what you deserve. Now shut up." The Filártigas claim that Joelito was tortured and killed in retaliation for his father's political activities and beliefs.

Shortly thereafter, Dr. Filártiga commenced a criminal action in the Paraguayan courts against Pena and the police for the murder of his son. As a result, Dr. Filártiga's attorney was arrested and brought to police headquarters where, shackled to a wall, Pena threatened him with death. This attorney, it is alleged, has since been disbarred without just cause.

During the course of the Paraguayan criminal proceeding, which is apparently still pending after four years, another man, Hugo Duarte, confessed to the murder. Duarte, who was a member of the Pena household, claimed that he had discovered his wife and Joelito in flagrante delicto, and that the crime was one of passion. The Filártigas have submitted a photograph of Joelito's corpse showing injuries they believe refute this claim. Dolly Filártiga, moreover, has stated that she will offer evidence of three independent autopsies demonstrating that her brother's death "was the result of professional methods of torture."

Despite his confession, Duarte, we are told, has never been convicted or sentenced in connection with the crime.

In July of 1978, Pena * * * entered the United States under a visitor's visa. He was accompanied by Juana Bautista Fernandez Villalba, who had lived with him in Paraguay. The couple remained in the United States beyond the term of their visas, and were living in Brooklyn, New York, when Dolly Filártiga, who was then living in Washington, D. C., learned of their presence. Acting on information provided by Dolly the Immigration and Naturalization Service arrested Pena and his companion, both of whom were subsequently ordered deported * * * following a hearing. They had then resided in the United States for more than nine months.

Almost immediately, Dolly caused Pena to be served with a summons and civil complaint at the Brooklyn Navy Yard, where he was being held pending deportation. The complaint alleged that Pena had wrongfully caused Joelito's death by torture and sought compensatory and punitive damages of $10,000,000. The Filártigas also sought to enjoin Pena's deportation to ensure his availability for testimony at trial. The cause of action is stated as arising under "wrongful death statutes; the U. N. Charter; the Universal Declaration on Human Rights; the U.N. Declaration Against Torture; the American Declaration of the Rights and Duties of Man; and other pertinent declarations, documents and practices constituting the customary international law of human rights and the law of nations," as well as 28 U.S.C. § 1350, Article II, sec. 2 and the Supremacy Clause of the U. S. Constitution. Jurisdiction is claimed under the general federal question provision, 28 U.S.C. § 1331 and, principally on this appeal, under the Alien Tort Statute, 28 U.S.C. § 1350.

Judge Nickerson stayed the order of deportation, and Pena immediately moved to dismiss the complaint on the grounds that subject matter jurisdiction was absent and for *forum non conveniens*. On the jurisdictional issue, there has been no suggestion that Pena claims diplomatic immunity from suit. The Filártigas submitted the affidavits of a number of distinguished international legal scholars, who stated unanimously that the law of nations prohibits absolutely the use of torture as alleged in the complaint.[4] Pena, in support of his motion to dismiss on the ground of *forum non conveniens*, submitted the affidavit of

---

4. Richard Falk, the Albert G. Milbank Professor of International Law and Practice at Princeton University, and a former Vice President of the American Society of International Law, avers that, in his judgment, "it is now beyond reasonable doubt that torture of a person held in detention that results in severe harm or death is a violation of the law of nations." Thomas Franck, professor of international law at New York University and Director of the New York University Center for International Studies offers his opinion that torture has now been rejected by virtually all nations, although it was once commonly used to extract confessions. Richard Lillich, the Howard W. Smith Professor of Law at the University of Virginia School of Law, concludes, after a lengthy review of the authorities, that officially perpetrated torture is "a violation of international law (formerly called the law of nations)." Finally, Myres MacDougal, a former Sterling Professor of Law at the Yale Law School, and a past President of the American Society of International Law, states that torture is an offense against the law of nations, and that "it has long been recognized that such offenses vitally affect relations between states."

his Paraguayan counsel, * * * who averred that Paraguayan law provides a full and adequate civil remedy for the wrong alleged. Dr. Filártiga has not commenced such an action, however, believing that further resort to the courts of his own country would be futile.

Judge Nickerson heard argument on the motion to dismiss * * *, and * * * dismissed the complaint on jurisdictional grounds. The district judge recognized the strength of appellants' argument that official torture violates an emerging norm of customary international law. Nonetheless, he felt constrained by *dicta* contained in two recent opinions of this Court, *Dreyfus v. von Finck*, 534 F.2d 24 (2d Cir.), *cert. denied*, 429 U.S. 835 (1976) ; *IIT v. Vencap, Ltd.*, 519 F.2d 1001 (2d Cir.1975), to construe narrowly "the law of nations," as employed in § 1350, as excluding that law which governs a state's treatment of its own citizens.

The district court continued the stay of deportation for forty-eight hours while appellants applied for further stays. These applications were denied by a panel of this Court on May 22, 1979, and by the Supreme Court two days later. Shortly thereafter, Pena and his companion returned to Paraguay.

II

Appellants rest their principal argument in support of federal jurisdiction upon the Alien Tort Statute, 28 U.S.C. § 1350, which provides: "The district courts shall have original jurisdiction of any civil action by an alien for a tort only, committed in violation of the law of nations or a treaty of the United States." Since appellants do not contend that their action arises directly under a treaty of the United States, a threshold question on the jurisdictional issue is whether the conduct alleged violates the law of nations. In light of the universal condemnation of torture in numerous international agreements, and the renunciation of torture as an instrument of official policy by virtually all of the nations of the world (in principle if not in practice), we find that an act of torture committed by a state official against one held in detention violates established norms of the international law of human rights, and hence the law of nations.

The Supreme Court has enumerated the appropriate sources of international law. The law of nations "may be ascertained by consulting the works of jurists, writing professedly on public law; or by the general usage and practice of nations; or by judicial decisions recognizing and enforcing that law." *United States v. Smith*, 18 U.S. (5 Wheat.) 153, 160–61 (1820) * * * In *Smith*, a statute proscribing "the crime of piracy [on the high seas] as defined by the law of nations," was held sufficiently determinate in meaning to afford the basis for a death sentence. The *Smith* Court discovered among the works of Lord Bacon, Grotius, Bochard and other commentators a genuine consensus that rendered the crime "sufficiently and constitutionally defined."

The Paquete Habana, 175 U.S. 677 (1900), reaffirmed that

> where there is no treaty, and no controlling executive or legislative act or judicial decision, resort must be had to the customs and usages of civilized nations; and, as evidence of these, to the works of jurists and commentators, who by years of labor, research and experience, have made themselves peculiarly well acquainted with the subjects of which they treat. Such works are resorted to by judicial tribunals, not for the speculations of their authors concerning what the law ought to be, but for trustworthy evidence of what the law really is.

Id. at 700. Modern international sources confirm the propriety of this approach [citing the Statute of the International Court of Justice, art. 38].

Habana is particularly instructive for present purposes, for it held that the traditional prohibition against seizure of an enemy's coastal fishing vessels during wartime, a standard that began as one of comity only, had ripened over the preceding century into "a settled rule of international law" by "the general assent of civilized nations." Thus it is clear that courts must interpret international law not as it was in 1789, but as it has evolved and exists among the nations of the world today.

The requirement that a rule command the "general assent of civilized nations" to become binding upon them all is a stringent one. Were this not so, the courts of one nation might feel free to impose idiosyncratic legal rules upon others, in the name of applying international law. Thus, in *Banco Nacional de Cuba v. Sabbatino,* 376 U.S. 398 (1964), the Court declined to pass on the validity of the Cuban government's expropriation of a foreign-owned corporation's assets, noting the sharply conflicting views on the issue propounded by the capital-exporting, capital-importing, socialist and capitalist nations.

The case at bar presents us with a situation diametrically opposed to the conflicted state of law that confronted the *Sabbatino* Court. Indeed, to paraphrase that Court's statement, *id.* at 428, there are few, if any, issues in international law today on which opinion seems to be so united as the limitations on a state's power to torture persons held in its custody.

The United Nations Charter (a treaty of the United States) makes it clear that in this modern age a state's treatment of its own citizens is a matter of international concern. It provides:

> With a view to the creation of conditions of stability and well-being which are necessary for peaceful and friendly relations among nations ... the United Nations shall promote ... universal respect for, and observance of, human rights and fundamental freedoms for all without distinctions as to race, sex, language or religion.

Id., Art. 55. And further:

All members pledge themselves to take joint and separate action in cooperation with the Organization for the achievement of the purposes set forth in Article 55.

Id., Art. 56.

While this broad mandate has been held not to be wholly self-executing, *Hitai v. Immigration and Naturalization Service*, 343 F.2d 466, 468 (2d Cir. 1965), this observation alone does not end our inquiry.[9] For although there is no universal agreement as to the precise extent of the "human rights and fundamental freedoms" guaranteed to all by the Charter, there is at present no dissent from the view that the guaranties include, at a bare minimum, the right to be free from torture. This prohibition has become part of customary international law, as evidenced and defined by the Universal Declaration of Human Rights, General Assembly Resolution 217 (III)(A) (Dec. 10, 1948) which states, in the plainest of terms, "no one shall be subjected to torture."[10] The General Assembly has declared that the Charter precepts embodied in this Universal Declaration "constitute basic principles of international law." G.A.Res. 2625 (XXV) (Oct. 24, 1970).

Particularly relevant is the Declaration on the Protection of All Persons from Being Subjected to Torture, General Assembly Resolution 3452, 30 U.N. GAOR Supp. (No. 34) 91, U.N.Doc. A/1034 (1975) * * *. The Declaration expressly prohibits any state from permitting the dastardly and totally inhuman act of torture. Torture, in turn, is defined as "any act by which severe pain and suffering, whether physical or mental, is intentionally inflicted by or at the instigation of a public official on a person for such purposes as ... intimidating him or other persons." The Declaration goes on to provide that "[w]here it is proved that an act of torture or other cruel, inhuman or degrading treatment or punishment has been committed by or at the instigation of a public official, the victim shall be afforded redress and compensation, in accordance with national law." This Declaration, like the Declaration of Human Rights before it, was adopted without dissent by the General Assembly.

These U.N. declarations are significant because they specify with great precision the obligations of member nations under the Charter. Since their adoption, "[m]embers can no longer contend that they do not know what human rights they promised in the Charter to promote." * * * Sohn, "A Short History of United Nations Documents on Human Rights," in The United Nations and Human Rights, 18th Report of the

---

9. We observe that this Court has previously utilized the U.N. Charter and the Charter of the Organization of American States, another non-self-executing agreement, as evidence of binding principles of international law. *See United States v. Toscanino*, 500 F.2d 267 (2d Cir. 1974). In that case, our government's duty under international law to refrain from kidnapping a criminal defendant from within the borders of another nation, where formal extradition procedures existed, infringed the personal rights of the defendant, whose international law claims were thereupon remanded for a hearing in the district court.

10. Eighteen nations have incorporated the Universal Declaration into their own constitutions. 48 Revue Internationale de Droit Penal Nos. 3 & 4, at 211 (1977).

Commission (Commission to Study the Organization of Peace ed. 1968). Moreover, a U.N. Declaration is, according to one authoritative definition, "a formal and solemn instrument, suitable for rare occasions when principles of great and lasting importance are being enunciated." 34 U.N. ESCOR, Supp. (No. 8) 15, U.N. Doc. E/CN.4/1/610 (1962) (memorandum of Office of Legal Affairs, U.N. Secretariat). Accordingly, it has been observed that the Universal Declaration of Human Rights "no longer fits into the dichotomy of 'binding treaty' against 'non-binding pronouncement,' but is rather an authoritative statement of the international community." E. SCHWELB, HUMAN RIGHTS AND THE INTERNATIONAL COMMUNITY 70 (1964). Thus, a Declaration creates an expectation of adherence, and "insofar as the expectation is gradually justified by State practice, a declaration may by custom become recognized as laying down rules binding upon the States." 34 U.N. ESCOR, *supra*. Indeed, several commentators have concluded that the Universal Declaration has become, *in toto*, a part of binding, customary international law.

Turning to the act of torture, we have little difficulty discerning its universal renunciation in the modern usage and practice of nations. *Smith, supra*, at 160–61. The international consensus surrounding torture has found expression in numerous international treaties and accords [citing the American Convention on Human Rights, Art. 5, ("No one shall be subjected to torture or to cruel, inhuman or degrading punishment or treatment"); the International Covenant on Civil and Political Rights, (identical language); the European Convention for the Protection of Human Rights and Fundamental Freedoms, Art. 3, (*semble*)]. The substance of these international agreements is reflected in modern municipal, *i.e.*, national law as well. Although torture was once a routine concomitant of criminal interrogations in many nations, during the modern and hopefully more enlightened era it has been universally renounced. According to one survey, torture is prohibited, expressly or implicitly, by the constitutions of over fifty-five nations, including both the United States and Paraguay. Our State Department reports a general recognition of this principle:

> There now exists an international consensus that recognizes basic human rights and obligations owed by all governments to their citizens. . . . There is no doubt that these rights are often violated; but virtually all governments acknowledge their validity.

Department of State, COUNTRY REPORTS ON HUMAN RIGHTS FOR 1979, at 1. We have been directed to no assertion by any contemporary state of a right to torture its own or another nation's citizens. Indeed, United States diplomatic contacts confirm the universal abhorrence with which torture is viewed:

> In exchanges between United States embassies and all foreign states with which the United States maintains relations, it has been the Department of State's general experience that no government has asserted a right to torture its own nationals. Where reports of

torture elicit some credence, a state usually responds by denial or, less frequently, by asserting that the conduct was unauthorized or constituted rough treatment short of torture.[15]

Memorandum of the United States as *Amicus Curiae* at 16 n.34.

Having examined the sources from which customary international law is derived, the usage of nations, judicial opinions and the works of jurists,[16] we conclude that official torture is now prohibited by the law of nations. The prohibition is clear and unambiguous, and admits of no distinction between treatment of aliens and citizens. Accordingly, we must conclude that the dictum in *Dreyfus v. von Finck, supra.,* to the effect that "violations of international law do not occur when the aggrieved parties are nationals of the acting state," is clearly out of tune with the current usage and practice of international law. The treaties and accords cited above, as well as the express foreign policy of our own government,[17] all make it clear that international law confers fundamental rights upon all people vis-a-vis their own governments. While the ultimate scope of those rights will be a subject for continuing refinement and elaboration, we hold that the right to be free from torture is now among them. We therefore turn to the question whether the other requirements for jurisdiction are met.

III

Appellee submits that even if the tort alleged is a violation of modern international law, federal jurisdiction may not be exercised consistent with the dictates of Article III of the Constitution. The claim is without merit. Common law courts of general jurisdiction regularly adjudicate transitory tort claims between individuals over whom they exercise personal jurisdiction, wherever the tort occurred. Moreover, as part of an articulated scheme of federal control over external affairs, Congress provided, in the first Judiciary Act, § 9(b), * * * for federal jurisdiction over suits by aliens where principles of international law are in issue. The constitutional basis for the Alien Tort Statute is the law of nations, which has always been part of the federal common law.

---

15. The fact that the prohibition of torture is often honored in the breach does not diminish its binding effect as a norm of international law. As one commentator has put it, "The best evidence for the existence of international law is that every actual State recognizes that it does exist and that it is itself under an obligation to observe it. States often violate international law, just as individuals often violate municipal law; but no more than individuals do States defend their violations by claiming that they are above the law." J. Brierly, THE OUTLOOK FOR INTERNATIONAL LAW 4–5 (Oxford 1944).

16. *See* note 4, *supra*: *see also Ireland v. United Kingdom,* Judgment of Jan. 18, 1978 (European Court of Human Rights) (holding that Britain's subjection of prisoners to sleep deprivation, hooding, exposure to hissing noise, reduced diet and standing against a wall for hours was "inhuman and degrading," but not "torture" within meaning of European Convention on Human Rights).

17. *E.g.,* 22 U.S.C. § 2304(a)(2) ("Except under circumstances specified in this section, no security assistance may be provided to any country the government of which engages in a consistent pattern of gross violations of internationally recognized human rights."); 22 U.S.C. § 2151(a). ("The Congress finds that fundamental political, economic, and technological changes have resulted in the interdependence of nations. The Congress declares that the individual liberties, economic prosperity, and security of the people of the United States are best sustained and enhanced in a community of nations which respect individual civil and economic rights and freedoms.")

It is not extraordinary for a court to adjudicate a tort claim arising outside of its territorial jurisdiction. A state or nation has a legitimate interest in the orderly resolution of disputes among those within its borders, and where the *lex loci delicti commissi* [the law of the place where the wrong was committed] is applied, it is an expression of comity to give effect to the laws of the state where the wrong occurred. Thus, Lord Mansfield in *Mostyn v. Fabrigas, 1 Cowp.* 161 (1774) , *quoted in McKenna v. Fisk*, 42 U.S. (1 How.) 241, 248 (1843), said:

> [I]f A becomes indebted to B, or commits a tort upon his person or upon his personal property in Paris, an action in either case may be maintained against A in England, if he is there found. . . . [A]s to transitory actions, there is not a colour of doubt but that any action which is transitory may be laid in any county in England, though the matter arises beyond the seas.

Mostyn came into our law as the original basis for state court jurisdiction over out-of-state torts, *McKenna v. Fisk, supra,* (personal injury suits held transitory); *Dennick v. Railroad Co.*, 103 U.S. 11 (1880) (wrongful death action held transitory), and it has not lost its force in suits to recover for a wrongful death occurring upon foreign soil, *Slater v. Mexican National Railroad Co.*, 194 U.S. 120 (1904), as long as the conduct complained of was unlawful where performed. Restatement (Second) of Foreign Relations Law of the United States § 19 (1965). Here, where *in personam* jurisdiction has been obtained over the defendant, the parties agree that the acts alleged would violate Paraguayan law, and the policies of the forum are consistent with the foreign law, state court jurisdiction would be proper. Indeed, appellees conceded as much at oral argument.

Recalling that *Mostyn* was freshly decided at the time the Constitution was ratified, we proceed to consider whether the First Congress acted constitutionally in vesting jurisdiction over "foreign suits," *Slater, supra,* * * * alleging torts committed in violation of the law of nations. A case properly "aris[es] under the . . . laws of the United States" for Article III purposes if grounded upon statutes enacted by Congress or upon the common law of the United States. *See Illinois v. City of Milwaukee*, 406 U.S. 91, 99–100 (1972); *Ivy Broadcasting Co., Inc. v. American Tel. & Tel. Co.*, 391 F.2d 486, 492 (2d Cir. 1968). The law of nations forms an integral part of the common law, and a review of the history surrounding the adoption of the Constitution demonstrates that it became a part of the common law of the United States upon the adoption of the Constitution. Therefore, the enactment of the Alien Tort Statute was authorized by Article III.

During the eighteenth century, it was taken for granted on both sides of the Atlantic that the law of nations forms a part of the common law. Under the Articles of Confederation, the Pennsylvania Court of Oyer and Terminer at Philadelphia, per McKean, Chief Justice, applied the law of nations to the criminal prosecution of the Chevalier de

Longchamps for his assault upon the person of the French Consul—General to the United States, noting that "[t]his law, in its full extent, is a part of the law of this state. . . ." *Respublica v. DeLongchamps,* 1 U.S. (1 Dall.) 113, 119 (1784). Thus, a leading commentator has written:

> It is an ancient and a salutary feature of the Anglo–American legal tradition that the Law of Nations is a part of the law of the land to be ascertained and administered, like any other, in the appropriate case. This doctrine was originally conceived and formulated in England in response to the demands of an expanding commerce and under the influence of theories widely accepted in the late sixteenth, the seventeenth and the eighteenth centuries. It was brought to America in the colonial years as part of the legal heritage from England. It was well understood by men of legal learning in America in the eighteenth century when the United Colonies broke away from England to unite effectively, a little later, in the United States of America.

Dickenson, "The Law of Nations as Part of the National Law of the United States," 101 U.PA.L.REV. 26, 27 (1952).

Indeed, Dickenson goes on to demonstrate, that one of the principal defects of the Confederation that our Constitution was intended to remedy was the central government's inability to "cause infractions of treaties or of the law of nations, to be punished." 1 Farrand, RECORDS OF THE FEDERAL CONVENTION 19 (Rev. ed. 1937) (Notes of James Madison). And, in Jefferson's words, the very purpose of the proposed Union was "to make us one nation as to foreign concerns, and keep us distinct in domestic ones." Dickenson, *supra.*

As ratified, the judiciary article contained no express reference to cases arising under the law of nations. Indeed, the only express reference to that body of law is contained in Article I, sec. 8, cl. 10, which grants to the Congress the power to "define and punish . . . offenses against the law of nations." Appellees seize upon this circumstance and advance the proposition that the law of nations forms a part of the laws of the United States only to the extent that Congress has acted to define it. This extravagant claim is amply refuted by the numerous decisions applying rules of international law uncodified in any act of Congress. *E.g., Ware v. Hylton,* 3 U.S. (3 Dall.) 199 (1796); *The Paquete Habana, supra; Sabbatino, supra.* A similar argument was offered to and rejected by the Supreme Court in *United States v. Smith, supra,* and we reject it today. As John Jay wrote in *The Federalist* No. 3, at 22 (1 Bourne ed. 1901), "Under the national government, treaties and articles of treaties, as well as the laws of nations, will always be expounded in one sense and executed in the same manner, whereas adjudications on the same points and questions in the thirteen states will not always accord or be consistent." Federal jurisdiction over cases involving international law is clear.

Thus, it was hardly a radical initiative for Chief Justice Marshall to state in *The Nereide,* 13 U.S. (9 Cranch) 388, 422 (1815), that in the absence of a congressional enactment,[20] United States courts are "bound by the law of nations, which is a part of the law of the land." These words were echoed in *The Paquete Habana, supra:* "international law is part of our law, and must be ascertained and administered by the courts of justice of appropriate jurisdiction, as often as questions of right depending upon it are duly presented for their determination." * * *

The Filártigas urge that 28 U.S.C. § 1350 be treated as an exercise of Congress's power to define offenses against the law of nations. While such a reading is possible, ... we believe it is sufficient here to construe the Alien Tort Statute, not as granting new rights to aliens, but simply as opening the federal courts for adjudication of the rights already recognized by international law. The statute nonetheless does inform our analysis of Article III, for we recognize that questions of jurisdiction "must be considered part of an organic growth, part of an evolutionary process," and that the history of the judiciary article gives meaning to its pithy phrases. *Romero v. International Terminal Operating Co.,* 358 U.S. 354, 360 (1959). The Framers' overarching concern that control over international affairs be vested in the new national government to safeguard the standing of the United States among the nations of the world therefore reinforces the result we reach today.

Although the Alien Tort Statute has rarely been the basis for jurisdiction during its long history,[21] in light of the foregoing discussion, there can be little doubt that this action is properly brought in federal court. This is undeniably an action by an alien, for a tort only, committed in violation of the law of nations. The paucity of suits successfully maintained under the section is readily attributable to the statute's requirement of alleging a "*violation* of the law of nations" (emphasis supplied) at the jurisdictional threshold. Courts have, accordingly, engaged in a more searching preliminary review of the merits than is required, for example, under the more flexible "arising under" formulation. Thus, the narrowing construction that the Alien Tort Statute has previously received reflects the fact that earlier cases did not involve such well-established, universally recognized norms of international law that are here at issue.

For example, the statute does not confer jurisdiction over an action by a Luxembourgeois international investment trust's suit for fraud, conversion and corporate waste. *IIT v. Vencap,* 519 F.2d 1001, 1015

---

20. The plainest evidence that international law has an existence in the federal courts independent of acts of Congress is the long-standing rule of construction first enunciated by Chief Justice Marshall: "an act of congress ought never to be construed to violate the law of nations, if any other possible construction remains...." *The Charming Betsy,* 6 U.S. (2 Cranch) 64, 67 (1804), quoted in *Lauritzen v. Larsen,* 345 U.S. 571, 578 (1953) .

21. Section 1350 afforded the basis for jurisdiction over a child custody suit between aliens in *Adra v. Clift,* 195 F. Supp. 857 (D.Md.1961), with a falsified passport supplying the requisite international law violation. In *Bolchos v. Darrel, 3* Fed. Cas. 810 (D.S.C.1795), the Alien Tort Statute provided an alternative basis of jurisdiction over a suit to determine title to slaves on board an enemy vessel taken on the high seas.

(1975). In *IIT*, Judge Friendly astutely noted that the mere fact that every nation's municipal law may prohibit theft does not incorporate "the Eighth Commandment, 'Thou Shalt not steal' . . . [into] the law of nations." It is only where the nations of the world have demonstrated that the wrong is of mutual, and not merely several, concern, by means of express international accords, that a wrong generally recognized becomes an international law violation within the meaning of the statute. Other recent § 1350 cases are similarly distinguishable.[23]

IIT adopted a dictum from *Lopes v. Reederei Richard Schroder,* 225 F. Supp. 292 (E.D.Pa.1963), to the effect that "a violation of the law of nations arises only when there has been 'a violation by one or more individuals of those standards, rules or customs (a) affecting the relationship between states or between an individual and a foreign state and (b) used by those states for their common good and/or in dealings inter se.'" *IIT, supra,* at 1015, quoting *Lopes, supra,* at 297. We have no quarrel with this formulation so long as it be understood that the courts are not to prejudge the scope of the issues that the nations of the world may deem important to their interrelationships, and thus to their common good. As one commentator has noted:

> the sphere of domestic jurisdiction is not an irreducible sphere of rights which are somehow inherent, natural, or fundamental. It does not create an impenetrable barrier to the development of international law. Matters of domestic jurisdiction are not those which are unregulated by international law, but those which are left by international law for regulation by States. There are, therefore, no matters which are domestic by their "nature." All are susceptible of international legal regulation and may become the subjects of new rules of customary law of treaty obligations.

Preuss, "Article 2, Paragraph 7 of the Charter of the United Nations and Matters of Domestic Jurisdiction," HAGUE RECEUIL (Extract, 149) at 8, *reprinted in* H. Briggs, THE LAW OF NATIONS 24 (1952). Here, the nations have made it their business, both through international accords and unilateral action,[24] to be concerned with domestic human rights viola-

---

23. *Dreyfus v. von Finck,* 534 F.2d 24 (2d Cir.), *cert. denied,* 429 U.S. 835 (1976), concerned a forced sale of property, and thus sought to invoke international law in an area in which no consensus view existed. *See Sabbatino, supra,* 376 U.S. at 428. Similarly, *Benjamins v. British European Airways,* 572 F.2d 913 (2d Cir. 1978), *cert. denied,* 439 U.S. 1114 (1979), held only that an air disaster, even if caused by "wilful" negligence, does not constitute a law of nations violation. *Id. at 916.* In *Khedivial Line, S. A. E. v. Seafarers' International Union,* 278 F.2d 49 (2d Cir. 1960), we found that the "right" to free access to the ports of a foreign nation was at best a rule of comity, and not a binding rule of international law.

The cases from other circuits are distinguishable in like manner. The court in *Huynh Thi Anh v. Levi,* 586 F.2d 625 (6th Cir. 1978), was unable to discern from the traditional sources of the law of nations "a universal or generally accepted substantive rule or principle" governing child custody, *id. at 629,* and therefore held jurisdiction to be lacking. Cf. *Nguyen Da Yen v. Kissinger,* 528 F.2d 1194, 1201 n.13 (9th Cir. 1975) ("the illegal seizure, removal and detention of an alien against his will in a foreign country would appear to be a tort . . . and it may well be a tort in violation of the 'law of nations'") (§ 1350 question not reached due to inadequate briefing). Finally, the district court in *Lopes v. Reederei Richard Schroder,* 225 F. Supp. 292 (E.D.Pa.1963) simply found that the doctrine of seaworthiness, upon which the plaintiff relied, was a uniquely American concept, and therefore not a part of the law of nations.

24. As President Carter stated in his address to the United Nations on March 17, 1977:

tions of this magnitude. The case before us therefore falls within the *Lopes/IIT* rule.

Since federal jurisdiction may properly be exercised over the Filárti-gas' claim, the action must be remanded for further proceedings. Appellee Pena, however, advances several additional points that lie beyond the scope of our holding on jurisdiction. Both to emphasize the boundaries of our holding, and to clarify some of the issues reserved for the district court on remand, we will address these contentions briefly.

IV

Pena argues that the customary law of nations, as reflected in treaties and declarations that are not self-executing, should not be applied as rules of decision in this case. In doing so, he confuses the question of federal jurisdiction under the Alien Tort Statute, which requires consideration of the law of nations, with the issue of the choice of law to be applied, which will be addressed at a later stage in the proceedings. The two issues are distinct. Our holding on subject matter jurisdiction decides only whether Congress intended to confer judicial power, and whether it is authorized to do so by Article III. The choice of law inquiry is a much broader one, primarily concerned with fairness; consequently, it looks to wholly different considerations. *See Lauritzen v. Larsen*, 345 U.S. 571 (1954). Should the district court decide that the *Lauritzen* analysis requires it to apply Paraguayan law, our courts will not have occasion to consider what law would govern a suit under the Alien Tort Statute where the challenged conduct is actionable under the law of the forum and the law of nations, but not the law of the jurisdiction in which the tort occurred.[25]

Pena also argues that "if the conduct complained of is alleged to be the act of the Paraguayan government, the suit is barred by the Act of State doctrine." This argument was not advanced below, and is there-fore not before us on this appeal. We note in passing, however, that we doubt whether action by a state official in violation of the Constitution and laws of the Republic of Paraguay, and wholly unratified by that nation's government, could properly be characterized as an act of state. *See Banco Nacionale de Cuba v. Sabbatino, supra; Underhill v. Hernandez,*

All the signatories of the United Nations Charter have pledged themselves to observe and to respect basic human rights. Thus, no member of the United Nations can claim that mistreatment of the citizens is solely its own business. Equally, no member can avoid its responsibilities to review and to speak when torture or unwarranted deprivation occurs in any part of the world.

Reprinted in 78 *Department of State Bull.* 322 (1977) * * *

25. In taking that broad range of factors into account, the district court may well decide that fairness requires it to apply Paraguayan law to the instant case. *See Slater v. Mexican National Railway Co.*, 194 U.S. 120, (1904). Such a decision would not retroactively oust the federal court of subject matter jurisdiction, even though plaintiff's cause of action would no longer properly be "created" by a law of the United States. *See American Well Works Co. v. Layne & Bowler Co.*, 241 U.S. 257, 260 (1916) (Holmes, J.). Once federal jurisdiction is established by a colorable claim under federal law at a preliminary stage of the proceeding, subsequent dismissal of that claim (here, the claim under the general international proscription of torture) does not deprive the court of jurisdiction previously established. *See Hagans v. Lavine*, 415 U.S. 528 (1974); *Romero v. International Terminal Operating Co.*, 358 U.S. 354 (1959); *Bell v. Hood*, 327 U.S. 678 (1946). Cf. *Huynh Thi Ahn, supra*, 586 F.2d at 633 (choice of municipal law ousts § 1350 jurisdiction when no international norms exist).

168 U.S. 250 (1897). Paraguay's renunciation of torture as a legitimate instrument of state policy, however, does not strip the tort of its character as an international law violation, if it in fact occurred under color of government authority. *See* Declaration on the Protection of All Persons from Being Subjected to Torture, *supra*; *cf. Ex parte Young,* 209 U.S. 123 (1908) (state official subject to suit for constitutional violations despite immunity of state.)

Finally, we have already stated that we do not reach the critical question of *forum non conveniens*, since it was not considered below. In closing, however, we note that the foreign relations implications of this and other issues the district court will be required to adjudicate on remand underscores the wisdom of the First Congress in vesting jurisdiction over such claims in the federal district courts through the Alien Tort Statute. Questions of this nature are fraught with implications for the nation as a whole, and therefore should not be left to the potentially varying adjudications of the courts of the fifty states.

In the twentieth century the international community has come to recognize the common danger posed by the flagrant disregard of basic human rights and particularly the right to be free of torture. Spurred first by the Great War, and then the Second, civilized nations have banded together to prescribe acceptable norms of international behavior. From the ashes of the Second World War arose the United Nations Organization, amid hopes that an era of peace and cooperation had at last begun. Though many of these aspirations have remained elusive goals, that circumstance cannot diminish the true progress that has been made. In the modern age, humanitarian and practical considerations have combined to lead the nations of the world to recognize that respect for fundamental human rights is in their individual and collective interest. Among the rights universally proclaimed by all nations, as we have noted, is the right to be free of physical torture. Indeed, for purposes of civil liability, the torturer has become like the pirate and slave trader before him *hostis humani generis*, an enemy of all mankind. Our holding today, giving effect to a jurisdictional provision enacted by our First Congress, is a small but important step in the fulfillment of the ageless dream to free all people from brutal violence.

NOTES AND QUESTIONS ON FILÁRTIGA

1. *After the decision.* By the time the Second Circuit issued its opinion, the Immigration and Naturalization Service had deported Peña-Irala back to Paraguay. He made no further appearance in the case and a default judgment was entered against him. On remand, the district court awarded the Filartigas over $10 million in compensatory and punitive damages. *Filartiga v. Pena–Irala,* 577 F.Supp. 860, 867 (E.D.N.Y. 1984). Significantly, in a choice of law analysis of the applica-

ble standard for punitive damages, the district court rejected the Paraguayan law's limitations on punitive damages and found that punitive damages must be awarded to further the ATS's remedial purposes.

To date, the Filartigas have never collected their judgment against Peña-Irala. Indeed, Dr. Filartiga was harassed in Paraguay (and also sued for defamation) in the immediate aftermath of the decision. But the family has never wavered in its belief in the case. In March 2004, just before the Supreme Court arguments in *Sosa v. Alvarez–Machain*, 542 U.S. 692 (2004), *infra*, Dolly Filartiga wrote in the *New York Times*:

> [M]y 17–year-old brother, Joelito, was tortured and killed by local police in Asuncion, Paraguay. At 3 that morning I was awakened by policemen, who took me to a neighbor's house and showed me my brother's beaten body. The chief inspector, Americo Peña-Irala, told me to take the body home and never talk about what had happened. I remember telling him, "Tonight you have power over me, but tomorrow I will tell the world."

> Little did I know that one day, I would not only be able to tell the world of Mr. Peña-Irala's brutality, but also that I would do so in an American court. * * *

> Although Mr. Peña-Irala was sent back to Paraguay and none of the $10 million judgment has yet been paid, our case established a remarkable precedent: from Ethiopia's Red Terror to Argentina's Dirty War to the Philippines' dictatorship under Ferdinand Marcos, in 19 instances survivors or victims' relatives have used this law to obtain a measure of justice.

> For my family, the court decision put us at risk but also gave protection—the Paraguayan government threatened us but wouldn't risk retaliating once we had the American legal system on our side. In Paraguay, the case remains a symbol of the injustice of the Stroessner dictatorship, and my brother is considered a martyr for human rights* * *.

> I came to this country in 1978 hoping simply to look a killer in the eye. With the help of American law, I got so much more. Eventually I received political asylum, then became a citizen. I am proud to live in a country where human rights are respected, where there is a way to bring to justice people who have committed horrible atrocities.

Dolly Filartiga, *American Courts, Global Justice*, N.Y. TIMES, March 30, 2004, at A21.

With few exceptions, victims have been unable to collect their judgments in ATS cases. Does this render ATS judgments ineffective, or is the formal recognition of a wrong and the establishment of responsibility sufficient?

2. *Evidence of international law.* Consider the range of authorities the *Filartiga* court consulted as evidence that the law of nations prohibit-

ed a government's torture of its own citizens: treaties, U.N. resolutions, domestic laws, the submissions of academic experts, and the defenses offered by non-conforming states. Should it have mattered that the U.S. had not yet ratified any human rights treaty prohibiting torture in 1980? And why didn't the pattern of state violations of the norm against torture undermine the existence of the norm?

3. *Customary international law as law of the United States.* The *Filartiga* court invoked a famously opaque passage in *The Paquete Habana*, 175 U.S. 677, 708 (1900):

> [i]nternational law is part of our law, and must be ascertained and administered by the courts of justice of appropriate jurisdiction, as often as questions of right depending upon it are duly presented for their determination. For this purpose, where there is no treaty, and no controlling executive or legislative act or judicial decision, resort must be had to the customs and usages of civilized nations; and as evidence of these, to the works of jurists and commentators, who by years of labor, research and experience, have made themselves peculiarly well acquainted with the subjects of which they treat. Such works are resorted to by judicial tribunals, not for the speculations of their authors concerning what the law ought to be, but for trustworthy evidence of what the law really is.

The U.S. courts' repeated approval of this language has generated the orthodoxy that customary international law is incorporated into federal common law, that it is enforceable in domestic courts even in the absence of direct legislative authorization, and that, like other forms of federal law, it constrains the actions of the states of the Union. That these principles should find acceptance and expression in the *Restatement (Third) of the Foreign Relations Law of the United States*—and that the judiciary should in turn invoke the Restatement's language—suggests at a minimum that they are not particularly radical, though it hardly immunizes them from criticism. Curtis A. Bradley & Jack L. Goldsmith, *Customary International Law as Federal Common Law: A Critique of the Modern Position*, 110 HARV. L. REV. 815 (1997). *See also* Curtis A. Bradley & Jack L. Goldsmith, *Sosa, Customary International Law, and the Continuing Relevance of Erie*, 120 Harv. L. Rev. 869 (2007).

4. *Incorporationism and interpretivism.* The *incorporationist* paradigm in *Paquete Habana* is not the only way to conceive the relationship between customary international law and the domestic law of the United States. There is in addition an *interpretativist* approach under which the statutes enacted by Congress "ought never to be construed to violate the law of nations if any other possible construction remains." *Murray v. The Schooner Charming Betsy*, 6 U.S. (2 Cranch) 64, 118 (1804). Like other canons of statutory construction, the *Charming Betsy* principle is easily dismissed as innocuous or meaningless. But this perspective masks the potential impact of the *Charming Betsy* principle; indeed, advocates, courts, and scholars routinely fail to appreciate the consequences of a

meaningful requirement that statutes be construed consistently with international law, even though those consequences are far from trivial. *The Charming Betsy* and its progeny offer a potentially potent though admittedly non-determinative principle, under which courts, advocates, and scholars faced with issues of statutory construction are obliged to consult international sources.

5. *Personal jurisdiction.* Successful ATS claims require that the court have personal jurisdiction over the defendants. Individual defendants residing in the U.S. are often targets of ATS suits (*e.g.* exiled Philippine president Ferdinand Marcos). Many ATS cases have relied on "tag" jurisdiction—*i.e.* serving a defendant with process while he is traveling in the United States—to obtain personal jurisdiction over the defendant. For example, in *Kadic v. Karadzic*, 70 F.3d 232, 248 (2d Cir. 1995), the Second Circuit upheld personal jurisdiction, even though the defendant, Bosnian Serb leader Radovan Karadzic, was only in the United States briefly and as a United Nations invitee. Should a defendant's temporary presence in the United States be a sufficient basis for a U.S. court to sit in judgment over alleged human rights violations in foreign countries? Does this give human rights lawyers, organizations and individual clients the power to cause embarrassment to foreign officials visiting the United States? *See Burnham v. Superior Court of California*, 495 U.S. 604, 619 (1990) (validating "tag" jurisdiction over a nonresident individual solely because he was served with process while visiting in the forum state).

6. *Are ATS cases political?* Some commentators have criticized ATS cases as being "political" and illegitimate. Other critics have characterized ATS litigation as a form of "plaintiffs' diplomacy." *See* Anne–Marie Slaughter & David Bosco, *Plaintiff's Diplomacy*, 79 FOREIGN AFF. 102 (Sept.—Oct. 2000). Are these critiques undermined by the fact that plaintiffs rarely, if ever, profit financially as a result of ATS litigation? What factors are important in determining the legitimacy of ATS litigation? Is ATS litigation rendered less legitimate because it often involves events occurring on foreign soil, by foreign (sometimes failed) governments?

7. *Translating Filartiga.* While no other country authorizes civil lawsuits exactly comparable to the ATS litigation, some countries do permit claims which are the functional equivalent of ATS claims. In her article, *Translating Filartiga: A Comparative and International Law Analysis of Domestic Remedies for International Human Rights Violations*, 27 YALE J. INT'L L. 1 (2002), Beth Stephens explores differences in legal procedure and culture in various countries and describes how criminal proceedings, administrative proceedings, and domestic tort law can respond to the same concerns raised in ATS lawsuits. She notes, for example, that

> [m]any civil law systems permit civil claims to be filed as an adjunct to a criminal prosecution. In France, for example, the victim of a crime can join the criminal prosecution as a *partie civile*, becoming a party to the case with the right to access to the proceedings, to seek

compensation for the harm caused, and to appeal an adverse decision. In Spain, compensation to the victim is automatically part of a criminal prosecution. Another variation permits private parties to initiate criminal proceedings, either by filing a formal request asking the public prosecutor to file charges or by pursuing an action as a private prosecutor. The case against Pinochet in Spain, for example, began when a private organization filed a criminal complaint against members of the Argentine military, which subsequently expanded to include charges against Pinochet. Civil claims can then be attached to these privately initiated prosecutions

Id. at 19.

And further that:

The goals of civil litigation closely parallel those sought in criminal prosecutions: punishment for past abuses; deterrence of future abuses; redress for victims, including compensation; and development of international law principles. Suits founded on domestic tort law can serve similar goals, even without labeling the bases for claims as international human rights abuses. Such actions have been filed in England, Canada, and Australia, asserting negligence claims arising out of corporate activities in foreign countries, where the firm is incorporated in the forum or has taken key decisions in its headquarters.

Id. at 39.

CHAPTER 2

LITIGATING HUMAN RIGHTS IN DOMESTIC COURTS

■ ■ ■

One of the most interesting ways to misunderstand the field of international human rights practice is to assume that international law (if it exists at all) is adjudicated (if it is adjudicated at all) only in international courts. The usual suspects in this scenario are the International Court of Justice or the various regional courts of human rights. To that list we might add the Rwandan and Yugoslavian War Crimes Tribunals, their predecessors at Nuremberg or Tokyo, or their successors in the International Criminal Court and the hybrid courts for Cambodia or Sierra Leone. Whatever else can be said about these institutions, at a minimum, they are doing what comes naturally: international law has its courts, and domestic law has its courts. The recent proliferation of international tribunals could even be interpreted as evidence of a continuing evolution toward a functional separation of international and domestic adjudication.

But there is much to be gained by looking through the other end of the telescope. Critical as these international institutions are, it is the domestic courts of each nation that offer the primary, daily line of defense in the judicial application of international human rights standards. Of course, domestic courts are not a single, homogeneous institution. They vary profoundly from country to country and from culture to culture. The very conception of the law and the role of lawyers varies dramatically around the world, as do the constitutional provisions on the status of international law within domestic law. Not all domestic judiciaries are independent or free of corruption. And no textbook can anticipate the full range of procedural or doctrinal steps that lawyers around the world must take to get international human rights law into their national courts. But the anecdotal evidence that domestic courts are the workhorses in this field of law is strong. In recent years, the Supreme Court of Argentina revoked a pardon of a former general accused of human rights abuse, potentially allowing his domestic prosecution for crimes against humanity during the Dirty War in that country. The Netherlands successfully prosecuted a Dutch citizen who had used his West African lumber company to smuggle weapons used by militias to commit atrocities against civilians. A Sri Lankan domestic court has found Sri Lankan soldiers liable under international standards for rape. The Constitutional Court of South Africa has been a leading institutional voice for the adjudication of economic, social, and cultural rights. The Supreme Court of the United States has ruled that provisions of the Geneva Conventions on the law of war apply to the U.S. treatment of detainees at Guantanamo Bay. These and scores of similar cases alert us to the fact that there is no clear or stable firebreak between international and domestic adjudication.

The materials in this chapter focus on the civil and criminal litigation of international human rights claims in the courts of the United States. This is not because American courts or judges have reached some pinnacle of refinement. To the contrary, the U.S. judiciary can be among the *least* receptive to international law argumentation, routinely exhibiting what might be called the "Blank Stare Phenomenon:" the lawyer who makes an argument on the basis of international law must be prepared to face the judge's blank stare, as though the advocate were suddenly speaking Russian to a cat.

The Blank Stare Phenomenon occurs because of three different, characteristic, and recurring issues that arise in one form or another whenever domestic courts are asked to apply international legal standards:

(i) *the problem of authority*. By what warrant or authority do domestic courts apply international law in the first place?

(ii) *the problem of proof*. To what evidence do the courts turn to determine the content of international law, especially the typically unwritten customary international law?

(iii) *the problem of restraint*. What devices must counsel anticipate that a reluctant court will use to avoid the application of international standards? Sometimes (and not infrequently) judges will be disqualified—or will disqualify themselves—in cases with significant elements of international law, and counsel must be prepared to respond when these prudential barriers are raised.

The modules in this chapter approach these questions in various settings, testing both the civil and the criminal uses of international human rights standards in the domestic courts and exploring the concept of each state's "universal jurisdiction."

Chapter 2

Module 1

Litigating Human Rights in Domestic Courts: The Alien Tort Statute

■ ■ ■

"The district courts shall have original jurisdiction of any civil action by an alien for a tort only, committed in violation of the law of nations or a treaty of the United States."

28 U.S.C. § 1350

Orientation

In this module, we consider one of the most dynamic areas of domestic human rights litigation: cases brought under the Alien Tort Statute ("ATS") (sometimes referred to as the Alien Tort Claims Act or "ATCA"). As noted in Chapter One, the ATS was part of the First Judiciary Act of 1789, the first law ever passed in the United States and the legislation that created the federal court system and defined its jurisdiction. The ATS provides for district court jurisdiction over claims brought by "alien[s]" for "tort[s] only, committed in violation of the law of nations or a treaty of the United States." 28 U.S.C. § 1350. Until 1980, the ATS was rarely invoked. This changed with the Second Circuit's landmark decision in *Filartiga v. Peña-Irala*, 630 F.2d 876 (2d Cir. 1980), *supra*, Chapter 1, which paved the way for the ATS to be used to vindicate human rights claims in U.S. courts.

Judge Henry Friendly once referred to the ATS as "a kind of legal Lohengrin; although it has been with us since the first Judiciary Act, § 9, 1 Stat. 73, 77 (1789), no one seems to know whence it came." *IIT v. Vencap, Ltd.*, 519 F.2d 1001, 1015 (2d Cir. 1975).[1] In recent years, much of the mystery surrounding the statute has been removed by considerable legal scholarship examining the historical origins of the ATS. This scholarship provides a richer context and suggests the probable Congressional intent of the statute. The Founders, in enacting the law as members of the First Congress, were concerned about the enforcement

---

1. "In the German legend, Lohengrin appears as if out of nowhere to rescue a maiden and break a curse, but after her inquiry into his cryptic origins, he vanishes again." *Flores v. Southern Peru Copper Corp.*, 343 F.3d 140, 149 n.16 (2d Cir. 2003).

of the "law of nations" by the federal courts for reasons important to the preservation of the nascent republic: avoiding the risk of wars caused by offending more powerful nations and adhering to a principled belief that the enforcement of the "law of nations" was an essential duty of international citizenship and the federal government. Anne–Marie Burley, *The Alien Tort Statute and the Judiciary Act of 1789: A Badge of Honor*, 83 AM. J. INT'L L. 461, 475–488 (1989).

In 1789, when referring to "torts ... committed in violation of the law of nations," the Founders likely believed that the ATS applied to at least three violations: piracy, violations of safe conducts (and other breaches of neutrality), and attacks on ambassadors. The Founders had little inkling that the "law of nations" would evolve over time to apply to a government's treatment of its own citizens. Whether the Founders intended for the ATS to remain limited only to the "law of nations" as understood in 1789, or whether they intended that it would be a dynamic concept, encompassing new violations of international law later recognized by the international community, is less clear.

Answers to these questions may lie in the legal culture that prevailed in the late 18th Century. During that period, many legal concepts that are familiar to today's lawyers were beginning to take shape. Much of that development was created by common law courts that fashioned new rules of civil liability based on a combination of existing precedents and overriding policy concerns. Thus, in 1789 there was no established list of "torts" committed in violation of the "law of nations" traceable to positive law sources. The Founders probably believed that those torts and the rules that would support their application would be forged by the courts.

Moreover, the Founders understood the English common law concept of transitory torts—the notion that a tortfeasor could be sued not only where the tort was committed, but also wherever the tortfeasor was found. In *Mostyn v. Fabrigas*, (1774) 98 Eng. Rep. 1021 (K.B.), Lord Mansfield applied the transitory tort doctrine to an assault and false imprisonment claim brought in London by a resident of the island of Minorca against the island's governor based on a tort committed there. Similarly, Oliver Ellsworth, the author of the ATS and a Senator from Connecticut, presided over a trial in Connecticut in 1786 in which he applied the transitory tort doctrine. *See Stoddard v. Bird*, 1 Kirby 65 (Conn. 1786).

In 1795, in one of the few pieces of direct evidence of the Founders' intent, Attorney General William Bradford issued an opinion finding that the ATS would be available to redress an attack, assisted by U.S. citizens, on British ships off the coast of Sierra Leone. Concluding that U.S. criminal statutes would not apply to this extraterritorial attack, Bradford opined: "[T]here can be no doubt that the company or individuals who have been injured by these acts of hostility have a remedy by a *civil* suit in the courts of the United States; jurisdiction being expressly given to these courts in all cases where an alien sues for a tort only, in violation of the laws of nations, or a treaty of the United States." Breach of Neutrality, 1 Op. Att'y Gen. 57, 59 (1795).

Some of the difficulty that currently surrounds the ATS is a product of the differences between the modern architecture of the federal courts and that which existed at the founding of the nation. Though the Founders had no reason to question the notion that federal courts would—like other courts—engage in common lawmaking, the decision in *Erie Railroad Co. v. Tompkins*, 304 U.S. 64 (1938) greatly circumscribed that authority. In *Erie*, the U.S. Supreme Court severely limited the extent to which federal courts could decide cases through the application of general common law principles. Nonetheless, even after *Erie*, the Supreme Court has affirmed that federal courts retain some authority to apply federal common law, especially in the area of foreign affairs. *Banco Nacional de Cuba v. Sabbatino*, 376 U.S. 398 (1964).

Between 1789 and 1980, while the ATS lay mostly dormant, the scope of customary international law expanded. After the trials of Nazi war criminals at Nuremberg, the idea that individuals bear direct responsibility for violations of international law became firmly established. Moreover, in the aftermath of World War II, the substantive scope and universal acceptance of international human rights norms increased at a rapid pace, giving individuals protections and not just imposing criminal obligations on them.

As noted in Chapter 1, the modern era of ATS litigation began with *Filartiga*. Following *Filartiga*'s lead, most of the ATS cases immediately post-*Filartiga* were filed against former foreign officials found in the United States who were implicated in human rights violations in their home countries. As time went on, however, ATS cases began to target not only individual torturers, those who aided and abetted or conspired with them, and their commanders, but also corporations and even U.S. officials alleged to have violated international human rights norms. The most important post-*Filartiga* case is *Sosa v. Alvarez–Machain*, 542 U.S. 692 (2004), *infra*. To date, *Sosa* remains the only Supreme Court decision interpreting the meaning and scope of the ATS. As of this writing, an intense legal struggle is being waged over the meaning and application of *Sosa*, especially in the corporate line of ATS cases.

In this module, we trace the development of ATS litigation after *Filartiga* and the issues these cases have generated. In the case study, we explore the cases brought against corporations for complicity in human rights violations. First, we include testimony from a prominent ATS trial as a reminder of the human suffering at the heart of these cases.

A TYPICAL ATS CASE: *ABEBE-JIRA v. NEGEWO*

Abebe-Jira v. Negewo, 72 F.3d 844 (11th Cir. 1996) is a good illustration of a typical case in the first generation of ATS litigation.[2] In

---

2. Many ATS cases present compelling accounts of serious human rights abuses and human suffering. For additional statements by ATS plaintiffs, students should visit the website of the Center for Justice and Accountability: www. cja.org.

the late 1970's, Kelbessa Negewo was the head of a local government unit in Addis Ababa under the military dictatorship then in power in Ethiopia. The case started when Edgegayehu Taye, a young Ethiopian woman, discovered that Negewo, the man who had tortured her in Addis Ababa more than a decade before, worked in the same Atlanta hotel that she did. Two other young Ethiopian women, Elizabeth Demissie and Hirute Abebe–Jira, confirmed that Negewo was the man who had directed the torture of all three women.

As in the *Filartiga* case, the women went to the Center for Constitutional Rights in New York and, with the ACLU as co-counsel, filed an ATS case in Atlanta, alleging that Negewo was responsible for their torture during the "Red Terror," which took place in 1977 and 1978 in Addis Ababa. During the "Red Terror," thousands of Ethiopians were rounded up and subjected to detention without charge or trial and tortured for their perceived opposition to the military junta in control of the country. *See* HUMAN RIGHTS WATCH, RECKONING UNDER THE LAW (1994).

During this period, many others were executed in the streets or were disappeared. For example, Ms. Demissie's father, a Supreme Court Justice in the Haile Selassie regime, was killed in the streets of Addis Ababa one night, and her 16-year-old sister, Haimanot, was taken from their joint cell the morning after their torture, without time for a final embrace, and after a short detention in another facility was "disappeared." After Elizabeth was released from detention, she and her mother scoured the country trying to find evidence of Haimanot's whereabouts. They were unable to obtain any information about what happened to her.

One of the unusual twists in this case was that Negewo represented himself at trial. This set the stage for an emotional confrontation between the three women and Negewo in court:

DIRECT TESTIMONY OF ELIZABETH DEMISSIE
MAY 17, 2003 TRANSCRIPT PAGES 76–87

Q: [W]hen you arrived at Kebele 10 What happened?[3]

A. Kelbessa told the guards "don't put them with the other prisoners."

Q. Where were you put?

A. What I recall is a very dingy place. * * * It's just a storage. * * * very dirty, spider webs everywhere.

    * * *

---

3. [Editors' note: Kebele 10 is a reference to a government building where Ms. Demisse was detained and tortured. A kebele was an administrative subdivision of Addis Abbaba.]

Q.   Was it just the two of you? [Elizabeth and her sister]

A.   Just the two of us.

     * * *

Q.   At some point did they come and take your sister away?

A.   At night. So one of the guards came and called my sister name.

Q.   What was your sister name?

A.   Haimanot.

Q.   How old was she at the time?

A.   She was 15 at the time.

     * * *

Q.   Now, how long was she outside of that cell?

A.   Could be two hours. * * *

     * * *

A.   When they brought her back * * * she couldn't walk. She beaten up. They beat her so hard she couldn't even walk, and so they had to carry her. And they just throw her inside that dingy room and told me I got to go to the office. * * *

Q.   Who was in the office when you arrived there?

A.   Kelbessa and four other, four or five other people. * * *

Q.   Where was Kelbessa?

     * * *

A.   He was sitting there and the others were. He was the boss. * * *

Q.   Did he say anything?

A.   He told me to take off my clothes.

Q.   Did you take of your clothes?

A.   Yes.

Q.   How did that make you feel?

A.   I was so ashamed and embarrassed, and I mean those people are strangers. And I didn't even take off my—take off my clothes in front of my brothers. So it was so embarrassing and it was a degrading experience. * * *

Q.   What did they do to you next?

A.   And they told me put my wrists together and my knees together and they tied it on this plastic wire and a string or—cable it's a cable wire. So they put my hands and my—close to my knees, and there was a small hole you can put the stick. I mean it's the pole, the wooden pole in between, in between my knees and hand, so they can have full control how to roll me around.

Q.   And did they put you in that position?

A.   Yeah. My head was facing the floor.

Q.   Who was in charge in that room?

A.   Kelbessa.

      * * *

Q.   What were they asking you?

A.   He asked me if I was a member of the EPRP,[4] and if I knew other peoples.

Q.   Other people who were members of the EPRP?

A.   Yeah, who are members of EPRP.

Q.   And Kelbessa was the interrogator in this action?

A.   Yes, he was.

Q.   Did they hit you at all?

A.   Yeah. * * *[M]ost of the time passed * * * by beating me in a state of—asking me any questions. That's their satisfaction I guess. They got satisfaction out of it. So what they did—at first I remember the first two strike was very painful and I screamed. So then they—they put socks. I mean they made it from socks. It's a kind of ball with socks. It's just covered with blood and vomit, and put it in my mouth so I cannot scream.

Q.   How long did the beatings go on?

A.   To me sound like forever, but it could be from one to two hours.

Q.   Did you see Kelbessa during this time?

A.   Yes.

Q.   Did you see his face?

A.   Yes. My position was so awkward. All my face is—my eyes is facing the—my top part is facing the floor, and I was upside down. What they had is my leg and my behind and my back. So it was so hard to know which one is which, but I believe everybody was there and that they participate. When they took break, they were talking. I mean they were just joking to each other as if nothing happened.

Q.   Did they laugh?

A.   They laughed. At one time I remember one person, it's a guard, he spit on me, and—this just disgusting creature. I mean they will just break you to pieces; just the verbal abuse.

Q.   When they took a break, did they leave you upside down?

A.   Yes.

Q.   Can you describe the physical pain?

---

4.   [Editors' note: The EPRP was the Ethiopian People's Revolutionary Party. The EPRP was in opposition to the military regime.]

A. I don't know if I can find the word really. Not in Amharic. It's not a language barrier. But it was so hard to express it in my language. It's the ultimate pain, really. It's hard to express pain.

Q. Did they bring you from that room back to the room you had been in?

A. Finally—I was weak. I could die on that pole. I mean in that position. So somehow it was just—they took that pole out and they thought they had—I mean, "you can take her to her cell now," and the two guards, they just took me because I couldn't walk then. And so I got to that dingy cell and my sister was lying there and moaning, crying .... I was in the same condition she was so I could not even help her out or I could not do anything about it. And, yeah, when they put me there, there is no way you can sleep because they hit your back and your behind, and it was so hard to sit. It was so hard to stand up. The only thing you can do is just lie down on your chest. And she was lying down there and I was beside her and we're crying, and wondering what's going to be next. I know that's going to be—it wasn't going to be the last time. Because you are so scared you cannot think the other things, not the physical things.

    * * *

Q. Was your sister taken from that room?

A. No. We spend the night crying and moaning and feeling our pain. And two days passed between—there was one day—I mean we stayed there another day and the next day they called her.

Q. Did the guards take her away?

A. The guard, the guard took her to—

Q. Did they take her out of your cell?

A. Yeah, they took her—I mean they called her. And she just tried to walk and which she did, and the next day I mean the swelling got better and she walked out and—

Q. After the day that your sister was taken from that place, have you ever seen you sister again?

A. No. I didn't know that was our last minute. I don't know what happened to her. I was waiting for her. So my mom even, she didn't know what happened to her. So she visit her in Higher 9. But she visited her there two days and third day when she went there they told her she wasn't there any more. There was no explanation. Nothing. Just she was not there. And I guess my mom, she didn't want to scare me or she just didn't want—and she didn't tell me what happened to my sister.

    * * *

Q. After your release in June of 1978, did you and your mother attempt to ascertain the whereabouts of your sister?

A. Yes.

Q. Did you go to other jails?

A. We filed a complaint to Kebeles to notify us what happened to my sister.

Q. Did you search for her?

A. We searched every prison you can think of, twenty-five higher—all highers and their subzones, and any jail you can think of in the city of Addis, because we didn't want to give up.

Q. Did the Kebeles ever give you an answer as to where your sister was?

A. No, they didn't. What they told us was she's not here any more.

Q. Did you ever get any explanation from anyone in the government?

A. No. That's why I need an explanation from Kelbessa today why it happened.

Q. Can you describe the continuing effects on you of your torture and detention in the years since 1978?

A. How the torture affects my life?

Q. Yes, your detention and the torture?

A. I believe it just changed me completely from where I was before prison, and I become very pessimistic person. What I see, everything so negative. And I feel like the whole world is in—a nightmare to live in this world. And really it didn't make any difference whether to live or to die, and I was in a constant fear.

When I was at home I thought all the things could happen again, but there was nothing to protect me. They put me down to pieces to I could not think my self as a human being again.

NEGEWO CROSS EXAMINATION MAY 17, 2003 TRANSCRIPT PAGES 95–96

Q. You were saying that your father and sister were killed by a security officer?

A. Yes.

Q. Why you claim that I'm responsible for that?

A. You know, I was hoping that you would tell me, but why I was thinking about—I mean why I assume or—I wasn't there but the pattern what the Kebeles do and their responsibility and their jurisdiction is well known. So my sister was taken from the prison where were together to your Kebele. You were a higher chairman for that Kebele. So if she isn't in your office and my mom saw her that day, and the following day she wasn't there, and tell me what's going to happen. I mean what was the situation then? People were executed. People were executed. You didn't see them the next day.

Q.   How did you know that people are executed?

A.   Nobody found her body. That's why I want you to know what happened to my sister. She was executed. That's fifteen years past.

Q.   How did you know?

A.   How did I know? I wasn't there.

Q.   Why do you relate to me?

A.   Because you are responsible. You are our chairman. You were the Higher 9 chairman. Everything passed through you.

Q.   How many people are supposed to be in the Higher 9?

A.   I don't have to know that. That's not my business to know.

Q.   Then you have to know who is responsible for?

A.   I don't work in the Kebeles, really.

Q.   Simply you are assuming that I have to be asking for your father and sister?

A.   I'm not assuming. They were under your—that's my father that was taken from home at night by Kebeles. They addressed themselves to my father. They said we want you for questioning to the Kebele. He didn't even get to the Kebele. They just shot him and kill him on the street, and there are the things that—what the Kebele do, they staple paper on their back and they said we are terror. So you're responsible for that. You were the Higher chairman.

After two days of the plaintiffs' emotional testimony, Judge Ernest Tidwell took the case under submission and several weeks later ruled for the women and awarded them each a judgment of $200,000 in compensatory damages and $300,000 in punitive damages for the torture and cruel, inhuman, and degrading treatment ("CIDT") to which Negewo had subjected them. *Abebe-Jiri v. Negewo*, 1993 WL 814304 (N.D. Ga. 1993). However, the trial court found insufficient evidence and denied relief with respect to the murder of Ms. Demissie's father and the disappearance of Haimanot.

The district court's decisions regarding the extra-judicial execution of Ms. Demissie's father and the disappearance and presumed execution of her sister reveal some of the evidentiary difficulties in ATS litigation. Demissie's father was left on an Addis Ababa street with a sign on his body typical of Red Terror victims, yet plaintiffs were unable to find witnesses to testify to these facts, though they were well known in the community. Similarly, to prove a disappearance, a plaintiff must demonstrate that the victim was in state custody, even if the state later refuses to acknowledge her detention or whereabouts. The plaintiffs could not supply evidence of these elements except through hearsay statements. The Eleventh Circuit affirmed the judgment, *Abebe-Jira v. Negewo*, 72

F.3d 844 (1996), and the Supreme Court denied Negewo's petition for *certiorari.*

The plaintiffs sought to execute their judgment against Negewo and obtained small amounts by garnishing his wages. He was fired from at least two jobs when employers learned about the case. Negewo later filed for bankruptcy to avoid the judgment, but the bankruptcy court found these debts to be non-dischargeable.

At the same time as the trial, unbeknownst to the plaintiffs, Negewo applied for and received American citizenship. Once this was discovered, the plaintiffs asked the INS to initiate denaturalization proceedings, and in the fall of 2004, an order denaturalizing Negewo, was issued. The INS then sought to deport him, and in the fall of 2005 Negewo was detained under the Intelligence Reform and Terrorism Prevention Act, Pub. L. No. 108–458, 118 Stat. 3638 (2004), which provides for the "deportability of aliens who have committed acts of torture or extrajudicial killings abroad," pending his deportation.

Ethiopia long sought Negewo's extradition. He was tried *in absentia* in Ethiopia, but the United States has no extradition treaty with Ethiopia. Moreover, the trials of former regime members in Ethiopia, which have been going on for more than a decade, raise a number of fair trial concerns. What should the United States do with defendants like Negewo? *See* William J. Aceves & Paul L. Hoffman, *Using Immigration Law to Protect Human Rights: A Legislative Proposal*, 20 MICH. J. INT'L L. 657 (1999). Should the United States screen all immigrants to exclude perpetrators of human rights violations? After 1994, it became possible for the United States to bring criminal prosecutions for extraterritorial torture. 18 U.S.C. § 2340A (2000). However, it is likely that, owing to the doctrine against *ex post facto* application of the law, prosecutions under this law will be limited to crimes committed after November 1994. Accordingly, for torturers like Negewo, prosecution in the United States is not an option. In this case, Negewo was deported on October 20, 2006, and is serving a life sentence in Ethiopia.

THE *KADIC* CASE: SUING NON–
STATE ACTORS

In the 1990's, the Bosnian war presented U.S. courts with difficult questions about the application of customary international law to non-state actors and the use of the ATS to remedy violations of the laws of war. The *Kadic* decision was the first to address these issues.

KADIC v. KARADZIC

70 F.3d 232 (2d Cir. 1995)

The plaintiffs-appellants are Croat and Muslim citizens of the internationally recognized nation of Bosnia–Herzegovina, formerly a republic of Yugoslavia. Their complaints, which we accept as true for purposes of this appeal, allege that they are victims, and representatives of victims, of various atrocities, including brutal acts of rape, forced prostitution, forced impregnation, torture, and summary execution, carried out by Bosnian–Serb military forces as part of a genocidal campaign conducted in the course of the Bosnian civil war. Karadzic, formerly a citizen of Yugoslavia and now a citizen of Bosnia–Herzegovina, is the President of a three-man presidency of the self-proclaimed Bosnian–Serb republic within Bosnia–Herzegovina, sometimes referred to as "Srpska," which claims to exercise lawful authority, and does in fact exercise actual control, over large parts of the territory of Bosnia–Herzegovina. In his capacity as President, Karadzic possesses ultimate command authority over the Bosnian–Serb military forces, and the injuries perpetrated upon plaintiffs were committed as part of a pattern of systematic human rights violations that was directed by Karadzic and carried out by the military forces under his command. The complaints allege that Karadzic acted in an official capacity either as the titular head of Srpska or in collaboration with the government of the recognized nation of the former Yugoslavia and its dominant constituent republic, Serbia. * * *

I. SUBJECT-MATTER JURISDICTION

* * * Our decision in *Filartiga* established that [the ATS] confers federal subject-matter jurisdiction when the following three conditions are satisfied: (1) an alien sues (2) for a tort (3) committed in violation of the law of nations (*i.e.*, international law). 630 F.2d at 887. The first two requirements are plainly satisfied here, and the only disputed issue is whether plaintiffs have pleaded violations of international law.

Because the Alien Tort Act requires that plaintiffs plead a "violation of the law of nations" at the jurisdictional threshold, this statute requires a more searching review of the merits to establish jurisdiction than is required under the more flexible "arising under" formula of section 1331. Thus, it is not a sufficient basis for jurisdiction to plead merely a colorable violation of the law of nations. There is no federal subject-matter jurisdiction under the Alien Tort Act unless the complaint adequately pleads a violation of the law of nations (or treaty of the United States).

Filartiga established that courts ascertaining the content of the law of nations "must interpret international law not as it was in 1789, but as it has evolved and exists among the nations of the world today." *Id.* at 881. * * * If this inquiry discloses that the defendant's alleged conduct violates "well-established, universally recognized norms of international law," *Id.* at 888, as opposed to "idiosyncratic legal rules," *id.* at 881, then federal jurisdiction exists under the Alien Tort Act.

Karadzic contends that appellants have not alleged violations of the norms of international law because such norms bind only states and persons acting under color of a state's law, not private individuals. In making this contention, Karadzic advances the contradictory positions that he is not a state actor, even as he asserts that he is the President of the self-proclaimed Republic of Srpska. * * * For their part, the Kadic appellants also take somewhat inconsistent positions in pleading defendant's role as President of Srpska (and also contending that "Karadzic is not an official of any government.") * * *

We do not agree that the law of nations, as understood in the modern era, confines its reach to state action. Instead, we hold that certain forms of conduct violate the law of nations whether undertaken by those acting under the auspices of a state or only as private individuals. An early example of the application of the law of nations to the acts of private individuals is the prohibition against piracy. *See United States v. Smith,* 18 U.S. (5 Wheat.) 153, 161 (1820). * * * Later examples are prohibitions against the slave trade and certain war crimes.

The liability of private persons for certain violations of customary international law and the availability of the Alien Tort Act to remedy such violations was early recognized by the Executive Branch in an opinion of Attorney General Bradford in reference to acts of American citizens aiding the French fleet to plunder British property off the coast of Sierra Leone in 1795. The Executive Branch has emphatically restated in this litigation its position that private persons may be found liable under the Alien Tort Act for acts of genocide, war crimes, and other violations of international humanitarian law. *See Statement of Interest of the United States* at 5–13.

The Restatement (Third) of the Foreign Relations Law of the United States (1986) ("*Restatement (Third)*") proclaims: "Individuals may be held liable for offenses against international law, such as piracy, war crimes, and genocide." The Restatement is careful to identify those violations that are actionable when committed by a state, *Restatement (Third)* § 702, and a more limited category of violations of "universal concern," *id.* § 404, partially overlapping with those listed in section 702. Though the immediate focus of section 404 is to identify those offenses for which a state has jurisdiction to punish without regard to territoriality or the nationality of the offenders, the inclusion of piracy and slave trade from an earlier era and aircraft hijacking from the modern era demonstrates that the offenses of "universal concern" include those capable of being committed by non-state actors. Although the jurisdiction authorized by section 404 is usually exercised by application of criminal law, international law also permits states to establish appropriate civil remedies, *id.* § 404 cmt. b, such as the tort actions authorized by the Alien Tort Act. Indeed, the two cases invoking the Alien Tort Act prior to *Filartiga* both applied the civil remedy to private action. *See Adra v. Clift*, 195 F. Supp. 857 (D. Md. 1961); *Bolchos v. Darrel*, 3 F. Cas. 810, 1 Bee 74 (D.S.C. 1795) (No. 1,607).

Karadzic disputes the application of the law of nations to any violations committed by private individuals, relying on *Filartiga* and the concurring opinion of Judge Edwards in *Tel-Oren* v. *Libyan Arab Republic*, 726 F.2d 774, 775 (D.C. Cir. 1984), *cert. denied*, 470 U.S. 1003 (1985). *Filartiga* involved an allegation of torture committed by a state official. Relying on the United Nations' Declaration on the Protection of All Persons from Being Subjected to Torture as a definitive statement of norms of customary international law prohibiting states from permitting torture, we ruled that *"official* torture is now prohibited by the law of nations." *Filartiga*, 630 F.2d at 884 (emphasis added). We had no occasion to consider whether international law violations other than torture are actionable against private individuals, and nothing in *Filartiga* purports to preclude such a result.

Nor did Judge Edwards in his scholarly opinion in *Tel-Oren* reject the application of international law to any private action. On the contrary, citing piracy and slave-trading as early examples, he observed that there exists a "handful of crimes to which the law of nations attributes individual responsibility," 726 F.2d at 795. Reviewing authorities similar to those consulted in *Filartiga*, he merely concluded that torture—the specific violation alleged in *Tel-Oren*—was not within the limited category of violations that do not require state action.

Karadzic also contends that Congress intended the state-action requirement of the Torture Victim Act to apply to actions under the Alien Tort Act. We disagree. Congress enacted the Torture Victim Act to codify the cause of action recognized by this Circuit in *Filartiga*, and to further extend that cause of action to plaintiffs who are U.S. citizens. *See* H.R. Rep. No. 367, 102d Cong., 2d Sess., at 4 (1991), *reprinted* in 1992 U.S.C.C.A.N. 84, 86 (explaining that codification of *Filartiga* was necessary in light of skepticism expressed by Judge Bork's concurring opinion in *Tel-Oren*). At the same time, Congress indicated that the Alien Tort Act "has other important uses and should not be replaced," because

> claims based on torture and summary executions do not exhaust the list of actions that may appropriately be covered [by the Alien Tort Act]. That statute should remain intact to permit suits based on other norms that already exist or may ripen in the future into rules of customary international law.

Id. The scope of the Alien Tort Act remains undiminished by enactment of the Torture Victim Act.

2. *Specific Application of Alien Tort Act to Appellants' Claims*

In order to determine whether the offenses alleged by the appellants in this litigation are violations of the law of nations that may be the subject of Alien Tort Act claims against a private individual, we must make a particularized examination of these offenses, mindful of the important precept that "evolving standards of international law govern who is within the [Alien Tort Act's] jurisdictional grant." *Amerada Hess*, 830 F.2d at 425. In making that inquiry, it will be helpful to group the appellants' claims into three categories: (a) genocide, (b) war crimes, and (c) other instances of inflicting death, torture, and degrading treatment.

(a) *Genocide.* In the aftermath of the atrocities committed during the Second World War, the condemnation of genocide as contrary to international law quickly achieved broad acceptance by the community of nations. In 1946, the General Assembly of the United Nations declared that genocide is a crime under international law that is condemned by the civilized world, whether the perpetrators are "private individuals, public officials or statesmen." G.A. Res. 96(I), 1 U.N. GAOR, U.N. Doc. A/64/Add.1, at 188–89 (1946). * * *

The Convention on the Prevention and Punishment of the Crime of Genocide, 78 U.N.T.S. 277, *entered into force* Jan. 12, 1951, for the *United States* Feb. 23, 1989 (hereinafter "Convention on Genocide"), provides a more specific articulation of the prohibition of genocide in international law. * * *

Especially pertinent to the pending appeal, the Convention makes clear that "[p]ersons committing genocide . . . shall be punished, whether they are constitutionally responsible rulers, public officials or private individuals." *Id*. art. IV (emphasis added). These authorities unambiguously reflect that, from its incorporation into international law, the proscription of genocide has applied equally to state and non-state actors.

The applicability of this norm to private individuals is also confirmed by the Genocide Convention Implementation Act of 1987, 18 U.S.C. § 1091 (1988), which criminalizes acts of genocide without regard to whether the offender is acting under color of law, *see id.* § 1091(a) ("[w]hoever" commits genocide shall be punished), if the crime is committed within the United States or by a U.S. national, *id.* § 1091(d). Though Congress provided that the Genocide Convention Implementation Act shall not "be construed as creating any substantive or procedural right enforceable by law by any party in any proceeding," *id.* § 1092, the legislative decision not to create a new private remedy does not imply that a private remedy is not already available under the Alien Tort Act. Nothing in the Genocide Convention Implementation Act or its legislative history reveals an intent by Congress to repeal the Alien Tort Act insofar as it applies to genocide, and the two statutes are surely not repugnant to each other. Under these circumstances, it would be improper to construe the Genocide Convention Implementation Act as repealing the Alien Tort Act by implication.

Appellants' allegations that Karadzic personally planned and ordered a campaign of murder, rape, forced impregnation, and other forms of torture designed to destroy the religious and ethnic groups of Bosnian Muslims and Bosnian Croats clearly state a violation of the international law norm proscribing genocide, regardless of whether Karadzic acted under color of law or as a private individual. The District Court has subject-matter jurisdiction over these claims pursuant to the Alien Tort Act.

(b) *War crimes.* Plaintiffs also contend that the acts of murder, rape, torture, and arbitrary detention of civilians, committed in the course of hostilities, violate the law of war. Atrocities of the types alleged here have long been recognized in international law as violations of the law of war. *See In re Yamashita,* 327 U.S. 1, 14 (1946). Moreover, international law imposes an affirmative duty on military commanders to take appropriate measures within their power to control troops under their command for the prevention of such atrocities. *Id.* at 15–16.

After the Second World War, the law of war was codified in the four Geneva Conventions, which have been ratified by more than 180 nations, including the United States. * * * [U]nder the law of war as codified in the Geneva Conventions, all "parties" to a conflict—which includes insurgent military groups—are obliged to adhere to these most fundamental requirements of the law of war.

The offenses alleged by the appellants, if proved, would violate the most fundamental norms of the law of war embodied in common article 3, which binds parties to internal conflicts regardless of whether they are recognized nations or roving hordes of insurgents. The liability of private individuals for committing war crimes has been recognized since World War I and was confirmed at Nuremberg after World War II. * * * The District Court has jurisdiction pursuant to the Alien Tort Act over appellants' claims of war crimes and other violations of international humanitarian law.

NOTES AND QUESTIONS ON KADIC

1. The Torture Victim Protection Act.[5] In 1992, Congress passed the Torture Victim Protection Act ("TVPA"). The TVPA was passed both to overcome any lingering uncertainty about ATS jurisdiction created by Judge Bork's opinion in *Tel-Oren* and to provide U.S. citizens with some of the benefits that aliens already enjoyed under the ATS. The TVPA expressly creates a cause of action for claims of torture and extra-judicial killings committed "under actual or apparent authority, or color of law, of any foreign nation." 28 U.S.C. § 1350 note (2000). Unlike the ATS, the TVPA allows U.S. citizens and non-citizens alike to make such claims. The statute contains explicit provisions governing exhaustion of

---

5. The text of the TVPA and excerpts from the House and Senate reports are in the Document Supplement.

plaintiffs must prove the following elements by a preponderance of the evidence: (1) A superior-subordinate relationship between existed between the defendant and the person or persons who committed torture, extrajudicial killing and/or crimes against humanity. (2) The defendant knew or should have known, in light of the circumstances, at the time that his subordinates had committed, were committing or were about to commit torture, extrajudicial killing and/or crimes against humanity. (3) The third element, the defendant failed to take all necessary and reasonable measures to prevent these abuses or failed to punish the subordinates after the commission of torture, extrajudicial killing and/or crimes against humanity.

Trial Proceedings Before the Honorable Jon Phipps McCalla, 1782–83 (Nov. 14, 2005), *available at* http://www.cja.org/cases/carranranscripts/ carranzatxt.

What differences do you see between the jury instructions in the *Marcos* case and those in the *Carranza* case? Which is more effective for holding defendants liable under a theory of command responsibility?

4. *Aftermath of Kadic.* On remand, the district court held a difficult, lengthy default hearing and entered a judgment of $15 billion for the class members. To date, plaintiffs have been unable to collect this judgment. In July 2008, after avoiding arrest for thirteen years, Karadzic was brought before the International Criminal Tribunal for the Former Yugoslavia.

FROM *FILARTIGA* TO *SOSA*

In the twenty-four years between *Filartiga* and *Sosa*, a substantial body of case law developed under the ATS. In fact, there have been three distinguishable generations of ATS cases. The initial cases in the 1980s typically involved suits against former foreign government officials who resided in or visited the United States. The most prominent cases involved former Argentine General Carlos Suarez–Mason, accused of mass killings and disappearances in that nation's Dirty War, and former President Ferdinand Marcos of the Philippines, accused of command responsibility for widespread torture, disappearances, summary executions, and arbitrary detention during his fourteen-year dictatorship.

In the mid–1990s, a new wave of cases emerged in which plaintiffs sued multinational corporations for complicity in human rights violations. The first and most prominent of these was *Doe v. Unocal*, a case charging the California-based oil company Unocal with complicity in forced labor, torture, rape and other human rights violations that occurred during the construction of a natural gas pipeline in Burma. *Doe v. Unocal Corp.*, 27 F. Supp. 2d. 1174 (C.D. Cal. 1998). By 2006, there were several dozen corporate complicity cases pending in U.S. courts. These cases are considered in the case study later in this module.

Finally, in *Sosa*, plaintiffs sought to use the ATS to hold U.S. officials accountable under international human rights law. The more recent human rights controversies created by the "war on terror" have generated a new generation of ATS cases against federal officials, most of which are still pending as of this writing.

Certain key issues recurred in ATS litigation in the run-up up to the Supreme Court's decision in *Sosa*.[6] Consider whether this case law remains untouched by *Sosa* or whether some or all pre-*Sosa* decisions became subject to challenge once the Supreme Court spoke.

Actionable Claims—One issue in every ATS case is whether the plaintiffs' claims qualify as violations of the "law of nations" within the meaning of the ATS. The most common test that has emerged asks whether the norm asserted was "specific, universal and obligatory." *In re Estate of Ferdinand Marcos (Marcos I)*, 25 F.3d 1467, 1475 (9th Cir. 1994). Over time, the courts have identified a number of claims that are actionable under the ATS: *See, e.g. Marcos I, supra,* 25 F.3d at 1475 (torture); *Kadic,* 70 F.3d at 241 (genocide, war crimes). Other cases have been rejected for not stating claims that were "specific, universal and obligatory." *Flores,* 414 F.3d at 255–66 (environmental claims); *but see Arias v. Dyncorp,* 517 F. Supp. 2d 221 (D.D.C. 2007) (permitting plaintiffs to proceed on their ATS claim for physical harm and property damage arising out of herbicide spraying).

The courts have been divided about the actionability of some claims, notably, cruel, inhuman and degrading treatment or punishment ("CIDT"). *Compare Forti v. Suarez–Mason,* 672 F.Supp. 1531, 1543 (N.D. Cal. 1987) (CIDT is not a sufficiently definite violation of international law), *with Abebe–Jira v. Negewo,* 72 F.3d 844, 845 (11th Cir. 1996) (affirming the lower court's decision that CIDT was actionable under the ATS). In *Xuncax v. Gramajo,* 886 F.Supp. 162, 187 (D. Mass. 1995), the court decided that CIDT claims were actionable under the ATS, but only to the extent that the cruel, inhuman or degrading treatment or punishment would have been domestically prohibited by the Fifth, Eighth and Fourteenth amendments to the United States Constitution. The *Xuncax* decision was premised on the reservations the U.S. has placed on its acceptance of the CIDT norm in human rights treaties it has ratified. Should U.S. endorsement of or resistance to a particular norm have a special bearing on its definition under international law in ATS litigation? Can the United States government block ATS claims by expressing the view that the norms plaintiffs rely on are not customary law?

Choice of Law—Though the early case law was uniform in finding that the ATS provided jurisdiction and a federal cause of action, it was not always clear what law applied to other issues in ATS cases. Choice of law issues arise in every transnational case, and ATS cases are no

---

6. For a more comprehensive treatment of these issues, see BETH STEPHENS, JUDITH CHOMSKY, JENNIFER GREEN, PAUL HOFFMAN & MICHAEL RATNER, INTERNATIONAL HUMAN RIGHTS LITIGATION IN U.S. COURTS, SECOND EDITION (2008).

exception. In *Filartiga*, the district court imposed punitive damages to further the purpose of the ATS, despite the fact that such damages were prohibited under Paraguayan law. *Filartiga v. Peña-Irala*, 577 F.Supp. 860, 866 (E.D.N.Y. 1984). In *Marcos*, after Ferdinand Marcos' death, the court applied Philippine law to allow the award of exemplary damages against an estate instead of the prevailing U.S. view that would have prohibited them. *Hilao v. Estate of Marcos*, 103 F.3d 767, 780 (9th Cir. 1996). This led to a $1.2 billion award of exemplary damages. Similar questions arise in the context of determining who has standing to sue under the ATS. *Cabello v. Fernandez–Larios*, 402 F.3d 1148 (11th Cir. 2005). What damages are available in ATS cases? Should the law of the state where the injury occurred provide the rules for executing "the law of nations" under the ATS? Should it make a difference if the nation is a "failed state" or if the regime involved does not enforce the law itself?

Statutes of Limitations—The ATS provides no statute of limitations. In early cases, the courts adopted the statute of limitations for domestic civil rights actions under 42 U.S.C. § 1983. *See Forti v. Suarez–Mason*, 672 F.Supp. 1531, 1547 (N.D. Cal. 1987). Following the passage of the Torture Victim Protection Act ("TVPA") in 1992, courts began to adopt that statute of limitations. In *Papa v. United States*, 281 F.3d 1004, 1012 (9th Cir. 2002), the Ninth Circuit adopted the ten-year statute of limitations in the TVPA (discussed *supra*), as opposed to the more restrictive state-law statute of limitations.

Statutes of limitations are often subject to equitable tolling provisions. The same is true in ATS and TVPA cases if "extraordinary circumstances" exist. *See Jean v. Dorelien*, 431 F.3d 776 (11th Cir. 2005) (suit against Haitian military official allowed to proceed, because the statute was tolled while the defendant was in power.) In *Arce v. Garcia*, 434 F.3d 1254 (11th Cir. 2006), the Eleventh Circuit upheld two tolling arguments: (1) that the ten-year statute of limitations did not begin to run until the defendants, Salvadoran generals who were former Ministers of Defense, had entered the U.S., and (2) that the limitations period could be further tolled for "extraordinary circumstances," because, even though both the plaintiffs and defendants resided in the U.S., the plaintiffs nevertheless legitimately feared retribution should they file an ATS case: the regime to which the defendants belonged remained in power and had intimidated witnesses. Only at the conclusion of the Salvadoran civil war would the statute of limitations begin to run. *Id.* at 1264–65. *See also Cabello v. Fernandez–Larios*, 402 F.3d 1148, 1155 (11th Cir. 2005) (for claims against a Chilean military officer, the statute of limitations was tolled until the first post-junta President was elected in 1990).

There is no statute of limitations for criminal prosecution of crimes against humanity. Should there be a statute of limitations for civil liability for equally serious human rights violations under the ATS? *See Handel v. Artukovic*, 601 F.Supp. 1421 (C.D. Cal. 1985).

Doctrines of Abstention and Immunity—In the early days of ATS litigation, important issues arose in the context of abstention doctrines which defendants claimed as a basis for the dismissal of ATS actions. The disposition of these defendants' arguments shows that the absention doctrines are intensely fact-dependent.

Act of State Doctrine—The "act of state" doctrine is a judicially-created means of maintaining the separation of powers by preventing the courts from sitting in judgment of the sovereign acts of foreign governments within their own territory. The Supreme Court, in *Banco Nacional de Cuba v. Sabbatino*, 376 U.S. 398 (1964), stated:

> "[T]he Judicial Branch will not examine the validity of a taking of property within its own territory by a foreign sovereign government, extant and recognized by this country at the time of suit, in the absence of a treaty or other unambiguous agreement regarding controlling legal principles, even if the complaint alleges that the taking violates customary international law."

Id. at 428.

In the period from *Filartiga* to *Sosa,* few claims were dismissed based upon the act of state doctrine. For the most part, the courts reasoned that acts of torture and other egregious human rights violations were not sovereign or public acts that were entitled to deference by the federal courts. The *Marcos* cases were initially dismissed based upon the act of state doctrine in 1986, but the Ninth Circuit reversed in a 1989 unpublished decision. *Hilao v. Marcos*, 878 F.2d 1438 (Table) (9th Cir. 1989); *see also Kadic*, 70 F.3d at 250 (finding that there is no act of state where an official's conduct violated the foreign state's fundamental laws and was "wholly unratified by that nation's government"). These decisions reflected a more general retreat from the application of the doctrine in transnational litigation. *See W.S. Kirkpatrick & Co., Inc. v. Environmental Tectonics Corp.*, 493 U.S. 400 (1990).

In *Doe v. Qi*, 349 F. Supp. 2d 1258 (N.D. Cal. 2004), plaintiffs, supporters of Falun Gong, a religion outlawed by the Chinese government, brought suit against local government officials in China for torture, CIDT and arbitrary detention. The court in *Qi* determined that "the evidence establishe[d] that the Defendants' alleged conduct was not 'wholly unratified' by the PRC. It was pursuant to policy and therefore constituted acts of state." *Id*. at 1295. Should it matter whether the Chinese government ratified acts of torture? Is that a defense or an essential element of the plaintiffs' claims?

Political question doctrine—The political question doctrine mandates that district courts decline to accept jurisdiction over a case involving issues constitutionally assigned to the political branches. *Baker v. Carr*, 369 U.S. 186 (1962). In determining whether a suit implicates a political question, courts typically look to various *Baker v. Carr* factors: (1) whether there is a textually demonstrable constitutional commitment of the issue to a coordinate branch of government; (2) whether there are judicially discoverable and manageable standards for resolving the claims; (3) whether the case is impossible to decide without an initial policy determination of a kind clearly for non-judicial discretion; (4) whether the court can undertake independent resolution of the case without expressing a lack of the respect due coordinate branches of government; (5) whether there exists an unusual need for unquestioning adherence to a political decision already made; or (6) whether there is the potential for embarrassment from multifarious pronouncements by various departments on one question. *Id.* at 217.

Until recently, the political question doctrine was not a substantial barrier to ATS cases despite Judge Robb's concurrence in the *Tel-Oren* case, discussed above. However, the D.C. Circuit has recently dismissed several cases against the federal government and its agents on the basis of the political question doctrine. *See, e.g., Harbury v. Hayden*, 522 F.3d 413 (D.C. Cir. 2008) (dismissing TVPA claim alleging that CIA agents tortured and killed a Guatemalan rebel fighter, because it would require the court to examine the wisdom of underlying policies); *Gonzalez-Vera v. Kissinger*, 449 F.3d 1260 (D.C. Cir. 2006) (dismissing ATS claim against United States for funding, assisting, aiding, and abetting the Pinochet government, because it would require examination of foreign policy decisions in Chile) *Bancoult v. McNamara*, 445 F.3d 427 (D.C. Cir. 2006) (dismissing ATS claim against the United States for forcibly removing island residents from their homes to build a military base because tactical measures used to depopulate the island are inextricably intertwined with underlying policy to create the base).

In some instances, the political question doctrine may pose a barrier to ATS suits against private corporations when a foreign policy interest of the United States is at issue. In *Corrie v. Caterpillar, Inc.*, 503 F.3d 974 (9th Cir. 2007), Palestinian Territories residents brought an ATS action against Caterpillar for manufacturing the bulldozers that Israeli Defense forces used to demolish their homes. The Ninth Circuit held that the political question doctrine barred the action, because deciding the case required looking beyond Caterpillar at whether the executive branch financed the sales as part of its military aid to Israel.

Courts may also consider whether a case involves a political question when the Executive branch submits a Statement of Interest (SOI) in a case to which it is not a party. In *Sarei v. Rio Tinto PLC*, 221 F. Supp. 2d 1116 (C.D. Cal. 2002), a district court dismissed a case against an international mining company based on a SOI submitted by the State Department indicating that the case would interfere with U.S. efforts to facilitate the ongoing peace process in Papua New Guinea. *Id.* at 1209. A three-panel judge reversed, reasoning that the case only touched upon foreign relations. *Sarei v. Rio Tinto, PLC*, 487 F.3d 1193 (9th Cir. 2007). The Ninth Circuit reheard the case en *banc in* October 2007, and a decision was pending when this book went to print.

Immunities—The courts have recognized other immunities as a bar to ATS claims. These include head of state immunity, *Tachiona v. Mugabe*, 169 F. Supp. 2d 259 (S.D.N.Y. 2001) (granting immunity to the sitting president of Zimbabwe); *Alicog v. Kingdom of Saudi Arabia*, 860 F.Supp. 379 (S.D. Tex. 1994) (granting immunity to the King of Saudi Arabia); diplomatic immunity, *Aidi v. Yaron*, 672 F.Supp. 516 (D.D.C. 1987) (granting immunity in a tort action to a diplomat who was accused of participating in massacres in Lebanon's refugee camps); *Tabion v. Mufti*, 73 F.3d 535 (4th Cir. 1996) (granting immunity to a diplomat in a contract dispute with his domestic servant). However, the courts have not recognized an immunity for former heads of state. *Marcos I*, 25 F.3d at 1472.

Forum Non Conveniens—Even where a district court determines that it has jurisdiction over a claim, the court may decline to exercise that jurisdiction if a more convenient forum is available. In deciding whether to dismiss a case on this ground, a court must (1) determine whether there is an adequate alternative forum to try the matter in another jurisdiction, and (2) if so, which forum will best serve public and private interests. *Aguinda v. Texaco, Inc.*, 303 F.3d 470, 476 (2d Cir. 2002). A resident U.S. plaintiff's choice of a U.S. forum is given great weight, and the burden is on the defendant to establish that the alternative forum is adequate. *Wiwa v. Royal Dutch Petroleum Co.*, 226 F.3d 88, 100–01 (2d Cir. 2000). Because of this preference, ATS cases involving foreign plaintiffs suing foreign defendants for harms occurring in a foreign country face the highest risk of a *forum non conveniens* dismissal. A foreign forum is generally considered adequate if the defendants are amenable to suit there, but there may be an exception if the plaintiff is highly unlikely to obtain justice because of conditions in the country. For example, in *Licea v. Curacao Drydock Co.*, 537 F. Supp. 2d 1270 (S.D. Fla. 2008), the court held that Curacao was an inadequate forum because plaintiffs were Cuban nationals that had been trafficked into the country by the defendant and fled the country at risk to their lives, eventually obtaining political asylum in the United States.

In ATS corporate cases, defendants frequently raise *forum non conveniens* arguments. *See, e.g., Aguinda v. Texaco, Inc.*, 303 F.3d 470 (2d Cir. 2002); *Wiva v. Royal Dutch Petroleum Co.*, 226 F.3d 88 (2d Cir. 2000). *Forum non conveniens* arguments have rarely been successful in ATS cases, the exception being *Aguinda*, which was transferred to Ecuadorian courts where it is still pending.

THE *SOSA* CASE

From 1980 to 2004, the Supreme Court declined to review nearly a dozen ATS cases decided by the courts of appeal. Although there was considerable uniformity of opinion among the appellate courts, it was only a matter of time before the Supreme Court would accept an ATS case and interpret the statute for the first time.

The *Sosa* case arose from an *en banc* decision in the Ninth Circuit in *Alvarez-Machain v. United States*, 331 F.3d 604 (9th Cir. 2003). The *Alvarez* case had a long and tangled history. The case arose from the 1985 torture and murder of Drug Enforcement Agency ("DEA") agent Enrique Camarena in Guadalajara, Mexico, by members of a drug cartel. After Agent Camarena's body was discovered, the United States government understandably sought to bring all those responsible for this crime to justice, preferably in the United States. The DEA launched Operation Leyenda for this purpose. In the 1980s, many of those responsible for Camarena's torture and execution were brought to justice in the United States or were convicted and imprisoned in Mexico.

One of the suspects who initially avoided apprehension was Dr. Humberto Alvarez–Machain. The United States alleged that Dr. Alvarez injected Camarena with a drug to keep him alive during his torture so that cartel members could determine the extent of Camarena's knowledge of the activities of the cartel. According to the U.S. government, it made informal attempts to arrange for Dr. Alvarez's informal rendition to the U.S., but these efforts failed. In early 1990, a Los Angeles-based grand jury indicted Dr. Alvarez for Agent Camarena's murder. An arrest warrant was issued by a federal district judge; however, this only authorized Alvarez's arrest within the territory of the United States.

On April 1, 1990, former police officers hired by the DEA and other Mexican nationals abducted Dr. Alvarez from his medical office in Guadalajara and hid him in a hotel in a nearby city overnight. The next morning, they flew him in a private plane to El Paso, Texas, where he was handed over to waiting DEA agents. Mexico formally protested Dr. Alvarez's abduction immediately and issued formal requests for the extradition of the DEA officials (Hector Berrellez and Antonio Garate–Bustamonte) responsible for the abduction.

Dr. Alvarez's appointed criminal defense lawyer filed a motion to dismiss the criminal charges against him, arguing, *inter alia*, that his abduction violated the U.S.-Mexico Extradition Treaty. The district judge granted this motion, though he found Dr. Alvarez's claims of mistreatment during the abduction unconvincing. *See United States v. Caro–Quintero*, 745 F.Supp. 599 (C.D. Cal. 1990). The Ninth Circuit affirmed. *United States v. Alvarez–Machain*, 946 F.2d 1466 (9th Cir. 1991). The U.S. Supreme Court reversed this decision, finding that the Extradition Treaty did not explicitly bar abductions and declining to read the treaty in the broad context of customary norms prohibiting one country from exercising law enforcement jurisdiction in the territory of another without the latter's consent. *United States v. Alvarez–Machain*, 504 U.S. 655 (1992).

Dr. Alvarez went to trial in November 1992 and, after the prosecution rested its case, the district judge granted a motion for acquittal under Rule 29 of the Federal Rules of Criminal Procedure, finding that the prosecution's cases was based on mere "speculation" and "wild hunches" and not on sufficient evidence. Dr. Alvarez was returned to Mexico that evening.

In 1993, Dr. Alvarez filed a civil suit under the ATS and the Federal Tort Claims Act ("FTCA"), seeking damages against the United States as well as all of the DEA officials and Mexican nationals involved in his abduction. Because Dr. Alvarez was suing the United States, he had to bring claims under the FTCA, as it is (with limited exceptions) the sole basis on which to bring tort claims against federal officials.[7] After interlocutory appeals, *Alvarez–Machain v. United States*, 107 F.3d 696 (9th Cir. 1996), and years of discovery, Dr. Alvarez prevailed against one of the Mexican nationals, Francisco Sosa, based on the ATS for arbitrary arrest and detention in violation of international human rights law and for the violation of Mexican sovereignty represented by the entire abduction operation. *Alvarez-Machain v. United States,* No. CV 93–4072 SVW, 1999 U.S. Dist. LEXIS 23304 (C.D. Cal. Mar. 18, 1999.) *Alvarez-Machain v. United States*, 331 F.3d 604, 631 (9th Cir. 2003). At the trial on damages, the district judge awarded him $25,000 in damages for the abduction. Because of the valid federal arrest warrant, the district judge cut off Dr. Alvarez's damages at the moment he was handed over to DEA agents in El Paso on April 2, 1990, and rejected the argument that Dr. Alvarez's detention actually lasted for 20 months until his release on December 14, 1992, making it a prolonged arbitrary detention in violation of international law. He was awarded damages for the less than 24 hours between his seizure and his arrest in El Paso the following day. *Id.*

In the Ninth Circuit, Sosa appealed from the $25,000 judgment against him, and Dr. Alvarez appealed the dismissal of the claims against the United States under the FTCA. On September 11, 2001, a panel of the Ninth Circuit affirmed the judgment against Sosa but reversed the summary judgment decision with respect to the United States, finding, based on the "headquarters doctrine," that the United States could be sued under the FTCA notwithstanding the exception for claims arising in foreign countries. The court found that since DEA officials had controlled the abduction operation from U.S. territory, the foreign country exception did not apply. *Alvarez–Machain v. United States*, 266 F.3d 1045 (9th Cir. 2001).

The Ninth Circuit reheard this decision *en banc* and, in June 2003, affirmed the judgment against Sosa by a 6–5 vote. *Alvarez–Machain v. United States*, 331 F.3d 604 (9th Cir. 2003). The panel found that Dr. Alvarez lacked standing to assert Mexico's sovereign claims relating to the abduction, *id.* at 616–17, but agreed that the abduction had violated his right to be free from arbitrary arrest and detention. The *en banc* panel also affirmed the decision in Dr. Alvarez's favor under the FTCA.

---

7. *See generally*, CIVIL ACTIONS AGAINST THE UNITED STATES, ITS AGENCIES, OFFICERS, AND EMPLOYEES, TRIAL PRACTICE SERIES (Jon L. Craig ed. 2002).

The court rejected the argument that the DEA's authorizing statute permitted the agency to conduct extraterritorial seizures, in part relying on Dr. Alvarez's argument that the statute had to be read in light of the customary law prohibition on extraterritorial law enforcement operations conducted without the consent of the territorial state. *Id.* at 629.

The stage was set for review by the Supreme Court. By this time, different interest groups began to see the potentially expansive implications of ATS ligation. The corporate community had the ATS on its radar screen because of cases like *Doe v. Unocal,* which had alleged corporate responsibility and liability for human rights violations associated with the building of an oil pipeline in Burma (Myanmar). ATS litigation also implicated the interests of the executive in prosecuting the "war on terror." Indeed, the United States, in its *amicus* brief, urged the court to take a restrictive view of the ATS to prevent the courts from impinging on the foreign policy prerogatives of the executive. The question of whether the United States could abduct Al Qaeda operatives or Osama Bin Laden himself was just below the surface of the case as it came before the Court in March 2004. Thus, the *Alvarez* case became enmeshed not only in the war on terror, but also in the debate about corporate accountability for complicity in human rights violations abroad.[8]

SOSA v. ALVAREZ–MACHAIN

542 U.S. 692 (2004)

JUSTICE SOUTER delivered the opinion of the Court.

The two issues are whether respondent Alvarez–Machain's allegation that the Drug Enforcement Administration instigated his abduction from Mexico for criminal trial in the United States supports a claim against the Government under the Federal Tort Claims Act (FTCA or Act), 28 U.S.C. § 1346(b)(1), §§ 2671–2680, and whether he may recover under the Alien Tort Statute (ATS), 28 U.S.C. § 1350. We hold that he is not entitled to a remedy under either statute. * * *

III

Alvarez has * * * brought an action under the ATS against petitioner, Sosa, who argues (as does the United States supporting him) that there is no relief under the ATS because the statute does no more than vest federal courts with jurisdiction, neither creating nor authorizing the courts to recognize any particular right of action without further congressional action. Although we agree the statute is in terms only jurisdictional, we think that at the time of enactment the jurisdiction enabled

---

8. Briefs available at http://sdshh.com/Unocal/index.html. *See generally* Ralph G. Steinhardt, *Laying One Bankrupt Critique to Rest: Sosa v. Alvarez–Machain and the Future of International Human Rights Litigation in U.S. Courts,* 57 VAND. L. REV. 2241 (2004).

federal courts to hear claims in a very limited category defined by the law of nations and recognized at common law. We do not believe, however, that the limited, implicit sanction to entertain the handful of international law *cum* common law claims understood in 1789 should be taken as authority to recognize the right of action asserted by Alvarez here.

A

Judge Friendly called the ATS a "legal Lohengrin," *IIT v. Vencap, Ltd.*, 519 F.2d 1001, 1015 (C.A. 2 1975); "no one seems to know whence it came," *ibid.*, and for over 170 years after its enactment it provided jurisdiction in only one case. The first Congress passed it as part of the Judiciary Act of 1789, in providing that the new federal district courts "shall also have cognizance, concurrent with the courts of the several States, or the circuit courts, as the case may be, of all causes where an alien sues for a tort only in violation of the law of nations or a treaty of the United States." Act of Sept. 24, 1789, ch. 20, § 9(b), 1 Stat. 79.

The parties and *amici* here advance radically different historical interpretations of this terse provision. Alvarez says that the ATS was intended not simply as a jurisdictional grant, but as authority for the creation of a new cause of action for torts in violation of international law. We think that reading is implausible. As enacted in 1789, the ATS gave the district courts "cognizance" of certain causes of action, and the term bespoke a grant of jurisdiction, not power to mold substantive law. The fact that the ATS was placed in § 9 of the Judiciary Act, a statute otherwise exclusively concerned with federal-court jurisdiction, is itself support for its strictly jurisdictional nature. Nor would the distinction between jurisdiction and cause of action have been elided by the drafters of the Act or those who voted on it. * * * In sum, we think the statute was intended as jurisdictional in the sense of addressing the power of the courts to entertain cases concerned with a certain subject.

But holding the ATS jurisdictional raises a new question, this one about the interaction between the ATS at the time of its enactment and the ambient law of the era. Sosa would have it that the ATS was stillborn because there could be no claim for relief without a further statute expressly authorizing adoption of causes of action. *Amici* professors of federal jurisdiction and legal history take a different tack, that federal courts could entertain claims once the jurisdictional grant was on the books, because torts in violation of the law of nations would have been recognized within the common law of the time. We think history and practice give the edge to this latter position.

1

"When the *United States* declared their independence, they were bound to receive the law of nations, in its modern state of purity and refinement." *Ware v. Hylton*, 3 Dall. 199, 281 (1796) (Wilson, J.). In the years of the early Republic, this law of nations comprised two principal elements, the first covering the general norms governing the behavior of national states with each other: *"the science which teaches the rights subsisting between nations or states, and the obligations correspondent to those rights,"* E. de Vattel, The Law of Nations, Preliminaries § 3 (J. Chitty et al. transl. and ed. 1883), or "that code of public instruction which defines the rights and prescribes the duties of nations, in their intercourse with each other," 1 J. Kent Commentaries on American Law *1. This aspect of the law of nations thus occupied the executive and legislative domains, not the judicial. *See* 4 W. Blackstone, Commentaries on the Laws of England 68 (1769) (hereinafter Commentaries).

The law of nations included a second, more pedestrian element, however, that did fall within the judicial sphere, as a body of judge-made law regulating the conduct of individuals situated outside domestic boundaries and consequently carrying an international savor. To Blackstone, the law of nations in this sense was implicated "in mercantile questions, such as bills of exchange and the like; in all marine causes, relating to freight, average, demurrage, insurances, bottomry . . .; [and] in all disputes relating to prizes, to shipwrecks, to hostages, and ransom bills." *Id.*, at 67. The law merchant emerged from the customary practices of international traders and admiralty required its own transnational regulation. And it was the law of nations in this sense that our precursors spoke about when the Court explained [that] the status of coast fishing vessels in wartime grew from "ancient usage among civilized nations, beginning centuries ago, and gradually ripening into a rule of international law. . . ." *The Paquete Habana*, 175 U.S. 677, 686 (1900).

There was, finally, a sphere in which these rules binding individuals for the benefit of other individuals overlapped with the norms of state relationships. Blackstone referred to it when he mentioned three specific offenses against the law of nations addressed by the criminal law of England: violation of safe conducts, infringement of the rights of ambassadors, and piracy. 4 Commentaries 68. An assault against an ambassador, for example, impinged upon the sovereignty of the foreign nation and if not adequately redressed could rise to an issue of war. *See* Vattel 463–464. It was this narrow set of violations of the law of nations, admitting of a judicial remedy and at the same time threatening serious consequences in international affairs, that was probably on minds of the men who drafted the ATS with its reference to tort.

2

Before there was any ATS, a distinctly American preoccupation with these hybrid international norms had taken shape owing to the distribution of political power from independence through the period of confederation. The Continental Congress was hamstrung by its inability to "cause infractions of treaties, or of the law of nations to be punished" and in 1781 the Congress implored the States to vindicate rights under the law of nations. In words that echo Blackstone, the congressional resolution called upon state legislatures to "provide expeditious, exemplary, and adequate punishment" for "the violation of safe conducts or passports, ... of hostility against such as are in amity... with the United States, ... infractions of the immunities of ambassadors and other public ministers ... [and] 'infractions of treaties and conventions to which the United States are a party.' " The resolution recommended that the States "authorise suits ... for damages by the party injured, and for compensation to the United States for damage sustained by them from an injury done to a foreign power by a citizen." ... Apparently only one State [Connecticut] acted upon the recommendation, *see* Public Records of the State of Connecticut, 1782, pp. 82, 83 (L. Larabee ed. 1982) (1942 compilation, exact date of Act unknown), but Congress had done what it could to signal a commitment to enforce the law of nations.

Appreciation of the Continental Congress' incapacity to deal with this class of cases was intensified by the so-called Marbois incident of May 1784, in which a French adventurer, DeLongchamps, verbally and physically assaulted the Secretary of the French Legion in Philadelphia. *See Respublica v. De Longchamps*, 1 Dall. 111 (O. T. Phila. 1784). Congress called again for state legislation addressing such matters, and concern over the inadequate vindication of the law of nations persisted through the time of the Constitutional Convention. * * *

The Framers responded by vesting the Supreme Court with original jurisdiction over "all Cases affecting Ambassadors, other public ministers and Consuls." U.S. Const., Art. III, § 2, and the First Congress followed through. The Judiciary Act reinforced this Court's original jurisdiction over suits brought by diplomats, *see* 1 Stat. 80, ch. 20, § 13, created alienage jurisdiction, § 11 and, of course, included the ATS, § 9.

3

Although Congress modified the draft of what became the Judiciary Act, it made hardly any changes to the provisions on aliens, including what became the ATS. There is no record of congressional discussion about private actions that might be subject to the jurisdictional provision, or about any need for further legislation to create private remedies; there is no record even of debate on the section. Given the poverty of drafting history, modern commentators have necessarily concentrated on the text, remarking on the innovative use of the word "tort." The historical scholarship has also placed the ATS within the competition between federalist and antifederalist forces over the national role in foreign relations. But despite considerable scholarly attention, it is fair to say that a consensus understanding of what Congress intended has proven elusive.

Still, the history does tend to support two propositions. First, there is every reason to suppose that the First Congress did not pass the ATS as a jurisdictional convenience to be placed on the shelf for use by a future Congress or state legislature that might, some day, authorize the creation of causes of action or itself decide to make some element of the law of nations actionable for the benefit of foreigners. The anxieties of the preconstitutional period cannot be ignored easily enough to think that the statute was not meant to have a practical effect. Consider that the principal draftsman of the ATS was apparently Oliver Ellsworth, previously a member of the Continental Congress that had passed the 1781 resolution and a member of the Connecticut Legislature that made good on that congressional request. Consider, too, that the First Congress was attentive enough to the law of nations to recognize certain offenses expressly as criminal, including the three mentioned by Blackstone. It would have been passing strange for Ellsworth and this very Congress to vest federal courts expressly with jurisdiction to entertain civil causes brought by aliens alleging violations of the law of nations, but to no effect whatever until the Congress should take further action. There is too much in the historical record to believe that Congress would have enacted the ATS only to leave it lying fallow indefinitely.

The second inference to be drawn from the history is that Congress intended the ATS to furnish jurisdiction for a relatively modest set of actions alleging violations of the law of nations. Uppermost in the legislative mind appears to have been offenses against ambassadors; violations of safe conduct were probably understood to be actionable, and individual actions arising out of prize captures and piracy may well have also been contemplated. But the common law appears to have understood only those three of the hybrid variety as definite and actionable, or at any rate, to have assumed only a very limited set of claims. As Blackstone had put it, "offences against this law [of nations] are principally incident to whole states or nations," and not individuals seeking relief in court.

4

The sparse contemporaneous cases and legal materials referring to the ATS tend to confirm both inferences, that some, but few, torts in violation of the law of nations were understood to be within the common law. * * *

Then there was the 1795 opinion of Attorney General William Bradford, who was asked whether criminal prosecution was available against Americans who had taken part in the French plunder of a British slave colony in Sierra Leone. 1 Op. Atty. Gen. 57. Bradford was uncertain, but he made it clear that a federal court was open for the prosecution of a tort action growing out of the episode:

> But there can be no doubt that the company or individuals who have been injured by these acts of hostility have a remedy by a civil suit in the courts of the United States; jurisdiction being expressly given to these courts in all cases where an alien sues for a tort only, in violation of the laws of nations, or a treaty of the United States. . . .

Although it is conceivable that Bradford (who had prosecuted in the Marbois incident) assumed that there had been a violation of a treaty, that is certainly not obvious, and it appears likely that Bradford understood the ATS to provide jurisdiction over what must have amounted to common law causes of action.

B

Against these indications that the ATS was meant to underwrite litigation of a narrow set of common law actions derived from the law of nations, Sosa raises two main objections. First, he claims that this conclusion makes no sense in view of the Continental Congress' 1781 recommendation to state legislatures to pass laws authorizing such suits. Sosa thinks state legislation would have been "absurd," if common law remedies had been available. Second, Sosa juxtaposes Blackstone's treatise mentioning violations of the law of nations as occasions for criminal remedies, against the statute's innovative reference to "tort," as evidence that there was no familiar set of legal actions for exercise of jurisdiction under the ATS. Neither argument is convincing.

The notion that it would have been absurd for the Continental Congress to recommend that States pass positive law to duplicate remedies already available at common law rests on a misunderstanding of the relationship between common law and positive law in the late 18th century, when positive law was frequently relied upon to reinforce and give standard expression to the "brooding omnipresence" of the common law then thought discoverable by reason. As Blackstone clarified the relation between positive law and the law of nations, "those acts of parliament, which have from time to time been made to enforce this universal law, or to facilitate the execution of [its] decisions, are not to be considered as introductive of any new rule, but merely as declaratory of the old fundamental constitutions of the kingdom; without which it must cease to be a part of the civilized world." 4 Commentaries 67. Indeed, Sosa's argument is undermined by the 1781 resolution on which he principally relies. Notwithstanding the undisputed fact (per Blackstone) that the common law afforded criminal law remedies for violations of the law of nations, the Continental Congress encouraged state legislatures to pass criminal statutes to the same effect, and the first Congress did the same, *supra*, at [79–80].

Nor are we convinced by Sosa's argument that legislation conferring a right of action is needed because Blackstone treated international law offenses under the rubric of "public wrongs," whereas the ATS uses a word, "tort," that was relatively uncommon in the legal vernacular of the day. It is true that Blackstone did refer to what he deemed the three principal offenses against the law of nations in the course of discussing criminal sanctions, observing that it was in the interest of sovereigns "to animadvert upon them with a becoming severity, that the peace of the world may be maintained," 4 Commentaries 68. But Vattel explicitly linked the criminal sanction for offenses against ambassadors with the requirement that the state, "at the expense of the delinquent, give full satisfaction to the sovereign who has been offended in the person of his minister." Vattel 463–464. The 1781 resolution goes a step further in showing that a private remedy was thought necessary for diplomatic offenses under the law of nations. And the Attorney General's Letter of 1795, as well as the two early federal precedents discussing the ATS, point to a prevalent assumption that Congress did not intend the ATS to sit on the shelf until some future time when it might enact further legislation.

In sum, although the ATS is a jurisdictional statute creating no new causes of action, the reasonable inference from the historical materials is that the statute was intended to have practical effect the moment it became law. The jurisdictional grant is best read as having been enacted on the understanding that the common law would provide a cause of action for the modest number of international law violations with a potential for personal liability at the time.

IV

We think it is correct, then, to assume that the First Congress understood that the district courts would recognize private causes of action for certain torts in violation of the law of nations, though we have found no basis to suspect Congress had any examples in mind beyond those torts corresponding to Blackstone's three primary offenses: violation of safe conducts, infringement of the rights of ambassadors, and piracy. We assume, too, that no development in the two centuries from the enactment of § 1350 to the birth of the modern line of cases beginning with *Filartiga v. Peña-Irala*, 630 F.2d 876 (C.A.2 1980), has categorically precluded federal courts from recognizing a claim under the law of nations as an element of common law; Congress has not in any relevant way amended § 1350 or limited civil common law power by another statute. Still, there are good reasons for a restrained conception of the discretion a federal court should exercise in considering a new cause of action of this kind. Accordingly, we think courts should require any claim based on the present-day law of nations to rest on a norm of international character accepted by the civilized world and defined with a specificity comparable to the features of the 18th-century paradigms we have recognized. This requirement is fatal to Alvarez's claim.

A

A series of reasons argue for judicial caution when considering the kinds of individual claims that might implement the jurisdiction conferred by the early statute. First, the prevailing conception of the common law has changed since 1789 in a way that counsels restraint in judicially applying internationally generated norms. When § 1350 was enacted, the accepted conception was of the common law as "a transcendental body of law outside of any particular State but obligatory within it unless and until changed by statute." *Black and White Taxicab & Transfer Co. v. Brown and Yellow Taxicab & Transfer Co.*, 276 U.S. 518, 533 (1928) (Holmes, J., dissenting). Now, however, in most cases where a court is asked to state or formulate a common law principle in a new context, there is a general understanding that the law is not so much found or discovered as it is either made or created. * * *

Second, along with, and in part driven by, that conceptual development in understanding common law has come an equally significant rethinking of the role of the federal courts in making it. *Erie R. Co. v. Tompkins*, 304 U.S. 64 (1938), was the watershed in which we denied the existence of any federal "general" common law, *id.*, at 78, which largely withdrew to havens of specialty, some of them defined by express congressional authorization to devise a body of law directly, *e.g.*, *Textile Workers v. Lincoln Mills of Ala.*, 353 U.S. 448 (1957) (interpretation of collective-bargaining agreements). Elsewhere, this Court has thought it was in order to create federal common law rules in interstitial areas of particular federal interest. And although we have even assumed competence to make judicial rules of decision of particular importance to foreign relations, such as the act of state doctrine, see *Banco Nacional de Cuba v. Sabbatino*, 376 U.S. 398, 427 (1964), the general practice has been to look for legislative guidance before exercising innovative authority over substantive law. It would be remarkable to take a more aggressive role in exercising a jurisdiction that remained largely in shadow for much of the prior two centuries.

Third, this Court has recently and repeatedly said that a decision to create a private right of action is one better left to legislative judgment in the great majority of cases. *Correctional Services Corp. v. Malesko*, 534 U.S. 61, 68 (2001). The creation of a private right of action raises issues beyond the mere consideration whether underlying primary conduct should be allowed or not, entailing, for example, a decision to permit enforcement without the check imposed by prosecutorial discretion. Accordingly, even when Congress has made it clear by statute that a rule applies to purely domestic conduct, we are reluctant to infer intent to provide a private cause of action where the statute does not supply one expressly. While the absence of congressional action addressing private rights of action under an international norm is more equivocal than its failure to provide such a right when it creates a statute, the possible collateral consequences of making international rules privately actionable argue for judicial caution.

Fourth, the subject of those collateral consequences is itself a reason for a high bar to new private causes of action for violating international law, for the potential implications for the foreign relations of the United States of recognizing such causes should make courts particularly wary of impinging on the discretion of the Legislative and Executive Branches in managing foreign affairs. It is one thing for American courts to enforce constitutional limits on our own State and Federal Governments' power, but quite another to consider suits under rules that would go so far as to claim a limit on the power of foreign governments over their own citizens, and to hold that a foreign government or its agent has transgressed those limits. *Cf. Sabbatino, supra,* at 431–432. Yet modern international law is very much concerned with just such questions, and apt to stimulate calls for vindicating private interests in § 1350 cases. Since many attempts by federal courts to craft remedies for the violation of new norms of international law would raise risks of adverse foreign policy consequences, they should be undertaken, if at all, with great caution. Cf. *Tel-Oren v. Libyan Arab Republic,* 726 F.2d 774, 813 (C.A.D.C. 1984) (Bork, J., concurring) (expressing doubt that § 1350 should be read to require "our courts [to] sit in judgment of the conduct of foreign officials in their own countries with respect to their own citizens").

The fifth reason is particularly important in light of the first four. We have no congressional mandate to seek out and define new and debatable violations of the law of nations, and modern indications of congressional understanding of the judicial role in the field have not affirmatively encouraged greater judicial creativity. It is true that a clear mandate appears in the Torture Victim Protection Act of 1991, 106 Stat. 73, providing authority that "establish[es] an unambiguous and modern basis for" federal claims of torture and extrajudicial killing, H. R. Rep. No. 102–367, pt. 1, p. 3 (1991). But that affirmative authority is confined to specific subject matter, and although the legislative history includes the remark that § 1350 should "remain intact to permit suits based on other norms that already exist or may ripen in the future into rules of customary international law," *id.,* at 4, Congress as a body has done nothing to promote such suits. Several times, indeed, the Senate has expressly declined to give the federal courts the task of interpreting and applying international human rights law, as when its ratification of the International Covenant on Civil and Political Rights declared that the substantive provisions of the document were not self-executing. 138 Cong. Rec. 8071 (1992).

B

These reasons argue for great caution in adapting the law of nations to private rights. Justice Scalia concludes that caution is too hospitable, and a word is in order to summarize where we have come so far and to focus our difference with him on whether some norms of today's law of nations may ever be recognized legitimately by federal courts in the absence of congressional action beyond § 1350. All Members of the Court agree that § 1350 is only jurisdictional. We also agree, or at least Justice Scalia does not dispute, that the jurisdiction was originally understood to be available to enforce a small number of international norms that a federal court could properly recognize as within the common law enforceable without further statutory authority. Justice Scalia concludes, however, that two subsequent developments should be understood to preclude federal courts from recognizing any further international norms as judicially enforceable today, absent further congressional action. As described before, we now tend to understand common law not as a discoverable reflection of universal reason but, in a positivistic way, as a product of human choice. And we now adhere to a conception of limited judicial power first expressed in reorienting federal diversity jurisdiction, *see Erie R. Co. v. Tompkins*, 304 U.S. 64 (1938), that federal courts have no authority to derive "general" common law.

Whereas Justice Scalia sees these developments as sufficient to close the door to further independent judicial recognition of actionable international norms, other considerations persuade us that the judicial power should be exercised on the understanding that the door is still ajar subject to vigilant doorkeeping, and thus open to a narrow class of international norms today. *Erie* did not in terms bar any judicial recognition of new substantive rules, no matter what the circumstances, and post-*Erie* understanding has identified limited enclaves in which federal courts may derive some substantive law in a common law way. For two centuries we have affirmed that the domestic law of the United States recognizes the law of nations. *See, e.g.*, *Sabbatino*, 376 U.S., at 423 ("[I]t is, of course, true that United States courts apply international law as a part of our own in appropriate circumstances"); *The Paquete Habana*, 175 U.S., at 700 ("International law is part of our law, and must be ascertained and administered by the courts of justice of appropriate jurisdiction, as often as questions of right depending upon it are duly presented for their determination").

We think an attempt to justify such a position would be particularly unconvincing in light of what we know about congressional understanding bearing on this issue lying at the intersection of the judicial and legislative powers. The First Congress, which reflected the understanding of the framing generation and included some of the Framers, assumed that federal courts could properly identify some international norms as enforceable in the exercise of § 1350 jurisdiction. We think it would be unreasonable to assume that the First Congress would have expected federal courts to lose all capacity to recognize enforceable international norms simply because the common law might lose some metaphysical cachet on the road to modern realism. Later Congresses seem to have shared our view. The position we take today has been assumed by some federal courts for 24 years, ever since the Second Circuit decided *Filartiga v. Peña-Irala*, 630 F.2d 876 (C.A. 2 1980), and for practical purposes the point of today's disagreement has been focused since the exchange between Judge Edwards and Judge Bork in *Tel-Oren v. Libyan Arab Republic*, 726 F.2d 774 (C.A.D.C. 1984). Congress, however, has not only expressed no disagreement with our view of the proper exercise of the judicial power, but has responded to its most notable instance by enacting legislation supplementing the judicial determination in some detail.

While we agree with Justice Scalia to the point that we would welcome any congressional guidance in exercising jurisdiction with such obvious potential to affect foreign relations, nothing Congress has done is a reason for us to shut the door to the law of nations entirely. It is enough to say that Congress may do that at any time (explicitly, or implicitly by treaties or statutes that occupy the field) just as it may modify or cancel any judicial decision so far as it rests on recognizing an international norm as such.

C

We must still, however, derive a standard or set of standards for assessing the particular claim Alvarez raises, and for this case it suffices to look to the historical antecedents. Whatever the ultimate criteria for accepting a cause of action subject to jurisdiction under § 1350, we are persuaded that federal courts should not recognize private claims under federal common law for violations of any international law norm with less definite content and acceptance among civilized nations than the historical paradigms familiar when § 1350 was enacted. *See, e.g., United States v. Smith,* 5 Wheat. 153, 163–180, n. a (1820) (illustrating the specificity with which the law of nations defined piracy). This limit upon judicial recognition is generally consistent with the reasoning of many of the courts and judges who faced the issue before it reached this Court. *See Filartiga, supra,* at 890 ("[F]or purposes of civil liability, the torturer has become—like the pirate and slave trader before him—*hostis humani generis,* an enemy of all mankind"); *Tel-Oren, supra,* at 781 (Edwards, J., concurring) (suggesting that the "limits of section 1350's reach" be defined by "a handful of heinous actions—each of which violates definable, universal and obligatory norms"); *see also In re Estate of Marcos Human Rights Litigation,* 25 F.3d 1467, 1475 (C.A.9 1994) ("Actionable violations of international law must be of a norm that is specific, universal, and obligatory"). And the determination whether a norm is sufficiently definite to support a cause of action should (and, indeed, inevitably must) involve an element of judgment about the practical consequences of making that cause available to litigants in the federal courts.

Thus, Alvarez's detention claim must be gauged against the current state of international law, looking to those sources we have long, albeit cautiously, recognized.

> [W]here there is no treaty, and no controlling executive or legislative act or judicial decision, resort must be had to the customs and usages of civilized nations; and, as evidence of these, to the works of jurists and commentators, who by years of labor, research and experience, have made themselves peculiarly well acquainted with the subjects of which they treat. Such works are resorted to by judicial tribunals, not for the speculations of their authors concerning what the law ought to be, but for trustworthy evidence of what the law really is.

The Paquete Habana, 175 U.S., at 700.

To begin with, Alvarez cites two well-known international agreements that, despite their moral authority, have little utility under the standard set out in this opinion. He says that his abduction by Sosa was an "arbitrary arrest" within the meaning of the Universal Declaration of Human Rights (Declaration). And he traces the rule against arbitrary arrest not only to the Declaration, but also to article nine of the International Covenant on Civil and Political Rights (Covenant), to which the United States is a party, and to various other conventions to which it is not. But the Declaration does not of its own force impose obligations as a matter of international law. And, although the Covenant does bind the United States as a matter of international law, the United States ratified the Covenant on the express understanding that it was not self-executing and so did not itself create obligations enforceable in the federal courts. Accordingly, Alvarez cannot say that the Declaration and Covenant themselves establish the relevant and applicable rule of international law. He instead attempts to show that prohibition of arbitrary arrest has attained the status of binding customary international law.

Here, it is useful to examine Alvarez's complaint in greater detail. As he presently argues it, the claim does not rest on the cross-border feature of his abduction. Although the District Court granted relief in part on finding a violation of international law in taking Alvarez across the border from Mexico to the United States, the Court of Appeals rejected that ground of liability for failure to identify a norm of requisite force prohibiting a forcible abduction across a border. Instead, it relied on the conclusion that the law of the United States did not authorize Alvarez's arrest, because the DEA lacked extraterritorial authority under 21 U.S.C. § 878, and because Federal Rule of Criminal Procedure 4(d)(2) limited the warrant for Alvarez's arrest to "the jurisdiction of the United States." It is this position that Alvarez takes now: that his arrest was arbitrary and as such forbidden by international law not because it infringed the prerogatives of Mexico, but because no applicable law authorized it.

Alvarez thus invokes a general prohibition of "arbitrary" detention defined as officially sanctioned action exceeding positive authorization to detain under the domestic law of some government, regardless of the circumstances. Whether or not this is an accurate reading of the Covenant, Alvarez cites little authority that a rule so broad has the status of a binding customary norm today. He certainly cites nothing to justify the federal courts in taking his broad rule as the predicate for a federal lawsuit, for its implications would be breathtaking. His rule would support a cause of action in federal court for any arrest, anywhere in the world, unauthorized by the law of the jurisdiction in which it took place, and would create a cause of action for any seizure of an alien in violation of the Fourth Amendment, supplanting the actions under Rev. Stat. § 1979, 42 U.S.C. § 1983 and *Bivens v. Six Unknown Fed. Narcotics Agents*, 403 U.S. 388 (1971), that now provide damages remedies for such violations. It would create an action in federal court for arrests by state officers who simply exceed their authority; and for the violation of any limit that the law of any country might place on the authority of its own officers to arrest. And all of this assumes that Alvarez could establish that Sosa was acting on behalf of a government when he made the arrest, for otherwise he would need a rule broader still.

Alvarez's failure to marshal support for his proposed rule is underscored by the Restatement (Third) of Foreign Relations Law of the United States (1987), which says in its discussion of customary international human rights law that a "state violates international law if, as a matter of state policy, it practices, encourages, or condones ... prolonged arbitrary detention." *Id.*, § 702. Although the RESTATEMENT does not explain its requirements of a "state policy" and of "prolonged" detention, the implication is clear. Any credible invocation of a principle against arbitrary detention that the civilized world accepts as binding customary international law requires a factual basis beyond relatively brief detention in excess of positive authority. Even the Restatement's limits are only the beginning of the enquiry, because although it is easy to say that some policies of prolonged arbitrary detentions are so bad that those who enforce them become enemies of the human race, it may be harder to say which policies cross that line with the certainty afforded by Blackstone's three common law offenses. In any event, the label would never fit the reckless policeman who botches his warrant, even though that same officer might pay damages under municipal law.

Whatever may be said for the broad principle Alvarez advances, in the present, imperfect world, it expresses an aspiration that exceeds any binding customary rule having the specificity we require. Creating a private cause of action to further that aspiration would go beyond any residual common law discretion we think it appropriate to exercise. It is enough to hold that a single illegal detention of less than a day, followed by the transfer of custody to lawful authorities and a prompt arraignment, violates no norm of customary international law so well defined as to support the creation of a federal remedy.

———————

JUSTICE SCALIA, with whom THE CHIEF JUSTICE and JUSTICE THOMAS join, concurring in part and concurring in the judgment.

I

The question at hand is whether the Alien Tort Statute (ATS), 28 U.S.C. § 1350, provides respondent Alvarez–Machain * * * a cause of action to sue in federal court to recover money damages for violation of what is claimed to be a customary international law norm against arbitrary arrest and detention. * * * The challenge posed by this case is to ascertain (in the Court's felicitous phrase) "the interaction between the ATS at the time of its enactment and the ambient law of the era." I begin by describing the general principles that must guide our analysis.

At the time of its enactment, the ATS provided a federal forum in which aliens could bring suit to recover for torts committed in "violation of the law of nations." The law of nations that would have been applied in this federal forum was at the time part of the so-called general common law.

General common law was not federal law under the Supremacy Clause, which gave that effect only to the Constitution, the laws of the United States, and treaties. U.S. Const., Art. VI, cl. 2. Federal and state courts adjudicating questions of general common law were not adjudicating questions of federal or state law, respectively—the general common law was neither. * * *

This Court's decision in *Erie R. Co. v. Tompkins,* 304 U.S. 64 (1938), signaled the end of federal-court elaboration and application of the general common law. * * * After the death of the old general common law in *Erie* came the birth of a new and different common law pronounced by federal courts. There developed a specifically federal common law (in the sense of judicially pronounced law) for a "few and restricted" areas in which "a federal rule of decision is necessary to protect uniquely federal interests, and those in which Congress has given the courts the power to develop substantive law." *Texas Industries, Inc. v. Radcliff Materials, Inc.,* 451 U.S. 630, 640 (1981). Unlike the general common law that preceded it, however, federal common law was self-consciously "made" rather than "discovered," * * *

Because post-*Erie* federal common law is made, not discovered, federal courts must possess some federal-common-law-making authority before undertaking to craft it. * * *

The general rule as formulated in *Texas Industries,* 451 U.S., at 640–641, is that "[t]he vesting of jurisdiction in the federal courts does not in and of itself give rise to authority to formulate federal common law." * * *

The rule against finding a delegation of substantive lawmaking power in a grant of jurisdiction is subject to exceptions, some better established than others. The most firmly entrenched is admiralty law, derived from the grant of admiralty jurisdiction in Article III, § 2, cl. 3, of the Constitution. * * * At the other extreme is *Bivens v. Six Unknown Fed. Narcotics Agents,* 403 U.S. 388 (1971), which created a private damages cause of action against federal officials for violation of the Fourth Amendment. We have said that the authority to create this cause of action was derived from "our general jurisdiction to decide all cases 'arising under the Constitution, laws, or treaties of the United States.'" *Correctional Services Corp. v. Malesko,* 534 U.S. 61, 66 (2001) (quoting 28 U.S.C. § 1331). While *Bivens* stands, the ground supporting it has eroded. * * *

II

* * *

None of the exceptions to the general rule against finding substantive lawmaking power in a jurisdictional grant apply. *Bivens* provides perhaps the closest analogy. That is shaky authority at best, but at least it can be said that *Bivens* sought to enforce a command of our *own* law—the *United States* Constitution. In modern international human rights litigation of the sort that has proliferated since *Filartiga v. Peña-Irala,* 630 F.2d 876 (C.A.2 1980), a federal court must first *create* the underlying federal command. * * * In Benthamite terms, creating a federal command (federal common law) out of "international norms," and then constructing a cause of action to enforce that command through the purely jurisdictional grant of the ATS, is nonsense upon stilts.

III

The analysis in the Court's opinion departs from my own in this respect: After concluding in Part III that "the ATS is a jurisdictional statute creating no new causes of action," the Court addresses at length in Part IV the "good reasons for a restrained conception of the *discretion* a federal court should exercise in considering a new cause of action" under the ATS (emphasis added). By framing the issue as one of "discretion," the Court skips over the antecedent question of authority. * * * On this point, the Court observes only that no development between the enactment of the ATS (in 1789) and the birth of modern international human rights litigation under that statute (in 1980) "has categorically *precluded* federal courts from recognizing a claim under the law of nations as an element of common law" (emphasis added). This turns our jurisprudence regarding federal common law on its head. The question is not what case or congressional action *prevents* federal courts from applying the law of nations as part of the general common law; it is what *authorizes* that peculiar exception from *Erie's* fundamental holding that a general common law *does not exist.*

The Court would apparently find authorization in the understanding of the Congress that enacted the ATS, that "district courts would recognize private causes of action for certain torts in violation of the law of nations." But as discussed above, that understanding rested upon a notion of general common law that has been repudiated by *Erie.* * * *

Because today's federal common law is not our Framers' general common law, the question presented by the suggestion of discretionary authority to enforce the law of nations is not whether to extend old-school general-common-law adjudication. Rather, it is whether to create new federal common law. The Court masks the novelty of its approach when it suggests that the difference between us is that I would "close the door to further independent judicial recognition of actionable international norms," whereas the Court would permit the exercise of judicial power "on the understanding that the door is still ajar subject to vigilant doorkeeping." The general common law was the old door. We do not close that door today, for the deed was done in *Erie*. Federal common law is a *new* door. The question is not whether that door will be left ajar, but whether this Court will open it.

Although I fundamentally disagree with the discretion-based framework employed by the Court, we seem to be in accord that creating a new federal common law of international human rights is a questionable enterprise. * * *

[The Court's discretionary concerns] are not, as the Court thinks them, reasons why courts must be circumspect in use of their extant general-common-law-making powers. They are reasons why courts cannot possibly be thought to have been given, and should not be thought to possess, federal-common-law-making powers with regard to the creation of private federal causes of action for violations of customary international law. * * *

The Ninth Circuit brought us the judgment that the Court reverses today. * * * But the verbal formula it applied is the same verbal formula that the Court explicitly endorses. Compare *ante*, (quoting *In re Estate of Ferdinand Marcos Human Rights Litigation*, 25 F.3d 1467, 1475 (C.A.9 1994), for the proposition that actionable norms must be " 'specific, universal, and obligatory' "), with 331 F.3d 604, 621 (C.A.9 2003) (en banc) (finding the norm against arbitrary arrest and detention in this case to be "universal, obligatory, and specific"); *id.*, at 619 ("[A]n actionable claim under the [ATS] requires the showing of a violation of the law of nations that is specific, universal, and obligatory" (internal quotation marks omitted)). Endorsing the very formula that led the Ninth Circuit to its result in this case hardly seems to be a recipe for restraint in the future. * * *

We Americans have a method for making the laws that are over us. We elect representatives to two Houses of Congress, each of which must enact the new law and present it for the approval of a President, whom we also elect. For over two decades now, unelected federal judges have been usurping this lawmaking power by converting what they regard as norms of international law into American law. Today's opinion approves that process in principle, though urging the lower courts to be more restrained. * * *

It would be bad enough if there were some assurance that future conversions of perceived international norms into American law would be approved by this Court itself. * * * But in this illegitimate lawmaking endeavor, the lower federal courts will be the principal actors; we review but a tiny fraction of their decisions. And no one thinks that all of them are eminently reasonable.

American law—the law made by the people's democratically elected representatives—does not recognize a category of activity that is so universally disapproved by other nations that it is automatically unlawful here, and automatically gives rise to a private action for money damages in federal court. That simple principle is what today's decision should have announced.

NOTES AND QUESTIONS ON SOSA

1. *Test for actionable claims.* What standard must ATS claims meet to be actionable after *Sosa?* At a minimum, plaintiffs must rely on a norm of customary law defined with specificity comparable to the 18th century paradigms which the Supreme Court recognized in its opinion. Were those paradigms more or less defined than customary human rights norms in the 21st century? In *United States v. Smith*, 18 U.S. 153, 162 (1820), the Supreme Court noted that there was some uncertainty about the definition of piracy but found, based largely on the works of scholars, that acts of robbery on the high seas were within the core meaning of piracy and affirmed a death sentence on that basis. What degree of uncertainty about the definition of a norm is acceptable after *Sosa?* Does *Sosa* alter the methodology by which the federal courts ascertain customary law? Are only certain customary norms actionable under the ATS now? Can a customary norm be actionable in some cases and not in others because of the "specificity" of the claim? In at least one post-*Sosa* case, defendants have argued that unratified treaties and U.N. declarations and resolutions are "illegitimate" indicators of actionable customary norms. Does *Sosa* support this argument?

2. *The "specific, universal, and obligatory" standard.* The Supreme Court noted that its decision was "generally consistent with the reasoning of many of the courts and judges who faced the issue before it reached this Court," citing *Filartiga, Marcos* and Judge Edwards' opinion in *Tel-Oren*. Plaintiffs in post-*Sosa* cases have argued that this part of the Court's opinion clearly signals that the "specific, universal and obligatory" standard recognized in many pre-*Sosa* cases still applies and that most of the norms recognized before *Sosa* remain actionable in the post-*Sosa* world (*e.g.* torture, extra-judicial killings, disappearances, genocide, crimes against humanity, war crimes, and slavery). *See Mujica v. Occidental Petroleum Corp.*, 381 F. Supp. 2d 1164, 1176 (C.D. Cal. 2005). Is this a fair reading of *Sosa?* Justice Souter's opinion indicates that the door is "ajar" to new claims under the ATS subject to "vigilant doorkeeping." To what extent did the majority endorse the pre-*Sosa* case law? How would you interpret the meaning of "ajar"? *See* Beth Stephens, *Sosa v. Alvarez–Machain: "The Door is Still Ajar" for Human Rights Litigation in U.S. Courts*, 70 BROOK. L. REV. 533 (2004–2005).

3. *A two-tiered test for ATS claims?* Defendants in post-*Sosa* cases have argued that there is a two-tiered test that any ATS claim must meet. First, the plaintiff must show that the norm she relies on is supported by the same evidence of uniformity and definiteness as the 18th century paradigms. Second, defendants argue, the court must

evaluate whether the "practical consequences" set forth in *Sosa* warrant the creation of a cause of action in that particular case or category of cases. *See, e.g., Mujica v. Occidental Petroleum*, 381 F. Supp. 2d 1164, 1181–82 (C.D. Cal. 2005) (appeal pending). Is this analysis required by *Sosa*? Is it consistent with *Sosa*? Plaintiffs contend that once they have alleged a "specific, universal and obligatory" customary norm with specificity comparable to the 18th century paradigms, the *Sosa* test is satisfied. Which of these views is more consistent with *Sosa*?

4.   *Cause of action.* Prior to *Sosa*, one of the unanswered questions in ATS cases was whether the ATS provided a cause of action for damages. *See, e.g., In re Estate of Ferdinand Marcos*, 25 F.3d 1467 (9th Cir. 1994) ("*Marcos I*") (the statute "creates a cause of action for violations of specific, universal, and obligatory international human rights standards"); *Abebe-Jira v. Negewo*, 72 F.3d 844 (11th Cir. 1996) (statute "provides both a private cause of action and a federal forum where aliens may seek redress for violations of international law"); *but see Tel-Oren v. Libyan Arab Republic*, 726 F.2d 774, 813–14 (D.C. Cir. 1984) (Bork, J., dissenting) (suggesting that without an express cause of action for damages in international or U.S. law, the ATS might be limited only to the handful of claims Blackstone had recognized: piracy, violations of safe conducts, and attacks on ambassadors).

The Supreme Court in *Sosa* rejected the idea that the ATS itself created a cause of action. Indeed, the Court termed this argument "frivolous," citing Professor William Casto. William R. Casto, *The Federal Courts' Protective Jurisdiction Over Torts Committed in Violation of the Law of Nations*, 18 CONN. L. REV. 467, 479–80 (1986). However, the Court went on to find that Congress intended that the federal courts hear and decide at least some claims based on the "law of nations" without further Congressional action. Does it matter that the Court has found that the ATS creates no causes of action? Where does the claim for relief come from in ATS cases after *Sosa*? *See, e.g.*, William R. Casto, *The New Federal Common Law of Tort Remedies for Violations of International Law*, 37 RUTGERS L. J 635 (2006).

5.   *Federal common law.* What does *Sosa* say about the status of federal common law in ATS cases? Which issues in an ATS case are governed by federal common law? Are customary international law or general principles of law relevant to a federal common law analysis under the ATS? Must a plaintiff prove, as some defendants suggest, that *all* rules applied in an ATS case satisfy the *Sosa* test? Is this contention consistent with the court's discussion of federal common law? (These issues are also considered *infra* in the case study on corporate human rights cases.)

6.   *Private actors.* Most of the defendants in ATS actions have been former foreign government officials. *See, e.g., Abebe–Jira v. Negewo*, 72 F.3d 844 (11th Cir. 1996). In *Kadic v. Karadzic*, 70 F.3d 232 (2d Cir. 1995), *supra*, the Second Circuit held that ATS actions could be brought

against a non-state actors, in that case the Bosnian–Serb president, for certain violations of international law. Footnote 20 of Justice Souter's majority opinion in *Sosa* reads:

> A related consideration is whether international law extends the scope of liability for a violation of a given norm to the perpetrator being sued, if the defendant is a private actor such as a corporation or individual. Compare *Tel-Oren* v. *Libyan Arab Republic*, 726 F.2d 774, 791–795 (D.C. Cir. 1984) (Edwards, J., concurring) (insufficient consensus in 1984 that torture by private actors violates international law), with *Kadic* v. *Karadzic*, 70 F.3d 232, 239–241 (2d Cir. 1995) (sufficient consensus in 1995 that genocide by private actors violates international law).

Many corporate defendants have argued that footnote 20 means that courts must find that a particular international law norm applies specifically to corporations before a court can enforce it in ATS cases against corporations. Is that a fair reading of footnote 20?

7. *Justice Breyer's concurrence.* In his concurring opinion, Justice Breyer noted the connection between universal criminal jurisdiction and civil tort recovery for similar harms.

> Today international law will sometimes reflect not only substantive agreement as to certain universally condemned behavior but also procedural agreement that universal jurisdiction exists to prosecute a subset of that behavior. See Restatement § 404, and Comment *a*; * * * The fact that this procedural consensus exists suggests that recognition of universal jurisdiction in respect to a limited set of norms is consistent with principles of international comity. That is, allowing every nation's courts to adjudicate foreign conduct involving foreign parties in such cases will not significantly threaten the practical harmony that comity principles seek to protect. That consensus concerns criminal jurisdiction, but consensus as to universal criminal jurisdiction itself suggests that universal tort jurisdiction would be no more threatening. * * * Thus, universal criminal jurisdiction necessarily contemplates a significant degree of civil tort recovery as well.

Sosa, 542 U.S. at 762–63. Should ATS jurisdiction be restricted by the scope of universal jurisdiction in criminal cases?

8. *A critique of the "modern position."* Some commentators have argued that according customary international law ("CIL") the domestic status of federal common law is inconsistent with the Constitution and the historical understanding of the general common law. They argue that pre-*Erie*, courts did not apply CIL as federal common law, but rather as general common law, which did not have the status of federal common law. Thus, when the court in *Filartiga* said that CIL "has always been part of the common law," it was referring to the general common law. This understanding of the existence of general common law was repudiated with the Supreme Court's decision in *Erie*, which required

that federal law had to be authorized in some manner by the U.S. Constitution or a federal statute. Critics argue that because nothing on the face of the Constitution or any federal statute authorizes the application of CIL by the judiciary, CIL has not been incorporated into the federal common law. *See* Curtis Bradley and Jack L. Goldsmith, III, *The Current Illegitimacy of International Human Rights Litigation*, 66 FORD-HAM L. REV. 319, 324–25 (1997); *see also* Owen C. Pell, *Historical Reparations Claims: The Defense Perspective*, in HOLOCAUST RESTITUTION: PERSPECTIVES ON THE LITIGATION AND ITS LEGACY (Roger Alford and Michael Bazyler, eds. 2006)

9. *Extraterritoriality*. In *amicus* briefs filed in the *Doe v. Unocal* and *In re South African Apartheid Litigation* cases after *Sosa*, the United States has argued that the ATS should not apply to human rights claims that occurred in the territory of other states. The argument is based on the general presumption against the extraterritorial application of all statutes and the contention that the Founders would not have wanted the federal courts to hear cases that might create international conflict at a time of national weakness. Is this argument plausible after *Sosa*?

10. *Expert declarations*. Expert declarations by international law scholars have been a feature of ATS cases since *Filartiga*. In *Filartiga*, the Second Circuit relied on such expert declarations in finding that torture violated the law of nations. 630 F.2d at 880 n. 4. After *Sosa*, what issues should be the subjects of scholarly declarations? Is it appropriate for scholars to express expert opinions on the meaning of *Sosa* or the manner in which international law is received in the American legal system? Should scholars be permitted to opine about which international norms meet the *Sosa* test? *See Flores v. Southern Peru Copper Corp.*, 343 F.3d 140, 171 (2d Cir. 2003) ("[A]lthough scholars may provide accurate descriptions of the *actual* customs and practices and legal obligations of States, only the courts may determine whether these customs and practices give rise to a rule of customary international law.")

11. *Transborder abduction claims*. Dr. Alvarez did not appeal the *en banc* Ninth Circuit decision that he lacked standing to assert a claim based on the invasion of Mexico's sovereignty. Do you think the Supreme Court would have sustained that claim? Is transborder abduction precluded as a basis for an ATS claim after *Sosa*? Suppose a potential client comes to you and tells you that he was the victim of a CIA rendition program. He was taken by U.S. agents from his home country to a foreign country where he was held for more than a year and was mistreated by his captors. After a year of detention and mistreatment, U.S. agents then returned him to his country. Do you think he has a claim for arbitrary arrest or detention? Any other claims? How do you think the Supreme Court would decide these claims after *Sosa*? What other facts would you like to know before you give your opinion? *See Arar v. Ashcroft*, 414 F. Supp. 2d 250 (E.D.N.Y. 2006).

12.   *Case selection.* Was the *Sosa* case a good case to bring under the ATS? What cases would you bring after *Sosa* if you were trying to develop a strategy for using the ATS to advance the cause of human rights? Was it a strategic error to bring an ATS case on behalf of Dr. Alvarez? How important do you think it is to have a sympathetic plaintiff like Dolly Filartiga or Elizabeth Demissie when bringing ATS claims?

13.   *Westfall Act.* Generally, the United States is immune from suit in the courts of the United States. The Federal Tort Claims Act (FTCA) waives sovereign immunity in suits "for * * * personal injury or death caused by the negligent or wrongful act or omission of any employee of the Government while acting within the scope of his office or employment, under circumstances where the United States, if a private person, would be liable to the claimant in accordance with the law of the place where the act or omission occurred." 28 U.S.C. § 1346(b)(1) (2000). Thus, if a human rights violation takes the form of a tort (*e.g.* false arrest) then the FTCA may be available as a remedy.

There are many statutory exceptions and limitations to overcome in FTCA actions. For example, "intentional torts" are actionable only if the federal official is an investigative or law enforcement officer. 28 U.S.C. § 2680(h). Another of the FTCA's limitations is a bar on suits for claims "arising in a foreign country," 28 U.S.C. § 2680(k). As a matter of statutory construction, the Supreme Court in *Sosa* unanimously interpreted this exception to bar claims based on any injury suffered in a foreign country, regardless of where the tortious act or omission occurred. The Court thereby rejected the so-called "headquarters doctrine," under which various circuit courts had found the foreign country exception inapplicable to torts planned and directed by government agents in the United States. *Sosa*, 542 U.S. at 712.

Further, when individual employees of the United States are sued for acts in their official capacity, the Westfall Act allows the United States to substitute itself as a defendant under the FTCA, unless the plaintiff is making a *Bivens* claim[9] under the U.S. Constitution or a claim under a federal statute providing an express cause of action. In *Sosa*, Dr. Alvarez named several federal officials involved in his kidnapping as defendants. The United States substituted itself as a defendant under the Westfall Act, thus transforming plaintiff's ATS claims against these defendants into a claim under the FTCA. *See Alvarez v. United States*, 331 F.3d 604, 631 (9th Cir. 2003) (*en banc*). The Ninth Circuit in *Alvarez* determined that the ATS was not the kind of statute that provided for an exception to substitution under the Westfall Act. *Id.* at 631. The Ninth Circuit ruled that individual federal officers and the United States can only be sued for torts in violation of the law of nations under the FTCA and not under the ATS.

---

9.   *See Bivens v. Six Unknown Fed. Narcotics Agents*, 403 U.S. 388 (1971). A Bivens claim is based on an implied cause of action for damages under the Constitution.

14. *Actions against state and local officials.* One unexplored area for further ATS litigation is the potential liability of state and local officials, or even private parties, where international law applies to non-state actors (*e.g.* slavery-like practices or human trafficking). Significantly, the sovereign immunity obstacle presented by the Westfall Act would not apply in these cases, because the officials sued would not be federal officials. In *Martinez v. City of Los Angeles,* 141 F.3d 1373 (9th Cir. 1998), an elderly Mexican man sued Los Angeles Police Department (LAPD) officers for causing him to be wrongfully detained for two months. In *Martinez,* the Ninth Circuit accepted the application of the ATS to LAPD officers but, as was the case in *Sosa,* took a narrow view of the scope of the arbitrary arrest norm in that case. What other opportunities exist for ATS litigation against state or local defendants in the United States? Do you think it would be a good strategy for U.S. civil rights lawyers to add ATS claims to their federal law claims in prisoners' rights or police abuse cases? What would such claims be, and, assuming they exist, would such claims raise additional questions? For example, are ATS claims subject to the same defenses and immunities that apply in civil rights actions brought under 42 U.S.C. § 1983 (*e.g.* qualified immunity, Eleventh Amendment immunity)?

15. *Advantages and disadvantages of ATS litigation.* For a summary of ATS case law and a discussion of the advantages and disadvantages of ATS litigation, see Sandra Coliver, Jennie Green & Paul Hoffman, *Holding Human Rights Violators Accountable By Using International Law in U.S. Courts: Advocacy Efforts and Complementary Strategies,* 19 EMORY INT'L L. REV. 169 (2005). The authors of this article list seven benefits of ATS cases: (1) ensuring that the U.S. does not remain a safe haven for human rights abusers; (2) holding individual perpetrators accountable for human rights abuses; (3) providing victims with some sense of official acknowledgment and reparation; (4) contributing to the development of international human rights law; (5) building a human rights constituency in the United States; (6) creating a climate of deterrence; and (7) encouraging similar efforts in other countries. *Id.* at 174–86.

FOREIGN SOVEREIGN IMMUNITY

One of the criticisms of ATS cases has been that they result in huge but uncollectible judgments. Unlike individual defendants, foreign states would surely have the funds necessary to satisfy such judgments. Why have human rights lawyers not sued the sovereign states responsible for human rights violations? The answer is that foreign sovereigns are generally immune from suit in the courts of other countries. This immunity doctrine is part of customary international law. In the United States, sovereign immunity is codified in the Foreign Sovereign Immunities Act of 1976 ("FSIA"). The FSIA is the exclusive means by which plaintiffs can obtain jurisdiction in U.S. courts over foreign sovereigns, their agents, or instrumentalities. The Supreme Court has held that the ATS is not an exception to the FSIA's exclusive regulation of suits against foreign sovereigns. *Argentine Republic v. Amerada Hess Shipping Corp.*, 488 U.S. 428 (1989).

Although foreign states are generally entitled to sovereign immunity, the FSIA also codifies a series of exceptions to that immunity. 28 U.S.C. § 1605(a) (2000).[10] In *Republic of Austria v. Altmann*, 541 U.S. 677, 697 (2004), the Supreme Court determined that the FSIA and its exceptions apply retroactively. As a result, a claimant who sued Austria for failing to return art looted by the Nazis during World War II could rely on one of the exceptions to immunity found in the FSIA for his suit against the Austrian government. *Id.* Since the passage of the FSIA, victims of human rights violations have attempted to use the waiver, non-commercial tort, commercial activities and terrorism exceptions to the FSIA to vindicate their rights, with mixed results.

A foreign sovereign can explicitly or implicitly waive its sovereign immunity under 28 U.S.C § 1605(a)(1). In *Siderman de Blake v. Republic of Argentina*, 965 F.2d 699 (9th Cir. 1992), the plaintiff filed suit for, among other things, the torture of Mr. Siderman by the Argentine government. Before the suit was filed, and as a part of its persecution of him because of his Jewish faith, Argentina had used a U.S. court to serve Mr. Siderman with papers making fraudulent criminal charges against him. In response to the Sidermans' suit, Argentina asserted the defense of sovereign immunity. The court accepted the Sidermans' argument that Argentina's use of the U.S. court system constituted an implied waiver of sovereign immunity for claims related to persecution. However, the *Siderman* case also rejected the argument that foreign states "waived" their sovereign immunity when they engaged in violations of *jus cogens* norms (*e.g.* torture). *Id.* at 718–19. Although the Sidermans succeeded in their claim of implicit waiver, courts have generally narrowly interpreted the implied waiver exception to immunity. *See Foremost–McKesson, Inc. v. Islamic Republic of Iran*, 905 F.2d 438, 444 (D.C. Cir. 1990).

---

10. 28 U.S.C. § 1605, General exceptions to the jurisdictional immunity of a foreign state:

(a) A foreign state shall not be immune from the jurisdiction of courts of the United States or of the States in any case—

(1) in which the foreign state has waived its immunity either explicitly or by implication * * *

(3) in which rights in property taken in violation of international law are in issue and that property or any property exchanged for such property is present in the United States in connection with a commercial activity carried on in the United States by the foreign state; or that property or any property exchanged for such property is owned or operated by an agency or instrumentality of the foreign state and that agency or instrumentality is engaged in a commercial activity in the United States; * * *

(5) not otherwise encompassed in paragraph (2) above, in which money damages are sought against a foreign state for personal injury or death, or damage to or loss of property, occurring in the United States and caused by the tortious act or omission of that foreign state or of any official or employee of that foreign state while acting within the scope of his office or employment. * * *

The tort exception has also successfully served as a vehicle for vindicating victims of certain narrowly defined human rights violations. *See Letelier v. Republic of Chile*, 748 F.2d 790 (2d Cir. 1984) (assassination of former Chilean official and U.S. citizen in Washington, D.C.); *Liu v. Republic of China*, 892 F.2d 1419 (9th Cir. 1989) (assassination of newspaper publisher in San Francisco); *Estate of Domingo v. Republic of Philippines*, 808 F.2d 1349 (9th Cir. 1987) (assassination of two Philippine trade union activists in Seattle). Suits claiming that extraterritorial human rights violations caused emotional distress in the United States and therefore fell within the FSIA's "tort" exception were unsuccessful. *See, e.g., Denegri v. Republic of Chile*, 1992 WL 91914 (D.D.C. Apr. 6, 1992).

Some plaintiffs have sought to hold foreign sovereigns liable for human rights violations under the "commercial activity" exception to the FSIA. Under this exception, a foreign sovereign doesn't have immunity for activities that are commercial in nature if there is a significant nexus between those activities, the injury, and the United States. 28 U.S.C. § 1605(a)(3)(2000). In *Saudi Arabia v. Nelson*, 507 U.S. 349, 354–55 (1993), an American working in a government-owned Saudi hospital asserted that the company's advertising, recruiting, hiring, and orientation in the U.S. provided a sufficient nexus to his detention and torture in Saudi Arabia. Nelson argued that "but for" his recruitment in the U.S., he would not have taken the job in Saudi Arabia, nor would he have been arrested and subsequently tortured there by Saudi officials. The Supreme Court rejected this argument, finding that the nexus between the "commercial activities" and Nelson's torture was not sufficient to overcome the immunity granted to Saudi Arabia under the FSIA, especially given the sovereign, and not commercial, nature of the police actions in question. 507 U.S. at 367. The *Nelson* case was instrumental in derailing an attempt to assert jurisdiction over the Burmese junta and its gas company in *Doe v. Unocal Corp.*, 963 F.Supp. 880, 887–88 (C.D. Cal 1997).

In a recent amendment to the FSIA, Congress has opened U.S. courts to human rights claims brought against states identified as "terrorist" states by the government. The Flatow Amendment (formally the Civil Liabilities for Acts of State Sponsored Terrorism), passed as part of the 1997 Omnibus Consolidated Appropriations Act,[11] denies sovereign immunity for personal injury or death caused by an act of torture, extra-judicial killing, aircraft sabotage, hostage taking, or the provision of material resources to a person who commits such acts, if that person was an official, employee, or agent of the foreign state and was acting within the scope of his or her position at the time. The exception is limited to foreign states that were included on the State Department's official list of countries designated as state sponsors of terrorism at the time the tort was committed. 28 U.S.C. § 1605(a)(7).

---

11. Civil Liability for Acts of State Sponsored Terrorism, Pub. L. No. 104–208, 589, 110 Stat. 3009—172 (1996) (codified at 28 U.S.C. 1605 note (2001)).

Even where the offending state was so designated, if the act occurred in that state, the plaintiff must first give the state a reasonable opportunity to arbitrate the claim, and the plaintiff or victim must have been a U.S. national when the act upon which the claim is based occurred. 28 U.S.C. § 1605(a)(7). Although this exception may seem a promising opportunity to get redress for acts of terrorism by a foreign sovereign, two D.C. Circuit Court decisions appear to have foreclosed litigation under § 1605(a)(7). In *Cicippio-Puleo v. Islamic Republic of Iran*, 353 F.3d 1024, 1032–33 (D.C. Cir. 2004), the court found that the terrorism exception did not impose liability or create a private right of action, but merely conferred subject matter jurisdiction on federal courts. The court went on to find that although the Flatow Amendment clearly created a cause of action, the cause of action could only be asserted against officials or agents of a foreign state in their individual capacity. Accordingly, neither the terrorism exception to FSIA nor the Flatow Amendment provided a cause of action against foreign states. The D.C. Circuit affirmed this reasoning in *Acree v. Republic of Iraq*, 370 F.3d 41 (D.C. Cir. 2004). The victims of the September 11th attacks have brought such claims against Iraq and Iran. *See In re Terrorist Attacks on Sept. 11, 2001*, 349 F. Supp. 2d 765 (S.D.N.Y. 2005) (bringing suit under the commercial activities exception, the state sponsor of terrorism exception, and the torts exception). *See* 28 U.S.C. 1605A (2008 amendments slightly revising these requirements).

Another issue that often arises in the FSIA cases is whether the FSIA only protects states, their agencies and instrumentalities, or whether individual defendants also benefit from its protections. In *Chuidian*, the Ninth Circuit found that, under some circumstances, the FSIA immunizes individuals, including sitting officials of national governments, who are sued in their official capacity. *Chuidian v. Philippine Nat'l Bank*, 912 F.2d 1095, 1003 (9th Cir. 1990).[12] However, in *In re Estate of Ferdinand Marcos*, 25 F.3d 1467, 1471 (9th Cir. 1994), the Ninth Circuit held that although officials may be covered by the FSIA, they are not protected for acts beyond the scope of their authority or for acts that violate the country's own laws. As the *Chuidian* court stated: "[W]here the officer's powers are limited by statute, his actions beyond those limitations are considered individual and not sovereign actions. The officer is not doing the business which the sovereign has empowered him to do." 912 F.3d at 1106. Further, if the official does not defend himself and defaults, a court may conclude that the official was acting outside the scope of his authority and thus is not protected by the FSIA. *See Doe v. Qi*, 349 F. Supp. 2d 1258 (N.D. Cal. 2004). Until recently, the courts typically found serious violations of international human rights to be beyond the scope of a former official's authority. The Ninth Circuit affirmed this principle in *In re Estate of Marcos*, 25 F.3d 1467 (9th Cir. 1994), stating,

---

12. *See also Belhas v. Ya'alon*, 515 F.3d 1279 (D.C. Cir. 2008); *Velasco v. Government of Indonesia*, 370 F.3d 392 (4th Cir. 2004); *Byrd v. Corporacion Forestal y Industrial de Olancho S.A.*, 182 F.3d 380 (5th Cir. 1999); *Keller v. Cent. Bank of Nigeria*, 277 F.3d 811 (6th Cir. 2002); *El-Fadl v. Cent. Bank of Jordan*, 75 F.3d 668 (D.C. Cir. 1996); *but see Enahoro v. Abubakar*, 408 F.3d 877 (7th Cir. 2005) (foreign officials are not within the protection of the foreign state, its agencies, or instrumentalities).

"Marcos' acts of torture, execution, and disappearance were * * * not taken within any official mandate and were therefore not the acts of an agency or instrumentality of a foreign state within the meaning of FSIA." *Id.* at 1472. *See* Joan Fitzpatrick, *The Future of the Alien Tort Claims Act of 1789: Lessons from In re Marcos Human Rights Litigation*, 67 St. John's L. Rev. 491 (1993).

However, more recent decisions call into question whether a government official can ever be held accountable for human rights violations committed in his official capacity. In *Belhas v. Ya'alon*, 515 F.3d 1279 (D.C. Cir. 2008), plaintiffs brought suit against Moshe Ya'alon, who served as the head of Israeli Army Intelligence from 1995–1998, alleging war crimes, extrajudicial killing, crimes against humanity, and cruel, inhuman and degrading treatment in connection with an Israeli military strike in Southern Lebanon. The D.C. Circuit found that Ya'alon's actions had been undertaken in his official capacity, stating, "We have no difficulty in holding that the district court properly ruled that the FSIA does not extend jurisdiction over this action against an officer for actions committed by the state in whose army he served." *See also Matar v. Dichter*, 500 F.Supp. 2d 284 (S.D.N.Y. 2007) (finding, despite allegations of war crimes, crimes against humanity, and extrajudicial killing, that the defendant had acted in his official capacity and was entitled to immunity under the FSIA); *Yousuf v. Samantar*, 2007 WL 2220579 (E.D. Va. Aug. 1, 2007). Given these decisions, can government officials ever be held liable under the ATS for international human rights violations committed in their official capacity? How would you reconcile these cases with decisions like *Filartiga*, *Abebe-Jira* and *Marcos*?

CASE STUDY: THE CORPORATE HUMAN RIGHTS CASES

Much of the current interest in the *Sosa* case concerns its implications for ATS cases against corporations for their complicity in human rights violations committed abroad. The first of the corporate human rights cases was *Doe v. Unocal Corp.*, 963 F.Supp. 880 (C.D. Cal. 1997). Villagers from the Tenasserim region of Burma brought the case claiming that Burmese soldiers subjected them to forced labor, forced relocation, torture, rape, and extra-judicial execution in connection with the construction of a natural gas pipeline from the Andaman Sea to market in Thailand. The pipeline project was a joint venture of Total (a French oil giant), MOGE (an instrumentality of the Burmese government), and Unocal, (a California-based oil and gas company). The villagers claimed that Unocal knew what the military was doing and even provided encouragement and practical assistance to the military in support of the human rights violations.

Initially, the district court denied the defendant's motions to dismiss claims against Unocal under the ATS. *Doe v. Unocal Corp.*, 963 F.Supp.

880 (C.D. Cal. 1997). However, in the summer of 2000, after several years of discovery, a different federal judge granted Unocal's motion for summary judgment. *Doe v. Unocal Corp.*, 110 F. Supp. 2d 1294 (C.D. Cal. 2000) (vacated by *Doe v. Unocal Corp.*, 403 F.3d 708 (9th Cir. 2005)). The plaintiffs appealed, and, in September 2002, the Ninth Circuit reversed the district court's summary judgment ruling. *Doe v. Unocal Corp.*, 395 F.3d 932 (9th Cir. 2002). The Ninth Circuit subsequently granted Unocal's petition for rehearing *en banc*, and the case was re-argued before an eleven-judge *en banc* panel in June 2003. *Doe v. Unocal Corp.*, 395 F.3d 978 (9th Cir. 2003) (noting the limited precedential value of the September 2002 decision). In January 2004, the Ninth Circuit withdrew the case from submission pending the Supreme Court's decision in the *Sosa* case. After *Sosa* was decided, the Ninth Circuit ordered supplemental briefing on the relevant consequences of the *Sosa* decision for the *Unocal* case. The case was set for re-argument, but parties concluded a monetary settlement days before the argument was scheduled. After the settlement, the district court's summary judgment ruling and the panel decision were vacated. *Doe v. Unocal Corp.*, 403 F.3d 708 (9th Cir. 2005).

The most important issue in the corporate complicity cases has been whether aiding and abetting liability exists under the ATS. In most cases, the corporate defendants are not alleged to have engaged in the human rights violations directly. Instead, the corporate defendants allegedly provided knowing practical assistance that had a substantial effect on the commission of the human rights violations by government actors. *See* RESTATEMENT TORTS (SECOND)§ 876(b)(1979).

The most recent circuit court case to address the issue of aiding and abetting liability for corporations is *Khulumani v. Barclay Nat'l Bank. Ltd.*, 504 F.3d 254 (2d Cir. 2007). In *Khulumani*, plaintiffs alleged that dozens of corporations had collaborated with the government of South Africa in maintaining its system of apartheid. The district court dismissed the cases on the ground that there was no aiding and abetting liability under the ATS after *Sosa*. *In re South African Apartheid Litigation*, 346 F. Supp. 2d 538 (S.D.N.Y. 2004). In October 2007, the Second Circuit reversed this decision in a *per curiam* decision, with each of the judges offering a separate opinion on aiding and abetting liability under the ATS.

KHULUMANI v. BARCLAY NAT'L. BANK LTD.

504 F.3d 254 (2d Cir. 2007)

PER CURIAM. The plaintiffs in this action bring claims under the Alien Tort Claims Act, 28 U.S.C. § 1350 (ATCA), against approximately fifty corporate defendants and hundreds of corporate Does. The plaintiffs argue that these defendants actively and willingly collaborated with the government of South Africa in maintaining a repressive, racially based system known as apartheid, which restricted the majority black African population in all areas of life while providing benefits for the minority white population. * * *

Two members of this panel join to vacate the district court's dismissal of the plaintiffs' ATCA claims because the district court erred in holding that aiding and abetting violations of customary international law cannot provide a basis for ATCA jurisdiction. We hold that in this Circuit, a plaintiff may plead a theory of aiding and abetting liability under the ATCA. The respective rationales of Judges Katzmann and Hall are set forth in separate concurring opinions. * * *

KATZMANN, CIRCUIT JUDGE, concurring:

Asking whether aiding and abetting international law violations * * * [is a] violation of the law of nations that [is] accepted by the civilized world and defined with a specificity comparable to the features of the 18th-century paradigms, the district court concluded that it is not, noting that it found little [in its review of international law] that would lead [it] to conclude that aiding and abetting international law violations is itself an international law violation that is universally accepted as a legal obligation, *id.* Although I believe the district court was correct to look to international law, I disagree with its analysis. * * *

The district court's conclusion that its jurisdiction under the ATCA should depend on whether international law specifically recognizes liability for aiding and abetting violations of the law of nations is consistent with our prior case law. We have repeatedly emphasized that the scope of the ATCA's jurisdictional grant should be determined by reference to international law.* * *

It is also consistent with the Supreme Court's opinion in *Sosa.* The Court observed in a footnote that whether a norm is sufficiently definite to support a cause of action raises a related consideration [of] whether international law extends the scope of liability for a violation of a given norm to the perpetrator being sued, if the defendant is a private actor such as a corporation or individual. *Sosa*, 542 U.S. at 732 & n. 20. While this footnote specifically concerns the liability of non-state actors, its general principle is equally applicable to the question of where to look to determine whether the scope of liability for a violation of international law should extend to aiders and abettors. Furthermore, in *Sosa,* the Supreme Court echoed our prior cases' emphasis on the narrowness of the ATCA's jurisdictional grant. I believe that we most effectively maintain the appropriate scope of this jurisdiction by requiring that the specific conduct allegedly committed by the defendants sued represents a violation of international law.

Most importantly, the district court's approach is consistent with *Sosa*'s broader characterization of the relationship between federal common law and international law. The ATCA's jurisdictional grant enable[s] federal courts to hear claims in a very limited category *defined by the law of nations. Id.* at 712 (emphasis added). Once a court determines that the defendants' alleged conduct falls within one of the modest number of international law violations with a potential for personal liability on the defendants' part, it then considers whether the common law would provide a cause of action to enable the plaintiffs to bring their claim. *Id.* at 724. The common law thus permits the independent judicial recognition of actionable international norms, but the courts must, as *Sosa* cautioned, be vigilant doorkeep[ers]. *Id.* at 729. * * * A federal court is free, in the exercise of its common-law discretion, to decline to provide a cause of action for a violation of international law. But to assure itself that it has jurisdiction to hear a claim under the ATCA, it should first determine whether the alleged tort was in fact committed in violation of the law of nations, 28 U.S.C. § 1350, and whether this law would recognize the defendants' responsibility for that violation. * * *

I conclude that the recognition of the individual responsibility of a defendant who aids and abets a violation of international law is one of those rules that States universally abide by, or accede to, out of a sense of legal obligation and mutual concern. *Flores*, 414 F.3d at 248. Recognized as part of the customary law which authorized and was applied by the war crimes trials following the Second World War, it has been frequently invoked in international law instruments as an accepted mode of liability. During the second half of the twentieth century and into this century, it has been repeatedly recognized in numerous international treaties, most notably the Rome Statute of the International Criminal Court, and in the statutes creating the International Criminal Tribunal for the Former Yugoslavia (ICTY) and the International Criminal Tribunal for Rwanda (ICTR).[5] Indeed, the United States concedes, and the defendants do not dispute, that the concept of criminal aiding and abetting liability is well established in international law. Brief for the United States as Amicus Curiae, at 21.

The London Charter, which established the International Military Tribunal at Nuremberg, was entered into by the allied powers of World War II, acting in the interests of all the United Nations, to establish a tribunal to punish violations of international law. We have previously recognized the London Charter as an authoritative source of customary international law. Moreover, other courts, international bodies, and scholars have recognized that the principles set out in the London Charter and applied by the International Military Tribunal are significant not only because they have garnered broad acceptance, but also because they were viewed as reflecting and crystallizing preexisting customary international law. * * *

The London Charter extended individual responsibility for crimes within its jurisdiction not only to "[l]eaders, organizers, [and] insti-

---

5. The district court seems to have dismissed the significance of some of these sources because they imposed criminal and not civil responsibility. *See In re S. African Apartheid Litig.*, 346 F.Supp.2d at 550. This distinction finds no support in our case law, which has consistently relied on criminal law norms in establishing the content of customary international law for purposes of the ATCA. In *Kadic*, for instance, we held that a defendant could be held liable under the ATCA based on international criminal law norms prohibiting genocide and war crimes. *Kadic*, 70 F.3d at 241–42. * * *

gators" but also to "accomplices participating in the formulation or execution of a common plan or conspiracy to commit" any of the crimes triable by the Tribunal. London Charter art. 6. While the Charter's language taken "literally . . . would seem to imply that the complicity rule did not apply to crimes perpetrated by individual action," as opposed to by common plan, in practice the Tribunal "applied general principles of criminal law regarding complicity." Accordingly, when the International Law Commission (ILC) formulated the principles recognized in the Charter . . . and in the judgment of the Tribunal at the direction of the General Assembly, *see* Nuremberg Principles Resolution I, it omitted any indication of a limitation on accomplice liability. Principle VII provides that [c]omplicity in the commission of a crime against peace, a war crime, or a crime against humanity . . . is a crime under international law. The ILC's formulation of the principles is considered to be an authoritative rendering of the formal holdings of the Nuremberg Tribunal and is consulted as an authoritative source of customary international law by the ICTY and ICTR. * * *

Having been accepted as one of the core principles of the post-World War II war crimes trials, the individual criminal responsibility of those who aid and abet violations of international law was repeatedly reflected in international treaties thereafter. These treaties include major agreements addressing fundamental human rights concerns such as torture, apartheid, slavery, and genocide. * * * More recently, aiding and abetting has been included in a number of the treaties concerning organized crime and terrorism, which have become prominent concerns of the international community. * * *

Aiding and abetting liability continues to be recognized and enforced in international tribunals. The Statutes creating the ICTY and ICTR were adopted by resolutions of the Security Council. In their respective sections on individual criminal responsibility, both statutes impose individual liability on any person "who planned, instigated, ordered, committed or otherwise aided and abetted in the planning, preparation or execution" of a crime.

As with the London Charter, the recognition of aiding and abetting liability in the ICTY Statute is particularly significant because the Individual Criminal Responsibility section of that statute was intended to codify existing norms of customary international law. In his report to the Security Council regarding the creation of the ICTY, the Secretary–General explained that "in assigning to the International Tribunal the task of prosecuting persons responsible for serious violations of international humanitarian law, the Security Council would not be creating or purporting to legislate that law. Rather, the International Tribunal would have the task of applying existing international humanitarian law." * * * Accordingly, the provision of aiding and abetting liability in the ICTY statute reflects a determination by both the Secretary–General and the Security Council, which approved the Secretary–General's report when it enacted the statute, that such liability is firmly established in customary international law. The inclusion of substantively identical language in the statute creating the ICTR presumably reflects a similar determination.

Consistent with its statutory authorization, the ICTY has recognized and applied aiding and abetting liability for violations of international law. *See, e.g., Furundzija,* Trial Chamber Judgment, 249, 275. Furthermore, it has done so only after confirming that such liability was part of customary law. * * * The Tribunal therefore conducted a probing and thoughtful analysis of international law sources in its early decisions to confirm that aiding and abetting liability is recognized in customary international law.

More recently, the Rome Statute of the International Criminal Court (Rome Statute), July 17, 1998, 2187 U.N.T.S. 90, provides that a person shall be criminally responsible and liable for punishment for a crime within the jurisdiction of the ICC if that person:

> (c) For the purpose of facilitating the commission of such a crime, aids, abets or otherwise assists in its commission or its attempted commission, including providing the means for its commission; [or]
>
> (d) In any other way contributes to the commission or attempted commission of such a crime by a group of persons acting with a common purpose. Such contribution shall be intentional and shall either:
>
> > (i) Be made with the aim of furthering the criminal activity or criminal purpose of the group, where such activity or purpose involves the commission of a crime within the jurisdiction of the Court; or
> >
> > (ii) Be made in the knowledge of the intention of the group to commit the crime[.]

Id. art. 25(3)(c), (d). The Rome Statute is particularly significant for the present inquiry because, unlike other sources of international legislation, it articulates the *mens rea* required for aiding and abetting liability. The Statute makes clear that, other than assistance rendered to the commission of a crime by a group of persons acting with a common purpose, a defendant is guilty of aiding and abetting the commission of a crime only if he does so "[f]or the purpose of facilitating the commission of such a crime." *Id.* art. 25(3)(c).

In drawing upon the Rome Statute, I recognize that it has yet to be construed by the International Criminal Court; its precise contours and the extent to which it may differ from customary international law thus remain somewhat uncertain. Nevertheless, the Statute has been signed by 139 countries and ratified by 105, including most of the mature democracies of the world. It may therefore be taken by and large * * * as constituting an authoritative expression of the legal views of a great number of States. *Furundzija,* Trial Chamber Judgment, 227.

Furthermore, the Rome Statute's *mens rea* standard is entirely consistent with the application of accomplice liability under the sources of international law discussed above. * * *

With respect to the *actus reus* component of the aiding and abetting liability, the international legislation is less helpful in identifying a specific standard. However, in the course of its analysis of customary international law, the ICTY concluded that "the *actus reus* of aiding and abetting in international criminal law requires practical assistance, encouragement, or moral support which has a *substantial effect* on the perpetration of the crime." *Furundzija*, Trial Chamber Judgment, 235 (second emphasis added). My research has uncovered nothing to indicate that a standard other than "substantial assistance" should apply.

Accordingly, I conclude that a defendant may be held liable under international law for aiding and abetting the violation of that law by another when the defendant (1) provides practical assistance to the principal which has a substantial effect on the perpetration of the crime, and (2) does so with the purpose of facilitating the commission of that crime. Furthermore, based on this review of international law's treatment of aiding and abetting liability over the past sixty years, I conclude that aiding and abetting liability, so defined, is sufficiently "well-established[ ][and] universally recognized" to be considered customary international law for the purposes of the ATCA. *See Kadic*, 70 F.3d at 239 (internal quotation marks omitted). * * *

HALL, CIRCUIT JUDGE, concurring:

As reflected in the *per curiam* opinion, I agree with Judge Katzmann with respect to the ultimate disposition of this appeal. The district court erred when it ruled that it lacked jurisdiction under the ATCA to determine plaintiffs' claims based on defendants' accessorial liability. * * * [T]he district court assumed that a federal court must look to international law to divine not only the applicable primary violation of international law cognizable under the ATCA, but also the standard for aiding and abetting liability. The district court went on to conclude that aiding and abetting liability did not exist as a matter of customary international law and thus that federal subject matter jurisdiction did not lie. This conclusion was error. As *Sosa* makes clear, a federal court must turn to international law to divine standards of primary liability under the ATCA. To derive a standard of accessorial liability, however, a federal court should consult the federal common law. * * *

In addition to its delineation of the standard by which federal courts derive primary violations of international law, the *Sosa* opinion also contains numerous dicta. In his concurring opinion, Judge Katzmann thoroughly summarizes these dicta. It remains inescapable, however, that *Sosa* at best lends Delphian guidance on the question of whether the federal common law or customary international law represents the proper source from which to derive a standard of aiding and abetting liability under the ATCA. Lacking the benefit of clear guidance,

I presume a federal court should resort to its traditional source, the federal common law, when deriving the standard. Because I find that federal common law provides a standard by which to assess aiding and abetting liability, I do not address the alternative argument that such a standard may be derived from international law.

It is a "hornbook principle that international law does not specify the means of its domestic enforcement." Brief for the International Law Scholars as Amici Curiae at 5–6; *see also* Brief for the United States of America as *Amicus Curiae* at 5 ("[A]lthough the substantive norm to be applied is drawn from international law or treaty, any cause of action recognized by a federal court is one devised as a matter of federal common law."). * * *

As *amicus* International Law Scholars persuasively argue, these "means of domestic enforcement" encompass at least some theories of accessorial liability, including aiding and abetting. I believe our Court should stand by this principle. Moreover, when international law and domestic law speak on the same doctrine, domestic courts should choose the latter. This, too, is a principle our Court should respect. Here, customary international law and the federal common law both include standards of aiding and abetting. In a situation such as this, I opt for the standard articulated by the federal common law. * * *

Until the Supreme Court provides us more explicit guidance regarding accessorial liability than it has to date, I remain convinced that our federal common law embodies a clearly extant standard of aiding and abetting liability. It is to this standard that federal courts should resort and to which I now turn.

The Supreme Court has described *Halberstam v. Welch*, 705 F.2d 472 (D.C.Cir.1983), "as a comprehensive opinion on the subject [of aiding and abetting]." *Cent. Bank, N.A. v. First Interstate Bank, N.A.*, 511 U.S. 164, 181 (1994). *Halberstam* relied heavily upon the Restatement (Second) of Torts to set the parameters of aiding and abetting liability. Section 876(b) of the Restatement provides: "For harm resulting to a third person from the tortious conduct of another, one is subject to liability if he ... (b) knows that the other's conduct constitutes a breach of duty and gives substantial assistance or encouragement to the other so to conduct himself." Based on the Restatement, *Halberstam* held that aiding and abetting included three elements:

> (1) the party whom the defendant aids must perform a wrongful act that causes an injury; (2) the defendant must be generally aware of his role as part of an overall illegal or tortious activity at the time that he provides the assistance; [and] (3) the defendant must knowingly and substantially assist the principal violation.

Halberstam, 705 F.2d at 477. The *Halberstam* Court then adopted and applied the factors enumerated in § 876 to assess whether the defendant's encouragement or assistance was sufficiently substantial to support liability. * * * In the almost quarter-century since *Halberstam* was decided, many state courts and Circuit Courts, including the Second Circuit, have adopted the Restatement's aiding and abetting standard. Following the lead of the *Halberstam* Court, I believe that § 876 provides the proper standard under which to assess whether a particular defendant may be held liable for aiding and abetting a primary violation of international law. I also agree with the *Halberstam* Court that a person who assists a tortious act may be liable for other reasonably foreseeable acts done in connection with it. *Id.* at 484.

Under a proper application of § 876 to ATCA civil aiding and abetting claims, liability should be found only where there is evidence that a defendant furthered the violation of a clearly established international law norm in one of three ways: (1) by knowingly and substantially assisting a principal tortfeasor, such as a foreign government or its proxy, to commit an act that violates a clearly established international law norm; (2) by encouraging, advising, contracting with, or otherwise soliciting a principal tortfeasor to commit an act while having actual or constructive knowledge that the principal tortfeasor will violate a clearly established customary international law norm in the process of completing that act; or (3) by facilitating the commission of human rights violations by providing the principal tortfeasor with the tools, instrumentalities, or services to commit those violations with actual or constructive knowledge that those tools, instrumentalities, or services will be (or only could be) used in connection with that purpose.

All members of this panel understand that corporations must transact business in a less than perfect world. I do not understand defendants to argue, however, that business imperatives require a license to assist in violations of international law. Rather, I understand defendants to express the concern that the recognition of ATCA aiding and abetting liability could expose corporations to liability for merely doing business in countries with repressive regimes or for participating in activities that, with twenty-twenty hindsight, can be said to have been indirectly linked to human rights abuses. I share Judge Katzmann's understanding, however, that private parties and corporate actors are subject to liability under the ATCA. * * * Defendants raise important concerns about such liability, but those concerns do not counsel in favor of the *per se* rejection of corporate liability, private party liability, and aiding and abetting liability under the ATCA. Instead, they require the narrow and careful extension of such liability to cases in which a defendant played a knowing and substantial role in the violation of a clearly recognized international law norm. Furthermore, the collateral consequences predicted by defendants and the dissent remain relevant considerations when making these judgments, as the common law nature of the inquiry allows for a limited but meaningful consideration of the practical consequences of extending ATCA liability in the context of each particular case.

Because I intend aiding and abetting liability to attach only in this limited way, I think it helpful to provide examples illustrating the three ways in which I believe a defendant may incur liability for aiding and abetting violations of customary international law. The first type of aiding and abetting liability is designed to capture the case of a principal tortfeasor who seeks assistance from a defendant to commit an act that violates international law norms, such as the extrajudicial killing of an opposition political figure. The second is designed to cover circumstances where the alleged aider and abettor is accused of having purchased security services with the knowledge that the security forces would, or were likely to, commit international law violations in fulfilling their mandate. The allegations raised in the cases of *Unocal,* 395 F.3d 932, and *Wiwa v. Royal Dutch Petroleum Co.,* No. 96–Civ–8386, 2002 WL 319887 (S.D.N.Y. Feb. 28, 2002), would be reached by this prong. In *Unocal,* the alleged aider and abettor corporation was accused of having purchased security services from a military government to further develop its oil operations, with the knowledge that the security forces would likely commit international law violations in fulfilling this mandate. 395 F.3d at 938–42. In *Wiwa,* the plaintiffs alleged that the defendants directed and aided government security forces in violating plaintiffs' rights by providing logistical support, transportation, and weapons to government security forces to ensure that the corporation's business activities could proceed as usual. *Wiwa,* 2002 WL 319887, at *2.

The Zyklon B Case provides a clear example of when liability would attach in the third circumstance, when a defendant provides "the tools, instrumentalities, or services to commit [human rights] violations with actual . . . knowledge that those tools, instrumentalities or services will be (or only could be) used in connection with that purpose." *See* Trial of Bruno Tesch and Two Others (The Zyklon B Case), 1 Law Reports of Trials of War Criminals 93 (1947) (British Military Ct., Hamburg, Mar. 1–8, 1946). In that case, Bruno Tesch was the sole owner of a firm that distributed Zyklon B, a highly dangerous poison gas, to Auschwitz and other concentration camps from 1941 to 1945. Zyklon B previously had been used as a disinfectant in public buildings. The evidence showed that Tesch himself proposed using the gas to exterminate human beings, undertook to train the S.S. in this "new method of killing," and was aware that, by June 1942, the gas was being used for such a purpose. *Id.* at 95. The Prosecutor successfully argued that knowingly to supply a commodity to a branch of the State which was using that commodity for the mass extermination of Allied civilian nationals was a war crime, and that the people who did it were war criminals for putting the means to commit the crime into the hands of those who actually carried it out. *Id.* at 94.

These examples are illustrative rather than exhaustive, and I offer them in an effort to provide greater substantive content for a doctrinal framework that, like most common law rules, is vague and abstract in its articulation of legal obligations and culpable conduct. Standards such as "substantial assistance" and "actual or constructive knowledge" are hardly newly minted, however, and judicial decisions interpreting the meaning of these standards in the context of individual cases will provide guidance to courts considering accessorial liability under the ATCA. Common law decisionmaking proceeds through the incremental, analogical application of broadly-stated principles, and it is therefore not amenable to the formulation of finely detailed rules in the manner of a regulatory code. Contrary to the dissent's suggestions, however, the contextual nature and factual sensitivity of common law judicial rule-making takes account of the practical problems that can result from ill-designed legal rules, and the flexibility of the common law process allows those problems to be addressed and avoided as they arise.

In the case at bar, plaintiffs have alleged, albeit in insufficiently specific terms, that the defendant corporations (a) knowingly and substantially assisted a principal tortfeasor to commit acts that violate clearly established international law norms, and (b) facilitated the commission of international law violations by providing the principal tortfeasors with the tools, instrumentalities, or services to commit those violations with actual or constructive knowledge that those tools, instrumentalities, or services would be (or only could be) used in connection with that purpose. Such allegations, if proven, clearly satisfy the standard for asserting ATCA liability under an aiding and abetting theory. * * *

KORMAN, DISTRICT JUDGE, concurring in part and dissenting in part:

* * * Judge Hall flatly ignores the holding of the Supreme Court that the second consideration in deciding whether to accept jurisdiction over a cause of action alleging a violation of the law of nations "is whether international law extends the scope of liability for a violation of a given norm to the perpetrator being sued, if the defendant is a private actor such as a corporation or individual." *Sosa,* 542 U.S. at 732 n.20, 124 S.Ct. 2739. Instead of undertaking an analysis of a given norm of international law to determine the scope of liability of a private actor, Judge Hall concludes that international law is irrelevant and that once a violation of a given norm is alleged, ATCA subjects a private party to liability if he aided-and-abetted that violation.

Judge Hall's concurring opinion is premised on the assumption that, even though the ATCA does not by its terms encompass aiding-and-abetting liability, it should be construed as if it contains such language. * * *

The language of the ATCA, like the language of the statute at issue in [*Boim v. Quranic Literacy Institute,* 291 F.3d 1000 (7th Cir. 2002)], can support the recognition of a cause of action for aiding-and-abetting. Nevertheless, it does so only if the plaintiff invokes an international law norm that provides for such liability. Nothing in the language of the ATCA supports the broad holding that Congress intended to provide a forum to adjudicate causes of action for aiding-and-abetting the violation of a norm when such conduct did not fall within the scope of the norm. Indeed, the same Congress that enacted the ATCA, without reference to aiding-and-abetting liability, explicitly made it a crime to aid-and-abet acts of piracy, a violation of the law of nations. This shows that, despite Judge Hall's suggestion to the contrary, the First Congress "knew how to impose aiding and abetting liability when it chose to do so," with respect to violations of the law of nations. * * *

The historical support for the proposition that the Founding Generation nevertheless understood that civil liability for aiding and abetting international law violations was contemplated under the ATCA is ambiguous at best. The lynchpin for this argument is Attorney General William Bradford's 1795 opinion, *Breach of Neutrality*, 1 Op. Atty. Gen. 57 (1795). In his opinion, Bradford specifically addressed a question posed to him, namely, whether American citizens who "voluntarily joined, conducted, aided, and abetted a French fleet in attacking the settlement, and plundering or destroying the property of British subjects on that coast" could be subject to criminal prosecution in the United States. *Id.* at 58. In responding to this question, Bradford expressed some doubt about a criminal prosecution, but he stated that

> there can be no doubt that the company or individuals who have been injured by these acts of hostility have a remedy by a civil suit in the courts of the United States; jurisdiction being expressly given to these courts in all cases where an alien sues for a tort only, in violation of the law of nations, or a treaty of the United States....

Id. at 59.

Because Bradford did not distinguish between primary and secondary liability, it is not possible to discern that, when he said a cause of action would lie for "these acts of hostility," he was focusing on aiding-and-abetting as opposed to direct participation in the conduct that violated a treaty of the United States. Indeed, because the conduct involved direct participation by American citizens, who acted with the intent to make the attack succeed, it seems likely that Bradford recognized all of the perpetrators as joint tortfeasors, as that term was understood at the time. * * *

In sum, Bradford's opinion and the cases cited by Judge Hall do not support the extraordinary proposition that Congress intended the ATCA to permit jurisdiction to be exercised over claims of aiding-and-abetting without regard to whether the conduct at issue violated an international law norm. Moreover, Judge Hall compounds his flawed discussion of this issue by adopting a standard for aiding-and-abetting that is vague and inappropriate in the present context. As if the language of section 876(b) of the Restatement (Second) of Torts imposing liability for "substantial assistance" was not vague enough, he endorses a five-factor test, first suggested by the Restatement and then adopted in *Halberstam,* to "assess whether the defendant's encouragement or assistance was sufficiently substantial to support liability." * * *

Such a five-prong test for determining whether assistance was substantial hardly provides the clear guidance necessary to those engaging in commercial transactions.

By incorporating a vague "substantial assistance" standard, this newly minted theory of aiding-and-abetting liability will create many practical problems harmful to the political and economic interests of the United States. As the United States observes in its *amicus* brief, the decision to embrace this broader scope of liability under the ATCA will generate tremendous uncertainty for private corporations, who will be reluctant to operate in countries with poor human rights records for fear of incurring legal liability for those regimes' bad acts. This uncertainty, in turn, will undermine efforts by the United States to encourage reform in those countries through active economic engagement, and will deter the free flow of trade and investment more generally. * * *

Unlike Judge Hall, Judge Katzmann looks to international law to resolve the issue of whether a private party or a corporation (he draws no distinction between the two) can be held liable for aiding-and-abetting a violation of international law otherwise applicable to state actors or to private parties acting under color of law. While Judge Katzmann properly looks to international law, he disregards the holding in *Sosa* and our own holdings in *Kadic* and *Wiwa,*, that require a norm-by-norm analysis to determine whether "international law extends the scope of liability for a violation of a *given* norm to the perpetrator being sued, if the defendant is a private actor such as a corporation or individual." *Sosa*, 542 U.S. at 732 n.20 (emphasis added). Judge Katzmann declines to undertake this analysis because that "is not how the inquiry is undertaken by international tribunals whose jurisdiction is limited by customary international law."

We do not enjoy the freedom to disregard the guidance of the Supreme Court and adopt the practice of international tribunals—particularly the unorthodox practices of the ITCY and the ICTR. Moreover, contrary to Judge Katzmann's suggestion, the jurisdiction of the post-apartheid international tribunals to which he refers, principally the ICTY, are conferred by the Security Council resolutions creating them. They are not limited by international law. Instead, these custom-made statutes, which address particular international crises are sometimes contrary to evolving norms of customary international law. * * *

More significantly, in the cases on which Judge Katzmann relies—those of the ICTY—the tribunal was not required to make any inquiry regarding the issue of whether international law extends the scope of liability for a given norm to the perpetrator being sued if the defendant is a private actor such as a corporation.

The Statute of the ICTY, article 5, followed the London Charter, the Judgment of the Nuremberg Tribunal construing it, and the tribunals empaneled pursuant to [Control Council Law ("CCL")] 10, all of which required a connection between crimes against humanity and war crimes. Because private parties are individually responsible for crimes committed in the course of a war, this connection made it unnecessary for the Nuremberg Tribunal or the CCL 10 tribunals to address the scope of liability of private actors as aiders-and-abetters. Thus, ICTY cases provide no support for failing to follow the instruction of the Supreme Court, one that is consistent with our own holding in *Kadic* and *Wiwa*, which requires an analysis of the particular norm the defendant is accused of violating to determine whether a private party may be held responsible as an aider-and-abettor.

While Judge Katzmann erroneously concludes that there was— during the period when the crimes alleged here took place—an independent norm of customary international law, making private actors legally responsible as aiders-and-abetters without regard to whether the particular norm they allegedly violated imposed such liability, he correctly rejects the "substantial assistance with knowledge" standard for this newly minted norm that Judge Hall finds in section 876(b) of the Restatement (Second) of Torts. Instead, he "conclude[s] that a defendant may be held liable under international law for aiding and abetting the violation of that law by another when the defendant (1) provides practical assistance to the principal which has a substantial effect on the perpetration of the crime, and (2) does so with the purpose of facilitating the commission of that crime." The basis for this formulation is article 25 of the Rome Statute. * * *

This article is significant because it makes clear that, other than assistance rendered to the commission of a crime by a group of persons acting with a common purpose, a defendant is guilty of aiding-and-abetting the commission of a crime *only* if he does so "[f]or the purpose of facilitating the commission of such a crime . . . including providing the means for its commission." *Id.* * * *

The Rome Statute has been signed by 139 countries and ratified by 105, including most of the mature democracies of the world. I agree that it reflects an international consensus on the issue of the appropriate standard for determining liability for aiding-and-abetting, it is consistent with our own domestic law, and it addresses the concern over the adoption of a substantial assistance with knowledge standard raised in the *amicus* brief filed by the United States. Indeed, the *amicus* brief appears to endorse the elements set out in article 25(3). * * * These considerations also obviate any concern regarding the failure of the United States to ratify the Treaty of Rome for reasons unrelated to the definition of aiding-and-abetting.

My point of disagreement with Judge Katzmann relates to the narrow issue of whether there was *any* well established[ ][and] universally recognized definition of aiding-and-abetting sufficient to be considered customary international law for the purposes of the ATCA during the apartheid era when the defendants allegedly violated customary international law. There was none and the absence of such a definition is significant for reasons already discussed.

Nevertheless, I concur in section II.B of his opinion that articulates the customary international law standard for aiding-and-abetting based on the Rome Statute. I do so because it provides a clear standard, adopted by a majority of the panel, for Judge Sprizzo to apply, in deciding whether to grant the plaintiffs' motion to file amended complaints. * * *

Judge Katzmann's opinion, however, does not end with section II.B. Thus, while he does not rely on post-apartheid decisions of the ICTY or the ICTR to support the standard that he enunciates for determining aiding-and-abetting liability, he does rely on those cases to suggest that "the substantial assistance with knowledge" standard for aiding-and-abetting may provide a foundation for future development of the law in this area. I discuss the cases on which he relies to demonstrate why, contrary to Judge Katzmann's gratuitous suggestion, they do not provide a reliable basis for a broader definition than the one proscribed in the Rome Statute. * * *

Conclusion

I dissent from the judgment reversing the dismissal of the complaint for the reasons I have elaborated above. Nevertheless, I concur in section II.A of Judge Katzmann's opinion that rejects Judge Hall's argument that the scope of liability for the violation of the norm of international law must be decided by reference to our own domestic law. * * *

POSTSCRIPT: *KHULUMANI v. BARCLAY NAT'L. BANK LTD.*

Following the fractured Second Circuit ruling, the defendants in the *apartheid* case filed a petition for *certiorari*. The plaintiffs opposed the petition on the grounds that the issues raised were not ripe, as the plaintiffs had been granted leave to amend their complaints, narrow their allegations, and plead specific connections between the corporation and the human rights violations at issue in the case. The Solicitor General, representing the United States, filed an *amicus* brief in support of the defendants. In its *amicus* brief, the government argued that "suits brought under the court of appeals' theory of liability will require federal courts to sit in judgment of the conduct of foreign states when Congress has determined those states should be immune from suit. Such litigation will inevitably give rise to tension in relations between the United States and the country whose conduct is at issue. Even when the government whose acts are under scrutiny has been removed from power, a suit brought in United States court to redress those wrongs is not a proper function of a United States court and will often be viewed by the foreign state's new government as an infringement of its sovereignty."

The government further argued that "[l]itigation such as this would also interfere with the ability of the U.S. government to employ the full range of foreign policy options when interacting with regimes whose policies the United States would like to influence. In general, the U.S. government supports open markets and trade and investment with other countries. But in certain circumstances, the U.S. government may determine that more limited commercial interaction is desirable in encouraging reform and pursuing other policy objectives."

Despite much anticipation on the part of the commentators and the strenuous urging of the Executive Branch, the Supreme Court did not grant the defendant's petition for *certiorari*. Four of the Justices were disqualified from deciding the matter due to investments in some of the defendant companies and family ties. Because it lacked the required quorum of six, the Supreme Court left the Second Circuit's decision undisturbed.

NOTES AND QUESTIONS ON *KHULUMANI v. BARCLAY NAT. BANK LTD.*

1. *Aiding and abetting.* What is the holding in *Khulumani* with respect to aiding and abetting? Is the holding limited to the finding that aiding and abetting liability exists under the ATS? Is there a holding with respect to the proper aiding and abetting standard that should be applied in ATS cases?

Judge Katzmann suggests that the standard for aiding and abetting should be drawn from international law and relies on the definition used in the Rome Statute, a treaty which articulates the *mens rea* requirement that a person is guilty of aiding and abetting the commission of a crime only if he does so "[f]or the purpose of facilitating the commission of [the] crime." Rome Statute, art. 25(3)(c). Is this any different from the *mens rea* requirement that the aider and abettor have knowledge that his actions will contribute to the commission of the crime? *See* GERHARD WERLE, PRINCIPLES OF INTERNATIONAL CRIMINAL LAW, at ¶ 306–307, 330 (2005) ("for the purpose of facilitating the commission of the crime" means only that the perpetrator be "aware that the consequence will occur in the ordinary course of events"). As noted by Judge Katzman, this language has yet to be construed by the International Criminal Court.

Judge Hall would look to the federal common law for the proper standard of aiding and abetting liability in ATS cases. This definition is reflected in the Restatement (Second) of Torts, § 876(b), and is mirrored in the aiding and abetting standard applied by the ICTY and ICTR, both of which are tasked with applying customary international law. This standard provides that "a third party is liable for harm caused by another if he 'knows that the other's conduct constitutes a breach of duty and gives substantial assistance or encouragement to the other so to conduct himself.' " Which source of law should the courts turn to for aiding and abetting standards?

In his concurring opinion, Judge Hall notes that Judge Katzmann declined to address whether federal common law provides a standard by which to determine aiding and abetting liability for this case, and states, "It is thus left to a future panel of this Court to determine whether international or domestic federal common law is the exclusive source from which to derive the applicable standard." 504 F.3d at 286 n.4.

How do you think the U.S. Supreme Court would decide this issue? Should there be a different rule for aiding and abetting in cases involving former foreign officials accused of complicity in human rights violations?

In an *amicus* brief filed in the *Apartheid* case, certain scholars contended that aiding and abetting was a general principle of law within the meaning of Article 38 of the Statute of the International Court of Justice. Should the courts use such general principles in ATS litigation? Would a federal common law approach, as adopted by Judge Hall, in which courts examine all of these sources and choose the principles most appropriate to vindicate the purposes of the ATS, be preferable? In doing so, should courts tailor those principles to take into account the "practical consequences" of the rules they adopt?

2. *Pleading aiding and abetting liability after Khulumani.* In *Khulumani*, the court granted the plaintiff's motion to amend the complaint and declined to determine whether the plaintiff's original complaint adequately pled a violation of international law, because it could not be sure the pleadings in the record before the court represented the final version of the plaintiff's allegations. How would you draft the new complaint based on a theory of aiding and abetting liability after *Khulumani*?

3. *Norm-by-norm analysis for aiding and abetting.* Judge Korman argued that it was insufficient to argue whether aiding and abetting was generally recognized under customary international law, and that courts were instead required to engage in a "norm-by-norm analysis" to determine whether aiding and abetting liability exists for a violation of a particular norm. Judge Katzmann took issue with this position, noting that this approach was inconsistent with the approach of the international tribunals, which treated aiding and abetting as a theory of liability for acts committed by a third party.

4. *Case-specific deference.* Footnote 21 of *Sosa* states:

Another possible limitation that we need not apply here is a policy of case-specific deference to the political branches. For example, there are now pending in federal district court several class actions seeking damages from various corporations alleged to have participated in, or abetted, the regime of apartheid that formerly controlled South Africa. *See In re South African Apartheid Litigation*, 238 F.Supp.2d 1379 (JPML 2002) (granting a motion to transfer the cases to the Southern District of New York). The Government of South Africa has said that these cases interfere with the policy embodied by its Truth and Reconciliation Commission, which "deliberately avoided a 'victors' justice' approach to the crimes of apartheid and chose instead one based on confession and absolution, informed by the principles of reconciliation, reconstruction, reparation and goodwill." The United States has agreed. In such cases, there is a strong argument that federal courts should give serious weight to the Executive Branch's view of the case's impact on foreign policy.

Not surprisingly, this footnote was the subject of debate in the *Apartheid* appeal and oral argument. In the Second Circuit, the South African government renewed its objections to the actions. However, the Chairperson of the Truth and Reconciliation Commission ("TRC"), Bishop Desmond Tutu, and several other members of the TRC filed an *amicus* brief supporting the actions. "We are compelled to make clear our collective view that it is fallacious to assert that actions for damages against corporations that participated in or aided and abetted violations of international law interfere with the policies embodied in the TRC. We respectfully submit that this assertion does not withstand even a cursory inspection." *TRC Brief* at 5. Because the plaintiffs were granted leave to amend their complaint, the Second Circuit did not reach the issue of case-specific deference in its decision, and instead remanded the question to the district court so that the court could "engage in the first instance in the careful case-by-case analysis that questions of this type require." *Khulumani*, 504 F.3d at 263.

How should federal courts respond to such arguments? How much deference should be afforded to the Executive Branch in this case? Consider Justice Powell's concurring statement in *First Nat'l City Bank v. Banco Nacional de Cuba*, 406 U.S. 759, 773 (1972), "I would be uncomfortable with a doctrine which would require the judiciary to receive the Executive's permission before invoking its jurisdiction. Such a notion, in the name of the doctrine of the separation of powers, seems to me to conflict with that very doctrine."

How much deference should be afforded to the wishes of foreign governments? Under the doctrine of international comity, courts may dismiss a case because it conflicts with the legislative, executive, or judicial acts of another country. Should courts simply accept a foreign government's assertion that such a conflict exists without scrutiny?

5. *Central Bank of Denver, N.A. v. First Interstate Bank of Denver, N.A.*, 511 U.S. 164 (1994). Defendants in ATS cases often argue that *Central Bank* precludes courts from recognizing aiding and abetting liability for claims brought under the ATS, because "where Congress has not explicitly provided for aider and abettor liability in civil causes of action, it should not be inferred." *In re S. African Apartheid Litig.*, 346 F. Supp. 2d at 550. Most courts have rejected this argument, finding the complex securities scheme at issue in *Central Bank* inapposite to ATS cases. *See, e.g., Presbyterian Church of Sudan v. Talisman Energy, Inc.*, 374 F.

Supp. 2d 331 (S.D.N.Y. 2005). In *Khulumani*, Judge Katzmann adopted a different approach, finding *Central Bank* inapplicable because the relevant norm in ATS cases are provided by the law of nations, which extends liability for the violation of its norms to aider and abettors.

6. *State Department statements of interest.* In several of the corporate accountability cases, the U.S. State Department has filed a Statement of Interest with the court suggesting that they should be dismissed due to the foreign policy concerns they raised. In *Filartiga*, the court gave great weight to the State Department's *amicus* brief, which argued that torture had become a violation of the "law of nations" and also that U.S. courts should be open for the redress of such claims. To date, there have been a variety of responses from the courts to these interventions. In *Doe v. Exxon–Mobil Corp.*, 393 F. Supp. 2d 20 (D.D.C. 2005), the district court dismissed the plaintiffs' ATS claims relating to events in Aceh, Indonesia, but retained jurisdiction over plaintiffs' state law claims, based in part on a Statement of Interest from the State Department.

What if the Executive statement is that the particular case or claim is inconsistent with U.S. foreign policy? In *Mujica v. Occidental Petroleum Corp.*, 381 F. Supp. 2d 1164 (C.D. Cal. 2005), the plaintiffs sued Occidental Petroleum for injuries resulting from the bombing of unarmed civilians by the security company hired by Occidental to protect their pipeline. Seven were killed in the operation, including six children. The district court dismissed plaintiffs' ATS claims based on the political question doctrine as a result of the foreign policy concerns expressed in a State Department intervention and dismissed plaintiffs' state law claims for similar reasons based on the "foreign affairs" doctrine as explained in *American Ins. Ass'n v. Garamendi*, 539 U.S. 396 (2003).

The foreign policy concerns in the Statement of Interest filed in the *Mujica* case included the following:

> Attached for the Court's information is a letter from U.S. Department of State Legal Adviser William H. Taft, to Daniel Meron, Principal Deputy Assistant Attorney General, Civil Division, U.S. Department of Justice, dated December 23, 2004, which sets forth the current views of the United States concerning the impact of this litigation on its foreign policy. As the Supreme Court has directed, it is appropriate for this Court to give these concerns great weight "as the considered judgment of the Executive on a particular question of foreign policy." *Republic v. Austria v. Altman*, 541 U.S. 677, (2004).

> The Legal Adviser
> Department of State Washington
> December 23, 2004

I am writing now to request that you bring the following views to Judge Rea's attention. We want to affirm at the outset, of course, that the State Department neither takes any position with respect to the merits of the litigation, nor do we condone or excuse any violations of human rights or humanitarian law which may have occurred in connection with the incidents on which the suit is based. Our views are confined to responding to the question posed to us by the court. For reasons stated below, and in light of the views communicated to us by the Colombian government, the State Department believes that the adjudication of this case will have an adverse impact on the foreign policy interests of the United States.

Allegations related to those involved in the suit before the court are currently being handled in the Colombian legal system. In May 2004, an administrative court in the Arauca Department of Colombia ruled that the Colombian government must pay approximately $700,000 in damages to the plaintiffs in this case. This decision is currently under appeal in the Colombian judicial system. In addition, certain Colombian military personnel who were allegedly involved in the incident in question have been dismissed from their positions and face criminal investigation. On January 3, 2003, the U.S. Embassy in Bogotá informed the Colombian government of the U.S. decision to suspend assistance to CACOM–1, the Colombian Air Force unit involved in the Santo Domingo incident.

The Department believes that foreign courts generally should resolve disputes arising in foreign countries, where such courts reasonably have jurisdiction and are capable of resolving them fairly. An important part of our foreign policy is to encourage other countries to establish responsible legal mechanisms for addressing and resolving alleged human rights abuses. Duplicative proceedings in U.S. courts second-guessing the actions of the Colombian government and its military officials and the findings of Colombian courts, and which have at least the potential for reaching disparate conclusions, may be seen as unwarranted and intrusive to the Colombian government. * * *

Colombia is one of the United States' closest allies in this hemisphere, and our partner in the vital struggles against terrorism and narcotics trafficking. Colombia's role in helping to maintain Andean regional security, our trade relationship, and our national interests in the security of U.S. persons and U.S. investments in Colombia, rank high on our foreign policy agenda. Important U.S. foreign policy objectives also include support for the rule of law and human rights in Colombia.

Lawsuits such as the one before Judge Rea have the potential for deterring present and future U.S. investment in Colombia. Reduced U.S. investment, particularly in the oil and other extractive industries, could harm Colombia's economy in several ways, including by increasing unemployment and reducing the Colombian government's revenues from taxes and royalties. Downturns in Colombia's economy could have harmful consequences for the United States and our interests in Colombia and the Andean region. Specifically, such downturns could damage the stability of Colombia, the Colombian government's U.S.—supported campaigns against terrorists and narcotics traffickers, regional security, our efforts to reduce the amount of drugs that reach the streets of the United States, promotion of the rule of law and human rights in Colombia, and protection of U.S. persons, government facilities, and investments. Finally, reduced U.S. investment in Colombia's oil industry may detract from the vital U.S. policy goal of expanding and diversifying our sources of imported oil.

I have attached two letters from the Colombian Ministry of Foreign Relations to the U.S. Ambassador in Colombia. The first letter (Attachment 1), dated February 25, 2004, informs the embassy that the Colombian judiciary is investigating the responsibility of Colombian officials in this case. The second letter (Attachment 2), dated March 12, 2004, states that "any decision in this case may affect the relations between Colombia and the [United States]."

We hope the Court will find the foregoing responsive to its request.

> Sincerely,
> William H. Taft, IV

Should the government's concerns lead to the dismissal of claims under the ATS? In what circumstances should a federal court defer to the views of the State Department when considering a motion to dismiss an ATS case? Should the views of foreign governments be given the same deference? Would this depend on whether the foreign government was an ally or an enemy? Would it depend on how democratic the foreign government was? Since *Filartiga* the Executive's attitudes toward ATS litigation have varied dramatically from one Administration to another. How should the courts respond to such changes of view? Is there a difference between Executive views on whether a particular norm (*e.g.* torture) is prohibited under customary law and the Executive's view of the proper interpretation of the ATS? *See, e.g., Barlow v. Collins*, 397 U.S. 159, 166 (1970).

7. *Holocaust Litigation.* One area of ATS litigation against corporations has been relatively successful. Starting in the mid–1990s, class actions were brought against Swiss banks and many other corporations for their complicity in the Holocaust. Though none of these cases has been tried to verdict, they have resulted in billions of dollars in settlements. *See generally*, MICHAEL J. BAZYLER, HOLOCAUST JUSTICE (2003). The success of these cases appears to have been the result of a unique confluence of legal and political efforts. *See* STUART E. EISENSTADT, IMPERFECT JUSTICE: LOOTED ASSETS, SLAVE LABOR, AND THE UNFINISHED BUSINESS OF WORLD WAR II (2003). Cases against Japanese companies involved in

human rights violations during World War II have not fared as well. *See, e.g., Hwang Geum Joo v. Japan,* 413 F.3d 45 (D.C. Cir. 2005) (dismissing sexual slavery cases based on the political question doctrine).

Practicum

During oral arguments in *Sosa,* Justice O'Connor asked whether the policy concerns expressed by the United States about the scope of the ATS had ever been addressed to Congress. To date, no Administration has sought amendment of the ATS.

In October 2005, Senator Dianne Feinstein introduced a bill to amend the ATS, though the effort was soon dropped. The text of the bill was as follows:

ALIEN TORT STATUTE REFORM ACT

S. 1874, 109th Congr. § 2 (2005)

SEC. 2. SUITS BY ALIENS.

Section 1350 of title 28, United States Code, is amended to read as follows:

Sec. 1350. Alien's action for tort

(a) Jurisdiction of District Courts—The district courts shall have original and exclusive jurisdiction of any civil action brought by an alien asserting a claim of torture, extrajudicial killing, genocide, piracy, slavery, or slave trading if a defendant is a direct participant acting with specific intent to commit the alleged tort. The district courts shall not have jurisdiction over such civil suits brought by an alien if a foreign state is responsible for committing the tort in question within its sovereign territory.

(b) Definitions—For the purposes of this section:

(1) DEFENDANT—The term "defendant" means any person subject to the jurisdiction of the district courts of the United States, including—

(A) a United States citizen;

(B) a natural person who is a permanent resident of the United States;

(C) a natural person who resides in the United States; or

(D) a partnership, corporation, or other legal entity organized under the laws of the United States or of a foreign state.

(2) FOREIGN STATE—The term "foreign state" has the meaning given that term in section 1603 of title 28, United States Code.

(3) EXTRAJUDICIAL KILLING—The term "extrajudicial killing"—

(A) means a deliberated killing, which—

(i) notwithstanding the jurisdictional limitations referred to in subsection (a), is carried out by an individual under actual or apparent authority, or color of law, of any foreign state;

(ii) is directed against another individual in the offender's custody or physical control; and

(iii) is not authorized by a previous judgment pronounced by a regularly constituted court affording all the judicial guarantees which are recognized as indispensable by civilized peoples; and

(B) does not include any such killing that, under international law, is lawfully carried out under the authority of a foreign state.

(4) GENOCIDE—The term "genocide" means, whether in time of peace or in time of war, an act carried out, or an attempt to carry out an act, with the specific intent to destroy, in whole or in substantial part, a national, ethnic, racial, or religious group as such, which—

(A) kills members of that group;

(B) causes serious bodily injury to members of that group;

(C) causes the permanent impairment of the mental faculties of members of the group through drugs, torture, or similar techniques;

(D) subjects the group to conditions of life that are intended to cause the physical destruction of the group in whole or in part;

(E) imposes measures intended to prevent births within the group; or

(F) transfers by force children of the group to another group.

(5) PIRACY—The term "piracy" means—

(A) any illegal acts of violence or detention, or any act of depredation, committed for private ends by the crew or the passengers of a private ship or a private aircraft, and directed—

(i) on the high seas, against another ship or aircraft, or against persons or property on board such ship or aircraft; or

(ii) against a ship, aircraft, persons, or property in a place outside the jurisdiction of any country;

(B) any act of voluntary participation in the operations of a ship or of an aircraft with knowledge of facts making it a pirate ship or aircraft; or

(C) any act of inciting or of intentionally facilitating an act described in subparagraph (A) or (B).

(6) SLAVE TRADING—The term "slave trading" includes—

(A) all acts involved in the capture, acquisition, or disposal of a person with intent to reduce such person to slavery;

(B) all acts involved in the acquisition of a slave with a view to selling or exchanging such slave;

(C) all acts of disposal by sale or exchange of a slave acquired with a view to being sold or exchanged; and

(D) in general, every act of trade or transport of slaves.

(7) SLAVERY—The term "slavery" means the status or condition of a person over whom any or all of the powers attaching to the right of ownership are exercised.

(8) TORTURE—

(A) IN GENERAL—Notwithstanding the jurisdictional limitations referred to in subsection (a), the term "torture" means any act, carried out by an individual under actual or apparent authority, or color of law, of any foreign state, directed against another individual in the offender's custody or physical control, by which severe pain or suffering (other than pain or suffering arising only from or inherent in, or incidental to, lawful sanctions), whether physical or mental, is intentionally inflicted on that individual for such purposes as obtaining from that individual or a third person information or a confession, punishing that individual for an act that individual or a third person has committed or is suspected of having committed, intimidating or coercing that individual or a third person, or for any reason based on discrimination of any kind.

(B) MENTAL PAIN OR SUFFERING—In subparagraph (A), mental pain or suffering refers to prolonged mental harm caused by or resulting from—

(i) the intentional infliction or threatened infliction of severe physical pain or suffering;

(ii) the administration or application, or threatened administration or application, of mind altering substances, or other procedures calculated to disrupt profoundly the senses or the personality;

(iii) the threat of imminent death; or

(iv) the threat that another individual will imminently be subjected to death, severe physical pain or suffering, or the administration or application of mind altering substances or other procedures calculated to disrupt profoundly the senses or personality.

(c) Liability for Damages—Any defendant who is a direct participant acting with specific intent to commit a tort referred to in subsection (a) against an alien shall be liable for damages to that alien or to any person who may be a claimant in an action for the wrongful death of that alien.

(d) Exhaustion of Remedies—A district court shall abstain from the exercise of jurisdiction over a civil action described in subsection (a) if the claimant has not exhausted adequate and available remedies in the place in which the injury occurred. Adequate and available remedies include those available through local courts, claims tribunals, and similar legal processes.

(e) Foreign Policy Interests of the United States—No court in the United States shall proceed in considering the merits of a claim under subsection (a) if the President, or a designee of the President, adequately certifies to the court in writing that such exercise of jurisdiction will have a negative impact on the foreign policy interests of the United States.

(f) Procedural Requirements—

(1) SPECIFICITY—In any action brought under this section, the complaint shall state with particularity specific facts that—

(A) describe each tort alleged to have been committed and demonstrate the reason or reasons why the tort action may be brought under this section, provided that if an allegation is made on information and belief, the complaint shall state with particularity all facts on which that belief is formed; and

(B) demonstrate that the defendant had the specific intent to commit the tort alleged to have been committed.

(2) MOTION TO DISMISS—In any action brought under this section, the court shall, on the motion of any defendant, dismiss the complaint if the requirements of subparagraphs (A) and (B) of paragraph (1) are not met.

(3) STAY OF DISCOVERY—In any action brought under this section, all discovery related to the merits of the claim and other proceedings shall be stayed during the pendency of any motion to dismiss, unless the court finds upon the motion of any party that particularized discovery is necessary to preserve evidence or to prevent undue prejudice to that party.

(4) PLAINTIFF IDENTITY—

(A) REQUIREMENT—Subject to subparagraph (B), in any action brought under this section, the first and last names of all plaintiffs shall be disclosed in the complaint filed with the court.

(B) EXCEPTION—A court may permit an anonymous filing of a complaint if a plaintiff's life or safety would be endangered by publicly disclosing the plaintiff's identity.

(g) Fees—Contingency fee arrangements are prohibited in any action brought under the jurisdiction provided in this section.

(h) Statute of Limitations—No action shall be maintained under this section unless it is commenced not later than 10 years from the date the injury occurred.

(i) Application of Other Laws—Nothing in this section may be construed to waive or modify the application of any provision of the Class Action Fairness Act of 2005 (Public Law 109–2; 119 Stat. 4) and any amendment made by that Act, or of title 28, United States Code, to any class action law suit brought under this section.

Students should convene as the Senate Judiciary Committee, which will engage in a debate and mark-up session on this proposed legislation. In the mock hearing, some class members should appear before the Committee representing the relevant interests: the executive branch of the U.S. government, human rights groups, religious groups, corporations, and foreign governments. Among the topics to consider are: (1) What norms would be actionable? (2) What remedies would be available? (3) Would the Executive Branch have a veto power over cases raising foreign policy concerns? (3) What statutes of limitation and tolling doctrines would apply? (4) Would treaty provisions have to have an additional express cause of action to be actionable under the ATS? For an idea of the range and substance of the various interests, students might review the numerous *amicus* briefs filed in the U.S. Supreme Court in the *Sosa* case.

CHAPTER 2

MODULE 2

BASIC PRINCIPLES OF INTERNATIONAL LAW IN U.S. COURTS

■ ■ ■

Orientation

In Module 1, we considered litigation under the Alien Tort Statute ("ATS"), a 200–year-old mandate from Congress to the courts to enforce the "law of nations." In this Module, we explore additional ways that international human rights law may be enforced in the courts of United States. Domestic human and civil rights lawyers frequently rely on international human rights arguments when they appear to offer more protection than domestic norms. In some cases, as in the case of the death penalty, recourse to international law may be a last resort. More frequently, litigators employ international arguments in tandem with domestic law arguments to provide the maximum chance of success given the uncertainties of litigation. They may also wish to contribute to the long-term project of incorporating international norms into the U.S. legal system.

In recent years, there has been a renewed interest in "bringing human rights home" in U.S. domestic litigation and advocacy. *See* BRINGING HUMAN RIGHTS HOME (Cynthia Soohoo, *et al.* eds., 2007). There are many reasons for this. Most importantly, international human rights law and institutions have grown and become stronger in the last sixty years. Today, there are many areas in which international human rights norms are more rights-protective than domestic civil rights norms, in part because the U.S. Supreme Court has taken a more restrictive view of civil rights than it did in prior decades. Additionally, lawyers and judges have become increasingly familiar with international human rights and thus more apt to make and accept arguments based on international authorities.

The growing practice of invoking international law in domestic litigation is not without its critics. Powerful forces within the political and legal culture of the United States oppose reliance on international norms, especially in constitutional litigation. These debates are not new;

indeed, they have taken place periodically since the creation of the Republic. Since September 11, 2001, the debate has taken on renewed urgency, as many observers have argued that the Bush Administration waged its "war on terrorism" in violation of human rights norms and have sought to use international human rights law in domestic courts to critique Executive Branch policy.

Before turning to the legal framework for using international law in U.S. courts, some historical background may be useful. Respect for international law has been embedded in American values and jurisprudence since the inception of the Republic. The Founders repeatedly stressed that the new American nation would have to play by international rules to establish itself as a legitimate sovereign on the world stage. The first Chief Justice of the United States, John Jay, noted in *Chisholm v. Georgia* that the United States "had, by taking a place among the nations of the earth, become amenable to the laws of nations." 2 U.S. (2 Dall.) 419, 474 (1793). According to Harold Koh, Dean of Yale Law School, "[t]he framers and early Justices understood that the global legitimacy of a fledgling nation crucially depended upon the compatibility of its domestic law with the rules of the international system within which it sought acceptance." Harold Hongju Koh, *"Agora: The United States Constitution and Federal Law: International Law as Part of Our Law"* 98 Am. J. Int'l. L. 43, 44 (2004).

In the first two centuries of American jurisprudence, cases at the intersection of human rights and international law were relatively rare. The cases that did arise stemmed from the slave trade, *The Nereide*, 13 U.S. (9 Cranch) 388 (1815); the laws of war, *The Paquete Habana*, 100 U.S. 677 (1900); and extradition treaties, *United States v. Rauscher*, 119 U.S. 407 (1886), among a handful of other areas. The modern course of international human rights jurisprudence did not begin until after World War II.

After the Second World War, the Nuremberg trials, and the ensuing human rights revolution, lawyers in the United States began to employ emerging international human rights norms on behalf of their clients. In the immediate aftermath of the war, the discrepancy between the U.N. Charter's promises of non-discrimination and the reality of *de jure* and *de facto* discrimination in post-war America led civil rights lawyers to turn to the UN Charter and the Universal Declaration of Human Rights (UDHR) in their struggle to dismantle American *apartheid*. Bert Lockwood, *The United Nations Charter and United States Civil Rights Litigation: 1946–1955*, 69 Iowa L. Rev. 901 (1984).

These early efforts led to a significant—though short-lived—victory in *Sei Fujii v. State of California*, 217 P.2d 481 (1950). In that case, the California Court of Appeals held that California's Alien Land Law, which prohibited Japanese citizens from owning land in California, was inconsistent with the UN Charter and UDHR and was thus superceded by the operation of the Supremacy Clause in Article VI of the U.S.

Constitution. The response to this decision was immediate and negative. The California Supreme Court found both the Charter and the UDHR, although worthy of the "greatest respect," to be "non-self-executing" and thus unenforceable in domestic courts. The Court chose instead to invalidate the Alien Land Law under the Equal Protection Clause of the Fourteenth Amendment. The backlash to the *Sei Fujii* decision cast a long shadow over early efforts to use international human rights law in U.S. courts.

These early efforts at incorporating international human rights norms into domestic litigation strategy also met with strong judicial and political resistance because of the turbulence that accompanied the incipient civil rights movement. International human rights law also became intertwined in the ideological battles of the Cold War. Once the UN Human Rights Commission began drafting a pair of binding Covenants intended to impose binding obligations on their parties, Senator John W. Bricker of Ohio introduced a proposal (known as the "Bricker Amendment") between 1951 and 1954 that would have amended Article VI of the Constitution to limit the domestic application of treaties and other international agreements. Most of Bricker's proposals would have barred U.S. courts from giving such treaties any legal effect in the absence of implementing legislation, effectively rendering them all "non-self-executing" and unenforceable in the courts. "My purpose in offering this resolution," Senator Bricker declared, "is to bury the so-called Covenant on Human Rights so deep that no one holding high public office will ever dare to attempt its resurrection." Louis Henkin, *U.S. Ratification of Human Rights Conventions: The Ghost of Senator Bricker*, 89 AM. J. INT'L L. 341, 349 (1995).

While Senator Bricker may have been supported by his constituents, he faced strong opposition from President Eisenhower, who viewed these proposed amendments as an encroachment on his foreign policy powers. David Sloss, *The Domestication of International Human Rights: Non–Self–Executing Declarations and Human Rights Treaties*, 24 YALE J. INT'L L. 129 (1999). In an attempt to defeat the amendment, the Eisenhower Administration promised that the United States would not sign any international covenants or conventions on human rights. As a result, the Bricker Amendment failed in the U.S. Senate in 1954 by a single vote. Although Senator Bricker's attempts to amend the Constitution failed, the effects of his movement linger on. When President Carter eventually submitted several major multilateral human rights treaties to the Senate for ratification in 1979, he did so with a package of reservations, understandings, and declarations ("RUDs") and the assurance that ratification of these treaties would not change U.S. law.

The apparent conflict between Article VI's pledge that treaties are the supreme "law of the land" and the reluctance of American law and society to implement that pledge in the area of human rights continues to bedevil human rights litigators. As a result of this continued ambivalence—and because the United States refrained from ratifying most of the major multilateral human rights treaties until the 1990s—most international human rights litigation in U.S. courts in the decades following World War II sought to enforce customary law.

The Supreme Court articulated the classic statement of the role of customary law in U.S. domestic courts in *The Paquete Habana,* 175 U.S. 677, 700 (1900). There, it stated:

> International law is part of our law, and must be ascertained and administered by the courts of justice of appropriate jurisdiction, as often as questions of right[s] depending upon it are duly presented for their determination. For this purpose, where there is no treaty, and no controlling executive or legislative act or judicial decision, resort must be had to the customs and usages of civilized nations; and, as evidence of these, to the works of jurists and commentators, who by years of labor, research and experience, have made them-selves peculiarly well acquainted with the subjects of which they treat. Such works are resorted to by judicial tribunals, not for the speculations of their authors concerning what the law ought to be, but for trustworthy evidence of what the law really is.

As we saw in the *Sosa* decision, *supra,* a six-Justice majority reiterated these basic principles. However, despite the fact that the Supreme Court has recognized customary law as "part of our law," the U.S. courts have often subjected claims based on customary international law to limitations similar to the non-self-executing treaty doctrine.

Congress sometimes incorporates international law directly into domestic legislation, making the enforcement of international law a matter of domestic law. For example, the Refugee Act of 1980 was intended to implement U.S. obligations under the Refugee Protocol of 1967. In litigation under the Refugee Act, courts frequently rely on international refugee law as the statute clearly reflects Congress's intent to abide by its international obligations. Other instances where Congress has incorporated international law directly into domestic legislation include the Genocide Convention Implementation Act, 18 U.S.C. § 1091, and the Torture Convention Implementation Act, 18 U.S.C. § 2340A(b) (2000). The Alien Tort Statute and the Torture Victim Protection Act may also be viewed as examples of domestic implementation of the "law of nations" and treaties of the United States by Congress.

Additionally, litigators often make indirect arguments derived from international law in domestic courts. For example, they may invoke the centuries-old interpretive canon favoring the interpretation of statutes to promote consistency with U.S. treaty obligations. As the Supreme Court stated in *Murray v. The Schooner Charming Betsy,* 6 U.S. (2 Cranch) 64, 118 (1804): "[A]n act of Congress ought never to be construed to violate the law of nations if any other possible construction remains, and consequently can never be construed to violate neutral rights, or to affect neutral commerce, further than is warranted by the law of nations as understood in this country." The *"Charming Betsy"* principle has often been employed in cases involving the interpretation of U.S. statutes. *See* Ralph G. Steinhardt, *The Role of International Law as a Canon of Domestic Statutory Construction*, 43 VAND. L. REV. 1103 (1990).

The Supreme Court has also relied on international norms in considering "evolving standards of decency" among civilized nations as part of its Eighth Amendment analysis. *Trop v. Dulles*, 356 U.S. 86, 101–103 (1958) (finding that stripping an individual of his citizenship was prohibited under the Eighth Amendment if it rendered him stateless). Although a majority of the justices have shown themselves willing to consider the experience of other legal systems in such analysis, there remains a great divide between the so-called "nationalists" (justices who deny any role for international law in constitutional analysis) and the "transnationalists" (justices who utilize such materials) over the proper sources for constitutional interpretation. This judicial debate reflects a larger societal debate, involving constitutional theory, sovereignty concerns, and the United States' role in the international community.

This Module begins with a consideration of the principles governing the use of treaty provisions and customary norms in U.S. courts (sections A and B). In section C, we consider the Refugee Act of 1980 and the Supreme Court's decision in *INS v. Cardoza–Fonseca* as an example of the direct incorporation of international norms in domestic legislation, and then we examine the *Charming Betsy* principle. We then consider the ongoing debate over the relevance of international and foreign law in constitutional interpretation (section D). Finally, we examine the role of international law in U.S. courts as a constraint on the government as it conducts its ongoing "war on terror." The ultimate question is what role international law will and should play in domestic litigation in the United States in the 21st century.

A.   THE ENFORCEMENT OF TREATIES

On its face, article VI, Section 2 of the U.S. Constitution, the Supremacy Clause, appears to grant judges broad authority to adjudicate claims arising under treaties to which the United States is a party:

> This Constitution, and the laws of the United States which shall be made in pursuance thereof; and all treaties made, or which shall be made, under the authority of the United States, shall be the supreme law of the land; and the judges in every state shall be bound thereby, anything in the Constitution or laws of any State to the contrary notwithstanding.

But this constitutional imperative has been sharply limited by the judge-made "non-self-executing" treaty doctrine, under which courts have held that they cannot enforce certain treaties or any of their provisions unless Congress has enacted separate "implementing legislation." *Foster v. Neilson*, 27 U.S. 253, 2 Pet. 253, 314 (1829). Although human rights litigators are often thwarted by this doctrine, there are many cases in which treaty provisions have provided the rule of decision in domestic cases.

We start with the *Asakura* case, in which a treaty formed the basis for a successful human rights claim. Following *Asakura*, we examine *Haitian Refugee Center v. Gracey* as an example of a case in which treaty claims were rejected based upon a finding that the treaty provisions in question were "non-self-executing." Finally, we examine the Supreme Court's recent decision in *Medellin v. Texas*, in which it broadly rejected the petitioner's claims that he had been denied rights guaranteed to him by the Vienna Convention.

ASAKURA v. CITY OF SEATTLE, ET AL.

265 U.S. 332 (1924)

MR. JUSTICE BUTLER delivered the opinion of the Court.

Plaintiff in error is a subject of the Emperor of Japan, and, since 1904, has resided in Seattle, Washington. Since July, 1915, he has been engaged in business there as a pawnbroker. The city passed an ordinance, which took effect July 2, 1921, regulating the business of pawnbroker and repealing former ordinances on the same subject. It makes it unlawful for any person to engage in the business unless he shall have a license, and the ordinance provides "that no such license shall be granted unless the applicant be a citizen of the United States." Violations of the ordinance are punishable by fine or imprisonment or both. Plaintiff in error brought this suit in the Superior Court of King County, Washington, against the city, its Comptroller and its Chief of Police to restrain them from enforcing the ordinance against him. He attacked the ordinance on the ground that it violates the treaty between the United States and the Empire of Japan, proclaimed April 5, 1911, 37 Stat. 1504 * * *. It was shown that he had about $5,000 invested in his business, which would be broken up and destroyed by the enforcement of the ordinance. The Superior Court granted the relief prayed. On appeal, the Supreme Court of the State held the ordinance valid and reversed the decree * * *.

Does the ordinance violate the treaty? Plaintiff in error invokes and relies upon the following provisions:

> The citizens or subjects of each of the High Contracting Parties shall have liberty to enter, travel and reside in the territories of the other to carry on trade, wholesale and retail, to own or lease and occupy houses, manufactories, warehouses and shops, to employ agents of their choice, to lease land for residential and commercial purposes, and generally to do anything incident to or necessary for trade

upon the same terms as native citizens or subjects, submitting themselves to the laws and regulations there established.... The citizens or subjects of each ... shall receive, in the territories of the other, the most constant protection and security for their persons and property....

Article 1.

A treaty made under the authority of the United States "shall be the supreme law of the land; and the judges in every State shall be bound thereby, any thing in the constitution or laws of any State to the contrary notwithstanding." Constitution, Art. VI, § 2.

The treaty-making power of the United States is not limited by any express provision of the Constitution, and, though it does not extend "so far as to authorize what the Constitution forbids," it does extend to all proper subjects of negotiation between our government and other nations. The treaty was made to strengthen friendly relations between the two nations. As to the things covered by it, the provision quoted establishes the rule of equality between Japanese subjects while in this country and native citizens. Treaties for the protection of citizens of one country residing in the territory of another are numerous, and make for good understanding between nations. The treaty is binding within the State of Washington. The rule of equality established by it cannot be rendered nugatory in any part of the United States by municipal ordinances or state laws. It stands on the same footing of supremacy as do the provisions of the Constitution and laws of the United States. It operates of itself without the aid of any legislation, state or national; and it will be applied and given authoritative effect by the courts.

The purpose of the ordinance complained of is to regulate, not to prohibit, the business of pawnbroker. But it makes it impossible for aliens to carry on the business. It need not be considered whether the State, if it sees fit, may forbid and destroy the business generally. Such a law would apply equally to aliens and citizens, and no question of conflict with the treaty would arise. The grievance here alleged is that plaintiff in error, in violation of the treaty, is denied equal opportunity * * *.

Decree reversed.

HAITIAN REFUGEE CENTER, INC. ET AL., v. GRACEY
600 F.Supp. 1396 (D.D.C. 1985)

The complaint in this case raises several challenges to the interdiction by United States officials of visaless aliens on the high seas. This program of interdiction was ordered by the President in 1981. The plaintiffs herein are the Haitian Refugee Center ("HRC"), a nonprofit membership corporation located in Miami, Florida, and two of its members. The defendants are the Commandant of the U.S. Coast Guard, and the Commissioner of the Immigration and Naturalization Service ("INS"). * * *

On September 29, 1981, President Reagan authorized the interdiction of certain vessels containing undocumented aliens on the high seas. The President had found that the illegal migration of many undocumented aliens into the United States was "a serious national problem detrimental to the interests of the United States", and that international cooperation to intercept vessels trafficking in such migrants was a necessary and proper means of ensuring the effective enforcement of United States immigration laws.

By Executive Order No. 12324, also dated September 29, 1981, President Reagan ordered the Secretary of State to enter into cooperative arrangements with appropriate foreign governments for the purpose of preventing illegal migration to the United States by sea. * * *

Executive Order 12324 also ordered the Secretary of Transportation to direct the Coast Guard "to return the vessel and its passengers to the country from which it came, when there is reason to believe that an offense is being committed against the United States immigration laws, or appropriate laws of a foreign country with which we have an arrangement to assist." The Order provided, however, "that no person who is a refugee will be returned without his consent." The Coast Guard actions were to be taken only outside United States territorial waters. * * *

The President also ordered the Attorney General, in consultation with the Secretaries of State and Transportation, to take appropriate steps "to ensure the fair enforcement of our laws relating to immigration . . . and the strict observance of our international obligations concerning those who genuinely flee persecution in their homeland."

On September 23, 1981, the United States and Haiti entered into a cooperative arrangement for the purpose of preventing illegal migration of undocumented Haitians to the United States by sea. The arrangement permits United States authorities to board Haitian flag vessels on the high seas, to inquire regarding the condition and destination of the vessels, and the status of those on board. If a violation of United States or appropriate Haitian law is discovered, the vessel and passengers may be returned to Haiti. The arrangement provided that "it is understood that under these arrangements the United States Government does not intend to return to Haiti any Haitian migrants whom the United States authorities determine to qualify for refugee status." The Government of Haiti also agreed that Haitians returned to their country who are not traffickers will not be subject to prosecution for illegal departure. Lastly, the United States agreed to the presence of a representative of the Navy of Haiti as liaison aboard any United States vessel engaged in the implementation of the cooperative arrangement. * * *

The United States is a party to the 1967 Protocol Relating to the Status of Refugees, which incorporates Articles 2 to 34 of the 1951 Convention Relating to the Status of Refugees. The Protocol defines a "refugee" as any person who, "owing to well-founded fear of being persecuted for reasons of race, religion, nationality, membership of a particular social group or political opinion is outside the country of his nationality and is unable or, owing to such fear, is unwilling to avail himself of the protection of that country."

Article 33 of the Convention, incorporated into the Protocol, provides as follows:

> No Contracting State shall expel or return ("refouler") a refugee in any manner whatsoever to the frontiers of territories where his life or freedom would be threatened on account of his race, religion, nationality, membership in a particular social group or political opinion.

The Protocol does not specify the procedures for determining refugee status. Those procedures are apparently left to each contracting nation. Although Congress has directed the Attorney General to establish procedures for use when an alien arrives in the United States or seeks admission to the United States from a foreign country, neither Congress nor the Attorney General has established any procedures for use on the high seas. * * *

In the present complaint, the plaintiffs attack the United States program of high seas interdiction of Haitians, which is carried out pursuant to the cooperative arrangement with Haiti. Alleging that "the human rights situation in Haiti [is] . . . very grave," and that "hundreds of thousands of Haitians have fled . . . to escape . . . political persecution," the plaintiffs bring several causes of action against the interdiction program. * * *

Count III—The United Nations Protocol and the Universal Declaration of Human Rights Do Not Provide Rights Upon Which Plaintiffs May Rely.

In Count III the plaintiffs invoke the 1967 United Nations Protocol Relating to the Status of Refugees and the Universal Declaration of Human Rights. Because neither document affords any rights to the interdicted Haitians, Count III cannot form the basis for any relief.

The plaintiffs claim that the program of interdiction violates the non-refoulement obligations of the United Nations Protocol. However, it has long been established that for a treaty to provide rights enforceable in a United States Court, the treaty must be one which is self-executing. *See Foster v. Neilson,* 27 U.S. (2 Pet.) 253, 314 (1829). "Unless a treaty is self-executing, it must be implemented by legislation before it gives rise to a private cause of action." *Mannington Mills, Inc. v. Congoleum Corp.,* 595 F.2d 1287, 1298 (3d Cir. 1979). * * *

The United Nations Protocol is not self-executing. *Bertrand v. Sava,* 684 F.2d 204, 218–19 (2d Cir. 1982). In *Bertrand,* the Second Circuit held that "the Protocol's provisions were not themselves a source of rights under our law unless and until Congress implemented them by appropriate legislation." This conclusion is compelled by the terms of the treaty itself, which provided that the signatories were to communicate to the United Nations the "laws and regulations which they adopt to ensure the application of the Present Protocol." * * *

Congress has implemented the Protocol, at least in part, through the Refugee Act of 1980. However, that statute does not provide any rights to aliens outside of the United States. Thus, the plaintiffs can find no relief in the United Nations Protocol. * * *

The *Medellin* Case (2008)

In 1963, the United States ratified the Vienna Convention on Consular Relations, Apr. 24, 1963, [1970] 21 U.S.T. 77, T.I.A.S. No. 6820, and its Optional Protocol Concerning Compulsory Settlement of Disputes, Apr. 24, 1963, [1970] 21 U.S.T. 325, T.I.A.S. No. 6820. Article 36(1) of the Vienna Convention provides *inter alia* that a foreign national detained by a government must be informed of his or her "right" to request assistance from the consul of his own state. The Optional Protocol to the Convention brings disputes arising out of the interpretation or application of the Convention within the jurisdiction of the International Court of Justice (ICJ) and allows any Party to the protocol to bring such a dispute before the court.[1] The UN Charter, pursuant to which the ICJ was established, provides in Article 94(1) that "[e]ach Member of the United Nations undertakes to comply with the decision of the [ICJ] in any case to which it is a party," provided that the parties have consented to the jurisdiction of the ICJ.

Beginning in the 1990s, non-citizens charged with criminal offenses in the United States began to bring claims in the United States courts alleging that the government had violated their rights under the Vienna Convention and had failed to inform them of their right to notify their foreign consulates of their arrest. In *Breard v. Greene,* the Supreme Court rejected an attempt by a Paraguayan national to enforce a procedural order issued by the ICJ requesting the U.S. courts to prevent Breard's execution before it ruled on the case. *Breard* v. *Greene,* 523 U.S. 371, 375 (1998) (*per curiam*). Following the Supreme Court's decision, the Governor of Virgina refused a request from the Secretary of State to stay Breard's execution, and Breard was executed before the ICJ completed its deliberations.

The ICJ more thoroughly considered the effect of the United States' "procedural default" rules on the rights conferred by the Vienna

---

1. The U.S. withdrew from the Optional Protocol as of 7 March 2005.

Convention when Germany initiated proceedings against the United States on behalf of two of its nationals, the LaGrand brothers, who had been sentenced to death for murder in Arizona. Although the U.S. courts again found that the defendants had procedurally defaulted their rights under the Vienna Convention by failing to raise their claims in state court, the ICJ was able to issue an opinion on the case before their execution. In *LaGrand*, the ICJ found that, because the U.S. had failed to inform the LaGrands of their rights under the Vienna Convention, its later application of the procedural default rule violated article 36(2) of the Convention. *Case Concerning the Vienna Convention on Consular Relations* (Germany v. United States of America), 2001 I.C.J. 466 (Judgment of June 27).

The ICJ ordered the United States to review and reconsider the convictions of the LaGrand brothers and to determine whether the failure of law enforcement authorities to inform them of their right to contact their consul had affected the outcome of the criminal proceedings. In response to the ICJ's ruling, the State Department sent a letter to the governor of Arizona "encouraging" him to consider the Vienna Convention during the clemency process. The governor refused the request and allowed the execution of the LaGrands to proceed.

Following the ICJ's decision in *LaGrand*, Mexico brought a claim against the United States before the ICJ on behalf of 52 Mexican nationals on death row who had not been informed of their consular rights under the Vienna Convention and who claimed that they had been prejudiced by the omission. In the *Case Concerning Avena and Other Mexican Nationals (Mex. v. U. S.)*, 2004 I.C.J. 12 (*Avena*), Mexico further claimed that the "procedural default" doctrine as applied by the U.S. courts violated the Vienna Convention, insofar as Article 36(2) of the Convention obligates States parties to provide "meaningful and effective review and reconsideration" of convictions and sentences tainted by violations of the Convention's consular notification rules. Affirming its holding in *LaGrand*, the ICJ found that the United States had violated the Vienna Convention with respect to all of the Mexican nationals and that it had violated the "meaningful reconsideration and review" provision of the Convention with respect to the three Mexican nationals who had exhausted their judicial remedies and were "procedurally barred" from raising further claims. The ICJ ordered the United States to provide, by means of its own choosing, review and reconsideration of the conviction and sentence of the Mexican defendants to determine whether they had been prejudiced by the failure of law enforcement officers to provide them with notice of their consular rights under the Convention. It specifically noted that clemency proceedings were not sufficient in themselves to provide an appropriate means of review and reconsideration. According to the ICJ, the United States had undertaken to comply with the rights guaranteed under the Vienna Convention "irrespective of the due process rights under U.S. constitutional law." Thus, defendants' Vienna Convention rights could be prejudiced even if the procedures afforded them satisfied the U.S. Constitution's due process requirements.

Jose Ernesto Medellin, a Mexican national who had lived in the United States since he was a child, was one of the criminal defendants at issue in Mexico's *Avena* claim before the ICJ. Medellin had been sentenced to death by a Texas court in 1997 for the rape and murder of two teenage girls by members of the "Black and Whites" gang in 1993. Following his apprehension by the police, Medellin was given *Miranda* warnings but was not informed of his Vienna Convention right to have the Mexican consulate notified of his detention. Medellin failed to raise his Vienna Convention claim until after he had been convicted by the Texas courts. Once he did, the state courts held that he had procedurally defaulted his Vienna Convention claim, as he had failed to raise it during his trial or on direct appeal. Medellin filed a habeas petition in federal district court, but it too was rejected on the ground that his claim was procedurally defaulted. After the ICJ's decision in *Avena*, Medellin appealed the rejection of his habeas petition to the Fifth Circuit. That court rejected Medellin's appeal, found that the Vienna Convention did not confer individually enforceable rights, and embraced the procedural default doctrine criticized by the ICJ, arguing that regardless of the ICJ's opinion, the Supreme Court had clearly held in *Breard* that Vienna Convention claims could be procedurally defaulted. *Medellín* v. *Dretke*, 371 F.3d 270, 280–81 (5th Cir. 2004).

In response to the conflicting decisions of the ICJ and Fifth Circuit, Medellin petitioned the Supreme Court for review. Before the Supreme Court could consider the petition, President Bush issued a Memorandum to the Attorney General stating that the United States would discharge its international obligations under *Avena* "by having State courts give effect to the decision." The Supreme Court dismissed Medellin's petition pending the response of the Texas state courts to that Memorandum. Medellin again filed a habeas petition in the Texas state courts, challenging his conviction and death sentence, but the Texas courts concluded that neither the ICJ's decision nor the President's Memorandum were binding on the state and that neither displaced Texas's procedural default rules. *Ex parte Medellín*, 223 S.W.3d 315, 322–323 (Tex. Crim. App. 2006). Medellin again petitioned the Supreme Court, which in March 2008 issued its decision on whether *Avena* or the President's Memorandum constituted directly enforceable federal law that pre-empts state procedural rules.

MEDELLIN v. TEXAS

128 S.Ct. 1346 (2008)

CHIEF JUSTICE ROBERTS delivered the opinion of the Court. * * *

II

Medellín first contends that the ICJ's judgment in *Avena* constitutes a "binding" obligation on the state and federal courts of the United

States. He argues that "by virtue of the Supremacy Clause, the treaties requiring compliance with the *Avena* judgment are *already* the 'Law of the Land' by which all state and federal courts in this country are 'bound.' " Accordingly, Medellín argues, *Avena* is a binding federal rule of decision that pre-empts contrary state limitations on successive habeas petitions.

No one disputes that the *Avena* decision—a decision that flows from the treaties through which the United States submitted to ICJ jurisdiction with respect to Vienna Convention disputes—constitutes an *international* law obligation on the part of the United States. But not all international law obligations automatically constitute binding federal law enforceable in United States courts. The question we confront here is whether the *Avena* judgment has automatic *domestic* legal effect such that the judgment of its own force applies in state and federal courts.

This Court has long recognized the distinction between treaties that automatically have effect as domestic law, and those that—while they constitute international law commitments—do not by themselves function as binding federal law. The distinction was well explained by Chief Justice Marshall's opinion in *Foster* v. *Neilson*, which held that a treaty is "equivalent to an act of the legislature," and hence self-executing, when it "operates of itself without the aid of any legislative provision." * * * When, in contrast, "[treaty] stipulations are not self-executing they can only be enforced pursuant to legislation to carry them into effect." *Whitney* v. *Robertson*, 124 U. S. 190, 194 (1888). In sum, while treaties "may comprise international commitments . . . they are not domestic law unless Congress has either enacted implementing statutes or the treaty itself conveys an intention that it be 'self-executing' and is ratified on these terms."

A treaty is, of course, "primarily a compact between independent nations." *Edye* v. *Robertson*, *Head Money Cases*, 112 U. S. 580, 598 (1884). It ordinarily "depends for the enforcement of its provisions on the interest and the honor of the governments which are parties to it." *Ibid.*; see also The Federalist No. 33, p. 207 (J. Cooke ed. 1961) (A. Hamilton) (comparing laws that individuals are "bound to observe" as "the supreme law of the land" with "a mere treaty, dependent on the good faith of the parties"). "If these [interests] fail, its infraction becomes the subject of international negotiations and reclamations. . . . It is obvious that with all this the judicial courts have nothing to do and can give no redress." *Head Money Cases, supra,* at 598. Only "[i]f the treaty contains stipulations which are self-executing, that is, require no legislation to make them operative, [will] they have the force and effect of a legislative enactment." *Whitney, supra,* at 194.

Medellín and his *amici* nonetheless contend that the Optional Protocol, United Nations Charter, and ICJ Statute supply the "relevant obligation" to give the *Avena* judgment binding effect in the domestic courts of the United States.[1] Because none of these treaty sources creates binding federal law in the absence of implementing legislation, and because it is uncontested that no such legislation exists, we conclude that the *Avena* judgment is not automatically binding domestic law.

A

The interpretation of a treaty, like the interpretation of a statute, begins with its text. Because a treaty ratified by the United States is "an agreement among sovereign powers," we have also considered as "aids to its interpretation" the negotiation and drafting history of the treaty as well as "the post-ratification understanding" of signatory nations.

As a signatory to the Optional Protocol, the United States agreed to submit disputes arising out of the Vienna Convention to the ICJ. The Protocol provides: "Disputes arising out of the interpretation or application of the [Vienna] Convention shall lie within the compulsory jurisdiction of the International Court of Justice." Art. I, 21 U. S. T., at 326. Of course, submitting to jurisdiction and agreeing to be bound are two different things. A party could, for example, agree to compulsory nonbinding arbitration. Such an agreement would require the party to appear before the arbitral tribunal without obligating the party to treat the tribunal's decision as binding.

The most natural reading of the Optional Protocol is as a bare grant of jurisdiction. It provides only that "[d]isputes arising out of the interpretation or application of the [Vienna] Convention shall lie within the compulsory jurisdiction of the International Court of Justice" and "may accordingly be brought before the [ICJ] . . . by any party to the dispute being a Party to the present Protocol." The Protocol says nothing about the effect of an ICJ decision and does not itself commit signatories to comply with an ICJ judgment. The Protocol is similarly silent as to any enforcement mechanism.

The obligation on the part of signatory nations to comply with ICJ judgments derives not from the Optional Protocol, but rather from Article 94 of the United Nations Charter—the provision that specifically addresses the effect of ICJ decisions. Article 94(1) provides that "[e]ach Member of the United Nations *undertakes to comply* with the decision of the [ICJ] in any case to which it is a party." The Executive Branch contends that the phrase "undertakes to comply" is not "an acknowledgment that an ICJ decision will have immediate legal effect in the courts of UN members," but rather "a *commitment* on the part of UN Members

---

1. The question is whether the *Avena* judgment has binding effect in domestic courts under the Optional Protocol, ICJ Statute, and UN Charter. Consequently, it is unnecessary to resolve whether the Vienna Convention is itself "self-executing" or whether it grants Medellín individually enforceable rights * * *.

to take *future* action through their political branches to comply with an ICJ decision."

We agree with this construction of Article 94. The Article is not a directive to domestic courts. It does not provide that the United States "shall" or "must" comply with an ICJ decision, nor indicate that the Senate that ratified the UN Charter intended to vest ICJ decisions with immediate legal effect in domestic courts. Instead, "[t]he words of Article 94 . . . call upon governments to take certain action." In other words, the UN Charter reads like "a compact between independent nations" that "depends for the enforcement of its provisions on the interest and the honor of the governments which are parties to it." *Head Money Cases*, 112 U. S., at 598.

The remainder of Article 94 confirms that the UN Charter does not contemplate the automatic enforceability of ICJ decisions in domestic courts. Article 94(2)—the enforcement provision—provides the sole remedy for noncompliance: referral to the United Nations Security Council by an aggrieved state.

The UN Charter's provision of an express diplomatic—that is, nonjudicial—remedy is itself evidence that ICJ judgments were not meant to be enforceable in domestic courts. And even this "quintessentially *international* remed[y]," * * * is not absolute. First, the Security Council must "dee[m] necessary" the issuance of a recommendation or measure to effectuate the judgment.* * * Second, as the President and Senate were undoubtedly aware in subscribing to the UN Charter and Optional Protocol, the United States retained the unqualified right to exercise its veto of any Security Council resolution. This was the understanding of the Executive Branch when the President agreed to the UN Charter and the declaration accepting general compulsory ICJ jurisdiction.

If ICJ judgments were instead regarded as automatically enforceable domestic law, they would be immediately and directly binding on state and federal courts pursuant to the Supremacy Clause. Mexico or the ICJ would have no need to proceed to the Security Council to enforce the judgment in this case. Noncompliance with an ICJ judgment through exercise of the Security Council veto—always regarded as an option by the Executive and ratifying Senate during and after consideration of the UN Charter, Optional Protocol, and ICJ Statute—would no longer be a viable alternative. There would be nothing to veto. In light of the UN Charter's remedial scheme, there is no reason to believe that the President and Senate signed up for such a result.

In sum, Medellín's view that ICJ decisions are automatically enforceable as domestic law is fatally undermined by the enforcement structure established by Article 94. His construction would eliminate the option of noncompliance contemplated by Article 94(2), undermining the ability of the political branches to determine whether and how to comply with an ICJ judgment. Those sensitive foreign policy decisions would instead be transferred to state and federal courts charged with applying an ICJ judgment directly as domestic law. And those courts would not be empowered to decide whether to comply with the judgment—again, always regarded as an option by the political branches—any more than courts may consider whether to comply with any other species of domestic law. This result would be particularly anomalous in light of the principle that "[t]he conduct of the foreign relations of our Government is committed by the Constitution to the Executive and Legislative—'the political'—Departments." * * *

D

In sum, while the ICJ's judgment in *Avena* creates an international law obligation on the part of the United States, it does not of its own force constitute binding federal law that pre-empts state restrictions on the filing of successive habeas petitions. * * * [A] contrary conclusion would be extraordinary, given that basic rights guaranteed by our own Constitution do not have the effect of displacing state procedural rules. Nothing in the text, background, negotiating and drafting history, or practice among signatory nations suggests that the President or Senate intended the improbable result of giving the judgments of an international tribunal a higher status than that enjoyed by "many of our most fundamental constitutional protections."

III

[The majority went on to determine that the President's 2005 Memorandum did not have the effect of rendering the *Avena* judgment binding on state courts, because the Executive Branch lacks the authority to unilaterally execute a non-self-executing treaty].

JUSTICE BREYER, with whom JUSTICE SOUTER and JUSTICE GINSBURG join, dissenting. * * *

The United States has signed and ratified a series of treaties obliging it to comply with ICJ judgments in cases in which it has given its consent to the exercise of the ICJ's adjudicatory authority. Specifically, the United States has agreed to submit, in this kind of case, to the ICJ's "compulsory jurisdiction" for purposes of "compulsory settlement." And it agreed that the ICJ's judgments would have "binding force ... between the parties and in respect of [a] particular case." President Bush has determined that domestic courts should enforce this particular ICJ judgment. And Congress has done nothing to suggest the contrary. Under these circumstances, I believe the treaty obligations, and hence the judgment, resting as it does upon the consent of the United States to the ICJ's jurisdiction, bind the courts no less than would "an act of the [federal] legislature." * * *

The critical question here is whether the Supremacy Clause requires Texas to follow, *i.e.*, to enforce, this ICJ judgment. The Court says "no." And it reaches its negative answer by interpreting the labyrinth of treaty provisions as creating a legal obligation that binds the United States internationally, but which, for Supremacy Clause purposes, is not automatically enforceable as domestic law. In the majority's view, the Optional Protocol simply sends the dispute to the ICJ; the ICJ statute says that the ICJ will subsequently reach a judgment; and the UN Charter contains no more than a promise to " 'undertak[e] to comply' " with that judgment. * * * Such a promise, the majority says, does not as a domestic law matter (in Chief Justice Marshall's words) "operat[e] of itself without the aid of any legislative provision." Rather, here (and presumably in any other ICJ judgment rendered pursuant to any of the approximately 70 U.S. treaties in force that contain similar provisions for submitting treaty-based disputes to the ICJ for decisions that bind the parties) Congress must enact specific legislation before ICJ judgments entered pursuant to our consent to compulsory ICJ jurisdiction can become domestic law.

In my view, the President has correctly determined that Congress need not enact additional legislation. The majority places too much weight upon treaty language that says little about the matter. * * * [W]e must look instead to our own domestic law, in particular, to the many treaty-related cases interpreting the Supremacy Clause. Those cases, including some written by Justices well aware of the Founders' original intent, lead to the conclusion that the ICJ judgment before us is enforceable as a matter of domestic law without further legislation.

A

Supreme Court case law stretching back more than 200 years helps explain what, for present purposes, the Founders meant when they wrote that "all Treaties ... shall be the supreme Law of the Land." * * *

Since *Foster* and *Pollard,* this Court has frequently held or assumed that particular treaty provisions are self-executing, automatically binding the States without more. See Appendix A, *infra* (listing, as examples, 29 such cases, including 12 concluding that the treaty provision invalidates state or territorial law or policy as a consequence). As far as I can tell, the Court has held to the contrary only in two cases: *Foster, supra,* which was later reversed, and *Cameron Septic Tank Co.* v. *Knoxville,* 227 U. S. 39 (1913), where specific congressional actions indicated that Congress thought further legislation necessary. The Court has found "self-executing" provisions in multilateral treaties as well as bilateral treaties. And the subject matter of such provisions has varied widely, from extradition, to criminal trial jurisdiction, to civil liability, to trademark infringement, to an alien's freedom to engage in trade, to immunity from state taxation, to land ownership, and to inheritance.

Of particular relevance to the present case, the Court has held that the United States may be obligated by treaty to comply with the judgment of an international tribunal interpreting that treaty, despite the absence of any congressional enactment specifically requiring such compliance. See *Comegys v. Vasse*, 1 Pet. 193, 211–212 (1828) (holding that decision of tribunal rendered pursuant to a United States–Spain treaty, which obliged the parties to "undertake to make satisfaction" of treaty-based rights, was "conclusive and final" and "not re-examinable" in American courts); see also *Meade v. United States*, 9 Wall. 691, 725 (1869) (holding that decision of tribunal adjudicating claims arising under United States–Spain treaty "was final and conclusive, and bar[red] a recovery upon the merits" in American court).

All of these cases make clear that self-executing treaty provisions are not uncommon or peculiar creatures of our domestic law; that they cover a wide range of subjects; that the Supremacy Clause itself answers the self-execution question by applying many, but not all, treaty provisions directly to the States; and that the Clause answers the self-execution question differently than does the law in many other nations. The cases also provide criteria that help determine *which* provisions automatically so apply—a matter to which I now turn.

B

1.   The case law provides no simple magic answer to the question whether a particular treaty provision is self-executing. But the case law does make clear that, insofar as today's majority looks for language about "self-execution" in the treaty itself and insofar as it erects "clear statement" presumptions designed to help find an answer, it is misguided.* * *

The many treaty provisions that this Court has found self-executing contain no textual language on the point. Few, if any, of these provisions are clear. Those that displace state law in respect to such quintessential state matters as, say, property, inheritance, or debt repayment, lack the "clea[r] state[ment]" that the Court today apparently requires.* * * This is also true of those cases that deal with state rules roughly comparable to the sort that the majority suggests require special accommodation. *See, e.g., Hopkirk v. Bell*, 3 Cranch 454, 457–458 (1806) (treaty pre-empts Virginia state statute of limitations). These many Supreme Court cases finding treaty provisions to be self-executing cannot be reconciled with the majority's demand for textual clarity. Indeed, the majority does not point to a single ratified United States treaty that contains the kind of "clea[r]" or "plai[n]" textual indication for which the majority searches. * * * And that is not because the United States never, or hardly ever, has entered into a treaty with self-executing provisions. * * *

[T]he issue whether further legislative action is required before a treaty provision takes domestic effect in a signatory nation is often a matter of how that Nation's domestic law regards the provision's legal status. And that domestic status-determining law differs markedly from one nation to another. As Justice Iredell pointed out 200 years ago, Britain, for example, taking the view that the British Crown makes treaties but Parliament makes domestic law, virtually always requires parliamentary legislation. On the other hand, the United States, with its Supremacy Clause, does not take Britain's view. And the law of other nations, the Netherlands for example, directly incorporates many treaties concluded by the executive into its domestic law even without explicit parliamentary approval of the treaty.

The majority correctly notes that the treaties do not explicitly state that the relevant obligations are self-executing. But given the differences among nations, why would drafters write treaty language stating that a provision about, say, alien property inheritance, is self-executing? How could those drafters achieve agreement when one signatory nation follows one tradition and a second follows another? Why would such a difference matter sufficiently for drafters to try to secure language that would prevent, for example, Britain's following treaty ratification with a further law while (perhaps unnecessarily) insisting that the United States apply a treaty provision without further domestic legislation? Above all, what does the absence of specific language about "self-execution" prove? It may reflect the drafters' awareness of national differences. It may reflect the practical fact that drafters, favoring speedy, effective implementation, conclude they should best leave national legal practices alone. It may reflect the fact that achieving international agreement on *this* point is simply a game not worth the candle.

In a word, for present purposes, the absence or presence of language in a treaty about a provision's self-execution proves nothing at all. At best the Court is hunting the snark. At worst it erects legalistic hurdles that can threaten the application of provisions in many existing commercial and other treaties and make it more difficult to negotiate new ones.* * *

2.   The case law also suggests practical, context-specific criteria that this Court has previously used to help determine whether, for Supremacy Clause purposes, a treaty provision is self-executing. The provision's text matters very much. * * * But that is not because it contains language that explicitly refers to self-execution. * * * Instead text and history, along with subject matter and related characteristics will help our courts determine whether, as Chief Justice Marshall put it, the treaty provision "addresses itself to the political ... department[s]" for further action or to "the judicial department" for direct enforcement.

In making this determination, this Court has found the provision's subject matter of particular importance. Does the treaty provision declare peace? Does it promise not to engage in hostilities? If so, it addresses itself to the political branches. Alternatively, does it concern the adjudication of traditional private legal rights such as rights to own property, to conduct a business, or to obtain civil tort recovery? If so, it may well address itself to the Judiciary. Enforcing such rights and setting their boundaries is the bread-and butter work of the courts.

One might also ask whether the treaty provision confers specific, detailed individual legal rights. Does it set forth definite standards that judges can readily enforce? Other things being equal, where rights are specific and readily enforceable, the treaty provision more likely "addresses" the judiciary. Alternatively, would direct enforcement require the courts to create a new cause of action? Would such enforcement engender constitutional controversy? Would it create constitutionally undesirable conflict with the other branches? In such circumstances, it is not likely that the provision contemplates direct judicial enforcement.

Such questions, drawn from case law stretching back 200 years, do not create a simple test, let alone a magic formula. But they do help to constitute a practical, context-specific judicial approach, seeking to separate run-of-the-mill judicial matters from other matters, sometimes more politically charged, sometimes more clearly the responsibility of other branches, sometimes lacking those attributes that would permit courts to act on their own without more ado. And such an approach is all that we need to find an answer to the legal question now before us.

C

* * * [T]he United States' treaty obligation to comply with the ICJ judgment in *Avena* is enforceable in court in this case without further congressional action beyond Senate ratification of the relevant treaties. The majority reaches a different conclusion because it looks for the wrong thing (explicit textual expression about self-execution) using the wrong standard (clarity) in the wrong place (the treaty language). Hunting for what the text cannot contain, it takes a wrong turn. It threatens to deprive individuals, including businesses, property owners, testamentary beneficiaries, consular officials, and others, of the workable dispute resolution procedures that many treaties, including commercially oriented treaties, provide. In a world where commerce, trade, and travel have become ever more international, that is a step in the wrong direction.

NOTES AND QUESTIONS ON THE SELF-EXECUTING TREATY DOCTRINE

1. *Routine enforcement.* The cases addressing the self-executing treaty doctrine often arise in a criminal setting, *see, e.g., United States v. Postal*, 589 F.2d 862 (5th Cir. 1979), and in extradition proceedings, *see, e.g., United States v. Rauscher*, 119 U.S. 407 (1886). But the relevance of the doctrine in international civil litigation is also clear. The non-discrimination provisions in Friendship, Commerce, and Navigation treaties like the one at issue in *Asakura* are routinely held to be self-executing. The same is true of bilateral extradition treaties. Executive agreements, though they are not treaties under the Treaty Power of the Constitution, are nonetheless considered "treaties" for purposes of the

Supremacy Clause, meaning that executive agreements are also subject to the self-executing treaty doctrine. This is significant because executive agreements can cover the range of issues in American foreign policy, including human rights. *See, e.g.* The Helsinki Accords, Conference on Security and Cooperation in Europe, Final Act, 14 INT'L LEG. MATS. 1292 (1975).

2. *Self-executing or not?* The language of Article 33 of the Refugee Convention is clear and suggests a categorical prohibition against the return of refugees. Why does the District Court in *Gracey* find this prohibition *not* judicially enforceable? Does the fact that the treaty may contemplate some discretion in the means of implementing the prohibition render it non-self-executing? Is *Gracey* consistent with *Asakura?*

3. *Self-executing treaties and the later-in-time rule.* A self-executing treaty is equivalent to a statute, meaning that, if there is a conflict between them, the one enacted later in time prevails to the extent of the conflict. The Supreme Court applied this rule in *Breard v. Greene*, 523 U.S. 371 (1998), a case involving a conflict between the Vienna Convention, which was ratified by the United States in 1969, and the Antiterrorism and Effective Death Penalty Act (AEDPA), a 1996 federal statute. In *Breard*, the Supreme Court considered whether a violation of the Vienna Convention provided the basis for federal habeas corpus relief, even though Breard had failed to raise his argument about the Vienna Convention in his state court proceeding (and had thus defaulted on the claim according to Virginia's procedural rules). Breard argued that his procedural default did not preclude consideration of his argument because the Vienna Convention was the "law of the land" under Article VI of the Constitution. The Court rejected this argument:

> The Vienna Convention—which arguably confers on an individual the right to consular assistance following arrest—has continuously been in effect since 1969. But in 1996, before Breard filed his habeas petition raising claims under the Vienna Convention, Congress enacted the Antiterrorism and Effective Death Penalty Act (AEDPA), which provides that a habeas petitioner alleging that he is held in violation of "treaties of the United States" will, as a general rule, not be afforded an evidentiary hearing if he "has failed to develop the factual basis of [the] claim in State court proceedings." Breard's ability to obtain relief based on violations of the Vienna Convention is subject to this subsequently-enacted rule, just as any claim arising under the United States Constitution would be. This rule prevents Breard from establishing that the violation of his Vienna Convention rights prejudiced him.

Breard, 523 U.S. at 376.

4. *Subsequent disposition of the issue in Gracey.* The specific issue before the district court in *Gracey*—whether Article 33 of the Refugee Convention is self-executing or not—continued to be the subject of litigation after the decision. In 1993, the U.S. Supreme Court decided

that nothing in Article 33 of the Refugee Convention limited the discretion of the President to interdict Haitians on the high seas and return them to Haiti. The analysis turned on a textual interpretation of Article 33 only. The self-execution issue was not addressed. *Sale v. Haitian Centers Council, Inc.*, 509 U.S. 155 (1993).

5.   *Is there a presumption that treaties are self-executing?* Some scholars read Justice Marshall's language in *Foster* to stand for the presumption that all treaties are self-executing and argue that *Foster* simply articulated an exception. *See, e.g.,* Louis Henkin, Foreign Affairs and the United States Constitution 200 (2d ed. 1996). *But see,* John C. Yoo, *Globalism and the Constitution: Treaties, Non–Self Execution, and the Original Understanding*, 99 Colum. L. Rev. 1955, 2090 (1999) (arguing that "Marshall's opinion . . . simply classifies treaties into two types—self-executing and non-self-executing—without stating that a general background rule existed that treaties are self-executing"). Indeed, Professor Yoo argues that the Constitution requires treaties to be non-self-executing to avoid separation of powers problems. Should courts begin their inquiry with a presumption in favor of or against self-execution? *See* Carlos Manuel Vazquez, *Treaty-Based Rights and Remedies of Individuals*, 92 Colum. L. Rev. 1082 (1992). Section 111(4)(c) of the Restatement (Third) of Foreign Relations suggests that there is a constitutional dimension to the doctrine of non-self executing treaties. The implication is that there are some treaties which, as a matter of U.S. constitutional law, require implementation through Congressional action, or which, if enforced by individuals in domestic courts, might invade the constitutional prerogatives of the Executive branch. What constitutional provisions would you consider particularly relevant in this regard?

6.   *From Asakura to Medellin.* Compare the decision in *Asakura v. City of Seattle*, which was decided in 1924, with the decision in *Medellin v. Texas*, which was decided in 2008. Do the differences in these opinions indicate a generational change in the recognition of treaties in U.S. law, or are the cases distinguishable as a matter of law?

7.   *Is intent relevant?* Some scholars have questioned whether an inquiry into the treaty parties' intent is appropriate at all. For example, David Sloss argues that treaty-makers have no authority to prevent a treaty from becoming domestic law after it is ratified. David Sloss, *Non-Self–Executing Treaties: Exposing a Constitutional Fallacy*, 36 U.C. Davis L. Rev. 1, 7 (2002). Professor Sloss rejects the Restatement approach:

> Although many lower court opinions and scholarly writings endorse the Restatement doctrine, either implicitly or explicitly, that doctrine cannot be reconciled with the text and structure of the United States Constitution. The Supreme Court has never endorsed the view that the treaty makers have an unlimited power to prevent a ratified treaty from becoming domestic law.* * * When the United States ratifies a treaty that creates primary international legal duties, the Supremacy Clause mandates automatic conversion of those

international duties into primary domestic law, except insofar as constitutional constraints preclude automatic conversion of a particular duty. Whether the treaty makers intended to create primary domestic law is irrelevant, because constitutional rules determine whether a particular provision of a ratified treaty creates primary domestic law; and the treaty makers do not have the power to alter those constitutional rules. * * *

Do you think courts should consider the treaty-makers' intent when interpreting treaties?

8. *Hawkins v. Comparet–Cassani*. The *Hawkins* case arose in the context of controversy over the use of stun gun technology in the criminal justice system. International human rights groups campaigned against the introduction of such technology as a mode of restraint on the grounds that its use constituted torture or cruel, inhuman or degrading treatment or punishment ("CIDT"). *Hawkins v. Comparet–Cassani*, 33 F. Supp.2d 1244 (C.D. Cal. 1999). Amnesty Int'l, Arming the Torturers: Electro-Shock Torture and the Spread of Stun Technology (1997). On January 25, 1999, a municipal court judge in Long Beach, California, ignited a national debate when she directed that a 50,000 volt shock be administered to a *pro se* criminal defendant who—facing life imprisonment under California's "three strikes" law for stealing medicine from a drug store—kept arguing his case after the judge directed him to stop. (He had been forced ahead of time to wear a stun belt at the hearing.) A sheriff's deputy triggered the shock by pressing a button. The media accounts of the impact of the stun belt on Hawkins created an uproar. In response, a local Los Angeles civil rights lawyer sued for an injunction against any future use of stun belts. In addition to constitutional arguments, the lawyer asserted claims based in treaties and customary law. The district court dismissed the plaintiff's international law claims finding that the treaties did not create a private right of action under which the plaintiff could state a claim.

The prohibition on torture at issue in *Hawkins* is categorical. What, if anything, prevents a district court judge from issuing an injunction prohibiting state or local authorities in Los Angeles from torturing inmates? Under the court's reasoning, it would not be empowered to enjoin the use of classic methods of torture (*e.g.* water torture or the rack) in Los Angeles County Jail, at least under the Torture Convention or customary law. Can this result be squared with Article III of the Constitution?

9. *Treaty interpretation*. Even if a treaty provision is self-executing, crucial issues of treaty interpretation can arise. For example, in the *Alvarez-Machain* case (*see* Module 2) it was assumed that the United States–Mexico extradition treaty was self-executing; however, the U.S. Supreme Court rejected the interpretation of the treaty adopted by the lower courts, finding that the treaty did not prohibit a state-sponsored abduction in lieu of formal extradition. *See United States v. Alvarez–*

Machain, 504 U.S. 655 (1992). The court rejected the argument that the treaty should be read in the context of the customary law prohibition on the exercise of law enforcement jurisdiction by one state in the territory of another state without the latter's consent.

10. *Alternative strategies.* Even if a treaty provision is found to be non-self-executing, there may be other means to enforce it. For example, plaintiffs may be able to raise treaty-based claims under habeas corpus statutes (28 U.S.C. § 2241(c)(3) provides that the writ of habeas corpus extends to prisoners who are "in custody in violation of the Constitution or laws or treaties of the United States"); or federal anti-discrimination statutes (42 U.S.C. § 1983 provides a cause of action for individuals who have been deprived under color of state law "of any rights, privileges, or immunities secured by the Constitution and laws" of the United States); or the Administrative Procedures Act (5 U.S.C. § 702 provides that a "person suffering legal wrong because of agency action, or adversely affected or aggrieved by agency action within the meaning of a relevant statute, is entitled to judicial review thereof."). It may also be possible to assert defenses in criminal proceedings based upon international law. Such defenses are often combined with claims that domestic statutes or the Constitution should be interpreted to be consistent with international treaty or customary norms. *See* Section C, *infra*.

Implied Cause of Action for Damages for a Treaty Violation

In *Asakura*, *supra*, the court enforced a treaty provision without considering whether the treaty provided a cause of action. If a treaty provision is found to be self-executing without the need for further Congressional action, is it still necessary to determine if there is an implied private right of action? Does the basic civil rights statute, 42 U.S.C. § 1983, supply a cause of action for the enforcement of treaties? In *Cornejo v. San Diego*, the Ninth Circuit addressed this issue after finding the relevant provisions of the Vienna Convention on Consular Relations to be self-executing.

CORNEJO v. COUNTY OF SAN DIEGO

504 F.3d 853 (9th Cir. 2007)

Cornejo is a national and citizen of Mexico. His First Amended Complaint alleges that when he was arrested, San Diego County Sheriff's Deputies Paul LaCroix, William McDaniel, and Jon Montion failed to inform him, and others similarly situated whom he seeks to make part of a class, of the individual right conferred by Article 36 * * * "to contact a consular official of his country." * * *

The district court * * * ruled that he could not state a claim under § 1983 for violations of the Vienna Convention because Article 36 does not provide for a private right of action[.] * * *

II

The Vienna Convention is a multilateral international agreement "that governs relations between individual nations and foreign consular officials. The United States ratified the Convention in 1969. Article 36 provides:

1. With a view to facilitating the exercise of consular functions relating to nationals of the sending State:

* * *

(b) if he so requests, the competent authorities of the receiving State shall, without delay, inform the consular post of the sending State if, within its consular district, a national of that State is arrested or committed to prison or to custody pending trial or is detained in any other manner. Any communication addressed to the consular post by the person arrested, in prison, custody or detention shall be forwarded by the said authorities without delay. The said authorities shall inform the person concerned without delay of his rights under this subparagraph;* * *

2. The rights referred to in paragraph 1 of this article shall be exercised in conformity with the laws and regulations of the receiving State, subject to the proviso, however, that the said laws and regulations must enable full effect to be given to the purposes for which the rights accorded under this article are intended.

Here, Mexico is the "sending State" and the United States is the "receiving State."

For any treaty to be susceptible to judicial enforcement it must both confer individual rights and be self-executing. There is no question that the Vienna Convention is self-executing. * * *

Therefore, the question here is whether Congress, by ratifying the Convention, intended to create private rights and remedies enforceable in American courts through § 1983 by individual foreign nationals who are arrested or detained in this country. * * *

It is clear from *Gonzaga University v. Doe*, 536 U.S. 273, 283 (2002), that "it is rights, not the broader or vaguer 'benefits' or 'interests,' that may be enforced under the authority of that section." Thus, an "unambiguously conferred right" phrased in terms of the person benefitted is essential before a statute—and by extension, a treaty having the force of federal law—may support a cause of action under § 1983.

"In construing a treaty, as in construing a statute, we first look to its terms to determine its meaning." As it is a treaty that is being construed, however, and a treaty is an agreement between States that implicates the foreign relations of the United States, we are also aided by canons that apply specially to international agreements. Among them: "While courts interpret treaties for themselves, the meaning given them by the departments of government particularly charged with their negotiation and enforcement is given great weight." *Sanchez–Llamas*, 126 S.Ct. at 2685. "An international agreement is to be interpreted in good faith in accordance with the ordinary meaning to be given to its terms in their context and in the light of its object and purpose." Restatement § 325(1). In that connection, the "context" of a treaty includes its preamble. Vienna Convention on the Law of Treaties ("Treaty Convention") art. 31(2), May 23, 1969, 1155 U.N.T.S. 331. "[S]ubsequent practice between the parties in the application of the agreement [is] to be taken into account in its interpretation." Restatement § 325(2).

Treaties customarily confer rights upon the States that are parties to them. While treaties *may* confer enforceable individual rights, most courts accept a "presumption" against inferring individual rights from international treaties.

Against this backdrop, Cornejo's most compelling argument is that Article 36 textually uses the word "rights" in reference to a detainee's being informed that he can, if he wants, have his consular post advised of his detention and have communications forwarded to it. This use of the word in paragraph 1(b) "arguably confers on an individual the right to consular assistance following arrest." *Breard*, 523 U.S. at 376. However, it says nothing about the nature of "his rights" or how, if at all, they may be invoked. This language, therefore, must be considered in light of what the Convention, and Article 36, are all about. * * *

Entitled "Communication and contact with nationals of the sending State," Article 36 appears in Section I of Chapter II of the Convention. Chapter II governs "Facilities, Privileges and Immunities Relating to Consular Posts, Career Consular Officers and Other Members of a Consular Post," while Section I concerns "Facilities, Privileges and Immunities Relating to a Consular Post." The lead sentence in paragraph 1 of Article 36, which is the paragraph that obliges authorities of a receiving State to notify a detained foreign national of "his rights" under sub-paragraph (1)(b), declares that the rights set forth in that section are "[w]ith a view to facilitating the exercise of consular functions relating to nationals of the sending State." Thus, the "rights" accorded under Article 36 are meant to facilitate the exercise of consular functions, an important one of which is to help nationals who run afoul of local law.

Accordingly, sub-paragraph 1(a) gives consular officials the right "to communicate with nationals of the sending State and to have access to them." The exchange of information provided for in sub-paragraph 1(b) supports the consular function and the rights conferred in sub-paragraph 1(a) upon consular officers to communication and access. And subparagraph 1(c) guarantees consular officials the right to visit a national of the sending State who is detained or incarcerated, as well as to converse and correspond with him and to arrange for his legal representation—if the national wants that kind of help and if the consulate wants to give it.

These "rights" are consistent with the articulated purpose of facilitating the exercise of consular functions, not with awarding compensation to individual detainees who receive no notification from their arresting officers. Requiring a receiving State to notify a foreign national that, if he wishes, it will inform the local consular post of an arrest or detention, and forward communications, enhances the ability of sending States to assist or protect their nationals. In this way, notification is a means of implementing the treaty obligations as between States* * * the right of assistance, as Article 36(1)(c) makes clear, belongs entirely to the sending State.

We conclude, therefore, that the unmistakable focus of Article 36 is on consular functions. The privileges discussed are explicitly those relating to *the consular post*. They are manifestly important, because Article 36 provides for communication and contact by sending States with their nationals who are in trouble in a foreign country. However, the signatory States did not choose to delegate enforcement of Article 36—even to their own consular officials. They plainly did not do so to individual foreign nationals. For all these reasons, we cannot see unambiguous clarity in the language of Article 36 implying that the States parties to the Convention conferred a private, judicially enforceable right upon individuals.

This conclusion is buttressed by the Convention as a whole, the contemporaneous understanding of Congress in ratifying it as well as the view of the Department of State, and the uniform practice of States implementing it over the years.

The Vienna Convention on Consular Relations is an agreement among States whose subject matter—"Consular Relations"—is quintessentially State-to-State. Except for its final provisions, the Convention's articles all have to do with consular posts.* * *

Cornejo suggests that the proviso in paragraph 2 manifests an intent to create privately enforceable rights. Nowhere does it say so. If anything, the fact that it talks in terms of how "rights referred to in paragraph 1 of this article shall be exercised" indicates the opposite, for it does not also say "and be compensated." The only articulated purpose is in paragraph 1, and it is to facilitate the exercise of consular functions relating to nationals of the sending State.

To the extent that Congressional intent in ratifying the Convention may be discerned, it, too, supports our interpretation. For example, the Report of the Committee on Foreign Relations recommending that the Senate give its advice and consent to ratification of the Convention emphasizes the preamble: "The general functional approach of the Convention is pointed up by the following preambular statement: '* * * the purpose of such privileges and immunities is not to benefit individuals but to ensure the efficient performance of functions by consular posts on behalf of their respective States.' "

The contemporaneous position of the United States Department of State, which is entitled to "great weight," also reinforces the view that the Convention as a whole, and Article 36 in particular, were not intended to create individually enforceable rights. For example, when the Senate was considering ratification, one of the deputy legal advisers to the State Department informed the Foreign Relations Committee that, "[i]f problems should arise regarding the interpretation or application of the convention, such problems would probably be resolved through diplomatic channels." Failing that, he represented, disputes would be submitted to the ICJ pursuant to the Optional Protocol. Since then, the Department has repeatedly asserted that "the only remedies for failures of consular notification under the Vienna Convention are diplomatic, political, or exist between states under international law." * * *

Finally, the government represents that none of the 170 States parties has permitted a private tort suit for damages for violation of Article 36. This is consistent with the State Department's position that the remedies "are diplomatic, political, or exist between states under international law." * * *

D. W. NELSON, SENIOR CIRCUIT JUDGE, dissenting:

The question that we should address, in accordance with Supreme Court precedent in *Gonzaga University v. Doe*, 536 U.S. 273 (2002), is whether Article 36(1)(b) of the Vienna Convention on Consular Relations was intended to confer individual rights that would be presumptively enforceable under 42 U.S.C. § 1983. Instead of addressing this question, the majority relies on an erroneous interpretation of *Gonzaga* and reframes the question as being "whether Congress, by ratifying the Convention, intended to create private rights and remedies enforceable in American courts through § 1983." The requirement that the appellant in this case, Cornejo, demonstrate that the ratifying Congress had an intent to create remedies enforceable in American courts through § 1983 finds no support in case law. Instead, such a remedy under § 1983 is presumptively available once Cornejo demonstrates that the ratifying Congress of the Vienna Convention had an intent to confer individual rights in Article 36(1)(b). Therefore, I respectfully dissent because it is clear that Article 36(1)(b) does confer individual rights and the presumption of a remedy under § 1983 has not been overcome.

In *Gonzaga*, the Supreme Court determined that "[§] 1983 provides a remedy only for the deprivation of rights, privileges, or immunities secured by the Constitution and laws of the United States." As a result, "it is rights, not the broader or vaguer 'benefits' or 'interests,' that may be enforced under the authority of [§ 1983]." The Court recognized the important distinction between the question of "whether a statutory violation may be enforced through § 1983 [and] whether a private right of action can be implied from a particular statute" that the majority seems to confuse. Parties suing under an implied right of action theory "must show that the statute manifests an intent to create not just a private *right* but also a private *remedy*." However, parties such as Cornejo, who are only seeking to enforce a statutory violation through § 1983, "do not have the burden of showing an intent to create a private remedy because § 1983 generally supplies a remedy for the vindication of rights secured by federal statutes." Instead, "[o]nce a plaintiff demonstrates that a statute confers an individual right, the right is presumptively enforceable by § 1983." Thus, the question of whether there was an intent under Article 36(1)(b) to create a private remedy, for which the majority places much weight, is irrelevant to the issue of whether Cornejo can enforce the treaty violation through § 1983. Instead, the only question relevant to Cornejo's claim is whether Article 36(1)(b) confers individual rights "on a particular class of persons."

II.   Text of Article 36(1)(b) of the Vienna Convention

To determine whether Article 36(1)(b) confers individual rights on a particular class of persons, we must first look to the language of the treaty. In order for the treaty to confer individual rights, "its text must be phrased in terms of the persons benefitted." * * *

Article 36(1)(b) speaks rather clearly in rights-conferring language as it "instructs authorities of a receiving State to notify an arrested foreign national of 'his rights' under the Convention 'without delay.' " * * *

Gonzaga does not require that the treaty say anything about the nature of his rights or how, if at all, they may be invoked. Instead, *Gonzaga* requires only that the rights be "conferr[ed] on a particular class of persons." In this case, the right is conferred on foreign nationals who are detained or arrested by competent authorities of the receiving State. These foreign nationals have a right to be informed that the competent authorities are required upon request of the foreign national to notify the sending State of the arrest or detention.

In spite of the clear language in Article 36(1)(b) referencing "his rights" and the conferral of the right on a particular class of persons, the majority contends that this right belongs entirely to the sending State. To support this contention, the majority looks to titles contained in the Vienna Convention and other subparagraphs within Article 36. However, such an interpretation is contrary to the clear language of Article 36(1)(b), which refers to "his rights" not to those of the sending State. If the drafters of the treaty intended that the rights in Article 36(1)(b) belong entirely to the State, it easily could have written language consistent with such a construction or simply omitted the last sentence of Article 36(1)(b). Instead, * * * the drafters of the treaty included this language to make clear that individuals have a right to be informed that competent authorities are required to notify their consulates if they so request.

III. EXTRATEXTUAL SOURCES OF INTERPRETATION OF ARTICLE 36(1)(B)

The majority seeks to buttress its conclusion that Article 36(1)(b) does not confer individual rights through an analysis of the Vienna "Convention as a whole, the contemporaneous understanding of Congress in ratifying it as well as the view of the Department of State, and the uniform practice of States implementing it over the years." According to *Gonzaga*, we do not need to address these sources because Article 36(1)(b) confers rights in "clear and unambiguous terms." In such cases, "no more . . . is required for Congress to create new rights." Nonetheless, evaluating these sources demonstrates that they support the interpretation of Article 36(1)(b) as conferring an individual right.

First, the majority states that "[e]xcept for its final provisions, the Convention's articles all have to do with consular posts." Assuming arguendo that this is the case, it does not foreclose the possibility that the drafters intended to protect the individual rights of foreign nationals in Article 36(1)(b) as made clear by the language of the provision. Instead, as will be discussed in greater detail below, the drafters understood Article 36(1)(b) to be a unique provision within the Vienna Convention that required extensive negotiations to secure passage.

Second, the majority relies on the Preamble to the Vienna Convention * * *. The majority contends that the language in the preamble stating that "the purpose of such privileges and immunities is not to benefit individuals" supports its contention that no part of the Vienna Convention, including Article 36(1)(b), was intended to confer individual rights.

The Seventh Circuit has explained, "[i]t is a mistake to allow general language of a preamble to create an ambiguity in specific statutory or treaty text where none exists. Courts should look to materials like preambles and titles only if the text of the instrument is ambiguous." [*Jogi v. Voges*, 480 F.3d 822 (7th Cir. 2007)] This explanation is consistent with a long-standing rule of statutory construction that a statute "clear and unambiguous in its enacting parts, may [not] be so controlled by its preamble as to justify a construction plainly inconsistent with the words used in the body of the statute." In other words, a preamble cannot be relied upon to create ambiguity in a statute.* * *

The majority also does not address an interpretation of the preamble that would be consistent with a rights-conferring Article 36(1)(b). The Seventh Circuit in *Jogi* explained, "the most reasonable understanding of this language is as a way of emphasizing that the Convention is not designed to benefit diplomats in their individual capacity, but rather to protect them in their official capacity." Thus, the language in the preamble explaining that "such privileges and immunities are not to benefit individuals" more reasonably refers to the fact that the privileges and immunities contained in the Vienna Convention are not intended to benefit consul in their individual capacity. Protecting the rights of detained foreign nationals is perfectly consistent with this interpretation of the Preamble.

Third, the majority relies on congressional intent in ratifying the Convention. The majority first looks to statements in the Report of the Committee on Foreign Relations describing the function of the Vienna Convention in terms of the preamble. As discussed above, the language in the preamble does not support the majority's conclusion that Article 36(1)(b) does not confer individual rights.* * *

I agree that the fact that the conferring of individual rights on a particular class of persons in the Convention establishes a presumptive right of enforcement under § 1983 was likely not foreseen by the congressional ratifiers. This presumptive enforcement right is a product of recent case law establishing § 1983 as the enforcement mechanism for federal statutes and treaties. However, this lack of foreseeability by the congressional ratifiers does not change the fact that the language of the statute that they ratified conferred rights to individual foreign nationals.* * *

Fourth, the majority contends that the contemporaneous position of the United States Department of State "reinforce[d] the view that the Convention as a whole, and Article 36 in particular, were not intended to create individually enforceable rights." The majority again confuses the *Gonzaga* standard. What is relevant under *Gonzaga* is whether the Convention creates individual rights, not whether it creates individually *enforceable* rights. * * * [T]he enforceability of the right under § 1983 is determined in accordance with a standard unrelated to the specific language in the treaty.

Relying on this misunderstanding of the *Gonzaga* standard, the majority continues by quoting a statement from one of the deputy legal advisers to the State Department to the Foreign Relations Committee when the Committee was considering ratification. * * * The majority then paraphrases the adviser as stating, "[f]ailing that, he represented, disputes would be submitted to the ICJ pursuant to the Optional Protocol." The majority ignores the context of these statements, which demonstrate that the adviser did not have in mind the issue of whether Article 36(1)(b) confers individual rights.* * *

A more reasonable interpretation of the response to the question than that offered by the majority is that the adviser was trying to assure the Senate that the ICJ would not have the authority to resolve disputes that the United States considered domestic. Instead, such disputes would be resolved through diplomatic channels or, in the case of international disputes, the International Court of Justice (ICJ).* * *

However, if we look at the mechanisms for resolving disputes cited by the State Department advisors, a decision of the ICJ provides support for an interpretation of Article 36(1)(b) as conferring individual rights. Although, the decisions of the ICJ have "no binding force except between the parties and in respect of that particular case," *see* ICJ

Statute, art. 34(1), they can provide persuasive support for a legal conclusion. In *LaGrand*, the ICJ held that Article 36(1)(b) "creates individual rights for the detained person in addition to the rights accorded the [sending State, and that consequently the reference to 'rights' in paragraph [b] must be read as applying not only to the rights of the sending State, but also to the rights of the detained individual]." *See LaGrand Case (Germany v. U.S.)*, 2001 I.C.J. 466, at ¶ 89 (June 27). Thus, on the basis of the ICJ process of resolution of conflicting interpretations of the Vienna Convention, Article 36(1)(b) does confer individual rights.

The ICJ's determination is consistent with the contemporaneous understanding of Secretary of State William P. Rodgers. In the Letter of Submittal of the Vienna Convention to President Nixon, Secretary of State Rodgers indicated that:

> [Article 36(1)(b)] requires that authorities of the receiving State inform the person detained of his right to have the fact of his detention reported to the consular post concerned and his *right* to communicate with that consular post. *If he so requests*, the consular post shall be notified without delay.

The majority dismisses this statement as "simply mirror[ing] the provision itself, which unquestionably refers to 'rights,' without shedding light on whether its intent was (or was not) to create privately enforceable rights." At the risk of sounding overly repetitive, all that *Gonzaga* requires to create a presumption of a remedy under § 1983 is that the statute confer an individual right, not a privately enforceable right. Thus, the fact that Secretary of State Rodgers understood Article 36(1)(b) to confer such rights is dispositive.

Further support for this conclusion is found in the U.S. Vienna Report, which was attached to the Letter of Submittal. The Report stated:

> The solution adopted by the Conference to the problem of adjusting the notification obligations of the receiving State to the *right of the individual* concerned to request notification lies in the final sentence of subparagraph 1(b). That sentence requires authorities of the receiving State to inform the person detained of his right to have the fact of his detention reported to the consular post concerned and of his right to communicate with that consular post.

The majority does not address these contemporaneous statements. Given that contemporaneous statements of the United States Department of State are entitled to "great weight" in the interpretation of treaties, the appropriate conclusion is that Article 36(1)(b) confers an individual right.

Finally, the majority relies on the legislative history of the Vienna Convention (the travaux preparatoires). * * * Specifically, the majority explains "there is no indication that States intended the enforcement of a 'right' to consular notification in the courts of the receiving State." The reasoning again demonstrates the majority's confusion with the *Gonzaga* standard. *Gonzaga* only requires an intent in the Vienna Convention to create a right, not an intent to enforce a right.* * *

In sum, I believe that the confusion in the majority opinion ultimately arises from the erroneous interpretation of *Gonzaga*. Contrary to the majority's view that there must be an intent to confer a privately enforceable individual right, *Gonzaga* only requires a demonstration that the statute confers an individual right.* * * For these reasons, I respectfully dissent.

NOTES AND QUESTIONS ON IMPLIED CAUSES OF ACTION

1.   *The Vienna Convention on Consular Relations.* As this book goes to press, the circuits are split on the question of whether Article 36 creates an individual right. The Seventh Circuit, in *Jogi v. Voges*, 480 F.3d 822, 835 (7th Cir. 2007), found that Article 36 of the Vienna Convention "grants private rights to an identifiable class of persons—aliens from countries that are parties to the Convention who are in the United States—and * * * its text is phrased in terms of the persons benefitted." The Fifth, Sixth, and Ninth Circuits have declined to find such a right. Lawyers following the split had hoped that the Supreme Court would settle this question when it granted *cert* in *State v. Sanchez-Llamas*, 108 P.3d 573 (Ore. 2005) and *Bustillo v. Johnson*, 65 Va. Cir. 69 (Va. 2004). However, in a consolidated decision (*Sanchez-Llamas v. Oregon*, 548 U.S. 331 (2006)), the Court assumed *without deciding* that Article 36 of the Vienna Convention granted the defendants individually enforceable rights but held that, even if there were an individual right, the defendants were not entitled to the relief they sought. In his dissent, Justice Breyer did analyze the individual rights question and found that Article 36 does create a judicially enforceable individual right.

2.   *Implied right of action.* In *Jogi v. Voges* (*Jogi I*) 425 F.3d 367, 380–85 (7th Cir. 2005), the Seventh Circuit found that Article 36 does convey an individual right. The court reasoned that "Article 36 ¶ 1(b) states, plainly enough, that authorities 'shall inform the person concerned without delay of his rights under this sub-paragraph.'" The court further reasoned that the "general language of a preamble [cannot be used to] create an ambiguity in specific statutory or treaty text where none exists." The court also cited Department of Homeland Security and State Department regulations and policies indicating that those government offices consider Article 36 to convey an individual right. Finally, the court acknowledged "that the international body with the authority to render binding interpretations of the Convention, the International Court of Justice (ICJ), has definitively announced that Article 36 gives rise to individually enforceable rights." The court then went on to consider "whether Jogi is entitled to enforce his individual

right under the Vienna Convention in a private action in court." On that question the court found an "implied private right of action to enforce the individual's Article 36 rights" and that federal courts had subject matter jurisdiction over such claims "under either the ATS or the general federal question statute, 28 U.S.C. § 1331."

The court later took the rare step of withdrawing its original opinion in *Jogi v. Voges* (*Jogi II*), 480 F.3d 822, 824–25 (7th Cir. 2007), upholding its individual right finding, but changing its holding with respect to the remedy structure. The court explained its decision as follows:

> In the interest of avoiding a decision on grounds broader than are necessary to resolve the case, especially in an area that touches so directly on the foreign relations of the United States, the panel has re-examined its earlier opinion and has decided to withdraw that opinion and substitute the following one. Briefly put, we are per-suaded that it is best not to rest subject matter jurisdiction on the ATS, since it is unclear whether the treaty violation Jogi has alleged amounts to a "tort." Both parties, as well as the United States, have suggested that jurisdiction is secure under 28 U.S.C. § 1331, and we agree with that position. Furthermore, rather than wade into the treacherous waters of implied remedies, we have concluded that Jogi's action rests on a more secure footing as one under 42 U.S.C. § 1983. At bottom, he is complaining about police action, under color of state law, that violates a right secured to him by a federal law (here, a treaty). We can safely leave for another day the question whether the Vienna Convention would directly support a private remedy.

3. *The Bivens analogy.* The Supreme Court found that it had the authority to imply a damage remedy for violations of the Fourth Amendment in *Bivens v. Six Unknown Named Agents Fed. Bureau of Narcotics*, 403 U.S. 388, 392 (1971) ("where federally protected rights have been invaded, it has been the rule from the beginning that courts will be alert to adjust their remedies so as to grant the necessary relief."). In *Handel v. Artukovic*, 601 F.Supp. 1421, 1427–28 (C. D. Cal. 1985), plaintiffs brought suit for deprivations of life and property suffered by Jews in Yugoslavia during World War II, in violation of both treaties and customary international law. The ACLU filed an *amicus* brief arguing, based on *Bivens*, that "the legal prohibition of such conduct entitles the plaintiffs to sue for damages, just as the rights guaranteed by treaties, statutes, and the Constitution may by their very nature justify private enforcement." The district court rejected this argument in the context of customary international law, citing "special factors counseling hesitation in the absence of affirmative action by Congress." *See also Corrie v. Caterpillar, Inc.*, 403 F. Supp.2d 1019 (W.D. Wash. 2005), *aff'd*, 503 F.3d 974 (9th Cir. 2007). The Supreme Court has used this "special factors" analysis to restrict the availability of implied rights of action derived from the Constitution in a number of areas.

4. *The issue of standing in other contexts.* In *Alvarez-Machain v. United States*, 331 F.3d 604, 616 (9th Cir. 2003) (*en banc*), *rev'd on other grounds*, 542 U.S. 692 (2004), the court found that Dr. Alvarez lacked standing to assert any of Mexico's sovereignty rights that may have been violated when he was kidnapped by U.S. agents from Mexican territory. Compare *United States v. Rauscher*, 119 U.S. 407 (1886), where a criminal defendant was permitted to raise the rule of specialty implied in the Webster–Ashburton Treaty of 1842 to prevent his trial on charges not specified in the U.S. extradition request.

Reservations, Understandings and Declarations ("RUDs")

Although the United States has ratified several important multilateral human rights treaties, it has done so subject to extensive qualifications known as reservations, understandings and declarations. The purpose of these RUD packages has generally been to limit U.S. treaty obligations to the content of existing U.S. domestic law. Other declarations establish that a treaty will be "non-self-executing." These RUDs have made it difficult for litigators to use treaty norms in domestic cases.

The legitimacy of RUDs has not been the subject of many published opinions. The discussion of these issues in the *Domingues* case, *infra*, is one of the most extensive to date. In *Domingues,* a defendant who was under eighteen at the time he committed his crime was facing the death penalty. He sought to use the prohibition on juvenile executions in Article 6(5) of the International Covenant on Civil and Political Rights ("ICCPR") to override Nevada's death penalty statute, which allowed juvenile executions in some cases.

DOMINGUES v. STATE

961 P.2d 1279 (Nev. 1998)

This case raises the single issue of whether [the Nevada juvenile death penalty statute] NRS 176.025 is superseded by an international treaty ratified by the United States, which prohibits the execution of individuals who committed capital offenses while under the age of eighteen. NRS 176.025 allows imposition of the death penalty on a defendant who was sixteen years old or older at the time that the capital offense was committed.* * *

In 1992, the United States Senate ratified the ICCPR, with the following pertinent reservation and declaration:

That the United States reserves the right, subject to its Constitutional constraints, to impose capital punishment on any person (other than a pregnant woman) duly convicted under existing or future laws permitting the imposition of capital punishment, including such punishment for crimes committed by persons below eighteen years of age. . . .

That the United States declares that the provisions of Articles 1 through 27 of the [ICCPR] *are not self-executing*.

* * * Domingues contends that pursuant to the ICCPR, imposition of the death sentence on one who committed a capital offense while under the age of eighteen is illegal. Although the United States Senate ratified the ICCPR with a reservation allowing juvenile offenders to be sentenced to death, Domingues asserts that this reservation was invalid and thus this capital sentencing prohibition set forth in the treaty is the supreme law of the land. Domingues contends that his death sentence, imposed for crimes he committed when he was sixteen years old, is thereby facially illegal. We disagree.

We conclude that the Senate's express reservation of the United States' right to impose a penalty of death on juvenile offenders negates Domingues' claim that he was illegally sentenced. Many of our sister jurisdictions have laws authorizing the death penalty for criminal offenders under the age of eighteen, and such laws have withstood Constitutional scrutiny. *See Stanford v. Kentucky*, 492 U.S. 361 (1989).* * *

NRS 176.025 provides that the death penalty shall not be imposed upon individuals who were under sixteen years of age at the time that the offense was committed. Because Domingues was sixteen at the time he committed a capital offense, we conclude that the death penalty was legally imposed upon him. Accordingly, we affirm the decision of the district court denying Domingues' motion to correct the sentence.

SPRINGER, C.J., dissenting:

The International Covenant on Civil and Political Rights, to which the United States is a "party," forbids imposing the death penalty on children under the age of eighteen. International treaties of this kind ordinarily become the "supreme law of the land." Under the majority's interpretation of the treaty, the United States, at least with regard to executing children, is a "party" to the treaty, while at the same time rejecting one of its most vital terms. Under Nevada's interpretation of the treaty, the United States will be joining hands with such countries as Iran, Iraq, Bangladesh, Nigeria and Pakistan in approving death sentences for children. I withhold my approval of the court's judgment in this regard.

ROSE, J., dissenting:

Following a brief hearing, the district court summarily concluded that the death sentence was facially valid in spite of an international treaty signed by the United States which prohibits the execution of individuals who were under eighteen years of age when the crime was committed. I believe this complicated issue deserved a full hearing, evidentiary if necessary, on the effect of our nation's ratification of the ICCPR and the reservation by the United States Senate to that treaty's provision prohibiting the execution of anyone who committed a capital crime while under eighteen years of age.

The penultimate issue that the district court should have considered is whether the Senate's reservation was valid. Article 4(2) of the treaty states that there shall be no derogation from Article 6 which includes the prohibition on the execution of juvenile offenders. Furthermore, there is authority to support the proposition that the Senate's reservation was invalid. *See, e.g.*, Restatement (Third) of the Foreign Relations Law of the United States § 313 (1987).

If the reservation was not valid, then the district court should determine whether the United States is still a party to the treaty. If the reservation was a *sine qua non* of the acceptance of the whole treaty by the United States, then the United State's ratification of the treaty could be considered a nullity. *See* William A. Schabas, *Invalid Reservations to the International Covenant on Civil and Political Rights: Is the United States Still a Party?*, 21 BROOK. J. INT'L. L. 277, 318–19 (1995). But, if the United States has shown an intent to accept the treaty as a whole, the result could be that the United States is bound by all of the provisions of the treaty, notwithstanding the reservation. *Id.*

These are not easy questions and testimony about the international conduct of the United States concerning the subjects contained in the treaty, in addition to expert testimony on the effect of the Senate's reservation may be necessary. A federal court that deals with federal law on a daily basis might be better equipped to address these issues; however, the motion is before the state court and it should do its best to resolve the matter. Accordingly, I would reverse the district court's denial of Domingues' motion and remand the case for a full hearing on the effect of the ICCPR on Domingues' sentence.

NOTES AND QUESTIONS ON RESERVATIONS, UNDERSTANDINGS AND DECLARATIONS

1. *Beazley v. Johnson.* The *Domingues* reasoning was subsequently adopted and expanded by the Fifth Circuit in *Beazley v. Johnson*, 242 F.3d 248 (5th Cir. 2001). *Beazley* also involved a prisoner's appeal of his death penalty sentence on the theory that he was under eighteen years old at the time of the offence, and that his sentence therefore violated the ICCPR. Notably, after the decision in *Dominguez* but before the decision in *Beazley*, the Human Rights Committee ("HRC")—the treaty body charged with interpreting the ICCPR—issued its General Comment 24 on the subject of reservations to the treaty. Without mentioning any specific states, it described some reservations—of the types used by the U.S.—as incompatible with the object and purpose of the treaty. Furthermore, the Human Rights Committee determined that incompati-

ble reservations are void, and it took the controversial step of deciding that the invalid reservations are severable. Thus, under the Human Rights Committee's approach, the reserving country remains a state party to the treaty without the illegal reservations.

2. *The debate: the legitimacy of reservations, understandings, and declarations.* There is a continuing debate as to whether the standard U.S. RUDs are consistent with international law and whether they are desirable as a matter of policy. Proponents of RUDs have argued that their use evinces a commitment on the part of the U.S. to adhere to the treaty. As a Carter Administration official stated in response to criticism of the RUDs proposed by the Administration:

> It is very easy to sign a human rights treaty without any reservations or understandings. Many authoritarian regimes have done so. The liberal democracies have not taken that approach.* * * One can almost judge those nations that take human rights obligations seriously by the manner in which they have approached the problems of reservations or understandings.* * * I would say that those Western liberal democracies that are entering a few reservations to make their law and the treaties compatible are doing a better job, a more serious job, and a more committed job because they are taking the treaties more seriously than those nations that become parties with no intention of conforming their practices to human rights treaty obligations and that make no statements indicating that they have any problems. From the government's perspective, if the United States did not care about complying with its treaty obligations, it could simply ratify human rights treaties with no reservations, declare them to be non-self-executing, and then refuse to enact implementing legislation to conform domestic law to the treaty requirements. The fact that the United States has adopted various RUDs, according to the government, demonstrates that the United States is serious about complying with its treaty obligations.

Arthur Rovine & Jack Goldklang, *Defense of Declarations, Reservations, and Understandings* in R. LILLICH, ED., U.S. RATIFICATION OF THE HUMAN RIGHTS TREATIES: WITH OR WITHOUT RESERVATIONS? 57 (1981).

Others have argued that RUDs serve to protect interests that are unique to the United States (*e.g.* free speech) or that they provide common ground for those politicians who view international law as a threat to U.S. sovereignty and those who want the U.S. to play a greater role in international law. *See* Curtis A. Bradley & Jack L. Goldsmith, *Treaties, Human Rights, and Conditional Consent*, 149 U. PA. L. REV. 399, 402 (2000).

Should human rights advocates urge the United States to ratify human rights treaties if they are accompanied by similar packages of RUDs? Is ratification in such circumstances an empty exercise? Are litigants seeking to rely on human rights law in their cases better or worse off because of U.S. ratification with RUDs?

3.   *Significance of international objections to RUDs.* The U.S. practice on RUDs has been criticized by UN bodies and U.S. allies, most notably in HRC General Comment 24, discussed above. Should U.S. courts adopt the Human Rights Committee's view and disregard U.S. RUDs? Do you think the United States would ratify any human rights treaties if U.S. RUDs could be found invalid and severable by an international body? Is it better to uphold RUDs and convince the U.S. to drop its objections over time?

4.   *What are the consequences of invalid RUDs?* In *Belilos v. Switzerland,* 132 Eur. Ct. H.R. (Ser. A) (1988), the European Court of Human Rights considered Switzerland's interpretive declaration (legally equivalent to a reservation) to Article 6 of the European Convention, involving the right to a fair trial. The Court held that the reservation was invalid under the Convention's rules on reservations and severed it from Switzerland's consent to be bound by the treaty. The effect was that Switzerland would be bound by the European Convention as though it had consented to the treaty without the reservation. For a detailed analysis of the *Belilos* case, see Richard W. Edwards, Jr., *Reservations to Treaties: The Belilos Case and the Work of the International Law Commission,* 31 U. TOL. L. REV. 195 (2002).

B.   THE ENFORCEMENT OF CUSTOMARY INTERNATIONAL LAW

In the last 25 years, human rights litigators have increasingly turned to customary international law in bringing claims challenging government action in the United States. One reason for this strategy is that the U.S. had, until recently, failed to ratify any of the major human rights treaties, and, even when the U.S. did ratify some of these treaties, it did so with a "non-self-executing" declaration. The United States has not expressed disagreement with the development of the most important international human rights norms. Indeed, the U.S. frequently criticizes other governments for their failure to abide by international human rights norms, such as the prohibitions against torture, extra-judicial executions, disappearances, forced labor, genocide, war crimes, and crimes against humanity.

Though much of this litigation has been under the statutory authorization of the ATS, *supra,* Module 1, litigators have also attempted to use customary law to challenge government action in a variety of other contexts. Such claims are based on the principle that customary law, like treaties, is federal law. Louis Henkin, *International Law as Law in the United States,* 82 MICH. L. REV. 1555 (1984). In other cases, litigators have used customary law or international documents which might be considered "soft law" or *lex ferenda* to supplement and bolster domestic law arguments.

In this section, we consider the various ways litigators have attempted to employ customary international law in the zealous representation of their clients' interests. The *Rodriguez-Fernandez* opinion, *infra*, is one of the relatively rare cases in which a claimant has prevailed against official action based upon customary international law. The case arose out of the Mariel Boatlift in 1980 when Cuban President Fidel Castro emptied Cuban prisons and allowed over 100,000 Cubans to make their way to the United States. Thousands of the Marielitos were detained in federal prisons and detention facilities for months while U.S. officials tried to respond to the crisis.

Rodriguez–Fernandez was one such Cuban detainee who filed a habeas petition from federal prison in Leavenworth, Kansas. Although the State Department made repeated efforts to repatriate him to Cuba, the Cuban government refused to accept him, and the U.S. government was unable to determine when it could carry out its order to deport him.

FERNANDEZ v. WILKINSON

505 F.Supp. 787 (D. Kansas 1980),
aff'd on other grounds, 654 F.2d 1382 (10th Cir. 1981)

We have declared that indeterminate detention of petitioner in a maximum security prison pending unforeseeable deportation constitutes arbitrary detention. Due to the unique legal status of excluded aliens in this country, it is an evil from which our Constitution and statutory laws afford no protection. Our domestic laws are designed to deter private individuals from harming one another and to protect individuals from abuse by the State. But in the case of unadmitted aliens detained on our soil, but legally deemed to be outside our borders, the machinery of domestic law utterly fails to operate to assure protection.

The *Amicus Curiae* in this case contends, and counsel for petitioner urges, that the continued detention of petitioner is in contravention of fundamental human justice as embodied in established principles of international law.* * * We agree that international law secures to petitioner the right to be free of arbitrary detention and that his right is being violated.* * *

International rules are generally binding upon nations only in cases where either: (1) the nation concerned has expressly consented to be bound by such rules, as by ratification of a treaty containing the rules; or (2) where it can be established through evidence of a wide practice by states that a customary rule of international law exists.

The most important source of international law is international treaties. At present, the United States has ratified and is a party to only a few human rights treaties. Petitioner does not assert that his detention is in direct violation of any treaty to which the United States is a party.* * *

The difficulty with international agreements as a legal source is that the courts are simply not bound by these documents unless they have been ratified by the United States. And we are signatory to very few international human rights agreements and ratifying state to even fewer such agreements. One important document by which the United States is bound is the United Nations Charter.* * * The Charter entered into force on October 24, 1945, and resolves to reaffirm faith in fundamental human rights and in the dignity of the human person. Almost all nations in the world are now parties to the UN Charter.

There are a great number of other international declarations, resolutions, and recommendations. While not technically binding, these documents establish broadly recognized standards. The most important of these is the Universal Declaration of Human Rights, adopted by the UN General Assembly in 1948.* * *

> It is a jurist's opinion that

> although the affirmations of the Declaration are not binding *qua* international convention within the meaning of Article 38, paragraph 1(a) of the Statute of the Court, they can bind states on the basis of custom within the meaning of the same Article, whether because they constitute a codification of customary law as was said in respect of Article 6 of the Vienna Convention on the Law of Treaties, or because they have acquired the force of custom through a general practice accepted as law, in the words of Article 38, paragraph 1(b), of the Statute.

Separate Opinion of Vice–President Ammoun in *Advisory Opinion on the Continued Presence of South Africa in Namibia (S.W. Africa)*, 1971 I.C.J. Reports 16, 76. Thus, it appears that the Declaration has evolved into an important source of international human rights law.

Articles 3 and 9 of the Declaration provide that "everyone has the right to life, liberty, and the security of person," and that "no one shall be subjected to arbitrary arrest, detention or exile."

The American Convention on Human Rights, cited by the *Amicus Curiae*, pertinently declares in Article 5 that "punishment shall not be extended to any person other than the criminal," and "all persons deprived of their liberty shall be treated with respect for the inherent dignity of the human person." In Article 7 of the Convention it is agreed:

> 1.   Every person has the right to personal liberty and security.

> 2.   No one shall be deprived of his physical liberty except for the reasons and under the conditions established beforehand by the Constitution of the State Party concerned or by a law established pursuant thereto.

3. No one shall be subject to arbitrary arrest or imprisonment.* * *

Two other principal sources of fundamental human rights are the European Convention for the Protection of Human Rights and Fundamental Freedoms (Rome 1950), and the International Covenant on Civil and Political Rights. Although the United States is not bound by either of these documents, they are indicative of the customs and usages of civilized nations.* * *

Principles of customary international law may be discerned from an overview of express international conventions, the teachings of legal scholars, the general custom and practice of nations and relevant judicial decisions. *Filartiga v. Pena–Irala*, 630 F.2d 876 (2d Cir. 1980). When, from this overview a wrong is found to be of mutual, and not merely several, concern among nations, it may be termed an international law violation, *Id*.

International law is a part of the laws of the United States which federal courts are bound to ascertain and administer in an appropriate case. Our review of the sources from which customary international law is derived clearly demonstrates that arbitrary detention is prohibited by customary international law. Therefore, even though the indeterminate detention of an excluded alien cannot be said to violate the United States Constitution or our statutory laws, it is judicially remedial as a violation of international law. Petitioner's continued, indeterminate detention on restrictive status in a maximum security prison, without having been convicted of a crime in this country or a determination having been made that he is a risk to security or likely to abscond, is unlawful; and as such amounts to an abuse of discretion on the part of the Attorney General and his delegates.* * *

We now return to the *Hawkins* case introduced in section A. After rejecting plaintiff's treaty-based arguments, the district judge considered whether the customary law prohibiting torture and other forms of cruel, inhuman or degrading treatment or punishment supported the issuance of an injunction against the use of stun-gun technology as a mode of restraint in court.

HAWKINS v. COMPARET–CASSANI

33 F. Supp. 2d 1244 (C.D. Cal. 1999)

Violations of jus cogens international law (Count I)

The plaintiff claims that the defendants' acts amount to torture under international law, and therefore the defendants violated *jus cogens* norms of international law. *Jus cogens* norms of international law comprise the body of laws that are considered so fundamental that they are binding on all nations whether the nations have consented to them or not. To determine the scope of *jus cogens* international law, courts look to several different sources including treaties, state practice, legal decisions, and works of noted jurists. In this regard, several courts have found that torture is a violation of *jus cogens* norms of international law. These cases define torture as:

> any act by which severe pain or suffering, whether physical or mental, is intentionally inflicted on a person for such purposes as obtaining from him or a third person information or a confession, punishing him for an act he or a third person has committed or is suspected of having committed, or intimidating or coercing him or a third person, or for any reason based on discrimination of any kind, when such pain or suffering is inflicted by or at the instigation of or with the consent or acquiescence of a public official or other person acting in an official capacity.

Siderman de Blake, 965 F.2d at 717 n.16, *quoting* The Convention Against Torture and Other Cruel, Inhuman or Degrading Treatment or Punishment, art 1, 39 U.N. GAOR Supp. (No. 51), 23 I.L.M. 1027 (1984).

All of the cases, however, that found a cognizable right under *jus cogens* norms of international law involved either acts committed on a foreign citizen or acts committed by a foreign government or government official. There is no reported case of a court in the United States recognizing a cause of action under *jus cogens* norms of international law for acts committed by United States government officials against a citizen of the United States. Therefore, the plaintiff is inviting this Court to define a new cause of action against state officers in the United States when they act against a citizen of this country.

It is clear that *jus cogens* norms of international law are part of the laws of the United States. *See The Paquete Habana*, 175 U.S. 677, 700, 44 L. Ed. 320, 20 S. Ct. 290 (1900). However, the law of nations does not in itself create a personal right of action for individual citizens. Instead, "whether and how the United States wished to react to such violations are domestic questions."

It is also clear, however, that federal courts may imply a personal right of action for violations of *jus cogens* norms of international law. In *Bivens*, the Supreme Court held that where federally protected rights are invaded then the "courts will be alert to adjust their remedies so as to grant the necessary relief." However, courts do not automatically recognize a *Bivens* claim anytime there is a federally protected right that does not have an express remedy. Instead, "federal courts also must consider whether there exist 'special factors counseling hesitation in the absence of affirmative action by Congress.' "

Here, * * * there are several factors which counsel against the Court implying a *Bivens* right of action in this case. First, in the Court's view, there are existing remedies for plaintiff's causes of action. Indeed, the plaintiff has filed several different claims under domestic laws such as the Eighth Amendment's prohibition of cruel and unusual punishment. Moreover, many of the claims barred in this Court due to Eleventh Amendment concerns could have been brought in a California state court.

Additionally, the Court notes * * * that Congress has acted in the field of torture. Congress enacted the Torture Victim Protection Act of 1991. This Act creates a private right of action for victims of torture taken under color of law in a foreign nation. Although this statute appears to be limited to acts of foreign officials, it represents congressional attempts to address the issue of a private remedy for acts of torture. Courts normally give great deference to congressional policy determinations regarding whether to afford individuals personal rights of action for particular violations. Likewise, this Court is hesitant to create a new cause of action in a circumstance where the Legislature has stated that domestic law affords adequate remedies.

Finally, this Court is also hesitant to interfere in an area that is traditionally entrusted to the legislative and executive branches. It is these two branches which must interpret what international obligations the United States will undertake and how to implement them domestically.

For these reasons, the Court finds that "the special factors counseling hesitation" the *Bivens* Court discussed are present in the current case. Therefore, the Court grants the defendants' motion to dismiss Count I of the plaintiff's amended complaint with prejudice.

Notes and Questions on the Enforcement of Customary International Law

1. *Subsequent history.* On appeal, the Tenth Circuit affirmed the result in *Rodriguez-Fernandez* but did so using the principle that federal statutes should be interpreted to be consistent with the customary norms on which the district court relied. *Rodriguez-Fernandez v. Wilkinson*, 654 F.2d 1382 (10th Cir. 1981). In subsequent years, many Marielitos were released or paroled in U.S. society. Some paroled Marielitos became re-offenders and were kept in detention after their sentences pending deportation. The courts rejected international law challenges to this form of indefinite detention based upon the "controlling" actions of the Executive Branch and the due process protections incorporated in administrative review provisions. *See e.g., Garcia–Mir v. Meese*, 788 F.2d 1446 (11th Cir. 1986); *Barrera-Echavarria v. Rison*, 44 F.3d 1441 (9th Cir. 1995) (*en banc*).

2. *Jus cogens norms.* Article 53 of the the Vienna Convention on the Law of Treaties recognizes that certain norms—*jus cogens* or peremptory

norms—are so fundamental to the international legal system that they may not be superceded by subsequent state practice or treaties. The Ninth Circuit described *jus cogens* norms, stating "As defined in the Vienna Convention on the Law of Treaties, a *jus cogens* norm, also known as a 'peremptory norm' of international law, 'is a norm accepted and recognized by the international community of states as a whole as a norm from which no derogation is permitted and which can be modified only by a subsequent norm of general international law having the same character.'" *Siderman de Blake v. Republic of Argentina*, 965 F.2d 699, 714 (9th Cir. 1992). "Whereas customary international law derives solely from the consent of states, the fundamental and universal norms constituting *jus cogens* transcend such consent.* * *" *Siderman*, 965 F.2d at 715. Should *jus cogens* norms be treated differently from ordinary customary norms in domestic litigation?

3. *Persistent objector.* "Although customary law may be built by the acquiescence as well as by the actions of states and become generally binding on all states, in principle a state that indicates its dissent from a practice while the law is still in the process of development is not bound by that rule even after it matures." RESTATEMENT (THIRD) OF FOREIGN RELATIONS LAW OF THE UNITED STATES, § 102, comment (d) (1986). Known in international law as the "persistent objector rule," this rule exempts a state from adhering to rules of customary law that develop despite the express and continuing objections of that state. In these instances, the emerging rule of customary international law will not bind the objecting state. Are there certain rules of customary law for which states should not be able to assert the "persistent objector rule"?

4. *Is Congress bound by customary international law?* The question of whether customary international law can trump federal statutes remains unsettled. The U.S. Supreme Court has yet to weigh in on the question, and circuit courts remain split. *Compare United States v. Javino*, 960 F.2d 1137, 1142–44 (2d Cir. 1992) (customary international law may override federal statutes) and *Beharry v. Reno*, 183 F. Supp. 2d 584, 586 (E.D.N.Y. 2002) *with Galo–Garcia v. Immigration & Naturalization Serv.*, 86 F.3d 916 (9th Cir. 1996) (where there is a extensive legislative scheme, customary international law is inapplicable and cannot confer jurisdiction) and *Committee of United States Citizens in Nicaragua v. Reagan*, 859 F.2d 929 (D.C. Cir. 1988) (federal statute overrides customary international law).

Courts appear to agree that a subsequent federal statute supersedes customary international law. However, some scholars have argued that customary international law supersedes prior federal legislation. *See* Louis Henkin, *The Constitution and United States Sovereignty: A Century of Chinese Exclusion and its Progeny*, 100 HARV. L. REV. 853, 872–78 (1987). On what rationale if any should customary law supercede prior federal statutes? Is this view likely to be accepted by the courts?

5. *Is the President bound by customary international law?* In *Garcia-Mir v. Meese, supra*, the Eleventh Circuit considered whether the Executive

could detain Marielito detainees indefinitely despite the customary international law prohibition on prolonged arbitrary detention. The court agreed that "[t]he public law of nations was long ago incorporated into the common law of the United States." *The Paquete Habana*, 175 U.S. 677, 700 (1900). However, the court noted that public international law is controlling only "where there is no treaty and no controlling executive or legislative act or judicial decision. . . ."*Id.* at 700.

The Eleventh Circuit found that the Attorney General's actions in creating a review program were "controlling" acts by the Executive and superceded customary law. The court also found that its own decision in *Jean v. Nelson*, 472 U.S. 846 (1985), was a "controlling" judicial act within the meaning of *The Paquette Habana*. In *Garcia-Mir*, the court held that the U.S. Attorney General could order the indefinite detention of Cuban nationals who could not be deported, despite its recognition that this type of prolonged arbitrary detention violated customary law. Several other courts have also determined that customary international law is unenforceable against the President or senior Executive officials. *See, e.g. Barrera–Echavarria v. Rison*, 44 F.3d at 1451 (9th Cir. 1995); *Gisbert v. United States Attorney General*, 988 F.2d 1437, 1448 (5th Cir. 1993).

Several scholars have criticized the court's decision in *Garcia-Mir*. *See, e.g.* Louis Henkin, Foreign Affairs and the United States Constitution 244–245 (2nd ed. 1996); Frederic Kirgis, *Federal Statutes, Executive Orders, and "Self–Executing Custom,"* 81 Am. J. Int'l. L. 371 (1987). Given the mandate in Article II that the President "shall take Care that the Laws be faithfully executed," is the President bound by customary international law?

C. SAILING ON THE *CHARMING BETSY*: INTERPRETING STATUTES IN LIGHT OF INTERNATIONAL LAW

In sections A and B, we considered the rules governing the circumstances in which treaty provisions or customary norms may be employed to supercede inconsistent domestic laws or official actions. In this section, we consider the principle that U.S. laws should be interpreted consistently with international treaties or customary law unless it is impossible to do so.

The *Charming Betsy* principle rests on the assumption that legislators intend to act consistently with international law when they legislate. Sometimes Congress acts to implement international obligations directly. The *Cardoza-Fonseca* case involves the interpretation of Congressional intent regarding the burden of proof in asylum proceedings under the Refugee Act of 1980. It came after the Court had upheld a stringent burden of proof on those seeking withholding of deportation in *INS v. Stevic*, 467 U.S. 407 (1984).

IMMIGRATION AND NATURALIZATION SERVICE v. CARDOZA-FONSECA

480 U.S. 421 (1987)

Since 1980, the Immigration and Nationality Act has provided two methods through which an otherwise deportable alien who claims that he will be persecuted if deported can seek relief. Section 243(h) of the Act, 8 U.S.C. § 1253(h), requires the Attorney General to withhold deportation of an alien who demonstrates that his "life or freedom would be threatened" on account of one of the listed factors if he is deported. In *INS v. Stevic*, 467 U.S. 407 (1984), we held that to qualify for this entitlement to withholding of deportation, an alien must demonstrate that "it is more likely than not that the alien would be subject to persecution" in the country to which he would be returned. The Refugee Act of 1980, also established a second type of broader relief. Section 208(a) of the Act, 8 U.S.C. § 1158(a), authorizes the Attorney General, in his discretion, to grant asylum to an alien who is unable or unwilling to return to his home country "because of persecution or a well-founded fear of persecution on account of race, religion, nationality, membership in a particular social group, or political opinion."

In *Stevic*, we rejected an alien's contention that the § 208(a) "well-founded fear" standard governs applications for withholding of deportation under § 243(h). Similarly, today we reject the Government's contention that the § 243(h) standard, which requires an alien to show that he is more likely than not to be subject to persecution, governs applications for asylum under § 208(a). Congress used different, broader language to define the term "refugee" as used in § 208(a) than it used to describe the class of aliens who have a right to withholding of deportation under § 243(h). The Act's establishment of a broad class of refugees who are eligible for a discretionary grant of asylum, and a narrower class of aliens who are given a statutory right not to be deported to the country where they are in danger, mirrors the provisions of the United Nations Protocol Relating to the Status of Refugees, which provided the motivation for the enactment of the Refugee Act of 1980. In addition, the legislative history of the 1980 Act makes it perfectly clear that Congress did not intend the class of aliens who qualify as refugees to be coextensive with the class who qualify for § 243(h) relief.* * *

II.

The Refugee Act of 1980 established a new statutory procedure for granting asylum to refugees. The 1980 Act added a new § 208(a) to the Immigration and Nationality Act of 1952, reading as follows:

The Attorney General shall establish a procedure for an alien physically present in the United States or at a land border or port of entry, irrespective of such alien's status, to apply for asylum, and the alien may be granted asylum in the discretion of the Attorney General if the Attorney General determines that such alien is a refugee within the meaning of section 1101(a)(42)(A) of this title. 94 Stat. 105, 8 U.S.C. § 1158(a).

Under this section, eligibility for asylum depends entirely on the Attorney General's determination that an alien is a "refugee," as that term is defined in § 101(a)(42), which was also added to the Act in 1980. The section provides:

The term 'refugee' means (A) any person who is outside any country of such person's nationality or, in the case of a person having no nationality, is outside any country in which such person last habitually resided, and who is unable or unwilling to return to, and is unable or unwilling to avail himself or herself of the protection of, that country because of persecution or a well-founded fear of persecution on account of race, religion, nationality, membership in a particular social group, or political opinion. . . .

94 Stat. 102, 8 U.S.C. § 1101(a)(42).

Thus, the "persecution or well-founded fear of persecution" standard governs the Attorney General's determination whether an alien is eligible for asylum.

In addition to establishing a statutory asylum process, the 1980 Act amended the withholding of deportation provision, § 243(h). Prior to 1968, the Attorney General had discretion whether to grant withholding of deportation to aliens under § 243(h). In 1968, however, the United States agreed to comply with the substantive provisions of Articles 2 through 34 of the 1951 United Nations Convention relating to the Status of Refugees. Article 33.1 of the Convention which is the counterpart of § 243(h) of our statute, imposed a mandatory duty on contracting States not to return an alien to a country where his "life or freedom would be threatened" on account of one of the enumerated reasons. Thus, although § 243(h) itself did not constrain the Attorney General's discretion after 1968, presumably he honored the dictates of the United Nations Convention. In any event, the 1980 Act removed the Attorney General's discretion in § 243(h) proceedings.

In *Stevic* we considered it significant that in enacting the 1980 Act Congress did not amend the standard of eligibility for relief under § 243(h). While the terms "refugee" and hence "well-founded fear" were made an integral part of the § 208(a) procedure, they continued to play no part in § 243(h). Thus we held that the prior consistent construction of § 243(h) that required an applicant for withholding of deportation to demonstrate a "clear probability of persecution" upon deportation remained in force. Of course, this reasoning, based in larger part on the plain language of § 243(h), is of no avail here since § 208(a) expressly provides that the "well-founded fear" standard governs eligibility for asylum.

The Government argues, however, that even though the "well-founded fear" standard is applicable, there is no difference between it and the "would be threatened" test of § 243(h). It asks us to hold that the only way an applicant can demonstrate a "well-founded fear of persecution" is to prove a "clear probability of persecution." The statutory language does not lend itself to this reading.

To begin with, the language Congress used to describe the two standards conveys very different meanings. The "would be threatened" language of § 243(h) has no subjective component, but instead requires the alien to establish by objective evidence that it is more likely than not that he or she will be subject to persecution upon deportation. *See Stevic, supra.* In contrast, the reference to "fear" in the § 208(a) standard obviously makes the eligibility determination turn to some extent on the subjective mental state of the alien.* * *

That the fear must be "well-founded" does not alter the obvious focus on the individual's subjective beliefs, nor does it transform the standard into a "more likely than not" one. One can certainly have a well-founded fear of an event happening when there is less than a 50% chance of the occurrence taking place. As one leading authority has pointed out: "Let us ... presume that it is known that in the applicant's country of origin every tenth adult male person is either put to death or sent to some remote labor camp. . . . In such a case it would be only too apparent that anyone who has managed to escape from the country in question will have 'well-founded fear of being persecuted' upon his eventual return." 1 A. Grahl–Madsen, The Status of Refugees in International Law 180 (1966).

This ordinary and obvious meaning of the phrase is not to be lightly discounted. With regard to this very statutory scheme, we have considered ourselves bound to "assume 'that the legislative purpose is expressed by the ordinary meaning of the words used.' "

The different emphasis of the two standards which is so clear on the face of the statute is significantly highlighted by the fact that the same Congress simultaneously drafted § 208(a) and amended § 243(h). In doing so, Congress chose to maintain the old standard in § 243(h), but to incorporate a different standard in § 208(a).* * * The contrast between the language used in the two standards, and the fact that Congress used a new standard to define the term "refugee," certainly indicate that Congress intended the two standards to differ.

III

The message conveyed by the plain language of the Act is confirmed by an examination of its history. Three aspects of that history are particularly compelling: The pre–1980 experience under § 203(a)(7), the only prior statute dealing with asylum; the abundant evidence of an intent to conform the definition of "refugee" and our asylum law to the United Nations Protocol to which the United States has been bound since 1968; and the fact that Congress declined to enact the Senate version of the bill that would have made a refugee ineligible for asylum unless "his deportation or return would be prohibited by § 243(h).* * *"

The United Nations Protocol

* * * If one thing is clear from the legislative history of the new definition of "refugee," and indeed the entire 1980 Act, it is that one of Congress' primary purposes was to bring United States refugee law into conformance with the 1967 United Nations Protocol Relating to the Status of Refugees, to which the United States acceded in 1968. Indeed, the definition of "refugee" that Congress adopted, is virtually identical to the one prescribed by Article 1(2) of the Convention which defines a "refugee" as an individual who "owing to a well-founded fear of being persecuted for reasons of race, religion, nationality, membership of a particular social group or political opinion, is outside the country of his nationality and is unable or, owing to such fear, is unwilling to avail himself of the protection of that country, or who, not having a nationality and being outside the country of his former habitual residence, is unable or, owing to such fear, is unwilling to return to it."

Not only did Congress adopt the Protocol's standard in the statute, but there were also many statements indicating Congress' intent that the new statutory definition of "refugee" be interpreted in conformance with the Protocol's definition. The Conference Committee Report, for example, stated that the definition was accepted "with the understanding that it is based directly upon the language of the Protocol and it is intended that the provision be construed consistent with the Protocol." It is thus appropriate to consider what the phrase "well-founded fear" means with relation to the Protocol.

The origin of the Protocol's definition of "refugee" is found in the 1946 Constitution of the International Refugee Organization (IRO). The IRO defined a "refugee" as a person who had a "valid objection" to returning to his country of nationality, and specified that "fear, based on reasonable grounds of persecution because of race, religion, nationality, or political opinions..." constituted a valid objection. The term was then incorporated in the United Nations Convention Relating to the Status of Refugees. The Committee that drafted the provision explained that "[the] expression 'well-founded fear of being the victim of persecution ...' means that a person has either been actually a victim of persecution or can show good reason why he fears persecution." The 1967 Protocol incorporated the "well-founded fear" test, without modification. The standard, as it has been consistently understood by those who drafted it, as well as those drafting the documents that adopted it, certainly does not require an alien to show that it is more likely than not that he will be persecuted in order to be classified as a "refugee."

In interpreting the Protocol's definition of "refugee" we are further guided by the analysis set forth in the Office of the United Nations High Commissioner for Refugees, Handbook on Procedures and Criteria for Determining Refugee Status (Geneva, 1979).[1] The Handbook explains that "[in] general, the applicant's fear should be considered well founded if he can establish, to a reasonable degree, that his continued stay in his country of origin has become intolerable to him for the reasons stated in the definition, or would for the same reasons be intolerable if he returned there."

The High Commissioner's analysis of the United Nations standard is consistent without examination of the origins of the Protocol's definition, as well as the conclusions of many scholars who have studied the matter. There is simply no room in the United Nations' definition for concluding that because an applicant only has a 10% chance of being shot, tortured, or otherwise persecuted, that he or she has no "well-founded fear" of the event happening. As we pointed out in *Stevic*, a moderate interpretation of the "well-founded fear" standard would indicate "that so long as an objective situation is established by the evidence, it need not be shown that the situation will probably result in persecution, but it is enough that persecution is a reasonable probability."

In *Stevic*, we dealt with the issue of withholding of deportation, or *non-refoulement*, under § 243(h). This provision corresponds to Article 33.1 of the Convention. Significantly though, Article 33.1 does not extend this right to everyone who meets the definition of "refugee." Rather, it provides that "[no] Contracting State shall expel or return ('refouler') a *refugee* in any manner whatsoever to the frontiers or territories where his *life or freedom would be threatened* on account of his race, religion, nationality, membership or a particular social group or political opinion" (emphasis added). Thus, Article 33.1 requires that an applicant satisfy two burdens: first, that he or she be a "refugee," *i.e.*, prove at least a "well-founded fear of persecution"; second, that the "refugee" show that his or her life or freedom "would be threatened" if deported. Section § 243(h)'s imposition of a "would be threatened" requirement is entirely consistent with the United States' obligations under the Protocol.

Section 208(a), by contrast, is a discretionary mechanism which gives the Attorney General the authority to grant the broader relief of asylum to refugees. As such, it does not correspond to Article 33 of the Convention, but instead corresponds to Article 34. That Article provides

---

1. We do not suggest, of course, that the explanation in the UN Handbook has the force of law or in any way binds the INS with reference to the asylum provisions of § 208(a). Indeed, the Handbook itself disclaims such force, explaining that "the determination of refugee status under the 1951 Convention and the 1967 Protocol ... is incumbent upon the Contracting State in whose territory the refugee finds himself."

that the contracting States "shall as far as possible facilitate the assimilation and naturalization of refugees...." Like § 208(a), the provision is precatory; it does not require the implementing authority actually to grant asylum to all those who are eligible. Also like § 208(a), an alien must only show that he or she is a "refugee" to establish eligibility for relief. No further showing that he or she "would be" persecuted is required.

Thus, as made binding on the United States through the Protocol, Article 34 provides for a precatory, or discretionary, benefit for the entire class of persons who qualify as "refugees," whereas Article 33.1 provides an entitlement for the subcategory that "would be threatened" with persecution upon their return. This precise distinction between the broad class of refugees and the subcategory entitled to § 243(h) relief is plainly revealed in the 1980 Act.

* * *

Our analysis of the plain language of the Act, its symmetry with the United Nations Protocol, and its legislative history, lead inexorably to the conclusion that to show a "well-founded fear of persecution," an alien need not prove that it is more likely than not that he or she will be persecuted in his or her home country. We find these ordinary canons of statutory construction compelling, even without regard to the long-standing principle of construing any lingering ambiguities in deportation statutes in favor of the alien.

Deportation is always a harsh measure; it is all the more replete with danger when the alien makes a claim that he or she will be subject to death or persecution if forced to return to his or her home country. In enacting the Refugee Act of 1980 Congress sought to "give the United States sufficient flexibility to respond to situations involving political or religious dissidents and detainees throughout the world." H.R. Rep., at 9. Our holding today increases that flexibility by rejecting the Government's contention that the Attorney General may not even consider granting asylum to one who fails to satisfy the strict § 243(h) standard. Whether or not a "refugee" is eventually granted asylum is a matter which Congress has left for the Attorney General to decide. But it is clear that Congress did not intend to restrict eligibility for that relief to those who could prove that it is more likely than not that they will be persecuted if deported.

The judgment of the Court of Appeals is *affirmed*.

NOTES AND QUESTIONS ON THE CHARMING BETSY PRINCIPLE

1. *The UNHCR Handbook.* In *Cardoza-Fonseca*, the Court sought guidance from the Office of the United Nations High Commissioner for Refugees, *Handbook on Procedures and Criteria for Determining Refugee*

Status for the Protocol's definition of "refugee." The Court emphasized that the UN *Handbook* did not have the force of law, nor did it bind the INS in any way. Nevertheless, the Court found the *Handbook* to be a useful tool for construing a term-of-art under the Protocol. How should courts use such resources? What weight, for example, should courts give to the International Committee for the Red Cross's *Commentary on the Geneva Conventions of 12 August 1949*—a series of four commentaries published between 1952 and 1959, which are intended to deal with "questions regarding the implementation and application of international humanitarian law"—when adjudicating Geneva Convention claims?

2. *Non-self-executing treaties as guides to interpretation of statutes.* Even if a treaty provision is non-self-executing, it is still an international obligation of the United States. Does this fact have significance in a litigation setting? Suppose a party invoked a treaty provision not as a rule of decision, but as a guide in the interpretation of the statute governing habeas corpus or the Eighth Amendment prohibition on cruel and unusual punishments. Amnesty International made this argument in the *Hawkins* case, *supra*, but the district court did not address it. Neither did the Ninth Circuit in affirming the preliminary injunction on constitutional grounds. *Hawkins v. Comparet–Cassani*, 251 F.3d 1230 (9th Cir. 2001). Why might the district court judge find international law irrelevant to his constitutional analysis?

3. *United States v. Smith.* In the early days of the Republic, Congress frequently incorporated the law of nations into federal statutes. In *United States v. Smith*, 18 U.S. 153 (1820), the Supreme Court considered the question of whether the incorporation of the customary law definition of piracy was sufficient to hang a convicted pirate. Despite some disagreements over the scope of "piracy" under customary law, the Court found that the defendant's actions were within the core of the accepted definitions and affirmed the death sentence. The existence of hard cases at the margins of a definition or a doctrine does not mean that no easy cases exist at the core.

4. *The Power to Define Offenses.* Article II gives Congress the power to define and punish offenses against the law of nations. Does this power limit the capacity of courts to embrace customary international law? In the D.C. Circuit decision in *Al Odah*, Judge Randolph noted in his concurring opinion that the "define and punish" clause "makes it abundantly clear that Congress—not the Judiciary—is to determine, through legislation, what international law is and what violations ought to be cognizable in the courts." *Al Odah v. United States*, 321 F.3d 1134, 1145 (D.C. Cir. 2003), at 1147 (Randolph, J., concurring), *rev'd sub nom. Rasul v. Bush*, 542 U.S. 466 (2004). What separation of powers issues are presented by judicial enforcement of customary law? *See* Donald J. Kochan, *Constitutional Structure as a Limitation on the Scope of the "Law of Nations" in the Alien Tort Claims Act*, 31 CORNELL INT'L L.J. 153 (1998).

In *Ma v. Reno*, plaintiff Ma, an alien who had completed a criminal sentence, was subsequently kept in detention while awaiting deportation. Because no country was willing to accept him, Ma's detention was effectively indefinite. The Ninth Circuit ordered his release. The decision in *Ma* was reviewed by the U.S. Supreme Court in *Zadvydas v. Davis*, 533 U.S. 678 (2001), and, though the Supreme Court did not rely on international law in its decision, relief was granted. *See* Ma v. Ashcroft, 257 F.3d 1095 (9th Cir. 2001).

MA v. RENO
208 F.3d 815 (9th Cir. 2000)

In interpreting the [immigration detention] statute to include a reasonable time limitation, we are also influenced by *amicus curiae* Human Rights Watch's argument that we should apply the well-established *Charming Betsy* rule of statutory construction which requires that we generally construe Congressional legislation to avoid violating international law. We have reaffirmed this rule on several occasions. In *United States v. Thomas*, 893 F.2d 1066, 1069 (9th Cir. 1990), we explained that we adhere to this principle "out of respect for other nations."

We recently recognized that "a clear international prohibition" exists against prolonged and arbitrary detention. *Martinez v. City of Los Angeles*, 141 F.3d 1373, 1384 (9th Cir. 1998).[1] Furthermore, Article 9 of the International Covenant on Civil and Political Rights (ICCPR), which the United States has ratified, provides that "no one shall be subjected to arbitrary arrest and detention."

In the present case, construing the statute to authorize the indefinite detention of removable aliens might violate international law. In *Martinez*, we expressed our approval of a district court decision in this circuit holding that "individuals imprisoned for years without being charged were arbitrarily detained" in violation of international law. Given the strength of the rule of international law, our construction of the statute renders it consistent with the *Charming Betsy* rule.

In the face of these compelling statutory arguments, we do not read [the statute] as authorizing the indefinite detention of removable aliens. Rather, we hold that the statute authorizes the Attorney General to detain removable aliens only for a reasonable time beyond the ninety day removal period. While we could reach this construction of the statute simply by invoking the doctrine of constitutional avoidance, it is not necessary to rest our decision on that legal principle. As the above

---

1. This court has held that within the domestic legal structure, international law is displaced by "a properly enacted statute, provided it be constitutional, even if that statute violates international law." *Alvarez-Mendez v. Stock*, 941 F.2d 956, 963 (9th Cir. 1991) (involving prolonged detention of excludable aliens); Those rulings, however, do not suggest that courts should refrain from applying the *Charming Betsy* principle. Rather, they stand for the proposition that when Congress has clearly abrogated international law through legislation, that legislation nonetheless has the full force of law. *See Restatement (Third) of International Law* § 115(1)(a).

discussion makes clear, ordinary tenets of statutory construction lead us to that same result. What constitutes a reasonable time will depend on the circumstances of the various cases. Here, we need not address all the conceivable situations that could arise to delay or preclude removal. We need hold only that where it is reasonably likely that an alien who has entered the United States cannot be removed in the reasonably foreseeable future, detention beyond the removal period is not justified.

In Ma's case, the district court did not err in concluding that there is not a reasonable likelihood that the INS will be able to remove Ma to Cambodia. Although the INS offered evidence that the State Department has submitted a proposal for a repatriation agreement to the Cambodian government, both sides agree that the United States has no functioning repatriation agreement with that country, that the Cambodian government does not presently accept the return of its nationals from the United States, and that it has not announced a willingness to enter into an agreement to do so in the foreseeable future, (or indeed at any time). In the absence of a repatriation agreement, extant or pending, we must affirm the district court's finding that there is no reasonable likelihood that the INS will be able to accomplish Ma's removal. Under these circumstances, the INS may not detain Ma any longer.

We stress that our decision does not leave the government without remedies with respect to aliens who may not be detained permanently while awaiting a removal that may never take place. All aliens ordered released must comply with the stringent supervision requirements set out in [the statute]. Ma will have to appear before an immigration officer periodically, answer certain questions, submit to medical or psychiatric testing as necessary, and accept reasonable restrictions on his conduct and activities, including severe travel limitations. More important, if Ma engages in any criminal activity during this time, including violation of his supervisory release conditions, he can be detained and incarcerated as part of the normal criminal process.

NOTES AND QUESTIONS ON INTERPRETING STATUTES IN LIGHT OF INTERNATIONAL LAW

1. *U.S. v. PLO.* In *United States v. Palestinian Liberation Organization*, 695 F. Supp. 1456 (S.D.N.Y. 1988), the court addressed the conflict between a U.S. statute requiring the closing of all offices of terrorist organizations and the United Nations Headquarters Agreement, which established an international enclave within the United States for the United Nations headquarters. The PLO was permitted to attend and participate at the UN as a permanent observer and was, thus, legally permitted to be present in the United States under the Headquarters Agreement, but not under the U.S. statute. The court held that the statute did not clearly indicate an intent to contravene U.S. international obligations under the United Nations Headquarters Agreement. Accordingly, the PLO office was not required under the statute to close.

2. *The Charming Betsy and constitutional interpretation.* Some advocates and scholars argue that the *Charming Betsy* principle should also apply to the interpretation of the Constitution. Is it reasonable to assume that the Founders intended that the Constitution should not conflict with international law in the same way this intent is ascribed to Congress? Does this give international law too much weight in constitutional interpretation? *See* Gordon A. Christenson, *Using Human Rights Law to Inform Due Process and Equal Protection Analysis*, 52 U. Cin. L. Rev. 3, 33 (1983). *See* Section D, *infra.*

3. *The Charming Betsy and state law.* Should the *Charming Betsy* principle apply to state statutes or constitutions? Under Article VI, international law trumps state law. Should the same principles apply? *See Sterling v. Cupp*, 625 P.2d 123 (Or. 1981).

4. *The Beharry case.* In *Beharry v. Reno*, 183 F. Supp. 2d 584 (E.D.N.Y. 2002), the defendant, Don Beharry, a lawful permanent resident in the United States and a citizen of Trinidad, was convicted of second-degree robbery for stealing $714.00 from a coffee shop. Mr. Beharry, who had moved to the United States when he was seven, resided in the U.S. for more than twenty-four years. His sister, mother, and six-year-old daughter also resided in the U.S. While in prison, Mr. Beharry made positive efforts to reform his life and secured a job at a non-profit computer recycling center, but, because of changes in the 1996 immigration law, Mr. Beharry, as an "aggravated felon," was not entitled to seek discretionary relief by presenting this information to an immigration judge.

District Court Judge Weinstein determined that international law, as evidenced by ratified and non-ratified treaties, the Universal Declaration of Human Rights, and customary international law, prohibited summary deportation and interference with the rights of children or the family. In setting forth his reasons, Judge Weinstein stated,

> United States courts should interpret legislation in harmony with international law and norms wherever possible. "An act of Congress ought never to be construed to violate the law of nations if any other possible construction remains." *Charming Betsy*, 6 U.S. at 118.* * * Where a statute appears to contradict international law, an appropriate remedy is to construe the statute so as to resolve the contradiction. Customary international law is legally enforceable unless superceded by a clear statement from Congress. Such a statement must be unequivocal. Mere silence is insufficient to meet this standard.

The Second Circuit reversed Judge Weinstein's decision without addressing the international law issues, on the ground that Mr. Beharry had failed to exhaust administrative remedies.

D. CONSTITUTIONAL INTERPRETATION: INCORPORATING INTERNATIONAL NORMS

In recent years, members of the Supreme Court have debated the relevance of international or foreign law to U.S. constitutional analysis. This debate closely mirrors the larger debates surrounding Constitutional interpretation—debates about sovereignty, excessive judicial discretion, and the United States' role in implementing international law. Justice Scalia's categorical response to this issue in *Stanford v. Kentucky* defines one end of the judicial spectrum:

> We emphasize that it is *American* conceptions of decency that are dispositive, rejecting the contention of petitioners and their various *amici* * * * that the sentencing practices of other countries are relevant. While "[t]he practices of other nations, particularly other democracies, can be relevant to determining whether a practice uniform among our people is not merely an historical accident, but rather so 'implicit in the concept of ordered liberty' that it occupies a place not merely in our mores, but, text permitting, in our Constitution as well," they cannot serve to establish the first Eighth Amendment prerequisite, that the practice is accepted among our people.

Stanford v. Kentucky, 492 U.S. 361, 369–370 n.1 (1989)(emphasis in original).

Justice Scalia's footnote in *Stanford* was one of the important early salvos in a running debate about whether and to what degree U.S. courts should consider the reasoning, policy consequences, or contextual similarities of international law or foreign legal sources generally when interpreting the U.S. Constitution. *See generally*, Harold Hongju Koh, *The Supreme Court Meets International Law*, 12 TULSA J. COMP. & INT'L L. 1 (2004). On the current Court, Chief Justice Roberts and Justices Scalia, Thomas and Alito appear to be squarely on the side of the "nationalists"—those who reject the notion of looking to foreign sources of law to interpret the U.S. Constitution. "Nationalist" judges and scholars believe that the extent and nature of incorporation of international standards into domestic law is exclusively a question for the political branches. They believe that for federal judges to incorporate international legal norms into U.S. jurisprudence without political branch authorization violates the principle that countries and their citizens accede to international law by consent, rather than by "judicial fiat."

Justices Breyer, Ginsburg, Kennedy, Souter, and Stevens, in various cases and to varying degrees, have shown themselves willing to engage foreign sources, not as binding sources of law, but for a broader understanding of abstract terms such as "cruel" or "unusual" punishment.

In broad terms, "transnationalist" judges and scholars believe that applying international law is properly part of the judicial role in an increasingly interconnected world. They assert both that international standards are relevant to domestic experience and that there is a national interest in maintaining a smoothly functioning international system. In recent years, these justices have invoked international human rights standards in opinions on substantive issues ranging from affirmative action, *Grutter v. Bollinger*, 539 U.S. 306 (2003), to the juvenile death penalty, *Roper v. Simmons*, 543 U.S. 558 (2003), to laws banning consensual homosexual conduct, *Lawrence v. Texas*, 539 U.S. 558 (2003). In *Sosa v. Alvarez–Machain*, 542 U.S. 692 (2004), *supra*, six of the justices affirmed many of the basic principles concerning the Judiciary's role in applying customary law in the federal courts.

ROPER v. SIMMONS

543 U.S. 551 (2005)

Justice Kennedy delivered the opinion of the Court.

* * * Our determination that the death penalty is disproportionate punishment for offenders under 18 finds confirmation in the stark reality that the United States is the only country in the world that continues to give official sanction to the juvenile death penalty. This reality does not become controlling, for the task of interpreting the Eighth Amendment remains our responsibility. Yet at least from the time of the Court's decision in *Trop* [*v. Dulles*, 356 U.S. 86 (1958)], the Court has referred to the laws of other countries and to international authorities as instructive for its interpretation of the Eighth Amendment's prohibition of "cruel and unusual punishments." 356 U.S., at 102–103 (plurality opinion) ("The civilized nations of the world are in virtual unanimity that statelessness is not to be imposed as punishment for crime"); *see also Atkins* [*v. Virginia*, 536 U.S. 304 (2002)], at 317, n. 21 (recognizing that "within the world community, the imposition of the death penalty for crimes committed by mentally retarded offenders is overwhelmingly disapproved"); [*Thompson v. Oklahoma*, 487 U.S. 815, 830–831, and n.31 (1988)] (plurality opinion) (noting the abolition of the juvenile death penalty "by other nations that share our Anglo–American heritage, and by the leading members of the Western European community," and observing that "[w]e have previously recognized the relevance of the views of the international community in determining whether a punishment is cruel and unusual"); *Enmund* [*v. Florida*, 458 U.S. 782 (1982)], at 796–797, n. 22 (observing that "the doctrine of felony murder has been abolished in England and India, severely restricted in Canada and a number of other Commonwealth countries, and is unknown in continental Europe"); *Coker* [*v. Georgia*, 433 U.S. 584 (1977)], at 596, n. 10 (plurality opinion) ("It is ... not irrelevant here that out of 60 major nations in the world surveyed in 1965, only 3 retained the death penalty for rape where death did not ensue").

As respondent and a number of *Amici* emphasize, Article 37 of the United Nations Convention on the Rights of the Child, which every country in the world has ratified save for the United States and Somalia, contains an express prohibition on capital punishment for crimes committed by juveniles under 18. United Nations Convention on the Rights of the Child, Art. 37.* * * No ratifying country has entered a reservation to the provision prohibiting the execution of juvenile offenders. Parallel prohibitions are contained in other significant international covenants. *See* ICCPR, Art. 6(5);* * * American Convention on Human Rights, Art. 4(5);* * * [and] African Charter on the Rights and Welfare of the Child, Art. 5(3).

Respondent and his *amici* have submitted, and petitioner does not contest, that only seven countries other than the United States have executed juvenile offenders since 1990: Iran, Pakistan, Saudi Arabia, Yemen, Nigeria, the Democratic Republic of Congo, and China. Since then each of these countries has either abolished capital punishment for juveniles or made public disavowal of the practice. In sum, it is fair to say that the United States now stands alone in a world that has turned its face against the juvenile death penalty.

Though the international covenants prohibiting the juvenile death penalty are of more recent date, it is instructive to note that the United Kingdom abolished the juvenile death penalty before these covenants came into being. The United Kingdom's experience bears particular relevance here in light of the historic ties between our countries and in light of the Eighth Amendment's own origins. * * * As of now, the United Kingdom has abolished the death penalty in its entirety; but, decades before it took this step, it recognized the disproportionate nature of the juvenile death penalty; and it abolished that penalty as a separate matter. * * * In the 56 years that have passed since the United Kingdom abolished the juvenile death penalty, the weight of authority against it there, and in the international community, has become well established.

It is proper that we acknowledge the overwhelming weight of international opinion against the juvenile death penalty, resting in large part on the understanding that the instability and emotional imbalance of young people may often be a factor in the crime. * * * The opinion of the world community, while not controlling our outcome, does provide respected and significant confirmation for our own conclusions.

Over time, from one generation to the next, the Constitution has come to earn the high respect and even, as Madison dared to hope, the veneration of the American people. The document sets forth, and rests upon, innovative principles original to the American experience, such as federalism; a proven balance in political mechanisms through separation of powers; specific guarantees for the accused in criminal cases; and broad provisions to secure individual freedom and preserve human dignity. These doctrines and guarantees are central to the American experience and remain essential to our present-day self-definition and national identity. Not the least of the reasons we honor the Constitution, then, is because we know it to be our own. It does not lessen our fidelity to the Constitution or our pride in its origins to acknowledge that the express affirmation of certain fundamental rights by other nations and peoples simply underscores the centrality of those same rights within our own heritage of freedom.

The Eighth and Fourteenth Amendments forbid imposition of the death penalty on offenders who were under the age of 18 when their crimes were committed. The judgment of the Missouri Supreme Court setting aside the sentence of death imposed upon Christopher Simmons is affirmed.

Justice Scalia, with whom the Chief Justice and Justice Thomas join, dissenting.

* * * Though the views of our own citizens are essentially irrelevant to the Court's decision today, the views of other countries and the so-called international community take center stage.

The Court begins by noting that Article 37 of the United Nations Convention on the Rights of the Child, which every country in the world has ratified save for the United States and Somalia, contains an express prohibition on capital punishment for crimes committed by juveniles under 18. The Court also discusses the International Covenant on Civil and Political Rights (ICCPR), which the Senate ratified only subject to a reservation that reads:

> The United States reserves the right, subject to its Constitutional restraints, to impose capital punishment on any person (other than a pregnant woman) duly convicted under existing or future laws permitting the imposition of capital punishment, including such punishment for crime committed by persons below eighteen years of age.

Unless the Court has added to its arsenal the power to join and ratify treaties on behalf of the United States, I cannot see how this evidence favors, rather than refutes, its position. That the Senate and the President (those actors our Constitution empowers to enter into treaties, see Art. II, § 2) have declined to join and ratify treaties prohibiting execution of under–18 offenders can only suggest that our country has either not reached a national consensus on the question, or has reached a consensus contrary to what the Court announces. That the reservation to the ICCPR was made in 1992 does not suggest otherwise, since the reservation still remains in place today. It is also worth noting that, in addition to barring the execution of under–18 offenders, the United Nations Convention on the Rights of the Child prohibits punishing them with life in prison without the possibility of release. If we are truly going to get in line with the international community, then the Court's reassurance that the death penalty is really not needed, since "the punishment of life imprisonment without the possibility of parole is itself a severe sanction" gives little comfort.

It is interesting that whereas the Court is not content to accept what the States of our Federal Union *say*, but insists on inquiring into what they *do* (specifically, whether they in fact *apply* the juvenile death penalty that their laws allow), the Court is quite willing to believe that every foreign nation—of whatever tyrannical political makeup and with however subservient or incompetent a court system—in fact *adheres* to a rule of no death penalty for offenders under 18. Nor does the Court inquire into how many of the countries that have the death penalty, but have forsworn (on paper at least) imposing that penalty on offenders under 18, have what no State of this country can constitutionally have: a *mandatory* death penalty for certain crimes, with no possibility of mitigation by the sentencing authority, for youth or any other reason. I suspect it is most of them. To forbid the death penalty for juveniles under such a system may be a good idea, but it says nothing about our system, in which the sentencing authority, typically a jury, always can, and almost always does, withhold the death penalty from an under–18 offender except, after considering all the circumstances, in the rare cases where it is warranted. The foreign authorities, in other words, do not even speak to the issue before us here.

More fundamentally, however, the basic premise of the Court's argument—that American law should conform to the laws of the rest of the world—ought to be rejected out of hand. In fact the Court itself does not believe it. In many significant respects the laws of most other countries differ from our law * * *. The Court-pronounced exclusionary rule, for example, is distinctively American. When we adopted that rule in *Mapp v. Ohio*, 367 U.S. 643, 655 (1961), it was "unique to American jurisprudence." Since then a categorical exclusionary rule has been "universally rejected" by other countries, including those with rules prohibiting illegal searches and police misconduct, despite the fact that "none of these countries appears to have any alternative form of discipline for police that is effective in preventing search violations." * * *

The Court has been oblivious to the views of other countries when deciding how to interpret our Constitution's requirement that "Congress shall make no law respecting an establishment of religion." Most other countries—including those committed to religious neutrality—do not insist on the degree of separation between church and state that this Court requires. For example, whereas "we have recognized special Establishment Clause dangers where the government makes direct money payments to sectarian institutions," countries such as the Netherlands, Germany, and Australia allow direct government funding of religious schools on the ground that "the state can only be truly neutral between secular and religious perspectives if it does not dominate the provision of so key a service as education, and makes it possible for people to exercise their right of religious expression within the context of public funding." * * *

And let us not forget the Court's abortion jurisprudence, which makes us one of only six countries that allow abortion on demand until the point of viability. Though the Government and *amici* in cases following *Roe v. Wade*, 410 U.S. 113 (1973), urged the Court to follow the international community's lead, these arguments fell on deaf ears. * * *

The Court should either profess its willingness to reconsider all these matters in light of the views of foreigners, or else it should cease putting forth foreigners' views as part of the *reasoned basis* of its decisions. To invoke alien law when it agrees with one's own thinking, and ignore it otherwise, is not reasoned decision making, but sophistry.

The Court responds that "[i]t does not lessen our fidelity to the Constitution or our pride in its origins to acknowledge that the express affirmation of certain fundamental rights by other nations and peoples simply underscores the centrality of those same rights within our own heritage of freedom." To begin with, I do not believe that approval by "other nations and peoples" should buttress our commitment to American principles any more than (what should logically follow) disapproval by "other nations and peoples" should weaken that commitment. More importantly, however, the Court's statement flatly misdescribes what is going on here. Foreign sources are cited today, *not* to underscore our "fidelity" to the Constitution, our "pride in its origins," and "our own [American] heritage." To the contrary, they are cited to *set aside* the centuries-old American practice—a practice still engaged in by a large majority of the relevant States—of letting a jury of 12 citizens decide whether, in the particular case, youth should be the basis for withholding the death penalty. What these foreign sources "affirm," rather than repudiate, is the Justices' own notion of how the world ought to be, and their diktat that it shall be so henceforth in America. The Court's parting attempt to downplay the significance of its extensive discussion of foreign law is unconvincing. "Acknowledgment" of foreign approval has no place in the legal opinion of this Court *unless it is part of the basis for the Court's judgment*—which is surely what it parades as today.

NOTES AND QUESTIONS ON INTERPRETING THE CONSTITUTION IN LIGHT OF INTERNATIONAL LAW

1. *Legislative attempts to limit indirect use of international norms.* The recent increase in the Court's use of international law to interpret domestic law has rallied some in Congress to introduce legislation to limit the practice. In 2005, Representative Ackerman of New York introduced H.R. Res. 1070, the "Constitution Restoration Act of 2005," designed "to limit the jurisdiction of Federal courts in certain cases and

promote federalism." Among other things, the resolution would prevent judges from using foreign law to interpret the Constitution and would subject judges who relied on these sources to impeachment and removal. On the same day, Senator Shelby of Alabama introduced S. Res. 520, a virtually identical resolution that would also prohibit judges from using foreign law to interpret the Constitution and subject those who did to impeachment and removal. Both resolutions languished in committee and were never put to a vote.

As noted in the beginning of this Module, there have been previous attempts by Congress to limit the impact of international law in the U.S. domestic legal system. What accounts for the stridency of this legislative response to these recent decisions? Do the recent decisions signal a willingness by a majority of the Court to consider international law and opinion in its Constitutional analysis? Would the same principles apply outside of the Eighth Amendment? How should creative lawyers use the discussion of international law and opinion in the recent cases to advance the general cause of human rights advocacy in U.S. domestic courts, state and federal?

2. *Lawrence v. Texas.* In *Lawrence v. Texas*, 539 U.S. 558 (2003), a case involving a Texas anti-sodomy law, the Court took issue with the international consensus conclusions drawn by Justice Burger in *Bowers v. Hardwick*, 478 U.S. 186 (1986). Justice Kennedy's opinion for the Court relies, in part, on foreign authority to emphasize this point:

> The sweeping references by Chief Justice Burger to the history of Western civilization and to Judeo–Christian moral and ethical standards did not take account of other authorities pointing in an opposite direction. A committee advising the British Parliament recommended in 1957 repeal of laws punishing homosexual conduct. Parliament enacted the substance of those recommendations 10 years later.

> Of even more importance, almost five years before *Bowers* was decided the European Court of Human Rights considered a case with parallels to *Bowers* and to today's case. An adult male resident in Northern Ireland alleged he was a practicing homosexual who desired to engage in consensual homosexual conduct. The laws of Northern Ireland forbade him that right. He alleged that he had been questioned, his home had been searched, and he feared criminal prosecution. The court held that the laws proscribing the conduct were invalid under the European Convention on Human Rights. *Dudgeon v. United Kingdom*, 45 Eur. Ct. H. R. (1981) ¶ 52. Authoritative in all countries that are members of the Council of Europe (21 nations then, 45 nations now), the decision is at odds with the premise in *Bowers* that the claim put forward was insubstantial in our Western civilization. * * *

> To the extent *Bowers* relied on values we share with a wider civilization, it should be noted that the reasoning and holding in

Bowers have been rejected elsewhere. Other nations, too, have taken action consistent with an affirmation of the protected right of homosexual adults to engage in intimate, consensual conduct. * * * The right the petitioners seek in this case has been accepted as an integral part of human freedom in many other countries. There has been no showing that in this country the governmental interest in circumscribing personal choice is somehow more legitimate or urgent.

Id. at 572, 576–77.

3. *Grutter v. Bollinger*. In *Grutter v. Bollinger*, 539 U.S. 306 (2003), the Court considered a challenge to the University of Michigan Law School's admissions policy, which took race into account as part of an effort to admit "a mix of students from varying backgrounds and experiences who will respect and learn from each other." During oral argument, Justice Ginsburg questioned whether there was anything that the Court could learn from looking to the experiences of other countries who had endorsed affirmative action programs. She posed the following question to the solicitor general:

We're part of a world, and this problem is a global problem. Other countries operating under the same equality norm have confronted it. Our neighbor to the north, Canada, has, the European Union, South Africa, and they have all approved this kind of, they call it positive discrimination.* * * They have rejected what you recited as the ills that follow from this. Should we shut that from our view at all or should we consider what judges in other places have said on this subject?

In her concurring opinion, Justice Ginsburg relied on international law to articulate the standard she would adopt for affirmative action programs. She stated:

The Court's observation that race-conscious programs "must have a logical end point," accords with the international understanding of the office of affirmative action. The International Convention on the Elimination of All Forms of Racial Discrimination, ratified by the United States in 1994, endorses "special and concrete measures to ensure the adequate development and protection of certain racial groups or individuals belonging to them, for the purpose of guaranteeing them the full and equal enjoyment of human rights and fundamental freedoms." But such measures, the Convention instructs, "shall in no case entail as a consequence the maintenance of unequal or separate rights for different racial groups after the objectives for which they were taken have been achieved." Id.; see also Art. 1(4) (similarly providing for temporally limited affirmative action); Convention on the Elimination of All Forms of Discrimination against Women, Annex to G.A. Res. 34/180, 34 U.N. GAOR Res. Supp. (No. 46) 194, U.N. Doc. A/34/46, Art. 4(1) (1979) (authorizing "temporary special measures aimed at accelerating de facto equality" that "shall be discontinued when the objectives of equality of opportunity and treatment have been achieved").

539 U.S. 306, at 344.

4. *The academic debate: international norms and constitutional interpretation*. These recent court decisions have generated considerable academic and public commentary. Compare, for instance, the following positions:

Harold Hongju Koh, *The United States Constitution and International Law: International Law as Part of Our Law*, 98 AM. J. INT'L L. 43 (2004):

> My point is simple: those who advocate the use of international law in U.S. constitutional interpretation are not mere "international majoritarians" who believe that American constitutional liberties should be determined by a worldwide vote. Rather, transnationalists suggest that particular provisions of our Constitution should be construed with decent respect for international and foreign comparative law. When phrases like "due process of law," "equal protection," and "cruel and unusual punishments" are illuminated by parallel rules, empirical evidence, or community standards found in other mature legal systems, that evidence should not simply be ignored. Wise American judges did not do so at the beginning of the Republic, and there is no warrant for them to start now.

Ernest A. Young, *Foreign Law and the Denominator Problem*, 119 HARV. L. REV. 148, 149 (2005).

> *Roper*'s "denominator problem" concerned whether foreign jurisdictions should count in Eighth Amendment cases. Justice Kennedy's claim that a domestic consensus rejected the juvenile death penalty was profoundly implausible given that twenty states retained the practice. But by shifting focus from the domestic to the international plane—where the United States stood as one jurisdiction against all the rest—the *Roper* majority made an implausible claim of "consensus" into a plausible one. Defenders of looking to foreign law typically describe that practice as a search for "persuasive authority"—an attempt, in Justice Breyer's words, to "learn something" from a "judge in a different country dealing with a similar problem." [H]owever * * * creating consensus by including foreign jurisdictions in the Eighth Amendment denominator goes considerably further and, in fact, gives the practices of those jurisdictions authoritative legal weight.

———————

E. INTERNATIONAL LAW AND THE WAR ON TERROR: IS THERE A ROLE FOR THE COURTS?

The "war on terror"[1] has generated substantial litigation raising profound issues about the role of international law in U.S. courts to restrain government conduct in a time of crisis. For example:

"Enemy combatants" detained at the U.S. military base in Guantanamo raised claims that they were being detained indefinitely in violation of international human rights law and that they were entitled to a hearing before a competent tribunal in which they could claim prisoner of war status under the Third Geneva Convention relative to the Treatment of Prisoners of War.

Revelations of prisoner abuse at the Abu Ghraib detention facility in Iraq and other detention facilities in Iraq and Afghanistan raised issues about the use of torture and cruel, inhuman and degrading treatment or punishment against detainees in U.S. custody.

Individuals subjected to the CIA's "rendition" program of seizing detainees and sending them to countries with a record of torturing suspects have asserted that the practice violated their rights under international human rights law.

Although international law issues have played prominent roles in several of the cases brought by litigators seeking to challenge the more controversial techniques used by the U.S. government in the "war on terror," in many of the cases, litigators have relied primarily on domestic law. For example, in the trilogy of Guantanamo cases decided by the Supreme Court in June 2004, counsel for several Guantanamo detainees and U.S. citizens who had been classified as "enemy combatants" under a Presidential Order argued that they had been improperly denied the right to challenge their detention under federal habeas corpus jurisdiction. These challenges rested on Constitutional, rather than international, norms.

In *Rumsfeld v. Padilla*, 542 U.S. 426 (2004), an American citizen, who had been arrested in 2002 at Chicago's O'Hare International Airport after returning from Pakistan and designated an "enemy combatant," filed a habeas corpus petition challenging the government's right to detain him *incommunicado* in a military brig, without access to a lawyer or the ability to see his family members. At issue in the case was whether the Executive had the right to detain a U.S. citizen apprehended on U.S. soil and to deny him any opportunity to challenge his designation by the Executive as an "enemy combatant," and whether the President's Order had illegally deprived Padilla of his right to due

---

1. For a comprehensive review of the international law issues and challenges posed by the "war on terror" *see* HELEN DUFFY, THE "WAR ON TERROR" AND THE FRAMEWORK OF INTERNATIONAL LAW (2005).

process. In a 5–4 decision, the Supreme Court ruled that Padilla had filed his petition in the wrong court, so he filed a second habeas petition in the Fourth Circuit, which it rejected in *Padilla v. Hanft*, 423 F.3d 386 (4th Cir. 2005). While Padilla awaited the Supreme Court's decision on his petition for certiorari to review the Fourth Circuit's decision, the government finally filed criminal charges against him and transferred him to civilian custody, a move widely seen as an attempt to avoid a Supreme Court decision on the merits of his case.

In *Hamdi v. Rumsfeld*, 542 U.S. 507 (2004), an American citizen captured by the U.S. military in Afghanistan and detained as an "enemy combatant" at a naval brig in Charleston, South Carolina, alleged that he was being detained in violation of the Fifth and Fourteenth Amendments to the U.S. Constitution, as he had been denied access to a lawyer and the right to challenge his classification as an enemy combatant. The Government countered that Congress had authorized its decision to detain U.S. citizens like Hamdi in the Authorization of Use of Military Force (AUMF), passed in the days following the terrorist attacks of September 11, 2001. The AUMF authorized the Executive to use "all necessary and appropriate force" against al Qaeda, its allies, and the Taliban. The Supreme Court, in a plurality opinion written by Justice O'Connor, held that the President did have congressional authorization to detain enemy combatants for the duration of active hostilities in Afghanistan, but a majority held in addition that U.S. citizens—like Hamdi—had a due process right to challenge the factual basis for his detention. As a result of the Court's decision in *Hamdi,* the Pentagon established Combatant Status Review Tribunals (CSRT) to "serve as a forum for detainees to contest their status as enemy combatants."[2] Hamdi was never tried for his alleged crimes. On October 9, 2004, he accepted a plea bargain, under which he would be deported to Saudi Arabia, renounce his U.S. citizenship, and refrain from traveling to certain countries.

In *Rasul v. Bush*, 542 U.S. 466 (2004), two Australian citizens and twelve Kuwaiti citizens being held as enemy combatants at Guantanamo Bay attempted to file habeas petitions in U.S. courts challenging their detention without trial, the limits on their access to counsel and to court in violation of the Constitution, treaties ratified by the United States, and customary international law. The Supreme Court found that Guantanamo was functionally under U.S. sovereignty and that the federal courts did have jurisdiction to hear their habeas corpus challenges to the legality of their detention. The Court remanded the case to permit the district court to consider the merits of the petitioners' claims.

---

2. "Combatant Status Review Tribunal order issued." U.S. Department of Defense News Release, 7 July 2004. According to the Order establishing Combatant Status Review Tribunal, "Following the hearing of testimony and the review of documents and other evidence, the Tribunal shall determine in closed session by majority vote whether the detainee is properly detained as an enemy combatant. Preponderance of the evidence shall be the standard used in reaching this determination, but there shall be a rebuttable presumption in favor of the Government's evidence."

The Evolution of "War on Terror" Cases—As a result of these decisions at the Supreme Court, detainees have pursued a variety of claims in the lower courts, especially habeas corpus claims, Geneva Convention claims, claims for torture and cruel, inhuman and degrading treatment, and claims of illegal rendition.

i. Habeas Corpus

In the wake of *Rasul*, over seventy additional detainees filed thirteen separate lawsuits in federal district court challenging their custody *inter alia* as violations of the Geneva Conventions. In the first post-*Rasul* decision, Judge Richard Leon dismissed the petitioners' claims, finding that the detainees had no rights under the Constitution to challenge their detention, because they were non-resident foreign nationals captured abroad and were being held in a location whose "ultimate sovereignty" was Cuba's; moreover, as "enemy combatants," rather than "prisoners of war," they had no rights under international law. *Khalid v. Bush*, 355 F. Supp. 2d 311, 314 (D.D.C. 2005). Judge Leon read *Rasul* largely as a mere jurisdictional decision which acknowledged that detainees had the right to petition federal courts for a writ of habeas corpus without finding that they had the right to be granted the writ.

Judge Joyce Green took a different view in *In Re Guantanamo Detainee Cases*, 355 F Supp. 2d 443 (D.D.C. 2005), in which she found that the Guantanamo Bay detainees had individually enforceable rights under the Third Geneva Convention. She determined under that Convention that the U.S. is required to treat Taliban fighters (but not members of Al–Qaeda) as prisoners of war and not as "enemy combatants" outside of the Convention's protections, until and unless a competent tribunal makes an individualized finding that they do not qualify for prisoner of war status.

Less than two years after the Supreme Court's decision in *Rasul*, and in the wake of the conflicting district court decisions in *Khalid* and *In Re Guantanamo Detainees*, Congress passed a series of laws, beginning with the Detainee Treatment Act in 2005 and continuing with the Military Commissions Act in 2006, which amended the federal habeas statute so as to strip the federal courts of jurisdiction to hear the petitions of the Guantanamo detainees. As a substitute for habeas review, the statutes created a limited review proceeding in the D.C. Circuit, where detainees could challenge their classification as enemy combatants, but subject to a host of conditions and presumptions favoring the government. In *Boumediene v. Bush*, 476 F.3d 981 (D.C. Cir. 2007), the D.C. Circuit held that the MCA effectively removed the federal courts' jurisdiction over habeas petitions filed by the Guantanamo detainees. However, in June 2008, the Supreme Court ruled, in a 5–4 opinion written by Justice Kennedy, that the DTA and the Military Commissions Act violated the Guantanamo detainees' constitutional right under the Suspension Clause to file habeas petitions in U.S. federal courts challenging the lawfulness of their detention, and that the

DTA review process was not an adequate substitute for habeas. That case, *Boumediene v. Bush*, 128 S.Ct. 2229 (2008), paved the way for the U.S. district courts to hear the more than 200 pending habeas petitions submitted by the Guantanamo detainees challenging their designation as enemy combatants.

ii.   The Geneva Conventions

Hamdan v. Rumsfeld. Salid Ahmed Hamdan, Osama bin Laden's personal driver, was captured in Afghanistan in November 2001 and transferred to Guantanamo Bay. Based on a finding by Executive Branch officials that he was a member of al-Qaeda or otherwise involved in terrorism against the U.S., Hamdan was designated to be tried for war crimes before a military commission. Pursuant to the Supreme Court's decision in *Hamdi*, Hamdan received a formal hearing before a Combatant Status Review Tribunal, which affirmed his status as an enemy combatant "either a member of or affiliated with Al Qaeda," for whom continued detention was required. Yet Hamdan submitted a habeas petition to the federal courts before his trial by military commission began, challenging the jurisdiction of the military commission on the grounds that the Geneva Conventions provided him with the right to seek "prisoner of war" status before a competent tribunal, and that the military commission's procedures did not provide him with the due process protections required by the Geneva Conventions. In making this argument, Hamdan also claimed that the Geneva Conventions were self-executing and provided him with protection even in the absence of domestic implementing legislation.

At the District Court, Judge James Robertson found that Hamdan could not be tried by a military commission until he had been afforded his rights under the Geneva Conventions. *Hamdan v. Rumsfeld*, 344 F. Supp. 2d 152, 165 (D.D.C. 2004). The court stated that,

> [b]ecause the Geneva Conventions were written to protect individuals, because the Executive Branch of our government has implemented the Geneva Conventions for fifty years without questioning the absence of implementing legislation, because Congress clearly understood that the Conventions did not require implementing legislation except in a few specific areas, and because nothing in the Third Geneva Convention itself manifests the contracting parties' intention that it not become effective as domestic law without the enactment of implementing legislation, I conclude that, insofar as it is pertinent here, the Third Geneva Convention is a self-executing treaty.

Accordingly, Hamdan could not be tried by a military commission unless a competent tribunal determined that he was not a prisoner of war under the 1949 Geneva Convention governing the treatment of prisoners.

The U.S. government appealed the decision, and the D.C. Circuit reversed the district court, stating that "[t]he Supreme Court's *Rasul* decision did give district courts jurisdiction over habeas corpus petitions filed on behalf of Guantanamo detainees such as Hamdan. But *Rasul* did not render the Geneva Convention judicially enforceable. That a court has jurisdiction over a claim does not mean the claim is valid. The availability of habeas may obviate a petitioner's need to rely on a private right of action, but it does not render a treaty judicially enforceable. We therefore hold that the 1949 Geneva Convention does not confer upon Hamdan a right to enforce its provisions in court."

The Supreme Court reversed, holding *inter alia* that the structure and procedure of the military commissions convened to try Hamdan violated the Uniform Code of Military Justice ("UCMJ") and the Geneva Conventions and therefore could not proceed. *Hamdan v. Rumsfeld*, 548 U.S. 557 (2006), *superceded by statute as stated in Boumediene v. Bush*, 128 S.Ct. 2229 (2008). Specifically, the authority to use military commissions is explicitly based on compliance with the American common law of war, the UCMJ, and with the rules and precepts of the law of nations. According to the Court, the Geneva Conventions apply to Hamdan, and common article 3 of the Conventions requires certain procedural safeguards that the commissions do not provide. Specifically, common article 3 prohibits "the passing of sentences and the carrying out of executions without previous judgment pronounced by a regularly constituted court affording all the judicial guarantees which are recognized as indispensable by civilized peoples." The Court determined that this standard is violated if the rules governing the commissions can be changed from time to time as the president thinks best; moreover, because the accused and his civilian counsel can be excluded from any part of the proceeding that the presiding officer decides to close, the accused cannot confront the evidence against him. The rules of evidence also allow a variety of hearsay and coerced testimony with no chance to challenge its veracity. The UCMJ also requires "procedural parity" between the commissions and the more formal court martial, a test that the current commissions fail.

A plurality of four justices ruled separately that "none of the overt acts that Hamdan is alleged to have committed violates the law of war," 548 U.S. at 600, and therefore are not triable through the law of war instrument of a military commission. In addition, the offence alleged must be both in a theater of war and during not before the relevant conflict:

> Hamdan's tribunal was appointed not by a military commander in the field of battle, but by a retired major general stationed away from any active hostilities. Hamdan is charged not with an overt act for which he was caught redhanded in a theater of war and which military efficiency demands be tried expeditiously, but with an agreement the inception of which long predated the attacks of September 11, 2001 and the AUMF. That may well be a crime, but

it is not an offense that by the law of war may be tried by military commission. None of the overt acts alleged to have been committed in furtherance of the agreement is itself a war crime, or even necessarily occurred during time of, or in a theater of, war.

548 U.S. at 612.

ALI v. RUMSFELD

In *Ali v. Rumsfeld*, some of the victims of abuse at Abu Ghraib prison in Iraq brought suit against the U.S. officials (civilian and military) with responsibility for the supervision of military detention facilities in that country. The case was consolidated with three other cases in which plaintiffs sought declaratory and monetary relief against former Secretary of Defense Donald Rumsfeld and high ranking military officials for alleged torture and abuse while they were detained by the U.S. military during the wars in Afghanistan and Iraq. How does the complaint in the case reflect the doctrines and precedents explored above?

Consolidated Amended Complaint for Declaratory
Relief and Damages, Filed January 2006

This suit alleges that widespread abuse was caused by the orders and derelictions of Defendant Rumsfeld and high-level commanders. First, Defendant Rumsfeld authorized an abandonment of our nation's inviolable and deep-rooted prohibition against torture and other cruel, inhuman or degrading treatment or punishment of detainees in U.S. military custody. His actions, orders and authorizations relating to interrogation precipitated further violations of law and caused an unlawful policy, pattern or practice of torture and other cruel, inhuman or degrading treatment of detainees, which was furthered and implemented by Defendants Sanchez, Karpinski and Pappas, and which caused the torture and abuse of Plaintiffs as part of the widespread pattern of abuse of countless other detainees in Iraq and Afghanistan.

In addition to their liability for torture and other abuse caused by their affirmative orders and authorizations, Defendants are also liable on the independent ground that they violated their legal duty to prevent and prohibit torture and other cruel, inhuman or degrading treatment by subordinates when they knew and had reason to know of it. Despite numerous credible reports of torture issued by governmental and non-governmental sources beginning in January 2002 and continuing throughout 2003, 2004, and thereafter, Defendants failed to take the reasonable, necessary, timely or adequate measures against subordinates to prohibit and prevent abuses as required by law. The vast majority of key command officials responsible for widespread and systemic torture and abuse have not been disciplined to this day. Defendants' failures violate their legal obligations as military commanders. Defendants acted with deliberate indifference to and conscious disregard of the high likelihood that Plaintiffs would be injured. * * *

The abuse and torture of Plaintiffs did not occur in the heat of battle or under exigent circumstances. Nor was torture deployed only against carefully selected individuals who possessed critical intelligence information. To the contrary, the International Committee of the Red Cross reported estimates by military intelligence that 70 to 90% of persons detained in Iraq had "been arrested by mistake;" the Army Inspector General estimated that 80% of detainees in Iraq "might be eligible for release" if their cases had been properly reviewed, and an internal military report cited estimates from the field that 85 to 90% of detainees at Abu Ghraib "were of no intelligence value." U.S. Army officers and assessment teams have variously concluded that 80% of detainees at one facility were "unnecessarily detained and were probably just victims of circumstance;" that detainees "happened to be in the wrong place at the wrong time," or were "randomly accused of crimes by vindictive neighbors and enemies;" and that U.S. military personnel "were picking up people for anything, just the drop of a hat."

The Defendants' unlawful policies and practices at issue in this suit, which caused Plaintiffs' injuries, continue. Thousands of Iraqi and Afghan civilians remain in U.S. military custody or control, and remain subject to the policies and practices at issue here.

Defendants have not been held legally accountable for their acts, omissions and failures of command. Plaintiffs have received no redress for their injuries and hence seek (1) a declaration that Defendants' acts alleged herein are unlawful, and that Defendant Rumsfeld and other Defendants are legally responsible for the violations of law that caused Plaintiffs' injuries, and (2) damages for the injuries Plaintiffs suffered. * * *

Representative Plaintiffs

Ali was subjected to torture and other cruel, inhuman or degrading treatment, including but not limited to severe beatings to the point of unconsciousness, stabbing and mutilation, isolation while naked and hooded in a wooden phone booth-sized box, prolonged sleep deprivation enforced by beatings, deprivation of adequate food and water, mock execution and death threats. During relevant time periods, Plaintiff Arkan M. Ali was under the control and authority of Defendants Rumsfeld, Sanchez, Karpinski and Pappas and their subordinates. * * *

Plaintiff Sherzad Kamal Khalid, age 35, is a citizen of Iraq who was detained by the U.S. military at various locations in Iraq for about two months from approximately July 2003 through September 2003. The U.S. military assigned to Plaintiff Khalid detainee number 12537. As further detailed below, during his detention by the U.S. military, Plaintiff Khalid was subjected to torture and other cruel, inhuman or degrading treatment, including but not limited to frequent and severe beatings, sexual abuse involving assault and threats of anal rape, deprivation of adequate food and water, mock executions, death threats, intentional exposure to dangerously high temperatures, and prolonged sleep deprivation enforced by beatings. During relevant time periods, Plaintiff Khalid was under the control and authority of Defendants Rumsfeld, Sanchez and Karpinski and their subordinates. * * *

Fifth Cause of Action Violation of the Geneva Conventions

The previous paragraphs are incorporated as if set forth fully herein.

Plaintiffs were tortured and subjected to other cruel, inhuman or degrading treatment during their detentions in U.S. custody in violation of specific provisions of the Third and Fourth Geneva Conventions, including but not limited to Article 3 Common to all Four Conventions.

Violations of these provisions of the Geneva Conventions are direct and enforceable treaty violations as well as violations of the law of nations.

Defendants are liable for violations of Plaintiffs' rights under the Geneva Conventions because Defendants formulated, authorized, approved, directed or ratified the torture and other cruel, inhuman or degrading treatment of Plaintiffs as part of a policy, pattern or practice. In addition, each Defendant is liable because his or her subordinates deliberately and intentionally engaged in the torture and other cruel, inhuman or degrading treatment of Plaintiffs while acting under the Defendant's effective command and control, and the Defendants knew and had reason to know of their subordinates' actions but failed to prevent or punish them.

Sixth Cause of Action Declaratory Relief for Violation of the Law of Nations, of the Geneva Conventions and of the Constitution.

The previous paragraphs are incorporated as if fully set forth herein.

There is a real and actual controversy between Plaintiffs and Defendant Rumsfeld as to whether he has violated the Plaintiffs' legal rights under the law of nations, binding treaties and the U.S. Constitution as a result of torture and other cruel, inhuman or degrading treatment or punishment of Plaintiffs while in U.S. custody.

Plaintiffs reasonably fear that they are at risk of and will again be subjected to Defendant Rumsfeld's unlawful and unconstitutional actions, and seek a judicial declaration that Defendant Rumsfeld's conduct deprived them of their rights under the law of nations, provisions of the Geneva Conventions, and the Fifth and Eighth Amendments to the U.S. Constitution.

The Court therefore should grant declaratory relief and any further necessary and proper relief as set forth below, pursuant to 28 U.S.C. §§ 2201, 2202.

IN RE IRAQ AND AFGHANISTAN DETAINEES LITIGATION

479 F. Supp. 2d 85 (D.D.C. 2007)

Opinion by HOGAN, C. J.:

Plaintiffs Arkan Mohammed Ali, Thahe Mohammed Sabar, Sherzad Kamal Khalid, Ali H., and Najeeb Abbas Ahmed are Iraqi citizens (collectively referred to as the "Iraqi plaintiffs") who were detained at Abu Ghraib prison or other military facilities in Iraq. Pllaintiffs Mehboob Ahmad, Said Nabi Siddiqi, Mohammed Karim Shirullah, and Haji Abdul Rahman are Afghani citizens (collectively referred to as the "Afghani plaintiffs") who were detained at military facilities in Afghanistan. The plaintiffs were detained for varying durations ranging from one month to one year, and several plaintiffs were detained on multiple occasions. Each plaintiff ultimately was released from custody without ever being charged with a crime. * * *

The plaintiffs assert that they were tortured and otherwise subjected to cruel, inhuman and degrading acts during their detentions.* * * Arkan Ali was beaten to unconsciousness, forcibly restrained and stabbed with a knife in his forearm, burned or shocked, locked for days in a phone-booth-sized wood box while stripped naked and hooded, urinated on, shackled with his hands behind his head while his head was stepped on and the shackles pulled, denied sleep and then dragged face down and beaten for falling asleep, chained to a metal container while kicked, spit on, choked, and threatened with a guard dog, threatened with death by having a gun placed to his head and a round chambered, mock executed by threat of being run down by a military vehicle, threatened with slaughter by sword, and denied food and water. * * * These are only some of the many examples of abuse allegedly inflicted on the plaintiffs, as described in their Amended Complaint. Each plaintiff avers that he suffered various injuries resulting from the torture and abuse, both physical and psychological harm. * * *

The plaintiffs advance six causes of action, five of which are premised on tort liability for violations of ((1) the *Fifth Amendment* right to due process, (2) the *Fifth Amendment* and *Eighth Amendment* prohibitions against cruel and unusual punishment, (3) the law of nations prohibition against torture, (4) the law of nations prohibition against cruel, inhuman or degrading treatment, and (5) the Geneva Convention Relative to the Protection of Civilian Persons in Time of War, "Geneva Convention IV"). The plaintiffs' sixth cause of action seeks declaratory relief for violations of the law of nations, Geneva Convention IV, and the United States Constitution. With regard to the constitutional violations, the plaintiffs argue that the Court should infer causes of action for tort liability pursuant to *Bivens v. Six Unknown Named Agents of Fed. Bureau of Narcotics.* The remaining tort claims involving violations of the law of nations and Geneva Convention IV are asserted pursuant to the Alien

Tort Statute, 28 U.S.C. § 1350, as well as directly under Geneva Convention IV. The plaintiffs assert that the defendants are liable for the plaintiffs' injuries because the defendants "issued orders and authorizations that caused the widespread torture and—wholly independent of those orders—failed in their legal duty to stop and prevent the torture and abuse of detainees they knew or had reason to know were being committed by subordinates under their command." According to the plaintiffs, "[e]ach Defendant had command and control over some or all of the military personnel who tortured and abused Plaintiffs." * * *

DISCUSSION

II. WHETHER THE WESTFALL ACT SHIELDS THE DEFENDANTS FROM LIABILITY

The plaintiffs' * * * tort claims assert liability pursuant to the Alien Tort Statute, 28 U.S.C. § 1350, for violations of international law and Geneva Convention. The defendants contend that they are absolutely immune from liability for such violations by the Federal Employees Liability Reform and Tort compensation Act of 1988, (codified at 28 U.S.C. §§ 2671, 2674, 2679), which is commonly referred to as the Westfall Act. The defendants take the position that absolute immunity is warranted because the Westfall Act applies to the plaintiffs' asserted international law claims and the defendants were acting within the scope of their employment. The plaintiffs challenge any such resort to the Westfall Act on the grounds that (1) the Act does not cover "intentional, egregious torts in violation of *jus cogens* norms such as the prohibition against torture and other cruel, inhuman or degrading treatment," (2) the defendants were acting outside the scope of their employment, and (3) the international law claims fall within the Westfall Act's exception for statutory violations.

The Westfall Act affords federal employees absolute immunity from tort liability for negligent or wrongful acts or omissions they commit while acting within the scope of their employment. 28 U.S.C. § 2679(b)(1). The purpose of the Westfall Act is "to relieve covered employees from the cost and effort of defending the lawsuit, and to place those burdens on the Government's shoulders." Accordingly, the Westfall Act provides that, if the Attorney General or his designee certifies that a federal employee was acting within the scope of his employment when an alleged act or omission occurred, then the lawsuit automatically is converted to one against the United States under the Federal Tort Claims Act, the federal employee is dismissed as a party, and the United States is substituted as the defendant.

A. Whether the Westfall Act Applies to Intentional Torts

The plaintiffs contest the notion that the Westfall Act applies to intentional torts that violate *jus cogens* norms that are recognized by the law of nations and Geneva Convention IV. The plaintiffs arrive at this conclusion by arguing that the Westfall Act statement that it applies to a "negligent or wrongful act or omission" is ambiguous. To be specific, the plaintiffs take issue with the term "wrongful"—which is not defined in the statute—and invite the Court to resort to the legislative history to discern what Congress intended by this term. The defendants oppose this tactic by arguing that it would be improper to consider the legislative history because the term "wrongful" should be interpreted according to its plain meaning.

The Court agrees with the defendants' approach. It has long been a canon of statutory interpretation that courts will resort to legislative history only when there is an ambiguity to be resolved. Otherwise, in the absence of such an ambiguity, the legislature is presumed to have intended what it plainly expressed. The mere fact that a term is undefined does not, by default, indicate an ambiguity that warrants resort to the statute's legislative history; to the contrary, an undefined term typically is construed according to its ordinary meaning.

The term "wrongful" ordinarily means "having no legal sanction." Merriam–Webster's Collegiate Dictionary 1368 (10th ed. 1999). The Westfall Act therefore applies to a federal employee's acts or omissions that have no legal sanction. It is axiomatic that intentional torts are not legally sanctioned, so it follows that the Westfall Act applies to intentional torts. This interpretation comports with legal precedent, according to which other courts have recognized application of the Westfall Act in the context of intentional tort claims.

In light of the foregoing discussion, the plaintiffs' argument that the statute does not cover intentional torts is contrary to the plain meaning of the statute as well as precedent concluding otherwise. This Court therefore finds that the Westfall Act applies to the intentional torts alleged by the plaintiffs in their Amended Complaint.

B.   Whether the Westfall Act Applies to Claims Asserting Violations of the Law of Nations and Geneva Convention IV

Although the Westfall Act broadly applies to negligent acts or omissions committed by federal employees during the scope of employment, there are two exceptions that preclude its application "when an injured plaintiff brings: (1) a *Bivens* action, seeking damages for a constitutional violation by a Government employee; or (2) an action under a federal statute that authorizes recovery against a Government employee." These are the only exceptions to the Westfall Act and the Supreme Court has indicated that it would be error to infer others. Consequently, the absolute immunity provided by the Westfall Act cannot be invoked by a defendant to shield himself from claims involving a *Bivens* remedy or claims premised on a statute that authorizes a private lawsuit against a federal employee.

The defendants maintain that they are entitled to absolute immunity under the Westfall Act for all claims asserted by the plaintiffs under the Alien Tort Statute for violations of the law of nations and Geneva Convention IV because those claims do not fall within either of these two exceptions to the Act. In opposition, the plaintiffs attempt to avoid application of the Westfall Act by defending their contrary approach, which argues that the claims for torture and abuse brought under the Alien Tort Statute and Geneva Convention IV do fall within the Act's exception for suits brought pursuant to a federal statute that authorizes recovery against a federal employee.* * *

The question whether the Alien Tort Statute falls within the statutory exception to the Westfall Act was answered by the Supreme Court's decision in *Sosa v. Alvarez–Machain*, 542 U.S. 692, 724 (2004), where it held that "the ATS is a jurisdictional statute creating no new causes of action." Accordingly, the plaintiffs cannot rely on the Alien Tort Statute to waive the Westfall Act because the plaintiffs have no claim for a violation of that statute itself. In other words, the Alien Tort Statute is not a federal statute that authorizes recovery against a federal employee. The plaintiffs, however, ask the Court simply to ignore the Supreme Court's holding in *Sosa* because "at the time Congress considered both the TVPA and the Westfall Act, it understood that the ATS provided a substantive cause of action for violations of the law of nations or treaties of the United States." This argument plainly is untenable given the binding effect *Sosa* has on this Court.

The plaintiffs' argument that Geneva Convention IV, a treaty, also falls within the statutory exception to the Westfall Act is equally unsound. Because the term "statute" is undefined, this Court will again resort to traditional canons of statutory interpretation and look to the plain meaning of the word. In this case, the term "statute" is generally recognized to mean "a law enacted by the legislative branch of a government." Merriam–Webster's Collegiate Dictionary at 1149. The Westfall Act exception for violations of statutes further states that it applies to statutes "of the United States." 28 U.S.C. § 2679(b)(2)(B). Thus, taken as a whole, the Westfall Act's exception unmistakably applies to a law enacted by the legislative branch of the United States, *i.e.*, Congress. Treaties are not enacted by the legislative branch. Treaties are international agreements made by the President with the advice and consent of Congress [sic] pursuant to Article II of the Constitution. Because Geneva Convention IV is not a law enacted by Congress it does not fall within the Westfall Act's exception for statutes. * * *

III.   WHETHER GENEVA CONVENTION IV AFFORDS THE PLAINTIFFS A PRIVATE RIGHT OF ACTION

In addition to invoking the Alien Tort Statute as authority for a cause of action for money damages to remedy alleged violations of Geneva Convention IV, the plaintiffs also assert that the treaty itself provides a private right to sue. The plaintiffs point to Articles 3, 27, 31, 32, 118 and 119 of Geneva Convention IV as self-executing provisions and rely principally on the decision in *Jogi v. Voges*, 425 F.3d 367 (7th Cir. 2005), to validate this contention. *Id.* at 79–80. The defendants counter that the D.C. Circuit's decision in *Hamdan v. Rumsfeld*, as well as other cited precedent, forecloses any notion that Geneva Convention IV affords private rights.

The Court is not convinced that Geneva Convention IV is self-executing and establishes individual rights that may be judicially enforced via private lawsuits in federal courts. "Absent authorizing legislation, an individual has access to courts for enforcement of a treaty's provisions only when the treaty is self-executing, that is, when it expressly or impliedly provides a private right of action." *Tel–Oren v. Libyan Arab Republic*, 726 F.2d 774, 808 (D.C. Cir. 1984) (*per curiam*) (Bork, J., concurring). First, the decision in *Jogi* is not as authoritative as the plaintiffs would like it to be with respect to interpretation of the treaty provisions at issue here. In *Jogi,* the Seventh Circuit considered a foreign national's claim that he was deprived of his right under the Vienna Convention on Consular Relations to contact his country's consulate for assistance after he pled guilty to aggravated battery with a firearm and was imprisoned. 425 F.3d at 369–70. The Seventh Circuit's determination that the Vienna Convention provided a private right of action was premised on an article in the treaty that stated that a person could request that authorities notify his consulate about his arrest or detention and expressly mandated that the "authorities shall inform the person concerned without delay *of his rights*" to make such a request. *Id.* at 374 (emphasis added). None of the provisions of Geneva Convention IV contain any such express or implied language indicating that persons have individual "rights" that may be enforced under the treaty. Instead, the provisions of Geneva Convention IV state general obligations with regard to the treatment of protected persons that are imposed on signatory States.

Second, the Court's position on this issue is bolstered by the language of the treaty itself. Judge Bork's concurrence in *Tel-Oren*, 726 F.2d at 809, explained that "[a] treaty that provides that party states will take measures through their own laws to enforce its proscriptions evidences its intent not to be self-executing." In this case, Article 146. of Geneva Convention 1V, which is located in Part IV titled "Execution of the Convention," states:

> The High Contracting Parties *undertake to enact any legislation* necessary to provide effective penal sanctions for persons committing, or ordering to be committed, any of the grave breaches of the present Convention defined in the following Article.

> Each High Contracting Party shall be under the obligation to search for persons alleged to have committed, or to have ordered to be committed, such grave breaches, and shall bring such persons, regardless of their nationality, before its own courts. It may also, if it prefers, and in accordance with the provisions of its own legislation, hand such persons over for trial to another High Contracting Party concerned, provided such High Contracting Party has made out a *prima facie* case.

Each High Contracting Party *shall take measures necessary* for the suppression of all acts contrary to the provisions of the present Convention other than the grave breaches defined in the following Article.

6 U.S.T. 3516, art. 146.

In addition, it is the law of this circuit that a treaty is not self-executing when the rights of individuals are intended to be vindicated through diplomatic recourse. Article 149 provides that any alleged violation of the treaty shall be subject to an "enquiry" at the request of a party to the conflict, which enquiry shall be undertaken according to procedures negotiated by the parties or determined by an agreed-upon umpire. *Id.* at art. 149. If a violation of the treaty is established, "the Parties to the conflict shall put an end to it and shall repress it with the least possible delay." *Id.* When considered as a whole, it is apparent from these provisions—which make clear that enforcement of Geneva Convention IV is to be left to the legislation and laws of the parties or to diplomatic enquiry—that the treaty is not intended to be self-executing, in which case the plaintiffs are not entitled to pursue private lawsuits against the defendants for alleged violations. This result is consonant with the recognized rule that "international agreements, even those directly benefitting private persons, generally do not create private rights or provide for a private cause of action in domestic courts." RESTATEMENT (THIRD) OF THE FOREIGN RELATIONS LAW OF THE UNITED STATES § 907 cmt. a (1987); *Hamdan I,* 415 F.3d at 39.

Third, other courts that have passed on the question of whether provisions of Geneva Convention IV are self-executing also concluded otherwise. *See Huynh Thi Anh v. Levi,* 586 F.2d 625, 629 (6th Cir. 1978) (stating that general language in Geneva Convention IV offered no evidence that the treaty "was intended to be self-executing or to create private rights or action in the domestic courts of the signatory countries, in the absence of further domestic legislative action"); *Iwanowa v. Ford Motor Co.,* 67 F. Supp. 2d 424, 439 n.16 (D.N.J. 1999) ("Had Iwanowa attempted to assert a claim under the Hague or Geneva Conventions, it would have been dismissed for lack of jurisdiction because only self-executing treaties, *i.e.,* those that do not require legislation to make them operative, confer rights enforceable by private parties."); *American Baptist Churches v. Meese,* 712 F. Supp. 756, 770 (N.D. Cal. 1989) (determining that Article I of Geneva Convention IV is not self-executing because it "does not impose any specific obligations on the signatory nations, nor does it provide any intelligible guidelines for judicial enforcement").

Fourth, the recently-enacted Military Commissions Act of 2006, confirms the Court's view that Geneva Convention IV is not self-executing. Section 5 of the Act states that "[n]o person may invoke the Geneva Conventions or any protocols thereto in any habeas corpus or other civil action or proceeding to which the United States, or a current or former officer, employee, member of the Armed Forces, or other agent of the United States is a party as a source of rights in any court of the United States or its States or territories." However, given that the other stated grounds support the Court's conclusion that Geneva Convention IV is not self-executing, it is not necessary to address at this time whether the Military Commissions Act of 2006 has retroactive application to the plaintiffs' lawsuit.

Because Geneva Convention IV manifests an intent to be enforced through legislation or diplomacy, it is not a self-executing treaty that provides a private right for the plaintiffs to sue the defendants for money damages. The plaintiffs' cause of action for violations of Geneva Convention IV therefore fails to state a claim for relief and will be dismissed. * * *

NOTES AND QUESTIONS ON THE WAR ON TERROR

1. *Is legislation needed?* The Ninth Circuit decided that the ATS is not an exception to the Westfall Act, which requires that tort claims against federal officials be brought exclusively under the Federal Tort Claims Act ("FTCA"). *Alvarez-Machain v. United States*, 331 F.3d 604 (9th Cir. 2003), a proposition the Supreme Court affirmed *Sosa, supra*. In *Rasul v. Rumsfeld*, a district judge determined that torture was within the scope of a federal officials' scope of authority for the purposes of the Westfall Act and required a former Guantanamo detainee to proceed under the FTCA and not under the ATS for his torture claim. *Rasul v. Rumsfeld*, 414 F. Supp. 2d 26, at 31 (D.D.C. 2006). Should the FTCA be amended to allow persons who have been subjected to human rights violations by the United States, its officials or agents, to file suit in U.S. courts for damages? How would you draft such legislation? Would you limit the amendment to actions occurring within U.S. territory? What exceptions to liability would you create?

2. *The extraterritoriality of the Constitution.* In a discussion omitted from the *Ali* excerpt above, the district court held that the plaintiffs did not assert a right protected by the Constitution and could not recover under *Bivens*. The Court determined that prohibitions on mistreatment in the Fifth and Eighth Amendments do not follow the flag when U.S. officials act abroad in regions where the United States is engaged in hostilities. *See Johnson v. Eisentrager*, 339 U.S. 763 (1950), and *United States v. Verdugo–Urquidez*, 494 U.S. 259 (1990). However, a majority of the Supreme Court rejected the notion that the Constitution has no application beyond the territorial borders of the United States in the *Boumediene v. Bush, supra*. There, Justice Kennedy, writing for the five-Justice majority, said, "[e]ven when the United States acts outside its borders, its powers are not 'absolute and unlimited,' but are subject 'to such restrictions as are expressed in the Constitution'" 553 U.S. ___,

128 S.Ct. 2229 (2008) (internal citation omitted) (finding that the Constitution does not necessarily cease to apply to noncitizens where *de jure* sovereignty of the United States ends and that the Suspension Clause, Art. I, sec. 9, cl. 2, has full effect at Guantanamo Bay). The precise implications of the Court's holding in *Boumediene* on the applicability of other constitutional protections, such as those afforded by the Fifth and Eighth amendments, have yet to be determined, but the opinion is a promising one for human rights advocates.

The plaintiffs' damages claim in *Ali* was further complicated by defendants' qualified immunity defense. The Court held in favor of Defendants' contention that, even if the courts were to find that U.S. officials are prohibited from engaging in such conduct under the U.S. Constitution, the law was not "clearly established" at the time of their actions and therefore they are immune from suit. A related argument was that "special factors counseling hesitation" should lead courts to refrain from implying a damages remedy because of the foreign policy and national security context of the cases. This argument was also accepted in the context of damages claims based on the CIA's rendition program in *Arar v. Ashcroft*, 414 F. Supp. 2d 250 (E.D. N.Y. 2006).

3. *TVPA claims?* Although there is nothing in the TVPA that excludes U.S. officials as defendants, the requirement that the defendant act "under the color of foreign law" poses a difficult barrier to such suits. When U.S. officials act in concert with foreign officials, are they acting "under the color of foreign law?" Would this apply to U.S. officials at Abu Ghraib prison? In *Schneider v. Kissinger*, the federal appellate court found that former Secretary of State Henry Kissinger could not be said to be acting under the color of foreign authority in allegedly inspiring the overthrow of President Salvador Allende's government in Chile. *Schneider v. Kissinger*, 310 F. Supp. 2d 251, 255 (D.D.C. 2004), aff'd 412 F.3d 190 (D.C. Cir. 2005); *see also Arar v. Ashcroft*, 414 F. Supp. 2d 250 (E.D. N.Y. 2006), *aff'd*, 532 F.3d 157 (2d Cir. 2008).

4. *Government contractors.* At the Abu Ghraib prison, a portion of the interrogation work was carried out by government contractors hired by the U.S. military. As a result, Abu Ghraib victims sued the civilian contractors—CACI International of Arlington, Virginia, and Titan Corporation of San Diego, California—alleging that three of their employees engaged in abusive behavior. The theory of the case is the same complicity theory of liability asserted in *Doe v. Unocal* and other corporate accountability cases brought under the ATS. However, a key issue in this case will be the government contractor defense. *See Boyle v. United Technologies*, 487 U.S. 500, 512 (1998) (suit against a contractor for design defects is subject to immunity because judgments against contractors would be borne by the government). *See also In re Agent Orange Product Liability Litigation*, 373 F. Supp. 2d 7 (E.D. N.Y. 2005). More recently, a number of cases have been filed against Blackwater for human rights violations committed against civilians in Iraq.

5. *State secrets privilege.* Under the "state secrets privilege," a court will dismiss a claim or suppress evidence where the government asserts that "there is a reasonable danger" that the litigation "will expose military matters which, in the interest of national security, should not be divulged." *United States v. Reynolds*, 345 U.S. 1 (1953). The United States has successfully invoked this privilege in recent ATS litigation. In *El-Masri v. United States*, 479 F.3d 296 (4th Cir. 2007), El–Masri filed claims against former Director of Central Intelligence, George Tenet, three corporate defendants, ten unnamed employees of the Central Intelligence Agency, and ten unnamed employees of the defendant corporations, for injuries he suffered when he was allegedly detained and beaten under the CIA's extraordinary rendition program. The United States intervened and asked the district court to dismiss the claims because, the government asserted, litigation of El–Masri's claims created an unreasonable risk that state secrets would be exposed. On this basis, the district court dismissed the case. The Fourth Circuit upheld the decision, reasoning that, although some information about the CIA's rendition program was publicly available, other facts central to the resolution of El–Masri's claims could not be litigated without risking disclosure of state secrets. Interestingly, the court found that, in addition to being well-grounded in common law, the state secrets privilege also has a constitutional dimension "because it allows the executive branch to protect information whose secrecy is necessary to its military and foreign-affairs responsibilities." *See also Mohamed v. Jeppesen Dataplan, Inc.*, 539 F. Supp. 2d 1128 (N.D. Cal. 2008) (dismissing the case for lack of subject matter jurisdiction because the "very subject matter of the case" was a state secret); *Al-Haramain Islamic Found., Inc. v. Bush*, 507 F.3d 1190 (9th Cir. 2007) (state secrets privilege used to suppress documents thereby precluding plaintiffs from establishing standing).

6. *Rendition.* In *Arar v. Ashcroft*, 414 F. Supp. 2d 250 (E.D.N.Y. 2006), Plaintiff Maher Arar, a native of Syria who immigrated to Canada when he was a teenager, was passing through John F. Kennedy Airport in New York City to catch a connecting flight to Montreal when he was detained by immigration officials and accused of being a member of a terrorist organization. Despite Arar's vigorous denials, U.S. officials sent Arar to Syria for interrogation by Syrian officials under a covert U.S. policy of "extraordinary rendition." Arar was detained and tortured for ten months. He was released in October 2005, without any charges filed against him, and he brought suit in the U.S. alleging, *inter alia*, violations of the TVPA and constitutional law. The district court dismissed all of Arar's claims.

The Foreign Affairs Reform and Restructuring Act ("FARRA") provides that "it shall be the policy of the United States not to expel, extradite, or otherwise effect the involuntary return of any person to a country in which there are substantial grounds for believing the person would be in danger of being subjected to torture." Pub. L. No. 105–277, div. G, Title XXII, § 2242, 112 Stat. 2681–822 (Oct. 21, 1998). The district court dismissed Arar's claims, stating first that the fact that the FARRA did not provide for a private cause of action militated against creating one under the TVPA. The court then went on to find that plaintiffs had not satisfied the "color of foreign law" requirement, because the U.S. defendants had not acted under color of Syrian law. Drawing upon the discussion of the "color of law" requirement in Module 1, do you think that U.S. defendants should be found to be acting under color of "foreign law" when they conspire with or aid and abet a foreign official by sending them suspects to be interrogated and who are subsequently tortured?

7. *Judicial abstention?* Do you agree with the district court's statement in *Arar v. Ashcroft* that "In the international realm * * * most, if not all, judges have neither the experience nor the background to adequately and competently define and adjudge the rights of an individual vis-a-vis the needs of officials acting to defend the sovereign interests of the United States"? What prevents a judge from adjudicating such claims? Can you think of any international standards that may enable a judge to "adequately and competently define and adjudge the rights of an individual" in these cases ?

Practicum

For many years, advocates in the civil rights and human rights communities have tried to integrate international human rights law into the ongoing work of domestic groups like the ACLU and the Legal Defense Fund, with some success. Some of these organizations resisted the incorporation of international law into their work for a variety of reasons, leading to a divide between groups with primarily an international focus (*e.g.* Amnesty International–USA and Human Rights Watch) and those with a domestic focus (*e.g.* the ACLU, NAACP, and MALDEF).

Given the growing recognition of the potential for the successful use of international human rights law in domestic civil rights and civil liberties work, you have been asked to create a long-term strategy for the successful marriage of international and domestic human rights strategies for the larger human rights and civil rights community. The request has come from a consortium of the most active donors to such causes. The donor community is interested in making sure that the substantial sums it intends to dispense to organizations in this community are well spent. The goal is for international human rights advocacy in the U.S. to have a greater impact, in conjunction with traditional domestic forms of advocacy, on the actual lives of the victims of human rights and civil rights violations. The time frame is the 75th anniversary of the UN Charter in 2020.

One important aspect of this strategy is litigation. The donor community wants to know what would be the most effective long-term strategy for achieving, in domestic civil rights litigation, a more effective use of the international human rights norms reflected in the human rights treaties ratified by the United States, especially the International Covenant on Civil and Political Rights, the Convention on the Elimination of All Forms of Racial Discrimination and the Convention Against Torture and Other Forms of Cruel, Inhuman and Degrading Treatment or Punishment.

In preparing this strategy, the donor community would like answers to the following questions:

1. Is litigation the most effective strategy for the incorporation of international human rights norms in actual U.S. civil rights and human rights work?

2. What other strategies (*e.g.* legislative, public advocacy) are required to make litigation a more effective strategy? Why? Are there some complementary strategies that would be more effective than others in advancing the litigation agenda for those donors who believe that success in court is critical to the ultimate success of this effort?

3. Is the time right to challenge in court the various reservations, declarations and understandings the U.S. has attached to its ratification of human rights treaties in court? Would a better strategy be to abolish or amend these caveats by Congress?

4. Are there some cases that ought to be brought even though they cannot be won at this time? What cases would these be, and why would they be worth bringing? Are there examples of such cases from the past?

5. To the extent that advances in litigating human rights issues in domestic courts are burdened by history, political, and legal culture, and current ideological divides in the U.S. body politic, what strategies could be employed to overcome these obstacles?

CHAPTER 2

MODULE 3

USING INTERNATIONAL HUMAN RIGHTS LAW IN DOMESTIC CRIMINAL PROSECUTIONS

■ ■ ■

Orientation

In Modules 1 and 2, we examined the ways that U.S. courts have used their *civil* jurisdiction to compensate the victims of human rights abuse. In this Module, we consider the extent of domestic courts' *criminal* jurisdiction to prosecute the perpetrators. In particular, we examine the power and the limits of using the international principle of "universal criminal jurisdiction" to ground a domestic prosecution. This is distinct from the international judicial framework for enforcing international criminal law, considered in Module 6, *infra*, which includes, among others, the International Criminal Court and the *ad hoc* Tribunals for the Former Yugoslavia and Rwanda. Important and revolutionary, these new international courts have advanced the post-Nuremberg dream of an effective international system of criminal justice, but they are insufficient standing alone. They simply do not have the capacity to end impunity everywhere for serious violations of human rights law. As a result, domestic courts will continue to be workhorses in the prosecution of international human rights criminals.

Currently, some 125 countries have legislation that authorizes criminal proceedings for at least some violations of human rights or humanitarian law, but they do so in different ways and to differing degrees.[1] Some use the explicit language of international human rights treaties and customary international law, and some simply criminalize the behavior without reference to international law. Some countries actively prosecute cases under their human rights legislation, others do not. The question arises: are states *required* or simply *allowed* to enact such laws? And what are the limits to the assertion of criminal jurisdiction when human rights standards are violated?

---

1. AMNESTY INTERNATIONAL, UNIVERSAL JURISDICTION: THE DUTY OF STATES TO ENACT AND ENFORCE LEGISLATION, 11 (Sept. 2001) ["AIUJ STUDY"].

Traditional principles of international law allow states to criminalize conduct (or assert "prescriptive jurisdiction") in five different circumstances:[2]

(1) *Territorial jurisdiction*: A state has jurisdiction to prohibit individuals or entities from committing certain actions within its territory. States may in particular exercise *objective territorial jurisdiction* over acts which occur outside of the state but have effects within it or *subjective territorial jurisdiction* over acts which occur inside their territory, regardless of where the effects are felt.

(2) *Active personality jurisdiction*: A state may criminalize the conduct of its own nationals, even if the crimes are committed abroad.

(3) *Passive personality jurisdiction*: A state may criminalize conduct that targets or victimizes its own nationals, even if the crimes are committed abroad. In the United States, the passive personality principle has been the most controversial of the five grounds for jurisdiction, because it requires no connection between the state and the criminal act except for the generally fortuitous fact that the victim is a citizen of the state exercising jurisdiction.

(4) *Protective jurisdiction*: A state may criminalize conduct that targets certain vital governmental functions, traditionally including such crimes as espionage, passport fraud, and counterfeiting.

(5) *Universal jurisdiction*: A state may criminalize conduct that has none of the four preceding connections to the state if it is so universally condemned that every state is authorized to vindicate the community interest in repressing it. Crucially, the crimes within a state's universal jurisdiction now overlap considerably with human rights standards and allow prosecution wherever the perpetrator is found. As shown below, this could include war crimes, crimes against humanity, genocide, torture, extrajudicial executions, and disappearances.

Of course, the fact that a state is allowed to criminalize an action does not mean that it is free to prosecute every case. Because most, though not all, international crimes are committed under the color of official authority, immunity is often an issue in universal jurisdiction cases. As shown below, traditional immunities can extend to heads of state, former heads of state, members of a national legislature, and diplomats, which routinely conflicts with the human rights project of ending impunity.

The Obligation to Extradite or Prosecute (aut dedere aut judicare)

In some situations, states have a treaty-based obligation to exercise universal jurisdiction. Each of the four Geneva Conventions of 1949,[3]

---

2. *See* IAN BROWNLIE, PRINCIPLES OF PUBLIC INTERNATIONAL LAW 299–305 (2003); RESTATEMENT (THIRD) OF THE FOREIGN RELATIONS LAW OF THE UNITED STATES § 401 *et seq.* (1987) (distinguishing jurisdiction to prescribe [*i.e.* to make a state's law applicable to the activities, relations or status of persons, or the interests of persons in things] from jurisdiction to adjudicate [*i.e.* to subject persons or things to the process of its courts or administrative tribunals] and jurisdiction to enforce [*i.e.* to induce or compel compliance or to punish noncompliance with its laws or regulations]).

3. Geneva Convention for the Amelioration of the Condition of the Wounded and Sick in Armed Forces in the Field, art. 49, Aug. 12, 1949, 75 U.N.T.S. 31 [First Geneva Convention];

which address aspects of the laws of war, requires states to extradite or prosecute those accused of committing "grave breaches" of the Geneva regime, regardless of the actor's nationality.[4] Typically however states have permissive authority to exercise universal jurisdiction. The Convention Against Torture and Other Cruel, Inhuman, or Degrading Treatment of Punishment, for example, requires that a state-party exercise its jurisdiction over those accused of torture committed on its territory, or committed by its nationals, or even if the accused is simply present in its territory if that state is not willing to extradite him or her. Under Article 7.1 of the Convention Against Torture, a state must either extradite or prosecute *(aut dedere aut punire)* any alleged torturer found in its jurisdiction.

There is considerable debate as to whether the *aut dedere aut punire* obligation applies even in the absence of a treaty. *See* General Assembly Resolution 60/22 (Jan. 6, 2006), Art. 5. But there is no doubt that states have authority under the principle of universal jurisdiction to prosecute individuals based on customary international law. For example, although the Genocide Convention does not explicitly provide for universal jurisdiction, customary international law enables states to exercise universal jurisdiction over those accused of genocide. *In Matter of Demjanuk*, 603 F.Supp. 1468 (N.D. Ohio 1985), *aff'd*, 776 F.2d 571 (6th Cir. 1985). Similarly, customary international law provides for universal jurisdiction over "crimes against humanity." *See Federation Nationale des Deportes et Internes Resistants et Patriots and Others v. Barbie, Cour de Cassation (Chambre Criminel)*, Judgment, 78 Int'l L. Rep. 125 (Oct. 6, 1983).

Whether states are permitted or required to prosecute is sometimes framed as an obligation *erga omnes, i.e.*, as an obligation that every state bears to the community of states.[5] In the human rights setting, an

---

Geneva Convention for the Amelioration of the Condition of Wounded, Sick and Shipwrecked Members of Armed Forces at Sea, art. 50, Aug. 12, 1949, 75 U.N.T.S. 85 [Second Geneva Convention]; Geneva Convention Relative to the Treatment of Prisoners of War, art. 129, Aug. 12, 1949, 75 U.N.T.S. 135 [Third Geneva Convention]; Geneva Convention Relative to the Protection of Civilian Persons in Time of War, art. 146, Aug. 12, 1949, 75 U.N.T.S. 287 [Fourth Geneva Convention].

4. *See Prosecution v. Refik Saric*, Danish High Court, Third Chamber, Eastern Division (Nov. 25, 1994) (Danish court convicted a Bosnian Muslim of committing grave breaches under the Third and Fourth Geneva Conventions for the torture of prisoners of war); summary *available at* http://www.icrc.ch/ihl-nat.nsf/46707c419d6bdfa24125673e00508145/9d9d5f3c500edb73c1256b51003bbf44?OpenDocument.

5. *See Barcelona Traction, Light & Power Co. Ltd.* (Belgium v. Spain), 1970 I.C.J. 3, 32, 33–34 (Feb. 5) "[A]n essential distinction should be drawn between the obligations of a State toward the international community as a whole, and those arising vis-à-vis another State. ... By their very nature the former are the concern of all States. In view of the importance of the rights involved, all States can be held to have an interest of a legal nature in their protection; they are obligations *erga omnes*. Such obligations derive, for example, in contemporary international law, from the outlawing of acts of aggression, and of genocide, as also from the principles and rules concerning the basic rights of the human person, including protection from slavery and racial discrimination. Some of the corresponding rights of protection have entered into the body of general international law; others are conferred by international instruments of a universal or quasi-universal character." *Id.*

obligation *erga omnes* might stem from the interest that all states have in ensuring protection against certain conduct, like torture, genocide, and crimes against humanity. Cooperating in the arrest, detention, and punishment of individuals who are involved in such crimes should satisfy the obligation.

We begin this Module with the *Pinochet* case and a consideration of the tension between the human rights project and traditional ideas about sovereignty and immunity. We conclude with contemporary proposals to bring order and international regulation to the exercise of universal jurisdiction by states. Along the way, we consider the existing landscape of universal jurisdiction cases and the policy debate that surrounds it.

Readings

A. THE PINOCHET PROCEEDINGS

On September 11, 1973, a military junta in Chile, headed by General Augusto Pinochet, led a coup d'etat against the democratically-elected socialist regime of President Salvador Allende. Upon seizing power, the junta immediately suspended the Constitution, outlawed leftist parties, and embarked on a campaign of terror against perceived political opponents. Just one month after the coup, a military task force, known as the "Caravan of Death," travelled from prison to prison removing political prisoners from jail only to execute and bury them in unmarked graves. Throughout the course of Pinochet's seventeen-year rule, thousands of individuals were abducted, tortured, disappeared, and executed in a widespread and systematic attempt to eliminate political opposition. *See* HUMAN RIGHTS WATCH, WHEN TYRANTS TREMBLE: THE PINOCHET CASE (1999), *available at* http://www.hrw.org/reports/1999/chile.

In 1978, the Chilean government gave itself amnesty for crimes committed between 1973–1978. Pinochet eventually agreed to hold elections under a new constitution that provided for a return to civilian rule. In 1988, he lost a plebiscite election but remained in power until 1990. He retained the title of Senator for Life, a position that, along with the amnesty law, provided him with legal immunity from prosecution for events which occurred during the junta's rule.

Less certain was whether the web of legal protection that Pinochet enjoyed in Chile would protect him when he left its territory. For years, Pinochet travelled internationally without fear of being subjected to prosecution abroad. However, in the mid–1990s, Spanish prosecutors began to use Spanish law to bring human rights violators to justice using the principles of universal jurisdiction. In 1996, the Progressive Union of Prosecutors of Spain filed criminal complaints against the military leadership in Argentina and Chile for their role in the disappearances of Spanish citizens in those countries. Richard A. Falk, *Assessing the Pinochet Litigation*, in UNIVERSAL JURISDICTION: NATIONAL COURTS AND THE PROSECUTION OF SERIOUS CRIMES UNDER INTERNATIONAL LAW 104 (Stephen Macedo ed., 2004). Those complaints and the *actio popularis*[6] charging several Argentine military officers with crimes of genocide were accepted by Judge Baltasar Garzón in June 1996. Maria del Carmen Marquez Carrasco & Joaquin Alcaide Fernandez, *Case Note, In Re Pinochet: Spanish National Court, Criminal Division (Plenary Session) Case 19/97, November 4, 1998* and *Case 1/98, November 5, 1998*, 93 A.J.I.L. 690, 692 (1999). Article 23 of the Organic Law of the Judicial Power gives Spanish courts jurisdiction over crimes committed by Spanish or foreign citizens outside of Spain when such crimes can be classified, according to Spanish criminal law, as genocide and terrorism, among others, as well as "any other [crime] which according to international treaties or conventions must be prosecuted in Spain." *Id*. at 692. The complaint fell by lot to Judge Garzón, who accepted the complaint and created an investigating team to inquire into the events that arose in Argentina. Despite Argentina's refusal to cooperate, Garzón issued an international arrest warrant for over one hundred Argentine officers. In May 1996, the Salvador Allende Foundation and the Chilean Group of Relatives of Detained and Disappeared Persons filed a second complaint accusing General Pinochet and others of the deaths and disappearances of Chileans. The two cases were consolidated under Judge Garzón. In the course of investigating Operation Condor, a coordinated effort by the South American militaries to disappear political opponents across borders, Judge Garzón issued an arrest warrant and a request for the extradition of General Pinochet.[7]

In October 1998, the United Kingdom agreed to enforce the international arrest warrant and detained Pinochet, who was in the United Kingdom for medical treatment. Judge Garzón's provisional warrant alleged Pinochet's responsibility for the execution of Spanish citizens between 1973 and 1983. Judge Garzón issued a second warrant a week later alleging that Pinochet was responsible for systematic acts in Chile of murder, torture, "disappearance," and illegal detention.

In response to these events, Pinochet initiated proceedings for *habeas corpus* and leave for judicial review of both provisional warrants in the British courts. On October 28, 1998, the Divisional Court quashed both warrants, finding that Pinochet "as a former head of state [was] clearly entitled to immunity [in U.K. courts] in relation to criminal acts

---

6. *Actio popularis* refers to legal actions brought by persons or groups in the name of, and for the benefit of, the general public, rather than a particular victim.

7. Naomi Roht–Arriaza, *The Pinochet Precedent and Universal Jurisdiction*, 35 NEW ENG. L. REV. 311, 312 (2001). *See generally*, NAOMI ROHT-ARRIRZA, THE PINOCHET EFFECT: TRANSNATIONAL JUSTICE IN THE AGE OF HUMAN RIGHTS (2005) (hereinafter "THE PINOCHET EFFECT"). For a comprehensive treatment of the Pinochet case, see also REED BRODY, THE PINOCHET PAPERS: THE CASE OF AUGUSTO PINOCHET IN SPAIN AND BRITAIN (2000). The Labour Party led by Prime Minister Tony Blair had replaced the Conservative Party by 1998 and had pledged itself to the enforcement of international law. The Labour Party's commitment to human rights was a crucial factor in Pinochet's arrest.

performed in the course of exercising public functions." *In re Pinochet Ugarte*, 38 I.L.M. 68, 83. On behalf of the government of Spain, the U.K. government appealed to the House of Lords. A panel of five judges considered submissions by the government of Spain, Pinochet, Amnesty International as intervenor, and Human Rights Watch, as *amicus curiae*.

On November 25, 1998, in a 3–2 ruling, the House of Lords held that Senator Pinochet was not entitled to immunity in relation to crimes under international law. *R. v. Bow Street Metropolitan Stipendiary Magistrate and Others, ex parte Pinochet Ugarte* (No.1) (Amnesty International and Others Intervening), [1998] 3 W.L.R 1456. Torture and crimes against humanity, the Lords concluded, were not "functions" of a head of state. This ruling was set aside, however, on the grounds that the judicial panel was improperly constituted. One of the judges, Lord Hoffman, had neglected to disclose his link as a director of the charitable parent organization of Amnesty International, an intervenor in the case.

The House of Lords convened another panel in January 1999, this time with seven judges, to determine whether the Spanish warrants to extradite Pinochet could be given effect under U.K. law or whether Pinochet was entitled to immunity as a former head of state. On March 24, 1999, in what would be the court's final decision on the matter, the Lords handed down their ruling. In a 6–1 decision, the court concluded that Pinochet was not entitled to immunity from prosecution for charges of torture, conspiracy to torture, and conspiracy to murder. This time, the Lords ruled on the narrower basis that the Torture Convention, as ratified by the U.K. and Chile, had eliminated immunity for torture. Employing the double-criminality rule, however, the Lords found that Pinochet could only be charged with crimes that occurred after 1998, the year in which Britain became party to the Convention Against Torture.

Each of the seven Lords wrote a separate opinion, illustrating their very different understandings of official immunity for violations of international law.

REGINA v. BOW STREET METROPOLITAN STIPENDIARY MAGISTRATE AND OTHERS, EX PARTE PINOCHET UGARTE

HOUSE OF LORDS, [2000] 1 A.C. 147
24 March 1999

JUDGMENT BY Lord Browne–Wilkinson:

My Lords, as is well known, this case concerns an attempt by the Government of Spain to extradite Senator Pinochet from this country to stand trial in Spain for crimes committed (primarily in Chile) during the period when Senator Pinochet was head of state in Chile. * * *

Torture

Apart from the law of piracy, the concept of personal liability under international law for international crimes is of comparatively modern growth. The traditional subjects of international law are states not human beings. But consequent upon the war crime trials after the 1939–45 World War, the international community came to recognise that there could be criminal liability under international law for a class of crimes such as war crimes and crimes against humanity. * * *

[T]he Republic of Chile accepted before your Lordships that the international law prohibiting torture has the character of *jus cogens* or a peremptory norm, *i.e.* one of those rules of international law which have a particular status. * * * The *jus cogens* nature of the international crime of torture justifies states in taking universal jurisdiction over torture wherever committed. International law provides that offences *jus cogens* may be punished by any state because the offenders are "common enemies of all mankind and all nations have an equal interest in their apprehension and prosecution." * * *

I have no doubt that long before the Torture Convention of 1984 state torture was an international crime in the highest sense. * * * But there was no tribunal or court to punish international crimes of torture. Local courts could take jurisdiction. But the objective was to ensure a general jurisdiction so that the torturer was not safe wherever he went. For example, in this case it is alleged that during the Pinochet regime torture was an official, although unacknowledged, weapon of government and that, when the regime was about to end, it passed legislation designed to afford an amnesty to those who had engaged in institution-alised torture. If these allegations are true, the fact that the local court had jurisdiction to deal with the international crime of torture was nothing to the point so long as the totalitarian regime remained in power: a totalitarian regime will not permit adjudication by its own courts on its own shortcomings. Hence the demand for some international machinery to repress state torture which is not dependent upon the local courts where the torture was committed. In the event, over 110 states (including Chile, Spain and the United Kingdom) became state parties to the Torture Convention. But it is far from clear that none of them practised state torture. What was needed therefore was an international system which could punish those who were guilty of torture and which did not permit the evasion of punishment by the torturer moving from one state to another. The Torture Convention was agreed not in order to create an international crime which had not previously existed but to provide an international system under which the international criminal—the torturer—could find no safe haven. * * *

Who is an "official" for the purposes of the Torture Convention?

The first question on the Convention is whether acts done by a head of state are done by "a public official or other person acting in an official capacity" within the meaning of Article 1. * * * It became clear during the argument that both the Republic of Chile and Senator Pinochet accepted that the acts alleged against Senator Pinochet, if proved, were acts done by a public official or person acting in an official capacity within the meaning of Article 1. In my judgment these concessions were correctly made. Unless a head of state authorising or promoting torture is an official or acting in an official capacity within Article 1, then he would not be guilty of the international crime of torture even within his own state. That plainly cannot have been the intention. In my judgment it would run completely contrary to the intention of the Convention if there was anybody who could be exempt from guilt. The crucial question is not whether Senator Pinochet falls within the definition in Article 1: he plainly does. The question is whether, even so, he is procedurally immune from process. To my mind the fact that a head of state can be guilty of the crime casts little, if any, light on the question whether he is immune from prosecution for that crime in a foreign state.* * *

State immunity * * *

The issue is whether international law grants state immunity in relation to the international crime of torture and, if so, whether the Republic of Chile is entitled to claim such immunity even though Chile, Spain and the United Kingdom are all parties to the Torture Convention and therefore "contractually" bound to give effect to its provisions from 8 December 1988 at the latest.

It is a basic principle of international law that one sovereign state (the forum state) does not adjudicate on the conduct of a foreign state. The foreign state is entitled to procedural immunity from the processes of the forum state. This immunity extends to both criminal and civil liability. State immunity probably grew from the historical immunity of the person of the monarch. In any event, such personal immunity of the head of state persists to the present day: the head of state is entitled to the same immunity as the state itself. The diplomatic representative of the foreign state in the forum state is also afforded the same immunity in recognition of the dignity of the state which he represents. This immunity enjoyed by a head of state in power and an ambassador in post is a complete immunity attaching to the person of the head of state or ambassador and rendering him immune from all actions or prosecutions whether or not they relate to matters done for the benefit of the state. Such immunity is said to be granted *ratione personae*.

What then when the ambassador leaves his post or the head of state is deposed? The position of the ambassador is covered by the Vienna Convention on Diplomatic Relations, 1961. After providing for immunity from arrest (Article 29) and from criminal and civil jurisdiction (Article 31), Article 39(1) provides that the ambassador's privileges shall be enjoyed from the moment he takes up post; and paragraph (2) provides:

When the functions of a person enjoying privileges and immunities have come to an end, such privileges and immunities shall normally cease at the moment when he leaves the country, or on expiry of a reasonable period in which to do so, but shall subsist until that time, even in case of armed conflict. However, with respect to acts performed by such a person in the exercise of his functions as a member of the mission, immunity shall continue to subsist.

The continuing partial immunity of the ambassador after leaving post is of a different kind from that enjoyed *ratione personae* while he was in post. Since he is no longer the representative of the foreign state he merits no particular privileges or immunities as a person. However in order to preserve the integrity of the activities of the foreign state during the period when he was ambassador, it is necessary to provide that immunity is afforded to his official acts during his tenure in post. If this were not done the sovereign immunity of the state could be evaded by calling in question acts done during the previous ambassador's time. Accordingly under article 39(2) the ambassador, like any other official of the state, enjoys immunity in relation to his official acts done while he was an official. This limited immunity, *ratione materiae*, is to be contrasted with the former immunity *ratione personae* which gave complete immunity to all activities whether public or private.

In my judgment at common law a former head of state enjoys similar immunities, *ratione materiae*, once he ceases to be head of state. He too loses immunity *ratione personae* on ceasing to be head of state. As ex-head of state he cannot be sued in respect of acts performed whilst head of state in his public capacity. Thus, at common law, the position of the former ambassador and the former head of state appears to be much the same: both enjoy immunity for acts done in performance of their respective functions whilst in office. * * *

The question then which has to be answered is whether the alleged organisation of state torture by Senator Pinochet (if proved) would constitute an act committed by Senator Pinochet as part of his official functions as head of state. It is not enough to say that it cannot be part of the functions of the head of state to commit a crime. Actions which are criminal under the local law can still have been done officially and therefore give rise to immunity *ratione materiae*. The case needs to be analysed more closely.

Can it be said that the commission of a crime which is an international crime against humanity and *jus cogens* is an act done in an official capacity on behalf of the state? I believe there to be strong ground for saying that the implementation of torture as defined by the Torture Convention cannot be a state function. * * *

The jurisdiction being established by the Torture Convention * * * is one where existing domestic courts of all the countries are being authorised and required to take jurisdiction internationally. The question is whether, in this new type of jurisdiction, the only possible view is that those made subject to the jurisdiction of each of the state courts of the world in relation to torture are not entitled to claim immunity.

I have doubts whether, before the coming into force of the Torture Convention, the existence of the international crime of torture as *jus cogens* was enough to justify the conclusion that the organisation of state torture could not rank for immunity purposes as performance of an official function. At that stage there was no international tribunal to punish torture and no general jurisdiction to permit or require its punishment in domestic courts. Not until there was some form of universal jurisdiction for the punishment of the crime of torture could it really be talked about as a fully constituted international crime. But in my judgment the Torture Convention did provide what was missing: a worldwide universal jurisdiction. Further, it required all member states to ban and outlaw torture: Article 2. How can it be for international law purposes an official function to do something which international law itself prohibits and criminalises? Thirdly, an essential feature of the international crime of torture is that it must be committed "by or with the acquiesence of a public official or other person acting in an official capacity." As a result all defendants in torture cases will be state officials. Yet, if the former head of state has immunity, the man most responsible will escape liability while his inferiors (the chiefs of police, junior army officers) who carried out his orders will be liable. I find it impossible to accept that this was the intention.

Finally, and to my mind decisively, if the implementation of a torture regime is a public function giving rise to immunity *ratione materiae*, this produces bizarre results. Immunity *ratione materiae* applies not only to ex-heads of state and ex-ambassadors but to all state officials who have been involved in carrying out the functions of the state. Such immunity is necessary in order to prevent state immunity being circumvented by prosecuting or suing the official who, for example, actually carried out the torture when a claim against the head of state would be precluded by the doctrine of immunity. If that applied to the present case, and if the implementation of the torture regime is to be treated as official business sufficient to found an immunity for the former head of state, it must also be official business sufficient to justify immunity for his inferiors who actually did the torturing. Under the Convention the international crime of torture can only be committed by an official or someone in an official capacity. They would all be entitled to immunity. It would follow that there can be no case outside Chile in which a successful prosecution for torture can be brought unless the State of Chile is prepared to waive its right to its officials' immunity. Therefore the whole elaborate structure of universal jurisdiction over torture committed by officials is rendered abortive and one of the main objectives of the Torture Convention—to provide a system under which there is no safe haven for torturers—will have been frustrated. In my judgment all these factors together demonstrate that the notion of continued immunity for ex-heads of state is inconsistent with the provisions of the Torture Convention.

For these reasons in my judgment if, as alleged, Senator Pinochet organised and authorised torture after 8 December 1988, he was not acting in any capacity which gives rise to immunity *ratione materiae* because such actions were contrary to international law, Chile had agreed to outlaw such conduct and Chile had agreed with the other parties to the Torture Convention that all signatory states should have jurisdiction to try official torture (as defined in the Convention) even if such torture were committed in Chile. * * *

For these reasons, I would allow the appeal so as to permit the extradition proceedings to proceed on the allegation that torture in pursuance of a conspiracy to commit torture, including the single act of torture which is alleged in charge 30, was being committed by Senator Pinochet after 8 December 1988 when he lost his immunity.

JUDGMENT BY: Lord Goff of Chieveley:

* * *

IV.   STATE IMMUNITY

Like my noble and learned friend, Lord Browne–Wilkinson, I regard the principles of state immunity applicable in the case of heads of state and former heads of state as being relatively non-controversial. * * * There can be no doubt that the immunity of a head of state, whether *ratione personae* or *ratione materiae*, applies to both civil and criminal proceedings. * * * However, a question arises whether any limit is placed on the immunity in respect of criminal offences. Obviously the mere fact that the conduct is criminal does not of itself exclude the immunity, otherwise there would be little point in the immunity from criminal process; and this is so even where the crime is of a serious character. It follows, in my opinion, that the mere fact that the crime in question is torture does not exclude state immunity. It has however been stated by [British international lawyer and diplomat] Sir Arthur Watts that a head of state may be personally responsible:

> for acts of such seriousness that they constitute not merely international wrongs (in the broad sense of a civil wrong) but rather international crimes which offend against the public order of the international community. * * * It can no longer be doubted that as a matter of general customary international law a head of state will personally be liable to be called to account if there is sufficient evidence that he authorised or perpetrated such serious international crimes.

So far as torture is concerned, however, there are two points to be made. The first is that it is evident from this passage that Sir Arthur is referring not just to a specific crime as such, but to a crime which offends against the public order of the international community, for which a head of state may be internationally * * * accountable. The instruments cited by him show that he is concerned here with crimes against peace, war crimes and crimes against humanity. Originally these were limited to crimes committed in the context of armed conflict, as in the case of the Nuremberg and Tokyo Charters, and still in the case of the Yugoslavia Statute, though there it is provided that the conflict can be international or internal in character. Subsequently, the context has been widened to include *inter alia* torture "when committed as part of a widespread or systematic attack against a civilian population" on specified grounds. * * * It follows that these provisions are not capable of evidencing any settled practice in respect of torture outside the context of armed conflict until well after 1989 which is the latest date with which we are concerned in the present case. The second point is that these instruments are all concerned with international responsibility before international tribunals, and not with the exclusion of state immunity in criminal proceedings before national courts. * * * It follows that, if state immunity in respect of crimes of torture has been excluded at all in the present case, this can only have been done by the Torture Convention itself.

V.   TORTURE CONVENTION

I turn now to the Torture Convention of 1984, which lies at the heart of the present case. This is concerned with the jurisdiction of national courts, but its "essential purpose" is to ensure that a torturer does not escape the consequences of his act by going to another country. * * * It is to be observed that no mention is made of state immunity in the Convention. Had it been intended to exclude state immunity, it is reasonable to assume that this would have been the subject either of a separate article, or of a separate paragraph in Article 7, introduced to provide for that particular matter. This would have been consistent with the logical framework of the Convention, under which separate provision is made for each topic, introduced in logical order.

VI.   THE ISSUE WHETHER IMMUNITY RATIONE MATERIAE HAS BEEN EXCLUDED UNDER THE TORTURE CONVENTION

(b) Waiver of immunity by treaty must be express

[I]n a treaty concluded between states, consent by a state party to the exercise of jurisdiction against it must * * * be express. In general, moreover, implied consent to the exercise of such jurisdiction is to be regarded only as an added explanation or justification for an otherwise valid and recognised exception, of which the only example given is actual submission to the jurisdiction of the courts of another state. * * * [I]n accordance both with international law, and with the law of this country which on this point reflects international law, a state's waiver of its immunity by treaty must * * * always be express. Indeed, if this was not so, there could well be international chaos as the courts of different state parties to a treaty reach different conclusions on the question whether a waiver of immunity was to be implied.

(c) The functions of public officials and others acting in an official capacity

However it is, as I understand it, suggested that this well-established principle can be circumvented in the present case on the basis that it is not proposed that state parties to the Torture Convention have agreed to waive their state immunity in proceedings brought in the states of other parties in respect of allegations of torture within the Convention. It is rather that, for the purposes of the Convention, such torture does not form part of the functions of public officials or others acting in an official capacity including, in particular, a head of state. Moreover since state immunity *ratione materiae* can only be claimed in respect of acts done by an official in the exercise of his functions as such, it would follow, for example, that the effect is that a former head of state does not enjoy the benefit of immunity *ratione materiae* in respect of such torture after he has ceased to hold office.

In my opinion, the principle which I have described cannot be circumvented in this way. I observe first that the meaning of the word "functions" as used in this context is well established. The functions of, for example, a head of state are governmental functions, as opposed to private acts; and the fact that the head of state performs an act, other than a private act, which is criminal does not deprive it of its governmental character. This is as true of a serious crime, such as murder or torture, as it is of a lesser crime.* * *

It was in answer to that question that the appellants advanced the theory that one draws the line at crimes which may be called "international crimes." If, however, a limit is to be placed on governmental functions so as to exclude from them acts of torture within the Torture Convention, this can only be done by means of an implication arising from the Convention itself. Moreover, as I understand it, the only purpose of the proposed implied limitation upon the functions of public officials is to deprive them, or as in the present case a former head of state, of the benefit of state immunity; and in my opinion the policy which requires that such a result can only be achieved in a treaty by express agreement, with the effect that it cannot be so achieved by implication, renders it equally unacceptable that it should be achieved indirectly by means of an implication such as that now proposed. * * *

VIII. CONCLUSION

For the above reasons, I am of the opinion that by far the greater part of the charges against Senator Pinochet must be excluded as offending against the double criminality rule; and that, in respect of the surviving charges—charge 9, charge 30 and charges 2 and 4 (in so far as they can be said to survive the double criminality rule)—Senator Pinochet is entitled to the benefit of state immunity *ratione materiae* as a former head of state. I would therefore dismiss the appeal of the Government of Spain from the decision of the Divisional Court. * * *

JUDGMENT BY Lord Millett: * * *

In my opinion, crimes prohibited by international law attract universal jurisdiction under customary international law if two criteria are satisfied. First, they must be contrary to a peremptory norm of international law so as to infringe a *jus cogens*. Secondly, they must be so serious and on such a scale that they can justly be regarded as an attack on the international legal order. Isolated offences, even if committed by public officials, would not satisfy these criteria. * * *

In my opinion, the systematic use of torture on a large scale and as an instrument of state policy had joined piracy, war crimes and crimes against peace as an international crime of universal jurisdiction well before 1984. I consider that it had done so by 1973. For my own part, therefore, I would hold that the courts of this country already possessed extra-territorial jurisdiction in respect of torture and conspiracy to torture on the scale of the charges in the present case and did not require the authority of statute to exercise it. I understand, however, that your Lordships take a different view, and consider that statutory authority is required before our courts can exercise extra-territorial criminal jurisdiction even in respect of crimes of universal jurisdiction. Such authority was conferred for the first time by section 134 of the Criminal Justice Act 1988, but the section was not retrospective. I shall accordingly proceed to consider the case on the footing that Senator Pinochet cannot be extradited for any acts of torture committed prior to the coming into force of the section.

The Torture Convention did not create a new international crime. But it redefined it. Whereas the international community had condemned the widespread and systematic use of torture as an instrument of state policy, the Convention extended the offence to cover isolated and individual instances of torture provided that they were committed by a public official. I do not consider that offences of this kind were previously regarded as international crimes attracting universal jurisdiction. The charges against Senator Pinochet, however, are plainly of the requisite character. The Convention thus affirmed and extended an existing international crime and imposed obligations on the parties to the Convention to take measures to prevent it and to punish those guilty of it. * * * [I]ts main purpose was to introduce an institutional mechanism to enable this to be achieved. Whereas previously states were entitled to take jurisdiction in respect of the offence wherever it was committed, they were now placed under an obligation to do so. Any state party in whose territory a person alleged to have committed the offence was found was bound to offer to extradite him or to initiate proceedings to prosecute him. The obligation imposed by the Convention resulted in the passing of section 134 of the Criminal Justice Act 1988.

I agree, therefore, that our courts have statutory extra-territorial jurisdiction in respect of the charges of torture and conspiracy to torture committed after the section had come into force and * * * the charges of conspiracy to murder where the conspiracy took place in Spain. * * *

The definition of torture, both in the Convention and section 134, is in my opinion entirely inconsistent with the existence of a plea of immunity *ratione materiae*. The offence can be committed only by or at the instigation of or with the consent or acquiescence of a public official or other person acting in an official capacity. The official or governmental nature of the act, which forms the basis of the immunity, is an essential ingredient of the offence. No rational system of criminal justice can allow an immunity which is coextensive with the offence. * * *

My Lords, the Republic of Chile was a party to the Torture Convention, and must be taken to have assented to the imposition of an obligation on foreign national courts to take and exercise criminal jurisdiction in respect of the official use of torture. I do not regard it as having thereby waived its immunity. In my opinion there was no immunity to be waived. The offence is one which could only be committed in circumstances which would normally give rise to the immunity. The international community had created an offence for which immunity *ratione materiae* could not possibly be available. International law cannot be supposed to have established a crime having the character of a *jus cogens* and at the same time to have provided an immunity which is co-extensive with the obligation it seeks to impose. * * *

For my own part, I would allow the appeal in respect of the charges relating to the offences in Spain and to torture and conspiracy to torture wherever and whenever carried out. But the majority of your Lordships think otherwise, and consider that Senator Pinochet can be extradited only in respect of a very limited number of charges. This will transform the position from that which the Secretary of State considered last December. I agree with my noble and learned friend, Lord Browne–Wilkinson, that it will be incumbent on the Secretary of State to reconsider the matter in the light of the very different circumstances which now prevail.

NOTES AND QUESTIONS ON THE PINOCHET PROCEEDINGS

1. *Is Pinochet a universal jurisdiction case?* While there are *dicta* in the *Pinochet* decision referencing universal jurisdiction, several commentators have observed that, strictly speaking, Pinochet's was not a universal jurisdiction case.

Notwithstanding the *dicta*, the issue was whether the United Kingdom's courts were competent to decide Spain's extradition request for the criminal charge of torture. The other issue was whether extradition should be granted in accordance with United Kingdom law. The United Kingdom is bound by the United Nation's Torture Convention and is obligated thereunder to prosecute or extradite. Spain, also a state party to the convention, sought extradition because its nationals were the victims of alleged crimes of torture. Thus, the *Pinochet* case, in the opinion of this writer, does not stand for the proposition of universal jurisdiction, nor for that matter is the extradition request from Spain for torture based on universal jurisdiction. The Torture Convention, however, implicitly allows universal jurisdiction.

M. Cherif Bassiouni, *The History of Universal Jurisdiction,* in UNIVERSAL JURISDICTION: NATIONAL COURTS AND THE PROSECUTION OF SERIOUS CRIMES UNDER INTERNATIONAL LAW 56 (Stephen Macedo ed. 2004). However, a subsequent decision by Spain's Constitutional Court held that Spanish courts may hear cases alleging crimes against humanity and genocide on the basis of universal jurisdiction. In reaching its decision, the Court approved the complaint filed in 1999 by Nobel Laureate Rigoberta Menchu, which had asked a Spanish court to investigate the genocide, torture, murder, and illegal imprisonment committed by Guatemalan security forces between 1978 and 1986—a period in which over 200,000 people were killed. The Constitutional Court's decision reversed a March 2003 decision by Spain's Supreme Court that had declined to hear the Guatemalan case because it was not tied to Spain's national interests. The Constitutional Court rejected this reasoning, making clear that "the principle of universal jurisdiction takes precedent over whether or not national interests are at stake." *Guatemala Genocide Case*, STC 237/2005, (26 September 2005).

2.   *The double criminality rule.* The double criminality rule in extradition law requires that the offense for which a person is being extradited be a recognizable criminal offense in the laws of both the sending and receiving state. What is the purpose of the double criminality requirement? How does it compare to the principle of legality, *nulla crimen sine lege, nulla poena sine lege*? The Lords applied the double-criminality rule in the *Pinochet* case to conclude that it was not until 1998, when the U.K. ratified the Torture Convention, that official extra-territorial torture was a criminal offense in both Spain and the U.K. This was so even though torture was a recognized criminal offense in both countries before 1998. Because the majority of the alleged crimes had occurred before 1998, the charges against Pinochet were drastically reduced. Is this an unduly narrow view of double criminality?

3.   *Pinochet's medical condition.* During the fall of 1998, Pinochet suffered two strokes. Though reluctant to raise the health issue initially, after the House of Lords' decision, the Chilean government had put Pinochet's health center stage. After receiving assurances of confidentiality, Pinochet consented to being examined by a team of doctors chosen by the U.K. The medical examination resulted in an opinion that he was

unfit to stand trial. PINOCHET EFFECT, *supra*, at 61–62. On March 2, 2000, U.K. Home Minister Jack Straw issued a final decision not to proceed with the extradition based on Pinochet's medical condition. The human rights organizations did not pursue appeals from this decision, and Pinochet returned to Chile. *Id.* at 63–64.

4. *The impact of the case in Chile.* The man who stepped off the plane in Chile on March 3, 2000, appeared far different from the decrepit, pitiable man Jack Straw had found unfit to stand trial. No longer in a wheelchair, Pinochet walked from the plane, lifted his cane to show everyone present that he could walk unaided, and strolled through the crowd who had gathered, greeting supporters by name. *Id.* at 68. By the time Pinochet returned home to Chile there were over 60 complaints filed in Chilean courts, and, by 2004, there were over 300 such complaints.

The Supreme Court of Justice, Chile's highest court, voted on August 8, 2000, to give Judge Juan Guzmán the authority to investigate charges relating to Pinochet's role in the deaths of 18 individuals committed in the course of Pinochet's infamous Caravan of Death. Relatives of the deceased cheered in the streets, but in July 2002 the Supreme Court dismissed the case, after determining that Pinochet was inflicted with vascular dementia. Twice more, in 2003, judges tried to strip Pinochet of his immunity for the murder of political opponents, but the higher courts would not permit it. After the verdict, Pinochet resigned from the Senate and attempted to live a quiet life, rarely making public appearances.

A few months after the Chilean courts affirmed his immunity from charges, Pinochet made one of his rare public appearances on a Miami-based television network, in which he appeared remarkably lucid. Prosecutors used this interview to prove that Pinochet was not mentally incompetent, and on May 28, 2004, the Court of Appeals in Chile agreed. The court revoked Pinochet's dementia status, and consequently his immunity from protection. On August 26, 2004, the Supreme Court of Justice affirmed the appellate decision, and Pinochet was stripped of his immunity from prosecution for 20 disappearances in conjunction with Operation Condor, a joint effort by South America's military dictators to help each other wipe out dissidents. This was followed by a September 14, 2005, decision by the Supreme Court, which stripped Pinochet of his immunity for a case involving the killing of 119 political opponents whose bodies were later found in neighboring Argentina. In October 2005, he was deemed fit to stand trial by the Supreme Court for charges relating to the disappearance of six dissidents in 1974. In December 2006, at the age of 91, General Pinochet suffered a heart attack and died while awaiting trial.

5. *Immunity.* The majority of the Lords in *Pinochet* found that former heads of state were only responsible for official acts, and then proceeded to employ different reasons for denying Pinochet former-

head-of-state immunity. Three Lords found that torture could not be a part of an official head of state function: Lord Browne–Wilkinson grounded the rule in the Torture Convention, Lord Hutton in customary law, and Lord Phillips in a rule that said former heads of state never have immunity. Two other judges, Lord Hope and Lord Saville, found that there was former-head-of-state immunity under international law, but that Chile had waived that immunity by ratifying the Torture Convention. Lord Millets' opinion went the farthest, finding that torture was prohibited in international law well before 1988 and that Pinochet did not have immunity for any of his alleged crimes. Only one judge, Lord Goff, would have awarded Pinochet complete immunity. He believed that states had to waive immunity explicitly and that the Torture Convention, at most, provided only an implied waiver. What guidance if any does *Pinochet* give for future prosecutions based on universal jurisdiction? How should the conflict between the sovereign interests justifying immunity and the need to end impunity for serious human rights violations be reconciled?

6. *Adolf Eichmann.* Israel's prosecution of Adolf Eichmann, one of the architects of the Holocaust, was an early example of a state invoking universal jurisdiction in part to prosecute a perpetrator of crimes against humanity and war crimes. In 1961, the Israeli Attorney General issued an indictment against Eichmann charging him with crimes against the Jewish people, crimes against humanity, and war crimes under Israel's Nazis and Nazi Collaborators (Punishment) Act. Israeli agents abducted Eichmann from Argentina, where he had fled after the war, and brought him to Israel to stand trial. He was convicted and executed for these crimes.

Addressing the principle of universal jurisdiction, the District Court of Jerusalem stated: "The State of Israel's 'right to punish' the accused derives, in our view, from two cumulative sources: a universal source (pertaining to the whole of mankind) which vests the right to prosecute and punish crimes of this order in every State within the family of nations; and a specific or national source. . . ." *Attorney Gen. of Isr. v. Eichmann*, 36 INT'L L. REP. 18, 50 (Isr. D.C. Jer. 1961), *aff'd*, 36 INT'L L. REP. 277 (Isr. S. Ct. 1962). The District Court went on to conclude, "Not only do all the crimes attributed to the appellant [Eichmann] bear an international character, but their harmful and murderous effects were so embracing and widespread as to shake the international community to its very foundations." The State of Israel therefore was entitled to try Eichmann, pursuant to the principle of universal jurisdiction and in the capacity of a guardian of international law and an agent for its enforcement. *Id.* at 299.

On appeal, the Supreme Court of Israel affirmed this reasoning, stating,

> [t]here is full justification for applying here the principle of universal jurisdiction since the international character of 'crimes against humanity' (in the wide meaning of the term) dealt with in this case is no longer in doubt, while the unprecedented extent of their

injurious and murderous effects is not to be disputed at the present time. In other words, the basic reason for which international law recognizes the right of each State to exercise such jurisdiction in piracy offences—notwithstanding the fact that its own sovereignty does not extend to the scene of the commission of the offence (the high seas) and the offender is a national of another State or is stateless—applies with even greater force to the above-mentioned crimes.

Eichmann, 36 INT'L L. REP. at 299. Eichmann was subsequently hanged.

B. UNIVERSAL JURISDICTION IN UNITED STATES COURTS

In *United States v. Yousef*, defendants were tried on charges relating to a conspiracy to bomb twelve United States commercial airliners in Southeast Asia. Yousef and another defendant were subsequently tried in a second trial for their involvement in the February 1993 bombing of the World Trade Center in New York City. In the district court, the government successfully argued that, even though the only overt acts cited in the airline conspiracy indictment were the bombings of a Manila theater and a Philippines Airlines plane without any connection to United States territory, U.S. courts had jurisdiction to try the defendants on the basis of universal jurisdiction. *United States v Yousef*, 927 F.Supp. 673, 681 (S.D.N.Y. 1996). Defendants appealed their conviction to the U.S. Court of Appeals for the Second Circuit, raising several questions of international law, among them, the question of whether universal jurisdiction was permissible in this case.

UNITED STATES v. YOUSEF
327 F.3d 56 (2d Cir. 2003)

B. EXERCISE OF UNITED STATES EXTRATERRITORIAL JURISDICTION AND CUSTOMARY INTERNATIONAL LAW

On appeal, Yousef challenges the District Court's jurisdiction * * * by arguing that customary international law does not provide a basis for jurisdiction over these counts and that United States law is subordinate to customary international law and therefore cannot provide a basis for jurisdiction. He particularly contests the District Court's conclusion that customary international law permits the United States to prosecute him under the so-called universality principle for the bombing of Philippine Airlines Flight 434 charged in Count Nineteen. Yousef claims that, absent a universally agreed-upon definition of "terrorism" and an international consensus that terrorism is a subject matter over which universal jurisdiction may be exercised, the United States cannot rest jurisdiction over him for this "terrorist" act either on the universality principle or on any United States positive law, which, he claims, necessarily is subordinate to customary international law.

Yousef's arguments fail. First, irrespective of whether customary international law provides a basis for jurisdiction over Yousef for Counts Twelve through Nineteen, United States law provides a separate and complete basis for jurisdiction over each of these counts and, contrary to Yousef's assertions, United States law is not subordinate to customary international law or necessarily subordinate to treaty-based international law and, in fact, may conflict with both. Further contrary to Yousef's claims, customary international law does provide a substantial basis for jurisdiction by the United States over each of these counts, although not (as the District Court held) under the universality principle.

While the District Court correctly held that jurisdiction was proper over each count, and we affirm the substance of its rulings in full, we hold that the District Court erred in partially grounding its exercise of jurisdiction over Count Nineteen—the bombing of Philippine Airlines Flight 434 while en route from Manila, the Philippines, via Cebu, to Japan—on the universality principle. * * *

iii. The Universality Principle Provides for Jurisdiction over Only a Limited Set of Acts Violating the Law of Nations

The District Court erred in holding that the universality principle provides a basis for jurisdiction over Yousef for the acts charged in Count Nineteen because the universality principle permits jurisdiction over only a limited set of crimes that cannot be expanded judicially, as discussed in full below. * * * Yousef argues that the District Court erred in finding that he was subject to universal jurisdiction because terrorist acts like his own are not universally condemned by the community of States and therefore not subject to jurisdiction under the universality principle. Although we are doubtful that the District Court's finding of universal jurisdiction relies on the notion that all acts of terrorism are universally condemned, we emphasize that the indefinite category of "terrorism" is not subject to universal jurisdiction. . . .

The universality principle permits a State to prosecute an offender of any nationality for an offense committed outside of that State and without contacts to that State, but only for the few, near-unique offenses uniformly recognized by the "civilized nations" as an offense against the "Law of Nations." The strictly limited set of crimes subject to universal jurisdiction cannot be expanded by drawing an analogy between some new crime such as placing a bomb on board an airplane and universal jurisdiction's traditional subjects. Nor * * * can universal jurisdiction be created by reliance on treatises or other scholarly works consisting of aspirational propositions that are not themselves good evidence of customary international law, much less primary sources of customary international law.

The class of crimes subject to universal jurisdiction traditionally included only piracy. *See, e.g., Arrest Warrant of 11 Apr. 2000*, 41 I.L.M. at 559 (separate opinion of ICJ President Guillaume) (stating that "universal jurisdiction is accepted in cases of piracy because piracy is carried out on the high seas, outside all State territory"). In modern times, the class of crimes over which States can exercise universal jurisdiction has been extended to include war crimes and acts identified after the Second World War as "crimes against humanity." *See, e.g., Demjanjuk v. Petrovsky*, 776F.2d 571, 582–83 (6th Cir. 1985), *vacated on other grounds*, 10 F.3d 338 (6th Cir. 1993).

The concept of universal jurisdiction has its origins in prosecutions of piracy, which States and legal scholars have acknowledged for at least 500 years as a crime against all nations both because of the threat that piracy poses to orderly transport and commerce between nations and because the crime occurs statelessly on the high seas.

Universal jurisdiction over violations of the laws of war was not suggested until the Second World War. Following the Second World War, the United States and other nations recognized "war crimes" and "crimes against humanity," including "genocide," as crimes for which international law permits the exercise of universal jurisdiction. *Demjanjuk*, 776 F.2d at 582. * * *

The historical restriction of universal jurisdiction to piracy, war crimes, and crimes against humanity demonstrates that universal jurisdiction arises under customary international law only where crimes (1) are universally condemned by the community of nations, and (2) by their nature occur either outside of a State or where there is no State capable of punishing, or competent to punish, the crime (as in a time of war).

Unlike those offenses supporting universal jurisdiction under customary international law—that is, piracy, war crimes, and crimes against humanity—that now have fairly precise definitions and that have achieved universal condemnation, "terrorism" is a term as loosely deployed as it is powerfully charged. * * *

We regrettably are no closer now than eighteen years ago to an international consensus on the definition of terrorism or even its proscription; the mere existence of the phrase "state-sponsored terrorism" proves the absence of agreement on basic terms among a large number of States that terrorism violates public international law. Moreover, there continues to be strenuous disagreement among States about what actions do or do not constitute terrorism, nor have we shaken ourselves free of the cliche that "one man's terrorist is another man's freedom fighter." We thus conclude that the statements of Judges Edwards, Bork, and Robb remain true today, and that terrorism—unlike piracy, war crimes, and crimes against humanity—does not provide a basis for

universal jurisdiction. [The court's discussion of the propriety of jurisdiction under other principles of prescriptive jurisdiction is omitted.]

NOTES AND QUESTIONS ON UNIVERSAL JURISDICTION IN U.S. COURTS

1. *The Court's definition of universal jurisdiction.* Consider the court's
statement, *supra*, that "universal jurisdiction arises under customary
international law only where crimes (1) are universally condemned by
the community of nations, and (2) by their nature occur either outside
of a State or where there is no State capable of punishing, or competent
to punish, the crime (as in a time of war)." Is that definition consistent
with international standards? What happens when the state is capable
and competent to punish the crime, but unwilling to do so?

2. *Terrorism and universal jurisdiction.* Do you agree that the international community's inability to agree upon a uniform definition of
terrorism necessarily precludes the invocation of universal jurisdiction?
Is it true that there is no consensus regarding the definition of any
"terrorist" acts?

3. *Universal jurisdiction statutes in the United States.* It is generally
understood that

> The United States does not recognize common law criminal juris-
> diction. That is, individuals cannot be prosecuted in the absence of
> criminal statutes that explicitly set forth the underlying offense.
> Even though crimes against humanity are recognized under inter-
> national criminal law, these international rules cannot provide the
> sole basis for criminal prosecutions in the United States. Explicit
> legislation is necessary to prosecute these offences.

William Aceves and Paul Hoffman, *Pursuing Crimes Against Humanity in
the United States*, in JUSTICE FOR CRIMES AGAINST HUMANITY 246 (Mark
Lattimer & Philippe Sands eds., 2003). The United States has enacted a
number of statutes that authorize courts to exercise universal criminal
jurisdiction: 18 U.S.C. § 32 (destruction of aircraft and aircraft facilities); 18 U.S.C. § 37 (violence at international airports); 18 U.S.C. § 112
(protection of foreign officials, official guests, and internationally protected persons); 18 U.S.C. § 878 (threats and extortion against foreign
officials, official guests, or internationally protected persons); 18 U.S.C.
§ 1116 (murder or manslaughter of foreign officials, official guests, or
internationally protected persons); 18 U.S.C. § 1203 (hostage-taking);
18 U.S.C. § 1651 (piracy under law of nations); 18 U.S.C. § 2280
(violence against maritime navigations); 18 U.S.C. § 2281 (violence
against maritime fixed platforms); 18 U.S.C. § 2340 (torture); 49 U.S.C.
§ 46502 (aircraft piracy). *Id.* at 252. Notably absent from this list is
genocide. The Genocide Convention Implementation Act, 18 U.S.C.
§ 1091–1093, imposes a significant jurisdictional limitation. Under subsection (d), prosecutions are limited to the following circumstances: (1)

the offence is committed within the United States; or (2) the alleged offender is a national of the United States. *Id.* at 248.

4. *"No safe haven."* Although the United States does not have statutes authorizing universal jurisdiction for certain egregious human rights violations, there have been significant efforts to ensure that those who perpetrate these crimes are not given safe haven in the United States. *See* William J. Aceves & Paul L. Hoffman, *Using Immigration Law to Protect Human Rights: A Critique of Recent Legislative Proposals*, 23 MICH. J. INT'L L. 733 (2002). These proposals have included (1) S. 1375, 106th Cong., (1999): Anti–Atrocity Alien Deportation Act; (2) H.R. 5285, 106th Cong, (2000): Serious Human Rights Abusers Accountability Act of 2000; (3) Human Rights Abusers Act of 2000; (4) H.R. 3058, 106th Cong., (2001): Anti–Atrocity Alien Deportation Act; (5) S. 864: Anti–Atrocity Alien Deportation Act of 2002. The common theme of these proposals is prohibiting human rights violators from seeking safe haven through the immigration system. Provisions in the proposed legislation included prohibiting perpetrators from gaining admission to the United States, removing those found already present, and barring perpetrators from receiving refugee and asylum status and withholding of removal. These bills, however, have faced criticisms from human rights organizations who argue that

> While the proposed restrictions targeted serious human rights abusers, they might also affect legitimate immigrants. The UNHCR [UN High Commissioner for Refugees] has expressed similar concerns, stating that "exclusion clauses should not become another avenue by which deserving cases are denied international protection." Human rights advocates criticized the exclusive focus on immigration restrictions, to the exclusion of criminal prosecution. An impunity regime focusing exclusively on immigration restrictions would provide only limited sanctions to serious human rights abusers. As noted by one commentator, "deportation is relocation of the criminal but not punishment of the crime. A person who comes * * * and then is told to move on has received a temporary haven and then a temporary inconvenience." * * * [I]mmigration and human rights advocates raised significant concerns about efforts to limit non-refoulement protection. They argued that restrictions on non-refoulement protection would violate U.S. obligations under the Refugee Convention and the Convention Against Torture.

Id. at 762. How should states fashion their immigration policies to address such concerns? Are universal jurisdiction statutes the solution? What other options are available?

5. *The United States, torture, and universal jurisdiction.* Amnesty International, in its report *"United States of America: A Safe Haven for Torturers,"*[1] discusses the principle of universal jurisdiction in light of the

---

1. AMNESTY INTERNATIONAL, UNITED STATES OF AMERICA: A SAFE HAVEN FOR TORTURERS (2002), *available at* http://www.amnestyusa.org/stoptorture/safehaven.pdf.

United States' obligations under the Convention against Torture, concluding that the United States should exercise universal jurisdiction over acts of torture, pursuant to its obligation to "extradite or prosecute" under CAT and 18 U.S.C. § 2340. The report issued several recommendations, among them: (1) The United States should immediately take into custody or take other legal measures to ensure the presence of any individual located in territory under its jurisdiction alleged to have committed acts of torture upon being satisfied after an examination of available information that the circumstances so warrant; (2) The United States should surrender any individual located in territory under its jurisdiction alleged to have committed acts of torture if it receives a valid request from an authorized international court or tribunal; (3) The United States should refer the case of any individual located in territory under its jurisdiction alleged to have committed acts of torture to the Justice Department for the purpose of prosecution if extradition or surrender are unavailable or not feasible; and (4) The United States should limit the scope of immigration relief available to individuals who have committed acts of torture.

In December 2006, a federal grand jury in Miami, Florida, indicted Charles Taylor, Jr., marking the first indictment for violations of the federal anti-torture statute. Federal authorities allege that Taylor ordered and committed torture while he served in Liberia as head commander of the Anti–Terrorist Unit known as the "Demon Forces" during his father's reign as President from 1997 to 2003. In October 2008, Taylor was convicted of torture and other crimes, for which he faces a possible life sentence.

6. *Universal jurisdiction and the ATS.* In the *Sosa* case, *Supra* Module 1, the European Commission filed an *amicus curiae* brief arguing that "in the absence of a traditional basis for prescriptive jurisdiction, the Alien Tort Statute should not be read to reach claims based on all violations of the law of nations, but only such conduct as the United States would have authority to regulate under principles of universal jurisdiction." In his concurring opinion in *Sosa v. Alvarez–Machain*, 542 U.S. 692, 762–63 (2004), Justice Breyer noted the connection between universal criminal jurisdiction and civil tort recovery for similar harms:

> Today international law will sometimes * * * reflect not only substantive agreement as to certain universally condemned behavior but also procedural agreement that universal jurisdiction exists to prosecute a subset of that behavior. That subset includes torture, genocide, crimes against humanity, and war crimes. * * * The fact that this procedural consensus exists suggests that recognition of universal jurisdiction in respect to a limited set of norms is consistent with principles of international comity. That is, allowing every nation's courts to adjudicate foreign conduct involving foreign parties in such cases will not significantly threaten the practical harmony that comity principles seek to protect. That consensus concerns criminal jurisdiction, but consensus as to universal crimi-

nal jurisdiction itself suggests that universal tort jurisdiction would be no more threatening. Thus, universal criminal jurisdiction necessarily contemplates a significant degree of civil tort recovery as well.

Is Justice Breyer correct that there is universal consensus with respect to criminal universal jurisdiction laws? Can you think of any objections that countries who endorse universal criminal jurisdiction principles may have to universal tort jurisdiction? Would you limit the ATS to include only those violations subject to universal jurisdiction standards? What claims are excluded with this approach?

7. *Comparative approaches to universal jurisdiction statutes.* There are several types of legislation that permit states to exercise universal jurisdiction.[2]

(a) *Express provisions.* A number of states have enacted legislation that expressly provides for universal jurisdiction over torture, either as part of their obligations under the Convention against Torture or to punish torture as a matter of international customary law.

(b) *Analogous crimes.* Other states may exercise universal jurisdiction over certain types of torture because their legislation permits the exercise of universal jurisdiction over analogous crimes under national law, such as rape or assault or murder, when the torture causes death. However, even if such legislation allows States to punish the perpetrators of some forms of torture, it is rarely comprehensive, as domestic definitions of crimes will not always mirror international definitions of torture. Moreover, such legislation may not incorporate all relevant principles of criminal responsibility, such as command or superior responsibility, or exclude impermissible defenses, such as superior orders.

(c) *Crimes defined in treaties.* Some states have legislation permitting their courts to exercise universal jurisdiction over crimes defined in treaties to which the state is a party. Such legislation may suffer from the flaws identified above.

(d) *Customary international law.* Other states have enacted laws permitting their courts to exercise universal jurisdiction over crimes under customary international law, although the failure to define torture as a crime under national law or to provide for penalties specifically applicable to torture may cause problems.

(e) *Direct incorporation.* Some states provide in their national constitutions or legislation that international law, either conventional or customary, is part of national law, either automatically through direct incorporation or after acceptance by the state. These states generally provide that international law takes precedence over national legislation. In some states, it is fairly clear that these provisions permit national courts to exercise universal jurisdiction to try persons suspected of torture. It is not always clear, however,

2. The discussion in this section is drawn from the AIUJ Study, *supra* note 1.

whether such provisions incorporate only the substantive criminal law provisions of treaties or also the procedural provisions, such as those concerning universal jurisdiction.

The variety of universal jurisdiction statutes suggests broad acceptance of this principle, but is the diversity in approaches to the exercise of universal jurisdiction problematic? Is the cause of international justice advanced if the domestic courts of different countries employ different definitions of international crimes or permit different defenses? Can you think of a solution to this dilemma?

8. *Regina v. Finta. Regina v. Finta*, [1994] 1 S.C.R. 701, illustrates some of the complications that arise when domestic courts take diverse approaches to universal jurisdiction. In that case, Imre Finta was accused of committing war crimes and crimes against humanity against Hungarian Jews in 1944, and he was prosecuted under Canada's Criminal Code. The Supreme Court of Canada found that the principle of universality constituted an exception to the principle of territoriality, thus providing Canadian courts with jurisdiction for war crimes and crimes against humanity. *Id.* at 811. Finta was eventually acquitted on all counts.

The court's discussion of the underlying violations at issue in the case applied a substantially narrower definition for war crimes and crimes against humanity than is generally recognized in international law:

> What distinguishes a crime against humanity from any other criminal offence under the Canadian *Criminal Code* is that the cruel and terrible actions which are essential elements of the offence were undertaken in pursuance of a policy of discrimination or persecution of an identifiable group or race. With respect to war crimes, the distinguishing feature is that the terrible actions constituted a violation of the laws of war. * * * Section 7(3.71), [which permits the prosecution of war crimes and crimes against humanity] cannot be aimed at those who killed in the heat of battle or in the defence of their country.

Id., at 814–17.

The Canadian Supreme Court's definition of crimes against humanity has been criticized for requiring a higher standard of proof than is required by international law—in effect, drastically limiting the types of international claims that can be brought in Canadian courts.[3] For example, contrary to the Court's definition, there is no requirement in international law that crimes against humanity be based on discrimination, nor is liability limited for defendants who "killed in the heat of battle or in defense of [their] country." Moreover, international law does not require that crimes against humanity contain the "essential elements" of being "cruel" and "terrible."

---

3. Judith Hippler Bello & Irwin Cotler, *International Decisions*, 90 A.J.I.L. 460, 468 (1996).

Is this simply one disadvantage to permitting national courts to apply international law? Do we risk improperly curtailing the scope of international law through the implementation of universal jurisdiction standards? What measures can states take to ensure that their universal jurisdiction statutes comport with international law standards? Is it permissible for domestic courts to narrow international law definitions to conform to domestically acceptable definitions? Is there harm in requiring universal jurisdiction suits brought in Canada for crimes against humanity to allege discrimination? Given the variety of legal systems, is variety in interpretation of international law standards inevitable?

9. *Proving the scope of universal jurisdiction.* How would a human rights lawyer go about proving universal condemnation of particular crimes at the jurisdictional stage of the litigation? What evidence should human rights lawyers use to prove that something is a "universal norm"? What if the perpetrator's home state declares an amnesty purporting to extinguish his or her liability for crimes subject to universal jurisdiction? *See "Ways and Means for Making the Evidence of Customary Law More Readily Available,"* YEARBOOK OF THE INTERNATIONAL LAW COMMISSION, 1950 Vol. II, Part II, at 367–74.

10. *Universal jurisdiction and extradition.* In October 1983, Israel issued an extradition request to the United States for John Demjanjuk who—the Israeli government alleged—had committed genocide and crimes against humanity in Germany during World War II. Based on testimony from several Holocaust survivors, Israel alleged that John Demjanjuk was, in fact, Ivan the Terrible, a notorious SS guard known to have committed acts of extreme brutality against Jewish prisoners. In 1985, a United States court authorized his extradition to Israel, relying, in part, on principles of universal jurisdiction. The District Court found that "International law provides that certain offenses may be punished by any state because the offenders are 'common enemies of all mankind and all nations have an equal interest in their apprehension and punishment.' * * * The power to try and punish an offense against the common law of nations, such as the law and customs of war, stems from the sovereign character of each independent state, not from the state's relationship to the perpetrator, victim or act." *In re Extradition of Demjanjuk,* 612 F.Supp. 544, 556 (N.D. Ohio 1985), *aff'd,* 776 F.2d 571 (6th Cir. 1985), *cert. denied,* 475 U.S. 1016 (1986). Demjanjuk was convicted in 1988, but five years later, five Israeli Supreme Court judges ruled that there was insufficient evidence to show that Demjanjuk was Ivan the Terrible and released him. *Demjanjuk v. Israel,* CA 347/88 *Dejankuk v. Israel* [1993] IsrSC 47(4) 221.

Currently, efforts are underway to extradite Hissene Habre, the former dictator of Chad, from Senegal to Belgium to answer for crimes against humanity, war crimes, and torture. As this book goes to press, Habre is living in Senegal. In 2000, Senegal indicted Habre on charges of crimes against humanity, war crimes, and torture. However, in March

2001, Senegal's highest court dismissed the charges, concluding that, because Senegal had not enacted legislation to implement the Convention Against Torture, it had no jurisdiction to adjudicate crimes that had not taken place in Senegal.

Prior to Senegal's dismissal of the case, twenty-one victims, including three Belgian citizens, had filed suit under Belgium's 1993 universal jurisdiction law. In October 2002, the government of Chad stated that it would waive any immunity Habre attempted to assert. After months of investigation, which included touring alleged torture sites and interviewing witnesses, Judge Fransen issued an indictment against the former dictator. In September 2005, another Belgian judge issued an international arrest warrant charging Habre with crimes against humanity, war crimes, and torture committed during his 1982–1990 rule. In January 2006 the African Union ("AU") asked a task force of legal experts to recommend where and how Habre should be tried. The Committee called on Senegal to prosecute Habre "in the name of Africa." Senegal's President declared that he would do so, but as yet the trial has not commenced and protests over Senegal's inaction have continued.[4] Notably, although Senegal appeared to receive European Union delegation led by the Registrar of the International Criminal Court in January 2008 to assist in the development of a prosecution strategy, the former coordinator of Habre's legal team was appointed as the Minister of Justice four months later.[5]

C. INTERNATIONAL LIMITS ON THE EXERCISE OF UNIVERSAL JURISDICTION

On April 11, 2000, Belgium issued an international arrest warrant for Abdulaye Yerodia Ndombasi, then the foreign minister of the Democratic Republic of Congo. The warrant, issued under Belgium's 1993 universal jurisdiction statute, alleged that prior to becoming foreign minister, Yerodia had incited racial hatred by publicly calling for the killing of Tutsis. His actions resulted in hundreds of deaths and, according to Belgium, constituted crimes against humanity and war crimes under the Geneva Conventions of 1949, the Additional Protocols I and II to those Conventions, and Belgium's universal jurisdiction law in place in 1999.

In response to Belgium's actions, the DRC instituted proceedings before the International Court of Justice ("ICJ") in *Case Concerning the*

----

4. Human Rights Watch, A.U. Summit: Experts to Study Habre Case, Panel to Consider Trial Venue in Africa and Belgium (2006) *available at* http://hrw.org/english/docs/2006/01/24/africa12518.htm.

5. Human Rights Watch, Chronology of the Habre Case, *available at* http://www.hrw.org/english/docs/2004/10/29/chad9579.htm.

Arrest Warrant of 11 April 2000, claiming that the warrant violated the foreign minister's immunity under international law. Although Mr. Yerodia was no longer Minister for Foreign Affairs as of November 2000, the case went forward on the merits to determine whether Belgium's issuing of an arrest warrant constituted an ongoing offense to the DRC itself. *Arrest Warrant of 11 April 2000 (Dem. Rep. Congo v. Belg.)*, 2002 I.C.J. 3, 8 (Feb. 14).

ARREST WARRANT OF 11 APRIL 2000

(Dem. Rep. Congo v. Belg.)
2002 I.C.J. 3 (Feb. 14)

[I]n its Application instituting these proceedings, the Congo originally challenged the legality of the arrest warrant of 11 April 2000 on two separate grounds: on the one hand, Belgium's claim to exercise a universal jurisdiction and, on the other, the alleged violation of the immunities of the Minister for Foreign Affairs of the Congo then in office. However, in its submissions in its Memorial, and in its final submissions at the close of the oral proceedings, the Congo invokes only the latter ground.

As a matter of logic, the second ground should be addressed only once there has been a determination in respect of the first, since it is only where a State has jurisdiction under international law in relation to a particular matter that there can be any question of immunities in regard to the exercise of that jurisdiction. However, in the present case, and in view of the final form of the Congo's submissions, the Court will address first the question whether, assuming that it had jurisdiction under international law to issue and circulate the arrest warrant of 11 April 2000, Belgium in so doing violated the immunities of the then Minister for Foreign Affairs of the Congo. * * *

The Court would observe at the outset that in international law it is firmly established that, as also diplomatic and consular agents, certain holders of high-ranking office in a State, such as the Head of State, Head of Government and Minister for Foreign Affairs, enjoy immunities from jurisdiction in other States, both civil and criminal. For the purposes of the present case, it is only the immunity from criminal jurisdiction and the inviolability of an incumbent Minister for Foreign Affairs that fall for the Court to consider. * * *

In customary international law, the immunities accorded to Ministers for Foreign Affairs are not granted for their personal benefit, but to ensure the effective performance of their functions on behalf of their respective States. In order to determine the extent of these immunities, the Court must therefore first consider the nature of the functions exercised by a Minister for Foreign Affairs. He or she is in charge of his or her Government's diplomatic activities and generally acts as its representative in international negotiations and intergovernmental meetings. Ambassadors and other diplomatic agents carry out their duties under his or her authority. His or her acts may bind the State represented, and there is a presumption that a Minister for Foreign Affairs, simply by virtue of that office, has full powers to act on behalf of the State (see, for example Article 7, paragraph 2 *(a)*, of the 1969 Vienna Convention on the Law of Treaties). In the performance of these functions, he or she is frequently required to travel internationally, and thus must be in a position freely to do so whenever the need should arise. He or she must also be in constant communication with the Government, and with its diplomatic missions around the world, and be capable at any time of communicating with representatives of other States. The Court further observes that a Minister for Foreign Affairs, responsible for the conduct of his or her State's relations with all other States, occupies a position such that, like the Head of State or the Head of Government, he or she is recognized under international law as representative of the State solely by virtue of his or her office. He or she does not have to present letters of credence: to the contrary, it is generally the Minister who determines the authority to be conferred upon diplomatic agents and countersigns their letters of credence. Finally, it is to the Minister for Foreign Affairs that *chargés d'affaires* are accredited.

The Court accordingly concludes that the functions of a Minister for Foreign Affairs are such that, throughout the duration of his or her office, he or she when abroad enjoys full immunity from criminal jurisdiction and inviolability. That immunity and that inviolability protect the individual concerned against any act of authority of another State which would hinder him or her in the performance of his or her duties.

In this respect, no distinction can be drawn between acts performed by a Minister for Foreign Affairs in an "official" capacity, and those claimed to have been performed in a "private capacity", or, for that matter, between acts performed before the person concerned assumed office as Minister for Foreign Affairs and acts committed during the period of office. Thus, if a Minister for Foreign Affairs is arrested in another State on a criminal charge, he or she is clearly thereby prevented from exercising the functions of his or her office. The consequences of such impediment to the exercise of those official functions are equally serious, regardless of whether the Minister for Foreign Affairs was, at the time of arrest, present in the territory of the arresting State on an "official" visit or a "private" visit, regardless of whether the arrest relates to acts allegedly performed before the person became the Minister for Foreign Affairs or to acts performed while in office, and regardless of whether the arrest relates to alleged acts performed in an "official" capacity or a "private" capacity. Furthermore, even the mere risk that, by traveling to or transiting another State a Minister for Foreign Affairs might be exposing himself or herself to legal proceedings could deter the Minister from traveling internationally when required to do so for the purposes of the performance of his or her official functions.

The Court will now address Belgium's argument that immunities accorded to incumbent Ministers for Foreign Affairs can in no case protect them where they are suspected of having committed war crimes or crimes against humanity. * * *

The Court has carefully examined State practice. * * * It has been unable to deduce from this practice that there exists under customary international law any form of exception to the rule according immunity from criminal jurisdiction and inviolability to incumbent Ministers for Foreign Affairs, where they are suspected of having committed war crimes or crimes against humanity. The Court has also examined the rules concerning the immunity or criminal responsibility of persons having an official capacity contained in the legal instruments creating international criminal tribunals, and which are specifically applicable to the latter. It finds that these rules likewise do not enable it to conclude that any such an exception exists in customary international law in regard to national courts.

Finally, none of the decisions of the Nuremberg and Tokyo international military tribunals, or of the International Criminal Tribunal for the former Yugoslavia, cited by Belgium deal with the question of the immunities of incumbent Ministers for Foreign Affairs before national courts where they are accused of having committed war crimes or crimes against humanity. The Court accordingly notes that those decisions are in no way at variance with the findings it has reached above. In view of the foregoing, the Court accordingly cannot accept Belgium's argument in this regard.

It should further be noted that the rules governing the jurisdiction of national courts must be carefully distinguished from those governing jurisdictional immunities: jurisdiction does not imply absence of immunity, while absence of immunity does not imply jurisdiction. Thus, although various international conventions on the prevention and punishment of certain serious crimes impose on States obligations of prosecution or extradition, thereby requiring them to extend their criminal jurisdiction, such extension of jurisdiction in no way affects immunities under customary international law, including those of Ministers for Foreign Affairs. These remain opposable before the courts of a foreign State, even where those courts exercise such a jurisdiction under these conventions.

The Court emphasizes, however, that the *immunity* from jurisdiction enjoyed by incumbent Ministers for Foreign Affairs does not mean that they enjoy *impunity* in respect of any crimes they might have committed, irrespective of their gravity. Immunity from criminal jurisdiction and individual criminal responsibility are quite separate concepts. While jurisdictional immunity is procedural in nature, criminal responsibility is a question of substantive law. Jurisdictional immunity may well bar prosecution for a certain period or for certain offences; it cannot exonerate the person to whom it applies from all criminal responsibility.

Accordingly, the immunities enjoyed under international law by an incumbent or former Minister for Foreign Affairs do not represent a bar to criminal prosecution in certain circumstances. First, such persons enjoy no criminal immunity under international law in their own countries, and may thus be tried by those countries' courts in accordance with the relevant rules of domestic law. Secondly, they will cease to enjoy immunity from foreign jurisdiction if the State which they represent or have represented decides to waive that immunity. Thirdly, after a person ceases to hold the office of Minister for Foreign Affairs, he or she will no longer enjoy all of the immunities accorded by international law in other States. Provided that it has jurisdiction under international law, a court of one State may try a former Minister for Foreign Affairs of another State in respect of acts committed prior or subsequent to his or her period of office, as well as in respect of acts committed during that period of office in a private capacity. Fourthly, an incumbent or former Minister for Foreign Affairs may be subject to criminal proceedings before certain international criminal courts, where they have jurisdiction. Examples include the International Criminal Tribunal for the former Yugoslavia, and the International Criminal Tribunal for Rwanda, established pursuant to Security Council resolutions under Chapter VII of the United Nations Charter, and the future International Criminal Court created by the 1998 Rome Convention. The latter's Statute expressly provides, in Article 27, paragraph 2, that "[i]mmunities or special procedural rules which may attach to the official capacity of a person, whether under national or international law, shall not bar the Court from exercising its jurisdiction over such a person." * * *

The Court is bound, however, to find that, given the nature and purpose of the warrant, its mere issue violated the immunity which Mr. Yerodia enjoyed as the Congo's incumbent Minister for Foreign Affairs. The Court accordingly concludes that the issue of the warrant constituted a violation of an obligation of Belgium towards the Congo, in that it failed to respect the immunity of that Minister and, more particularly, infringed the immunity from criminal jurisdiction and the inviolability then enjoyed by him under international law. * * *

The Court accordingly considers that Belgium must, by means of its own choosing, cancel the warrant in question and so inform the authorities to whom it was circulated.

NOTES AND QUESTIONS ON INTERNATIONAL LIMITS ON THE EXERCISE OF UNIVERSAL JURISDICTION

1. *Failing to address universal jurisdiction.* The ICJ had a clear opportunity to decide whether States are authorized by international law to invoke the principle of universal jurisdiction. Several judges argued, in separate opinions, that the court should have first taken up the question of whether Belgium could legitimately invoke universal jurisdiction before proceeding to determine whether the Congolese foreign minister was entitled to immunity from prosecution. Why might the ICJ have declined to resolve the issue?

2. *Treaties as evidence for universal jurisdiction.* In *Pinochet Revisited*, INT'L & COMP. L. QTRLY 959 (2002), Campbell McLachlan discusses the ICJ judges' diverging viewpoints on universal jurisdiction and the reliance on international conventions as evidence of the existence of universal jurisdiction:

> What is the proper role of the national court in the emerging international criminal justice system to police international crimes unconnected to its jurisdiction? * * * [T]he *obiter dicta* of the judges in *Congo v. Belgium* reveal the Court at its most divided. The President and Judges Ranjeva and Rezek express the view that international law prohibits the exercise of such jurisdiction. Judges Higgins, Buergenthal, Kooijmans, and Koroma take the opposite view. Much of the analysis centered on the series of international conventions on international crimes, which are commonly referred to as providing for "universal jurisdiction". But, as Judge Higgins observed extra-judicially: "this is not treaty-based universal jurisdiction (and so the question of such a treaty basis 'passing into' general international law does not arise). * * * [The Conventions] provide for various bases of jurisdiction coupled with the *aut dedire aut punire* principle—that is, that a state party to the treaty undertakes to try an offender found on its territory, or to extradite him for trial." As she observes in the Joint Separate Opinion: "By the loose use of language the latter has come to be referred to as 'universal jurisdiction,' though this is really an obligatory territorial jurisdiction over persons, albeit in relation to acts committed elsewhere. These conventions, then, do not provide for universal jurisdiction in absentia. On the contrary, they represent a carefully negotiated array of permitted jurisdictional bases and an obligation imposed upon the state where the alleged offender is present to extradite or prosecute. In this way, no safe haven from jurisdiction is allowed for offenders."

Id. at 963–64.

3. *Immunity for functionally similar positions.* The Court in the *DRC* case reasoned by analogy to determine that former foreign ministers should be afforded immunity for their "official acts." Citing the New

York Convention on Special Missions of December 8, 1969, which affords immunities to heads of state, the court reasoned that foreign ministers and Heads of State are functionally similar. This functionality argument differs from the traditional basis for granting immunity, which is grounded in state sovereignty. As one commentator has noted, "[F]oreign ministers, although senior and important figures, do not symbolize or personify their States in the way that Heads of State do. Accordingly, they do not enjoy in international law any entitlement to special treatment by virtue of qualities of sovereignty or majesty attaching to them personally."[1] Should senior government officials be afforded the same level of immunity as Heads of State? What factors should be taken into account when deciding which officials should receive this immunity?

4. *Immunity for other officials.* Should this immunity be extended to incumbent Ministers of Internal Affairs? In December 2005, survivors of a massacre in Andijan, Uzbekistan, together with victims of torture, filed suit in Germany against Zokirjon Almatov, Uzbekistan's Minister of Internal Affairs. Their complaint alleges Almatov's responsibility for torture and crimes against humanity, and stems, in part, from the events of May 2005, in which troops from the Ministry of Internal Affairs surrounded a group of thousands of protesters and opened fire on the crowd without warning. Hundreds were killed and wounded. The complaint further alleges that Almatov is responsible for acts of torture committed in Jaslyk prison, a detention facility run by the Ministry of Internal Affairs. Despite the fact that German law recognizes universal jurisdiction for torture and crimes against humanity, as this book goes to press, the federal prosecutor of Germany had yet to decide whether to prosecute.

5. *Ratione personae and ratione materiae. Ratione personae* is a well-established principle in international law according to which certain categories of state officials (such as heads of state or diplomats) are protected from prosecution while they are in office. It is grounded in notions of sovereignty and recognition of the state's need to protect officials as they perform their duties on behalf of the state. Indeed, even in the *Pinochet* case, the Lords acknowledged that if Pinochet were President at the time of Spain's extradition request, he would be immune from prosecution. Under the holding in *Arrest Warrant*, this protection has been extended to foreign ministers.

However, the ICJ's statements with regard to former government officials present the greater challenge to advocates of universal jurisdiction. Immunity for former state officials, as opposed to incumbent officials, is based on functional immunity, or *ratione materiae*. Under the *ratione materiae* principle, acts undertaken by state officials in their official capacity are understood to be acts which are attributed directly to the

---

1. A. Watts, *The Legal Position in International Law of Heads of States, Heads of Governments and Foreign Ministers*, 247 RECUEIL DES COURS: COLLECTED COURSES OF THE HAGUE ACADEMY OF INTERNATIONAL LAW 9, 102–103 (1994).

state: individual liability never arises. As a result, when state officials leave office, they cannot be extradited to a foreign court to answer for their actions any more than the state itself could be extradited.

While technically *dicta*, the court's statements are likely to have a significant impact on future litigation. Foreign ministers are entitled to absolute immunity for all official and personal acts so long as they hold office. Once they leave office, they are entitled to immunity for any actions they undertook in their official capacity while in office. Under the ICJ's decision, former foreign ministers potentially enjoy immunity for their participation in crimes against humanity and war crimes—crimes which nations agree have attained the status of *jus cogens*—so long as those crimes were committed in a public capacity. The court's explanation of immunity for former officials has the potential to sharply limit the efforts of foreign courts to hold former officials accountable for international crimes perpetrated in their official capacity. Efforts to bring former foreign ministers to account for egregious international law violations under universal jurisdiction principles will challenge human rights lawyers to distinguish between official and private acts and to think creatively about the intersections of customary international law and immunity.

6. *Immunity and customary international law.* The court's understanding of the *ratione materiae* principle appears to be inconsistent with customary international law in one important respect: it fails to recognize that some violations of international law, in addition to being imputed to the state, also provide for criminal liability for the individual. A state official who commits genocide or crimes against humanity or torture can be held criminally liable in his or her individual capacity. Indeed, some of these crimes, such as those arising under the Torture Convention, require state action. Since Nuremberg, it has been no defense for state officials to claim that they were acting in their official capacity in committing certain violations of international law. One potential solution to the ICJ's limitation on prosecuting former foreign ministers, subscribed to by three ICJ judges, is that international crimes such as genocide, torture, and crimes against humanity should not be regarded as "official acts" because they are not normal state functions. Under the ICJ decision, categorizing a former foreign minister's crimes as "private acts," as opposed to "official acts" would preclude immunity.

However, Professor Antonio Cassese has pointed out that categorizing international crimes as "private acts" does nothing but create an artificial legal construct. Antonio Cassese, *When May Senior State Officials Be Tried for International Crimes? Some Comments on* The Congo v. Belgium Case, 13 EUR. J. INT'L L. 853 (2002), *available at* http://www.ejil.org/journal/curdevs/sr31.html. If international crimes are "private acts," the "the crimes for which Joachim von Ribbentrop (Reich Minister for Foreign Affairs from 1938 to 1945) was sentenced to death, namely crimes against humanity and war crimes, should be regarded as private acts." *Id.* A more realistic understanding of *ratione materiae* immunity for universal jurisdiction purposes would acknowledge the reality that the crimes are "official acts," but would also recognize that customary international law eliminates immunity for these crimes. Indeed, several courts have prohibited state officials from asserting official capacity as a defense to war crimes, crimes against humanity, or genocide.

7. *Limiting the reach of universal jurisdiction in Belgium.* At one time, Belgium had one of the most robust universal jurisdiction laws in the world and a judiciary intent on using it to bring perpetrators of egregious human rights violations to justice. However, in July 2003, under intense pressure from the United States, the Belgian Parliament repealed its universal jurisdiction statute. Under current law, Belgian courts only have jurisdiction over international crimes if the accused or the victim is Belgian, if the accused or victim resides in Belgium, or if Belgium is required by a treaty to exercise jurisdiction over the case. In its present state, the law has significantly limited the reach of universal jurisdiction in Belgian courts. The law does, however, preserve a small number of cases that were initiated prior to the law's repeal. Among these cases is that of ex-Chadian dictator Hissene Habre, cases concerning the Rwandan genocide, and cases concerning the killing of two priests in Guatemala.

D. "LEGISLATIVE" PROPOSALS

PRINCETON PROJECT ON UNIVERSAL JURISDICTION

http:/lapa.princeton.edu/nosteddocs/unive_jur.pdf

The participants in the Princeton Project on Universal Jurisdiction propose the following principles for the purposes of advancing the continued evolution of international law and the application of international law in national legal systems:

Principle 1—Fundamentals of Universal Jurisdiction

1. For purposes of these Principles, universal jurisdiction is criminal jurisdiction based solely on the nature of the crime, without regard to where the crime was committed, the nationality of the alleged or convicted perpetrator, the nationality of the victim, or any other connection to the state exercising such jurisdiction.

2. Universal jurisdiction may be exercised by a competent and ordinary judicial body of any state in order to try a person duly accused of committing serious crimes under international law as specified in Principle 2(1), provided the person is present before such judicial body.
* * *

4. In exercising universal jurisdiction or in relying upon universal jurisdiction as a basis for seeking extradition, a state and its judicial

organs shall observe international due process norms including but not limited to those involving the rights of the accused and victims, the fairness of the proceedings, and the independence and impartiality of the judiciary (hereinafter referred to as "international due process norms"). * * *

Principle 2—Serious Crimes Under International Law

1.   For purposes of these Principles, serious crimes under international law include: (1) piracy; (2) slavery; (3) war crimes; (4) crimes against peace; (5) crimes against humanity; (6) genocide; and (7) torture. * * *

Principle 3—Reliance on Universal Jurisdiction in the Absence of National Legislation

With respect to serious crimes under international law as specified in Principle 2(1), national judicial organs may rely on universal jurisdiction even if their national legislation does not specifically provide for it.

Principle 4—Obligation to Support Accountability

1.   A state shall comply with all international obligations that are applicable to: prosecuting or extraditing persons accused or convicted of crimes under international law in accordance with a legal process that complies with international due process norms, providing other states investigating or prosecuting such crimes with all available means of administrative and judicial assistance, and undertaking such other necessary and appropriate measures as are consistent with international norms and standards. * * *

Principle 5—Immunities

With respect to serious crimes under international law as specified in Principle 2(1), the official position of any accused person, whether as head of state or government or as a responsible government official, shall not relieve such person of criminal responsibility nor mitigate punishment.

Principle 6—Statutes of Limitations

Statutes of limitations or other forms of prescription shall not apply to serious crimes under international law as specified in Principle 2(1).

Principle 7—Amnesties

1.   Amnesties are generally inconsistent with the obligation of states to provide accountability for serious crimes under international law as specified in Principle in 2(1).

2.   The exercise of universal jurisdiction with respect to serious crimes under international law as specified in Principle 2(1) shall not be precluded by amnesties which are incompatible with the international legal obligations of the granting state. * * *

Principle 9—Non Bis In Idem / Double Jeopardy

1. In the exercise of universal jurisdiction, a state or its judicial organs shall ensure that a person who is subject to criminal proceedings shall not be exposed to multiple prosecutions or punishment for the same criminal conduct where the prior criminal proceedings or other accountability proceedings have been conducted in good faith and in accordance with international norms and standards. Sham prosecutions or derisory punishment resulting from a conviction or other accountability proceedings shall not be recognized as falling within the scope of this Principle.

Principle 10—Grounds for Refusal of Extradition

1. A state or its judicial organs shall refuse to entertain a request for extradition based on universal jurisdiction if the person sought is likely to face a death penalty sentence or to be subjected to torture or any other cruel, degrading, or inhuman punishment or treatment, or if it is likely that the person sought will be subjected to sham proceedings in which international due process norms will be violated and no satisfactory assurances to the contrary are provided. * * *

Principle 11—Adoption of National Legislation

A state shall, where necessary, enact national legislation to enable the exercise of universal jurisdiction and the enforcement of these Principles.

Principle 12—Inclusion of Universal Jurisdiction in Future Treaties

In all future treaties, and in protocols to existing treaties, concerned with serious crimes under international law as specified in Principle 2(1), states shall include provisions for universal jurisdiction.

Principle 13—Strengthening Accountability and Universal Jurisdiction

1. National judicial organs shall construe national law in a manner that is consistent with these Principles. * * *

Principle 14—Settlement of Disputes

1. Consistent with international law and the Charter of the United Nations, states should settle their disputes arising out of the exercise of universal jurisdiction by all available means of peaceful settlement of disputes and in particular by submitting the dispute to the International Court of Justice.

NOTES AND QUESTIONS ON "LEGISLATIVE" PROPOSALS

1. *Objection to the principles.* Only one of the participants at the Princeton conference decided not to endorse the Princeton Principles.

That participant was Lord Browne–Wilkinson, the senior law lord who had written the lead opinion permitting Pinochet's extradition to Spain. He filed a dissenting statement[1] in which he explained his concerns with the Principles as adopted:

> I am strongly in favour of universal jurisdiction over serious international crimes, if by those words, one means the exercise by an international court or by the courts of one state of jurisdiction over the nationals of another state with the prior consent of that state, *i.e.* in cases such as the ICC and Torture Convention. But the Princeton Principles propose that individual national courts should exercise such jurisdiction against nationals of a state which has not agreed to such jurisdiction. Moreover the Principles do not recognize any form of sovereign immunity. If the law were to be so established, states antipathetic to Western powers would be likely to seize both active and retired officials and military personnel of such Western powers and stage a show trial for alleged international crimes. Conversely, zealots in Western States might launch prosecutions against, for example, Islamic extremists for their terrorist activities. It is naïve to think that, in such cases, the national state of the accused would stand by and watch the trial proceed: resort to force would be more probable. In any event the fear of such legal actions would inhibit the use of peacekeeping forces when it is otherwise desirable and also the free interchange of diplomatic personnel. I believe that the adoption of such universal jurisdiction without preserving the existing concepts of immunity would be more likely to damage than to advance chances of international peace.

Are Lord Browne–Wilkinson's concerns well-founded?

2. *Jus cogens.* The Principles do not limit the crimes which are subject to universal jurisdiction to *jus cogens* crimes. They refer instead refer to "serious crimes under international law." Is the more flexible definition of a "serious crime" desirable? Should universal jurisdiction be limited to only *jus cogens* crimes? Why or why not?

3. *Amnesty International's Fourteen Principles of Universal Jurisdiction.* Amnesty International has also proposed a set of principles to govern the practice of universal jurisdiction, entitled *Amnesty International's Fourteen Principles of Universal Jurisdiction.*[2] Consider some of the differences between the Princeton Principles and Amnesty's Principles:

> (a) *Differences in purpose*: Amnesty's principles were drafted to launch a worldwide campaign for its members to lobby all governments to enact or amend universal jurisdiction legislation for the listed crimes and then to implement it. *See generally,* Amnesty

---

1. Stephen Macedo, *Introduction* in UNIVERSAL JURISDICTION: NATIONAL COURTS AND THE PROSECUTION OF SERIOUS CRIMES UNDER INTERNATIONAL LAW 6 (Stephen Macedo ed., 2004), citing Letter to William J. Butler, Commentary to the Princeton Principles at 20.

2. *Available at* http://www.amnesty.org/en/library/info/10R53/001/1999.

International, Universal Jurisdiction, *available at* http://www. amnesty.org/en/international-justice/issues/universal-jurisdiction.   In contrast with Amnesty's Principles, which amount to more of a blueprint for establishing more uniform universal jurisdiction, Princeton's Principles are more similar to an academic Restatement, providing, in part, guiding principles for decision-making by states that have already endorsed universal jurisdiction in their legislation.

(b) *Differing perspectives*: Amnesty International is a international non-governmental organization dedicated to promoting human rights, whereas Princeton convened its meeting under more academic auspices. How might the principles promulgated by each group reflect any political proclivities and constraints faced by academia and the NGO community?

(c) *Specific differences*: Amnesty Principle 14 provides that national legislatures should ensure that judges, prosecutors, and defense lawyers receive effective training in human rights law, international humanitarian law, and international criminal law, while the Princeton Principles are silent on this issue. Does effective litigation under universal jurisdiction in fact require specialized training?

In some instances, Amnesty's 14 Principles may provide greater protections for defendants. For example, Amnesty's 14 Principles provide for "public trials in the presence of international monitors" (Principle 10) whereas Princeton Principles state only that a state and its judicial organs shall "observe international due process norms" including rights of both victims and the accused.

E.   THE POLICY DEBATE OVER UNIVERSAL JURISDICTION

HENRY KISSINGER, THE PITFALLS OF UNIVERSAL JURISDICTION: RISKING JUDICIAL TYRANNY
FOREIGN AFFAIRS (JULY/AUGUST 2001)

In less than a decade, an unprecedented movement has emerged to submit international politics to judicial procedures. It has spread with extraordinary speed and has not been subjected to systematic debate, partly because of the intimidating passion of its advocates. To be sure, human rights violations, war crimes, genocide, and torture have so disgraced the modern age and in such a variety of places that the effort to interpose legal norms to prevent or punish such outrages does credit to its advocates. The danger lies in pushing the effort to extremes that risk substituting the tyranny of judges for that of governments; historically, the dictatorship of the virtuous has often led to inquisitions and even witch-hunts.

The doctrine of universal jurisdiction asserts that some crimes are so heinous that their perpetrators should not escape justice by invoking doctrines of sovereign immunity or the sacrosanct nature of national frontiers. Two specific approaches to achieve this goal have emerged recently. The first seeks to apply the procedures of domestic criminal justice to violations of universal standards, some of which are embodied in United Nations conventions, by authorizing national prosecutors to bring offenders into their jurisdictions through extradition from third countries. The second approach is the International Criminal Court (ICC), the founding treaty for which was created by a conference in Rome in July 1998 and signed by 95 states, including most European countries. * * *

The very concept of universal jurisdiction is of recent vintage. The sixth edition of Black's Law Dictionary, published in 1990, does not contain even an entry for the term. The closest analogous concept listed is *hostes humani generis* ("enemies of the human race"). Until recently, the latter term has been applied to pirates, hijackers, and similar outlaws whose crimes were typically committed outside the territory of any state. The notion that heads of state and senior public officials should have the same standing as outlaws before the bar of justice is quite new.

In the aftermath of the Holocaust and the many atrocities committed since, major efforts have been made to find a judicial standard to deal with such catastrophes: the Nuremberg trials of 1945–46, the Universal Declaration of Human Rights of 1948, the genocide convention of 1948, and the anti-torture convention of 1988. * * * In the 1990s, international tribunals to punish crimes committed in the former Yugoslavia and Rwanda, established ad hoc by the U.N. Security Council, have sought to provide a system of accountability for specific regions ravaged by arbitrary violence.

But none of these steps was conceived at the time as instituting a "universal jurisdiction." It is unlikely that any of the signatories of * * * the U.N. conventions * * * thought it possible that national judges would use them as a basis for extradition requests regarding alleged crimes committed outside their jurisdictions. The drafters almost certainly believed that they were stating general principles, not laws that would be enforced by national courts. * * * Even with respect to binding undertakings such as the genocide convention, it was never thought that they would subject past and future leaders of one nation to prosecution by the national magistrates of another state where the violations had not occurred. Nor, until recently, was it argued that the various U.N. declarations subjected past and future leaders to the possibility of prosecution by national magistrates of third countries without either due process safeguards or institutional restraints.

Yet this is in essence the precedent that was set by the 1998 British detention of former Chilean President Augusto Pinochet as the result of an extradition request by a Spanish judge seeking to try Pinochet for crimes committed against Spaniards on Chilean soil. For advocates of universal jurisdiction, that detention—lasting more than 16 months—was a landmark establishing a just principle. But any universal system should contain procedures not only to punish the wicked but also to constrain the righteous. It must not allow legal principles to be used as weapons to settle political scores. Questions such as these must therefore be answered: What legal norms are being applied? What are the rules of evidence? What safeguards exist for the defendant? And how will prosecutions affect other fundamental foreign policy objectives and interests?

A Dangerous Precedent

It is decidedly unfashionable to express any degree of skepticism about the way the Pinochet case was handled. For almost all the parties of the European left, Augusto Pinochet is the incarnation of a right-wing assault on democracy because he led a coup d'etat against an elected leader. At the time, others, including the leaders of Chile's democratic parties, viewed Salvador Allende as a radical Marxist ideologue bent on imposing a Castro-style dictatorship with the aid of Cuban-trained militias and Cuban weapons. This was why the leaders of Chile's democratic parties publicly welcomed—yes, welcomed—Allende's overthrow. (They changed their attitude only after the junta brutally maintained its autocratic rule far longer than was warranted by the invocation of an emergency.)

Disapproval of the Allende regime does not exonerate those who perpetrated systematic human rights abuses after it was overthrown. But neither should the applicability of universal jurisdiction as a policy be determined by one's view of the political history of Chile. The appropriate solution was arrived at in August 2000 when the Chilean Supreme Court withdrew Pinochet's senatorial immunity, making it possible to deal with the charges against him in the courts of the country most competent to judge this history and to relate its decisions to the stability and vitality of its democratic institutions.

On November 25, 1998, the judiciary committee of the British House of Lords (the United Kingdom's supreme court) concluded that "international law has made it plain that certain types of conduct . . . are not acceptable conduct on the part of anyone." But that principle did not oblige the lords to endow a Spanish magistrate—and presumably other magistrates elsewhere in the world—with the authority to enforce it in a country where the accused had committed no crime, and then to cause the restraint of the accused for 16 months in yet another country in which he was equally a stranger. It could have held that Chile, or an international tribunal specifically established for crimes committed in Chile on the model of the courts set up for heinous crimes in the former Yugoslavia and Rwanda, was the appropriate forum.

The unprecedented and sweeping interpretation of international law in *Ex parte Pinochet* would arm any magistrate anywhere in the world with the power to demand extradition, substituting the magistrate's own judgment for the reconciliation procedures of even incontestably democratic societies where alleged violations of human rights may have occurred. It would also subject the accused to the criminal procedures of the magistrate's country, with a legal system that may be unfamiliar to the defendant and that would force the defendant to bring evidence and witnesses from long distances. Such a system goes far beyond the explicit and limited mandates established by the U.N. Security Council for the tribunals covering war crimes in the former Yugoslavia and Rwanda as well as the one being negotiated for Cambodia.

Perhaps the most important issue is the relationship of universal jurisdiction to national reconciliation procedures set up by new democratic governments to deal with their countries' questionable pasts. One would have thought that a Spanish magistrate would have been sensitive to the incongruity of a request by Spain, itself haunted by transgressions committed during the Spanish Civil War and the regime of General Francisco Franco, to try in Spanish courts alleged crimes against humanity committed elsewhere.

The decision of post-Franco Spain to avoid wholesale criminal trials for the human rights violations of the recent past was designed explicitly to foster a process of national reconciliation that undoubtedly contributed much to the present vigor of Spanish democracy. Why should Chile's attempt at national reconciliation not have been given the same opportunity? Should any outside group dissatisfied with the reconciliation procedures of, say, South Africa be free to challenge them in their own national courts or those of third countries?

It is an important principle that those who commit war crimes or systematically violate human rights should be held accountable. But the consolidation of law, domestic peace, and representative government in a nation struggling to come to terms with a brutal past has a claim as well. The instinct to punish must be related, as in every constitutional democratic political structure, to a system of checks and balances that includes other elements critical to the survival and expansion of democracy.

Another grave issue is the use in such cases of extradition procedures designed for ordinary criminals. If the Pinochet case becomes a precedent, magistrates anywhere will be in a position to put forward an extradition request without warning to the accused and regardless of the policies the accused's country might already have in place for dealing with the charges. The country from which extradition is requested then faces a seemingly technical legal decision that, in fact, amounts to the exercise of political discretion—whether to entertain the claim or not.

Once extradition procedures are in train, they develop a momentum of their own. The accused is not allowed to challenge the substantive merit of the case and instead is confined to procedural issues: that there was, say, some technical flaw in the extradition request, that the judicial system of the requesting country is incapable of providing a fair hearing, or that the crime for which the extradition is sought is not treated as a crime in the country from which extradition has been requested—thereby conceding much of the merit of the charge. Meanwhile, while these claims are being considered by the judicial system of the country from which extradition is sought, the accused remains in some form of detention, possibly for years. Such procedures provide an opportunity for political harassment long before the accused is in a position to present any defense. It would be ironic if a doctrine designed to transcend the political process turns into a means to pursue political enemies rather than universal justice.

The Pinochet precedent, if literally applied, would permit the two sides in the Arab–Israeli conflict, or those in any other passionate international controversy, to project their battles into the various national courts by pursuing adversaries with extradition requests. When discretion on what crimes are subject to universal jurisdiction and whom to prosecute is left to national prosecutors, the scope for arbitrariness is wide indeed. So far, universal jurisdiction has involved the prosecution of one fashionably reviled man of the right while scores of East European communist leaders—not to speak of Caribbean, Middle Eastern, or African leaders who inflicted their own full measures of torture and suffering—have not had to face similar prosecutions.

Some will argue that a double standard does not excuse violations of international law and that it is better to bring one malefactor to justice than to grant immunity to all. This is not an argument permitted in the domestic jurisdictions of many democracies—in Canada, for example, a charge can be thrown out of court merely by showing that a prosecution has been selective enough to amount to an abuse of process. In any case, a universal standard of justice should not be based on the proposition that a just end warrants unjust means, or that political fashion trumps fair judicial procedures. * * *

AN INDISCRIMINATE COURT * * *

The doctrine of universal jurisdiction is based on the proposition that the individuals or cases subject to it have been clearly identified. In some instances, especially those based on Nuremberg precedents, the definition of who can be prosecuted in an international court and in what circumstances is self-evident. But many issues are much more vague and depend on an understanding of the historical and political context. It is this fuzziness that risks arbitrariness on the part of prosecutors and judges years after the event and that became apparent with respect to existing tribunals.

For example, can any leader of the United States or of another country be hauled before international tribunals established for other purposes? This is precisely what Amnesty International implied when, in the summer of 1999, it supported a "complaint" by a group of European and Canadian law professors to Louise Arbour, then the prosecutor of the International Criminal Tribunal for the Former Yugoslavia (ICTY). The complaint alleged that crimes against humanity had been committed during the NATO air campaign in Kosovo. Arbour ordered an internal staff review, thereby implying that she did have jurisdiction if such violations could, in fact, be demonstrated. Her successor, Carla Del Ponte, in the end declined to indict any NATO official because of a general inability "to pinpoint individual responsibilities," thereby implying anew that the court had jurisdiction over NATO and American leaders in the Balkans and would have issued an indictment had it been able to identify the particular leaders allegedly involved. * * *

The pressures to achieve the widest scope for the doctrine of universal jurisdiction were demonstrated as well by a suit before the European Court of Human Rights in June 2000 by families of Argentine sailors who died in the sinking of the Argentine cruiser General Belgano during the Falklands War. The concept of universal jurisdiction has moved from judging alleged political crimes against humanity to second-guessing, 18 years after the event, military operations in which neither civilians nor civilian targets were involved. * * *

MODEST PROPOSALS

The precedents set by international tribunals established to deal with situations where the enormity of the crime is evident and the local judicial system is clearly incapable of administering justice, as in the former Yugoslavia and Rwanda, have shown that it is possible to punish without removing from the process all political judgment and experience. * * * Until then, the United States should go no further toward a more formal system than one containing the following three provisions. First, the U.N. Security Council would create a Human Rights Commission or a special subcommittee to report whenever systematic human rights violations seem to warrant judicial action. Second, when the government under which the alleged crime occurred is not authentically representative, or where the domestic judicial system is incapable of sitting in judgment on the crime, the Security Council would set up an ad hoc international tribunal on the model of those of the former Yugoslavia or Rwanda. And third, the procedures for these international tribunals as well as the scope of the prosecution should be precisely defined by the Security Council, and the accused should be entitled to the due process safeguards accorded in common jurisdictions.

In this manner, internationally agreed procedures to deal with war crimes, genocide, or other crimes against humanity could become institutionalized. Furthermore, the one-sidedness of the current pursuit of universal jurisdiction would be avoided. This pursuit could threaten the very purpose for which the concept has been developed. In the end, an excessive reliance on universal jurisdiction may undermine the political will to sustain the humane norms of international behavior so necessary to temper the violent times in which we live.

KENNETH ROTH, THE CASE
FOR UNIVERSAL JURISDICTION
FOREIGN AFFAIRS
(SEPTEMBER/OCTOBER 2001)

Behind much of the savagery of modern history lies impunity. Tyrants commit atrocities, including genocide, when they calculate they can get away with them. Too often, dictators use violence and intimidation to shut down any prospect of domestic prosecution. Over the past decade, however, a slowly emerging system of international justice has begun to break this pattern of impunity in national courts.

The United Nations Security Council established international war crimes tribunals for the former Yugoslavia in 1993 and Rwanda in 1994 and is now negotiating the creation of mixed national-international tribunals for Cambodia and Sierra Leone. In 1998, the world's governments gathered in Rome to adopt a treaty for an International Criminal Court (ICC) with potentially global jurisdiction over genocide, war crimes, and crimes against humanity.

With growing frequency, national courts operating under the doctrine of universal jurisdiction are prosecuting despots in their custody for atrocities committed abroad. Impunity may still be the norm in many domestic courts, but international justice is an increasingly viable option, promising a measure of solace to victims and their families and raising the possibility that would-be tyrants will begin to think twice before embarking on a barbarous path.

In "The Pitfalls of Universal Jurisdiction" (July/August 2001), former Secretary of State Henry Kissinger catalogues a list of grievances against the juridical concept that people who commit the most severe human rights crimes can be tried wherever they are found. But his objections are misplaced, and the alternative he proposes is little better than a return to impunity.

Kissinger begins by suggesting that universal jurisdiction is a new idea, at least as applied to heads of state and senior public officials. However, the exercise by U.S. courts of jurisdiction over certain heinous crimes committed overseas is an accepted part of American jurisprudence, reflected in treaties on terrorism and aircraft hijacking dating from 1970. Universal jurisdiction was also the concept that allowed Israel to try Adolf Eichmann in Jerusalem in 1961. * * *

As for the many formal treaties on human rights, Kissinger believes it "unlikely" that their signatories "thought it possible that national judges would use them as a basis for extradition requests regarding alleged crimes committed outside their jurisdictions." To the contrary, the Torture Convention of 1984, ratified by 124 governments including the United States, requires states either to prosecute any suspected torturer found on their territory, regardless of where the torture took place, or to extradite the suspect to a country that will do so. Similarly, the Geneva Conventions of 1949 on the conduct of war, ratified by 189 countries including the United States, require each participating state to "search for" persons who have committed grave breaches of the conventions and to "bring such persons, regardless of nationality, before its own courts." What is new is not the concept of extraterritorial jurisdiction but the willingness of some governments to fulfill this duty against those in high places. * * *

National courts come under Kissinger's fire for selectively applying universal jurisdiction. He characterizes the extradition request by a Spanish judge seeking to try former Chilean President Augusto Pinochet for crimes against Spanish citizens on Chilean soil as singling out a "fashionably reviled man of the right." But Pinochet was sought not, as Kissinger writes, "because he led a coup d'etat against an elected leader" who was a favorite of the left. Rather, Pinochet was targeted because security forces under his command murdered and forcibly "disappeared" some 3,000 people and tortured thousands more.

Furthermore, in recent years national courts have exercised universal jurisdiction against a wide range of suspects: Bosnian war criminals, Rwandan *genocidaires,* Argentine torturers, and Chad's former dictator. It has come to the point where the main limit on national courts empowered to exercise universal jurisdiction is the availability of the defendant, not questions of ideology.

Kissinger also cites the *Pinochet* case to argue that international justice interferes with the choice by democratic governments to forgive rather than prosecute past offenders. In fact, Pinochet's imposition of a self-amnesty at the height of his dictatorship limited Chile's democratic options. Only after 16 months of detention in the United Kingdom diminished his power was Chilean democracy able to begin prosecution. Such imposed impunity is far more common than democratically chosen impunity.

Kissinger would have had a better case had prosecutors sought, for example, to overturn the compromise negotiated by South Africa's Nelson Mandela, widely recognized at the time as the legitimate representative of the victims of apartheid. Mandela agreed to grant abusers immunity from prosecution if they gave detailed testimony about their crimes. In an appropriate exercise of prosecutorial discretion, no prosecutor has challenged this arrangement, and no government would likely countenance such a challenge.

Kissinger legitimately worries that the nations exercising universal jurisdiction could include governments with less-entrenched traditions of due process than the United Kingdom's. But his fear of governments robotically extraditing suspects for sham or counterproductive trials is overblown. Governments regularly deny extradition to courts that are unable to ensure high standards of due process. And foreign ministries, including the U.S. State Department, routinely deny extradition requests for reasons of public policy.

If an American faced prosecution by an untrustworthy foreign court, the United States undoubtedly would apply pressure for his or her release. If that failed, however, it might prove useful to offer the prosecuting government the face-saving alternative of transferring the suspect to the ICC, with its extensive procedural protections, including deference to good-faith investigations and prosecutions by a suspect's own government. Unfortunately, the legislation being pushed by ICC opponents in Washington would preclude that option. * * *

As a nation committed to human rights and the rule of law, the United States should be embracing an international system of justice, even if it means that Americans, like everyone else, might sometimes be scrutinized.

Notes and Questions on the Policy Debate

1. *Politics and universal jurisdiction.* Does Kissinger make a convincing case that United States officials may be subjected to "political" prosecutions based on universal jurisdiction? Is the response that such prosecutions are based on universal standards a sufficient answer? Do you think that prosecutions based on universal jurisdiction advance or hinder the development of an international legal framework in which there will be "no safe haven" for human rights violators?

2. *Universal jurisdiction and national reconciliation.* In his article, *supra*, Kissinger argues that "the decision of post-Franco Spain to avoid wholesale criminal trials for the human rights violations of the recent past was designed explicitly to foster a process of national reconciliation that undoubtedly contributed much to the present vigor of Spanish democracy." Several democracies in transition have chosen to forgo criminal trials in favor of truth commissions or amnesty laws, wagering that the benefits of future peace are worth the cost of permitting certain individuals to go unpunished. Chile made a similar decision, deciding to grant immunity for the military junta's worst human rights violators. South Africa also chose to forgo trials and instituted the Truth and Reconciliation Commission, which granted amnesty to individuals who testified truthfully before the Commission. Are national courts operating under principles of universal jurisdiction obligated to respect other nations' amnesty legislation? Would an individual who had come forward and confessed to crimes against humanity, before a TRC be subject to prosecution when traveling to a country with a universal jurisdiction statute? What factors should states consider before exercising universal jurisdiction in such situations? Should they inquire into whether the reconciliation process was successful, or whether it provided victims with some kind of redress?

Over the years, the Inter–American Court of Human Rights ("IACHR") has issued a number of decisions striking down the amnesty laws of various Latin American countries when defendants attempted to raise amnesty as a defense to alleged violations of the American Convention on Human Rights. For example, in 1992, the IACHR found that the amnesty laws enacted in Uruguay and Argentina were incompatible with the American Convention on Human Rights.[3] In 2001, the IACHR affirmed its position in the *Barrios Altos* case declaring that two amnesty laws implemented by the government of Peruvian President Alberto Fujimori were incompatible with the state's obligations under the American Convention on Human Rights. *Barrios Altos Case*, Interpretation of the Judgment on the Merits (Art. 67 American Convention on Human Rights), Judgment of Sept. 3, 2001, Inter–Am. Ct. H.R. (ser. C) No. 83 (Sept. 3, 2001). Should courts exercising universal jurisdiction adopt the same approach with respect to amnesty laws?

<hr>

Practicum

On a hypothetical private visit to Europe, in February 2003, assume that Henry Kissinger was wandering along the coast of France and made the mistake of accidentally crossing the Belgium border. It turns out that a Belgian investigating magistrate had issued a secret arrest warrant for Kissinger's arrest for his alleged involvement in crimes against humanity committed by the Pinochet regime in Chile in 1973.

The charges against Kissinger allege that he, as U.S. Secretary of State in 1993, gave Pinochet the "go ahead" to overthrow the elected government of Salvador Allende, and that Kissinger tacitly approved the executions of dozens of officials of the Allende regime, including a series of extra-judicial killings which has been called the "Caravan of Death." (The general background for the "Caravan" is discussed in *Estate of Cabello v. Fernandez-Larios*, 157 F. Supp. 2d 1345 (S.D. Fla. 2001)). The allegations in the charges against Kissinger state that the Chilean military orchestrated the disappearance and extra-judicial murder of at least twenty-five officials of the Allende regime in the "Caravan of Death" and that Kissinger's "green light" to the Pinochet regime led directly to the regime embarking on this systematic elimination of its perceived enemies. Kissinger is not alleged to have specifically approved the particular killings involved in the "Caravan of Death," but rather to have been informed that the Pinochet regime intended to eliminate some of its opponents, and to have subsequently indicated to Pinochet that the U.S. would not oppose such actions. [This hypothetical is *not* based on actual allegations made against Kissinger. *See, e.g.*, CHRISTOPHER HITCHENS, THE TRIAL OF HENRY KISSINGER (2001).]

Two low level Belgian law enforcement officials who knew about the arrest warrant happened upon Kissinger and arrested him. Kissinger

---

3. Report No. 28/92, Cases 10.147, 10.181, 10.240, 10.262, 10.309 and 10.311 (Argentina), Oct. 2, 1992 and Report No. 29/92, Cases 10.029, 10.036, 10.145, 10.305, 10.372, 10.373, 10.374 and 10.375 (Uruguay), Oct. 2, 1992 in OEA/Ser.L/V/III.27, doc. 10, Inter–Am. C.H.R, Annual Report 1992. The Annual Reports of the Commission are accessible on the Commission's web site, *available at* http://www.cidh.oas.org.

has now been indicted for crimes against humanity for his role in the Caravan of Death, and a Belgian magistrate has upheld his continued detention.

The United States has raised a diplomatic furor, but, so far, the Belgian government has stood firm against U.S. pressure. However, it has agreed to allow the International Court of Justice to decide the legality of the arrest and of Belgium's assertion of universal jurisdiction over the alleged crimes under international customary law.

Belgium has asserted universal jurisdiction over these claims pursuant to its 1999 law, *la loi relative à la répression des violations graves du droit international humanitaire* (Act Concerning the Punishment of Grave Breaches of International Law). Article 7 of the 1999 law provides in relevant part: "The Belgian courts shall be competent to deal with breaches provided for in the present Act, irrespective of where such breaches have been committed."

Breaches covered by the 1999 law include "all of the acts of genocide in Article II of the Genocide Convention and Article 6 of the Rome Statute" and crimes against humanity. Under the law, a

> [c]rime against humanity committed in peace time or in time of war, shall constitute a crime under international law and be punishable in accordance with the provisions of the present Act. In accordance with the Statute of the International Criminal Court, a crime against humanity means any of the following acts, committed as part of a widespread or systematic attack directed against any civilian population, with knowledge of the attack: (1) murder; (2) extermination; (3) enslavement; (4) deportation or forcible transfer [of population]; (5) imprisonment or other severe deprivation of physical liberty in violation of fundamental rules of international law; (6) torture; (7) rape, sexual slavery, enforced prostitution, forced pregnancy, enforced sterilization, or any other form of sexual violence of comparable gravity; (8) persecution against any identifiable group or collectivity on political, racial, national, ethnic, cultural, religious, gender or other grounds that are universally recognized as impermissible under international law, in connection with any act referred to in the Article.

Discuss the objections that will be raised by the U.S. in this hypothetical case, including its arguments that Mr. Kissinger enjoys immunity under international law, and that the principle of universal jurisdiction cannot be extended to allow Belgium to assert criminal jurisdiction over Mr. Kissinger, a United States citizen, for his alleged complicity in crimes committed by the Chilean military in Chile and against Chilean nationals.

Discuss Belgium's available responses to these objections, as well as its support for the propositions that the principle of universal jurisdiction allows Belgium to try Mr. Kissinger for his alleged crimes consistent with international law, and that under the circumstances, Mr. Kissinger enjoys no immunity from arrest or trial.

CHAPTER 3

ADVANCING HUMAN RIGHTS CLAIMS IN INTERGOVERNMENTAL ORGANIZATIONS

■ ■ ■

The organizing principle behind international law—the idea that has given international law its essential character—is that it is a "horizontal" legal order: there is no central sovereign, no legislature with global authority to pass laws for the governments and peoples of the world, and no centralized police force or executive body to enforce the law. Instead, the legal order rests at least fictively on the will of co-equal states, who make the rules for themselves. Admittedly, some states are extremely powerful and others are not, so there is something mildly hallucinatory about the assumption that international law is made by co-equal states, but, if anything, that element of *realpolitik* simply reinforces the difference between international law and other forms of law.

One of the real-world consequences of this "horizontality" is that international law is better at stating authoritative expectations than imposing punishments. Another is that it preserves more state power than it constrains. It does this by defining and protecting a zone of discretion within which states can act as they choose, beyond international scrutiny. When skeptics observe that international law is not really "law," they presumably mean at a minimum that it has none of the coercive characteristics that define more familiar forms of law, like criminal law or administrative law at the domestic level, which better fit the vertical form.

If that skepticism were fully persuasive, the materials in this chapter would be inexplicable. Each of the modules below explores the ways that states themselves have set up intergovernmental institutions for the advancement and protection of human rights. In each case, governments have agreed to soften the barrier of sovereignty and allow the development and promotion of international human rights standards by these institutions. They may do this for example by establishing a treaty regime and empowering an intergovernmental institution to supervise or publicize the parties' compliance through formal reporting mechanisms (Module 4); or by establishing international courts to adjudicate the human rights responsibilities of state officials (Module 6) or even governments themselves (Module 7). Alternatively, they may identify global issues around a single human rights "theme" and jointly empower a person or a group to address it (Module 5). The common ground among these modules is that each offers an enforcement setting established by states, and each is fundamentally distinct from the domestic courts explored in the prior chapter.

These approaches and institutions are not always successful, but no law can prevent its own violation. The existence of contract law does not mean that contracts are never broken. The laws criminalizing murder do not stop homicides. In the face of apparent violations, it's always relevant to ask, "what are the consequences? What sanctions are legitimate for this violation of the law?" You may think of the following materials as an exploration of the sanctions that are available within intergovernmental institutions when one of their members departs from the authoritative expectations expressed in international human rights law.

CHAPTER 3

MODULE 4

STATE-REPORTING MECHANISMS IN THE UNITED NATIONS

■ ■ ■

Orientation

The adoption of the Universal Declaration of Human Rights in 1948 made it difficult for a state to assert that its treatment of its own citizens was exempt from international scrutiny. The widespread devastation and abuses of World War II had led the international community—the survivors—to recognize a two-way connection between international peace and security on one hand and respect for human rights on the other. By declaring the need to develop a "common standard of achievement for all peoples and all nations," the UN declined to perpetuate a legal system in which the rights of individuals were ancillary to the obligations states owed to one another. The human rights of people, regardless of citizenship, was to be a primary subject of international law and therefore properly discussed, monitored, and developed by states and their representatives. Although many governments continue to argue against international "interference" in their domestic affairs, the Universal Declaration established an aspirational—and gradually a legal—framework for denying the premise that human rights were strictly domestic in the first place. In this Module, we review the principal powers of the United Nations under treaties and under the Charter itself.

Treaty bodies. Although progress could be glacial, the Universal Declaration cleared the way for members of the United Nations to negotiate a range of international treaties covering a panoply of civil, political, economic, social, and cultural rights. As noted in Chapter 1, in 1966, after several years of negotiation, the UN General Assembly adopted and opened for signature the International Covenant on Civil and Political Rights (ICCPR) and the International Covenant on Economic, Social, and Cultural Rights (ICESCR). At roughly the same time, the General Assembly approved the International Convention on the

Elimination of Racial Discrimination (1965) (CERD); followed several years later by the Convention on the Elimination of Discrimination Against Women (1979) (CEDAW); the Convention Against Torture and Other Forms of Cruel, Inhuman, or Degrading Treatment or Punishment (1984) (CAT); the Convention on the Rights of the Child (1989) (CRC); the Convention on the Protection of the Rights of All Migrant Workers and Members of Their Families (2003) (CMW); and the Convention on the Rights of Persons with Disabilities (2008) (CRPD). Each of these conventions has entered into force, generally with vast numbers of signatures and ratifications but sometimes with significant reservations.

One common procedural feature of each of these conventions—and a matter of crucial importance to human rights lawyers—was the creation of a committee to review each party's compliance with its terms. For all parties, review begins with the submission of a report to the relevant Committee. Under some of these treaties (or pursuant to an optional protocol), governments may subject themselves to further scrutiny and authorize a Committee to receive petitions filed by individuals who claim that their treaty rights were violated by the government. Thus for example, individual petitions may be filed against governments accepting this form of jurisdiction in the Human Rights Committee (established under the ICCPR), the Committee against Torture (established under the CAT), and the Committee on the Elimination of Racial Discrimination (established under CERD). Although the work of these committees has been criticized over the years, their reports and decisions or recommendations have been instrumental in advancing the goals of the treaty regimes. The Committees' work has added texture and sweep to the bare-bones texts of these instruments.

Charter bodies. It is important to distinguish those human rights institutions created by separate treaties negotiated under the umbrella of the United Nations from those institutions created within the United Nations itself. Often, these Charter-based mechanisms may seem impenetrable and driven by political or diplomatic constraints; nevertheless, they constitute an important component in the global trend toward publicizing human rights violations and bringing pressure to bear on abusive governments and individuals. Increasingly, human rights NGOs have considered these mechanisms an important part of their advocacy strategies.

The UN Charter created three bodies that would come to address human rights issues regularly: the Security Council, which could—subject to the veto of one of the five Permanent Members—respond to human rights-based threats to the peace under Chapter VII of the Charter; the General Assembly; and the Economic and Social Council (ECOSOC). In 1946, pursuant to Article 68 of the Charter, ECOSOC created the Commission on Human Rights (not to be confused with the Committee on Human Rights established under the ICCPR, *supra*). For much of its history, the human rights work of the Commission was dominated by its Sub–Commission on the Promotion and Protection of

Minorities, a body of largely-independent human rights experts, who were generally more proactive and aggressive in the protection of human rights than the diplomats who served on the parent Commission.

In 2005, responding to the UN Secretary General's call to reform the Commission, the General Assembly created the UN Human Rights Council and brought it under the General Assembly as a way of giving it a higher profile. In addition, it approved a process of *universal periodic review* (UPR), a peer-review mechanism under which the human rights record of every UN member is reviewed every five years. The status and impact of NGOs were also enhanced through an interactive dialogue with thematic rapporteurs (see Module 5, *infra*) involving both governments and civil society.

All four of these bodies—the Security Council, the General Assembly, ECOSOC, and the Human Rights Council—can in principle and practice consider thematic issues and individual country situations, and each is authorized to adopt resolutions and take other decisions with varying normative power. Although much of their work is procedural, opaque, and preparatory, member states do wrangle over important substantive issues as well, like the mandates of special rapporteurs, the content of country-specific resolutions, and the need for new human rights instruments like treaties and declarations.

For many, the UN has the quality of *kabuki* theater: long on stylized talk and short on real action. It is criticized for being dominated by diplomats too eager to please and too slow to criticize. But the human rights lawyer who learns its nuances and utilizes its strengths will find value, both as a source of tools to be used in other forums and as a worthy venue for increasing pressure on governments to live up to their treaty commitments.

This Module covers the UN treaty-based mechanisms and the UN Charter mechanisms, focusing with respect to the former on both the individual petition system and the state reporting system in two illustrative treaty bodies: the Committee against Torture and the Human Rights Committee. With respect to the Charter-based mechanisms, the module explores the resolution process within the UN's subsidiary human rights bodies as well as the individual-state petition mechanisms.

A.   TREATY–BASED MECHANISMS: THE INDIVIDUAL–STATE PETITION

A.S. v. SWEDEN
Communication No. 149/1999
U.N. Doc. CAT/C/25/D/149/1999

1.1. The author of the communication is A.S., an Iranian citizen currently residing with her son in Sweden, where she is seeking refugee status. The author and her son arrived in Sweden on 23 December 1997 and applied for asylum on 29 December 1997. Ms. S. claims that she would risk torture and execution upon return to the Islamic Republic of Iran and that her forced return to that country would therefore constitute a violation by Sweden of article 3 of the Convention.[1] The author is represented by counsel.

1.2. In accordance with article 22, paragraph 3, of the Convention, the Committee transmitted communication No. 149/1999 to the State party on 12 November 1999. Pursuant to rule 108, paragraph 9, of the Committee's rules of procedure, the State party was requested not to expel the author to Iran pending the consideration of her case by the Committee. In a submission dated 12 January 2000 the State party informed the Committee that the author would not be expelled to her country of origin while her communication was under consideration by the Committee.

2.1. The author submits that she has never been politically active in Iran. In 1981, her husband, who was a high-ranking officer in the Iranian Air Force, was killed during training in circumstances that remain unclear; it has never been possible to determine whether his death was an accident. According to the author, she and her husband belonged to secular-minded families opposed to the regime of the mullahs.

2.2. In 1991, the Government of the Islamic Republic of Iran declared the author's late husband a martyr. The author states that martyrdom is an issue of utmost importance for the Shia Muslims in Iran. All families of martyrs are supported and supervised by a foundation, the *Bonyad-e Shahid*, the Committee of Martyrs, which constitutes a powerful authority in Iranian society. Thus, while the author and her two sons' material living conditions and status rose considerably, she had to submit to the rigid rules of Islamic society even more conscientiously than before. One of the aims of *Bonyad-e Shahid* was to convince the martyrs' widows to remarry, which the author refused to do.

2.3. At the end of 1996 one of the leaders of the *Bonyad-e Shahid*, the high-ranking Ayatollah Rahimian, finally forced the author to marry him by threatening to harm her and her children, the younger of whom is handicapped. The Ayatollah was a powerful man with the law on his side. The author claims that she was forced into a so-called *sighe* or *mutah* marriage, which is a short-term marriage, in the present case stipulated for a period of one and a half years, and is recognized legally only by Shia Muslims. The author was not expected to live with her *sighe* husband, but to be at his disposal for sexual services whenever required.

2.4. In 1997, the author met and fell in love with a Christian man. The two met in secret, since Muslim women are not allowed to have

---

1. Article 3 of the Convention Against Torture states: "No State Party shall expel, return ("refouler") or extradite a person to another State where there are substantial grounds for believing that he would be in danger of being subjected to torture."

relationships with Christians. One night, when the author could not find a taxi, the man drove her home in his car. At a roadblock they were stopped by the Pasdaran (Iranian Revolutionary Guards), who searched the car. When it became clear that the man was Christian and the author a martyr's widow, both were taken into custody at Ozghol police station in the Lavison district of Tehran. According to the author, she has not seen the man since, but claims that since her arrival in Sweden she has learned that he confessed under torture to adultery and was imprisoned and sentenced to death by stoning.

2.5. The author says that she was harshly questioned by the Zeinab sisters, the female equivalents of the Pasdaran who investigate women suspected of "un-Islamic behaviour", and was informed that her case had been transmitted to the Revolutionary Court. When it was discovered that the author was not only a martyr's widow but also the *sighe* wife of a powerful ayatollah, the Pasdaran contacted him. The author was taken to the ayatollah's home where she was severely beaten by him for five or six hours. After two days the author was allowed to leave and the ayatollah used his influence to stop the case being sent to the Revolutionary Court.

2.6. The author states that prior to these events she had, after certain difficulties obtained a visa to visit her sister-in-law in Sweden. The trip was to take place the day after she left the home of the ayatollah. According to the information submitted, the author had planned to continue from Sweden to Canada where she and her lover hoped to be able to emigrate since he had family there, including a son. She left Iran with her younger son on a valid passport and the visa previously obtained, without difficulty.

2.7. The author and her son arrived in Sweden on 23 December 1997 and applied for asylum on 29 December 1997. The Swedish Immigration Board rejected the author's asylum claim on 13 July 1998. On 29 October 1999, the Aliens Appeal Board dismissed her appeal.

2.8. The author submits that since her departure from Iran she has been sentenced to death by stoning for adultery. Her sister-in-law in Sweden has been contacted by the ayatollah who told her that the author had been convicted. She was also told that the authorities had found films and photographs of the couple in the Christian man's apartment, which had been used as evidence.

2.9. The author draws the attention of the Committee to a report from the Swedish Embassy in Iran which states that chapter I of the Iranian *hudud* law "deals with adultery, including whoring, and incest, satisfactory evidence of which is a confession repeated four times or testimony by four righteous men with the alternative of three men and two women, all of whom must be eyewitnesses. Capital punishment follows in cases of incest and other specified cases, *e.g.* when the adulterer is a non-Muslim and the abused a Muslim woman. Stoning is called for when the adulterer is married". The report further underlines that even if these strict rules of evidence are not met, the author can still be sentenced to death under the criminal law, where the rules of evidence are more flexible. * * *

4.2. As to the merits of the communication, the State party explains that when determining whether article 3 of the Convention applies, the following considerations are relevant; (a) the general situation of human rights in the receiving country, although the existence of a consistent pattern of gross, flagrant or mass violations of human rights is not in itself determinative; and (b) the personal risk of the individual concerned of being subjected to torture in the country to which he/she would be returned.

4.3. The State party is aware of human rights violations taking place in Iran, including extrajudicial and summary executions, disappearances, as well as widespread use of torture and other degrading treatment.

4.4. As regards its assessment of whether or not the author would be personally at risk of being subjected to torture if returned to Iran, the State party draws the attention of the Committee to the fact that several of the provisions of the Swedish Aliens Act reflect the same principle as the one laid down in article 3, paragraph 1 of the Convention. The State party recalls the jurisprudence of the Committee according to which, for the purposes of article 3, the individual concerned must face a foreseeable, real and personal risk of being tortured in the country to which he or she is returned. The State party further refers to the Committee's general comment on the implementation of article 3 of the Convention which states that the risk of torture must be assessed on grounds that go beyond mere theory or suspicion, although the risk does not have to meet the test of being highly probable. * * *

4.6. In its decision of 13 July 1998, the Swedish Immigration Board noted that apart from giving the names of her *sighe* husband and her Christian friend, the author had in several respects failed to submit verifiable information such as telephone numbers, addresses and names of her Christian friend's family members. The Immigration Board found it unlikely that the author claimed to have no knowledge of her Christian friend's exact home address and noted in this context that the author did not even want to submit her own home address in Iran. * * *

4.8. Finally, the Immigration Board questioned the credibility of the author's account of her marriage to the ayatollah, her relationship with the Christian man and the problems that had emerged as a result of it. * * *

4.10. In addition to the decisions of the Immigration Board and the Aliens Appeal Board, the State party refers to the UNHCR Handbook on Procedures and Criteria for Determining Refugee Status, according to which "the applicant should: (i) (t)ell the truth and assist the examiner to the full in establishing the facts of his case, [and] (ii) (m)ake an effort to support his statements by any available evidence and give a satisfactory explanation for any lack of evidence. If necessary he must make an effort to procure additional evidence". According to the UNHCR Handbook, the applicant should be given the benefit of the doubt, but only when all available evidence has been obtained and checked and when the examiner is satisfied as to the applicant's general credibility.

4.11. In the present case, the State party first reminds the Committee that the author has refused to provide verifiable information and that her reasons for doing so, *i.e.* that she was forbidden by her friend to do so and that new tenants are now occupying her apartment in Tehran, are not plausible.

4.12. Second * * * the State party notes that although the author claims that the authorities in Iran are in possession of a film showing her last meeting with her friend, no additional information has been provided by the author on this issue.

4.13. A third reason for doubting the author's credibility is that the author has not submitted any judgement or other evidence to support her claim that she has been sentenced for adultery by a Revolutionary Court. In addition, the author has not given any explanation as to why her sister-in-law was not able to obtain a copy of the Revolutionary Court's judgement when she visited Iran. Further, the State party notes that according to information available to it, the Revolutionary Courts in Iran have jurisdiction over political and religious crimes, but not over crimes such as adultery. *Hudud* crimes, *i.e.* crimes against God, including adultery, are dealt with by ordinary courts.

4.14. The State party further draws to the attention of the Committee that the author left Tehran without any problems only a few days after the incident which allegedly led to her detention, which would indicate that she was of no interest to the Iranian authorities at the moment of her departure. * * *

4.15. The State party also draws the Committee's attention to the fact that the author has not cited any medical report in support of her statement that she was severely beaten by Ayatollah Rahimian only a few days before her arrival in Sweden. In addition, according to information received by the State party, the head of the *Bonyad-e Shahid* was, until April 1999, Hojatolleslam Mohammad Rahimian, but he does not hold the title of ayatollah. * * *

4.17. On the basis of the above, the State party maintains that the author's credibility can be questioned, that she has not presented any evidence in support of her claim and that she should therefore not be given the benefit of the doubt. In conclusion, the State party considers that the enforcement of the expulsion order to Iran would, under the present circumstances, not constitute a violation of article 3 of the Convention.

5.1. In her submissions dated 4 February and 6 March 2000, counsel disputes the arguments of the State party regarding the failure of the author to submit written evidence. Counsel states that the author has provided the only written evidence she could possibly obtain, *i.e.* her identity papers and documentation showing that she is the widow of a martyr. Counsel states that the ayatollah conducted the *sighe* or *mutah* wedding himself with no witnesses or written contract. As to her failure to provide the immigration authorities with a written court verdict, counsel submits that the author only has second-hand information about the verdict, as it was passed after her departure from Iran. She cannot, therefore, submit a written verdict. Counsel further disputes that the author's sister-in-law should have been able to obtain a copy of the verdict while visiting Iran. She further states that the author's sister-in-law long ago ended all contacts with the author because she strongly resents the fact that the author has had a relationship with any man after the death of her husband.

5.2. Counsel acknowledges that crimes such as adultery are handled by ordinary courts. However, she draws the attention of the Committee to the fact that the jurisdictional rules are not as strict in Iran as for example in the State party and that the prosecuting judge can choose the court. In addition, for a martyr's widow to ride alone with a Christian man in his car would probably fall under the heading of "un-islamic behaviour" and as such come under the jurisdiction of the Revolutionary Court. Even if this were not the case, counsel reminds the Committee that the author has only been informed that she has been sentenced to death by stoning by a court. Not being a lawyer, and in view of what she was told during her interrogation by the Zeinab sisters, the author assumes that the sentence was handed down by the Revolutionary Court and this assumption should not be taken as a reason for questioning the general veracity of her claim.

5.3. Counsel states that the author has given credible explanations for not being able or not wishing to provide the Swedish authorities with certain addresses and telephone numbers. * * *

5.4. Counsel underlines that the fact that the Swedish authorities do not find the author's explanations credible is a result of speculation based on the supposition that all people behave and think according to Swedish or Western standards. The authorities do not take into account the prevailing cautiousness in Iran with respect to giving personal information, particularly to public officials. * * *

5.6. Counsel notes that the State party observes that the author has not cited any medical certificate attesting to injuries resulting from the beatings she was subjected to by her *sighe* husband. Counsel reminds the Committee that the author left Iran the following day and that her main preoccupation was to arrive safely in Sweden. Counsel further states that most Iranian women are used to violence by men and they do not or cannot expect the legal system to protect them, despite the positive changes which have recently taken place in Iran in this respect. As an example, counsel states that an Iranian woman wishing to report a rape must be examined by the courts' own doctors as certificates by general doctors are not accepted by courts. * * *

5.8. Counsel notes that the State party has confirmed that the author's *sighe* husband was the head of the *Bonyad-e Shahid*, which should support the author's claim; he was generally referred to as "Ayatollah", even though his title was Hojatolleslam. Counsel reminds the Committee that there are only some 10 real ayatollahs in Iran. The great majority of mullahs are of the rank of hojatolleslam. However, mullahs who have gained power, particularly political power, are often referred to as Ayatollah out of courtesy, an illustrative example being Ayatollah Khamenei whose office demanded the rank of an ayatollah but who was in fact only hojatolleslam when he was appointed.

5.9. With reference to the State party's argument that the author left Iran without difficulty, counsel points out that this is consistent with the author's version of the events leading to her flight. She has maintained that at the time of her departure she was not yet of interest to the Iranian authorities since her *sighe* husband had suppressed the Pasdaran report to the Revolutionary Court. * * *

5.12. Counsel further encloses a letter dated 27 December 1999 from the leading Swedish expert on Islam, Professor Jan Hjärpe, who confirms the author's account concerning the institution of *sighe* or *mutah* marriages and the legal sanctions provided for in cases of adultery.

5.13. Counsel draws the attention of the Committee to the fact that the immigration authorities in examining the author's case have not considered the situation of women in Iran, existing legislation and its application, or the values of the Iranian society. Counsel states that the argumentation of the authorities, based almost exclusively on the author's failure to submit certain verifiable information, seems to be a pretext for refusing the author's application. In conclusion, counsel submits that according to the information provided by the author, there exist substantial grounds to believe that the author would be subjected to torture if returned to Iran and that the author has provided reasonable explanations for why she has not been able to or not wished to furnish certain details. * * *

7.6. With reference to the Committee's request for additional information, counsel states that the author's older son, born in 1980, tried to seek asylum in Sweden from Denmark in March 2000. In accordance with the Dublin Convention, after a short interview, he was sent back to Denmark where he is still waiting to be interrogated by Danish immigration authorities. Since his case had not yet been examined by the Danish authorities, counsel requested Amnesty International to interview him.

7.7. The records of the interview confirm statements made by the author regarding her *sighe* marriage and of her being called to the

Bonyad-e Shahid office several times a week. The son also states that when his mother left she had told him that he had to leave school and hide with close relatives of hers in Baghistan. He received private teaching to become a veterinary surgeon and subsequently enrolled in University. On 25 January 2000 he was summoned to the university information office by the intelligence service, Harasar, from where two men took him to the *Bonyad-e Shahid* office in Tehran where he was detained, interrogated, threatened and beaten. He claims that the interrogators wanted to know his mother's whereabouts and that they threatened to keep him and beat him until his mother came "crawling on all fours" and then they would "carry out her sentence". The author's son claims that it was during the interrogation that he fully realized his mother's situation, although he had not spoken to her since she left the country.

7.8. In conclusion, counsel maintains that although it has not been possible to obtain direct written evidence, for the reasons given above, the chain of circumstantial evidence is of such a nature that there can be no reason to doubt the author's credibility. Reference is further made to a recent judgement of the European Court of Human Rights dated 11 July 2000, regarding an Iranian woman asylum-seeker who allegedly had committed adultery and who feared death by stoning, whipping or flogging if returned. As in the case of the author no written evidence existed in the form of a court judgement, but the Court stated that it is not persuaded that the situation in the applicant's country of origin has evolved to the extent that adulterous behaviour is no longer considered a reprehensible affront to Islamic law. It has taken judicial notice of recent surveys of the current situation in Iran and notes that punishment of adultery by stoning still remains on the statute book and may be resorted to by authorities.[1] The Court ruled that to expel the applicant would be a violation of the European Convention for the Protection of Human Rights and Fundamental Freedoms.

7.9. The State party made additional submissions on 19 September and 19 October 2000. With reference to the Committee's request for additional information, the State party reiterates its view that the burden is on the author to present an arguable case. It maintains that the author has not given any evidence in support of her claim and therefore there are serious reasons to doubt the veracity of those claims. * * *

8.2. The issue before the Committee is whether the forced return of the author to the Islamic Republic of Iran would violate the obligation of Sweden under article 3 of the Convention not to expel or to return a person to another State where there are substantial grounds for believing that he or she would be in danger of being subjected to torture. * * *

8.4. From the information submitted by the author, the Committee notes that she is the widow of a martyr and as such supported and supervised by the *Bonyad-e Shahid* Committee of Martyrs. It is also noted

---

1. *Jabari v. Turkey* (para. 40), European Court of Human Rights, 11 July 2000.

that the author claims that she was forced into a *sighe* or *mutah* marriage and to have committed and been sentenced to stoning for adultery. Although treating the recent testimony of the author's son, seeking asylum in Denmark, with utmost caution, the Committee is nevertheless of the view that the information given further corroborates the account given by the author.

8.5. The Committee notes that the State party questions the author's credibility primarily because of her failure to submit verifiable information and refers in this context to international standards, *i.e.* the UNHCR Handbook on Procedures and Criteria for Determining Refugee Status, according to which an asylum-seeker has an obligation to make an effort to support his/her statements by any available evidence and to give a satisfactory explanation for any lack of evidence.

8.6. The Committee draws the attention of the parties to its general comment on the implementation of article 3 of the Convention in the context of article 22, adopted on 21 November 1997, according to which the burden to present an arguable case is on the author of a communication. The Committee notes the State party's position that the author has not fulfilled her obligation to submit the verifiable information that would enable her to enjoy the benefit of the doubt. However, the Committee is of the view that the author has submitted sufficient details regarding her *sighe* or *mutah* marriage and alleged arrest, such as names of persons, their positions, dates, addresses, name of police station, *etc.*, that could have, and to a certain extent have been, verified by the Swedish immigration authorities, to shift the burden of proof. In this context the Committee is of the view that the State party has not made sufficient efforts to determine whether there are substantial grounds for believing that the author would be in danger of being subjected to torture.

8.7. The State party does not dispute that gross, flagrant or mass violations of human rights have been committed in Iran. The Committee notes, *inter alia*, the report of the Special Representative of the Commission on Human Rights on the situation of human rights in Iran (E/CN.4/2000/35) of 18 January 2000, which indicates that although significant progress is being made in Iran with regard to the status of women in sectors like education and training, "little progress is being made with regard to remaining systematic barriers to equality" and for "the removal of patriarchal attitudes in society". It is further noted that the report, and numerous reports of non-governmental organizations, confirm that married women have recently been sentenced to death by stoning for adultery.

9. Considering that the author's account of events is consistent with the Committee's knowledge about the present human rights situation in Iran, and that the author has given plausible explanations for her failure or inability to provide certain details which might have been of relevance to the case, the Committee is of the view that, in the

prevailing circumstances, the State party has an obligation, in accordance with article 3 of the Convention, to refrain from forcibly returning the author to Iran or to any other country where she runs a risk of being expelled or returned to Iran. * * *

Notes and Questions on the Individual Petition Mechanism

1. *Burden of proof.* In *A.S. v. Sweden*, the Committee determined that the author had presented sufficient evidence to meet her burden of showing there were substantial grounds for believing she would be subjected to torture upon being returned to Iran. It was Sweden's position that the evidence presented by the author was unverifiable, and therefore insufficient to meet her burden. The Committee disagreed, finding that Sweden should have tried to determine whether the author's claims could be substantiated. Where an Article 3 case is based primarily on the oral testimony of an author, should the burden shift so easily to the government? Who is in a better position to substantiate the testimony of an author in these cases, the author or the government? How should the particular circumstances in which an Article 3 case arises affect your answers to these questions?

2. *Judicial review by an international treaty body.* From the case excerpted above, one can see how the Committee can act as a kind of supra-national court that sits in judgment of the highest national courts. Many states are uncomfortable with giving a body of this nature this kind of power. Can such a body adequately review and consider questions of fact that are thoroughly briefed and considered through the presentation of evidence in a lower court? What about questions of law? Does the Committee in *A.S. v. Sweden* make a distinction between questions of fact and those of law?

Judicial review by an international adjudicatory body gives rise to recurring questions. For example, would adoption of standards used by international judicial tribunals (as opposed to the less rigorous standards used by treaty bodies) make individual-state complaint mechanisms under UN human rights treaties more or less effective? *See generally* Mojtaba Kazazi, Burden of Proof and Related Issues: A Study on Evidence Before International Tribunals (1996); Fact-Finding by International Tribunals (Richard Lillich ed., 1992); D. Sandifer, Evidence Before International Tribunals (1975).

Viewed in the context of the membership of treaty bodies, these concerns become particularly acute. Treaty bodies are made up of independent experts nominated and elected by governments but not all experts are truly "independent." They are nominated for membership by governments; therefore, most have a certain ideology, philosophy, or legal bias that has been, in a sense, pre-approved by the nominating state. Some are chosen strictly on the basis of their ability to forward a particular state's political agenda within the Committee's work. Although there is a certain level of accountability created by regular elections and limited terms of membership, some see the inherently political nature of Committee membership as a hindrance to the effective functioning of the treaty body mechanism. *See* Craig Scott, *Bodies of Knowledge: A Diversity Promotion Role for the UN High Commissioner for Human Rights, in* THE FUTURE OF UN HUMAN RIGHTS TREATY MONITORING 403 (Philip Alston & J. Crawford eds., 2000)(discussing the diversity of expertise and experience among different committees' membership).

3. *The cultural challenges of international adjudication.* Note that the author in *A.S. v. Sweden* did not deny either (a) being part of a *sighe* or *mutah* marriage to a Ayatollah Rahimian, or (b) engaging in an "adulterous" affair. Although the author claims that she was forced into the marriage, in your view, did she present sufficient evidence to establish this fact? Assuming she did not, and she entered into this marriage of her own free will, under Iranian law, she was guilty of adultery, the punishment for which is death by stoning. Of course, the implicit assumption underlying this decision is that death by stoning constitutes torture under the Convention. Islamic law establishes punishments that many consider to be violations of basic human rights. Nevertheless, some Islamic states continue to implement these punishments and maintain that international human rights standards must account for varied cultural and religious practices. In paragraph 2.5 above, the Committee notes that the author was questioned by the Zeinab sisters, "who investigate women suspected of 'un-Islamic behaviour'." Does the Committee's use of quotation marks around the phrase "un-Islamic behaviour" reflect a bias in its consideration of this case?

The debate over cultural and religious relativism in human rights is a serious one, particularly after 9/11, the U.S-proclaimed global war on terror, and the drive to promote democracy around the world. Clearly the development of democratic institutions must account for local cultural and religious traditions, but how does one account for local traditions that are in conflict with perceptions of human rights in western democracies? For democracy and human rights advocates, some cases are fairly straightforward—punishing thieves with amputation, for instance. But how does one reconcile the conflict between the manner in which Islamic inheritance law treats women and generally "accepted" principles of non-discrimination? *See generally* ABDULLAHI AHMED AN–NA'IM, TOWARD AN ISLAMIC REFORMATION: CIVIL LIBERTIES, HUMAN RIGHTS, AND INTERNATIONAL LAW (1990).

4. *U.S. interpretation of the CAT.* While the United States has not accepted the jurisdiction of the Committee Against Torture to hear individual petitions, it has implemented its obligation under article 3 through regulations that prohibit the return of an individual to a state where it is more likely than not he or she will be tortured. *See* U.S. DEPT. OF STATE, Second Periodic Report to the Committee Against Torture, ¶¶ 30–43 (2005); Initial Report to the Committee Against Torture,

paras. 156–177. In ratifying the Convention Against Torture, the United States submitted a general understanding whereby it "does not consider this Convention to restrict or prohibit the United States from applying the death penalty consistent with the Fifth, Eighth and/or Fourteenth Amendments to the Constitution of the United States. . . ." Given its narrow understanding of the scope of the CAT (*e.g.*, not including the death penalty), would the United States have an obligation not to return a person like A.S. to Iran? Would a different mode of execution make a difference in your analysis? *See generally* AMNESTY INTERNATIONAL, CONSTITUTIONAL PROHIBITIONS ON THE DEATH PENALTY (1999); AMNESTY INTERNATIONAL, INTERNATIONAL STANDARDS ON THE DEATH PENALTY (1998); WILLIAM A. SCHABAS, THE DEATH PENALTY AS CRUEL TREATMENT AND TORTURE (1996).

5. *The challenges of investigation.* Place yourself in the position of counsel for the petitioner in *A.S. v. Sweden.* How do you go about assembling evidence to support the information provided to the Swedish immigration authorities? How can non-governmental organizations be used for this purpose? How do you represent your client without jeopardizing the safety of her friends and family in Iran? For information related to the investigation of human rights claims, see OFFICE OF THE HIGH COMMISSIONER FOR HUMAN RIGHTS, ISTANBUL PROTOCOL: MANUAL ON THE EFFECTIVE INVESTIGATION AND DOCUMENTATION OF TORTURE AND OTHER CRUEL, INHUMAN OR DEGRADING TREATMENT OR PUNISHMENT, U.N. Sales No. E.01.-XIV.1 (1999); OFFICE OF THE HIGH COMMISSIONER FOR HUMAN RIGHTS, TRAINING MANUAL ON HUMAN RIGHTS MONITORING, U.N. Sales No. E.01.-XIV.2 (2001); OFFICE OF THE HIGH COMMISSIONER FOR HUMAN RIGHTS, HUMAN RIGHTS IN THE ADMINISTRATION OF JUSTICE: A MANUAL ON HUMAN RIGHTS FOR JUDGES, PROSECUTORS, AND LAWYERS, U.N. Sales No. E.02.XIV.3 (2003); LAWYERS COMMITTEE FOR HUMAN RIGHTS, WHAT IS A FAIR TRIAL? A BASIC GUIDE TO LEGAL STANDARDS AND PRACTICE (2000); ASIAN HUMAN RIGHTS COMMISSION, HUMAN RIGHTS MONITORING AND FACT-FINDING (2000); AMNESTY INTERNATIONAL, UKWELI: MONITORING AND REPORTING HUMAN RIGHTS VIOLATIONS IN AFRICA. A HANDBOOK FOR COMMUNITY ACTIVISTS (2002).

6. *The Committee on Economic, Social and Cultural Rights.* When adopted, the International Covenant on Economic, Social and Cultural Rights (IESCR) did not include an individual-state complaint mechanism. The Committee on Economic, Social and Cultural Rights had only the power to consider state reports under the Covenant. Unlike the obligations assumed under the International Covenant on Civil and Political Rights, which are of immediate impact, the IESCR requires the "progressive realization of" economic, social, and cultural rights. Notwithstanding the vagaries of this standard, many governments and NGOs have been advocating the negotiation and adoption of an Optional Protocol that would give the Committee the power to consider individual-state petitions. In response, a working group of the Commission on Human Rights was established to "consider options" regarding the elaboration of an optional protocol. After several sessions of the working group, the newly created Human Rights Council expanded the

mandate of the working group and instructed it to actually come up with an Optional Protocol. Eventually, in 2008, the Working Group agreed on an Optional Protocol to be presented to the Human Rights Council for its consideration. *See UN Human Rights Council, Report of the Open–Ended Working Group on an Optional Protocol to the International Covenant on Economic, Social and Cultural Rights on its fifth session*, Annex I, U.N. Doc. A/HRC/8/7 (May 23, 2008). The Optional Protocol is primarily procedural in nature, giving the Committee on Economic, Social and Cultural Rights the authority to consider individual-state petitions. How would you envision such an individual-state petition mechanism functioning in the absence of immediate obligations?

Through adopting general comments, the Committee on Economic, Social and Cultural Rights has articulated its view of the content, as well as the means to achieve progressive realization, of the rights included in the IESCR. For instance, in General Comment 12, the Committee stated that the "right to adequate food, like any other human right, imposes three types of obligations on States parties [to the IESCR]: the obligation to *respect*, to *protect* and to *fulfill*. In turn, the obligation to *fulfill* incorporates both an obligation to *facilitate* and an obligation to *provide*." *UN Econ. & Soc. Council, Substantive Issues Arising in the Implementation of the International Covenant on Economic, Social, and Cultural Rights*, General Comment 12, ¶ 15, U.N. Doc. No. E/C.12/199/5. The Committee went on to state that any person or group "who is a victim of the violation of the right to adequate food should have access to effective judicial or other appropriate remedies at both national and international levels . . . [and] victims of such violations are entitled to adequate reparation. . . ." *Id.* at ¶ 32.

For some states, General Comment 12 was controversial. Many argue that the Committee glosses over the important caveat in the IESCR that all rights established there are to be "progressively realized." Through the Committee's attempt to define the right to adequate food as an obligation to respect, to protect and to fulfill, as well as to make such a right justiciable, some states party to the IESCR argue that the Committee is creating obligations that governments did not undertake upon ratifying the treaty. Moreover, critics point to the General Comment's lack of citation to the travaux preparatoires of the IESCR, the language of the treaty, or to state practice under the treaty—standard tools of treaty interpretation. Instead, the Committee arrives at conclusions of law as if they were widely accepted, without providing adequate support for its interpretations. Others argue, however, that the Committee was established as the authoritative interpretive body for the IESCR, and—as a body of experts—is authorized to provide guidance to states in the implementation of the obligations they assumed under the treaty.

General Comment 12 shows the difficulty of creating an individual-state complaint mechanism for the IESCR. For example, how will the Committee apply agreed standards to allegations of violations of a right to adequate food against countries in different stages of development?

Should a different standard be applied to Bangladesh than would be applied to Canada? If so, where in the text of the Covenant would you find support for this position? One solution proposed to this problem is to require the Committee to draft and apply benchmarks for the progressive realization of economic, social, and cultural rights. Would this satisfy the concerns of skeptics, or would it raise a different set of problems?

Practicum

In September 1999, Moscow was rocked by several explosions, killing numerous residents. First, a bomb went off in a shopping arcade near the Kremlin, killing one and injuring forty. Then, two bombs exploded in multi-story apartment buildings, killing hundreds of sleeping residents.

President Boris Yeltsin blamed terrorists who, he claimed, had declared war on the Russian people. "The bandits are operating secretly like wild animals which creep around by night, killing people who are sleeping, planting bombs in densely-populated areas, where there are many children and women and old people," he said. "They are afraid to claim responsibility for this, concealing their names and faces, but we already know on whose conscience these evil acts lie." After holding an emergency meeting with senior ministers and the Moscow Mayor, Yuri Luzhkov, he ordered heightened security in a number of cities and at sensitive installations around Russia.

Although he denied any responsibility for these acts, a Chechen warlord, Shamil Basaylev (who was suspected of fomenting rebellion in Dagestan as well as in Chechnya), was largely believed by Russian authorities to be behind the bombings. Heightened security led to large-scale repression of civil liberties throughout Moscow immediately after the explosions. People who looked and spoke like they were from the Caucuses or Central Asia—where Chechnya and Dagestan are located—were harassed, arrested and abused by police on a routine basis.

Vukovich is a 35 year-old Muslim, born in Tashkent, Uzbekistan, to an ethnic-Uzbek mother and an ethnic-Russian father. Because he only recently moved to Moscow from Uzbekistan, he had a temporary residence permit and no Russian Federation passport. On October 1, 1999, he was late for work, and while he was hurrying to catch a bus, he was stopped by two police officers, asked for his papers, and then immediately arrested.

Upon his arrest, Vukovich was not informed of the charges on which he had been detained. In fact, he was held for more than three weeks in a Moscow jail without any indication of the crime for which he was being detained. He was both verbally and physically abused by police during lengthy interrogations, locked in a small cell with ten other prisoners, denied access to a toilet, and received barely edible food. Vukovich's confinement caused him both physical and emotional suffering. In addition, he lost his job and his apartment based on his disappearance. He was released without being charged with a crime.

Ivanova is a 28 year-old Russian journalist who writes for a Moscow daily newspaper. The paper has been acclaimed by many as aggressive and free-thinking, and Ivanova in particular has proved to be an irritant to Russian authorities, especially on matters related to the treatment of minorities and so-called "break-away republics."

A mutual friend of Ivanova and Vukovich informed Ivanova of Vukovich's treatment at the hands of the Moscow police immediately after he was released from jail. The two met, and Ivanova wrote a stinging editorial criticizing everyone from President Yeltsin to Mayor Luzhkov to the police officers who imprisoned Vukovich. In the article, she also criticized the Russian government for what she called its "illegal occupation" of Chechnya and Dagestan. In one noteworthy sentence, she wrote "I am not surprised that Islamic fundamentalists were bombing targets in Moscow. If I were in their position, I too, might take such measures against Russians in the fight to liberate my people."

After the article was published, Ivanova's newspaper was shut down, and Ivanova was arrested. She was not mistreated, but she was charged with violating an old, Soviet-era criminal statute which made unlawful the publication of "any statement which may cause damage to the State, or which may lead to racial intolerance." She was convicted and sentenced to 5 years in prison—the judge did not indicate which clause of the statute she was found to have violated.

Both Vukovich and Ivanova filed legal actions against the government in the Russian courts, but neither was successful. In fact, after several years of litigation, both left the country as a result of harassment and a continuing fear for their own safety.

Vukovich and Ivanova have each filed individual petitions against the Russian Federation in the UN Human Rights Committee, based on allegations of unlawful harassment and abuse by Russian authorities after the bombings in Moscow. Each alleges that the Russian Federation violated its obligations under the International Covenant on Civil and Political Rights.

You represent one of the parties above—Vukovich, Ivanova, or the Russian Federation for purposes of filing a complaint before the UN Human Rights Committee. On behalf of Vuckovich or Ivanova, what articles would you allege have been violated? What arguments would you marshal in support of your claims? On behalf of the Russian Federation, how would you argue that you have not violated your obligations under the ICCPR?

B. TREATY–BASED MECHANISMS: STATE REPORTS

INTERNATIONAL COVENANT ON CIVIL AND POLITICAL RIGHTS

G.A. Res. 22200 A (XXI) (16 December 1966), *entered into force* 23 March 1976

Article 40

1. The States Parties to the present Covenant undertake to submit reports on the measures they have adopted which give effect to the rights recognized herein and on the progress made in the enjoyment of those rights:

(a) Within one year of the entry into force of the present Covenant for the States Parties concerned;

(b) Thereafter whenever the Committee so requests.

2. All reports shall be submitted to the Secretary–General of the United Nations, who shall transmit them to the Committee for consideration. Reports shall indicate the factors and difficulties, if any, affecting the implementation of the present Covenant.

3. The Secretary–General of the United Nations may, after consultation with the Committee, transmit to the specialized agencies concerned copies of such parts of the reports as may fall within their field of competence.

4. The Committee shall study the reports submitted by the States Parties to the present Covenant. It shall transmit its reports, and such general comments as it may consider appropriate, to the States Parties. The Committee may also transmit to the Economic and Social Council these comments along with the copies of the reports it has received from States Parties to the present Covenant.

5. The States Parties to the present Covenant may submit to the Committee observations on any comments that may be made in accordance with paragraph 4 of this article.

INITIAL REPORT OF THE UNITED STATES TO THE HUMAN RIGHTS COMMITTEE

U.N. Doc. CCPR/C/81/Add.4 (Aug. 24, 1994)

Article 7—Freedom from torture, or cruel, inhuman or degrading treatment or punishment

149. Torture. U.S. law prohibits torture at both the federal and state levels. As this report is being prepared, the U.S. is completing the process of ratifying the UN Convention against Torture and Other Cruel, Inhuman or Degrading Treatment or Punishment. Torture has

always been prohibited by the Eighth Amendment to the U.S. Constitution. As a consequence, torture is unlawful in every jurisdiction of the United States, and [e]xcessive bail shall not be required, nor excessive fines imposed, nor cruel and unusual punishments inflicted. U.S. Constitution, Amendment VIII.

150.   Cruel, inhuman or degrading treatment or punishment. The Eighth Amendment to the U.S. Constitution (applicable to actions of the federal government) and the Fourteenth Amendment (making the Eighth Amendment applicable to the states) prohibit cruel and unusual punishment. Cruel and unusual punishments include uncivilized and inhuman punishments, punishments that fail to comport with human dignity, and punishments that include physical suffering. *Furman v. Georgia*, 408 U.S. 238 (1972). Since the prohibition of cruel, inhuman or degrading treatment or punishment and the promotion of humane treatment consistent with human dignity are intertwined, the discussion in this section relates also to paragraph 1 of article 10 [which provides that "All persons deprived of their liberty shall be treated with humanity and with respect for the inherent dignity of the human person."]. Because the scope of the constitutional protections differs from the provisions of article 7, the U.S. conditioned its ratification upon a reservation discussed below.

151.   Basic rights of prisoners. The U.S. Supreme Court has applied the constitutional prohibition against cruel and unusual punishment not only to the punishments provided for by statute or imposed by a court after a criminal conviction, but also to prison conditions and treatment to which a prisoner is subjected during the prisoner's period of incarceration. *See Estelle v. Gamble*, 429 U.S. 97 (1976). Prisoners may not be denied an "identifiable human need such as food, warmth, or exercise." *Rhodes v. Chapman*, 452 U.S. 337 (1981). Accordingly, prisoners must be provided "nutritionally adequate food, prepared and served under conditions which do not present an immediate danger to the health and well being of the inmates who consume it." Ramos v. Lamm, 639 F.2d 559 (10th Cir. 1980), *cert. denied*, 450 U.S. 1041 (1981). Prisoners must also be provided medical care, although an inadvertent failure to provide medical care does not rise to the level of a constitutional violation. Rather, it is prison officials' "deliberate indifference to a prisoner's serious illness or injury" that constitutes cruel and unusual punishment. *Estelle v. Gamble*, 429 U.S. 97 (1976). Prison officials have a duty to protect prisoners from violence inflicted by fellow prisoners. *Hudson v. Palmer*, 468 U.S. 517 (1984). Because prisons are by definition dangerous places, prison administrators are responsible to victims only if they had prior knowledge of imminent harm. Finally, prisoners must not be subject to excessive use of force. Force may be applied "in a good faith effort to maintain or restore discipline", but may not be used "maliciously and sadistically to cause harm". *Whitley v. Albers*, 475 U.S. 312, 320–21 (1986). It does not matter whether the force results in serious injury. *Hudson v. McMillian*, 112 S.Ct. 995 (1992).

152. The Department of Justice can criminally prosecute any prison official who wilfully causes a convicted prisoner to be subjected to cruel and unusual punishment under 18 U.S.C. section 241 and/or section 242. In addition, certain federal and state statutes call for affirmative protection of the interests of prisoners. For example, 18 U.S.C. section 4042 imposes a duty upon the Attorney General to provide suitable quarters and provide for the safekeeping, care, and subsistence of all persons charged with or convicted of offences against the United States, and to provide for the protection, instruction, and discipline of such persons.

153. The Attorney General may also initiate civil actions under the Civil Rights of Institutionalized Persons Act when there is reason to believe that a person, acting on behalf of a state or locality, has subjected institutionalized persons * * * to "egregious or flagrant conditions which deprive such persons of any rights, privileges or immunities secured or protected by the Constitution or laws of the United States causing such persons to suffer grievous harm." 42 U.S.C. section 1997a.

154. Prisoners who have been subjected to cruel and unusual punishment may file a civil suit to recover damages from the individuals who inflicted such punishment. * * *

155. <u>Solitary confinement and special security measures.</u> Convicted prisoners may be subjected to special security measures and segregation (*i.e.*, physical separation from the general prison population) only in unusual circumstances. Such measures may be employed for punitive reasons or as a means of maintaining the safety and security of inmates and staff in the institution. No conditions of confinement, including segregation, may violate the proscription of the Eighth Amendment, nor may they violate the prisoners' rights to due process and access to the courts under the Fifth and Fourteenth Amendments.

156. All correctional systems in the U.S. have codes of conduct that govern inmate behaviour, and all have systems for imposing sanctions when inmates violate this code. * * *

157. Segregation is one of the sanctions that may be imposed upon an inmate who, it has been determined, has violated the code of conduct. Before this sanction may be imposed, the inmate is entitled to due process protection emanating from the Fifth and Fourteenth Amendments of the Constitution and recognized by the Supreme Court in *Wolff v. McDonnell*, 418 U.S. 539 (1974). * * *

158. Inmates may also be separated from the general prisoner population as the result of a classification decision. Prison administrators may determine that, based on a host of factors, an inmate's presence in general population would pose a substantial threat of harm to him/herself or others and the inmate therefore must be removed. * * *

160. Segregation is not solitary confinement. The segregation unit in a prison separates, or segregates, certain prisoners from those who are in general population. Inmates in segregation are not permitted to

eat in the dining hall; rather, they are served in their cells. They are not permitted to report to their work assignments, nor are they permitted to attend school. They are permitted to exercise (though they may not be permitted to do so out of doors) and they are permitted to read and to correspond. Depending upon the reason for their segregation, they may be permitted to listen to the radio and watch television if available. Some rights and privileges may not be abridged by virtue of an inmate's placement in segregation, whatever the reason for such placement. First, they must be permitted to correspond with persons outside the prison in the same fashion as prisoners in general population. Second, they must be allowed visits with friends or relatives, and to make telephone calls. Inmates must also be permitted access to the law library, their legal papers, and their attorney. Finally, they must be given appropriate medical care, food, clothing, and other basic necessities.

161.   Inmates held in segregation have limited contact with other inmates and with staff, but under no circumstances will they be denied all human contact. For the duration of their stay in segregation, inmates are carefully monitored by medical and mental health personnel to ensure they do not suffer detrimental effects. * * *

176.   U.S. reservation. The extent of the constitutional provisions discussed above is arguably narrower in some respects than the scope of article 7. For example, the Human Rights Committee adopted the view that prolonged judicial proceedings in cases involving capital punishment might constitute cruel, inhuman or degrading treatment or punishment in contravention of this standard. The Committee has also indicated that the prohibition may extend to such other practices as corporal punishment and solitary confinement.

177.   As such proceedings and practices have repeatedly withstood judicial review of their constitutionality in the United States, it was determined to be appropriate for the United States to condition its acceptance of the United Nations Convention against Torture and Other Cruel, Inhuman or Degrading Treatment or Punishment on a formal reservation to the effect that the United States considers itself bound to the extent that "cruel, inhuman treatment or punishment" means the cruel and unusual treatment or punishment prohibited by the Fifth, Eighth and/or Fourteenth Amendments to the Constitution of the United States. For the same reasons, and to ensure uniformity of interpretation as to the obligations of the United States under the Covenant and the Torture Convention on this point, the United States took the following reservation to the Covenant:

> "The United States considers itself bound by Article 7 to the extent that 'cruel, inhuman or degrading treatment or punishment' means the cruel and unusual treatment or punishment prohibited by the Fifth, Eighth and/or Fourteenth Amendments to the Constitution of the United States." * * *

Article 10—Treatment of persons deprived of their liberty

259. <u>Humane treatment and respect</u>. As discussed in connection with article 7, the Fifth, Eighth and Fourteenth Amendments to the U.S. Constitution, as well as federal and state statutes, regulate the treatment and conditions of detention of persons deprived of their liberty by state action. In addition, as discussed below, at both the federal and state levels a number of mechanisms exist to ensure that, through enforcement of their constitutional and statutory rights, prisoners are treated with humanity and respect for their dignity, commensurate with their status.

260. In all criminal correctional systems, the policies and practices of prison staff are governed by official regulations. These regulations are based on U.S. and state constitutional requirements, and, with the exception of rules dealing exclusively with staff or security issues, are generally available to inmates through inmate libraries. Few if any systems' regulations comply with every provision of the United Nations Standard Minimum Rules for the Treatment of Prisoners and the Code of Conduct for Law Enforcement Officials, but most do substantially comply. For example, most U.S. department of corrections' regulations do not incorporate the United Nations standard that no male staff shall enter a women's institution unless accompanied by a woman. None the less, the important underlying issue of sexual abuse is addressed through staff training and through criminal statutes prohibiting such activity. For example, federal correctional officers are given training regarding appropriate behaviour towards inmates of the opposite sex, and 18 U.S.C. section 2243 provides that anyone who engages in a sexual act with a person in a federal prison may be subject to a fine and/or a term of imprisonment.

261. As evidenced by the many successful suits that have been brought to enforce detainees' rights, the actual practice of detention in the United States frequently does not meet constitutional standards. Overcrowding in county jails is a perpetual problem, especially as the federal government often must rely upon those jails for pretrial detention. When prison policies are, on their face, inconsistent with constitutional provisions, or when the conduct of staff does not comport with policy, prisoners generally can bring their complaints to the attention of prison administrators through internal grievance procedures. A prisoner can also file suit in the appropriate federal or state court. Additionally, there are less formal mechanisms of complaint, such as writing letters to government representatives or to private activists apprising them of inmate concerns. Inmates are also afforded liberal access to the media through both written correspondence (28 C.F.R. section 540.20 (C)) and in-person interviews. In many instances these informal mechanisms give rise to internal and outside investigations of prison conditions and procedures. * * *

276. Complaints. The Department of Justice receives and acts on complaints sent directly from both federal and state prisoners. Such letters are received regularly both by the Civil Rights Division and by the Federal Bureau of Investigation (FBI). All letters from prisoners are carefully reviewed to determine if they state a basis for a criminal investigation. Those which complain about conditions of confinement are referred to the Civil Rights Division's Special Litigation Section to determine if any civil action may be warranted pursuant to the Civil Rights of Institutionalized Persons Act. * * *

Pursuant to the Civil Rights of Institutionalized Persons Act, 42 U.S.C. section 1997e, the Attorney General has authority to investigate various public facilities where she believes that conditions are subjecting confined individuals to a pattern or practice of deprivations of their constitutional rights. Since the passage of the statute in 1980, some 150 institutions have been investigated.

281. Prosecutions. Abuses do sometimes occur in jails and prisons in the United States. The states can and do prosecute their abusive prison officials. In addition, the Department of Justice has conducted prosecutions in a variety of cases involving federal and state prison officials. * * *

282. Since October 1988, the Department of Justice has filed charges in approximately 126 cases of official misconduct. These cases involved approximately 180 police officers. About 15 of the cases in-volved officials violating the civil rights of a prisoner or person in jail; approximately 55 officials were involved in such cases.

283. Segregation of the accused from the convicted. A suspect detained pending trial is entitled to greater rights and privileges than convicted persons and may not be punished. To ensure these rights and privileges are provided, accused persons are, to the extent practicable, segregated from convicted persons. *United States v. Lovett*, 328 U.S. 303 (1946). Such separation is required by federal law, 18 U.S.C. section 3142, and many state laws contain similar provisions. Separation of federal detainees is accomplished by housing pretrial detainees in sepa-rate units within Metropolitan Correctional or Detention Centres, or in local jails, or in federal correctional institutions. *See* 28 C.F.R. section 551.104. When consistent with the security and good order of the correctional facility, and where it appears to present no danger to the detainee, a pretrial detainee, at the detainee's request, may be intermin-gled with convicted prisoners in order to participate in programmes. Most state and county corrections policies require separation of individ-uals based upon their conviction status, whenever practicable. When possible, pretrial detainees are separated from convicted offenders. Due to overcrowding in most correctional systems, the separation of pretrial and convicted offenders is not always possible due to space constraints. Moreover, in the military justice system, segregation of the accused from

the convicted cannot always be guaranteed in light of military exigencies.

284.   U.S. understanding. Because of the above and related concerns, the United States included in its instrument of ratification the following statement of understanding:

> "The United States understands the reference to 'exceptional circumstances' in paragraph 2(a) of Article 10 to permit the imprisonment of an accused person with convicted persons where appropriate in light of an individual's overall dangerousness, and to permit accused persons to waive their right to segregation from convicted persons." * * *

287.   Reform and rehabilitation. While there is no right under the U.S. Constitution to rehabilitation, *Coakley v. Murphy*, 884 F.2d 1218 (9th Cir. 1989), all prison systems have as one of their goals the improvement of prisoners to facilitate their successful reintegration into society. For example, the Federal Bureau of Prisons' mission is to protect society by confining offenders in the controlled environments of prisons and community-based facilities that are safe, humane, and appropriately secure, and which provide work and other self-improvement opportunities to assist offenders in becoming law-abiding citizens. Moreover, Bureau of Prisons regulations require virtually all BOP institutions to provide a range of academic, occupational, and leisure-time activities to allow inmates to improve their knowledge and skills. 28 C.F.R. section 544.80–544.83.

288.   While the extent of educational, vocational, and treatment programmes varies among prison systems, such programmes are an integral part of every correctional institution. * * * While not required by the Constitution, prisoners are usually compensated for their services, though the pay is modest. Correctional institutions employ prisoners in industry (manufacturing furniture and many other items), data processing, and maintenance and repair. Inmates with a low security classification may be released during the day to work on community projects such as maintaining state and federal parks and public roads. Some federal correctional institutions are located on the grounds of military bases and the inmates provide support services to the military such as lawn maintenance. Some correctional institutions allow private businesses to employ prisoners, but such arrangements are complicated as to appropriate compensation for the prisoners. *See Gilbreath v. Cutter Biological, Inc.*, 931 F.2d 1320 (9th Cir. 1991). * * *

291.   All prisons have education programmes and inmates are strongly encouraged to participate. Federal law requires the Bureau of Prisons to operate a mandatory functional literacy programme for inmates to ensure that inmates possess reading and mathematical skills equivalent to the eighth grade level. Further, non-English-speaking federal inmates must participate in an English as a second language programme until they also meet the literacy requirements. 18 U.S.C.

section 3624(f). In addition to basic educational programmes including the preparation for the Federal Education Development certificate, many prisons offer university courses by correspondence or by bringing college instructors to the prison. Staff encourage inmates to enroll in such programmes, and they assist inmates in exploring sources of funding. *See* e.g. 28 C.F.R. section 544.20–21. * * *

294.   In furtherance of the programmes described above and in order to protect the safety of prisoners and staff alike, prison administrators have found it useful to classify prisoners and house prisoners with others who share some important characteristics. For example, it would be dangerous to house young, inexperienced, non-violent offenders with older men who have spent a great deal of their lives in prison for the commission of violent, predatory crimes. Accordingly, prisoners are classified at a particular security level prior to their admission into a correctional institution. Classification decisions are based on age, prior criminal history, offence giving rise to the imprisonment, history of escape or violence, history of prison misconduct, as well as the prisoner's needs regarding treatment, education, and release planning.

HUMAN RIGHTS VIOLATIONS IN THE UNITED STATES: A REPORT ON U.S. COMPLIANCE WITH THE INTERNATIONAL COVENANT ON CIVIL AND POLITICAL RIGHTS

Human Rights Watch, American Civil Liberties Union (1993)

Conditions of Confinement in U.S. Prisons

The most significant human rights abuses in the U.S. stem from its exploding prison population. Since 1973, the nation's prison population has tripled. In an attempt to control crime, the nation embarked on a vast effort to confine offenders in prison facilities whenever identified, arrested an sentenced. Currently, about 1.3 million men and women are confined to prison and jail facilities at any given time, and perhaps ten times as many in the course of a year. As a result, U.S. incarceration rates are among the highest in the world. The Justice Department's latest reports how that in 1992 there was a 6.8 percent increase in the states' prison population and a 12.1 growth in the number of federal inmates. This means that every week about 1,200 more inmates than the week before had to be housed, fed and clothed in the nation's prison facilities. Despite on-going prison construction all over the country, its pace has not kept up with the steady increase in prison population. * * *

Lack of privacy and space is only one result of overcrowded prison facilities. Common sense dictates that when prison authorities decide to double or triple-bunk in an open dormitory setting, guards' ability to monitor and observe the prisoners is greatly reduced. Overcrowding also means deteriorating physical conditions and sanitation, as well as reduced levels of basic necessities such as staff supervision and the delivery of health care services. Moreover, crowding is directly linked to the spread of airborne diseases such as tuberculosis. U.S. prisoners are therefore subjected to a regime which endangers their basic human rights to a safe and healthy custodial environment. These aspects and results of overcrowding violate the Article 10 right to be treated with humanity and respect.

Article 10, paragraph 2 of the ICCPR mandates separate treatment for pre-trial detainees, who, in the U.S. and many other countries are innocent under the law until proven guilty. Thus, under the Covenant, accused prisoners should receive treatment which is better, or at least not worse than, the conditions for sentenced prisoners. Most pre-trial detainees in the U.S. are held in local jails, facilities which tend to be older, more crowded more dilapidated and sometimes more dangerous than the prisons. In fact, jailed detainees are more apt to suffer abuse than are sentenced inmates in prison facilities. These conditions violate Article 10, paragraph 2.

Violence and Personal Safety

Related to overcrowding is the endemic violence and threat of violence that pervades U.S. prisons. Both inmate-on-inmate violence and assaults by the staff are extremely serious problems. These facilities are dangerous places. In addition to prisoners being forced to live with other offenders who have committed serious and often violent crimes, prison conditions, policies and practices make these facilities into more dangerous places than they need be.

Racial hostility and animosity aggravate the situation. Prison gangs organized on racial and ethnic lines compete with one another for resources and control, with a frequent result of tension and then violence. Supervision by an underpaid and undertrained largely white rural guard force does not help matters. * * *

The failure to protect prisoners' personal safety is directly related to the pervasive overcrowding situation discussed above. The lack of space and privacy increases tension and stress. Overcrowding also depletes resources necessary to keep prisoners occupied and to maintain adequate staff supervision and control. In spite of these problems, U.S. prison authorities are continuing to provide dormitory housing for increasing numbers of more dangerous prisoners, because of the great cost savings involved. * * *

The use of weapons and even deadly force on unarmed sentenced prisoners is a frequent occurrence in prisons across the country. Excessive use of force has been found in many cases. In *Wilson v. Lambert*, a prisoner was beaten by guards when he refused to return to a housing unit where he was threatened with sexual assault. He won on his Eighth

Amendment claim and damages were awarded. *Brown v. Triche*, involved a handcuffed inmate who was pushed against a wall, hit several times in the face and hit or kicked in the neck when he failed to sit down as ordered by a staff member. * * *

Human rights abuses in "supermax" facilities

Perhaps one of the most troubling aspects of the human rights situation in U.S. prisons is a trend that could be labeled "Marionization." In 1983, the federal prison at Marion, Illinois, implemented a series of extraordinary security measures in order to stem the tide of violence, injury and death that occurred at that facility. Since then, at least 36 states have followed suit in establishing similar facilities, dubbed "super-maxs" or "maxi-maxis." They have been established in Southport, New York; Pelican Bay, California; Florence, Arizona; and Ely, Nevada, among other places. The federal system is constructing a new maxi-max in Florence, Colorado. All of these facilities purport to house the most feared and dangerous prisoners of their state.

Conditions in these prisons are particularly harsh and security is exceptionally strict. Placement can often amount to solitary confinement for years on end. * * *

An observer from the ACLU's National Prison Project gave this description of living conditions at California's version of the "supermax":

> Twenty-two-and-a-half hours a day are spent in the cells. The "free" hour and a half is spent in an "exercise yard" which is essentially a small bare concrete room with high ceilings. Handcuffed and in waist chains, prisoners are put under double escort when they go to the "yard," and once there, they are continually monitored by cameras while they exercise in solitude. Officers communicate with prisoners though disembodied speakers in the walls. The ceiling is covered with heavy mesh on one side and heavy plastic on the other, and the resulting filtered light allowed through the screen is the closest the prisoners in the SHU [special housing unit] ever get to feeling the sunlight. Every move is monitored by a closed-circuit camera. Activity is severely limited. There are no training programs for prisoners, no correspondence courses, and no vocational training.

> Inside the SHU, four 500–foot long corridors are monitored by video cameras. Every 100 feet there are "crash gates" which can be closed during an emergency. All staff carry pocket alarms, which if activated, set off red lights in the hallways. Each set of four corridors is overseen from a control room where all camera are monitored.

> Each concrete cell contains a concrete stool, concrete bed, heavy stainless steel. Nothing is allowed on the walls. The cells of SHU prisoners are lined with opaque materials, so that prisoners cannot

see out. Prisoners never walk freely, they never emerge from their cells without being handcuffed and in chains. They shuffle to the law library single file, chained to each other at the ankles. Prisoners eat on trays of food which are passed through a slot in the cell door. Toothpaste is removed from the tube. There is no unread mail. * * *

U.S. law justifies this brutal treatment by pointing to the dangerous violence-prone nature of the prisoners confined to these prisons. * * * The ACLU and Human Rights Watch have argued that no matter how dangerous a prisoner may be, certain basic rights must be guaranteed in the course of an inmate's confinement.[1]

Women Prisoners

Women account for about 6% of total state prison inmates and about 7% of total federal prison inmates. Since 1980, however, the number of female inmates has been growing at a faster rate than that of men.

Because of the relatively low number of women inmates, the number of female prisons is low. Consequently many women are housed far from their homes and, as a result, receive few visits. This is a particularly serious problem for women serving sentences in the federal system, because there are only ten federal prisons in the entire country that house women convicts. Women prisoners from Washington, D.C., are confined to federal facilities located in other states, hundreds or even thousands of miles from their homes; male inmates, in contrast, are housed within a 15–mile radius of Washington, D.C.

Female prisoners generally have fewer educational, recreational, and vocational opportunities than their male counterparts. On-site visits by Human Rights Watch confirm this assessment. In the federal camp in Danbury, which is adjacent to a larger male prison, women get the lower-paying, less-skilled jobs. In a plant making equipment for the department of Defense, men perform a variety of electronic jobs, while women do the packing. In the federal institution in Marianna, Florida, female inmates in a prison that held eighty-four prisoners at the time of our visit informed us that they had fewer educational opportunities and recreational facilities than the male prisoners held in a larger institution next door. In *Glover v. Johnson*, the court found that vocational programs were more numerous for men and provided men with more marketable skills than programs for women. These gender inequalities in prison facilities and programs violate U.S. anti-discrimination law as well as Article 26, the ICCPR's broad anti-discrimination provision. The failure to adequately enforce these laws violates Article 126, which requires "effective protection against discrimination," and Article 2,

---

1. The application of Article 7's ban on "inhuman or degrading treatment" would be critical here, since it goes well beyond the narrowly-construed Eighth Amendment ban on "cruel and unusual punishments." . . .

which requires effective remedies for violations of Covenant rights, as well as enforcement of those remedies. * * *

CONCLUDING OBSERVATIONS OF THE HUMAN RIGHTS COMMITTEE: UNITED STATES OF AMERICA

U.N. Doc. CCPR/C/79/Add.50; A/50/40 (Oct. 3, 1995)

267.   The Committee expresses its appreciation at the high quality of the report submitted by the State party, which was detailed, informative and drafted in accordance with the guidelines. * * *

268.   The Committee appreciates the participation of a high-level delegation which included a substantial number of experts in various fields relating to the protection of human rights in the country. The detailed information provided by the delegation in its introduction of the report, as well as the comprehensive and well-structured replies provided to questions raised by members, contributed to making the dialogue extremely constructive and fruitful.

269.   The Committee notes with appreciation that the Government gave publicity to its report, thus enabling non-governmental organizations to become aware of its contents and to make known their particular concerns. In addition, a number of representatives of these organizations were present during the Committee's consideration of the report. * * *

285.   The Committee is concerned about conditions of detention of persons deprived of liberty in federal or state prisons, particularly with regard to planned measures which would lead to further overcrowding of detention centres. The Committee is also concerned at the practice which allows male prison officers access in women's detention centres and which has led to serious allegations of sexual abuse of women and the invasion of their privacy. The Committee is particularly concerned at the conditions of detention in certain maximum security prisons, which are incompatible with article 10 of the Covenant and run counter to the United Nations Standard Minimum Rules for the Treatment of Prisoners and the Code of Conduct for Law Enforcement Officials. * * *

297.   The Committee urges the State party to take all necessary measures to prevent any excessive use of force by the police; that rules and regulations governing the use of weapons by the police and security forces be in full conformity with the United Nations Basic Principles on the Use of Force and Firearms by Law Enforcement Officials; that any violations of these rules be systematically investigated in order to bring those found to have committed such acts before the courts; and that those found guilty be punished and the victims be compensated. Regula-

tions limiting the sale of firearms to the public should be extended and strengthened. * * *

299. The Committee expresses the hope that measures be adopted to bring conditions of detention of persons deprived of liberty in federal or state prisons in full conformity with article 10 of the Covenant. Legislative, prosecutorial and judicial policy in sentencing must take into account that overcrowding in prisons causes violation of article 10 of the Covenant. Existing legislation that allows male officers access to women's quarters should be amended so as to provide at least that they will always be accompanied by women officers. Conditions of detention in prisons, in particular in maximum security prisons, should be scrutinized with a view to guaranteeing that persons deprived of their liberty be treated with humanity and with respect for the inherent dignity of the human person, and implementing the United Nations Standard Minimum Rules for the Treatment of Prisoners and the Code of Conduct for Law Enforcement Officials therein. Appropriate measures should be adopted to provide speedy and effective remedies to compensate persons who have been subjected to unlawful or arbitrary arrests as provided in article 9, paragraph 5, of the Covenant. * * *

304. The Committee recommends that measures be taken to ensure greater public awareness of the provisions of the Covenant and that the legal profession as well as judicial and administrative authorities at federal and state levels be made familiar with these provisions in order to ensure their effective application.

THIRD PERIODIC REPORT OF THE UNITED STATES TO THE HUMAN RIGHTS COMMITTEE

U.N. Doc. CCPR/C/USA/3 (Nov. 28, 2005)

470. The Committee expresses the hope that measures [will] be adopted to bring conditions of detention of persons deprived of liberty in federal or state prisons in full conformity with Article 10 of the Covenant. Legislative, prosecutorial and judicial policy in sentencing must take into account that overcrowding in prisons causes violation of Article 10 of the Covenant.

471. Comment: All prisons in the United States are subject to the strictures of the federal Constitution and federal civil rights laws. Prisons must ensure that "inmates receive adequate food, clothing, shelter, and medical care and must 'take reasonable measures to guarantee the safety of inmates.'" *Farmer v. Brennan*, 511 U.S. 825, 832–33 (1994). The Americans with Disabilities Act and the Rehabilitation Act generally require prison physical spaces and programs to be accessible to inmates with impairments, subject to appropriate security and safety concerns, and the Individuals with Disabilities in Education Act requires prisons to provide inmates with appropriate special educational services.

472. As noted, the federal Constitution prohibits prison conditions, including overcrowding, when such constitutes "cruel and unusual punishment." *Rhodes v. Chapman*, 452 U.S. 337, 352(1981). However, in making such a determination, "courts cannot assume that state legislatures and prison officials are insensitive to the requirements of the Constitution or to the perplexing sociological problems of how best to achieve the goals of the penal function in the criminal justice system: to punish justly, to deter future crime, and to return imprisoned persons to society with an improved chance of being useful, law-abiding citizens." *Id.* Overcrowding, standing alone, does not violate federal law. Nor does the United States agree that overcrowding, standing alone, violates Article 10(1).

473. [According to the Committee,] existing legislation that allows male officers access to women's quarters should be amended so as to provide at least that they will always be accompanied by women officers.

474. Comment: It is not the practice of the federal Bureau of Prisons or of most state corrections departments to restrict corrections officers to work only with inmates of the same sex. Furthermore, requiring female officers always to be present during male officers' access to women's quarters would be extremely burdensome on prison resources. Appropriate measures are taken, however, to protect female prisoners. Staff are trained to respect offenders' safety, dignity, and privacy, and procedures exist for investigation of complaints and disciplinary action—including criminal prosecution—against staff who violate applicable laws and regulations.

475. [According to the Committee,] conditions of detention in prisons, in particular in maximum security prisons, should be scrutinized with a view to guaranteeing that persons deprived of their liberty be treated with humanity and with respect for the inherent dignity of the human person, and implementing the United Nations Standard Minimum Rules for the Treatment of Prisoners and the Code of Conduct for Law Enforcement Officials therein.

476. Comment: All prisoners in the United States are guaranteed treatment that does not constitute cruel and unusual punishment prohibited by the United States Constitution. Also, see the response to Question 10, supra. It is also worth noting that the United Nations Standard Minimum Rules for the Treatment of Prisoners and the Code of Conduct for Law Enforcement Officials are non-binding recommendations.

NOTES AND QUESTIONS ON STATE REPORTS

1. *Reporting treaty violations.* In 1995, Human Rights Watch and the ACLU drew on the report excerpted above in filing a direct submission to the Human Rights Committee, specifically to assist it in its consider-

ation of the U.S. Report. In this joint submission, the NGOs criticized the United States for being open about "abuses that are largely in the past, like slavery," and "vague or silent about ongoing human rights violations * * * a favorite dodge of nations wishing to avoid serious human rights scrutiny * * *." They also roundly criticized the United States for its declaration that Articles 1 through 27 are not "self-executing," thereby denying Americans the right to invoke the treaty in U.S. courts, "a right they would have had if the U.S. government had either declared the covenant to be self-executing or if implementing legislation had been enacted to create causes of action under the treaty."

In addition to their obligation to report on their progress in implementing obligations under the ICCPR, do states also have an obligation to "candidly" report violations of the treaty?

2. *Committee recommendations.* After the oral presentation of a state's report, the responsible treaty body issues a series of "concluding observations" which often provide comments on the quality of the report and presentation as well as recommendations which, in the committee's view, will strengthen compliance with the state's obligations under the relevant treaty. In the case of the United States, you will note from the "Third Periodic Report," *supra*, that the U.S. responded to those recommendations in its next submission to the Committee.

Note, in particular, the U.S. response to the Committee's comment that overcrowding of prisons results in a violation of article 10 of the ICCPR. On what does the Committee base its charge that overcrowding violates article 10? Are you satisfied with the U.S. government's response to the Committee's comment? Consider the reservations, understandings, and declarations made by the United States in submitting its instrument of ratification. Does this change your view? How does the Human Rights Watch/ACLU Report's treatment of this issue affect your response? As a purely legal matter, should it?

3. *Sexual abuse in prison.* The Committee expressed concern over the practice of allowing men access to female prison facilities, which it said had led to serious allegations of sexual abuse. Accordingly, the Committee recommended that the U.S. government implement measures to require male officials to be accompanied by female officials when in female prison facilities. How does the U.S. government respond to this recommendation? Consider the following excerpt from the Second Periodic Report to the Committee Against Torture of the United States:

> 97. *Sexual abuse in prison.* The Prison Rape Elimination Act of 2003 (PREA) was enacted to address the problem of sexual assault of persons in the custody of U.S. correctional agencies. On September 4, 2003, President George W. Bush signed PREA into law. The purpose of the Act is to:
>
> (a) establish a zero-tolerance standard for the incidence of rape in prisons in the United States;

(b) make the prevention of rape a top priority in each prison system;

(c) develop and implement national standards for the detection, prevention, reduction, and punishment of prison rape;

(d) increase the available data and information on the incidence of prison rape, consequently improving the management and administration of correctional facilities;

(e) standardize the definitions used for collecting data on the incidence of prison rape;

(f) increase the accountability of prison officials who fail to detect, prevent, reduce, and punish prison rape;

(g) protect the Eighth Amendment rights of federal, state, and local prisoners;

(h) increase the efficiency and effectiveness of federal expenditures through grant programs such as those dealing with health care; mental health care; disease prevention; crime prevention, investigation, and prosecution; prison construction, maintenance, and operation; race relations; poverty; unemployment; and homelessness; and

(i) reduce the costs that prison rape imposes on interstate commerce. * * *

138.   Illustrative of the problem of sexual abuse in correctional facilities are *United States v. Arizona* and *United States v. Michigan*, both cases filed under CRIPA in 1997 and dismissed in 1999 and 2000 respectively; the Civil Rights Division [of the Justice Department] sought to remedy a pattern or practice of sexual misconduct against female inmates by male staff, including sexual contact and unconstitutional invasions of privacy. The cases were dismissed after the state prisons agreed to make significant changes in conditions of confinement for female inmates.

Is this a better response to the recommendation of the Human Rights Committee? Why would the U.S. discuss sensitivity training in a response to the Human Rights Committee, but then—in a report to the Committee Against Torture—discuss laws put in place to punish sexual abuse?

4.   *Supermax facilities*. So-called "supermax" facilities are maximum security prisons where the most dangerous (and notorious) prisoners are housed. Notably, neither of the U.S. reports to the Human Rights Committee or to the Committee Against Torture addresses supermax facilities in any detail. In one short paragraph, the U.S. noted:

For certain violent inmates, supermaximum security ("supermax") facilities may be necessary, for among other reasons, to protect the safety of the community at large and of other members of the prison population. As discussed in the preceding paragraphs, U.S.

law requires that prisons throughout the United States satisfy U.S. constitutional requirements. When they fail to do so, a variety of remedies are available. * * * For example, in March 2003, the ACLU and others settled a lawsuit brought against Wisconsin's Department of Corrections regarding conditions at its supermax prison in Boscobel, Wisconsin. The settlement agreement included a ban on seriously mentally ill prisoners being housed in the facility; a modest improvement to exercise provision and rehabilitation programs; and a reduction in the use of restraints and electro-shock control devices.

U.S. State Dept., Second Periodic Report of the United States to the Committee Against Torture, U.N. Doc. CAT/C/48/Add.3 (June 2005), ¶ 95. Yet, consider the following description of the federal ADX Florence facility:

> Dubbed by the Guinness World Records as the most secure prison in the world, the 37 acre complex comprises four separate detention facilities, each with a different grade of security. Supermax is equipped with motion detectors, 1,400 steel remote-controlled steel doors, laser beams, barbed wire fences, pressure pads and attack dogs.

> The prison opened in 1994 with the aim of incarcerating its inmates in solitary confinement for most of the day and keeping them in extreme conditions. The result is debilitating, say security officials, leading former prisoners to describe it as a living tomb.

> Most of the prisoners are held in solitary confinement for 23 hours every day. For one hour each day they are allowed to exercise in a concrete chamber, fettered by leg irons and handcuffs. Prisoners stay in sound-proofed cells measuring seven feet by twelve. Each cell is bolted shut with a steel door.

> Stark cells are lit by neon lighting and contain a bed, desk and stool. A shaft of natural light filters through a narrow slit window.

> US security experts describe a highly-controlled environment designed to cut the prisoner off from the outside world and one another. * * *

> The psychological effect of long-term solitary confinement is profound, leading to prisoners suffering from hallucinations, anxiety, depression and self-harm. One former prisoner David Clark told *The Guardian* in 2002 of extreme restraint methods used by the prison, even during family visits.

> "Your family has to look at you chained up like Hannibal Lecter or something. They have to look at you in pain, squirming," he said. * * *

Edna Fernandes, *Supermax Prison, the Alcatraz of the Rockies*, TIMES ONLINE, May 4, 2006, http://www.timesonline.co.uk/tol/news/world/us_and_americas/article713240.ece.

How might it be argued that the use—or misuse—of supermax facilities such as Florence ADX violates either the ICCPR or the Torture Convention? Could it be argued that the continued use of these facilities by the United States is a violation of its obligations under these instruments, or do U.S. reservations, understandings, and declarations effectively insulate it from this charge?

5. *The "mea culpa."* In 1999, the United States submitted its Initial Report to the Committee Against Torture, the treaty monitoring body created under the Convention Against Torture and Other Forms of Cruel, Inhuman or Degrading Treatment. In it, the United States recognized:

> continuing allegations of specific types of abuse and ill-treatment in particular cases, the existence of areas of concern in the context of the criminal justice system, and obstacles to full achievement of the goals and objectives of the Convention. These include allegations and instances (and in some cases even patterns or practices) of:
>
> - police abuse, brutality and unnecessary or excessive use of force, including inappropriate use of devices and techniques such as tear gas and chemical (pepper) spray, tasers or "stun guns," stun belts, police dogs, handcuffs and leg shackles;
> - racial bias and discrimination against members of minorities, as reflected, *inter alia*, in statistical disparities in instances (as well as allegations) of harassment and abuse;
> - sexual assault and abuse of prisoners by correctional officers and other prisoners;
> - ill-treatment of and discrimination against prisoners in custody, including inadequate medical care, especially for those with mental illnesses or who are HIV-positive;
> - lack of police accountability, including failure to discipline, prosecute and punish police misconduct;
> - overcrowding of prison facilities;
> - excessively harsh conditions and unnecessarily stringent procedures in "supermaximum" security facilities for violent prisoners, including wrongful confinement to such units;
> - confinement of children in substandard or abusive correctional facilities;
> - under-funding of governmental agencies, including correctional institutions.

Do you think this mea culpa of sorts should satisfy the concerns of NGOs like Human Rights Watch? What value does the government's candor in 1999 represent for the elimination of torture in or by the United States after 9/11?

6. *General Comment 24 of the Human Rights Committee.* In addition to considering state reports and individual petitions, treaty bodies regularly

release "general comments" addressing matters of procedure, laying out reporting guidelines, or opining on issues of treaty interpretation. In 1994, the Human Rights Committee adopted General Comment 24, addressing the subject of reservations made by States Parties to the International Covenant on Civil and Political Rights. In it, the Human Rights Committee concluded that the provisions of the Vienna Convention on the Law of Treaties, which make the legality of one state's reservation turn on the reactions of other states, pertaining the role of State objections in relation to reservations "are inappropriate to address the problem of reservations to human rights treaties." It went on to note:

> It necessarily falls to the Committee to determine whether a specific reservation is compatible with the object and purpose of the Covenant. This is in part because, as indicated above, it is an inappropriate task for States parties in relation to human rights treaties, and in part because it is a task that the Committee cannot avoid in the performance of its functions.

Human Rights Committee, General Comment 24(52), U.N. Doc. CCPR/C/21/Rev.1/Add.6 (1994). Why are human rights treaties different from other treaties? How do these differences justify a departure from widely accepted reservations law and practice as reflected in the Vienna Convention on the Law of Treaties?

The United States, as well as the United Kingdom and France, lodged written objections to the Committee's observations in General Comment 24. *See* Report of the Human Rights Committee (United States and the United Kingdom), U.N. Doc. A/50/40 (3 October 1995); Report of the Human Rights Committee (France), U.N. Doc. A/51/40 (16 September 1996). The United States asserted, "The Committee's position, while interesting, runs contrary to the Covenant scheme and international law." The United Kingdom concluded that the correct approach to the validity of reservations is "to apply the general rules relating to reservations laid down in the Vienna Convention in a manner which takes full account of the particular characteristics of the treaty in question," not, as the Committee asserted, to reject the Vienna Convention's applicability altogether.

Some years later, support for the position of these states parties to the Covenant came from the International Law Commission, which concluded that the system for determining the validity of reservations to treaties developed under the Vienna Convention on the Law of Treaties was just as valid for human rights instruments as it is for other treaties. *See Report of the International Law Commission on the Work of its Forty-ninth Session*, U.N. Doc. A/52/10 (1997). *See also* Ryan Goodman, *Human Rights Treaties, Invalid Reservations and State Consent*, 96 Am. J. Int'l L. 531 (2002); Elena A. Baylis, *General Comment 24: Confronting the Problem of Reservations to Human Rights Treaties*, 17 Berkeley J. Int'l L. 277 (1999).

7. *The persistent objector doctrine and General Comment 24.* Another controversial aspect of General Comment 24 was the Human Rights Committee's conclusion that "provisions in the Covenant that represent customary international law . . . may not be the subject of reservations." Can this assertion be squared with the "persistent objector" principle? *See* Ted Stein, *The Approach of the Different Drummer: The Principle of the Persistent Objector in International Law,* 26 HARV. INT'L L.J. 457 (1985).

By way of example, the United States has repeatedly asserted that it cannot be bound by any customary international legal principle that prohibits the execution of juvenile offenders (under the age of 18), based on its status as a persistent objector. In part, the United States has relied on its reservation to article 6(5) of the ICCPR that would otherwise obligate it to prohibit this practice. Is this assertion valid in light of General Comment 24? *See generally* Amnesty International, *The Exclusion of Child Offenders from the Death Penalty Under General International Law* (2003); Curtis A. Bradley, *The Juvenile Death Penalty and International Law,* 52 DUKE L.J. 485 (2002); Connie de la Vega & Jennifer Brown, *Can a United States Treaty Reservation Provide a Sanctuary for the Juvenile Death Penalty?,* 32 U.S.F. L.REV. 735 (1998); Margaret Thomas, Comment: *"Rogue States" Within American Borders: Remedying State Noncompliance with the International Covenant on Civil and Political Rights,* 90 CAL. L. REV. 165 (2002); Erica Templeton, *Note: Killing Kids: The Impact of Domingues v. Nevada on the Juvenile Death Penalty as a Violation of International Law,* 41 B.C. L. REV. 1175 (2000).

In *Roper v. Simmons,* 543 U.S. 551 (2005), the U.S. Supreme Court held that "evolving standards of decency" require that the juvenile death penalty be considered cruel and unusual punishment under the Eighth Amendment. Yet, the Executive Branch continues to maintain its position as a persistent objector to the development of a customary international law prohibition on the execution of juvenile offenders. Clearly, the U.S. system of separation of powers creates complications for the observance or formulation of customary international law—while the Executive Branch asserts persistent objector status, the U.S. Supreme Court is free to overturn existing precedent and bring U.S. law into compliance with the developing customary norm. Nevertheless, the case raises an interesting point—can the judiciary's statement on a matter of domestic law "interrupt" and, therefore, invalidate the consistency of the executive branch's continuing objections? Why would the U.S. continue to object to language in UN documents that characterizes the execution of juvenile offenders as a violation of customary international law? Now that the U.S. Supreme Court has spoken on the matter, is there any need for continued, persistent objection to the development of a customary norm?

8. *Increasing public awareness of treaty obligations.* In its concluding observations regarding the U.S. Report, the Human Rights Committee recommended that the United States take measures to ensure greater awareness of the ICCPR among the legal profession, as well as state and

federal judicial and administrative authorities. How would greater awareness increase implementation of the United States' obligations under the Covenant?

9. *The self-executing treaty doctrine.* In ratifying the ICCPR, the United States included an understanding that the treaty's provisions are "not self-executing," *i.e.*, that the treaty does not create rights directly enforceable in U.S. courts. This understanding of the ICCPR has been affirmed by U.S. courts dismissing suits attempting to enforce the treaty against the United States. *See United States ex. rel. Perez v. Warden*, 286 F.3d 1059, 1063 (8th Cir. 2002) (denying federal prisoners the right to assert the ICCPR in habeas corpus proceedings); *Beazley v. Johnson*, 242 F.3d 248, 267–68 (5th Cir. 2001) (rejecting prisoner's claim that the ICCPR voided the state law that allowed petitioner to receive the death penalty for an offense that he committed when he was 17 years old); *Buell v. Mitchell*, 274 F.3d 337, 372 (6th Cir. 2001) (rejecting prisoner's contention that death penalty violated U.S. obligations under the ICCPR); *United States v. Duarte–Acero*, 208 F.3d 1282, 1287 (11th Cir. 2000) (rejecting defendant's claim that double jeopardy guarantee in ICCPR protected prisoner from prosecution in U.S. because prisoner had already been convicted and served time in Colombia).

The United States has adopted the same understanding in ratifying the Convention Against Torture as well as the Convention on the Elimination of Racial Discrimination. How does this substantial limitation on the legal effect of these human rights treaties affect your response to the questions above?

10. *Treaty body reform.* While most observers consider the practice of reviewing state reports by treaty bodies a worthwhile endeavor, many observers recognize serious shortcomings. Separate treaty bodies review reports under different treaties that in many ways overlap in subject matter. The treaty bodies are under-staffed and under-funded, yet their workload increases every year, particularly as individual-state petition mechanisms gain popularity with advocates. Only a short time after being empowered to do so, the Committee on the Elimination Against Racial Discrimination and the Committee on the Elimination of Discrimination Against Women are considering increasing numbers of individual-state petitions. And the problem will become more acute as the Committee under the Covenant on Economic, Social and Cultural Rights begins to hear individual petitions under its Optional Protocol.

In a report prepared for the Office of the U.N. High Commissioner for Human Rights, Professor Anne Bayefsky observed:

> Ultimately, the human rights treaty system will remain inefficient and inadequate in the absence of consolidation of the treaty bodies. Some limited amendment is, therefore, unavoidable. The treaty bodies cannot handle in a timely manner the number of reports which the system now requires or produces, even if there was a general amnesty—which in practice is now the case. The average

consideration by each treaty body of a state for six or seven hours once every five years has not maximized constructive interaction. Six different working methods, documents, practices, rules of procedure, and reporting guidelines do not serve users. There is substantive overlap of treaty rights and freedoms, and inevitable overlap of reporting and dialogue. Examination of a single state in light of all human rights information, encourages a coherent understanding of problems and needs. It means the concrete application of the "universal, indivisible, interdependent and interrelated" nature of rights. It integrates programmatic advice from the international level and matches the crosscutting character of human rights for operational agencies or organs at the national level. Consolidation would conform to the overall goal of modern UN reform which seeks to adopt a global approach to the needs of each country.

Anne F. Bayefsky, The UN Human Rights Treaty System: Universality at the Crossroads (April 2001), *available at* http://www.yorku.ca/hrights/ Report/finalreport.pdf. Professor Bayefsky recommends consolidation of the treaty bodies not only to increase efficiency, but to promote "universality" in the consideration of state reports. What concerns—both legal and otherwise—would need to be met in carrying out such consolidation? Can you envision other ways to improve the reporting system that might raise fewer concerns?

Practicum

According to the Secretary General of the United Nations, as of February 2008, 185 states are parties to the United Nations Convention on the Elimination of All Forms of Discrimination against Women (CEDAW), making it one of the most widely adopted human rights treaties in history. It is also one of the most heavily reserved. In recent years, international human rights lawyers have struggled to determine the legal effects of these various reservations under the Vienna Convention on the Law of Treaties. They have also struggled with the basic strategic decision of whether it is better to get a handful of "pure" ratifications or a lot of reserved ones. This exercise is designed to show how difficult these doctrinal and strategic issues are.

First, please read the excerpts from the General Comment Number 24, *supra* adopted by the UN Human Rights Committee in 1994. Then, please consider the following six articles of CEDAW:

Article 1: For the purposes of the present Convention, the term "discrimination against women" shall mean any distinction, exclusion or restriction made on the basis of sex which has the effect or purpose of impairing or nullifying the recognition, enjoyment or exercise by women, irrespective of their marital status, on a basis of equality of men and women, of human rights and fundamental freedoms in the political, economic, social, cultural, civil or any other field.

Article 2: States Parties condemn discrimination against women in all its forms, agree to pursue by all appropriate means and without delay a policy of eliminating discrimination against women and, to this end, undertake: * * *

(c) To establish legal protection of the rights of women on an equal basis with men and to ensure through competent national tribunals and other public institutions the effective protection of women against any act of discrimination; * * *

(e) To take all appropriate measures to eliminate discrimination against women by any person, organization or enterprise;

(f) To take all appropriate measures, including legislation, to modify or abolish existing laws, regulations, customs and practices which constitute discrimination against women; * * *

Article 7: States Parties shall take all appropriate measures to eliminate discrimination against women in the political and public life of the country and, in particular, shall ensure to women, on equal terms with men, the right:

(a) To vote in all elections and public referenda and to be eligible for election to all publicly elected bodies;

(b) To participate in the formulation of government policy and the implementation thereof and to hold public office and perform all public functions at all levels of government; * * *

Article 16. States Parties shall take all appropriate measures to eliminate discrimination against women in all matters relating to marriage and family relations and in particular shall ensure, on a basis of equality of men and women: * * *

(f) The same rights and responsibilities with regard to guardianship, wardship, trusteeship and adoption of children, or similar institutions where these concepts exist in national legislation; in all cases the interests of the children shall be paramount; * * *

Article 28: * * *

2. A reservation incompatible with the object and purpose of the present Convention shall not be permitted. * * *

Article 29: 1. Any dispute between two or more States Parties concerning the interpretation or application of the present Convention which is not settled by negotiation shall, at the request of one of them, be submitted to arbitration. If within six months from the date of the request for arbitration the parties are unable to agree on the organization of the arbitration, any one of those parties may refer the dispute to the International Court of Justice by request in conformity with the Statute of the Court.

2.   Each State Party may at the time of signature or ratification of the present Convention or accession thereto declare that it does not consider itself bound by paragraph 1 of this article. * * *

Finally, consider two of the reservations to CEDAW entered by the government of Kuwait at the time of its accession:

The Government of Kuwait enters a reservation regarding article 7(a), inasmuch as the provision contained in that paragraph conflicts with the Kuwaiti Electoral Act, under which the right to be eligible for election and to vote is restricted to males. * * *

The Government of the State of Kuwait declares that it does not consider itself bound by the provision contained in article 16(f) inasmuch as it conflicts with the provisions of the Islamic Shariah, Islam being the official religion of the State.

Several states adopted reservations similar to the Kuwaiti package, but the government of Finland, among others, responded to each of these in similar terms:

In their present formulation the reservations are clearly incompatible with the object and purpose of the Convention and therefore inadmissible under article 28 paragraph 2, of the Convention. Therefore, the Government of Finland objects to these reservations. The Government of Finland further notes that the reservations made by the Government of Kuwait are devoid of legal effect.

For this practicum, students will represent either the government of Kuwait or an NGO that follows women's issues in Kuwait. The students representing Kuwait should prepare a report to the Committee on the Elimination of Discrimination Against Women under article 18 of the Convention. The students representing the NGO should prepare a shadow report for submission to the Committee. Each group should focus on the issue of gender equality, placing particular emphasis on whether or not Kuwaiti law complies with the obligations assumed by Kuwait under CEDAW. After each student's oral presentation, the remainder of the students will serve as members of the CEDAW Committee—each from a different country (and associated legal perspective)—and negotiate a series of conclusions and recommendations based on the two reports.

C.   CHARTER–BASED MECHANISMS: THE COMMISSION ON HUMAN RIGHTS AND THE HUMAN RIGHTS COUNCIL

Under the UN Charter, the Economic and Social Committee was created to perform studies and make recommendations on a variety of issues, including most notably, "respect for, and observance of, human rights * * * for all." In 1946, the Commission on Human Rights was created as a functional commission of ECOSOC, and it subsequently took primary responsibility for UN activities in the human rights field. The Commission was composed of fifty-three states, each of which would serve for a three-year term. Its annual meetings in Geneva were attended by over 3,000 delegates from member and observer states, as well as from non-governmental organizations.

The Commission on Human Rights had the mandate to examine, monitor, and report on both worldwide human rights violations (*e.g.*, by theme) and country-specific human rights situations. It performed these functions primarily by appointing rapporteurs or establishing working groups, as well as by focusing on particular issues or countries during its regular session. Its deliberations would culminate in the adoption of resolutions, statements, and decisions to express the views of the international community on a variety of human rights issues.

The proceedings of the Commission on Human Rights were intensely political, and each session resulted in the adoption of over one hundred resolutions that were non-binding in nature and regularly ignored by the world's worst human rights abusers. Indeed, any international lawyer seeing Commission negotiations for the first time would likely be aghast at the sloppy use of language and legal principles, the bilateral grudges masquerading as human rights issues, and the hypocritical grand-standing by notorious human rights abusers. Diplomatic gamesmanship caused many observers to see the Commission as a failed institution.

By 2004, criticism of the Commission had reached new heights. Two years earlier, Libya has been chosen as the human rights body's chair. Then, as violence escalated in Darfur, Sudan was reelected to a seat on the Commission. Zimbabwe too was elected to sit on the Commission, as was Cuba. Responding to the widespread dissatisfaction with the Commission, then UN Secretary General Kofi Annan observed,

> the Commission's capacity to perform its tasks has been increasingly undermined by its declining credibility and professionalism. In particular, States have sought membership of the Commission not to strengthen human rights but to protect themselves against criticism or to criticize others. As a result, a credibility deficit has developed, which casts a shadow on the reputation of the United Nations system as a whole.

In larger freedom: towards development, security and human rights for all, Report of the Secretary General, U.N. Doc. A/59/2005 (March 21, 2005), ¶ 182. To remedy these defects, the Secretary–General called for the creation of a smaller, more transparent, and more disciplined body.

After months of heated negotiations, the UN General Assembly adopted a resolution in April 2006 replacing the Commission with a Human Rights Council. In creating the Council, UN member states tried to craft the new body in such a way as to correct the failings of the Commission:

- The Council is a subsidiary organ of the General Assembly, rather than of ECOSOC. This was meant to provide more direct control over the Council by the broad membership of the UN, rather than by the subset of its members that sit on ECOSOC. Moreover, Council members are elected by the General Assembly (all UN member states). This reform was intended to ensure that the Council's membership is representative of the will of the entire UN, rather than simply of ECOSOC members.

- The Council consists of 47 members, 6 fewer than the Commission. By reducing the number of seats available, the reformers' intent was to improve the focus and efficiency of the Council as well as to limit the opportunity for politicization.

- The Council meets regularly throughout the year. This reform was also intended to reduce the politicization of the Council and make it more nimble and responsive than the Commission.

- A new Universal Periodic Review mechanism was created. Under this mechanism, all member States will have their human rights records regularly considered by the Council through interactive dialogue. Universal Periodic Review was created to respond to critics of the Commission's previous "name and shame" practice, whereby individual countries were singled out for criticism while others were not—arguably, for political reasons.

As discussed in the notes and questions below, many have questioned whether these reforms have worked. In fact, the United States voted against the resolution creating the Council and has decided not to run for membership based on its view that the Council is no better—and is in many ways worse—than the Commission. Similarly, many UN watchers have been disappointed with the Council's performance in its short life. As of yet, there is no consensus on whether the Council will be an effective mechanism for the promotion and protection of human rights.

With lawyers' persistent advocacy, skilled diplomacy, and a working knowledge of its mechanisms, the Commission on Human Rights could be a modestly effective platform for publicizing human rights violations. The Council retains many of the Commission's most useful mechanisms and, accordingly, remains a valuable tool in the human rights lawyer's toolbox. And, with the Council's new Universal Periodic Review mechanism, lawyers have an additional forum for advocacy at their disposal.

Ideally, the Council will speak for the international community with the moral authority and influence that the United Nations can bring to a conversation about human rights—not only with governments, but also with human rights defenders, political dissidents, and human rights victims throughout the world. Time will tell whether it fulfills this mission.

Case Study

The year 2004 was, in many ways, a turning point for the Commission on Human Rights, and the case of Sudan best exemplifies the challenges of using the UN human rights machinery to effect change. For many, the Commission's treatment of Sudan reflected the need for a drastic change in the UN human rights machinery—membership, mandate, and mission.

The Situation of Human Rights in Sudan

Since Sudan obtained independence from the United Kingdom in 1956, the country has been embroiled in almost continuous conflict. The only period of relative calm was from 1972 to 1983, when the non-Muslim, non-Arab South was granted autonomy. When the Arab, Muslim ruling government revoked the South's autonomy in 1983, the North–South civil war began again, continuing until 2004, when the insurgent Sudan People's Liberation Movement/Army (SPLA) and the Khartoum government agreed to a cease-fire and had nearly achieved a comprehensive peace settlement.

As peace talks between the SPLA and the Sudanese government progressed in 2003, conflict erupted in the western region of Darfur. Fueled by ethnic tensions, competition for resources, and an imbalance of power, by mid–2004 the Darfur conflict had left thousands dead and some 830,000 uprooted from their homes.[1] According to numerous sources, the Sudanese government was arming Arab militias (so-called "Janjaweed") and encouraging the systematic rape and murder of non-Arab, African civilians in Darfur. Moreover, accounts indicated that the Sudanese air force was conducting surveillance and bombing villages, after which Janjaweed and Sudanese armed forces would attack the villages.

As a result of the conflict, hundreds of thousands of Sudanese civilians were displaced from their homes and farms. For several months, the Sudanese government obstructed international humanitarian assistance to displaced civilians. Even where the government allowed access, it was controlled in a manner that rendered assistance ineffective. By the beginning of the 2004 session of the UN Commission on Human Rights, the human rights and humanitarian situation in Darfur had reached crisis proportions. *See* Emily Wax, *Chad Broken by Strain of Suffering; Sudanese Refugees Seeking Aid Find Only Shared Misery*, Wash. Post, Mar. 11, 2004, at A1; Press Release, Human Rights Watch, *Sudan: Rights Defenders in Darfur Detained* (Mar. 9, 2003); Eric Reeves, Editorial,

---

1. *Darfur Rising: Sudan's New Crisis*, International Crisis Group, 25 March 2004.

Unnoticed Genocide, WASH. POST, Feb. 25, 2004, at A25; McLaughlin, Abraham & Meera Selva, *Sudan's Refugees Wait and Hope*, CHRISTIAN SCI. MONITOR (Boston, Mass.), Feb. 18, 2004, at 6; Editorial, *Sudan's Ethnic Cleansing*, BOSTON GLOBE, Feb. 8, 2004, at H10; Amnesty Int'l, *Darfur:"Too many people killed for no reason."* AI Index: AFR 54/008/2004. Further information on the human rights situation in Darfur is in Module 7(c), *infra*.

On the tenth anniversary of the Rwandan Genocide, Secretary General of the United Nations, Kofi Annan addressed the Commission on Human Rights to launch an Action Plan to Prevent Genocide. Excerpts of the speech are reprinted below:

THE SECRETARY–GENERAL'S ADDRESS TO THE COMMISSION ON HUMAN RIGHTS
(delivered Apr. 7, 2004)[1]

It is good that we have observed those minutes of silence together. We must never forget our collective failure to protect a least eight hundred thousand defenceless men, women and children who perished in Rwanda ten years ago.

Such crimes cannot be reversed. Such failures cannot be repaired. The dead cannot be brought back to life. So what can we do?

First, we must all acknowledge our responsibility for not having done more to prevent or stop the genocide. Neither the United Nations Secretariat, nor the Security Council, nor Member States in general, nor the international media, paid enough attention to the gathering signs of disaster. Still less did we take timely action.

When we recall such events and ask "why did no one intervene?", we should address the question not only to the United Nations, or even to its Member States. No one can claim ignorance. All who were playing any part in world affairs at that time should ask, "what more could I have done? How would I react next time—and what am I doing now to make it less likely there will be a next time?"

[Editor's Note: The Secretary General went on to identify four of the five elements of his Action Plan to Prevent Genocide: preventing armed conflict, protection of civilians in armed conflict, ending impunity, and early and clear warning.]

That brings me to the fifth and final heading of the action plan, which is the need for swift and decisive action when, despite all our efforts, we learn that genocide is happening, or about to happen.

Too often, even when there is abundant warning, we lack the political will to act.

---

1. *Available at* http://www.un.org/apps/sg/printsgstats.asp?nid=862.

Anyone who embarks on a genocide commits a crime against humanity. Humanity must respond by taking action in its own defence. Humanity's instrument for that purpose must be the United Nations, and specifically the Security Council.

In this connection, let me say here and now that I share the grave concern expressed last week by eight independent experts appointed by this Commission at the scale of reported human rights abuses and at the humanitarian crisis unfolding in Darfur, Sudan.

Last Friday, the United Nations Emergency Relief Coordinator reported to the Security Council that "a sequence of deliberate actions has been observed that seem aimed at achieving a specific objective: the forcible and long-term displacement of the targeted communities, which may also be termed 'ethnic cleansing.'" His assessment was based on reports from our international staff on the ground in Darfur, who have witnessed first hand what is happening there, and from my own Special Envoy for Humanitarian Affairs in Sudan, Ambassador Vraalsen who has visited Darfur.

Mr. Chairman, such reports leave me with a deep sense of foreboding. Whatever terms it uses to describe the situation, the international community cannot stand idle.

At the invitation of the Sudanese government, I propose to send a high-level team to Darfur to gain a fuller understanding of the extent and nature of this crisis, and to seek improved access to those in need of assistance and protection. It is vital that international humanitarian workers and human rights experts be given full access to the region, and to the victims, without further delay. If that is denied, the international community must be prepared to take swift and appropriate action.

By "action" in such situations I mean a continuum of steps, which may include military action. But the latter should always be seen as an extreme measure, to be used only in extreme cases. * * *

But let us not wait until the worst has happened, or is already happening. Let us not wait until the only alternatives to military action are futile hand wringing or callous indifference. Let us, Mr. Chairman, be serious about preventing genocide.

Only so we can honor the victims whom we remember today. Only so can we save those who might be victims tomorrow. * * *

RESOLUTION ON THE SITUATION OF
HUMAN RIGHTS IN THE SUDAN

Commission on Human Rights resolution 2004/128,
U.N. Doc. No. E/CN.4/2004/L.11/Add.8
(Adopted Apr. 23, 2004, by recorded vote of 50 votes to 1, with 2 abstentions)

1.   The Commission on Human Rights is deeply concerned about the situation in the Sudan and in particular in Darfur–Western Sudan. The Commission welcomes the inclusion of the N'djamena peace talks on 8 April 2004 between the Government of the Sudan and the armed groups under the auspices of H.E. President Idris Dedy of Chad, in the presence of international and regional representatives, including the African Union, United Nations agencies, the European Union, the United States of America and international non-governmental organizations.

2.   The Commission welcomes:

(a) The full involvement of the Commission of the African Union in the peaceful resolution to the conflict in Darfur and calls upon the African Union and its member States to continue their pivotal role in ensuring the effective and speedy implementation of the N'djamena agreement;

(b) The visit by the African Union team to the Sudan at the invitation of the Government with a view to assessing the situation and ensuring respect for human rights and humanitarian law, and the positive response of the Government of the Sudan to the request of the African Commission on Human and Peoples' Rights to dispatch to Darfur a delegation from the Commission which includes the Commissioner in charge of refugees and internally displaced persons.

3.   The Commission welcomes the ongoing peace talks at Naivasha, Kenya, aiming at the conclusion of a comprehensive and lasting peace agreement and expresses its firm belief that human rights should be an integral part of such agreement. The Commission expresses its firm belief that a peaceful settlement to the conflict in the Sudan, which is a responsibility of all parties to the peace talks, will greatly contribute to respect for human rights in the Sudan.

4.   The Commission shares the grave concern of the Secretary–General of the United Nations, Mr. Kofi Annan, concerning the scale of reported human rights abuses and the humanitarian situation in Darfur–Western Sudan and welcomes his decision to send a high-level team to Darfur, at the invitation of the Government of the Sudan, to gain a fuller understanding and to establish the facts of the situation in the area.

5.   The Commission calls on all parties to the N'djamena ceasefire agreement to fully respect the agreement and to ensure that all armed groups under their control comply with the agreement. The Government of the Sudan shall commit itself to neutralizing the armed militias.

6.   The Commission calls upon the parties to the conflict in Darfur to observe the humanitarian ceasefire and to grant immediate, full, safe and unhindered access to Darfur and elsewhere in the Sudan aimed at delivering humanitarian assistance to all civilians in need and to cooperate closely with the United Nations Office for Humanitarian Affairs and Operation Lifeline Sudan as a further sign of consolidation of the progress already achieved in many regions.

7.   The Commission expresses its solidarity with the Sudan in overcoming the current situation. The Commission reiterates the important role played by the African Union and its various mechanisms in helping to reach a peaceful settlement of this question. The Commission further appreciates the leadership of H.E. Idris Deby, President of Chad, in hosting and chairing the N'djamena peace talks and expresses its confidence that his sincerity and integrity will enable him to bring this process to a satisfactory conclusion.

8.   The Commission calls upon the international community to continue providing relief assistance to the affected population in Darfur and to enhance the efforts of the Government of the Sudan, supported by the African Union, in the peace process.

9.   The Commission calls on the Government of the Sudan to actively promote and protect human rights and international humanitarian law throughout the country; the Commission also calls on the international community to expand its support for these activities and to continue its support for the peace process in the Sudan.

10.   The Commission requests that Chairman of the Commission to appoint an independent expert on the situation of human rights in the Sudan for a period of one year and requests him/her to submit an interim report to the General Assembly at its fifty-ninth session and to report to the Commission at its sixty-first session on the situation of human rights in the Sudan. The Commission requests the Secretary–General to provide all necessary assistance to the independent expert to enable him/her to fully discharge his/her mandate.

11.   The Commission recommends the following draft decision to the Economic and Social Council for adoption:

"The Economic and Social Council, taking note of Commission on Human Rights decision 2004/128 of 23 April 2004, endorses the Commission's request to appoint an independent expert on the situation of human rights in the Sudan for a period of one year and its request to the independent expert to submit an interim report to the General Assembly at its fifty-ninth session and to report to the Commission at its sixty-first session on the situation of human rights in the Sudan.

The Council also endorses the Commission's request to the Secretary–General to provide all necessary assistance to the independent expert to enable him/her to discharge the mandate fully."

NOTES AND QUESTIONS ON THE *UN RESPONSE TO SUDAN*

1. *Commission [in]action on Sudan.* When you read the resolution on the Situation of Human Rights in the Sudan adopted by the Commission on Human Rights, how does it compare to the Secretary General's address to the Commission two weeks before? Is the resolution an accurate reflection of the facts or the sentiments expressed by the Secretary General?

Note that the resolution was adopted by a vote of 50 votes to 1, with 2 abstentions. One might think a resolution of this nature would be adopted by consensus; however, the context in which this resolution was tabled and adopted was extremely controversial and is worth studying to understand the political dynamic of the Commission on Human Rights.

During the 2003 session of the Commission, the Sudanese delegation was successful in defeating a resolution on the situation of human rights in Sudan, tabled by the European Union, for the first time in ten years. The resolution was defeated largely due to coordinated action by the Africa Group which argued that progress in peace talks between the SPLA and the Government of Sudan warranted eliminating the resolution, and equally important, the progress of a Special Rapporteur who had been reporting on the human rights situation there for the previous decade. At the 2004 session, however, escalating violence in Darfur and the Sudanese government's apparent active participation in human rights and humanitarian law violations created renewed pressure for the Commission to adopt a resolution under Item 9 of the Commission agenda—the so-called "name and shame" item reserved for critical country-specific resolutions.

Indeed, as the session progressed, increasing UN, NGO, and media attention to the situation in Darfur, capped off by the Secretary General's speech, made passage of an EU-sponsored, critical resolution on Sudan more and more likely. Even influential members of the Africa Group, like South Africa, seemed ready to reverse the position they took the year before and support a resolution in 2004.

On the day before scheduled action on the Sudan resolution, the EU Presidency (Ireland) concluded a deal with the Sudanese delegation, whereby references critical of the government would be dropped from the resolution in exchange for the creation of an "Independent Expert." As part of this deal, the resolution would be adopted as a consensus "Chairman's Statement." Not surprisingly, some states (even some within the EU) were furious at this development: a watered-down Chair's Statement that applauded the activities of the Sudanese government and neglected to identify its contribution to the crisis in Darfur was unacceptable.

As a result, the United States began a series of procedural maneuvers in order to introduce amendments to the Chair's Statement and reintroduce the critical language removed through the EU's negotiations with Sudan. Both amendments failed. The United States then called for a vote on the Statement as a whole and voted against it; however, the resolution passed by an overwhelming majority. Finally, the United States reintroduced the originally tabled Item 9 resolution for action by the Commission, but its effort was defeated by a procedural motion by the Congo to adjourn debate.

Although the U.S. delegation had no expectation that its procedural maneuvers would succeed, it felt it was important to take a stand on the situation in Darfur. As Ambassador Rich Williamson, Head of the U.S. Delegation, stated before the voting began,

> Mr. Chairman, ten years from now, the 60th Commission on Human Rights will be remembered for one thing and one thing alone: Did we have the courage and strength to take strong action against the "ethnic cleansing" in Darfur. We will be asked, "Where were you at the time of the ethnic cleansing? What did you do?"
>
> Mr. Chairman, the horrific events in Darfur demand strong action. I ask my colleagues to reflect on the "ethnic cleansing" that is going on. Reflect on the 30,000 dead and the 900,000 internally displaced people living now in intolerable and dangerous conditions. * * *
>
> The U.N. Commission on Human Rights cannot do everything. It cannot unilaterally stop the carnage. But that does not mean we must not do what we can.
>
> Mr. Chairman, the Commission can shine light on the desperate situation in Darfur. We can condemn the violence. We can and must stand tall and strong for an end to ethnic violence.

Richard S. Williamson, Ambassador, General Statement on item 3 and 9 on Sudan (Ap. 23, 2004), *available at* http://geneva.usmission.gov/humanrights/2004/statements/0423Sudan.htm.

Viewed in this light, was the adoption of the Chair's Statement on Sudan a success or a failure of the Commission? Consider the statement of Joanna Weschler, Human Rights Watch's UN Representative, made in the midst of the controversy over the EU's secretly negotiated deal with Sudan: "Darfur presents a critical test of the Commission's credibility." *See* Press Release, Human Rights Watch, U.N.: Darfur Poses Critical Test for Rights Body, (Apr. 20, 2004), *available at* http://www.hrw.org/english/docs/2004/04/20/sudan8466.htm. Did the Commission pass Weschler's test?

2. *Action by the High Commissioner.* During the 2004 session of the Commission on Human Rights, the Acting High Commissioner for Human Rights dispatched a team to Sudan to meet with government officials in Khartoum and to visit Darfur in order to make an assessment of the human rights and humanitarian situation there. The Acting High Commissioner's report, released on May 7, 2004, noted that "the Government appears to have sponsored a militia composed of a loose

collection of fighters, apparently of Arab background, known as the 'Janjaweed.' With the active support of the regular army, the Janjaweed have attacked villages, targeting those suspected of supporting the rebels and committing numerous human rights violations." UN Econ. & Soc. Council, Comm' on Human Rights, *Report of the United Nations High Commissioner for Human Rights and Follow-up to the World Conference on Human Rights: Situation of human rights in the Darfur region of the Sudan*, U.N. Doc. E/CN.4/2005/3 (May 7, 2004).

3. *The suffering and the negotiations continue.* Since 2004, the situation in Darfur has, if anything, gotten worse. Even after the signing of the Darfur Peace Agreement in 2007, the security situation in the region deteriorated. By many accounts, violations of human rights and international humanitarian law by all parties to the conflict have increased. From 2004 to 2008, the Human Rights Council passed resolutions, the Secretary–General and various special rapporteurs drafted reports, and a "High–Level Mission" mandated by the Human Rights Council released a scathing report on the situation in Sudan. Yet the human rights violations continue unabated. Bleak as this outlook may be, can you identify the value all of this material might have for a human rights lawyer? If not useful now, are there conditions under which this material would have greater value in the future?

4. *Sudan and the Genocide Convention.* In his speech to the Commission, excerpted above, the Secretary General stated, "Whatever terms it uses to describe the situation, the international community cannot stand idle." Before the Secretary–General and the U.S. Secretary of State visited Darfur, there was a great deal of speculation as to whether the situation there would be described as genocide. Why should this matter? Given your understanding of international law and obligations on the subject (*see, e.g.,* UN Convention on Genocide, Jan. 12, 1951, 78 UNTS 277, *entered into force* Jan. 12, 1951), does it matter what language—legal or otherwise—the international community uses to describe the situation in Darfur? Does characterizing the situation in Darfur as "genocide" create legal obligations for Sudan?

In testimony before the Senate Foreign Relations Committee in September 2004, then Secretary of State Colin Powell stated, "We concluded—I concluded—that genocide has been committed in Darfur and that the government of Sudan and the Janjaweed bear responsibility—and genocide may still be occurring." Glenn Kessler and Colum Lynch, *U.S. Calls Killings In Sudan Genocide*, WASH. POST, at A1 (Sept. 10, 2004). Does this statement create obligations for the United States as a party to the Genocide Convention? What about other UN Member States more broadly, or for the Security Council?

5. *The responsibility to protect.* At the World Summit in September 2005, the outcome document recognized that "[e]ach individual State has the responsibility to protect its populations from genocide, war crimes, ethnic cleansing and crimes against humanity. This responsibility

entails the prevention of such crimes, including their incitement, through appropriate and necessary means." 2005 World Summit Outcome, UN Doc. A/RES/60/1, ¶ 138 (Oct. 24, 2005). Notably, the Summit outcome document also recognized the responsibility of the international community "to use appropriate diplomatic, humanitarian and other peaceful means, in accordance with Chapters VI and VIII of the UN Charter, to help to protect populations from genocide, war crimes, ethnic cleansing and crimes against humanity." *Id.*, at ¶ 139.

The legal components of the Responsibility to Protect are fully explored in Module 17 below. But it is clear that Sudan presents a serious challenge to the meaning and status of the doctrine.

6. *Commission vs. Council: Has anything changed?* The proceedings of the Commission on Human Rights were—and the proceedings of the Council so far have been—intensely political. States devote enormous resources both to campaigning for a seat and, once there, to assemble the votes necessary to convene special sessions, reject or adopt resolutions, or control the mandates of its various special mechanisms.

Reforms in the Council were intended to correct failings in the Commission, but have they? The Council reports to the UN General Assembly, but the dynamics have not changed—certain human rights situations (such as Israel and the Occupied Territories) are highlighted to the exclusion of many others. Membership is smaller, but states continue to act in regional groups to block censure of governments from their region. The Council meets throughout the year, but its various resolutions and reports continue to be ignored by the world's worst human rights abusers.

The failings of the Commission, and now the Council, lead to inevitable questions about their value as institutions. Since it is clear that human rights can never truly be divorced from politics and power, why continue the yearly ritual through which "universal" criticism appears to fall on deaf ears? Investigations are performed, reports prepared, resolutions adopted, yet widespread and systematic human rights abuses persist. Responding to these criticisms, the focus of the Council has shifted more toward cooperation, *i.e.*, working with states to determine how UN resources might be targeted toward improving the human rights of their citizens. Is this the panacea for the Council's ills?

7. *Universal periodic review.* One innovation added to the UN human rights machinery is the Universal Periodic Review (UPR) mechanism of the new Human Rights Council. Under UPR, all UN member states must submit information—which could take the form of a national report—to a working group of the Council, which will consider it in conjunction with other information on the state concerned prepared by the Office of the High Commissioner for Human Rights and by NGOs. After an interactive dialogue with the state under review, a report will be submitted for adoption by the Council, which will include recommendations.

8. *Country-specific resolutions.* Some countries see country-specific resolutions as a means of expressing the international community's condemnation of a particular country's abusive policies and practices. For others, country-specific resolutions are mere attempts to justify moral indignation and cultural ignorance at the expense of those states that lack the influence to prepare a proper defense. Still others see these resolutions as political hypocrisy: Why censure Iran but not Saudi Arabia? Why Sudan but not Pakistan? These inconsistencies have led many to question whether the practice of negotiating country-specific resolutions should be shelved altogether.

Although country-specific resolutions are non-binding, their adoption sends a strong political message to those states singled out for condemnation. Governments sometimes try to meet the specific benchmarks incorporated into these resolutions in order to convince members to forgo adopting a resolution, or at least moderating the language, that addresses its domestic human rights situation. This was particularly the case with the resolution addressing the states comprising the former Yugoslavia—as the situation there improved between the time the Commission first considered the matter in the early 90s and 2002, the tone and substance of the Commission's resolutions changed considerably. Even the title of the resolution was revised to reflect the decision to shift criticism away from any one particular state. *Compare Situation of human rights in the territory of the former Yugoslavia* (CHR Res. 1993/7) with *Situation of human rights in parts of south-eastern Europe* (CHR Res 2002/13).

9. *The UN General Assembly and human rights.* The Human Rights Council is not the only UN body to consider human rights issues. During the UN General Assembly, which meets every fall in New York, a wide range of human rights issues is considered by the General Assembly's Third Committee, and many country-specific and thematic resolutions are adopted in the area of human rights. In the past, there was a large degree of overlap between Third Committee and Commission resolutions. Compare Resolution on the situation of human rights in Turkmenistan, UN Doc. E/CN.4/RES/2003/11 (2003), with Resolution on the situation of human rights in Turkmenistan, UN Doc. A/Res/58/194 (2003). Indeed, by making the new Human Rights Council a subsidiary organ of the UN General Assembly, it is hoped some of this overlap can be eliminated.

There are, however, reasons for the parallel work of the two bodies. Sometimes, parallel resolutions are adopted in order to keep up the pressure on a particular country to improve its human rights situation, as was the case with Turkmenistan. In other circumstances, events might lead a country to choose to advance a resolution in the General Assembly, rather than wait for a session of the Council. This was the case when Canada promoted a successful resolution on Iran after the death of a Canadian–Iranian photographer in Iran and the subsequent diplomatic dispute between the two countries. *See* Kathleen Harris, *Ottawa's*

UN Draft Sparks Rage in Iran, Tᴏʀᴏɴᴛᴏ Sᴜɴ, Nov. 25, 2003, at 34; Evelyn Leopold, *UN Panel Backs Call to Rebuke Iran Abuses*, Tᴏʀᴏɴᴛᴏ Sᴛᴀʀ, Nov. 22, 2003, at A12. In previous sessions of the Commission on Human Rights, the EU successfully tabled a human rights resolution on Iran, but the EU had stopped advancing the resolution, in part, based on its determination of near certain failure. In the General Assembly, however, the Canadians were successful. Why?

The Commission on Human Rights was made up of 53 states, the majority of which were from the developing world. Many of these states opposed—and continue to oppose—country-specific resolutions as being inconsistent with the spirit of cooperation they feel the United Nations should embody. In other words, they contend that states should not be criticized for human rights violations, but instead should be provided assistance and encouragement to improve the situations in their countries. (It is interesting to note, however, that the same states that take this "principled" stand regularly vote in favor of a number of resolutions that criticize Israel for its actions in the Occupied Territories.) Moreover, representatives in Geneva (where the Council meets) often receive no instructions from their home capitals, and, personal rivalries, alliances, and petty grudges can drive negotiating and voting positions, regardless of a delegate's national position on an issue. As a result of this dynamic, many resolutions can be blocked through diplomatic stonewalling in Geneva.

The General Assembly in New York, however, can be a different environment. First, it is made up of more than three times as many states, many of whom are willing to take principled stands on human rights issues, regardless of regional blocs. Second, the General Assembly is made up of six separate committees, some of which are more important to states than the Third Committee, which handles human rights issues. Accordingly, their actions in one committee may leave them open to retribution in another committee, thus causing them to think carefully about the impact a position in the Third Committee might have on their interests in another. Third, because the Security Council is in New York, there is a higher degree of "adult supervision" over committee work in the General Assembly, *i.e.*, both capitals and New York Permanent Representatives (who tend to be well-connected diplomats) ensure that their delegations act consistently with their national positions, not according to personal foibles. This characteristic of New York delegations also makes states more receptive to high-level diplomatic lobbying in capitals.

It is important to note that the Geneva–New York dynamic cuts both ways. Where many Western countries sought a resolution on the situation of human rights in Iran, the Canada-led effort was successful in the UNGA where it would not likely have been in the Commission. In another context, when the Mexican Government pushed for the creation of a working group to elaborate a draft convention on the rights of persons with disabilities—an initiative opposed by Western governments—it also decided to work within the UNGA instead of the Commission. Much to the disappointment of Western governments who felt another international human rights instrument was unnecessary, Mexico was successful, and the working group was established. *See* G.A. Res. 56/168, UN GAOR, 56th Sess., UN Doc. A/CN/56/198 (2001). Ultimately, the new treaty on the rights of disabled people was adopted and opened for signature.

10. *The UN and NGOs.* Non-governmental organizations (NGOs) play a vital role in the United Nations. Often serving as the "conscience" of the international community, they are ever-watchful of the words and deeds of member states within the institution. Those NGOs with consultative status (through a process established by ECOSOC Resolution 1996/31) maintain a permanent presence at the UN and have access to all formal meetings of states. They lobby delegates in the hallways, make statements during meetings, and, at times, observe negotiations over text. As a result of their growing political influence in national capitals, many NGOs are able to influence the positions taken by their home governments in important UN negotiations. Can you identify any problems posed by the role played by NGOs in the United Nations? Do you think NGOs should be provided a greater role in the UN, *e.g.*, should they be given the capacity to vote or sponsor resolutions? Negotiate treaties?

11. *The UN, the United States, and Cuba.* It should be clear by now that multilateral human rights work can be high political theater. Perhaps nowhere was this more apparent than in the yearly debate over the Commission on Human Rights Resolution on the situation of human rights in Cuba. For years, the United States was the lead sponsor of a resolution that criticized the Castro regime for widespread violations of human rights on the small island nation. For several years before the Council was created, other countries took the lead in promoting the resolution in the Commission, yet many still saw it as a U.S.-driven exercise. Although the margin by which the resolution passed varied from year to year, the resolution was regularly adopted by the Commission.

Each year in Geneva, U.S. and Cuba would act out their bilateral relationship on the UN stage. Cuban delegates would give lengthy, passionate speeches denouncing every element of U.S. policy that would fit into the time allotted, primarily for the audience watching on television in Havana, Fidel Castro foremost among them. The U.S. delegation would respond in kind, and the room would be filled to capacity for the vote on the resolution. Before the session, the Cuban Foreign Minister would travel the globe lobbying against the resolution with promises of Cuban development assistance in the form of Cuban doctors. The United States would also engage in a high-level lobbying campaign before the vote.

At the 2003 session of the CHR, the U.S.-Cuba battle reached an all time high–or low, given your perspective. After the resolution was adopted, a Cuban delegate assaulted a Cuban–American NGO representative, which led to the U.S. ambassador (an ex-U.S. Marine) giving chase and assisting UN security in apprehending the Cuban delegate. Shortly thereafter, the Cuban delegation introduced a resolution on the U.S. detention facility at Guantanamo Bay. At the last minute, Cuba withdrew the resolution after determining the U.S. had assembled a sufficient number of votes to defeat the resolution.

Now that the U.S. has decided not to participate in the Council, the body no longer adopts resolutions on Cuba, and accordingly, there is no special rapporteur to report on the human rights situation there. As a result, some of the drama delegates could previously look forward to in Geneva has been lost.

12.   *The Security Council and Human Rights.* The UN Security Council is granted authority under Chapter VII of the UN Charter to address threats to peace and security. Because the Security Council is the only UN mechanism that can issue resolutions that have the force of law, this authority is not used lightly. Many human rights advocates have argued that the Security Council should take a more active role in considering human rights issues. From time to time, the Security Council has invited the UN High Commissioner for Human Rights to brief the Council, but there has been substantial institutional reluctance for the Security Council to do much more than this.

In light of the Council's Charter-mandated authority, under what circumstances can you see the Security Council acting on the basis of human rights violations? When the Security Council adopted a resolution on the situation in Sudan in 2004, it was careful to frame the resolution in the context of a Chapter VII threat to international peace and security. *See* Security Council Resolution 1574 (2004), UN Doc. No. S/Res/1574 (19 November 2004). In your view, would a human rights-based argument have been sufficient to obtain a Security Council resolution authorizing the use of force in Afghanistan before 9/11? Iraq? Sudan? Burma? Zimbabwe?

Practicum

For years, the human rights situation in Egypt has steadily deteriorated. Civil and political rights are continually under threat, and activists expect matters to get worse. Many of these issues are raised in reports prepared by NGOs and in the annual U.S. Human Rights Reports issued by the State Department. While Egypt has not previously been the subject of a resolution at the UN Human Rights Council, some NGOs have managed to persuade the European Union to sponsor a resolution this year.

Students should be assigned to represent various members of the Council that will negotiate a resolution addressing the human rights situation in Egypt. One or more students (on behalf of the EU) should prepare a draft resolution that will be considered by the rest of the class. Students should be assigned countries with a specific interest in either the adoption or rejection of such a resolution. For instance, students could represent the United States, Egypt, Guatemala, Syria, Norway and Canada. Students should assume that Egypt is a member of the Council for purposes of this practicum and, therefore, can call for a vote on the resolution, but it is unclear whether it has the votes it needs to defeat the resolution. As a result, the students should strive for a consensus document that incorporates all members' concerns.

D.   CHARTER–BASED MECHANISMS: THE 1503 PROCEDURE

In 1970, the UN Economic and Social Council (ECOSOC) adopted Resolution 1503 (XLVIII), which established a confidential procedure (now known as the "1503 procedure") by which "situations which appear to reveal a consistent pattern of gross and reliably attested violations of human rights and fundamental freedoms" could be addressed by the Commission on Human Rights and its subsidiary Sub–Commission on the Promotion and Protection of Human Rights. Through the 1503 procedure, NGOs would file a "communication" with the UN High Commissioner for Human Rights, which in turn, would transmit the communication to the government concerned to permit it to respond. Although the Human Rights Commission has been replaced by the Human Rights Council and the Sub–Commission has been eliminated, a complaints procedure was retained. The new "Human Rights Council Complaint Procedure" is intended to be more efficient and streamlined.

Each year, a Working Group on Communications (made up of five independent experts designated by a Human Rights Council Advisory Committee) considers communications and government responses (to those that are not screened out as "manifestly ill-founded or anonymous"), to assess the admissibility and the merits of the communications received. If deemed admissible, the communication is transmitted to the Working Group on Situations, which is comprised of five members appointed by the regional groups from among States sitting on the Human Rights Council. The Working Group on Situations, in turn, examines the communications, the replies of states, as well as the recommendations made by the Working Group on Communications. The Working Group on Situations will then present the Council with a report on any "consistent patterns of gross and reliably attested violations of human rights and fundamental freedoms" and make recommendations to the Council on the course of action to take. The Council can then choose any number of ways to address a situation brought to its attention, ranging from keeping the matter "under consideration" to appointing a special rapporteur to investigate the situation to requesting that the situation be made public.

Notably, all documents submitted under this procedure, as well as the meetings of both Working Groups, are kept confidential. The identity of those states being examined becomes public only if the Council decides to do so.

The secrecy with which this kind of a complaints mechanism is conducted as well as its non-binding nature have lead many to question its value as a tool for human rights advocates. Nevertheless, as monolithic and distant governments may seem, they care about their appearance before international human rights bodies like the Human Rights Council. States respond carefully to allegations made through this procedure and, at times, will take steps to ameliorate situations that come before the Council. The Human Rights Council Complaint Procedure should therefore be considered as part of any UN advocacy strategy.

ACCUSATION FOR VIOLATION OF HUMAN RIGHTS: A COMMUNICATION AGAINST THE UNITED STATES OF AMERICA UNDER ECOSOC RESOLUTION 1503 (XLVIII)

I emigrated from my native country (Cuba) in the year of 1980, due to political reasons, to this country of liberty, hope, and great opportunities (the United States of America), in search of asylum, peace, democracy, and well being for myself and my family, with the bad luck that by mistake I came to a country where repression, and discrimination are predominant, and where the Human Rights of immigrants are violated because of race, sex, language, religion and other conditions without distinction.

On 11–17–88, I committed a small infraction against the American laws, and on 12–22–89 was sentenced indiscriminately by a criminal court to serve for such crime, the exaggerated and inhuman sentence of 5 years in prison, which I completed on 8–10–92. That same day when I fulfilled the sentence that had been imposed on me, I was picked by the authorities of the US Immigration and Naturalization Service. * * * I have been unjustly denied my liberty for 7 months, this after having completed my sentence, and for the only and exclusive reason of being a Cuban immigrant, since no person from a different citizenship as mine is incarcerated again (like us Cubans), in order to serve another sentence for the same crime, and even a longer one than the one imposed by the criminal courts, because their judicial situation is immediately resolved (they are either granted conditional freedom under bond, or deported to their country of origin).

Many are the injustice, abuses, maltreatment, and constitutional violations committed by the judicial authorities of the USA against the Cuban community incarcerated in the prisons of this country, which are too many to enumerate, and for which reason we claim for justice before the United Nations. * * *

The Universal Declaration of Human Rights consists of 30 articles and I, as a juridical person, accuse the Department of Justice, or the "US Immigration and Naturalization Service" of violating my rights under articles 1, 2, 3, 5, 6 and 7. * * *

RESPONSE OF THE UNITED STATES TO COMMUNICATIONS FROM FIVE CUBAN NATIONALS UNDER ECOSOC RESOLUTION 1503 (MAY 1993)

The Government of the United States welcomes the opportunity to respond to * * * communications from five Cuban nationals who came to the United States illegally during the 1980 Mariel Boatlift. The circumstances under which these individuals arrived in the United States, and under which they are detained, are sufficiently similar to warrant a combined response. Accordingly, this response will set forth: (1) the factual and legal background of the Mariel Boatlift; (2) the treatment of the Mariel Cubans by the Government of the United States; and (3) the specific issues raised by these individual communications.

At the outset, however, the Government of the United States would cite the pertinent sections both of ECOSOC Resolution 1503 (XLVIII), under which government comments on this communication are being solicited, as well as Sub-commission Resolution 1 (XXIV), whereby standards for admissibility of communications are laid out:

[The working group should meet] with a view to bringing to the attention of the Sub-commission those communications, together with replies of governments, if any, which appear to reveal a consistent pattern of gross and reliably attested violations of human rights and fundamental freedoms within the terms of reference of the Sub-commission.

ECOSOC Resolution 1503 (XLVIII)

1. Standards and Criteria

(B) Communications shall be admissible only if, after consideration thereof, together with the replies of any of the governments concerned, there are reasonable grounds to believe that they may reveal a consistent pattern of gross and reliably attested violations of human rights and fundamental freedoms. * * *

4. Existence of Other Remedies

(B) Communications shall be inadmissible if domestic remedies have not been exhausted, unless it appears that such remedies would be ineffective or unreasonably prolonged. Any failure to exhaust remedies should be satisfactorily established.

The United States Government respectfully states that the communications in question are inadmissible. First, the communications fail to reveal the required consistent pattern of gross and reliably attested violations of human rights. The petitions in question deal with the circumstances of only a small number of individuals, and do not demonstrate any human rights abuse, let alone a systemic pattern. As discussed more fully below, the treatment of more than 125,000 Mariel Cubans by the Government of the United States, all of whom came to the United States illegally, has been extraordinarily generous. Nearly all have been afforded the opportunity to obtain permanent residence and citizenship, and only approximately 125 persons admitting to serious criminal acts in Cuba prior to their arrival or suffering from serious mental disorders have never been released into U.S. society. Aside from these few, the Government of the United States currently detains only those who committed crimes or otherwise seriously violated the terms under which they were released into U.S. society.

Second, the communications do not establish the exhaustion of domestic remedies, or allege that the pursuit of such remedies would be futile. Indeed, as set forth below, the United States has established effective and humane procedures under which those Mariel Cubans who remain in detention have their cases frequently reviewed to determine possible release. In addition, the detainees may invoke habeas corpus procedures available under U.S. law. The communications do not demonstrate, or even allege, that the individuals in question have exhausted these remedies.

For these reasons, the Government of the United States requests that these communications be deemed inadmissible. Nevertheless, in an effort to be as responsive as possible, the Government of the United States would like to take this opportunity to address briefly the substantive issues raised by the communications.

History of the Mariel Boatlift. These communications involve Cuban nationals who came to the United States in 1980 as part of a mass exodus of more than 125,000 Cubans from Mariel, Cuba, to the United States. The 1980 exodus was triggered by the occupation of the Peruvian embassy in Havana by over 10,000 Cubans who desired to leave that country. On April 14, 1980, the President of the United States authorized the admission to the United States as refugees of up to 3,500 of those who had taken refuge in the Peruvian embassy, provided that they met the requirements of applicable U.S. immigration and refugee laws. Shortly thereafter, the Cuban government announced that all Cubans wishing to go to the United States were free to board boats at the port of Mariel. This announcement effectively precluded any orderly processing of these individuals by U.S. immigration authorities.

Boat owners in Miami at once began to shuttle back and forth between Florida and Cuba to transport such individuals to the United States. The United States government moved to halt this activity, on grounds that the incoming Cubans had no right to enter the United States without proper documentation. * * *

Eventually, unable to stem the growing number of vessels participating in the boatlift, the U.S. Navy and Coast Guard undertook rescue operations and began directing inbound vessels to Key West, Florida, in an effort to keep control over arriving Cubans. On May 2, 1980, the President of the United States invoked his powers under the U.S. Migration and Refugee Assistance Act of 1962 to make ten million dollars available for processing, transporting, and caring for the arriving Cubans. Throughout the course of the boatlift, the President increased the amount of emergency funding available to deal with the evolving crisis.

In the midst of these chaotic events, the United States government became aware that the Cuban government had intermingled common criminals and persons with serious mental health problems with those who were leaving Cuba in the boatlift. On May 2, 1980, the United States government announced that it would carefully screen the recent arrivals, and that it would return those with criminal records and certain others back to Cuba. * * *

At the same time, the President announced that for humanitarian reasons the United States would accept certain pre-screened escapees from Cuba–specifically, those who had sought refugee status in the United States Interest Section or in the Peruvian embassy in Havana, political prisoners whom Castro had held for many years, and close family members of those individuals. In June 1980, the President directed that Cubans identified as having committed serious crimes in Cuba were to be securely confined and ordered that exclusion proceedings be initiated against those who have violated U.S. law while waiting to be reprocessed or relocated. The President later reiterated that the United States government would not allow those persons to be resettled or relocated in the United States. The boats continued to come, however, until shortly after September 26, 1980, when Castro closed Mariel harbor and ordered all boats awaiting passengers to depart. In total, more than 125,000 Cubans arrived in the United States during the Mariel Boatlift.

<u>U.S. Treatment of the Mariel Cubans.</u> Although each of the more than 125,000 Mariel Cubans were "excludable" aliens under the U.S. Immigration and Nationality Act with no right to enter the United

States, the U.S. Attorney General exercised his parole authority under the Act to allow 123,000 to be released—or "paroled"—into U.S. society.

Of those individuals detained upon completion by the United States government of its initial screening process in August 1981, only about 1,800 remained in detention because of suspected or admitted criminal backgrounds that would make them ineligible for admission to the United States. A number of others were detained because of serious medical or psychiatric problems.

Some of those who initially were released committed crimes in the United States, and some of their sponsorship arrangements—required as a condition of their release—broke down. As a result, the INS on November 12, 1980, issued guidelines providing for revocation of parole in sponsorship breakdown cases "if the alien has no means of support, no fixed address and no sponsor" and in criminal cases "if an alien is convicted of a serious misdemeanor or felony." The INS twice revised these guidelines, so that in March 1983 parole of any Mariel Cuban would be revoked if he or she had been "convicted in the United States of a felony or a serious misdemeanor and completed the imprisonment portion of [his] sentence" or if he or she "presents a clear and imminent danger to the community or himself."

Initially, the Government of Cuba refused to take back any of its own nationals who were excluded from the United States and held in detention. Since this refusal created the possibility that some of the Mariel Cubans would face indefinite detention, an undesirable outcome, the U.S. Attorney General adopted a status review plan. * * *

On December 28, 1987, the U.S. Department of Justice issued regulations on Mariel Cuban parole determinations that set out the framework of the current Cuban review plan. Under the regulations, in the case of detainees whose parole has been revoked, the review process is ordinarily to begin within three months of revocation of previous parole; in the case of those who have previously been reviewed and continued in detention, a subsequent review is to commence within one year of a refusal to grant parole. In addition, the director of the Cuban review plan ("the director") may schedule a review of a detainee at any time he deems such a review to be warranted.

The INS establishes a file on each detainee including his record of institutionalization in Cuba, his history of reviews under the Cuban review plan, his criminal record in the United States, U.S. Public Health Service reports, and any outstanding warrants. The review plan process consists of two INS officers who review the file of each detainee and, if they cannot recommend release on the basis of the file alone, conduct a personal interview of the detainee. The detainee may bring a person of his choice to the interview and may submit any information either orally or in writing that he believes demonstrates that it is in the public interest that he be released. If the INS panel recommends that the detainee be released on parole, a written recommendation (including a brief statement of the factors which were deemed material to the recommendation) goes to the Associate Commissioner for Enforcement or his designee (currently the director). The Associate Commissioner or his designee, in the exercise of his discretion, then decides whether or not granting immigration parole would be in the public interest. Before recommending release, the INS panel must conclude that:

(1) The detainee is presently a non-violent person;

(2) The detainee is likely to remain non-violent;

(3) The detainee is not likely to pose a threat to the community following his release; and

(4) The detainee is not likely to violate the conditions of his parole.
  * * *

Detainees who are approved for parole by the Associate Commissioner are released after a suitable sponsorship or placement has been found for them, which may include placement by the U.S. Public Health Service or the U.S. Community Relations Service in an approved halfway house or community project or placement with a close relative who is a lawful permanent resident or a citizen of the United States. Paroled detainees are required to abide by any special conditions that may have been placed on their immigration parole. The sponsorship/placement requirement and conditions placed on parole are intended to minimize danger to public safety and order and to maximize the chances that the detainee will successfully integrate into the community.
* * *

The United States submits that its treatment of Mariel Cubans has been generous and fair. Of the over 125,000 who entered the United States illegally, the vast majority have been given the opportunity to obtain permanent resident status in the U.S., and eventually citizenship. Only a small minority who suffer from serious mental illness or have committed serious crimes and/or violated the terms of their release into society have been detained by the INS pending return to Cuba, and they are regularly considered for release.

Information on Individual Petitioners and Response to Allegations. The United States submits that the petitioners have been treated fairly. While petitioners would obviously have preferred not to be detained, their detention as excludable aliens is entirely justified as a means of protecting U.S. society and sovereignty.

Approximately 61 percent of the Mariel Cubans housed by the Bureau of Prisons are in so-called "general population" status. That means that they eat their meals, exercise and work with other detainees for approximately eight hours a day. The remaining 39 percent, who have engaged in disruptive behavior or asked for personal protection are placed in the more restrictive administrative housing units for Mariel Cubans. Their movement is more limited, and they usually take their meals in their cells. They nonetheless usually enjoy one or two hours of supervised exercise every day.

Conditions inside the Cuban units of the various detention facilities are identical to those afforded the general population. Contrary to the petitioners' allegations, three meals a day, exercise opportunities and basic toilet articles are provided to all detainees, although persons in administrative detention status may not be allowed to have certain articles that could be used as weapons, such as razor blades. While housed in general population status, Cuban detainees have full access to the complete range of education and employment opportunities available to federally sentenced inmates. Program and work opportunities are somewhat more limited for inmates housed in secure Cuban units; the operation of the secure units, however, is intended to reflect a general population status while ensuring the degree of security necessary to protect the safety of individuals and property. Within the secure Cuban units, employment is available for institutional maintenance activities, special work details, and in federal prison industries. The educational opportunities available to Cubans within secure Cuban units include adult basic education, English as a second language, general equivalency diploma, and drug abuse education/counseling. Some of the facilities also offer behavioral therapy, acculturation, and group communication activities.

For Cuban detainees with release decisions who are in need of a more intensive drug treatment program, the Bureau of Prisons is operating a comprehensive drug abuse program at the Federal Correctional Institute in Englewood, Colorado. Cuban detainees in need of acute medical or mental health care are transferred to a Bureau of Prisons medical center for federal prisoners for evaluation and/or treatment. * * *

Notes and Questions on the *1503 Procedure*

1. *Recent Supreme Court rulings.* In 2005, in *Clark v. Martinez*, 543 U.S. 371 (2005) (per Scalia, J.), the Supreme Court held that the detention of two deportable Mariel Cubans was unreasonable in light of the fact they were not likely to be readmitted to Cuba. The Court relied on its earlier opinion in *Zadvydas v. Davis*, 533 U.S. 678 (2001) finding that an admitted immigrant could be detained for deportation for more than 90 days, but only as long as "reasonably necessary" to remove him from the country, and not longer than six months if the alien could demonstrate that there was "no significant likelihood of removal in the reasonably foreseeable future." 533 U.S., at 701. The government argued the Court should not apply the *Zadvydas* standard because the Mariel Cubans at issue in *Clark* were paroled into the United States by the Attorney General. The Court, however, found that the requirement

that immigrants be held no longer than necessary for deportation applies to both admissible and inadmissible immigrants without distinction. Within months, inadmissible aliens were receiving parole into the United States from federal courts nationwide. *See, e.g., Morales-Fernandez v. INS*, 418 F.3d 1116 (10th Cir. 2005); *Baez v. Bureau of ICE*, 150 Fed.Appx. 311 (5th Cir. 2005); *Perez-Aquillar v. Ashcroft*, 130 Fed. Appx. 432 (11th Cir. 2005).

Notably, the Court in *Clark* did not address either international law in the opinion or any of the international adjudications of these issues (*see, e.g.*, Rafael Ferrer–Mazorra et al., (Case No. 9903), No. 51/01, Inter–Am. C.H.R. (2001); Response of the Government of the United States to Inter–American Commission on Human Rights Report 85/00 of October 23, 2000 Concerning Mariel Cubans (Case 9903), Inter–Am. C.H.R. (2001)). Also of note is the failure of the United States to release any of the nearly 1000 Marielitos still held in U.S. prisons, several years after the Court's opinion in *Clark*. Moreover, a 2004 report of the Government Accountability Office noted that U.S. Immigration and Customs Enforcement has failed to implement the *Zadvydas* opinion. *See Government Accountability Office, Immigration Enforcement: Better Data and Controls are Needed to Assure Consistency with the Supreme Court Decision on Long–Term Alien Detention* (2004); *available at*, http://www.gao.gov/new.items/d04434.pdf.

2. *Proceedings before the Commission.* The 1503 communication and response excerpted above represent one of several exchanges between Mariel Cubans and the United States—twenty-three communications were filed against the United States before the Sub–Commission. While each petition included varied allegations, all were premised on the common claim that the administrative detention of the Mariel Cubans constituted a prolonged, arbitrary detention in violation of international law. This claim clearly had resonance with the members of the Sub–Commission, as the petitions were repeatedly "held over," by the Sub–Commission, then eventually submitted to the Commission on Human Rights for action. This was the only matter against the United States that proceeded all the way to the Commission. In the end, by a vote of 45–2–6, the Commission voted to dismiss the petitions, with only China and Cuba voting against dismissal.

3. *Prolonged arbitrary detention.* In your view, did the United States adequately address the allegation that the detentions of the Mariel Cubans constituted prolonged, arbitrary detention? How does the United States argue that its treatment of the Mariel Cubans is consistent with international law? What evidence does it present? Where in international law could you find support for the position asserted in the communication?

If you conclude, as the Sub–Commission did, that the communications had merit, try viewing the position of the United States as matter of policy, not law. If, under U.S. law, a conviction is a sufficient basis for deportation (a legitimate exercise of national sovereignty under international law), and no country—including Cuba—was willing to accept these individuals, what options were available to U.S. authorities? Should these individuals, some of whom had records as violent criminals, have been released into U.S. society?

––––––––––

Practicum

For centuries, female infanticide has been practiced with regularity in India. Some forms of the practice include discerning the sex of an unborn fetus, then, if the child is determined to be a girl, taking measures to effect an abortion. In other forms, female infants are killed by midwives, some of whom charge twice as much to dispose of the child as to deliver it. As one couple admitted, "To have one girl in India is bad luck, a second daughter is a catastrophe. We couldn't afford a second girl so we killed her, poisoned her; she died within an hour, after screaming for 15 minutes."

In many large cities in India, neighborhoods near hospitals are filled with prenatal clinics that provide ultrasounds to enable expecting mothers to abort female fetuses. Through passage of the Pre–Natal Diagnostic Techniques Act in 1994, the Indian Parliament made misuse of diagnostic techniques criminal, but reports indicate that enforcement is lax, penalties are ineffective, and the Act has served only to drive the practice underground.

The causes of the practice are numerous and complex, finding root in religion, tradition, culture, and economics. Whatever the causes, it is argued that modern Indian society continues to place a higher value on male children, thereby encouraging the practice of female infanticide. In turn, inequalities and discrimination are perpetuated through a practice which, it is argued, has been legitimized by government inaction.

Assume that the American Federation of Churches has filed a petition against the Government of India under the so-called "1503 procedure" before the UN's new "Human Rights Complaint Procedure" mechanism, alleging the Indian government is in violation of its obligations under international law for failing to prevent—or even curb—the practice of female infanticide. Although the Federation is concerned with female infanticide generally, it should focus its petition on the practice of selectively aborting female fetuses. The Government of India must respond. Both parties should address (a) the question of admissibility; (b) the substantive international law arguments; and (c) India's responsibility for the practice's existence. Assume domestic remedies have been exhausted.

CHAPTER 3

MODULE 5

THEMATIC REPORTING MECHANISMS IN THE UNITED NATIONS

■ ■ ■

Orientation

The previous module identified the various United Nations mechanisms that exist to address human rights situations in particular *countries*. The UN also offers a variety of mechanisms for addressing recurring *themes* or issues in the protection of human rights around the world. These "thematic mechanisms" take the form of Special Rapporteurs, Representatives or Working Groups, generally with a mandate to investigate and report on particular types of human rights violations, ranging from disappearances and violence against women to contemporary forms of slavery and the right to health. These thematic mechanisms are typically authorized to receive complaints from individuals or organizations and to communicate with governments about them; indeed, governments routinely receive communications from the thematic mechanisms requesting information on what the government has done or is doing about particular cases or widespread situations. In addition, Special Rapporteurs or Representatives are generally authorized to conduct site visits as part of their investigations, although some governments have refused to allow them in. The negative inferences drawn from non-cooperation, combined with the constant pressure created by aggressive, industrious Rapporteurs, can be crucial for advocates, and the thematic mechanisms have on occasion demonstrably improved the human rights situation of groups and individuals around the world. Equally important, the thematic mechanisms can provide a platform for the development of substantive human rights norms, for example by focusing attention on the meaning of "due diligence" or erecting the conceptual foundation for treating rape as a war crime in certain circumstances.

The existing thematic mechanisms[1] were created primarily by the Commission on Human Rights and continued by the new Council on

---

1. As of the date of publication, there are thirty thematic mechanisms–twenty-eight created by the Commission, beginning in 1980 with the Working Group on Enforced or Involuntary Disappearances, and two—the Special Rapporteurs on Contemporary Forms of Slavery (2007) and Adequate Housing (2008)—created by the Council.

Human Rights.[2] Traditionally, the thematic mechanisms created by the Commission focused primarily on civil and political rights, but as the broader human rights agenda has shifted towards economic, social, and cultural rights, the thematic mechanisms have kept pace, and there is now an agenda item and parallel Working Group or Special Rapporteur to address almost every high-profile human rights issue—from extreme poverty to toxic waste to torture.

In addition to the mechanisms created by the Commission/Council, other UN institutions have either been created specifically to address thematic human rights issues or have become increasingly involved in human rights issues over the past several years. Of particular importance is the Office of the High Commissioner for Human Rights ("OHCHR"), created at the World Conference on Human Rights in 1994 to coordinate UN action on the promotion and protection of human rights. Since 1994, OHCHR has expanded substantially to support the mandate of the High Commissioner and the work of its special mechanisms, as well as to mainstream human rights into the work of UN field presences.[3]

Given this institutional framework, how can a human rights advocate use the UN thematic mechanisms?

1. *Investigating and reporting on conditions in particular countries.* The mechanisms are authorized to seek and receive information and can be used to publicize an individual case or human rights situation in a particular country. Because Special Rapporteurs and Representatives are in regular contact with governments, advocates can urge them to bring certain cases to the attention of government officials. They also regularly include information regarding individual cases in their annual reports.

2. *Collecting and archiving the global evidence.* The reports of the thematic mechanisms may be a valuable and comprehensive source of information about patterned human rights abuses in countries around the world. Because these mechanisms draw on information from varied sources in preparing their reports, lawyers should look to these publica-

---

2. In April 2004, the UN General Assembly adopted a resolution replacing the much-criticized Commission with the Human Rights Council. The organizational change was not entirely cosmetic: although all of the Commission's thematic mechanisms were simply carried over to the Council, the Council was made a subsidiary organ of the General Assembly, rather than of the UN Economic and Social Council, giving it at least on paper a higher profile within the United Nations bureaucracy. As noted in the prior module, the Council has hardly been immune from criticism.

3. A growing part of the High Commissioner's budget is spent on implementing programs throughout the world. For 2007, OHCHR had available over $170 million for activities. Office of the High Commissioner for Human Rights, Annual Report 2007, 138 (April 2008). These funds supported eleven OHCHR country offices, nine regional offices and thirteen human rights advisors in UN country teams; OHCHR also supported human rights components in seventeen peace missions. *Id.* at A7. The OHCHR is funded by the UN regular budget and by voluntary contributions; the UN regular budget generally covers approximately one-third of the OHCHR's activities, with the remaining two-thirds covered by voluntary contributions. The United States has traditionally been the largest contributor to the OHCHR through voluntary contributions and, since 2005, has been advocating an increase in funding for the OHCHR from the UN regular budget.

tions for factual support and guidance when preparing a case, a petition, or an advocacy strategy.

3. *Developing legal norms.* The work of the thematic mechanisms has contributed to the development of both international and domestic human rights law. Because many Rapporteurs and Representatives are themselves prominent lawyers and scholars, their statements and analysis can constitute valuable evidence of a principle of international human rights law that must be proved in court. At the legislative phase, the work of Special Rapporteurs can also serve as a tool for governments drafting domestic law in a manner that incorporates (or is consistent with) international human rights standards. And when international norms themselves are inadequate to address a contemporary human rights problem, the thematic mechanisms can play a profound role in concentrating the community mind and developing the law.

The materials that follow illustrate each of these functions. You will focus on the work of the Special Rapporteur for Violence Against Women, who proved instrumental not only in raising the public consciousness on this particular abuse, but who also immeasurably advanced the legal analysis of the issue.

Readings

A.   INVESTIGATING AND REPORTING ON CONDITIONS IN PARTICULAR COUNTRIES

There are two primary mechanisms available to Special Rapporteurs to investigate and report on cases of human rights violations relevant to their specific mandate.

The first is through receiving information about individual cases and communicating them to governments. Some governments take these communications seriously and either initiate an investigation based on the Rapporteur's communication or provide information about the case in response to it. Other governments ignore these requests entirely or provide cursory responses that fail to address the allegations in any substantive way. The Rapporteurs' yearly reports detail the extent to which governments have or have not provided responses. That communication process (and the prospect of public exposure behind it) provides a valuable mechanism to human rights advocates who choose to publicize a particular human rights case or exert pressure on a government to investigate a case. Although the Special Rapporteur has no independent enforcement powers, the communications process allows her to exert diplomatic pressure on a country where human rights violations have taken place. In addition, the accumulation of communications against a country creates a useful record of consistent violations that may be relied upon as evidence in other forums of a widespread, consistent practice in the target state.

The second mechanism is the country visit. Although Special Rapporteurs are occasionally denied entry to countries, many requests for invitations are accepted and provide valuable insight into the human rights situation in a country. On these investigatory visits, the Special Rapporteur meets with a broad spectrum of individuals and groups with an interest in the issues she has a mandate to investigate. This includes government officials, victims, NGOs, and human rights defenders. The dialogue that takes place on these visits is valuable not only for advocates, but also for governments that are willing to undertake changes to improve the human rights situation. Often, the Special Rapporteur makes specific recommendations for improvement based on her visit as well as on her experience with other countries.

The reports of the Special Rapporteur are generally made public and, as with the annual report, are submitted to the body that created her mandate. The states that are identified in these reports are given an opportunity to respond to allegations at regular sessions of the UN body to which the Special Rapporteur reports. There is considerable pressure for the country to respond in substance and, equally important, to describe the steps taken to remedy the problems identified in the report. Although some countries are more receptive to the reports than others, the process is important in maintaining diplomatic pressure on countries where human rights violations are common. The human rights advocate should see these visits as an opportunity to engage directly with a Special Rapporteur to ensure that human rights concerns are investigated and addressed in the published report.

As you read the following excerpts from the reports of a Special Rapporteur, consider both the substance of the issues that are identified and the pressure points that the process offers to advocates.

---

1. COMMUNICATIONS TO GOVERNMENTS

REPORT OF THE SPECIAL RAPPORTEUR ON VIOLENCE AGAINST WOMEN, ITS CAUSES AND CONSEQUENCES (MS. RADHIKA COOMARASWAMY): INTEGRATION OF THE HUMAN RIGHTS OF WOMEN AND THE GENDER PERSPECTIVE: VIOLENCE AGAINST WOMEN

U.N. Doc. E/CN.4/1999/68/Add.1 (11 January 1999)

Guatemala

5. By letter dated 30 July 1998 the Special Rapporteur informed the Government that she had received reports alleging that at approxi-

mately 3 a.m. on 17 June 1998, men armed with grenades, machetes and firearms assaulted a group of 30 members of Mama Maquin, a women's organization which works with returned refugees and displaced people in Guatemala, as they were returning from a meeting in the returned refugee community of Victoria 20 de Enero, Ixcan municipality, El Quiche department. It is reported that the assailants beat several women with the broadsides of their machetes and stole their personal goods. They allegedly tore up the papers from the meeting and cursed the women and their organization. According to information received, the same day members of Mama Maquin in Guatemala City received death threats and messages of intimidation from unidentified men urging them to give up their struggle on behalf of returned refugee women. The information suggests that these actions are connected to their activities as defenders of women's rights in Guatemala. The Special Rapporteur expressed the hope that the Government would investigate the allegations and take immediate action to bring the alleged perpetrators to trial, in order to comply with its international obligations.

6.   The Government replied that it had contacted Mama Maquin and held meetings to investigate the facts. A complaint will be submitted by Mama Maquin to the District Attorney's Office (Fiscalía Distrital) of the Public Ministry of Alta Verapez, and the organization will present the case during the week of 23 to 28 November 1998. The Government has guaranteed that representatives of the Office for the Defence of Women of the Office of the General Attorney for Human Rights (Defensoría de la Mujer de la Procuraduría de los Derechos Humanos) and the Unit for Women of the Prosecutor General's Office (la Unidad de la Mujer de la Procuraduría General de la Nación) will accompany Mama Maquin to this hearing. * * *

Peru

19.   By letter dated 9 November 1998 the Special Rapporteur informed the Government that she had received reports alleging that the climate of harassment and the pressure exerted against human rights defenders in Peru has been worsening. A number of female human rights activists have been subjected to harassment, abductions, attacks and death threats, including Ms. Delia Revoredo Marsano de Mur, Ms. Elba Greta Minaya Calle and Ms. Sofia Macher.

20.   Since early 1998 another prominent women's rights activist, currently campaigning against forced sterilization, Ms. Giulia Tamayo León, has allegedly been subjected to several incidents threatening her personal security and that of her family, including physical assault, intrusion upon private property and anonymous threatening telephone calls. Women's groups have been campaigning against a law authorizing the sterilization of women as a means of family planning which was introduced in 1995. The law has allegedly been used to put pressure in particular on poor indigenous women to be sterilized. Furthermore, it is

argued that the real motive for the law is not to enhance women's reproductive rights but to reduce birth rates. It is alleged that the incidents against Ms. Tamayo León were attempts by the authorities to intimidate and force her to stop her work against violence against women in the health and public sectors and other issues of women's rights.* * *

REPORT OF THE SPECIAL RAPPORTEUR ON VIOLENCE AGAINST WOMEN, ITS CAUSES AND CONSEQUENCES (MS. RADHIKA COOMARASWAMY): INTEGRATION OF THE HUMAN RIGHTS OF WOMEN AND THE GENDER PERSPECTIVE: VIOLENCE AGAINST WOMEN

U.N. Doc. No. E/CN.4/2000/68/Add.1 (27 January 2000)

Peru

Follow-up to previously transmitted communications

106.   By letter dated 13 August 1999, the Government responded to a letter from the Special Rapporteur sent on 9 November 1998 regarding the harassment of human rights defenders (see E/CN.4/1999/68/Add.1, paras. 19–20). Concerning Ms. Giulia Tamayo Léon, the Government indicated that the 40th Provincial Procurator's Office took up the case on 25 November 1998 and ordered a police investigation. On 20 July 1999, a decision was made to close the file on the investigation provisionally, as it had been impossible to identify the perpetrators of the act, without prejudice to the issuing of an order for the continuation of investigations aimed at identifying and/or finding the offenders. In its reply the Government did not give any information on the three other individuals who were mentioned in the same letter. * * *

REPORT OF THE SPECIAL RAPPORTEUR ON VIOLENCE AGAINST WOMEN, ITS CAUSES AND CONSEQUENCES (MS. RADHIKA COOMARASWAMY): INTEGRATION OF THE HUMAN RIGHTS OF WOMEN AND THE GENDER PERSPECTIVE: VIOLENCE AGAINST WOMEN

U.N. Doc. E/CN.4/2001/73/Add.1 (13 February 2001)

Sri Lanka

51.   In a letter dated 14 March 2000 the Special Rapporteur expressed her concern regarding cases of gang rape and murder of women and girls that are reportedly being committed by the security forces. In addition to rape cases in the North and East, she reported

that she had received information about political violence in the South that has affected women victims.

52.   On 14 March 1999 the Special Rapporteur also issued a press release in this regard.

53.   The following information in regard to individual cases was transmitted:

(a) Sarathambal Saravanabavanthakurukal, aged 29, was reportedly gang raped and then killed by Sri Lankan navy personnel on 28 December 1999 in Pungudutivu, near the Jaffna peninsula. Her body was reportedly found the following morning under leaves not far from her home near Kannaki Amman Temple. According to reports received, apart from a few high-profile cases which have been investigated thoroughly and the perpetrators brought to trial, cases of rape and murder of women and girls by Sri Lankan military personnel have often gone unpunished. In this context the Special Rapporteur is encouraged that on 30 December 1999, President Chandrika Kumaratunga ordered an immediate investigation into the case. However, it is alleged that the suspects have been transferred from the area to avoid prosecution and that very little is being done to pursue the matter;

(b) Ida Caremelitta was allegedly gang raped by five soldiers and then killed during the night of 12 July 1999 in Pallimunai village on Mannar Island. Five masked and heavily armed men reportedly entered the house while her family were sleeping and took Ms. Caremelitta outside and violently raped and killed her. The post-mortem report indicates that Ms. Caremelitta had been repeatedly raped and her body had been sexually mutilated;

(c) On 6 October 1998 Ms. Pushpamalar, aged 12, was allegedly detained whilst returning from school and raped by a soldier in Sangathaanai, Chavakachcheri, east of Jaffna. Following the assault she was admitted to hospital;

(d) Anoja Weerasinghe's house was reportedly attacked on two separate occasions, on 24 December 1999 and 2 January 2000. The first attack was with stones and caused a few broken windows, the second attack was more severe and led to the burning down of a part of her house. Concern has been expressed that the two incidents are related to her political involvement over the last 22 years. Ms. Weerasinghe recently played the lead role in a film version of "The Trojan Women", an anti-war play. Her political involvement has also encompassed speaking in support of the United National Party and peacefully picketing in Veyangoda on 17 November 1999 to protest the physical attacks against actors and actresses. She has also participated in news conferences, one of which was on 18 January, immediately following the attack. The actors supporting the UNP also organized a picket line in Colombo on that day.

54. By letter dated 6 April 2000 the Government responded to the communication sent on 14 March 2000 concerning four cases of violence against women.

55. Regarding the case of Saravana Bhawanandan Kurukkal Saaradambaal, the Government stated that her brother had reported the murder to the Kayts police. On directions given by the Inspector–General of Police on 5 January 2000, investigators of the Criminal Investigations Department (CID) proceeded to Kyts, Jaffna, and took over the investigation which had been started by the Kayts police. The incident reportedly took place on 28 December 1999. At around 9.30 p.m., four armed men came to the house and took away the deceased. After the abductors left, the brother, with the assistance of the neighbours, searched the area, without success. Upon making a complaint to army personnel attached to a nearby camp, they too joined in the search. The following morning the complainant found the body of the deceased. The post-mortem examination showed that the deceased had been raped. There is no conclusive information relating to the identity of the perpetrators, but investigations are continuing.

56. Regarding the case of Fareed Ida Carmaleeta Laila, the Government reported that pursuant to instructions given to the Inspector–General of Police by the President on 15 July 1999, the CID [Criminal Investigations Department] commenced investigation into the alleged rape and murder of Fareed Ida Carmeleeta Laila. Investigations revealed that there was a prima facie case that she had been raped and murdered. A second post-mortem was conducted to obtain more accurate and scientific proof by a consultant forensic pathologist. Criminal investigations revealed that two armed persons had forced their way into the house of the victim. It is suspected that the intruders thereafter raped and murdered the victim. Eleven members of an army detachment in the vicinity of the victim's house were arrested and arraigned for an identification parade. Two of the soldiers were identified by witnesses as the two persons who went into the house of the victim on the day of the incident. They are Dayantha Upul Gurusinghe and Raja Somarantne. Upon identification of the two suspects, the magistrate remanded them in custody. They have been denied bail and are still in remand. The CID also found several pieces of cartridge from an automatic firearm. The findings of the government analyst reveals that the cartridge had been fired from the firearms used by the suspects. The CID is continuing its investigation, and is due to seek the advice of the Attorney–General.

57. Concerning the cases of Ms. Pushpamalar and Anoja Weerasinghe, the Government responded that investigations were continuing and detailed reports would be submitted in due course. The Government stated that it paid particular attention to acts of violence being committed by armed forces and police personnel in areas affected by conflict. It indicated that it refutes the accusation that only a few high-profile cases had been investigated. The Government states that every

case of alleged criminal conduct committed by the armed forces and police has been investigated and the perpetrators prosecuted, although there may have been unavoidable legal delays.

---

2. COUNTRY MISSIONS

REPORT OF THE SPECIAL RAPPORTEUR ON VIOLENCE AGAINST WOMEN, ITS CAUSES AND CONSEQUENCES (MS. RADHIKA COOMARASWAMY):

INTEGRATION OF THE HUMAN RIGHTS OF WOMEN AND THE GENDER PERSPECTIVE: VIOLENCE AGAINST WOMEN

**Report of the Mission to
the United States of Violence Against
Women in State and Federal Prisons**

U.N. Doc. E/CN.4/1999/68/Add.2 (4 January 1999)

1. At the invitation of the Government of the United States of America, transmitted by letter dated 15 May 1998, the Special Rapporteur on violence against women, its causes and consequences visited Washington D.C. and the States of New York, Connecticut, New Jersey, Georgia, California, Michigan and Minnesota from 31 May to 18 June 1998 to study the issue of violence against women in the state and federal prisons in each of the states mentioned. * * *

10. The present report is intended as a case-study to complement the Special Rapporteur's previous report on violence against women perpetrated and/or condoned by the State, presented to the Commission on Human Rights at its fifty-fourth session (E/CN.4/1998/54). The Special Rapporteur chose the United States of America because of serious allegations of sexual misconduct by male corrections officers in United States prisons which had been received, and also because of the several existing programmes and activities, both at federal and state levels, to prevent and combat violence in women's prisons. It is from the practical experience of such initiatives that the Special Rapporteur hoped to gain a deeper understanding of the causes and consequences of violence against women in prisons and detention facilities and of the effective measures to eliminate such violence. The Special Rapporteur also studied issues concerning access to health care and parenting/family programmes for incarcerated women and sought to evaluate positive initiatives undertaken by prison authorities to address the issues of violence against women in prisons. * * *

IV. GENERAL FINDINGS

A. Diversity and the lack of minimum standards

49. The first finding that the Special Rapporteur would like to highlight is the extraordinary diversity of conditions in United States

prisons. The Special Rapporteur was astonished that the prisons that she saw on video in Michigan and the prison that she toured in Minnesota were in the same country. Diversity is an important part of federalism in the United States context; however, there is diversity even within the states. Officials at Valley State Prison in California told the Special Rapporteur that many of the charges of sexual misconduct were frivolous, while across the street, in the Central California Women's Facility, sensitization training on sexual misconduct was being vigorously pursued. Further, 10 cases involving sexual misconduct had been prosecuted, leading to a conviction in one case. Although criminal prosecution was not successful in the other cases, the services of the accused were terminated. In Georgia, the Special Rapporteur was informed that there were 159 counties and that there was no uniformity within the state in terms of policing and correctional institutions.

50.   There is a need to develop minimum standards with regard to state practices in women's prisons, especially in the area of sexual misconduct. * * *

B.   Use of instruments of restraint

51.   In addition to the lack of minimum standards, the Special Rapporteur discovered the use of practices that contravened the Standard Minimum Rules on the Treatment of Prisoners. Rule 33 states clearly that instruments of restraint should not be used as punishment and that chains or irons should never be used as restraints. The Special Rapporteur was informed that there were large-scale violations of this provision in United States prisons. Reportedly, women refugees and asylum seekers coming into the United States are, in many cases, shackled at the airport even when there is no criminal sanction against them. In INS detention centres, prisoners are taken to their interviews in leg-irons.

52.   Convicts may be restrained in certain circumstances. * * * Amnesty International reports that mentally disturbed prisoners have been bound, spread-eagled on boards for prolonged periods without proper medical authorization. Amnesty International, *United States of America–Rights for All*, AI Index AMR/51/35/98, 1998, p. 65. According to Amnesty International, there are no nationally binding minimum standards regarding the use of restraints in the United States.

53.   Women in labour are also shackled during transport to hospital and soon after the baby is born. The Special Rapporteur heard of one case where shackles were kept on even during delivery.

54.   The use of these instruments violates international standards and may be said to constitute cruel and unusual practices. Some States, such as Minnesota, have abandoned the use of four-point restraints and instead use a "chair" with a straightjacket. In some cases, the chair is only used with the presence of a round-the-clock nurse. The chair can be abused and Amnesty International has chronicled these abuses in detail. *Ibid*, p. 67. The use of gas and chemical sprays, such as shown on

video to the Special Rapporteur in Michigan, and electroshock devices is also widespread in the United States. The abuse of restraints is of major concern to the Special Rapporteur. Many NGOs gave her evidence of such practices and she was able to see some of them on video in Michigan. The use of restraints without medical supervision and for prolonged periods is a clear violation of international standards.

C.   Sexual misconduct

55.   The Special Rapporteur interviewed women who had been subjected to some form of sexual abuse in practically all the facilities except in Minnesota. Sexual misconduct covers a whole range of abusive sexual practices in the context of custody. Rape does occur, but it is a fairly rare phenomenon. The more common types of sexual misconduct are sex in return for favours or consensual sex. Given the power imbalance inherent in prison/prisoner relationships and the hierarchy within the prison, relationships between prison guards and prisoners corrupt the prison environment and tend to exploit the women. Sanctioned sexual harassment, *i.e.* women being pat-frisked by men and monitored in their rooms and in the showers by male corrections officers, is also prevalent. * * *

56.   From the literature received by the Special Rapporteur and from discussions she had in the United States, it is clear that sexual misconduct by male corrections officers against women inmates is widespread. National mobilization by prisoners' groups and the prisoners themselves seems to have led to fresh and innovative attempts to deal with the problem. Although the Standard Minimum Rules for the Treatment of Prisoners requires that women prisoners be supervised only by women officers, the Supreme Court has deemed such a standard as unconstitutional under Title VII of the Civil Rights Act of 1964, the equal employment opportunity statute. Accordingly, it was found that the employment and career opportunities of female corrections officers would be curtailed if such a standard were implemented since there are only a small number of women's prisons. As a result, the United States continues to have male corrections officers supervising women prisoners. The United Nations Human Rights Committee has also expressed concern about male prison officers guarding women in United States prisons. *Official Records of the General Assembly*, Fiftieth Session, Supplement No. 40 (A/50/40), vol. I, paras. 285, 299.

57.   The presence of male corrections officers in housing units and elsewhere creates a situation in which sexual misconduct is more pervasive than if women were guarded by female officers. Although there have been cases of sexual misconduct on the part of female corrections officers, such cases were the exception rather than the rule. Corrections officers told the Special Rapporteur that men were necessary in women's prisons because they provided positive male role models. They argued that the key to success was in the professionalism of the officers and not their gender. They also said that the presence of women in male

correctional institutions has a calming effect on the men. They argued that the prison should be seen as a microcosm of society, with both males and females providing good role models. In response, the Special Rapporteur would point to the prevalence in United States society of violence against women generally, and sexual violence specifically, which raises particular worries about the use of male guards in female facilities.

58.   The Special Rapporteur found that the reality in women's prisons failed to match the ideal described above. One of the many cases she heard about was that concerning prisoner S. who, in 1995, was cleaning the back stairs of the compound when officer X grabbed and fondled her and kissed her. After that, he insisted on regular sexual encounters in different parts of the prison compound, and she complied because she was too frightened to refuse. She performed all the sexual acts that he demanded. In February 1996, when she tried to break off the relationship, he threatened her and threatened her daughter. She therefore continued. Finally, the FBI, with the cooperation of S., began investigations against the officer and subsequently had him removed.

59.   Though sexual misconduct remains a serious problem in United States women's prisons, recent court cases and awareness-raising campaigns have resulted in some encouraging changes, especially in the State of Georgia. The warden at Bedford in New York informed the Special Rapporteur of the increased understanding of the issues, which has reportedly led to positive changes. The Federal Government prohibits sexual intercourse or sexual contact with a prisoner by a prison employee. Under Title 18 of United States Code, section 2241, sexual intercourse by the use or threatened use of force is a felony with the maximum penalty being life imprisonment. Section 2243 prohibits consensual sexual contact between a person in custodial, supervisory or disciplinary authority and the person supervised. According to Human Rights Watch, 27 states and the District of Columbia have expressly criminalized sexual intercourse with, or sexual touching of a prisoner by prison staff. These developments took place in the 1990s after many complaints had been made by prisoners and NGOs interested in prisoners' rights. The Prevention of Custodial Sexual Assault by Correctional Staff is a bill currently being discussed in the Congress; it would provide funds to state governments for setting up prevention programmes with regard to custodial sexual assault, including the maintenance of databases.[1]

60.   The State of Georgia has set up procedures to deal with sexual misconduct which may be relevant elsewhere. The development of these procedures was a response to the *Cason v. Seckinger* case [231 F.3d 777 (11th Cir. 2000),] in which 10 women, identified only as Jane Does, brought a class-action suit complaining of rape, sexual assault, coerced sexual activity, involuntary abortions and retaliation. The shocking

---

1. [Editors' note: *See* The Prison Rape Elimination Act of 2003, 111 Stat. 972, which was designed to address the problem of sexual assault and rape in all correctional systems in the United States.]

revelations forced the court and the Department of Corrections to make sweeping changes. First, they closed the prison and created new prisons for the women. They argued that only women should guard women, but this was successfully opposed by trade unions. They created gender-specific posts and ordered that men entering the women's housing units had to announce themselves. There are notices all over the prison citing the *Cason* case and demanding compliance.

61.   Corrections officers have to sign statements that they agree with the *Cason* conditions. Staff failing to report sexual misconduct may also be punished. A special unit has been set up in the Georgia Department of Corrections to deal exclusively with allegations of sexual misconduct. If the allegations are found to be true, the unit will terminate the person's contract and turn the case over to the prosecutor's office. Pre-screening of corrections officers has been introduced to assess their behaviour in this regard. Corrections officers are now given eight hours of training on sexual misconduct and eight hours of training on sexual harassment. All inmates in Georgia prisons interviewed by the Special Rapporteur told her that after *Cason*, they had seen a welcome change with regard to the attitude of corrections officers.

62.   Georgia's response in this case was commendable. Unfortunately, no figures in respect to the number of individuals terminated or prosecuted could be provided to the Special Rapporteur. The NGOs welcomed the reforms instituted after *Cason*; they reported, however, that although the framework was now in place, action was not being taken. Women rarely come forward since they fear retaliation; further, women ask, who would believe a felon? Nevertheless, the reorganization in Georgia as a direct result of the *Cason* class action suit was unique.

63.   Though the *Cason* provisions address unwanted sexual advances, there remains the problem of the right of women prisoners to privacy. The Special Rapporteur's visit and discussions with women in prisons all over the country have convinced her that the presence of male corrections officers in women's housing units is a direct violation of the right to privacy. The modesty panels on showers and shower curtains in some prisons are inadequate to ensure privacy. Women complained to the Special Rapporteur that they were watched in the toilet, in the showers and while they were undressing. They reported that the male presence was extremely intrusive. In addition, in most of the prisons, men reportedly pat-frisk the women, while women guards conducted strip-searches. In Connecticut, women inmates reported that they don't go to the cafeteria to avoid being pat-frisked by male guards. Many inmates reported that they felt that pat-frisks by men were very intrusive. * * *

E.   Parenting

69.   Despite the fact that the overwhelming number of women in prisons are mothers, there is no consistency among the states and even within institutions in dealing with this issue. Georgia does not encourage

bonding between an inmate and her child, since officials believe that such a bond is not in the best interests of the child. Georgia prefers to put the child in foster care. However, Pulaski State Prison in Georgia has a dynamic warden; Pulaski has a children's centre and is attempting to arrange transport for children to visit their mothers. Although in other prisons in Georgia, basic visiting rights are permitted and nurseries are provided, there were no creative programmes that encouraged mother-child bonding. The same was true in California and Michigan.

70.   Bedford, New York, and Minnesota, on the other hand, encourage the link between mother and child with creative programmes. In Bedford, children are transported once a week to visit their mothers. There are trailer units where some inmates can spend time, including weekends, with their children. There is a programme whereby mothers can record themselves reading a children's story and the cassette sent to the child. There is also a programme on long-distance mothering to help inmates with children cope with their problems. However, it must be recognised that these programmes are run by private Christian charities and are not a part of government policy. In Minnesota, weekend visits are also encouraged, and there are separate apartments where inmates can spend a longer time with their children.

71.   One of the most difficult problems attendant upon putting mothers in jail is the destruction of the family unit. The foster care option may lead to the permanent break-up of the family. For many inmates, children are a life-sustaining force. To break that bond is punishment of the worst kind. The location of many prisons in some cases prevents visitation by children who cannot afford to visit at regular intervals.

72.   When one mother was arrested, her son went berserk. At the time, he was 12 years old. He ended up in a juvenile penitentiary with 71 charges, from burglary to grand larceny, against him. By September 1997, he was one of the most wanted men in America. A minister brought him into a rehabilitation programme. He is now a leading athlete and member of the Olympic team. Explaining his early life of crime, he said, "I wanted my mama. When she was taken in, I had nothing to live for." The effect of large-scale incarceration of African American women is having a major impact on the African American family. Research and analysis in this regard should be pursued. The Special Rapporteur was quite moved, in speaking to many of the inmates, by the importance they placed on their children. It is necessary to develop parenting programmes in prisons throughout the United States along the lines of those started in New York and Minnesota.

F.   Grievance procedures

73.   In each institution the Special Rapporteur visited, she asked staff as well as inmates, about the grievance procedure within the institution. With the exceptions of Minnesota and Georgia (after *Cason*),

no states have grievance procedures that rely on outside monitoring. Most grievances are addressed within the institution, with a great deal of discretion vested in the warden. Many grievances are dealt with through informal counseling by the officers within the institution, with the assistance of the warden. The Special Rapporteur feels that in situations of a captive population, the need for outside review cannot be underestimated.

74.   Most of the inmates said that they had no faith in internal grievance procedures. They were also afraid of retaliation. If someone brings a charge of sexual misconduct against an officer, she is usually removed to administrative segregation or solitary confinement, allegedly "for her own protection." Such segregation is experienced as punitive. Additionally, many inmates reported that staff in the administrative segregation, out of loyalty to the accused officer, are often abusive to the inmate who has complained. It is for reasons such as this that outside review should be an essential part of the monitoring of inmates' complaints. * * *

I.   Privatization of prisons

79.   The privatization of prisons raises particular concerns for the safety and well-being of prisoners in general, and of women prisoners in particular. The only private facility visited by the Special Rapporteur was the INS facility in Elizabeth, New Jersey. The emphasis of the facility seemed to be on security more than anything else, despite the fact that many inmates were not violent offenders. Rather, many of the inmates were immigrants in the country illegally and awaiting deportation. There were no projects for the women and no programmes. Most of the women spent their time sleeping, since there was very little activity. The Special Rapporteur is concerned that private prisons will not provide the humanitarian and rehabilitation programmes that are now essential aspects of prison life. If privatization is to be allowed, there must be strict guidelines and oversight so that the profit motive does not interfere with health and medical services, education, training and cultural programmes for inmates. * * *

_____

NOTES AND QUESTIONS ON THE SPECIAL RAPPORTEURS

1.   *Interpreting the Special Rapporteur's mandate.* The resolution creating the Special Rapporteur on Violence Against Women authorized her to:

> Seek and receive information on violence against women, its causes and its consequences, from Governments, treaty bodies, specialized agencies, other special rapporteurs responsible for various human rights questions and intergovernmental and non-governmental organizations, including women's organizations, and to respond effectively to such information [and]

Recommend measures, ways and means, at the national, regional and international levels, to eliminate violence against women and its causes, and to remedy its consequences.

UN Commission on Human Rights, *Question of integrating the rights of women into the human rights mechanisms of the United Nations and the elimination of violence against women*, Resolution 1994/45 (1994). How does Ms. Coomaraswamy's discussion of parenting in U.S. prisons fit within this mandate? Could her mandate extend to investigating the pornography industry?

2. *Identifying best practices.* Review the report on women in U.S. prisons with an eye to listing the best practices the Special Rapporteur has identified. What is the legal and strategic value of pointing these out?

3. *NGO engagement.* The information on which Special Rapporteurs base their inquiries to governments is often provided by domestic and international NGOs. This is inevitable since Special Rapporteurs are not paid for their work and have virtually no staff. The NGOs not only provide information about particular individual cases of abuse, they also offer guidance on which countries should be the subject of country visits. In the report on women in U.S. prisons, the Special Rapporteur drew particular attention to the prior work of Amnesty International and Human Rights Watch. *See also* Human Rights Watch, NOWHERE TO HIDE (1998); Amnesty International, NOT PART OF MY SENTENCE: VIOLATIONS OF THE HUMAN RIGHTS OF WOMEN IN CUSTODY (1999). What standards should the Special Rapporteur apply in determining which NGO reports to use and which ones to ignore?

4. *State cooperation.* The excerpts above provide insight into the thematic Special Rapporteurs' investigative and reporting role. Note however that these materials reflect exchanges with governments that are cooperative: Guatemala, Peru, and Sri Lanka each provided detailed responses to the Special Rapporteur's inquiry and in certain cases launched investigations into the alleged violations. With respect to her request to visit the United States, the government extended the Special Rapporteur an invitation to visit and investigate prison conditions in several parts of the country. Although she was able to visit several facilities in New York, Connecticut, New Jersey, Georgia, and California, and was granted broad access to both prison facilities and individual prisoners, the Governor of Michigan cancelled Ms. Coomaraswamy's plans to meet with state representatives and to visit women's prisons located in that state. As noted by Ms. Coomaraswamy,

> This refusal was particularly disturbing since she had received serious allegations about misconduct in Florence Crane Women's Facility, Camp Branch facility for Women and Scott Correctional Facility for women. The Special Rapporteur nevertheless continued with her journey to Michigan and had meetings with lawyers, academics, former guards and former prisoners. She was also able

to speak to some prison inmates on the phone to hear their complaints. Given the seriousness of the allegations, corroborated by diverse sources, the Special Rapporteur decided that these allegations should form part of her report despite the lack of cooperation from Michigan State authorities.

Report of the Special Rapporteur on violence against women, its causes and consequences, Ms. Radhika Coomaraswamy, UN ESCOR, Comm'n on Human Rights, 55th Sess., para. 145, UN Doc. E/CN.4/1999/68/Add.2 (1999).

In many circumstances, governments do not welcome the Special Rapporteurs: many requests for information about individual cases go unanswered, and requests for country visits are either denied or access is severely restricted. Institutionally, how could the United Nations improve compliance with its thematic mechanisms? Is there a role for the Security Council? What are the legal and political obstacles to creating such an enforcement mechanism?

5. *Standing invitations to Special Rapporteurs.* Increasingly, governments extend standing invitations to UN thematic mechanisms as a way of showing their transparency and their willingness to engage the international community on its human rights concerns. As of March 2008, fifty-seven states had issued standing invitations. Some of these states, like Liechtenstein and Iceland, have little to fear from international scrutiny of their human rights records. Others who have issued standing invitations, however, such as Iran, Turkey, and Georgia, face greater exposure on human rights issues. Why would these countries take that risk when they are under no obligation to issue such invitations?

6. *Relationship to other international bodies.* The treatment of women in U.S. prisons was also taken up by the UN Committee Against Torture when the U.S. presented its initial report to the Committee. *Consideration of Reports Submitted by States Parties under Art. 19 of the Convention*, Comm. Against Torture, 24th Sess., UN Doc. CAT/C/SR.424, 427 & 431 (2001), reviewing *Initial Reports of States Parties Due in 1995: United States of America (09/02/2000)*, Comm. Against Torture, 24th Sess., UN Doc. CAT/C/28/Add.5 (2000). *See also Report of the Committee against Torture, 23rd session (8–19 November 1999), 24th session (1–19 May 2000)*, Comm. Against Torture, 24th Sess., paras. 175–180, UN Doc. A/55/44 (2000).

7. *Domestic implementation.* Although the U.S. Department of Justice has the legal tools to investigate and prosecute violations of the rights of prisoners, including women prisoners, critics assert that the federal government has been either politically unwilling or financially unable to put an end to the wide range of abuses throughout the vast U.S. prison system. These problems are magnified at the state level, where funding may be more scarce and a "get tough on crime" stance has taken precedence over the protection of individual rights. Indeed, in recent

years the problem has gotten even more difficult to manage with increased privatization of the prison function. How would you craft each of the observations made by the Special Rapporteur above as violations of the United States' international human rights obligations? Remembering that the U.S. has signed, but not ratified, the Convention on the Elimination of Discrimination Against Women, how would you craft your argument as a violation of U.S. obligations under both treaty and customary international law? Assuming you are acting as counsel for a woman who has suffered an actual injury-in-fact, what international forums would be available for your claim? What are the pros and cons of each forum?

8. *The Special Rapporteurs and Guantanamo Bay.* On June 25, 2004, several Special Rapporteurs issued a Joint Statement on the Protection of Human Rights and Fundamental Freedoms in the Context of Anti-terrorism Measures, requesting that the Special Rapporteur on the Independence of Judges, the Chairperson–Rapporteur of the Working Group on Arbitrary Detentions, the Special Rapporteur on the Right of Everyone to the Highest Attainable Standard of Physical and Mental Health, and the Special Rapporteur on Torture and other Cruel, Inhuman or Degrading Treatment or Punishment, be permitted to visit those persons arrested, detained, or tried on grounds of alleged terrorism or other violations in Iraq, Afghanistan, and the Guantanamo Bay military base in order to ascertain whether the detainees' international human rights were being respected. *See Joint Statement by Participants at the Eleventh Annual Meeting of the Special Rapporteurs/Representatives, Independent Experts and Chairpersons of the Working Groups of the Special Procedures of the Commission on Human Rights and of the Advisory Services Programme*, in *Report of the United Nations High Commissioner for Human Rights and Follow-up to the World Conference on Human Rights: Effective Functioning of Human Rights Mechanisms*, Annex. II, at 20, U.N. Doc. E/CN.4/2005/5 (2004) (reiterating concern that anti-terrorism measures may have violated the enjoyment of human rights and fundamental freedoms, and requesting that Working Groups and Special Rapporteurs be permitted to visit detention facilities in Iraq, Afghanistan, and Guantanamo Bay).

You can review the mandates of each of these mechanisms. *See* Office of the United Nations High Commissioner on Human Rights: Human Rights Bodies: Special Procedures: Thematic Mandates: www2.ohchr.org/english/bodies/chr/special/themes.htm. Is this an appropriate use of each of the mandates? Does the U.S. position that the fight against terrorism is governed by international humanitarian law and not human rights law—and, therefore, lies outside the mandate of the special mechanisms—affect your answer?

B.   COLLECTING AND ARCHIVING THE GLOBAL EVIDENCE

Special Rapporteurs often prepare reports that highlight a specific aspect of the human rights abuse within their mandates. Because these reports draw on the Special Rapporteur's experience in investigating individual human rights abuses and carrying out country missions, they can provide valuable evidence of a regional, national, or international pattern or practice of human rights abuse.

REPORT OF THE SPECIAL RAPPORTEUR ON VIOLENCE AGAINST WOMEN, ITS CAUSES AND CONSEQUENCES   (MS. RADHIKA COOMARASWAMY):

CULTURAL PRACTICES IN THE FAMILY THAT ARE VIOLENT TOWARDS WOMEN

U.N. Doc. E/CN.4/2002/83 (31 January 2002)

1.   Throughout the world, there are practices in the family that are violent towards women and harmful to their health. Young girls are circumcised, live under severe dress codes, given in prostitution, denied property rights and killed for the sake of honour in the family. These practices and many others constitute a form of domestic violence but have avoided national and international scrutiny because they are seen as cultural practices that deserve tolerance and respect. The universal standards of human rights are often denied full operation when it comes to the rights of women. Cultural relativism is therefore often an excuse to allow for inhumane and discriminatory practices against women in the community. In the next century, the problems posed by cultural relativism, and the implications for women's rights, will be one of the most important issues in the field of international human rights.

2.   The Convention on the Elimination of Discrimination against Women is extremely clear. Article 5 states:

State Parties shall take all appropriate measures:

(a) To modify the social and cultural patterns of conduct of men and women, with a view to achieving the elimination of prejudices and customary and all other practices which are based on the idea of the inferiority or the superiority of either of the sexes or on stereotyped roles for men and women....

3.   Article 2 of the Convention states: "State Parties condemn discrimination against women in all its forms, agree to pursue by all appropriate means and without delay a policy of eliminating discrimination against women...."

4.   The Declaration on the Elimination of Violence against Women, solemnly proclaimed by the General Assembly in its resolution 48/104,

also states clearly, in article 4, "States should condemn violence against women and should not invoke any custom, tradition or religious consideration to avoid their obligations with respect to its elimination".

5. Despite these international norms and standards, the tension between universal human rights and cultural relativism is played out in the everyday lives of millions of women throughout the globe. The situation is made more complex by the fact that women also identify with their culture and are offended by the arrogant gaze of outsiders who criticize their way of doing things. Since their sense of identity is integrally linked to the general attitude towards their community, their sense of dignity and self-respect often comes from being members of the larger community. In minority communities and third world communities that already suffer from discrimination, this sense of identity poses major problems for women. Some women have told the Special Rapporteur that they do not mind wearing the veil because they see the veil as subversive against imperialism. Cultural markers and cultural identity that allow a group to stand united against the oppression and discrimination of a more powerful ethnic or political majority often entail restrictions on the rights of women. Many indigenous communities do not allow women civil rights or property rights and yet they themselves are often a threatened community, very vulnerable to the dictates of the more powerful groups in their respective societies. For this reason, the issue of cultural relativism requires a measure of sensitivity. Women's rights must be vindicated but women should win those rights in a manner that allows them to be full participants in a community of their choosing. Without respecting their right to community, any attempt to struggle for women's rights might create a backlash that will marginalize the women fighting for equal rights.

6. Nevertheless, many of the practices enumerated in the next section are unconscionable and challenge the very concept of universal human rights. Many of them involve "severe pain and suffering" and may be considered "torture like" in their manifestation. Others such as property and marital rights are inherently unequal and blatantly challenge the international imperatives towards equality. The right to be free from torture is considered by many scholars to be *jus cogens*, a norm of international law that cannot be derogated from by nation States. So fundamental is the right to be free from torture that, along with the right to be free from genocide, it is seen as a norm that binds all nation States, whether or not they have signed any international convention or document. Therefore those cultural practices that involve "severe pain and suffering" for the woman or the girl child, those that do not respect the physical integrity of the female body, must receive maximum international scrutiny and agitation. It is imperative that practices such as female genital mutilation, honour killings, Sati or any other form of cultural practice that brutalizes the female body receive international attention, and international leverage should be used to ensure that these practices are curtailed and eliminated as quickly as possible. * * *

II. CULTURAL PRACTICES IN THE FAMILY THAT VIOLATE WOMEN'S RIGHTS

11.   There are many cultural practices throughout the world that are violent toward women. In this section some of the more disturbing violations are described, in order to highlight the nature of the problem.

A.   Female genital mutilation

12.   Female genital mutilation (FGM), a deeply rooted traditional practice, is believed to have started in Egypt some 2,000 years ago. It is estimated that more than 135 million girls and women in the world have undergone FGM and 2 million girls a year are at risk of mutilation. FGM is practised in many African countries including Chad, Côte d'Ivoire, Ethiopia, Kenya, Mali, Nigeria, Sierra Leone, the Sudan, Uganda and the United Republic of Tanzania. In the Middle East, FGM is practised in Egypt, Oman, the United Arab Emirates and Yemen. It has also been reported in Asian countries such as India, Indonesia, Malaysia and Sri Lanka. Immigrants from these countries perform FGM in Australia, Canada, Denmark, France, Italy, the Netherlands, Sweden, the United Kingdom and the United States of America. It is suspected that FGM is performed among some indigenous groups in Central and South America.

13.   The methods and types of mutilation differ according to each country and ethnic group. But, FGM may be broadly classified into four groups:

   (i) *Circumcision*, or cutting of the prepuce or hood of the clitoris, known in Muslim countries as *sunna* (tradition). This is the mildest form, of FGM and affects only a small proportion of women. It is the only form of mutilation to be correctly termed circumcision, but there has been a tendency to group all kinds of mutilations under the misleading term "female circumcision".

   (ii) *Excision*, meaning the cutting of the clitoris and all or part of the labia minora.

   (iii) *Infibulation*, the cutting of the clitoris, labia minora and at least the anterior two thirds and often the whole of the labia majora. The two sides of the vulva are then pinned together by silk or catgut sutures, or with thorns, leaving a small opening for the passage of urine or menstrual blood. These "operations" are done with special knives, razor blades, scissors or pieces of glass and stone. The girl's legs are then bound together from hip to ankle and she is kept immobile for up to 40 days to permit the formation of scar tissue.

   (iv) *Intermediate*, meaning the removal of the clitoris and some or all of the labia minora. Sometimes, slices of the labia majora are removed. The practice varies according to the demands of the girl's relatives.

14.   The main reasons given for the continuation of this practice are custom and tradition. In societies where FGM is practised, a girl is not considered an adult or a complete woman until she goes through the "operation." Some societies believe that all persons are hermaphroditic and the removal of the clitoris makes the female a "pure woman". It is said also to test a woman's ability to bear pain and defines her future roles in life and marriage while preparing her for the pain of childbirth. FGM is also a result of the patriarchal power structures which legitimize the need to control women's lives. It arises from the stereotypical perception of women as the principal guardians of sexual morality, but with uncontrolled sexual urges. FGM reduces a woman's desire for sex, reduces the chances of sex outside marriage and thus promotes virginity. It is also deemed necessary by society to enhance her husband's sexual pleasure. A husband may reject a woman who has not gone through the "operation." Health reasons are also put forward as justifications for FGM. Unmutilated women are considered unclean. It is believed that FGM enhances fertility. It is considered that the clitoris is poisonous and that it could prick the man or kill a baby at childbirth. In some FGM-practising societies, there is a belief that the clitoris could grow and become like a man's penis. Even though FGM pre-dates Islam, religious reasons are given for the continuation of FGM in some societies. * * *

B.   *Honour killings*

21.   Honour killings in Pakistan (originally a Baloch and Pashtun tribal custom) have recently received international attention. Honour killings are now reported not only in Balochistan, the North–West Frontier Province and Upper Sind, but in Punjab province, as well. They are also reported in Turkey (eastern and south-eastern Turkey but also in Istanbul and Izmir in western Turkey), Jordan, Syria, Egypt, Lebanon, Iran, Yemen, Morocco and other Mediterranean and Gulf countries. It also takes place in countries such as Germany, France and the United Kingdom within the migrant communities.

22.   Honour killings are carried out by husbands, fathers, brothers or uncles, sometimes on behalf of tribal councils. The killing is mainly carried out by under-aged males of the family to reduce the punishment. They are then treated as heroes. The action is further endorsed by their fellow inmates in prison, if they are sent there, who wash these young boys' feet and tell them that they are now "complete" men. The act is regarded as a rite of passage into manhood. Ironically, it is not unheard of for female relatives to either carry out the murder or be accomplice to it.

23.   It should be stated here that it is extremely difficult to collect accurate statistical data on honour killings in any given community. As honour killings often remain a private family affair, there are no official statistics on practice or frequency and the real number of such killings is vastly greater than those reported. The Washington Post Foreign Ser-

vice reports that 278 murders were reported in Punjab in 1999. The Special Task Force for Sindh of the Human Rights Commission of Pakistan received reports of 196 cases of honour killings in 1998 and more than 300 in 1999. Every year more than 1,000 women are killed in the name of honour in Pakistan alone. During the summer of 1997, Khaled Al–Qudra, then Attorney–General in the Palestinian National Authority stated that he suspected that 70 per cent of all murders in Gaza and the West Bank were honour killings. They are usually attributed to natural causes. In Lebanon, 36 honour crimes were reported between 1996 and 1998, in Jordan 20 honour killings in 1998 and in Egypt 52 similar crimes in 1997. In Iraq more than 4000 women have been killed since 1991. The same report stated that between 1996 and 1998 in Bangladesh, about 200 women were attacked with acid by husbands or close relatives, but the number of deaths is unknown. In the West there are honour killings among immigrant communities. In the United Kingdom, INTERIGHTS has a special project that documents forced marriage cases and the threat of honour killings to British women who come from immigrant communities.

24.   In a frequently cited case, a teenager's throat was slit in a town square in Turkey because a love ballad was dedicated to her over the radio. Other reasons include bringing food late, answering back, undertaking forbidden family visits *etc.* These women's lives are circumscribed by traditions which enforce extreme seclusion and submission to men. Male relatives virtually own them and punish contraventions of their proprietorship with violence.

25.   It is not necessarily for love, shame, jealousy or social pressure that these crimes are committed. Economic and social issues also contribute to the rise in honour killings. Amnesty International claims that factors such as the progressive brutalization of society due to conflict and war, increased access to heavy weapons, economic decline and social frustration also lead to increased resort to the honour killing system.

26.   Cleansing one's honour of shame is typically handled by shedding the blood of a loved one; the person being murdered is typically a female, the murderer is typically a male relative, and the punishment of the male is typically minimal. Most significantly, the murderer is revered and respected as a true man.

27.   Honour is a magic word, which can be used to cloak the most heinous of crimes. The concept of honour is especially powerful because it exists beyond reason and beyond analysis. But what masquerades as "honour" is really men's need to control women's sexuality and their freedom. These murders are not based on religious beliefs but, rather, deeply rooted cultural ones. Family status depends on honour. In patriarchal and patrilineal societies maintaining the honour of the family is a woman's responsibility. In these societies, the concept of women as commodities and not as human beings endowed with dignity and rights equal to those of men is deeply embedded. Women are seen as the

property of men and they have to be obedient and passive, not assertive and active. Their assertion is considered as an element which would result in an imbalance of power relations within the parameters of the family unit.

28.   Women are seen to embody the honour of the men to whom they "belong". As such they must guard their virginity and chastity. Honour killings in West Asia have their roots in the crude Arabic expression "a man's honour lies between the legs of a woman". By controlling women's sexuality and reproduction, they become the custodians of cultural and ethnic purity. But, male control extends not just to a woman's body and her sexual behaviour, but also to all of her behaviour, including her movements and language. In any one of these areas, defiance by women translates into undermining male honour. The woman's body is considered to be the "repository of family honour". Alarmingly, the number of honour killings is on the rise as the perception of what constitutes honour and what damages it widens. * * *

34.   Honour crimes are not confined to Muslim communities only. They occur in various parts of the world. In Brazil, men who kill their spouse after the wife's alleged adultery are able to obtain an acquittal based on the theory that the killing was justified to defend the man's "honour". Enormous pressure by women's groups resulted in the honour defence being removed from the books or judges' instructions to juries. However, juries continue to acquit men whom they feel have killed their wives for reasons of honour. * * *

E.   Caste

49.   In Bangalore, India, when a social worker, who belonged to a low caste, prevented a child marriage, she was gang raped by five upper-caste men. They were acquitted after a three year trial because the judge ruled that they could not possibly have raped a lower-caste woman.

50.   According to a Human Rights Watch report more than 250 million people worldwide suffer because of caste-based discrimination. It calls caste "a hidden apartheid of segregation," modern-day slavery. Caste is descent-based and hereditary. Exploitation and violence based on birth are found in many parts of the world. The most talked-about community are the Dalits or so-called untouchables of India. The Indian caste system, which is perhaps the world's longest surviving social hierarchy, is a feature of its social life. Corollaries to this caste system are found in other parts of South Asia, such as Nepal, Pakistan, Sri Lanka and Bangladesh.

51.   Caste-based divisions of labour are central to several ethnic groups in many African countries. Burkina Faso, Senegal (Jaam), Nigeria (Osu), Burundi, Mali, Cameroon, Mauritania, Guinea, Guinea Bissau, Côte d'Ivoire, Sierra Leone, Gambia, Mauritius and Liberia are some of the countries in which marginalization because of social hierar-

chy is rampant. The Buraku or Eta of Japan are another group of people who are subject to exploitation and violence because of their birth into so called "unclean" communities. Caste differentiation is also perpetuated by the Asian and African diaspora.

52.   Caste-based discrimination places culturally defined limits upon the individual in terms of mobility and interaction. Lower-caste people are excluded from villages and communities, which forces them to beg and scavenge in the streets. The upper castes have little or no interaction with lower-caste people in their day-to-day lives. The forms of discrimination vary according to each country and community, but are mostly exclusion from schools, religious sites and other public facilities, being forced to wear specific caste attire and to undertake specific occupations such as grave digging, sanitation jobs, manual scavenging and leather work, and being prevented from having physical interaction with so-called upper castes.

53.   Lower-caste women often suffer double and triple discrimination because of their caste, class and gender. They face targeted violence, even rape and death, from State actors and powerful members of dominant castes, used to inflict political lessons and crush dissent within the community; or the women are used as pawns to capture their men folk. These women are gang raped, forced into prostitution, stripped, paraded around naked, made to eat excrement or even murdered for no crime of theirs. The hypocrisy of the caste system is revealed during these crimes, as "untouchability" does not operate then. The women also face discrimination through the payment of unequal wages, or work in slave-like conditions in bonded labour. They also face sexual discrimination in the workplace. Young girls are married off at an early age mainly as protection against sexual assault from upper-caste men.

54.   There are formal protections in law, but discrimination persists. Women suffer more because of their inability to access legal protection. Many women do not approach the police for fear of dishonour or that they will be dismissed or suffer further abuse. Many Dalit women demanded that caste-based bias, atrocities and rape be recognized as racism at the World Conference against Racism in Durban, but were unfortunately not very successful.

F.   Marriage

55.   In many societies, young girls are prepared for marriage from a very early age. Girls are schooled from birth to be respectful, hardworking and self-sacrificing; respectful of their parents' wishes and choice of a groom; hardworking to ensure that the housework will be done and all other members of the family will be looked after; and self-sacrificing even to the extent of sacrificing their own lives.

56. Girls may be wed in some countries even before reaching puberty. There is great community pressure for daughters to be married at an early age. This could be because virginity is more readily

guaranteed when the girl is younger. Also, the husband and his family can control a young girl more easily. This also gives a longer reproductive period for the girl to produce more children, or specifically more sons. Childhood or early marriages are disadvantageous for young girls for many reasons. As most girls are still receiving schooling when they are given in marriage, they have to curtail their education. If the marriage is patrilocal, the bride must go and live in her husband's house among strangers. She will have to submit to sex with an older man and her immature body must endure the dangers of repeated pregnancies and childbirth.

57.   Forced marriages are a common occurrence in these societies. Relentless pressure and emotional blackmail are used by parents and relatives to force the young girl into an unwanted marriage. Their more extreme forms can involve threatening behaviour, abduction, imprisonment, physical violence, rape, and in some cases, murder. Forced marriages must be distinguished from arranged marriages, which operate successfully within many communities. According to the report of the Working Group on Forced Marriage, a forced marriage is a marriage conducted without the valid consent of both parties, where duress is a factor. It is a violation of internationally recognized human rights standards and cannot be justified on religious or cultural grounds. While both men and women experience forced marriages, it is primarily seen as an issue of violence against women. Marriages are forced upon young women for various reasons. Strengthening family links, protecting perceived cultural and religious ideals, preventing "unsuitable" relationships, protecting family honour and controlling female behaviour and sexuality are some of the reasons given by the Working Group on Forced Marriage. In some cases, if the woman or her family refuses a marriage proposal, the man or his family kidnaps the woman and attempts to formalize the marriage forcefully or rape her. They may also resort to character assassination by spreading rumours about her conduct. Acid attacks are another common act of violence against women when they spurn the advances or marriage proposal of a man. This practice is common in India and Bangladesh. In Sindh, to keep daughters in the paternal family, they are sometimes married to paternal cousins 10 to 20 years younger than themselves. The girl sometimes has to raise her would-be husband. If there are no such cousins the woman has to undergo the ceremony of *haq-baksh-wai*, which is marriage with the Quran. In the same area, another custom, called swara, is practised whereby women are used as a commodity to settle disputes between tribes or clans. The receiving tribe can marry those women or keep them as sex slaves. * * *

IV.   STATE RESPONSIBILITY

109.   In the past, States have been reluctant to intervene with regard to cultural practices in the family, often stating that this is a "private" matter and the State has no obligation in the domain of the "domestic". Throughout the world, domestic violence has rarely been

prosecuted because of this private/public differentiation. However, since the 1980s, international standards have emerged that are very clear on the matter of domestic violence and the duties of States to eradicate violence in the family.

110. The Declaration on the Elimination of Violence against Women states clearly:

> States should condemn violence against women and should not invoke any custom, tradition or religious consideration to avoid their obligations with respect to its elimination. States should pursue by all appropriate means and without delay a policy of eliminating violence against women.

The Declaration goes on to say that States should "exercise due diligence to prevent, investigate and, in accordance with national legislation, punish acts of violence against women, whether those acts are perpetrated by the State or by private actors."

111. The Declaration also specifies the type of action a State should take to eliminate violence in the home: it must develop appropriate penal legislation; it must consider developing national plans of action to eliminate violence against women; in the light of the available resources it must provide social services for women victims of violence; it must take measures to ensure that public officials entrusted with implementing the laws have adequate training to sensitize them to the needs of women, and it must ensure that adequate resources are set aside in the government budget to combat violence in the family. All these provisions are also contained in general recommendation 19 of the Committee on the Elimination of Discrimination against Women, where the legal obligation of State parties to the Convention on the Elimination of All Forms of Discrimination against Women is spelled out with regard to violence against women. Both these documents make it clear that, at the beginning of the twenty-first century, the action of State parties may be measured against international standards that clearly articulate a strategy for the elimination of violence against women in the family. By arguing that custom, tradition and religion cannot be invoked by State parties to defend violence against women in the family, international standards reject the cultural relativist argument that cultural practices that are violent towards women in the family should be shielded from international scrutiny.

NOTES AND QUESTIONS ON COLLECTING AND ARCHIVING EVIDENCE

1. *Different obligations under different international instruments.* The Special Rapporteur analyzes cultural practices against the international standards laid out in the Declaration on the Elimination of Violence Against Women and the Convention on the Elimination of Discrimination Against Women (CEDAW). Under the Declaration, governments

inter alia "should not invoke any custom, tradition or religious consideration to avoid their obligations with respect to [the] elimination of violence against women." Under the Convention, by contrast, governments are required to (i) "take all appropriate measures * * * to modify the social and cultural patterns of conduct of men and women, with a view to achieving the elimination of prejudices and customary and all other practices which are based on the idea of the inferiority or the superiority of either of the sexes or on stereotyped roles for men and women" and (ii) "to pursue by all appropriate means and without delay a policy of eliminating discrimination against women." Considering two different hypothetical states—one that is a party to CEDAW and one that is not—how would you describe to a client the different legal status and the substantive content of these two instruments?

2.   *Domestic violence as discrimination.* In her 1996 report, the Special Rapporteur defined domestic violence "as violence that occurs within the private sphere, generally between individuals who are related through intimacy, blood, or law." In what sense can domestic violence against women be considered a form of *discrimination* within the reach of CEDAW? *See* Committee on the Elimination of Discrimination Against Women, General Recommendation 19, U.N. Doc. No. A/47/38 (1992):

1.   Gender-based violence is a form of discrimination that seriously inhibits women's ability to enjoy rights and freedoms on a basis of equality with men. * * *

6.   The Convention in Article 1 defines discrimination against women. The definition of discrimination includes gender-based violence, that is, violence that is directed against a woman because she is a woman or that affects women disproportionately. It includes acts that inflict physical, mental or sexual harm or suffering, threats of such acts, coercion and other deprivations of liberty. Gender-based violence may breach specific provisions of the Convention, regardless of whether those provisions expressly mention violence.

3.   *Gender violence and refugee law.* Consider how the Special Rapporteur's report might be useful to a lawyer seeking asylum for a client. Specifically, how could the practices described in the Special Rapporteur's report—FGM, honor killings, caste, and marriage—be framed so as to meet the standard necessary for protection as a refugee?

The 1951 Convention relating to the Status of Refugees[1] defines a refugee as a person "outside of his or her country of nationality who is unable or unwilling to return because of persecution or a well-founded fear of persecution on account of race, religion, nationality, membership in a particular social group, or political opinion." *Id.*, art. 1, § A(2). In the United States, the Refugee Act of 1980[2] implements U.S. obligations under the 1951 Convention *via* the 1967 Protocol Relating to the Status

---

1.   189 U.N.T.S. 150.
2.   Pub. L. No. 96–212, 94 Stat. 102 (1980).

of Refugees.[3] Neither the 1951 Convention nor the Refugee Act lists persecution on the basis of gender as a basis for refugee status, but—in part as a result of the Special Rapporteur's work—women who suffer gender-based violence can potentially qualify under any of the five categories depending on the facts of the individual case, especially claims falling under the "social group" category. In its Guidelines on the Protection of Refugee Women (1991), for example, the UN High Commissioner for Refugees urged "acceptance of the principle that women fearing persecution or severe discrimination on the basis of their gender should be considered a member of a social group for the purposes of determining refugee status."

The asylum decision of *In re Fauziya Kasinga*, 21 I. & N. Dec. 357 (BIA 3298, 1996), illustrates the point. In *Kasinga*, a 19–year-old native and citizen of Togo, a member of the Tchamba–Kunsuntu Tribe of northern Togo, sought asylum in the United States on the ground that she would be subjected to FGM if she were returned to Togo. In that country, her father had protected her from the practice but had died, and her aunt now insisted that she undergo the ritual. In *Kasinga*, the Board of Immigration Appeals ruled that FGM could be the basis for a grant of asylum under section 208 of the Immigration and Nationality Act, 8 U.S.C. § 1158 (1994). That determination rested on seven essential findings:

> First, the record before us reflects that the applicant is a credible witness. Second, FGM, as practiced by the Tchamba–Kunsuntu Tribe of Togo and documented in the record, constitutes persecution. Third, the applicant is a member of a social group consisting of young women of the Tchamba–Kunsuntu Tribe who have not had FGM, as practiced by that tribe, and who oppose the practice. Fourth, the applicant has a well-founded fear of persecution. Fifth, the persecution the applicant fears is "on account of" her social group. Sixth, the applicant's fear of persecution is country-wide. Seventh, and finally, the applicant is eligible for and should be granted asylum in the exercise of discretion.

Other provisions of U.S. law respond sharply to the practice.[4]

Can the *Kasinga* approach apply to the much larger population of women who face not FGM but domestic violence generally? In *Matter of*

---

3. 19 U.S.T. 6223, 606 U.N.T.S. 267.

4. *See e.g.,* Illegal Immigration Reform and Immigrant Responsibility Act of 1996, Pub. L. 104–208, § 645, 110 Stat. 3009–546, 18 U.S.C. § 116 (1996) (imposing fines and up to five years imprisonment for FGM, unless the procedure is medically necessary to protect a young person's health); Illegal Immigration Reform and Immigrant Responsibility Act, 8 U.S.C. § 1374, (1996) (directing the Immigration and Naturalization Service to provide information to all aliens issued U.S. visas on the health and psychological effects of FGM, and on the legal consequences of FGM under criminal or child-protection statutes); Public Health Services Act, 42 U.S.C. § 241 (1996) (requiring the Department of Health and Human Services to compile data on FGM and to engage in education and outreach to relevant communities); Foreign Relations and Intercourse, Female Genital Mutilation, 22 U.S.C. § 262k–2(a) (1996) (requiring U.S. executive directors of international financial institutions, such as the World Bank, to oppose non-humanitarian loans to countries that have not undertaken educational measures designed to prevent FGM).

R–A–, Int. Dec. 3403 (BIA 1999), a U.S. immigration judge granted asylum to a Guatemalan refugee who had fled domestic violence, and the Board of Immigration Appeals reversed. The case then followed an odyssey of administrative review, reaching the Attorney General's office twice. Yule Kim, *Asylum Law and Female Genital Mutilation: Recent Developments* (2008), http://www.fas.org/sgp/crs/misc/RS22810.pdf.

4. *Translating international obligations into governmental policies.* If you were a lawyer in a government that had ratified CEDAW without reservations, what policy programs would you advise the government to pursue to eradicate widely-held cultural or religious beliefs and practices that perpetuated violence against women?

5. *Illegal reservations.* As noted in Module 4, CEDAW is one of the most widely adopted human rights treaties. It is also one of the most heavily reserved. In recent years, international human rights lawyers have struggled to determine the legal effects of these various reservations under Articles 19–21 of the Vienna Convention on the Law of Treaties (VCLT), which is in the Document Supplement. Under Article 19,

> A State may, when signing, ratifying, accepting, approving or acceding to a treaty, formulate a reservation unless:
>
> (a) the reservation is prohibited by the treaty;
>
> (b) the treaty provides that only specified reservations, which do not include the reservation in question, may be made; or
>
> (c) in cases not falling under sub-paragraphs (a) and (b), the reservation is incompatible with the object and purpose of the treaty.

Some parties to CEDAW have adopted reservations to CEDAW specifically to preserve certain traditional cultural or religious practices even if they discriminate against women. Consider for example Kuwait's reservation to Article 16(f) of CEDAW, which prohibits discrimination "in all matters relating to marriage and family relations and in particular * * * rights and responsibilities with regard to guardianship, wardship, trusteeship and adoption of children."

> The Government of the State of Kuwait declares that it does not consider itself bound by the provision contained in article 16(f) inasmuch as it conflicts with the provisions of the Islamic Shariah, Islam being the official religion of the State.

Is Kuwait's reservation legal or not under the VCLT? And who (or what) determines its legality? If it is an illegal reservation, does that mean that Kuwait is not a party to CEDAW at all or that other states and intergovernmental bodies may ignore the reservation altogether? The CEDAW Committee, like the Human Rights Committee under the International Covenant on Civil and Political Rights, has suggested that it—and not governments—has the final say on whether a reservation is consistent with the object and purpose of a treaty or not. *See* Human

Rights Committee, *General Comment No. 24* (1994), U.N. Doc. CCPR/C/ 21/Rev.1/Add.6 (1994). *General Recommendations Made by the Committee on the Elimination of Discrimination Against Women, General Comment No 4* (sixth session, 1987); *General Recommendation No. 20* (11th session, 1992); Office of the High Commissioner for Human Rights; *Report of the Meeting of the Working Group on Reservations*, HRI/MC/2006/5 (2006). As a strategic matter, is it better get a handful of "pure" CEDAW ratifications or a lot of reserved ones?

C. DEVELOPING LEGAL NORMS

On occasion, a Special Rapporteur may provide the conceptual scaffolding for a strategy to develop the law in ways that enhance the legal protections against abuse. In connection with their regular reporting duties, for example, they may offer non-binding but authoritative interpretations of treaties and customary international law. They may also identify gaps in international and domestic law that facilitate or perpetuate the abuse and may call for reform at the appropriate level. In what specific ways do the following reports identify and accelerate normative development?

REPORT OF THE SPECIAL RAPPORTEUR ON VIOLENCE AGAINST WOMEN, ITS CAUSES AND CONSEQUENCES   (MS. RADHIKA COOMARASWAMY):

FURTHER PROMOTION AND ENCOURAGEMENT OF HUMAN RIGHTS AND FUNDAMENTAL FREEDOMS, INCLUDING THE QUESTION OF THE PROGRAMME AND METHODS OF WORK OF THE COMMISSION ALTERNATIVE APPROACHES AND WAYS & MEANS WITHIN THE UNITED NATIONS SYSTEM FOR IMPROVING THE EFFECTIVE ENJOYMENT OF HUMAN RIGHTS AND FUNDAMENTAL FREEDOMS

U.N. Doc. E/CN.4/1996/53 (6 February 1996)

III.   DOMESTIC VIOLENCE AS A VIOLATION OF HUMAN RIGHTS

29.   The Special Rapporteur, in her preliminary report, outlined in detail the international human rights standards with regard to violence against women. It, therefore, suffices to state that domestic violence, defined as violence that occurs within the domestic sphere perpetrated by both private and State actors, constitutes a violation of the human rights of women. State policies, manifested by both State action and inaction, may perpetuate and/or condone violence within the domestic sphere, although it is the duty of States to ensure that there exists no impunity for the perpetrators of such violence. "In the case of

intimate violence, male supremacy, ideology and conditions, rather than a distinct, consciously coordinated military establishment, confer upon men the sense of entitlement, if not the duty, to chastise their wives. Wife-beating is, therefore, not an individual, isolated, or aberrant act, but a social license, a duty or sign of masculinity, deeply ingrained in culture, widely practised, denied and completely or largely immune from legal sanction." It is, therefore, argued that the role of State inaction in the perpetuation of the violence combined with the gender-specific nature of domestic violence require that domestic violence be classified and treated as a human rights concern rather than as a mere domestic criminal justice concern.

30. Under international human rights law, Governments are not only obliged to refrain from committing human rights violations but also to prevent and respond to human rights abuses, without discrimination. In the past, however, a narrow interpretation of international human rights protections has overlooked the issue of State inaction to prevent and punish violations committed by private actors, despite provisions in, *inter alia*, the International Covenant on Civil and Political Rights, which require States to respect and ensure, among other things, the right to life, the right to be free from torture and cruel, inhuman or degrading treatment and the security of person.

31. Increasingly, however, international legal interpretations and norms are evolving to define more clearly the positive role and responsibility of the State in preventing abuses perpetrated by para-State or private actors. The concept of State responsibility has developed to recognize that States also have an obligation to take preventive and punitive steps where human rights violations by private actors occur. In this context, the Human Rights Committee has clearly stated that a State not only has a duty to protect its citizens from such violations but also to investigate violations when they occur and to bring the perpetrators to justice. At the regional level, the Inter–American Convention on the Prevention, Punishment and Eradication of Violence Against Women (the "Convention of Belém do Pará") is the first regional human rights treaty to focus exclusively on gender-based violence and to prohibit violence within the home.

A. Due diligence

32. It follows from the above that, by definition, a State can be held complicit where it fails systematically to provide protection from private actors who deprive any person of his/her human rights.

33. However, unlike for direct State action, the standard for establishing State complicity in violations committed by private actors is more relative. Complicity must be demonstrated by establishing that the State condones a pattern of abuse through pervasive non-action. Where States do not actively engage in acts of domestic violence or routinely disregard evidence of murder, rape or assault of women by their intimate partners, States generally fail to take the minimum steps

necessary to protect their female citizens' rights to physical integrity and, in extreme cases, to life. This sends a message that such attacks are justified and will not be punished. To avoid such complicity, States must demonstrate due diligence by taking active measures to protect, prosecute and punish private actors who commit abuses.

34.   In 1992, the Committee on the Elimination of Discrimination against Women (CEDAW) adopted General Recommendation 19, in which it confirmed that violence against women constitutes a violation of human rights and emphasized that "States may also be responsible for private acts if they fail to act with due diligence to prevent violations of rights or to investigate and punish acts of violence, and for providing compensation." The Committee also made recommendations on measures States should take to provide effective protection of women against gender-based violence, including, *inter alia*:

(i) Effective legal measures, including penal sanctions, civil remedies and compensatory provisions to protect women against all kinds of violence, including, inter alia, violence and abuse in the family, sexual assault and sexual harassment in the workplace;

(ii) Preventive measures, including public information and education programmes to change attitudes concerning the roles and status of women;

(iii) Protective measures, including refuges, counselling, rehabilitation action and support services for women who are the victims of violence or who are at risk of violence.

35.   The Declaration on the Elimination of Violence Against Women also calls on States to "pursue by all appropriate means and without delay a policy of eliminating violence against women" and, among other things, to "exercise due diligence to prevent, investigate and, in accordance with national legislation, punish acts of violence against women, whether those acts are perpetrated by the State or by private persons (art. 4)."

36.   The Inter–American Court of Human Rights has issued a judgement in the case of *Velásquez-Rodríguez*, which articulates one of the most significant assertions of State responsibility for acts by private individuals; this represents an authoritative interpretation of an international standard on State duty. The opinion of the Court could also be applied, by extension, to article 2 of the International Covenant on Civil and Political Rights (ICCPR), which requires States parties to ensure to all individuals the rights recognized in that Covenant. In the same case, the Inter–American Court further reaffirmed that States are "obliged to investigate every situation involving a violation of the rights protected by [international law]." It discussed the scope of the duty of States, under article 1 of the American Convention on Human Rights, "to ensure" the rights within the treaty to all persons within their jurisdiction. The Court stated that a State "has failed to comply with [this] duty . . . when the State allows private persons or groups to act freely and with

impunity to the detriment of the rights recognized by the Convention." Moreover, the Court required Governments to:

> Take reasonable steps to prevent human rights violations and to use the means at its disposal to carry out a serious investigation of violations committed within this jurisdiction, to identify those responsible, to impose the appropriate punishment and to ensure the victim adequate compensation.

This includes "ensur[ing] that any violations are considered and treated as illegal acts." Consistent with this reasoning, States should be held accountable for consistent patterns of non-enforcement of criminal law. Thus, what would otherwise be wholly private conduct is transformed into a constructive act of State, "because of the lack of due diligence to prevent the violation or respond to it as required by the [American Convention]."

37.   The Court also clearly stated that a single violation of human rights or just one investigation with an ineffective result does not establish a lack of due diligence by a State. Rather, the test is whether the State undertakes its duties seriously. Such seriousness can be evaluated through the actions of both State agencies and private actors on a case-by-case basis. The due diligence requirement encompasses the obligation both to provide and enforce sufficient remedies to survivors of private violence. Thus, the existence of a legal system criminalizing and providing sanctions for domestic assault would not in itself be sufficient; the Government would have to perform its functions to "effectively ensure" that incidents of family violence are actually investigated and punished.

38.   For example, actions by State employees, the police, justice, health and welfare departments, or the existence of government programmes to prevent and protect women victims of violence are all concrete indications for measuring due diligence. Individual cases of policy failure or sporadic incidents of non-punishment would not meet the standard to warrant international action.

39.   When setting out the international legal framework relevant to domestic violence in her preliminary report, the Special Rapporteur wrote, with regard to State responsibility:

> In the context of norms recently established by the international community, a State that does not act against crimes of violence against women is as guilty as the perpetrators. States are under a positive duty to prevent, investigate and punish crimes associated with violence against women.

REPORT OF THE SPECIAL RAPPORTEUR ON VIOLENCE AGAINST WOMEN, ITS CAUSES AND CONSEQUENCES (MS. RADHIKA COOMARASWAMY):

ECONOMIC AND SOCIAL POLICY AND ITS IMPACT ON VIOLENCE AGAINST WOMEN

U.N. Doc. E/CN.4/2000/68/Add.5 (24 February 2000)

B.   Economic status and dependence

8.   Economic and social policies that continue to ensure women's economic dependence on men often result in violence against women. Of the world's 1.3 billion poor, 70 per cent are women. A major factor underlying violence against women is their low economic and social status relative to men and their dependence on men to provide protection and the means of survival. If women have independent means they can often walk away from situations of abuse.

9.   Women's multiple roles as producers, home managers, mothers and community organizers are ignored. The importance of reproductive activity is undervalued. By raising and caring for children, by preparing food and organizing the household, women ensure the sustenance of society and of the workforce necessary to carry out productive activities.

10.   Even when women are involved in productive activity, this is overlooked. Despite the fact that more than half of Asia's working women and about three quarters of the female working population in sub-Saharan Africa are involved in the agricultural sector; despite the fact that women produce 70 per cent of Africa's food, most of women's work remains invisible. This is because women's work is frequently not evaluated through the market. As food production is mainly for home consumption, and household work, childcare and cooking are not sold on the market, there is no measurement of women's contribution to the economy. Attempts to place a monetary value on this "invisible" work have resulted in figures indicating that annually US$11 trillion worth of women's contribution is overlooked.

11.   In developed countries, women do 51 per cent of all work; in developing countries as much as 53 per cent. Women do two thirds of all unpaid work, while men do two thirds of all paid work. In industrialized countries, women who are employed and have a child aged under 15 have the longest working day, amounting to 11 hours. When a woman takes up employment, the unpaid work she previously was responsible for still remains and she will have to work on average one hour additionally per day.

12.   Their low economic status has serious consequences for the social and legal status of women. In regions with high rates of female participation in the workforce, women's status is raised, which has direct consequences on their ability to lead a life without fear of violence. In addition, women's low economic status allows for practices in the family

that result in violence against women. Female infanticide, widow murder, neglect of girl children and dowry-deaths are related to the economic potential of women. Where women generally do not contribute to the monetary income of the household, they are regarded solely as a financial burden. The capacity to earn income makes a woman a valuable asset. When a woman is able to provide for herself, she will have respect within the family and she will also be more likely to leave a violent relationship, as she has the means to support herself.

C.   Women's legal status

13.   Low economic and social status has serious consequences for the legal position of women. Laws in many countries ensure that women remain in an economic[ally] dependent situation. Society and Government view men as the representatives and heads of household. Such an assumption places the ever-increasing number of female-headed households at a disadvantage. In countries such as Nigeria, women have the legal status of a minor. Women who choose to live alone, who are widowed, divorced or lesbians, and women with children outside marriage are at a severe disadvantage, as they do not share the same rights as men. When married, women become the property of their husband; only through him or through their father or sons do women have access to land. By themselves, they are not able to sign legal contracts or file for divorce. Without a man, women-headed households are severely limited in their access to means to support themselves.

14.   Unequal ownership rights leave women dependent on men. In Cameroon there is no legal provision for women to own property. Following traditional laws, a woman does not inherit land since she will marry and then be provided for by her husband outside her community. When her husband dies, again she will not inherit as the land returns to the husband's family. In many African countries formal law has no provision for women's inheritance rights; in others customary law is an obstacle to women making use of legal provisions. Widows are often left without the means to support themselves financially or to obtain necessary medical care, and may be made to leave their marital home. Where women are made recipients of property or funds, they may incur the anger of other family members. They suffer from (threats of) violence or even death: Uganda and Nigeria can both offer examples of abused widows.

15.   In Nigeria, 90 per cent of land and property are in the name of men. Accommodation grants from the employer can only be received by men as women are expected to move in with the husband. Single mothers fall through this safety net. In Nigeria, landlords are reluctant to give accommodation to single women or mothers, who have the reputation of being promiscuous. Should they become homeless, women are at a great risk of becoming victims of violence such as rape.

16. When women do not hold any land, they are frequently unable to obtain credit, even when they are legally able to do so, as land is

required as collateral. This is the case in Nigeria, where women are effectively barred from obtaining credit, as they do not possess land, a house or other property. In South Africa, in order to obtain credit from public banks often requires the husband's signature and surety.

17.   Not being a full member of society in legal terms prevents female heads of household from being able to support their family. Housing in the formal sector may not be available or affordable and the family may be exposed to the vagaries of the informal housing sector. But married women also are affected by this situation, as they are dependent on their husbands in legal and economic terms. Where the husband does not allocate the resources equally, women are at a severe disadvantage and powerless. In cases of domestic violence, the inability to live life independently without a husband or father may force women to stay with their batterers.

18.   Social, economic and legal dependence is an extremely important factor to be taken into account when trying to place violence in its social and economical context. Violence is often a means by which the dominant person asserts power. In equal relationships no one partner is dependent on the other one, as both have sufficient power—in economic, as well as in social and legal, terms—to leave the relationship and live independently.

D. Consequences

19.   The undervaluing of women by the legal and economic structures of society has important consequences. Premature death is the most fatal consequence of the undervaluing of women. A troubling statistic indicates that millions of women are missing in less developed countries owing to female foeticide, female infanticide, purposeful malnourishment and starvation, neglected health problems and murders, some of which related to dowry—so-called dowry deaths. In Pakistan, every day one woman dies from "stove death." While in Europe and North America for every 100 men there are 106 women, there are only 97 women in less developed countries. In Africa there are 102 women. On the basis of this ratio, it can reasonably be said that there are 30 million women missing in India and 38 million women missing in China alone. Another study shows that the countries with the highest proportion of missing women are Bangladesh and Pakistan, where the number of missing women amounts to 10 per cent of the total number of women.

20.   In many countries, a family requires a son to continue the family name and inherit the family land. In Chinese tradition, a son is also essential because only a male child can appease the spirits of the ancestors by sacrificing money and incense. Without a son, the parent's spirits will have to wander the earth, never finding rest. As China strictly enforces its one-child policy, parents prefer their only child to be a son. In India a son is required to light the father's cremation fire.

21. Raising a daughter is considered an investment the family will not profit from. Once married, she will become a member of another family and cheap labour. Additionally, on a daughter's marriage the future husband and his family need to be given a dowry by her parents. This can be very expensive, and, especially where there are several daughters, can cause families to become heavily indebted. Although originally intended to ensure the bride's financial independence, the system has been corrupted and the dowry now only serves as a source of enrichment for the husband. If the woman's family fails to pay the full dowry or does not meet demands for further payments, dowry deaths are a frequent consequence. Husbands and mothers-in-law burn the woman alive in a "cooking accident" or murder her otherwise. The husband is permitted to remarry and receive a second dowry. It is in fact the case that in regions where the dowry system is common there is often a highly increased mortality rate for women. This contrasts with regions where a bride price is customary, such as in southern and western regions of Africa. Here families have a financial incentive to ensure their daughters' survival and there is no excessive female mortality. This does not, however, hinder the husband mistreating his wife. As he had to pay a bride price, he regards his wife as a commodity he has paid for and therefore she has to be at his service, which includes sexual activity when and as he requests.

22.   Since the introduction of the capacity to detect the sex of a child before birth through ultrasound techniques, many abortions are being carried out because the child is of the "wrong sex." In Bombay, India, 96 per cent of aborted foetuses are female. Improvements in technology have been a mixed blessing in this respect. The population imbalance that will result in the next century from technological innovation and the undervaluing of women is a serious consequence that requires State intervention.

23.   In societies with greater gender equality, infant boys have a 20 to 30 per cent higher mortality rate than girls. In Bangladesh, female infant mortality is nearly twice that of male infants. In China, it is more than double that of boys, and is concentrated in the first year of life. In India, as well, female mortality is highest among infants, but remains higher than male mortality up to the age of 35. In all three countries, the mortality rate increases for girls from large families. In India and Bangladesh, first-born girls have better chances of survival (although lower than boys), than in China, where even first-born girls have drastically reduced survival chances. For later-born girls survival chances decrease rapidly in all three countries.

24.   All this illustrates clearly the extent to which women's lives are disregarded. They are valued so little that death and murder are not seen as reprehensible. The reason for this can partly be found in the status of women, which is inferior to men's in social, cultural, economic and legal terms in most societies.

25. Gender equality is obviously not merely a question of financial wealth, but rather of political commitment. Increasing female literacy can easily be achieved when Governments demonstrate the will. In 1992 China, Sri Lanka and Zimbabwe had female literacy rates of between 70 and 86 per cent, although their gross national product (GNP) per capita was only US$480 to 580. In comparison, Gabon and Saudi Arabia, with GNP per capita around 10 times higher, only had literacy rates of 48 per cent and 46 per cent, respectively. The impact Governments' attitudes and policies have on women's lives is thus crucial for their well-being.

NOTES AND QUESTIONS ON NORMATIVE DEVELOPMENT

1. *State responsibility and domestic violence.* How does the due diligence standard, as developed by the Special Rapporteur, undermine the received distinction between private acts and public responsibility? One of the orthodoxies of traditional international law is that, except in limited circumstances defined by treaty, an act or omission is a violation only if it can be attributed to a state actor. That state action requirement does not apply to acts of slavery, genocide, certain war crimes, and crimes against humanity, but, according to the Special Rapporteur, in what circumstances is a government responsible under international law for acts of domestic violence by its private citizens? And in articulating this normative approach, was she writing on a blank slate, or was there existing international authority for her analysis?

2. *Expanding the approach from CEDAW to other human rights treaty regimes.* The United States is currently not a party to the Convention on the Elimination of Discrimination Against Women, but it is a party to the Convention Against Torture and the International Covenant on Civil and Political Rights. What are the consequences of the Special Rapporteur's analysis of due diligence for U.S. implementation of these treaties? For an analysis of this topic by the Special Rapporteur on Torture, *see* Report of the Special Rapporteur, Mr. Nigel S. Rodley, submitted pursuant to Commission on Human Rights resolution 1992/32, U.N. Doc. E/CN.4/1995/34, paras. 15–24 (12 January 1995).

3. *The U.S. Violence Against Women Act.* In 1994, Congress enacted the Violence Against Women Act (VAWA), which created a federal civil remedy for victims of gender motivated violence. *See* Violence Against Women Act of 1994, Pub. L. No. 103–322, tit. IV, 108 Stat. 1902 (1994) (codified as amended in scattered sections of 8, 18, and 42 U.S.C.). In an action filed by women victims of violence under the statute, the defendants moved to dismiss the case, arguing that the citizen suit provision was unconstitutional. Eventually, the case came before the Supreme Court, which held that the section was unconstitutional. *United States v. Morrison*, 529 U.S. 598 (2000). Several international law scholars

and human rights experts filed a brief *amicus curiae*, arguing that the VAWA's citizen suit provision was within the federal government's authority as implementing legislation for the international obligations of the United States. *See* Brief of Amici Curiae International Law Scholars and Human Rights Experts, *United States v. Morrison*, 529 U.S. 598 (2000) (No. 99–0005, 99–0029), *available at* 1999 WL 1032805. Their argument was based, *inter alia*, on U.S. ratification of the International Covenant on Civil and Political Rights as well as customary international law, which they argued clearly recognizes a woman's right to live free of gender-based violence. In its decision, the U.S. Supreme Court did not address any of the arguments made by these *amici*. Congress did not reference any international obligations of the United States in adopting the statute. Was that fatal to the *amicus* argument? On what legal basis should the Court have paid closer attention to international law arguments? *See generally*, Ana Maria Merico–Stephens, *Of Federalism, Human Rights, and the Holland Caveat: Congressional Power to Implement Treaties*, 25 Mich. J. Int'l L. 265 (2004); G. Kristian Miccio, *With All Due Deliberate Care: Using International Law and the Federal Violence Against Women Act to Locate the Contours of State Responsibility for Violence Against Mothers in the Age of* Deshaney, 29 Colum. Hum. Rts. L. Rev. 641 (1998).

4. *Economic development and violence against women.* Ms. Coomaraswamy's discussion of economic and social policy and its impact on violence against women would have wide-ranging implications if adopted as a foundation for international development policy. For instance, according to the Special Rapporteur, the continued diminished legal status, combined with their low economic status, makes women more susceptible to violence, particularly in the form of infanticide. And she identifies various ways that the process of globalization perpetuates the low social, economic, and cultural status of women and thereby contributes to violence against women. For a similar analysis of the place of women in development, see the Third Report of the Independent Expert on the Right to Development, Mr. Arjun Sengupta, submitted in accordance with Commission resolution 2000/5, UN Doc. E/CN.4/2001/WG.18/2, para 27; *see also* "Human rights and extreme poverty: report submitted by Ms. A–M. Lizin, independent expert, pursuant to Commission resolution 1999/26," UN Doc. E/CN.4/2000/52, paras. 56–60, 97, 99–102 (providing specific recommendations for improving the conditions for women in the context of development policy and practice). Assuming you are a policy-maker at the World Bank, the International Monetary Fund or any of the other international financial institutions, how would you translate the Special Rapporteur's analysis into action and especially legal reform? How would you argue that gender equity would actually increase economic development, based on Ms. Coomaraswamy's analysis?

5. *Violence, culture, and sociology.* In 2003, Dr. Yakin Erturk, a professor of sociology and the head of the Gender and Women's Studies Programme at the Middle East Technical University (METU), Ankara,

Turkey, took over the position of Special Rapporteur from Ms. Coomaraswamy. In her first thematic report to the Human Rights Council, she took on the issue of cultural practices that lead to violence against women from a different perspective—that of a sociologist. Rather than stress state *legal* responsibility for cultural practices that result in violence against women, she developed a series of recommendations based on "dismantling cultural paradigms." In Dr. Erturk's view, the global agenda to recognize and enforce the rights of women has been slowed by interpretations of culture that either justify violations in the name of culture or to condemn cultures as inherently primitive and violent toward women. In her words, "Both variants of cultural essentialism ignore the universal dimensions of patriarchical culture that subordinates, albeit differently, women in all societies and fails to recognize women's active agency in resisting and negotiating culture to improve their terms of existence." *Report of the Special Rapporteur on violence against women, its causes and consequences,* Yakin Erturk, UN Doc. A/HRC/4/34 (Jan. 2007), para. 68.

Clearly, Dr. Erturk has taken a different approach to the issue of violence against woman than her jurist predecessor. However, there is substantial value to a sociologist's perspective, particularly when crafting policy targeted at reducing a particular human rights problem, in this case, violence against women. One area where law and sociology intersect is in the process of developing "indicators" to guide policy. Statistics and indicators—the data necessary to measure trends—are the province of sociologists, not lawyers, but, in the area of human rights, indicators often have a legal component. For example, in measuring the extent to which women's rights are being protected in a particular country, one would look to legal protections that exist as well as enforcement of those protections. Is harmful conduct prohibited? Does the prohibition track with a government's international obligations? Where these indicators are lacking, the policy prescription is to ratify treaties, recognize international standards, pass implementing legislation, and prosecute violators. For a discussion of proposed indicators in the area of violence against women, see *Report of the Special Rapporteur on violence against women, its causes and consequences,* Yakin Erturk, UN Doc. A/HRC/7/6/Add.5 (Feb. 2008).

6. *Additional readings.* For a general discussion and evaluation of the special mechanisms of the U.N. system, see *Report of the United Nations High Commissioner for Human Rights and Follow-up to the World Conference on Human Rights: Effective Functioning of Human Rights Mechanisms,* UN ESCOR, Comm'n on Human Rights, 61st Sess., UN Doc. E/CN.4/2005/5 (2004); Amnesty International, *The United Nations Human Rights Thematic Mechanisms 2002,* AI Index: IOR 40/009/2002 (2002); INTERNATIONAL HUMAN RIGHTS MONITORING MECHANISMS: ESSAYS IN HONOUR OF JAKOB TH. MÖLLER (Gudmundur Alfredsson ed., 2001); Patrick James

Flood, Evaluating the Effectiveness of UN Human Rights Institutions (1998).

Practicum

Pursuant to a resolution of the UN Human Rights Council, you have just been appointed Special Rapporteur on Human Rights and HIV/AIDS. Your mandate is as follows:

(a) Investigate and examine the human rights implications of HIV/ AIDS, in particular, violations of the right to be free from all forms of discrimination;

(b) Investigate, monitor, examine, and receive communications and gather information on the human rights situation of persons infected by, or suspected of being infected by, HIV/AIDS in particular countries;

(c) Make recommendations and proposals on adequate measures at the national, regional, and international levels to eliminate human rights violations committed against person with HIV/AIDS, and to remedy the social, economic and cultural consequences of the global epidemic.

During your first year, you would like to accomplish three goals. The first is to establish the legal framework and rationale for addressing the HIV/AIDS epidemic within the framework of existing international human rights norms. Drawing on various international legal principles and instruments, you wish to build the legal foundation for your future work. Your second goal is to carry out a country visit, in particular, you wish to travel to South Africa to address the human rights implications of HIV/AIDS in that country. You have requested an invitation from the Government of South Africa, but your request has been refused. Given the substantial HIV/AIDS problem in that country, as well as the controversial comments of the President on the subject, you have decided nevertheless to prepare a report on the country. By doing so, you expect to raise the profile of the issue in South Africa as well as the profile of your office. Finally, you would like to prepare a set of recommendations for national, regional, and international action to combat the negative human rights implications of the HIV/AIDS epidemic. This could consist of recommendations for national legislation and action (including model legislation), regional programs and international cooperation. Where national institutions exist, you wish to recommend how to improve them; where they do not exist, you should recommend how they should be created. You should also prepare a survey of the regional and international institutions relevant to combatting this problem, and how they can be strengthened, modified and improved.

At the end of the year, you will have to present each of these reports to Human Rights Council and be prepared to defend your analysis and conclusions before representatives of the international community at the UN Human Rights Council.

Three students should undertake to prepare each of the three reports identified above. At a mock session of the UN Human Rights Council, the remainder of the class should represent various government officials—from both the developed and developing world—who will prepare various questions for the Special Rapporteur. Students should take into account the perspective of the government each represents in preparing these questions. Because South Africa will be specifically targeted by one of the reports, on student should represent the South African delegation to the Council.

CHAPTER 3

MODULE 6

INTERNATIONAL CRIMINAL TRIBUNALS

▪ ▪ ▪

Orientation

"The privilege of opening the first trial in history for crimes against the peace of the world imposes a grave responsibility. The wrongs which we seek to condemn and punish have been so calculated, so malignant, and so devastating, that civilization cannot tolerate their being ignored, because it cannot survive their being repeated. That four great nations, flushed with victory and stung with injury stay the hand of vengeance and voluntarily submit their captive enemies to the judgment of the law is one of the most significant tributes that Power has ever paid to Reason."[1]

With these eloquent words, United States Supreme Court Justice Robert Jackson opened the Nuremberg war crimes trials in November 1945. The Nuremberg judgment that followed was a watershed event in the development of international accountability for human rights violations, but Justice Jackson's hope that the rule of law could end the scourge of such crimes has not been fulfilled. The years since Nuremberg have proven to be some of the bloodiest in history. Across the globe, millions of people have been brutalized and killed because of racial, ethnic, religious, and political animus.

In the aftermath of Nuremberg, hopes were high that an international criminal tribunal could be created to assure accountability for international crimes. For years, these hopes went unrealized. In the last decade, however, largely due to the extraordinary mobilization of international civil society, a functioning permanent International Criminal Court ("ICC") now exists. This module explores and assesses these extraordinary developments.

---

1. Opening Statement for the United States of America by Robert H. Jackson, Chief of Counsel for the United States, Nov. 21, 1945, reprinted in ROBERT H. JACKSON, *THE NUREMBERG CASE* 30 (1947).

THE LONDON CHARTER AND LEGACY OF THE NUREMBERG TRIBUNAL

In the aftermath of World War II, the Allies were faced with the decision of what to do with Axis leaders. Here, unlike other wars, these leaders had not only fought a cataclysmic war, they had also orchestrated, ordered, implemented, and ratified the Holocaust—an outrage against their own civilians and those in the territories they had conquered. The crimes committed—crimes against peace, war crimes, and crimes against humanity—were so abhorrent that the Allies considered their prosecution to be in the interest of the entire international community. The decision to forego vengeance and to pursue prosecution under the law fundamentally shaped modern humanitarian law.

The jurisdiction of the Nuremberg Tribunal was established by Article 6 of the London Charter of the International Military Tribunal, 8 Aug. 1945, which provided jurisdiction to "try and punish persons who * * * whether as individuals or as members of organizations, committed any of the following crimes:

Article 6

The following acts, or any of them, are crimes coming within the jurisdiction of the Tribunal for which there shall be individual responsibility:

(a) CRIMES AGAINST PEACE: namely, planning, preparation, initiation or waging of a war of aggression, or a war in violation of international treaties, agreements or assurances, or participation in a common plan or conspiracy for the accomplishment of any of the foregoing;

(b) WAR CRIMES: namely, violations of the laws or customs of war. Such violations shall include, but not be limited to, murder, ill-treatment or deportation to slave labor or for any other purpose of civilian population of or in occupied territory, murder or ill-treatment of prisoners of war or persons on the seas, killing of hostages, plunder of public or private property, wanton destruction of cities, towns or villages, or devastation not justified by military necessity;

(c) CRIMES AGAINST HUMANITY: namely, murder, extermination, enslavement, deportation, and other inhumane acts committed against any civilian population, before or during the war; or persecutions on political, racial or religious grounds in execution of or in connection with any crime within the jurisdiction of the Tribunal, whether or not in violation of the domestic law of the country where perpetrated."

The London Charter not only defined these crimes, it also established that acting pursuant to superior orders was no defense to egregious violations of international law. Indeed, the Nuremberg Judgment established that such a defense was prohibited by the law of nations.

Facing the monumental and unprecedented task of pursuing justice for some of the century's most horrific crimes, the Allies understood the importance of conducting fair and impartial trials. Justice Jackson remarked on the magnitude of this responsibility in his opening statement:

> We must never forget that the record on which we judge these defendants today is the record on which history will judge us tomorrow. To pass these defendants a poisoned chalice is to put it to our own lips as well. We must summon such detachment and intellectual integrity to our task that this Trial will commend itself to posterity as fulfilling humanity's aspirations to do justice.

To ensure the fairness of the proceedings, Article 16 of the London Charter guaranteed certain fundamental rights to the accused. These due process rights included the right to be presented with an indictment written in a language which the defendants understood and within a reasonable time before trial; the right to give an explanation in response to the charges; the right to have the proceedings translated into a language that the accused understood; the right to assistance of counsel; and the right to present evidence and cross-examine witnesses.[2] That Nazi war criminals were tried by a tribunal and that they had certain legal rights before that tribunal reflected the moral and strategic power of the rule of law and lay the groundwork for the international justice tribunals that have followed.

Critics argue that the Nuremberg Tribunal did not go far enough in protecting the due process rights of defendants. Specifically, they argue that the prosecutions rested on *ex post facto* laws: the doctrine of *nullum crimen sine lege, nulla poena sine lege*—literally translated as "unless there is a law, there can be no crime; unless there is a law, there can be no punishment"—prohibits the prosecution of individuals for crimes not clearly established by existing law. "Crimes against humanity" and "war crimes," many pointed out,[3] were defined at Nuremberg for the first time. Others argued that the prosecutor's ability to introduce *ex parte* affidavits of individuals who were available to testify in lieu of their live testimony significantly undermined the right of defendants to cross-examine the witnesses against them. Michael P. Scharf, *A Critique of the Yugoslavia War Crimes Tribunal*, 25 DENV. J. INT'L L. & POL'Y 305, 309 (1997). The Nuremberg Tribunal also permitted trials *in absentia* and had no Appellate Chamber, preventing even those defendants sentenced to death from obtaining any post-conviction relief or review. Quite apart

---

2. *See* Diane Marie Amann, *Harmonic Convergence? Constitutional Criminal Procedure in an International Context*, 75 IND. L.J. 809, 819–820 (2000).

3. Michael Scharf & Valerie Epps, *The International Trial of the Century? A "Cross–Fire" Exchange on the First Case Before the Yugoslavia War Crimes Tribunal*, 29 CORNELL INT'L L.J. 635, 644 (1996).

from specific fairness concerns, critics observe that the entire Nuremberg process smacked of "victor's justice."

FROM NUREMBERG TO THE AD HOC INTERNATIONAL CRIMINAL TRIBUNALS

Notwithstanding these criticisms, the basic principles in the Nuremberg Judgment were affirmed by the UN General Assembly as reflecting principles of customary international law, thus providing a firm foundation for the later development of a permanent international criminal tribunal.[4] The Allies also established the International Military Tribunal for the Far East (also referred to as the "Tokyo War Crimes Tribunal").[5] The tribunal, which operated from 1946–1948, tried twenty-eight high-ranking Japanese officials, including former premiers and military leaders for crimes against peace, war crimes, and crimes against humanity committed during WWII. These included the Rape of Nanking, during which Japanese troops invaded the Chinese city of Nanking, killing roughly 250,000 people and raping 20,000 women. Eleven judges, nine from nations that signed the Instrument of Surrender, presided over the trials, in which five were sentenced to death and eighteen were sentenced to prison.[6]

In addition to the trial and conviction of the major war criminals at Nuremberg and Tokyo, an extensive body of jurisprudence developed from war crimes prosecuted under Control Council Order No. 10. The Order authorized prosecutions by Allied military tribunals in their separate zones of occupation, and it expanded the definition of crimes against humanity to include "atrocities and offenses, including but not limited to murder, extermination, enslavement, deportation, imprisonment, torture, rape, or other inhumane acts committed against any civilian population, or persecutions on political, racial or religious grounds whether or not in violation of the domestic laws of the country where perpetrated." The American Military Tribunal at Nuremberg tried 142 defendants in twelve trials pursuant to Control Council Order No. 10.

In addition to affirming the Nuremberg principles at the UN, the international community pushed international law further by recognizing the crime of genocide, which had not previously been an explicit

---

4. *See* Affirmation of the Principles of International Law recognized by the Charter of the Nuremberg Tribunal, G.A. Res. 95 (I), UN GAOR,1st Sess., UN Doc. A/236 1946, *affirming* "the principles of international law recognized by the Charter of the Nuremberg Tribunal and the judgment of the Tribunal."

5. Charter of the International Military Tribunal for the Far East, Jan. 19, 1946, amended Apr. 26, 1946, T.I.A.S. No. 1589.

6. The Tokyo War Crimes Tribunal did not account for all instances of sexual crimes committed by the Axis Powers during WWII. Notably absent from the proceedings is any prosecution of Japan's widespread practice of sexual slavery to "comfort" their soldiers. Although Japan ratified the Rome Statute in 2007, thereby accepting the jurisdiction of the International Criminal Court, it has yet to publicly accept responsibility for its use of sexual slavery during WWII.

part of the Tribunal's mandate. In 1948, the UN General Assembly adopted the Convention on the Prevention and Punishment of the Crime of Genocide, which defined genocide as acts "committed with the intent to destroy, in whole or in part, a national, ethnical, racial or religious group, as such."[7] Notably, "genocide, whether committed in time of peace or in time of war, is a crime under international law which [the parties to the Convention] undertake to prevent and punish."[8]

The next year, in 1949, the Diplomatic Conference held in Geneva adopted four Conventions known as the "Geneva Conventions," which further updated and codified changes in the laws of war in the aftermath of World War II.[9] These conventions supplemented the body of international humanitarian law developed in the century before World War II.

These normative developments did not lead to the creation of new international institutions for the prosecution of offenders. In the immediate aftermath of World War II, UN bodies worked to formulate workable definitions of international crimes and a permanent international criminal court. By 1954, the International Law Commission had prepared a draft code of crimes.[10] But progress stopped there, and the idea of an international criminal court languished throughout the Cold War.

THE *AD HOC* INTERNATIONAL CRIMINAL TRIBUNALS

It took two additional genocides to put the establishment of an international criminal tribunal back on track. One might credit the advent of "around the clock" international media coverage with exposing the horrors in the former Yugoslavia and forcing governments to act, albeit belatedly. A more cynical view might be that focusing on the creation of the International Criminal Tribunal for Yugoslavia ("ICTY") enabled governments to avoid the difficult decision to deploy soldiers while the genocide continued. Similarly, in creating the International Criminal Tribunal for Rwanda ("ICTR"), the international community may have acted more out of embarrassment over its inaction during genocide, rather than its commitment to international justice.

Despite these controversies, the ICTY and the ICTR were created to try the perpetrators of the genocides, to resolve conflicts, and to

---

7. Convention on the Prevention and Punishment of the Crime of Genocide, G.A. Res. 260A (III), art. 2 (Dec. 9, 1948).

8. *Id.* art. 1.

9. *See* Convention for the Amelioration of the Condition of the Wounded and Sick in Armed Forces in the Field, Aug. 12, 1949, No. 970, 75 U.N.T.S. 31; Convention for the Treatment of Prisoners of War, Aug. 12, 1949, No. 972, 75 U.N.T.S. 135; Convention Re Amelioration of the Condition of the Wounded, Sick and Shipwrecked members of Armed Forces at Sea, Aug. 12, 1949, No. 971, 75 U.N.T.S. 85; Convention Relative to the Protection of Civilian Persons in Time of War, Aug. 12, 1949, No. 973, 75 U.N.T.S. 287.

10. International Law Commission, *Draft Code of Offences Against the Peace and Security of Mankind*, [1954] 2 Y.B. Int'l L. Comm'n 150, UN Doc. A/CN.4/SER.A/1954/Add.1.

promote reconciliation. First, they seek justice by demonstrating that the crime of genocide requires investigation, documentation, and prosecution. Second, they deter future conflict and war crimes by demonstrating that no one is above the rule of law and that such heinous violations of international law will be tried and punished. Third, they provide an alternative to war for redressing serious human rights abuses by one group against another. Fourth, they create and elucidate a rule of law under humanitarian and international criminal law. The tribunals also preserve a lasting factual record of the crimes that occurred, thereby chronicling history for future generations to safeguard against revisionist history and denial. Finally, the international tribunals challenge a culture of impunity, which perpetuates instability and civil unrest, and deters economic growth, the creation of sustainable infrastructure, and the ability of affected communities to pursue social healing.

The International Criminal Tribunal for the Former Yugoslavia

Beginning in 1991, the Socialist Federal Republic of Yugoslavia began to disintegrate with the secession of Slovenia and Croatia. Over the next several years, a series of wars spread from Slovenia to Croatia to Bosnia and Herzegovina, which with its large Muslim population, exacerbated the ethnic character of the conflict, and added a religious component.

Responding to growing reports of widespread violations of humanitarian and human rights law in Yugoslavia, the UN Security Council formed an independent Commission of Experts to investigate. The Commission confirmed that gross and systematic violations, especially mass rape and ethnic cleansing, were occurring with impunity. Based on the findings of the Commission, the Security Council took the innovative action of creating an *ad hoc* international criminal tribunal to prosecute war crimes in the former Yugoslav republic *while* the conflict persisted.

The Security Council based its authority to act on Chapter VII of the UN Charter, which provides that it has power to "take measures necessary to maintain international peace and security." The Council also cited Article 29 of the Charter, which provides that it may create subsidiary bodies through Chapter VII when necessary to perform its duties.[11]

On May 25, 1993, the UN Security Council unanimously passed Resolution 827, thereby creating the ICTY to prosecute "[p]ersons responsible for serious violations of International Humanitarian Law Committed in the Territory of the Former Yugoslavia since 1991."[12] The creation of an *ad hoc* tribunal through the Security Council's Chapter VII powers was not only unprecedented, it also offered a potentially more realistic conflict resolution mechanism than the domi-

---

11. The Secretary General, *Report of the Secretary–General Pursuant to Paragraph 2 of Security Council Resolution 808*, ¶ ¶ 27–28, UN Doc. S/25704 (1993).

12. Statute of the International Criminal Tribunal for the former Yugoslavia, art. I, May 25, 1993, 32 I.L.M. 1192 ("ICTY Statute"); *see also* S.C. Resolution 827, at 29, UN Doc. S/Res/827/1993 (May, 25 1993).

nant alternative—to enact and adopt a treaty concerning the conflict. Moreover, unlike the treaty process, the Chapter VII action was automatically binding upon all UN member states.

Under the ICTY Statute, the Tribunal's jurisdiction encompassed the most serious human rights abuses, including grave breaches of the Geneva Conventions (Art. 2 of the ICTY statute), violations of the laws and customs of war (Art. 3), crimes against humanity (Art. 5), and genocide (Art. 4). The ICTY's mandate gave the tribunal *primacy* over domestic and municipal judicial systems. That is, the ICTY's jurisdiction took precedence over that of any national or municipal court in the region if either were to assert jurisdiction over the same person accused of the same crime. Member states were also required to cooperate with the Tribunal's investigations and prohibited from hindering the enforcement of its judgments. This served as a necessary tool for the purposes of investigation and the issuance of warrants. It also protected the integrity of the ICTY's investigations and judgments to the extent possible.

The Challenge to the ICTY's Legitimacy: The *Tadic* Case

The main architects of the genocide in Yugoslavia initially evaded arrest, so the first prosecution was against a relatively small fish: Dusko Tadic, a low-level detention facility guard in Bosnia. Tadic was charged with thirty-one counts of crimes against humanity and grave breaches of the Geneva Conventions, including the murder, rape and torture of Muslim men and women at the Omarska detention camp. After he was arrested by German authorities, the ICTY requested that Tadic be sent to the Hague for trial, resting its request on the principle of the ICTY's international primacy.[13] Tadic challenged the legitimacy and "constitutionality" of the tribunal, as defendants had at Nuremberg. The Tribunal, however, rejected these challenges.

The Prosecutor v. Tadic, Case No. IT–94–1, Decision on the Defense Motion for Interlocutory Appeal on Jurisdiction, ¶ ¶ 27–48 (Appeals Chamber) (2 Oct. 1995)

[Appellant's] arguments raise a series of constitutional issues which all turn on the limits of the power of the Security Council under Chapter VII of the Charter of the United Nations and determining what action or measures can be taken under this Chapter, particularly the establishment of an international criminal tribunal. * * *

1. The Power of the Security Council to Invoke Chapter VII

Article 39 opens Chapter VII of the Charter of the United Nations and determines the conditions of application of this Chapter. It provides:

---

13. Compare this with the principle of complementarity, discussed later in this module, which is the foundation of the work of the International Criminal Court.

The Security Council shall determine the existence of any threat to the peace, breach of the peace, or act of aggression and shall make recommendations, or decide what measures shall be taken in accordance with Articles 41 and 42, to maintain or restore international peace and security. * * *

3. *The Establishment of the International Tribunal as a Measure under Chapter VII*

As with the determination of the existence of a threat to the peace, a breach of the peace or an act of aggression, the Security Council has a very wide margin of discretion under Article 39 to choose the appropriate course of action and to evaluate the suitability of the measures chosen, as well as their potential contribution to the restoration or maintenance of peace. But here again, this discretion is not unfettered; moreover, it is limited to the measures provided for in Articles 41[1] and 42[2]. Indeed, in the case at hand, this last point serves as a basis for the Appellant's contention of invalidity of the establishment of the International Tribunal.

In its Resolution 827, the Security Council considers that "in the particular circumstances of the former Yugoslavia," the establishment of the International Tribunal "would contribute to the restoration and maintenance of peace" and indicates that, in establishing it, the Security Council was acting under Chapter VII. However, it did not specify a particular Article as a basis for this action.* * *

   a. *What Article of Chapter VII Serves as a Basis for the Establishment of a Tribunal?*

      * * *

Obviously, the establishment of the International Tribunal is not a measure under Article 42, as these are measures of a military nature, implying the use of armed force. Nor can it be considered a "provisional measure" under Article 40. These measures, as their denomination indicates, are intended to act as a "holding operation," producing a "stand-still" or a "cooling-off" effect, "without prejudice to the rights, claims or position of the parties concerned." (United Nations Charter, Art. 40.) They are akin to emergency police action rather than to the activity of a judicial organ dispensing justice according to law. Moreover, not being enforcement action, according to the language of Article 40 itself ("before making the recommendations or deciding upon the measures provided for in Article 39"), such provisional measures are

---

1. [Editor's note: Article 41 provides that "The Security Council may decide what measures not involving the use of armed force are to be employed to give effect to its decisions, and it may call upon the Members of the United Nations to apply such measures. These may include complete or partial interruption of economic relations and of rail, sea, air, postal, telegraphic, radio, and other means of communication, and the severance of diplomatic relations."]

2. [Editor's note: Article 42 provides that "Should the Security Council consider the measures provided for in Article 41 would be inadequate or have proved to be inadequate, it may take such action by air, sea, or land forces as may be necessary to maintain or restore international peace and security. Such action may include demonstrations, blockade, and other operations by air, sea, or land forces of Members of the United Nations."]

subject to the Charter limitation of Article 2, paragraph 7, and the question of their mandatory or recommendatory character is subject to great controversy; all of which renders inappropriate the classification of the International Tribunal under these measures.

Prima facie, the International Tribunal matches perfectly the description in Article 41 of "measures not involving the use of force." Appellant, however, has argued before both the Trial Chamber and this Appeals Chamber, that:

> ... "[I]t is clear that the establishment of a war crimes tribunal was not intended. The examples mentioned in this article focus upon economic and political measures and do not in any way suggest judicial measures." (Brief to Support the Motion [of the Defense] on the Jurisdiction of the Tribunal before the Trial Chamber of the International Tribunal, 23 June 1995 (Case No. IT–94–1–T), at ¶ 3.2.1.)

It has also been argued that the measures contemplated under Article 41 are all measures to be undertaken by Member States, which is not the case with the establishment of the International Tribunal.

The first argument does not stand by its own language. Article 41 reads as follows:

> The Security Council may decide what measures not involving the use of armed force are to be employed to give effect to its decisions, and it may call upon the Members of the United Nations to apply such measures. These may include complete or partial interruption of economic relations and of rail, sea, air, postal, telegraphic, radio, and other means of communication, and the severance of diplomatic relations.

It is evident that the measures set out in Article 41 are merely illustrative examples which obviously do not exclude other measures. All the Article requires is that they do not involve "the use of force." It is a negative definition.

That the examples do not suggest judicial measures goes some way towards the other argument that the Article does not contemplate institutional measures implemented directly by the United Nations through one of its organs but, as the given examples suggest, only action by Member States, such as economic sanctions (though possibly coordinated through an organ of the Organization). However, as mentioned above, nothing in the Article suggests the limitation of the measures to those implemented by States. The Article only prescribes what these measures cannot be. Beyond that it does not say or suggest what they have to be.* * *

Logically, if the Organization can undertake measures which have to be implemented through the intermediary of its Members, it can *a fortiori* undertake measures which it can implement directly via its organs, if it happens to have the resources to do so. It is only for want of such resources that the United Nations has to act through its Members. But it is of the essence of "collective measures" that they are collectively undertaken. Action by Member States on behalf of the Organization is but a poor substitute *faute de mieux*, or a "second best" for want of the first. This is also the pattern of Article 42 on measures involving the use of armed force.

In sum, the establishment of the International Tribunal falls squarely within the powers of the Security Council under Article 41.* * *

The first ground of Appeal: unlawful establishment of the International Tribunal, is accordingly dismissed.

NOTES AND QUESTIONS ON THE *ICTY*

1. *The legal basis for the tribunal.* Are there any limits on the Security Council's authority to create judicial tribunals to enforce international humanitarian or human rights law? Do you see any due process problems in trying suspected war criminals in a tribunal created by a political body based on findings that massive human rights violations had occurred?

2. *Complicity.* At the trial level, Dusko Tadic was acquitted of the murder of five Muslim men in a Bosnian village (specifically murder as a crime against humanity), because it could not be proven that he, or the armed group of which he was a member, actually shot the victims. The Appeals Chamber concluded that the armed group had been the cause of deaths and that Tadic was guilty by virtue of being part of a joint criminal enterprise. Some commentators have pointed out that the Appeals Chamber "largely did not address the objections to this extended form of complicity. Instead, it called upon World War II-era cases to justify the doctrine's existence as a matter of customary international law and to elucidate its elements." Allison Marston Danner & Jenny S. Martinez, *Guilty Associations: Joint Criminal Enterprise, Command Responsibility, and the Development of International Criminal Law*, 93 CAL. L. REV. 75, 104, 109 (2005).

3. *Aftermath.* In 2008, as the ICTY began to complete its work, some respected observers lamented the fact "that several high-ranking officials, who had been indicted by the tribunal, remained at large, especially Radovan Karadzic, the former president of the self-proclaimed Republika Srpska," and Ratko Mladic, the former Bosnian Serb Army commander. *See* Dianne Orentlicher, *Shrinking the Space for Denial: The Impact of the ICTY in Serbia*, Open Society Justice Initiative (2008). In July 2008, however, the ICTY announced that Karadzic had been captured in Serbia, over thirteen years after the issuance of the first indictment against him. *See* Office of the Prosecutor, *Statement of the Office of the Prosecutor on the Arrest of Radovan Karadzic* (21 July 2008), *available at* http://www.un.org/icty/pressreal/2008/pr1274e.htm. Karadzic

was transferred to The Hague, where on August 1, 2008, the indict-ment—containing charges of genocide, crimes against humanity, and war crimes—was read in his presence. Specifically, Karadzic is accused *inter alia* of having directed the massacre of 8,000 Muslim boys and men at Srebenica in 1995 and the 43–month siege of Sarajevo that killed over 10,000 Bosnian Muslims. Karadzic claimed that the U.S. diplomats who had orchestrated the Dayton Peace Accord had cut a deal with him, according to which he was to refrain from public life in exchange for non-prosecution. Richard Holbrooke, the lead U.S. negotiator at Day-ton, roundly denied that assertion.

The International Criminal Tribunal for Rwanda

In the spring of 1994, genocide ravaged the African nation of Rwanda. Despite numerous warnings in advance of the genocide, the international community failed to take action to prevent the slaughter of hundreds of thousands of men, women, and children. Although the international community maintained a presence in Rwanda via the United Nations Assistance Mission for Rwanda (UNAMIR), its legal mandate was to aid in and enforce the implementation of the Arusha Accords (intended to end Rwanda's three-year civil war). It was there-fore restricted by its rules of engagement (permitted to fire only when fired upon), and unable to defend the great majority of Tutsis and Hutu moderates who were murdered.[1]

The genocide in Rwanda began on the night of April 6, 1994. Shortly thereafter, the UN Secretary General began to receive pleas from observers and officials to reinforce and arm UNAMIR and modify its mandate so as to address the chaos.[2] The Secretary General present-ed the Security Council with three alternative courses of action, to which the Council responded by voting to decrease the number of UNAMIR personnel to 270 staff.[3] All other international personnel were with-drawn by their governments, leaving the victims of the genocide be-hind.[4]

The genocide in Rwanda unfolded at an astonishing pace. Within 100 days, hundreds of thousands of persons perceived to be ethnic Tutsis or Tutsi sympathizers were maimed, raped, and/or killed, often with rudimentary weapons, such as machetes. An additional four million

---

1. *See* UNSCOR, 48th Sess., 3288th mtg., UN Doc. S/RES/872 (1993).

2. Special Report of the Secretary General on the United Nations Assistance Mission for Rwanda, S/1994/470, ¶ 13 (2004).

3. S/RES/912 (1994).

4. Countries providing personnel to UNAMIR included: Argentina, Australia, Austria, Bangla-desh, Belgium, Brazil, Canada, Chad, Congo, Djibouti, Egypt, Ethiopia, Fiji, Germany, Ghana, Guinea, Guinea Bissau, Guyana, India, Jordan, Kenya, Malawi, Mali, Netherlands, Niger, Nigeria, Pakistan, Poland, Romania, Russian Federation, Senegal, Slovak Republic, Spain, Switzerland, Togo, Tunisia, United Kingdom, Uruguay, Zambia, and Zimbabwe.

people fled to neighboring countries, including Burundi, Zaire, Tanzania, and Uganda.

Having stood idly by while the genocide raged, the UN again acted pursuant to its Chapter VII powers and established the *ad hoc* International Criminal Tribunal for Rwanda (the "ICTR") to prosecute the masterminds of the atrocities.[5] Like the ICTY, the ICTR's jurisdiction was targeted. The ICTR could only exercise jurisdiction over persons responsible for serious violations of international humanitarian law committed in the territory of Rwanda and over Rwandan citizens responsible for violations committed in both Rwanda and in neighboring states.[6] The ICTR's subject matter jurisdiction was also limited to those crimes enumerated in articles two through four of its Statute, including: genocide (Art. 2), crimes against humanity (Art. 3), and violations of Article 3 common to the Geneva Conventions and Additional Protocol II (Art. 4). Due to the internal nature of the Rwandan genocide, the international category of war crimes did not fall within the ICTR's jurisdiction. Finally, its Statute temporally limits the ICTR's jurisdiction to crimes committed between January 1, 1994, and December 31, 2004.[7]

Rwanda's civil war and genocide left its infrastructure ill-equipped to provide a suitable seat for the tribunal. Security for victims, witnesses, and staff also created a concern. Accordingly, the Security Council decided to seat the ICTR in Arusha, Tanzania, rather than in Rwanda or the territories where the crimes were committed.[8] This decision was the result of balancing a preference to conduct proceedings in Rwanda against considerations of justice and fairness, administrative efficiency and economy, access to witnesses, and the conclusion of appropriate arrangements between the United Nations and the State of the seat.

The ICTR has not encountered the same difficulty in apprehending suspects as the ICTY. The ICTR began its first case in January 1997. As of June 2008, the ICTR had handed down 41 judgments, 28 cases were in progress at the trial level, and two were pending on appeal, with 86 accused to be brought before the ICTR by the end of the year. Two cases have been transferred to France and one to the Netherlands for prosecution before domestic courts. Thirty case files were submitted to

---

5. Statute of the International Criminal Tribunal for Rwanda, S.C. Res. 955, 49th Sess., 3453rd mtg., U.N. Doc. S/RES/955 (1994)("ICTR Statute").

6. In extending the territorial jurisdiction of the ICTR beyond the territorial bounds of Rwanda, the Security Council hoped to enable the prosecution of serious crimes that occurred in refugee and IDP (Internally Displaced Persons) camps located in neighboring countries and committed in connection with the Rwandan genocide. *See* Report of the Secretary–General Pursuant to ¶ 5 of Security Council Resolution 955 (1994), UN Doc. S/1995/134, 13 February 1995, ¶ 13 ("S.G.Report").

7. "Although the crash of the aircraft carrying the Presidents of Rwanda and Burundi on 6 April 1994 is considered to be the event that triggered the civil war and the acts of genocide that followed, the Council decided that the temporal jurisdiction of the Tribunal would commence on 1 January 1994, in order to capture the planning stage of the crimes." *S.G. Report*, ¶ 14.

8. The "seat" of the ICTR refers to where trial chambers are located and where trials are held. To expedite the tribunal's operations, a temporary office for initial investigations and prosecutions was installed in the UNICEF building in Kigali, and the ICTR shared its Prosecutor, prosecutorial staff, and Appeals Chamber with the ICTY in the Hague. *S.G. Report* ¶ ¶ 15–17, 36.

Rwandan authorities for prosecution before Rwandan national courts. Thirteen accused remained at large.[9]

NOTES AND QUESTIONS ON THE *ICTR*

1. *Liability for inaction or complicity?* UNAMIR's presence in Rwanda during the genocide is widely criticized. It should be noted, however, that the 270 members of UNAMIR who remained in Rwanda despite the UN's decision not to heed the UNAMIR Commander's requests for reinforcements, aided thousands of Tutsi and Hutu moderates during the genocide. Twenty-seven UNAMIR personnel lost their lives. UNAMIR Commander Romeo Dallaire later stated that "[t]he killings could have been prevented if there had been the international will to accept the costs of doing so * * *."[10]

The UN has been subjected to more than criticism for its response to the Rwandan genocide. The wife of Rwandan Constitutional Court President Joseph Kavaruganda, who was deemed a Tutsi sympathizer and murdered during the genocide, brought suit against the UN for its complicity in the Rwandan genocide. She claims that Commander Dallaire assigned UN troops from Ghana to protect her family after he received intelligence regarding a plot to assassinate her husband and other Tutsi leaders and Hutu moderates. Instead, she alleges, the Ghanian UN troops handed her family over to the *genocidaires* and drank and socialized with them as her husband was murdered and while she and her daughters were tortured. A second plaintiff, Louise Mushikiwabo, also brought claims against the UN for the death of her brother, the only Tutsi minister in the Rwandan government, and other murdered family members. She also claims that UN troops were assigned to protect her family in response to information about an assassination plot against them but that the Ghanian troops fled when the killers arrived.[11] *See* CHRISTIAN C. SHERER, GENOCIDE AND CRISIS IN AFRICA: CONFLICT ROOTS, MASS VIOLENCE, AND REGIONAL WAR, 139–160 n.1(2002); Louise Mushikiwabo, *One Woman's Quest for Justice*, MAGAZINE: THE TRIBUNALS, Crimes of War Project: 2001, *available at*: http://www.crimesofwar.org/tribun-mag/rwandatestim_print.html.

The ICTR indicted Major Protais Mpiranya, the Commander of the Presidential Guard within the High Command of the Rwandan Army,

---

9. Report of the International Criminal Tribunal for the Prosecution of Persons Responsible for Genocide and Other Serious Violations of International Humanitarian Law Committed in the Territory of Rwanda and Rwandan Citizens Responsible for Genocide and Other Such Violations Committed in the Territory of Neighbouring States between 1 January and 31 December 1994, UN Doc. A/62/284–S/2007/502 (21 August 2007).

10. Romeo Dallaire and Bruce Poulin, *"Rwanda: From Peace Agreement to Genocide,"* CANADIAN DEFENCE QUARTERLY, 24, no. 3, March 1995.

11. Louise Mushikiwabo also filed suit under the ATCA against an individual leader of the Rwandan political party, the Coalition pour la Defense de la Public ("CDR"), for his role in ordering and conspiring to commit genocide. *See Mushikiwabo v. Barayagwiza*, 1996 WL 164496 (S.D.N.Y. 1996) (unpublished).

for conspiring to commit genocide by ordering the death of Kavarugan-da and other Tutsi and Hutu moderate officials. *See Prosecutor v. Bizimungu, et al.*, ICTR-2000–56–I. However, many critics of the UN's response to the Rwandan genocide have sought a measure of UN accountability, including the payment of reparations to the family members of victims.

Should the ICTR also prosecute the commanding officers of those Ghanian UN troops (or the troops themselves) who allegedly failed to protect Rwandans during the genocide? Is it significant that some members of the Belgian constituency of the UN Mission, who were also protecting Tutsis and Hutu moderates, were executed by the Rwandan Army while the troops belonging to the Ghanian constituency of the UN Mission were released? Should the UN itself be amenable to suit for extracting troops from areas surrounded by *genocidaires*, with the knowledge that extracting such troops would mean certain death for the thousands of Tutsi and Hutu moderates they were protecting? Should an international peacekeeping force enjoy immunity from prosecution for conduct during the course of their mission?

2.   *Contributing to culture and education in Rwanda.* Some critics state that the ICTR's location across the border in Arusha, Tanzania, leaves ordinary Rwandans unaware of the legal processes taking place and unable to be confident that the perpetrators of the genocide are being prosecuted. Others argue that the ICTR's decision to conduct its proceedings in English and French, rather than in Kinyarwanda, the national language of Rwanda, leaves the impression that the ICTR is unconcerned with the people with the greatest stake in the accountability trials. Responding to these concerns is the ICTR's Outreach Program, the focal point of which is the *Umuzanzu mu Bwiyunge*, or Information Centre, in Kigali, Rwanda. There, Rwandans can access briefings, lectures, workshops, and films for information about the tribunal. Should these resources have been spent on constructing a seat for the tribunal in Rwanda?

The Workings of the Ad Hoc Tribunals

Both *ad hoc* tribunals got off to a slow start. The first few years were spent organizing the courts, the Office of the Prosecutor, and the defense bar.[12] Additionally, a great deal of time was spent marshalling resources for the courts and creating the rules of evidence and procedure. One particular issue in the drafting of the rules was whether to adopt a civil or common law system. The rules struck a balance in legal traditions, and the Tribunal's proceedings became an amalgam of common law and civil law features. (Defense lawyers from the civil law tradition needed to learn the art of cross-examination, while lawyers

---

12.   Thomas S. Warrick in consultation with M. Cherif Bassiouni, *Organization of the International Criminal Court: Administrative and Financial Issues*, 25 DENV. J. INT'L L. & POL'Y 333, 334–35 (1997).

from the common law tradition had to adjust to the absence of a jury and the admissibility of a wider range of evidence than would ordinarily be permitted in jury trials.) Other practical considerations included: leasing property for the Tribunals from national governments; drafting regulations governing the employment of staff; implementing technology for communication and the collection and storage of evidence; and recruiting Court officers and support staff reflecting diversity by geographic origin and gender.

NOTES AND QUESTIONS ON THE WORKINGS OF THE AD HOC TRIBUNALS

1. *Rules of evidence and procedure.* At the ICTY, the judges were responsible for drafting the Rules of Procedures and Evidence. Relying heavily on proposals submitted by a UN working group composed of criminal and international lawyers, NGOs, and governments, they adopted a short but broad list of evidentiary rules, including *inter alia*, rules pertaining to the testimony of witnesses, false testimony, confessions, evidence of patterns of conduct, experts, evidence obtained by illegal means, special rules for evidence in sexual assault cases, and the lawyer-client privilege.[13]

Under Rule 89, judges admit evidence so long as it is relevant and its probative value is not substantially outweighed by the need to ensure a fair trial. In this sense, it is very similar to Federal Rule of Evidence 403. The rule governing exclusion of evidence is similarly succinct. Evidence can be excluded "if obtained by methods which cast substantial doubt on its reliability or if its admission is antithetical to, and would seriously damage, the integrity of the proceedings."

Among the most controversial evidentiary issues are the permissibility of hearsay evidence and anonymous witnesses, *infra*. The ICTY Rules of Evidence do not exclude hearsay evidence, an omission that many argue unfairly deprives a defendant of his right to cross-examine the declarant. Others defend the ICTY's decision to admit hearsay, arguing that the judge's ability to exclude unreliable, overly prejudicial evidence provides sufficient protection for the defendant.

2. *Fair trial rights.* Article 21 of the ICTY Statute and Article 20 of the ICTR Statute are virtually identical and derive from the due process protections in Article 14 of the International Covenant on Civil and Political Rights. The Article 14 guarantee of a fair trial and due process under the law is widely understood to have achieved the status of customary international law. A defendant in proceedings before the ICTY and the ICTR is thus entitled to a fair and public hearing, to be informed promptly of the charges against him in a language he under-

---

13. *See* ICTY R. P. & EVID. 89–99; ICTR R. P. & EVID, 89–98; JUDGE RICHARD MAY & MARIEKE WIERDA, INTERNATIONAL CRIMINAL EVIDENCE (2002); SALVATORE ZAPPALA, HUMAN RIGHTS IN INTERNATIONAL CRIMINAL PROCEEDINGS (2003).

stands, to be tried without undue delay, to examine witnesses against him, to legal assistance, and not to be compelled to testify against himself.

3. *Equality of arms.* In *Prosecutor v. Tadic*, the ICTY determined that the right to a fair trial included equality of arms. Drawing on Article 20(1), Article 21 (4)(b), and the jurisprudence of the European Court of Human Rights, the Appeals Chamber concluded that "[t]he principle of equality of arms means that the Prosecution and the Defence must be equal before the Trial Chamber. It follows that the Chamber shall provide every practicable facility it is capable of granting under the Rules and Statute when faced with a request by a * * * party for assistance in presenting its case[.]"

Equality of arms is a procedural protection given to the accused to ensure substantial parity in legal proceedings. In *Prosecutor v. Kayishema*, Case No. ICTR–95–I-T, Trial Chamber, Judgment, ¶¶ 20, (May 21, 1999), the defendant argued that, in accordance with the "equality of arms," he should be provided with equivalent assistance in preparing his case from investigators, lawyers, and consultants as had been provided to the prosecution. *Id.*, ¶ 55–60. Affirming the Trial Chamber, the Appeals Court found that equality of arms referred to equality of rights, not resources. *Id.*, ¶ 60.

4. *The right to self-representation.* Article 21(4)(d) of the ICTY Statute guarantees the accused the right to self-representation, a right well-established in international law as set forth in ICCPR Article 14(3)(d). In granting former Serbian President Slobodan Milosevic's request to represent himself at trial, the Trial Chamber relied, in part, on remarks made by the Secretary General, in which he stated that the "International Tribunal must fully respect the rights of the accused:* * * in particular, [rights] contained in article 14 of the International Covenant on Civil and Political Rights."[14] The Trial Chamber also appointed two attorneys as *amicus curiae* to assist Milosevic in his defense. However, after several months of delay due to Milosevic's health problems and his refusal to cooperate, the ICTY found that Milosevic should be assigned counsel in the "interests of justice." In order to preserve Milosevic's right to self-representation, the assigned counsel would only act when Milosevic was physically incapable of acting in his own defense, and Milosevic retained full control over the decisions in the case.[15] He died mid-trial on March 13, 2006.

5. *Exclusionary rule.* Both the ICTY and the ICTR have exclusionary provisions built into their rules. The language in the ICTY Rules and the ICTR Rules is identical, providing, "[n]o evidence shall be

---

14. *Prosecutor v. Milosevic*, Case No. IT–02–54–T, Reasons for Decision on the Prosecution Motion Concerning Assignment of Counsel, ¶ 40 (Apr. 4, 2003).

15. *Prosecutor v. Milosevic*, Case No. IT–02–54–AR73.7, Decision on Interlocutory Appeal of the Trial Chamber's Decision on The Assignment of Defense Counsel, ¶¶ 19–20 (Nov. 1, 2004); *see* Kate Kerr, *Note, Fair Trials at International Criminal Tribunals: Examining the Parameters of the International Right to Counsel*, 36 GEO. J. INT'L L. 1227 (2005).

admissible if obtained by methods which cast substantial doubt on its reliability or if its admission is antithetical to, and would seriously damage, the integrity of the proceedings."[16] In *Prosecutor v. Delalic*,[17] the ICTY applied the exclusionary rule to exclude evidence obtained in violation of the right to counsel. Zdravko Mucic, the defendant in *Delalic*, was apprehended in Austria and interrogated by Austrian police. Because Austrian law failed to provide a right to counsel in preliminary investigations, Mucic was not permitted access to a lawyer. The Trial Chamber refused to admit the statements that Mucic made to the Austrian authorities, stating "the Austrian rights of the suspect are so fundamentally different from the rights under the International Tribunal's Statute and Rules as to render the statement made under it inadmissible."[18]

6. *Obtaining evidence.* Obtaining evidence poses a complex problem for the *ad hoc* tribunals, including the challenge of obtaining reliable eyewitness testimony. The dangers of relying on eyewitness testimony by traumatized witnesses is examined in Diane Marie Amann, *International Decision, Prosecutor v. Kupreskic,* 96 Am. J. Int'l L. 439 (2002).

7. *The duty of states to cooperate.* Upon whose efforts do the tribunals rely to unearth evidence? Can the tribunals' investigators contact witnesses and obtain other evidence over the objections of the countries in which they were located? These question were addressed in *Prosecutor v. Blaskic*, Case No. IT–95–24–T, Judgment on the Request of the Republic of Croatia for Review of the Decisions of Trial Chamber II of 18 July 1997 (Oct. 29, 1997).

In *Blaskic*, the court found that member states owed a duty to cooperate with the evidence-gathering efforts of the ICTY and ICTR and that the Security Council could enforce court orders to cooperate. In connection with its investigation of Tihomir Blaskic, a Bosnian Croat wanted by the ICTY for ethnic cleansing, the Tribunal issued a *subpoena duces tecum* to the Government of Croatia. Croatia argued that the Tribunal did not have the authority to issue such a subpoena and refused to comply. The Appeals Chamber agreed with the Trial Chamber, finding that because the Tribunal had been established by Security Council Resolution, the Tribunal had the legal authority to issue binding orders to states. As a result, failure to comply with an order by the Tribunal could subject states to potential enforcement action by the Security Council.

8. *Plea bargaining.* Plea bargaining is not a universal practice. In some cultures the idea of negotiating with a criminal defendant about

---

16. ICTY R. P. & Evid; ICTR R. P. & Evid; The International Criminal Court is similarly required to exclude evidence obtained in violation of the statute or internationally recognized human rights standards if: "(a) The violation casts substantial doubt on the reliability of the evidence; or (b) The admission of such evidence would be antithetical to and would seriously damage the integrity of the proceedings." Rome Statute, art. 69(7).

17. *Prosecutor v. Delalic* ("Celebici Case"), Case No. IT–96–21–A, *Decision on Zdravko Mucic's Motion for the Exclusion of Evidence,* ¶ 40 (Sept. 2, 1997).

18. *Id.,* ¶ 52.

criminal responsibility and his or her sentence is anathema.[19] However, the Tribunals could not possibly try all potential defendants; indeed, in Rwanda, with more than 100,000 potential defendants in custody, it would take many lifetimes to try the accused. This reality led to the adoption of other methods of handling the mass of cases, such as the Rwandan Gacaca, or local village courts.[20]

While initially rejecting plea bargaining as incompatible with its mandate, the ICTY has increasingly used plea bargains to manage its substantial caseload. In *Plavsic*, the ICTY engaged in "charge bargaining," agreeing to drop the charge of genocide in return for a guilty plea on a single count of crimes against humanity, a lesser charge. *See* Michael P. Scharf, *Trading Justice for Efficiency: Plea–Bargaining and International Tribunals*, 2 J. INT'L CRIM. JUST. 1070 (2004).

How would you resolve the problem of having too many defendants and not enough judicial resources? This problem is especially grave where the acts charged include genocide. Should those who commit the worst crimes be able to negotiate a more lenient sentence by a plea bargain? Does resort to plea bargains distort the historical record? Can this problem be minimized by requiring an apology or other public conciliatory statement on the record by the accused? *See* Diane Marie Amann, *Group Mentality, Expressivism, and Genocide*, 2 INT'L CRIM. L. REV. 93 (2002).

9. *Death penalty*. There is no customary international norm forbidding the death penalty in all circumstances. Some human rights treaties even provide for the imposition of the death penalty with important limitations. In the last several decades, the abolition of the death penalty, *de jure* or *de facto*, has grown to the point that more than half of the world's nation-states may be considered abolitionist, especially those in Europe and Latin America.[21] Whatever the status of the death penalty under customary law, it is not permitted under the ICTY and ICTR statutes: the maximum sentence is life without the possibility of parole. This prohibition was not without objection. In fact, Rwanda was so committed to retaining the death penalty as a potential punishment for those convicted by the ICTR, that it voted against the Security Council resolution authorizing the tribunal, even though it had requested the tribunal in the first place. Is it fair that the biggest fish, being tried by the ICTR, do not face the death penalty, while the smaller fish being tried in the Rwandan courts, do?

---

19.   Ethan A. Nadelmann, *The Role of the United States in the International Enforcement of Criminal Law*, 31 HARV. INT'L L.J. 37, 49 (1990); Nancy Amoury Combs, *Copping a Plea to Genocide: The Plea Bargaining of International Crimes*, 151 U. PA. L. REV. 1 (2002).

20.   *See* Amnesty Int'l, *Gacaca: A Question of Justice*, AI Index 47/007/2002, Dec. 17, 2002. See Module 7(C), *infra*.

21.   *See* Amnesty Int'l, *Facts and Figures on the Death Penalty*, http://www.amnesty.org/en/library/info/ACT50/006/2005/en (last visited July, 4, 2008).

CASE STUDIES

CASE STUDY 1: WITNESS PROTECTION AND DUE PROCESS

One of the early controversies in the ICTY was the possible conflict between the rights of witnesses and the fair trial rights of defendants. Under Article 21 of the ICTY Statute, fair trial rights of defendants are to be guaranteed, but under Article 22 of the ICTY Statute, witnesses are entitled to protection. The apparent conflict arose in the early years in the context of anonymous witnesses. Under the rules, the court could issue orders for the protection of witnesses, including granting witnesses complete anonymity. This led to a debate reflected in the following excerpts.

Monroe Leigh, *The Yugoslav Tribunal: Use of Unnamed Witnesses Against Accused*, 90 Am. J. Int'l L. 235 (1996)

On August 10, 1995, a trial chamber of the International Criminal Tribunal for the Former Yugoslavia issued two rulings in the first case brought under the Statute establishing the Tribunal, *Prosecutor v. Tadic.* * * * In a second ruling—a procedural one—the trial chamber authorized the prosecutor to withhold from the accused and his counsel the identity of a number of witnesses against the accused. It is the thesis of this commentator, who has been and remains a strong supporter of the Tribunal, that this * * * ruling, if acted upon, will deny the accused the "fair trial" and the right "to examine * * * witnesses against him" which are required by the Statute as well as by international law.* * *

In its * * * ruling, the trial chamber acted upon the Chief Prosecutor's request for a number of measures for the protection of victims and witnesses. Among these the most important were requests that certain victims and witnesses be heard *in camera* (*i.e.*, in closed session); that certain victims and witnesses be assigned pseudonyms; that their true names be expunged from the public record and included only in sealed records not disclosed to the public or the media, and also that their testimony be given by closed-circuit television with image- and voice-altering devices; and finally that the identities of several victims and witnesses not be disclosed to the accused or his counsel. With a few exceptions, not here relevant, the trial chamber granted all of these requests for protective measures, many of which defense counsel did not object to.* * *

No provision of the Statute or of the Tribunal's Rules of Procedure and Evidence specifically authorizes the withholding of the names of victims and witnesses. Although the Statute provides in Article 21(4)(e) that the accused shall be entitled "to examine, or have examined, the witnesses against him," there is in the Statute no specific right of "confrontation" in the sense that right is guaranteed by the Sixth Amendment to the U.S. Constitution. On the other hand, it can be argued that the right to examine or cross-examine witnesses cannot be effective without the right to know the identity of adverse witnesses. It is an almost impossible task to cross-examine an adverse witness effectively without knowing that witness's name, background, habitual residence or whereabouts at the time of the events to which he testifies—or, indeed, to prepare to conduct such an examination in a professionally responsible manner.

Article 21(2) of the Yugoslav Statute provides that the accused "shall be entitled to a fair and public hearing"—language taken verbatim from the International Covenant on Civil and Political Rights and the earlier European Convention for the Protection of Human Rights and Fundamental Freedoms. But in Article 21(2) this language is qualified by a subject-to clause, which reads, "subject to article 22 of the Statute"—a limitation that has no analog in the earlier conventions. And when one turns to Article 22 of the Statute, one finds language that is unfortunately not free from ambiguity. It reads as follows: "The International Tribunal shall provide in its rules of procedure and evidence for the protection of victims and witnesses. Such protection measures shall include, but shall not be limited to, the conduct of *in camera* proceedings and the protection of the victim's identity." * * *

Judge Stephen, in his separate opinion, concluded that neither the Statute nor the Tribunal's Rules give support to the idea that the use of unnamed witnesses against the accused can be reconciled with the requirement of a fair trial. Therefore, in his view, the Statute and the Rules should not be interpreted as allowing identity to be withheld from the accused and his counsel.* * *

The plausibility of Judge Stephen's reading is reinforced by the fact that the Rules of Procedure clearly do not contemplate so drastic a procedure as withholding from the accused the names of his accusers. Indeed, such inferences as can be drawn from Rules 69 and 75, which deal specifically with the protection of victims and witnesses, point in the opposite direction. Thus, Rule 69(A), which contemplates nondisclosure "[i]n exceptional circumstances," limits this possibility "until such person is brought under the protection of the Tribunal." * * *

Similarly, Rule 75, which is captioned "Measures for the Protection of Victims and Witnesses," provides in Subrule A that any such measures must be "consistent with the rights of the accused."

The balance of Rule 75 deals specifically with *in camera* proceedings, preventing disclosure of the identity and whereabouts to the public and the media through such means as expunging names and identifying information from the public records, the use of image- and voice-altering devices or closed-circuit television, and the assignment of pseudonyms. Nowhere in the midst of this Rule 75 specificity is it specified that the identities of victims and witnesses may be withheld from the accused.

Finally, it should be pointed out that Rule 70, which deals in detail with confidentiality of information obtained from confidential sources, provides in Subrule (F) that nothing in earlier sections shall impair the Trial Chamber's power to exclude evidence "if its probative value is substantially outweighed by the need to ensure a fair trial." Subrule 89(D) contains similar cautionary language.* * *

There can be no question that the Trial Chamber had to deal with an issue of transcendent difficulty. Terrorist activities and ethnic tensions * * * are an ever-present threat to the orderly administration of justice. Nevertheless, it is * * * of even greater importance that the International Tribunal at The Hague * * * establish itself as the preeminent defender of human rights and particularly of the right of every accused to a fair trial according to the most exacting standards of due process required by contemporary international law.* * *

From a legal policy point of view, it seems obvious that the Tribunal's priority should be to do justice to Tadic and at the same time maintain its credibility. It can most readily achieve both objectives if it decides on appeal that Judge Stephen's interpretation of the Statute is correct. It is also the interpretation that is most nearly consistent with international law as reflected in the International Covenant on Civil and Political Rights, the European Convention for the Protection of Human Rights and Fundamental Freedoms, and the Universal Declaration of Human Rights. It seems to me axiomatic that the Tribunal should presume that the Security Council in establishing the Tribunal intended that its Statute should be interpreted in a way that is consistent with international law. * * *

Christine M. Chinkin, *Due Process and Witness Anonymity*, 91 AM. J. INT'L L. 75 (1997)

Monroe Leigh strongly criticized the pretrial ruling * * * in *Prosecutor v. Tadic*, which held that "the identities of several victims and witnesses can be indefinitely withheld from the accused and his counsel." Mr. Leigh claims that the majority's ruling will deny the accused a fair trial and *may* lead to the conviction of accused persons on the basis of tainted evidence. I would argue that he has failed to take into account the full details of the chamber's judgment, which recognized in particular that the accused's right to know and confront prosecution witnesses is not absolute but may have to be balanced against other important interests.

It is undoubted that those accused of offenses under the jurisdiction of the Tribunal must receive a fair trial in accordance with the human rights standards laid down in international instruments. * * * This is required by the Statute of the Tribunal (Article 21). Accordingly, in drafting the Rules of Evidence and Procedure of the Tribunal, the judges incorporated throughout guarantees for the conduct of proceedings in accordance with international standards of fair trial and due process. The credibility and legitimacy of the Tribunal depend upon its fulfilling these guarantees, as does its value in setting precedents for future war crimes trials at either the international or the domestic level.

Nevertheless, the requirements of a fair trial cannot be determined in the abstract.* * * Among the Tribunal's unique characteristics is the "affirmative obligation to protect witnesses and victims" mandated by Article 22 and fleshed out by Rules 69 and 75. Accordingly, the chamber held that the safety of victims and witnesses must be balanced against the right of the accused to a fair trial. It "had to take into account the most conspicuous aspects of the armed conflict" in former Yugoslavia, including the spread of "terror and anguish" among the civilian population. This factor was especially significant since prosecutions at the Tribunal, unlike those at Nuremberg, "would, to a considerable degree, be dependent on eyewitness testimony." However, unlike many domestic jurisdictions confronting the issue of witness security, the Tribunal cannot operate an effective protection program that extends across national boundaries to the many places where witnesses are now located. The Victims and Witnesses Unit set up within the Registry of the Tribunal under Rule 34 has very limited resources and can offer only minimal counseling and protection to witnesses while they are present in The Hague to give evidence.

The interest in the safety of victims and witnesses also forms part of the broader interest of the international community in the pursuit of justice. The Security Council established the Tribunal under Chapter VII of the United Nations Charter to "put an end to such crimes and to take effective measures to bring to justice the persons who are responsible for them." The Tribunal's functions have been described as three-fold: to do justice, to deter further crimes and to contribute to the restoration and maintenance of international peace. Its jurisdiction signals to the international community the unacceptability under international law of atrocities committed during armed conflict. If the unwillingness of witnesses to testify prevents it from successfully prosecuting those who have been indicted, those objectives are undermined. The crucial question, therefore, is whether a fair trial includes an absolute right to know the identity of one's accuser.* * *

The chamber sought guidance in national jurisprudence and in that of the European Commission and Court of Human Rights.* * * The European Court, in *Kostovski v. The Netherlands*, had concluded that the disadvantages that an accused must face when addressing the evidence of an anonymous witness can be counterbalanced by safeguards provided by the trial court.* * *

The [*Tadic*] chamber explicitly recognized the need to balance competing interests. It did not accord blanket anonymity to all who might claim it. It drew upon case law from various jurisdictions and listed in the judgment factors to be weighed against the accused's right to a fair trial. First, there must be a real fear for the safety of the witness. The chamber added that "the ruthless character of an alleged crime justifies such fear of the accused and his accomplices." Second, the prosecutor must demonstrate the importance of the witness to proving the counts of the indictment to which the evidence relates. Third, there must be no evidence to suggest that the witness is untrustworthy. Fourth, the Tribunal itself is in no position to offer protection to the witnesses or their families after receiving their testimony.

These factors are sufficiently flexible to allow the particular facts of each claim to be taken into account. In some cases the identity of the accuser may be crucial to the establishment of guilt, while in others it may not be. For example, where a charge is based upon command authority, it will be necessary for the prosecution to establish that violations of the laws of war occurred in a particular location and that they can be linked to the accused's authority. In these circumstances the identity of the individual witnesses testifying to the occurrence of particular events would be less relevant than their location and the chain of command.

The chamber also provided guidelines to be followed when evidence is taken from an anonymous witness. The judges must know each witness's identity and must be able to observe the witnesses' demeanor to assess the reliability of testimony.* * * The defense must be given ample opportunity to question the witness on issues unrelated to identity and current whereabouts. * * * Finally, the anonymity is not to be permanent, but will last only so long as there is reason to fear for the witness's security.

Many of the arguments presented to the Tribunal in support of anonymity related specifically to charges of sexual abuse. Indeed, the Secretary–General of the United Nations stated that protection should be provided to victims "especially in cases of rape or sexual assault." While the Tribunal did not limit its ruling to these cases, it was aware of the particular features of such trials and referred to the attention given in the Rules of Procedure and Evidence to crimes committed against women. This context cannot be ignored when assessing the chamber's ruling. Rape is notoriously under-reported and convictions are hard to secure in domestic criminal courts. Unless one believes that many women put themselves through the ordeal of a rape trial to make false accusations against men, this is a cause for concern. Writers have described the re-traumatization of a victim through having to confront her alleged rapist at trial, and describe what he did to her in the face of hostile defense questioning. Societal pressures may also weigh against an admission of having been raped. In the *Tadic* trial, the subsequent refusal to testify of one of the witnesses accorded anonymity by the chamber underlines the reality of these fears.* * *

The argument that human rights standards have been defined by men in accordance with male assertions of what constitutes the most fundamental guarantees required by individuals is highlighted in the conflict between the rights of the accused to a fair trial and the right of the victim to equality before the law and to be free from fear of further abuse. Women typically feature in a criminal trial as victims and witnesses, while more men than women appear as accused. It is not surprising that the guarantee of a fair trial is seen by many as more fundamental than the victim's interests, and those of other potential victims. Leigh argues that the Tribunal must "establish itself as the preeminent defender of human rights and particularly of the right of every accused to a fair trial according to the most exacting standards of due process required by contemporary international law." For many women, the Tribunal's jurisdiction over rape (as a crime against humanity) and the willingness of the prosecution to bring indictments for "forcible sexual penetration" (as a grave breach of the Geneva Conventions, torture, enslavement and crimes against humanity) are of paramount importance in breaking the long silence about the incidence of violent sexual abuse in armed conflict. This move forward will be prejudiced if fear prevents witnesses from giving their testimony.* * *

The chamber's decision is carefully constructed to give appropriate weight to both sets of interests and not to give automatic priority to those of the accused. In conjunction with the further protections accorded to victims of sexual assault in Rule 96 of the Rules of Procedure and Evidence, the decision is to be welcomed for its recognition that individual rights cannot always be absolute but must be weighed against those of other individuals. It also provides guidance for trials of charges of sexual abuse that might be followed by domestic criminal courts and thus improve the chances of convictions for these serious offenses.

Unlike Nuremberg, where the Allied forces were in complete control of the security situation in post-war Germany, the ICTY and ICTR are not in a position to offer complete security guarantees to witnesses, even though they operate pursuant to Security Council resolutions. Moreover, the government of Yugoslavia, at least when Milosevic was still in power, was overtly hostile to the work of the Tribunal. On the other hand, was it reasonable to assume that some witnesses might give false testimony because of ethnic hatred or allegiance? Would you trust the prosecution and court to ensure that witnesses were not giving false testimony? Is cross-examination and investigation of witnesses by defense counsel the only way to ensure a fair trial? Is defense counsel able to test the first hand knowledge and internal consistency of the witness's testimony without knowing the witness's name?

One witness in the *Tadic* trial, Witness L, was granted complete anonymity. Witness L turned out to have given false testimony about his background at the trial, demonstrating the potential for abuse in granting such anonymity.[22] On the other hand, it was the prosecution that detected the false testimony and provided the information to the court for action. Upon discovery of the deception, Witness L's testimony was stricken.

CASE STUDY 2:

THE JURISPRUDENCE OF RAPE AND OTHER SEXUAL VIOLENCE

The *ad hoc* tribunals have provided a rich jurisprudence—principles of international criminal law building upon the foundation of Nuremberg and other well-established norms of customary and conventional law. This case study examines the way these new international tribunals have contributed to the evolution of a new international jurisprudence relating to rape and gender violence, especially the understanding that such wrongs can constitute crimes against humanity, war crimes, grave breaches of the Geneva Conventions, torture, and genocide. These developments in turn contributed to the enumeration of crimes in the Rome Statute defining the jurisdiction of the International Criminal Court.

The use of sexual violence in armed conflict has historically been obscured by the myth that rape is a private, lust-induced act of renegade soldiers. However, sexual violence—whether on a mass scale or as a solitary criminal act—rises to the level of a war crime when it is executed as part of a military strategy of "ethnic cleansing," or is used to terrorize, torture, or displace a population.

1. THE HISTORICAL DEVELOPMENT OF RAPE AS A WAR CRIME

Rape has been proscribed as a violation of the laws of war for centuries. As far back as 1385, rape was categorized as a war crime punishable by death in the military codes of Richard II as well as the 1419 military code of Henry the V.[23] The Hague Conventions adopted before World War I, set forth the rules for conducting war and mandated that individuals could be prosecuted for crimes which

---

22. Robert M. Hayden, *Biased "Justice:" Humanrightsism and the International Criminal Tribunal for the Former Yugoslavia*, 47 CLEV. ST. L. REV. 549, 562 (1999); Sara Stapleton, *Note, Ensuring a Fair Trial in the International Criminal Court: Statutory Interpretation and the Impermissibility of Derogation*, 31 N.Y.U. J. INT'L L. & POL. 535, 569 (1999).

23. Theodor Meron, *Rape as a Crime Under International Humanitarian Law*, 87 AM. J. INT'L L. 424, 425 (1993); Kelly D. Askin, *Prosecuting Wartime Rape and Other Gender–Related Crimes under International Law: Extraordinary Advances, Enduring Obstacles*, 21 BERKELEY J. INT'L L. 288, 299 (2003).

"shocked the conscience of mankind." Frances T. Pilch, *The Crime of Rape in International Humanitarian Law*, 9 U.S.A.F.A. J. LEG. STUD. 99, 103 (1999). Similarly, while the Nuremberg Tribunal did not expressly list rape as one of the crimes under its jurisdiction, evidence of widespread rape and sexual violence was weighed by the Tribunal in determining sentences for the accused. Moreover, sexual violence and wartime rape arguably fell within the ambit of Article 6(c) of the Nuremberg Charter, which defined "crimes against humanity" as including "inhumane acts committed against any civilian population."[24] In the following excerpt, the ICTR Trial chamber traced the history of the proscription of rape in armed conflict and found that it was prohibited under customary international law.

Prosecutor v. Furundzija, Case No. ICTR–95–17/1–T, Judgment, ¶ ¶ 168–172 (10 Dec. 1998)

C.   Rape and Other Serious Sexual Assaults in International Law

   1.   *International Humanitarian Law*

   The prohibition of rape and serious sexual assault in armed conflict has * * * evolved in customary international law. It has gradually crystallized out of the express prohibition of rape in article 44 of the Lieber Code [during the U.S. Civil War] and the general provisions contained in article 46 of the regulations annexed to Hague Convention IV, read in conjunction with the 'Martens clause' laid down in the preamble to that Convention. While rape and sexual assaults were not specifically prosecuted by the Nuremberg Tribunal, rape was expressly classified as a crime against humanity under article II(1)(c) of Control Council Law No. 10. The Tokyo International Military Tribunal convicted Generals Toyoda and Matsui of command responsibility for violations of the laws or customs of war committed by their soldiers in Nanking, which included widespread rapes and sexual assaults. The former Foreign Minister of Japan, Hirota, was also convicted for these atrocities. This decision and that of the United States Military Commission in *Yamashita*, along with the ripening of the fundamental prohibition of "outrages upon personal dignity" laid down in common article 3 into customary international law, has contributed to the evolution of universally accepted norms of international law prohibiting rape as well as serious sexual assault. These norms are applicable in any armed conflict.

   It is indisputable that rape and other serious sexual assaults in armed conflict entail the criminal liability of the perpetrators.

   2.   *International Human Rights Law*

   No international human rights instrument specifically prohibits rape or other serious sexual assaults. Nevertheless, these offences are implicitly prohibited by the provisions safeguarding physical integrity,

---

   24. Samantha I. Ryan, *Comment, From the Furies of Nanking to the Eumenides of the International Criminal Court; The Evolution of Sexual Assaults as International Crimes*, 11 PACE INT'L L. REV. 447, 459 (1999).

which are contained in all of the relevant international treaties. The right to physical integrity is a fundamental one, and is undeniably part of customary international law.

In certain circumstances, however, rape can amount to torture and has been found by international judicial bodies to constitute a violation of the norm prohibiting torture * * *.

3. *Rape Under the Statute*

The prosecution of rape is explicitly provided for in Article 5 of the Statute of the International Tribunal as a crime against humanity. Rape may also amount to a grave breach of the Geneva Conventions, a violation of the laws or customs of war or an act of genocide, if the requisite elements are met, and may be prosecuted accordingly.

NOTES AND QUESTIONS ON THE HISTORICAL DEVELOPMENT OF RAPE AS A WAR CRIME

Conceptualizing the crime of rape. Rape was historically criminalized as an outrage upon dignity, because it branded the victim (always seen to be a woman) as unchaste, impure, and dishonorable and thus unworthy of marriage. Rape could even be viewed as a crime against the chattel of a man or the honor of the man. Human rights activists have criticized these conceptualizations as archaic and discriminatory, and as a dismissal of the brutality of rape and sexual assault, which can destroy a person physically, mentally, and spiritually. *See* Samantha I. Ryan, *From the Furies of Nanking to the Eumenides of the International Criminal Court; The Evolution of Sexual Assaults as International Crimes*, 11 PACE INT'L L. REV. 447, 461 (1999). What types of prosecutorial problems could you envision in conceptualizing rape and other sexual violence as an "outrage upon personal dignity" instead of a violent crime?

---

2. THE DOCTRINAL EVOLUTION OF "RAPE" AT THE *AD HOC* TRIBUNALS

Under the ICTY and ICTR Statutes, rape is included as a crime against humanity.[25] In addition, the ICTR explicitly enumerates rape as an "outrage[] upon personal dignity" in violation of Article 3 Common to the Geneva Conventions and Additional Protocol II.[26] However, it was the ICTR Trial Chamber Judgment in *Prosecutor v. Akayesu* that provided the first concrete definition of rape for the *ad hoc* tribunals.

---

25. ICTY Statute, art. 5(g); ICTR Statute, art. 3(g).

26. ICTR Statute, art. 4(e).

PROSECUTOR v. AKAYESU

Case No. ICTR–96–4–T, Judgment, ¶¶ 686–688 (Sept. 2, 1998)

[T]he Tribunal must define rape, as there is no commonly accepted definition of the term in international law. The Tribunal notes that many of the witnesses have used the term "rape" in their testimony. At times, the Prosecution and the Defense have also tried to elicit an explicit description of what happened in physical terms, to document what the witnesses mean by the term "rape." The Tribunal notes that while rape has been historically defined in national jurisdictions as non-consensual sexual intercourse, variations on the form of rape may include acts which involve the insertion of objects and/or the use of bodily orifices not considered to be intrinsically sexual. An act such as that described by Witness KK in her testimony—the Interahamwes (militias formed by the Hutu ethnic majority) thrusting a piece of wood into the sexual organs of a woman as she lay dying—constitutes rape in the Tribunal's view.

The Tribunal considers that rape is a form of aggression and that the central elements of the crime of rape cannot be captured in a mechanical description of objects and body parts. The Tribunal also notes the cultural sensitivities involved in public discussion of intimate matters and recalls the painful reluctance and inability of witnesses to disclose graphic anatomical details of sexual violence they endured. The United Nations Convention Against Torture and Other Cruel, Inhuman and Degrading Treatment or Punishment does not catalogue specific acts in its definition of torture, focusing rather on the conceptual framework of state-sanctioned violence. The Tribunal finds this approach more useful in the context of international law. Like torture, rape is used for such purposes as intimidation, degradation, humiliation, discrimination, punishment, control or destruction of a person. Like torture, rape is a violation of personal dignity, and rape in fact constitutes torture when it is inflicted by or at the instigation of or with the consent or acquiescence of a public official or other person acting in an official capacity.

The Tribunal defines rape as a physical invasion of a sexual nature, committed on a person under circumstances which are coercive. The Tribunal considers sexual violence, which includes rape, as any act of a sexual nature which is committed on a person under circumstances which are coercive. Sexual violence is not limited to physical invasion of the human body and may include acts which do not involve penetration or even physical contact. The incident described by Witness KK in which the Accused ordered the Interahamwe to undress a student and force her to do gymnastics naked in the public courtyard of the bureau communal, in front of a crowd, constitutes sexual violence. The Tribunal notes in this context that coercive circumstances need not be evidenced by a show of physical force. Threats, intimidation, extortion and other forms of duress which prey on fear or desperation may constitute coercion, and coercion may be inherent in certain circumstances, such as armed conflict or the military presence of Interahamwe among refugee Tutsi women at the bureau communal. Sexual violence falls within the scope of "other inhumane acts," set forth Article 3(i) of the Tribunal's Statute, "outrages upon personal dignity," set forth in Article 4(e) of the Statute, and "serious bodily or mental harm," set forth in Article 2(2)(b) of the Statute.

THE PROSECUTOR v. FURUNDZIJA

Case No. ICTY–95–17/1–T, Judgment, ¶¶ 174–186 (Dec. 10, 1998)

The Definition of Rape

The Trial Chamber notes the unchallenged submission of the Prosecution in its Pre-trial Brief that rape is a forcible act: this means that the act is "accomplished by force or threats of force against the victim or a third person, such threats being express or implied and must place the victim in reasonable fear that he, she or a third person will be subjected to violence, detention, duress or psychological oppression." This act is the penetration of the vagina, the anus or mouth by the penis, or of the vagina or anus by other object. In this context, it includes penetration, however slight, of the vulva, anus or oral cavity, by the penis, and sexual penetration of the vulva or anus is not limited to the penis.* * *

Trial Chamber I of the ICTR has held in *Akayesu* that to formulate a definition of rape in international law one should start from the assumption that "the central elements of the crime of rape cannot be captured in a mechanical description of objects or body parts." According to that Trial Chamber, in international law it is more useful to focus "on the conceptual framework of State sanctioned violence." It then went on to state the following:

> Like torture, rape is used for such purposes as intimidation, degradation, humiliation, discrimination, punishment, control or destruction of a person. Like torture, rape is a violation of personal dignity, and rape in fact constitutes torture when inflicted by or at the instigation of or with the consent or acquiescence of a public official or others person acting in an official capacity. The Chamber defines rape as a physical invasion of a sexual nature, committed on a person under circumstances which are coercive.

This definition has been upheld by Trial Chamber II *quater* of the International Tribunal in *Delalic*.* * *

Whenever international criminal rules do not define a notion of criminal law, reliance upon national legislation is justified, subject to the following conditions: (i) unless indicated by an international rule, reference should not be made to one national legal system only, say that of common-law or that of civil-law States. Rather, international courts must draw upon the general concepts and legal institutions common to all the major legal systems of the world. This presupposes a process of identification of the common denominators in these legal systems so as to pinpoint the basic notions they share; (ii) since "international trials exhibit a number of features that differentiate them from national criminal proceedings," account must be taken of the specificity of international criminal proceedings when utilizing national law notions. In this way a mechanical importation or transposition from national law into international criminal proceedings is avoided, as well as the attendant distortions of the unique traits of such proceedings.* * *

It is apparent from our survey of national legislation that, in spite of inevitable discrepancies, most legal systems in the common and civil law worlds consider rape to be the forcible sexual penetration of the human body by the penis or the forcible insertion of any other object into either the vagina or the anus. A major discrepancy may, however, be discerned in the criminalization of forced oral penetration: some States treat it as sexual assault, while it is categorized as rape in other States. Faced with this lack of uniformity, it falls to the Trial Chamber to establish whether an appropriate solution can be reached by resorting to the general principles of international criminal law or, if such principles are of no avail, to the general principles of international law.

The Trial Chamber holds that the forced penetration of the mouth by the male sexual organ constitutes a most humiliating and degrading attack upon human dignity. The essence of the whole corpus of international humanitarian law as well as human rights law lies in the protection of the human dignity of every person, whatever his or her gender. The general principle of respect for human dignity is the basic underpinning and indeed the very *raison d'être* of international humanitarian law and human rights law; indeed in modern times it has become of such paramount importance as to permeate the whole body of international law. This principle is intended to shield human beings from outrages upon their personal dignity, whether such outrages are carried out by unlawfully attacking the body or by humiliating and debasing the honor, the self-respect or the mental well being of a person. It is consonant with this principle that such an extremely serious sexual outrage as forced oral penetration should be classified as rape.

Moreover, the Trial Chamber is of the opinion that it is not contrary to the general principle of *nullum crimen sine lege* to charge an accused with forcible oral sex as rape when in some national jurisdictions, including his own, he could only be charged with sexual assault in respect of the same acts. It is not a question of criminalizing acts which were not criminal when they were committed by the accused, since forcible oral sex is in any event a crime, and indeed an extremely serious crime. Indeed, due to the nature of the International Tribunal's subject-matter jurisdiction, in prosecutions before the Tribunal forced oral sex is invariably an aggravated sexual assault as it is committed in time of armed conflict on defenseless civilians; hence it is not simple sexual assault but sexual assault as a war crime or crime against humanity. Therefore so long as an accused, who is convicted of rape for acts of forcible oral penetration, is sentenced on the factual basis of coercive oral sex—and sentenced in accordance with the sentencing practice in the former Yugoslavia for such crimes, pursuant to Article 24 of the Statute and Rule 101 of the Rules—then he is not adversely affected by the categorization of forced oral sex as rape rather than as sexual assault. * * *

Thus, the Trial Chamber finds that the following may be accepted as the objective elements of rape:

   (i) the sexual penetration, however slight:

      (a) of the vagina or anus of the victim by the penis of the perpetrator or any other object used by the perpetrator; or

      (b) of the mouth of the victim by the penis of the perpetrator;

   (ii) by coercion or force or threat of force against the victim or a third person.

———————————

In *Prosecutor v. Kunarac*, Case No. IT–96–23 & 23/1, Judgment (22 Feb. 2001) ("*Foca*"), the Trial Chamber broadened *Furundzija*'s definition of rape as "sexual penetration, however slight: (a) of the vagina or anus of the victim by the penis of the perpetrator or any other object used by the perpetrator; or (b) of the mouth of the victim by the penis of the perpetrator; where such sexual penetration occurs without the consent of the victim. Consent for this purpose must be consent given voluntarily, as a result of the victim's free will, assessed in the context of the surrounding circumstances. The *mens rea* is the intention to effect this sexual penetration, and the knowledge that it occurs without the consent of the victim." *Foca* ¶ 460 (internal quotation marks omitted).

On appeal, the *Foca* Appeals Chamber adopted this definition and added that "there are factors 'other than force' which would render an act of sexual penetration non-consensual or non-voluntary on the part of the victim. A narrow focus on force or threat of force could permit perpetrators to evade liability for sexual activity to which the other party had not consented by taking advantage of coercive circumstances without relying on physical force." *Prosecutor v. Kunarac*, Case No. IT–96–23 & 23/1, Judgment on Appeal (June 12, 2002). Notably, the circumstances giving rise to rape charges as crimes against humanity or war crimes "will be almost universally coercive" such that "true consent will not be possible." *Id.*

———————————

What is the difference between the ICTR's definition under *Akayesu* and the ICTY's definition under *Furundzija* and *Foca*? Which approach is preferable in determining whether rape has occurred in the context of an armed conflict?

———————

3. RAPE AS GENOCIDE

Under Article 2 of the ICTR Statute and Article 4 of the ICTY Statute, rape and sexual violence constitute genocide if such acts were committed with the specific intent to destroy, in whole or in part, a particular group as such.[27] Sexual violence may reflect the "intent to destroy" through actions such as sexual mutilation or impregnating women of the targeted group in order to prevent births within that group. The Trial Chamber in *Akayesu* certainly found that sexual violence, including rape, played an essential role in the Rwandan genocide: "Sexual violence was a step in the process of the destruction of the Tutsi group—destruction of the spirit, of the will to live, and of life itself."[28] As the *Akayesu* court found:

> With regard * * * to * * * rape and sexual violence, the Chamber wishes to underscore the fact that in its opinion, they constitute genocide in the same way as any other act as long as they were committed with the specific intent to destroy, in whole or in part, a particular group, targeted as such. Indeed, rape and sexual violence certainly constitute infliction of serious bodily and mental harm on the victims and are even, according to the Chamber, one of the worst ways of inflicting harm on the victim as he or she suffers both bodily and mental harm. In light of all the evidence before it, the Chamber is satisfied that the acts of rape and sexual violence described above, were committed solely against Tutsi women, many of whom were subjected to the worst public humiliation, mutilated, and raped several times, often in public, in the Bureau Communal premises or in other public places, and often by more than one assailant. These rapes resulted in physical and psychological destruction of Tutsi women, their families and their communities. *Sexual violence was an integral part of the process of destruction, specifically targeting Tutsi women and specifically contributing to their destruction and to the destruction of the Tutsi group as a whole.*

Akayesu, Judgment, ¶ ¶ 731–34 (emphasis added).

———————

27. The elements of genocide under Article 2 (3)(a) of the ICTR Statute are: The accused committed one or more of the following acts with the intent to destroy, in whole or in part, a national, ethnical, racial or religious group, as such: (1) killing members of the group; (2) causing serious bodily or mental harm to members of the group; (3) deliberately inflicting on the group conditions of life calculated to bring about its physical destruction in whole or in part; (4) imposing measures intended to prevent births within the group; or (5) forcibly transferring children of the group to another group.

28. *Akayesu* Judgment at ¶ ¶ 731–33.

Acts of sexual mutilation also constitute genocide under Article 2(2)(d) of the ICTR Statute, which prohibits measures intended to prevent births within the targeted group.[29] As the *Akayesu* court found:

> For purposes of interpreting Article 2(2)(d) of the Statute, the Chamber holds that the measures intended to prevent births within the group, should be construed as sexual mutilation, the practice of sterilization, forced birth control, separation of the sexes and prohibition of marriages. In patriarchal societies, where membership of a group is determined by the identity of the father, an example of a measure intended to prevent births within a group is the case where, during rape, a woman of the said group is deliberately impregnated by a man of another group, with the intent to have her give birth to a child who will consequently not belong to its mother's group.

> Furthermore, the Chamber notes that measures intended to prevent births within the group may be physical, but can also be mental. For instance, rape can be a measure intended to prevent births when the person raped refuses subsequently to procreate, in the same way that members of a group can be led, through threats or trauma, not to procreate.

Akayesu, Judgment, ¶ ¶ 507–08.

Rape can also constitute genocide under Article 2(2)(e) of the ICTR Statute and Article 4(2)(e) of the ICTY Statute if that act results in the forcible transfer of children from the group to another group. This requirement is satisfied, for example, if the victim subsequently becomes pregnant with the perpetrator's child.

---

4. SEXUAL VIOLENCE, INCLUDING RAPE, AS A CRIME AGAINST HUMANITY

Sexual violence, including rape, can constitute a crime against humanity pursuant to Article 5(g) of the ICTY Statute and Article 3(g) of the ICTR Statute. *See Akayesu* Judgment at ¶ 598. Generally, "crimes against humanity" refers to inhumane acts, constituting a serious attack on human dignity and committed against civilians as part of a widespread or systematic attack. Thus, to constitute a crime against humanity, the *actus reus* of rape must be committed as part of a widespread or systematic attack and not as a random inhumane act. *Id.* ¶ 579. "Widespread" has been defined as a massive, frequent, large-scale action, carried out collectively with considerable seriousness and directed against multiple victims. *Id.* ¶ 580; *Musema* Judgment, ¶ 204. "Systematic" has been defined as an organized action, following a regular pattern, on the basis of a common policy and involving substantial public or

---

29. *Akayesu* Judgment, ¶ 507; *Rutaganda* Judgment, ¶ 53; *Prosecutor v. Musema*, Judgment, Case No. ICTR–96–13–A, ¶ 158 (Jan. 27, 2000). ("*Musema* Judgment").

private resources. The policy need not be formally adopted as a policy of a state, but a preconceived plan or policy must have existed. *Id.*

This approach is consistent with the precedent of the ICTY. For example, in *Prosecutor v. Karadzic and Mladic*,[30] the Trial Chamber stated:

> On the basis of the features of all these sexual assaults, it may be inferred that they were part of a widespread policy of "ethnic cleansing": the victims were mainly "non-Serbian" civilians, the vast majority being Muslims. Sexual assault occurred in several regions of Bosnia and Herzegovina, in a systematic fashion and using recurring methods (*e.g.*, gang rape, sexual assault in camps, use of brutal means, together with other violations of international humanitarian law). They were performed together with an effort to displace civilians and * * * to increase the shame and humiliation of the victims and of the community they belonged to in order to force them to leave. It would seem that the aim of many rapes was enforced impregnation; several witnesses also said that the perpetrators of sexual assault—often soldiers—had been given orders to do so and that camp commanders and officers had been informed thereof and participated therein.

Id. at ¶ 64 (quoted in Kelly D. Askin, *Developments in International Criminal Law: Sexual Violence in Decisions and Indictments of the Yugoslav and Rwandan Tribunals: Current Status*, 93 AM. J. INT'L L. 97, 114 (1999)).

Similarly, in *Prosecutor v. Tadic*, the Trial Chamber found that a formal policy is not necessary. Rather, it found that a sufficient policy "can be deduced from the way in which the acts occur. Notably, if the acts occur on a widespread or systematic basis, that demonstrates a policy to commit those acts, whether formalized or not." *Tadic* Judgment, ¶ 653.

---

5. SEXUAL VIOLENCE, INCLUDING RAPE, AS TORTURE

Both *ad hoc* tribunals have found that rape and other sexual violence may constitute torture under international humanitarian law and qualify in that category as one of the crimes within their jurisdiction.

PROSECUTOR v. DELALIC ("CELEBICI JUDGMENT")
Case No. IT–96–21, Judgment, ¶¶ 475–96, (Nov. 16, 1998)

The crime of rape is not itself expressly mentioned in the provisions of the Geneva Conventions relating to grave breaches, nor in common article 3, and hence its classification as torture and cruel treatment. It is

---

30. Case No. IT–95–5–R61, IT–95–18–R61, Review of the Indictment Pursuant to Rule 61, (July 11, 1996).

the purpose of this section to consider the issue of whether rape constitutes torture, under the above mentioned provisions of the Geneva Conventions. In order to properly consider this issue, the Trial Chamber first discusses the prohibition of rape and sexual assault in international law, then provides a definition of rape and finally turns its attention to whether rape, a form of sexual assault, can be considered as torture.* * *

[T]he Inter–American Commission on Human Rights (hereafter "Inter–American Commission") * * * recently issued [a] decision[] on the question of whether rape constitutes torture in the case of *Fernando and Raquel Mejia v. Peru.*** * Peruvian military personnel, armed with submachine guns and with their faces covered, entered the Mejia home. They abducted Fernando Mejia, a lawyer, journalist and political activist, on suspicion of being a subversive and a member of the Tupac Amaru Revolutionary Movement. Shortly thereafter, one of these military personnel re-entered the home, apparently looking for identity documents belonging to Mr. Mejia. While his wife, Raquel Mejia, was searching for these documents, she was told that she was also considered a subversive, which she denied. The soldier involved then raped her. About 20 minutes later the same soldier returned, dragged her into her room and raped her again. Raquel Mejia spent the rest of the night in a state of terror. Her husband's body, which showed clear signs of torture, was subsequently found on the banks of the Santa Clara River.

The Inter–American Commission found that the rape of Raquel Mejia constituted torture in breach of Article 5 of the American Convention of Human Rights. In reaching this conclusion, the Inter–American Commission found that torture under article 5 has three constituent elements. First, there must be an intentional act through which physical or mental pain and suffering is inflicted on a person; secondly, such suffering must be inflicted for a purpose; and, thirdly, it must be inflicted by a public official or by a private person acting at the instigation of a public official. * * *

In finding that the second element of torture had also been met, the Inter–American Commission found that Raquel Mejia was raped with the aim of punishing her personally and intimidating her. Finally, it was held that the third requirement of the definition of torture was met as the man who raped Raquel Mejia was a member of the security forces.* * *

The view that rape constitutes torture, is further shared by the United Nations Special Rapporteur on Torture [who] stated that rape or other forms of sexual assault against women in detention were a particularly ignominious violation of the inherent dignity and the right to physical integrity of the human being, they accordingly constituted an act of torture. In his first report he also listed various forms of sexual aggression as methods of torture, which included rape and the insertion of objects into the orifices of the body. * * *

In view of the above discussion, the Trial Chamber therefore finds that the elements of torture, for the purposes of applying Articles 2 and 3 of the Statute, may be enumerated as follows:

(i) There must be an act or omission that causes severe pain or suffering, whether mental or physical,

(ii) which is inflicted intentionally,

(iii) and for such purposes as obtaining information or a confession from the victim, or a third person, punishing the victim for an act he or she or a third person has committed or is suspected of having committed, intimidating or coercing the victim or a third person, or for any reason based on discrimination of any kind,

(iv) and such act or omission being committed by, or at the instigation of, or with the consent or acquiescence of, an official or other person acting in an official capacity.

Accordingly, whenever rape and other forms of sexual violence meet the aforementioned criteria, then they shall constitute torture, in the same manner as any other acts that meet this criteria.

Subsequent decisions, such as the ICTY Trial Chamber decision in *Kvočka*, clarified that there is no state actor requirement for sexual violence, including rape, to constitute torture as a violation of international humanitarian law.

PROSECUTOR v. KVOČKA

Case No. It–98–30/1–T, Judgment, ¶¶ 137–41 (2 Nov. 2001)

(b) *Torture*

(i) *No State Actor Requirement*

Torture has been defined by the Tribunal jurisprudence as severe mental or physical suffering deliberately inflicted upon a person for a prohibited purpose, such as to obtain information or to discriminate against the victim. Differing views have been expressed in the jurisprudence of the Tribunal as to whether the suffering must be inflicted by a public agent or the representative of a public authority in order to meet the definition of torture.

The *Kunarac* Judgment departed from the previous definitions of torture set forth by the Trial Chambers of the ICTY and the ICTR, in ruling that, in contrast to international human rights law, international humanitarian law does not require the involvement of a state official or of any other authority-wielding person in order for the offence to be regarded as torture.

The Trial Chamber is persuaded by the reasoning of the *Kunarac* Trial Chamber that the state actor requirement imposed by international human rights law is inconsistent with the application of individual criminal responsibility for international crimes found in international humanitarian law and international criminal law.

The Trial Chamber also agrees with the *Celebici* Trial Chamber that the prohibited purposes listed in the Torture Convention as reflected by customary international law "do not constitute an exhaustive list, and should be regarded as merely representative," and notes that the *Furundzija* Trial Chamber concluded that humiliating the victim or a third person constitutes a prohibited purpose for torture under international humanitarian law.

The Trial Chamber applies the following definition of torture to this case:

(i) Torture consists of the infliction, by act or omission, of severe pain or suffering, whether physical or mental;

(ii) the act or omission must be intentional; and

(iii) the act or omission must be for a prohibited purpose, such as obtaining information or a confession, punishing, intimidating, humiliating, or coercing the victim or a third person, or discriminating, on any ground, against the victim or a third person.

NOTES AND QUESTIONS ON SEXUAL VIOLENCE AS TORTURE

1. *Prosecuting rape.* Why would the prosecutor indict a defendant for rape as torture if rape is also enumerated as a crime against humanity under the *ad hoc* tribunal statutes? What if the victims of a conflict are not civilians, but imprisoned combatants, raped in jail as part of a systematic attack? Could such crimes be prosecuted under the statutes of the ICTY and ICTR?

2. *Human rights law vs. international humanitarian law?* What do you make of the Tribunal's distinction between "torture" for purposes of international human rights law, which in its view includes a state action requirement, and "torture" for purposes of international humanitarian law (traditionally called the "law of war"), which in its view does not? Does common article 3 of the Geneva Conventions, with its reference to non-international conflict, justify the distinction?

3. *Sexual violence and peremptory norms.* On 19 June 2008, the UN Security Council conducted an open debate on Women, Peace and Security, with a focus on sexual violence in situations of armed conflict. Following the debate, the Security Council adopted a unanimous resolution, noting that "rape and other forms of sexual violence can constitute a war crime, a crime against humanity, or a constitutive act with respect to genocide." S/RES/1820 (19 June 2008), at ¶ 4. As you read the following excerpt, written by a former prosecutor of gender crimes at

the *ad hoc* tribunals, consider whether the prohibition on rape during armed conflict has risen to the level of *jus cogens* and what legal difference that designation would make.

Patricia Viseur Sellers, *Sexual Violence and Peremptory Norms: The Legal Value of Rape*, 34 CASE W. RES. J. INT'L L. 287 (2002)

* * * The modern concept of peremptory norms is defined in Article 53 of the Vienna Convention [on the Law of Treaties, which states that a "peremptory norm of general international law is a norm accepted and recognized by the international community of states as a whole as a norm from which no derogation is permitted, and which can be modified only by a subsequent norm of general international law having the same character."] * * *

A *jus cogens* norm automatically renders what is contrary to it illegal. The modern examples of this grandiose supreme legal entity are the crimes of genocide and piracy and the crimes and the human rights violations of slavery and torture. One could readily agree that today, no state or states could collude and enter into a treaty to commit genocide or piracy against a third country. All states have obligations *vis a vis* peremptory norms. In that way, peremptory norms or *jus cogens* function to identify and to uphold what is deemed to be the most serious and essential values of the community of states.* * *

First, it is fair to say there exists no acknowledged, exhaustive list of peremptory norms. What remains debate-free is that torture, genocide, and slavery are accepted as peremptory norms that can only be modified by a subsequent norm having the same character. States, according to non-deroga[ble] obligations, cannot commit nor condone other states that torture, commit genocide, or enslave.* * *

It can be posited, that acts of sexual violence are already characterized as components of *jus cogens* obligations. Sexual violence has been held to satisfy elements of torture in several cases under the jurisprudence of the European Court of Human Rights, the Inter–American Court of Human Rights, the Inter–American Commission [and] the Yugoslav Tribunal.* * * [R]ape has been recognized under human rights and humanitarian law as an act satisfying the *actus reus* of torture, an accepted peremptory norm.

Similarly, one can demonstrate that sexual violence, including rape, is a component of genocide and therefore resides within its peremptory norm protection [as demontrated by] [t]he Rwandan Tribunal's jurisprudence in *Akayesu*.* * *

Moreover, sexual violence including rape can be evidence of enslavement, an accepted form of the peremptory norm of slavery, * * * [a]s in *Kunarac*, [where] Bosnian women were held in a series of detention centers and women were reduced to slavery. Ownership of the women, an element of enslavement, was primarily shown by the relentless and unconditional sexual access that the accused had to the women.

Thus, rape has been interpreted to establish conduct that proves elements of torture, slavery, and genocide under the jurisprudence of the *ad hoc* criminal tribunals and by regional human rights courts. It seems uncontested that acts of sexual violence fit within the prism of peremptory norms. I readily applaud that eminent jurisprudence; however, I suggest the result is a form of legal piggybacking. Prohibitions of sexual violence do not rise on their own volition, but enter by way of a non-explicit sexual crime, to reach the glory of *jus cogens*.

Beyond these true advances, and the incorporation of sex-based crimes in the Rome Statute, the community of states has not expressed a more poignant interest in accepting prohibition of rape, in and of itself, as a peremptory norm. These advances have not triggered articulation of any overriding community interest or obligations. States still do not "act obligated" in the face of present day massive trafficking of eastern European women or Asian women throughout Europe, that is essentially institutionalized rape. Therefore, my specific question still remains. Under international law as recognized by the community of states, can the prohibition of rape, standing alone, be deemed a peremptory norm?

---

6. SEXUAL VIOLENCE FALLING OUTSIDE THE DEFINITION OF RAPE

Rape falls explicitly within the *ad hoc* tribunals' jurisdiction as a crime against humanity. Further, the *ad hoc* tribunals have found rape to constitute genocide and torture. The jurisdiction of the tribunals, however, is not limited to instances of sexual violence that constitute rape. The ICTY and the ICTR have jurisdiction over other forms of sexual violence under the "other inhumane acts" prong of crimes against humanity if the conduct constituting the alleged sexual violence is of "comparable seriousness" to other enumerated crimes against humanity. As indicated in the *Furundzija* Judgment at ¶ 186,

> international criminal rules punish not only rape but also any serious sexual assault falling short of actual penetration. It would seem that the prohibition embraces all serious abuses of a sexual nature inflicted upon the physical and moral integrity of a person by means of coercion, threat of force or intimidation in a way that is degrading and humiliating for the victim's dignity. As both these categories of acts are criminalized in international law, the distinction between them is one that is primarily material for the purposes of sentencing. *See also Tadic* Judgment ¶ ¶ 728–29.

PROSECUTOR v. ELIEZER NIYITEGEKA

Case No. ICTR–96–14–T, ¶¶ 462–467, Judgment and Sentence (16 May 2003)

* * * [T]he Chamber [has] found that on 22 June 1994, at Kazirandimwe Hill, the Accused * * * was rejoicing when Kabanda [a prominent Tutsi] was killed, decapitated, castrated and his skull pierced through the ears with a spike.* * * Kabanda's genitals were hung on a spike, and visible to the public. The Chamber finds that the jubilation of the Accused, particularly in light of his leadership role in the attack, at the decapitation and castration of Kabanda, and the piercing of Kabanda's skull, supported and encouraged the attackers, and thereby aided and abetted the commission of these crimes.

* * * [T]he Chamber [has also] found that on 28 June 1994, near the Technical Training College, the Accused ordered Interahamwe to undress the body of a Tutsi woman, whom he called "Inyenzi", who had just been shot dead, to fetch and sharpen a piece of wood, which he then instructed them to insert into her genitalia. This act was then carried out by the Interahamwe, in accordance with his instructions. * * *

The Chamber finds that the acts committed with respect to Kabanda and the sexual violence to the dead woman's body are acts of seriousness comparable to other acts enumerated in * * * Article [3], and would cause mental suffering to civilians, in particular, Tutsi civilians, and constitute a serious attack on the human dignity of the Tutsi community as a whole.

Given the Accused's leadership role in attacks against Tutsi, his acts of shooting at Tutsi refugees, his act of procurement of weapons and gendarmes for attacks against Tutsi, his planning of attacks against Tutsi during meetings, his acts of incitement against Tutsi, * * * the fact that Kabanda was generally regarded as a prominent Tutsi, and the characterization of the dead woman by the Accused as "Inyenzi" or Tutsi, * * * the Chamber finds that the Accused intended these acts to be perpetrated on the bodies of Kabanda and the dead woman, and knew that these acts were part of a widespread and systematic attack against the civilian Tutsi population on ethnic grounds.

The Chamber finds that by his act of encouragement during the killing, decapitation and castration of Kabanda, and the piercing of his skull, and his association with the attackers who carried out these acts, and his ordering of Interahamwe to perpetrate the sexual violence on the body of the dead woman, the Accused is individually criminally responsible, pursuant to Article 6(1) of the Statute, for inhumane acts committed as part of a widespread and systematic attack on the civilian Tutsi population on ethnic grounds and as such constitute a crime against humanity, as provided in Article 3(i) of the Statute. Accordingly, the Chamber finds that the Accused is guilty of Crime against Humanity (Other Inhumane Acts) as charged in Count 8 of the Indictment.

Rape is explicitly listed as a crime against humanity in Article 7(g) of the *ad hoc* tribunal statutes, but Article 7(g) of the Rome Statute also enumerates sexual slavery, enforced prostitution, forced pregnancy, enforced sterilization, and any other sexual violence of comparable gravity as separate crimes against humanity. Rome Statute, art. 7(g).

NOTES AND QUESTIONS ON SEXUAL VIOLENCE FALLING OUTSIDE THE DEFINITION OF RAPE

1. *Other forms of sexual violence.* Combatants have long used acts of sexual violence as weapons of war, including sexual slavery, forced impregnation, and sexual violence. "In Rwanda, Hutu men crossed an additional boundary: they often forced Tutsi women to marry them * * * and force them to perform household duties and sexual acts.* * * Many of the Hutu men who forced the women into marriage were members of the Interahamwe, the Hutus' trained youth militia." *See* Monkia Satya Kalra, *Forced Marriage: Rwanda's Secret Revealed*, 7 U.C. DAVIS J. INT'L L. & POL'Y 197 (2001). What separates sexual violence from other forms of violence prosecutable as crimes against humanity at the *ad hoc* tribunals?

2. *Sexual violence at Abu Ghraib.* During the war in Iraq, United States military officers engaged in abusive practices in Iraqi prisons, most notoriously in Abu Ghraib. For example, Army Pfc. Lynndie England posed in pictures in which she held a naked Iraqi soldier on a leash, another in which she smiled, pointing at a naked detainee's genitals with a cigarette in her mouth. And, in another she posed with a group of naked detainees who were stacked in a pyramid. Do these acts constitute sexual violence prosecutable under "other inhumane acts" prong of crime against humanity? Do these acts constitute torture?

3. *Evidentiary issues in rape and other sexual assault cases.* Recognizing the unique issues that arise in sexual violence cases, both for the victim and for the court, the ICTY and the ICTR have adopted special rules of evidence and procedure for such cases. Under these rules, corroboration of the victim's testimony is not required. The rules also mandate that consent shall not be a defense if the victim was subjected to threats of violence or detention, or if the victim reasonably believed that, if the victim did not submit, another would be endangered. Moreover, the rules exclude admission of the victim's sexual history and provide for alternate ways for the victim to give testimony, for example, in closed hearings. *See* ICTY R. P. & EVID 96; ICTR R. P. & EVID 96; *See also Prosecutor v. Kunarac*, Case No. IT–96–23 & 23/1, Judgment, ¶ ¶ 440–64 (Feb. 22, 2001). Are defendant's rights compromised by giving such protections to victims of sexual crimes? Could the defense of consent ever be established in the circumstances of these conflicts?

OTHER INTERNATIONAL CRIMINAL TRIBUNALS

Since the creation of the ICTY and ICTR, other international criminal tribunals have been created to address particular situations. The UN created the Special Court for Sierra Leone to prosecute those that bore the most responsibility for the mass amputations, killings, and rapes that occurred during Sierra Leone's decade-long civil war in the 1990s. Additionally, in 2003, the UN reached a tentative agreement with the Cambodian government to create a hybrid criminal tribunal to try former Khmer Rouge leaders, who were responsible for the deaths of over one million Cambodians in the 1970s. Finally, a special court was established to address the human rights abuses that occurred in East Timor, Indonesia, surrounding its movement toward independence. The Special Court for Sierra Leone, which incorporates international legal standards into local justice systems, may provide an important model for future international justice efforts.

CASE STUDY: THE SPECIAL COURT FOR SIERRA LEONE

From 1991 to 2002, Sierra Leone was embroiled in a brutal armed conflict between armed rebels (the Revolutionary United Front (RUF) led by Foday Sankoh) and the Sierra Leonean government forces. The conflict was characterized by widespread attacks on civilians including execution, forced amputations, torture, rape, and the conscription of children. While the majority of the violations were committed by the rebels, charges were also leveled at government forces.

The Special Court for Sierra Leone was established in 2002 under an agreement between Sierra Leone and the United Nations. Under its mandate, the Special Court is authorized to "prosecute persons who bear the greatest responsibility for serious violations of international humanitarian law and Sierra Leonean law."[29]

This court is viewed as a "hybrid" because it reflects both national and international influences in its subject matter jurisdiction, its judges, and its location. In addition to the international offences of crimes against humanity, war crimes, and other serious international humanitarian law violations concerning civilians and child soldiers, the Special Court has jurisdiction over domestic criminal offenses under Sierra Leonean law, including sexual offences against girls and the wanton destruction of property.

The mix of international and national judges is another important contribution of the hybrid model. One of the three trial judges on the Special Court is Sierra Leonean, as are two of the five Appellate Judges.[30] The remaining international judges were appointed by the UN Secretary General in consultation with Sierra Leone.

Rather than being removed geographically from the conflict, the Special Court is located in Freetown, Sierra Leone, keeping the process

---

29. Statute of the Special Court for Sierra Leone (SCSL Statute), art. 1(1), Jan. 16, 2002.

30. Controversy surrounded the appointment of Geoffrey Robertson as President of the Special Court, the only non-Sierra Leonean among the three "national" judges appointed by the Govern-

close to the people most affected by the conflict and strengthening respect for the rule of law in post-conflict Sierra Leone. The location allows the Special Court to engage in outreach activities, such as public screenings of video summaries of court proceedings and town hall meetings, helping to ensure that the court remains accessible and meaningful to the people of Sierra Leone.

One commentator has noted that hybrid courts increase the legitimacy of the judicial process and contribute to the incorporation of international norms into domestic systems in ways that remote tribunals cannot.[31] The drawbacks of the hybrid court appear less related to its structure and more related to the problem of obtaining the funds needed to continue operations. There are of course the traditional problems that plague *ad hoc* tribunals, such as delays in establishing the court and the potential for the politicization of the process by the Security Council, which authorized the tribunals.

The existence of the International Criminal Court (ICC) does not diminish the need for hybrid tribunals. To the contrary, hybrid and domestic courts are necessary to supplement the work of the ICC. First, the jurisdiction of the ICC only extends to crimes committed after 2002, when the Rome Statute entered into force. Hybrid and domestic courts can adjudicate cases that are temporally beyond the jurisdiction of the ICC. Second, because the ICC is mandated to prosecute only those bearing the greatest responsibility for the enumerated crimes,[32] relying solely on the ICC would leave an "impunity gap." Capable and willing national judicial systems, as well as *ad hoc* tribunals, can fill that gap.

The Special Court was not the sole mechanism created to ease the transition to the new government. The Lome Peace Accords, which ended the conflict in Sierra Leone, included a provision granting amnesty to those who had participated in the conflict, as well as an agreement, inspired by the South African Truth and Reconciliation Commission (TRC), to establish a Truth and Reconciliation Commission for Sierra Leone. Until 2004, the TRC fulfilled its mandate in parallel with the work of the Special Court.

The Special Court and the TRC at times came to different conclusions on significant issues. For example, the Tribunal considered itself to be not bound by the amnesty clause of the Lome Agreements,[33] while

---

ment of Sierra Leone, because of Robertson's prior publications on the culpability of some of the Revolutionary United Front (RUF) indictees. An Appeals Chamber issued an order preventing him from hearing any cases involving RUF indictees. *See* James Cockayne, Note and Comment, *Special Court for Sierra Leone*, 2 J. INT'L CRIM. JUST. 1154 (2004). For additional discussion of the problem of judicial impartiality in Sierra Leone, see Diane Marie Amann, *Impartiality Deficit and International Criminal Judging, in* ATROCITIES AND INTERNATIONAL ACCOUNTABILITY: BEYOND TRANSITIONAL JUSTICE (William A. Schabas, Ramesh Thakur & Edel Hughes eds., 2007).

31. *See* Laura A. Dickinson, *The Promise of Hybrid Courts*, 97 AM. J. INT'L L. 295 (2003).

32. Crimes under the ICC's jurisdiction include genocide, crimes against humanity, and war crimes.

33. *Prosecutor v. Allieu Kondewa*, Case No. SCSL–04–14–T–128–7347 (May 25, 2004) *available at* http://www.sc-sl.org/CDF-decisions.html.

the TRC concluded that it was "unable to condemn the resort to amnesty by those who negotiated the Lome Peace Agreement, . . . [when] in all good faith, [the Government] believed that the RUF would not agree to end hostilities if the Agreement were not accompanied by a form of pardon or amnesty."[34] Notwithstanding the different approaches of the two bodies, this parallel approach to seeking justice and truth simultaneously is an important addition to the arsenal of international justice mechanisms.[35] In addition, the hybrid nature of the tribunal provides a method of infusing international norms into national legal systems, making the judicial process accessible and meaningful for the affected population, and strengthening the rule of law.

NOTES AND QUESTIONS ON OTHER INTERNATIONAL TRIBUNALS

1. *Cambodia.* From 1975 until 1979, under the leadership of Pol Pot, the Khmer Rouge controlled Cambodia. The Khmer Rouge attempted to establish an agrarian communist society, expelling thousands from their homes and forcing them to work in the fields. During this period, two million Cambodians lost their lives. On March 17, 2003, the UN and the Cambodian government concluded a draft agreement setting forth the framework for the establishment of a tribunal to try crimes committed during the Khmer Rouge regime. The final agreement was ratified by Cambodia's National Assembly on October 5, 2004.[36] Under the final agreement, the jurisdiction of the court extends to genocide, crimes against humanity, and grave breaches of the 1949 Geneva Conventions. The court is staffed by both Cambodian and international judges. A common obstacle facing hybrid courts is the struggle for adequate funding. The Extraordinary Chambers in the Courts of Cambodia (ECCC) has had insufficient funds to carry out its mandate. The ECCC has also faced intense scrutiny from civil society, the UN, and other monitoring organizations to ensure its adherence to international standards for fair trials. After appointing judges and finalizing procedural rules, the tribunal began its first proceedings against five former leaders of the Khmer Rouge in late 2007.[37] *"Recent*

---

34. WITNESS TO TRUTH: REPORT OF THE SIERRA LEONE TRUTH AND RECONCILIATION COMMISSION, vol. 1, ch. 6, at 4 (2004), *available at* http://www.trcsierraleone.org/pdf/FINAL% 20VOLUME%2 0ONE/VOLUME% 20ONE.pdf [hereinafter "Witness to Truth"] at 4.

35. For a detailed discussion of the interrelation between the Special Court for Sierra Leone and the Sierra Leone Truth and Reconciliation Commission, *see* William A. Schabas, *Amnesty, the Sierra Leone Truth and Reconciliation Commission and the Special Court for Sierra Leone*, 11 U.C. DAVIS J. INT'L L. & POL'Y 145 (2004); *See also* Michael Nesbitt, *Lessons from the Sam Hinga Norman Decision of the Special Court for Sierra Leone: How Trials and Truth Commissions Can Co–Exist*, 8 GERMAN L.J. 977 (2007).

36. *See,* the "Agreement between The United Nations and The Royal Government of Cambodia Concerning The Prosecution Under Cambodian Law Of Crimes Committed During The Period Of Democratic Kampuchea," entered into force on 29 April 2005, UN Doc.A/RES57/228B(Annexe) (13 May 2005).

37. For a list of indictments issued by the ECCC, *see* http://www.cambodia.gov.kh/krt/english/indictments.htm.

Developments at the ECCC: August 2007," Open Society Justice Initiative (August 2, 2007).

2. *East Timor*. When East Timor voted for independence in a 1999 referendum, ending a 24–year occupation by Indonesia, Indonesian forces launched a systematic campaign of destruction that lead to the deaths of 200,000 East Timorese. In 2000, the UN Security Council, acting pursuant to its Chapter VII authority, established a hybrid East Timorese/Indonesian court, the Special Panels for Serious Crimes, to try those responsible. The Special Panels were staffed by both East Timorese and international judges. Unfortunately, the Special Panels were significantly undermined by Indonesia's refusal to extradite 339 indictees to East Timor for prosecution. The Special Panel's mandate expired in May 2005. In the end, eighty-seven defendants were tried and eighty-four defendants were convicted of crimes against humanity.

Responding to international pressure, Indonesia also established an *ad hoc* court in Jakarta, the Human Rights Court for East Timor, to try individuals accused of crimes committed in East Timor. Indonesian political and military leaders resisted the idea of sending their generals to a foreign court and argued that Indonesia could be trusted to try the alleged perpetrators themselves. The trial of eighteen suspects indicted on charges of crimes against humanity ended in 2004 with disappointing results. All sixteen Indonesian defendants were freed, one of the East Timorese defendants was freed, and the remaining East Timorese defendant was freed on appeal. In February 2005, the UN established a Commission of Experts to determine whether the two tribunals met international standards of due process of law and to evaluate the extent to which the tribunals have been able to achieve accountability for the violations of international law committed in East Timor, and to make recommendations to the Secretary–General to ensure that those responsible for the violations of international law are held accountable. See Herbert D. Bowman, *Letting the Big Fish Get Away: The United Nations Justice Effort in East Timor*, 18 EMORY INT'L L. REV. 371 (2004); *see also* Coalition for International Justice, Frequently Asked Questions: East Timor, *available at* http://www.justiceinitiative.org/db/resource2/fl?file_id=13322.

THE INTERNATIONAL CRIMINAL
COURT (ICC)

1. INTRODUCTION

Former UN Secretary General, Kofi Annan, declared the ICC to be a "gift of hope to future generations, and a giant step forward in the march towards universal human rights and the rule of law."[38]

---

38. Kofi Annan, United Nations Secretary–General, Statement at the Ceremony Held at Campidoglio Celebrating the Adoption of the Statute of the International Criminal Court (18 July 1998), *available at* http://www.un.org/icc /speeches/718sg.htm).

The Rome Statute of the International Criminal Court, establishing the first permanent international criminal court, was adopted on July 17, 1998, at the United Nations Diplomatic Conference of Plenipotentiaries on the Establishment of an International Criminal Court.[39] This marked the culmination of decades of discussion, which began with the International Law Commission's Draft Code of Offenses Against the Peace and Security of Mankind (1954) and continued among academics and delegations from states and civil society at the Ad Hoc and Preparatory Commission for the Establishment of an International Criminal Court. The Preparatory Commission then considered rules, procedures, and practical considerations for a permanent court. Unlike the ICTY and ICTR, which were set up within the framework of the UN, an independent ICC would be treaty-based, consisting of an Assembly of States Parties that signed and ratified the Rome Statute.

The ICC was founded on the principle of *complementarity*, as enumerated in Article I of the Rome Statute, which declares that the ICC's jurisdiction is "complementary to national criminal jurisdictions." That provision is intended to assure that national governments bear the initial and primary authority (and obligation) to investigate and prosecute international crimes committed in their territories or by their nationals. If a particular government fails to discharge that obligation, the ICC's authority may be triggered. Thus for example, under the Rome Statute, the principle of *aut dedere aut judicare*, requires states to prosecute or extradite a person suspected of certain categories of crimes proscribed by international law, and thereby meets their responsibility to eradicate impunity within their borders. As a consequence, even where all other admissibility requirements are met, prosecution before the ICC may occur only when the concerned state is *unwilling or unable* to prosecute. The ICC is meant to serve victims and communities affected by atrocities when there is no functioning or effective judicial system at the national level in which accountability can be assured.

LUIS MORENO–OCAMPO, CHIEF PROSECUTOR OF THE INTERNATIONAL CRIMINAL COURT, IRAQ RESPONSE[40]

The Office of the Prosecutor

The Hague, 9 February 2006

Thank you for your communication concerning the situation in Iraq. The Office of the Prosecutor has received over 240 communications concerning the situation in Iraq.* * *

---

39. United Nations Conference of Plenipotentiaries on the Establishment of an International Criminal Court, *available at* http://www.un.org/icc/index.htm (last visited Oct. 19, 2008).

40. *Available at* http://www.icc-cpi.int/library/organs/otp/OTP_letter_to_senders_re_Iraq_9_February_2006.pdf

Mandate of the Office

In accordance with Article 15 of the Rome Statute, my duty is to analyse information received on potential crimes, in order to determine whether there is a reasonable basis to proceed with an investigation. * * * I am required to consider three factors. First, I must consider whether the available information provides a reasonable basis to believe that a crime within the jurisdiction of the Court has been or is being committed. Where this requirement is satisfied, I must then consider admissibility before the Court, in light of the requirements relating to gravity and complementarity with national proceedings. Third, if these factors are positive, I must give consideration to the interests of justice.* * *

Personal and Territorial Jurisdiction

The events in question occurred on the territory of Iraq, which is not a State Party to the Rome Statute and which has not lodged a declaration of acceptance under Article 12(3), thereby accepting the jurisdiction of the Court. Therefore, in accordance with Article 12, acts on the territory of a non-State Party fall within the jurisdiction of the Court only when the person accused of the crime is a national of a State that has accepted jurisdiction (Article 12(2)(b)). As I noted in my first public announcement on communications, we do not have jurisdiction with respect to actions of non-State Party nationals on the territory of Iraq. Some communications submitted legal arguments that nationals of States Parties may have been accessories to crimes committed by nationals of non-States Parties. * * *

Allegations concerning Legality of the Conflict

Many of the communications received related to concerns about the legality of the armed conflict. While the Rome Statute includes the crime of aggression, it indicates that the Court may not exercise jurisdiction over the crime until a provision has been adopted which defines the crime and sets out the conditions under which the Court may exercise jurisdiction with respect to it (Article 5(2)). * * *

Allegations concerning Genocide and Crimes against Humanity

Very few factual allegations were submitted concerning genocide or crimes against humanity. The Office collected information and examined the allegations. The available information provided no reasonable indicia that Coalition forces had "intent to destroy, in whole or in part, a national, ethnical, racial or religious group as such", as required in the definition of genocide (Article 6). Similarly, the available information provided no reasonable indicia of the required elements for a crime against humanity, *i.e.* a widespread or systematic attack directed against any civilian population (Article 7).

Allegations concerning War Crimes

1. *Allegations concerning the targeting of civilians or clearly excessive attacks*

* * * Under international humanitarian law and the Rome Statute, the death of civilians during an armed conflict, no matter how grave and regrettable, does not in itself constitute a war crime. * * * A crime occurs if there is an intentional attack directed against civilians (principle of distinction) (Article 8(2)(b)(i)) or an attack is launched on a military objective in the knowledge that the incidental civilian injuries would be clearly excessive in relation to the anticipated military advantage (principle of proportionality) (Article 8(2)(b)(iv)). * * *

Several communications expressed concerns about the use of cluster munitions. The Rome Statute contains a list of weapons whose use is prohibited *per se* (Article 8(2)(b)(xvii)-(xx)). Cluster munitions are not included in the list and therefore their use *per se* does not constitute a war crime.* * *

The Office examined all communications and readily-available information, applied rules of source evaluation and measurement, prepared tables of allegations and conducted pattern analysis on 64 incidents of potential relevance. The available information established that a considerable number of civilians died or were injured during the military operations. The available information did not indicate intentional attacks on a civilian population. With respect to Article 8(2)(b)(iv) allegations,[41] the available material with respect to the alleged incidents was characterized by (1) a lack of information indicating clear excessiveness in relation to military advantage and (2) a lack of information indicating the involvement of nationals of States Parties. * * *

Drawing on all the additional information collected, the Office examined several incidents in greater detail. A variety of techniques were employed in analyzing the information. The resulting information did not allow for the conclusion that there was a reasonable basis to believe that a clearly excessive attack within the jurisdiction of the Court had been committed. After exhausting all measures appropriate during the analysis phase, the Office determined that, while many facts remained undetermined, the available information did not provide a reasonable basis to believe that a crime within the jurisdiction of the Court had been committed. As stipulated in Article 15(6) of the Statute, the conclusion may be reviewed in the light of new facts or evidence.

2. *Allegations concerning wilful killing or inhuman treatment of civilians*

During the course of analysis, allegations came to light in the media concerning incidents of mistreatment of detainees and wilful killing of

---

41. [Editor's note. Article 8(2)(b)(iv) of the Rome Statute defines as a war crime "intentionally launching an attack in the knowledge that such attack will cause incidental loss of life or injury to civilians or damage to civilian objects or widespread long-term and severe damage to the natural environment which would be clearly excessive in relation to the concrete and direct overall military advantage anticipated."]

civilians. General allegations included brutality against persons upon capture and initial custody, causing death or serious injury.* * * The Office collected information with respect to these incidents as well as with respect to the relevant national criminal proceedings undertaken by the governments of States Parties.* * * After analyzing all the available information, it was concluded that there was a reasonable basis to believe that crimes within the jurisdiction of the Court had been committed, namely wilful killing and inhuman treatment. The information available at this time supports a reasonable basis for an estimated 4 to 12 victims of wilful killing and a limited number of victims of inhuman treatment, totaling in all less than 20 persons.

Admissibility

Even where there is a reasonable basis to believe that a crime has been committed, this is not sufficient for the initiation of an investigation by the International Criminal Court. The Statute then requires consideration of admissibility before the Court, in light of the gravity of the crimes and complementarity with national systems. While, in a general sense, any crime within the jurisdiction of the Court is "grave", the Statute requires an additional threshold of gravity even where the subject-matter jurisdiction is satisfied. This assessment is necessary as the Court is faced with multiple situations involving hundreds or thousands of crimes and must select situations in accordance with the Article 53 criteria.* * *

The Office considers various factors in assessing gravity. A key consideration is the number of victims of particularly serious crimes, such as wilful killing or rape. The number of potential victims of crimes within the jurisdiction of the Court in this situation–4 to 12 victims of wilful killing and a limited number of victims of inhuman treatment— was of a different order than the number of victims found in other situations under investigation or analysis by the Office. It is worth bearing in mind that the OTP is currently investigating three situations involving long-running conflicts in Northern Uganda, the Democratic Republic of Congo and Darfur. Each of the three situations under investigation involves thousands of wilful killings as well as intentional and large-scale sexual violence and abductions. Collectively, they have resulted in the displacement of more than 5 million people. Other situations under analysis also feature hundreds or thousands of such crimes.

Taking into account all the considerations, the situation did not appear to meet the required threshold of the Statute. In light of the conclusion reached on gravity, it was unnecessary to reach a conclusion on complementarity. It may be observed, however, that the Office also collected information on national proceedings, including commentaries from various sources, and that national proceedings had been initiated with respect to each of the relevant incidents.

Conclusion

For the above reasons, in accordance with Article 15(6) of the Rome Statute, I wish to inform you of my conclusion that, at this stage, the Statute requirements to seek authorization to initiate an investigation in the situation in Iraq have not been satisfied. This conclusion can be reconsidered in the light of new facts or evidence. I wish to remind you, in accordance with Rule 49(2) of the Rules of Procedure and Evidence, that should you have additional information regarding crimes within the jurisdiction of the Court, you may submit it to the Office of the Prosecutor. * * *

I thank you very much for providing information regarding alleged crimes to the Office of the Prosecutor of the International Criminal Court. * * *

Luis Moreno–Ocampo

Chief Prosecutor of the International Criminal Court

---

2. STRUCTURE OF THE INTERNATIONAL CRIMINAL COURT

As of June 1, 2008, there were 106 members of the Assembly of States Parties ("ASP") to the ICC and 139 signatories to the Rome Statute.[42] The Assembly of States Parties consists of those states that have signed and ratified the Rome Statute. The ASP decides on such items as the adoption of normative texts and the budget, and it elects the judges, the Chief Prosecutor, and Deputy Prosecutors. According to Article 112(7), each State Party has one vote, and every effort must be made to reach decisions by consensus. If consensus cannot be reached, decisions are taken by vote.[43]

In addition to the ASP, Article 34 of the Rome Statute structures the Court into four Organs: (a) the Presidency; (b) an Appeals Division, a Trial division, and the Pre–Trial Chambers; (c) the Office of the Prosecutor (OTP); and (d) the Registry. The Presidency consists of the President of the Court and two Vice–Presidents elected by an absolute majority of the Court's 18 judges to three-year terms and eligible for re-election to one additional three year term. The Presidency is authorized to administer the Court, but the OTP remains independent. Article 38. The Court's judges are nominated and elected by secret ballot by the ASP, taking into consideration representation of the principal legal systems of the world, equitable geographic representation, and fair representation of female and male judges. Article 36(8)(a).

---

42. The complete list of States Parties to the Rome Statute can be found at http://www.icc-cpi.int/asp/statesparties.html.

43. *See* the Assembly of States Parties, *available at* http://www.untreaty.unorg/cod/icc/asp/aspfra.htm.

The Appeals Division of Chambers consists of the President of the Court and four other Judges. The Trial Division and the Pre–Trial Chambers each consist of at least six judges. Judges serving on the Appeals division remain there the full length of their terms, while Judges in the trial and pre-trial divisions serve three years in one division before they may be switched to the other. Judges serving on a full time basis may not engage in any activity likely to intervene with their judicial functions or affect confidence in their independence. Articles 39, 40.

The Office of the Prosecutor (OTP) is divided into components in accordance with the Rome Statute. The Immediate Office of the Prosecutor (IOP) serves the Chief Prosecutor in daily functions and policy issues. The Jurisdiction, Complementarity and Cooperation Division (JCCD) analyzes referrals and communications, with support from the Investigations Division, and helps secure the cooperation needed for the activities of the Office.[44] The Investigations Division, headed by a Deputy Prosecutor, is responsible for the conduct of investigations (such as collecting and examining evidence, and questioning persons being investigated, as well as victims and witnesses) with respect to both incriminating and exonerating facts. The Investigations Division includes teams of "staff members who are nationals of countries targeted by the investigations, taking care not to recruit individuals whose background or political affiliation may compromise the integrity and objectivity of the investigations."[45] The Prosecutions Division of the OTP is led by another Deputy Prosecutor. Although it has a role in the investigative process, it is principally responsible for the litigation of cases before the various Chambers of the Court.

The final organ of the court is the Registry, which is responsible for the "non-judicial aspects of the administration and servicing of the Court," as well as for the Victims Participation and Reparations Section, Office of Public Counsel for Victims, defense counsel, and the detention unit. Article 43(1), (6), 68(4); Rules of Procedure and Evidence Article 21(2).[46] It also serves as a channel of communication between the Court and states, inter-governmental organizations (IGOs) and non–governmental organizations (NGOs).[47] Art. 43(6), 68(4). The Registry is headed by a Registrar, who is elected by a secret ballot majority of the Judges upon consideration of the recommendation from the Assembly of State Parties. The Registrar's term lasts five years and may be renewed once upon re-election. Article 43(4), (5).

---

44. *See* "Annex to the Paper on Some policy issues Before the Office of the Prosecutor: Referrals and Communications," *available at* http://www.icc-cpi.int/library/organs/otp/policy_annex_final_210404.pdf (last visited Apr. 1, 2006).

45. Paper on Some Policy Issues Before the Office of the Prosecutor 9 (Sept. 2003), *available at* http://www.icc-cpi.int/library/organs/otp/030905_Policy_Paper.pdf (last visited Apr.1, 2006) [hereinafter "OTP Policy Paper"]

46. See also, The Registry, http://www.icc-cpi.int/organs/registry.html (last visited Apr. 1, 2006).

47. *See* The Registry Functions, http://www.icc-cpi.int/registry/regfuncs.html (last visited Apr. 1, 2006).

Unique to the International Criminal Court is its authority to offer civil redress to victims of atrocities once the perpetrator of a crime has been convicted. Reparations for victims may include restitution, indemnification, and rehabilitation. To obtain reparations, victims must apply through the Registry. The Court has the option of granting individual or collective reparations and ordering payment through the Victim's Trust Fund. The Trust Fund is capable of adapting to the cultural and social norms of the communities or individuals to whom redress may be awarded. Considering that justice may be best served in some communities through mechanisms that encompass principles of restorative justice ordered by the Court under Article 75 (2), the Trust Fund serves to provide victims and communities with the resources necessary to rebuild lives and infrastructure often destroyed when human rights are violated on a mass basis.[48] The Fund may provide, for example, child soldiers with an opportunity to receive re-training, which may enable them to lead productive lives once the conflict ends. Rape victims may be provided with trauma counseling or medical care for long term or terminal illnesses contracted from their assailant. In other cases, a village may have been destroyed in fighting, and money may be needed to rebuild it.[49]

NOTES AND QUESTIONS ON THE ICC GENERALLY

1. *Iraq and the ICC.* After reading the Chief Prosecutor's response to the communications regarding military operations in Iraq, do you think his decision not to pursue the situation in Iraq is proper? Although neither the United States nor Iraq is currently a party to the Rome Statute, could a future Iraqi government consent to ICC jurisdiction over U.S. citizens serving in that country?

2. *Right of self-representation.* The ICC has departed from the ICTY's jurisprudence on many issues, one of which is the issue of self-representation. Under Rule 22(1) of the ICC Rules of Procedure, defense counsel must be competent in criminal law and procedure and possess relevant experience in criminal proceedings. "After all, the most competent of defendant[s], and most academically trained, such as Milosevic and Seselj (both of whom are lawyers), would, notwithstanding their own training, have difficulty following the rules of procedure of an international court, as well as standard international criminal law practices." Michael P. Scharf & Christopher M. Rassi, *Do Former Leaders Have an International Right to Self–Representation in War Crimes Trials,* 20 OHIO

------

48. Victims Trust Fund, *available at*: http://www.icc-cpi.int/vtf.html (last visited Apr. 1, 2005). Article 75(2) states, "The court may make an order directly against a convicted person specifying appropriate reparations to, or in respect of, victims, including restitution, compensation and rehabilitation." *See also*, Article 79.

49. Victims Trust Fund, *available at*: http://www.icc-cpi.int/vtf.html (last visited January 16, 2005).

St. J. on Disp. Resol. 3, 27–28 (2005). Should a defendant be required to accept the assistance of a qualified defense lawyer if he or she would prefer to represent himself or herself?

3. *Exclusionary rule.* The ICC has adopted the approach of the *ad hoc* tribunals with respect to the exclusionary rule. Article 69(7) of the Rome Statute requires the Court to exclude evidence obtained in violation of the statute or internationally recognized human rights standards if: "(a) The violation casts substantial doubt on the reliability of the evidence; or (b) The admission of such evidence would be antithetical to and would seriously damage the integrity of the proceedings." The ICC has not yet had occasion to rule on the admission of evidence, but Article 69(7) enables the court to balance its interests in obtaining justice for the victims and ensuring that evidence used in furtherance of this goal is not itself procured through human rights violations.

3. DECIDING TO EXERCISE JURISDICTION (OR NOT)

Should the Office of the ICC Prosecutor seek to bring charges against all alleged perpetrators? The Statute provides in Article 5 that "[t]he jurisdiction of the Court shall be limited to the most serious crimes of concern to the international criminal community as a whole." Article 17 states that the Court (which includes the Office of the Prosecutor) shall determine that a case is inadmissible where "the case is not of sufficient gravity to justify further action by the Court." What factors should determine the "gravity" of a case? As a procedural matter, under Article 13, the court may exercise its jurisdiction only when (1) "one or more such crimes is referred to the Prosecutor by a State Party;" (2) "one or more such crimes is referred to the Prosecutor by the Security Council acting under Chapter VII of the Charter of the United Nations;" or (3) "the Prosecutor has initiated an investigation (*proprio motu*) in respect of such a crime [on the basis of information on crimes within the jurisdiction of the Court]."

In addition, "[t]he Statute gives to the Prosecutor the power *not* to investigate or *not* to prosecute when such an investigation or prosecution would not serve the interests of justice." OTP Policy Paper, at 7 (emphasis added); Rome Statute Article 53. The phrase "interests of justice" is not clearly defined in the Rome Statute. Article 53 aims to prevent prosecution and investigation from undermining the best interests of victims, communities, and governments, or worse, placing them at risk for more violence. The Prosecutor is not required to establish that an investigation or prosecution is in the interests of justice. Rather, he or she shall proceed with an investigation unless there are specific circumstances which provide substantial reasons to believe it is not in the interests of justice to do so at that time, considering the gravity of the crime, the interests of victims, or the age and infirmity of the alleged perpetrator. The OTP is guided by the objective of ending impunity by prosecuting serious crimes of concern to the international community. To date, no decision has been made by the Prosecutor not to proceed because an investigation or prosecution would not serve the interests of justice. *See*, the 2007 OTP *"Policy Paper on the Interests of Justice,"* www.icc-cpi.int/library/organs/otp/ICC–OTP–InterestsOfJustice.pdf.

Three States Parties have referred situations to the office of the Prosecutor. In January 2004, the Republic of Uganda referred the situation concerning the Lord's Resistance Army (LRA). The government of Uganda is engaged in a twenty-year old conflict with a rebel group that targets the civilian population with rape, mutilation, executions, and abductions. The LRA also kidnaps children and forcefully conscripts them into the fighting in order to have a continuous supply of soldiers. On May 6, 2005, the Office of the Prosecutor issued five arrest warrants for the senior commanders of the LRA, including its leader, Joseph Kony.

In April 2004, the Democratic Republic of Congo referred the situation within its territory concerning mass murder, summary execution, rape, torture, forced displacement, and the illegal use of child soldiers. The ICC announced its first arrest in this case on March 17, 2006. With the cooperation of the Congolese and French governments, Thomas Lubanga, the leader of the UPC and commander-in-chief of its military wing the Forces Patriotiques pour la liberation du Congo, was arrested. Lubanga is alleged to have been involved in forcefully conscripting children under the age of fifteen and forcing them to participate in hostilities.

In January 2005, the Central African Republic referred the situation concerning war crimes and crimes against humanity, especially against women, committed in armed conflict in its territory between October 2002 and March 2003. In May 2008, a Trial Chamber of the ICC issued an arrest warrant for Jean-Pierre Bemba Gombo for these crimes.

In October 2004, the International Commission of Inquiry on Darfur, Sudan, was established by UN Secretary–General Kofi Annan. The Commission reported to the UN in January 2005 that there was reason to believe that crimes against humanity and war crimes had been committed in Darfur and recommended that the situation be referred to the ICC. The United Nations Security Council subsequently adopted Resolution 1593, referring the situation concerning Darfur to the Prosecutor, who initiated an investigation pursuant to Article 53 of the Rome Statute and Article 104 of the Rules of Evidence. The Resolution requires Sudan and all other parties to the conflict in Darfur to cooperate with the Court. It also invites the Court and the African Union to discuss practical arrangements that will facilitate the work of the Prosecutor and the Court, including the possibility of conducting proceedings in the region.

In July 2008, in an unprecedented step, the ICC Prosecutor, Luis–Moreno Ocampo, asked the Court's Pre–Trial Chamber I to issue an arrest warrant against President Omar Hassan Ahmed al-Bashir, a sitting head of state who has held office in Sudan since 1989. The warrant rests on ten counts of genocide, crimes against humanity, and war crimes. Three years after the UN Security Council asked him to investigate Darfur, the Prosecutor presented his summary of the case against al-Bashir, alleging that he masterminded and implemented a plan to destroy in substantial part the Fur, Masalit, and Zaghawa ethnic groups, over two million of whom had fled from government-organized violence to displaces persons cams, where they were also systematically attacked. Moreno–Ocampo said that "al Bashir organized the destitution, insecurity, and harassment of the survivors. He did not need bullets. He used other weapons: rapes, hunger, and fear. As efficient, but silent." *See* ICC Press Release, ICC–OTP–20080712–PR341–ENG (July 14, 2008), *available at* http://www.icc-cpi.int/press/pressreleases/406.html. The re-trial Chamber will issue a warrant against al-Bashir if it determines that the Prosecutor's evidence establishes "reasonable grounds to believe" that he has committed the crimes alleged.

In the aftermath of the Prosecutor's decision, the government of Sudan has sought to convince African states on the UN Security Council to pursue the Council's Chapter VII authority to defer the prosecution for 12 months, pursuant to Article 16 of the Rome Statute. As this book goes to print, the Security Council has declined to exercise that authority, preferring instead to reaffirm the mandate for peacekeepers in Darfur and rejecting efforts by Libya and South Africa to adopt language halting the Court's consideration of the Prosecutor's indictment request.

Notes and Questions on the Exercise of Jurisdiction

1. *Current candidates for ICC referral.* What other contemporary situations do you think should be referred to the ICC for investigation? Taking into account the States Parties to the Rome Statute and the makeup of the Security Council, what is the most likely method by which the Court will obtain jurisdiction?

2. *"Interests of justice."* In determining what is "in the interest of justice," should the ICC Prosecutor ever take into consideration national decisions to promote reconciliation by means of truth commission and amnesty programs? *See Human Rights Watch Policy Paper: The Meaning of "The Interests of Justice" in Article 53 of the Rome Statute* (June 2005). http://hrw.org/campaigns/icc/docs/ij070505.pdf. Compare with the OTP's 2007 Policy Paper on the Interests of Justice, referenced above.

3. *"A close call for the ICC."* In June 2008, the ICC's first trial was nearly derailed by the Prosecutor's misuse of a unique evidentiary tool.

The defendant, Thomas Lubanga Dyilo—the alleged leader of the Union of Conglolese Patriots (UPC)—had been accused of war crimes, but Trial Chamber I ordered his release, citing concerns that he would not be able to get a fair trial. Just weeks earlier, the prosecution had revealed that it had obtained hundreds of documents from the UN but would be unable to reveal them to the Chamber or to the defense, because the documents had been obtained pursuant to confidentiality agreements with the UN. Article 54 of the Rome Statute and Rule 154 of the ICC's Rules of Procedure and Evidence allow the OTP to enter into these confidentiality agreements, but the evidence so obtained can only be used to gather new evidence and not as the basis for a charge or in trial. Concerned that the evidence would be used unfairly or illegally, the Trial Chamber ordered Lubanga's release. The OTP filed an immediate appeal and soon persuaded the UN to abandon its prior position and allow the Chamber and the defense to view the evidence. With disaster narrowly averted, the Prosecutor asserted confidently that Lubanga's trial would begin in 2009.

---

4. CHECKS, BALANCES, AND LIMITATIONS

The Rome Statute imposes certain checks and balances to preserve justice and efficiency throughout court proceedings. These checks also serve to prevent the OTP, Chambers, the Registry, States Parties, and intergovernmental organizations from influencing decisions on legal issues, including admissibility and jurisdiction.

Opponents of the Court criticize the grant of *proprio motu* power to the Prosecutor, alleging that it provides ample opportunity for abuse of prosecutorial discretion. On the contrary, it is argued that the ability to initiate an investigation *proprio motu* is necessary in order to preserve the Prosecutor's independence from politically motivated decisions not to refer situations and information to the Court. Under Article 15, the Prosecutor must request authorization for an investigation from the Pre–Trial Chamber. The Pre–Trial Chamber must decide that there is a reasonable basis to proceed based on the information presented by the Prosecutor *and* that the case falls within the jurisdiction of the Court before it may authorize an investigation. Questions of admissibility and jurisdiction in the Pre–Trial Chamber are rendered without prejudice to later findings of the Court, and the decision of the Pre–Trial Chamber must be concurred in by a majority of its judges. Article 57. After receiving authorization from the Pre–Trial Chamber, if pursuit of the investigation furthers the "interests of justice," and only after the Prosecutor obtains evidence sufficient to prosecute an individual, the Prosecutor can then submit the charges to the Pre–Trial Chamber for confirmation. Only then may a case be initiated without referral from a State Party or the Security Council.

Although the UN and the ICC are independent of one another, the Security Council in connection with Resolution 1593 (referring the Darfur situation to the OTP) invites the Prosecutor to deliver a report every six months on actions taken pursuant to the Resolution. The Prosecutor's first two reports issued to the Security Council outline the progress of the OTP's investigation and the legal basis upon which the Court has and will continue to proceed.[50] Neither the Resolution nor the Prosecutor's reports mention oversight by the United Nations, in accordance with the need for independence of the OTP.

Nevertheless, the United Nations Security Council is entitled under Article 16 to postpone any prosecutorial investigation for twelve months. The Security Council may renew the postponement each year without limitation.

The selection procedures for judges and independent prosecutors add additional layers of accountability to the ICC. The maximum term a judge may serve is nine years.

Perhaps the most important accountability measure provided by the Rome Statute is found in Article 46, which provides for the removal of judges and/or prosecutors who have engaged in misconduct or who are unable to exercise the functions required in the Statute. A judge is removed upon a two-thirds majority vote of the Assembly of State Parties, while the Prosecutor and deputy prosecutors may be removed upon a simple majority vote of the Assembly of State Parties. These votes are taken by secret ballot.

From a practical standpoint, the OTP is limited by its independence from States Parties and political organizations. A national prosecutor has power within her territory that includes law enforcement agencies and a national prosecution system subject to the rule of law. By contrast, the international prosecutor faces a unique challenge. Consider this excerpt from the *Paper on Some Policy Issues before the Office of the Prosecutor*,[51] which highlights the challenges unique to the OTP of the ICC:

> Given the nature of the crimes within the jurisdiction of the Court, the Prosecutor may be called upon to act in a situation of violence over which the State authorities have no control. His Office can be present in the country concerned only at great risk. The protection of witnesses, gathering of evidence and arrest of suspects will be difficult if not impossible. The Prosecutor may also be asked to act in a situation where those who have the monopoly of force in a State are the ones to commit the crimes. It goes without saying that

---

50. Report of the Prosecutor of the International Criminal Court, Mr. Luis Moreno–Ocampo, to the Security Council Pursuant to UNSC Resoluton 1593 (June 29, 2005), *available at* http://www.icc-cpi.int/library/cases/ICC_Darfur_UNSC_Report_29–06–05_EN.pdf (last visited January 24, 2006); Second Report of the Prosecutor of the International Criminal Court, Mr. Luis Moreno–Ocampo, to the Security Council Pursuant to UNSC Resolution 1593 (Dec. 31, 2005), *available at* http://www.icc-cpi.int/library/organs/otp/LMO_UNSC_ReportB_En.pdf (last visited January 24, 2006).

51. *Available at* http://www.icc-cpi.int/library/organs/otp/030905_Policy_Paper.pdf

in such a case the enforcement authorities in that State will not be at the Prosecutor's disposal. * * *

The Prosecutor will encourage States and civil society to take ownership of the Court. The external relations and outreach strategy of the Office will develop a network of relationships between the Prosecutor, national authorities, multi-lateral institutions, non-governmental organizations and other entities and bodies, to ensure that in any kind of situation in which the Prosecutor is called upon to act, practical resources are made available to enable an investigation to be mounted. Agreements with states will be necessary, supporting the Court's efforts by providing security, police and investigative teams, and giving intelligence and other evidence. The investigation of financial transactions, for example for the purchase of arms used in murder, may well provide evidence proving the commission of atrocities. Here again the interaction between State authorities and the Office of the Prosecutor will be crucial: national investigative authorities may pass to the Office evidence of financial transactions, which will be essential to the Court's investigations of crimes within the Court's jurisdiction; for its part, the Office may have evidence of the commission of financial crimes which can be passed to national authorities for domestic prosecutions. Such prosecutions will be a key deterrent to the commission of future crimes, if they can curb the source of funding. And all assistance of this kind provided by national authorities to the Office of the Prosecutor will help to keep the Court cost-effective. * * *

As the OTP recognizes in its policy paper, state cooperation may be nonexistent, and the OTP must therefore rely on assistance from other actors. From what sources might the Prosecutor draw for intelligence and practical assistance? Can you envision the role of other States (in whose jurisdiction an investigation is not taking place)? Of NGOs? Of private enterprise? Who might have relevant information spanning a particular region, inclusive of many actors and groups, and collected over decades?

---

5. THE ICC AND THE UNITED STATES

The United States' relationship with the ICC is complicated. Although President Bill Clinton signed the Rome Statute on December 31, 2000, President George W. Bush withdrew the United States' signature on May 6, 2002. As you will see from the excerpts below, U.S. opposition to the ICC is motivated primarily by concerns over politically-motivated prosecutions of U.S. military personnel and political officials serving around the world. As you read this section, consider whether the risk is real or perceived. Does the fact that the U.S. actively engages in a variety of high risk environments around the world create greater political exposure than for other governments? Or do the checks and balances and practical limitations of the ICC reduce the risk to acceptable levels?

STATEMENT OF HON. DAVID J. SCHEFFER, AMBASSADOR–AT LARGE FOR WAR CRIMES ISSUES[52]

Thank you for the opportunity to discuss with the committee the developments in Rome this summer relating to the establishment of a permanent international criminal court.* * * Mr. Chairman, no one can survey the events of this decade without profound concern about worldwide respect for internationally recognized human rights. We live in a world where entire populations can still be terrorized and slaughtered by nationalistic butchers and undisciplined armies. We have witnessed this in Iraq, in the Balkans, and in Central Africa. Internal conflicts dominate the landscape of armed struggle, and impunity too often shields the perpetrators of the most heinous crimes against their own people and others. As the most powerful nation committed to the rule of law, we have a responsibility to confront these assaults on humankind. One response mechanism is accountability, namely to help bring the perpetrators of genocide, crimes against humanity, and war crimes to justice. If we allow them to act with impunity, then we will only be inviting a perpetuation of these crimes far into the next millennium. Our legacy must demonstrate an unyielding commitment to the pursuit of justice.

That is why, since early 1995, U.S. negotiators labored through many *ad hoc* and preparatory committee sessions at the United Nations in an effort to craft an acceptable statute for a permanent international criminal court using as a foundation the draft statute prepared by the International Law Commission in 1994. Our experience with the establishment and operation of the International Criminal Tribunals for the former Yugoslavia and Rwanda had convinced us of the merit of creating a permanent court that could be more quickly available for investigations and prosecutions and more cost efficient in its operation.* * *

Our delegation included highly talented and experienced lawyers and other officials from the Departments of State and Justice, the Office of the Secretary of Defense, the Joint Chiefs of Staff, the U.S. mission to the United Nations, and from the private sector. America can be proud of the tireless work and major contributions that these individuals made to the negotiations.

---

52. *Is a UN International Criminal Court in the U.S. National Interest?* Hearing Before the Subcomm. on Int'l Operations of the Senate Comm. on Foreign Relations, 105th Cong. 12–15 (1998) (statement of David Scheffer, Ambassador At–Large for War Crimes Issues, U.S. Dept. of State).

Among the objectives we achieved in the statute of the Court were the following:

- an improved regime of complementarity, meaning deferral to national jurisdictions, that provides significant protection, although not as much as we had sought;

- a role preserved for the UN Security Council, including the affirmation of the Security Council's power to intervene to halt the Court's work;

- sovereign protection of national security information that might be sought by the Court;

- broad recognition of national judicial procedures as a predicate for cooperation with the Court;

- coverage of internal conflicts, which comprise the vast majority of armed conflicts today;

- important due process protections for defendants and suspects;

- viable definitions of war crimes and crimes against humanity, including the incorporation in the statute of elements of offenses (We are not entirely satisfied with how the elements have been incorporated in the treaty, but at least they will be a required part of the Court's work. We also were not willing to accept the wording proposed for war crimes covering the transfer of population into occupied territory);

- some progress on recognition of gender issues;

- acceptable provisions based on command responsibility and superior orders;

- rigorous qualifications for judges;

- acceptance of the basic principle of state party funding;

- an Assembly of States Parties to oversee the management of the Court;

- reasonable amendment procedures; and

- a sufficient number of ratifying states before the treaty can enter into force, namely 60 governments have to ratify the treaty.

The U.S. delegation also sought to achieve other objectives in Rome that in our view are critical. I regret to report that certain of these objectives were not achieved and therefore we could not support the draft that emerged on July 17th.

First, while we successfully defeated initiatives to empower the Court with universal jurisdiction, a form of jurisdiction over nonparty states was adopted by the conference despite our strenuous objections.* * * We sought an amendment to the text that at a minimum, would have required that only the consent of the state of nationality of the perpetrator be obtained before the Court could exercise jurisdiction.

We are left with consequences that do not serve the cause of international justice.* * * Since most atrocities are committed internally and most internal conflicts are between warring parties of the same nationality, the worst offenders of international humanitarian law can choose never to join the treaty and be fully insulated from its reach absent a Security Council referral. Yet multinational peacekeeping forces operating in a country that has joined the treaty can be exposed to the Court's jurisdiction even if the country of the individual peacekeeper has not joined the treaty. Thus, the treaty purports to establish an arrangement whereby U.S. armed forces operating overseas could be conceivably prosecuted by the international court even if the United States has not agreed to be bound by the treaty. Not only is this contrary to the most fundamental principles of treaty law, it could inhibit the ability of the United States to use its military to meet alliance obligations and participate in multinational operations, including humanitarian interventions to save civilian lives. Other contributors to peacekeeping operations will be similarly exposed.* * *

Our position is clear. Official actions of a non-party state should not be subject to the Court's jurisdiction if that country does not join the treaty, except by means of Security Council action under the UN Charter. Otherwise, the ratification procedure would be meaningless for governments. In fact, under such a theory, two governments could join together to create a criminal court and purport to extend its jurisdiction over everyone everywhere in the world.* * * The United States has long supported the right of the Security Council to refer situations to the Court with mandatory effect, meaning that any rogue state could not deny the Court's jurisdiction under any circumstances. We believe this is the only way under international law and the UN Charter to impose the Court's jurisdiction on a non-party state. In fact, the treaty reaffirms this Security Council referral power.* * *

The treaty also creates a *proprio motu*, or self-initiating prosecutor, who on his or her own authority, with the consent of two judges, can initiate investigations and prosecutions without referral to the Court of a situation either by a government that is a party to the treaty or by the Security Council. We opposed this proposal, as we are concerned that it will encourage overwhelming the Court with complaints and risk diversion of its resources, as well as embroil the Court in controversy, political decisionmaking, and confusion.

In addition, we are disappointed with the treatment of the crime of aggression. We and others had long argued that such a crime had not been defined under customary international law for purposes of individual criminal responsibility. We also insisted, as did the International Law Commission in 1994, that there had to be a direct linkage between a prior Security Council decision that a State had committed aggression and the conduct of an individual of that State. The statute of the Court now includes a crime of aggression, but leaves it to be defined by a subsequent amendment to be adopted 7 years after entry into force of the treaty.* * *

Finally, we were confronted on July 17th with a provision stipulating that no reservations to the treaty would be allowed. We had long argued against such a prohibition and many countries had joined us in that concern. We believe that at a minimum there were certain provisions of the treaty, particularly in the field of state cooperation with the Court, where domestic constitutional requirements and national judicial procedures might require a reasonable opportunity for reservations that did not defeat the intent or purpose of the treaty.

Mr. Chairman, the administration hopes that in the years ahead other governments will recognize the benefits of potential American participation in the Rome treaty and correct the flawed provisions in the treaty.* * * The hard reality is that the international court will have no jurisdiction over crimes committed prior to its actual operation. So more ad hoc judicial mechanisms will need to be considered. We trust our friends and allies will show as much resolve to pursue the challenges of today as they have to create the future international court.

KENNETH ROTH, YES A WORLD COURT, WASHINGTON POST, (JUNE 26, 2000), at A23

The debate over a permanent international criminal court is coming to a head. The Clinton administration is threatening to walk out of UN deliberations in New York unless its proposal to exempt U.S. citizens is accepted by June 30. The vehemence of U.S. objections is founded in part on important misconceptions. These are illustrated by Fred Hiatt's column "Internationally: War Crimes Sanctimony" [op-ed, June 19].

By providing a forum to prosecute the authors of genocide, war crimes and crimes against humanity, the court is designed to curtail the impunity that has fueled the worst atrocities of our time. Hiatt charges that the court will in fact have the opposite effect by discouraging military intervention to stop such crimes. The remote possibility that the court could prosecute American military personnel, he contends, might ensure that the United States "never stages a humanitarian intervention again." * * *

Recent history refutes that claim. The Pentagon willingly participated in bombing campaigns over Serb depredations in Bosnia in 1995 and Kosovo in 1999. Yet in each case, U.S. troops were subject to prosecution by the Yugoslav War Crimes Tribunal. Indeed, the tribunal arguably posed a greater threat to U.S. forces than the international criminal court, because any tribunal decision to prosecute would have superseded the views of U.S. authorities. The court, by contrast, must defer to conscientious investigations by national authorities, even if they decide against prosecution.

Hiatt compares political supervision of the court unfavorably to that of the Yugoslav tribunal. The tribunal, he asserts, must be "sensitive to political ramifications" of its actions because it was created by the UN Security Council. But the court, he claims, "will operate with almost no external checks and balances." Here again he is mistaken.

The Security Council's capacity to rein in a hypothetical runaway tribunal is limited by the veto power of the council's permanent members. China or Russia, as well as Britain and France, could single-handedly block U.S. efforts to curb an inappropriate tribunal prosecution. The prosecutor of the international criminal court, by contrast, can be dismissed for misconduct by a simple majority of the governments that ratify the court's treaty. Moreover, before the need for such a political check even arose, a defendant alleging inappropriate prosecution by the court would be entitled to review by up to three separate judicial panels.

For an example of the caution that marks these international proceedings, consider the tribunal's treatment of NATO's bombing campaign in Yugoslavia. As Human Rights Watch documented in an extensive report, NATO's violations of international humanitarian law were responsible for roughly half the 500 civilian deaths caused by NATO bombs. Yet, after careful reasoning, the tribunal found no basis to charge war crimes. The best way to ensure similar caution by the international court is for the U.S. government to embrace it and play a central role in shaping its culture, as it did with the tribunal, rather than snub it.

Many U.S. opponents of the international criminal court focus on its power to prosecute nationals of states that do not ratify its treaty. But that is no different from treaties on terrorism and drug trafficking that permit prosecution of offenders regardless of the views of their native states.

[Some] would prefer a court that is restricted to cases referred by the victim state or the Security Council. But victim states are often ruled by their abusers, who are not about to turn themselves in for prosecution. And the permanent members of the Security Council have been so preoccupied with protecting friends and allies that they have blocked the establishment of international tribunals for such worthy candidates as the Iraqi government or the Khmer Rouge. The broader jurisdiction of the international criminal court is needed.

The court has more than adequate guarantees against the unwarranted prosecution of an American. But the U.S. government wants more: an ironclad guarantee against any prosecution of an American, whether warranted or not. Such an exemption would sabotage this landmark institution for combating the worst human rights crimes of our era. It would be antithetical to American ideals of justice and to the universality that is key to the court's legitimacy. It should not be sought or granted.

NOTES AND QUESTIONS ON THE ICC AND THE UNITED STATES

1. *Signing and unsigning.* As indicated by Ambassador Scheffer's testimony, the approach of the Clinton administration was to remain engaged in the creation of the ICC, working to incorporate safeguards that were compatible with the United States' understanding of due process protections. Though President Clinton referred to the treaty as "flawed," he vowed to work to correct it before submitting it to the Senate for ratification. Almost immediately after taking office, President Bush took the unprecedented step of "unsigning" the treaty, making clear that the United States was no longer interested in staying engaged in the development of what the new Administration perceived as a fundamentally flawed court. Rather than "unsign" the treaty, could the Bush administration have remained a signatory while protecting the U.S. from the flaws in the Statute? The current list of U.S. objections to the ICC may be found on the State Department website: http://www.state.gov/t/pm/rls/fs/23428.htm (last visited July 4, 2008); For additional discussion on the political and constitutional concerns underlying the U.S. position on the ICC, *see* Diane Marie Amann & M.N.S. Sellers, *The United States of America and the International Criminal Court*, 50 Am. J. Comp. L. 381 (2002).

2. *Responding to U.S. concerns.* The American Non–Governmental Organizations Coalition for the International Criminal Court ("AM-ICC") counters the State Department's objections to the ICC. AMICC notes that "The ICC Statute limits the Court's jurisdiction over persons to the two most traditional bases: crimes occurring on the territory of a state party or by an accused who is the national of a state party." AMICC, AMICC RESPONSE TO THE U.S. ADMINISTRATION INTERNATIONAL CRIMINAL COURT POLICY (2005) *available at* http://www.amicc.org/docs/AMICC_USpolicy.pdf. Additionally, AMICC points out that the Court's subject matter jurisdiction is limited to the most heinous crimes such as crimes against humanity, genocide, war crimes, and crimes of aggression.

According to the AMICC, another factor that mitigates the United State's concerns regarding the ICC's jurisdiction is that it is "a court of last resort" operating under the principles of complementarity. The ICC may only take a case when it can be shown "that the state in question is incapable of acting, has no independent judicial system, or has invoked complementarity in bad faith."

The AMICC also states that the U.S. concerns about new crimes and its concerns about jurisdiction over, and the definition of, acts of aggression fail to consider that any member state of the ICC may opt out of the provision providing jurisdiction over the crime of aggression if and when the Statute is amended to include it.

According to AMICC, U.S. concerns over a lack of due process rights are similarly misplaced. All but one of the protections provided by the United States Bill of Rights are guaranteed by the Rome Statute. The only difference is that there is no right to a jury at the ICC. Rather, defendants are tried by judges in a fashion similar to American military courts.

3. *Similarities and differences between ICC and U.S. criminal proceedings.* The Rome Statute has incorporated numerous principles of criminal law that are present in the American legal system, though there are significant differences. For example, all accused in both systems are entitled to the presumption of innocence. An accused cannot be found guilty without having the necessary *mens rea*, defined as intent or knowledge depending on the level of culpability, and *actus reus* under the Rome Statute. Article 30. The ICC's pre-trial procedures are also similar to American pre-trial procedures. The accused has *Miranda* rights, protections from searches and seizures without a warrant, and the right to attend a pretrial hearing in which the charges are brought against him. A difference in ICC procedure is that the defense is allowed two chances to prove its case and challenge the prosecution's evidence: at the pretrial hearing *and* at trial. Articles 61(6), 65(1)(c)(iii), 67(1)(e). Unlike in U.S. law, appellate review may be requested by either party on the grounds of factual error. Articles 81, 82.

The ICC has no juvenile court. It does not exercise jurisdiction over anyone accused of committing a crime prior to 18 years of age. Article 26. Do the differences mean that ICC norms would run afoul of core U.S. due process norms? *Compare* Lee A. Casey, *Assessments of the United States Position: The Case Against the International Criminal Court*, 25 FORD-HAM INT'L L.J. 840, 861–64 (2002) *with* Gregory S. Gordon, *Toward an International Criminal Procedure: Due Process Aspirations and Limitations*, 45 COL. J. TRANSNATIONAL L. 635, 663–67 (2007).

4. *Bilateral immunity/Article 98 agreements.* Despite the checks and balances outlined above, the United States has sought and entered into numerous bilateral immunity agreements, in which nations have agreed to waive their ability to bring charges against United States citizens before the ICC.[53] According to the State Department, the Authority to enter into these bilateral agreements is provided by Article 98 of the Rome Statute.

Critics cite Article 98 Agreements as a tactic to undermine the effectiveness of the International Criminal Court. They also cite the

---

53. As of December 11, 2006, the U.S. reported that 102 countries have signed U.S. bilateral immunity agreements. Full list *available at* http://www.iccnow.org/documents/CICCFS_BIAstatus. current.pdf; *see also* Richard Boucher, U.S. Department of State Spokesman, *U.S. signs 100th Article 98 Agreement,* Press Release (May 3, 2005), *available at* http://www.state.gov/r/pa/ prs/ps/2005/45573. htm Of these, 42 are states parties to the ICC. A listing by region is available at http://www.iccnow. org/documents/CICCFS_BIAstatus_08Jan06.pdf.; *see also* http://www.ll.georgetown.edu/intl/guides /article_98.cfm.

United States' failed threat to veto the UN mission to East Timor unless American citizens were granted immunity from the ICC, and its July 12, 2002, successful negotiation of a year-long grant of immunity during the peacekeeping mission in Bosnia-Herzegovina. Another effort by the United States to immunize U.S. citizens from possible ICC jurisdiction is the American Service Members' Protection Act ("ASPA"), which was signed into law by President Bush on August 2, 2002. 22 U.S.C. §§ 7421–7433 (2002). This law "authorizes the withdrawal of U.S. military assistance from certain non-NATO allies supporting the Court." The ASPA also prohibits U.S. governmental entities, including courts from rendering assistance, cooperation and support to the ICC, and it prohibits agents of the ICC from conducting any investigative activity within the U.S. The President has the authority to waive application of the law if he determines it to be in the U.S. national interest.

In 2006, the Senate Foreign Relations Subcommittee on Western Hemisphere, Peace Corps and Narcotics Affairs held a Hearing on "The Impact on Latin America of the American Servicemembers' Protection Act," to discuss the consequences of withholding military assistance in Latin America.[54] After the hearing, Senator Norm Coleman wrote an article for the Washington Times in which he stated, "[T]he American Servicemembers' Protection Act [carried] some unintended consequences that directly counter U.S. interests. The panelists at my hearing agreed * * * that in most Latin American nations the political costs of signing an immunity agreement with [the] U.S. far outweigh the benefits of continued U.S. aid." He also noted that General Bantz Craddock, the commander of U.S. Southern Command has cautioned that "Restrictions in military and economic aid could also result in loss of U.S. diplomatic influence in the region.* * * [A]ny real or perceived vacuum created by the U.S. could be filled by worrisome actors in the region or beyond, that may not share our democratic values. * * *" Norm Coleman, *Finding a Better Way to Protect Troops*, WASHINGTON TIMES, Mar. 19, 2006. Whether the U.S. will simply extend waivers to a greater number of countries or seek a different source of leverage remains to be seen.

Partly in response to concerns about weakening military relationships, the President has exercised his authority to waive application of the ASPA's prohibition on military training programs to countries which have not signed Article 98 agreements, like Mexico. Then in 2008, the President signed into law the FY 2008 Defense Authorization Bill containing a two-line amendment which partially repealed the ASPA. This amendment introduced by Senator James Inhofe (R–OK) permits International Military Education and Training ("IMET") assistance to ICC member states who do not have an Article 98 Agreement with the United States. President Bush also issued waivers for the twenty-one ICC member countries that were previously being denied IMET because

---

54. *The Impact on Latin America of the Servicemembers' Protection Act: Hearing Before the S. Comm. on Foreign Relations*, 109th Cong. (2006).

of their refusal to sign an Article 98 Agreement with the United States, a legally redundant move in light of the 2008 Defense Authorization Bill.

5. *The Nethercutt Amendment.* On December 7, 2004, President Bush signed into law the Nethercutt Amendment to the Foreign Appropriations bill. The Amendment suspended Economic Support Fund assistance to any member nation of the ICC that has not signed an Article 98 agreement with the United States. Money from the Economic Support Fund is provided to nations to support anti-terrorism measures, peacekeeping initiatives, drug interdiction initiatives, and democracy building programs. An exemption is provided in the bill that allows the President to exempt members of NATO, major non-NATO allies (Argentina, Australia, Egypt, Israel, Japan, Jordan, New Zealand, and the Republic of Korea) and Millennium Fund Countries if the President determines that it is in the U.S. national interest.[55] The Nethercutt Amendment reads, in part:

> LIMITATION ON ECONOMIC SUPPORT FUND ASSISTANCE FOR CERTAIN FOREIGN GOVERNMENTS THAT ARE PARTIES TO THE INTERNATIONAL CRIMINAL COURT SEC. 574.
>
> (a) None of the funds made available in this Act in title II under the heading "Economic Support Fund" may be used to provide assistance to the government of a country that is a party to the International Criminal Court and has not entered into an agreement with the United States pursuant to Article 98 of the Rome Statute preventing the International Criminal Court from proceeding against United States personnel present in such country.[56]

6. *Darfur.* Despite American objections to the ICC, on March 31, 2005, the United Nations Security Council adopted Resolution 1593 which referred the Darfur situation to the ICC. S.C. Res. 1593, UN Doc. S/RES/1593 (Mar. 21, 2005). The Resolution includes a provision, at the United States' request, that exempts citizens of non-State parties from ICC prosecution for activities in Sudan. Despite obtaining this provision, however, the United States still abstained on the vote, explaining that while it "strongly supported bringing to justice those responsible for the crimes and atrocities that had occurred in Darfur and ending the climate of impunity there," it maintained its "long-standing and firm objections and concerns regarding the Court. United Nations Press Release," "Security Council Refers Situation in Darfur, Sudan, to Prosecutor of International Criminal Court," UN Doc. SC/8351 (Mar. 31,

---

55. In September 2000, the United Nations unanimously approved of the Millennium Declaration in which it outlined a vision to fight world poverty, drastically reduce world hunger and infant mortality rates, improve the environment in developing nations, and fight the spread of disease. Under the Millennium Challenge Act of 2003, the United States created the Millennium Challenge Account ("MCA") and the Millennium Challenge Corporation ("MCC"). The MCC administers the MCA. In 2004 $1.3 billion was appropriated to fund the MCA.

56. "An Act Making Appropriations For Foreign Operations, Export Financing, and Related Programs for the Fiscal Year Ending September 30, 2006, and for Other Purposes," Pub. L. No. 109–102, § 574, 110 Stat. 2229 (2005).

2005). Given U.S. concerns about the ICC, why do you think it chose not to veto S.C. Resolution 1593?

7. *The ICC's limited resources.* The Chief Prosecutor stated that his office will be occupied with the Democratic Republic of Congo, Uganda, and now Darfur, for years to come. With three cases from Africa requiring the Prosecutor's attention, is this truly an international court? How would you address the issues raised in the *OTP Policy Paper* and *Annex* regarding the OTP's resources, protection of staff and witnesses, state cooperation, and enforcement of Court orders?

8. *ICC Review Conference.* A review conference for the ICC will take place in 2009, where parties to the treaty will review and recommend modifications to the Rome Statute. Only parties to the Statute are eligible to participate in this formal review where one topic likely to be addressed is the definition for the crime of "aggression."[57] However, some claim that "[e]ven in a limited observer role, with neither voting status nor the ability to table amendments, the U.S. could be effective. The U.S. could participate in the pre-negotiations leading up to the 2009 review conference, where representatives from the U.S. military and diplomatic communities could address discussions defining crimes." *See* Victoria K. Holt & Elisabeth W. Dallas, On Trial: The U.S. Military and the ICC, 64 (Mar. 2006), *available at* http://www.stimson.org/fopo/pdf/US_Military_and_the_ICC_FINAL_website.pdf. Does the ability to participate in the formal review process give the United States greater incentive to become a party to the treaty?

Practicum

INTERNATIONAL CRIMINAL COURT
Senate Foreign Relations Committee Hearings

Context:

The Senate Foreign Relations Committee has decided to hold hearings on whether the United States should ratify the Rome Statute for the International Criminal Court or continue to oppose the Court in its foreign policy. Each of you has been given the role of presenting written testimony on this issue. You should be prepared to summarize your written testimony in the Committee hearing and respond to any questions the Senators may have.

Roles:

John Bolton, former U.S. Ambassador to the United Nations: He will present the views of the Bush Administration on the Court and will argue against ratification and for an aggressive campaign against the

---

57. *See* Stephen Rickard, *Protect U.S. Interests More Effectively by Supporting the International Criminal Court, in* Restoring American Leadership, *available at* http://www.americanprogress.org/atf/cf/E9245FE4–9A2B–43C7–A521–5D6FF2E06E03/Chapter4RALICC.pdf (last visited Apr. 1, 2006).

Court on the grounds primarily that the ICC presents a threat to U.S. citizens, especially its soldiers, and to America's allies, especially Israel.

David Scheffer: the former Ambassador for War Crimes in the Clinton Administration and one of the participants in the Rome Conference in 1998. He will present the argument that the U.S. should push for changes in the Rome Statute that would alleviate legitimate U.S. concerns and enable the U.S. to play a constructive role in building the ICC, so that the United States would eventually be able to ratify the Rome Statute.

Kenneth Roth, Executive Director of Human Rights Watch will represent a coalition of human rights groups, including Amnesty International and Human Rights Watch. He will express the views of human rights NGOs on the above issues which are strongly in support of U.S. ratification of the ICC and against U.S. efforts to undermine its effectiveness.

Louise Arbour, the former UN High Commissioner for Human Rights. She will present arguments on behalf of the United Nations in favor of U.S. ratification and in opposition to U.S. efforts to undermine the ICC. She is expected to outline the emerging new international order based on the rule of law and the ICC's place in it and try to convince the U.S. that its national interests favor ratification.

Each of these presentations should analyze specific provisions of the Rome Statute in order to make the overall points you want to make in playing your roles. Each presentation should address at least the following issues:

Would American soldiers engaged in peacekeeping operations in other countries face a serious threat of prosecution under the Rome Statute?

What are the short-term and long-term U.S. national interests *vis-a-vis* the ICC?

Are there any problems with the Rome Statute that might be addressed within the current framework of the treaty?

You should not feel limited by these questions, and you may address any other issue you believe is appropriate to convince the Senators.

Senator Assignments: Several students should be assigned the roles of Senators on the Senate Foreign Relations Committee and be prepared to ask penetrating questions of the speakers. At the end of the presentations, each Senator should be prepared to state his or her position and the reasons for it.

CHAPTER 3

MODULE 7

HOLDING GOVERNMENTS ACCOUNTABLE THROUGH REGIONAL SYSTEMS FOR THE PROTECTION OF HUMAN RIGHTS

■ ■ ■

One of the most profound attacks on the principle of state sovereignty was mounted by governments themselves. By creating international organizations with the power to set human rights standards and to oversee member-states' compliance with those standards, governments relinquished a measure of their traditional right to be left alone. Judging from the enforcement mechanisms that eventually emerged, governments were more comfortable giving apparent power to regional organizations than to global organizations, perhaps because each state's influence could be greater in regional organizations or perhaps because the cultural and legal differences with neighboring states were less significant (or at least more familiar). It is at least equally conceivable that governments had no intention of surrendering real power to any supranational organization and that whatever doctrinal and institutional innovation has occurred was in spite of, rather than because of, the member-states' positions. But, whatever the actual motivation behind the empowerment of regional human rights organizations may have been, contemporary human rights advocacy draws heavily on regional doctrine and procedure.

If the first line of human rights defense is the national system of internalization and enforcement in each country, and the safety net is the universal system under the auspices of the United Nations, the regional systems–currently in Europe, the Americas, and Africa—offer an intermediate level of protection covering almost half of humanity. In this chapter, we emphasize these three systems, noting how each has developed an institutional character and expertise and how they have evolved over time, often in conscious response to one another's successes and failures. The materials that follow also invite a critical understanding of the most visible gaps in regional protection—in Asia and the Arab world—a contemporary clinic in the fits-and-starts development of common standards and institutions across vastly different cultures.

Ultimately, it is a mistake to think too simply about the phenomenon of regionalism in the protection of human rights. After all, the proliferation of human rights bodies could lead to the balkanization of doctrine, inconsistent enforcement, and patchy accountability. And, even more conceptually, differences among the regions could subvert the asserted universality of human rights norms. On the other hand, these problems may be more theoretical than real: there can be little doubt that the regional systems for the protection of human rights have played an historic role in legitimizing human rights as a proper matter for international concern and no doubt that the human rights advocate's toolkit includes the authority and the remedies offered by the regional organizations.

CHAPTER 3

MODULE 7A

THE EUROPEAN SYSTEMS

■ ■ ■

Orientation

The citizens of Europe live under a highly developed and integrated regime of regional human rights law, but there is no single system for the protection of human rights on the continent. There are instead at least three separate European institutions, with different but often overlapping memberships, with the protection of human rights at or near the center of their mandates. The work of these institutions covers a wide range of substantive rights and includes procedural innovations, like a right of individual access to a regional human rights court, the judgments of which are routinely respected by governments. In this module, we explore the doctrine and procedure of these various European institutions and the extent to which member states incorporate European human rights law into their domestic legal systems. Crucial as that understanding is to the contemporary human rights lawyer, it is equally important to understand the mixture of idealism and *realpolitik* that created these institutions in the first place. Certainly after the fall of the Soviet Union, newly independent states understood that their access to the economic benefits of joining "Europe" explicitly depended on their commitment to the protection of human rights. As a result, over time, human rights law has offered the only successful ideology of unification and reconciliation in Europe, a continent divided—and haunted—by wars and cycles of human rights abuse for centuries. Any observer with a decent sense of history might be shocked that there is now a meaningful regime of human rights law, stretching for thousands of miles from Iceland to the Russian Pacific, covering almost one billion people.

This chapter examines each of the three dominant European institutions for the protection of human rights:

(i) the *Council of Europe*, now with 47 members,[1] was established in Western Europe after World War II to defend human rights,

---

1. All membership data in this introduction are as of June 2008.

parliamentary democracy and the rule of law, by *inter alia* developing continent-wide agreements to standardize the law and legal practices across the continent. Headquartered in Strasbourg, the Council of Europe is now understood as the gateway to the European Union, *infra*, and has therefore grown rapidly since the demise of the Soviet Union and the rise of newly independent states in central and Eastern Europe. In addition to developing treaties like the European Convention for the Protection of Human Rights and Fundamental Freedoms ("European Convention"), which established the European Court of Human Rights, the Council of Europe has formulated over 200 treaties covering a full range of human rights concerns;[2]

(ii) the *European Union*, now with 27 members, was originally designed to facilitate economic and commercial integration in Western Europe by creating a customs union and a common market. The member states established various institutions to which they delegated authority over issues of joint interest to be resolved at the continental level, including *inter alia* the European *Commission*, headquartered in Brussels, independent of governments, with various regulatory powers; the European *Court of Justice* in Luxembourg ("ECJ"), assuring a measure of uniformity in the interpretation of European law in the various member states and assuring that governments and the EU institutions themselves abide by European law; and the European *Parliament* and the *Council* of the European Union, which through a complicated formula share power in the setting of policy and the adoption of European law. Although the human rights provisions of the early EU treaties were rudimentary, the EU has become a dominant actor in the harmonization of member states' domestic laws around a common human rights standard, and the ECJ now routinely applies international human rights law in its decisions;

(iii) the *Organization for Security and Cooperation in Europe*, now with 56 members including European states, Canada, and the United States, offers a forum for the diplomatic resolution of security issues, which are broadly conceived to include human rights, democracy, and the rule of law. The OSCE has developed a range of institutions for addressing conflicts with human rights components, but none is a court or court-equivalent. Human rights lawyers must be aware nevertheless of the pressure points offered by the OSCE in the identification and solution of abuses on a wide or otherwise destabilizing scale.

These institutions assure that the protection of human rights in Europe has not only a layered institutional structure but a cultural significance

---

2. *See* conventions.coe.int/Treaty/Commun/ListeTraites.asp?CM=8&CL=ENG. As shown elsewhere in this chapter, other regional systems for the protection of human rights, especially in Africa and the Americas, have developed law and expertise—especially with respect to peoples' rights, economic, social, and cultural rights, and various remedies—that dwarf developments in Europe.

as well. They give political legitimacy to the ability of one state to raise with another state an individual case or a situation concerning human rights.

Readings

THE COUNCIL OF EUROPE MACHINERY

DINAH SHELTON, THE BOUNDARIES OF HUMAN RIGHTS JURISDICTION IN EUROPE

13 DUKE J. COMP. & INT'L. L. 95, 96–109
(2003)

[In 1949], ten northern and western European countries[1] created the Council of Europe, the first post-war European regional organization. Europe had been the theater of the greatest atrocities of the Second World War and felt compelled to press for international human rights guarantees as part of its reconstruction. Faith in western European traditions of democracy, the rule of law and individual rights inspired belief that a regional system could be successful in avoiding future conflict and in stemming post-war revolutionary impulses backed by the Soviet Union.[2] The Statute of the Council provides that each Member State must "accept the principles of the rule of law and of the enjoyment by all persons within its jurisdiction of human rights and fundamental freedoms."[3] * * *

A year later, these same states, self-described as "like-minded and hav[ing] a common heritage of political traditions, ideals, freedom and the rule of law," agreed to take the "first steps for the collective enforcement of certain of the rights stated in the Universal Declaration (of Human Rights)" and adopted the Convention for the Protection of Human Rights and Fundamental Freedoms (hereinafter European Convention [or ECHR]).[4] Today, membership in the Council is *de facto* conditioned upon adherence to the European Convention and cooperation with its supervisory machinery,[5] a condition met by all of the [47]

---

1. The original Member States of the Council of Europe and drafters of the European Convention on Human Rights are Belgium, Denmark, France, Ireland, Italy, Luxembourg, Netherlands, Norway, Sweden and the United Kingdom.

2. In the preamble to the European Convention on Human Rights, the contracting parties declare that they are "reaffirming their profound belief in those Fundamental Freedoms which are the foundation of justice and peace in the world and are best maintained on the one hand by an effective political democracy and on the other by a common understanding and observance of the human rights upon which they depend." * * *

3. Statute of the Council of Europe, May 5, 1949, art. 3, E.T.S. No. 1, Gr. Brit. T.S. No. 51 (Cmnd. 8969).

4. On the origins and legislative history of the Convention, see A.H. ROBERTSON & J.G. MERRILLS, HUMAN RIGHTS IN EUROPE 1 (3rd ed. 1993); COUNCIL OF EUROPE, COLLECTED EDITION OF THE 'TRAVAUX PRÉPARATOIRES' OF THE EUROPEAN CONVENTION ON HUMAN RIGHTS (8 vols., 1975–85).

5. Vienna Declaration of the Heads of State and Government of the Council of Europe, Oct. 9, 1993, reprinted in D. HUBER, A DECADE WHICH MADE HISTORY: THE COUNCIL OF EUROPE 1989–1999 247

Member States.[6] In addition, accession requires free and fair elections based upon national suffrage, freedom of expression, protection of national minorities and observance of the principles of international law. Several new Member States also have entered into additional and specific commitments during the examination of their request for membership.

The drafters of the European Convention focused their attention primarily on developing control machinery to supervise implementation and to enforce the initially short list of guaranteed rights. * * * The European Convention initially established two institutions whose mandate was "to ensure the observance of the engagements undertaken by the High Contracting Parties:" the European Commission of Human Rights and the European Court of Human Rights. The former Commission and Court were replaced on November 1, 1998, with the entry into force of Protocol 11[7] and the inauguration of a new full-time Court. The European Convention also confers some supervisory functions relating to the enforcement of the rights it guarantees on the Committee of Ministers, the governing body of the Council of Europe. * * *

The Court today is composed "of a number of members equal to that of the High Contracting Parties" to the European Convention.[8] The judges are elected for a six-year renewable period by the Parliamentary Assembly[9] of the Council of Europe from a list of three nominees submitted by each Member State. The judges serve in their individual capacities and must be persons of "high moral character," who "possess the qualifications required for appointment to high judicial office or be persons of recognized competence."[10] The judges do not have to be nationals of the Member States of the Council of Europe. They serve full-time during their term and may not undertake any activity incompatible with their judicial functions. * * * The permanent Court has its

(1999). *See also* Declaration on Compliance with Commitments Accepted by Member States of the Council of Europe, adopted by the Comm. of Ministers on Nov. 10, 1994, reprinted in Council of Europe, Information Sheet No. 35, app. I, 146 (1995).

6. [As of 2008, forty-seven nations are members of the Council of Europe: Albania, Andorra, Armenia, Austria, Azerbaijan, Belgium, Bosnia and Herzegovina, Bulgaria, Croatia, Cyprus, Czech Republic, Denmark, Estonia, Finland, France, Georgia, Germany, Greece, Hungary, Iceland, Ireland, Italy, Latvia, Liechtenstein, Lithuania, Luxembourg, Malta, Moldova, Monaco, Montenegro, Netherlands, Norway, Poland, Portugal, Romania, Russian Federation, San Marino, Serbia and Montenegro, Slovakia, Slovenia, Spain, Sweden, Switzerland, "The former Yugoslav Republic of Macedonia," Turkey, Ukraine, and the United Kingdom.]

7. Protocol No. 11 to the European Convention for the Protection of Human Rights and Fundamental Freedoms, May 11, 1994 (Nov. 1, 1998), E.T.S. 155, reprinted in 33 I.L.M. 960 (1994). [hereinafter ECHR].

8. ECHR, *supra*, art. 20.

9. The Parliamentary Assembly is one of the Council of Europe's two main statutory organs and represents the main political tendencies in its Member States. The Assembly sees its role as primary in extending European co-operation to all democratic states throughout Europe. The Parliamentary Assembly's members and substitutes are elected or appointed by national parliaments of Council of Europe Member States from among their own parliamentarians. Each country has between 2 and 18 representatives depending on the size of its population. National delegations to the Assembly are supposed to ensure a fair representation of the political parties or groups in their parliaments.

10. ECHR, *supra*, art. 21(1).

seat in Strasbourg, also the seat of the Council of Europe, and judges are expected to live in the area. The Court has a Registry and legal secretaries to assist it. The Registrar is the chief clerk of the Court.

Although the European Convention initially created an independent Commission and Court, the drafters made the Court's jurisdiction optional. They also established, but again made optional, the world's first individual petition procedure for human rights violations. The "normal" procedure thus envisaged was one of inter-state complaints brought through the Commission to the Committee of Ministers. The Commission would meet in closed sessions, undertake fact-finding, attempt a friendly settlement of the matter, and report its findings to the Committee of Ministers for decision. Only the Commission or the state could refer a matter to the Court, if the state in question had accepted the Court's jurisdiction. Enforcement of judgments of the Court and decisions of the Committee of Ministers lay with the Committee itself, which could suspend a state from its rights of representation or ask it to withdraw from the Council for serious violations of its obligations.

During the intervening half century, this rather modest system has undergone evolutionary, sometimes revolutionary changes. The Council of Europe has adopted 13[11] protocols to the European Convention, and in the process expanded the list of guaranteed civil and political rights. The first Protocol added a right to property, a right to education and the undertaking by the Contracting Parties to hold free and secret elections at reasonable intervals.[12] Protocol No. 4 enlarged the list further by prohibiting deprivation of liberty for failure to comply with contractual obligations, by guaranteeing the right to liberty of movement, and by barring forced exile of nationals and the collective expulsion of aliens.[13] Protocol No. 6 abolished the death penalty except during wartime[14] and Protocol No. 7 requires states to accord aliens various due process safeguards before they may be expelled from a country where they reside.[15] The instrument also provides for rights of appeal in criminal proceedings, compensation in cases of miscarriage of justice, protection against double jeopardy, and equality of rights and responsibilities between spouses. Protocol No. 12 augments the non-discrimination guarantee in Convention Art. 14 by providing that "the enjoyment of any right set forth by law shall be secured without discrimination on any ground," adding that "no one shall be discrimi-

---

11. [Editors' note: There are now 14 protocols to the European Convention.]

12. Protocol No. 1 to the European Convention for the Protection of Human Rights and Fundamental Freedoms, adopted March 20, 1951, (entered into force May 18, 1954), E.T.S. 9.

13. Protocol No. 4 to the European Convention for the Protection of Human Rights and Fundamental Freedoms, Sept. 16, 1963, (entered into force May 2, 1968), E.T.S. 46.

14. Protocol No. 6 to the European Convention for the Protection of Human Rights and Fundamental Freedoms, April 28, 1983, (entered into force March 1, 1985), E.T.S. 114, reprinted in 22 I.L.M. 539 (1983).

15. Protocol No. 7 to the European Convention for the Protection of Human Rights and Fundamental Freedoms, Nov. 22, 1984, (entered into force Nov. 1, 1988), E.T.S. 117, reprinted in 24 I.L.M. 435 (1985).

nated against by any public authority."[16] Protocol No. 13, adopted by the Committee of Ministers [in] 2002, abolishes the death penalty under all circumstances.

Other protocols gradually enhanced the role and status of the individual before the Court and eliminated the discretion of Member States to accept the jurisdiction of the Court and the right of individual petition. In 1990, Protocol No. 9 enabled individuals to take cases to the Court in certain circumstances.[17] Protocol No. 11 fundamentally restructured the system, eliminating the Commission and providing the new full-time Court with compulsory jurisdiction over interstate and individual cases brought against Contracting Parties to the Convention. Today the states are locked into a system of collective responsibility for the protection of human rights, a system in which the jurisdiction of the Court provides the centerpiece. Pursuant to Article 34 of the Convention, the Court now may receive applications from "any person, nongovernmental organization or group of individuals claiming to be the victim of a violation ... of the rights set forth in the Convention or the protocols thereto."[18] * * *

CASE STUDY: FREE SPEECH UNDER THE EUROPEAN CONVENTION

JERSILD v. DENMARK
APPLICATION No. 36/1993/431/510
EURO. CT. H.R. SEPT. 23, 1994

Mr. Jens Olaf Jersild, a Danish national, is a journalist and lives in Copenhagen. He was at the time of the events giving rise to the present case, and still is, employed by Danmarks Radio (Danish Broadcasting Corporation, which broadcasts not only radio but also television programmes), assigned to its Sunday News Magazine. The latter is known as a serious television programme intended for a well-informed audience, dealing with a wide range of social and political issues, including xenophobia, immigration and refugees.

On 31 May 1985 the newspaper *Information* published an article describing the racist attitudes of members of a group of young people, calling themselves "the Greenjackets" at Osterbro in Copenhagen. In the light of this article, the editors of the Sunday News Magazine decided to produce a documentary on the Greenjackets. Subsequently the applicant contacted representatives of the group, inviting three of

---

16. Protocol No. 12 to the European Convention for the Protection of Human Rights and Fundamental Freedoms, Nov. 4, 2000, (not yet in force), E.T.S. 177.

17. Protocol No. 9 to the European Convention for the Protection of Human Rights and Fundamental Freedoms, Nov. 6, 1990, (entered into force Oct. 1, 1994), E.T.S. 140, reprinted in 30 I.L.M. 693 (1991).

18. ECHR, *supra*, art. 34.

them together with Mr. Per Axholt, a social worker employed at the local youth centre, to take part in a television interview. During the interview, which was conducted by the applicant, the three Greenjackets made abusive and derogatory remarks about immigrants and ethnic groups in Denmark. It lasted between five and six hours, of which between two and two-and-a-half hours were video-recorded. * * * The applicant subsequently edited and cut the film of the interview down to a few minutes. On 21 July 1985 this was broadcast by Danmarks Radio as a part of the Sunday News Magazine. The programme consisted of a variety of items, for instance on the martial law in South Africa, on the debate on profit-sharing in Denmark and on the late German writer Heinrich Böll. The transcript of the Greenjackets item reads as follows [(I): TV presenter; (A): the applicant; (G): one or other of the Green-jackets [*in italics*]]:

(I) In recent years, a great deal has been said about racism in Denmark. The papers are currently publishing stories about distrust and resentment directed against minorities. Who are the people who hate the minorities? Where do they come from? What is their mentality like? Mr. Jens Olaf Jersild has visited a group of extremist youths at Osterbro in Copenhagen.

(A) The flag on the wall is the flag of the Southern States from the American Civil War, but today it is also the symbol of racism, the symbol of the American movement, the Ku Klux Klan, and it shows what Lille Steen, Henrik and Nisse are. Are you a racist?

(G) *Yes, that's what I regard myself as. It's good being a racist. We believe Denmark is for the Danes.*

(A) Henrik, Lille Steen and all the others are members of a group of young people who live in Studsgardsgade, called STUDSEN, in Osterbro in Copenhagen. It is public housing, a lot of the inhabitants are unemployed and on social security; the crime rate is high. Some of the young people in this neighbourhood have already been involved in criminal activities and have already been convicted.

(G) *It was an ordinary armed robbery at a petrol station.*

(A) What did you do?

(G) *Nothing. I just ran into a petrol station with a . . . gun and made them give me some money. Then I ran out again. That's all.*

(A) What about you, what happened?

(G) *I don't wish to discuss that further.*

(A) But, was it violence?

(G) *Yes.*

(A) You have just come out of . . . you have been arrested, what were you arrested for?

(G) *Street violence.*

(A) What happened?

(G) *I had a little fight with the police together with some friends.*

(A) Does that happen often?

(G) *Yes, out here it does.*

(A) All in all, there are 20–25 young people from STUDSEN in the same group. They meet not far away from the public housing area near some old houses which are to be torn down. They meet here to reaffirm among other things their racism, their hatred of immigrants and their support for the Ku Klux Klan.

(G) *The Ku Klux Klan, that's something that comes from the States in the old days during—you know—the civil war and things like that, because the Northern States wanted that the niggers should be free human beings, man, they are not human beings, they are animals, right, it's completely wrong, man, the things that happened. People should be allowed to keep slaves, I think so anyway.*

(A) Because blacks are not human beings?

(G) *No, you can also see that from their body structure, man, big flat noses, with cauliflower ears, etc., man. Broad heads and very broad bodies, man, hairy, you are looking at a gorilla and compare it with an ape, man, then it is the same [behaviour], man, it's the same movements, long arms, man, long fingers etc., long feet.*

(A) A lot of people are saying something different. There are a lot of people who say, but . . .

(G) *Just take a picture of a gorilla, man, and then look at a nigger, it's the same body structure and everything, man, flat forehead and all kinds of things.*

(A) There are many blacks, for example in the USA, who have important jobs.

(G) *Of course, there is always someone who wants to show off, as if they are better than the white man, but in the long run, it's the white man who is better.*

(A) What does Ku Klux Klan mean to you?

(G) *It means a great deal, because I think what they do is right. A nigger is not a human being, it's an animal, that goes for all the other foreign workers as well, Turks, Yugoslavs and whatever they are called.*

(A) Henrik is 19 years old and on welfare. He lives in a rented room in Studsgardsgade. Henrik is one of the strongest supporters of the Klan, and he hates the foreign workers, "Perkerne" [a very derogatory word in Danish for immigrant workers].

(G) *They come up here, man, and sponge on our society. But we, we have enough problems in getting our social benefits, man, they just get it. Fuck, we can argue with those idiots up there at the social benefit office to get our money, man, they just get it, man, they are the first on the housing list, they get better flats than us, man, and some of our friends who have children, man, they are living in the worst slum, man, they can't even get a shower in their flat, man, then those "Perkere"-families, man, go up there with seven kids, man, and they just get an expensive flat, right there and then. They get everything paid, and things like that, that can't be right, man, Denmark is for the Danes, right? It is the fact that they are "Perkere", that's what we don't like, right, and we don't like their mentality–I mean they can damn well, I mean ... what's it called ... I mean if they feel like speaking Russian in their homes, right, then it's okay, but what we don't like is when they walk around in those Zimbabwe-clothes and then speak this hula-hula language in the street, and if you ask them something or if you get into one of their taxis then they say: I don't know where it is, you give directions right.*

(A) It is not so that perhaps you are a bit envious that some of the "Perkere" as you call them have their own shops, and cars, they can make ends ...

(G) *It's drugs they are selling, man, half of the prison population in "Vestre" are in there because of drugs, man, half of those in Vestre prison anyway, they are the people who are serving time for dealing drugs or something similar. They are in there, all the "Perkere", because of drugs, right. [That] must be enough, what's it called, there should not be drugs here in this country, but if it really has to be smuggled in, I think we should do it ourselves, I mean, I think it's unfair that those foreigners come up here to ... what's it called ... make Denmark more drug dependent and things like that. We have painted their doors and hoped that they would get fed up with it, so that they would soon leave, and jumped on their cars and thrown paint in their faces when they were lying in bed sleeping.*

(A) What was it you did with that paint–why paint?

(G) *Because it was white paint, I think that suited them well, that was the intended effect.*

(A) You threw paint through the windows of an immigrant family?

(G) *Yes.*

(A) What happened?

(G) *He just got it in his face, that's all. Well, I think he woke up, and then he came out and shouted something in his hula-hula language.*

(A) Did he report it to the police?

(G) *I don't know if he did, I mean, he won't get anywhere by doing that.*

(A) Why not?

(G) *I don't know, it's just kid's stuff, like other people throwing water in people's faces, he got paint in his. They can't make anything out of that.*

(A) Per Axholt, known as "Pax" [(P)], is employed in the youth centre in Studsgardsgade. He has worked there for several years, but many give up a lot sooner because of the tough environment. Per Axholt feels that the reasons why the young people are persecuting the immigrants is that they are themselves powerless and disappointed. What do you think they would say that they want, if you asked them?

(P) Just what you and I want. Some control over their lives, work which may be considered decent and which they like, a reasonable economic situation, a reasonably functioning family, a wife or a husband and some children, a reasonable middle-class life such as you and I have.

(A) They do many things which are sure to prevent them from getting it.

(P) That is correct.

(A) Why do you think they do this?

(P) Because they have nothing better to do. They have been told over a long period that the means by which to achieve success is money. They won't be able to get money legitimately, so often they try to obtain it through criminal activity. Sometimes they succeed, sometimes not, and that's why we see a lot of young people in that situation go to prison, because it doesn't work.

(A) How old were you when you started your criminal activities?

(G) *I don't know, about 14 I guess.*

(A) What did you do?

(G) *The first time, I can't remember, I don't know, burglary.*

(A) Do you have what one might call a criminal career?

(G) *I don't know if you can call it that.*

(A) You committed your first crime when you were 14.

(G) *Well, you can put it that way, I mean, if that is a criminal career. If you have been involved in crime since the age of 15 onwards, then I guess you can say I've had a criminal career.*

(A) Will you tell me about some of the things you have done?

(G) *No, not really. It's been the same over and over again. There has been pinching of videos, where the "Perkere" have been our customers, so they have money. If people want to be out here and have a nice time and be racists and drink beer, and have fun, then it's quite obvious you don't want to sit in the slammer.*

(A) But is the threat of imprisonment something that really deters people from doing something illegal?

(G) *No, it's not prison, that doesn't frighten people.*

(A) Is that why you hear stories about people from out here fighting with knives etc., night after night. Is the reason for this the fact that they are not afraid of the police getting hold of them?

(G) *Yes, nothing really comes of it, I mean, there are no bad consequences, so probably that's why. For instance fights and stabbings and smashing up things ... If you really get into the joint it would be such a ridiculously small sentence, so it would be, I mean . . . usually we are released the next day. Last time we caused some trouble over at the pub, they let us out the next morning. Nothing really comes of it. It doesn't discourage us, but there were five of us, who just came out and then we had a celebration for the last guy, who came out yesterday, they probably don't want to go in again for some time so they probably won't commit big crimes again.*

(A) You would like to move back to Studsgardsgade where you grew up, but we know for sure that it's an environment with a high crime rate. Would you like your child to grow up like you?

(G) *No, and I don't think she will. Firstly, because she is a girl, statistics show that the risk is not that high, I mean they probably don't do it, but you don't have to be a criminal because you live in an environment with a high crime rate. I just wouldn't accept it, if she was mugging old women and stealing their handbags.*

(A) What if she was among those beating up the immigrants etc. What then?

(G) *That would be okay. I wouldn't have anything against that. . . .*

(I) We will have to see if the mentality of this family changes in the next generation. Finally, we would like to say that groups of young people like this one in STUDSEN at Osterbro, have been formed elsewhere in Copenhagen.

Following the programme no complaints were made to the Radio Council, which had competence in such matters, or to Danmarks Radio but the Bishop of Alborg complained to the Minister of Justice. After undertaking investigations the Public Prosecutor instituted criminal proceedings in the City Court of Copenhagen against the three youths interviewed by the applicant, charging them with a violation of Article 266(b) of the Penal Code. * * *

The applicant was charged, under Article 266(b) in conjunction with Article 23, with aiding and abetting the three youths; the same charge was brought against the head of the news section of Danmarks Radio, Mr. Lasse Jensen. In the City Court, counsel for the applicant and Mr. Jensen called for their acquittal. He argued that the conduct of the applicant and Mr. Jensen could in no way be compared to that of the other three defendants, with whose views they did not sympathise. They sought merely to provide a realistic picture of a social problem; in fact the programme only provoked resentment and aroused pity in respect of the three other defendants, who had exposed themselves to ridicule on their own terms. Accordingly, it was by no means the intention of Danmarks Radio to persuade others to subscribe to the same views as the Greenjackets, rather the contrary. Under the relevant law a distinction had to be drawn between the persons who made the statements and the programme editors, the latter enjoying a special freedom of expression. Having at that time a broadcasting monopoly, Danmarks Radio was under a duty to impart all opinions of public interest in a manner that reflected the speaker's way of expressing himself. The public also had an interest in being informed of notoriously bad social attitudes, even those which were unpleasant. The programme was broadcast in the context of a public debate which had resulted in press comments, for instance in Information, and was simply an honest report on the realities of the youths in question. Counsel, referring inter alia to the above-mentioned article in Information, also pointed to the fact that no consistent prosecution policy had been followed in cases of this nature.

On 24 April 1987 the City Court convicted the three youths, one of them for having stated that "niggers" and "foreign workers" were "animals", and two of them for their assertions in relation to drugs and "Perkere". The applicant was convicted of aiding and abetting them, as was Mr. Jensen, in his capacity as programme controller; they were sentenced to pay day-fines (dagsboder) totalling 1,000 and 2,000 Danish kroner, respectively, or alternatively to five days' imprisonment (hoefte). As regards the applicant, the City Court found that, following the article in *Information* of 31 May 1985, he had visited the Greenjackets and after a conversation with Mr. Axholt, amongst others, agreed that the three youths should participate in a television programme. The object of the programme had been to demonstrate the attitude of the Greenjackets to the racism at Osterbro, previously mentioned in the article in *Information*, and to show their social background. Accordingly, so the City Court held, the applicant had himself taken the initiative of making the television programme and, further, he had been well aware in advance that discriminatory statements of a racist nature were likely to be made during the interview. The interview had lasted several hours, during which beer, partly paid for by Danmarks Radio, was consumed. In this connection the applicant had encouraged the Greenjackets to express their racist views, which in so far as they were broadcast on television, in itself constituted a breach of Article 266(b) of the Penal Code. The statements were broadcast without any counter-balancing comments, after the recordings had been edited by the applicant. He was accordingly guilty of aiding and abetting the violation of Article 266(b).

The applicant and Mr. Jensen, but not the three Greenjackets, appealed against the City Court's judgment to the High Court of Eastern Denmark. They essentially reiterated the submissions made before the City Court and, in addition, the applicant explained that, although he had suspected that the Greenjackets' statements were punishable, he had refrained from omitting these from the programme, considering it crucial to show their actual attitude. He assumed that they were aware that they might incur criminal liability by making the statements and had therefore not warned them of this fact.

By judgment of 16 June 1988 the High Court, by five votes to one, dismissed the appeal. The dissenting member was of the view that, although the statements by the Greenjackets constituted offences under Article 266(b) of the Penal Code, the applicant and Mr. Jensen had not transgressed the bounds of the freedom of speech to be enjoyed by television and other media, since the object of the programme was to inform about and animate public discussion on the particular racist attitudes and social background of the youth group in question.

[T]he applicant and Mr. Jensen appealed from the High Court judgment to the Supreme Court which by four votes to one dismissed the appeal in a judgment of 13 February 1989. The majority held:

> The defendants have caused the publication of the racist statements made by a narrow circle of persons and thereby made those persons liable to punishment and have thus, as held by the City Court and the High Court, violated Article 266(b) in conjunction with Article 23 of the Penal Code. [We] do not find that an acquittal of the defendants could be justified on the ground of freedom of expression in matters of public interest as opposed to the interest in the protection against racial discrimination. [We] therefore vote in favour of confirming the judgment [appealed from].
>
> * * *

When the Supreme Court has rendered judgment in a case raising important issues of principle it is customary that a member of the majority publishes a detailed and authoritative statement of the reasons for the judgment. * * * As regards the conviction of the applicant and Mr. Jensen, the majority had attached importance to the fact that they had caused the racist statements to be made public. The applicant's item had not been a direct report on a meeting. He had himself contacted the three youths and caused them to make assertions such as those previously made in *Information*, which he knew of and probably expected them to repeat. He had himself cut the recording of the interview, lasting several hours, down to a few minutes containing the crude comments. The statements, which would hardly have been punishable under Article 266(b) of the Penal Code had they not been made to a wide circle of people, became clearly punishable as they were broadcast on television on the applicant's initiative and with Mr. Jensen's approval. It was therefore beyond doubt that they had aided and abetted the dissemination of the statements. Acquitting the applicant and Mr. Jensen could only be justified by reasons clearly outweighing the wrongfulness of their actions. In this connection, the interest in protecting those grossly insulted by the statements had to be weighed up against that of informing the public of the statements. Whilst it is desirable to allow the press the best possible conditions for reporting on society, press freedom cannot be unlimited since freedom of expression is coupled with responsibilities.

In striking a balance between the various interests involved, the majority had regard to the fact that the statements, which were brought to a wide circle of people, consisted of series of inarticulate, defamatory remarks and insults spoken by members of an insignificant group whose opinions could hardly be of interest to many people. Their news or information value was not such as to justify their dissemination and therefore did not warrant acquitting the defendants. This did not mean that extremist views could not be reported in the press, but such reports must be carried out in a more balanced and comprehensive manner than was the case in the television programme in question. Direct reports from meetings which were a matter of public interest should also be permitted. The minority, on the other hand, considered that the right to information overrode the interests protected by Article 266(b) of the Penal Code.

Relevant domestic law

A. *The Penal Code.* At the relevant time Article 266(b) of the Penal Code provided:

> Any person who, publicly or with the intention of disseminating it to a wide circle ("videre kreds") of people, makes a statement, or other communication, threatening, insulting or degrading a group of persons on account of their race, colour, national or ethnic origin or belief shall be liable to a fine or to simple detention or to imprisonment for a term not exceeding two years.

Article 23, paragraph 1, reads:

> A provision establishing a criminal offence shall apply to any person who has assisted the commission of the offence by instigation, advice or action. The punishment may be reduced if the person in question only intended to give assistance of minor importance or to strengthen an intent already resolved or if the offence has not been completed or an intended assistance failed.

B. *The 1991 Media Liability Act.* The 1991 Media Liability Act, which entered into force * * * after the events giving rise to the present case, lays down rules inter alia on criminal liability in respect of television broadcasts. Section 18 provides:

> A person making a statement during a non-direct broadcast (forskudt udsendelse) shall be responsible for the statement under general statutory provisions, unless:
>
> (1) the identity of the person concerned does not appear from the broadcast; or
>
> (2) [that person] has not consented to the statement being broadcast; or
>
> (3) [he or she] has been promised that [he or she] may take part [in the broadcast] without [his or her] identity being disclosed and reasonable precautions have been taken to this effect.
>
> In the situations described in paragraph 1, sub-paragraphs (1) to (3) above, the editor is responsible for the contents of the statements even where a violation of the law has occurred without intent or negligence on his part. * * *

Pursuant to section 22:

> A person who reads out or in any other manner conveys a text or statement, is not responsible for the contents of that text or statement.

Instruments of the United Nations

Provisions relating to the prohibition of racial discrimination and the prevention of propaganda of racist views and ideas are to be found in a number of international instruments, for example the 1945 United Nations Charter, the 1948 Universal Declaration of Human Rights and the 1966 International Covenant on Civil and Political Rights. The most directly relevant treaty is the 1965 International Convention on the Elimination of All Forms of Racial Discrimination ("the UN Convention"), which has been ratified by a large majority of the Contracting States to the European Convention, including Denmark. Articles 4 and 5 of that Convention provide:

Article 4

States Parties condemn all propaganda and all organizations which are based on ideas or theories of superiority of one race or group of persons of one colour or ethnic origin, or which attempt to justify or promote racial hatred and discrimination in any form, and undertake to adopt immediate and positive measures designed to eradicate all incitement to, or acts of, such discrimination and, to this end, with due regard to the principles embodied in the Universal Declaration of Human Rights and the rights expressly set forth in Article 5 of this Convention, *inter alia*:

a.   shall declare an offence punishable by law all dissemination of ideas based on racial superiority or hatred, incitement to racial discrimination, as well as acts of violence or incitement to such acts against any race or group of persons of another colour or ethnic origin, and also the provision of any assistance to racist activities, including the financing thereof; * * *

Article 5

In compliance with the fundamental obligation laid down in ... this Convention, States Parties undertake to prohibit and to eliminate racial discrimination in all its forms and to guarantee the right of everyone, without distinction as to race, colour, or national or ethnic origin, to equality before the law, notably in the enjoyment of the following rights: ... (d) ... viii. the right to freedom of opinion and expression; ...

The effects of the "due regard" clause in Article 4 ha[ve] given rise to differing interpretations and the UN Committee on the Elimination of Racial Discrimination ("the UN Committee"—set up to supervise the implementation of the UN Convention) was divided in its comments on the applicant's conviction. The present case had been presented by the

Danish Government in a report to the UN Committee. Whilst some members welcomed it as "the clearest statement yet, in any country, that the right to protection against racial discrimination took precedence over the right to freedom of expression", other members considered that "in such cases the facts needed to be considered in relation to both rights". * * *

JUDGMENT

The applicant maintained that his conviction and sentence for having aided and abetted the dissemination of racist remarks violated his right to freedom of expression within the meaning of Article 10 of the [European] Convention, which reads:

> 1. Everyone has the right to freedom of expression. This right shall include freedom to hold opinions and to receive and impart information and ideas without interference by public authority and regardless of frontiers. This Article shall not prevent States from requiring the licensing of broadcasting, television or cinema enterprises.

> 2. The exercise of these freedoms, since it carries with it duties and responsibilities, may be subject to such formalities, conditions, restrictions or penalties as are prescribed by law and are necessary in a democratic society, in the interests of national security, territorial integrity or public safety, for the prevention of disorder or crime, for the protection of health or morals, for the protection of the reputation or rights of others, for preventing the disclosure of information received in confidence, or for maintaining the authority and impartiality of the judiciary.

The Government contested this contention whereas the Commission[1] upheld it.

It is common ground that the measures giving rise to the applicant's case constituted an interference with his right to freedom of expression. It is moreover undisputed that this interference was "prescribed by law", the applicant's conviction being based on Articles 266(b) and 23(1) of the Penal Code. In this context, the Government pointed out that the former provision had been enacted in order to comply with the UN Convention. The Government's argument, as the Court understands it, is that, whilst Article 10 of the Convention is applicable, the Court, in applying paragraph 2, should consider that the relevant provisions of the Penal Code are to be interpreted and applied in an extensive manner, in accordance with the rationale of the UN Convention. In other words, Article 10 should not be interpreted in such a way as to limit, derogate from or destroy the right to protection against

---

1. [Editors' note: At the time of this decision (*i.e.*, prior to Protocol 11), individual petitions under the European Convention were filed with the European Commission, which in limited circumstances could then bring the cases to the European Court of Human Rights. In this case, the Commission ruled by twelve votes to four that Denmark had violated Article 10 of the European Convention by convicting the journalists. It then initiated these proceedings before the Court.]

racial discrimination under the UN Convention. Finally it is uncontested that the interference pursued a legitimate aim, namely the "protection of the reputation of rights of others".

The only point in dispute is whether the measures were "necessary in a democratic society". The applicant and the Commission were of the view that, notwithstanding Denmark's obligations as a Party to the UN Convention, a fair balance had to be struck between the "protection of the reputation or rights of others" and the applicant's right to impart information. According to the applicant, such a balance was envisaged in a clause contained in Article 4 of the UN Convention to the effect that "due regard" should be had to "the principles in the Universal Declaration of Human Rights and the rights ... in Article 5 of [the UN] Convention". The clause had been introduced at the drafting stage because of concern among a number of States that the requirement in Article 4(a) that "States Parties ... shall declare an offence punishable by law all dissemination of ideas based on racial superiority or hatred" was too sweeping and could give rise to difficulties with regard to other human rights, in particular the right to freedom of opinion and expression. * * *

The applicant and the Commission emphasised that, taken in the context of the broadcast as a whole, the offending remarks had the effect of ridiculing their authors rather than promoting their racist views. The overall impression of the programme was that it sought to draw public attention to a matter of great public concern, namely racism and xenophobia. The applicant had deliberately included the offensive statements in the programme, not with the intention of disseminating racist opinions, but in order to counter them through exposure. The applicant pointed out that he tried to show, analyse and explain to his viewers a new phenomenon in Denmark at the time, that of violent racism practised by inarticulate and socially disadvantaged youths. Joined by the Commission, he considered that the broadcast could not have had any significant detrimental effects on the "reputation or rights of others". The interests in protecting the latter were therefore outweighed by those of protecting the applicant's freedom of expression. In addition the applicant alleged that had the 1991 Media Liability Act been in force at the relevant time he would not have faced prosecution since under the Act it is in principle only the author of a punishable statement who may be liable. This undermined the Government's argument that his conviction was required by the UN Convention and "necessary" within the meaning of Article 10.

The Government contended that the applicant had edited the Greenjackets item in a sensationalist rather than informative manner and that its news or information value was minimal. Television was a powerful medium and a majority of Danes normally viewed the news programme in which the item was broadcasted. Yet the applicant, knowing that they would incur criminal liability, had encouraged the Greenjackets to make racist statements and had failed to counter these statements in the programme. It was too subtle to assume that viewers would not take the remarks at their face value. No weight could be attached to the fact that the programme had given rise to only a few complaints, since, due to lack of information and insufficient knowledge of the Danish language and even fear of reprisals by violent racists, victims of the insulting comments were likely to be dissuaded from complaining. The applicant had thus failed to fulfil the "duties and responsibilities" incumbent on him as a television journalist. The fine imposed upon him was at the lower end of the scale of sanctions applicable to Article 266(b) offences and was therefore not likely to deter any journalist from contributing to public discussion on racism and xenophobia; it only had the effect of a public reminder that racist expressions are to be taken seriously and cannot be tolerated.

The Government moreover disputed that the matter would have been dealt with differently had the 1991 Media Liability Act been in force at the material time. The rule that only the author of a punishable statement may incur liability was subject to exceptions; how the applicant's case would have been considered under the 1991 Act was purely a matter of speculation. The Government stressed that at all three levels the Danish courts, which were in principle better placed than the European Court to evaluate the effects of the programme, had carried out a careful balancing exercise of all the interests involved. The review effected by those courts had been similar to that carried out under Article 10; their decisions fell within the margin of appreciation to be left to the national authorities and corresponded to a pressing social need.

The Court would emphasise at the outset that it is particularly conscious of the vital importance of combating racial discrimination in all its forms and manifestations. It may be true, as has been suggested by the applicant, that as a result of recent events the awareness of the dangers of racial discrimination is sharper today than it was a decade ago, at the material time. Nevertheless, the issue was already then of general importance, as is illustrated for instance by the fact that the UN Convention dates from 1965. Consequently, the object and purpose pursued by the UN Convention are of great weight in determining whether the applicant's conviction, which—as the Government have stressed—was based on a provision enacted in order to ensure Denmark's compliance with the UN Convention, was "necessary" within the meaning of Article 10(2).

In the second place, Denmark's obligations under Article 10 must be interpreted, to the extent possible, so as to be reconcilable with its obligations under the UN Convention. In this respect it is not for the Court to interpret the "due regard" clause in Article 4 of the UN Convention, which is open to various constructions. The Court is however of the opinion that its interpretation of Article 10 of the European Convention in the present case is compatible with Denmark's obligations under the UN Convention.

A significant feature of the present case is that the applicant did not make the objectionable statements himself but assisted in their dissemination in his capacity of television journalist responsible for a news programme of Danmarks Radio. In assessing whether his conviction and sentence were "necessary", the Court will therefore have regard to the principles established in its case law relating to the role of the press[.]

The Court reiterates that freedom of expression constitutes one of the essential foundations of a democratic society and that the safeguards to be afforded to the press are of particular importance. Whilst the press must not overstep the bounds set, *inter alia*, in the interest of "the protection of the reputation and right of others", it is nevertheless incumbent on it to impart information and ideas of public interest. Not only does the press have the task of imparting such information and ideas: the public also has a right to receive them. Were it otherwise, the press would be unable to play its vital role of "public watchdog". Although formulated primarily with regard to the print media, these principles doubtless apply also to the audio-visual media.

In considering the "duties and responsibilities" of a journalist, the potential impact of the medium concerned is an important factor and it is commonly acknowledged that the audio-visual media have often a much more immediate and powerful effect than the print media[.] The audio-visual media have means of conveying through images meanings which the print media are not able to impart.

At the same time, the methods of objective and balanced reporting may vary considerably, depending among other things on the media in question. It is not for this Court, nor for the national courts for that matter, to substitute their own views for those of the press as to what technique of reporting should be adopted by journalists. In this context the Court recalls that Article 10 protects not only the substance of the ideas and information expressed, but also the form in which they are conveyed.

The Court will look at the interference complained of in the light of the case as a whole and determine whether the reasons adduced by the national authorities to justify it are relevant and sufficient and whether the means employed were proportionate to the legitimate aim pursued. In doing so the Court has to satisfy itself that the national authorities did apply standards which were in conformity with the principles embodied in Article 10 and, moreover, that they based themselves on an acceptable assessment of the relevant facts. The Court's assessment will have regard to the manner in which the Greenjackets feature was prepared, its contents, the context in which it was broadcast and the purpose of the programme. Bearing in mind the obligations on States under the UN Convention and other international instruments to take effective measures to eliminate all forms of racial discrimination and to prevent and combat racist doctrines and practices, an important factor in the Court's evaluation will be whether the item in question, when considered as a whole, appeared from an objective point of view to have had as its purpose the propagation of racist views and ideas.

The national courts laid considerable emphasis on the fact that the applicant had himself taken the initiative of preparing the Greenjackets feature and that he not only knew in advance that racist statements were likely to be made during the interview but also had encouraged such statements. He had edited the programme in such a way as to include the offensive assertions. Without his involvement, the remarks would not have been disseminated to a wide circle of people and would thus not have been punishable. The Court is satisfied that these were relevant reasons for the purposes of paragraph 2 of Article 10.

On the other hand, as to the contents of the Greenjackets item, it should be noted that the TV presenter's introduction started by a reference to recent public discussion and press comments on racism in Denmark, thus inviting the viewer to see the programme in that context. He went on to announce that the object of the programme was to address aspects of the problem, by identifying certain racist individuals and by portraying their mentality and social background. There is no reason to doubt that the ensuing interviews fulfilled that aim. Taken as a whole, the feature could not objectively have appeared to have as its purpose the propagation of racist views and ideas. On the contrary, it clearly sought—by means of an interview—to expose, analyse and explain this particular group of youths, limited and frustrated by their social situation, with criminal records and violent attitudes, thus dealing with specific aspects of a matter that already then was of great public concern.

The Supreme Court held that the news or information value of the feature were not such as to justify the dissemination of the offensive remarks. However, * * * the Court sees no cause to question the Sunday News Magazine staff members' own appreciation of the news or information value of the impugned item, which formed the basis for their decisions to produce and broadcast it. Furthermore, it must be borne in mind that the item was broadcast as a part of a serious Danish news programmes and was intended for a well-informed audience.

The Court is not convinced by the argument, also stressed by the national courts, that the Greenjackets item was presented without any attempt to counterbalance the extremist views expressed. Both the TV presenter's introduction and the applicant's conduct during the interviews clearly dissociated him from the persons interviewed, for example by describing them as members of "a group of extremist youths" who supported the Klu Klux Klan and by referring to the criminal records of some of them. The applicant also rebutted some of the racist statements for instance by recalling that there were black people who had important jobs. It should finally not be forgotten that, taken as a whole, the filmed portrait surely conveyed the meaning that the racist statements were part of a generally anti-social attitude of the Greenjackets. Admittedly the item did not explicitly recall the immorality, dangers and unlawfulness of the promotion of racial hatred and of ideas of superiority of one race. However, in view of the above-mentioned counter-balancing elements and the natural limitations on spelling out such elements in a short item within a longer programme as well as the journalist's discretion as to the form of expression used, the Court does not consider the absence of such precautionary reminders to be relevant.

News reporting based on interviews, whether edited or not, constitutes one of the most important means whereby the press is able to play its vital role of "public watchdog." The punishment of a journalist for assisting in the dissemination of statements made by another person in an interview would seriously hamper the contribution of the press to discussion of matters of public interest and should not be envisaged unless there are particularly strong reasons for doing so. In this regard the Court does not accept the Government's argument that the limited nature of the fine is relevant; what matters is that the journalist was convicted.

There can be no doubt that the remarks in respect of which the Greenjackets were convicted were more than insulting to members of the targeted groups and did not enjoy the protection of Article 10. However, even having regard to the manner in which the applicant prepared the Greenjackets item, it has not been shown that, considered as a whole, the feature was such as to justify also his conviction of, and punishment for, a criminal offence under the Penal Code.

It is moreover undisputed that the purpose of the applicant in compiling the broadcast in question was not racist. Although he relied on this in the domestic proceedings, it does not appear from the reasoning in the relevant judgments that they took such a factor into account. Having regard to the foregoing, the reasons adduced in support of the applicant's conviction and sentence were not sufficient to establish convincingly that the interference thereby occasioned with the enjoyment of his right to freedom of expression was "necessary in a democratic society"; in particular the means employed were disproportionate to the aim of protecting "the reputation or rights of others". Accordingly the measures gave rise to a breach of Article 10 of the Convention. * * *

For these reasons, THE COURT

1. Holds by 12 votes to seven that there has been a violation of Article 10 of the Convention;

2. Holds by 17 votes to two that Denmark is to pay the applicant, within three months, 1,000 (one thousand) Danish kroner in compensation for pecuniary damage; and, for costs and expenses; * * *

3. Dismisses unanimously the remainder of the claim for just satisfaction.

NOTES AND QUESTIONS ON JERSILD

1. *Damages.* Jersild asked the Court for "just satisfaction" under Article 50 of the European Convention, according to which:

> If the Court finds that a decision or a measure taken by a legal authority or any other authority of a High Contracting Party, is completely or partially in conflict with the obligations arising from the * * * Convention, and if the internal law of the said Party allows only partial reparation to be made for the consequences of this decision or measure, the decision of the Court shall, if necessary, afford just satisfaction to the injured party.

The Court awarded 1000 Dkr as reimbursement for the fine that had been imposed upon him, and certain costs and expenses. As to his request for 20,000 Dkr in compensation for non-pecuniary damage, and specifically the damage to his professional reputation, the Court determined that the finding of a violation of Article 10 constituted adequate just satisfaction.

2. *Reconciling freedom and respect.* How can the freedom of expression protected in Article 10 of the European Convention be reconciled with Article 4 of the Convention on the Elimination of All Forms of Racial Discrimination, which prohibits the dissemination of ideas based on racial superiority or hatred? In answering that question (and judging from the Court's analysis in *Jersild*), how relevant is the journalist's subjective intent in disseminating the statements? How relevant is the fact that the journalist's fine in Denmark was relatively small? Note also that the Court found significance in the fact that the program was intended for a sophisticated and well-informed television audience. Would the result be the same if the program had aired on a channel dominated by "reality shows" or programs intended for a younger or less-educated audience?

3. *Subsidiarity and the "margin of appreciation."* *Jersild* demonstrates that primary responsibility for enforcing the rights of the Convention falls on the individual states themselves. The Convention offers "machinery of last resort" that is secondary (or "subsidiary") to national protection. In fact, by far the most common reason that a complaint under the Convention goes nowhere is that there are no grounds for invoking *international* remedies given the protections assured under *domestic* law. The Convention regime includes a measure of structural deference to the national authorities' interpretations of their domestic law under the international standard. In *Jersild*, three levels of Danish courts had all agreed on the effects of the program and had carefully balanced the interests involved. According to the Danish government, these decisions fell within the *margin of appreciation* to be left to the national authorities. One of the dissents in *Jersild* rests on this ground, and, though the argument did not prevail in the majority on these facts, it was plainly sound in its premise.

By contrast, in *Handyside v. United Kingdom*, 1 Eur. H.R. Rep. 737 (1976), the ECHR endorsed the British government's censorship of a book on the grounds that it was obscene and destructive of the morals of adolescents. Because there was no unified European conception of morals, the Court had to defer to the primary state's decisions: "By reason of their direct and continuous contact with the vital forces of their countries, State authorities are in principle in a better position than the international judge to give an opinion on the exact content of these requirements as well as on the 'necessity' of a 'restriction' or 'penalty' intended to meet them." *Id.* ¶ 48.

Admittedly, the margin of appreciation can vary with context: there is limited deference to regulations or policies that impinge on the most intimate aspects of private life (like sexual orientation and identity) and greater discretion in matters affecting national security. But *Handyside* and *Jersild* are both freedom-of-expression cases. Why did the margin of appreciation "work" in one case and not the other?

4. *The effects of the margin of appreciation.* Does the very existence of a margin of appreciation in international adjudication undermine the universality of human rights? *See* Eyal Benvenisti, *Margin of Appreciation, Consensus, and Universal Standards*, 31 N.Y.U. J. INT'L L. & POL. 843, 843 (1999) ("each society is entitled to certain latitude in resolving the inherent conflicts between individual rights and national interests or among different moral convictions"). Do we need to distinguish between a universal "core" understanding of rights and a penumbra of state-to-state difference at the margins of a right? As a lawyer, how would you go about proving what was at the "core" and what was at the "margin"?

5. *Imagining a contrary result in Jersild.* Seven judges, in two separate opinions, dissented in *Jersild*. *See Jersild v. Denmark*, Application No. 36/1993/431/510 (Euro. Ct. H.R. 1994)(Joint Dissenting Opinions of Judges Ryssdal, Bernhardt, Spielman and Loizou, and of Judges Gölcüklü, Russo and Valticos). Even if you agree with the result in *Jersild*–indeed *especially* if you agree with the result in *Jersild*–try to outline the most persuasive human rights arguments under the Convention for the dissent.

6. *The right of individual petition.* Protocol 11 made the power of individual petition compulsory and continent-wide, and so, for the first time in history, 800 million people have direct access to an international court for the resolution of human rights complaints against their own or any other government that is a party to the treaty.

7. *Hate speech.* The *Jersild* decision is about the rights of the press to report the racist statements made by others. Why do you suppose the underlying right of the Greenjackets to express hateful opinions was not at issue? Would their opinions be protected under the First Amendment to the Constitution of the United States? *See Virginia v. Black*, 538 U.S. 343 (2003). *Dambrot v. Cent. Mich. Univ.*, 55 F.3d 1177 (6th Cir. 1995); *Levin v. Harelston*, 966 F.2d 85 (2d Cir. 1992); *IOTA XI Chapter of Sigma*

Chi Fraternity v. George Mason Univ., 993 F.2d 386 (4th Cir. 1993). *See generally* Harold Hongju Koh, *On American Exceptionalism*, 55 STAN. L. REV. 1479, 1483 (2003) ("the U.S. First Amendment is far more protective than other countries' laws of hate speech, libel, commercial speech, and publication of national security information."); Mari Matsuda, *Public Responses to Racist Speech: Considering the Victim's Story*, 87 MICH. L. REV. 2320 (1989). In this connection, note that Article 20 of the International Covenant on Civil and Political Rights bans propaganda for war as well as "national, racial or religious hatred that constitutes incitement to discrimination, hostility or violence." In giving its advice and consent to the ratification of the Covenant, the Senate adopted a reservation "[t]hat Article 20 does not ... restrict the right of free speech and association protected by the Constitution and laws of the United States." 138 CONG. REC. at S4781, S4783 (1992); 1992 WL 65154. Why are free speech rights so different in Europe and the United States? Does the difference undermine the inference of a customary international norm of free speech?

8. *The culture of compliance*. It is generally asserted that the members of the Council of Europe routinely comply with the decisions of the European Court of Human Rights, as they are obliged to do under Article 53 of the European Convention ("[t]he High Contracting Parties undertake to abide by the decision of the Court in any case to which they are parties."). Acknowledging that the remedies ordered by the Court can vary from case to case, the compliance record over time is remarkable and consistent. It includes the payment of damages or restitution, but it also includes more far-reaching remedies: the modification of criminal records; the acceleration of administrative and judicial proceedings; and the repeal or revision of existing national legislation. *Norris v. Ireland*, [1988] ECHR 10581/83 (Ireland repealed its laws prohibiting gay sex between men as a result of the ECHR decision); *Ireland v. United Kingdom* [1978] ECHR 5310/71 (the United Kingdom revised its national security measures against terrorists). The United Kingdom severely curtailed corporal punishment in schools, to the extent that corporal punishment would be inhuman or degrading, largely as a result of ECtHR decisions such as *Case of Campbell and Cosans* (1982). *See generally* Douglass Cassell, *International Human Rights Law in Practice: Does International Human Rights Law Make a Difference?* 2 CHI. J. INT'L L. 121, 132 n. 34–38 (2001). Two prominent skeptics have argued that the assertedly high rate of compliance by states with decisions of the ECHR is difficult to substantiate. Eric A. Posner & John C. Yoo, *Judicial Independence in International Tribunals*, 93 CALIF. L. REV. 1, 65 (2005). But, at its website, the Court maintains a list of measures adopted by states in compliance with the Court's judgments (www.coe.int).

The overwhelming consistency with which "loser" states comply with the Court's judgments is difficult to explain in a world that takes a simplistic view of states' self-interest. What accounts for the culture of compliance that induces governments to respect adverse judgments from the European Court of Human Rights? What is Denmark's self-interest in complying with the Court's judgment in *Jersild*? The Danish government might well have made the political calculation that the Council of Europe's Committee of Ministers would not agree with the court, or, at a minimum, it might have delayed compliance until that vote had been taken. But in the words of now-Judge Rosalyn Higgins:

> states which are the subject of adverse findings by the court have virtually without exception been prepared to take the action necessary to bring themselves back into a position of compliance with the convention. Thus after the adverse findings in the *Golder* case, the UK government altered prison regulations to remove the rights of prison authorities to control the communication of a prisoner with his or her lawyer.

The decisions of the Court (and the old Commission) interpreting article 3, which prohibits torture or inhuman or degrading treatment, are especially effective and therefore especially challenging to the skeptic: when the European institutions have found a violation of article 3— whether in the context of prison conditions and mental institutions, corporal punishment in schools, racial discrimination, the war on terrorism, or extradition and deportation—the governments have always responded; indeed, through the friendly settlement mechanism, many governments have simply reformed a practice in such a way that the application could be withdrawn. Is it just civic faith that convinces a government to respect the Court's judgment even when it's adverse?

LEYLA SAHIN v. TURKEY

European Court of Human Rights Application no. 44774/98
10 November 2005

The applicant * * * comes from a traditional family of practising Muslims and considers it her religious duty to wear the Islamic headscarf. * * * [In] August 1997 the applicant, then in her fifth year at the Faculty of Medicine at Bursa University, enrolled at the Cerrahpasa Faculty of Medicine at Istanbul University. She says that she wore the Islamic headscarf during the four years she spent studying medicine at the University of Bursa and continued to do so until February 1998. On 23 February 1998 the Vice Chancellor of Istanbul University issued a circular, the relevant part of which provides:

> By virtue of the Constitution, the law and regulations, and in accordance with the case-law of the Supreme Administrative Court and the European Commission of Human Rights and the resolutions adopted by the university administrative boards, students whose 'heads are covered' (wearing the Islamic headscarf) and students (including overseas students) with beards must not be admitted to lectures, courses or tutorials. Consequently, the name

and number of any student with a beard or wearing the Islamic headscarf must not be added to the lists of registered students. However, if students whose names and numbers are not on the lists insist on attending tutorials and entering lecture theatres, they must be advised of the position and, should they refuse to leave, their names and numbers must be noted and they must be informed that they are not entitled to attend lectures. If they refuse to leave the lecture theatre, the teacher shall record what has happened in a report explaining why it was not possible to give the lecture and shall bring the matter to the attention of the university authorities as a matter of urgency so that disciplinary measures can be taken.

On 12 March 1998, in accordance with the aforementioned circular, the applicant was denied access by [proctors] to a written examination on oncology because she was wearing the Islamic headscarf. [T]he secretarial offices of the chair of orthopaedic traumatology [later] refused to allow her to enroll because she was wearing a headscarf. On 16 April 1998 she was refused admission to a neurology lecture and on 10 June 1998 to a written examination on public health, again for the same reason.

[The applicant challenged the circular on the grounds that] its implementation infringed her rights guaranteed by Articles 8, 9 and 14 of the [European] Convention and Article 2 of Protocol No. 1, in that there was no statutory basis for the circular and the education authority had no regulatory power in this sphere.

[T]he Istanbul Administrative Court dismissed her application, holding that by virtue of section 13(b) of the Higher–Education Act (Law no. 2547) a university vice chancellor, had power to regulate students' dress in order to maintain order. * * *

In May 1998 disciplinary proceedings were brought against the applicant [at the university] as a result of her failure to comply with the rules on dress [and for joining in] an unauthorised assembly gathered outside the deanery * * * to protest the rules on dress. [She was] suspended from the university [and her] application to have the disciplinary penalty quashed was dismissed by the Istanbul Administrative Court, which held [that] the impugned measure could not be regarded as illegal. [Following an amnesty law subsequently entered into force] the applicant was granted amnesty releasing her from all the disciplinary penalties and their effects. * * *

The Turkish Republic was founded on the principle that the State should be secular (*laik*). After the proclamation of the Republic on 29 October 1923, the public and religious spheres were separated through a series of revolutionary reforms: the abolition of the caliphate [in] 1923; the repeal of the constitutional provision declaring Islam the religion of the State [in] 1928; and, lastly, [in] 1937 a constitutional amendment according constitutional status to the principle of secularism[2]. The

---

2. [*See* Article 2 of the Turkish Constitution, which provides: "The Republic of Turkey is a democratic, secular (*laik*) and social State based on the rule of law that is respectful of human rights

principle of secularism was inspired by developments in Ottoman society in the period between the nineteenth century and the proclamation of the Republic.

The main feature of the republican system was the status accorded to women's rights, with women being granted equality in the enjoyment of individual rights. The process began [in] 1926 with the adoption of the Civil Code, which provided for equality of the sexes in the enjoyment of civic rights, in particular as regards divorce and succession. Subsequently, through a constitutional amendment [in] 1934 (Article 10 of the 1924 Constitution), women obtained equal political power with men. [3]

At the time of the Ottoman Empire both the central government and religious groups required people to dress in accordance with their religious affiliations. The reforms introduced by the Republic on the question of dress were inspired by the evolution of society in the nineteenth century and sought first and foremost to create a religion-free zone in which all citizens were guaranteed equality, without distinction on the grounds of religion or denomination. [The ideas that women should be freed from religious constraints and that society should be modernized come from this common origin. Significant advances in women's rights were made during this period, including equality of treatment in education, the introduction of a ban on polygamy in 1914, and the transfer of jurisdiction in matrimonial cases to the secular courts that had been established in the nineteenth century.]

The first enactment [to regulate dress] was the Headgear Act of 28 November 1925 (Law no. 671), which treated dress as an issue relating to modernity. Similarly, a ban was imposed on wearing religious attire other than in places of worship or at religious ceremonies, irrespective of the religion or belief concerned, by the Dress (Regulations) Act of 3 December 1934 (Law no. 2596). Under the Education Services (Merger) Act of 3 March 1924 (Law no. 430), religious schools were closed and all schools came under the control of the Ministry for Education. * * *

Wearing the Islamic headscarf to school and university is a recent phenomenon in Turkey, which began in the 1980s. There has been extensive discussion on the issue and it continues to be the subject of lively debate in Turkish society. Those in favour of the headscarf see wearing it as a duty and/or a form of expression linked to religious identity, whereas those against regard it as a symbol of a political Islam that is seeking to establish a regime based on religious precepts and threatens to cause civil unrest and undermine the rights acquired by

---

in a spirit of social peace, national solidarity and justice, adheres to the nationalism of Atatürk and is underpinned by the fundamental principles set out in the Preamble."]

3. [Article 10 provides: "All individuals shall be equal before the law without any distinction based on language, race, colour, sex, political opinion, philosophical belief, religion, membership of a religious sect or other similar grounds. Men and women shall have equal rights. The State shall take action to achieve such equality in practice. No privileges shall be granted to any individual, family, group or class. State bodies and administrative authorities shall act in compliance with the principle of equality before the law in all circumstances. * * *"]

women under the republican system. The accession to power [in] 1996 of a coalition government comprising the Islamist *Refah Partisi*, and the centre-right *Dogru Yol Partisi*, has given the debate strong political overtones. The ambivalence displayed by the leaders of the *Refah Partisi*, including the then Prime Minister, over their attachment to democratic values, and their advocacy of a plurality of legal systems functioning according to different religious rules for each religious community was perceived in Turkish society as a genuine threat to republican values and civil peace. * * *

On 10 December 1982 the Higher–Education Authority issued a circular on the wearing of headscarves in higher-education institutions. The Islamic headscarf was banned in lecture theatres. In a judgment of 13 December 1984, the Supreme Administrative Court held that the regulations were lawful, noting:

> Beyond being a mere innocent practice, wearing the headscarf is in the process of becoming the symbol of a vision that is contrary to the freedoms of women and the fundamental principles of the Republic.

[In 1989 the Constitutional Court invalidated a provision of the Higher–Education Act which had provided that "[m]odern dress or appearance shall be compulsory in the rooms and corridors of institutions of higher education, preparatory schools, laboratories, clinics and multidisciplinary clinics. A veil or headscarf covering the neck and hair may be worn out of religious conviction." That provision was held to be contrary to Articles 2 (secularism), 10 (equality before the law) and 24 (freedom of religion) of the Constitution. It also found that it could not be reconciled with the principle of sexual equality implicit, *inter alia*, in republican and revolutionary values.]

In their judgment, the Constitutional Court judges explained, firstly, that secularism had acquired constitutional status by reason of the historical experience of the country and the particularities of Islam compared to other religions; secularism was an essential condition for democracy and acted as a guarantor of freedom of religion and of equality before the law. It also prevented the State from showing a preference for a particular religion or belief; consequently, a secular State could not invoke religious conviction when performing its legislative function. [They stated, *inter alia*:

> Secularism is the civil organiser of political, social and cultural life, based on national sovereignty, democracy, freedom and science. Secularism is the principle which offers the individual the possibility to affirm his or her own personality through freedom of thought and which, by the distinction it makes between politics and religious beliefs, renders freedom of conscience and religion effective. In societies based on religion, which function with religious thought and religious rules, political organisation is religious in character. In a secular regime, religion is shielded from a political role. It is not a

tool of the authorities and remains in its respectable place, to be determined by the conscience of each and everyone.]

Stressing its inviolable nature, the Constitutional Court observed that freedom of religion, conscience and worship, which could not be equated with a right to wear any particular religious attire, guaranteed first and foremost the liberty to decide whether or not to follow a religion. It explained that, once outside the private sphere of individual conscience, freedom to manifest one's religion could be restricted on public-order grounds to defend the principle of secularism.

Everyone was free to choose how to dress, as the social and religious values and traditions of society also had to be respected. However, when a particular dress code was imposed on individuals by reference to a religion, the religion concerned was perceived and presented as a set of values that were incompatible with those of contemporary society. In addition, in Turkey, where the majority of the population were Muslims, presenting the wearing of the Islamic headscarf as a mandatory religious duty would result in discrimination between practising Muslims, non-practising Muslims and non-believers on grounds of dress with anyone who refused to wear the headscarf undoubtedly being regarded as opposed to religion or as irreligious.

The Constitutional Court also said that students had to be able to work and pursue their education together in a calm, tolerant and mutually supportive atmosphere without being deflected from that goal by signs of religious affiliation. It found that, irrespective of whether the Islamic headscarf was a precept of Islam, granting legal recognition to a religious symbol of that type in institutions of higher education was not compatible with the principle that State education must be neutral, as it would be liable to generate conflicts between students with differing religious convictions or beliefs.

[The Court then undertook a comparative analysis of regulations governing the wearing of Islamic headscarves across Europe. It noted that "Turkey, Azerbaijan and Albania ... are the only member States to have introduced regulations on wearing the Islamic headscarf in universities. In France, where secularism is regarded as one of the cornerstones of republican values, legislation was passed [in 2004] regulating, in accordance with the principle of secularism, the wearing of signs or dress manifesting a religious affiliation in State primary and secondary schools.... In other countries (Austria, Germany, the Netherlands, Spain, Sweden, Switzerland and the United Kingdom), in some cases following a protracted legal debate, the State education authorities permit Muslim pupils and students to wear the Islamic headscarf. In Germany, where the debate focused on whether teachers should be allowed to wear the Islamic headscarf, the Constitutional Court stated ... that the lack of any express statutory prohibition meant that teachers were entitled to wear the headscarf. Consequently, it imposed a duty on the Länder [the state or provincial government] to lay down rules on dress if they wished to prohibit the wearing of the Islamic headscarf in State schools. * * * In the United Kingdom a tolerant attitude is shown to pupils who wear religious signs. Difficulties with respect to the Islamic headscarf are rare. The issue has also been debated in the context of the elimination of racial discrimination in schools in order to preserve their multicultural character. * * * In Spain, there is no express statutory prohibition on pupils' wearing religious head coverings in State schools. * * * In Finland and Sweden the veil can be worn at school. However, a distinction is made between the *burka* (the term used to describe the full veil covering the whole of the body and the face) and the *niqab* (a veil covering all the upper body with the exception of the eyes). * * * In the Netherlands, where the question of the Islamic headscarf is considered from the standpoint of discrimination rather than of freedom of religion, it is generally tolerated."]

ALLEGED VIOLATION OF ARTICLE 9 OF THE CONVENTION

The applicant submitted that the ban on wearing the Islamic headscarf in institutions of higher education constituted an unjustified interference with her right to freedom of religion, in particular, her right to manifest her religion. She relied on Article 9 of the Convention, which provides:

> 1. Everyone has the right to freedom of thought, conscience and religion; this right includes freedom to change his religion or belief and freedom, either alone or in community with others and in public or private, to manifest his religion or belief, in worship, teaching, practice and observance.

> 2. Freedom to manifest one's religion or beliefs shall be subject only to such limitations as are prescribed by law and are necessary in a democratic society in the interests of public safety, for the protection of public order, health or morals, or for the protection of the rights and freedoms of others.

The Court must consider whether the applicant's right under Article 9 was interfered with and, if so, whether the interference was "prescribed by law", pursued a legitimate aim and was "necessary in a democratic society" within the meaning of Article 9 § 2 of the Convention.

The applicant said that her manner of dressing had to be treated as obedience to a religious rule which she regarded as "recognised practice". She maintained that the restriction and her resulting exclusion from the University of Istanbul was a clear interference with her right to freedom to manifest her religion.

"Prescribed by law"

[The Court determined that the prohibition on the headscarf was "prescribed by law," within the meaning of the Convention, reiterating "its settled case-law that the expression 'prescribed by law' requires firstly that the impugned measure should have a basis in domestic law. It also refers to the quality of the law in question, requiring that it be accessible to the persons concerned and formulated with sufficient precision to enable them–if need be, with appropriate advice–to foresee, to a degree that is reasonable in the circumstances, the consequences which a given action may entail and to regulate their conduct. * * * Further, as regards the words "in accordance with the law" and "prescribed by law" which appear in Articles 8 to 11 of the Convention, the Court observes that it has always understood the term 'law' in its 'substantive' sense, not its 'formal' one; it has included both 'written law', encompassing enactments of lower ranking statutes (*De Wilde, Ooms and Versyp v. Belgium*, judgment of 18 June 1971, Series A no 12, p. 45, § 93) and regulatory measures taken by professional regulatory bodies under independent rule-making powers delegated to them by parliament (*Bartold v. Germany*, judgment of 25 March 1985, Series A no. 90, p. 21, § 46), and unwritten law."]

Legitimate aim

* * * Having regard to the circumstances of the case and the terms of the domestic courts' decisions, the Court finds that the impugned interference primarily pursued the legitimate aims of protecting the rights and freedoms of others and of protecting public order.

"Necessary in a democratic society"

The Court reiterates that as enshrined in Article 9, freedom of thought, conscience and religion is one of the foundations of a "democratic society" within the meaning of the Convention. This freedom is, in its religious dimension, one of the most vital elements that go to make up the identity of believers and their conception of life, but it is also a precious asset for atheists, agnostics, sceptics and the unconcerned. The pluralism indissociable from a democratic society, which has been dearly won over the centuries, depends on it. That freedom entails, *inter alia*, freedom to hold or not to hold religious beliefs and to practise or not to practise a religion. * * * While religious freedom is primarily a matter of individual conscience, it also implies, *inter alia*, freedom to manifest one's religion, alone and in private, or in community with others, in public and within the circle of those whose faith one shares. Article 9 lists the various forms which manifestation of one's religion or belief may take, namely worship, teaching, practice and observance. * * *

Article 9 does not protect every act motivated or inspired by a religion or belief (see, among many other authorities, *Kalaç v. Turkey*, judgment of 1 July 1997, Reports of Judgments and Decisions 1997–IV, p. 1209, § 27; *Arrowsmith v. the United Kingdom*, no. 7050/75, Commission decision of 12 October 1978, Decisions and Reports (DR) 19, p. 5; *C. v. the United Kingdom*, no. 10358/83, Commission decision of 15 December

1983, DR 37, p. 142; and *Tepeli and Others v. Turkey* (dec.), no. 31876/96, 11 September 2001).

In democratic societies, in which several religions coexist within one and the same population, it may be necessary to place restrictions on freedom to manifest one's religion or belief in order to reconcile the interests of the various groups and ensure that everyone's beliefs are respected. [This follows both from paragraph 2 of Article 9 and the State's positive obligation under Article 1 of the Convention to secure to everyone within its jurisdiction the rights and freedoms defined in the Convention.]

The Court has frequently emphasised the State's role as the neutral and impartial organiser of the exercise of various religions, faiths and beliefs, and stated that this role is conducive to public order, religious harmony and tolerance in a democratic society. It also considers that the State's duty of neutrality and impartiality is incompatible with any power on the State's part to assess the legitimacy of religious beliefs or the ways in which those beliefs are expressed and that it requires the State to ensure mutual tolerance between opposing groups (*United Communist Party of Turkey and Others v. Turkey*, judgment of 30 January 1998, Reports 1998 I, § 57). Accordingly, the role of the authorities in such circumstances is not to remove the cause of tension by eliminating pluralism, but to ensure that the competing groups tolerate each other.

Pluralism, tolerance and broad-mindedness are hallmarks of a "democratic society". Although individual interests must on occasion be subordinated to those of a group, democracy does not simply mean that the views of a majority must always prevail: a balance must be achieved which ensures the fair and proper treatment of people from minorities and avoids any abuse of a dominant position (see, *mutatis mutandis*, *Young, James and Webster v. the United Kingdom*, judgment of 13 August 1981, Series A no. 44, p. 25, § 63; and *Chassagnou and Others v. France* [GC], nos. 25088/94, 28331/95 and 28443/95, § 112, ECHR 1999 III). Pluralism and democracy must also be based on dialogue and a spirit of compromise necessarily entailing various concessions on the part of individuals or groups of individuals which are justified in order to maintain and promote the ideals and values of a democratic society. Where these "rights and freedoms" are themselves among those guaranteed by the Convention or its Protocols, it must be accepted that the need to protect them may lead States to restrict other rights or freedoms likewise set forth in the Convention. It is precisely this constant search for a balance between the fundamental rights of each individual which constitutes the foundation of a "democratic society."

Where questions concerning the relationship between State and religions are at stake, on which opinion in a democratic society may reasonably differ widely, the role of the national decision-making body must be given special importance. This will notably be the case when it comes to regulating the wearing of religious symbols in educational institutions, especially * * * in view of the diversity of the approaches taken by national authorities on the issue. It is not possible to discern throughout Europe a uniform conception of the significance of religion in society (*Otto-Preminger–Institut v. Austria*, judgment of 20 September 1994, Series A no. 295 A, p. 19, § 50) and the meaning or impact of the public expression of a religious belief will differ according to time and context. Rules in this sphere will consequently vary from one country to another according to national traditions and the requirements imposed by the need to protect the rights and freedoms of others and to maintain public order. Accordingly, the choice of the extent and form such regulations should take must inevitably be left up to a point to the State concerned, as it will depend on the domestic context concerned.

This margin of appreciation goes hand in hand with a European supervision embracing both the law and the decisions applying it. The Court's task is to determine whether the measures taken at [the] national level were justified in principle and proportionate. In delimiting the extent of the margin of appreciation in the present case the Court must have regard to what is at stake, namely the need to protect the rights and freedoms of others, to preserve public order and to secure civil peace and true religious pluralism, which is vital to the survival of a democratic society.

The Court notes that in the decisions of *Karaduman v. Turkey* (no. 16278/90, Commission decision of 3 May 1993, DR 74, p. 93) and *Dahlab v. Switzerland* (no. 42393/98, ECHR 2001 V) the Convention institutions found that in a democratic society the State was entitled to place restrictions on the wearing of the Islamic headscarf if it was incompatible with the pursued aim of protecting the rights and freedoms of others, public order and public safety. In the *Dahlab* case, which concerned the teacher of a class of small children, the Court stressed among other matters the "powerful external symbol" which her wearing a headscarf represented and questioned whether it might have some kind of proselytising effect, seeing that it appeared to be imposed on women by a religious precept that was hard to reconcile with the principle of gender equality.

[T]he Court has also previously stated that the principle of secularism in Turkey is undoubtably one of the fundamental principles of the State, which are in harmony with the rule of law and respect for human rights[.] In a country like Turkey, where the great majority of the population belong to a particular religion, measures taken in universities to prevent certain fundamentalist religious movements from exerting pressure on students who do not practise that religion or on those who belong to another religion may be justified under Article 9(2) of the Convention. In that context, secular universities may regulate manifestation of the rites and symbols of the said religion by imposing restrictions as to the place and manner of such manifestation with the aim of ensuring peaceful co-existence between students of various faith and thus protecting public order and the beliefs of others. * * *

[T]he interference caused by the circular of 23 February 1998 imposing restrictions as to place and manner on the rights of students such as Ms. Sahin to wear the Islamic headscarf on university premises * * * was based in particular on the two principles—secularism and equality—which reinforce and complement each other. In its judgment of 7 March 1989, the Constitutional Court stated that secularism in Turkey was, among other things, the guarantor of democratic values, the principle that freedom of religion is inviolable—to the extent that it stems from individual conscience—and the principle that citizens are equal before the law. [Secularism prevented the State from manifesting a preference for a particular religion or belief; it thereby guided the State in its role of impartial arbiter, and necessarily entailed freedom of religion and conscience. It also served to protect the individual not only against arbitrary interference by the State but from external pressure from extremist movements. The Constitutional Court added that freedom to manifest one's religion could be restricted in order to defend those values and principles.] The notion of secularism appears to the Court to be consistent with the values underpinning the Convention and it accepts that upholding that principle may be regarded as necessary to protect the democratic system in Turkey. The Court must now determine whether in the instant case there was a reasonable relationship of proportionality between the means employed and the legitimate objectives pursued by the interference. [The Court] notes at the outset that it is common ground that practising Muslim students in Turkish universities are free, within the limits imposed by educational organisational constraints, to manifest their religion in accordance with habitual forms of Muslim observance. In addition, the resolution adopted by Istanbul University on 9 July 1998 shows that various other forms of religious attire are also forbidden on the university premises. * * * Furthermore, the process whereby the regulations that led to the decision of 9 July 1998 were implemented took several years and was accompanied by a wide debate within Turkish society and the teaching profession. The two highest courts, the Supreme Administrative Court and the Constitutional Court, have managed to establish settled case-law on this issue. It is quite clear that throughout that decision-making process the university authorities sought to adapt to the evolving situation in a way that would not bar access to the university to students wearing the veil, through continued dialogue with those concerned, while at the same time ensuring that order was maintained and in particular that the requirements imposed by the nature of the course in question were complied with. * * * In the light of the foregoing and having regard to the Contracting States' margin of appreciation in this sphere, the Court finds that the interference in issue was justified in principle and proportionate to the aim pursued. Consequently, there has been no breach of Article 9 of the Convention.

1. *Protecting some speech but not all speech.* Can *Jersild* and its values be squared with the approach to good faith religious expression taken in *Sahin*? Are the cases irreconcilable or distinguishable? What (or whose) rights *were* protected in *Sahin*? *See* Natan Lerner, *How Wide the Margin of Appreciation? The Turkish Headscarf Case, the Strasbourg Court, and Secularist Tolerance,* 13 WILLAMETTE J. INT'L L. & DISP. RESOL. 65 (2005); Jonathan Zugden, *A Certain Lack of Empathy, available at* http://www.hrw.org/english/docs/2004/07/01/turkey8985.htm.

2. *Articulating the critique.* If an appeal were possible from a judgment of the European Court of Human Rights, how would you structure the appellate argument in *Sahin*?

3. *Additional categories of violations at issue in Sahin.* It is conceivable that other categories of rights might have been advanced in *Sahin, e.g.,* the right to education, the right to privacy, gender equality. How should the court have disposed of these claims?

REFORM OF THE EUROPEAN COURT OF HUMAN RIGHTS

It is routinely observed that the European Court of Human Rights is a victim of its own success, especially after the structural and procedural reforms of Protocol 11, *supra*. Current reform proposals take many forms, including the amendment of the European Convention (*see* Protocol 14, *infra*) and reconsideration of the Court's working methods (*see* The Woolf Commission Report, *infra*). Do the proposed changes, especially the articulation of a new admissibility criterion under Protocol 14, address the root causes of the Court's current problems? Can you imagine other reforms that might ease the burden of success?

JOINT COMMITTEE ON HUMAN RIGHTS OF THE HOUSE OF LORDS AND THE HOUSE OF COMMONS

Protocol No. 14 to the European Convention on Human Rights
First Report of Session 2004–05 (December 2004)

8. Protocol 14 and the Committee of Ministers Recommendations accompanying it are the culmination of a lengthy process of consultation and deliberation aimed at guaranteeing the long-term effectiveness of the European Court of Human Rights in the face of concerns that, on present trends, it will soon be unable to cope with its rapidly expanding case-load.

9. The Convention's control mechanism was last radically reformed by Protocol 11, which was agreed by member states in 1994 and

came into force on 1 November 1998. Those reforms were designed to simplify the Convention system in order to speed up proceedings and help the system to deal with the large rise in the number of individual applications.[8] The reforms have greatly increased the productivity of the Court,[9] but it rapidly became apparent that further reform of the Convention system was going to be necessary in order to deal with the continued increase in the Court's workload.

10.   The main reason for the rise in the number of individual applications before the Court is the enlargement of the Council of Europe. It now has 46 member states, bringing to 800 million the total number of citizens with the right to make an application to the Court.[10] Not surprisingly, the rapid expansion of the Council of Europe's membership has led to a dramatic increase in the number of new applications.[11] Despite the reforms introduced by Protocol 11, the current Convention system cannot cope with this level of caseload. The number of applications which can be disposed of is far exceeded by the number of new applications made, resulting in a growing backlog of cases: by the end of 2003, some 65,000 applications were pending before the Court.

11.   In addition to the current backlog, it is envisaged that the number of applications will continue to grow. In addition to the obvious effect of enlargement, a number of other factors point to a likely increase in future: growing awareness of the Convention in the new member states; the entry into force of Protocol 12 (containing the general nondiscrimination provision); the ratification of additional protocols by States not currently parties to them; the Court's continuing development of the Convention as a "living instrument"; and eventually, possibly, the accession of the EU to the Convention system.

12.   Against this background, the Council of Europe initiated a process of further reform of the Convention machinery in 2000, in order to preserve the long-term effectiveness of the Convention system.
* * *

15.   The [continent-wide process of consultation and analysis] identified two principal contributors to the Court's excessive caseload. First, the very large proportion of cases which are declared inadmissible (in 2003, 96% of applications considered were declared inadmissible). Second, the significant number of cases which concern repetitive violations

---

8. The main simplification was the creation of a single full-time Court and the abolition of both the European Commission of Human Rights and the quasi-judicial role played by the Committee of Ministers.

9. The new Court gave 61,633 judgments in the five years since 1998, compared to 38,389 judgments in the preceding forty-four years.

10. Thirteen new states parties have ratified the Convention since Protocol No. 11 was opened for signature, bringing some 240 million more individuals within the scope of the Convention's protection.

11. In 2003 39,000 new applications were lodged with the Court, compared to 18,164 in 1998 (the year in which the previous reforms were implemented).The increase has been dramatic: as recently as 1990, for example, only 5, 279 applications were received.

following an earlier judgment in a pilot case (in 2003, some 60% of the 703 judgments given by the Court concerned such repetitive cases).

16.   The procedural reforms contained in the Protocol are mainly designed to address the problem that a great deal of the Court's time is spent processing cases which are either inadmissible or repeat violations following pilot judgments. The purpose is to enable the Court to concentrate on the most important cases.

17.   In drawing up the reforms contained in Protocol 14, certain features of the Convention system were seen as being essential to retain. First, the right of individual petition (the principle that any person claiming to be victim of a breach of Convention rights and freedoms can refer the matter to the Court), was regarded as sacrosanct. Second, the judicial character of European supervision was also seen as being non-negotiable. These therefore provide important standards according to which the reforms are to be judged.

18.   In order to reduce the time spent by the Court on clearly inadmissible applications and repetitive applications, the reforms introduce amendments to the Convention machinery in four main areas:

> The process for filtering out unmeritorious cases

> A new admissibility criterion

> Measures for dealing with repetitive cases

> Execution of judgments.

Filtering out unmeritorious cases

19.   The principal provision designed to increase the Court's filtering capacity is the introduction of a single-judge formation of the Court,[14] competent to declare applications inadmissible, or strike them out of the Court's list of cases, "where such a decision can be taken without further examination."[15] These words are intended to convey that the single judge will take such decisions only in clear-cut cases, where the inadmissibility of the application is manifest from the outset. The decision of the single judge is to be final.[16] If the single judge does not declare an application inadmissible or strike it out, it is forwarded to a committee or chamber for further examination.[17] * * *

A new admissibility requirement

21.   Probably the most controversial reform, because of its potential impact on the right of individual petition, is the introduction of a new admissibility requirement. The Court shall declare an application inadmissible if it considers that: "the applicant has not suffered a significant disadvantage, unless respect for human rights as defined in the Conven-

---

14.   New Article 26(1) ECHR, as amended by Article 6 of the amending protocol.

15.   New Article 27(1) ECHR, as amended by Article 7 of the amending protocol.

16.   New Article 27(2) ECHR.

17.   New Article 27(3) ECHR.

tion and the Protocols thereto requires an examination of the application on the merits and provided that no case may be rejected on this ground which has not been duly considered by a domestic tribunal."[20]

22. What is meant by a "significant disadvantage" is not elaborated by the Protocol. It is left for the Court to establish relevant criteria on a case-by-case basis.

23. The Protocol provides for three main safeguards designed to avoid rejection of cases warranting an examination on the merits. First, even where the individual applicant has not suffered a significant disadvantage, the application will not be declared inadmissible if respect for human rights as defined in the Convention requires an examination on the merits. This reflects the wording which circumscribes the Court's power to strike applications out of its list of cases.[21]

24. Second, the new admissibility requirement is subject to a condition that no application may be declared inadmissible on this ground if it has not been duly considered by a domestic tribunal. This safeguard was proposed by the Parliamentary Assembly.[22]

25. Third, for two years following the entry into force of the Protocol, only Chambers and the Grand Chamber will be able to apply the new admissibility criterion.[23] Single judge formations and committees will not be apply it. This is to allow time for the development of clear guidance in the case-law as to how the requirement should be applied in different contexts, and avoid the danger of inconsistent application by different single judges or committees.

Measures for dealing with repetitive cases

26. The main measure for dealing with repetitive cases is the powers of the competence of the three-judge committees to enable them, unanimously, to declare applications admissible and decide them on their merits, when the questions they raise concerning the interpretation or application of the Convention are covered by well-established case-law of the Court.[24] The state concerned may contest the application of the new power, for example by disputing the "well established" character of the case-law, or seeking to distinguish the issue in the case from such case-law. If the State agrees with the Committee's position, however, the committee will give its judgment on all aspects of the case (admissibility, merits and just satisfaction) very rapidly.

Execution of judgments

27. The Protocol seeks to improve the process for the execution of the Court's judgments by strengthening the means given to the Committee of Ministers.

---

20. New Article 35(3)(b), as amended by Article 12 of the amending protocol.

21. Article 37(1) ECHR.

22. Parliamentary Assembly of the Council of Europe, Opinion No. 251 (2004) (28 April 2004), para 14 (vi).

23. Article 20(2) of the amending protocol.

24. New Article 28(1)(b) ECHR, as amended by Article 8 of the amending protocol.

28.   First, it is to be empowered to ask the Court to interpret a final judgment, for the purpose of facilitating the supervision of its execution.[25]

29.   Second, it is given the power to bring a form of infringement proceedings before the Court. If it considers that a State is refusing to abide by a final judgment of the Court, it may refer to the Court the question whether that State has failed to fulfil its obligation under Article 46(1). If the Court finds a violation of that obligation, it shall refer it back to the Committee of Ministers for consideration of the measures to be taken.[26]

Miscellaneous other reforms to the Convention machinery

30.   In addition to the four main areas identified above, Protocol 14 introduces a number of other miscellaneous reforms to the Convention machinery, some of which are worthy of mention.

31.   It provides that judges of the Court are to be elected for a single nine-year term, in order to reinforce their independence and impartiality.[27]

32.   It revises the system for the appointment of ad hoc judges in a Chamber or the Grand Chamber, where the judge elected in respect of the state concerned is entitled to sit as an *ex officio* member of the Chamber or Grand Chamber but that judge is unable to sit or there is no such judge. Under the previous system, the State concerned could choose an ad hoc judge after the beginning of proceedings. This was criticised, including by the Parliamentary Assembly, on the ground that it was not compatible with basic standards of judicial independence and impartiality. The new provision provides for the President to choose the ad hoc judge from a list submitted in advance by the state concerned.[28]

33.   It also introduces an amendment with a view to the possible accession of the EU to the Convention.[29]

REVIEW OF THE WORKING METHODS OF THE EUROPEAN COURT OF HUMAN RIGHTS

[The Woolf Commission Report]
December 2005

[At the invitation of the Secretary General of the Council of Europe and the President of the European Court of Human Rights, a commission of prominent jurists was appointed "to consider what steps can be taken by the President, judges and staff of the European Court of

---

25. New Article 46(3) ECHR, as amended by Article 16 of the amending protocol.
26. New Article 46(4) and (5) ECHR, as amended by Article 16 of the amending protocol.
27. New Article 223(1) ECHR, as amended by Article 2 of the amending protocol.
28. New Article 26(4) ECHR, as amended by Article 6 of the amending protocol.
29. New Article 59(2) ECHR, as amended by Article 17 of the amending protocol.

Human Rights [*i.e., without amending the European Convention itself as in Protocol 14, supra*] to deal most effectively and efficiently with its current and projected caseload, and to make recommendations accordingly to the Secretary General of the Council of Europe and to the President of the Court." The Executive Summary of the report follows:]

The European Court of Human Rights is faced with an enormous and ever-growing workload. 44,100 new applications were lodged last year, and the number of cases pending before the Court–now at 82,100– is projected to rise to 250,000 by 2010. It is clear that something must be done, in the short term, if the Court is not to be overwhelmed by its own workload. The purpose of this Review is to suggest administrative steps that can be taken, without amending the Convention, to allow the Court to cope with its current and projected caseload, and pending more fundamental reform.

A number of key principles were applied in the course of this Review:

— First, it was considered that it should be the responsibility of the individual applicant to submit a properly completed application form, and provide the Court with all the information required for processing the application.

— Secondly, there should be greater information and education at national level on the jurisdiction and purpose of the Court, and on the Court's admissibility criteria.

— Thirdly, there should be increased recourse to national ombudsmen and other methods of alternative dispute resolution.

— Fourthly, the Court's priority should be to deal, without delay, with admissible cases that raise new or serious Convention issues. It therefore follows that clearly inadmissible cases and repetitive cases should be handled in a way that has the minimum impact on the Court's time and resources.

— Fifthly and finally, the management and organisation of the Registry should ensure that the Court's workload is processed as efficiently and effectively as possible. * * *

The Review's main recommendations are as follows:

1) The Court should **redefine what constitutes an application**. It should only deal with properly completed application forms which contain all the information required for the Court to process the application. This would simplify the task of the Registry, as it would not have to register and store letters from potential applicants. It would also reduce the total number of applications dealt with by the Court, and would also make the processing of applications much simpler.

2) **Satellite Offices of the Registry** should be established in key countries that produce high numbers of inadmissible applications. The satellite offices would provide applicants with information as to the Court's admissibility criteria, and the availability, locally, of ombudsmen

and other alternative methods of resolving disputes. This could divert a significant number of cases away from the Court. Satellite offices would also be responsible for the initial processing of applications. They would then send applications, together with short summaries in either French or English, to the relevant division in Strasbourg. This would enable Strasbourg lawyers to prepare draft judgments more quickly.

3) The Council of Europe, the Court and its satellite offices should encourage greater use of **national Ombudsmen and other methods of Alternative Dispute Resolution.** This would divert from the Court a large number of complaints that should never have come to it in the first place, and would in many cases provide a more appropriate route for the practical resolution of grievances. The Court should also establish a specialist **'Friendly Settlement Unit'** in the Registry, to initiate and pursue proactively a greater number of friendly settlements.

4) The Court should deliver a greater number of **Pilot Judgments**, and then deal summarily with repetitive cases. Cases that are candidates for a pilot judgment should be given priority, and all similar cases stayed pending outcome of that case. The question of how much compensation to award successful litigants takes up a disproportionate amount of judges' time. The Court should therefore establish an 'Article 41 Unit', which would give guidance as to rates of compensation. Where possible, issues of compensation should be remitted to domestic courts for resolution.

5) A second Deputy Registrar, responsible for management of the Court's lawyers and staff, should be appointed. The **'Deputy Registrar for Management'** would be responsible for recruitment and training, career development, and the setting and oversight of targets. This would allow for more effective management of the overall functioning of the Court.

6) There should be a **Central Training Unit for lawyers,** and divisions should be restructured to allow for a more efficient division of labour between lawyers. The Court should continue to develop its case-weighting system, and should undertake a review of the target system.

7) There should be a **formal induction programme** for new judges and, where necessary, **intensive language training**. This would make it more likely that judges were able to start off 'on the right foot'.

Urgent action is needed to enable the Court to keep abreast of its workload. These recommendations do not provide the panacea but, taken together, should provide the Court with some very real assistance, and enable it to cope with its workload pending a more fundamental review of the Convention system.

CONCLUDING NOTE ON THE COUNCIL OF EUROPE

The preceding Council of Europe materials have focused on the role of the European Court of Human Rights in a particular substantive setting. But human rights lawyers should also appreciate the breadth of the Council's human rights concerns and the variety of its institutions for addressing them. Although the international judicial model for the protection of human rights is far advanced in Europe, it is a mistake to assume that litigation is the exclusive or preferred technique within the Council of Europe. To the contrary, as noted by Professor Dinah Shelton, "The Council of Europe has moved from a system of human rights protection based solely on litigation to a complex network of interlocking bodies focused on standard-setting, prevention, monitoring and enforcement." The Council of Europe has several constituent bodies, other than the European Court of Human Rights, with specific human rights mandates. For example, the *Secretary-General*, which heads the administrative Secretariat, is empowered by the European Convention to have member-states explain how Convention standards are implemented into domestic law and practice. The *Parliamentary Assembly*, composed of members from the national parliaments of the member-states, has created a mechanism for monitoring, verifying, and—when appropriate—sanctioning each member-state's compliance with its human rights obligations under Council of Europe instruments. The *Congress of Local and Regional Authorities*, with the European Charter of Local Self–Government at its core, represents the interests of Europe's regions and municipalities, promoting democracy at the local and regional levels. In 1999, the Council created the office of *Commissioner for Human Rights*, "a non-judicial institution to promote education in, awareness of and respect for human rights, as embodied in the human rights instruments of the Council of Europe."[1] The *Committee of Ministers*, which is in many respects the organization's decision-making body, is composed of the foreign ministers of each member-state (or their Strasbourg-based deputies). It is responsible for supervising the execution of the judgments of the European Court of Human Rights, including remedial measures and legislative reform.

Even a partial list of the Council of Europe's substantive human rights concerns would have to include *inter alia* privacy; fair trial rights; the independence of the judiciary; the protection of journalists; gender equality; domestic violence; human cloning; democracy and electoral integrity; and the nested problems of racism, xenophobia, anti-Semitism, and intolerance. Consider also the Council's work with respect to:

A. *Torture.* The Council of Europe developed the European Convention for the Prevention of Torture and its Protocols,[2] which

---

1. Committee of Ministers Res. (99) 50, *On the Council of Europe Commission for Human Rights*, (7 May 1999), at art. 1.

2. European Convention for the Prevention of Torture and Inhuman or Degrading Treatment or Punishment, Nov. 26, 1987, entered into force Feb. 1, 1989, *reprinted in* 27 I.L.M. 1152 (1988).

adopted an innovative regime of inspections wherever people are detained. Specifically, the Committee for the Prevention of Torture is authorized to arrange *ad hoc* visits "as appear to it to be required in the circumstances" to any place of detention–including prisons and police stations but also including mental hospitals and military barracks.

B. *Economic, social, and cultural rights*. The European Social Charter[3] was one of the first international treaties to focus exclusively on economic, social, and cultural rights, including workers rights, health, education, and social security. As amended, the Charter establishes the European Committee of Social Rights which receives periodic reports from states and which is now authorized to receive collective complaints from certain specified non-state actors.[4]

C. *Minority rights*. Conscious of the history of discrimination against minorities within Europe, the Council of Europe has paid particular attention to the rights of minorities, adopting both conventions for the protection of particular rights, like minority languages,[5] and more general "framework" statements of principles.[6] Typically, compliance is supervised through state reports to the Committee of Ministers, assisted by an advisory committee of independent experts.

D. *Human trafficking*. In 2008, the Council of Europe's Convention on Action against Trafficking in Human Beings[7] came into effect, setting out measures to prevent trafficking in human beings, prosecute the traffickers, and protect the victims of this modern form of slavery. A Group of Experts on Action against Trafficking in Human Beings ("GRETA") will monitor the implementation of the Convention.

E. *Extraordinary rendition*. Under Council of Europe instruments, member-states are prohibited from direct violations of human rights and from indirect facilitation of violations by non-members. In the war on terrorism, that includes participating in secret detentions and illegal transfers of detainees, and the Parliamentary Assembly of the Council of Europe has reported repeatedly on member-states' facilitation of non-member's violation of detainees' human rights. *Compare Soering v. the United Kingdom*, 11 Eur. Ct. H.R. (ser. A) (1989), holding that the United Kingdom's extradition of a young German national to the United States to face charges of capital

---

3. European Social Charter, Oct. 18, 1961, entered into force Feb. 26, 1965, 529 U.N.T.S. 89.

4. Additional Protocol to the European Social Charter Providing for a System of Collective Complaints, Nov. 9, 1995, entered into force January 7, 1998, E.T.S. 158.

5. European Charter for Regional or Minority Languages, Nov. 5, 1992, entered into force March 1, 1998, E.T.S. 148.

6. Framework Convention for the Protection of National Minorities, Feb. 1, 1995, entered into force Feb. 1, 1998, E.T.S. 15.

7. Convention on Action against Trafficking in Human Beings, May 16, 2005, entered into force Feb. 1, 2008, E.T.S. No. 197.

murder violated its obligations under Article 3 of the European Convention, which prohibits inhuman and degrading treatment.

THE EUROPEAN UNION MACHINERY

Historically, the primary concern of the European Union ("EU") and its predecessor institutions[1] has been economic integration, including the creation of a customs union, or a single European market, or the harmonization of commercial and company laws in each of its member states. Law students in the United States typically study the EU in connection with international trade law or business transactions or comparative law, and certainly the focus of the North American press has been on the European market as the great counter-force to, and the political rationale for, the North American Free Trade Agreement. But, in the human rights field, the European Union has been secondary: human rights are recognized in only a limited way in the original instrument that made up the European Community.[2]

Over time however, human rights concerns have become more important within the community than the isolated provisions of the Treaty of Rome suggest. There is now a Community Ombudsman to redress individual complaints about illegal administration by EU institutions. The Amsterdam Agreement of 1997 reaffirms the role of human rights standards in the decision-making of the EU.[3] In the Charter of Fundamental Rights (2001), the EU formalized its competence to address European human rights issues. The continuing conversation on a draft Constitution for Europe includes the desirability of a charter of rights and a provision allowing the EU to accede to the European

---

1. The history of the European Union complicates its nomenclature. The Treaty of Rome (1957) established the European Economic Community ("EEC"), one of three European Communities, the other two being the European Coal and Steel Community and the European Atomic Energy Community. The forces for continental integration intensified over the subsequent decades, and the EEC increasingly dealt with non-economic matters. From the common market and customs union of the 1950's grew a robust, continent-wide political, regulatory, and financial system balanced by strong principles of subsidiarity. Under the Treaty of Maastricht (1992), the member states resolved themselves into the European Union, with enhanced centralized powers.

2. *See, e.g.*, Treaty of Rome, Treaty Establishing the European Economic Community, Mar. 25, 1957, 298 U.N.T.S. 11, at Article 7, which prohibits discrimination among European community citizens; Article 48, which establishes the right to freedom of movement for workers within the community; and Article 119, which provides that men and women should receive equal pay for equal work.

3. Article 6 of the Treaty on the European Union is central to the protection of fundamental human rights within the EU, providing in part that:

1. The Union is founded on the principle of liberty, democracy, respect for human rights and fundamental freedoms and the rule of law, principles which are common to the Member States.

2. The Union shall respect fundamental rights, as guaranteed by the European Convention for the Protection of Human Rights and Fundamental Freedoms signed in Rome on 4 November 1950 and as they result from the constitutional traditions common to the Member States, as general principles of Community law. * * *

4. The Union shall provide itself the means necessary to attain its objectives and carry through its policies.

Convention, meaning that the *Council of Europe* text would come to bind the *EU* bodies.

Perhaps most significantly, as shown in the *Nold* case, *infra* the European Court of Justice ("ECJ") routinely applies human rights principles in its interpretation of Community law. From the legal practitioner's standpoint, the fact that human rights norms might actually constrain the daily operation of the regulatory state gives them a relevance that is at once profound and under-appreciated. Nor should we underestimate the power of the rule-of-law ideology as an instrument of political integration in Europe after the Cold War. The human rights consensus at work in the evolution of EU law generally helps member-states and their citizens adjust to the fact that the European Union tends to operate less democratically than the member governments themselves. As Professor Schwarze notes:

> The Court of Justice has concentrated on transferring to the Community level the principles of the rule of law and of the liberty of citizens which lend legitimacy to state power at a national level, and has thereby strengthened the supranational authority of the Community legal order. From this point of view, the case law of the Court can also contribute to improving the legitimacy of the Community in the eyes of citizens and thus politically to promoting integration to a significant extent.

J. SCHWARZE, EUROPEAN ADMINISTRATIVE LAW 1464–65 (1992). In other words, the EU Court, and the other EU institutions like the Commission and the Council, gain legitimacy by assuring that their decisions conform to widely-held principles of law and human rights. Especially as former Soviet bloc states seek admission to the "club" of Europe, adherence to the European Convention on Human Rights is seen as a precondition. Historically, no country has joined the EU without being a member of the Council of Europe first.

LAURENCE R. HELFER & ANNE–MARIE SLAUGHTER, TOWARD A THEORY OF EFFECTIVE SUPRANATIONAL ADJUDICATION

107 YALE L.J. 273, 290–92 (1997)

The European Court of Justice was established by the Treaty of Rome as a court of limited international jurisdiction charged with interpreting and applying the treaty in disputes between member states of the European Community or between the Commission of the Community and one or more member states.[1] At the outset, the ECJ's powers

---

1. *See* Treaty of Rome art. 169 (permitting the Commission of the Community to refer cases of noncompliance with its opinions to the Court of Justice); *Id*. art. 170 (permitting member states to bring before the Commission of the Community and the Court of Justice other member states that have allegedly failed to fulfill treaty obligations).

appeared no greater than those of the ICJ; it had jurisdiction over disputes between states, but no direct means of enforcing its decisions. Yet, over a forty-year period, the ECJ succeeded in transforming the Treaty of Rome and secondary Community legislation into law directly enforceable in cases brought by private parties in the domestic courts. European Union law is supreme over domestic law and recognized as such by domestic courts—not, in most cases, by action of domestic constitutions or legislative provisions, but by decree of the ECJ itself, a decree ultimately accepted even by the highest national courts.

The task facing the ECJ was the penetration of national legal systems. It accomplished this task by exploiting a relatively obscure provision in the Treaty of Rome, Article 177, which allowed all national courts, and required national courts of last resort, to refer cases involving the application of European law to the ECJ for a preliminary ruling on the European law issues.[2] The ostensible purpose of this provision was to ensure uniformity of interpretation of the treaty by ensuring that [what was originally] six * * * sets of national judges did not develop divergent interpretations of the treaty and Community secondary legislation. In one of the earliest referrals, however, the ECJ took matters into its own hands and declared the doctrine of "direct effect," holding that certain provisions of the Treaty of Rome are directly applicable to individuals within national legal systems.[3] Individuals could thus invoke these provisions in national court against contrary provisions of national law; the national court was then to refer the issue to the ECJ for resolution.

Over the course of several decades, the number of references from national courts to the ECJ steadily increased, effectively providing the ECJ with domestic enforcement mechanisms for its judgments. The doctrine of direct effect was quickly followed by the doctrine of supremacy of European Community law over conflicting national law, a much more direct enforcement mechanism than the system of national implementing legislation that the treaty's drafters originally envisioned. Other ECJ innovations included implied powers for Community lawmaking, preemption of conflicting national legislation, and the development of a human rights jurisprudence to check potential excesses of Community law and actors. Acceptance of these doctrines by national courts has given the judgments of the ECJ in cases referred to it under Article 177 roughly the same effect as judgments issued by domestic courts in the member states of the European Union. Individuals, corporations, and

---

2. Article 177 of the Treaty of Rome provides: "The Court of Justice shall be competent to make a preliminary decision concerning * * * the validity and interpretation of acts of the institutions of the Community; and * * *the interpretation of the statutes of any bodies set up by an act of the Council.* * *" Treaty of Rome art. 177. Any court of a member state may refer a case involving such issues to the ECJ. Further, national courts of last resort, "from whose decisions no appeal lies under municipal law," must refer cases raising questions of European law to the ECJ. *Id.* Article 171 requires member states to "take the measures required for the implementation of the judgment" of the ECJ. *Id.*, art. 171.

3. *See* Case 26/62, *N.V. Algemene Transp. & Expeditie Onderneming Van Gend & Loos v. Nederlandse administratie der belastingen*, 1963 E.C.R. 1, 12.

government agencies anticipate the ECJ's position on important economic and political questions; its decisions are carefully reported and analyzed not only in legal reporters, but also in major national newspapers. Indeed, the ECJ's success has been such that it has been widely credited with transforming the Treaty of Rome from an international instrument into the "constitution" of the European Community.

J. NOLD v. COMMISSION OF THE EUROPEAN COMMUNITIES

European Court of Justice
[1974] ECR 491, 2 CMLR 338
14 May 1974

1. By application lodged on 31 January 1973, * * * Nold, a limited partnership carrying on a wholesale coal and construction materials' business in Darmstadt, [Germany] requested * * * that the court should annul the Commission's Decision of 21 December 1972 authorizing new terms of business [in the coal supply sector.] * * *

12. The applicant asserts * * * that certain of its fundamental rights have been violated, in that the restrictions introduced by the new trading rules authorized by the Commission have the effect, by depriving it of direct supplies, of jeopardizing both the profitability of the undertaking and the free development of its business activity, to the point of endangering its very existence. In this way, the Decision is said to violate, in respect of the applicant, a right akin to a proprietary right, as well as its right to the free pursuit of business activity, as protected by the [basic law] of the Federal Republic of Germany and by the constitutions of other Member States and various international treaties, including in particular the convention for the protection of human rights and fundamental freedoms of 4 November 1950 and the protocol to that convention of 20 March 1952.

13. As the court has already stated, fundamental rights form an integral part of the general principles of law, the observance of which it ensures. In safeguarding these rights, the court is bound to draw inspiration from constitutional traditions common to the Member States, and it cannot therefore uphold measures which are incompatible with fundamental rights recognized and protected by the constitutions of those states. Similarly, international treaties for the protection of human rights on which the Member States have collaborated or of which they are signatories, can supply guidelines which should be followed within the framework of Community law. The submissions of the applicant must be examined in the light of these principles.

14. If rights of ownership are protected by the constitutional laws of all the Member States and if similar guarantees are given in respect of their right freely to choose and practice their trade or profession, the

rights thereby guaranteed, far from constituting unfettered prerogatives, must be viewed in the light of the social function of the property and activities protected thereunder. For this reason, rights of this nature are protected by law subject always to limitations laid down in accordance with the public interest. Within the Community legal order it likewise seems legitimate that these rights should, if necessary, be subject to certain limits justified by the overall objectives pursued by the Community, on condition that the substance of these rights is left untouched. As regards the guarantees accorded to a particular undertaking, they can in no respect be extended to protect mere commercial interests or opportunities, the uncertainties of which are part of the very essence of economic activity.

15. The disadvantages claimed by the applicant are in fact the result of economic change and not of the contested Decision. It was for the applicant, confronted by the economic changes brought about by the recession in coal production, to acknowledge the situation and itself carry out the necessary adaptations.

17. The action must accordingly be dismissed.

NOTES AND QUESTIONS ON THE EU AND HUMAN RIGHTS

1. *Proliferation of courts, balkanization of law.* The contribution that the EU system might make in the articulation of international and domestic standards should not be underestimated. But does the proliferation of human rights tribunals threaten to balkanize the substantive norms of human rights law? The possibility of divergence is not remote:

> in a case concerning the powers of European Commission officials to enter premises to obtain evidence of infringement of the competition rules, the ECJ held that the inviolability of the home could not be invoked to resist the exercise of those powers in regard to the business premises of undertakings. The ECHR, on the other hand, held that Article 8 of the Convention was wide enough to encompass both the home when used for business purposes and professional premises. However, the ECJ went on to rule that an intervention in a person's private activities must in any event have a legal basis, be justified on grounds laid down by law, and not be arbitrary or disproportionate in its application.

Francis G. Jacobs, *Judicial Dialogue and the Cross–Fertilization of Legal Systems: The European Court of Justice,* 38 TEX. INT'L L.J. 547 (2003); *see also* Koen Lenaerts, *Interlocking Legal Orders in the European Union and Comparative Law,* 52 INT'L & COMP. L.Q. 873, 905 (2003).

2. *Modalities of protecting human rights within the EU.*

A. *Preventive diplomacy and the protection of minorities.* In 1993, the European Union adopted a plan for the protection of minorities in the new (*i.e.* post-Cold War) Europe. Named after its proponent, French Prime Minister Edouard Balladur, the Plan was the first major initiative of the EU's common foreign and security policy following the adoption of the Maastricht Treaty. Through a series of bilateral treaties, the Plan effectively linked a non-member's admission to the EU with that country's willingness and ability to protect minorities within its borders and to resolve ethnic conflicts peacefully.

B. *Regulation/harmonization and the rights of disabled people.* With respect to the rights of disabled people, the various EU institutions, including the Council, the Commission, and the Committee of Ministers, have adopted a variety of resolutions endorsing policies of non-discrimination and equal opportunity in different areas of life (*e.g.*, education, employment, and access to information technology). *See e.g.*, Council Resolution 1999/C186/02 of 17 June 1999 on equal employment opportunities for people with disabilities. Beyond the right of non-discrimination, however, the EU has attempted to implement a harmonized policy of accommodation, rehabilitation, and integration of disabled people into the life of their communities and has mainstreamed the rights of the disabled in its own decision-making. *See, e.g.*, Council Directive 2000/78/EC of 27 November 2000, establishing a general framework for equal treatment in employment and occupation, at Article 5:

> In order to guarantee compliance with the principle of equal treatment in relation to persons with disabilities, reasonable accommodation shall be provided. This means that employers shall take appropriate measures, where needed in a particular case, to enable a person with a disability to have access to, participate in, or advance in employment, or to undergo training, unless such measures would impose a disproportionate burden on the employer. This burden shall not be disproportionate when it is sufficiently remedied by measures existing within the framework of the disability policy of the Member State concerned.

C. *Protecting human rights through information-gathering and dissemination.* Not all of the EU's human rights work is a matter of adjudication as in *Nold*, or in the form of high diplomacy and linkage as in the Balladur Plan, or in the form of regulation and harmonization, as in the rights of the disabled. Consider for example the European Monitoring Centre on Racism and Xenophobia ("EUMC"), whose prime objective is to "[p]rovide the Community and its Member States with objective, reliable and comparable data at the European level on the phenomena of racism, xenophobia and Antisemitism in order to help them take measures or formulate courses of action within their respective spheres of competence." The EUMC has become a clearing-house for studying the extent of racism and xenophobia in its many forms, including Antisemitism and Islamophobia, and to disseminate information, data, and best practices to the member states.

THE OSCE MACHINERY

The Organization for Security and Cooperation in Europe ("OSCE") describes itself as the "largest regional security organization in the world," and it is certainly a political force to be reckoned with. Its membership includes the United States and Canada, Western and Eastern Europe, the Baltic States, Russia and Ukraine, and the other republics of the former Soviet Union.[4] Begun during the détente phase of the Cold War, the OSCE–then known as the *Conference* on Economic Security and Cooperation ("CSCE")–offered an on-going forum for political dialogue between East and West. With the demise of the Soviet Union in the 1990's, the organization morphed into a more formal instrument for early warning and prevention of conflict in the region, crisis management, and post-conflict rehabilitation.

Despite the absence of judicial institutions and mandatory reporting mechanisms, the OSCE works in part because it operates on the basis of a broad conception of "security." It has no military or intelligence forces under its command, and no centralized or hierarchical power separate from the members themselves, but it has developed an institutional structure (and a specialized lingo) for addressing *three dimensions* of security: the "politico-military dimension," "the economic and environmental dimension," and the "human dimension." From this perspective, the protection of national minorities, democratization, and the rule of law are no less security-related than arms control and counter-terrorism. The essentially diplomatic dynamic of the OSCE is effective because of perceived linkages between human rights, democratic pluralism, and the rule of law on one hand, with other items on the members' agenda like trade and commerce, security, and the environment.

The human rights work of the organization originated in a general statement on human rights embodied in Principle VII of the Helsinki Final Act of 1975:

Respect for human rights and fundamental freedoms, including the freedom of thought, conscience, religion or belief–

> The participating States will respect human rights and fundamental freedoms, including the freedom of thought, conscience,

---

4. As of June 2008, the 56 members of the OSCE were Albania, Andorra, Armenia, Austria, Azerbaijan, Belarus, Belgium, Bosnia and Herzegovina, Bulgaria, Canada, Croatia, Cyprus, Czech Republic, Denmark, Estonia, Finland, France, Georgia, Germany, Greece, Holy See, Hungary, Iceland, Ireland, Italy, Kazakhstan, Kyrgyzstan, Latvia, Liechtenstein, Lithuania, Luxembourg, former Yugoslav Republic of Macedonia, Malta, Moldova, Monaco, Montenegro, Netherlands, Norway, Poland, Portugal, Romania, Russian Federation, San Marino, Serbia, Slovak Republic, Slovenia, Spain, Sweden, Switzerland, Tajikistan, Turkey, Turkmenistan, Ukraine, United Kingdom, United States of America and Uzbekistan.

religion or belief, for all without distinction as to race, sex, language or religion.

> They will promote and encourage the effective exercise of civil, political, economic, social, cultural and other rights and freedoms all of which derive from the inherent dignity of the human person and are essential for his free and full development.

> Within this framework the participating States will recognize and respect the freedom of the individual to profess and practice, alone or in community with others, religion or belief acting in accordance with the dictates of his own conscience.

> The participating States on whose territory national minorities exist will respect the right of persons belonging to such minorities to equality before the law, will afford them the full opportunity for the actual enjoyment of human rights and fundamental freedoms and will, in this manner, protect their legitimate interests in this sphere.

> The participating States recognize the universal significance of human rights and fundamental freedoms, respect for which is an essential factor for the peace, justice and well-being necessary to ensure the development of friendly relations and co-operation among themselves as among all States.

> They will constantly respect these rights and freedoms in their mutual relations and will endeavour jointly and separately, including in co-operation with the United Nations, to promote universal and effective respect for them.

> They confirm the right of the individual to know and act upon his rights and duties in this field.

> In the field of human rights and fundamental freedoms, the participating States will act in conformity with the purposes and principles of the Charter of the United Nations and with the Universal Declaration of Human Rights. They will also fulfil their obligations as set forth in the international declarations and agreements in this field, including inter alia the International Covenants on Human Rights, by which they may be bound.

The collection of rights in the Helsinki Final Act nourished a generation of dissidents in the Warsaw Pact states. CSCE review conferences became a venue for criticism—of martial law in Poland, of systematic rural destruction in Romania, of repression of dissidents in the Czech Republic.

Since the formalization (and renaming) of the organization in 1994, the human rights portfolio of the organization has grown through the development of the so-called Human Dimension Mechanism ("HDM"), which consists in a system of bilateral, multilateral, and conference-wide negotiations, supplemented by third-party mediation and fact-finding processes. In fact, over the years, the OSCE has established a variety of

HDM institutions focused on the promotion and protection of human rights, including the Office for Democratic Institutions and Human Rights ("ODIHR"), the OSCE Representative on Freedom of the Media, and the High Commissioner for National Minorities. The organization also operates a series of field missions in OSCE participating states that have protecting human rights, strengthening rule of law, and promoting democracy as part of their mandates. The OSCE has also established two mechanisms to monitor the implementation of the commitments of member states in the field of human rights and democracy—the so-called Vienna and Moscow Mechanisms. The Vienna Mechanism permits a participating State to raise questions relating to human rights concerns in other OSCE States. The Moscow Mechanism builds on this by providing for the creation of an *ad hoc* mission of independent experts to investigate and assist in the resolution of the concerns identified. The Moscow Mechanism was used for example by ten states (Germany, the United States, Austria, Canada, the United Kingdom, Greece, Ireland, Italy, Norway and Sweden) in response to Turkmenistan's investigation of a reported attack on President Niyazov in 2002.

As a result of the invocation of the Moscow Mechanism, an OSCE rapporteur was appointed "to investigate all matters relating to the conduct of the investigations, including allegations of torture, and resulting developments which may constitute a serious threat to the fulfillment by Turkmenistan of its OSCE commitments in the human dimension." In February 2003, the rapporteur submitted a report of his fact-finding "mission" concerning the ongoing repression since the murder attempt against President Niyazov. Although the rapporteur was not permitted to visit Turkmenistan by the Turkmen government, the report nevertheless concluded:

> Large-scale violations of all the principles of due process of law, like arbitrary detentions or show trials took place. Not only has torture been used to obtain confessions, but the forced use of drugs was a means of criminalizing the detainees, entailing lethal risks for them. A multiform collective repression fell on the "enemies of the people", whereas forced displacement is officially announced in arid regions of the country, especially against peoples targeted on the ground of their ethic origin. Even if the death penalty has been legally abolished, in practice, the survival expectancy of political detainees and displaced persons seems very low. Certain personalities, who were detained incommunicado, may have already been eliminated.

Notably, the rapporteur did not even contact the lawyers for individuals detained by the Turkmen government, for fear of compromising their safety. Such are the hazards of investigating human rights violations in a country like Turkmenistan.

The protection of national minorities

Perhaps the most striking example of the "human dimension" of security within the OSCE region is the treatment of national minorities.

Ethnic tension has been the most frequent source of conflict within the OSCE region. One need only consider the conflict in the Balkans in the 1990s to see how the lack of respect for the rights of minorities can cause conflict and regional instability. Over time, the OSCE has co-alesced around the idea that the questions relating to national minorities can only be resolved in a democratic political framework based on the rule of law, with a functioning independent judiciary. In Chapter IV of the Copenhagen Document, for example, the organization attempted to articulate a common approach to the treatment of identity groups, including minorities, based on the principle that "to belong to a national minority is a matter of a person's individual choice and no disadvantage may arise form the exercise of such choice." At a minimum, minorities are entitled to equal protection and non-discrimination, but democratic pluralism—for all of its potential messiness—is no less essential. The idea is that, of all the simplistic ways to misunderstand democracy, majority rule tops the list. Democracy is best preserved, according to this document, when persons belonging to national minorities have the right "freely to express, preserve, and develop their ethnic, cultural, linguistic or religious identity and to maintain and develop their culture in all aspects, free of any attempts at assimilation against their will." This general idea brings with it some specific protections, like the right to use one's native tongue; to establish special educational, cultural, and religious institutions; to practice and profess one's religion; to maintain contact with other members of one's group both inside the country and abroad; and to work with NGOs.

Recognizing the need for action on this front, OSCE participating states created the post of High Commissioner for National Minorities in 1992 to "provide 'early warning' and, as appropriate, 'early action' at the earliest possible stage in regard to tensions involving national minority issues that have the potential [to escalate] into a conflict within the CSCE area, affecting peace, stability, or relations between participating States." CSCE HELSINKI DOCUMENT 1992: THE CHALLENGES OF CHANGE, DECISIONS at ¶ 23.

The mandate of the High Commissioner is unique, not only for its focus on minorities, but because it is designed to provide him or her maximum flexibility to reduce tensions by advocating on behalf of threatened national minorities. The High Commissioner does this through quiet diplomacy, not through press conferences and sensational reports, which allows him or her to gain the confidence of the main actors and to make progress where sensitive issues warrant discretion.

An important component of the High Commissioner's work is the ability to travel throughout the OSCE region and engage directly with government, civil society and—most important—members of national minority groups themselves. Through these consultations, he or she can identify particular areas of concern and formulate approaches to improving the treatment of minorities. In recent years, the High Commissioner has worked with Hungary to revise its status law and encouraged the adoption of bilateral agreements with neighboring Romania and Slovakia to reduce inter-ethnic relations; with Kyrgyzstan to develop a national policy on integration of minorities through education; and with the former Yugoslav Republic of Moldova to increase the number ethnic Albanians who have access to higher education.

In addition to carrying out country visits and engaging bilaterally with governments, the High Commissioner prepares thematic recommendations for all OSCE participating states. In the past, he has focused *inter alia* on policing in multi-ethnic societies, the use of minority languages in broadcasting, minority participation in the elections process, and increasing the participation of ethnic minorities in public life. These recommendations constitute valuable tools for advocates in the region because they reflect international standards and best practice for guaranteeing the rights of minorities. Notably, these documents are not a collection of mere hortatory principles drafted by consensus; they include concrete, operational recommendations that are readily implemented by states with the political will to protect minorities.

Election-observing and democracy

Over the three decades of its existence, the CSCE/OSCE has developed particular expertise in elections; indeed, the OSCE stamp of approval is generally considered the gold standard for elections. Guided by the general principle that everyone has the right to participate in free and fair elections, the OSCE has comprehensively identified the legal, institutional and operational elements necessary to ensure that this right is respected in practice. This includes *inter alia* an independent elections commission, secret balloting, universal and equal suffrage, a free media, and the right to establish political parties. In practice, an OSCE elections observation mission maintains vigilance throughout the election to guard against violations of fundamental civil and political rights, administrative constraints on political participation, ballot-box stuffing, and voter intimidation. Clearly, human rights lawyers and experts have an important role to play not only by identifying and pursuing the component rights of the right to vote in elections, but also by providing expert advice and guidance to elections officials where there the political will exists to strengthen democratic institutions.

The institution with responsibility for observing and monitoring elections, as well as providing guidance, recommendations and technical assistance to improve the quality of elections, is the Office for Democratic Institutions and Human Rights (ODIHR). When a participating state invites the OSCE to observe its elections, ODIHR deploys a multidisciplinary team months in advance of election day, which includes elections, political and legal analysts; logistics officers; and administrative staff. These activities are coordinated by a Head of Mission who provides regular reports to ODIHR headquarters in Warsaw. Just prior to the election, ODIHR sends a substantial team of short-term observers drawn from throughout the OSCE region to observe the voting and counting of ballots. After the election, the OSCE publishes a final report, and ODIHR continues to engage with local election authorities to encourage the implementation of any recommendations made in its final report.

A common misperception is that the OSCE only sends election observation missions to countries whose elections are not perceived as free and fair. In recent years, however, ODIHR has shifted some of its focus to elections in established democracies. For example, the OSCE sent a mission to the United States in 2004 to observe the Presidential elections. *See* OSCE/ODIHR Election Observation Mission Final Report: United States of America 2 November 2004 Elections (31 March 2005). The report concluded that the elections "mostly met the OSCE commitments included in the 1990 Copenhagen Document," but raised concerns over the redrawing of congressional districts, conflicts of interest presented by state and county election officials running for office and campaigning for candidates, alleged vote suppression among minorities, and non-transparent certification procedures for electronic voting machines.

Human trafficking

The OSCE has recognized that the trafficking of human beings is a transnational crime, a modern form of slavery, and that states have an obligation under international human rights law to combat it. In 2003, the OSCE adopted an Action Plan to Combat Trafficking in Human Beings, which called on participating states to prevent trafficking, to prosecute traffickers, and to protect trafficked persons. In 2004, the OSCE appointed a Special Representative on Trafficking in Human Beings to assist participating States in the implementation of the Action Plan. Part of the Special Representative's mandate includes country visits and the identification of best practices, as the following report suggests.

ORGANIZATION FOR SECURITY AND CO-OPERATION IN EUROPE SPECIAL REPRESENTATIVE ON COMBATING TRAFFICKING IN HUMAN BEINGS ["THB"] COUNTRY VISIT TO DENMARK (7–9 JUNE 2005)
Vienna, December 2005

Denmark is mainly a country of transit and destination for women and children from Eastern Europe, the Baltic States, the former Soviet Union, Thailand, and Africa. Tourist visas, au pair arrangements, training programs, bogus asylum applications, marriages of convenience and mail-order-bride systems are among the means employed to get victims of trafficking into the country. Women from Nigeria and Thailand are often "hidden" within their own communities, which makes identification particularly difficult for social service providers and authorities.

Initially the Danish authorities viewed human trafficking as a problem related to sexual exploitation. So far, no cases of trafficking for labour exploitation have been disclosed.

Denmark has had a National Action Plan (NAP) to Combat Trafficking in Women since 2002, which focuses on two main areas: support to victims of trafficking, mostly with a view to returning them to their home countries, and to preventive measures. What is lacking in the NAP is a focus on child trafficking, on other forms of trafficking (*i.e.*, trafficking for labour exploitation/forced and bonded labour), as well as on long term protection and assistance for victims of trafficking. The government is aware of the fact that the current NAP is not comprehensive enough, and has initiated discussions with key interlocutors to consider the inclusion of child protection issues into a new plan. On the other hand, the NAP provides for funds allocated to the activities mentioned as well as for monitoring by the Danish Centre for Research on Social Vulnerability. The Centre's remit includes documentation, monitoring of THB at national level, and provides a platform for sharing experience among government agencies and NGOs. Further, it has been requested to compile a report on the progress made in implementing the NAP and to give recommendations to the government. In the long run, these functions could be transferred to a National Rapporteur with a broader mandate.

The inter-ministerial group for anti-trafficking, established within the Ministry of Gender Equality, should be chaired by a national governmental coordinator in order to strengthen national and international cooperation of anti-trafficking measures and activities.

Denmark supports a number of anti-trafficking programs in countries of origin focusing on activities in the field of prevention and protection of victims, such as cooperation and networking with embassies. Denmark is funding activities in countries of origin via the Ministry of Foreign Affairs. The approach is comprehensive and includes: assessment of the situation, long-term commitment (*i.e.* a three year program), yearly consultation with potential partners and relevant authorities via field missions, and involvement of relevant implementing agencies (i.e. IOs and NGOs).

Legal background and law enforcement

Denmark has ratified the UN Protocol [to Prevent, Suppress and Punish Trafficking in Persons, especially Women and Children], but opted out of the EC Directive on Temporary Residence Permit for Trafficked Persons. Since June 2002, the Danish law on trafficking in human beings covers all forms of exploitation and provides for a maximum sentence of eight years. Victims of trafficking are granted a reflection period of 15 days before having to decide, whether they wish to collaborate with the authorities. This period can be extended for the duration of the judicial procedure, if deemed necessary by law enforcement. However, the final decision on extensions lies with the immigration services on the basis of a humanitarian visa on "extraordinary conditions"; yet, to date, there has been no such case. A legal counsel can be retained at the expense of the state, but only if law enforcement has recognised the individual in question as a victim. This situation may weaken the position of the victim since s/he is made fully dependent on recognition by the authorities before getting access to services and information. In addition, Danish authorities are reluctant to grant long-term stays for victims of trafficking and to render appropriate assistance and protection to trafficked persons. This practice may become an obstacle to the successful prosecution of traffickers.

When potential cases of THB are investigated by the police, a specialized unit, called SOCA, is responsible for monitoring and coordinating the gathering of information at national and international level. There is a need to strengthen training and awareness raising of law enforcement officials at the local level where inquiries into THB cases are initiated. This would facilitate the identification of victims of trafficking, as well as contribute to more prosecutions under the trafficking law(s) as opposed to other related offences such as pimping.

Trafficking in children

Since 1999, Save the Children Denmark received information of at least 14 cases of trafficking in children from Russia, Latvia, Lithuania, Poland, Slovakia, Romania, Nigeria, and Ecuador. In 2003, the same organization came across 205 cases, followed by 26 new cases in 2004 of trafficking in children for petty crime, involving boys from the Balkan region and Lithuania However, these cases have not led to further investigation by the authorities. * * * Denmark has no tailor-made facilities and specialized services for child victims of trafficking. NGOs suspect that bogus family reunifications are used to camouflage trafficking in minors for the purpose of abusing the social security system. Similarly, Danish citizens marry foreign women with a child/children with a view to sexually abusing the child/children. A national network to combat trafficking in children, consisting of NGOs, public social service providers, the municipality of Copenhagen, police and other authorities has been initiated by Save the Children, which also organised a two-day workshop for professionals providing assistance.

Disappearance of unaccompanied minors is an issue of concern, along with the fact that social service providers have noticed worrying trends of vulnerable behaviour among unaccompanied minors, such as the use of mobile phones to communicate with unknown persons shortly after their arrival to the country. The special vulnerability of unaccompanied minors calls for clear procedures along with a referral mechanism, and the establishment of specialized services for minors-victims of trafficking. Individual risk assessment should be part of the standard procedures for minors prior to returning them to their countries of origin.

Services for victims of trafficking

Victim identification is usually the responsibility of law enforcement agencies, while the immigration service is responsible for the assessment of cases including the final decision on the granting of residence permits. Approximately 42 women have been sheltered at safe houses from October 2003 to May 2005, most of whom were referred by the police. Psychological and legal counselling, accommodation, medical care, etc., are provided by social services and NGOs funded by the government. Most victims of trafficking have opted to return to their countries of origin, which may be partly due to the obstacles to obtaining temporary residence permits and the lack of long term social inclusion.

The Danish Government supports a number of awareness raising programs at national level, hotline services, and the dissemination of information (in several languages) on assistance and on the legal rights of potential victims. In general, there is good cooperation between NGOs and the government, and in particular with law enforcement.

Current problems and areas for follow-up

There is a need to address the following problems:

> Government authorities consider trafficking in human beings mainly from an illegal migration perspective, which implies a lack of understanding for the complexity of the problem and uncertainty as to the measures required to deal with it within a multi-disciplinary framework;

> the need to raise the knowledge base on victim identification and service provision for government authorities, in particular law enforcement and immigration officials, regarding trafficked persons;

> the need to strengthen a victim centred approach, when it comes to victim protection and assistance, including the need to expand and to institutionalise cooperation between authorities and NGOs, as the service providers for victims of trafficking;

> the need to strengthen national anti-trafficking structures aimed at closer cooperation between the different interlocutors, based on a better understanding of the scale and nature of the problem at national level;

> the need to establish a specific protection scheme for victims of trafficking with the granting of a reflection period followed by a temporary (and if necessary, a permanent) residence permit;

> the need to develop a protection scheme for victims of trafficking which is not conditional to cooperation with the judiciary;

> the need to establish comprehensive national referral mechanisms in order to provide appropriate assistance to victims;

> the need to raise awareness of the problem of child trafficking, in particular among persons responsible for child care and protection;

> the need for regular training in victim identification and service provision for government authorities, in particular law enforcement and immigration officials dealing with trafficked persons, in cooperation with NGOs, social service providers and relevant interlocutors, such as health and labour inspectors;

> the need to strengthen the capacity of NGOs and social services to provide appropriate assistance to victims of trafficking;

> the need to earmark appropriate funds for the protection services;

> the need to establish multi-disciplinary teams/units of NGOs, law enforcement and other relevant authorities, working together on individual cases;

> the need for clear time frames for the implementation of the anti-trafficking measures laid down in the National Action Plan with a clear division of labour, budgeting and a self-monitoring mechanism;

> the need to establish/strengthen a coordination mechanism at inter-ministerial and operational level designed for better coordination among the different authorities and services, including the appointment of a national coordinator.

NOTES AND QUESTIONS ON THE OSCE

1. *The link between security and human rights advocacy.* Because of its preference for diplomatic rather than judicial approaches to human rights violations, the OSCE may appear to be less relevant to a lawyer with a client to represent. But human rights advocates should not underestimate the power of the OSCE as a forum for addressing more systematic abuses and for preventing conflict that arises out of some unredressed human rights crisis. As Professor Shelton has observed,

> The OSCE has a comparative advantage in conflict prevention because the Council of Europe is not a security organization and its mandate is limited. The OSCE has also taken action on some situations where the Council of Europe and the United Nations have been inactive, such as with regard to citizenship and language laws in Estonia and Latvia, and the language law in Slovakia. On the other hand, the complaints procedure of the European Convention has no parallel in the OSCE. The political character of OSCE commitments precludes judicial enforcement or complaints procedures, but allows rapid response in periods of crisis. It can thus be seen to supplement, but not replace the pre-existing European system.

Dinah Shelton, *The Boundaries of Human Rights Jurisdiction in Europe*, 13 DUKE J. COMP. & INT'L L. 95, 122 (2003).

2. *Other principles of the OSCE.* As noted, Principle VII of the Helsinki Final Act addresses "respect for human rights and fundamental freedoms, including the freedom of thought, conscience, religion, or belief," but other bedrock principles of the OSCE may involve human rights as well, including Principle II, "Refraining from the threat or use of force;" Principle V, "Peaceful settlement of disputes;" Principle VIII, "Equal rights and self-determination of peoples;" and Principle X, "Fulfilment in good faith of obligations under international law."

3. *Human rights diplomacy.* A quick glance at the mandates for various OSCE field missions presents an interesting study in human rights diplomacy within the OSCE. Consider first Belarus. The 2006 presidential elections in Belarus were clearly rigged in favor of President Lukashenko, an unreconstructed Communist dictator who uses violence and intimidation to crush political opposition. As a result, both the U.S. and the EU imposed travel and financial restrictions on Belarusian regime officials. The OSCE maintains a field presence in Minsk, the present mandate of which is to: "Assist the Belarusian Government in further promoting institution building, in further consolidating the Rule of Law and in developing relations with civil society, in accordance with OSCE principles and commitments." OSCE Permanent Council Decision No. 526, 429th Plenary Meeting, Doc No. PC.DEC/526 (Dec. 30, 2002) ¶ 2. Compare this to the mandate for the OSCE Center in Dushanbe, Tajikistan: "promote ways and means for the OSCE to assist in the development of a legal framework and democratic political institutions and processes including the respect of human rights. * * *" OSCE Permanent Council Decision No. 500, Doc. No. PC.DEC/500/Corr.1 (Oct. 31, 2002) ¶ 2. How would you articulate the practical differences that these different formulations make in the power of the OSCE field mission?

Assume that you are working in the OSCE field offices in Belarus and Tajikistan during a violent police crack-down on demonstrators who have taken to the street to protest a new, restrictive media law. Given a range of possible actions in the office's official capacity, what would each mandate permit you to do? Recognizing that the very existence of the office might be at stake, could you register complaints with the government? Express solidarity with the protesters through public remarks? Convene civil society and political opposition groups to document and publicize the abuses? Prepare a report for presentation to the OSCE Permanent Council?

4. *The long-term power of short-term hypocrisy.* The Soviet Union may have thought that it got the better end of the deal in the Helsinki Accords, because the agreement obliged the West to acknowledge national boundaries within Eastern Europe–a long-term strategic goal of the U.S.S.R. In exchange, the Soviet Union was obliged to give what it probably thought was lip service to human rights ideals. Thirteen years later, the Soviet empire fell apart, as though the Soviet system for all its power could not survive the power of the ideas in the Helsinki Final Act.

As noted by Vaclav Havel, a playwright and dissident who eventually became the president of Czechoslovakia,

> [The Helsinki Accords] were important for all the so-called dissident movements in the Soviet Bloc. They offered something that no one, probably, initially, knew they were offering. They offered a basic argument, one that is difficult to dismiss: and that is the idea of human and civil rights in the form of agreements and the closing text from Helsinki. There, communist governments guaranteed certain rights and freedoms, even though those governments, of course, had no intention of respecting them. But, nevertheless, they signed it. They had their reasons for signing it then. And these movements were based on that [sic] they took them literally and they referred to these agreements. That was one source of the idea of resistance which was non-violent and even legalistic, I'd say. All we wanted was for the government to abide by these valid laws and international treaties.

www.cnn.com/SPECIALS/cold.war/episodes/19/interviews/havel/.

5. *Assessing the effectiveness of the OSCE.* After the fall of the Soviet Union, many held out hope that the ex-Soviet states would become democracies and that the OSCE would facilitate if not drive the transition. Some members, like the Baltic States, have made the transition; however, others in Central Asia have not fared as well. Throughout Central Asia, human rights abuses and dictatorial forms of government continue. So is the OSCE a success story or not?

At a minimum, the Human Dimension Mechanism gave political legitimacy to the ability of one state to raise with another state an individual case or a situation concerning human rights. Of course, problems remain, but the failure of the organization to fix the former Yugoslavia or to prevent human rights abuses in Chechnya should not blind us to the reality of its confidence-building measures in some of the ethnic hot-spots of Europe: Slovakia and Romania with regard to the Hungarian minorities; in the Baltic states and Ukraine with regard to the Russian minorities; and in Macedonia with regard to the Albanian minority.

Practicum

Legal Background to Sex Trafficking in Europe

The United States government and the NGO community estimate that between 600,000 and 800,000 people worldwide are trafficked each year. Eighty percent of the victims are women. Over the last three decades, Europe has experienced a surge in human trafficking, partly as a consequence of more open borders. The increasing flow of trafficked people—generally from the former Soviet satellite states to the more affluent central and western European nations—has resulted from a confluence of factors: changed gender roles, an increase in demand for sex-related services, economic downturns that disproportionately affect women, and a desire among women to escape abusive environments.

The various European institutions have identified sex trafficking as a pressing human rights issue and have adopted numerous initiatives to address it. For example, the Charter of Fundamental Rights of the European Union prohibits slavery and forced labor (Article 5), and the Treaty on the European Union (Title VI(3)) includes provisions on police and judicial cooperation intended to improve efforts to prevent and combat crime, including trafficking in persons. The Council of the European Union has also adopted a Framework Decision (2002) on combating trafficking in human beings which requires EU member states to make trafficking a punishable offense, establishes penalties for the crime, and provides for civil liability in trafficking cases. Similarly, the Council of Europe has developed a convention designed to prevent and combat trafficking through discouraging demand as well as protecting and providing legal redress for victims.

Human Rights Standards for Admission to the EU

Admission to the European Union is based on the criteria developed at the Copenhagen European Council in 1993, which requires, among other things, that the state seeking admission have achieved "stability of institutions guaranteeing democracy, the rule of law, human rights and respect for and protection of minorities."

Trafficking in Takania

The southeastern European country of Takania has one of the largest markets in the sex trade. Conservative estimates have the industry netting a profit of $3.6 billion in 2005 with over 5,000 women working as sex slaves.

In the summer of 2005, security forces in Takania found five women–from the former Soviet state of Okraine–who had been imprisoned for 10 months in an underground, windowless, 40–square-foot cell in a Takanian resort town. The women had been lured by the promise of legitimate jobs as waitresses. But, when they arrived in Takania, they had been forced into prostitution and grossly abused if they refused to provide sex to customers. One woman told officials that she had boiling water poured over her legs and genitals when she had refused to have sex with a client. All five women described similar and worse treatment.

This discovery highlighted a major issue of concern for the Takanian government and its human rights activists: the country had become a prominent destination in the underground European sex trafficking industry. As a member of the Council of Europe and a participating state in the OSCE, and as a party to several international agreements against human trafficking, Takania is under pressure to take active steps to curb the industry. The failure to do so threatens Takania's overriding foreign policy goal: admission to the European Union.

The government of Takania has sought outside assistance in the development of a plan for tackling the trafficking problem, both for its own sake and in order to gain admission to the EU. Students will assume the role of private sector advisors to the Government of Takania and develop a comprehensive strategy and action plan addressing this crisis. The strategy should focus on international obligations and commitments assumed by governments in this area and the specific implementation of these international standards in states seeking admission to the EU.

As a participating state in the OSCE, Takania is committed to all of the OSCE instruments addressing trafficking in persons. *See, e.g.,* OSCE Action Plan To Combat Trafficking in Human Beings. Moreover, as a member state of the Council of Europe, Takania is similarly obligated to the implementation of Council instruments and directives. *See, e.g.,* Council Framework Decision of 19 July 2002 on combating trafficking in human beings; Council Directive of 29 April 2004 on the residence permit issued to third-country nationals who are victims of trafficking in human beings or have been the subject of an action to facilitate illegal immigration, who cooperate with the competent authorities.

In addition, Takania is a party to each of the following instruments:

(1) The United Nations Protocol to Prevent, Suppress and Punish Trafficking in Persons, Especially Women and Children, supplementing the United Nations Convention against Transnational Organized Crime;

(2) The Charter of Fundamental Rights of the European Union, Chapter 1, Art.5;

(3) Treaty on European Union, Title VI (3) (Provisions on police and judicial cooperation in criminal matters);

(4) The Council of Europe: Action Against Trafficking in Human Beings, CETS 197.

CHAPTER 3

MODULE 7B

THE INTER-AMERICAN HUMAN RIGHTS SYSTEM

■ ■ ■

Orientation

In 1948; when the Organization of American States ("OAS") was formed, its founding members recognized the link between human rights and international peace and security. Not only did the OAS Charter create an Inter–American Commission on Human Rights, but, in that same year, the American Declaration on the Rights and Duties of Man was adopted by the OAS General Assembly. At the time, these initial steps toward a regional human rights system seemed small, but, in the decades to follow, the human rights organs of the OAS would prove instrumental in the promotion and protection of human rights in the region. The relationship between peace, security and human rights would become all too clear as many states in the Americas became caught in a repeating cycle of war and human rights abuses.

For human rights lawyers, the Inter–American system has proved to be a valuable asset—as a forum for advancing the claims of victims, for publicizing abuses, and for pressuring governments to act. The Inter–American Commission on Human Rights has performed numerous on-site investigations of widespread abuses that have formed the basis for domestic prosecutions, international censure, and national reconciliation processes in post-conflict situations. The Commission and the Inter–American Court of Human Rights have developed ground-breaking jurisprudence in the field of human rights law and provided protection and compensation for human rights victims. Moreover, within the OAS, states negotiated and adopted a series of regional instruments that have formed the basis of domestic law as well as the development of international human rights standards.

The obstacles to these regional successes have been—and to some extent remain—considerable. For many countries, colonialism had lasting, disastrous effects that permeate economic, cultural, and political life. Similarly, some OAS member states share the historical legacy of slavery.

As a consequence, racism and racial discrimination can block full social integration and equality for all peoples. In addition, the human rights organs of the OAS lack sufficient resources to fulfil their mandates efficiently; compliance with Commission recommendations and Court judgments is inconsistent; and few OAS conventions have been widely ratified. And, while the human rights situation has improved, widespread abuses continue to plague many countries in the region.

Of course, these shortcomings should come as no surprise: despite the many attributes the region shares, there are many differences and conflicts that hinder cooperation and foster inequality. The region is dominated by the economic, political, and military power of the United States. Many states in the region have also experienced decades of corruption and incompetent governance, as well as failed economic management. As a result, human rights and fundamental freedoms have not always been a priority; indeed, political and economic failures have contributed to the development of a culture of impunity in some countries.

Given these formidable challenges, the promise of a region where states share and observe the same values with regard to human rights, monitored and enforced by a powerful international institution, remains elusive. Nevertheless, the Inter–American System is worth understanding for the opportunities it provides advocates, its contribution to the development of human rights law, and the pressure points it offers for the promotion and protection of human rights in the Americas.

OAS Human Rights Instruments

The principal human rights instruments within the Americas are the American Declaration on the Rights and Duties of Man, Nov. 22, 1969, O.A.S.T.S. No. 36, 1144 U.N.T.S 123 ("the Declaration"), adopted by resolution of the OAS General Assembly in 1948, and the American Convention on Human Rights, July 18, 1978, O.A.S.T.S. No. 36, 1144 U.N.T.S. 123 ("the Convention"), which was adopted in 1969 but did not enter into force until 1978. The Convention applies only to those states that have signed and ratified it, and the Declaration applies to all states within the OAS.

Like the Universal Declaration of Human Rights, the American Declaration sets forth a wide range of human rights, covering civil, political, economic, social, and cultural rights. Notably, the Declaration not only establishes the rights of citizens and the duties of states to respect those rights, but it also purports to establish the duties of citizens, such as to work, to serve the community, and to vote.

One president of the Inter–American Court has observed that the American Declaration has made four key contributions to the development of the Inter-American human rights system: the concept that human rights inhere to the individual; the concept of the integral nature of all human rights (civil, political, economic, social and cultural);

the normative basis of protection for states not party to the Convention; and the correlation between rights and duties. *See* Antonio Augusto Cancado Trindade, *Current State and Perspectives of the Inter–American System of Human Rights at the Dawn of the New Century*, 8 TUL. J. INT'L & COMP. L. 5, 78 (2000). Although there is disagreement as to the legal status of the American Declaration (*i.e.*, as creating legal obligations or as an aspirational document), its contribution to the jurisprudence of the Inter–American human rights system is beyond question.

The entry into force of a legally binding Convention thirty years after the adoption of the American Declaration was a logical and important step forward. The Convention transformed the Declaration's hortatory statements into obligations to be implemented into the domestic legal systems of states parties, and it created an Inter–American Court to consider the complaints of individuals whose human rights have been violated. As of 2008, 24 states had ratified the Convention. Trinidad and Tobago suspended its ratification in 1998. Notably, neither the United States nor Canada is party to the Convention.

The Convention devotes itself almost entirely to civil and political rights, including only one article (art. 26) by which states commit themselves to taking measures, "with a view to achieving progressively" the realization of economic, social, and cultural rights. In addition to setting forth a full panoply of generally accepted individual human rights (as well as the concomitant obligation of states to respect those rights), the Convention included somewhat controversial provisions. For instance, article 4 notes that the right to life "shall be protected by law, and in general, from the moment of conception,"[1] and article 21 purports to establish the "right to property" as a human right.

After the Convention entered into force, the OAS negotiated and adopted two protocols to the Convention: the Additional Protocol to the American Convention on Human Rights in the Area of Economic, Social and Cultural Rights (Protocol of San Salvador): Nov. 17, 1988, entered into force Nov. 16, 1999, O.A.S.T.S. No. 69, 28 I.L.M. 156; and the Protocol to the American Convention on Human Rights to Abolish the Death Penalty: June 8, 1990, entered into force Oct. 6, 1993, O.A.T.S. No. 73, 29 I.L.M. 1447. In addition to the Declaration and Convention, the OAS has adopted various instruments related to human rights, which have received varied levels of support. (*See, e.g.* Inter–American Convention Against Corruption, March 29, 1996, O.A.S., 35 I.L.M. 724; Inter–American Convention Against the Illicit Manufacturing of and Trafficking in Firearms, Ammunition, Explosives, and Other Related Material, Nov. 11, 1997, O.A.S., AGIRES. 1999 (XXXIV–0/04)(2004); and Convention to Prevent and Punish the Acts of Terrorism Taking the Form of Crimes Against Persons and Related Extortion that Are of

---

1. For an interesting discussion of Article 4, *see* JOCELYN E. GETGEN, *Reproductive Injustice: An Analysis of Nicaragua's Complete Abortion Ban*, 41 CORNELL INT'L L.J. 143, 167 (2008) (noting that this protection of fetal rights has not been found to be inconsistent with a woman's right to obtain a safe and legal abortion.)

International Significance, Feb. 2, 1971, 27 U.S.T. 3949, O.A.S.T.S. 37); the Inter–American Convention to Prevent and Punish Torture: Dec. 9, 1985, O.A.S.T.S. No. 67, 25 I.L.M. 519; the Inter–American Convention on Forced Disappearance of Persons: June 9, 1994, 33 I.L.M. 1529; the Inter–American Convention on the Prevention, Punishment and Eradication of Violence against Women: June 9, 1994, entered into force March 5 1995, O.A.S.Doc A–61, 33 I.L.M. 1534; and the Inter–American Convention on the Elimination of All Forms of Discrimination against Persons with Disabilities: June 7, 1999, OEADOC A.G/Res. 1608, (XXIX–0199).

In addition to these binding instruments, the member states of the OAS have been negotiating a Draft American Declaration on the Rights of Indigenous Peoples since 1989. Even though negotiations will not lead to a legally binding document, the process has been long and contentious. Issues of self-determination, cultural dominance, and rights to land and resources figure prominently in the Draft Declaration. Indigenous peoples view this process as a means to achieve recognition of their status as peoples with a collective right to self-determination and control over land and resources. Governments, on the other hand, see the process as a threat to their sovereignty, both over political processes and economic resources. Decisions of the Commission and Court, such as *The Case of the Mayagna (Sumo) Awas Tingni Community v. Nicaragua*, Case No. 79 (Judgment of Aug. 31, 2001), have affirmed the rights of indigenous peoples, particularly as they lose their ancestral lands and cultural traditions throughout the Americas at an alarming rate.

Inter-American Commission on Human Rights

Created by the OAS Charter "to promote the observance and protection of human rights and to serve as a consultative organ of the Organization in these matters," the Commission is the principal human rights mechanism in the Inter-American human rights system. Its regulations and statute authorize the Commission to consider petitions against OAS member states and to prepare reports on the human rights situation in any OAS member state. In addition, involving governments that are the Commission can forward cases to the Inter–American Court, where the Commission represents the petitioner.

Given the multitude of roles the Commission plays—investigator, adjudicator, advocate—it occupies a unique position in the human rights world. On the one hand, its broad expertise and access to information enhance its ability to fulfill the Commission's mandate; on the other, its cross-cutting roles have given rise to charges of a lack of impartiality by states appearing before it. This charge has increased in resonance in recent years as resource constraints have required the Commission to prioritize its work in ways some criticize as politically motivated. Of course, with an enormous backlog of pending individual-state petitions and a skeletal professional staff, choices are necessary and rarely meet with universal approval.

Since its inception, the Commission's consideration of individual-state petitions has grown to be the most vibrant mechanism within the Inter-American human rights system. The Commission publishes a yearly report on its activities, in which its decisions in these matters figure prominently. Although not binding, the Commission's recommendations have often led to the resolution of disputes and are increasingly relied on by other international tribunals as an important source of human rights law.

The Commission's individual-petition mechanism is open to any person, group of persons, or non-governmental organization recognized in any of the OAS member states. Third parties are also permitted to file petitions before the Commission. Indeed, there is no requirement that a victim consent to, or even have knowledge of, a petition filed on his or her behalf. The petition need only contain some basic biographical information and a statement of facts on which the allegations are based.

For a petition to be admissible (the first stage of Commission review before addressing the merits), the petitioner must establish either that all available and effective domestic remedies have been exhausted, or that one of the statutory exceptions to the exhaustion requirement is met. This basic principle of international legal procedure is often debated before the Commission, because the regularly asserted exceptions—lack of due process, denial of access to remedies, and unwarranted delay—are often difficult to assess and vary widely from state to state. This determination also implicates the Commission's "fourth instance" principle, *i.e.*, that it will not sit in review of the decisions of national courts, unless it is alleged that a state violated the petitioner's right to a fair trial or to due process. The mandate of the Commission is to interpret and apply international human rights as set forth in the Declaration and the Convention, not to review the correctness of the decisions of national courts.

A petition must also be timely (filed within six months after the exhaustion of domestic remedies) and not duplicative of a petition pending or already examined by the Commission or another international review mechanism (*e.g.*, the UN's 1503 procedure). Finally, in reviewing admissibility, the Commission must determine that a petition is not "manifestly groundless," *i.e.*, it does not state facts that—if proved—would establish a violation of the American Declaration or Inter–American Convention. Because most cases before the Commission do not involve factual disputes (a record before national courts has already been developed), this review is often folded into the Commission's determination on the merits.

In reviewing a petition's merits, the Commission is authorized to interpret and apply the American Declaration on the Rights and Duties of Man and the Inter–American Convention on Human Rights, but the Convention applies only to those states that are parties to it. As to all others, the Commission can only consider the American Declaration.

The Commission has interpreted its jurisdiction broadly however, looking to other sources of international law to "inform" its interpretation of the provisions of the American Declaration. Not surprisingly, many states have objected strenuously to this practice, seeing it as an unauthorized expansion of the Commission's mandate, particularly where issues of international humanitarian law (*e.g.* the laws of war) are concerned, an area arguably not covered by the American Declaration.

The Commission's rules allow two stages of briefing. The government is given the opportunity to reply to the petition, then each party is given another opportunity to file briefs: the petitioner responds to the government, and the government may file another reply. Because Commission proceedings tend to be informal, requests for extensions of time and for further briefing are often approved. The Commission is authorized to perform factual investigations and to hold hearings where evidence can be presented. Either party may also invoke the Commission's friendly settlement mechanism, but neither is obligated to agree to negotiate a resolution to the dispute.

The Commission is empowered only to make recommendations to states, not to issue legally binding judgments. While many states view the Commission's recommendations as strictly advisory, others have passed legislation that gives these recommendations the force of law and allows enforcement in domestic courts. Although no mechanism exists to enforce Commission recommendations, the Commission presents an analysis in its annual report of compliance by states with its recommendations. *See, e.g.,* Annual Report of the Inter–American Commission on Human Rights, 23 Feb. 2005, OEA/Ser.L/V/II.122 Doc. 5 Rev.1 at ¶¶ 53–59.

In addition to considering individual-state petitions, the Commission is given broad authority to investigate and report on human rights abuses in OAS member states. It has used this authority aggressively, reporting on abuses throughout the Americas. Commission reports have proved instrumental in increasing public awareness of human rights situations and in pressuring governments to increase accountability and provide redress to victims. Human rights advocates have been positively effective by influencing the Commission's decision to report on a particular country and assisting with the investigation that precedes the Commission's report. The investigatory and reporting authority of the Commission should not be neglected by advocates when considering means to publicize and affect change in the human rights situation in OAS member states.

Inter-American Court of Human Rights

The Inter–American Court has jurisdiction only over cases concerning states that are parties to the Inter–American Convention and who have accepted its jurisdiction. A case can only be submitted to the Court by either a state or the Commission after full consideration before the Commission. Although individual petitioners have standing to participate in Court proceedings, they do not have the right to submit a case to the Court directly.

The Court can be a crucial mechanism for human rights advocates, as it is given broad powers under the Convention. Unlike recommendations of the Commission, decisions of the Court are legally binding on a state which has been found to violate its obligations under the Convention. The Court is provided explicit authority to order a government to take provisional measures, and it can order states to pay compensation to individuals whose rights have been violated, as well as attorneys' fees and costs. Although there is no specific means to enforce Court orders identified in the Convention, the OAS General Assembly exerts considerable political pressure against recalcitrant states, which can be effective.

In addition to considering individual petitions forwarded by the Commission, the Court is authorized to resolve disputes arising between states parties to the Convention, but this mechanism has never been invoked. The Court also has broad advisory jurisdiction to render opinions upon the request of a State party to the Convention or of any of the OAS organs, including the Commission. The advisory jurisdiction of the Court has been used to issue opinions on, *inter alia*, derogation from treaty obligations (OC–3/83), freedom of expression and the practice of law (OC–5/85), and consular notification (OC–16/99). These advisory opinions have made a substantial contribution to the development of international human rights law, but very few contentious cases have been submitted for the Court's review. This appears to be changing, as the Commission has begun to refer more cases to the Court each year. We should expect this trend to continue, so long as the Commission and Court have sufficient resources to handle their increasing dockets.

As you read the cases excerpted below, consider the value of the Inter–American human rights system as both a normative body that has contributed to the development of human rights law and as a tool for increasing awareness of human rights abuses throughout the hemisphere. While the system has its shortcomings and failures, it is important for advocates to give careful consideration to the role it can play in any advocacy strategy.

Readings

VELASQUEZ-RODRIGUEZ CASE

Judgment of July 29, 1988, Inter–Am.Ct.H.R. (Ser. C) No. 4 (1988)

1. The Inter–American Commission on Human Rights (hereinafter "the Commission") submitted the instant case to the Inter–American Court of Human Rights (hereinafter the "Court") on April 24, 1986. It

originated in a petition * * * against the State of Honduras (hereinafter "Honduras" or "the Government"), which the Secretariat of the Commission received on October 7, 1981.

2.   In submitting the case, the Commission invoked Articles 50 and 51 of the American Convention on Human Rights (hereinafter "the Convention" or "the American Convention") and requested that the Court determine whether the State in question had violated Articles 4 (Right to Life), 5 (Right to Humane Treatment) and 7 (Right to Personal Liberty) of the Convention in the case of Angel Manfredo Velásquez Rodríguez (also known as Manfredo Velásquez). In addition, the Commission asked the Court to rule that "the consequences of the situation that constituted the breach of such right or freedom be remedied and that fair compensation be paid to the injured party or parties."

3.   According to the petition * * * and the supplementary information received subsequently, Manfredo Velasquez, a student at the National Autonomous University of Honduras, "was violently detained without a warrant for his arrest by members of the National Office of Investigations (DNI) and G–2 of the Armed Forces of Honduras." The detention took place in Tegucigalpa on the afternoon of September 12, 1981. According to the petitioners, several eyewitnesses reported that Manfredo Velasquez and others were detained and taken to the cells of Public Security Forces Station No. 2 located in the Barrio El Manchen of Tegucigalpa, where he was "accused of alleged political crimes and subjected to harsh interrogation and cruel torture." The petition added that on September 17, 1981, Manfredo Velásquez was moved to the First Infantry Battalion, where the interrogation continued, but that the police and security forces denied that he had been detained. * * *

[Exhaustion of Domestic Remedies]

56.   The Court will first consider the legal arguments relevant to the question of exhaustion of domestic remedies and then apply them to the case.

57.   Article 46(1)(a) of the Convention provides that, in order for a petition or communication lodged with the Commission in accordance with Articles 44 or 45 to be admissible, it is necessary "that the remedies under domestic law have been pursued and exhausted in accordance with generally recognized principles of international law."

58.   The same article, in the second paragraph, provides that this requirement shall not be applicable when

"a. the domestic legislation of the state concerned does not afford due process of law for the protection of the right or rights that have allegedly been violated;

b.   the party alleging violation of his rights has been denied access to the remedies under domestic law or has been prevented from exhausting them; or

c. there has been unwarranted delay in rendering a final judgment under the aforementioned remedies."

59. In its Judgment of June 26, 1987, the Court decided, *inter alia*, that "the State claiming non-exhaustion has an obligation to prove that domestic remedies remain to be exhausted and that they are effective".

60. Concerning the burden of proof, the Court did not go beyond the conclusion cited in the preceding paragraph. The Court now affirms that if a State which alleges non-exhaustion proves the existence of specific domestic remedies that should have been utilized, the opposing party has the burden of showing that those remedies were exhausted or that the case comes within the exceptions of Article 46(2). It must not be rashly presumed that a State Party to the Convention has failed to comply with its obligation to provide effective domestic remedies.

61. The rule of prior exhaustion of domestic remedies allows the State to resolve the problem under its internal law before being confronted with an international proceeding. This is particularly true in the international jurisdiction of human rights, because the latter reinforces or complements the domestic jurisdiction. * * *

62. It is a legal duty of the States to provide such remedies, as this Court indicated in its Judgment of June 26, 1987, when it stated:

> The rule of prior exhaustion of domestic remedies under the international law of human rights has certain implications that are present in the Convention. Under the Convention, States Parties have an obligation to provide effective judicial remedies to victims of human rights violations (Art. 25), remedies that must be substantiated in accordance with the rules of due process of law (Art. 8(1)), all in keeping with the general obligation of such States to guarantee the free and full exercise of the rights recognized by the Convention to all persons subject to their jurisdiction (Art. 1). (Velásquez Rodríguez Case, Preliminary Objections, supra 23, para. 91).

63. Article 46(1)(a) of the Convention speaks of "generally recognized principles of international law." Those principles refer not only to the formal existence of such remedies, but also to their adequacy and effectiveness, as shown by the exceptions set out in Article 46(2).

64. Adequate domestic remedies are those which are suitable to address an infringement of a legal right. A number of remedies exist in the legal system of every country, but not all are applicable in every circumstance. If a remedy is not adequate in a specific case, it obviously need not be exhausted. A norm is meant to have an effect and should not be interpreted in such a way as to negate its effect or lead to a result that is manifestly absurd or unreasonable. For example, a civil proceeding specifically cited by the Government, such as a presumptive finding of death based on disappearance, the purpose of which is to allow heirs to dispose of the estate of the person presumed deceased or to allow the

spouse to remarry, is not an adequate remedy for finding a person or for obtaining his liberty.

65. Of the remedies cited by the Government, habeas corpus would be the normal means of finding a person presumably detained by the authorities, of ascertaining whether he is legally detained and, given the case, of obtaining his liberty. The other remedies cited by the Government are either for reviewing a decision within an inchoate proceeding (such as those of appeal or cassation) or are addressed to other objectives. If, however, as the Government has stated, the writ of habeas corpus requires the identification of the place of detention and the authority ordering the detention, it would not be adequate for finding a person clandestinely held by State officials, since in such cases there is only hearsay evidence of the detention, and the whereabouts of the victim is unknown.

66. A remedy must also be effective–that is, capable of producing the result for which it was designed. Procedural requirements can make the remedy of habeas corpus ineffective: if it is powerless to compel the authorities; if it presents a danger to those who invoke it; or if it is not impartially applied. * * *

70. In its conclusions, the Government stated that some writs of habeas corpus were granted from 1981 to 1984, which would prove that this remedy was not ineffective during that period. It submitted various documents to support its argument. * * *

72. The Commission maintained that, in cases of disappearances, the fact that a writ of habeas corpus or amparo has been brought without success is sufficient to support a finding of exhaustion of domestic remedies as long as the person does not appear, because that is the most appropriate remedy in such a situation. It emphasized that neither writs of habeas corpus nor criminal complaints were effective in the case of Manfredo Velásquez. The Commission maintained that exhaustion should not be understood to require mechanical attempts at formal procedures; but rather to require a case-by-case analysis of the reasonable possibility of obtaining a remedy. * * *

74. The record before the Court shows that the following remedies were pursued on behalf of Manfredo Velásquez:

"a. Habeas Corpus

   i. Brought by Zenaida Velásquez against the Public Security Forces on September 17, 1981. No result.

   ii. Brought by Zenaida Velásquez on February 6, 1982. No result.

   iii. Brought by various relatives of disappeared persons on behalf of Manfredo Velásquez and others on July 4, 1983. Denied on September 11, 1984.

b. Criminal Complaints

    i.   Brought by the father and sister of Manfredo Velásquez before the First Criminal Court of Tegucigalpa on November 9, 1982. No result.

    ii. Brought by Gertrudis Lanza González, joined by Zenaida Velásquez, before the First Criminal Court of Tegucigalpa against various members of the Armed Forces on April 5, 1984. The court dismissed this proceeding and the First Court of Appeals affirmed on January 16, 1986, although it left open the complaint with regard to General Gustavo Alvarez Martínez, who was declared a defendant in absence."

75. Although the Government did not dispute that the above remedies had been brought, it maintained that the Commission should not have found the petition admissible, much less submitted it to the Court, because of the failure to exhaust the remedies provided by Honduran law, given that there are no final decisions in the record that show the contrary. * * *

76. The record * * * contains testimony of members of the Legislative Assembly of Honduras, Honduran lawyers, persons who were at one time disappeared, and relatives of disappeared persons, which purports to show that in the period in which the events took place, the legal remedies in Honduras were ineffective in obtaining the liberty of victims of a practice of enforced or involuntary disappearances (hereinafter "disappearance" or "disappearances"), ordered or tolerated by the Government. The record also contains dozens of newspaper clippings which allude to the same practice. According to that evidence, from 1981 to 1984 more than one hundred persons were illegally detained, many of whom never reappeared, and, in general, the legal remedies which the Government claimed were available to the victims were ineffective. * * *

78. The evidence offered shows that lawyers who filed writs of habeas corpus were intimidated, that those who were responsible for executing the writs were frequently prevented from entering or inspecting the places of detention, and that occasional criminal complaints against military or police officials were ineffective, either because certain procedural steps were not taken or because the complaints were dismissed without further proceedings. * * *

80. The testimony and other evidence received and not refuted leads to the conclusion that, during the period under consideration, although there may have been legal remedies in Honduras that theoretically allowed a person detained by the authorities to be found, those remedies were ineffective in cases of disappearances because the imprisonment was clandestine; formal requirements made them inapplicable in practice; the authorities against whom they were brought simply ignored them, or because attorneys and judges were threatened and intimidated by those authorities. * * *

81. Aside from the question of whether between 1981 and 1984 there was a governmental policy of carrying out or tolerating the disappearance of certain persons, the Commission has shown that although writs of habeas corpus and criminal complaints were filed, they were ineffective or were mere formalities. The evidence offered by the Commission was not refuted and is sufficient to reject the Government's preliminary objection that the case is inadmissible because domestic remedies were not exhausted.

[Pattern and Practice Liability]

82. The Commission presented testimony and documentary evidence to show that there were many kidnappings and disappearances in Honduras from 1981 to 1984 and that those acts were attributable to the Armed Forces of Honduras (hereinafter "Armed Forces"), which was able to rely at least on the tolerance of the Government. Three officers of the Armed Forces testified on this subject at the request of the Court. * * *

95. The Court received testimony which indicated that somewhere between 112 and 130 individuals were disappeared from 1981 to 1984. A former member of the Armed Forces testified that * * * the number might be 140 or 150. * * *

99. According to testimony on the modus operandi of the practice of disappearances, the kidnappers followed a pattern: they used automobiles with tinted glass (which requires a special permit from the Traffic Division), without license plates or with false plates, and sometimes used special disguises, such as wigs, false mustaches, masks, *etc*. The kidnappings were selective. The victims were first placed under surveillance, then the kidnapping was planned. Microbuses or vans were used. Some victims were taken from their homes; others were picked up in public streets. On one occasion, when a patrol car intervened, the kidnappers identified themselves as members of a special group of the Armed Forces and were permitted to leave with the victim. * * *

100. A former member of the Armed Forces, who said that he belonged to Battalion 316 (the group charged with carrying out the kidnappings) and that he had participated in some kidnappings, testified that the starting point was an order given by the chief of the unit to investigate an individual and place him under surveillance. According to this witness, if a decision was made to take further steps, the kidnapping was carried out by persons in civilian clothes using pseudonyms and disguises and carrying arms. The unit had four double-cabin Toyota pick-up trucks without police markings for use in kidnappings. * * *

103. The former member of the Armed Forces confirmed the existence of secret jails and of specially chosen places for the burial of those executed. He also related that there was a torture group and an interrogation group in his unit, and that he belonged to the latter. The torture group used electric shock, the water barrel and the "capucha."

They kept the victims nude, without food, and threw cold water on them. He added that those selected for execution were handed over to a group of former prisoners, released from jail for carrying out executions, who used firearms at first and then knives and machetes. * * *

104.   The current Director of Intelligence denied that the Armed Forces had secret jails, stating that it was not its modus operandi. He claimed that it was subversive elements who do have such jails, which they call "the peoples' prisons." He added that the function of an intelligence service is not to eliminate or disappear people, but rather to obtain and process information to allow the highest levels of government to make informed decisions. * * *

107.   According to the testimony of his sister, eyewitnesses to the kidnapping of Manfredo Velásquez told her that he was detained on September 12, 1981, between 4:30 and 5:00 p.m., in a parking lot in downtown Tegucigalpa by seven heavily-armed men dressed in civilian clothes. * * *

108.   This witness informed the Court that Col. Leonidas Torres Arias, who had been head of Honduran military intelligence, announced in a press conference in Mexico City that Manfredo Velásquez was kidnapped by a special squadron commanded by Capt. Alexander Hernández, who was carrying out the direct orders of General Gustavo Alvarez Martínez. * * *

113.   The former member of the Armed Forces who claimed to have belonged to the group that carried out kidnappings told the Court that, although he did not take part in the kidnapping of Manfredo Velásquez, Lt. Flores Murillo had told him what had happened. According to this testimony, Manfredo Velásquez was kidnapped in downtown Tegucigalpa in an operation in which Sgt. José Isaías Vilorio, men using the pseudonyms Ezequiel and Titanio, and Lt. Flores Murillo himself, took part. The Lieutenant told him that during the struggle Ezequiel's gun went off and wounded Manfredo in the leg. They took the victim to INDUMIL (Military Industries) where they tortured him. They then turned him over to those in charge of carrying out executions who, at the orders of General Alvarez, Chief of the Armed Forces, took him out of Tegucigalpa and killed him with a knife and machete. They dismembered his body and buried the remains in different places. * * *

[The Burden of Proof]

122.   Before weighing the evidence, the Court must address some questions regarding the burden of proof and the general criteria considered in its evaluation and finding of the facts in the instant proceeding.

123.   Because the Commission is accusing the Government of the disappearance of Manfredo Velásquez, it, in principle, should bear the burden of proving the facts underlying its petition.

124.   The Commission's argument relies upon the proposition that the policy of disappearances, supported or tolerated by the Govern-

ment, is designed to conceal and destroy evidence of disappearances. When the existence of such a policy or practice has been shown, the disappearance of a particular individual may be proved through circumstantial or indirect evidence or by logical inference. Otherwise, it would be impossible to prove that an individual has been disappeared.

125.   The Government did not object to the Commission's approach. Nevertheless, it argued that neither the existence of a practice of disappearances in Honduras nor the participation of Honduran officials in the alleged disappearance of Manfredo Velásquez had been proven.

126.   The Court finds no reason to consider the Commission's argument inadmissible. If it can be shown that there was an official practice of disappearances in Honduras, carried out by the Government or at least tolerated by it, and if the disappearance of Manfredo Velásquez can be linked to that practice, the Commission's allegations will have been proven to the Court's satisfaction, so long as the evidence presented on both points meets the standard of proof required in cases such as this. * * *

130.   The practice of international and domestic courts shows that direct evidence, whether testimonial or documentary, is not the only type of evidence that may be legitimately considered in reaching a decision. Circumstantial evidence, indicia, and presumptions may be considered, so long as they lead to conclusions consistent with the facts.

131.   Circumstantial or presumptive evidence is especially important in allegations of disappearances, because this type of repression is characterized by an attempt to suppress all information about the kidnapping or the whereabouts and fate of the victim. * * *

133.   The above principle is generally valid in international proceedings, but is particularly applicable in human rights cases.

134.   The international protection of human rights should not be confused with criminal justice. States do not appear before the Court as defendants in a criminal action. The objective of international human rights law is not to punish those individuals who are guilty of violations, but rather to protect the victims and to provide for the reparation of damages resulting from the acts of the States responsible.

135.   In contrast to domestic criminal law, in proceedings to determine human rights violations the State cannot rely on the defense that the complainant has failed to present evidence when it cannot be obtained without the State's cooperation.

136.   The State controls the means to verify acts occurring within its territory. Although the Commission has investigatory powers, it cannot exercise them within a State's jurisdiction unless it has the cooperation of that State.

137.   Since the Government only offered some documentary evidence in support of its preliminary objections, but none on the merits, the Court must reach its decision without the valuable assistance of a

more active participation by Honduras, which might otherwise have resulted in a more adequate presentation of its case.

138.   The manner in which the Government conducted its defense would have sufficed to prove many of the Commission's allegations by virtue of the principle that the silence of the accused or elusive or ambiguous answers on its part may be interpreted as an acknowledgment of the truth of the allegations, so long as the contrary is not indicated by the record or is not compelled as a matter of law. This result would not hold under criminal law, which does not apply in the instant case (supra 134 and 135). The Court tried to compensate for this procedural principle by admitting all the evidence offered, even if it was untimely, and by ordering the presentation of additional evidence. This was done, of course, without prejudice to its discretion to consider the silence or inaction of Honduras or to its duty to evaluate the evidence as a whole. * * *

[Factual Findings]

147.   The Court now turns to the relevant facts that it finds to have been proven. They are as follows:

"a.   During the period 1981 to 1984, 100 to 150 persons disappeared in the Republic of Honduras, and many were never heard from again * * *;

b.   Those disappearances followed a similar pattern, beginning with the kidnapping of the victims by force, often in broad daylight and in public places, by armed men in civilian clothes and disguises, who acted with apparent impunity and who used vehicles without any official identification, with tinted windows and with false license plates or no plates * * * ;

c.   It was public and notorious knowledge in Honduras that the kidnappings were carried out by military personnel or the police, or persons acting under their orders * * * ;

d.   The disappearances were carried out in a systematic manner, regarding which the Court considers the following circumstances particularly relevant:

i.   The victims were usually persons whom Honduran officials considered dangerous to State security * * *;

ii.   The arms employed were reserved for the official use of the military and police, and the vehicles used had tinted glass, which requires special official authorization. In some cases, Government agents carried out the detentions openly and without any pretense or disguise; in others, government agents had cleared the areas where the kidnappings were to take place and, on at least one occasion, when government agents stopped the kidnappers they were allowed to continue freely on their way after showing their identification * * *;

ii. The kidnappers blindfolded the victims, took them to secret, unofficial detention centers and moved them from one center to another. They interrogated the victims and subjected them to cruel and humiliating treatment and torture. Some were ultimately murdered and their bodies were buried in clandestine cemeteries * * *;

iv. When queried by relatives, lawyers and persons or entities interested in the protection of human rights, or by judges charged with executing writs of habeas corpus, the authorities systematically denied any knowledge of the detentions or the whereabouts or fate of the victims. That attitude was seen even in the cases of persons who later reappeared in the hands of the same authorities who had systematically denied holding them or knowing their fate * * *;

v. Military and police officials as well as those from the Executive and Judicial Branches either denied the disappearances or were incapable of preventing or investigating them, punishing those responsible, or helping those interested discover the whereabouts and fate of the victims or the location of their remains. The investigative committees created by the Government and the Armed Forces did not produce any results. The judicial proceedings brought were processed slowly with a clear lack of interest and some were ultimately dismissed * * *;

e. On September 12, 1981, between 4:30 and 5:00 p.m., several heavily-armed men In civilian clothes driving a white Ford without license plates kidnapped Manfredo Velásquez from a parking lot in downtown Tegucigalpa. Today, nearly seven years later, he remains disappeared, which creates a reasonable presumption that he is dead * * *;

f. Persons connected with the Armed Forces or under its direction carried out that kidnapping * * *;

g. The kidnapping and disappearance of Manfredo Velásquez falls within the systematic practice of disappearances referred to by the facts deemed proved in paragraphs a-d. To wit:

i. Manfredo Velásquez was a student who was involved in activities the authorities considered "dangerous" to national security * * *;

ii. The kidnapping of Manfredo Velásquez was carried out in broad daylight by men in civilian clothes who used a vehicle without license plates * * * ;

iii. In the case of Manfredo Velásquez, there were the same type of denials by his captors and the Armed Forces, the same omissions of the latter and of the Government in investigating and revealing his whereabouts, and the same ineffectiveness of the courts where three writs of habeas corpus and two criminal complaints were brought * * *;

h. There is no evidence in the record that Manfredo Velásquez had disappeared in order to join subversive groups, other than a letter from the Mayor of Langue, which contained rumors to that effect. The letter itself shows that the Government associated him with activities it considered a threat to national security. However, the Government did not corroborate the view expressed in the letter with any other evidence. Nor is there any evidence that he was kidnapped by common criminals or other persons unrelated to the practice of disappearances existing at that time."

148. Based upon the above, the Court finds that the following facts have been proven in this proceeding: (1) a practice of disappearances carried out or tolerated by Honduran officials existed between 1981 and 1984; (2) Manfredo Velásquez disappeared at the hands of or with the acquiescence of those officials within the framework of that practice; and (3) the Government of Honduras failed to guarantee the human rights affected by that practice.

[Disappearances as a Violation of International Human Rights Law]

149. Disappearances are not new in the history of human rights violations. However, their systematic and repeated nature and their use not only for causing certain individuals to disappear, either briefly or permanently, but also as a means of creating a general state of anguish, insecurity and fear, is a recent phenomenon. Although this practice exists virtually worldwide, it has occurred with exceptional intensity in Latin America in the last few years.

150. The phenomenon of disappearances is a complex form of human rights violation that must be understood and confronted in an integral fashion.

151. The establishment of a Working Group on Enforced or Involuntary Disappearances of the United Nations Commission on Human Rights, by Resolution 20 (XXXVI) of February 29, 1980, is a clear demonstration of general censure and repudiation of the practice of disappearances, which had already received world attention at the UN General Assembly (Resolution 33/173 of December 20, 1978), the Economic and Social Council (Resolution 1979/38 of May 10, 1979) and the Subcommission for the Prevention of Discrimination and Protection of Minorities (Resolution 5B (XXXII) of September 5, 1979). The reports of the rapporteurs or special envoys of the Commission on Human Rights show concern that the practice of disappearances be stopped, the victims reappear and that those responsible be punished.

152. Within the inter-American system, the General Assembly of the Organization of American States (OAS) and the Commission have repeatedly referred to the practice of disappearances and have urged that disappearances be investigated and that the practice be stopped. * * *

153. International practice and doctrine have often categorized disappearances as a crime against humanity, although there is no treaty in force which is applicable to the States Parties to the Convention and which uses this terminology (Inter-American Yearbook on Human Rights, 1985, pp. 368, 686 and 1102). The General Assembly of the OAS has resolved that it "is an affront to the conscience of the hemisphere and constitutes a crime against humanity" (AG/RES.666, *supra*) and that "this practice is cruel and inhuman, mocks the rule of law, and undermines those norms which guarantee protection against arbitrary detention and the right to personal security and safety" (AG/RES.742, *supra*).

154. Without question, the State has the right and duty to guarantee its security. It is also indisputable that all societies suffer some deficiencies in their legal orders. However, regardless of the seriousness of certain actions and the culpability of the perpetrators of certain crimes, the power of the State is not unlimited, nor may the State resort to any means to attain its ends. The State is subject to law and morality. Disrespect for human dignity cannot serve as the basis for any State action.

155. The forced disappearance of human beings is a multiple and continuous violation of many rights under the Convention that the States Parties are obligated to respect and guarantee. The kidnapping of a person is an arbitrary deprivation of liberty, an infringement of a detainee's right to be taken without delay before a judge and to invoke the appropriate procedures to review the legality of the arrest, all in violation of Article 7 of the Convention. * * *

156. Moreover, prolonged isolation and deprivation of communication are in themselves cruel and inhuman treatment, harmful to the psychological and moral integrity of the person and a violation of the right of any detainee to respect for his inherent dignity as a human being. Such treatment, therefore, violates Article 5 of the Convention, which recognizes the right to the integrity of the person. * * *

157. The practice of disappearances often involves secret execution without trial, followed by concealment of the body to eliminate any material evidence of the crime and to ensure the impunity of those responsible. This is a flagrant violation of the right to life, recognized in Article 4 of the Convention. * * *

158. The practice of disappearances, in addition to directly violating many provisions of the Convention, such as those noted above, constitutes a radical breach of the treaty in that it shows a crass abandonment of the values which emanate from the concept of human dignity and of the most basic principles of the inter-American system

and the Convention. The existence of this practice, moreover, evinces a disregard of the duty to organize the State in such a manner as to guarantee the rights recognized in the Convention, as set out below.

159.   The Commission has asked the Court to find that Honduras has violated the rights guaranteed to Manfredo Velasquez by Articles 4, 5 and 7 of the Convention. The Government has denied the charges and seeks to be absolved.

160.   This requires the Court to examine the conditions under which a particular act, which violates one of the rights recognized by the Convention, can be imputed to a State Party thereby establishing its international responsibility.

[State Responsibility]

161.   Article 1(1) of the Convention provides:

"Article 1. Obligation to Respect Rights

The States Parties to this Convention undertake to respect the rights and freedoms recognized herein and to ensure to all persons subject to their jurisdiction the free and full exercise of those rights and freedoms, without any discrimination for reasons of race, color, sex, language, religion, political or other opinion, national or social origin, economic status, birth, or any other social condition."

162.   This article specifies the obligation assumed by the States Parties in relation to each of the rights protected. Each claim alleging that one of those rights has been infringed necessarily implies that Article 1(1) of the Convention has also been violated. * * *

164.   Article 1(1) is essential in determining whether a violation of the human rights recognized by the Convention can be imputed to a State Party. In effect, that article charges the States Parties with the fundamental duty to respect and guarantee the rights recognized in the Convention. Any impairment of those rights which can be attributed under the rules of international law to the action or omission of any public authority constitutes an act imputable to the State, which assumes responsibility in the terms provided by the Convention.

165.   The first obligation assumed by the States Parties under Article 1(1) is "to respect the rights and freedoms" recognized by the Convention. The exercise of public authority has certain limits which derive from the fact that human rights are inherent attributes of human dignity and are, therefore, superior to the power of the State. * * *

166.   The second obligation of the States Parties is to "ensure" the free and full exercise of the rights recognized by the Convention to every person subject to its jurisdiction. This obligation implies the duty of the States Parties to organize the governmental apparatus and, in general, all the structures through which public power is exercised, so that they are capable of juridically ensuring the free and full enjoyment of human rights. As a consequence of this obligation, the States must

prevent, investigate and punish any violation of the rights recognized by the Convention and, moreover, if possible attempt to restore the right violated and provide compensation as warranted for damages resulting from the violation.

167.   The obligation to ensure the free and full exercise of human rights is not fulfilled by the existence of a legal system designed to make it possible to comply with this obligation—it also requires the government to conduct itself so as to effectively ensure the free and full exercise of human rights. * * *

169.   According to Article 1(1), any exercise of public power that violates the rights recognized by the Convention is illegal. Whenever a State organ, official or public entity violates one of those rights, this constitutes a failure of the duty to respect the rights and freedoms set forth in the Convention.

170.   This conclusion is independent of whether the organ or official has contravened provisions of internal law or overstepped the limits of his authority: under international law a State is responsible for the acts of its agents undertaken in their official capacity and for their omissions, even when those agents act outside the sphere of their authority or violate internal law.

171.   This principle suits perfectly the nature of the Convention, which is violated whenever public power is used to infringe the rights recognized therein. If acts of public power that exceed the State's authority or are illegal under its own laws were not considered to compromise that State's obligation under the treaty, the system of protection provided for in the Convention would be illusory.

172.   Thus, in principle, any violation of rights recognized by the Convention carried out by an act of public authority or by persons who use their position of authority is imputable to the State. However, this does not define all the circumstances in which a State is obligated to prevent, investigate and punish human rights violations, nor all the cases in which the State might be found responsible for an infringement of those rights. An illegal act which violates human rights and which is initially not directly imputable to a State (for example, because it is the act of a private person or because the person responsible has not been identified) can lead to international responsibility of the State, not because of the act itself, but because of the lack of due diligence to prevent the violation or to respond to it as required by the Convention.

173.   Violations of the Convention cannot be founded upon rules that take psychological factors into account in establishing individual culpability. For the purposes of analysis, the intent or motivation of the agent who has violated the rights recognized by the Convention is irrelevant—the violation can be established even if the identity of the individual perpetrator is unknown. What is decisive is whether a violation of the rights recognized by the Convention has occurred with the support or the acquiescence of the government, or whether the State

has allowed the act to take place without taking measures to prevent it or to punish those responsible. Thus, the Court's task is to determine whether the violation is the result of a State's failure to fulfill its duty to respect and guarantee those rights, as required by Article 1(1) of the Convention.

174.   The State has a legal duty to take reasonable steps to prevent human rights violations and to use the means at its disposal to carry out a serious investigation of violations committed within its jurisdiction, to identify those responsible, to impose the appropriate punishment and to ensure the victim adequate compensation.

175.   This duty to prevent includes all those means of a legal, political, administrative and cultural nature that promote the protection of human rights and ensure that any violations are considered and treated as illegal acts, which, as such, may lead to the punishment of those responsible and the obligation to indemnify the victims for damages. It is not possible to make a detailed list of all such measures, since they vary with the law and the conditions of each State Party. Of course, while the State is obligated to prevent human rights abuses, the existence of a particular violation does not, in itself, prove the failure to take preventive measures. On the other hand, subjecting a person to official, repressive bodies that practice torture and assassination with impunity is itself a breach of the duty to prevent violations of the rights to life and physical integrity of the person, even if that particular person is not tortured or assassinated, or if those facts cannot be proven in a concrete case.

176.   The State is obligated to investigate every situation involving a violation of the rights protected by the Convention. If the State apparatus acts in such a way that the violation goes unpunished and the victim's full enjoyment of such rights is not restored as soon as possible, the State has failed to comply with its duty to ensure the free and full exercise of those rights to the persons within its jurisdiction. The same is true when the State allows private persons or groups to act freely and with impunity to the detriment of the rights recognized by the Convention.

177.   In certain circumstances, it may be difficult to investigate acts that violate an individual's rights. The duty to investigate, like the duty to prevent, is not breached merely because the investigation does not produce a satisfactory result. Nevertheless, it must be undertaken in a serious manner and not as a mere formality preordained to be ineffective. An investigation must have an objective and be assumed by the State as its own legal duty, not as a step taken by private interests that depends upon the initiative of the victim or his family or upon their offer of proof, without an effective search for the truth by the government. This is true regardless of what agent is eventually found responsible for the violation. Where the acts of private parties that violate the Convention are not seriously investigated, those parties are aided in a

sense by the government, thereby making the State responsible on the international plane.

178.   In the instant case, the evidence shows a complete inability of the procedures of the State of Honduras, which were theoretically adequate, to carry out an investigation into the disappearance of Manfredo Velásquez, and of the fulfillment of its duties to pay compensation and punish those responsible, as set out in Article 1(1) of the Convention.

179.   As the Court has verified above, the failure of the judicial system to act upon the writs brought before various tribunals in the instant case has been proven. Not one writ of habeas corpus was processed. No judge had access to the places where Manfredo Velasquez might have been detained. The criminal complaint was dismissed.

180.   Nor did the organs of the Executive Branch carry out a serious investigation to establish the fate of Manfredo Velasquez. There was no investigation of public allegations of a practice of disappearances nor a determination of whether Manfredo Velásquez had been a victim of that practice. The Commission's requests for information were ignored to the point that the Commission had to presume, under Article 42 of its Regulations, that the allegations were true. The offer of an investigation in accord with Resolution 30/83 of the Commission resulted in an investigation by the Armed Forces, the same body accused of direct responsibility for the disappearances. This raises grave questions regarding the seriousness of the investigation. The Government often resorted to asking relatives of the victims to present conclusive proof of their allegations even though those allegations, because they involved crimes against the person, should have been investigated on the Government's own initiative in fulfillment of the State's duty to ensure public order. This is especially true when the allegations refer to a practice carried out within the Armed Forces, which, because of its nature, is not subject to private investigations. No proceeding was initiated to establish responsibility for the disappearance of Manfredo Velásquez and apply punishment under internal law. All of the above leads to the conclusion that the Honduran authorities did not take effective action to ensure respect for human rights within the jurisdiction of that State as required by Article 1(1) of the Convention.

181.   The duty to investigate facts of this type continues as long as there is uncertainty about the fate of the person who has disappeared. Even in the hypothetical case that those individually responsible for crimes of this type cannot be legally punished under certain circumstances, the State is obligated to use the means at its disposal to inform the relatives of the fate of the victims and, if they have been killed, the location of their remains.

182.   The Court is convinced, and has so found, that the disappearance of Manfredo Velásquez was carried out by agents who acted under cover of public authority. However, even had that fact not been

proven, the failure of the State apparatus to act, which is clearly proven, is a failure on the part of Honduras to fulfill the duties it assumed under Article 1(1) of the Convention, which obligated it to ensure Manfredo Velásquez the free and full exercise of his human rights.

183. The Court notes that the legal order of Honduras does not authorize such acts and that internal law defines them as crimes. The Court also recognizes that not all levels of the Government of Honduras were necessarily aware of those acts, nor is there any evidence that such acts were the result of official orders. Nevertheless, those circumstances are irrelevant for the purposes of establishing whether Honduras is responsible under international law for the violations of human rights perpetrated within the practice of disappearances.

184. According to the principle of the continuity of the State in international law, responsibility exists both independently of changes of government over a period of time and continuously from the time of the act that creates responsibility to the time when the act is declared illegal. The foregoing is also valid in the area of human rights although, from an ethical or political point of view, the attitude of the new government may be much more respectful of those rights than that of the government in power when the violations occurred.

185. The Court, therefore, concludes that the facts found in this proceeding show that the State of Honduras is responsible for the involuntary disappearance of Angel Manfredo Velásquez Rodríguez. Thus, Honduras has violated Articles 7, 5 and 4 of the Convention.

Notes and Questions on Velasquez-Rodriguez

1. *The obligation to investigate and prosecute. Velasquez–Rodriguez* was ground-breaking both for its holding and the evidence on which it was based: the Government of Honduras was responsible for the disappearance of Velasquez and, even in the absence of direct evidence implicating Honduras, its responsibility lay in part in its failure to investigate the allegations that persons acting under color of its authority had kidnapped and killed Velasquez. Where does the Court find such an obligation to investigate and prosecute? How far does this obligation extend, *i.e.*, does the Court indicate the measures—if Honduras had taken them—that would have satisfied this obligation? If the acts complained of in *Velasquez–Rodriguez* were the responsibility of private actors, would Honduras still have been responsible for a violation of the American Convention for failing to adequately investigate and prosecute?

2. *Problems of proof.* International human rights bodies are often faced with difficult evidentiary questions. Evidence of abuses is often in the control of a recalcitrant state that will resist all attempts from the

victim to obtain the evidence. Neither the Inter-American Court nor the Commission has the authority to compel the production of documents or witnesses; indeed, the rules of evidence are considerably more relaxed than in most domestic courts, and states routinely refuse to respond to petitions, let alone engage in the discovery of evidence. From that perspective, consider the evidence presented by the Commission on Velasquez' behalf. Would such evidence have been admissible in a domestic proceeding, as in a U.S. court? What is the Court's justification for not only allowing such evidence but using it to shift the burden of proof from the petitioner to the state?

3. *Exhaustion of domestic remedies.* How does the Court address Honduras' argument that Velasquez's case was barred due to a failure to exhaust his domestic remedies? How might this rationale be applied in other situations in countries with judiciaries that function at a higher level of predictability and efficiency? For example, in death penalty cases in the United States, the appellate process is rather extensive, encompassing direct and habeas corpus appeals at both the state and federal levels. How would you craft an argument that would permit Commission review before the full panoply of appellate procedures has been completed? For one approach to addressing this issue, see *Gary T. Graham (Shaka Sankofa) v. United States*, Case 11.193, Inter–Am., OEA/Ser.LJ v./II.118, C.H.R., doc.5, rev.2.

4. *Establishing an international norm.* In addition to having significant juridical significance, the *Velasquez-Rodriguez* case had important normative value as well. A few years after the decision, the OAS undertook the negotiation and eventual adoption of the Inter–American Convention on Forced Disappearance of Persons, which entered into force on June 9, 1994, and relies on many of the principles enunciated by the Court in *Velasquez-Rodriguez*. A similar convention was adopted by the UN General Assembly in December, 2006. Currently, seventy-three States have signed on to the agreement, with four having ratified it. *See* International Convention for the Protection of All Persons from Enforced Disappearance, UN Doc. A/RES/61/177 (2006).

5. *Velasquez-Rodriguez twenty years later.* Since the *Velasquez-Rodriguez* case, the Inter–American Court and Commission have applied its holding that states have a responsibility to investigate properly and to capture, prosecute, and adequately punish the perpetrators of human rights violations in a variety of situations. For example, in its decision in *Case of the Rochela Massacre v. Colombia* (Judgment of May 11, 2007) Ser. C No. 163., the Court ordered Colombia to pay $7.8 million in damages to the relatives of 12 judicial workers killed in a 1989 massacre by paramilitary groups supporting the Colombian army. The judicial workers were investigating previous massacres allegedly committed by the paramilitaries and members of the Army. Applying its previous due diligence jurisprudence, the Court found that Colombia's failure to provide the survivors of the massacre and the relatives of the victims with effective judicial resources in conformity with due process of law

violated the state's obligation to guarantee the free and full exercise of their rights under the Inter–American Convention. The Court further found that Colombia's failure to undertake effective investigations into the massacre violated the rights of the victims, survivors, and society to know the truth about the incident and to prevent further serious human rights abuses from occurring. According to the Court, Colombia's lack of due diligence was "manifested in the unreasonable length of the proceedings [18 years in some cases], the failure to adopt the necessary measures to protect against the threats [against the judges and some witnesses] which arose during the investigations; the delays, obstacles and obstructions which arose during the proceedings, and the grave omissions in the development of logical lines of investigation." *Id*. at ¶ 155. The court reaffirmed that the due diligence obligation "requires that the body investigating a violation of human rights use all available means to carry out all such steps and inquiries as are necessary to achieve the goal pursued within a reasonable time," and that the obligation is particularly important in the case of serious human rights violations such as the Rochela massacre. *Id*. at ¶ 156. Colombia's superficial investigation of low-level actors involved in a massacre, when the evidence strongly suggested that it had been planned and executed by a vast network of state and non-state actors including senior military leaders, was insufficient to satisfy its obligations under the Convention.

The Inter–American Court further expanded on its due diligence jurisprudence in the years following *Velasquez*, finding that the Convention gives rise to an obligation on the part of the state not only to investigate previously committed crimes, but also to take proper precautions to prevent crimes that it should know are likely to occur. In one of the earliest post-*Velasquez* cases, a candidate for the presidency of Nicaragua brought a claim arguing that the government violated its duty to attempt to prevent attacks on his livelihood by militia groups while he campaigned in the Nicaraguan countryside. *Aleman Lacayo (Nicaragua)*, Provisional Measures, Inter–Am Ct HR, Order of February 2, 1996, Ser. E. The Court agreed, ordering that the government adopt measures necessary to protect his life and personal integrity, to investigate the attack on his life, and to prosecute those responsible for it.

6. *Velasquez-Rodriguez beyond the Americas.* The Inter–American Court's decision in *Velasquez-Rodriguez* has resonated outside the Inter–American system in other international human rights tribunals. For example, the European Court of Human Rights has agreed that states have a positive obligation to investigate and prosecute serious human rights violations. In *Osman v. United Kingdom*, the Court held that in some circumstances, state authorities have a "positive obligation * * * to take preventive operational measures to protect an individual whose life is at risk from the criminal acts of another individual." 1998–VIII Eur. Ct. H.R. (1998). The Court held that such a due diligence responsibility is triggered when "authorities knew or ought to have known at the time of the existence of a real and immediate risk to the life of an identified

individual . . . [and failed] to take measures within the scope of their powers which, judged reasonably, might have been expected to avoid that risk." *Id.* at ¶ 115. This high threshold for finding that such an obligation exists has led the Court to reject a number of cases alleging state failure to exercise "due diligence." For example, in *Osman*, the court found that the state had not failed to fulfill a positive obligation to prevent an individual from killing the applicant's husband, as the police had no prior knowledge that the future killer was mentally ill or that he had previously harassed his eventual victim. *Id.*at ¶ ¶ 118–121. However, in *Akkoç v. Turkey*, the court held that the Turkish government had violated a trade union member's right to life insofar as it knew that he and his wife had received death threats and had failed to protect him and then had undertaken only the most superficial of investigations into his murder. *Akkoç v. Turkey*, Eur. Ct. H.R. (2000), ¶ 77. Further, the European Court of Human Rights has found that that states are responsible for taking measures to "provide effective protection, in particular, of children and other vulnerable persons to prevent ill-treatment of which the authorities had or ought to have had knowl-edge," and that the United Kingdom's social workers' failure to protect children from an abusive parent despite their awareness that the chil-dren were in danger and had been abused in the past, amounted to a violation of their rights. *Z and Others v. United Kingdom*, Eur. Ct. H.R. (2001), ¶ 73.

The *Velasquez-Rodriguez* decision has also had a powerful effect on the jurisprudence of the African Commission on Human and Peoples' Rights. In one decision, the Commission found that Nigeria had imper-missibly allowed an oil consortium to exploit the Ogoniland region's oil reserves with no regard to the health or environment of the local communities in violation of the population's rights under the African Charter. *See The Social and Economic Rights Action Center and the Center for Economic and Social Rights v. Nigeria*, African Commission on Human and Peoples' Rights, Comm. No. 155/96 (2001). Finding that the govern-ment had a positive duty to protect the people of Ogoniland from the dangerous effects of pollution and environmental degradation, the Commission stated, "the Nigerian Government has given the green light to private actors, and the oil Companies in particular, to devastatingly affect the well-being of the Ogonis. By any measure of standards, its practice falls short of the minimum conduct expected of governments, and therefore, is in violation of Article 21 of the African Charter." *Id.* at ¶ 58. Further, it held that the Nigerian Government "should not destroy or contaminate food sources. It should not allow private parties to destroy or contaminate food sources, and prevent peoples' efforts to feed themselves" *Id.* at ¶ 65.

Finally, the UN Human Rights Committee has also concurred with the holding in *Velasquez-Rodriguez*, finding that Article 2 of the ICCPR imposes an obligation on states to take the necessary steps to prevent violations of human rights by private actors. Human Rights Committee,

General Comment 31, Nature of the General Legal Obligation on States Parties to the Covenant, UN Doc. CCPR/C/21/Rev.1/Add.13 (2004) ¶ 8.

CASE STUDY: CHALLENGING THE DEATH PENALTY IN THE UNITED STATES

For the last several years, human rights lawyers have used the available mechanisms of the Inter–American Commission on Human Rights to pursue claims related to the use of the death penalty in the United States. Although advocates have had little practical success in restraining the use of the "ultimate punishment" in individual cases, they have contributed to a substantial body of jurisprudence purporting to establish international legal standards limiting the use of capital punishment.

As you read the following excerpts, evaluate both the Commission's reasoning and the value these cases represent for advocates opposed to capital punishment. Is the Commission taking liberties with its mandate, going beyond its authority to interpret the American Declaration, and arrogating to itself the authority to make recommendations? Is it worth the time and effort to pursue these cases when the United States and its constituent states routinely proceed with executions in contravention of Commission recommendations to either delay executions or vacate death sentences? How can decisions like these be used by advocates to support defendants in individual cases, or, more broadly, in domestic and international campaigns against capital punishment?

ROACH AND PINKERTON v. UNITED STATES

Case No. 9647, Inter–Am. Comm'n H.R. Res. No 3/87 (September 22, 1987)

3. James Terry Roach was convicted of the rape and murder of a fourteen year old girl and the murder of her seventeen year old boyfriend. Roach committed these crimes at the age of seventeen and was sentenced to death in the General Session Court, Richland County, South Carolina, on 16 December 1977. Roach petitioned the United States Supreme Court for a writ of certiorari on three separate occasions. All petitions were denied. Roach also exhausted all appeals to the state and federal courts, and on 10 January 1986 he was executed.

4. Jay Pinkerton was convicted of murder and attempted rape which he committed at the age of seventeen. The death sentence was appealed to the Texas Supreme Court which affirmed the trial court's decision. The United States Supreme Court denied Pinkerton's writ of certiorari on 7 October 1985. Pinkerton was executed on 15 May 1986.

5. On 23 February 1987, the U.S. Supreme Court announced that it would decide in its next term the case of *Thompson v. Oklahoma*,

thereby, for the first time, taking up the issue of the execution of juvenile offenders. The constitutional issue presented is whether the execution of a juvenile offender violates the U.S. Constitution's prohibition on cruel and unusual punishment.

6.   In their complaint to the Commission, the petitioners allege that the United States has violated Article I (right to life), Article VII (special protection of children), and Article XXVI (prohibition against cruel, infamous or unusual punishment) of the American Declaration of the Rights and Duties of Man by executing persons for crimes committed before their eighteenth birthday. The Petitioners allege a violation of their right to life guaranteed under the American Declaration, as informed by customary international law, which prohibits the execution of persons who committed crimes under the age of eighteen. * * *

43.   The American Declaration is silent on the issue of capital punishment. * * *

44.   The American Convention on the other hand, refers specifically to capital punishment in five of its provisions. * * *

45.   The international obligation of the United States of America, as a member of the Organization of American States (OAS), under the jurisdiction of the Inter–American Commission on Human Rights is governed by the Charter of the OAS (Bogotá, 1948), as amended by the Protocol of Buenos Aires on 27 February 1967, ratified by the United States on 23 April 1968.

46.   The United States is a member State of the Organization of American States, but is not a State party to the American Convention on Human Rights, and, therefore, cannot be found to be in violation of Article 4(5) of the Convention, since as the Commission stated in Case 2141 (United States), para. 31: "it would be impossible to impose upon the United States Government or that of any other State member of the OAS, by means of 'interpretation,' an international obligation based upon a treaty that such State has not duly accepted or ratified."

47.   As a consequence of articles 3(j), 16, 51(e), 112 and 150 of the Charter, the provisions of other instruments of the OAS on human rights acquired binding force. Those instruments, approved with the vote of the U.S. Government, are the following:

 — American Declaration of the Rights and Duties of Man (Bogotá, 1948)

 — Statute and Regulations of the IACHR

48.   The Statute provides that, for the purpose of such instruments, the IACHR is the organ of the OAS entrusted with the competence to promote the observance of and respect for human rights. For the purpose of the Statute, human rights are understood to be the rights set forth in the American Declaration in relation to States not parties to the American Convention on Human Rights (San José, 1969).

49.   The central violation denounced in the petition concerns a violation of the right to life, Article I of the Declaration, which states: "Every human being has the right to life ..." Since the Declaration is silent on the issue of capital punishment, Petitioners, in connection with Article I, seek an affirmative response to the question: Is there a norm of customary international law which prohibits the imposition of the death penalty on persons who committed capital crimes before completing eighteen years of age?

50.   The elements of a norm of customary international law are the following:

a) a concordant practice by a number of states with reference to a type of situation falling within the domain of international relations;

b) a continuation or repetition of the practice over a considerable period of time;

c) a conception that the practice is required by or consistent with prevailing international law; and

d) general acquiescence in the practice by other states.

51.   The evidence of a customary rule of international law requires evidence of widespread state practice. Article 38 of the Statute of the International Court of Justice (I.C.J.) defines "international custom, as evidence of a general practice accepted as law." The customary rule, however, does not bind States which protest the norm. In the *Fisheries Case (United Kingdom v. Norway)* the I.C.J. found that although the * * * ten-mile rule has been adopted by certain States both in their national law and in their treaties and conventions, and although certain arbitral decisions have applied it as between these States, other States have adopted a different limit. Consequently, the ten-mile rule has not acquired the authority of a general rule of law. How many states need to engage in the state practice for it to acquire the authority of a customary norm has never been definitively established, but it is clear that while a universal practice is not necessary, the practice must be common and widespread.

52.   The U.S. Government, in December 1977, transmitted the American Convention on Human Rights, *inter alia*, to the U.S. Senate for advice and consent to ratification subject to specified reservations. As regards the issue in question, the U.S. Government proposed reservations to Articles 4 and 5 which were presented as follows:

Article 4 deals with the right to life generally, and includes provisions on capital punishment. Many of the provisions of Article 4 are not in accord with United States law and policy, or deal with matters in which the law is unsettled. The Senate may wish to enter a reservation as follows: "United States adherence to Article 4 is subject to the Constitution and other law of the United States."

[Article (5)], [p]aragraph 5 requires that minors subject to criminal proceedings are to be separated from adults and brought before specialized tribunals as speedily as possible. * * * With respect to paragraph (5), the law reserves the right to try minors as adults in certain cases and there is no present intent to revise these laws. The following statement is recommended:

"The United States * * * with respect to paragraph (5), reserves the right in appropriate cases to subject minors to procedures and penalties applicable to adults."

53.   Since the United States has protested the norm, it would not be applicable to the United States should it be held to exist. For a norm of customary international law to be binding on a State which has protested the norm, it must have acquired the status of *jus cogens*.[1] Petitioners do not argue that a rule prohibiting the execution of juvenile offenders has acquired the authority of *jus cogens*, a peremptory norm of international law from which no derogation is permitted. The Commission, however, is not a judicial body and is not limited to considering only the submissions presented by the parties to a dispute.

54.   The concept of *jus cogens* is derived from ancient law concepts of a "superior order" of legal norms, which the laws of man or nations may not contravene. The norms of *jus cogens* have been described by publicists as comprising "international public policy." They are "rules which have been accepted, either expressly by treaty or tacitly by custom, as being necessary to protect the public interest of the society of States or to maintain the standards of public morality recognized by them." * * *

55.   The Commission finds that in the member States of the OAS there is recognized a norm of *jus cogens* which prohibits the State execution of children. This norm is accepted by all the States of the inter-American system, including the United States. The response of the U.S. Government to the petition in this case affirms that "[A]ll states, moreover, have juvenile justice systems; none permits its juvenile courts to impose the death penalty."

56.   The Commission finds that this case arises, not because of doubt concerning the existence of an international norm as to the prohibition of the execution of children but because the United States disputes the allegation that there exists consensus as regards the age of majority. Specifically, what needs to be examined is the United States law and practice, as adopted by different states, to transfer adolescents charged with heinous crimes to adult criminal courts where they are tried and may be sentenced as adults.

57.   Since the federal Government of the United States has not preempted this issue, under the U.S. constitutional system the individual

---

1.   The concept of *jus cogens* is included in Article 53 of the Vienna Convention on the Law of Treaties which states: "A treaty is void if, at the time of its conclusion, it conflicts with a peremptory norm of general international law. For the purposes of the present Convention, a peremptory norm of general international law is a norm accepted and recognized by the international community of states as a whole as a norm from which no derogation is permitted and which can be modified only by a subsequent norm of general international law having the same character."

states are free to exercise their discretion as to whether or not to allow capital punishment in their states and to determine the minimum age at which a juvenile may be transferred to an adult criminal court where the death penalty may be imposed. Thirteen states and the U.S. capital have abolished the death penalty entirely. As regards the other states which have enacted death penalty statutes since the *Furman* decision,[2] these states have adopted death penalty statutes which either 1) prohibit the execution of persons who committed capital crimes under the age of eighteen, or 2) allow for juveniles to be transferred to adult criminal courts where they may be sentenced to the death penalty. It is the discretion and practice of this second group of states which has become the subject of our analysis. Whereas approximately ten retentionist states have now enacted legislation barring the execution of under-18 offenders, a hodge-podge of legislation characterizes the other states which allow transfer of juvenile offenders to adult courts from age 17 to as young as age 10, and some states have no specific minimum age. The Indiana state statute which allows a ten year old to be judged before an adult criminal court and potentially sentenced to death shocks this Commission.

58.   The juvenile justice system was established in the United States at the turn of the century as a result of reformist efforts to mitigate the harshness of the adult criminal justice system. Under common law, children under the age of seven were conclusively presumed to have no criminal capacity and for children from age seven to fourteen, the presumption was rebuttable and the child could be convicted of a crime and executed. By a long series of statutory changes this age has been steadily increased, and the age of criminal incapacity is now set at 14 in most states. Consequently a child below the statutory age may be prosecuted by an adult criminal court but would not be adjudged responsible for a crime, the child would be adjudged a juvenile delinquent.

59.   The Commission is convinced by the U.S. Government's argument that there does not now exist a norm of customary international law establishing 18 to be the minimum age for imposition of the death penalty. Nonetheless, in light of the increasing numbers of States which are ratifying the American Convention on Human Rights and the United Nations Covenant on Civil and Political Rights, and modifying their domestic legislation in conformity with these instruments, the norm is emerging. As mentioned above, thirteen states and the U.S. capital have abolished the death penalty entirely and nine retentionist states have abolished it for offenders under the age of 18.

60.   The Commission, however, does not find the age question dispositive of the issue before it, which is whether the absence of a federal prohibition within U.S. domestic law on the execution of juve-

---

2.   [Eds. note. *Furman v. Georgia*, 408 U.S. 238 (1972) (invalidity the death penalty as cruel and unusual punishment on the facts presented.]

niles, who committed serious crimes under the age of 18, is in violation of the American Declaration.

61.   The Commission finds that the diversity of state practice in the U.S.—reflected in the fact that some states have abolished the death penalty, while others allow a potential threshold limit of applicability as low as 10 years of age—results in very different sentences for the commission of the same crime. The deprivation by the State of an offender's life should not be made subject to the fortuitous element of where the crime took place. Under the present system of laws in the United States, a hypothetical sixteen year old who commits a capital offense in Virginia may potentially be subject to the death penalty, whereas if the same individual commits the same offense on the other side of the Memorial Bridge, in Washington, D.C., where the death penalty has been abolished for adults as well as for juveniles, the sentence will not be death.

62.   For the federal Government of the United States to leave the issue of the application of the death penalty to juveniles to the discretion of state officials results in a patchwork scheme of legislation which makes the severity of the punishment dependent, not, primarily, on the nature of the crime committed, but on the location where it was committed. Ceding to state legislatures the determination of whether a juvenile may be executed is not of the same category as granting states the discretion to determine the age of majority for purposes of purchasing alcoholic beverages or consenting to matrimony. The failure of the federal government to preempt the states as regards this most fundamental right—the right to life—results in a pattern of legislative arbitrariness throughout the United States which results in the arbitrary deprivation of life and inequality before the law, contrary to Articles I and II of the American Declaration of the Rights and Duties of Man, respectively.
* * *

WILLIAM ANDREWS v. UNITED STATES
Case 11,139, Report N° 57/96, Inter–Am. Comm'n H.R.,
OEA/Ser.L/V/II.95 Doc. 7 rev. at 570 (1997)

2.   On July 28, 1992 the Commission received a petition * * *, on behalf of William Andrews which alleged that he was an African–American male born in Jonesboro, Louisiana, was now a prisoner on death row in Draper Correctional Institution, Draper, Utah, and was scheduled to be executed at or about 12:01 a.m on July 30, 1992. The petition alleged that in 1974, Mr. Andrews was convicted of three counts of first degree murder and two counts of aggravated robbery in the State of Utah, and that he was subsequently sentenced to death on all three counts by the same jury which convicted him.

3.   The petitioners further alleged that both the victims and the jurors were Caucasian, and the sole black member of the jury pool was

stricken peremptorily by the prosecution during jury selection. Mr. Andrews had left the premises prior to the offenses, and [he alleged] that his co-defendant, fatally shot the victims. His co-defendant, also African–American was executed by the State of Utah in 1987.

4.   It is further alleged that a napkin (note) was found among the jurors during a recess of the trial, which stated "Hang the Nigger's" and that Mr. Andrews' attorney requested a mistrial and a right to question jurors concerning the note, but this request was denied by the trial judge. Instead the trial judge admonished the jurors to "ignore communications from foolish people." That the denial of the right to question the jury about the note and the mistrial coupled with the known racist Mormon Church doctrine was ground for a mistrial and at minimum, a further inquiry into the authorship, and source of the note, exposure of the note to members of the jury or their response to it. * * *

143.   Did the action of the United States in trying, convicting, sentencing, and executing William Andrews on July 30, 1992 constitute violations of the American Declaration of the Rights and Duties of Man, in particular, Article I, the right to life, liberty and personal security, Article II, the right to equality before the law and Article XXVI, the right to an impartial hearing, and not to receive cruel, infamous or unusual punishment? * * *

146.   The Commission finds that the petitioners have established a *prima facie* case of human rights violations of the American Declaration and have met their burden of proof. The petitioners' main contentions are that 1) William Andrews' right to life was violated; 2) he was not treated equally at trial because of his race; 3) he did not receive an impartial hearing and he was subjected to cruel, infamous or unusual punishment. The issue of impartiality will be dealt with first; second, the issue of equality; third, the issue of the right to life; and finally, the issue of cruel, infamous or unusual punishment.

A.   Did Mr. Andrews Have a Fair and Impartial Hearing?

147.   Article XXVI of the American Declaration, paragraph 2 provides: "Every person accused of an offense has the right to be given an impartial and public hearing, and to be tried by courts previously established in accordance with pre-existing laws, and not to receive cruel, infamous or unusual punishment." This Article refers to four rights:

i) every accused person is presumed to be innocent until proved guilty,

ii) every person accused of an offense has the right to be given an impartial and public hearing,

iii) and to be tried by courts previously established in accordance with pre-existing laws,

iv) and not to receive cruel, infamous or unusual punishment.
* * *

149. The Commission has noted the petitioners' argument and their evidence: exhibits reflecting a copy of the "napkin" depicting the racial notation; a copy of the transcript of the afternoon Session of the Court Proceeding questioning the bailiff as to the origin of the napkin; LDS Church Historical Department, 1971 census page 206, which shows that the jury venire was drawn from Davis County, in the State of Utah where the petitioner was tried.

155. Mr. Andrews has had several reviews of his case by the United States' Courts to no avail. The Supreme Court of Utah held that the following admonishment by the trial court to the jury when they returned to trial was sufficient to cure any prejudice which might have occurred: " . . . Occasionally some foolish person will try to communicate with you. Please disregard the communications from foolish persons and ignore the same. . . . Just ignore communications from foolish people."

156. The United States Supreme Court denied Mr. Andrew's motion for certiorari. However, two of the Justices, Marshall and Brennan in the Supreme Court dissented. The note was referred to as "a vulgar incident of lynch-mob racism reminiscent of Reconstruction days." Justice Marshall referred to the denial of due process by stating that Mr. Andrews merely sought an evidentiary hearing to determine the origins of the note, and that "the Constitution [of the United States], not to mention common decency, require[d] no less than this modest procedure." Justice Marshall stated:

> Was it one or more of [Mr. Andrews'] jurors who drew a black man hanging on a gallows and attached the inscription, "Hang the niggers"? How many other jurors saw the incendiary drawing before it was turned over to the bailiff? Might it have had any effect on the deliberations? * * *

159. The international standard on the issue of "judge and juror impartiality" employs an objective test based on "reasonableness, and the appearance of impartiality." The United Nations Committee to Eliminate Racial Discrimination has held that a reasonable suspicion of bias is sufficient for juror disqualification, and stated that: "it is incumbent upon national judicial authorities to investigate the issue and to disqualify the juror if there is a suspicion that the juror might be biased." The Commission notes that in the European System of Human Rights an objective test was enunciated in the cases of *Piersack v. Belgium,*[1] and *Gregory v. United Kingdom.*[2]

---

1. 5 HRR 169 (1982). The European Court of Human Rights held that there was a violation of Article 6 of the European Convention which guarantees the right to a fair and impartial trial. The European Commission stated that: "Whilst impartiality normally denotes absence of prejudice or bias, its existence or otherwise can . . . be tested in various ways. A distinction can be drawn in this context between a subjective approach, that is endeavoring to ascertain the personal conviction of a given judge in a given case, and an objective approach, that is determining whether he offered guarantees sufficient to exclude any legitimate doubt in this respect."

2. 16 H.R.L.J. 238 (1995). In this case an Afro–Caribbean male, had been convicted of armed robbery. During jury deliberations, the trial judge received a handwritten note for a juror stating:

160.   In the case of *Remli v. France* the European Court of Human Rights referred to the principles laid down in its case-law concerning the independence and impartiality of tribunals, which applied to jurors as they did to professional and lay judges and found that there had been a violation of Article 6(1) of the European Convention For the Protection of Human Rights and Fundamental Freedoms.[3] That Article provides that: "In the determination of his civil rights and obligations or of any criminal charge against him, everyone is entitled to a fair and public hearing ... by an independent and impartial tribunal established by law...."

161.   The European Court considered that Article 6(1) of the Convention imposed an obligation on every national court to check whether, as constituted, it was "an impartial tribunal" within the meaning of that provision where, as in the instant case, that was disputed on a ground that did not immediately appear to be manifestly devoid of merit. In *Remli's* case the Rhone Assize Court had not made any such check, thereby depriving Mr. Remli of the possibility of remedying, if it had proved necessary, a situation contrary to the requirements of the Convention.[4]

162.   The Commission has noted the United States Government's argument that the admonishment by the trial court to the jury to disregard communications from foolish people was appropriate. It has also noted its argument that the jury was not racist because Mr.

"Jury showing racial overtones 1 member to be excused." The trial judge redirected the jury, and did not hold an evidentiary hearing. The European Commission found the case admissible and found that the defendant essentially makes the case that it was clear from the jury note that there was, at the very least, a strong objective indication of racial bias within the jury. It looked at the international standard and stated:

> [i]f the possibility of bias on the part of the juror comes to the attention of the trial judge in the course of a trial, the trial judge should consider whether there is actual bias or not (a subjective test). If this has not been established, that trial judge or appeal court must then consider whether there is "a real danger of bias affecting the mind of the relevant juror or jurors"(objective test). Note, the real danger test originated in the English common law in the case of *R. v. Gough*, 4 A.E.R.481 (Court of Appeal, Criminal Division 1992).

However, the European Commission concluded that the judge's detailed and careful redirection of the jury was sufficient. The *Gregory's* case is now before the European Court of Human Rights.

3. [1996] HRCD Vol. VII No. 7, European Court of Human Rights: Judgments, at 608–613. Judgment was delivered on April 23, 1996. The case involves the trial of an Algerian national in France for escape, during which a prison guard was struck and killed. The applicant and another person (both of them were of North African origin) were tried and convicted for intentional homicide and attempted escape in the Rhone Assize Court. The applicant was sentenced to life imprisonment on April 14, 1989. He submitted evidence that during his trial, a person overheard one of the jurors say, "What's more, I'm a racist." That person so certified in writing, and defense counsel asked that the court take formal note of the racist remark, and that the court append the written statement to the record. The trial court refused the first request but granted the second. As to the first request, the Assize Judge stated that it was "not able to take formal note of events alleged to have occurred out of its presence."

4. In *Remli's* case the Rhone Assize Court dismissed their application without even examining the evidence submitted to it, on the ground that it was "not able to take formal note of events alleged to have occurred out of its presence." Nor had it ordered that evidence should be taken to verify what had been reported and, if had been established, take formal note of it as requested by the defence, although it could have done so. The applicant had been unable either to have the juror in question replaced by one of the additional jurors or to rely on the fact in issue in support of his appeal on points of law. Nor had he been able to challenge the juror, since the jury had been finally empaneled and no appeal lay against the Assize Court's judgment other than on points of law. *Id.* at 612.

Andrews' co-defendant, Keith Roberts, who was African American, and whose counsel was African American and also charged with murder, was not convicted of murder, nor sentenced to death; and the attorneys for the other two co-defendants were not African American. The Commission finds that these factors are not dispositive of whether the United States violated the Articles of the American Declaration as pertaining to Mr. William Andrews' right to an "impartial hearing." The Commission has also noted that Mr. Andrews' other co-defendant who was African American was convicted and sentenced to death by the State of Utah, and executed in 1987.

163. The United States Government's evidence produced at the hearing on the merits of the case before the Commission through the testimony of its own witness Mr. Yocum, Assistant Attorney General of Utah substantiates the petitioners' case. Mr. Yocum testified that the jury members were not questioned by the trial judge about the note. The trial judge held a hearing, but only the bailiff was questioned. The judge denied the motion for a mistrial and proceeded to trial with the same members of the jury.

164. Conclusion: The Commission finds that the United States has not disputed that a napkin was found by one of the jurors, and given to the bailiff (who took the jurors to lunch in a restaurant) with words written in black stating "hang the nigger's" and a figure drawn in black hanging therefrom. Nor has it disputed that the napkin was brought to the attention of the trial judge who questioned the bailiff as to its origin.

165. The Commission finds that in assessing the totality of the facts in an objective and reasonable manner the evidence indicates that Mr. Andrews did not receive an impartial hearing because there was a reasonable appearance of "racial bias" by some members of the jury, and the omission of the trial court to voir dire the jury tainted his trial and resulted in him being convicted, sentenced to death and executed. The record before the Commission reflects ample evidence of "racial bias."

166. First, Mr. Andrews was a black male, and was tried by an all white jury some of whom were members of the Mormon Church and adhered to its teachings that black people were inferior beings.[5] The transcript reveals that the bailiff testified that when the juror told him he had some evidence for him, both the bailiff and some of the other jurors thought that it was one of the juror's jokes which they were humoring and there was discussion among the jurors concerning the "napkin."

167. Second, * * * the conduct and manner, in which the note was handed to the bailiff by the juror [evinces "racial bias."] * * * The note depicts racial words "hang the nigger's," written on the napkin that was given to the Court. * * * The trial transcript states "Hang the

---

5. In Davis County, Utah, 73.9% of the people who resided there were Mormons.

Niggers," and the drawing on the napkin was described by the bailiff as "a gallows and a stick figure hanging therefrom."

168.   Third, the admonishment by the trial court to the jury was inadequate. The trial judge at the very least if he did not want to grant a mistrial, should have conducted an evidentiary hearing of the jury members to ascertain whether some of them had seen the note and * * * had been influenced by it. The trial judge instead warned them against foolish people, and questioned the bailiff and left such an important and fundamental issue for the bailiff, whom he instructed to admonish the juror who found the note. The trial judge appeared to be more concerned to continue the trial with the same members of the jury without questioning them, as to whether they had seen the note, and denied both motions to sequester the jury and for a mistrial.

169.   Fourth, in addition to the note being found, there is language in the trial transcript which indicates the concern expressed by the defense attorneys, that two things had occurred during the trial, "the talk in the hallway, and the note," which would influence the jury members in their deliberations and in making their decisions, and which language had become accumulative.

170.   It should be noted that while it is not the function of the Inter–American Commission on Human Rights to act as a quasi-judicial fourth instance court and to review the holdings of the domestic courts of the OAS member states, it is mandated by its Statute and its Regulations to examine petitions alleging violations of human rights under the American Declaration against member States who are not parties to the American Convention.

171.   The Commission finds that Mr. Andrews did not receive an impartial trial because there was evidence of "racial bias" present during his trial, and because the trial court failed to conduct an evidentiary hearing of the jury in order to ascertain whether members of the jury found the napkin as the juror claimed or whether the jurors themselves wrote and drew the racial words on the napkin. If the note did not originate from the jurors and was "found" by the juror then the trial court could have inquired of the jurors by conducting an evidentiary hearing as to whether they would be influenced or their judgment impaired by the napkin depicting the racial words and drawing so that they would be unable to try the case impartially. Had the Court conducted the hearing it would have had the possibility of remedying, if it had proved necessary so to do, a situation contrary to the requirements of the American Declaration.

172.   Therefore, the Commission finds the United States in violation of Article XXVI, paragraph 2, of the American Declaration, because Mr. Andrews had the right to receive an impartial hearing as provided by the Article, and he did not receive an impartial trial in United States Courts. In capital punishment cases, the States Parties have an obligation to observe rigorously all the guarantees for an impartial trial.

B.   Did Mr. Andrews Receive Equal Treatment Without Distinction as to Race?

173.   Article II provides: "All persons are equal before the law and have the rights and duties established in this Declaration, without distinction as to race, sex, language, creed or any other factor." This Article has been defined as "the right of everyone to equal protection of the law without discrimination." This right to equality before the law means not that the substantive provisions of the law will be the same for everyone, but that the application of the law should be equal for all without discrimination. The provision was intended to ensure equality, not identity of treatment, and would not preclude reasonable differentiations between individuals or groups of individuals.

174.   The Commission finds that on the basis of the above definitions and interpretations, Mr. Andrews had a right to an impartial hearing as required by Article XXVI of the American Declaration. He also had a right to be treated equally at law without discrimination. The facts reveal that he was not treated equally at law without discrimination, and he did not receive an impartial hearing at trial because of evidence of "racial bias" during his trial. Therefore, the Commission finds that the United States violated Mr. Andrews' right to equality at law pursuant to Article II of the American Declaration.

C.   Was Mr. Andrews' Right to Life Violated?

175.   With regard to the petitioner's claim that the United States violated Article I of the American Declaration, Article I provides: "Every human being has the right to life, liberty and the security of his person." Article I is silent on the issue of the death penalty. However, when the definitive draft of the "Project of Declaration of the International Rights and Duties of Man, formulated by the Inter–American Juridical Committee," was presented for consideration by the Ninth International Conference of American States in 1948, the original Article I, provided:

> Every person has the right to life. This right extends to the right to life from the moment of conception; to the right to life of incurables, imbeciles and the insane. Capital punishment may only be applied in cases in which it has been prescribed by pre-existing law for crimes of exceptional gravity.

176.   The explanation given for the amendment of the last part of Article I was stated by the Committee as follows:

> The Committee is not taking sides in favor of the death penalty but rather admitting the fact that there is a diversity of legislation in this respect, recognizes the authority of each State to regulate this question.

> The Committee must note that several constitutions of America based on generous humanitarian conceptions, forbid the legislator to impose the said penalty.

177. Thus, the construction of Article I of the Right to Life of the American Declaration does not define nor sanction capital punishment by a member State of the OAS. However, it provides that a member State can impose capital punishment if it is prescribed by pre-existing law for crimes of exceptional gravity. Therefore, inherent in the construction of Article I, is a requirement that before the death penalty can be imposed and before the death sentence can be executed, the accused person must be given all the guarantees established by pre-existing laws, which includes guarantees contained in its Constitution, and its international obligations, including those rights and freedoms enshrined in the American Declaration. These guarantees include, the right to life, and not to be arbitrarily deprived of one's life, the right to due process of law, the right to an impartial and public hearing, the right not to receive cruel, infamous, or unusual punishment, and the right to equality at law. Evidence produced to the Commission was sufficient to prove that Mr. Andrews did not receive an impartial trial because the trial court failed to grant Mr. Andrews an evidentiary hearing for the reasons discussed above. The Commission therefore finds, that Mr. Andrews' right to life was violated because he was tried by an impartial and incompetent court which did not provide him with equal treatment at law. Therefore, the Commission finds for the reasons discussed above that Mr. Andrews' right to life was violated by the United States pursuant to Article I of the American Declaration. * * *

GARZA v. UNITED STATES

Case No. 12, 243, Inter–Am. Comm'n H.R. Report No. 52/01 (April 4, 2001)

2. The petition was filed on behalf of Juan Raul Garza (the "Petitioner"), an inmate on Federal death row in the United States. In their petition and subsequent observations, the Petitioner's representatives have alleged that Mr. Garza's death sentence violates his right to life under Article I of the American Declaration of the Rights and Duties of Man (the "American Declaration" or the "Declaration"), and that the procedures employed by the State in sentencing Mr. Garza to death violate his right to equal protection of the law under Article II of the Declaration, his right to a fair trial under Article XVIII of the Declaration and his right to due process under Article XXVI of the Declaration. In particular, the petition contests the introduction during the sentencing phase of the Petitioner's criminal proceeding of evidence of four unadjudicated murders that Mr. Garza was alleged to have perpetrated in Mexico, which evidence was considered by the jury in determining whether Mr. Garza should be sentenced to death. The petition also indicated that, according to information provided by the United States at that time, Mr. Garza's execution date might be set for February 2000. * * *

3.   In the present Report, having examined the information and arguments provided by the parties, the Commission decided to admit the case in relation to Articles I, XVIII, and XXVI of the Declaration, with the exception of further claims under Articles I and II of the Declaration raised by the Petitioner in observations dated September 22, 2000, which the Commission declared to be inadmissible. In addition, after considering the merits of the case, the Commission found the State responsible for violations of Articles I, XVIII and XXVI of the American Declaration, in connection with the procedure followed by the State in sentencing the Petitioner to death. Accordingly, the Commission recommended that the State provide Mr. Garza with an effective remedy, which includes commutation of his death sentence. The Commission also decided to recommend that the State review its laws, procedures and practices to ensure that persons who are accused of capital crimes are tried and sentenced in accordance with the rights under the American Declaration, including in particular prohibiting the introduction of evidence of unadjudicated crimes during the sentencing phase of capital trials. * * *

24.   With respect to the merits of the case, the Petitioner's representatives indicate that Mr. Garza is a U.S. national who was tried and convicted by a jury in the United States District Court, Southern District of Texas, under U.S. Federal law on three counts of killing in the furtherance of a continuing criminal enterprise, among other offenses, and sentenced by the same jury to death. They also confirm that in his proceedings before the Commission, Mr. Garza does not challenge these convictions, but rather takes issue with the punishment that he has received for these crimes. * * *

70.   Before addressing the merits of the present case, the Commission wishes to reaffirm and reiterate its well-established doctrine that it will apply a heightened level of scrutiny in deciding capital punishment cases. The right to life is widely-recognized as the supreme right of the human being, and the *conditio sine qua non* to the enjoyment of all other rights. The Commission therefore considers that it has an enhanced obligation to ensure that any deprivation of life that an OAS member state proposes to perpetrate through the death penalty complies strictly with the requirements of the applicable inter-American human rights instruments, including the American Declaration. This "heightened scrutiny test" is consistent with the restrictive approach taken by other international human rights authorities to the imposition of the death penalty, and has been articulated and applied by the Commission in previous capital cases before it.

71.   The Commission also notes that this heightened scrutiny test applicable to death penalty cases is not precluded by the Commission's fourth instance formula, according to which the Commission in principle will not review the judgments issued by domestic courts acting within their competence and with due judicial guarantees. In particular, where a possible violation of an individual's rights under applicable

Inter–American human rights instruments is involved, the Commission has consistently held that the fourth instance formula has no application and the Commission may consider the matter.

72.   The Commission will therefore review the allegations of the Petitioner's representatives in the present case with a heightened level of scrutiny, to ensure in particular that the right to life, the right to due process, and the right to a fair trial as prescribed under the American Declaration have been properly respected by the State. * * *

87.   Article I of the Declaration provides as follows:

Right to life, liberty and person security:

Every human being has the right to life, liberty and the security of his person.

88.   In addressing the allegations raised by the Petitioner's representatives in this case, including their claim that Mr. Garza's death penalty violates Article I of the American Declaration, the Commission first wishes to clarify that in interpreting and applying the Declaration, it is necessary to consider its provisions in the context of the international and Inter-American human rights systems more broadly, in the light of developments in the field of international human rights law since the Declaration was first composed and with due regard to other relevant rules of international law applicable to member states against which complaints of violations of the Declaration are properly lodged.[1] The Inter–American Court of Human Rights recently reiterated its endorsement of an evolutive interpretation of international human rights instruments, which takes into account developments in the corpus juris gentium of international human rights law over time and in present-day conditions.[2] * * *

95.   The Commission is unable to conclude, however, based upon the information before it, that the international legal norms binding upon the State by way of Article I of the American Declaration precluded the United States from applying the death penalty in the circumstances of Mr. Garza's case. In particular, the Commission cannot find on the evidence in the record that the State abolished the death penalty under its law so as to preclude it from applying this penalty to Mr. Garza's crimes. Rather, the evidence indicates that the death penalty

---

1.   See I/A Court H.R., Interpretation of the American Declaration of the Rights and Duties of Man Within the Framework of Article 64 of the American Convention on Human Rights, Advisory Opinion OC–10/89 of July 14, 1989, Inter–Am.Ct.H.R. (Ser. A) N° 10 (1989), ¶ 37 (pointing out that in determining the legal status of the American Declaration, it is appropriate to look to the inter-American system of today in the light of the evolution it has undergone since the adoption of the Declaration, rather than to examine the normative value and significance which that instrument was believed to have had in 1948). *See also* ICJ, Legal Consequences for States of the Continued Presence of South Africa in Namibia (South West Africa) notwithstanding Security Council Resolution 276 (1970), Advisory Opinion, I.C.J. Reports 1971, p. 16 ad 31 stating that "an international instrument must be interpreted and applied within the overall framework of the juridical system in force at the time of the interpretation").

2.   Advisory Opinion OC–16/99, *supra*, ¶ 114, citing, inter alia, the decisions of the European Court of Human Rights in *Tryer v. United Kingdom* (1978), *Marckx v. Belgium* (1979), and *Louizidou v. Turkey* (1995).

continued to be applied in the United States as early as 1976, albeit at the state level. Further, the Commission is not satisfied based upon the information available that the norms of international law under Article I of the Declaration, as informed by current developments in international human rights law, prevented the State from prescribing the penalty for the crimes for which Mr. Garza was tried and convicted. In particular, the Commission does not find before it sufficient evidence establishing the existence of an international legal norm binding upon the United States, under Article I of the Declaration or under customary international law, that prohibited the extension of the death penalty to Mr. Garza's crimes, provided that they are properly considered to be of a "most serious" nature. The Commission notes further in this connection that Mr. Garza was convicted, among other offenses, of multiple homicides in the course of a continuing criminal enterprise, convictions with which he has not taken issue in these proceedings. The Commission cannot find that crimes of this nature do not constitute "most serious crimes" to which the death penalty may be imposed without rendering the execution arbitrary contrary to Article I of the Declaration. For similar reasons, the Commission cannot conclude that the State's decision to seek the death penalty in the circumstances of Mr. Garza's crimes lacked sufficient justification so as to be rendered arbitrary under Article I of the Declaration.

96. Based upon the foregoing analysis and the record in the present matter, therefore, the Commission does not find a violation of Mr. Garza's rights under Article I of the Declaration in relation to the application per se of the death penalty in the circumstances of his case.

97. Articles XVIII and XXVI of the Declaration provide as follows:

> Right to a fair trial.
>
> Article XVIII. Every person may resort to the courts to ensure respect for his legal rights. There should likewise be available to him a simple, brief procedure whereby the courts will protect him from acts of authority that, to his prejudice, violate any of his fundamental constitutional rights.
>
> Right to due process of law.
>
> Article XXVI. Every accused person is presumed to be innocent until proven guilty.
>
> Every person accused of an offense has the right to be given an impartial and public hearing, and to be tried by courts previously established in accordance with pre-existing laws, and not to receive cruel, infamous or unusual punishment.

98. * * * [T]he Petitioner's representatives have challenged the procedure employed by the State in sentencing Mr. Garza to death under Articles XVIII and XXVI of the American Declaration in two respects, both of which relate to the introduction during Mr. Garza's

sentencing hearing of evidence of unadjudicated murders alleged to have been committed by Mr. Garza in Mexico. * * *[3]

99. First, the Petitioner's representatives argue that evidence of the four unadjudicated murders in Mexico should not have been introduced at all for the purposes of sentencing, essentially because consideration of evidence of this nature failed to satisfy the standard of due process applicable when trying individuals for capital crimes.

100. In this connection, the Commission reiterates the fundamental significance of ensuring full and strict compliance with due process protections in trying individuals for capital crimes, from which there can be no derogation. The Commission has recognized previously that, due in part to its irrevocable and irreversible nature, the death penalty is a form of punishment that differs in substance as well as in degree in comparison with other means of punishment, and therefore warrants a particularly stringent need for reliability in determining whether death is the appropriate punishment in a given case. Further, the Inter–American Court of Human Rights recently noted the existence of an "internationally recognized principle whereby those States that still have the death penalty must, without exception, exercise the most rigorous control for observance of judicial guarantees in these cases," such that "[i]f the due process of law, with all its rights and guarantees, must be respected regardless of the circumstances, then its observance becomes all the more important when that supreme entitlement that every human rights treaty and declaration recognizes and protects is at stake: human life." The U.S. Supreme Court has similarly emphasized in addressing allegations of due process violations in capital cases that it is of vital importance to a defendant and to the community more broadly that any decision to impose the death penalty be, and appear to be, based on reason rather than caprice or emotion.

101. Consistent with these fundamental principles, the Commission considers that Articles I, XVIII and XXVI of the Declaration must be interpreted and applied in the context of death penalty prosecutions so as to give stringent effect to the most fundamental substantive and procedural due process protections. The essential requirements of substantive due process in turn include the right not to be convicted of any act or omission that did not constitute a criminal offense, under national or international law, at the time it was committed, and the right not to be subjected to a heavier penalty than the one that was applicable at the

---

3. [Editors' Note: 21 U.S.C. § 848(j) relaxes the rules of evidence governing the admission of evidence at criminal trials. For purposes of sentencing, section 848(j) allows the jury to consider information that is relevant to statutory mitigating or aggravating factors, "except that information may be excluded if its probative value is substantially outweighed by the danger of unfair prejudice, confusion of the issues, or misleading of the jury." 21 U.S.C. § 848(j). In this case, the United States introduced evidence that Mr. Garza had committed four additional murders in Mexico. The record presented to the Commission reflected that Mexican authorities had been unable to solve the murders, and that the U.S. government sent U.S. Customs agents to Mexico to re-investigate these murders. According to the Petitioners, the prosecution offered no physical evidence tying Mr. Garza to the crimes; instead relying on the testimony of three accomplices, each of whom was offered substantially reduced sentences in exchange for their testimony.]

time when the criminal offense was committed. The requisite procedural due process protections include most fundamentally the right of a defendant to be presumed innocent until proven guilty according to law, the right to prior notification in detail of the charges against him, the right to adequate time and means for the preparation of his defense, the right to be tried by a competent, independent and impartial tribunal, previously established by law, the right of the accused to defend himself personally or to be assisted by legal counsel of his own choosing and to communicate freely and privately with his counsel, and the right not to be compelled to be a witness against himself or to plead guilty.

102.   The Commission considers that these protections apply to all aspects of a defendant's criminal trial, regardless of the manner in which a state may choose to organize its criminal proceedings. Consequently, where, as in the present case, the State has chosen to establish separate proceedings for the guilt/innocence and sentencing stages of a criminal prosecution, the Commission considers that due process protections nevertheless apply throughout.

103.   It is in light of the above principles that the Commission has analyzed the allegations of the Petitioner's representatives regarding the conduct of Mr. Garza's sentencing proceeding. In this respect, several facts, as described previously, are particularly relevant to determining this aspect of his claim. First, the parties agree that during Mr. Garza's sentencing hearing, the prosecution introduced evidence relating to four additional murders that Mr. Garza was alleged to have committed in Mexico. Mr. Garza was never previously charged or convicted of these crimes; indeed the Mexican authorities were not able to resolve or prosecute them, which resulted in their "unadjudicated" status. Moreover, the Petitioner's representatives have alleged, and the State has not disputed, that these murders could not have been prosecuted under U.S. Federal law at the time that they were committed, as they did not occur within the special maritime or territorial jurisdiction of the United States, a prerequisite for prosecuting the crime of murder under U.S. federal law. The evidence presented by the prosecution consisted of the testimony of several alleged accomplices to these murders, who agreed to testify in exchange for substantial reductions in their sentences.

104.   It also appears to be common ground, as supported by the record and judicial decisions in Mr. Garza's case, that the jury was required to conclude, and in fact did conclude "beyond a reasonable doubt" on the evidence presented that Mr. Garza committed each of these four murders. Finally, it is apparent from the record that the jury considered Mr. Garza's responsibility for these additional murders in determining whether he should be sentenced to the death penalty.

105.   Based upon these facts, the Commission can only conclude that during his criminal proceeding, Mr. Garza was not only convicted and sentenced to death for the three murders for which he was charged

and tried in the guilt/innocence phase of his proceeding; he was also convicted and sentenced to death for the four murders alleged to have been committed in Mexico, but without having been properly and fairly charged and tried for these additional crimes. Considered in this light, in the Commission's view, the introduction of evidence of this nature and in this manner during Mr. Garza's sentencing hearing was inconsistent with several fundamental principles underlying Articles XVIII and XXVI of the Declaration.

106.   First, based upon the record in this case, the United States would have been prevented from prosecuting Mr. Garza for these additional crimes under the *nullum crimen sine lege* principle, as U.S. federal law did not render conduct of this nature perpetrated in Mexico as a crime under U.S. law at the time that Mr. Garza was alleged to have committed them. To this extent, then, the State appears to be seeking to do indirectly what it cannot do directly, namely secure responsibility and punishment on the part of Mr. Garza for four murders through a sentencing hearing, which are otherwise outside of U.S. federal jurisdiction to prosecute.

107.   In addition, it cannot be said that Mr. Garza was tried for these four additional murders before an impartial tribunal. Rather, the Commission is of the view that the jury that sentenced Mr. Garza could not reasonably have been considered impartial in determining his criminal liability for the four unadjudicated murders in Mexico when the same jury had just convicted Mr. Garza of three murders. The Commission has previously articulated the international standard on the issue of "judge and juror impartiality" as employing an objective test based on "reasonableness and the appearance of impartiality".[4] In the Commission's view, it cannot reasonably be contended that the facts concerning these additional four murders were presented to an untainted, unbiased jury in a forum in which the full protections of the rights under the American Declaration were afforded to Mr. Garza. To the contrary, presentation of evidence of prior criminal conduct is generally considered to be irrelevant and highly prejudicial to the determination of guilt for a current criminal charge. This conclusion is corroborated by the State's own Federal Rules of Evidence, which preclude the introduction of evidence of prior crimes during the guilt/innocence phase of a criminal trial, unless it is relevant to proof of motive, intent, preparation, plan, knowledge, identity, or absence of mistake or accident.

108.   Further, the prejudice resulting from the determination of Mr. Garza's guilt for four additional murders during his sentencing hearing was compounded by the fact that lesser standards of evidence were applicable during the sentencing process. As the Petitioner's representatives have pointed out, the application of strict rules of evidence during trials of criminal charges, where the onus is solely upon the prosecution, is generally intended to protect the defendant from convic-

---

4. *Andrews v. US, supra,* ¶ 159.

tion based upon information that is prejudicial or unreliable. Such protections were not, however, applicable when the jury found Mr. Garza responsible for the four murders in Mexico * * *. Consequently, Mr. Garza was not afforded the strictest and most rigorous standard of due process when his liability for the four foreign murders was determined.

109.   The State appears to argue in this respect that the unadjudicated murders were simply another aggravating factor properly taken into account in determining the appropriate sentence for Mr. Garza. The Commission must emphasize, however, that a significant and substantive distinction exists between the introduction of evidence of mitigating and aggravating factors concerning the circumstances of an offender or his or her offense * * * and an effort to attribute to an offender individual criminal responsibility for violations of additional serious offenses that have not, and indeed could not under the State's criminal law, be charged and tried pursuant to a fair trial offering the requisite due process guarantees. The State itself asserts that the purpose of a sentencing hearing is to determine the appropriate punishment for a defendant's crime, not to prove guilt. Yet proving Mr. Garza's guilt for the four unadjudicated murders so as to warrant imposition of the death penalty was, by the Government's own admission, precisely the intended and actual effect of its effort in introducing evidence in this regard during Mr. Garza's sentencing hearing.

110.   Based upon the foregoing, the Commission considers that the State's conduct in introducing evidence of unadjudicated foreign crimes during Mr. Garza's capital sentencing hearing was antithetical to the most basic and fundamental judicial guarantees applicable in attributing responsibility and punishment to individuals for crimes. Accordingly, the Commission finds that the State is responsible for imposing the death penalty upon Mr. Garza in a manner contrary to his right to a fair trial under Article XVIII of the American Declaration, as well as his right to due process of law under Article XXVI of the Declaration.

111.   The Commission also concludes that, by sentencing Mr. Garza to death in this manner, and by scheduling his execution for December 12, 2000 and thereby exhibiting its clear intention to implement Mr. Garza's sentence, the State had placed Mr. Garza's life in jeopardy in an arbitrary and capricious manner, contrary to Article I of the Declaration. In addition, to execute Mr. Garza pursuant to this sentence would constitute a further deliberate and egregious violation of Article I of the American Declaration. * * *

NOTES AND QUESTIONS ON THE *U.S. DEATH PENALTY*
UNDER INTER-AMERICAN STANDARDS

1. *Juvenile death penalty in the U.S. Supreme Court.* The year after the Commission's opinion in *Roach & Pinkerton*, the U.S. Supreme Court decided in *Thompson v. Oklahoma*, 487 U.S. 815 (1988), that it violated the Eighth Amendment of the Constitution to execute a person who had committed a crime below the age of fifteen. Then, in its next term, the U.S. Supreme Court held that the execution of persons aged sixteen or seventeen at the time of the crime did not violate the Eighth Amendment. *Stanford v. Kentucky*, 492 U.S. 361 (1989). Does the Commission's basis for finding a violation of the American Declaration in *Roach & Pinkerton* remain valid after these two Supreme Court decisions?

In 1999 the U.S. Supreme Court denied *certiorari* in *Domingues v. Nevada*, a case in which petitioners alleged that the execution of an individual who committed murder at the age of sixteen would violate, *inter alia*, U.S. treaty obligations, customary international law, and *jus cogens*. 961 P.2d 1279 (Nev. 1998) *cert. denied*, 526 U.S. 1156 (U.S. Nov. 1, 1999) (No. 98–8327). The petitioners also filed a petition for relief before the Inter–American Commission on Human Rights, making many of the same arguments but couched in terms of the American Declaration. *See* Annual Report of the Inter–American Commission on Human rights, OAS Doc. OEA/Ser./L/V/II.111 (16 Apr. 2001). The Commission issued a request that the United States take precautionary measures to prevent the execution of Mr. Domingues.

Ultimately, in *Roper v. Simmons*, 543 U.S. 551 (2005), the U.S. Supreme Court held, under the "evolving standards of decency test," that the execution of offenders who were under eighteen at the time of the crime constitutes cruel and unusual punishment under the Eighth Amendment to the Constitution. Notably, the Court observed that only seven other countries (Iran, Pakistan, Saudi Arabia, Yemen, Nigeria, the Democratic Republic of the Congo, and China) have recently executed juvenile offenders, and—since 1990—each of these countries has abolished or publicly disavowed the practice. In Justice Kennedy's words, writing for the majority, "In sum, it is fair to say that the United States stands alone in a world that has turned its face against the juvenile death penalty." *Id.* at 577.

2. *Jus cogens.* In a dissenting opinion in *Roach & Pinkerton*, Dr. Marco Gerardo Monroy Cabra took issue with the majority's determination that the question before the Commission was whether the absence of a prohibition on the execution of persons who committed crimes under the age of eighteen "is inconsistent with human rights standards applicable to the United States under the inter-American system." According to Dr. Cabra, the Commission is only authorized to interpret the American Declaration as to practices of states not party to the American Convention, not to issue advisory opinions as to whether the

United States has violated customary or *jus cogens* norms of international law. In your opinion, did the Commission go beyond its authority in finding a "norm of *jus cogens* which prohibits the execution of children" in the member states of the OAS? Was it necessary for the Commission to reach this conclusion given the basis on which it ultimately found a violation of the American Declaration?

3. *Authority to interpret.* The question of what law the Commission has the authority to interpret and apply comes up regularly in the Commission's proceedings. For instance, in *Abella v. Argentina*, Inter.-Am. Comm'n H.R., Case No. 11.137 (1997), the Commission found that it could interpret and apply international humanitarian law (traditionally known as the law of war), including the four Geneva Conventions on the laws of war, in interpreting the terms of the American Declaration and Inter–American Convention. It found this authority primarily in article 29(b) of the American Convention, which provides that no provision of the Convention shall be interpreted as "restricting the enforcement or exercise of any right or freedom recognized by virtue of the laws of any State Party of another convention which one of the said states is a party." But what about states *not* party to the American Convention? Should the Commission have the authority to interpret and apply instruments other than the American Declaration to the conduct of OAS member states? Why or why not?

4. *Precautionary measures in the IACHR.* Article 25 of the Commission's Rules of Procedure authorizes the Commission to "indicate provisional measure," *i.e.*, to adopt interim measures during the pendency of the case:

> 25. (1) In serious and urgent cases, and whenever necessary according to the information available, the Commission may, on its own initiative or at the request of a party, request that the State concerned adopt precautionary measures to prevent irreparable harm to persons.

> (2) If the Commission is not in session, the President, or, in his or her absence, one of the Vice–Presidents, shall consult with the other members, through the Executive Secretariat, on the application of the provision in the previous paragraph. If it is not possible to consult within a reasonable period of time under the circumstances, the President or, where appropriate, one of the Vice–President shall take the decision on behalf of the Commission and shall so inform its members.

> (3) The Commission may request information from the interested parties on any matter related to the adoption and observance of the precautionary measures.

> (4) The granting of such measures and their adoption by the State shall not constitute a prejudgment on the merits of a case.

Other international and regional courts and tribunals have similar provisions in their governing instruments that provide authority to grant or indicate provisional or interim measures.

Generally, precautionary measures have been adopted in two primary settings: "as an injunctive measure to prevent prejudice to the positions of parties in a particular complaint until the Commission has decided upon the merits of the matter; and as a protective mechanism to preclude the imminent perpetration of human rights violations against the life or personal integrity of a person or group of persons." BRIAN D. TITTEMORE, *Guantanamo Bay and the Precautionary Measures of the Inter–American Commission on Human Rights: A Case for International Oversight in the Struggle Against Terrorism*, 6 HUM. RTS. L. REV. 378, 381 (2006).

Often, in capital punishment cases, the Commission requests that a State take "precautionary measures" to prevent an execution while the Commission considers the petition. In the *Garza* case, the United States challenged its authority to make such requests on the basis that the American Convention authorizes the Commission only to make "recommendations," but not to request precautionary measures. In the alternative, the United States noted that even if it did have this authority, such requests were really in the nature of recommendations and therefore entirely non-binding in nature. In its opinion, the Commission responded:

117. With respect to the State's submissions on the non-binding nature of the Commission's precautionary measures, the Commission previously expressed in this Report its profound concern regarding the fact that its ability to effectively investigate and determine capital cases has frequently been undermined when states have scheduled and proceeded with the execution of condemned persons, despite the fact that those individuals have proceedings pending before the Commission. It is for this reason that in capital cases the Commission requests precautionary measures from states to stay a condemned prisoner's execution until the Commission has had an opportunity to investigate his or her claims. Moreover, in the Commission's view, OAS member states, by creating the Commission and mandating it through the OAS Charter and the Commission's Statute to promote the observance and protection of human rights of the American peoples, have implicitly undertaken to implement measures of this nature where they are essential to preserving the Commission's mandate. Particularly in capital cases, the failure of a member state to preserve a condemned prisoner's life pending review by the Commission of his or her complaint emasculates the efficacy of the Commission's process, deprives condemned persons of their right to petition in the inter-American human rights system, and results in serious and irreparable harm to those individuals, and accordingly is inconsistent with the state's human rights obligations.

Can a state be found to have "implicitly undertaken to implement measures of this nature" where it has previously expressed no intent to be bound by such an obligation? How does the Commission's conclusion comport with your understanding of the powers of a sovereign state under international law, particularly with regard to its treaty practice? On the other hand, are certain implied powers necessary in order for a body to fulfill its mandate to "promote the observance and protection of human rights."? *See Precautionary Measures in Guantanamo Bay, Cuba*, Inter–Am. Comm'n H.R., March 13, 2002.

5. *Attempts to enforce the Garza decision in the U.S. courts.* After the Commission issued its opinion in the *Garza* case, petitioners attempted to obtain a stay of execution from the U.S. federal courts based on the Commission's conclusion that Garza's death sentence was a violation of the American Declaration. *See Garza v. Lappin*, 253 F.3d 918 (7th Cir. 2001). The court held that Garza had not presented a "substantial ground on which relief could be granted" (the standard for *habeas* relief under 18 U.S.C. § 2241) because he could not show that the Commission's report created an enforceable obligation "that the United States was bound by treaty to honor." *Id*. at 923. According to the court, "The Commission's power is only to make 'recommendations,' which according to the plain language of the term, are not binding." *Id*. at 924.

6. *Equality of arms.* Although the Commission did not address the issue in its opinion in the *Garza* case, the petitioner relied heavily on the claim that Mr. Garza's rights to a fair trial and to due process were violated because, at trial, there was no "equality of arms." The principle of equality of arms requires that each party be afforded a reasonable opportunity to present his case under conditions that do not place him at a substantial disadvantage *vis-à-vis* his opponent. *See, e.g,. Dombo Beheer v. The Netherlands*, ECHR (1993) Series A, No. 27, para. 33; *The Prosecutor v. Dusko Tadic*, ICTY (Case No. IT–94–1–A), Judgment (15 June 1999). According to the petitioner in *Garza*, the defendant was placed at a substantial disadvantage at the sentencing phase of his trial because he did not have the resources or opportunity to assemble evidence to rebut the prosecution's allegations that he was responsible for the four additional, unadjudicated murders. Because the United States has a mutual legal assistance treaty with Mexico, the petitioners contended that the prosecution received assistance from Mexican authorities that was unavailable to the defendant. The United States responded by relying on the case law, which it argued establishes the principle of equality of arms as requiring procedural equality, not substantive equality. In other words, so long as both sides are placed on an equal footing before the court, there is no violation of the principles of equality of arms.

Assuming the United States had the better of the argument, and that all that is required for equality of arms is procedural equality, where do you draw the line between procedure and substance? Can a case present a substantive disparity so great that procedural equality is irrelevant? In light of the facts before the Commission, do you think *Garza* was such a case? Why do you think the Commission dodged the "equality of arms" issue and decided the opinion the way that it did?

7. *The "fourth instance formula."* Under its "fourth instance formula," the Commission has determined that its task is

> to ensure the observance of the obligations undertaken by the States parties to the Convention, but it cannot serve as an appellate court to examine alleged errors of internal law or fact that may have been committed by the domestic courts acting within their jurisdiction. Such examination would be in order only insofar as the mistakes entailed a possible violation of any of the rights set forth in the Convention.

Santiago Marzioni v. Argentina, Case 11.673, Report No. 39/96, Inter–Am.C.H.R., OEA/Ser.L/V/II.95 Doc. 7 rev. at 76, para. 51 (1997). Can you see how the distinctions drawn by the Commission in the *Santiago Marzioni* case are not always easy to draw in human rights cases?

For instance, in *Andrews v. United States*, Case 11139, *supra*, the Commission found that a trial court's refusal to declare a mistrial or to allow defense counsel to question the jury after a note was found among the jurors that stated "Hang the Nigger's" violated articles I, II, and XXVI of the American Declaration. The petitioner in *Andrews* made many of the same arguments presented before the Commission during the course of extensive appeals in both the state and federal courts, arguing that the improprieties in his trial constituted violations of the state and U.S. Constitution. These claims were all rejected, and Andrews' death sentence was upheld. How is the Commission's finding that the American Declaration was violated distinct from its acting as an appellate court? Is this a matter of substance or semantics?

Practicum

Maria Sanchez–Espinoza is a 32–year old married woman presently living with a distant cousin in Mexico City, Mexico. Until recently, she lived with her husband, Carlos, and four children in a ramshackle house in the city's slums. Fearing for her life, and the safety of her children, she packed up the few belongings she could carry and escaped to her cousin's house in the dead of night with her children.

For the last twelve years, Ms. Sanchez–Espinoza has been beaten by her husband on an almost daily basis. During the evening, Carlos would come home drunk and on the basis of his complaints about her—the house, the kids, his dinner—he would "punish" her. Sometimes the beatings would come for no reason at all. Ms. Sanchez–Espinoza would be performing household chores and suddenly feel a blow to the back of her head. Other times, the beatings would be accompanied by sexual assault. If Ms. Sanchez–Espinoza resisted her husband's advances, she would be beaten even more severely. Some beatings were so severe that she required medical attention. On two occasions she was hospitalized.

Over the course of their marriage, Ms. Sanchez–Espinoza complained to the police about her husband's behavior on several occasions. She tried to file a complaint at the local police station but was refused. Ms. Sanchez–Espinoza attempted to speak with the commanding officer at the local police station but was refused a meeting. She even wrote a letter to the President of Mexico but received a perfunctory reply telling her to bring the matter up at the local police station. Routinely, when she complained to the police, she was told this was a "domestic matter" with which the police would not interfere.

Ms. Sanchez–Espinoza also tried to get help from government-run social services agencies. She sought counseling as well as medical and legal assistance, but was repeatedly told that services were unavailable for financial reasons or that her situation was not severe enough to merit assistance. One night, after a particularly severe beating, she went to a battered woman's shelter, but the next day, Carlos discovered her whereabouts and forcibly took her home with him. One lawyer she spoke with informed her that if she attempted to pursue legal action, it was almost certain the courts would do nothing, and it would be impossible to keep Carlos from retaliating.

On the night Ms. Sanchez–Espinoza left her home to live with her cousin, her husband had discovered she had been talking to the police. Apparently, the brother of one of Carlos' friends was a police officer who informed him of her visits. He also told Carlos that the police were getting tired of her visits and that "he should keep his wife in line." Upon returning home from a night of heavy drinking, Carlos challenged his wife with what he had been told. In the course of the beating that ensued, Carlos threatened to kill his wife and hurt the children. When he grew tired and passed out, Ms. Sanchez–Espinoza escaped with her children. Since she left, Carlos has been asking all of her family and friends where she is, but they have maintained silence. Ms. Sanchez–Espinoza fears it is only a matter of time before he finds out where she his hiding.

Ms. Sanchez–Espinoza has come to you for legal assistance. You have determined that pursuing legal action through the Mexican courts would be futile, and have therefore decided to look to the inter-American human rights system. Part of your decision is based on the need to publicize Ms. Sanchez–Espinoza's case in order to force the Mexican government to provide her with protection. Students should prepare briefs for submission to the Inter–American Commission on Human Rights on behalf of Ms. Sanchez–Espinoza and the Mexican government.

CHAPTER 3

MODULE 7C

THE AFRICAN SYSTEM FOR THE PROTECTION OF HUMAN RIGHTS

■ ■ ■

"This must be a world of democracy and respect for human rights, a world freed from the horrors of poverty, hunger, deprivation and ignorance, relieved of the threat and the scourge of civil wars and external aggression and unburdened of the great tragedy of millions forced to become refugees."

Nelson Mandela, accepting the Nobel Peace Prize (1993)

Orientation

International human rights lawyers routinely encounter certain recurring distinctions: civil and political rights *versus* economic and social rights; individual rights *versus* group rights; rights *versus* duties. The African regional system for the protection of human rights invites us to reconsider some of these received distinctions and to take account of the variety of institutional approaches that may succeed (or not) in a range of cultures and settings. The African experience offers multi-layered case studies in both the effectiveness and the limitations of human rights advocacy across a wide variety of issues, including the increased enforcement of women's rights, the dismantling of *apartheid* in South Africa, the response after the fact to the genocide in Rwanda, the accountability trials of leaders like Charles Taylor, the legal response to the HIV/AIDS epidemic, and the inaction of the international community in Darfur. Because of the tendency in the industrialized, developed states to focus on the human rights failures in Africa—in short, to "pathologize" the continent—western analysts may lose sight of certain best practices which can be extracted from its history,[1] especially with regard to

---

1. *See, e.g.*, O.C. Okafor & S.C. Agbakwa, *Re-Imagining International Human Rights Education in our Time: Beyond Three Constitutive Orthodoxies* 14 LEIDEN J. INT'L L. 563–90, 576 (2001) ("by constructing the Third World in virtually absolute terms, as a hellish place, the Western 'teacher' of human rights, *i.e.* the [international human rights education] enthusiast, justifies and secures her or

559

"standard-setting (*i.e.* normative development), case law (*i.e.* jurisprudential development) and enforcement mechanisms (*i.e.* institutional development)." Mashood Baderin, *Recent Developments in the African Regional Human Rights System*, 5 HUM. RTS. L. REV. 117 (2005). The following materials attempt to right the balance by noting the power and the limits of human rights law in modern Africa, the legacy of colonialism and exploitation, and the complexity of reconciling multiple rights-in-conflict.

The African regional system originated under the auspices of the Organization of African Unity ("OAU"), which was created in 1963 to address the abolition of colonialism and *apartheid*, among other things. The OAU was not primarily a human rights organization however, and, aside from a reference to the Universal Declaration of Human Rights in the Preamble to the OAU Charter,[2] there were few explicit references to "human rights" in the Charter itself. By the late 1970's, that changed for a variety of reasons, including

> the increased emphasis on human rights internationally at the time (as in the foreign policy of President Carter of the United States of America), the use to which the concept of human rights was put in international bodies such as the United Nations and the OAU to condemn the *apartheid* practices in South Africa, and abhorrence at the human rights violations in some newly independent African states, including Uganda, Central African Republic, and Equatorial Guinea.[3]

The challenge was to draft a continent-wide treaty that echoed the common core of protections in the various regional and universal human rights instruments, but which also gave voice to the unique values and histories of African nations, individuals, and peoples. The result was the African Charter on Human and Peoples' Rights ("African Charter"),[4] which is the foundational document of the African regional human rights system.

In 2002, the OAU was transformed into the African Union ("AU"), whose Constitutive Act, excerpted below, places human rights prominently on the regional agenda.[5] The economic development program of the AU, known as the New Partnership for Africa's Development ("NEPAD"), contains a particularly strong commitment to human rights. Section 10 of NEPAD's constitutive instrument makes an explicit connection among human rights, economic development, and regional security.

---

his own existence and position, as well as secures the unidirectional flow of human rights knowledge from the Western world (the teachers) to the Third World (the students).").

2.   479 U.N.T.S. 39 (1963).

3.   Christof Heyns, *The African Regional Human Rights System: The African Charter*, 108 PENN. ST. L. REV. 679, 685 (2004).

4.   African Charter on Human and People's Rights, OAU Doc./CAB/LEG/67/3/rev.5, *opened for signature* in 1981, entered into force in 1986. The African Charter is also known as the "Banjul Charter."

5.   Constitutive Act of the African Union CAB/LEG/23.15 (May 26, 2001).

In the light of Africa's recent history, respect for human rights has to be accorded an importance and urgency all of its own. One of the tests by which the quality of a democracy is judged is the protection it provides for each individual citizen and for the vulnerable and disadvantaged groups. Ethnic minorities, women and children have borne the brunt of the conflicts raging on the continent today. We undertake to do more to advance the cause of human rights in Africa generally and, specifically, to end the moral shame exemplified by the plight of women, children, the disabled and ethnic minorities in conflict situations in Africa.[6]

NEPAD is not merely normative or aspirational. At its center is an innovative institutional component, the African Peer Review Mechanism ("APRM"), which is empowered *inter alia* to address the human rights practices of member states. "[D]esigned and implemented by Africans for Africa, * * * [APRM] is a mutually agreed instrument voluntarily acceded to by member-States of the African Union, mainly for the purpose of self-monitoring. * * * The APRM provides an opportunity for the systematic assessment of the performance of the State by its peers with the ultimate goal of helping it to adopt best practices, improve its policy making process and comply with established standards and principles."[7]

Substantive individual rights. In many respects, the protections in the African Charter are consistent with, if not identical to, the protections in the other regional treaty regimes. Here, for example, will be found the prohibition of torture and cruel, human, or degrading treatment;[8] a prohibition on arbitrary arrest and detention;[9] a right to due process of law;[10] and guarantees of "[f]reedom of conscience [and] the profession and free practice of religion...."[11]

But the African Charter also articulates a greater range of economic, social, and cultural rights than is found in the basic European and

---

6. NEPAD, Declaration on Democracy, Political, Economic, and Corporate Governance, AHG/235 (XXXVIII) Annex I, *available at* www.nepad.org/2005/files/documents/2.pdf.

7. APRM Country Review Report of the Republic of Rwanda i (November 2005), *available at* www.nepad.org/2005/files/aprm/FINAL_RWANDA_REPORT_SEPT_22_2006.pdf.

8. African Charter, at art. 5:

Every individual shall have the right to the respect of the dignity inherent in a human being and to the recognition of his legal status. All forms of exploitation and degradation of man particularly slavery, slave trade, torture, cruel, inhuman or degrading punishment and treatment shall be prohibited.

9. African Charter, at art. 6:

Every individual shall have the right to liberty and to the security of his person. No one may be deprived of his freedom except for reasons and conditions previously laid down by law. In particular, no one may be arbitrarily arrested or detained.

10. African Charter, at art. 7(1):

Every individual shall have the right to have his cause heard. This comprises: (a) the right to an appeal to competent national organs against acts of violating his fundamental rights as recognized and guaranteed by conventions, laws, regulations and customs in force; (b) the right to be presumed innocent until proved guilty by a competent court or tribunal; (c) the right to defense, including the right to be defended by counsel of his choice; (d) the right to be tried within a reasonable time by an impartial court or tribunal.

11. African Charter, at art. 8.

American Conventions, including *inter alia* the right to work, the right to health, and the right to education;[12] indeed, the Preamble to the African Charter makes an explicit connection between both categories of rights, noting that "civil and political rights cannot be dissociated from economic, social and cultural rights in their conception as well as universality and that the satisfaction of economic, social and cultural rights is a guarantee for the enjoyment of civil and political rights." In addition, the member states are obliged to recognize all the rights in the Charter, regardless of category, and they "undertake to adopt legislative or other measures to give effect to them." African Charter, art. 1. A court— whether international or domestic—will generally not direct a legislature to adopt a statute (let alone draft the legislation itself), but these rights are increasingly justiciable, judging from the recent African experience. As suggested below, the principles of "progressive realization" and non-discrimination may offer a strategy for using the courts to enforce even those economic, social, and cultural rights that have traditionally been discounted as non-justiciable. For example, because individuals are entitled to enjoy rights regardless of category "without distinction of any kind such as race, ethnic group, color, sex, language, religion, political or any other opinion, national and social origin, fortune, birth or other status," African Charter, art. 2, the courts may well adjudicate disputes involving the discriminatory administration of the right to housing, education, food, and medical care.

Peoples' rights. The African Charter is also unique in its wide endorsement of peoples' rights. Although the term "peoples" is not defined in the treaty, the collective entitlements themselves are specified in greater detail than in either the European or the American Conventions and include a people's right "to free themselves from the bonds of domination by resorting to any means recognized by the international community." Consider for example:

Article 19

All peoples shall be equal; they shall enjoy the same respect and shall have the same rights. Nothing shall justify the domination of a people by another.

---

12. Consider for example:

Article 15

Every individual shall have the right to work under equitable and satisfactory conditions, and shall receive equal pay for equal work.

Article 16

1. Every individual shall have the right to enjoy the best attainable state of physical and mental health. 2. States Parties to the present Charter shall take the necessary measures to protect the health of their people and to ensure that they receive medical attention when they are sick.

Article 17

1. Every individual shall have the right to education. 2. Every individual may freely, take part in the cultural life of his community. 3. The promotion and protection of morals and traditional values recognized by the community shall be the duty of the State.

Article 20

1. All peoples shall have the right to existence. They shall have the unquestionable and inalienable right to self-determination. They shall freely determine their political status and shall pursue their economic and social development according to the policy they have freely chosen. 2. Colonized or oppressed peoples shall have the right to free themselves from the bonds of domination by resorting to any means recognized by the international community. 3. All peoples shall have the right to the assistance of the States parties to the present Charter in their liberation struggle against foreign domination, be it political, economic or cultural.

Article 22

1. All peoples shall have the right to their economic, social and cultural development with due regard to their freedom and identity and in the equal enjoyment of the common heritage of mankind. 2. States shall have the duty, individually or collectively, to ensure the exercise of the right to development.

Article 24

All peoples shall have the right to a general satisfactory environment favorable to their development.

What entity might be held responsible for enforcing these rights? In some cases, the state itself is explicitly identified as having the duty to enforce a peoples' right to economic development. But against itself for not spending enough on economic empowerment of the poor? Against donor or creditor countries? Are there circumstances in which individuals or companies or the media might be deemed to have violated these rights? And thinking broadly, consider the possibility that these rights might be enforced or internalized without going through a courtroom at all.

Duties. Unlike other human rights instruments, the African Charter links the "enjoyment of rights and freedoms" to "the performance of duties on the part of everyone." African Charter, Preamble. Under Article 27(1), for example, "[e]very individual shall have duties towards his family and society, the State and other legally recognized communities and the international community." Article 29 specifies a broad range of these obligations:

> The individual shall also have the duty: 1. to preserve the harmonious development of the family and to work for the cohesion and respect of the family; to respect his parents at all times, to maintain them in case of need; 2. To serve his national community by placing his physical and intellectual abilities at its service; 3. Not to compromise the security of the State whose national or resident he is; 4. To preserve and strengthen social and national solidarity, particularly when the latter is threatened; 5. To preserve and strengthen the

national independence and the territorial integrity of his country and to contribute to its defence in accordance with the law; 6. To work to the best of his abilities and competence, and to pay taxes imposed by law in the interest of the society; 7. to preserve and strengthen positive African cultural values in his relations with other members of the society, in the spirit of tolerance, dialogue and consultation and, in general, to contribute to the promotion of the moral well being of society; 8. To contribute to the best of his abilities, at all times and at all levels, to the promotion and achievement of African unity.

With a few exceptions,[13] these duties are not conceived as a *quid pro quo* for the recognition of human rights: it's not as though an individual forfeits her right to be free of torture or to participate in public life if she fails to maintain her parents in case of need. But the drafters of the African Charter were attempting to forge a post-colonial understanding of citizenship and viewed the treaty as a means of expressing that social contract.

On the other hand, the African Charter has been criticized for favoring the rights of governments in ways that overly restrict the exercise of human rights. In addition to the specification of individual duties, critics point to the related problem of so-called "claw-back" provisions in the African Charter. These provisions

> permit the routine breach of Charter obligations for reasons of public utility or national security and confine many of the Charter's protections to rights as they are defined and limited by domestic legislation. This effectively allows governments to determine the scope of human rights protections themselves. * * * By contrast, most international human rights conventions contain specific derogation clauses. Under these clauses, certain rights are declared non-derogable under all circumstances while precise conditions and legal requirements for permissible derogation are laid out for others. There is little room for arbitrariness under such well-defined standards, whereas the opportunities for discretionary abuse under the Charter's "claw-back clauses" are broad and well-used.

Nsongurua Udombana, *Toward the African Court on Human and Peoples' Rights: Better Late Than Never*, 3 YALE H. R. & DEV. L.J. 45, 63 (2000).[14] *But see* African Commission on Human and Peoples Rights, *Media Rights Agenda and Constitutional Rights Project v. Nigeria*, Comm. Nos. 105/93, 128/94, 130/94 and 152/96 (1998).

---

13. *See, e.g.*, African Charter, art. (1) ("Every individual shall have the right to free association *provided that he abides by the law*") (emphasis supplied).

14. *See, e.g.*, African Charter, art. 8 ("Freedom of conscience, the profession and free practice of religion shall be guaranteed. No one may, *subject to law and order*, be submitted to measures restricting the exercise of these freedoms"); Article 9(2) ("Every individual shall have the right to express and disseminate his opinions *within the law*"); Article 14 ("The right to property shall be guaranteed. It may only be encroached upon *in the interest of public need or in the general interest of the community and in accordance with the provisions of appropriate laws*.") (emphasis supplied in all cases).

Enforcement. The dominant supervisory body under the African Charter has historically been the African Commission on Human and Peoples' Rights ("African Commission" or "ACHPR"), which reports to the Assembly of Heads of State and Government of the AU. The eleven-member African Commission is empowered *inter alia* to receive a variety of "communications" alleging violations of the African Charter: inter-state communications under Articles 48–49, and individual or organizational communications under Article 55. The African Commission has generally operated confidentially, but increasingly its work product is being published and incorporated—as shown below—into a recognizably African human rights jurisprudence. The Commission may also establish Working Groups, Focal Points, Special Mechanisms, or Special Rapporteurs and has exercised that authority repeatedly to address various human rights issues.[15] The Commission is also empowered to initiate proceedings in the African Court on Human and Peoples' Rights, which came into being under the terms of a special protocol which entered into force in 2004.[16]

The differences between the African Court and its counterparts in the European and Inter–American systems are instructive. For example, unlike the Inter–American Court, the African Court of Human Rights is in principle empowered to hear cases brought directly by individuals and non-governmental organizations. But unlike the European Court as reformed, only individuals or NGOs that have been granted observer status have this power. Protocol for Establishment of an African Court, art 5(3), art. 34(6). As a consequence, unless the African states recognize the competence of the African Court to hear individual or NGO petitions, cases that originate with the Commission will dominate the Court's docket. But the African court's substantive reach is in principle broader than either of the other regional courts: quite apart from the rights that are unique to the African Charter, the Inter–American and European courts are limited by their governing conventions and protocols, while the African Court is empowered to apply *any* human rights instrument that is ratified by all the states concerned, including universal treaties like the Convention against Torture, or regional instruments dealing for example with the rights of refugees[17] or children[18] or women.[19]

---

15. The African Commission has for example established special mechanisms to deal with (i) Extra-judicial, Summary or Arbitrary Executions, (ii) Freedom of Expression, (iii) Human Rights Defenders, (iv) Prisons and Conditions of Detention, (v) Refugees and Internally Displaced Persons, and (vi) the Rights of Women. (Available at http://www.achpr.org/english/_info/news_en.html).

16. Protocol to the African Charter on Human and Peoples' Rights on the Establishment of an African Court on Human and Peoples' Rights, OAU Doc. CAB/LEG/66/5, *adopted* 10 June 1998.

17. *See, e.g.,* Convention governing the Specific Aspects of the Refugee Problems in Africa, adopted 1 September 1969, entered into force 20 June 1974, 1001 U.N.T.S. 45.

18. *See, e.g.,* African Charter on the Rights and Welfare of the Child, adopted July 1990, entered into force 29 November 1999, OAU Doc. CAB/LEG/TSG/Rev.1.

19. *See, e.g.,* Protocol to the African Charter on Human and Peoples' Rights on the Rights of Women in Africa, adopted in July 2003, and entered into force on November 25, 2005, *available at* http://www.achpr.org/english/_info/women_en.html.

In the materials that follow, you will encounter a range of African institutions enforcing regional and international human rights law: a domestic court, the African Commission on Human and Peoples' Rights, and the AU's African Peer Review Mechanism. Consider in each case both the substantive rights at issue and the procedural or institutional means of respecting, protecting, promoting, fulfilling, and enforcing them.

Readings

THE GOVERNMENT OF THE REPUBLIC OF SOUTH AFRICA ET AL. v. GROOTBOOM, ET AL.

Constitutional Court of South Africa (CCT11/00)
[2000] ZACC 19; 2001 (1) SA 46 (2000)

The people of South Africa are committed to the attainment of social justice and the improvement of the quality of life for everyone. The Preamble to our Constitution records this commitment. The Constitution declares the founding values of our society to be "[h]uman dignity, the achievement of equality and the advancement of human rights and freedoms." This case grapples with the realisation of these aspirations for it concerns the state's constitutional obligations in relation to housing: a constitutional issue of fundamental importance to the development of South Africa's new constitutional order. The issues here remind us of the intolerable conditions under which many of our people are still living. * * * It is also a reminder that unless the plight of these communities is alleviated, people may be tempted to take the law into their own hands in order to escape these conditions. The case brings home the harsh reality that the Constitution's promise of dignity and equality for all remains for many a distant dream. People should not be impelled by intolerable living conditions to resort to land invasions. Self-help of this kind cannot be tolerated, for the unavailability of land suitable for housing development is a key factor in the fight against the country's housing shortage.

The group of people with whom we are concerned in these proceedings lived in appalling conditions, decided to move out and illegally occupied someone else's land. They were evicted and left homeless. The root cause of their problems is the intolerable conditions under which they were living while waiting in the queue for their turn to be allocated low-cost housing. They are the people whose constitutional rights have to be determined in this case. Mrs. Irene Grootboom and the other respondents [510 children and 390 adults] were rendered homeless as a result of their eviction from their informal homes situated on private land earmarked for formal low-cost housing. They applied to the Cape of Good Hope High Court (the High Court) for an order requiring government to provide them with adequate basic shelter or housing until they obtained permanent accommodation and were granted certain relief. The appellants were ordered to provide the respondents who were children and their parents with shelter. The judgment provisionally concluded that "tents, portable latrines and a regular supply of water (albeit transported) would constitute the bare minimum." The appellants who represent all spheres of government responsible for housing challenge the correctness of that order. * * *

The cause of the acute housing shortage lies in apartheid. A central feature of that policy was a system of influx control that sought to limit African occupation of urban areas. Influx control was rigorously enforced in the Western Cape, where government policy favoured the exclusion of African people in order to accord preference to the coloured community: a policy adopted in 1954 and referred to as the "coloured labour preference policy." In consequence, the provision of family housing for African people in the Cape Peninsula was frozen in 1962. This freeze was extended to other urban areas in the Western Cape in 1968. Despite the harsh application of influx control in the Western Cape, African people continued to move to the area in search of jobs. Colonial dispossession and a rigidly enforced racial distribution of land in the rural areas had dislocated the rural economy and rendered sustainable and independent African farming increasingly precarious. Given the absence of formal housing, large numbers of people moved into informal settlements throughout the Cape peninsula. The cycle of the apartheid era, therefore, was one of untenable restrictions on the movement of African people into urban areas, the inexorable tide of the rural poor to the cities, inadequate housing, resultant overcrowding, mushrooming squatter settlements, constant harassment by officials and intermittent forced removals. The legacy of influx control in the Western Cape is the acute housing shortage that exists there now. * * * Hundreds of thousands of people in need of housing occupied rudimentary informal settlements providing for minimal shelter, but little else.

Mrs. Grootboom and most of the other respondents previously lived in an informal squatter settlement called Wallacedene. It lies on the edge of the municipal area of Oostenberg, which in turn is on the eastern fringe of the Cape Metro. The conditions under which most of the residents of Wallacedene lived were lamentable. A quarter of the households of Wallacedene had no income at all, and more than two thirds earned less than R500 per month. About half the population were children; all lived in shacks. They had no water, sewage or refuse removal services and only 5% of the shacks had electricity. The area is partly waterlogged and lies dangerously close to a main thoroughfare. Mrs. Grootboom lived with her family and her sister's family in a shack about twenty metres square. Many had applied for subsidised low-cost housing from the municipality and had been on the waiting list for as long as seven years. Despite numerous enquiries from the municipality no definite answer was given. Clearly it was going to be a long wait.

Faced with the prospect of remaining in intolerable conditions indefinitely, the respondents began to move out of Wallacedene at the end of September 1998. They put up their shacks and shelters on vacant land that was privately owned and had been earmarked for low-cost housing. They called the land "New Rust."

They did not have the consent of the owner and on 8 December 1998 he obtained an ejectment order against them in the magistrates' court. The order was served on the occupants but they remained in occupation beyond the date by which they had been ordered to vacate. Mrs. Grootboom says they had nowhere else to go: their former sites in Wallacedene had been filled by others. The eviction proceedings were renewed in March 1999. The respondents' attorneys in this case were appointed by the magistrate to represent them on the return day of the provisional order of eviction. Negotiations resulted in the grant of an order requiring the occupants to vacate New Rust and authorising the sheriff to evict them and to dismantle and remove any of their structures remaining on the land on 19 May 1999. The magistrate also directed that the parties and the municipality mediate to identify alternative land for the permanent or temporary occupation of the New Rust residents.

The municipality had not been party to the proceedings but it had engaged attorneys to monitor them on its behalf. It is not clear whether the municipality was a party to the settlement and the agreement to mediate. Nor is it clear whether the eviction was in accordance with the provisions of the Prevention of Illegal Eviction from and Unlawful Occupation of Land Act of 1998. The validity of the eviction order has never been challenged and must be accepted as correct. However, no mediation took place and on 18 May 1999, at the beginning of the cold, windy and rainy Cape winter, the respondents were forcibly evicted at the municipality's expense. This was done prematurely and inhumanely: reminiscent of apartheid-style evictions. The respondents' homes were bulldozed and burnt and their possessions destroyed. Many of the residents who were not there could not even salvage their personal belongings.

The respondents went and sheltered on the Wallacedene sports field under such temporary structures as they could muster. Within a week the winter rains started and the plastic sheeting they had erected afforded scant protection. The next day the respondents' attorney wrote to the municipality describing the intolerable conditions under which his clients were living and demanded that the municipality meet its constitutional obligations and provide temporary accommodation to the respondents. The respondents were not satisfied with the response of the municipality and launched an urgent application in the High Court on 31 May 1999. As indicated above, the High Court granted relief to the respondents and the appellants now appeal against that relief. * * *

The relevant constitutional provisions and their justiciability

The key constitutional provisions at issue in this case are section 26 and section 28(1)(c).

Section 26 provides:

> (1) Everyone has the right to have access to adequate housing.

> (2) The state must take reasonable legislative and other measures, within its available resources, to achieve the progressive realisation of this right.

> (3) No one may be evicted from their home, or have their home demolished, without an order of court made after considering all the relevant circumstances. No legislation may permit arbitrary evictions.

Section 28(1)(c) provides:

> (1) Every child has the right * * * (c) to basic nutrition, shelter, basic health care services and social services.

These rights need to be considered in the context of the cluster of socio-economic rights enshrined in the Constitution. They entrench the right of access to land, to adequate housing and to health care, food, water and social security. They also protect the rights of the child and the right to education.

While the justiciability of socio-economic rights has been the subject of considerable jurisprudential and political debate, the issue of whether socio-economic rights are justiciable at all in South Africa has been put beyond question by the text of our Constitution as construed in [prior judgments of this Court, which ruled that:]

> [T]hese rights are, at least to some extent, justiciable. * * * [M]any of the civil and political rights entrenched in the [constitutional text before this Court for certification in that case] will give rise to similar budgetary implications without compromising their justiciability. The fact that socio-economic rights will almost inevitably give rise to such implications does not seem to us to be a bar to their justiciability. At the very minimum, socio-economic rights can be negatively protected from improper invasion.

Socio-economic rights are expressly included in the Bill of Rights; they cannot be said to exist on paper only. Section 7(2) of the Constitution requires the state "to respect, protect, promote and fulfil the rights in the Bill of Rights" and the courts are constitutionally bound to ensure that they are protected and fulfilled. The question is therefore not whether socio-economic rights are justiciable under our Constitution, but how to enforce them in a given case. This is a very difficult issue which must be carefully explored on a case-by-case basis. To address the challenge raised in the present case, it is necessary first to consider the terms and context of the relevant constitutional provisions and their application to the circumstances of this case. Although the judgment of the High Court in favour of the appellants was based on the right to shelter (section 28(1)(c) of the Constitution), it is appropriate to consider the provisions of section 26 first so as to facilitate a contextual evaluation of section 28(1)(c). * * *

Our Constitution entrenches both civil and political rights and social and economic rights. All the rights in our Bill of Rights are inter-related and mutually supporting. There can be no doubt that human dignity, freedom and equality, the foundational values of our society, are denied those who have no food, clothing or shelter. Affording socio-economic rights to all people therefore enables them to enjoy the other rights enshrined in Chapter 2 [of the Constitution, which contains the Bill of Rights]. The realisation of these rights is also key to the advancement of race and gender equality and the evolution of a society in which men and women are equally able to achieve their full potential. * * *

The relevant international law and its impact

During argument, considerable weight was attached to the value of international law in interpreting section 26 of our Constitution. Section 39 of the Constitution[1] obliges a court to consider international law as a tool to interpretation of the Bill of Rights. In *Makwanyane*,[2] [this Court] said:

> . . . public international law would include non-binding as well as binding law. They may both be used under the section as tools of interpretation. International agreements and customary international law accordingly provide a framework within which [the Bill of Rights] can be evaluated and understood, and for that purpose, decisions of tribunals dealing with comparable instruments, such as the United Nations Committee on Human Rights, the Inter–American Commission on Human Rights, the Inter–American Court of Human Rights, the European Commission on Human Rights, and the European Court of Human Rights, and, in appropriate cases, reports of specialised agencies such as the International Labour Organisation, may provide guidance as to the correct interpretation of particular provisions of [the Bill of Rights].

The relevant international law can be a guide to interpretation but the weight to be attached to any particular principle or rule of international law will vary. However, where the relevant principle of international law binds South Africa, it may be directly applicable.

The *amici*[3] submitted that the International Covenant on Economic, Social and Cultural Rights (the Covenant)[4] is of significance in

---

1. Section 39 of the Constitution provides [in part]:

(1) When interpreting the Bill of Rights, a court, tribunal or forum

(a) must promote the values that underlie and open and democratic society based on human dignity, equality and freedom;

(b) must consider international law; and

(c) may consider foreign law.

2. [*S v. Makwanyane and Another, 1995 (3) SA 391 (CC), 1995 (6) BCLR 665 (CC)*]

3. [Editors' note: The South African Human Rights Commission, the Community Law Centre of the University of the Western Cape, and GM Budlender of the Legal Resources Centre had been admitted as *amici curiae* in these proceedings before the Constitutional Court.]

4. The Covenant was signed by South Africa on 3 October 1994 but has as yet not been ratified.

understanding the positive obligations created by the socio-economic rights in the Constitution. Article 11.1 of the Covenant provides:

> The States Parties to the present Covenant recognize the right of everyone to an adequate standard of living for himself and his family, including adequate food, clothing and housing, and to the continuous improvement of living conditions. The States Parties will take appropriate steps to ensure the realization of this right, recognizing to this effect the essential importance of international co-operation based on free consent.

This Article must be read with Article 2.1 which provides:

> Each State Party to the present Covenant undertakes to take steps, individually and through international assistance and co-operation, especially economic and technical, to the maximum of its available resources, with a view to achieving progressively the full realization of the rights recognized in the present Covenant by all appropriate means, including particularly the adoption of legislative measures.

The differences between the relevant provisions of the Covenant and our Constitution are significant in determining the extent to which the provisions of the Covenant may be a guide to an interpretation of section 26. These differences, in so far as they relate to housing, are:

> (a) The Covenant provides for a *right to adequate housing* while section 26 provides for the *right of access* to adequate housing.

> (b) The Covenant obliges states parties to take *appropriate* steps which must include legislation while the Constitution obliges the South African state to take *reasonable* legislative and other measures.

The obligations undertaken by states parties to the Covenant are monitored by the United Nations Committee on Economic, Social and Cultural Rights (the committee). The *amici* relied on the relevant general comments issued by the committee concerning the interpretation and application of the Covenant, and argued that these general comments constitute a significant guide to the interpretation of section 26. In particular they argued that in interpreting this section, we should adopt an approach similar to that taken by the committee in paragraph 10 of general comment 3 issued in 1990, in which the committee found that socio-economic rights contain a minimum core:

> On the basis of the extensive experience gained by the Committee, as well as by the body that preceded it, over a period of more than a decade of examining States parties' reports the Committee is of the view that minimum core obligation to ensure the satisfaction of, at the very least, minimum essential levels of each of the rights is incumbent upon every State party. Thus, for example, a State party in which any significant number of individuals is deprived of essential foodstuffs, of essential primary health care, of basic shelter and housing, or of the most basic forms of education, is *prima facie*, failing to discharge its obligations under the Covenant. If the

Covenant were to be read in such a way as not to establish such a minimum core obligation, it would be largely deprived of its *raison d'etre*. By the same token, it must be noted that any assessment as to whether a State has discharged its minimum core obligation must also take account of resource constraints applying within the country concerned. Article 2(1) obligates each State party to take the necessary steps "to the maximum of its available resources". In order for a State party to be able to attribute its failure to meet at least its minimum core obligations to a lack of available resources it must demonstrate that every effort has been made to use all resources that are at its disposition in an effort to satisfy, as a matter of priority, those minimum obligations.

It is clear from this extract that the committee considers that every state party is bound to fulfil a minimum core obligation by ensuring the satisfaction of a minimum essential level of the socio-economic rights, including the right to adequate housing. Accordingly, a state in which a significant number of individuals is deprived of basic shelter and housing is regarded as *prima facie* in breach of its obligations under the Covenant. A state party must demonstrate that every effort has been made to use all the resources at its disposal to satisfy the minimum core of the right. However, it is to be noted that the general comment does not specify precisely what that minimum core is.

The concept of minimum core obligation was developed by the committee to describe the minimum expected of a state in order to comply with its obligation under the Covenant. It is the floor beneath which the conduct of the state must not drop if there is to be compliance with the obligation. Each right has a "minimum essential level" that must be satisfied by the states parties. The committee developed this concept based on "extensive experience gained by [it] * * * over a period of more than a decade of examining States parties' reports." The general comment is based on reports furnished by the reporting states and the general comment is therefore largely descriptive of how the states have complied with their obligations under the Covenant. The committee has also used the general comment "as a means of developing a common understanding of the norms by establishing a prescriptive definition." Minimum core obligation is determined generally by having regard to the needs of the most vulnerable group that is entitled to the protection of the right in question. It is in this context that the concept of minimum core obligation must be understood in international law. * * *

The determination of a minimum core in the context of "the right to have access to adequate housing" presents difficult questions. This is so because the needs in the context of access to adequate housing are diverse: there are those who need land; others need both land and houses; yet others need financial assistance. There are difficult questions relating to the definition of minimum core in the context of a right to have access to adequate housing, in particular whether the minimum core obligation should be defined generally or with regard to specific groups of people. As will appear from the discussion below, the real question in terms of our Constitution is whether the measures taken by the state to realise the right afforded by section 26 are reasonable. There may be cases where it may be possible and appropriate to have regard to the content of a minimum core obligation to determine whether the measures taken by the state are reasonable. However, even if it were appropriate to do so, it could not be done unless sufficient information is placed before a court to enable it to determine the minimum core in any given context. In this case, we do not have sufficient information to determine what would comprise the minimum core obligation in the context of our Constitution.

Analysis of section 26

The right delineated in section 26(1) is a right of "access to adequate housing" as distinct from the right to adequate housing encapsulated in the Covenant. This difference is significant. It recognises that housing entails more than bricks and mortar. It requires available land, appropriate services such as the provision of water and the removal of sewage and the financing of all of these, including the building of the house itself. For a person to have access to adequate housing all of these conditions need to be met: there must be land, there must be services, there must be a dwelling. Access to land for the purpose of housing is therefore included in the right of access to adequate housing in section 26. A right of access to adequate housing also suggests that it is not only the state who is responsible for the provision of houses, but that other agents within our society, including individuals themselves, must be enabled by legislative and other measures to provide housing. The state must create the conditions for access to adequate housing for people at all economic levels of our society. State policy dealing with housing must therefore take account of different economic levels in our society. * * *

The state's obligation to provide access to adequate housing depends on context, and may differ from province to province, from city to city, from rural to urban areas and from person to person. Some may need access to land and no more; some may need access to land and building materials; some may need access to finance; some may need access to services such as water, sewage, electricity and roads. What might be appropriate in a rural area where people live together in communities engaging in subsistence farming may not be appropriate in an urban area where people are looking for employment and a place to live.

Subsection (2) speaks to the positive obligation imposed upon the state. It requires the state to devise a comprehensive and workable plan to meet its obligations in terms of the subsection. However subsection (2) also makes it clear that the obligation imposed upon the state is not an absolute or unqualified one. The extent of the state's obligation is defined by three key elements that are considered separately: (a) the obligation to "take reasonable legislative and other measures"; (b) "to achieve the progressive realisation" of the right; and (c) "within available resources." * * *

Reasonable legislative and other measures

A reasonable programme * * * must clearly allocate responsibilities and tasks to the different spheres of government and ensure that the appropriate financial and human resources are available. * * * [A] co-ordinated state housing programme must be a comprehensive one determined by all three spheres of government in consultation with each other. * * * Each sphere of government must accept responsibility for the implementation of particular parts of the programme but the national sphere of government must assume responsibility for ensuring that laws, policies, programmes and strategies are adequate to meet the state's section 26 obligations. * * * It should be emphasised that national government bears an important responsibility in relation to the allocation of national revenue to the provinces and local government on an equitable basis. Furthermore, national and provincial government must ensure that executive obligations imposed by the housing legislation are met.

The measures must establish a coherent public housing programme directed towards the progressive realisation of the right of access to adequate housing within the state's available means. The programme must be capable of facilitating the realisation of the right. The precise contours and content of the measures to be adopted are primarily a matter for the legislature and the executive. They must, however, ensure that the measures they adopt are reasonable. In any challenge based on section 26 in which it is argued that the state has failed to meet the positive obligations imposed upon it by section 26(2), the question will be whether the legislative and other measures taken by the state are reasonable. A court considering reasonableness will not enquire whether other more desirable or favourable measures could have been adopted, or whether public money could have been better spent. The question would be whether the measures that have been adopted are reasonable. It is necessary to recognise that a wide range of possible measures could be adopted by the state to meet its obligations. Many of these would meet the requirement of reasonableness. Once it is shown that the measures do so, this requirement is met.

The state is required to take reasonable legislative and other measures. Legislative measures by themselves are not likely to constitute constitutional compliance. Mere legislation is not enough. The state is obliged to act to achieve the intended result, and the legislative measures will invariably have to be supported by appropriate, well-directed policies and programmes implemented by the executive. These policies and programmes must be reasonable both in their conception and their implementation. The formulation of a programme is only the first stage in meeting the state's obligations. The programme must also be reasonably implemented. An otherwise reasonable programme that is not implemented reasonably will not constitute compliance with the state's obligations.

In determining whether a set of measures is reasonable, it will be necessary to consider housing problems in their social, economic and historical context and to consider the capacity of institutions responsible for implementing the programme. The programme must be balanced and flexible and make appropriate provision for attention to housing crises and to short, medium and long term needs. A programme that excludes a significant segment of society cannot be said to be reasonable. Conditions do not remain static and therefore the programme will require continuous review. * * *

Progressive realisation of the right

The extent and content of the obligation consist in what must be achieved, that is, "the progressive realisation of this right." It links subsections (1) and (2) by making it quite clear that the right referred to is the right of access to adequate housing. The term "progressive realisation" shows that it was contemplated that the right could not be realised immediately. But the goal of the Constitution is that the basic needs of all in our society be effectively met and the requirement of progressive realisation means that the state must take steps to achieve this goal. It means that accessibility should be progressively facilitated: legal, administrative, operational and financial hurdles should be examined and, where possible, lowered over time. Housing must be made more accessible not only to a larger number of people but to a wider range of people as time progresses. The phrase is taken from international law and Article 2.1 of the Covenant in particular. The committee has helpfully analysed this requirement in the context of housing as follows:

> Nevertheless, the fact that realization over time, or in other words progressively, is foreseen under the Covenant should not be misinterpreted as depriving the obligation of all meaningful content. It is on the one hand a necessary flexibility device, reflecting the realities of the real world and the difficulties involved for any country in ensuring full realization of economic, social and cultural rights. On the other hand, the phrase must be read in the light of the overall objective, indeed the raison d'être, of the Covenant which is to establish clear obligations for States parties in respect of the full realization of the rights in question. It thus imposes an obligation to move as expeditiously and effectively as possible towards that goal. Moreover, any deliberately retrogressive measures in that regard would require the most careful consideration and would need to be fully justified by reference to the totality of the rights provided for in the Covenant and in the context of the full use of the maximum available resources.

Although the committee's analysis is intended to explain the scope of states parties' obligations under the Covenant, it is also helpful in plumbing the meaning of "progressive realisation" in the context of our Constitution. The meaning ascribed to the phrase is in harmony with the context in which the phrase is used in our Constitution and there is no reason not to accept that it bears the same meaning in the Constitution as in the document from which it was so clearly derived.

Within available resources

The * * * obligation to take the requisite measures * * * does not require the state to do more than its available resources permit. This means that both the content of the obligation in relation to the rate at which it is achieved as well as the reasonableness of the measures employed to achieve the result are governed by the availability of resources. Section 26 does not expect more of the state than is achievable within its available resources. * * * There is a balance between goal and means. The measures must be calculated to attain the goal expeditiously and effectively but the availability of resources is an important factor in determining what is reasonable.

Description and evaluation of the state housing programme

In support of their contention that they had complied with the obligation imposed upon them by section 26, the appellants placed evidence before this Court of the legislative and other measures they had adopted. There is in place both national and provincial legislation concerned with housing. It was explained that in 1994 the state inherited fragmented housing arrangements which involved thirteen statutory housing funds, seven ministries and housing departments, more than twenty subsidy systems and more than sixty national and regional parastatals operating on a racial basis. These have been rationalised. The national Housing Act provides a framework which establishes the responsibilities and functions of each sphere of government with regard to housing. The responsibility for implementation is generally given to the provinces. Provinces in turn have assigned certain implementation functions to local government structures in many cases. All spheres of government are intimately involved in housing delivery and the budget allocated by national government appears to be substantial. There is a single housing policy and a subsidy system that targets low-income earners regardless of race. The White Paper on Housing aims to stabilise the housing environment, establish institutional arrangements, protect consumers, rationalise institutional capacity within a sustainable long-term framework, facilitate the speedy release and servicing of land and co-ordinate and integrate the public sector investment in housing. In addition, various schemes are in place involving public/private partnerships aimed at ensuring that housing provision is effectively financed. * * *

What has been done in execution of this programme is a major achievement. Large sums of money have been spent and a significant number of houses has been built. Considerable thought, energy, resources and expertise have been and continue to be devoted to the process of effective housing delivery. It is a programme that is aimed at achieving the progressive realisation of the right of access to adequate housing.

A question that nevertheless must be answered is whether the measures adopted are reasonable within the meaning of section 26 of the Constitution. Allocation of responsibilities and functions has been coherently and comprehensively addressed. The programme is not haphazard but represents a systematic response to a pressing social need. It takes account of the housing shortage in South Africa by seeking to build a large number of homes for those in need of better housing. The programme applies throughout South Africa and although there have been difficulties of implementation in some areas, the evidence suggests that the state is actively seeking to combat these difficulties. * * *

The national government bears the overall responsibility for ensuring that the state complies with the obligations imposed upon it by section 26. The nationwide housing programme falls short of obligations imposed upon national government to the extent that it fails to recognise that the state must provide for relief for those in desperate need. They are not to be ignored in the interests of an overall programme focussed on medium and long-term objectives. It is essential that a reasonable part of the national housing budget be devoted to this, but the precise allocation is for national government to decide in the first instance.

This case is concerned with the Cape Metro and the municipality. The former has realised that this need has not been fulfilled and has put in place its land programme in an effort to fulfil it. This programme, on the face of it, meets the obligation which the state has towards people in the position of the respondents in the Cape Metro. Indeed, the amicus accepted that this programme "would cater precisely for the needs of people such as the respondents, and, in an appropriate and sustainable manner." However, as with legislative measures, the existence of the programme is a starting point only. What remains is the implementation of the programme by taking all reasonable steps that are necessary to initiate and sustain it. And it must be implemented with due regard to the urgency of the situations it is intended to address.

Effective implementation requires at least adequate budgetary support by national government. This, in turn, requires recognition of the obligation to meet immediate needs in the nationwide housing programme. Recognition of such needs in the nationwide housing programme requires it to plan, budget and monitor the fulfilment of immediate needs and the management of crises. This must ensure that a significant number of desperate people in need are afforded relief, though not all of them need receive it immediately. Such planning too will require proper co-operation between the different spheres of government.

In conclusion it has been established in this case that as of the date of the launch of this application, the state was not meeting the obligation imposed upon it by section 26(2) of the Constitution in the area of the Cape Metro. In particular, the programmes adopted by the state fell short of the requirements of section 26(2) in that no provision was made for relief to the categories of people in desperate need identified earlier.
* * *

Consideration is now given to whether the state action (or inaction) in relation to the respondents met the required constitutional standard. It is a central feature of this judgment that the housing shortage in the area of the Cape Metro in general and Oostenberg in particular had reached crisis proportions. Wallacedene was obviously bursting and it was probable that people in desperation were going to find it difficult to resist the temptation to move out of the shack settlement onto unoccupied land in an effort to improve their position. This is what the respondents apparently did.

Whether the conduct of Mrs. Grootboom and the other respondents constituted a land invasion was disputed on the papers. There was no suggestion however that the respondents' circumstances before their move to New Rust was anything but desperate. There is nothing in the papers to indicate any plan by the municipality to deal with the occupation of vacant land if it occurred. If there had been such a plan the appellants might well have acted differently.

The respondents began to move onto the New Rust Land during September 1998 and the number of people on this land continued to grow relentlessly. I would have expected officials of the municipality responsible for housing to engage with these people as soon as they became aware of the occupation. I would also have thought that some effort would have been made by the municipality to resolve the difficulty on a case-by-case basis after an investigation of their circumstances before the matter got out of hand. The municipality did nothing and the settlement grew by leaps and bounds.

There is, however, no dispute that the municipality funded the eviction of the respondents. The magistrate who ordered the ejectment of the respondents directed a process of mediation in which the municipality was to be involved to identify some alternative land for the occupation for the New Rust residents. Although the reason for this is unclear from the papers, it is evident that no effective mediation took place. The state had an obligation to ensure, at the very least, that the eviction was humanely executed. However, the eviction was reminiscent of the past and inconsistent with the values of the Constitution. The respondents were evicted a day early and to make matters worse, their possessions and building materials were not merely removed, but destroyed and burnt. I have already said that the provisions of section 26(1) of the Constitution burdens the state with at least a negative obligation in relation to housing. The manner in which the eviction was carried out resulted in a breach of this obligation.

In these circumstances, the municipality's response to the letter of the respondents' attorney left much to be desired. It will be recalled that the letter stated that discussions were being held with officials from the Provincial Administration in order to find an amicable solution to the problem. There is no evidence that the respondents were ever informed of the outcome of these discussions. The application was then opposed and argued on the basis that none of the appellants either individually or jointly could do anything at all to alleviate the problem. The Cape Metro, the Western Cape government and the national government were joined in the proceedings and would all have been aware of the respondents' plight.

In all these circumstances, the state may well have been in breach of its constitutional obligations. It may also be that the conduct of the municipality was inconsistent with the provisions of the Prevention of Illegal Eviction from and Unlawful Occupation of Land Act. In addition, the municipality may have failed to meet the obligations imposed by the provisions of sections 2(1)(b), 2(1)(h)(i) and 9(1)(e) of the Housing Act. However no argument was addressed to this Court on these matters and we are not in a position to consider them further.

This judgment must not be understood as approving any practice of land invasion for the purpose of coercing a state structure into providing housing on a preferential basis to those who participate in any exercise of this kind. Land invasion is inimical to the systematic provision of adequate housing on a planned basis. It may well be that the decision of a state structure, faced with the difficulty of repeated land invasions, not to provide housing in response to those invasions, would be reasonable. Reasonableness must be determined on the facts of each case.

Summary and conclusion

This case shows the desperation of hundreds of thousands of people living in deplorable conditions throughout the country. The Constitution obliges the state to act positively to ameliorate these conditions. The obligation is to provide access to housing, health-care, sufficient food and water, and social security to those unable to support themselves and their dependants. The state must also foster conditions to enable citizens to gain access to land on an equitable basis. Those in need have a corresponding right to demand that this be done. * * *

[I]t is an extremely difficult task for the state to meet these obligations in the conditions that prevail in our country. This is recognised by the Constitution which expressly provides that the state is not obliged to go beyond available resources or to realise these rights immediately. I stress however, that despite all these qualifications, these are rights, and the Constitution obliges the state to give effect to them. This is an obligation that courts can, and in appropriate circumstances, must enforce.

Neither section 26 nor section 28 entitles the respondents to claim shelter or housing immediately upon demand. The High Court order ought therefore not to have been made. However, section 26 does oblige the state to devise and implement a coherent, co-ordinated programme designed to meet its section 26 obligations. The programme that has been adopted and was in force in the Cape Metro at the time that this application was brought, fell short of the obligations imposed upon the state by section 26(2) in that it failed to provide for any form of relief to those desperately in need of access to housing.

In the light of the[se] conclusions * * *, it is necessary and appropriate to make a declaratory order. The order requires the state to act to meet the obligation imposed upon it by section 26(2) of the Constitution. This includes the obligation to devise, fund, implement and supervise measures to provide relief to those in desperate need.

———————

NOTES AND QUESTIONS ON GROOTBOOM

1. *International "versus" domestic sources of human rights law.* Grootboom is a decision by a domestic court, interpreting and applying a domestic constitutional provision. By what authority and to what effect did the Court consult international legal standards? How, if at all, might a human rights advocate use *Grootboom*'s approach to the justiciability of socio-economic rights *beyond* South Africa?

2. *Identifying the "minimum core" right.* In *Grootboom*, the Court declared that the "[m]inimum core obligation is determined generally by having regard to the needs of the most vulnerable group that is entitled to the protection of the right in question." Does such a definition "aim too low" in the articulation and enforcement of economic, social, and cultural rights? What are the alternative formulations of the "minimum core" obligation? The minimum consensus among governments? The minimum needed for the most deprived to survive? *See* Katharine G. Young, *The Minimum Core of Economic and Social Rights: A Concept in Search of Content*, 33 YALE J. INT'L L. 113 (2008).

3. *Framing the relief in Grootboom.* List the different elements of a housing policy that would be "reasonable" according to the Court in *Grootboom*. Does the Court's reference to "available means" imply that budgetary restraints offer an effective defense for the government?

4. *Equity among the rights-bearers.* The Court in *Grootboom* was concerned about preferential remedies:

Although the conditions in which the respondents lived in Wallacedene were admittedly intolerable and although it is difficult to level any criticism against them for leaving the Wallacedene shack settlement, it is a painful reality that their circumstances were no worse than those of thousands of other people, including young children, who remained at Wallacedene. It cannot be said, on the evidence before us, that the respondents moved out of the Wallacedene settlement and occupied the land earmarked for low-cost housing development as a deliberate strategy to gain preference in the allocation of housing resources over thousands of other people who remained in intolerable conditions and who were also in urgent need of housing relief. It must be borne in mind however, that the effect of any order that constitutes a special dispensation for the respondents on account of their extraordinary circumstances is to accord that preference.

Conceptually and practically, how might a human rights advocate work around this problem?

THE OAU CHARTER ON HUMAN AND PEOPLES' RIGHTS (1981) SELECT PROVISIONS ON THE AFRICAN COMMISSION ON HUMAN AND PEOPLES' RIGHTS

OAU Doc. CAB/LEG/67/3 rev. 5

Article 45—[The Functions of the African Commission]

The functions of the Commission shall be:

1. To promote Human and Peoples' Rights and in particular:

    (a) to collect documents, undertake studies and researches on African problems in the field of human and peoples' rights, organize seminars, symposia and conferences, disseminate information, encourage national and local institutions concerned with human and peoples' rights, and should the case arise, give its views or make recommendations to Governments.

    (b) to formulate and lay down, principles and rules aimed at solving legal problems relating to human and peoples' rights and fundamental freedoms upon which African Governments may base their legislations [*sic*].

    (c) co-operate with other African and international institutions concerned with the promotion and protection of human and peoples' rights.

2. Ensure the protection of human and peoples' rights under conditions laid down by the present Charter.

3.   Interpret all the provisions of the present Charter at the request of a State party, an institution of the OAU or an African Organization recognized by the OAU.

4.   Perform any other tasks which may be entrusted to it by the Assembly of Heads of State and Government.

Article 47—[Inter–State Communications]

If a State Party to the present Charter has good reasons to believe that another State Party to this Charter has violated the provisions of the Charter, it may draw, by written communication, the attention of that State to the matter. This Communication shall also be addressed to the Secretary General of the OAU and to the Chairman of the Commission. Within three months of the receipt of the Communication, the State to which the Communication is addressed shall give the enquiring State, written explanation or statement elucidating the matter. This should include as much as possible, relevant information relating to the laws and rules of procedure applied and applicable and the redress already given or course of action available.

Article 55—[Other Communications (emphasis supplied)]

1.   Before each Session, the Secretary of the Commission shall make a list of the Communications other than those of State Parties to the present Charter and transmit them to Members of the Commission, who shall indicate which Communications should be considered by the Commission.

2.   A Communication shall be considered by the Commission if a simple majority of its members so decide.

Article 56—[Admissibility of Communications under Article 55]

Communications relating to Human and Peoples' rights referred to in Article 55 received by the Commission, shall be considered if they:

1.   Indicate their authors even if the latter requests anonymity;

2.   Are compatible with the Charter of the Organisation of African Unity or with the present Charter;

3.   Are not written in disparaging or insulting language directed against the State concerned and its institutions or to the Organisation of African Unity;

4.   Are not based exclusively on news disseminated through the mass media;

5.   Are sent after exhausting local remedies, if any, unless it is obvious that this procedure is unduly prolonged;

6.   Are submitted within a reasonable period from the time local remedies are exhausted or from the date the Commission is seized with the matter; and

7. Do not deal with cases which have been settled by those States involved in accordance with the principles of the Charter of the United Nations, or the Charter of the Organisation of African Unity or the provisions of the present Charter.

DECISION ON COMMUNICATION
NO. 245/2002
ZIMBABWE HUMAN RIGHTS
NGO FORUM/ZIMBABWE
TWENTY–FIRST ACTIVITY
REPORT OF THE AFRICAN COMMISSION
ON HUMAN AND PEOPLES' RIGHTS (2007)[1]

The communication is submitted by the Zimbabwe Human Rights NGO Forum, a coordinating body and a coalition of twelve Zimbabwean NGO human rights based in Zimbabwe. The complainant states that in February 2000, the country held a Constitutional Referendum in which the majority of Zimbabweans voted against the new government * * *. The complainant [further] alleges that following the Constitutional Referendum there was political violence, which escalated with farm invasions, by war veterans and other landless peasants. That during the period between February and June 2000 when Zimbabwe held its fifth parliamentary elections, ZANU (PF) [the party of Zimbabwean President Robert Mugabe] supporters engaged in a systematic campaign of intimidation aimed at crushing support for opposition parties.

It is alleged that violence was deployed by the party as a systematic political strategy in the run up to the Parliamentary elections. The complainant also alleges that in the 2 months before the Parliamentary elections, * * * political violence targeted especially white farmers and black farmers workers, teachers, civil servants and rural villagers believed to be supporting opposition parties. Such violence included dragging farm workers and villagers believed to be supporters of the opposition from their homes at night, forcing them to attend reeducation sessions and to sing ZANU (PF) songs. The Complainant alleges that men, women and children were tortured and there were cases of rape. Homes and businesses in both urban and rural areas were burnt and looted and opposition members were kidnapped, tortured and killed. It is also alleged that ZANU (PF) supporters invaded numerous secondary schools; over 550 rural schools were disrupted or closed as teachers, pupils and rural opposition members numbering 10,000 fled violence, intimidation and political reeducation. Other civil servants in rural areas such as doctors and nurses were targeted for supposedly being pro-Movement for Democratic Change (MDC). * * * The com-

---

1. *Available at* http://www.achpr.org/english/activity_ reports/21% 20Activity% 20Report.pdf.

plainant also allege[s] that following the elections, MDC contested the validity of the outcome of the elections in 38 constituencies won by ZANU (PF), and this prompted another wave of violence.

The complainant claims that human rights abuses were reported in most of those cases that were brought before the High Court. However, those individuals that testified in the elections challenges before the Harare High Court, were subjected to political violence on returning home and thus forcing some to refrain from testifying and others to flee their homes due to fear of being victimized. * * * The complainant also alleges that the primary instigators of this violence were war veterans who operated groups of militias comprising * * * ZANU (PF) youth and supporters. They also allege that the State was involved in this violence through Zimbabwe Republic Police (ZRP), the Zimbabwe National Army (ZNA) and the Central Intelligence Organisation (CIO) specifically through facilitating farm invasions.

The complainant states that prior to the June 2000 parliamentary elections, the ZRP on numerous occasions turned a blind eye to violence perpetrated against white farmers and MDC supporters. It is alleged that the police forces have generally failed to intervene or investigate the incidents of murder, rape, torture or the destruction of property committed by the war veterans. Furthermore, a General Amnesty for Politically Motivated Crimes gazetted on 6th October 2000 absolved most of the perpetrators from prosecution. While the Amnesty excluded those accused of murder, robbery, rape, indecent assault, statutory rape, theft, possession of arms or any offence involving fraud or dishonesty, very few persons accused of these crimes have been prosecuted. * * *

Admissibility

The law relating to the admissibility of communications brought pursuant to Article 55 of the African Charter is governed by the conditions stipulated in Article 56 of the African Charter. This Article lays down seven conditions, which generally must be fulfilled by a complainant for a communication to be declared admissible. In the present communication, the Respondent State submitted that the communication should be declared inadmissible by virtue of the fact that the communication did not satisfy the requirements contained in Articles 56(4) and (5) of the African Charter.

Article 56(4) of the African Charter provides that: "Communications . . . received by the Commission shall be considered if they: (4) are not based exclusively on news disseminated through the mass media." The Respondent State alleged that the statement of facts submitted by the complainant was based on information disseminated through the mass media which information should be considered cautiously. * * * The Respondent State maintained that during the period prior to, during and following the Referendum, there was a concerted effort by the "so called independent press" and the international press to publish false stories in order to tarnish Zimbabwe's image. * * *

The African Commission has had the opportunity to review the documents before it as submitted by the complainant. While it may be difficult to ascertain the veracity of the statements allegedly made to the complainant by the alleged victims, it is however evident through the judgment of the High Court of Zimbabwe that the communication did not rely "exclusively on news disseminated through the mass media" as the Respondent State would like the African Commission to believe. Besides, this Commission has held in Communications 147/95 and 149/9615, that "while it would be dangerous to rely exclusively on news disseminated through the mass media, it would be equally damaging if the African Commission were to reject a communication because some aspects of it are based on news disseminated through the mass media. This is borne out of the fact that the Charter makes use of the word 'exclusively' ". Based on this reasoning, the African Commission is of the opinion that the communication is not based "exclusively on news disseminated through the mass media. The operative term being 'exclusively' ".

The other provision of the Charter in contention between the parties is Article 56(5) of the African Charter. This []article provides that * * * communications * * * received by the Commission shall be considered if they: (5) are sent after exhausting local remedies, if any, unless it is obvious that this procedure is unduly prolonged. The Respondent State submitted in this regard that the complainant failed to exhaust domestic remedies by virtue of failing to pursue the alternative remedy of lodging a complaint with the Office of the Ombudsman, which is mandated to investigate human rights violations. The African Commission holds that the internal remedy to which Article 56(5) refers entails remedies sought from courts of a judicial nature, and the Office of the Ombudsman is certainly not of that nature. * * *

[T]he Commission is of the opinion that there are no domestic remedies available to all the persons referred to in [the Communication], who as victims, were effectively robbed of any remedies that might have been available to them by virtue of Clemency Order No 1 of 2000. The Clemency Order granted pardon to every person liable to criminal prosecution for any politically motivated crime committed between 1 January 2000 and July 2000. The Order also granted a remission of the whole or remainder of the period of imprisonment to every person convicted of any politically motivated crime committed during the stated period.

In terms of the Clemency Order, "a politically motivated crime" is defined as: "(a) Any offence motivated by the object of supporting or opposing any political purpose and committed in connection with: (i) The Constitutional referendum held on the 12th and 13th of February 2000; or (ii) The general Parliamentary elections held on 24th and 25th June 2000; whether committed before, during or after the said referendum or elections." The only crimes exempted from the Clemency Order were murder, robbery, rape, indecent assault, statutory rape, theft, possession of arms and any offence involving fraud or dishonesty.

The complainant averred that the exceptions in the Clemency Order were a hoodwink; that even where reports were made by victims of criminal acts not covered by the Clemency Order, arrests were never made by the police neither were investigations undertaken and therefore there was no prosecution of the perpetrators of the violence, concluding that, the Clemency Order was constructively, a blanket amnesty. The complainant argued further that it could not challenge the Clemency Order in a court of law because the President of Zimbabwe, who was exercising his prerogative powers in terms of the Constitution of Zimbabwe, ordered it.

Additionally, the complainant argued * * * that it was not possible to exhaust domestic remedies during the period in question because there was pervasive violence; and gross and massive human rights violations took place on a large scale and more particularly, politically motivated violence. * * * Furthermore, the complainant argued that the violence was extended to some members of the Judiciary. The complainant submitted that during the time in question, some members of the judiciary were threatened, several magistrates were assaulted while presiding over politically sensitive matters and several Supreme Court judges were forced to resign. According to the complainant, there were instances where persons approached the courts and sought to interdict the government of Zimbabwe or the persons who had forcefully settled themselves on private properties; court orders were granted but subsequently they were ignored because the government of Zimbabwe said it could not allow itself to follow court decisions that went against government policy. The complainant asserted that in the overall context of such a situation there was no realistic hope of getting a firm and fair hearing from judicial system that had been so undermined by the Respondent State. * * *

Responding to the complainant's submission relating to the effect of the Clemency Order, the Respondent State submitted that the victims of the criminal acts covered by the Clemency Order could have and could still institute civil suits and sought to be compensated, which according to the Respondent State, would be more beneficial to the victims than the imprisonment of the perpetrators of the crimes. * * * The Respondent State also submitted that the complainant had the right and could have challenged the legality of the Clemency Order in Court. * * * The Respondent State argued that challenging the legality of Clemency Order would have eventually paved the way for prosecuting the persons that committed those criminal acts covered by the Clemency Order; therefore by neglecting to challenge the legality of the President's prerogative, the complainant had failed to exhaust local remedies. * * * The Respondent State also submitted that if all else was not possible, the complainant could have instituted private prosecutions against those persons alleged to have committed crimes and had not been prosecuted by the State in accordance with * * * the Constitution of Zimbabwe. * * *

The African Commission holds the view that by pardoning "every person liable for any politically motivated crime * * *" the Clemency Order had effectively foreclosed the complainant or any other person from bringing criminal action against persons who could have committed the acts of violence during the period in question and upon which this communication is based. By so doing, the complainant had been denied access to local remedies by virtue of the Clemency Order. Exhaustion of local remedies does not mean that the complainants are required to exhaust any local remedy, which may be impractical or even unrealistic. Ability to choose which course of action to pursue when wronged is essential and clearly in the instant communication the one course of action that was practical and therefore realistic for the victims to pursue—that of criminal action was foreclosed as a result of the Clemency Order. * * *

The Respondent State also submitted that the complainant failed to exhaust domestic remedies when they did not challenge the legality of the President's prerogative to issue a Clemency Order. The African Commission is of the view that asking the complainant to challenge the legality of the Clemency Order in the Constitutional Court of Zimbabwe would require the complainant to engage in an exercise that would not bring immediate relief to the victims of the violations. The African Commission is aware that the situation prevailing in Zimbabwe at the time in question was perilous and therefore required the State machinery to act fast and firmly in cases such as this in order to restore the rule of law. To therefore ask victims in this matter to bring a constitutional matter before being able to approach the domestic courts to obtain relief for criminal acts committed against them would certainly result into going through an unduly prolonged procedure in order to obtain a remedy, an exception that falls within the meaning of Article 56(5) of the African Charter. * * *

The responsibility of maintaining law and order in any country lies with the State specifically with the police force of that State. As such, it is the duty of the State to ensure through its police force that where there is a breakdown of law and order, the perpetrators are arrested and brought before the domestic courts of that country. Therefore any criminal processes that flow from this action, including undertaking investigations to make the case for the prosecution are the responsibility of the State concerned and the State cannot abdicate that duty. To expect victims of violations to undertake private prosecutions where the State has not instituted criminal action against perpetrators of crimes or even follow up with the Attorney General what course of action has been taken by the State as the Respondent State seems to suggest in this matter would be tantamount to the State relinquishing its duty to the very citizens it is supposed to protect. Thus, even if the victims of the criminal acts did not institute any domestic judicial action, as the guardians of law and order and protectors of human rights in the country, the Respondent State is presumed to be sufficiently aware of the situation prevailing in its own territory and therefore holds the ultimate responsibility of harnessing the situation and correcting the wrongs complained of. * * *

It is apparent to the African Commission that the human rights situation prevailing at the time this communication was brought was grave and the numbers of victims involved were numerous. Indeed the Respondent State concedes that its criminal justice system could not have been expected to investigate and prosecute all the cases reported and ensure that remedies are given. This admission on part of the Respondent State points to the fact that domestic remedies may have been available in theory but as a matter of practicality were not capable of yielding any prospect of success to the victims of the criminal assaults. Thus, for the reasons outlined above, the African Commission declares this communication admissible. * * *

The Law–Merits

* * *

Regarding the Clemency Order No 1 of 2000 granting a general amnesty for politically motivated crimes committed in the period preceding the June 2000 general elections, the complainant submitted that by failing to secure the safety of its citizens and by granting a general amnesty, the Respondent State had failed to respect the obligations imposed on it under Article 1 of the African Charter. Any violation of the provisions of the African Charter automatically means a violation of Article 1 of the African Charter and that goes to the root of the African Charter since the obligations imposed by Article 1 of the African Charter are peremptory. * * *

On the Clemency Order No. 1 of 2000, the Respondent State emphasised that the prerogative of clemency or amnesty is recognised as an integral part of constitutional democracies. To ensure that those who had committed more serious offences did not go unpunished, the Clemency Order excluded crimes such as murder, rape, robbery, indecent assault, statutory rape, theft and possession of arms. The State further noted that a decision by the Commission that the Clemency Order was an abdication of Zimbabwe's obligations under the Charter would amount to undermining the whole notion of the clemency prerogative worldwide adding that Clemency Orders are the prerogatives of the Head of State and this discretion was exercised reasonably under Clemency Order No 1 of 2000. * * *

The complainant submits that by virtue of Clemency Order No 1 of 2000, the victims of human rights abuses could not seek redress for the human rights violations they suffered because they could not challenge the Clemency order. The Clemency Order granted pardon to every person liable to criminal prosecution for any politically motivated crime committed between January and July 2000. The Respondent State emphasised that the prerogative of clemency is recognised as an integral part of constitutional democracies. * * * The Respondent State further noted that a decision by the African Commission that the Clemency Order is an abdication of Zimbabwe's obligations under the African Charter would amount to undermining the whole notion of the clemency prerogative worldwide. * * *

Having concluded that it has the competence to rule on the question of the Clemency Order, the African Commission would now determine whether the Clemency Order as issued by the Respondent State violated the latter's obligation under the African Charter. The Clemency Order granted pardon to every person liable to criminal prosecution for any politically motivated crime committed between January and July 2000. The Order also granted a remission of the whole or remainder of the period of imprisonment to every person convicted of any politically motivated crime committed during the stated period. * * * The question for the African Commission is to determine whether the clemency order in question is a negation of the State's responsibility under Article 1 of the African Charter.

The term clemency is a general term for the power of an executive to intervene in the sentencing of a criminal defendant to prevent injustice from occurring. The exercise of executive clemency is inherent in many, if not, all constitutional democracies of the world. National governments have chosen to implement clemency for a number of reasons. For instance, executive clemency exists to afford relief from undue harshness or evident mistake in the operation or enforcement of the criminal law. The administration of justice by the courts is not necessarily always just or certainly considerate of circumstances which may properly mitigate guilt. To afford remedy, it has always been thought essential to vest in some authority other that the courts, power to ameliorate or avoid particular criminal judgments. * * *

Clemency orders are not peculiar to Zimbabwe. These are resorted to the world over generally in the interest of peace and security. In the history of Zimbabwe, it is a well known fact that Clemency orders have been resorted to as a process of easing tension and creating a new beginning. For instance, at Independence in 1979/80, amnesty was resorted to by former colonial regime in order to create an environment for the new independent dispensation and to reduce the tension between the nationalists and the former white rule[r]s. In the process, members of the former white regime who had been guilty of massive killings were beneficiaries of clemency. In another incident, following the civil war in the southern part of Zimbabwe involving two former nationalists movements, ZANU (PF) and the opposition (PF) ZAPU, an amnesty was resorted to in order to create an environment for a Peace Accord in 1987, which brought about permanent peace to Zimbabwe. The result was the release of several thousands of people including those who were guilty of massive human rights violations including murder, treason, and terrorism. Also generally, clemency is granted annually to serving prisoners for the purpose of giving them a new beginning, including those released on the humanitarian grounds.

Generally however, a Clemency power is used in a situation where the President believes that the public welfare will be better served by the pardon, or to people who have served part of their sentences and lived within the law, or a belief that a sentence was excessive or unjust or again for personal circumstances that warrant compassion. In all these situations, the President exercises a near absolute discretion. * * *

Over the years however, * * * Clemency powers have been the subject of considerable scrutiny by international human rights bodies and legal scholars. It is generally believed that the single most important factor in the proliferation and continuation of human rights violations is the persistence of impunity, be it of a *de jure* or *de facto* nature. Clemency, it is believed, encourages *de jure* as well as *de facto* impunity and leaves the victims without just compensation and effective remedy. *De jure* impunity generally arises where legislation provides indemnity from legal process in respect of acts to be committed in a particular context or exemption from legal responsibility in respect of acts that have in the past been committed, for example, as in the present case, by way of clemency (amnesty or pardon). *De facto* impunity occurs where those committing the acts in question are in practice insulated from the normal operation of the legal system. That seems to be the situation with the present case.

There has been consistent international jurisprudence suggesting that the prohibition of amnesties leading to impunity for serious human rights has become a rule of customary international law. In a report entitled "Question of the impunity of perpetrators of human rights violations (civil and political)", prepared by Mr. Louis Joinet for the Sub-commission on Prevention of Discrimination and Protection of Minorities, * * * it was noted that "amnesty cannot be accorded to perpetrators of violations before the victims have obtained justice by means of an effective remedy" and that "the right to justice entails obligations for the State: to investigate violations, to prosecute the perpetrators and, if their guilt is established, to punish them".

In his report, Mr. Joinet drafted a set of principles for the protection and promotion of human rights through action to combat impunity, in which he stated that "there can be no just and lasting reconciliation unless the need for justice is effectively justified" and that "national and international measures must be taken * * * with a view to securing jointly, in the interests of the victims of human rights violations, observance of the right to know and, by implication, the right to the truth, the right to justice and the right to reparation, without which there can be no effective remedy against the pernicious effects of impunity." The Report went on to state that "even when intended to establish conditions conducive to a peace agreement or to foster national reconciliation, amnesty and other measures of clemency shall be kept within certain bounds, namely: (a) the perpetrators of serious crimes under international law may not benefit from such measures until such time as the State has met their obligations to investigate violations, to take appropriate measures in respect of the perpetrators, particularly in the area of justice, by ensuring that they are prosecuted, tried and duly punished, to provide victims with effective remedies and reparation for the injuries suffered, and to take acts to prevent the recurrence of such atrocities."

In its General Comment No. 20 on Article 7of the ICCPR, the UN Human Rights Committee noted that "amnesties are generally incompatible with the duty of States to investigate such acts; to guarantee freedom from such acts within their jurisdiction; and to ensure that they do not occur in the future. States may not deprive individuals of the right to an effective remedy, including compensation and such full rehabilitation as may be possible". In the case of *Hugo Rodríguez v. Uruguay*, [Communication No. 322/1988, U.N. Doc. CCPR/C/51/ D/322/1988 (1994)], the Committee reaffirmed its position that amnesties for gross violations of human rights are incompatible with the obligations of the State party under the Covenant and expressed concern that in adopting the amnesty law in question, the State party contributed to an atmosphere of impunity which may undermine the democratic order and give rise to further human rights violations. The 1993 Vienna Declaration and Programme of Action supports this stand and stipulates that "States should abrogate legislation leading to impunity for those responsible for grave violations of human rights such as torture and prosecute such violations, thereby providing a firm basis for the rule of law".[1]

Importantly, the international obligation to bring to justice and punish serious violations of human rights has been recognized and established in all regional human rights mechanisms. The Inter–American Commission and Court of Human Rights have also decided on the question of amnesty legislation. The Inter–American Commission on Human Rights has condemned amnesty laws issued by democratic successor Governments in the name of reconciliation, even if approved by a plebiscite, and has held them to be in breach of the 1969 American Convention on Human Rights, in particular the duty of the State to respect and ensure rights recognized in the Convention (article 1(1)), the right to due process of law (article 8) and the right to an effective judicial remedy (article 25). The Commission held further that amnesty laws extinguishing both criminal and civil liability disregarded the legitimate rights of the victims' next of kin to reparation and that such measures would do nothing to further reconciliation. Of particular interest are the findings by the Inter–American Commission on Human Rights that "amnesty" legislation enacted in Argentina and Uruguay violated basic provisions of the American Convention on Human Rights.

---

1. *See* The Vienna Declaration and Programme of Action, Section II, para. 60, at www.unhchr. ch/huridocda/huridoca.nsf/(Symbol)/A.CONF.157.23.en.

In these cases, the Inter–American Commission held that the legal consequences of the amnesty laws denied the victims the right to obtain a judicial remedy. The effect of the amnesty laws was that cases against those charged were thrown out, trials already in progress were closed, and no judicial avenue was left to present or continue cases. In consequence, the effects of the amnesty laws violated the right to judicial protection and to a fair trial, as recognized by the American Convention and in the present case, the African Charter. * * *

The Inter–American Court stated in its first judgment that states must prevent, investigate and punish any violation of the rights recognized by the Convention.[2] This has been re-emphasized in subsequent cases. In the *"Street Children" Case*, the Court reiterated "that Guatemala is obliged to investigate the facts that generated the violations of the American Convention in the instant case, identify those responsible and punish them."[3] * * * The European Court of Human Rights on its part has recognized that where the alleged violations include acts of torture or arbitrary killings, the state is under a duty to undertake an investigation capable of leading to the identification and punishment of those responsible.[4]

The African Commission has also held amnesty laws to be incompatible with a State's human rights obligations.[5] Guideline No. 16 of the Robben Island Guidelines adopted by the African Commission * * * states that "in order to combat impunity States should: (a) ensure that those responsible for acts of torture or ill-treatment are subject to legal process; and (b) ensure that there is no immunity from prosecution for nationals suspected of torture, and that the scope of immunities for foreign nationals who are entitled to such immunities be as restrictive as is possible under international law."[6]

The UN Special Rapporteur on Torture has also expressed his opposition to the passing, application and non-revocation of amnesty laws (including laws in the name of national reconciliation, the consolidation of democracy and peace, and respect for human rights), which prevent torturers from being brought to justice and hence contribute to

---

2. *Velasquez Rodriguez v. Honduras*, Judgment of July 29, 1988, Inter–Am.Ct.H.R. (Ser. C) No. 4 (1988). ¶ 166.

3. *Hilaire, Constantine and Benjamin et al. Case*, Judgment of June 21, 2002, Inter–Am. Ct. H.R., (Ser. C) No. 94 (2002) or the *"Street Children" Case*, Judgment of May 26, 2001, Inter–Am. Ct. H.R., (Ser. C) No. 77 (2001), ¶ 101 and operative clause 8.

4. European Court of Human Rights Case *Zeki Aksoy v. Turkey*, 18 December 1996, ¶ 98. See also, *Aydin v. Turkey*, App. No. 23178/94 Judgment of 25 September 1997, ¶ 103; *Selçuk and Asker v. Turkey*, App. Nos. 23184/94 and 23185/94 Judgment of 24 April 1998, ¶ 96; *Kurt v.Turkey*, App. No. 24276/94 Judgment of 25 May 1998, ¶ 139; and *Keenan v. United Kingdom*, App. No. 27229/95 Judgment of 3 April 2001, ¶ 122.

5. *See also Various communications v. Mauritania Communications* 54/91, 61/91, 96/93, 98/93, 164/97–196/97, 210/98 and *Jean Yokovi Degli on behalf of Corporal N. Bikagni, Union Interafricaine des Droits de l'Homme, Commission International de Juristes v. Togo Communications* 83/92, 88/93, 91/93.

6. *Guidelines and Measures for the Prohibition and Prevention of Torture, Cruel, Inhuman or Degrading Treatment or Punishment in Africa* (The Robben Island Guidelines), African Commission on Human and Peoples' Rights, 32nd Session, 17—23 October, 2002: Banjul, The Gambia. *See also Various communications v. Mauritania Communications* 54/91, 61/91, 96/93, 98/93, 164/97–196/97, 210/98.

a culture of impunity. He called on States to refrain from granting or acquiescing in impunity at the national level, *inter alia*, by the granting of amnesties, such impunity itself constituting a violation of international law. * * *

[T]his Commission is of the opinion that by passing the Clemency Order No. 1 of 2000, prohibiting prosecution and setting free perpetrators of "politically motivated crimes," including alleged offences such as abductions, forced imprisonment, arson, destruction of property, kidnappings and other human rights violations, the State did not only encourage impunity but effectively foreclosed any available avenue for the alleged abuses to be investigated, and prevented victims of crimes and alleged human rights violations from seeking effective remedy and compensation.

This act of the state constituted a violation of the victims' right to judicial protection and to have their cause heard under Article 7 (1) of the African Charter. The protection afforded by Article 7 is not limited to the protection of the rights of arrested and detained persons but encompasses the right of every individual to access the relevant judicial bodies competent to have their causes heard and be granted adequate relief. If there appears to be any possibility of an alleged victim succeeding at a hearing, the applicant should be given the benefit of the doubt and allowed to have their matter heard. Adopting laws such as the Clemency Order No. 1 of 2000, that have the effect of eroding this opportunity, renders the victims helpless and deprives them of justice. * * *

In light of the above, the African Commission holds that by enacting Decree No. 1 of 2000 which foreclosed access to any remedy that might be available to the victims to vindicate their rights, and without putting in place alternative adequate legislative or institutional mechanisms to ensure that perpetrators of the alleged atrocities were punished, and victims of the violations duly compensated or given other avenues to seek effective remedy, the Respondent State did not only prevent the victims from seeking redress, but also encouraged impunity, and thus reneged on its obligation in violation of Articles 1 and 7 (1) of the African Charter. The granting of amnesty to absolve perpetrators of human rights violations from accountability violates the right of victims to an effective remedy.

For these reasons, the African Commission:

Holds that the Republic of Zimbabwe is in violation of Articles 1 and 7(1) of the African Charter;

Calls on the Republic of Zimbabwe to establish a Commission of Inquiry to investigate the causes of the violence which took place from February–June 2000 and bring those responsible for the violence to justice, and identify victims of the violence in order to provide them with just and adequate compensation.

Request[s] the Republic of Zimbabwe to report to the African Commission on the implementation of this recommendation during the presentation of its next periodic report.

NOTES AND QUESTIONS ON THE AFRICAN COMMISSION

1. *Powers of the African Commission.* The African Charter identifies the powers of the African Commission, including certain promotional activities (art. 45(1)); receiving and considering the biannual reports of member states on their efforts to comply with the African Charter (art. 62); and receiving both state-to-state communications (arts. 47–49) and "other" communications, generally from individuals and organizations (art. 55). The Commission has no free-standing enforcement powers of its own under the Charter, though its own Rules of Procedure allow for the grant or "indication" of provisional or interim measures in limited circumstances (which were famously ignored in Nigeria's execution of Ogoni activist Ken Saro–Wiwa). Reading the African Charter in the Documents Supplement, who (or what) *could* enforce the decision of the African Commission in *Zimbabwean Human Rights NGO Forum*?

2. *Expertise of the African Commission.* Over the course of its existence, the African Commission has considered a wide range of human rights issues: freedom of expression, treatment of detainees, fair trial rights; contemporary forms of slavery; anti-personnel mines; the electoral process; HIV/AIDS; and a variety of economic and social and cultural rights. Like the Inter–American Court of Human Rights in *Velasquez–Rodriguez, supra,* the African Commission has also recognized an affirmative duty of states to protect people from violations of human rights by private actors. *See, e.g., Malawi African Ass'n & Others v. Mauritania,* Comm. No. 54/91, 61/91, 98/93, 164–196/97, & 210/98, Thirteenth Annual Activity Report (1999) (finding Mauritania under an obligation to enforce against private parties the laws abolishing slavery). In a particularly striking example of this analysis, the Commission ruled that the government of Nigeria had violated multiple rights through its own actions and by failing to protect the Ogoni people from environmental degradation by petroleum companies in the Niger Delta. *Social & Economic Rights Action Center (SERAC) v. Nigeria,* Comm. No. 155/96, *available at* http://www.escr_net.org/usr_doc/serac.pdf. The *SERAC* decision is particularly remarkable because the Commission inferred an implicit right to "housing or shelter" from the Charter's explicit provisions on health, property and family life, and it recognized an implicit right to food in the right to human dignity *inter alia.*

3. *Procedures of the African Commission.* At a minimum, advocates with potential cases in the African Commission must be familiar with the African Charter's admissibility criteria (Article 56, *supra*). What is the rationale for each criterion, and how might you revise the standards if

you were writing on a clean slate? Advocates must also be familiar with the Commission's Rules of Procedure and its Guidelines for Submission of Communications, *available at* www.achpr.org/english/_info/guidelines_ communications_en.html.

4. *The power of the African Commission's rules of interpretation.* The "claw-back" provisions of the African Charter arguably subordinate international human rights standards to domestic law. *See, e.g.,* African Charter, art. 9(2) ("Every individual shall have the right to express and disseminate his opinions *within the law*") (emphasis supplied). But, in Articles 60 and 61, the Charter also requires the Commission to "draw inspiration" from a wide range of international human rights instruments law. The Commission has used that interpretive mandate to establish that "[i]nternational human rights standards must always prevail over contradicting national law." Otherwise, "[t]o allow national law to have precedence over the international law of the Charter would defeat the purpose of the rights and freedoms enshrined in the Charter. Any limitation on the rights of the Charter must be in conformity with the provisions of the Charter." *Media Rights Agenda and Constitutional Rights Project v. Nigeria,* Communications 105/93, 128/94, 130/94, and 152/96, at ¶ 66. For the same reason, the Commission has concluded that declared national emergencies cannot justify derogation. *Id.* at ¶ 67 ("In contrast to other international human rights instruments, the African Charter does not contain a derogation clause. Therefore limitations on the rights and freedoms enshrined in the Charter cannot be justified by emergencies or special circumstances.").

5. *Analyzing the Zimbabwean NGO decision: exhaustion of remedies.* In its defense, the government of Zimbabwe pointed out numerous internal or domestic remedies that remained open to the complainants. The argument was sound in its premise: under Article 50 of the African Charter (and under general principles of international law), domestic remedies must be exhausted before a complaint is admissible and international remedies can be triggered. What is the rationale for such a rule? Equally important, according to the Commission, what are the limits on the exhaustion rule? What sources does the African Commission consider in applying the rule, and why are they authoritative?

6. *Analyzing the Zimbabwean NGO decision: amnesties for human rights violations.* When is amnesty for human rights violations itself a violation of international human rights law? If, after a period of wide-spread abuses and chaotic national violence, a nation decided—in the interest of peace and reconciliation and following a representative and democratic process—to grant amnesty to human rights abusers on all sides, would that violate international human rights law? Was that possibility at issue in the *Zimbabwean NGO* case? *See* United Nations Principles of International Cooperation in the Detection, Arrest, Extradition, and Punishment of Persons Guilty of War Crimes and Crimes Against Humanity, G.A. Res. 3074 (XXVIII) ¶ 8, UN Doc. A/9030/add.l ("States shall not take any legislative or other measures which may be prejudicial to the

international obligations they have assumed in regard to the detection, arrest, extradition and punishment of persons guilty of war crimes and crimes against humanity."). Other authorities, including decisions from the European and Inter–American Courts of Human Rights, are cited in the African Commission's decision itself. *See generally* Dinah L. Shelton, REGIONAL PROTECTION OF HUMAN RIGHTS 433–74 (2008).

   7. *Enforcement: continuing abuses in Zimbabwe*. The 2008 elections in Zimbabwe were marked by the same kinds of political violence as occurred in 2000. *See* Human Rights Watch, *"Bullets for Each of You:" State–Sponsored Violence Since Zimbabwe's March 29 Elections*, available at hrw.org/reports/2008/zimbabwe0608/. By 2008, Zimbabwe's isolation within the African Union and other international fora had become nearly complete, leaving human rights advocates little leverage to protect rights or lives, let alone to effect change in Zimbabwe's government.

THE AFRICAN UNION
THE CONSTITUTIVE ACT OF 2001

Article 3

* * *

The objectives of the Union shall be to * * * (e) [e]ncourage international cooperation, taking due account of the Charter of the United Nations and the Universal Declaration of Human Rights; * * * (h) [p]romote and protect human and peoples' rights in accordance with the African Charter on Human and Peoples' Rights and other relevant human rights instruments.

Article 4

The Union shall function in accordance with the following principles: * * * (g) [n]on-interference by any Member State in the internal affairs of another; (h) [t]he right of the Union to intervene in a Member State pursuant to a decision of the Assembly in respect of grave circumstances, namely war crimes, genocide and crimes against humanity; * * * (*l*) [p]romotion of gender equality; (m) [r]espect for democratic principles, human rights, the rule of law and good governance; (n) [p]romotion of social justice to ensure balanced economic development; (o) [r]espect for the sanctity of human life, condemnation and rejection of impunity and political assassination, acts of terrorism and subversive activities; (p) [c]ondemnation and rejection of unconstitutional changes of governments. * * *

Article 23(2)

[A]ny Member State that fails to comply with the decisions and policies of the Union may be subjected to * * * sanctions, such as the denial of transport and communications links with other Member States, and other measures of a political and economic nature to be determined by the Assembly. * * *

Article 30

Governments which shall come to power through unconstitutional means shall not be allowed to participate in the activities of the Union.

THE AFRICAN UNION
AFRICAN PEER REVIEW MECHANISM ("APRM"): COUNTRY REVIEW REPORT OF THE REPUBLIC OF RWANDA NOVEMBER 2005[1]

Introduction

1. The Republic of Rwanda is located in Central Africa. It was gripped by periodic political crises for decades until 1994, when the instability reached its peak and the country sank into three months of genocide. About a million people were killed and another three million fled into exile in neighbouring countries. Nevertheless, from its dramatic recovery, rehabilitation, economic reforms, through broad-based participation, decentralisation and experiments with a traditional form of transitional justice, Rwanda offers much peer learning for other African countries.

2. The APRM's Mission found that the effects of genocide still permeate Rwanda's policy and development framework, but the negative impacts are gradually being reversed in the effort to rebuild the country. The Review Mission was guided by the Rwanda Country Self–Assessment Report (CSAR), the Programme of Action (POA), the Country Background Document (CBD) and the Country Issues Paper (CIP).

3. Rwanda signed a Memorandum of Understanding on the African Peer Review Mechanism (the MOU) on 9 March 2003, committing itself to "provide all necessary resources to facilitate the processes involved at the national level, access to all the required information and stakeholders". An important milestone in the exercise was marked by the APRM Country Support Mission, which took place from 21 to 24 June 2004. Rwanda submitted its CSAR and the preliminary POA to the APRM Secretariat in March 2005.

4. Between 18 and 30 April 2005, a Country Review Mission took place to discuss extensively the CSAR, Action Plan and the CIP, and to

---

1. *Available at* http://www.eisa.org/29/apr./pdf/countries_Rwanda_aprm_report.pdf.

ascertain that Rwanda's National Assessment Process was technically competent, credible and free of political manipulation. All of Rwanda's twelve provinces were visited in order to interact widely with stakeholders, in addition to exchanging views with the Head of State, H.E. Paul Kagame, government officials, parliamentarians, civil society and the private sector in the capital. Following the CRM, the Panel's Report of Rwanda was drafted, highlighting the findings on the state of governance in the four thematic areas to be taken up by the Heads of State in the spirit of peer learning and peer pressure.

Democracy and Good Political Governance

5.   Rwanda has ratified almost all the standards and codes provided in the APRM Questionnaire and in doing so demonstrates a good example of political will to adhere to the rule of law and good political governance. (Important exceptions are the CEDAW–OP and the African Charter on the Rights and Welfare of the Child.) The tardiness in the ratification of some optional protocols, as well as compliance of ratified standards and codes are explained by lack of resources and insufficient capacity. Rwanda also faces the challenge of intra- and inter-state conflicts, stemming mainly from ethnic, religious and other divisions in society; socio-economic inequality and poverty; illicit small arms circulation and trade; drug trafficking; a high level of illiteracy; and, most importantly, land and resource distribution. The National Unity and Reconciliation Commission (NURC) and Gacaca courts are two examples of the institutions established to mitigate conflict.

6.   Efforts are being made to promote constitutional democracy in Rwanda, as shown through the adoption of a Constitution through a referendum, which provides for the establishment of an independent judiciary, a Human Rights Commission, the Institution of Ombudsman and other institutions. There is, however, a concern about the opening up of political space for competition of ideas and power, the voting system used in local communities and the capacity of the Electoral Commission.

7.   Considerable progress has been made in implementing decentralisation through a participatory bottom-up approach to development across different sectors. This is well demonstrated by the participation of cooperatives and associations in sector committees with local councils, although real fiscal power is still to be ceded to the local authorities.

8.   The Government is trying to promote economic and social rights by creating public works to encourage employment. Compulsory universal and free primary education is being provided. The 2003 Constitution of Rwanda also recognises the rights of her citizens and duties relating to health.

9.   Rwanda is making progress with freedom of expression, of the Press and information and association, respectively. For example, a new Press law was established in 2003, and a High Council of the Press

(HCP) was set up to authorise and approve various permits, including starting a private radio station. It has not been possible to confirm whether freedom of expression is being promoted or undermined by the regulatory regime supervised by the HCP. This would need an opinion survey on press freedoms in Rwanda.

10.   The Government is taking steps to facilitate equal access to justice by restructuring the justice sector, mobile courts, women's rights and associations, in addition to Gacaca courts and mediation committees. The Gacaca courts are not only an instrument of administering justice, but also a mechanism for promoting community dialogue, reconciliation and national unity. However, their sustainability in reaching their primary objective still needs to be ensured.

11.   The independence of the judiciary is compromised through the appointment of the Superior Council of the Judiciary. This is because there is no Judicial Service Commission that underscores the role peers play in judicial appointments and regulations of the conduct of members of the judiciary, as is the norm in international law. Instead, the Supreme Council of the Judiciary plays the role of the Judicial Service Commission.

12.   The Constitution provides for an independent civil service. The Rwandan Public Service is being reformed through various initiatives that examine its organisation, the conditions of recruitment, staff training and the adoption of new operating procedures. Although elected representatives at the local level can monitor services, this is not a sufficient mechanism. Rwanda is, therefore, advised to continue to reinforce civic education to involve the public more effectively in civil service delivery. The Government has launched various initiatives through institutional decisions and conducted a campaign to organise and mobilise the society to curb corruption. The need to create an institution comprising all existing agencies dealing with corruption should be pursued without delay.

13.   The Constitution outlaws any form of discrimination based on gender, disability, language or social status. At the political level, the Constitution sets aside 30% of the seats in Parliament for women. All political parties are required by law to reserve 30% of their posts for women. Nonetheless, women still face societal discrimination. Gaps still exist with regard to control and ownership of key resources and means of production, as evidenced in the socio-economic section of this report. Women are yet to be fully integrated into local government processes.

14.   Rwanda has signed the Convention of the Rights of the Child (CRC) and ratified the same in 2002. The Government is encouraged to ratify the African Charter on the Rights and Welfare of the Child, and to design a global policy that enhances the integration of youth into society and permits them to develop to the full measure of their capacities. Notably, government expenditure on education accounts for 25% of the Government's non-recurrent expenditure.

15.   Articles 14 and 76.4 of the Constitution provide that the State must safeguard the well-being of genocide survivors, the disabled, the destitute and the elderly, as well as other vulnerable groups. In this context, the vulnerable groups in Rwanda are the Batwa, genocide orphans, street children, widows and refugees from neighbouring states. Although the Government has achieved a great deal in this area, Rwandan authorities are advised to put more effort into providing education, health and housing for displaced persons and/or refugees, and to initiate in-depth dialogue with the Batwa on the state of their welfare.

Economic Governance and Management

16.   Rwanda is broadly on course to become largely compliant with Best Practices for Budget Transparency. The CRM learned, for example, that the Treasury Committee that meets every Thursday attempts to close the gaps between planned expenditures and actual allocations. Many other gaps in fiscal and budgetary practices are likely to be closed as a result of ongoing economic reforms. Donors have a major responsibility of enhancing the predictability of assistance in order for major instruments of development planning, such as the Medium–Term Expenditure Framework (MTEF), to take root in Rwanda.

17.   Rwanda is advised to develop an explicit small and medium/micro-enterprise policy, possibly as a private sector counterpart of the Common Development Fund, and this activity is proposed in the Action Plan. It was confirmed during the CRM that the long-delayed Organic Budget Law (OBL) had been passed by Parliament, paving the way for implementation of financial instructions that will provide the operational details. The three-year rolling MTEF is in effect, and could become an important tool in enhancing economic governance and management.

18.   The soundness and sustainability of public finances are highly vulnerable. In the long run, the high average level of grants over total revenue (average 77.8% over 1992–2004) has changed little in the past five years—by just 1% (it averaged 76.8% over 2000–2004). The key constraint is the sources of funding for the two reforms and their implementation. It is recommended that information on tax procedures and the appeals process be rendered more accommodating and be widely disseminated.

19.   The Government of Rwanda has ratified the African Union's Convention on Preventing and Combating Corruption, and has yet to ratify the United Nations Convention on Combating Corruption. The CRM found that the Government maintains a zero-tolerance policy against all forms of corruption (political, administrative and economic) and at all levels of government. Nonetheless, the Government is advised to guard against potential legal loopholes, avoid duplication of mandates and achieve effectiveness through rationalisation of proliferating anti-corruption bodies. * * *

Corporate Governance

21.   Corporate governance is fairly new in Rwanda. There is no capital market in Rwanda in the conventional sense. The private sector is in its infancy and the involvement of the State as producer and provider of economic essential services was widespread until recently. The monetary and financial market is dominated by nine banks and six insurance companies in which the State continues to be a major shareholder.

22.   Rwanda has ratified or adopted a significant number of key international standards and codes in corporate governance. Nevertheless, official reaffirmation of adhesion to these principles notwithstanding, there is an overall lack of awareness of corporate governance. It is advised that an Inter-ministerial Task Force be established to review the state of the implementation of all the standards and codes. It is recommended that Rwanda proceeds with a large consultation for the formulation of a comprehensive strategy on corporate governance with the support of the appropriate organisations.

23.   Although a regulatory framework promoting good corporate governance exists in Rwanda, the CRM ascertained that much still needs to be done to establish and enforce these legislative obligations and duties, as well as to update and expand them. In this regard, all private initiatives for reporting and commenting on business activities, including financial and economic journalism, should be encouraged for the sake of a higher level of transparency. * * *

Socio–Economic Development

25.   In this objective, Rwanda has also demonstrated considerable political will to adhere to international and regional standards and codes by ratifying all the standards and codes provided in the APRM Questionnaire. There are ongoing efforts at implementation, but capacity remains a constraint. In Rwanda's own assessment, challenges in the implementation process include a lack of resources to package and disseminate information, and a lack of awareness by the public as well as social and cultural traditions that hinder or slow down the process of change.

26.   In spite of Rwanda's legacy of genocide, as well as the fact that large sections of the population are living below the poverty line, and that the numbers of orphans and persons living with HIV/AIDS are alarming, Rwanda has made some significant progress in building the foundation for socio-economic development. Rwanda has done this by establishing institutional, policy and legal frameworks such as the Vision 2020, Poverty Reduction Strategy Programme, Sector Strategies, Poverty Observatory Unit, Gender Monitoring Unit, a Community Development Fund, and Women Councils. Rwanda has also relied on traditional practices such as Gacaca, Ubudehe, [and] Umuganda * * *, which promote socio-economic development through a culture of broad-based

participation and community mobilisation. Unfortunately, many of the institutions, such as the Women Councils, are lacking in capacity and therefore not operating effectively. The Gender Monitoring Unit is also still not fully operational.

27. To date, some sectors have witnessed encouraging results, namely gender equality and education. Nonetheless, Rwanda is still struggling with poverty reduction and maternal and child health indicators. These indicators (relevant to the Millennium Development Goals) have not shown any signs of improvement over the past five years. The HIV prevalence rate of 13% is also very high for a small country that relies heavily on its human resources for growth and development. Even with this limited manpower, capacity is a major constraint, as skills are limited. Fortunately, Rwanda is a beneficiary of substantial external support to combat HIV/AIDS, but it is also recommended that should Rwanda allocate more resources to the construction of antiretroviral treatment centres and continue to work at obtaining reliable HIV/AIDS data.

28. The promotion of women in all areas of society and broad-based participation of all stakeholders in the country are hailed in the socio-economic section report as two best practices from which other countries can learn. On access to basic utilities, Rwanda has found innovative approaches, such as the Imidugugu (communal setting) to bridge the problem of water and extraction of methane from Lake Kivu to bridge the problem of energy. Rwanda has also embarked on an ambitious twenty-year information and communications technology plan and is also taking serious measures to address the land problem. On access to markets and finance, legal instruments have been established and initial results are being observed, for example, the burgeoning micro-credit institutions and the recent performance of the coffee industry. The Government is encouraged to maintain its impetus with regard to implementation, and to ensure that access to basic amenities is not limited to the urban areas.

Overarching Issues

29. The issue of land, which is linked to high population growth and density, is a critical one for Rwanda, particularly where conflict, land use and environmental protection are concerned. The Government is encouraged to establish a clear land and population policy that includes a plan to create more off-farm employment for the youth and rural populations.

30. Another overarching issue of concern is the complexity of Rwanda's steady move towards multi-party and political pluralism. The Rwandese political system or culture is characterised by consensus rather than "voluntary participation" by political parties. Removing all restrictions on political rights and freedoms, while ensuring that political parties are able to operate freely but along non-ethnic or racial lines,

would, in the long run, benefit democracy in Rwanda, rather than adhering to a tight framework within which parties can operate.

31.   While the Gacaca courts are viewed by the Government and some segments of Rwandans as the main alternative means for dispute resolution and a much-needed way to achieve justice and reconciliation, there are serious concerns about their legitimacy and ability to win trust and confidence in dispensing justice, while strictly conforming to contemporary international human rights norms and standards. The real challenge for Rwanda in the short-to-medium term is how to build capacity in the judiciary sector, so that the lessons and value added from reviving the Gacaca system can be institutionalised.

32.   It is clear that Rwanda has made a significant effort in establishing institutions and mechanisms to promote good governance and socio-economic development. Nonetheless, an emerging challenge throughout the four thematic areas is the lack of capacity within institutions to perform their tasks effectively. Rwanda is advised to initiate extensive capacity building from national to local levels in terms of training and skills development. In this regard, the Human and Institutional Capacity Development Agency (HIDA) should be effectively strengthened. It is highly recommended that civil society, the private sector and development partners complement the Government's efforts in this regard.

33.   The reliance on external assistance has been underscored in the main report. An overarching issue is how effectively this aid is being utilised. While the CRM is led to believe that Rwanda has made a serious effort to use external aid appropriately in the form of social services, the traditional justice system, infrastructural development, decentralisation, policy reforms, and the like, it would be helpful to the country to see specific data on the proportions of aid funds that are allocated to poverty-reducing sectors and the proportion of the same aid money that returns to the donor country or institution.

Notes and Questions on the African Peer Review Mechanism

1.   *Human rights and economic renewal.* The APRM is an integral part of the New Partnership for African Development ("NEPAD"), which was established to "develop an integrated socio-economic *development framework* for Africa" (*available at* http://www.nepad.org/2005/files/home.php) (emphasis supplied). What is the practical, strategic, or normative connection between the protection of human rights and the economic development of Africa?

2.   *The breadth of the APRM's human rights jurisdiction.* Taking the Rwandan report as illustrative, list the human rights that fall within the APRM's mandate.

3. *Assessing the APRM.* The APRM is an essentially political process, involving self-reporting to peer governments. What is the argument that these characteristics make it (i) stronger or (ii) weaker than an international court as a means of enforcing international human rights standards?

4. *Best practices.* The APRM Panel devotes much of its analysis identifying Rwanda's "best practices." Why do "best practices" matter? Why might a human rights advocate be suspicious of the very notion of "best practices," especially in a state-to-state peer review mechanism?

5. *Proliferation and its discontents.* Consider this observation from one prominent African human rights lawyer and scholar:

> The continuous creation of new mechanisms for the protection of human rights in Africa is not necessarily helping the situation. Instead of focusing on getting the mechanism created by the African Charter, the African Commission, to function properly, new mechanisms are created, such as the African Human Rights Court. Even before the African Human Rights Court is established, the NEPAD African Peer Review Mechanism is developed, and so forth. In themselves all of these mechanisms could be a viable starting point, but the current proliferation of mechanisms means that there is a lack of focus of resources and effort, with the result that none of them might be in a position to make any difference. The question should be asked which mechanism is mostly likely to make a significant impact on human rights in Africa, and that particular mechanism should be supported and developed until it is functioning properly before other mechanisms are created.

Christof Heyns, *The African Regional Human Rights System: The African Charter*, 108 PENN. ST. L. REV. 679, 702 (2004).

CASE STUDY: DARFUR
TESTING THE AFRICAN UNION
AND THE INTERNATIONAL COMMUNITY

REPORT OF THE [U.N.] INTERNATIONAL
COMMISSION OF INQUIRY ON DARFUR
EXECUTIVE SUMMARY
25 JANUARY 2005[1]

Acting under Chapter VII of the United Nations Charter, on 18 September 2004, the Security Council adopted resolution 1564 requesting, *inter alia*, that the Secretary–General "rapidly establish an interna-

---

1. *Available at* http://www.un.org/news/dh/sudan/com_ing_darfur.pdf.

tional commission of inquiry in order immediately to investigate reports of violations of international humanitarian law and human rights law in Darfur by all parties, to determine also whether or not acts of genocide have occurred, and to identify the perpetrators of such violations with a view to ensuring that those responsible are held accountable". * * * In order to discharge its mandate, the Commission endeavoured to fulfil four key tasks: (1) to investigate reports of violations of international humanitarian law and human rights law in Darfur by all parties; (2) to determine whether or not acts of genocide have occurred; (3) to identify the perpetrators of violations of international humanitarian law and human rights law in Darfur; and (4) to suggest means of ensuring that those responsible for such violations are held accountable. While the Commission considered all events relevant to the current conflict in Darfur, it focused in particular on incidents that occurred between February 2003 and mid-January 2005. * * *

I.   Violations of international human rights law and international humanitarian law

In accordance with its mandate to "investigate reports of violations of human rights law and international humanitarian law", the Commission carefully examined reports from different sources including Governments, inter-governmental organizations, United Nations bodies and mechanisms, as well as nongovernmental organizations. The Commission took as the starting point for its work two irrefutable facts regarding the situation in Darfur. Firstly, according to United Nations estimates there are 1,65 million internally displaced persons in Darfur, and more than 200,000 refugees from Darfur in neighbouring Chad. Secondly, there has been large-scale destruction of villages throughout the three states of Darfur. The Commission conducted independent investigations to establish additional facts and gathered extensive information on multiple incidents of violations affecting villages, towns and other locations across North, South and West Darfur. The conclusions of the Commission are based on the evaluation of the facts gathered or verified through its investigations.

Based on a thorough analysis of the information gathered in the course of its investigations, the Commission established that the Government of the Sudan and the Janjaweed are responsible for serious violations of international human rights and humanitarian law amounting to crimes under international law. In particular, the Commission found that Government forces and militias conducted indiscriminate attacks, including killing of civilians, torture, enforced disappearances, destruction of villages, rape and other forms of sexual violence, pillaging and forced displacement, throughout Darfur. These acts were conducted on a widespread and systematic basis, and therefore may amount to crimes against humanity.

The extensive destruction and displacement have resulted in a loss of livelihood and means of survival for countless women, men and children. In addition to the large scale attacks, many people have been arrested and detained, and many have been held incommunicado for prolonged periods and tortured. The vast majority of the victims of all of these violations have been from the Fur, Zaghawa, Massalit, Jebel, Aranga and other so-called "African" tribes.

In their discussions with the Commission, Government of the Sudan officials stated that any attacks carried out by Government armed forces in Darfur were for counter-insurgency purposes and were conducted on the basis of military imperatives. However, it is clear from the Commission's findings that most attacks were deliberately and indiscriminately directed against civilians. Moreover even if rebels, or persons supporting rebels, were present in some of the villages—which the Commission considers likely in only a very small number of instances—the attackers did not take precautions to enable civilians to leave the villages or otherwise be shielded from attack. Even where rebels may have been present in villages, the impact of the attacks on civilians shows that the use of military force was manifestly disproportionate to any threat posed by the rebels.

The Commission is particularly alarmed that attacks on villages, killing of civilians, rape, pillaging and forced displacement have continued during the course of the Commission's mandate. The Commission considers that action must be taken urgently to end these violations. While the Commission did not find a systematic or a widespread pattern to these violations, it found credible evidence that rebel forces, namely members of the SLA and JEM, also are responsible for serious violations of international human rights and humanitarian law which may amount to war crimes. In particular, these violations include cases of murder of civilians and pillage.

II. Have acts of genocide occurred?

The Commission concluded that the Government of the Sudan has not pursued a policy of genocide. Arguably, two elements of genocide might be deduced from the gross violations of human rights perpetrated by Government forces and the militias under their control. These two elements are, first, the *actus reus* consisting of killing, or causing serious bodily or mental harm, or deliberately inflicting conditions of life likely to bring about physical destruction; and, second, on the basis of a subjective standard, the existence of a protected group being targeted by the authors of criminal conduct. However, the crucial element of genocidal intent appears to be missing, at least as far as the central Government authorities are concerned. Generally speaking the policy of attacking, killing and forcibly displacing members of some tribes does not evince a specific intent to annihilate, in whole or in part, a group distinguished on racial, ethnic, national or religious grounds. Rather, it would seem that those who planned and organized attacks on villages pursued the intent to drive the victims from their homes, primarily for purposes of counter-insurgency warfare. The Commission does recognise that in some instances individuals, including Government officials, may commit acts with genocidal intent. Whether this was the case in Darfur, however, is a determination that only a competent court can make on a case by case basis.

The conclusion that no genocidal policy has been pursued and implemented in Darfur by the Government authorities, directly or through the militias under their control, should not be taken in any way as detracting from the gravity of the crimes perpetrated in that region. International offences such as the crimes against humanity and war crimes that have been committed in Darfur may be no less serious and heinous than genocide.

III.   Identification of perpetrators

The Commission has collected reliable and consistent elements which indicate the responsibility of some individuals for serious violations of international human rights law and international humanitarian law, including crimes against humanity or war crimes, in Darfur. In order to identify perpetrators, the Commission decided that there must be "a reliable body of material consistent with other verified circumstances, which tends to show that a person may reasonably be suspected of being involved in the commission of a crime." The Commission therefore makes an assessment of likely suspects, rather than a final judgment as to criminal guilt.

Those identified as possibly responsible for the above-mentioned violations consist of individual perpetrators, including officials of the Government of Sudan, members of militia forces, members of rebel groups, and certain foreign army officers acting in their personal capacity. Some Government officials, as well as members of militia forces, have also been named as possibly responsible for joint criminal enterprise to commit international crimes. Others are identified for their possible involvement in planning and/or ordering the commission of international crimes, or of aiding and abetting the perpetration of such crimes. The Commission also has identified a number of senior Government officials and military commanders who may be responsible, under the notion of superior (or command) responsibility, for knowingly failing to prevent or repress the perpetration of crimes. Members of rebel groups are named as suspected of participating in a joint criminal enterprise to commit international crimes, and as possibly responsible for knowingly failing to prevent or repress the perpetration of crimes committed by rebels.

The Commission has decided to withhold the names of these persons from the public domain. This decision is based on three main grounds: 1) the importance of the principles of due process and respect for the rights of the suspects; 2) the fact that the Commission has not been vested with investigative or prosecutorial powers; and 3) the vital need to ensure the protection of witnesses from possible harassment or intimidation. The Commission instead will list the names in a sealed file that will be placed in the custody of the UN Secretary–General. The Commission recommends that this file be handed over to a competent Prosecutor (the Prosecutor of the International Criminal Court, according to the Commission's recommendations), who will use that material as he or she deems fit for his or her investigations. A distinct and very voluminous sealed file, containing all the evidentiary material collected by the Commission, will be handed over to the High Commissioner for Human Rights. This file should be delivered to a competent Prosecutor.

IV. Accountability mechanisms

The Commission strongly recommends that the Security Council immediately refer the situation of Darfur to the International Criminal Court, pursuant to article 13(b) of the ICC Statute. As repeatedly stated by the Security Council, the situation constitutes a threat to international peace and security. Moreover, as the Commission has confirmed, serious violations of international human rights law and humanitarian law by all parties are continuing. The prosecution by the ICC of persons allegedly responsible for the most serious crimes in Darfur would contribute to the restoration of peace in the region.

The alleged crimes that have been documented in Darfur meet the thresholds of the Rome Statute as defined in articles 7 (1), 8 (1) and 8 (f). There is an internal armed conflict in Darfur between the governmental authorities and organized armed groups. A body of reliable information indicates that war crimes may have been committed on a large-scale, at times even as part of a plan or a policy. There is also a wealth of credible material which suggests that criminal acts were committed as part of widespread or systematic attacks directed against the civilian population, with knowledge of the attacks. In the opinion of the Commission therefore, these may amount to crimes against humanity.

The Sudanese justice system is unable and unwilling to address the situation in Darfur. This system has been significantly weakened during the last decade. Restrictive laws that grant broad powers to the executive have undermined the effectiveness of the judiciary, and many of the laws in force in Sudan today contravene basic human rights standards. Sudanese criminal laws do not adequately proscribe war crimes and crimes against humanity, such as those carried out in Darfur, and the Criminal Procedure Code contains provisions that prevent the effective prosecution of these acts. In addition, many victims informed the Commission that they had little confidence in the impartiality of the Sudanese justice system and its ability to bring to justice the perpetrators of the serious crimes committed in Darfur. In any event, many have feared reprisals in the event that they resort to the national justice system.

The measures taken so far by the Government to address the crisis have been both grossly inadequate and ineffective, which has contributed to the climate of almost total impunity for human rights violations in

Darfur. Very few victims have lodged official complaints regarding crimes committed against them or their families, due to a lack of confidence in the justice system. Of the few cases where complaints have been made, most have not been properly pursued. Furthermore, procedural hurdles limit the victims' access to justice. Despite the magnitude of the crisis and its immense impact on civilians in Darfur, the Government informed the Commission of very few cases of individuals who have been prosecuted, or even disciplined, in the context of the current crisis.

The Commission considers that the Security Council must act not only against the perpetrators but also on behalf of the victims. It therefore recommends the establishment of a Compensation Commission designed to grant reparation to the victims of the crimes, whether or not the perpetrators of such crimes have been identified. It further recommends a number of serious measures to be taken by the Government of the Sudan, in particular (i) ending the impunity for the war crimes and crimes against humanity committed in Darfur; (ii) strengthening the independence and impartiality of the judiciary, and empowering courts to address human rights violations; (iii) granting full and unimpeded access by the International Committee of the Red Cross and United Nations human rights monitors to all those detained in relation to the situation in Darfur; (iv) ensuring the protection of all the victims and witnesses of human rights violations; (v) enhancing the capacity of the Sudanese judiciary through the training of judges, prosecutors and lawyers; (vi) respecting the rights of IDPs and fully implementing the Guiding Principles on Internal Displacement, particularly with regard to facilitating the voluntary return of IDPs in safety and dignity; (vii) fully cooperating with the relevant human rights bodies and mechanisms of the United Nations and the African Union; and (viii) creating, through a broad consultative process, a truth and reconciliation commission once peace is established in Darfur.

The Commission also recommends a number of measures to be taken by other bodies to help break the cycle of impunity. These include the exercise of universal jurisdiction by other States, re-establishment by the Commission on Human Rights of the mandate of the Special Rapporteur on human rights in Sudan, and public and periodic reports on the human rights situation in Darfur by the High Commissioner for Human Rights.

In July 2007, after years of delay and ineffective negotiation with the Government of Sudan, the African Union Mission in Sudan (AMIS) and the United Nations developed a path-breaking hybrid mission in Darfur—the United Nations–African Mission to Darfur (UNAMID)— which places military forces in the area, subject to a strict legal mandate. Among its purposes, UNAMID is intended to "contribute to the restoration of necessary security conditions for the safe provision of humanitarian assistance and to facilitate full humanitarian access throughout Darfur" and to "contribute to the protection of civilian populations under imminent threat of physical violence and prevent attacks against civilians, within its capability and areas of deployment, without prejudice to the responsibility of the Government of the Sudan."

UNITED NATIONS–AFRICAN UNION MISSION TO DARFUR (UNANAMID)

REPORT OF THE SECRETARY–GENERAL AND THE CHAIRPERSON OF THE AFRICAN UNION COMMISSION ON THE HYBRID OPERATION IN DARFUR S/2007/307/REV.1 (5 JUNE 2007)

In order to achieve these broad goals, the operation's tasks would include the following: * * *

(i) To promote the re-establishment of confidence, deter violence and assist in monitoring and verifying the implementation of the redeployment and disengagement provisions of the Darfur Peace Agreement, including by actively providing security and robust patrolling of redeployment and buffer zones, by monitoring the withdrawal of long-range weapons, and by deploying hybrid police, including formed police units, in areas where internally displaced persons are concentrated, in the demilitarized and buffer zones, along key routes of migration and in other vital areas, including as provided for in the Darfur Peace Agreement; * * *

(iii) To monitor, verify and promote efforts to disarm the Janjaweed and other militias; * * *

(vi) To contribute to the creation of the necessary security conditions for the provision of humanitarian assistance and to facilitate the voluntary and sustainable return of refugees and internally displaced persons to their homes; * * *

(viii) To monitor through proactive patrolling the parties' policing activities in camps for internally displaced persons, demilitarized and buffer zones and areas of control;

(ix) To support, in coordination with the parties, as outlined in the Darfur Peace Agreement, the establishment and training of community police in camps for internally displaced persons, to support capacity-building of the Government of the Sudan police in Darfur, in accordance with international standards of human rights and accountability, and to support the institutional development of the police of the movements;

(x) To support the efforts of the Government of the Sudan and of the police of the movements to maintain public order and build the capacity of Sudanese law enforcement in this regard through specialized training and joint operations;

(c) [With respect to] Rule of law, governance, and human rights:

(i) To assist in the implementation of the provisions of the Darfur Peace Agreement and any subsequent agreements relating to human rights and the rule of law and to contribute to the creation of an environment conducive to respect for human rights and the rule of law, in which all are ensured effective protection;

(ii) To assist all stakeholders and local government authorities, in particular in their efforts to transfer resources in an equitable manner from the federal Government to the Darfur states, and to implement reconstruction plans and existing and subsequent agreements on land use and compensation issues;

(iii) To support the parties to the Darfur Peace Agreement in restructuring and building the capacity of the police service in Darfur, including through monitoring, training, mentoring, co-location and joint patrols;

(iv) To assist in promoting the rule of law, including through institution-building, and strengthening local capacities to combat impunity;

(v) To ensure an adequate human rights and gender presence capacity, and expertise in Darfur in order to contribute to efforts to protect and promote human rights in Darfur, with particular attention to vulnerable groups;

(vi) To assist in harnessing the capacity of women to participate in the peace process, including through political representation, economic empowerment and protection from gender-based violence;

(vii) To support the implementation of provisions included in the Darfur Peace Agreement and any subsequent agreements relating to upholding the rights of children;

(d) Humanitarian assistance: to facilitate the effective provision of humanitarian assistance and full access to people in need.

NOTES AND QUESTIONS ON THE CRISIS IN DARFUR

1. *Understanding the UN Commission's legal conclusions.* The Commission of Inquiry included some of the most highly respected human rights lawyers in the world. As a legal matter, why did they conclude that "no genocidal policy has been pursued and implemented in Darfur by the Government authorities, directly or through the militias under their control"? The government of the United States disagreed and continues to disagree. *See, e.g.,* Testimony of U.S. Secretary of State

Colin L. Powell before the Senate Foreign Relations Committee, *available at* http://www.state.gov/secretary/former/powell/remarks/36042. htm. ("Genocide has been committed in Darfur and * * * the Government of Sudan and the Janjaweed bear responsibility—and that genocide may still be occurring.") Under the Genocide Convention, contained in the Document Supplement, what consequences follow from a determination that genocide has occurred or is continuing to occur in Darfur?

2. *ICC Proceedings.* On February 27, 2007, pursuant to Article 58(7) of the Rome Statute, the Office of the Prosecutor requested a chamber of the International Criminal Court to issue arrest warrants to for Ahmad Muhammad Harun, former Minister of State for the Interior, and Ali Muhammad Ali Abd–Al–Rahman (also known as Ali Kushayb), a Janjaweed leader, for crimes against humanity and war crimes. After a lengthy investigation, the Prosecutor concluded that

> there are reasonable grounds to believe that [Harun and Ali Kushayb] bear criminal responsibility in relation to 51 counts of alleged crimes against humanity and war crimes. * * * The vast majority of attacks in Darfur were carried out by the Militia/Janjaweed and the Armed Forces, and were directed at areas inhabited by mainly Fur, Masalit and Zaghawa tribes. The attackers did not target any rebel presence. Rather, they targeted civilian residents based on the rationale that they were supporters of the rebel forces. This strategy became the justification for the mass murder, summary execution, and mass rape of civilians who were known not to be participants in any armed conflict. The strategy included the forced displacement of entire villages and communities. * * * Thousands of civilians died in Darfur either from direct violence or as a result of disease, starvation and the conditions of life imposed by the crimes. Rape is widespread. The conflict has resulted in more than 2 million internally displaced persons and over two hundred thousands refugees. Our evidence exposes the facts and the suffering of the victims in Darfur as conveyed by the witnesses we interviewed. Based on their stories we built a judicial investigation to unveil the truth, to prosecute the most responsible and to contribute to the prevention of future crimes.

Transcript of the Prosecutor's Opening Remarks, ICC–OTP–20070227– 208–En. In April 2007, the judges of the International Criminal Court issued the arrest warrants as requested. As of this writing, both defendants remained at large.

In July 2008, the ICC Prosecutor presented evidence that the President of Sudan, Omar Hassan Ahmad al Bashir, had committed genocide, crimes against humanity, and war crimes in Darfur. It is the first time in history that an international arrest warrant has been requested against a sitting head of state. As of this writing, he remains in power.

3. *The crisis continues.* The various legalisms of the UN Commission of Inquiry, the ICC arrest warrants, and the UNAMID mandate should not obscure the reality that a human rights crisis continues in Darfur as this book goes to press.

THE AFRICAN COURT OF HUMAN AND PEOPLES' RIGHTS

INTRODUCTORY NOTE ON INSTITUTIONAL INNOVATION WITHIN THE CONTINENT

There are many international courts that have focused much or all of their work on human rights issues in Africa. The International Court of Justice at the Hague, considered the "the principal judicial organ of the United Nations" under the UN Charter, has occasionally had human rights cases on a variety of continents, including Africa.[1] The first investigations by the Office of the Prosecutor at the International Criminal Court involved cases in Darfur, Congo, and Uganda. The United Nations also established the International Criminal Tribunal for Rwanda, which has made significant contributions to the jurisprudence of international human rights and humanitarian law since its creation in 1994. *See* Module 6, *supra*. And the first hybrid court in the world, combining both domestic and United Nations elements, was created with "the power to prosecute persons who bear the greatest responsibility for serious violations of international humanitarian law and Sierra Leonean law committed in the territory of Sierra Leone since 30 November 1996, including those leaders who, in committing such crimes, have threatened the establishment of and implementation of the peace process in Sierra Leone."[2] The Permanent Court of Arbitration at the Hague has established an Eritrea–Ethiopia Claims Commission which has developed a body of innovative jurisprudence *inter alia* on the proof and remediation of violations of international humanitarian law.[3]

But shifting the focus from these international tribunals to continental and sub-continental courts within Africa reveals that Africa actually leads the world in developing innovative regional courts with poten-

---

1. *See, e.g., Armed Activities on the Territory of the Congo (Democratic Republic of the Congo v. Rwanda),* 2006 I.C.J. 27; *Armed Activities on the Territory of the Congo (D.R. Congo v. Uganda),* 2005 I.C.J. 1; *Arrest Warrant of 11 April 2000 (D.R. Congo v. Belg.),* 2002 I.C.J. 11; *Legal Consequences for States of the Continued Presence of South Africa in Namibia (South–West Africa) Notwithstanding Security Council Resolution 276,* Advisory Opinion, 1971 I.C.J. 16; *South West Africa Cases (Eth. v. S. Afr, Lib. v. S. Afr.),* Second Phase, 1966 I.C.J. 6; *Western Sahara,* Advisory Opinion, 1975 I.C.J. 12.

2. *See* Statute of the Special Court for Sierra Leone at art. 1, *available at* http://www.sc-sl.org/documents/scsi-statute.html. In April 2006, Charles Taylor, former President of Liberia, made his first appearance before the Special Court.

3. *See, e.g.,* Eritrea–Ethiopia Claims Commission, *Partial Award (Civilian Claims),* 44 I.L.M. 630 (2005).

tial jurisdiction over human rights cases. And the creation of these courts within Africa—with their successes and their failures—offers a virtual laboratory in institutional development. "Africa is the continent that by far has given birth to the largest number of international judicial bodies. Yet, at the same time, a larger than usual part of these have been non-starters or, after a hesitant beginning, have been derelict, or remained only a project on paper." Project on International Courts and Tribunals, African International Courts and Tribunals, *available at* http:// www.aict-ctia.org/aict_about.html. Before focusing on the AU's African Court of Human Rights, it is important to understand the range of sub-continental courts within Africa and their potential human rights trajectories. These include but are not limited to:[4]

> *The Economic Community of West African States* (ECOWAS). ECOWAS was created in 1975 as a means of regional economic integration, but it has gradually assumed a wider range of responsibilities. After a long gestation period, an ECOWAS Community Court of Justice (CCJ) came into existence,[5] but it was not until 2005 that human rights issues were explicitly brought within its jurisdiction, and legal and natural persons were empowered to bring suit in the CCJ. Since that time, human rights claims have proliferated: in 2008, for example, a former slave successfully sued the government of Niger in the CCJ, claiming that it failed to implement the law against slavery. In a previous case, Nigerian politicians sued the Nigerian government claiming violation of their human rights in the determination of election results. Whether the CCJ will become a force in the protection of human rights—and specifically whether the member states will support it with adequate material resources—remains to be seen.

> *The Southern African Development Community* (SADC).[6] Like the European Union, the SADC began its institutional life as an instrument for regional economic integration and development, and, like the European Court of Justice, the SADC Tribunal has jurisdiction over controversies involving the interpretation or application of the Community Treaty and related instruments. By a special protocol, natural and juristic individuals may bring cases before the Tribunal

---

4. Sub-continental courts other than those listed in the text exist, at least on paper, including the Instance Judiciaire of the Arab Maghreb Union (IJAMU), the Court of Justice of the Common Market for Eastern and Southern Africa (COMESA), the Court of Justice of the Economic Community of Central African States (ECCAS), the Court of Justice of the Central African Economic and Monetary Community (CEMACCJ), and the Court of Justice of the Organization for the Harmonization of African Business Law.

5. The countries subject to the jurisdiction of the CCJ include Benin, Burkina Faso, Cape Verde, Côte d'Ivoire, Gambia, Ghana, Guinea, Guinea–Bissau, Liberia, Mali, Niger, Nigeria, Senegal, Sierra Leone, and Togo. Some of these states also belong to the West African Economic and Monetary Union, which, though its has its own Court of Justice, has no jurisdiction over human rights matters. Additional information about the current human rights workload of the CCJ may be found at www.aict-ctia.org/courts_subreg/ecowas/ecowas_home.html.

6. The countries subject to the jurisdiction of the SADC Court of Justice include Angola, Botswana, DRC, Lesotho, Madagascar, Malawi, Mauritius, Mozambique, Namibia, South Africa, Swaziland, Tanzania, Zambia, Zimbabwe.

against member-states for violations of Community law once national remedies have been exhausted. The working assumption is that the Tribunal's jurisprudence will accelerate and unify the member-states' economic development. To that end, the Tribunal is empowered to apply SADC law but also general principles of international law and principles from individual states' municipal legal systems, presumably including the human rights provisions in the members' constitutional law. In other words, just as the European Court of Justice has developed a coherent body of European administrative law with human rights at its core, it is possible that the SADC Tribunal—which received its first complaint in October 2007—will do the same.

The East African Economic Community (EAEC). The Treaty for the Establishment of the East African Economic Community[7] established an East African Court of Justice (EACJ) with jurisdiction over the interpretation and application of the treaty. Partner States, the Secretary–General of the EAEC, and, in limited circumstances, individuals were empowered to use the Court to enforce the treaty against member-states, but only for violations of the treaty itself—a largely economic and commercial instrument. On the other hand, the treaty does require states to "take such * * * measures that shall eliminate prejudices against women and promote the equality of the female gender with that of the male gender in every respect," Art. 121(e), and specifies that one of the objectives of a common foreign and security policy within the Community is to "develop and consolidate democracy and the rule of law and respect for human rights and fundamental freedoms," Art. 123(3)(c). The potential for bringing cases under these human rights provisions is entirely untested: the EACJ received its first case in December 2005 and was reconstituted in July 2007.

PROJECT ON INTERNATIONAL COURTS AND TRIBUNALS THE AFRICAN COURT OF HUMAN AND PEOPLES' RIGHTS[1]

The African Court on Human and Peoples' Rights (ACtHPR) is the most recent of the three regional human rights judicial bodies. Envisioned by the African Charter on Human and Peoples' Rights concluded in 1981, its structure was not planned until the Organization of African Unity (OAU) promulgated a protocol for its creation in 1998. The

---

7. Treaty for the Establishment of the East African Economic Community, entered into force July 7, 2000. The countries subject to the jurisdiction of the East African Court of Justice include Burundi, Kenya, Rwanda, Uganda and the United Republic of Tanzania.

1. *Available at* http://www.pict-pcti.org/courts/ACHPR.html.

Protocol to the African Charter on Human and Peoples' Rights Establishing the ACtHPR entered into force on January 25, 2004, upon its ratification by fifteen member states. * * *

Unlike the European and Inter–American systems for the protection of human rights, where the ECHR and the IACHPR are integral parts of the cardinal instrument of the system *ab initio*, in the case of Africa, the establishment of a regional judicial body to ensure the implementation of the fundamental agreement is rather an afterthought. Before the adoption of the ACtHPR Protocol, the protection of rights listed in the African Charter rested solely with the African Commission on Human and Peoples' Rights, a quasi-judicial body * * * with no binding powers. In particular, under the African Charter, the Commission's functions are limited to examining state reports, considering communications alleging violations, and interpreting the Charter at the request of a State party, the OAU, or any organization recognized by the OAU. The scantiness of the enforcement and compliance control mechanism contained in the African Charter, however, is hardly surprising. At the time the OAU adopted the African Charter, very few African States (*i.e.*, Gambia, Senegal, and Botswana), could vaunt of a democratic regime respectful of at least the fundamental human rights.

In the second half of the 1990s, advancements of democracy in several African states (*e.g.*, Namibia, Malawi, Benin, South Africa, Tanzania, Mali, and Nigeria) and the weak record of the African Commission heightened the need for stronger domestic and regional guarantees for the protection of human rights, making the establishment of the ACtHPR possible. Such a renewed impetus toward more effective protection of human rights accounts also for certain features of the ACtHPR which set it apart, not only from its American and European congeners, but from all other judicial bodies. In particular, the Protocol provides that actions may be brought before the Court on the basis of any instrument, including international human rights treaties, which have been ratified by the State party in question (article 3.1). Furthermore, the Court can apply as sources of law any relevant human rights instrument ratified by the State in question, in addition to the African Charter (article 7). In other words, the ACtHPR could become the judicial arm of a panoply of human rights agreements concluded under the aegis of the United Nations (*e.g.*, the International Covenant on Civil and Political Rights, the Convention on the Elimination of all Forms of Discrimination against Women, or the Convention on the Rights of the Child) or of any other relevant legal instrument codifying human rights (e.g., the various conventions of humanitarian law, those adopted by the International Labour Organization, and even several environmental treaties). Very few of those agreements contain judicial mechanisms of ensuring their implementation, and therefore, at least potentially, several African states could end up with a dispute settlement and implementation control system stronger and with more bite than the one ordinarily provided for by those treaties for the rest of the world.

Another peculiarity of the ACtHPR concerns the standing of individuals and NGOs. Unlike any other judicial body, advisory opinions can be asked for by not only member States and OAU organs, but by any African NGO that has been recognized by the OAU, provided that at the time of ratifying of the Protocol or thereafter, the State at issue has made a declaration accepting the jurisdiction of the Court to hear such cases. Again, this is another provision that, if the OAU recognizes NGOs liberally, might eventually strengthen the ACtHPR's promotional function. In the area of contentious jurisdiction, individuals also can bring cases if the above declaration has been made by the State at issue. This is a step forward from the Inter–American Court, where individuals have no standing at all, but it is still far from the progressive attitude of the new European Court of Human Rights.

With the transformation of the OAU into the African Union (AU), and a renewed emphasis on democratization and the protection of human rights on the Continent, the necessary ratifications of the ACtHPR Charter came swiftly. Pursuant to the Constitutive Act of the African Union, the ACtHPR was originally to be one of two separate courts for the reconstituted organization. However, in July 2004 the AU determined that the ACtHPR should be merged with the African Court of Justice. * * * Meanwhile, despite the non-ratification of the Protocol on the Court of Justice, the AU elected the first eleven judges to the ACtHPR on January 22, 2006. * * * The states of the Eastern Region of the AU (Comoros, Djibouti, Eritrea, Ethiopia, Kenya, Madagascar, Mauritius, Rwanda, Seychelles, Somalia, Sudan, Tanzania and Uganda) chose the seat of the Court to be in Arusha, Tanzania. Thus, unless the African Commission on Human and Peoples' Rights moves from its current location in the Gambia, the seat of the ACtHPR will be on the other side of the continent from the Commission, alienating the latter from the Court.

Practicum

GACACA COURTS IN RWANDA

In this exercise, you will be asked to analyze the international legality of the *gacaca* ("ga-cha-cha") court system, a traditional form of community justice in Rwanda, adapted by the Rwandan government to try people responsible for genocide and related crimes in that country's holocaust. The institutional setting for your work will be a "communication" to the African Commission for Human and Peoples' Rights under Article 55 of the African Charter. Students will serve variously as (i) counsel for the party filing the communication, (ii) counsel for the government of Rwanda, and (iii) members of the Commission.

MARY KIMANI, *COMMUNITY FREES FOUR GENOCIDE SUSPECTS DURING PILOT GACACA JUSTICE PROCESS*

INTERNEWS (30 May 2001)

Four suspects who had been detained in Gitarama prison for more than four years on genocide charges were released last Thursday by their community in a preliminary session of a justice system known as Gacaca. Under the preliminary Gacaca sessions, a genocide suspect is brought before members of the community where the crimes were allegedly committed and the charges read out. If no one in the community has evidence against the suspect, then he or she is freed. If there is testimony that the suspect participated in the genocide, the case is deferred and the suspect goes back to detention, pending the convening of a proper Gacaca session.

The Gitarama four were from the first seven cases heard in a preliminary Gacaca session at Nogwe commune in Gitarama province. Some 30 more cases were heard before the day's session was concluded. The suspects whose cases were heard during preliminary Gacaca sessions are detainees without case files or those whose case files are incomplete. Similar preliminary trials have been conducted countrywide. The preliminary sessions are being used as a test of the process' viability. In time, suspects with complete case files will be brought before the communal courts.

The commune court in Gitarama sat in a grass patch on a small hill next to a road. There was no formal arrangement, just a few seats for visitors who included Belgian and French embassy officials. Each detainee stood before approximately 2000 local residents while Jean Barushinana, the region's prosecutor, read out their names, age and asked the community if anyone knew of any reason why the person should be detained.

The first case was that of 18–year–old Byumbu Aron. He was arrested when he was only 14 and charged with murder. Aron, who looked perplexed, fearful and worried, stood silently before the crowd to await their ruling. Barushinana asked those who knew Aron to tell the rest of the community if there was anything for which he ought to be held accountable. The scene was reminiscent of an auction yard. The prosecutor once more asked if there were any charges against Aron. Barushinana asked the question a second and third time. He then asked those who survived the genocide if they recognized Aron or had anything to say against him. The question was met with silence. "We have established that there is nothing against him and as soon as the paperwork is completed tomorrow he will be free to go home," Barushinana said.

Next came Rose Murekatete, aged 58. She had been in jail for five years. She stood before the crowd clutching a small black bible. No one in the crowd had anything to say against her and she was released amid clapping and cheers from the crowd. Two other women, Saverine Nyiraminani and Venancie Nyirakamengeri, followed Murekatete. However, four women stood up and spoke against Nyiraminani. "Her behavior during the genocide was not good, she helped kill people," one of the women said. One woman said that her son was killed after Nyiraminani led the killers to his hideout. The four women were asked to document their claims and were strongly warned that false testimony was an offense for which they could be jailed.

Nyiraminani was taken back to jail. Her case will be dealt with later, in a proper Gacaca session.

When it came to Nyirakamengeri's turn to face the community, it was alleged that four children who had been hidden in her house were taken by militiamen and killed elsewhere. The children's relatives alleged that Nyirakamengeri had asked the militiamen to kill the children; others claimed that her husband, who was implicated in other killings, took the children away and had them killed with her acquiescence. However, no one testified that Nyirakamengeri was directly involved in the children's deaths. In her defense, Nyirakamengeri said unknown people, who included a former mayor, took the children away.

The former mayor was also among the prisoners and was called to give his version of the events. He said that a group of men had approached him, demanding that the children be handed over. He said he did not identify the men. The former mayor and Nyirakamengeri were taken back to jail, pending further investigations.

The community released two more people, Florence Mukanyagezi and Emmanel Rwabuhungu. The last of the seven was 80–year–old Jacque Munyesanga, who could hardly stand and leaned heavily on his staff. There were many people in the crowd with claims against Munyesanga. One man stood up and stated that Munyesanga was responsible for the deaths in his family. He added that he had evidence to prove his claims. Munyesanga was ordered to remain in prison until the evidence produced was assessed.

———————

PENAL REFORM INTERNATIONAL INTEGRATED REPORT ON GACACA RESEARCH AND MONITORING (PILOT PHASE) JANUARY 2002–DECEMBER 2004 (DECEMBER 2005)[1]

In 1994, approximately one million[2] Tutsis and so-called "moderate" Hutus opposed to the massacres were killed in the space of three months. This genocide was planned and perpetrated by the former government of President Habyarimana. The country was devastated, and nearly three million people were forced into exile. Institutions responsible for law enforcement, such as the justice system, the courts, the police and the prisons ... all ceased to function. The new government believed that peace and national unity could only be achieved by striking at the roots of genocide and, in particular, the "culture of impunity." The solution of a general amnesty was immediately dismissed and both the authorities representing the Rwandan people and the international community agreed that the perpetrators of the genocide must be tried. But exactly how could impunity be successfully combated while also attempting to reconcile two communities? How could such an endeavor succeed when so many had participated in the atrocities?

As of June 30, 2005, the International Criminal Tribunal for Rwanda, which is based in Arusha, Tanzania, had tried only twenty-four out of sixty former government officials detained there in the space of eleven years. Only a few isolated cases have been tried in foreign courts.
* * *

In the aftermath of the genocide, more than 120,000 people were arrested and imprisoned in Rwanda for the crime of genocide, while the prisons were built to hold only 18,000. Rwanda was going to have to try these individuals even when the entire judicial system had been destroyed by the events of 1994: court buildings had been sacked, all qualified personnel had either been killed, accused of genocide, or had fled the country. By the end of 1994, Rwanda had no more than twenty magistrates for the entire country. Thanks to generous assistance from various United Nations agencies, foreign governments and NGOs, the Rwandan government would attempt to rebuild the infrastructure of the

---

1. *Available at* http://www.penalreform.org/integrated-report-on-gacaca-research-and-monito ring-pilot-phase-january–2002–december.html.

2. According to figures published by the Rwandan government in December 2001, during the period from 1 October 1990 to 31 December 1994, the number of genocide victims reached 1,074,017, 93.7% of whom were Tutsi.

judicial system and to quickly train new personnel who, whether qualified or not, would be in charge of handling the prosecution.

Genocide trials began in December 1996 in a climate of extreme
tension. Confronted with considerable logistic and financial problems,
Rwanda has nevertheless made concrete progress, and five years later,
the number of trials increased eight-fold. However, regardless of their
efforts to reconstruct the judicial system, the authorities are still at an
impasse. At the rate of 1,000 verdicts per year, it will take more than a
century in the regular court system to empty the country's prisons and
cachots (jails).

The government would thus reach the conclusion that the judicial
system could not be the sole solution. Starting in 1998, it would look
elsewhere for answers—a step that would lead the authorities to propose
a new justice system that, this time, would be in essence participatory
and inspired by tradition. After several amendments to the initial project
brought before the parliament in July 1999, and discussions with the
international community, the first "*Gacaca* Law" was adopted and published in March 2001.

The *Gacaca* courts would introduce a unique and innovative character to matters of transitional justice. For the first time, an entire
population would be entrusted with the responsibility for judging persons accused of the crime of genocide and other crimes against humanity. * * *

Up until the colonial period, the *Gacaca* was a traditional method of
conflict resolution among members of the same lineage. When social
norms were violated or conflicts arose (land disputes, damage to property, marital problems, and struggles over inheritance . . .), the parties
were brought together during informal and non-permanent sessions
presided over by the elders (Inyangamugayo). The primary objective
during these *Gacaca* sessions was, in addition to ending the violation of
shared values, to restore the social order by reintegrating the transgres-
sors into the community. The principal goal of the traditional *Gacaca*
was thus "not to determine guilt nor to apply State law . . . but to
restore social harmony and social order in a given society, and to re-
include the person who was the source of the disorder."[3]

It must however be made clear that the most serious cases were not
presented before the *Gacaca*. Blood crimes, in particular, were not
handled by the *Gacaca*. In such cases, the operative concept was that of
vengeance, to the degree that it was understood as a religious duty.
During the colonial period, a western-style judicial system was introduced in Rwanda, but the *Gacaca* remained an integral part of traditional practice. * * *

Authorized by the law to carry out investigations, to issue summons-
es, to order preventive detentions, but also to impose sentences, the

---

3. Stef Vandeginste, Justice, Reconciliation and Reparation after Genocide and Crimes against
Humanity. The proposed establishment of popular *Gacaca* Tribunals in Rwanda, Addis Ababa,
Conference, 8–12 November 1999.

current *Gacaca* courts combine the powers of the former traditional *Gacaca* tribunals with those of regular courts and even those of the State Prosecutor. These are, therefore, veritable criminal courts, endowed with ample jurisdictional competences. However, only a massive and voluntary participation by the population can establish legitimacy of these courts, as well as permit them to function such that the principal of procedural due process is respected.

In resorting to this hybrid and innovative system, the government anticipated the following advantages:

— The acceleration of trials: neither victims nor suspects should have to wait for years to see justice done,

— The relief of the prison system and the reduction of penitentiary costs, with releases occurring as a result of the acceleration of trials,

— The establishment of the truth, the participation of the entire community being perceived as the best way to reveal the truth,

— The eradication of the culture of impunity, the purpose of the *Gacaca* being to judge both genocide crimes and crimes against humanity,

— The reconciliation of the Rwandan people. The *Gacaca* should contribute to the reestablishment of social ties that were severely damaged by the genocide. * * *

In keeping with the spirit that presides over any pilot phase, the first *Gacaca* Law of 2001 underwent, as a result of the difficulties encountered on the ground, a certain number of changes that were framed in a new organic law that was passed in 2004. Two aspects of this law warrant particular attention.

On the Categorization of Penalties Incurred

In order to distinguish between the different levels of participation in the genocide, the accused—according to the 2004 law—are placed in one of three designated categories, whereas the 2001 law contained four.

First category: the planners, organizers, and ringleaders of the genocide; those who acted in positions of authority; well-known murderers, as well as those guilty of sexual torture or rape. The penalty incurred in this category can extend to the death penalty. The redefinition of category 1 that was worked into the 2004 law was rather an expansion of this category, to which "acts of tortures" was added, including those which did not result in death, as well as "dehumanizing acts on dead bodies". At the time, [we] expressed [our] concern with regard to this extensive redefinition, which ran the risk of increasing the backlog in the regular courts and the prisons.

Second category: those who committed or assisted in the commission of murder or attacks against persons that resulted in death;

those who, with the intent to kill, inflicted injuries or committed other acts of serious violence that did not result in death. The maximum punishment incurred in this category is 25 to 30 years' imprisonment.

Third category: those who committed serious attacks without the intent to cause death of their victims. In actuality, the third category proved difficult to manage; it was thus eliminated under the 2004 law and the defendants associated with this category were henceforth placed in category 2.

Fourth category: those who committed offenses against property. With the 2004 law and the disappearance of the third category, this has become *de facto* category 3. The penalty incurred at this level consists of reparation for damages to property.

It must also be underscored that, aside from capital punishment (for convicted persons in the first category) and deprivation of liberty, the law requires that the accused in category 1 suffer a permanent and total loss of civil liberties. Those in category 2 are to suffer a partial loss of civil liberties (right to vote, eligibility for public service or teaching or medical staff positions in either the private or public sector, etc.). With regard to the sentencing of persons between the ages of 14 and 18 at the time of the crime, these individuals incur only half the penalty of an adult having committed similar crimes. Minors who were less than 14 years of age at the time of the crime cannot be prosecuted. Moreover, among the most important elements pertaining to the jurisdiction of these *Gacaca* courts, it is worth mentioning that they are not authorized to impose the death penalty. The prosecution of criminals in the first category who are subject to capital punishment is relegated exclusively to the jurisdiction of professional judges in the regular courts. * * *

On the Structure of the Courts

In the law of January 26, 2001, the structure of the courts was designed to reflect the administrative structure. In other words, each court would correspond to an administrative division: the cell (between 150 and 300 people on average), the sector (which encompasses several cells), the district and the province. With the 2004 law, the organization of the courts was simplified with a view to reducing the number of judges by improving their instructions and training, and consequently, their motivation. The district and provincial courts were thus eliminated.

Each court is composed of a General Assembly (at the cell level, this encompasses the entire population over the age of 18; at the sector level, it encompasses the seats of the cell court of the particular sector, the seat of the sector court and the appeals court, comprised of anywhere from 50 to 60 elected judges), of the Seat (originally 19 judges, and later 9 under the 2004 law) and the Coordinating Committee (originally 5 people chosen from among the judges, and later only 3 under the 2004 law).

The process itself is divided into three phases which were maintained under the 2004 reform:

— The entire process begins with the *gathering of information*: the General Assemblies of the cell-level courts are responsible for establishing a certain number of lists intended to retrace as closely as possible the actual events of the genocide as they occurred in their area:

    — the list of persons residing in the cell before and during the 1994 genocide,

    — the list of persons who died in the cell,

    — the list of persons residing in the cell who died outside of it,

    — the list of goods damaged,

    — the list of the accused who committed crimes of genocide inside the cell.

— This is followed by the fundamental phase of *categorization*. This task is carried out by the seat of the cell-level courts which must, based on information gathered, place the accused in one of three categories set out by the law. Thus, both the referral of a case to the regular court (for category 1) or to a *Gacaca* trial court (cell or sector), and the range of applicable penalties (death penalty, life or a determined period of imprisonment, reparations) are dependent upon categorization.

Finally, the *sentence* is handed down by the court competent court, according to the category into which the accused has been placed: the cell-level courts handle third category cases and second category cases from the sector level. First category cases are referred to the regular courts.

AMNESTY INTERNATIONAL
RWANDA: GACACA: A QUESTION OF JUSTICE (2002)

AFR 47/007/2002

Amnesty International has a number of human rights concerns regarding the constitution of the *Gacaca* Jurisdictions and the fairness of their proceedings. The fact that the *Gacaca* Jurisdictions are a hierarchical network of community-based judicial hearings makes them even more dependent on the human rights environment in which they are located than the ordinary jurisdictions, which are based on an established body of law and legal procedure. * * * The Rwandese government has repeatedly violated an individual's right to be presumed innocent until guilt is proven in a court of law whose proceedings meet minimum standards of fair trial. Tens of thousands of Rwandese have been arrested and detained for prolonged periods of time with little or no judicial investigation of the accusations leading to their arrest and detention or trial in a court of law. * * *

[T]he lack of fair trial guarantees in the legislation establishing the *gacaca* tribunals refers as much to the government's presumption of detainees' guilt as it does to the lack of resources to provide a fair trial. Government action, or the lack thereof, with respect to the presumption of innocence of genocide suspects until they are convicted in a court of law that meets prescribed standards of fairness, has established a negative precedent for the effective operation of the *Gacaca* Jurisdictions. Government precedent obviously affects the public mindset regarding guilt and innocence and the character of their participation in the *gacaca* hearings.

There are few legislative safeguards guaranteeing an "equality of arms" between parties in cases before gacaca benches. Government authorities insist that the identity and structure of gacaca as a community forum ensures a procedurally equal position for both plaintiff and defendant. * * *Their focus is on the communal investigation of genocide offences that were committed within their communities. Though they are legally established judicial bodies, they were not created to duplicate courtroom procedure wherein both parties mobilize all the resources at their disposal. Despite government disavowals, the prosecution enjoys a number of other advantages. A majority of cases will be judged on the basis of case-files prepared and passed on to the gacaca benches by the Public Prosecutor's Offices. Lay judges, with virtually no legal training, may be unwilling to challenge the information contained in them. Likewise, it will be difficult for defendants, without counsel, to effectively counter cases prepared by state authorities with infinitely more resources at their disposal. * * *

The fact that *gacaca* sessions are located in local communities and managed by community members can further advantage the prosecution. Community power wielders, or those close to them, who have engineered the arrest and detention of individuals for economic gain or personal enmity can similarly use their power to influence who speaks and what they say during the *gacaca* hearings. * * *

There is no clear, definitive statement in the *gacaca* legislation that states when defendants are informed of the charges and case against them. Defendants require adequate time and facilities to prepare their defence, particularly as they are responsible for it. There is also no provision enabling the *gacaca* benches to adjourn proceedings if defendants have not been given sufficient time or the materials to prepare their case. * * *

Community members—*gacaca* judges, general assembly members and those testifying—will be subject to considerable political, social, economic and psychological pressures emanating from within polarized communities torn by the genocide and all that has preceded it. Collusion between members of *gacaca* organs could secure the removal of members they dislike or who threaten their designs and negatively affect the availability and testimony of witnesses. The impartiality of appointed *Gacaca* Jurisdiction members cannot be assured in a socio-political environment characterized by the intense politicisation of personal disputes and dissatisfaction or dissent with the current government, transforming both into a vicious cycle of accusations and counter-accusations of genocide or treason.

The competence of the *gacaca* judges is questionable. Most of them have no legal or human rights background. The highly abbreviated training they have received is grossly inadequate to the task at hand, given the range, character and complexity of crimes committed during the genocide. Their concomitant lack of legal objectivity, moreover, could make it more difficult for them to resist governmental and local interference in *gacaca* proceedings or their own subjective experience of what occurred. * * *

Amnesty International appreciates the legislation's provisions regarding the mandated public dimension of *gacaca* hearings and judgments. It is vitally important that *gacaca* sessions and hearings remain completely open to not only community members but also all interested parties, particularly human rights monitors.

Amnesty International recognizes the value of the confession and guilty-plea procedure established in the organic law that set up the special genocide chambers in the ordinary jurisdictions and maintained in the law establishing the *Gacaca* Jurisdictions. At the same time, Amnesty International has received reports of genocide confessions obtained by torture or under duress. . . . Inhumane treatment, the lack of food, sleep or communication with others including those in the outside world have also led to confessions. Detention in Rwanda's overcrowded prisons, in and of itself, may have led individuals to confess to crimes they did not commit.

The *gacaca* legislation does not forbid the retrial of individuals who have already been tried and acquitted by ordinary jurisdictions. Moreover, *gacaca* counsellors assisting the first phase of the *gacaca* sessions have stated that individuals acquitted by the ordinary jurisdictions can be placed on the lists of genocide suspects these sessions are preparing and retried if new facts emerge. * * *

Amnesty International is concerned that appeal to a higher *Gacaca* Jurisdiction may not adequately address an individual's rights to have his or her conviction and sentence reviewed. The fact that Category 2 offenders can receive sentences of up to life imprisonment in province-level *Gacaca* Jurisdictions heightens its concern. * * *

Reasons have already been elucidated that document Amnesty International's concerns for the safety of all those involved in the *gacaca* sessions and hearings: the poor human rights record of the Rwandese government, the intense politicisation of personal issues and the existent polarization within Rwandese communities. It is within this context that Rwandese are asked to publicly denounce or defend genocide suspects within their communities. The fact that these public revelations will occur almost simultaneously in over 10,000 locations presents the Rwandese authorities with a seeming insoluble security problem, one in which government authorities frankly admit they have no answer.

Partially in response to the critique of human rights NGOs, the Rwandan Parliament revised the organic law governing *gacaca* courts in 2007, the relevant provisions of which follow:

LAW NO. 10/2007 (1 MARCH 2007)[1]

Article 3: Conditions for being a member of the bench of Gacaca Court

Members of the benches of Gacaca Courts are Rwandans of integrity elected by the General Assemblies of their Cells of residence. A person of integrity is any Rwandan meeting the following conditions:

1) not to have participated in genocide;

2) to be free from the spirit of sectarianism;

3) not to have been definitively sentenced to a penalty of at least six (6) months of imprisonment;

4) to be of high morals and conduct;

5) to be truthful;

6) to be honest;

7) to be characterised by a spirit of speech sharing;

8) to be free from genocide ideology. Ideology of genocide consists in behaviour, a way of speaking, written documents and any other actions meant to wipe out human beings on the basis of their ethnic group, origin, nationality, region, colour of skin, physical traits, sex, language, religion or political opinions.

Any person of integrity who is at least twenty-one (21) years old and meeting all the conditions required by this organic law, can be elected a member of an organ of a Gacaca Court without any discrimination whatsoever, such as that based on sex, origin, religion, opinion or social position. * * *

Article 11: Categories of the accused

Following acts of participation in offences referred to in article one of [the law] establishing the organisation, competence and functioning of

----

1. *Available at* http://www.inkiko-gacaca.gov.rw/pdf/6.0"N " 10.2007?20version"finale.pdf.

Gacaca courts charged with prosecuting and trying the perpetrators of the crime of genocide and other crimes against humanity, committed between October 1, 1990 and December 31, 1994, the accused may be classified in one of the following categories:

First Category:

1. The person whose criminal acts or criminal participation place among planners, organisers, incitators [*sic*], supervisors, and ringleaders of the crime of genocide or crimes against humanity, together with his or her accomplices;

> 1) the person who, at that time, was in the organs of leadership, at national, prefecture, sub-prefecture and commune levels, leaders of political parties, members of the high command of the army and gendarmerie, of communal police, leaders of religious denominations, or illegal militia groups and who committed those offences or encouraged other people to commit them, together with his or her accomplices;

> 2) the person who committed acts of rape or sexual torture, together with his or her accomplices;

The Prosecutor General of the Republic shall publish, at least twice a year, the list of persons classified in the first category, forwarded to him or her by Gacaca Courts of the Cell.

Second Category:

> 1) the well known murderer who distinguished himself or herself in the area where he or she lived or wherever he or she passed, because of the zeal which characterized him or her in the killings or excessive wickedness with which they were carried out, together with his or her accomplices;

> 2) the person who committed acts of torture against others, even though they did not result in[] death, together with his or her accomplices;

> 3) the person who committed dehumanising acts on the dead body, together with his or her accomplices.

> 4) the person whose criminal acts or criminal participation place among the killers or authors of serious attacks against others, causing death, together with his or her accomplices;

> 5) the person who injured or committed other acts of serious attacks, with intention to kill them, but who did not attain his or her objective, together with his or her accomplices;

> 6) the person who committed or participated in criminal acts against persons, without any intention of killing them, together with his or her accomplices.

Third Category:

The person who only committed offences against property. However, if the author of the offence and the victim have agreed on an amicable settlement on their own initiative, or before the public authority or witnesses, before this organic law came into force, he or she cannot be prosecuted. * * *

Article 19: Persons authorized to appeal in Gacaca Courts

The defendant, plaintiff or any other interested person may appeal against a judgment passed by a Gacaca Court, in the interest of justice.

Article 20: Reasons for the review of the judgement

A judgement can be subject to review when:

1) a person was acquitted in a judgement passed in the last resort by an ordinary court, but is thereafter found guilty by a Gacaca Court;

2) a person was convicted in a judgement passed in the last resort by an ordinary court, but is thereafter found innocent by a Gacaca Court;

3) a judgement was passed in the last resort by a Gacaca Court, and later on there are [sic] new evidence proving contrary to what the initial judgment of that Gacaca Court was grounded;

4) a person was given a sentence that is contrary to legal provisions of the charges against him or her.

Persons entitled to lodge a review of the judgement are the defendant, the plaintiff or any other person acting in the interest of justice. The Gacaca Court of Appeal is the only competent court to review judgements passed in the last resort.

———————

1.   Group 1: draft a communication to the African Commission, in conformity with the African Charter and the Commission's Rules of Procedure, *available at* www.achpr.org/english/_info/guidelines_communi cations_en.html, challenging the legality of the *gacaca* courts, and prepare for a hearing on the communication before the Commission.

2.   Group 2: prepare a response to the communication (or if time is limited, anticipate the most likely allegations of the communication and respond), and prepare for a hearing on the communication before the Commission.

3.   Group 3: acting as members of the African Commission, hold a hearing on the issues of procedure and substance raised by the communication and prepare a disposition.

———————

CHAPTER 3

MODULE 7D

REGIONAL PROSPECTS IN ASIA AND THE ARAB WORLD

■ ■ ■

Orientation

It is one thing for a lawyer to engage a body of existing human rights law, articulated by an established regional institution, interpreting a broad-gauged treaty, adopted and implemented by consensus among the member states. It is quite another to be present before the creation of such an institution, when the applicable human rights norms are not fully settled, and the organizational arrangements for enforcing them are hypothetical and remote. The lawyer's role in the latter scenario is necessarily more creative, more political, and less certain.

This final module on the regional protection of human rights addresses these challenges and centers on the reality that a majority of the world's population lives under no regional human rights system. Some of the most populous countries in the world—China, India, Indonesia—are not members of any regional organization that includes protecting human rights among its essential purposes. Of course, all human beings are covered by the global protections within the United Nations system and customary international law. And the domestic law of every individual state, combined with the work of national human rights institutions ("NHRIs"), also protects the human rights of citizens, at least on paper. But the three major regional systems—Europe, the Americas, and Africa—are of no direct use to people in other regions, like Asia and the Middle East.

It is not the case that there are no international human rights instruments in these two vaguely-defined regions. As shown below, a variety of declarations and charters express a general understanding of human rights with a regional accent. And in one sub-region, southeast Asia, considerable attention has focused recently on the development of a human rights commission, with lawyers in the region extracting lessons from the successes and failures of the commissions on other continents. Still the question persists: why have these countries *not* adopted a system among themselves to protect human rights? If a global system, for all of its gaps, can be adopted among a greater number of states, with profound differences in language, culture, ideology, religion, and history, why can't a smaller number of states, bound by geopolitical proximity, find sufficient common ground to create their own regional systems?

One possible answer is that the governments in these regions are not convinced that a regional system is necessary: between the global system and the various domestic legal systems, human rights are adequately protected in their view. The value added by an intermediate level of protection is simply insufficient to justify the costs. Another possible reason is that the regional systems to date have required a greater and more concrete surrender of sovereignty than has the global system. Other explanations may fall within the expertise of anthropologists, political scientists, and area specialists, rather than lawyers, especially lawyers outside the region. At a minimum, however, it is necessary for the contemporary human rights lawyer to understand the reach of existing regional arrangements in these places and how his or her legal skills might be used to develop institutions that are both effective and appropriate.

CASE STUDY 1:

ASEAN: TOWARDS A HUMAN RIGHTS COMMISSION IN SOUTHEAST ASIA

In August 1967, at the height of the Vietnam War, five states (Indonesia, Malaysia, Philippines, Singapore, and Thailand) created the Association of Southeast Asian Nations (ASEAN). To some extent, ASEAN offered a regional economic bloc to improve trade and a security bloc to check the spread of communism in the region, but its powers were limited, and it offered more of a forum for the discussion of common issues than a mechanism for resolving them. ASEAN's founding document, the Bangkok Declaration, 6 INT'L LEG. MATS. 1233 (1967), identified ASEAN's primary goals as advancing trade and economic development, social progress and cultural development among its member states; promoting peace and stability within the region; and maintaining respect for justice and the rule of law. "Justice and the rule of law" is a broad concept of course, but nothing in the Bangkok Declaration referred specifically to human rights.

ASEAN has grown over the last forty years to include ten nations,[1] and its mandate has evolved over time. In 1993, ASEAN foreign

---

1. Brunei Darussalam, Cambodia, Indonesia, Lao People Democratic Republic, Malaysia, Burma (Myanmar), Philippines, Singapore, Thailand and Vietnam.

ministers meeting in Singapore agreed that the institution should consider a regional mechanism for human rights. But "considering" a
commission and creating it are two different things. As Professor Li-ann
Thio observed in 1999:

> Human rights have not figured prominently on the agenda of the
> [then] nine-member Association for Southeast Asian States * * *
> since its inception in 1967. Rather, the pursuit of regional security
> and cooperative measures for promoting trade and economic devel-
> opment have been paramount ASEAN objectives. By insisting on a
> strict separation between human rights policy and trade issues,
> ASEAN has marginalized human rights and has consistently op-
> posed the use by foreign states or international organizations of
> economic or other forms of pressure to induce change in human
> rights practices. ASEAN member states display an antipathy towards
> critical scrutiny of their human rights records—for example, in
> reports from the United States Department of State or non-govern-
> mental organizations like Amnesty International and Human Rights
> Watch. ASEAN's general response has been that this constitutes
> foreign intervention in domestic matters, which undermines state
> sovereignty and violates the sacred principle of nonintervention in
> internal affairs. Within the context of ASEAN itself, an emphasis on
> harmony, compromise and consensus in ordering interstate rela-
> tions helps to preserve a fraternal silence with respect to the human
> rights violations of member states. ASEAN policy (or lack thereof)
> towards human rights has been one of reticence and non-engage-
> ment.

Li-ann Thio, *Implementing Human Rights in ASEAN Countries: "Promises to
Keep and Miles to Go Before I Sleep,"* 2 YALE H.R. & DEV. L.J., 1, 2 (1999).
See also Maznah Mohamad, *Towards a Human Rights Regime in Southeast
Asia: Charting the Course of State Commitment*, 24 CONTEMP. SOUTHEAST ASIA
(2002).

In 1995, human rights advocates within the member states banded
together to establish the Working Group for an ASEAN Human Rights
Mechanism ("Working Group"). Even as it tried to develop a formal
mechanism with general jurisdiction, the Working Group identified
particular human rights problems in the region, leading ASEAN to
adopt a Declaration on the Elimination of Violence Against Women in
the ASEAN Region (2004), *available at* http://www.aseansec.org/16189.
htm, and a Declaration Against Trafficking in Persons Particularly
Women and Children (2004), *available at* http://www.aseansec.org/16793.
htm. The apparent consensus on these principles—driven by the realities of gender-based violence and sex trafficking in the region—led the
Working Group to propose a Commission on the Promotion and
Protection of the Rights of Women and Children with "sufficient power
and scope to investigate non-compliance of international and regional
human rights norms with respect to the promotion and protection of
the rights of women and children, in particular engaging in the thematic

reporting of the most urgent instances of non-compliance with human rights norms concerning women and children."[2]

The Working Group's long institutional efforts were rewarded in November 2007, when the members of ASEAN signed the organization's first Charter, *infra*, which called for the establishment of a human rights commission "[i]n conformity with the purposes and principles of the ASEAN Charter relating to the promotion and protection of human rights and fundamental freedoms." ASEAN Charter, art. 14, ¶ 1, *available* at http://www.aseansec.org/ASEAN_charter.pdf.Id., at art. 14, ¶ 1. As this book goes to press, six states have ratified the Charter, and the Working Group has recommended a time-line for the final development of an ASEAN Human Rights Commission. The recent history within ASEAN thus provides another example not only of regional intergovernmental organizations expanding their focus from economic matters to human rights but also the long-term power of civil society to propel the development of substantive legal norms and institutional innovation.

BANGKOK DECLARATION

6 Int'l Leg. Mats. 1233 (1967)

* * * Considering that the countries of South-East Asia share a primary responsibility for strengthening the economic and social stability of the region and ensuring their peaceful and progressive national development, and that they are determined to ensure their stability and security from external interference in any form or manifestation in order to preserve their national identities in accordance with the ideals and aspirations of their peoples; * * *

[T]he aims and purposes of the Association [of Southeast Asian Nations] shall be:

1.   To accelerate the economic growth, social progress and cultural development in the region through joint endeavours in the spirit of equality and partnership in order to strengthen the foundation for a prosperous and peaceful community of South–East Asian Nations;

2.   To promote regional peace and stability through abiding respect for justice and the rule of law in the relationship among countries of the region and adherence to the principles of the United Nations Charter;

3.   To promote active collaboration and mutual assistance on matters of common interest in the economic, social, cultural, technical, scientific and administrative fields;

----

2. Summary of Proceedings, 7th workshop on the ASEAN Regional Mechanism on Human Rights, Sec. 3, ¶ 30(a), *available at* http://www.siiaonline.org/files/7th_WS_summary_proceedings.final.pdf (June 12–13, 2008).

4.   To provide assistance to each other in the form of training and research facilities in the educational, professional, technical and administrative spheres;

5.   To collaborate more effectively for the greater utilization of their agriculture and industries, the expansion of their trade, including the study of the problems of international commodity trade, the improvement of their transportation and communications facilities and the raising of the living standards of their peoples; * * * [and]

7.   To maintain close and beneficial cooperation with existing international and regional organizations with similar aims and purposes, and explore all avenues for even closer cooperation among themselves.

CHARTER OF THE ASSOCIATION OF SOUTHEAST ASIAN NATIONS (2007)[3]

Preamble

WE, THE PEOPLES of the Member States of the Association of Southeast Asian Nations (ASEAN), as represented by the Heads of State or Government of Brunei Darussalam, the Kingdom of Cambodia, the Republic of Indonesia, the Lao People's Democratic Republic, Malaysia, the Union of Myanmar, the Republic of the Philippines, the Republic of Singapore, the Kingdom of Thailand and the Socialist Republic of Viet Nam: * * *

Mindful of the existence of mutual interests and interdependence among the peoples and Member States of ASEAN which are bound by geography, common objectives and shared destiny;

United by a common desire and collective will to live in a region of lasting peace, security and stability, sustained economic growth, shared prosperity and social progress, and to promote our vital interests, ideals and aspirations; * * *

Adhering to the principles of democracy, the rule of law and good governance, respect for and protection of human rights and fundamental freedoms; * * *

Hereby decide to establish, through this Charter, the legal and institutional framework for ASEAN, and to this end, the Heads of State or Government of the Member States of ASEAN, assembled in Singapore on the historic occasion of the 40th anniversary of the founding of ASEAN, have agreed to this Charter. * * *

Article 1: *Purposes*

The Purposes of ASEAN are:

---

3.   *Available at* http://www.aseansec.org/ASEAN_charter.pdf

1.   To maintain and enhance peace, security and stability and further strengthen peace-oriented values in the region;

2.   To enhance regional resilience by promoting greater political, security, economic and socio-cultural cooperation;

3.   To preserve Southeast Asia as a Nuclear Weapon–Free Zone and free of all other weapons of mass destruction;

4.   To ensure that the peoples and Member States of ASEAN live in peace with the world at large in a just, democratic and harmonious environment;

5.   To create a single market and production base which is stable, prosperous, highly competitive and economically integrated with effective facilitation for trade and investment in which there is free flow of goods, services and investment; facilitated movement of business persons, professionals, talents and labour; and freer flow of capital;

6.   To alleviate poverty and narrow the development gap within ASEAN through mutual assistance and cooperation;

7.   To strengthen democracy, enhance good governance and the rule of law, and to promote and protect human rights and fundamental freedoms, with due regard to the rights and responsibilities of the Member States of ASEAN; * * *

Article 14: ASEAN Human Rights Body

1.   In conformity with the purposes and principles of the ASEAN Charter relating to the promotion and protection of human rights and fundamental freedoms, ASEAN shall establish an ASEAN human rights body.

2.   This ASEAN human rights body shall operate in accordance with the terms of reference to be determined by the ASEAN Foreign Ministers Meeting.

————

**WORKING GROUP FOR AN
ASEAN HUMAN RIGHTS MECHANISM
SUMMARY PROCEEDINGS,
7TH WORKSHOP ON THE ASEAN REGIONAL
MECHANISM ON HUMAN RIGHTS**

Singapore (June 12–13, 2008)

A. Conclusions

14.   The Workshop congratulates ASEAN on the incorporation of a human rights body pursuant to Art 14 of the ASEAN Charter and recognizes that its establishment is a breakthrough for human rights in the region. The Workshop further recognizes ASEAN's commitments to its Joint Communiqués beginning in 1993, particularly on establishing an appropriate regional mechanism on human rights.

15.   While ASEAN member countries have shown their commitment to promote and protect human rights, and in particular, the rights of women, children and migrant workers, through various declarations, plans of action, laws, policies and mechanisms both at regional and national levels, gaps remain at ground level which require enhanced action and vigilance on the part of governments and civil society in promoting and protecting human rights. It is important to emphasize that all should strive to implement what have already been declared and agreed upon by ASEAN member countries.

16.   Further, ASEAN member countries which have not ratified the ASEAN Charter must do so as soon as possible and civil society groups, NHRIs and other stakeholders in these countries must work for the ratification of the ASEAN Charter by their respective governments. In addition, it is not necessary for ASEAN governments and civil society to wait for the ratification of the ASEAN Charter before taking action pursuant to its human rights provisions since these are based on existing agreements or commitments of ASEAN member countries.

17.   Civil society, NHRIs and other stakeholders should have important roles to play in consultations and in providing inputs to the HLP[1] which will draft the TOR [Terms of Reference] for the ASEAN Human Rights body. The HLP should facilitate meaningful and comprehensive consultations and work in a transparent manner.

18.   There remain many challenges or constraints to the eventual establishment of the ASEAN Human Rights body. In particular,

i.   There is a variety of opinions on whether the ASEAN Human Rights body should be composed of government representatives or of independent experts.

ii. Most participants believe that there should be independent powers, which includes to investigate, monitor and report, as well as the obligation on the member countries to provide the access, while other participants believe that less intrusive powers should be provided.

iii. Some participants believe that ASEAN should move as a whole in establishing the ASEAN Human Rights body while other participants believe that member countries who are ready and able to move first could do so.

19.   There is a variety of opinions on how to proceed with the possible establishment of a possible ASEAN Commission on the Promotion and Protection of the Rights of Women and Children in light of the advent of the ASEAN Charter.

B.   General Recommendations

20.   The Workshop considers that human rights issues in ASEAN should be viewed in light of a broader ASEAN agenda as human rights

---

1.   [Editors' note: ASEAN Foreign Ministers are to convene a High Level Panel ("HLP") to draft the Terms of Reference for the Commission.]

issues crosscut into the ASEAN Political and Security Community, Economic Community and Socio–Cultural Community.

21.   The Workshop recognizes that for effective recognition and protection of human rights to take place within ASEAN, the establishment of an ASEAN Human Rights body should also be accompanied by renewed efforts to strengthen the body of substantive international, regional and national human rights norms. Accordingly, the Workshop encourages the ASEAN governments:

a.   to abide by and strengthen existing human rights norms in international law;

b.   to take steps to sign, ratify and implement existing international human rights instruments with possible withdrawal of reservations where they have yet to do so;

c.   to increase cooperation and engagement with regional and international human rights organizations and mechanisms for strengthened and improved compliance with international human rights instruments;

d.   to continue to strengthen and affirm the human rights principles found in the ASEAN Charter, the VAP[2] and in other ASEAN instruments;

e.   to continue in a step-by-step, multi-track and building block approach in developing principles of regional human rights norms which should be consistent with the standards set in international human rights instruments;

f.   to facilitate ASEAN's human rights programmes and to enhance the functions of the ASEAN Secretariat accordingly;

g.   to establish NHRIs in accordance with the Paris Principles,[3] if they have not done so;

h.   to welcome dialogue between ASEAN and NHRIs, which could possibly be called as "National Human Rights Institutions Dialogue with ASEAN" (NIDA); and

i.   to increase cooperation and engagement with domestic human rights organizations.

22.   The Workshop recommends that the HLP address the issue of the possible establishment of the Commission on the Promotion and Protection of the Rights of Women and Children which should not

---

2.   [Editors' note: The Vientiane Action Plan ("VAP") was developed in 2004 to map the future development of ASEAN. According to the Singapore Institute of International Affairs, the VAP "reveals an unprecedented emphasis on human rights and obligations, as well as on the active facilitation of good governance and the empowerment of civil society." SIIA, VIENTIANE ACTION PROGRAMME: 2004–2010 (November 2004), *available at* http://www.siiaonline.org/?q=vientiane-action-programme–2004–2010–november–2004.]

3.   [Editors' note: Principles Relating to the Status and Functioning of National Institutions for Protection and Promotion of Human Rights ("Paris Principles"), endorsed by the UN Commission on Human Rights, Res. 1992/54 (March 1992), and by the UN General Assembly, A/RES/48/134 (December 1993).]

result in its lesser status in the event that two commissions/bodies are established.

23.   While the Migrant Worker Declaration[4] is a landmark document, there is a need for follow up efforts, including consideration of a binding legal instrument on the rights of migrant workers. In particular, it is important for civil society to help the ASEAN Secretariat implement the Migrant Worker Declaration pending the possible concretization of a binding instrument.

C.   Specific Recommendations

24.   The Workshop welcomes the possible timeline that the TOR should be finalized and the ASEAN Human Rights body established by the end of 2009 as proposed by a participant from Thailand, factoring in effective consultation with civil society.

25.   The Workshop welcomes the convening of the HLP which is to draft the TOR that will spell out the mandate and scope of an ASEAN Human Rights body. In furtherance of this objective, the Workshop considers that the HLP should bear the following principles in mind in the course of drafting the TOR, wherein, inter alia, the TOR could empower an ASEAN Human Rights body that is:

i.   mandated to carry out state and/or thematic reporting coupled with an optional protocol to conduct investigations upon complaints by individuals in accordance to international standards and broadly, with the power to assess situations and advise member countries;

ii. with the power to promote and protect human rights;

iii. to provide for effective implementation of the ASEAN Human Rights body's findings and adequate resources for its operations.

iv. to provide that the appointment of its members should be carried out in consultation with civil society groups, NHRIs and other stakeholders transparently.

v.   to provide public education with respect to human rights;

vi. to study and promote relevant human rights treaties;

vii. to promulgate human rights declarations on behalf of ASEAN;

viii. to consult with NGOs, NHRIs and other stakeholders;

ix. to appoint a human rights coordinator to advocate in development and work of ASEAN councils, networks of existing NHRIs; and

x.   to engage in capacity building in the implementation and encouraging compliance with human rights treaties.

---

4.   [Editors' note: Human rights advocates within ASEAN have paid particular attention to the protection of migrant workers within the region. In January 2007, the member states adopted the Declaration on the Protection and Promotion of the Rights of Migrant Workers in an effort to recognize the contributions of migrant workers to the economy of the region and to protect workers against abuse and violence.]

a.   Accordingly, the TOR should provide adequate provisions for its own amendment so as to facilitate the gradual development of the ASEAN Human Rights body.

b.   The TOR should provide the ASEAN Human Rights body with sufficient powers and scope to examine and develop regional human rights norms which should at least be consistent with international human rights standards.

c.   The TOR should address the issue of follow up of recommendations-consultations with whatever human rights body.

31.   The Workshop recognizes that the ASEAN Charter is but a seminal and significant beginning for the promotion and protection of human rights in the region.

NOTES AND QUESTIONS ON DEVELOPMENTS IN ASIA

1.   *Drafting a proposed statute for the ASEAN commission.* Before reading the Working Group's draft charter for the proposed commission, *infra*, identify the four or five most prominent issues that must be addressed in such a document and frame out the possible language for doing so. Are there any parts of the experience of the African, American, and European commissions that seem especially useful at this stage of the Southeast Asian process?

2.   *Developing an effective strategy.* At the June 2008 meeting of the Working Group, Raymond Lim, Singapore's Transport Minister, emphasized the difficulties in establishing a regional human rights body, stressing that the body should be achieved gradually and warning against artificial deadlines. He noted the importance of taking account of the political realities and diversity within the region in order to garner support from all ASEAN states. *See* Summary of Proceedings, 7th Workshop on the ASEAN Regional Mechanism on Human Rights, Sec. 1, ¶ 4, *available at* http://www.siiaonline.org/files/7th_WS_Summary_Proceedings.final.pdf (June 12–13, 2008). Taking the minister's concerns at face value, and drawing on the experience of the other regional organizations, what is the lawyerly argument that the proposed commission is essentially incremental and evolutionary?

3.   *NGO activity.* In 1998, a variety of human rights NGOs and activists adopted the Asian Human Rights Charter, *available at* http://material.ahrchk.net/charter/, which addresses a comprehensive range of human rights standards, urges the adoption of a meaningful enforcement structure, and articulates the relationship between the Asian initiative and universal human rights. It continues to be an organizational focal point for NGO activism in the region, even if few states in the region have responded to it.

4. *Regional activity in South Asia*. In 1985, the South Asian states of Bangladesh, Bhutan, India, Maldives, Nepal, Pakistan and Sri Lanka established the South Asian Association for Regional Cooperation ("SAARC"), primarily for the advancement of economic and social cooperation. Recently, high level working groups have been established within the organization to strengthen cooperation in the areas of information and communications technology, biotechnology, intellectual property rights, and energy, but human rights *per se* have not emerged as a particular concern. As has been the case with the ASEAN Working Group, however, NGOs and advocates in South Asia established the South Asian Forum for Human Rights, which continues its efforts to focus popular and governmental attention on human rights, peace and democracy.

5. *Asia–Pacific Economic Cooperation*. Asia–Pacific Economic Cooperation (APEC) is a forum with twenty-one "member economies" from around the Pacific Rim,[5] which exists for the purpose of "facilitating economic growth, cooperation, trade and investment in the Asia–Pacific region." APEC imposes no treaty obligations on its members and operates exclusively on the basis of consensus and voluntary commitments. The APEC Secretariat estimates that APEC member economies account for roughly 41% of the world's population, 55% of world GDP and 49% of world trade. APEC Secretariat, *About APEC*, *available at* http://www.apec.org/apec/about_apec.html). The members have emphasized efforts to develop fair and transparent markets for trade and investment, fight corruption and terrorism, and protect intellectual property rights, but human rights has not been a targeted topic within the forum.

———

WORKING GROUP FOR AN
ASEAN HUMAN RIGHTS MECHANISM
DRAFT AGREEMENT ON THE
ESTABLISHMENT OF THE ASEAN
HUMAN RIGHTS COMMISSION[6]

Article I

The Contracting States aim to establish a regional human rights mechanism to promote and protect human rights.

Article 2

Inspiration shall be drawn from international law on human rights, universally recognised human rights standards and principles, and

---

5. As of June 2008, APEC's 21 member economies are Australia; Brunei Darussalam; Canada; Chile; People's Republic of China; Hong Kong, China; Indonesia; Japan; Republic of Korea; Malaysia; Mexico; New Zealand; Papua New Guinea; Peru; The Republic of the Philippines; The Russian Federation; Singapore; Chinese Taipei; Thailand; United States of America; Vietnam.

6. *available at* http://www.aseanhrmech.org/downloads/draft-agreement.pdf.

regional and national laws, policies and practices consistent with international law. The relevant instruments of international law include the 1948 Universal Declaration on Human Rights, the 1986 United National Declaration on the Right to Development, the 1993 Vienna Declaration and Programme of Action of the World Conference on Human Rights and the treaties to which the Contracting States have acceded. * * *

Article 3

The Contracting States hereby establish a permanent human rights commission for the region, which shall be called the ASEAN Human Rights Commission (hereinafter referred to as "the Commission"). * * *

Article 7

1. The members of the Commission shall be elected in a personal capacity by the Ministers of Foreign Affairs of the Contracting States which have ratified this Agreement, from a list of candidates proposed by their governments. Members of civil society, including non-governmental organisations, shall be consulted in the choice of candidates.

Article 10

The Contracting States which have ratified this Agreement shall provide the Commission with adequate resources required to accomplish the tasks assigned to it. * * *

Article 11

The main function of the Commission shall be to promote and protect human rights in the region. In the exercise of its mandate, it shall have the following functions and powers:

1. to develop an awareness of human rights among the peoples of the region;

2. to recommend to the governments of the Contracting States which have ratified this Agreement, when it considers such action advisable, the adoption of measures in favour of human rights;

3. to prepare such studies or reports as it considers advisable to the performance of its duties;

4. to request the governments of the Contracting States which have ratified this Agreement to provide it with information the measure adopted by them in relation to human rights;

5. to investigate on its own initiative (alleged) violations of human rights by a Contracting State or States which have ratified this Agreement in accordance with established rules of procedure;

6. to respond to inquiries from Contracting States which have ratified this Agreement on matters concerning human rights and, where possible, to provide those States with the advisory services they request;

7. to take action on petitions and communications pursuant to its authority, under the provisions of Articles 10 and 11 of this Agreement;

8. to interpret all the provisions of the present Agreement at the request of a Contracting State or States which have ratified this Agreement;

9. to submit an annual report to the Ministers of Foreign Affairs of the Contracting States which have ratified this Agreement and to make it available to the public; and

10. to perform any other tasks concerning the promotion and protection of human rights which may be entrusted to it by the Heads of State and Government and the Ministers of Foreign Affairs of the Contracting States which have ratified this Agreement.
* * *

Article 12

Any person or group of persons, or any non-governmental organisation recognised in one or more Contracting States which have ratified this Agreement, may lodge petition(s) with the Commission containing complaints of violation of human rights by a Contracting State or States which have ratified this Agreement.

Article 13

Any Contracting State which has ratified this Agreement may send communication(s) to the Commission alleging that another Contracting State which has ratified this Agreement has committed a violation of human rights.

————

Notes and Questions on Asian Values

1. *Cultural relativism and Asian values.* Quite apart from the difficulty of defining "Asia," some regional critics of the international human rights regime have suggested that it rests on values that are antithetical to Asian values. Amartya Sen, *Human Rights and Asian Values: What Lee Kuan Yew and Le Peng Don't Understand about Asia*, 217 The New Republic 2–3 (1997); Rendell Perenboom, *Beyond Universalism and Relativism: The Evolving Debates About "Values in Asia,"* 14 Ind. Int'l & Comp. L. Rev. 1 (2003). The argument is regularly but not exclusively invoked by apologists for repressive regimes.

Human rights doctrine is now so powerful, but also so unthinkingly imperialist in its claim to universality, that it has exposed itself to serious intellectual attack. These challenges have raised important questions about whether human rights norms deserve the authority they have acquired: whether their claims to universality are justified, or whether they are just another cunning exercise in Western moral imperialism.* * * This challenge within has been amplified by a challenge from without: the critique of Western human rights standards by some political leaders in the rising economies of East Asia. Whereas the Islamic challenge to human rights can be explained in part by the failure of Islamic societies to benefit from the global economy, the Asian challenge is a consequence of the region's staggering economic success. Because of Malaysia's robust economic growth, for example, its leaders feel confident enough to reject Western ideas of democracy and individual rights in favor of an Asian route to development and prosperity—a route that depends on authoritarian government and authoritarian family structures.

The same can be said about Singapore, which successfully synthesized political authoritarianism with market capitalism. Singapore's Senior Minister Lee Kuan Yew has been quoted as saying that Asians have "little doubt that a society with communitarian values where the interests of society take precedence over that of the individual suits them better than the individualism of America." Singaporeans often cite rising divorce and crime rates in the West to illustrate that Western individualism is detrimental to the order necessary for the enjoyment of rights themselves.

An "Asian model" supposedly puts community and family ahead of individual rights and order ahead of democracy and individual freedom. In reality, of course, there is no single Asian model: each of these societies has modernized in different ways, within different political traditions, and with differing degrees of political and market freedom. Yet it has proven useful for Asian authoritarians to argue that they represent a civilizational challenge to the hegemony of Western models.

Michael Ignatieff, *The Attack on Human Rights*, FOREIGN AFFAIRS, Nov./Dec. 2001, at 107. How should a human rights lawyer go about determining whether a particular human rights norm violates Asian culture or not?

———

CASE STUDY 2:

INSTITUTIONALIZING HUMAN RIGHTS IN THE ARAB AND ISLAMIC WORLD

One of the difficulties in studying regional approaches to human rights is the sheer arbitrariness of geographical labels. For example, according to the United Nations, the Arab Charter, *infra*, is an "Asian" regional instrument, and the "Asian" membership of various UN institutions refers to some 40 states, including states like Oman, Bahrain, United Arab Emirates, Iran, and Iraq. DINAH L. SHELTON, REGIONAL

PROTECTION OF HUMAN RIGHTS 1051, 1055–56 (2008). This casebook treats Arab and Islamic nations separately from Asia however, because, when it comes to human rights, they have treated themselves separately. In 1990, the Organisation of the Islamic Conference adopted the Cairo Declaration of Human Rights in Islam (CDHRI), *infra*, which provides "general guidance for Member States in the field of human rights" and affirms Islamic Shari'ah as its sole source. CDHRI, pmbl., U.N. Doc. A/CONF. 157/PC/62/add. 18 (1992). In 1994, the League of Arab States—a smaller organization—adopted the Arab Charter on Human Rights ("Arab Charter"), which affirmed the principles contained in the UN Charter, the International Bill of Rights, and the Cairo Declaration. The Arab Charter, as revised in 2004, provides for the election of a seven-person Committee of Experts on Human Rights to consider states' reports, and it entered into force in March 2008, sixty days after its ratification by seven states: the United Arab Emirates, Jordan, Bahrain, Algeria, Syria, Palestine, and Libya. The UN High Commissioner for Human Rights, initially welcomed the revised Arab Charter, believing that it reflected a regional commitment to the core human rights principles embodied in the UDHR, but she also echoed the criticism that it restricts the international standards for the rights of women, children, and noncitizens and that it unacceptably equates Zionism with racism.

CAIRO DECLARATION ON HUMAN RIGHTS IN ISLAM
UN Doc. A/CONF.157/PC/62/Add.18 (1993)

Reaffirming the civilizing and historical role of the Islamic Ummah which God made the best nation that has given mankind a universal and well-balanced civilization in which harmony is established between this life and the hereafter and knowledge is combined with faith; and the role that this Ummah should play to guide a humanity confused by competing trends and ideologies and to provide solutions to the chronic problems of this materialistic civilization. * * *

Believing that fundamental rights and universal freedoms in Islam are an integral part of the Islamic religion and that no one as a matter of principle has the right to suspend them in whole or in part or violate or ignore them in as much as they are binding divine commandments, which are contained in the Revealed Books of God and were sent through the last of His Prophets to complete the preceding divine messages thereby making their observance an act of worship and their neglect or violation an abominable sin, and accordingly every person is individually responsible—and the Ummah collectively responsible—for their safeguard.

Article 1

(a) All human beings form one family whose members are united by submission to God and descent from Adam. All men are equal in terms of basic human dignity and basic obligations and responsibilities, without any discrimination on the grounds of race, colour, language, sex, religious belief, political affiliation, social status or other considerations. True faith is the guarantee for enhancing such dignity along the path to human perfection.

(b) All human beings are God's subjects, and the most loved by him are those who are most useful to the rest of His subjects, and no one has superiority over another except on the basis of piety and good deeds.

Article 2

(a) Life is a God-given gift and the right to life is guaranteed to every human being. It is the duty of individuals, societies and states to protect this right from any violation, and it is prohibited to take away life except for a Shari'ah-prescribed reason.

(b) It is forbidden to resort to such means as may result in the genocidal annihilation of mankind.

(c) The preservation of human life throughout the term of time willed by God is a duty prescribed by Shari'ah.

(d) Safety from bodily harm is a guaranteed right. It is the duty of the state to safeguard it, and it is prohibited to breach it without a Shari'ah-prescribed reason.

Article 3

(a) In the event of the use of force and in case of armed conflict, it is not permissible to kill non-belligerents such as old men, women and children. The wounded and the sick shall have the right to medical treatment; and prisoners of war shall have the right to be fed, sheltered and clothed. It is prohibited to mutilate dead bodies. It is a duty to exchange prisoners of war and to arrange visits or reunions of the families separated by the circumstances of war. * * *

Article 5

(a) The family is the foundation of society, and marriage is the basis of its formation. Men and women have the right to marriage, and no restrictions stemming from race, colour or nationality shall prevent them from enjoying this right.

(b) Society and the State shall remove all obstacles to marriage and shall facilitate marital procedure. They shall ensure family protection and welfare.

Article 6

(a) Woman is equal to man in human dignity, and has rights to enjoy as well as duties to perform; she has her own civil entity and financial independence, and the right to retain her name and lineage.

(b) The husband is responsible for the support and welfare of the family.

Article 7

(a) As of the moment of birth, every child has rights due from the parents, society and the state to be accorded proper nursing, education and material, hygienic and moral care. Both the fetus and the mother must be protected and accorded special care.

(b) Parents and those in such like capacity have the right to choose the type of education they desire for their children, provided they take into consideration the interest and future of the children in accordance with ethical values and the principles of the Shari'ah.

(c) Both parents are entitled to certain rights from their children, and relatives are entitled to rights from their kin, in accordance with the tenets of the Shari'ah. * * *

Article 9

(a) The quest for knowledge is an obligation, and the provision of education is a duty for society and the State. The State shall ensure the availability of ways and means to acquire education and shall guarantee educational diversity in the interest of society so as to enable man to be acquainted with the religion of Islam and the facts of the Universe for the benefit of mankind. * * *

Article 10

Islam is the religion of unspoiled nature. It is prohibited to exercise any form of compulsion on man or to exploit his poverty or ignorance in order to convert him to another religion or to atheism.

Article 11

(a) Human beings are born free, and no one has the right to enslave, humiliate, oppress or exploit them, and there can be no subjugation but to God the Most–High.

(b) Colonialism of all types being one of the most evil forms of enslavement is totally prohibited. Peoples suffering from colonialism have the full right to freedom and self-determination. It is the duty of all States and peoples to support the struggle of colonized peoples for the liquidation of all forms of colonialism and occupation, and all States and peoples have the right to preserve their independent identity and exercise control over their wealth and natural resources.

Article 12

Every man shall have the right, within the framework of Shari'ah, to free movement and to select his place of residence whether inside or outside his country and, if persecuted, is entitled to seek asylum in another country. The country of refuge shall ensure his protection until he reaches safety, unless asylum is motivated by an act which Shari'ah regards as a crime.

Article 13

Work is a right guaranteed by the State and Society for each person able to work. Everyone shall be free to choose the work that suits him best and which serves his interests and those of society. The employee shall have the right to safety and security as well as to all other social guarantees. He may neither be assigned work beyond his capacity nor be subjected to compulsion or exploited or harmed in any way. He shall be entitled—without any discrimination between males and females—to fair wages for his work without delay, as well as to the holidays, allowances and promotions which he deserves. For his part, he shall be required to be dedicated and meticulous in his work. Should workers and employers disagree on any matter, the State shall intervene to settle the dispute and have the grievances redressed, the rights confirmed and justice enforced without bias.

Article 14

Everyone shall have the right to legitimate gains without monopolization, deceit or harm to oneself or to others. Usury (riba) is absolutely prohibited.

Article 15

(a) Everyone shall have the right to own property acquired in a legitimate way, and shall be entitled to the rights of ownership, without prejudice to oneself, others or to society in general. Expropriation is not permissible except for the requirements of public interest and upon payment of immediate and fair compensation

(b) Confiscation and seizure of property is prohibited except for a necessity dictated by law.

Article 16

Everyone shall have the right to enjoy the fruits of his scientific, literary, artistic or technical production and the right to protect the moral and material interests stemming therefrom, provided that such production is not contrary to the principles of Shari'ah.

Article 17

(a) Everyone shall have the right to live in a clean environment, away from vice and moral corruption, an environment that would foster his self-development; and it is incumbent upon the State and society in general to afford that right.

(b) Everyone shall have the right to medical and social care, and to all public amenities provided by society and the State within the limits of their available resources.

(c) The State shall ensure the right of the individual to a decent living which will enable him to meet all his requirements and those of his dependents, including food, clothing, housing, education, medical care and all other basic needs.

Article 18

(a) Everyone shall have the right to live in security for himself, his religion, his dependents, his honour and his property.

(b) Everyone shall have the right to privacy in the conduct of his private affairs, in his home, among his family, with regard to his property and his relationships. It is not permitted to spy on him, to place him under surveillance or to besmirch his good name. The State shall protect him from arbitrary interference.

(c) A private residence is inviolable in all cases. It will not be entered without permission from its inhabitants or in any unlawful manner, nor shall it be demolished or confiscated and its dwellers evicted.

Article 19

(a) All individuals are equal before the law, without distinction between the ruler and the ruled.

(b) The right to resort to justice is guaranteed to everyone.

(c) Liability is in essence personal.

(d) There shall be no crime or punishment except as provided for in the Shari'ah.

(e) A defendant is innocent until his guilt is proven in a fair trial in which he shall be given all the guarantees of defence.

Article 20

It is not permitted without legitimate reason to arrest an individual, or restrict his freedom, to exile or to punish him. It is not permitted to subject him to physical or psychological torture or to any form of humiliation, cruelty or indignity. Nor is it permitted to subject an individual to medical or scientific experimentation without his consent or at the risk of his health or of his life. Nor is it permitted to promulgate emergency laws that would provide executive authority for such actions.

Article 21

Taking hostages under any form or for any purpose is expressly forbidden.

Article 22

(a) Everyone shall have the right to express his opinion freely in such manner as would not be contrary to the principles of the Shari'ah.

(b) Everyone shall have the right to advocate what is right, and propagate what is good, and warn against what is wrong and evil according to the norms of Islamic Shari'ah.

(c) Information is a vital necessity to society. It may not be exploited or misused in such a way as may violate sanctities and the dignity of Prophets, undermine moral and ethical values or disintegrate, corrupt or harm society or weaken its faith.

(d) It is not permitted to arouse nationalistic or doctrinal hatred or to do anything that may be an incitement to any form of racial discrimination.

Article 23

(a) Authority is a trust; and abuse or malicious exploitation thereof is absolutely prohibited, so that fundamental human rights may be guaranteed.

(b) Everyone shall have the right to participate, directly or indirectly in the administration of his country's public affairs. He shall also have the right to assume public office in accordance with the provisions of Shari'ah.

Article 24

All the rights and freedoms stipulated in this Declaration are subject to the Islamic Shari'ah.

Article 25

The Islamic Shari'ah is the only source of reference for the explanation or clarification to any of the articles of this Declaration.

Notes and Questions on the Cairo Declaration

1. *The Cairo Declaration and the UDHR.* In 1981, the Iranian representative to the United Nations argued that the Universal Declaration of Human Rights "represented a secular understanding of the Judeo–Christian tradition, could not be implemented by Muslims, and did not accord with the system of values recognized by the Islamic Republic of Iran; his country would therefore not hesitate to violate its provisions, since it had to choose between violating the divine law of the country and violating secular conventions." UN GAOR 3d Comm., 39th Sess., 65th mtg. at 20, UN Doc. A/C.3/39/SR.65 (1984). It has become common for human rights advocates to emphasize the discrepancies between the Cairo Declaration and the Universal Declaration of Human Rights. *See, e.g.,* Europe News, *Cairo Declaration on Human Rights in Islam Diverges from the Universal Declaration of Human Rights in Key Respects, available at* http://europenews.dk/en/node/3847. These are generally portrayed as restrictions or qualifications in the Cairo Declaration that cannot be found in the UDHR. Comparing these documents carefully, identify the more restrictive provisions for yourself, and then determine whether there are any provisions of the Cairo Declaration that are

arguably *more* protective of human rights than the corresponding provisions of the UDHR.

2. *The declaratory power of governments.* International law certainly privileges the power of governments to define the requirements of international law. What power do the members of the Organisation of the Islamic Conference (OIC) have to declare the requirements of Islam?

3. *Evolution of human rights within Islam.* Almost fifteen years separate the Cairo Declaration from the Arab Charter, which follows. Checking the two instruments against one another (and acknowledging that they come from two different organizations—the OIC and the Arab League), what substantive and procedural evolution, if any, can you identify?

THE ARAB CHARTER ON HUMAN RIGHTS

September 15, 1994
reprinted in 18 HUM. RTS. L.J. 151 (1997)

The Governments of the member States of the League of Arab States[1]

* * * *Reaffirming* the principles of the Charter of the United Nations and the Universal Declaration of Human Rights, as well as the provisions of the United Nations International Covenants on Civil and Political Rights and Economic, Social and Cultural Rights and the Cairo Declaration on Human Rights in Islam

Article 1

(a) All peoples have the right of self-determination and control over their natural wealth and resources and, accordingly, have the right to freely determine the form of their political structure and to freely pursue their economic, social and cultural development.

(b) Racism, zionism, occupation and foreign domination pose a challenge to human dignity and constitute a fundamental obstacle to the realization of the basic rights of peoples. There is a need to condemn and endeavour to eliminate all such practices.

Article 2

Each State Party to the present Charter undertakes to ensure to all individuals within its territory and subject to its jurisdiction the right to enjoy all the rights and freedoms recognized herein, without any distinction on grounds of race, colour, sex, language, religion, political opinion, national or social origin, property, birth or other status and without any discrimination between men and women. * * *

---

1. The 22 member States of the League of Arab States are: Jordan, United Arab Emirates, Bahrain, Tunisia, Algeria, Djibouti. Saudi Arabia, Sudan, Syrian Arab Republic. Somalia. Iraq, Oman. Palestine, Qatar, Comoros, Kuwait, Lebanon, Libyan Arab Jamahiriya, Egypt, Morocco, Mauritania, and Yemen.

Article 4

(a) No restrictions shall be placed on the rights and freedoms recognized in the present Charter except where such is provided by law and deemed necessary to protect the national security and economy, public order, health or morals or the rights and freedoms of others.

(b) In time of public emergency which threatens the life of the nation, the States Parties may take measures derogating from their obligations under the present Charter to the extent strictly required by the exigencies of the situation.

(c) Such measures or derogations shall under no circumstances affect or apply to the rights and special guarantees concerning the prohibition of torture and degrading treatment, return to one's country, political asylum, trial, the inadmissibility of retrial for the same act, and the legal status of crime and punishment.

Article 5

Every individual has the right to life, liberty and security of person. These rights shall be protected by law.

Article 6

There shall be no crime or punishment except as provided by law and there shall be no punishment in respect of an act preceding the promulgation of that provision. The accused shall benefit from subsequent legislation if it is in his favour.

Article 7

The accused shall be presumed innocent until proved guilty at a lawful trial in which he has enjoyed the guarantees necessary for his defence.

Article 8

Everyone has the right to liberty and security of person and no one shall be arrested, held in custody or detained without a legal warrant and without being brought promptly before a judge.

Article 9

All persons are equal before the law and everyone within the territory of the State has a guaranteed right to legal remedy.

Article 10

The death penalty may be imposed only for the most serious crimes and anyone sentenced to death shall have the right to seek pardon or commutation of the sentence. * * *

Article 12

The death penalty shall not be inflicted on a person under 18 years of age, on a pregnant woman prior to her delivery or on a nursing mother within two years from the date on which she gave birth.

Article 13

(a) The States parties shall protect every person in their territory from being subjected to physical or mental torture or cruel, inhuman or degrading treatment. They shall take effective measures to prevent such acts and shall regard the practice thereof, or participation therein, as a punishable offence.

(b) No medical or scientific experimentation shall be carried out on any person without his free consent.

Article 14

No one shall be imprisoned on the ground of his proven inability to meet a debt or fulfil any civil obligation.

Article 15

Persons sentenced to a penalty of deprivation of liberty shall be treated with humanity.

Article 16

No one shall be tried twice for the same offence. Anyone against whom such proceedings are brought shall have the right to challenge their legality and to demand his release. Anyone who is the victim of unlawful arrest or detention shall be entitled to compensation.

Article 17

Privacy shall be inviolable and any infringement thereof shall constitute an offence. This privacy includes private family affairs, the inviolability of the home and the confidentiality of correspondence and other private means of communication.

Article 18

Everyone shall have the inherent right to recognition as a person before the law.

Article 19

The people are the source of authority and every citizen of full legal age shall have the right of political participation, which he shall exercise in accordance with the law.

Article 20

Every individual residing within the territory of a State shall have the right to liberty of movement and freedom to choose his place of residence in any part of the said territory, within the limits of the law.

Article 21

No citizen shall be arbitrarily or unlawfully prevented from leaving any Arab country, including his own, nor prohibited from residing, or compelled to reside, in any part of his country.

Article 22

No citizen shall be expelled from his country or prevented from returning thereto.

Article 23

Every citizen shall have the right to seek political asylum in other countries in order to escape persecution. This right shall not be enjoyed by persons facing prosecution for an offence under the ordinary law. Political refugees shall not be extraditable.

Article 24

No citizen shall be arbitrarily deprived of his original nationality, nor shall his right to acquire another nationality be denied without a legally valid reason.

Article 25

Every citizen has a guaranteed right to own private property. No citizen shall under any circumstances be divested of all or any part of his property in an arbitrary or unlawful manner.

Article 26

Everyone has a guaranteed right to freedom of belief, thought and opinion.

Article 27

Adherents of every religion have the right to practise their religious observances and to manifest their views through expression, practice or teaching, without prejudice to the rights of others. No restrictions shall be imposed on the exercise of freedom of belief, thought and opinion except as provided by law.

Article 28

All citizens have the right to freedom of peaceful assembly and association. No restrictions shall be placed on the exercise of this right unless so required by the exigencies of national security, public safety or the need to protect the rights and freedoms of others. * * *

Article 34

The eradication of illiteracy is a binding obligation and every citizen has a right to education. Primary education, at the very least, shall be compulsory and free and both secondary and university education shall be made easily accessible to all.

Article 35

Citizens have a right to live in an intellectual and cultural environment in which Arab nationalism is a source of pride, in which human rights are sanctified and in which racial, religious and other forms of discrimination are rejected and international cooperation and the cause of world peace are supported.

Article 36

Everyone has the right to participate in cultural life, as well as the right to enjoy literary and artistic works and to be given opportunities to develop his artistic, intellectual and creative talents.

Article 37

Minorities shall not be deprived of their right to enjoy their culture or to follow the teachings of their religions.

Article 38

(a) The family is the basic unit of society, whose protection it shall enjoy.

(b) The State undertakes to provide outstanding care and special protection for the family, mothers, children and the aged.

Article 39

Young persons have the right to be afforded the most ample opportunities for physical and mental development.

Article 40

(a) The States members of the League's Council which are parties to the Charter shall elect a Committee of Experts on Human Rights by secret ballot.

(b) The Committee shall consist of seven members nominated by the member States Parties to the Charter. The initial elections to the Committee shall be held six months after the Charter's entry into force. The Committee shall not include more than one person from the same State.

(c) The Secretary–General shall request the member States to submit their candidates two months before the scheduled date of the elections.

(d) The candidates, who must be highly experienced and competent in the Committee's field of work, shall serve in their personal capacity with full impartiality and integrity.

(e) The Committee's members shall be elected for a three-year term which, in the case of three of them, shall be renewable for one further term, their names being selected by lot. The principle of rotation shall be observed as far as possible.

(f) The Committee shall elect its chairman and shall draw up its rules of procedure specifying its method of operation.

(g) Meetings of the Committee shall be convened by the Secretary–General at the Headquarters of the League's Secretariat. With the Secretary–General's approval, the Committee may also meet in another Arab country if the exigencies of its work so require.

Article 41

1. The States Parties shall submit reports to the Committee of Experts on Human Rights in the following manner:

(a) An initial report one year after the date of the Charter's entry into force.

(b) Periodic reports every three years.

(c) Reports containing the replies of States to the Committee's questions.

2. The Committee shall consider the reports submitted by the member States Parties to the Charter in accordance with the provisions of paragraph 1 of this article.

3. The Committee shall submit a report, together with the views and comments of the States, to the Standing Committee on Human Rights at the Arab League.

STATEMENT BY THE UN HIGH COMMISSIONER FOR HUMAN RIGHTS ON THE ENTRY INTO FORCE OF THE ARAB CHARTER ON HUMAN RIGHTS (30 JANUARY 2008)[1]

On 24 January 2008 * * *, I welcomed the 7th ratification required to bring the Arab Charter on Human Rights into force. While emphasizing universal human rights, I noted that regional systems of protection and promotion can help further strengthen the enjoyment of human rights. As the 1993 Vienna Declaration and Programme of Action affirmed, "regional arrangements play a fundamental role in promoting and protecting human rights. They should reinforce universal human rights standards, as contained in international human rights instruments, and their protection."

Throughout the development of the Arab Charter, my office shared concerns with the drafters about the incompatibility of some of its provisions with international norms and standards. These concerns included the approach to death penalty for children and the rights of women and non-citizens. Moreover, to the extent that it equates Zionism with racism, we reiterated that the Arab Charter is not in conformity with General Assembly Resolution 46/86, which rejects that Zionism is a form of racism and racial discrimination. OHCHR does not endorse these inconsistencies. We continue to work with all stakeholders in the region to ensure the implementation of universal human rights norms.

---

1. *Available at* www.unhchr.ch/huricane/huricane.nsf/view01/6C211162E43235FAC12573E00056 E19D?opendocument

NOTES AND QUESTIONS ON THE ARAB CHARTER

1. *The logistics of change.* In trying to account for these developments, consider the following description of the drafting process:

> The redrafting process is * * * worthy of note since it involved the Arab League, arguably for the first time, agreeing to be inclusive, by consulting outside experts and non-governmental organizations. In 2003, the Council [of the Arab League] instructed the Arab Standing Committee on Human Rights to "modernize the Arab Charter on Human Rights. . . ." The Committee produced an initial version that was largely inconsistent with international human rights standards. The Arab League, under pressure from the UN and the Office of the High Commissioner for Human Rights (OCHCR) agreed to allow independent experts to prepare a new draft. The OCHCR reached a bilateral agreement with the Arab League to assemble a group of "independent Arab experts" as a Committee of Experts to carry out the task. All of the Committee's members, consisting of two women and three men from Algeria, Egypt, Qatar, Saudi Arabia, and Tunisia, were drawn from the United Nations human rights bodies.

Mervat Rishmawi, *The Revised Arab Charter on Human Rights: A Step Forward?*, 5 HUM. RTS. L. REV. 361 (2005).

2. *Bringing the new Charter into conformity with international law.* It is conceivable that the Committee of Experts established under Article 40 will interpret the Charter in light of international legal standards and thereby gradually close whatever gaps exist between the two. *See* the preamble to the Arab Charter, *supra.* Thinking proactively however, what specific optional protocols to the Arab Charter would you advise to assure that congruity?

3. *Appreciating the complexity of Islam.* The scholarship on the relationship between Islam and contemporary human rights law is vast. *See generally* ABDULLAHI AHMED AN-NA'IM, TOWARD AN ISLAMIC REFORMATION: CIVIL LIBERTIES, HUMAN RIGHTS AND INTERNATIONAL LAW(1990); Ann Elizabeth Mayer, *Universal versus Islamic Human Rights: A Clash of Cultures or a Clash with a Construct?*, 15 MICH. J. INT'L L. 307 (1994); MASHOOD A. BADERIN, INTERNATIONAL HUMAN RIGHTS AND ISLAMIC LAW (2003). In reviewing the latter work, Professor Mayer observes:

> Often, when writing on this topic, authors fail to attend to the actual political struggles going on within Muslim countries over rights * * *. [A]uthors often refer to current national versions of Islam at the same time that they cite from works such as accounts of the life of the Prophet or the legal theories and scholarly treatises of medieval jurists—treating both contemporary and medieval material as equally authoritative. In addition, they may refer haphazardly to diverse contemporary Muslim thinkers, statements by govern-

ment officials, legislative measures and case law in Muslim countries, and other current sources, all without proposing a coherent methodological approach to the enormous range of such source material. * * *

Another common flaw in the literature on Islam and human rights is that authors fail to treat fairly and comprehensively the range of opinions among contemporary Muslims regarding human rights, there being a prevailing inclination to endorse one point of view and to depict Muslims as sharing a unified outlook. Most frequently, this outlook turns out to be one that precludes endorsing the UN human rights system. Thus the literature often portrays Muslims as concurring that international law is excessively "Western" or "too secular." In this vein, and based on his assumption that he can speak for all Muslims, Baderin deprecates "current international human rights interpretations, some of which are considered by Muslims as insensitive to Islamic religious and moral viewpoints". He also writes as if all Muslims would concur in his belief that, in case of any clashes, Islamic law should prevail over human rights, as countries like Iran and Saudi Arabia would insist. Baderin refuses to admit that a large percentage of people living in Muslim countries—especially those who would be harmed thereby—would deplore upholding conservative readings of Islamic requirements at the expense of their human rights.

As persons familiar with contemporary debates within Muslim societies about human rights can confirm, Muslims do not necessarily agree that Islamic law, correctly understood, requires forfeiting any human rights. The Iranian Nobel laureate Shirin Ebadi, a vigorous and popular supporter of international human rights law and its universal applicability, is only one example of a believing Muslim who scoffs at governments' claims that their violations of human rights flow from their dedication to Islamic values. Ebadi speaks for Muslims who insist that the mandates of Islam have been wrongly conflated with old customs and traditions that are incompatible with human rights.

Ann Elizabeth Mayer, *Book Review*, 99 Am. J. Int'l L. 302, 303–304 (2005).

ABDULLAHI A. AN–NA'IM, ISLAM AND HUMAN RIGHTS: BEYOND THE UNIVERSALITY DEBATE

94 Am. Soc'y Int'l L. Proc. 95, 97–99 (2000)

Islam, Sharia and Human Rights

Like other believers, Muslims have always sought to experience their faith in terms of individual and collective conformity with its normative system, commonly known as *sharia*, which is supposed to regulate their daily lives as Muslims. While Muslims tend to ascribe divine authority to historical formulations of *sharia* by jurists of the eighth and ninth centuries, it is clear that the precise content of that normative system has always been, and will continue to be, the product of human understanding in specific historical context. As a scholar of Islamic studies recently explained, "Although the law [*sharia*] is of divine provenance, the actual construction of the law is a human activity, and its results represent the law of God as humanly understood. Since the law does not descend from heaven ready-made, it is the human understanding of the law—the human *fiqh* [literally, understanding]—that must be normative for society."[1]

While readily understandable, the common confusion between *sharia* as divinely ordained, on the one hand, and human efforts to discover what it means, on the other, needs to be clarified if Islam itself is to play a positive role in the lives of Muslims today. Given drastic changes in the social, economic, and political circumstances of Islamic societies throughout the world, an understanding of *sharia* that was developed more than a thousand years ago is bound to face some practical difficulties today. Yet, significant reform of any problematic aspect of *sharia* cannot occur as long as preexisting human formulations of it are taken to be divine. As a result of this "man-made" deadlock, Muslims everywhere continue to subscribe to a conception of *sharia* that none of them are willing or able to live by. For example, religious condemnation of *ribba* (usury) is understood to mean that the payment of any interest on loans is totally prohibited. Similarly, religious objections to *gharar* (uncertainty and speculation in commercial dealings) is taken to invalidate contracts of insurance where the obligations of the parties are contingent on whether or not something happens in the future. In practice, however, Muslim individuals and their governments routinely charge and pay interest on loans, and conclude and enforce contracts of insurance because it is impossible to have viable economic systems today without these practices. This discrepancy between theory and practice can be bridged through an appreciation of the fact that all specific definitions of concepts such as *ribba* and *gharar* are necessarily the product of human understanding in specific historical context, not direct divine decree.

Failing to distinguish between the two meanings of human rights noted earlier, some Muslims claim that historical formulations of *sharia* have always secured human rights in theory, though such a situation may not have materialized in practice. In my view, by securing a relatively advanced degree of protection for the rights of women and non-Muslims, historical formulations of *sharia* did provide for better protection of human rights than other normative systems in the past. For example, from the very beginning, *sharia* was understood to require an independent legal personality for women, and the protection of certain minimum rights for them in inheritance and family relations, beyond what was possible under other major normative systems until

---

1. BERNARD WEISS, THE SPIRIT OF ISLAMIC LAW 116 (1998).

the nineteenth century. Similarly, *sharia* guarantees specific rights for the so-called People of the Book (mainly Christians and Jews) more than what had been provided for under other major normative systems in the past. However, since the rights of women and non-Muslims under *sharia* are not equal to those of men and Muslims, respectively, the level of protection of rights under *sharia* is not sufficient when judged by the standards set by the UDHR, which require equal rights for all human beings, without distinction on such grounds as sex, religion, or belief.

A possible response to this criticism of *sharia* is the argument that Muslims (and other believers) should strive to live by the dictates of their religion, not according to some fallible, humanly devised set of human rights norms. However, since divine commands are always understood and applied by human beings, the contrast between orthodox perceptions of "the dictates of religion" and new or unorthodox views on the matter is really between two human understandings of what the religion requires of its adherents. Accordingly, a reinterpretation of Islamic sources that demonstrates agreement with human rights norms should be considered on its own terms, rather than dismissed as un-Islamic because it is inconsistent with previously established human understandings of *sharia*. For Muslims, a reinterpretation should be accepted or rejected in terms of its own foundation in Islamic sources, instead of being rejected simply because it is new or unorthodox. Space does not permit a detailed discussion of possible Islamic reform methodologies that can achieve consistency between human rights and modern understandings of *sharia*. What I wish to emphasize here is the possibility of establishing the religious legitimacy of such an interpretation through what might be called an anthropological approach to Islam. * * *

[T]his approach is premised on an organic and dynamic relationship between the sacred texts of a religion, the Qur'an and Sunna (traditions of the Prophet) in the case of Islam, on the one hand, and the comprehension, imagination, judgment, behavior, and practical experience of human beings, on the other. Such an approach is not only justified, but in fact required by the terms of the Qur'an, which in numerous verses invites individuals, or the community, to reflect and reason independently. Indeed, verse 12 of chapter 2 and verse 43 of chapter 3 proclaim that human reflection and understanding is the whole purpose of revealing the Qur'an. The rich diversity of opinion among Muslim jurists over almost every significant legal principle or issue of public policy clearly indicates a dynamic relationship between the Qur'an and Sunna, on the one hand, and human comprehension, imagination and experience, on the other.

Since the historical context of the community and the personal experiences of individual believers substantially influence human perception and behavior, drastic changes in the conditions of individual and communal life should lead to reconsideration of the meaning and implications of the divine message. By the same token, one must appreciate the differential impact of these factors on the perception and orientation of each community of Muslims today. To emphasize the importance of the specific historical context within which Islamic principles are understood and practiced is to call for clear understanding of the nature of these factors and careful consideration of their consequences for each society. In other words, one should address these issues for each Islamic society in its own context, instead of treating all such societies in the same way.

This contextualization is particularly important because of the role of the state as the framework for the articulation and implementation of public policy for Islamic societies today. Whatever role *sharia* may play in the lives of contemporary Muslims, that role will necessarily be mediated through the agency of their respective national states, rather than by the autonomous action of the global Muslim community as such. As an essentially political institution, any state has to balance a variety of competing claims and interests. It is true that some of those claims and interests will probably reflect the religious sentiments of the population. But in view of the religious and political diversity of the population of Islamic countries today, and the complexity of their regional and global economic and security concerns, it is totally unrealistic to expect any state to be solely motivated by the religious sentiments of even the vast majority of its population.

In addition to the above-mentioned elements of internal discourse and its processes, consideration must also be given to factors and processes of cross-cultural dialogue. First, the realities of global interaction and interdependence mean that cross-cultural dialogue is already taking place in different ways among various participants, and around a variety of national and international concerns. The question here is to what extent these processes can be used to promote acceptance of international human rights norms within different religious communities. Second, as is the case with all forms of human communication, the nature and outcomes of such dialogue are conditioned by the perspectives or agendas of different participants, their perceptions of historical and current power relations, levels of trust or misapprehension, and other features of both the immediate and the broader contexts. Moreover, these factors tend to interact over time not only in the context of experience but in that of shifting perceptions of self-interest, mounting or diminishing solidarity, and other variable factors. Third, with regard to the relationship between religion and human rights in particular, it is important to understand the synergy between internal discourse and cross-cultural dialogue, as these two aspects of the process can reinforce or undermine each other, depending on the interaction of the contextual factors indicated above. While the preceding remarks may indicate the sort of factors and considerations that I believe should be taken into account, I can only conclude by calling for further exploration of local and global conditions that are likely either to facilitate or to hinder the legitimation of human rights within different religious traditions in general.

CHAPTER 4

HUMAN RIGHTS IN THE MARKETPLACE

■ ■ ■

This chapter explores the effects of international human rights law on some the most powerful economic forces in the world: international capital, international labor, and the multinational institutions that dominate the international economy. The particular settings for analyzing this relationship vary and include the human rights obligations of multinational corporations (Module 8), the large international financial institutions (like the World Bank and the International Monetary Fund) and the World Trade Organization (Module 9), and the International Labour Organisation (Module 10). The fact that it is now meaningful to speak of these institutions as having human rights obligations (or of contributing to the development and enforcement of human rights standards) shows just how much the law governing this field has changed: it is now anachronistic to speak of international human rights law as governing only the obligations of state actors. To the contrary: non-state actors—including multinational corporations and intergovernmental economic institutions—now have enforceable obligations to protect human rights and can play a profound role in articulating human rights standards in a variety of forms and in numerous commercial settings.

CHAPTER 4

MODULE 8

MULTINATIONAL CORPORATIONS AND HUMAN RIGHTS

■ ■ ■

Orientation[1]

Corporate law and international human rights law have historically evolved in isolation from one another. In practice, the transnational corporation has remained relatively immune from effective international regulation of any variety, let alone the obligation to protect human rights, and human rights lawyers have traditionally considered governments—not private companies—to be the principal targets for concern. With a handful of exceptions, international human rights instruments have traditionally addressed the conduct of governments, and instruments treating the transnational corporation, when they exist at all, have addressed restrictive or corrupt business practices and have neglected any obligation a corporation might have to protect the civil and political rights of individuals in the society at large.

In part, the distance between these two legal cultures reflects matters of apparent principle: one received orthodoxy locates rights in a "public" realm, binding only on governments in their dealings with individuals, and corporate profits in a "private" realm, governed only by the rules of the marketplace. Certainly, the state-centeredness of international law, though qualified constantly, has never been so compromised as to equate the corporation with the state that gives it existence or to trigger state-like obligations on corporations to respect human rights standards. A separate orthodoxy, grounded in the bedrock conception of an "exclusive domestic jurisdiction," treats the protection of human rights as properly within the reach of modern international law and the regulation of corporate conduct as a matter of domestic law.

As a result of these lawyerly habits of mind, the distinction between corporate practice and international human rights law may have come to seem both inevitable and proper. In its received form, however, it has

---

1. This module is adapted from Ralph Steinhardt, "Corporate Responsibility and the International Law of Human Rights: The New *Lex Mercatoria*," in NON-STATE ACTORS AND HUMAN RIGHTS (Alston, ed. 2005).

become dysfunctional. Over the last decade, prominent transnational companies have adopted codes of conduct which make the protection of at least some human rights an explicit corporate objective. Coalitions in apparel, textiles, and footwear have adopted industry-wide standards to govern international labor practices. Various global standards for social accountability have been created to guide and assess corporate compliance with international human rights norms across industrial and geographical boundaries. Many companies now advertise their international human rights policies. Corporate officers periodically gather at human-rights roundtables and affirm the strategic value of a public commitment to such rights, even as a self-styled "progressive" stream of corporate and management scholarship offers a theoretical foundation for understanding the economic self-interest of corporate social responsibility.

These developments may simply reflect a new way for one corporation to compete with another, but entrepreneurialism alone is inadequate to account for the sea change in the corporate culture: national, state, and municipal legislation increasingly regulates the market through "human rights conditionality," barring corporate presence in certain countries where human rights are not respected, or requiring certain labor practices, or linking government contracts and other benefits to a corporation's compliance with international human rights norms. And now overarching those regulatory initiatives is the prospect of civil liability, as various domestic courts have ruled that corporations may in principle be obliged to pay substantial awards of damages for their complicity in abuses by the governments with which they do business. On the international plane, multilateral and bilateral investment agreements increasingly oblige transnational corporations to protect the human rights of workers and other citizens, even as international financial institutions, like the World Bank and the regional development banks, episodically adopt rights-based policies with consequences for the transnational corporation.

The rough coherence of these developments with one another and within the larger framework of international law suggests that corporate counsel and management ignore this recent history at their peril. But it is a mistake to assume that change is occurring only within the corporate world. In fact, the international human rights movement is in a reciprocal process of transformation. A movement that has focused almost exclusively on state actors must now grapple with the range of complex relationships among governments, people, and organizations. Human rights advocacy, which has traditionally emphasized such rights as bodily integrity and political expression, has broadened its focus to include economic concerns like the rights of labor, the transparency of government operations, and the protections of private property. The recommendations of human rights advocates and non-governmental organizations increasingly reflect sophisticated economic models of advocacy, explicitly defending the long-term profitability of human rights protection and unifying the rights of political dissidents with the interests of transnational corporations under the rubric of "the rule of law."

This module explores this emerging, controversial order and the legal premises on which it rests, suggesting that the corporate human rights movement consists of four separate but compatible regimes of doctrine and practice:

(i) *a market-based regime*, under which corporations compete for consumers and investors by attempting to conform to international human rights standards or a substantial subset of them;

(ii) *a regime of domestic regulation*, exemplified by directives and legislation in the United States which, through human rights conditionality, recruit the transnational corporation as an instrument of foreign policy;

(iii) *a regime of civil liability*, enforced through private lawsuits in domestic courts and exemplified by recent actions under the Alien Tort Statute, such as *Doe v. Unocal, Presbyterian Church v. Talisman*, and the Holocaust litigation; and

(iv) *a regime of international regulation and quasi-regulation by intergovernmental organizations*, which have attempted to channel corporate conduct in ways that are thought to be socially responsible.

Although each of these regimes is grounded in international and domestic law, the field of corporate responsibility continues to be in flux.

In fact, crucial as these developments are, it is important to acknowledge the most pointed objections to them, *e.g.*, that social responsibility movements subvert the implicit promise of corporations to their shareholders or require expertise that corporations cannot be expected to have; that none of the four regimes is conspicuously successful in protecting human rights, and none adequately distinguishes degrees of corporate culpability or gives adequate advance notice of the corporation's human rights responsibilities; that *Unocal* and its progeny impose a uniquely American form of liability that disadvantages U.S. corporations in the global marketplace; and that imposing greater human rights obligations just as corporations are voluntarily beginning to undertake them demonstrates the truism that no good deed goes unpunished.

It is equally important to recognize potential objections from the human rights perspective, especially the argument that the current body of corporate human rights concerns is pretextual, unambitious, skewed towards labor rights, and unenforceable. Many human rights advocates resist any argument to the effect that a corporate human rights agenda is "good business" because that argument commodifies basic principles of human dignity and thus surrenders the moral high ground. In this view, corporations should protect human rights because it is the right thing to do, whether it is profitable or not. Moreover, critics argue, shifting the focus to economic rights or forcing all human rights under the "rule of law" rubric undermines whatever coherence the human rights movement has achieved over the last half-century.

These objections are far from trivial, though in our view they are insufficient to derail the corporate human rights initiative altogether. Instead, they define and illuminate a middle path, maintaining the general impetus towards corporate responsibility in the human rights field but justifying a global standard that is so grounded in international law as to offer corporations a measure of protection from aggressive or idiosyncratic approaches to human rights.

Finally, it should be noted that the corporate responsibility initiative shares some essential characteristics with the ancient *lex mercatoria*: a set of good mercantile practices, growing out of the needs and customs of the marketplace, that ultimately gave rise to law in more recognizable and more enforceable form, like the Uniform Commercial Code and the Customs and Usages governing Documentary Letters of Credit. In short, *lex mercatoria* consisted in a body of authority that was (and remains to this day) transnational in scope, grounded in good faith, reflective of market practices, and later codified in the commercial law of the various nations and in international law.

If a new law of corporate human rights responsibility emerges from this "buzzing, blooming confusion" of developments and initiatives, it would not be the first time that law had gradually crystallized from commercial practices that were grounded in what the entrepreneurial class considered to be its own long-term self-interest.

CASE STUDIES: FOUR REGIMES OF PRINCIPLE AND PRACTICE

1. A MARKET REGIME: HUMAN RIGHTS ENTREPRENEU-RIALISM

The evidence of corporations' market-driven commitment to human rights takes many forms:

(i) *"Rights–Sensitive" Product Lines and Branding*. Many transnational companies have determined that a profitable contingent of consumers will pay a premium for some assurance that the goods they purchase are not produced or marketed in violation of the rights of workers and communities. Starbucks has periodically offered "fair trade" coffees, noting in print on every cup that the production and marketing of its products harm neither coffee workers nor the environment. Chiquita, having adopted an independently-verifiable social and environmental standard for its banana farms in Latin America, has marketed an "Ethical Banana" in response to consumer demand, especially in Europe.[2] And, aware of the problem of "conflict diamonds," the World Diamond Council developed a protocol for assuring that the profits from the sale of gems do not support governments or paramilitary groups that abuse civilians[3] and promoted the "Kimberley Process"— international negotiations on the creation of a reliable and permanent system of combating the illicit trade in diamonds. Similarly, the apparel industry—often in partnership with human rights NGOs—has adopted various workplace codes of conduct and principles of monitoring in order to eliminate sweatshop practices.[4] The awareness that rights-sensitive product lines and branding offer a competitive advantage is thus established across industry types and political borders, even if its translation into corporate practice is only episodic.

(ii) *Unilateral Codes of Conduct.* Beginning in the early 1990s, a handful of companies began unilaterally to adopt statements of general business principles, which purported to institutionalize the company's commitment to good practices. In 1991, for example, Levi Strauss adopted its "Global Sourcing and Operating Guidelines," which declared that "we will favor business partners who share our commitment to contribute to improving community conditions" and "may withdraw production from [any factory that violates these standards] or require that a contractor implement a corrective action plan within a specified time period." The company also adopted "Country Assessment Guidelines," to enable it to assess the possibility of harm to its reputation from doing business in a particular country. Among the criteria used in the Guidelines is "whether the [h]uman rights environment would prevent us from conducting business activities in a manner that is consistent with the Global Sourcing Guidelines and other company policies." The company's well-publicized decision to withdraw from Burma in 1992 gave effect to these policies.[5] Similar statements of policy followed from Reebok and The Body Shop, among many others. Whether these initial,

---

2. The standard is administered by the Rainforest Alliance, an international non-profit organization responsible for certifying farms under its Better Banana Project (BBP). Complying with the BBP reportedly cost Chiquita more than $20 million in capital expenditure, and millions more in annual operating costs, but Chiquita's quality director in Europe judged the money to have been well-invested: "Many of our retail customers would not be doing business with us unless we had a really thorough and deeply rooted programme like this," *quoted at* http://www.ethicalperformance. co.uk/bestpractice/casestudy.php?articID=8.

3. World Diamond Council, Joint Resolution of the World Federation of Diamond Bourses and the International Diamond Manufacturers Association (19 July 2000). The Kimberley Process Certification Scheme has been specifically approved by the United Nations in recognition that it

can help to ensure the effective implementation of relevant resolutions of the Security Council containing sanctions on the trade in conflict diamonds and act as a mechanism for the prevention of future conflicts, and calls for the full implementation of existing Council measures targeting the illicit trade in rough diamonds, particularly conflict diamonds which play a role in fuelling conflict.

UN Doc. A/62/L.16 (Nov. 21. 2007).

4. *See, e.g.,* in Europe, the Clean Clothes Campaign, *Code of Labour Practices for the Apparel Industry Including Sportswear, available at* http://www.cleanclothes.org/cccodes.htm; in the United States, the Fair Labor Association, *Workplace Code of Conduct* and *Principles of Monitoring, available at* http://www.fairlabor.org/.

5. "Under current circumstances, it is not possible to do business in Myanmar without directly supporting the military government and its pervasive violations of human rights." T. Smith, *Transnational Influence: The Power of Business, in* HUMAN RIGHTS: THE NEW CONSENSUS 151 (1994).

unilateral corporate commitments made any immediate or verifiable difference in the lives of workers or of citizens is inevitably a matter for speculation. But the fact that *other* companies—like Royal Dutch Shell, Exxon–Mobil, Nike, Liz Claiborne—adopted similar policies suggests that the advantages of human rights entrepreneurialism were not lost on competitors or the commercial world generally.

(iii) *Social Accountability Auditing and Certification.* In an effort to standardize the various corporate codes and to define corporate social responsibility across firms and across industry sectors, some multinational companies—often in partnership with human rights organizations and trade unions—have adopted verifiable standards governing conditions in the workplace. Social Accountability (SA) 8000, for example, offers a voluntary process under which independent auditors may certify that a company complies with standards in nine essential areas: child labor, forced labor, health and safety, freedom of association, freedom from discrimination, disciplinary practices, work hours, compensation, and management systems to assure compliance.[6] The standards themselves are drawn from conventions of the International Labour Organisation, the Universal Declaration on Human Rights, and the U.N. Convention on the Rights of the Child, *inter alia*. Like other auditable standards, including ISO 9000 (establishing quality control standards) and ISO 14001 (establishing environmental management standards), SA 8000 and similar standards allow companies to differentiate themselves from their uncertified competitors. Admittedly, SA 8000 may be objectionable on the ground that it purports to quantify the unquantifiable or requires for its success a consumer who is both insensible to price and implausibly well-informed. But the practical value of industry certification standards may lie in their potential to alter the commercial relationship between a company and its suppliers, who, because the standards apply upstream, have a clear competitive incentive to seek, receive, and advertise certification.

(iv) *Ethical investment organizations and shareholder pressure.* Human rights concerns are present in the investment market as well as the consumer market. Individual and institutional investors have increasingly followed "social" or "ethical" criteria, both in screening their initial investments and—perhaps more effectively—in voting their shares as stockholders, with the result that management must increasingly respond to investors' calls for "sustainable business," *i.e.*, business "that enhances long-term shareholder value by addressing the needs of all relevant stakeholders and adding economic, environmental, and social value through its core business functions."[7] Major stock markets have

---

6. SA 8000 was developed by the Council on Economic Priorities Accreditation Agency, now Social Accountability International. The text of SA 8000 is available at http://www.sa-intl.org (visited 8 May 2008). As of this writing, over 700 firms, in over 35 countries and representing over 30 industries, have been certified under SA 8000. Factory certification is valid for three years, with surveillance audits at six-month intervals.

7. *Tim Dickson, The* Financial Case for Behaving Responsibly, FINANCIAL TIMES (August 19, 2002), at 5.

also developed social indices for the guidance of investors, such as the Dow Jones STOXX Sustainability Index and the London FTSE4Good index. Major investment houses have also developed ethical-investment mutual funds (*e.g.*, Dreyfus' Third Century Fund and Merrill Lynch's Ecological Trust), and an ethical consulting industry has emerged to assist companies manage risk by adhering to the norms of corporate citizenship.

HESS CORPORATION, CORPORATE POLICIES

http://www.hess.com/ehs/policies.htm

The following are formal Hess policies that provide our employees with guidance and Company-wide expectations regarding environment, health, safety and social responsibility:

* * *

Corporate Social Responsibility Policy: Hess Corporation and its subsidiaries conduct business consistent with our long established values which encompass product quality, service to our customers and making positive contributions to the communities where we do business. Corporate social responsibility is an extension of the way we have done, and will continue to do, our business. We reaffirm our commitment and will:

— Maintain the highest standards of business and personal integrity as detailed in our Business Practice Guide.

— Respect the law in the countries and communities where we operate and accept and uphold the principles contained in the United Nations Universal Declaration of Human Rights.

— Maintain our commitment to an equal employment opportunity workforce and encourage diversity.

— Build cooperative relationships with our customers, suppliers, host governments, other companies and communities concerning these issues.

— Identify and understand the potential social and cultural impacts of our operations in new areas prior to making major investments.

— Identify and assess our contribution to social and cultural changes in the areas where we operate and develop appropriate strategies to respect the rights and cultures of local communities.

— Routinely monitor, assess and report on our conformity with this policy.

Voluntary Initiatives: Hess supports several international voluntary initiatives designed to protect the environment and promote universal human rights. These include:

— *United Nations Universal Declaration of Human Rights*: Comprised of 30 articles covering fundamental freedoms ranging from the right to nationality to the right to equality before the law, the Universal Declaration of Human Rights was established in 1948 by the UN General Assembly. It serves as the international standard and codification of human rights norms.

* * *

— *United Nations Global Compact*—The UN Global Compact is a voluntary initiative that seeks to provide a global framework to promote sustainable growth and good citizenship through adherence to 10 principles encompassing environment, human rights and anti-corruption.

— *Voluntary Principles on Security and Human Rights*: The Voluntary Principles on Security and Human Rights is a voluntary guide for companies to assure the safety and security of their operations while respecting human rights and fundamental freedoms. Voluntary Principles participants include the Governments of the United States, United Kingdom, the Netherlands and Norway, companies in the extractive and energy sectors, and non-governmental organizations. The participants recognize the importance of the promotion and protection of human rights throughout the world and the constructive role business and civil society play—including non-governmental organizations, labor/trade unions, and local communities—can play in advancing these goals.

— *Extractive Industries Transparency Initiative*: 3.5 billion people live in countries rich in oil, gas and minerals. With good governance the exploitation of these resources can generate large revenues to foster growth and reduce poverty. However, when governance is weak, it may result in poverty, corruption, and conflict. The Extractive Industries Transparency Initiative (EITI) aims to strengthen governance by improving transparency and accountability in the extractives sector. The EITI sets a global standard for companies to publish what they pay and for governments to disclose what they receive.

THE VOLUNTARY PRINCIPLES ON SECURITY AND HUMAN RIGHTS[1]

http://www.voluntaryprinciples.org

Acknowledging that security is a fundamental need, shared by individuals, communities, businesses and governments alike, and acknow-

---

1. [Editors' note: As of this writing, the corporations participating in the Voluntary Principles are Amerada Hess Corporation, Anglo Gold Ashanti, Anglo American,BG Group, BHP Billiton, BP, ChevronTexaco, ConocoPhillips, ExxonMobil, Freeport McMoRan Copper and Gold, Hydro, Marathon Oil, Newmont Mining Corporation, Occidental Petroleum Corporation, Rio Tinto, Shell,

ledging the difficult security issues faced by Companies operating globally, we recognize that security and respect for human rights can and
should be consistent;

Understanding that governments have the primary responsibility to
promote and protect human rights and that all parties to a conflict are
obliged to observe applicable international humanitarian law, we recognize that we share the common goal of promoting respect for human
rights, particularly those set forth in the Universal Declaration of
Human Rights, and international humanitarian law;

Emphasizing the importance of safeguarding the integrity of company personnel and property, Companies recognize a commitment to act
in a manner consistent with the laws of the countries within which they
are present, to be mindful of the highest applicable international standards, and to promote the observance of applicable international law
enforcement principles (e.g., the U.N. Code of Conduct for Law Enforcement Officials and the U.N. Basic Principles on the Use of Force
and Firearms by Law Enforcement Officials), particularly with regard to
the use of force;

Taking note of the effect that Companies' activities may have on local
communities, we recognize the value of engaging with civil society and
host and home governments to contribute to the welfare of the local
community while mitigating any potential for conflict where possible;

* * *

We hereby express our support for the following voluntary principles regarding security and human rights in the extractive sector. * * *

Interactions Between Companies and Public Security

Although governments have the primary role of maintaining law
and order, security and respect for human rights, Companies have an
interest in ensuring that actions taken by governments, particularly the
actions of public security providers, are consistent with the protection
and promotion of human rights. In cases where there is a need to
supplement security provided by host governments, Companies may be
required or expected to contribute to, or otherwise reimburse, the costs
of protecting Company facilities and personnel borne by public security.
While public security is expected to act in a manner consistent with local
and national laws as well as with human rights standards and international humanitarian law, within this context abuses may nevertheless
occur.

In an effort to reduce the risk of such abuses and to promote
respect for human rights generally, we have identified the following

StatoilHydro, and Talisman Energy. On the evolution and meaning of the Voluntary Principles
generally, *see* Bennett Freeman, Maria B. Pica, & Christopher N. Camponovo, *A New Approach to
Corporate Responsibility: The Voluntary Principles on Security and Human Rights*, 24 HASTINGS INT'L &
COMP. L. REV. 423 (2001).]

voluntary principles to guide relationships between Companies and public security regarding security provided to Companies:

Security Arrangements

• Companies should consult regularly with host governments and local communities about the impact of their security arrangements on those communities.

• Companies should communicate their policies regarding ethical conduct and human rights to public security providers, and express their desire that security be provided in a manner consistent with those policies by personnel with adequate and effective training. * * *

Deployment and Conduct
* * *

• Equipment imports and exports should comply with all applicable law and regulations. Companies that provide equipment to public security should take all appropriate and lawful measures to mitigate any foreseeable negative consequences, including human rights abuses and violations of international humanitarian law.

• Companies should use their influence to promote the following principles with public security: (a) individuals credibly implicated in human rights abuses should not provide security services for Companies; (b) force should be used only when strictly necessary and to an extent proportional to the threat; and (c) the rights of individuals should not be violated while exercising the right to exercise freedom of association and peaceful assembly, the right to engage in collective bargaining, or other related rights of Company employees as recognized by the Universal Declaration of Human Rights and the ILO Declaration on Fundamental Principles and Rights at Work. * * *

Consultation and Advice * * *

• In their consultations with host governments, Companies should take all appropriate measures to promote observance of applicable international law enforcement principles, particularly those reflected in the U.N. Code of Conduct for Law Enforcement Officials and the U.N. Basic Principles on the Use of Force and Firearms.

• Companies should support efforts by governments, civil society and multilateral institutions to provide human rights training and education for public security as well as their efforts to strengthen state institutions to ensure accountability and respect for human rights.

Responses to Human Rights Abuses

• Companies should record and report any credible allegations of human rights abuses by public security in their areas of operation to appropriate host government authorities. Where appropriate, Companies should urge investigation and that action be taken to prevent any recurrence.

● Companies should actively monitor the status of investigations and press for their proper resolution.

● Companies should, to the extent reasonable, monitor the use of equipment provided by the Company and to investigate properly situations in which such equipment is used in an inappropriate manner.

● Every effort should be made to ensure that information used as the basis for allegations of human rights abuses is credible and based on reliable evidence. The security and safety of sources should be protected. Additional or more accurate information that may alter previous allegations should be made available as appropriate to concerned parties.

Interactions Between Companies and Private Security

Where host governments are unable or unwilling to provide adequate security to protect a Company's personnel or assets, it may be necessary to engage private security providers as a complement to public security. In this context, private security may have to coordinate with state forces, (law enforcement, in particular) to carry weapons and to consider the defensive local use of force. Given the risks associated with such activities, we recognize the following voluntary principles to guide private security conduct:

● Private security should observe the policies of the contracting Company regarding ethical conduct and human rights; the law and professional standards of the country in which they operate; emerging best practices developed by industry, civil society, and governments; and promote the observance of international humanitarian law. * * *

● Private security should act in a lawful manner. They should exercise restraint and caution in a manner consistent with applicable international guidelines regarding the local use of force, including the UN Principles on the Use of Force and Firearms by Law Enforcement Officials and the UN Code of Conduct for Law Enforcement Officials, as well as with emerging best practices developed by Companies, civil society, and governments.

● Private security should have policies regarding appropriate conduct and the local use of force (*e.g.*, rules of engagement). Practice under these policies should be capable of being monitored by Companies or, where appropriate, by independent third parties. Such monitoring should encompass detailed investigations into allegations of abusive or unlawful acts; the availability of disciplinary measures sufficient to prevent and deter; and procedures for reporting allegations to relevant local law enforcement authorities when appropriate.

- All allegations of human rights abuses by private security should be recorded. Credible allegations should be properly investigated. In those cases where allegations against private security providers are forwarded to the relevant law enforcement authorities, Companies should actively monitor the status of investigations and press for their proper resolution.

- Consistent with their function, private security should provide only preventative and defensive services and should not engage in activities exclusively the responsibility of state military or law enforcement authorities. Companies should designate services, technology and equipment capable of offensive and defensive purposes as being for defensive use only.

- Private security should (a) not employ individuals credibly implicated in human rights abuses to provide security services; (b) use force only when strictly necessary and to an extent proportional to the threat; and (c) not violate the rights of individuals while exercising the right to exercise freedom of association and peaceful assembly, to engage in collective bargaining, or other related rights of Company employees as recognized by the Universal Declaration of Human Rights and the ILO Declaration on Fundamental Principles and Rights at Work.

- In cases where physical force is used, private security should properly investigate and report the incident to the Company. Private security should refer the matter to local authorities and/or take disciplinary action where appropriate. Where force is used, medical aid should be provided to injured persons, including to offenders.

- Private security should maintain the confidentiality of information obtained as a result of its position as security provider, except where to do so would jeopardize the principles contained herein.

To minimize the risk that private security exceed their authority as providers of security, and to promote respect for human rights generally, we have developed the following additional voluntary principles and guidelines:

- Where appropriate, Companies should include the principles outlined above as contractual provisions in agreements with private security providers and ensure that private security personnel are adequately trained to respect the rights of employees and the local community. To the extent practicable, agreements between Companies and private security should require investigation of unlawful or abusive behavior and appropriate disciplinary action. Agreements should also permit termination of the relationship by Companies where there is credible evidence of unlawful or abusive behavior by private security personnel. * * *

- Companies should review the background of private security they intend to employ, particularly with regard to the use of excessive force. Such reviews should include an assessment of previous services provided to the host government and whether these services raise concern about the private security firm's dual role as a private security provider and government contractor.

• Companies should consult with other Companies, home country officials, host country officials, and civil society regarding experiences with private security. Where appropriate and lawful, Companies should facilitate the exchange of information about unlawful activity and abuses committed by private security providers.

FAIR LABOR ASSOCIATION
WORKPLACE CODE OF CONDUCT[2]

Forced Labor: There shall not be any use of forced labor, whether in the form of prison labor, indentured labor, bonded labor or otherwise.

Child Labor: No person shall be employed at an age younger than 15 (or 14 where the law of the country of manufacture allows) or younger than the age for completing compulsory education in the country of manufacture where such age is higher than 15.

Harassment or Abuse: Every employee shall be treated with respect and dignity. No employee shall be subject to any physical, sexual, psychological or verbal harassment or abuse.

Nondiscrimination: No person shall be subject to any discrimination in employment, including hiring, salary, benefits, advancement, discipline, termination or retirement, on the basis of gender, race, religion, age, disability, sexual orientation, nationality, political opinion, or social or ethnic origin.

Health and Safety: Employers shall provide a safe and healthy working environment to prevent accidents and injury to health arising out of, linked with, or occurring in the course of work or as a result of the operation of employer facilities.

Freedom of Association and Collective Bargaining: Employers shall recognize and respect the right of employees to freedom of association and collective bargaining.

Wages and Benefits: Employers recognize that wages are essential to meeting employees' basic needs. Employers shall pay employees, as a floor, at least the minimum wage required by local law or the prevailing industry wage, whichever is higher, and shall provide legally mandated benefits.

Hours of Work: Except in extraordinary business circumstances, employees shall (i) not be required to work more than the lesser of (a) 48 hours

---

2. *Available at* www.fairlabor.org/all/code (including the Principles of Monitoring referred to below).

per week and 12 hours overtime or (b) the limits on regular and overtime hours allowed by the law of the country of manufacture or, where the laws of such country do not limit the hours of work, the regular work week in such country plus 12 hours overtime and (ii) be entitled to at least one day off in every seven day period.

Overtime Compensation: In addition to their compensation for regular hours of work, employees shall be compensated for overtime hours at such premium rate as is legally required in the country of manufacture or, in those countries where such laws do not exist, at a rate at least equal to their regular hourly compensation rate.

Any Company that determines to adopt the Workplace Code of Conduct shall, in addition to complying with all applicable laws of the country of manufacture, comply with and support the Workplace Code of Conduct in accordance with the attached Principles of Monitoring and shall apply the higher standard in cases of differences or conflicts. Any Company that determines to adopt the Workplace Code of Conduct also shall require its licensees and contractors and, in the case of a retailer, its suppliers to comply with applicable local laws and with this Code in accordance with the Principles of Monitoring and to apply the higher standard in cases of differences or conflicts.

NOTES AND QUESTIONS ON THE MARKET REGIME

1. *The variety of voluntary instruments.* How would you articulate the substantive legal differences among these three "market-based" instruments? What accounts for those differences?

2. *Justifying corporate responsibility norms.* It is fundamental that governments bear the primary legal responsibility for respecting, protecting, and promoting human rights. It is equally fundamental that corporations must abide by the domestic law of the states in which they operate. What is the justification for imposing *any* international legal obligations on private companies to protect human rights? One contemporaneous school of management theory has challenged the notion that corporations owe anything other than legal, profitable operations to anyone other than stockholders, noting in the famous phrase of Milton Friedman that "the social responsibility of business is to increase its profits." On the other hand, over the last decade, many prominent transnational corporations have adopted statements of general business principles, like the Hess policy, *supra*, which typically include the protection of at least some human rights, especially of workers, and industry-wide coalitions have committed themselves to similar precepts. Because they are defended in part as attempts to attract both customers and investors, these statements of principle implicitly repudiate the assumption that social responsibility is inherently unprofitable, but, for that

reason, they also provoke the suspicion that the corporate commitment to human rights is neither altruistic nor particularly credible.

These market-based initiatives have provoked their share of cynicism not least because the companies alleged to be complicit in abuses are frequently the very companies that adopt human rights principles with the greatest public fanfare, and there is nothing other than the market to "enforce" these various standards. But, even if accurate, this critique misses the essential characteristic of the market-based regime, namely that it is compelled not so much by law as by potentially powerful commercial incentives. As articulated by the UN High Commissioner for Human Rights, the commercial advantages of corporate compliance with human rights standards include:

(1) ensuring compliance with local and international laws;

(2) satisfying consumer concerns;

(3) promoting the rule of law, by contributing to 'the development of legal systems in which contracts are enforced fairly, bribery and corruption are less prevalent and all business entities have equal access to legal process and equal protection under law';

(4) building community goodwill;

(5) improving supply chain management by selecting business partners that are well-managed and reliable;

(6) enhancing risk management by assuring more stable and productive business operations;

(7) keeping markets open;

(8) increasing worker productivity and retention; and

(9) applying corporate values in a way that maintains 'the faith of employees and external stakeholders in company integrity'.

UN High Commissioner for Human Rights, *Business and Human Rights: A Progress Report, available at* http://www.unhchr.ch/business.htm. Are you convinced? How would you go about confirming whether these advantages actually follow from a corporation's commitment to social responsibility?

3. *Legal value of the marketplace instruments.* As a matter of law, what does it mean for a multinational corporation to "accept and uphold the principles contained in the United Nations Universal Declaration of Human Rights" as in the Hess Corporation policy? What are the legal obligations—if any—of a corporation that adheres to the Voluntary Principles, which refer to the UN Code of Conduct for Law Enforcement Officials and the UN Basic Principles on the Use of Force and Firearms by Law Enforcement Officials. [Both of these United Nations documents are in the Documents Supplement.] If your conclusion is that these voluntary codes of conduct are purely public relations documents, is that necessarily useless to a lawyer? If you were a lawyer for a corporation considering the adoption of such a code, with the profes-

sional obligation to represent your client's interest zealously, what would your advice be?

4. *Using hypocrisy.* From one perspective, some of the most profound advances in human rights law have been the result of rank hypocrisy. If we assume for example that governments endorsed the Universal Declaration of Human Rights in 1948 precisely because it was non-binding and that they had no intention of reforming their existing human rights practices, the Declaration has nonetheless ratcheted towards law and become an authoritative interpretation of states' human rights obligations under the UN Charter. At a minimum, it qualifies as primary evidence of customary human rights law. Similarly, if the Soviet Union had no intention of abiding by the human rights standards of the Helsinki Accords in 1976, the agreement nonetheless released ideas with force in eastern Europe, giving rise to the Solidarity Movement in Poland and the fall of Communism a decade later. Does that history affect your assessment of the corporate codes in any way?

5. *Precursors to the corporate human rights movement.* The recent effort by corporations to compete for sales and capital through a public commitment to international human rights—"human rights entrepreneurialism"—had its precursors in the anti-apartheid and pro-environment movements. The Sullivan Principles, first articulated in 1977, amounted to a voluntary code of conduct for companies doing business in South Africa under the apartheid regime. The principles required integrated workplaces, fair employment practices, and affirmative action, and a signatory company's compliance with these principles was assessed by independent auditors. The Sullivan Principles not only offered an alternative to divestment, as urged by some stockholders and activists, it also blunted the periodic efforts to impose economic sanctions on South Africa or to ban foreign companies from doing business there. The principles also gave companies an objective, common standard under which their presence in South Africa might be defended in the competition for a good corporate image. In 1984, with some 125 signatories, the principles were expanded to require companies to take more aggressive action against apartheid, tantamount to corporate civil disobedience. The principles provided a benchmark for the managers of municipal pension funds and university endowments and were ultimately incorporated in an executive order adopted by President Reagan. Exec. Order 12352, 50 Fed. Reg. 36861 (1985). They also served as the model for the MacBride Principles, which articulated a code of conduct for companies doing business in Northern Ireland. But by 1987, with only glacial change in South Africa, even the drafters of the Sullivan Principles considered them a failure and urged corporations to withdraw from South Africa altogether.

6. *Socially-responsible investing ("SRI").* One study for the Organization for Economic Cooperation and Development concluded in 2006 that more than $5 trillion in assets were managed by SRI funds around the world. But the profitability and the effectiveness of ethical invest-

ment are difficult to measure. Some data suggest that high-profile corporate scandals in 2002 led to an increase in SRI and that socially responsible mutual funds significantly out-performed diversified funds. *See* Social Investment Forum, *Market Slump Providing Unexpected Boost to Socially Responsible Mutual Funds* (July 2002), *available at* http://www.tbli. org/newsletter/0208_newsletter.html. There is also anecdotal evidence that pension fund managers exert ethical leverage through negative screening and divestment. Consider for example the Norwegian Government Pension Fund, one of the largest investment funds in the world (valued at roughly $400 billion and growing). The Norwegian Parliament adopted ethical standards for the investment of that fund, administered by the Ministry of Finance, to assure that no investment contributed to unethical acts, such as violations of fundamental humanitarian principles, serious violations of human rights, gross corruption, or severe environmental degradation. *See* http://www.norway.org/business/ businessnews/ethicoil.html. In June 2006, the Fund withdrew over $400 million from shares in Wal–Mart on human rights grounds. *See Norway Keeps Nest Egg from Some U.S. Companies*, N.Y. TIMES (June 4, 2007). Similarly, in 2002, the largest pension fund in the United States decided to pull out of four East Asian countries—Thailand, the Philippines, Malaysia, and Indonesia—despite the fact that these countries had some of the best performing economies in Asia, and it did so primarily because of its human rights concerns in those nations, especially reports of forced labor, discrimination, and interference with the freedom of association. *See* Lesley Curwen & Manuela Saragosa, *Major Pension Fund Quits Asian Countries: Malaysia's Human Rights Record Prompted Calpers Exit*, BBC WORLD BUSINESS REPORT (February 21, 2002). "Conscientious proxy statements" and shareholder resolutions led to substantial corporate pullouts from Burma in the 1990s and from South Africa in the 1980s, and high-profile investigations of child labor practices led to a restructuring of supply chain relationships in many industries explicitly in order to maintain share value. For a more contemporary example of this corporate behavior, *see* "Gap Pulls 'Child Labour Clothing' " (BBC News October 28, 2007).

7. *The Rise and Convergence of NGOs.* An integral part of human rights entrepreneurialism has been the rise of non-governmental organizations that are specifically devoted to assuring that human rights norms are respected in the marketplace. Some NGOs have developed standard reporting guidelines (*e.g.*, Global Reporting Initiative), and others have emerged to report on companies' social performance (*e.g.*, Global Witness, the Investor Responsibility Research Center, the Ecumenical Council for Corporate Responsibility). Non-governmental organizations with traditional human rights mandates, such as Amnesty International and Human Rights Watch, have increasingly criticized private companies for their role in human rights abuse, as have consumer, labor, religious, and cultural NGOs. These groups may be especially effective in organizing publicity campaigns and boycotts in response to perceived instances of

corporate irresponsibility. Perhaps more telling are the non-adversarial relationships that have developed between human rights NGOs and business leadership NGOs, which have jointly engaged in public information and outreach campaigns. *See, e.g.*, Amnesty International and the Prince of Wales International Business Leaders Forum, *Business and Human Rights: A Geography of Corporate Risk*, available at http://www.iblf.org/resources/general.jsp?id=69. Even before the traditional human rights NGOs focused on the issue, business groups were developing norms of corporate citizenship and modes of implementation. The Caux Roundtable, comprised of senior business leaders from Europe, Japan, and North America, was one of the first organizations of any sort to articulate *Principles for Business*—an aspirational set of recommendations covering a wide range of corporate behavior.

8. *Historical antecedents.* There is nothing particularly modern about the perspective that corporations can be complicit in the violation of human rights. *See, e.g.*, Adam Hochschild, King Leopold's Ghost: A Story of Greed, Terror, and Heroism in Colonial Africa (1999) (describing the role of various private entities, in relationship with the King of Belgium, in the exploitation of the Congo); Teemu Ruskola, *Conceptualizing Corporations and Kinship: Comparative Law and Development Theory in a Chinese Perspective*, 52 Stanford L. Rev. 1599, 1677 *et seq.* (2002) (describing the depredations of the British East India Company).

---

2. A REGIME OF DOMESTIC REGULATION

Supplementing—and perhaps provoking—the market-based, self-regulating mechanisms just described are domestic regulatory initiatives which require or encourage the protection of human rights in the marketplace by companies. In a variety of countries, the last decade has seen the proliferation of legislation that attempts to recruit the transnational corporation as an instrument of foreign policy. This legislation may for example (i) bar any corporate presence in, or transactions with, certain countries where human rights are not respected; or (ii) require certain corporate practices (especially with respect to workers' rights); or (iii) condition government contracts, market access, and other benefits on a corporation's compliance with international human rights norms; or (iv) require transparency and disclosure to the consuming and investing public about the human rights consequences of its business decisions. As the following examples from the United States suggest, this domestic legislation is typically episodic and limited either geographically to particular countries (like Burma or South Africa under *apartheid*) or substantively to particular human rights violations (like forced labor). There is no domestic legislation anywhere in the world that defines a comprehensive, enforceable code of human rights conduct for multinational corporations, though it is possible to identify common themes or approaches in this body of law and to mark its slow evolution towards breadth and definition.

One statutory precedent in the United States offers an instructive if cautionary tale in the move towards legislating corporations' human rights responsibilities: the Foreign Corrupt Practices Act of 1977 ("FCPA").[1] The FCPA prohibited any publicly-traded company in the United States from paying bribes to a foreign official. Growing out of a series of bribery scandals that had compromised U.S. foreign relations with Chile, Italy, the Netherlands, and Japan, the FCPA was initially resisted by American businesses on the ground that it would subject them to a unique form of liability and thereby put them at a distinct competitive disadvantage. But by the early 1990s,

> attitudes began to change. It was becoming increasingly clear that the dimensions of the bribery problem were much greater than many thought. In addition to recognizing the debilitating effect on government and on public trust in government, widespread bribery came to be seen as leading itself to a serious misallocation of resources. Developing nations in particular could ill afford such waste. The adverse effect of official corruption on investments was also becoming increasingly apparent. An IMF study suggested that there was a demonstrable inverse relationship between the level of corruption prevalent in a country and the level of investment as a percent of domestic product.[2]

In quick succession, public and private actors embraced the principles (if not the details) of the FCPA.

Thus, instead of illustrating the tendency of the United States to legislate morality extraterritorially—hurting only U.S. companies in the process—the FCPA offered an organizing principle for a new business culture; indeed, the FCPA is now routinely cited by U.S. firms as the exemplar of progressive legislation, protecting them from the importuning of foreign officials and improving the quality of competition in the global marketplace. Certainly issues of interpretation and application persist, and what change has occurred took a generation to achieve, but the FCPA does provide a striking example of how domestic legislation can give rise to a consensus for change and international standard-setting, so long as it is grounded in both moral and economic principle and so long as it is not persistently overbroad.

The preliminary outlines of a similar legislative and cultural dynamic are discernible with respect to human rights in the marketplace:

(i) *Transactional controls: imports, exports, and sanctions.* Legislation and executive regulation clearly provide for the imposition of trade sanctions on particular countries where human rights abuses are profound and widespread, as in Burma and apartheid South Africa. During the Cold

---

1.   Foreign Corrupt Practices Act, codified at 15 U.S.C. § 78m, § 78dd–1 & 2, and §§ 78ff.

2.   ALAN SWAN & JOHN MURPHY, CASES AND MATERIALS ON THE REGULATION OF INTERNATIONAL BUSINESS AND ECONOMIC RELATIONS 831 (2d ed. 1999).

War, especially after 1974 when the Jackson–Vanik Amendment to the Trade Act was adopted, the United States could use human rights concerns—especially emigration—to restrict trade with communist countries. The sanctions for these pervasive violations generally run state-to-state, but multinational corporations are clearly affected by them, and they may even be complicit in the conditions that trigger the sanctions in the first place. When the commerce is itself a form of human rights abuse for example—as in human trafficking—a range of trade sanctions may be imposed. As shown in module 10, Congress has also linked trade preferences with the protection of "internationally recognized worker rights." Executive regulation has similarly targeted the importation of goods that are "mined, produced, or manufactured wholly or in part by forced or indentured child labor."[3]

(ii) *Administrative law: linking government benefits to social performance criteria*. One way that domestic legislation can induce compliance with human rights standards is to assure that no public money is spent facilitating or enabling human rights violations, even if that effect is achieved indirectly through the operations of private companies. For example, certain provisions of U.S. law make workers' rights relevant to government decision-making, especially in foreign aid and public-sector financing. Amendments to the Foreign Assistance Act of 1961 for example bar funding any program of the Agency for International Development which contributes to the denial of "internationally recognized worker rights," 22 U.S.C. 2151 *et seq.* (1992), and require executive officers "to use the voice and vote of the United States to urge [international financial institutions] * * * to adopt policies to encourage borrowing countries to guarantee internationally recognized worker rights." 22 U.S.C. 1621 (1996). Incentives for the development of a private sector in former communist states were similarly made contingent on the protection of internationally recognized workers' rights.[4]

Other, more specific categories of human rights abuse are also targeted: the President may use his or her expansive authority under the International Emergency Economic Powers Act, *infra*, for example to combat trafficking in persons, and countries that violate international religious freedom may find that their companies are denied U.S. government contracts and a comprehensive range of other benefits. International Religious Freedom Act of 1998, 22 U.S.C. 6401, 6445.

Legislation linking government decision-making to human rights more broadly conceived is rare, but it exists. The Human Rights and Security Assistance Act, 22 U.S.C. 2304 (a)(2), for example, provides that "no security assistance may be provided to any country the government of which engages in a consistent pattern of gross violations of internationally recognized human rights. * * * [T]he term 'gross violations of internationally recognized human rights' includes torture or cruel,

---

3. Exec. Order 13126, Prohibition of Acquisition of Products Produced by Forced or Indentured Child Labor, 64 Fed. Reg. 32383 (1999).

4. *See, e.g.*, Support for East European Democracy Act of 1989, 22. U.S.C. 5421 (1989).

inhuman, or degrading treatment or punishment, prolonged detention without charges and trial, causing the disappearance of persons by the abduction and clandestine detention of those persons, and other flagrant denial of the right to life, liberty, or the security of person."

Similarly, the statute governing the Export–Import Bank of the United States generally requires that the decision to extend credit to a particular applicant or to finance a particular transaction abroad be guided by exclusively commercial considerations and good banking practice, but the statute also provides in part:

> *Only in cases where the President ... determines that such action would be in the national interest where such action would clearly and importantly advance United States policy in such areas as* international terrorism, nuclear proliferation, environmental protection and *human rights* (including child labor), *should the Export–Import Bank deny applications for credit for nonfinancial or non-commercial considerations.*[5]

Known as the "Chafee Amendment," this provision is hardly a model of clarity, but it assures at a minimum that the Export–Import Bank does not subsidize or underwrite egregious departures from the international law of human rights: an application for credit may be denied on otherwise impermissible non-commercial grounds if the President determines that such action "would clearly and importantly advance" the human rights policy of the United States.

(iii) *Holocaust restitution.* Over the last decade, in Europe and the United States, legislation has proliferated for the purpose of assuring that survivors of the Nazi Holocaust are offered compensation from the companies that were complicit in genocide, crimes against humanity, war crimes, and other egregious violations of human rights. Some of these laws require disclosure of business in Europe during the Nazi regime, especially in the insurance sector. Some allow the state insurance commissioner to suspend the operating license of any insurer that fails to pay any valid claim from a Holocaust survivor until that claim is paid. The broadest laws provide a cause of action to recover damages from corporations for the violation of some human rights standard, typically the use of slave labor. The constitutionality of state and local statutes with foreign policy implications remains contested, as suggested in the *Crosby* case, *infra*.

Although the evolving regime of domestic regulation can only be suggested by these examples, certain themes emerge. First, domestic legislation creates an increasingly dense regulatory environment in which corporate operations in violation of at least certain human rights standards pose legal risks to the company itself. The laws establishing U.S. import controls for example adopt a meaningful form of "human rights conditionality" in the international marketplace, even though they target only specific labor practices used in the production of particular goods introduced into the American market. Rights-sensitive export

---

5.   12 U.S.C. 635(b)(1)(B) (emphasis supplied).

controls by contrast are not necessarily limited to labor rights, but they tend to be limited geographically and politically, targeting only the most offensive states that also happen to have weak import markets (*e.g.* Sudan and Burma but not China and Russia). Broader-gauged legislation linking trade and human rights is unlikely to emerge until there is consensus on two recurring issues: whether human rights conditions are better advanced by "constructive engagement" with an abusive government or by its economic isolation, and whether human rights conditionality can be squared with the trade liberalization regime of the World Trade Organization. On the other hand, the trade statutes clearly are useful as a means of advancing an important if limited subset of human rights in an important if limited subset of states. And the disclosure provisions of national and state securities laws offer an untested but potentially powerful vehicle for improving corporate compliance with a broader range of human rights norms, driven by the markets' demand for information and transparency.

There is in addition this crucial historical perspective: experience with the FCPA and with the Depression-era securities laws suggests that the time lag between the adoption of legislation and the evolution of a responsive business culture can be measured in decades, and progress is almost never linear. But if the economic health of the market improves as that culture evolves, the stimulus provided by the threat of public enforcement of domestic law is gradually internalized by the corporate actors themselves: in that sense the market regime and the regime of domestic regulation may prove to be mutually reinforcing.

INTERNATIONAL EMERGENCY ECONOMIC POWERS ACT

50 U.S.C. 1701 *et seq.*

§ 1701. *Unusual and extraordinary threat; declaration of national emergency; exercise of Presidential authorities*

(a) Any authority granted to the President by section 1702 of this title may be exercised to deal with any unusual and extraordinary threat, which has its source in whole or substantial part outside the United States, to the national security, foreign policy, or economy of the United States, if the President declares a national emergency with respect to such threat.

(b) The authorities granted to the President by section 1702 of this title may only be exercised to deal with an unusual and extraordinary threat with respect to which a national emergency has been declared for purposes of this chapter and may not be exercised for any other purpose. Any exercise of such authorities to deal with any new threat shall be based on a new declaration of national emergency which must be with respect to such threat.

§ 1702. *Presidential authorities*

(a)(1) At the times and to the extent specified in section 1701 of this title, the President may, under such regulations as he may prescribe, by means of instructions, licenses, or otherwise

(A) investigate, regulate, or prohibit—

(i) any transactions in foreign exchange,

(ii) transfers of credit or payments between, by, through, or to any banking institution, to the extent that such transfers or payments involve any interest of any foreign country or a national thereof,

(iii) the importing or exporting of currency or securities, by any person, or with respect to any property, subject to the jurisdiction of the United States;

(B) investigate, block during the pendency of an investigation, regulate, direct and compel, nullify, void, prevent or prohibit, any acquisition, holding, withholding, use, transfer, withdrawal, transportation, importation or exportation of, or dealing in, or exercising any right, power, or privilege with respect to, or transactions involving, any property in which any foreign country or a national thereof has any interest by any person, or with respect to any property, subject to the jurisdiction of the United States; and

(C) when the United States is engaged in armed hostilities or has been attacked by a foreign country or foreign nationals, confiscate any property, subject to the jurisdiction of the United States, of any foreign person, foreign organization, or foreign country that he determines has planned, authorized, aided, or engaged in such hostilities or attacks against the United States; and all right, title, and interest in any property so confiscated shall vest, when, as, and upon the terms directed by the President, in such agency or person as the President may designate from time to time, and upon such terms and conditions as the President may prescribe, such interest or property shall be held, used, administered, liquidated, sold, or otherwise dealt with in the interest of and for the benefit of the United States, and such designated agency or person may perform any and all acts incident to the accomplishment or furtherance of these purposes. * * *

———

The President has periodically exercised his authority under the International Emergency Economic Powers Act ("IEEPA") to advance certain human rights policies of the United States. *See, e.g.*, Exec. Order 12532, 50 Fed. Reg. 36861 (Sept. 9, 1985) (imposing sanctions on South Africa), *revoked by* Exec. Order 12769, 56 Fed. Reg. 31855 (July 10,

1991); Exec. Order 13047, 62 Fed. Reg. 28301 (May 20, 1997) (banning new investment in Burma); Exec. Order 13088, 64 Fed. Reg. 24021 (June 9, 1998) (prohibiting new investment in the Republic of Serbia in response to the situation in Kosovo); Exec. Order 13213, 66 Fed. Reg. 28829 (May 22, 2001) (banning all rough diamond shipments from Sierra Leone for an indefinite period). Congress has occasionally adopted legislation in connection with IEEPA to address human rights concerns in particular countries. *See, e.g.*, Sudan Peace Act of 2002, 50 U.S.C. 1701 note. Sanctions may also be imposed to advance national security and foreign policy interests which are secondarily related to human rights, including the effort to combat terrorism and the proliferation of weapons of mass destruction. *See, e.g.*, Iran and Libya Sanctions Act of 1996, 50 U.S.C. 1701 note.

————

BURMESE FREEDOM AND DEMOCRACY ACT OF 2003

50 U.S.C. § 1701 note

Sec. 2. *Findings.* Congress makes the following findings:

(1) The State Peace and Development Council (SPDC)[, the governing body in Burma,] has failed to transfer power to the National League for Democracy (NLD) whose parliamentarians won an overwhelming victory in the 1990 elections in Burma.

(2) The SPDC has failed to enter into meaningful, political dialogue with the NLD and ethnic minorities and has dismissed the efforts of United Nations Special Envoy ... to further such dialogue....

(4) On May 30, 2003, the SPDC, threatened by continued support for the NLD throughout Burma, brutally attacked NLD supporters, killed and injured scores of civilians, and arrested democracy advocate Aung San Suu Kyi and other activists.

(5) The SPDC continues egregious human rights violations against Burmese citizens, uses rape as a weapon of intimidation and torture against women, and forcibly conscripts child-soldiers for the use in fighting indigenous ethnic groups.

(6) The SPDC is engaged in ethnic cleansing against minorities within Burma, including the Karen, Karenni, and Shan people, which constitutes a crime against humanity and has directly led to more than 600,000 internally displaced people living within Burma and more than 130,000 people from Burma living in refugee camps along the Thai–Burma border.

* * *

(10) The International Labor Organization (ILO), for the first time in its 82–year history, adopted in 2000, a resolution recommending that governments, employers, and workers organizations take appropriate measures to ensure that their relations with the SPDC do

not abet the government-sponsored system of forced, compulsory, or slave labor in Burma, and that other international bodies reconsider any cooperation they may be engaged in with Burma and, if appropriate, cease as soon as possible any activity that could abet the practice of forced, compulsory, or slave labor.

* * *

(12) Investment in Burmese companies and purchases from them serve to provide the SPDC with currency that is used to finance its instruments of terror and repression against the Burmese people.

(13) * * * [T]he American Apparel and Footwear Association [has] expressed its "strong support for a full and immediate ban on U.S. textiles, apparel and footwear imports from Burma" and called upon the United States Government to "impose an outright ban on U.S. imports" of these items until Burma demonstrates respect for basic human and labor rights of its citizens. * * *

Sec. 3. *Ban against trade that supports the military regime of Burma.*

(a) General ban.—

(1) In general.—Notwithstanding any other provision of law, until such time as the President determines and certifies to Congress that Burma has met the conditions described in paragraph (3), beginning 30 days after the date of the enactment of this Act [July 28, 2003], the President shall ban the importation of any article that is a product of Burma. * * *

(3) Conditions described.—The conditions described in this paragraph are the following:

(A) The SPDC has made substantial and measurable progress to end violations of internationally recognized human rights including rape, and the Secretary of State, after consultation with the ILO Secretary General and relevant nongovernmental organizations, reports to the appropriate congressional committees that the SPDC no longer systematically violates workers rights, including the use of forced and child labor, and conscription of child-soldiers.

(B) The SPDC has made measurable and substantial progress toward implementing a democratic Government including—

(i) releasing all political prisoners;

(ii) allowing freedom of speech and the press;

(iii) allowing freedom of association;

(iv) permitting the peaceful exercise of religion; and

(v) bringing to a conclusion an agreement between the SPDC and the democratic forces led by the NLD and Burma's ethnic nationalities on the transfer of power to a civilian government accountable to the Burmese people through democratic elections under the rule of law. * * *

(b) Waiver authorities.—The President may waive the prohibitions described in this section for any or all articles that are a product of Burma if the President determines and notifies the [appropriate Congressional committees] that to do so is in the national interest of the United States.

Sec. 4.   *Freezing assets of the Burmese regime in the United States.*

(a) Reporting requirement.—Not later than 60 days after the date of enactment of this Act [July 28, 2003], the President shall take such action as is necessary to direct, and promulgate regulations to the same, that any United States financial institution holding funds belonging to the SPDC or the assets of those individuals who hold senior positions in the SPDC or its political arm, the Union Solidarity Development Association, shall promptly report those funds or assets to the Office of Foreign Assets Control.

(b) Additional authority.—The President may take such action as may be necessary to impose a sanctions regime to freeze such funds or assets, subject to such terms and conditions as the President determines to be appropriate. * * *

Sec. 5.   *Loans at international financial institutions.* The Secretary of the Treasury shall instruct the United States executive director to each appropriate international financial institution in which the United States participates, to oppose, and vote against the extension by such institution of any loan or financial or technical assistance to Burma until such time as the conditions described in section 3(a)(3) are met. * * *

Sec. 8.   *Support democracy activists in Burma.*

(a) In general.—The President is authorized to use all available resources to assist Burmese democracy activists dedicated to nonviolent opposition to the regime in their efforts to promote freedom, democracy, and human rights in Burma, including a listing of constraints on such programming.

(b) Reports. * * *

(3) Report on trade sanctions.—Not later than 90 days before the date on which the import restrictions contained in section 3(a)(1) are to expire, the Secretary of State, in consultation with the United States Trade Representative and the heads of appropriate agencies, shall submit to the [appropriate Congressional committees] a report on—

(A) bilateral and multilateral measures undertaken by the United States Government and other governments to promote human rights and democracy in Burma;

(B) The extent to which actions related to trade with Burma taken pursuant to this Act have been effective in—

(i) improving conditions in Burma, including human rights violations, arrest and detention of democracy activists, forced and child labor, and the status of dialogue between the SPDC and the NLD and ethnic minorities;

(ii) furthering the policy objections of the United States toward Burma; and

(C) the impact of actions relating to trade take pursuant to this Act on other national security, economic, and foreign policy interests of the United States, including relations with countries friendly to the United States.

Congress has repeatedly approved the renewal of the import restrictions specified in Section 3 of the Burmese Freedom and Democracy Act of 2003, *supra*. *See, e.g.* Block Burmese JADE (Junta's Anti–Democratic Efforts) Act of 2008, Pub. L. 110–286 (2008). In 2000, the Supreme Court addressed the issue of whether an earlier version of federal sanctions precluded the various states from adopting their own sanctions regimes against companies doing business in Burma:

CROSBY ET AL. v. NAT'L FOREIGN TRADE COUNCIL
530 U.S. 363 (2000)

Justice SOUTER delivered the opinion of the Court.

The issue is whether the Burma law of the Commonwealth of Massachusetts, restricting the authority of its agencies to purchase goods or services from companies doing business with Burma,[1] is invalid under the Supremacy Clause of the National Constitution owing to its threat of frustrating federal statutory objectives. We hold that it is.

I

In June 1996, Massachusetts adopted "An Act Regulating State Contracts with Companies Doing Business with or in Burma (Burma)." The statute generally bars state entities from buying goods or services from any person (defined to include a business organization) identified on a "restricted purchase list" of those doing business with Burma. Although the statute has no general provision for waiver or termination of its ban, it does exempt from boycott any entities present in Burma solely to report the news, or to provide international telecommunication goods or services, or medical supplies. * * * There are three exceptions to the ban: (1) if the procurement is essential, and without the restricted bid, there would be no bids or insufficient competition; (2) if the

---

1. The Court of Appeals noted that the ruling military government of "Burma changed [the country's] name to Burma in 1989," but the court then said it would use the name Burma since both parties and *amici curiae*, the state law, and the federal law all do so. We follow suit, noting that our use of this term, like the First Circuit's, is not intended to express any political view.

procurement is of medical supplies; and (3) if the procurement efforts elicit no "comparable low bid or offer" by a person not doing business with Burma, meaning an offer that is no more than 10 percent greater than the restricted bid. To enforce the ban, the Act requires petitioner Secretary of Administration and Finance to maintain a "restricted purchase list" of all firms "doing business with Burma."

In September 1996, three months after the Massachusetts law was enacted, Congress passed a statute imposing a set of mandatory and conditional sanctions on Burma. *See* Foreign Operations, Export Financing, and Related Programs Appropriations Act, 1997, § 570, 110 Stat. 3009–166 to 3009–167 (enacted by the Omnibus Consolidated Appropriations Act, 1997, § 101(c), 110 Stat. 3009–121 to 3009–172). The federal Act has five basic parts, three substantive and two procedural.

First, it imposes three sanctions directly on Burma. It bans all aid to the Burmese Government except for humanitarian assistance, counter-narcotics efforts, and promotion of human rights and democracy. The statute instructs United States representatives to international financial institutions to vote against loans or other assistance to or for Burma, and it provides that no entry visa shall be issued to any Burmese government official unless required by treaty or to staff the Burmese mission to the United Nations. These restrictions are to remain in effect "[u]ntil such time as the President determines and certifies to Congress that Burma has made measurable and substantial progress in improving human rights practices and implementing democratic government."

Second, the federal Act authorizes the President to impose further sanctions subject to certain conditions. He may prohibit "United States persons" from "new investment" in Burma, and shall do so if he determines and certifies to Congress that the Burmese Government has physically harmed, rearrested, or exiled Daw Aung San Suu Kyi (the opposition leader selected to receive the Nobel Peace Prize), or has committed "large-scale repression of or violence against the Democratic opposition." "New investment" is defined as entry into a contract that would favor the "economical development of resources located in Burma," or would provide ownership interests in or benefits from such development, but the term specifically excludes (and thus excludes from any Presidential prohibition) "entry into, performance of, or financing of a contract to sell or purchase goods, services, or technology."

Third, the statute directs the President to work to develop "a comprehensive, multilateral strategy to bring democracy to and improve human rights practices and the quality of life in Burma." He is instructed to cooperate with members of the Association of Southeast Asian Nations (ASEAN) and with other countries having major trade and investment interests in Burma to devise such an approach, and to pursue the additional objective of fostering dialogue between the ruling State Law and Order Restoration Council (SLORC) and democratic opposition groups.

As for the procedural provisions of the federal statute, the fourth section requires the President to report periodically to certain congressional committee chairmen on the progress toward democratization and better living conditions in Burma as well as on the development of the required strategy. And the fifth part of the federal Act authorizes the President "to waive, temporarily or permanently, any sanction [under the federal Act] . . . if he determines and certifies to Congress that the application of such sanction would be contrary to the national security interests of the United States."

On May 20, 1997, the President issued the Burma Executive Order, Exec. Order No. 13047. He certified * * * that the Government of Burma had "committed large-scale repression of the democratic opposition in Burma" and found that the Burmese Government's actions and policies constituted "an unusual and extraordinary threat to the national security and foreign policy of the United States," a threat characterized as a national emergency. The President then prohibited new investment in Burma "by United States persons," any approval or facilitation by a United States person of such new investment by foreign persons, and any transaction meant to evade or avoid the ban. The order generally incorporated the exceptions and exemptions addressed in the statute. Finally, the President delegated to the Secretary of State the tasks of working with ASEAN and other countries to develop a strategy for democracy, human rights, and the quality of life in Burma, and of making the required congressional reports.

II

Respondent National Foreign Trade Council * * * is a nonprofit corporation representing companies engaged in foreign commerce; 34 of its members were on the Massachusetts restricted purchase list in 1998. Three withdrew from Burma after the passage of the state Act, and one member had its bid for a procurement contract increased by 10 percent under the provision of the state law allowing acceptance of a low bid from a listed bidder only if the next-to-lowest bid is more than 10 percent higher.

In April 1998, the Council filed suit in the United States District Court for the District of Massachusetts, seeking declaratory and injunctive relief against the petitioner state officials charged with administering and enforcing the state Act. * * * The Council argued that the state law unconstitutionally infringed on the federal foreign affairs power, violated the Foreign Commerce Clause, and was preempted by the federal Act. After detailed stipulations, briefing, and argument, the District Court permanently enjoined enforcement of the state Act, holding that it "unconstitutionally impinge[d] on the federal government's exclusive authority to regulate foreign affairs." *National Foreign Trade Council v. Baker*, 26 F. Supp.2d 287, 291 (D. Mass.1998).

The United States Court of Appeals for the First Circuit affirmed on three independent grounds. [*National Foreign Trade Council v. Natsios*,

181 F.3d 38 (1st Cir. 1999)], at 45. It found the state Act unconstitution-ally interfered with the foreign affairs power of the National Govern-ment[;] violated the dormant Foreign Commerce Clause, U.S. Const. Art. I, § 8, cl. 3; and was preempted by the congressional Burma Act. The State's petition for certiorari challenged the decision on all three grounds and asserted interests said to be shared by other state and local governments with similar measures. * * * We granted certiorari * * *, and now affirm.

III

A fundamental principle of the Constitution is that Congress has the power to preempt state law. Art. VI, cl. 2; *Gibbons v. Ogden,* 9 Wheat. 1, 211 (1824). Even without an express provision for preemption, we have found that state law must yield to a congressional Act in at least two circumstances. When Congress intends federal law to "occupy the field," state law in that area is preempted. And even if Congress has not occupied the field, state law is naturally preempted to the extent of any conflict with a federal statute. We will find preemption where it is impossible for a private party to comply with both state and federal law, and where "under the circumstances of [a] particular case, [the chal-lenged state law] stands as an obstacle to the accomplishment and execution of the full purposes and objectives of Congress." What is a sufficient obstacle is a matter of judgment, to be informed by examining the federal statute as a whole and identifying its purpose and intended effects:

> For when the question is whether a Federal act overrides a state law, the entire scheme of the statute must of course be considered and that which needs must be implied is of no less force than that which is expressed. If the purpose of the act cannot otherwise be accomplished—if its operation within its chosen field else must be frustrated and its provisions be refused their natural effect—the state law must yield to the regulation of Congress within the sphere of its delegated power.

Savage [v. Jones, 225 U.S. 501, 533 (1912).]

Applying this standard, we see the state Burma law as an obstacle to the accomplishment of Congress's full objectives under the federal Act. We find that the state law undermines the intended purpose and "natural effect" of at least three provisions of the federal Act, that is, its delegation of effective discretion to the President to control economic sanctions against Burma, its limitation of sanctions solely to United States persons and new investment, and its directive to the President to proceed diplomatically in developing a comprehensive, multilateral strategy towards Burma. * * *

A

First, Congress clearly intended the federal act to provide the President with flexible and effective authority over economic sanctions against Burma. Although Congress immediately put in place a set of initial sanctions (prohibiting bilateral aid, support for international financial assistance, and entry by Burmese officials into the United States), it authorized the President to terminate any and all of those measures upon determining and certifying that there had been progress in human rights and democracy in Burma. It invested the President with the further power to ban new investment by United States persons, dependent only on specific Presidential findings of repression in Burma. And, most significantly, Congress empowered the President "to waive, temporarily or permanently, any sanction [under the federal act] * * * if he determines and certifies to Congress that the application of such sanction would be contrary to the national security interests of the United States."

This express investiture of the President with statutory authority to act for the United States in imposing sanctions with respect to the government of Burma, augmented by the flexibility to respond to change by suspending sanctions in the interest of national security, recalls Justice Jackson's observation in *Youngstown Sheet & Tube Co. v. Sawyer*, 343 U.S. 579, 635 (1952): "When the President acts pursuant to an express or implied authorization of Congress, his authority is at its maximum, for it includes all that he possesses in his own right plus all that Congress can delegate." * * * [T]he President's power in the area of foreign relations is least restricted by Congress. * * * Within the sphere defined by Congress, then, the statute has placed the President in a position with as much discretion to exercise economic leverage against Burma, with an eye toward national security, as our law will admit. And it is just this plenitude of Executive authority that we think controls the issue of preemption here. The President has been given this authority not merely to make a political statement but to achieve a political result, and the fullness of his authority shows the importance in the congressional mind of reaching that result. It is simply implausible that Congress would have gone to such lengths to empower the President if it had been willing to compromise his effectiveness by deference to every provision of state statute or local ordinance that might, if enforced, blunt the consequences of discretionary Presidential action.

And that is just what the Massachusetts Burma law would do in imposing a different, state system of economic pressure against the Burmese political regime. * * * [T]he state statute penalizes some private action that the federal Act (as administered by the President) may allow, and pulls levers of influence that the federal Act does not reach. But the point here is that the state sanctions are immediate, * * * and perpetual, there being no termination provision. * * * This unyielding application undermines the President's intended statutory authority by making it impossible for him to restrain fully the coercive power of the national economy when he may choose to take the discretionary action open to him, whether he believes that the national interest requires sanctions to be lifted, or believes that the promise of lifting sanctions would move the Burmese regime in the democratic direction. Quite simply, if the Massachusetts law is enforceable the President has less to offer and less economic and diplomatic leverage as a consequence. In *Dames & Moore v. Regan*, 453 U.S. 654 (1981), we used the metaphor of the bargaining chip to describe the President's control of funds valuable to a hostile country; here, the state Act reduces the value of the chips created by the federal statute. It thus "stands as an obstacle to the accomplishment and execution of the full purposes and objectives of Congress."

B

Congress manifestly intended to limit economic pressure against the Burmese Government to a specific range. The federal Act confines its reach to United States persons, imposes limited immediate sanctions, places only a conditional ban on a carefully defined area of "new investment," and pointedly exempts contracts to sell or purchase goods, services, or technology. * * *

The State has set a different course, and its statute conflicts with federal law at a number of points by penalizing individuals and conduct that Congress has explicitly exempted or excluded from sanctions. While the state Act differs from the federal in relying entirely on indirect economic leverage through third parties with Burmese connections, it otherwise stands in clear contrast to the congressional scheme in the scope of subject matter addressed. It restricts all contracts between the State and companies doing business in Burma, except when purchasing medical supplies and other essentials (or when short of comparable bids). It is specific in targeting contracts to provide financial services, and general goods and services, to the Government of Burma, and thus prohibits contracts between the State and United States persons for goods, services, or technology, even though those transactions are explicitly exempted from the ambit of new investment prohibition when the President exercises his discretionary authority to impose sanctions under the federal Act.

As with the subject of business meant to be affected, so with the class of companies doing it: the state Act's generality stands at odds with the federal discreteness. The Massachusetts law directly and indirectly imposes costs on all companies that do any business in Burma, save for those reporting news or providing international telecommunications goods or services, or medical supplies. It sanctions companies promoting the importation of natural resources controlled by the government of Burma, or having any operations or affiliates in Burma. The state Act thus penalizes companies with pre-existing affiliates or investments, all of which lie beyond the reach of the federal act's restrictions on "new investment" in Burmese economic development. The state Act, moreover, imposes restrictions on foreign companies as well as domestic, whereas the federal Act limits its reach to United States persons.

The conflicts are not rendered irrelevant by the State's argument that there is no real conflict between the statutes because they share the same goals and because some companies may comply with both sets of restrictions. The fact of a common end hardly neutralizes conflicting means, and the fact that some companies may be able to comply with both sets of sanctions does not mean that the state Act is not at odds with achievement of the federal decision about the right degree of pressure to employ. "[C]onflict is imminent" when "two separate remedies are brought to bear on the same activity," *Wisconsin Dept. of Industry v. Gould, Inc.*, 475 U.S. 282, 286 (1986). Sanctions are drawn not only to bar what they prohibit but to allow what they permit, and the inconsistency of sanctions here undermines the congressional calibration of force.

C

Finally, the state Act is at odds with the President's intended authority to speak for the United States among the world's nations in developing a "comprehensive, multilateral strategy to bring democracy to and improve human rights practices and the quality of life in Burma." Congress called for Presidential cooperation with members of ASEAN and other countries in developing such a strategy, directed the President to encourage a dialogue between the government of Burma and the democratic opposition, and required him to report to the Congress on the progress of his diplomatic efforts. As with Congress's explicit delegation to the President of power over economic sanctions, Congress's express command to the President to take the initiative for the United States among the international community invested him with the maximum authority of the National Government, *cf. Youngstown Sheet & Tube Co.*, 343 U.S. at 635, in harmony with the President's own constitutional powers, U.S. Const., Art. II, § 2, cl. 2 ("[The President] shall have Power, by and with the Advice and Consent of the Senate, to make Treaties" and "shall appoint Ambassadors, other public Ministers and Consuls"); § 3 ("[The President] shall receive Ambassadors and other public Ministers"). This clear mandate and invocation of exclusively national power belies any suggestion that Congress intended the President's effective voice to be obscured by state or local action.

Again, the state Act undermines the President's capacity, in this instance for effective diplomacy. It is not merely that the differences between the state and federal Acts in scope and type of sanctions threaten to complicate discussions; they compromise the very capacity of the President to speak for the Nation with one voice in dealing with other governments. We need not get into any general consideration of limits of state action affecting foreign affairs to realize that the President's maximum power to persuade rests on his capacity to bargain for the benefits of access to the entire national economy without exception for enclaves fenced off willy-nilly by inconsistent political tactics. When such exceptions do qualify his capacity to present a coherent position on behalf of the national economy, he is weakened, of course, not only in dealing with the Burmese regime, but in working together with other nations in hopes of reaching common policy and "comprehensive" strategy.

While the threat to the President's power to speak and bargain effectively with other nations seems clear enough, the record is replete with evidence to answer any skeptics. First, in response to the passage of the state Act, a number of this country's allies and trading partners filed formal protests with the National Government ([*e.g.*] * * * Japan, the European Union (EU), and ASEAN). * * *

Second, the EU and Japan have gone a step further in lodging formal complaints against the United States in the World Trade Organization (WTO), claiming that the state Act violates certain provisions of the Agreement on Government Procurement, and the consequence has been to embroil the National Government for some time now in international dispute proceedings under the auspices of the WTO. In their brief before this Court, EU officials point to the WTO dispute as threatening relations with the United States, and note that the state Act has become the topic of "intensive discussions" with officials of the United States at the highest levels, those discussions including exchanges at the twice yearly EU–U.S. Summit.

Third, the Executive has consistently represented that the state Act has complicated its dealings with foreign sovereigns and proven an impediment to accomplishing objectives assigned it by Congress. Assistant Secretary of State Larson, for example, has directly addressed the mandate of the federal Burma law in saying that the imposition of unilateral state sanctions under the state Act "complicates efforts to build coalitions with our allies" to promote democracy and human rights in Burma. "[T]he EU's opposition to the Massachusetts law has meant that U.S. government high level discussions with EU officials often have focused not on what to do about Burma, but on what to do about the Massachusetts Burma law." This point has been consistently echoed in the State Department. * * *

This evidence in combination is more than sufficient to show that the state Act stands as an obstacle in addressing the congressional obligation to devise a comprehensive, multilateral strategy. * * *

V

Because the state Act's provisions conflict with Congress's specific delegation to the President of flexible discretion, with limitation of sanctions to a limited scope of actions and actors, and with direction to develop a comprehensive, multilateral strategy under the federal Act, it is preempted, and its application is unconstitutional, under the Supremacy Clause.

NOTES AND QUESTIONS ON THE REGIME OF DOMESTIC REGULATION

1. *Triggering the IEEPA.* In what statutorily-defined circumstances may the President exercise the various regulatory powers specified in the IEEPA? In what circumstances would a foreign government's human rights policies constitute "an unusual and extraordinary threat to the national security and foreign policy of the United States?"

2. *Effectiveness of sanctions.* In 2008, as this book goes to press, the Burmese junta remains in power, five years after the Burmese Freedom and Democracy Act. What lessons can be drawn from this experience? What additional information would you like to know before drawing any conclusions?

3. *Federal pre-emption and the "vertical" separation of powers.* Why would the National Foreign Trade Council and its members care about the Massachusetts law in the first place? After all, the federal and state laws had the same policy objective. Why isn't that overlap sufficient to save the state law, according to the *Crosby* court?

The recent resurrection of federalism by the Supreme Court might have suggested that the ability of a state to apply its own law even in international cases would enjoy a kind of renaissance. *Compare, e.g., United States v. Lopez,* 514 U.S. 549 (1995) (invalidating federal Gun–Free School Zones Act on the ground that it exceeded Congress' authority over interstate commerce); *Alden v. Maine,* 527 U.S. 706 (1999) (invalidating overtime provisions of federal Fair Labor Standards Act, as applied to state workers, on the ground that Congress had no power to subject the state to suit in state courts without the state's consent). But *Crosby* suggests that, when the state law interferes too much in the conduct of foreign relations, or undermines the president's powers in foreign relations, it will be invalidated despite the recent trend towards state power. *See also American Ins. Ass'n v. Garamendi,* 539 U.S. 396 (2003). In *Garamendi,* the Supreme Court invalidated California's Holocaust Victim Insurance Relief Act of 1999, which required any insurer doing business in California to disclose information about all policies sold in Europe between 1920 and 1945 by that company or any "related" entities. The Court held that the state law interfered with the national government's conduct of foreign relations and was therefore pre-empted.

Crosby and *Garamendi* relied heavily on *Zschernig v. Miller,* 389 U.S. 429 (1968), in which the state courts of Oregon had applied an Oregon escheat statute to deny an inheritance to a resident of a Communist bloc country. That ruling was based on the claimant's failure to demonstrate either that his country would allow U.S. nationals to inherit estates or that any payments he might receive from the Oregon estate would not be confiscated by his home government. The Supreme Court reversed on the ground that the state statute required Oregon courts to "launc[h] inquiries into the type of governments that obtain in particular foreign nations," rendering "unavoidable judicial criticism of nations established on a more authoritarian basis than our own." That prospect had a "direct impact upon foreign relations" and threatened to "impair the effective exercise of the Nation's foreign policy." On that basis, the statute was held to be unconstitutional as applied.

After *Zschernig*, *Crosby*, and *Garamendi*, are there any circumstances under which a state (or a city) might impose human rights responsibilities on companies?

4. *"Horizontal" separation of powers.* Is it possible for Congress to interfere too much by statute with the executive branch's prerogatives in matters of foreign affairs?

5. *Securities regulation and disclosure.* Nations with strong capital markets have experimented with requiring social disclosure as a way of promoting corporate responsibility. In 2002, for example, France adopted legislation that required all French companies to report on the "sustainability" of their practices, including human rights compliance and environmental impacts. No enforcement measures were specified in the French legislation, but other nations have experimented with social disclosure as a way of bringing market pressure to bear on corporate decision-making. The United Kingdom amended its Pension Act to require fund trustees to disclose their policy on social, environmental, and ethical issues, and, the United States Commission on International Religious Freedom has endorsed the use of disclosure statements to help investors decide if they wished to purchase the securities of companies thought to be complicit in the violation of religious freedoms in Sudan.

The legal infrastructure for requiring corporate disclosure is already in place in the leading capital markets of the world. The U.S. Securities and Exchange Commission, for example, is authorized by statute to issue disclosure regulations as "necessary or appropriate in the public interest for the protection of investors." If companies wish to raise capital in U.S. markets, they must file a disclosure statement for investors, and false or incomplete disclosure can lead to substantial penalties and criminal proceedings against the company and its directors and managers, as well as civil liability. The legislative history of the Securities Act of 1933 provides for the "use of disclosure as a regulatory means to foster greater public accountability in the corporate enterprise."

As investors begin to care more about the human rights records of public companies, the SEC may find an opening for exercising its regulatory powers and expanding the requirements for "social disclosure," including information on the countries in which a company does business, information on its domestic and global labor practices, and information on its domestic and global environmental effects. *See* Cynthia Williams, *The SEC and Corporate Social Transparency*, 112 HARV. L. REV. 1197 (1999). Because contingent liabilities must be disclosed, the securities laws also leverage the rise of civil lawsuits against corporations for human rights abuse (as described below).

---

3. A REGIME OF CIVIL LIABILITY

In the United States, civil liability lawsuits have periodically required changes in the corporate culture, inducing corporations to improve the design of their products or their manufacturing and marketing practices. Commonly, lawsuits initially filed under tort or contract theories generate momentum for more comprehensive statutory reforms, as in the areas of products liability and occupational safety and health. A similar dynamic may be developing with respect to corporations and human rights. Various domestic courts have ruled that corporations may be obliged in principle to pay substantial damage awards for their complicity in abuses by the governments with which they do business or for committing international wrongs that do not require state action. A corporation engaged in the slave trade or piracy on the high seas would presumably face international and domestic liability in some form. In a series of cases arising out of World War II, Holocaust survivors sued companies that relied on slave labor, *see, e.g., In re World War II Era Japanese Forced Labor Litigation*, 164 F.Supp. 2d 1160 (N.D. Cal. 2001), *aff'd sub nom., Deutsch v. Turner Corp.*, 317 F.3d 1005 (9th Cir. 2003), *opinion amended and superseded on denial of rehearing by Deutsch v. Turner Corp.*, 324 F.3d 692 (9th Cir. 2003); or seized the property of Jews, *see, e.g., Bodner v. Banque Paribas*, 114 F. Supp. 2d 117 (E.D.N.Y. 2000); or manufactured goods the sole purpose of which was the destruction of the Jews, *see, e.g., Burger–Fischer v. Degussa AG*, 65 F. Supp. 2d 248 (D.N.J. 1999). Some of these cases settled through the payment of compensation to the plaintiffs.

As shown in Module 1, *supra*, in the United States, these and similar cases tend to be filed under the Alien Tort Statute ("ATS"), 28 U.S.C. 1350, which provides that "the district courts shall have original jurisdiction of any civil action for a tort only, committed in violation of the law of nations or a treaty of the United States." The ATS became a vehicle for the protection of human rights in 1980 with the decision of the Second Circuit Court of Appeals in *Filartiga v. Pena–Irala*, 630 F.2d 876 (2d Cir. 1980). Over the last decade, ATS actions have been filed in U.S. federal court against some of the largest multinational companies for their alleged complicity in human rights violations around the world. Some of these cases have been dismissed on *forum non conveniens* or jurisdictional or political or factual grounds, but a majority of courts has ruled that private companies are not *in principle* immune from liability under international law. To the contrary, in *Doe v. Unocal, supra* and similar cases, the courts have ruled that the plaintiffs were entitled to try to prove their case, implicitly rejecting the prophylactic rule proposed by the defendants to the effect that private corporations do not act under color of law and therefore cannot violate the law of nations or a treaty of the United States.

As the following pair of cases suggests, there continues to be controversy over the extent to which—and the circumstances under which—corporations face civil liability under international law.

PRESBYTERIAN CHURCH OF SUDAN, ET AL. v. TALISMAN ENERGY, INC.

244 F. Supp. 2d 289 (S.D.N.Y. 2003)

This action arises out of the alleged activities of Talisman in southern Sudan. Plaintiffs claim that Talisman, a large Canadian energy company, collaborated with Sudan in "ethnically cleansing" civilian populations surrounding oil concessions located in southern Sudan in order to facilitate oil exploration and extraction activities. This policy of "ethnic cleansing" was aimed at non-Muslim, African residents of southern Sudan, and entailed extrajudicial killing, forced displacement, military attacks on civilian targets, confiscation and destruction of property, kidnappings, rape, and the enslavement of civilians. * * * Plaintiffs note that in 1997, Sudan was classified by the United States as a state sponsor of terrorism pursuant to the International Emergency Economic Powers Act, 50 U.S.C. § 1701 et seq., based, *inter alia*, on its record of terrorism and on the prevalence of human rights violations including slavery and restrictions on religious freedom. * * *

Plaintiffs contend that the current conflict in Sudan has evolved into an "oil war" for control of valuable petroleum resources in the south. * * * According to plaintiffs, the Government's oil development policy and its violent campaign against ethnic and religious minorities were inextricably linked from the beginning. Plaintiffs allege that the Government saw its oil reserves as potential sources of capital to purchase missiles, tanks, bombers, helicopters, and other sophisticated armaments needed to intensify its "jihad" against the southern population. The Sudanese government realized it would be unable to successfully develop its oil reserves without outside aid. Plaintiffs describe the resulting arrangement between the Government and oil companies thusly:

> In exchange for oil concessions, the Government promised to clear the area around the oil fields of the local population. The oil companies agreed to invest in the infrastructure, such as transportation, roads and airfields and communications facilities, to support exploration and the Government would use that same infrastructure to support its genocidal military campaign of ethnic cleansing against the local population. Under this unholy alliance, the oil companies would be able to maximize security around the oil installations and Sudan would get the capital necessary to wage a full scale war against the south.

Amended Complaint, at ¶ 21. * * *

Plaintiffs contend that Talisman worked with the Government to devise a plan of security for the oil fields and related facilities. Talisman hired its own military advisors to coordinate military strategy with the Government. Specifically, Talisman would have regular meetings with Sudan's army intelligence unit and the Ministry of Energy and Mining during which the parties would discuss "how to dispose of civilians" in areas in which Talisman intended to operate. Based on the joint Talisman–Government strategy, "Government troops and allied militia engaged in an ethnic cleansing operation to execute, enslave or displace the non-Muslim, African Sudanese civilian population from areas that are near the pipeline or where Talisman wanted to drill." *Id.*, at ¶ 26. Talisman was and is aware that Government's "protection" of oil operations entailed "ethnic cleansing" or genocide, including the murder of substantial numbers of civilians (including women and children); the destruction of civilian residences and villages; and the capture and enslavement of civilians who survived the military attacks. Defendants' concerted actions are purportedly demonstrated by, *inter alia*, a May 7, 1999 communication from the Government's Petroleum Security Office in Khartoum to a satellite office in Heglig. This directive, denominated as "very urgent," reads as follows:

> In accordance with directives of His Excellency the Minister of Energy and Mining and fulfilling the request of the Canadian Company ... the armed forces will conduct cleaning up operations in all villages from Heglig to Pariang.

Id. at ¶ 27. Plaintiffs claim that thousands of villages and at least seventeen churches were destroyed in the areas surrounding Talisman's oil fields. * * * In addition to this alleged direct support, Talisman also allegedly indirectly supported the Government's genocidal campaign. Plaintiffs note that Talisman, through [a joint venture with the government], built a network of all-weather roads. These roads were used by Government forces to launch military offensives against civilian targets. Similarly, Talisman expanded an existing dirt runway in Heglig to accommodate large transport planes. This runway was later regularly used, with Talisman's knowledge, for military purposes, including bombing and strafing attacks on civilian areas. * * *

Plaintiffs also cite statements made by non-governmental organizations, United States government officials, United Nations officials, and others attesting to the gross human rights violations committed by Sudan. These statements also allege that the oil exploration and extraction activities taking place in Sudan are fueling the war on civilians. For example, plaintiffs cite a statement by the United Nations Commission on Human Rights: "[L]ong-term efforts by the various Governments of the Sudan to protect oil production have included a policy of forcible population displacement in order to clear oil producing areas and transportation routes of southern civilians." * * *

Legal Analysis

* * * The primary basis for asserting the Court's jurisdiction is 28 U.S.C. § 1350, otherwise known as the Alien Tort Claims Act ("ATCA"). The ATCA itself is succinct and simple on its face:

> The district courts shall have original jurisdiction of any civil action by an alien for a tort only, committed in violation of the law of nations or a treaty of the United States.

28 U.S.C. § 1350. Notwithstanding its brevity, however, the ATCA has dramatically altered the legal landscape. The statute was passed by the first Congress as part of the Judiciary Act of 1789. * * * Despite the fact that the ATCA has existed for over two hundred years, little is known of the framers' intentions in adopting it—the legislative history of the Judiciary Act does not refer to section 1350. * * *

In order to be actionable under the Alien Tort Claims Act, a defendant's conduct must violate "well-established, universally recognized norms of international law." *Kadic v. Karadzic*, 70 F.3d 232, 239 (2d Cir.1995) (quoting *Filartiga v. Pena–Irala*, 630 F.2d 876, 888 (2d Cir.1980)). Courts must "interpret international law not as it was in 1789, but as it has evolved and exists among the nations of the world today." *See Kadic*, 70 F.3d at 238. * * *

The allegations in the Amended Complaint include charges of genocide, war crimes, torture, and enslavement. It is not disputed that such acts violate universally-recognized norms of international law (though Talisman contends that corporations are not legally capable of violating international law). States practicing, encouraging, or condoning genocide, slavery or the slave trade, extrajudicial killings, torture, or systematic racial discrimination violate international law. Individuals committing such acts may also be liable under international law. *See, e.g., Kadic v. Karadzic*, 70 F.3d 232 (2d Cir.1995) (holding that individuals may violate international law by committing acts of genocide, war crimes, or torture). * * * The Amended Complaint is rife with accusations which, if proven true, would constitute behavior manifestly in violation of the most basic rules of international law and, indeed, of civilized conduct. Such acts violate peremptory norms, or *jus cogens*. See Restatement (Third) of Foreign Relations § 702 cmt. n (1987) (stating that acts of genocide, slavery, and extrajudicial killing violate *jus cogens* norms). * * * [T]hese acts are offenses of universal concern by virtue of the "depths of depravity the conduct encompasses, the often countless toll of human suffering the misdeeds inflict upon their victims, and the consequential disruption of the domestic and international order they produce." *Tachiona v. Mugabe*, 234 F.Supp.2d 401, 415–16 (S.D.N.Y. 2002).[2]. * * *

---

2. Of course, while *jus cogens* violations are actionable under the ATCA, a *jus cogens* violation is not required. Under the ATCA, any violation of a specific, universal, and obligatory international norm is actionable, whether it is *jus cogens* or not.

Talisman contends [however] that the Court lacks subject matter jurisdiction because corporations are legally incapable of violating the laws of nations. It argues that international law applies to states and in some cases to individuals, but that "the law of nations simply does not encompass principles of corporate liability." Talisman relies primarily on affidavits submitted by two renowned international law scholars, James Crawford and Christopher Greenwood. Both scholars, consulting a variety of international sources, conclude that there is no basis in existing international law for the liability of corporations. Nonetheless, a considerable body of United States and international precedent indicates that corporations may be liable for violations of international law. * * * Messrs. Crawford and Greenwood, while citing a variety of international law sources, fail to cite a single United States case upholding their position. In fact, numerous Second Circuit cases, as well as cases from courts outside the Second Circuit, make it clear that corporations can be held liable for *jus cogens* violations. Indeed, since *Filartiga*, the Second Circuit has led the nation in ATCA jurisprudence. Clear and consistent Second Circuit precedent demonstrates that corporations may be held liable for *jus cogens* violations of international law. * * *

In [*Bigio v. Coca–Cola Co.*, 239 F.3d 440 (2d Cir.2000)], Canadian citizens and an Egyptian corporation sued the Coca–Cola Company and the Coca–Cola Export Company, both Delaware corporations. The plaintiffs in *Bigio* stated that the Egyptian government had unlawfully seized their property in Egypt because they were Jewish. Coca–Cola then allegedly purchased or leased the plaintiffs' property with full knowledge of the unlawful manner in which it was seized.... The Second Circuit emphasized the centrality of the question of subject matter jurisdiction, stating that the "first issue we must address is whether Coca–Cola can have violated 'the law of nations' if it acted solely as a non-governmental entity." *Bigio*, 239 F.3d at 447. The Second Circuit noted that the plaintiffs only alleged that Coca–Cola had acquired property that it knew had been discriminatorily expropriated. The Second Circuit rightly pointed out that although such discriminatory expropriation was "reprehensible," it was not an act of "universal concern" or a *jus cogens* violation. Additionally, the Second Circuit found that the *Bigio* plaintiffs had not alleged that Coca–Cola conspired with the Egyptian government in conducting the unlawful expropriation.

The Second Circuit's reasoning in *Bigio* is instructive. Although it ultimately held that the district court lacked subject matter jurisdiction under the ATCA, it did so because it was unclear that the acts allegedly committed by Coca–Cola actually violated international law. At the very least, the court held, the acts alleged to have been committed by Coca–Cola only violated international law when committed by state actors. The *Bigio* court contrasted these acts with slave trading, genocide, and war crimes. * * * The clear implication is that subject matter jurisdiction would have existed if the *Bigio* plaintiffs had alleged *jus cogens* violations such as enslavement, genocide, or war crimes—exactly the acts alleged in the instant case—rather than procurement of unlawfully expropriated property. * * *

[T]his Court is obliged to follow international law as interpreted by the Supreme Court and Second Circuit. In light of the precedent cited above, the Court must reject Talisman's claim that it is legally incapable of violating the law of nations. A further examination of international legal precedent similarly reveals that Talisman's position is "anachronistic." * * * Historically, states, and to a lesser extent individuals, have been held liable under international law. However, substantial international and United States precedent indicates that corporations may also be held liable under international law, at least for gross human rights violations. Extensive Second Circuit precedent further indicates that actions under the ATCA against corporate defendants for such substantial violations of international law, including *jus cogens* violations, are the norm rather than the exception. Such a result should hardly be surprising. A private corporation is a juridical person and has no *per se* immunity under U.S. domestic or international law. As noted above, a corporation may be imputed with having the requisite specific intent to commit a criminal action. Given that private individuals are liable for violations of international law in certain circumstances, there is no logical reason why corporations should not be held liable, at least in cases of *jus cogens* violations. * * *

[T]he concept of complicit liability for conspiracy or aiding and abetting is well-developed in international law, especially in the specific context of genocide, war crimes, and the like. The Statute of the International Military Tribunal, the body that tried Nazi war criminals, stated that "[l]eaders, organizers, instigators and accomplices participating in the formulation or execution of a common plan or conspiracy to commit any of the foregoing crimes are responsible for all acts performed by any persons in execution of such a plan." *Agreement for the Prosecution and Punishment of Major War Criminals of the European Axis, and Establishing the Charter of the International Military Tribunal*, art. 6, 82 U.N.T.S. 279. Allied Control Council Law No. 10, used to prosecute German war criminals domestically, created criminal liability not only for principals who committed acts of genocide or war crimes but also for those who were connected with any plans or enterprises involving the commission of such crimes. Such complicity could include corporate liability. Talisman cites the *von Weizsacker* case, in which a banker was acquitted of crimes against humanity for making loans that were used by an enterprise which exploited slave labor. However, unlike the facts in that case, here plaintiffs allege that Talisman worked directly with the government in its policy of "ethnic cleansing" and provided material aid to its efforts. In such cases, liability may follow. For example, the supplier of Zyklon B, the poison used for mass execution in many German concentration camps, was condemned by a British military court for violations of "the laws and usages of war." *United Kingdom v. Tesch*, 1 L. Rep. Tr. War.Crim. 93 (1947). The Statute of the International Criminal Tribunal for the former Yugoslavia ("ICTY") and the International Criminal Tribunal for Rwanda ("ICTR") similarly establish criminal liability for those who have "planned, instigated, ordered, committed, or otherwise aided and abetted in the planning, preparation or execution of a crime." * * *

[T]he Court finds that the Amended Complaint adequately sets forth that Talisman acted under color of law. The case cited by Talisman with respect to whether or not Talisman acted under color of law is *NCAA v. Tarkanian*, 488 U.S. 179 (1988). This case examined whether a state university's compliance with NCAA rules and regulations turned the NCAA's conduct into state action. A far more relevant and recent case is *Wiwa v. Royal Dutch Petroleum Co.*, No. 96 Civ. 8386, 2002 WL 319887 (S.D.N.Y. Feb. 28, 2002). Unlike *NCAA*, which analyzed general color of law principles, *Wiwa* concerned whether the human rights violations of a foreign state could be imputed to a corporation operating in that country. The facts in *Wiwa* are nearly identical to those here. Looking at 42 U.S.C. § 1983 jurisprudence as a guide, Judge Wood held that the "relevant test in this case is the 'joint action' test, under which private actors are considered state actors if they are 'willful participant[s] in joint action with the State or its agents.'" The *Wiwa* court also noted that "[W]here there is a substantial degree of cooperative action between the state and private actors in effecting the deprivation of rights, state action is present."

The *Wiwa* court held that a substantial degree of cooperative action was present between the corporate defendants and the government of Nigeria. This substantial degree of cooperative action included payments to the Nigerian government, corporate contracts for the purchase of arms, and coordination with the Nigerian government with respect to certain military attacks on civilians. Likewise, in this case plaintiffs allege that Talisman paid Sudan for "protection" knowing that such protection included unlawful acts; that it purchased dual use military equipment and permitted the Sudanese military to use certain facilities to launch unlawful attacks on civilians; and that it helped plan a strategy involving "ethnic cleansing." Just as in *Wiwa*, plaintiffs have adequately pled a "substantial degree of cooperation" between Talisman and Sudan. Therefore, the Court finds that Talisman can be treated as a state actor for purposes of the ATCA (though it reiterates, as noted *supra*, that such a finding is not necessary in light of the nature of plaintiffs' allegations). * * *

For the reasons set forth above, Talisman's motion to dismiss the Amended Complaint is denied.

FLORES v. S. PERU COPPER CORP.

414 F.3d 233 (2d Cir. 2003)

Plaintiffs in this case are residents of Ilo, Peru, and the representatives of deceased Ilo residents. They brought personal injury claims under the ATCA against Southern Peru Copper Corporation ("SPCC"), a United States company, alleging that pollution from SPCC's copper mining, refining, and smelting operations in and around Ilo caused plaintiffs' or their decedents' severe lung disease. The ATCA states that "[t]he district courts shall have original jurisdiction of any civil action by an alien for a tort only, committed in violation of the law of nations or a treaty of the United States." Plaintiffs claimed that defendant's conduct violates the "law of nations"—commonly referred to as "international law" or, when limited to non-treaty law, as "customary international law." In particular, they asserted that defendant infringed upon their customary international law "right to life," "right to health," and right to "sustainable development."

The United States District Court for the Southern District of New York held that plaintiffs had failed to establish subject matter jurisdiction or to state a claim under the ATCA because they had not alleged a violation of customary international law—i.e., that they had not "demonstrated that high levels of environmental pollution within a nation's borders, causing harm to human life, health, and development, violate well-established, universally recognized norms of international law." The Court further held that even if plaintiffs had alleged a violation of customary international law, the case would have to be dismissed on *forum non conveniens* grounds because Peru provides an adequate alternative forum for plaintiffs' claims and because the relevant public and private interest factors weigh heavily in favor of the Peruvian forum. Accordingly, the District Court granted defendant's motion to dismiss. * * *

SPCC's operations emit large quantities of sulfur dioxide and very fine particles of heavy metals into the local air and water. Plaintiffs claim that these emissions have caused their respiratory illnesses and that this "egregious and deadly" local pollution constitutes a customary international law offense because it violates the "right to life," "right to health," and right to "sustainable development."[1] * * * The District Court held that plaintiffs had failed to state a claim under the ATCA because they had not pleaded a violation of any cognizable principle of customary international law. The Court noted that it did not need to reach the question of *forum non conveniens* because it had determined that it lacked subject matter jurisdiction, but it nonetheless concluded that, even if plaintiffs had pleaded a violation of customary international law, dis-

---

1. On appeal, plaintiffs only pursue their claims that defendant's conduct violates customary international law rights to life and health; they no longer base their argument on a right to "sustainable development."

missal on the ground of *forum non conveniens* would have been appropriate.

In its analysis, the District Court discussed the requirements for a claim under the ATCA. It noted that "[t]he ATCA provides for federal court jurisdiction where a plaintiff's claim involves a violation of [i] a treaty of the United States or [ii] the law of nations, which consists of rules that 'command the general assent of civilized nations.'" Because plaintiffs did not claim any violation of a United States treaty, the Court turned to the issue of whether plaintiffs had alleged a violation of customary international law. The District Court noted that, in order to allege a violation of customary international law, "a plaintiff must demonstrate that a defendant's alleged conduct violated 'well-established, universally recognized norms of international law'" (quoting *Filartiga*, 630 F.2d at 888; citing *Kadic v. Karadzic*, 70 F.3d 232, 239 (2d Cir.1995)). * * *

On appeal, plaintiffs claim that the District Court erred in declining to recognize customary international law rights to life and health and in concluding that such rights were not sufficiently determinate to constitute "well-established, universally recognized norms of international law." *Filartiga*, 630 F.2d at 888. They also challenge the District Court's refusal to accord sufficient probative value to the numerous professorial affidavits, conventions, and declarations of multinational organizations that plaintiffs submitted in support of their claims. With respect to defendant's *forum non conveniens* claim, plaintiffs claim that the District Court erred in concluding that Peru provides an adequate alternative forum.

DISCUSSION

* * * In determining whether a particular rule is a part of customary international law—*i.e.*, whether States universally abide by, or accede to, that rule out of a sense of legal obligation and mutual concern—courts must look to concrete evidence of the customs and practices of States. As we have recently stated, "we look primarily to the formal lawmaking and official actions of States and only secondarily to the works of scholars as evidence of the established practice of States." *United States v. Yousef*, 327 F.3d 56, 103 (2d Cir.2003). * * *

A. The Rights to Life and Health Are Insufficiently Definite to Constitute Rules of Customary International Law

As an initial matter, we hold that the asserted "right to life" and "right to health" are insufficiently definite to constitute rules of customary international law. As noted above, in order to state a claim under the ATCA, we have required that a plaintiff allege a violation of a "clear and unambiguous" rule of customary international law. *Kadic*, 70 F.3d at 239 (holding that federal jurisdiction lies under the ATCA if "the defendant's alleged conduct violates 'well-established, universally recognized norms of international law' . . . as opposed to 'idiosyncratic legal rules'" (quoting *Filartiga*, 630 F.2d at 888, 881)); *cf. Beanal v. Freeport–McMoran, Inc.*, 197 F.3d 161, 167 (5th Cir.1999) (stating that customary international law cannot be established by reference to "abstract rights and liberties devoid of articulable or discernable standards and regulations"); *Hilao v. Estate of Marcos (In re Estate of Ferdinand Marcos, Human Rights Litig.)*, 25 F.3d 1467, 1475 (9th Cir.1994) (stating that a rule of customary international law must be "specific, universal, and obligatory").

Far from being "clear and unambiguous," the statements relied on by plaintiffs to define the rights to life and health are vague and amorphous. For example, the statements that plaintiffs rely on to define the rights to life and health include the following:

> Everyone has the right to a standard of living adequate for the health and well-being of himself and of his family. . . .

Universal Declaration of Human Rights, Art. 25 (1948).

> The States Parties to the present Covenant recognize the right of everyone to the enjoyment of the highest attainable standard of physical and mental health.

International Covenant on Economic, Social, and Cultural Rights, Art. 12, opened for signature Dec. 19, 1966, 993 U.N.T.S. 3.

> Human beings are . . . entitled to a healthy and productive life in harmony with nature.

Rio Declaration on Environment and Development ("Rio Declaration"), United Nations Conference on Environment and Development, June 13, 1992, Principle 1.

These principles are boundless and indeterminate. They express virtuous goals understandably expressed at a level of abstraction needed to secure the adherence of States that disagree on many of the particulars regarding how actually to achieve them. But in the words of a sister circuit, they "state abstract rights and liberties devoid of articulable or discernable standards and regulations." *Beanal*, 197 F.3d at 167. The precept that "[h]uman beings are * * * entitled to a healthy and productive life in harmony with nature," Rio Declaration, Principle 1, for example, utterly fails to specify what conduct would fall within or outside of the law. Similarly, the exhortation that all people are entitled to the "highest attainable standard of physical and mental health," International Covenant on Economic, Social, and Cultural Rights, Art. 12, proclaims only nebulous notions that are infinitely malleable.

In support of plaintiffs' argument that the statements and instruments discussed above are part of customary international law, plaintiffs attempt to underscore the universality of the principles asserted by pointing out that they "contain no limitations as to how or by whom these rights may be violated." However, this assertion proves too much; because of the conceded absence of any "limitations" on these "rights," they do not meet the requirement of our law that rules of customary international law be clear, definite, and unambiguous.

For the foregoing reasons, plaintiffs have failed to establish the existence of a customary international law "right to life" or "right to health."

B.   Plaintiffs Have Not Submitted Evidence Sufficient to Establish that Customary International Law Prohibits Intranational Pollution.

Although customary international law does not protect a right to life or right to health, plaintiffs' complaint may be construed to assert a claim under a more narrowly-defined customary international law rule against intranational pollution.[2] However, the voluminous documents and the affidavits of international law scholars submitted by plaintiffs fail to demonstrate the existence of any such norm of customary international law. * * *

The treaties on which plaintiffs principally rely include: the International Covenant on Civil and Political Rights; the American Convention on Human Rights; the International Covenant on Economic, Social and Cultural Rights; and the United Nations Convention on the Rights of the Child. The only treaty relied on by plaintiffs that the United States has ratified is the non-self-executing International Covenant on Civil and Political Rights ("ICCPR"), opened for signature Dec. 19, 1966, 999 U.N.T.S. 171.[3] * * * Plaintiffs rely on Article 6(1) of the ICCPR, which states that "[e]very human being has the inherent right to life" that "shall be protected by law," and that "[n]o one shall be arbitrarily deprived of his life." As noted above, the "right to life" is insufficiently definite to give rise to a rule of customary international law. Because no other provision of the ICCPR so much as suggests an international law norm prohibiting intranational pollution, the ICCPR does not provide a basis for plaintiffs' claim that defendant has violated a rule of customary international law.

Plaintiffs also rely on the unratified International Covenant on Economic, Social and Cultural Rights ("ICESCR"). This instrument arguably refers to the topic of pollution in article 12, which "recognize[s] the right of everyone to the enjoyment of the highest attainable standard of physical and mental health," and instructs the States parties to take the steps necessary for "[t]he improvement of all aspects of environmental and industrial hygiene," id. art. 12(2)(b). Although article 12(2)(b) instructs States to take steps to abate environmental pollution within their borders, it does not mandate particular measures or specify what levels of pollution are acceptable. Instead, it is vague and aspirational, and there is no evidence that the States parties have taken

---

2. Because plaintiffs do not allege that defendants' conduct had an effect outside the borders of Peru, we need not consider the customary international law status of transnational pollution.

3. The United States Senate gave its advice and consent to ratification of the ICCPR on April 2, 1992, see International Covenant on Civil and Political Rights, 102d Cong., 138 Cong. Rec. S4781, S4784, and it was ratified by the President on June 8, 1992, see I United Nations, Multilateral Treaties Deposited with the Secretary General 165 (2003). However, the treaty was ratified with numerous reservations conforming the United States' obligations under the ICCPR to the requirements of the Constitution, and with the declaration that the ICCPR is not self-executing. Id. Accordingly, this treaty does not create a private cause of action in United States courts.

significant uniform steps to put it into practice. Finally, even if this provision were sufficient to create a rule of customary international law, the rule would apply only to state actors because the provision addresses only "the steps to be taken by the States Parties," ICESCR art. 12(2), and does not profess to govern the conduct of private actors such as defendant SPCC. * * *

Plaintiffs [also] rely on several resolutions of the United Nations General Assembly in support of their assertion that defendant's conduct violated a rule of customary international law. These documents are not proper sources of customary international law because they are merely aspirational and were never intended to be binding on member States of the United Nations. * * * General Assembly resolutions and declarations do not have the power to bind member States because the member States specifically denied the General Assembly that power after extensively considering the issue—first at the Dumbarton Oaks Conference, held in Washington in 1944, then at the Yalta conference in 1945, and finally at the United Nations' founding conference, held in San Francisco in 1945. * * * In sum, as described in THE LAW OF NATIONS, the classic handbook by Professors Brierly and Waldock:

> [A]ll that the General Assembly can do is to discuss and recommend and initiate studies and consider reports from other bodies. It cannot act on behalf of all the members, as the Security Council does, and its decisions are not directions telling the member states what they are or are not to do.

J.L. Brierly, THE LAW OF NATIONS 110 (Sir Humphrey Waldock ed., 6th ed. 1963). Because General Assembly documents are at best merely advisory, they do not, on their own and without proof of uniform state practice, evidence an intent by member States to be legally bound by their principles, and thus cannot give rise to rules of customary international law.

Our position is consistent with the recognition in *Filartiga* that the right to be free from torture embodied in the Universal Declaration of Human Rights has attained the status of customary international law. *Filartiga* cited the Universal Declaration for the proposition that torture is universally condemned, reasoning that "a [United Nations] declaration may by custom become recognized as [a] rule[ ]" of customary international law. The Court explained that non-binding United Nations documents such as the Universal Declaration "create[ ] an expectation of adherence," but they evidence customary international law only "insofar as the expectation is gradually justified by State practice." In considering the Universal Declaration's prohibition against torture, the *Filartiga* Court cited extensive evidence that States, in their domestic and international practices, repudiate official torture. In particular, it recognized that torture is prohibited under law by, *inter alia*, the constitutions of fifty-five States, and noted the conclusion expressed by the Executive Branch of our government—the political branch with principal responsi-

bility for conducting the international relations of the United States—
that "[t]here now exists an international consensus" against official
torture that "virtually all governments acknowledge." Accordingly, although *Filartiga* did indeed cite the Universal Declaration, this non-
binding General Assembly declaration was only relevant to *Filartiga*'s
analysis insofar as it accurately described the actual customs and practices of States on the question of torture.

In the instant case, the General Assembly documents relied on by
plaintiffs do not describe the actual customs and practices of States.
Accordingly, they cannot support plaintiffs' claims. * * *

Plaintiffs [also] submitted to the District Court several affidavits by
international law scholars in support of their argument that strictly
intranational pollution violates customary international law. After careful
consideration, the District Court declined to afford evidentiary weight to
these affidavits. It determined that the affidavits "are even less probative
[than plaintiffs' documentary evidence] of the existence of universal
norms, especially considering the vigorous academic debate over the
content of international law." It explained further:

> The Second Circuit in *Filartiga* stated that courts should determine
> whether a rule is well-established and universally recognized by
> consulting, among other sources, " 'the works of jurists, writing
> professedly on public law.' " In this case, plaintiffs and defendant
> have submitted multiple affidavits by professors, explaining why or
> why not plaintiffs' claims are supported by customary international
> law. The affidavits serve essentially as supplemental briefs, provid-
> ing arguments and citations which for the most part also appear in
> the parties' main briefs. I doubt that such academic exercises in
> advocacy are the sort of scholarly writings the Second Circuit had in
> mind when it identified the sources that could serve as evidence of
> customary international law.

Plaintiffs argue on appeal that the District Court did not accord proper
weight to the statements of their experts. They maintain that "[t]he
authority of scholars, [and] jurists . . . has long been recognized by the
Supreme Court and this Court as authoritative sources for determining
the content of international law."

In its seminal decision in *Paquete Habana*, the Supreme Court
designated "the works of jurists [*i.e.*, scholars] and commentators" as a
possible source of customary international law. 175 U.S. at 700. However, the Court expressly stated that such works "are resorted to by
judicial tribunals, not for the speculations of their authors concerning
what the law ought to be, but for trustworthy evidence of what the law
really is." Accordingly, under *Paquete Habana*, United States judicial
tribunals may only "resort[ ] to" the works of "jurists and commentators" insofar as such works set forth the current law as it "really is."
Conversely, courts may not entertain as evidence of customary international law "speculations" by "jurists and commentators" about "what the

law ought to be." * * * [Nothing in] *Paquete Habana* recognizes as a source of customary international law the policy-driven or theoretical work of advocates that comprises a substantial amount of contemporary international law scholarship. Nor do these authorities permit us to consider personal viewpoints expressed in the affidavits of international law scholars. In sum, although scholars may provide accurate descriptions of the actual customs and practices and legal obligations of States, only the courts may determine whether these customs and practices give rise to a rule of customary international law.

We have reviewed the affidavits submitted by plaintiffs and agree with the District Court's conclusion that they are not competent evidence of customary international law.

In addition to the types of evidence discussed above, plaintiffs direct the Court's attention to a varied assortment of other instruments that neither give rise to, nor evidence, concrete, international legal obligations. Plaintiffs argue that all of the items of evidence they have submitted, when taken together, prove that local environmental pollution violates customary international law. However, because each of the instruments and affidavits plaintiffs rely on provides no evidence that intranational pollution violates customary international law, plaintiffs' claims fail whether these instruments and affidavits are considered individually or cumulatively. * * *

NOTES AND QUESTIONS ON THE REGIME OF CIVIL LIABILITY

1. *Identifying the actionable wrongs.* Why is the genocide alleged in *Talisman* actionable and the environmental degradation alleged in *Flores* is not? Specifically, how would you describe the differences between the causes of action (and the evidence of the norms' status) in the two cases? Must a norm qualify as *jus cogens* before it is actionable under the Alien Tort Statute against a corporation? Is it relevant that, at the time of the suits, Sudan was considered a pariah state by the government of the United States and Peru was considered an ally?

2. *Corporations and the war on terrorism.* In *Ibrahim v. Titan Corp.*, 391 F. Supp.2d 10 (D.D.C. 2005), seven Iraqi nationals alleged that they (or their late husbands) were tortured while held in detention by the U.S. military at the Abu Ghraib prison in Iraq. Plaintiffs invoked the ATS against two private government contractors that had provided interpreters and interrogators at Abu Ghraib. Concluding that torture is a violation of international law only when committed by state actors, the court dismissed the action under the ATS. Plaintiffs could not sue the United States government directly, because it enjoys sovereign immunity for "any claim arising out of the combatant activities of the military ... forces ... during time of war," 28 U.S.C. § 2680(j). Should government contractors get the same immunity as the government itself? *See Boyle v.*

United Techs. Corp., 487 U.S. 500 (1988). Should the political question doctrine, *supra* Module 2, pose a prophylactic barrier to such lawsuits?

How would you resolve the following case under the ATS? Jeppesen Dataplan, Inc., is a subsidiary of Boeing Company. Three victims of the United States government's unlawful "extraordinary rendition" program allege that Jeppesen knowingly provided direct flight services to the CIA, enabling the clandestine transportation of Binyam Mohamed, Abou Elkassim Britel and Ahmed Agiza to secret overseas locations where they were allegedly subjected to torture and other forms of cruel, inhuman and degrading treatment. *See* Amnesty International, *Below the Radar: Secret Flights to Torture and "Disappearance"* (Apr. 5, 2006), *available at* http://web.amnesty.org/library/Index/ENGAMR510512006.

3.   *Corporations and terrorism.* In *Almog v. Arab Bank, PLC,* 471 F. Supp. 2d 257 (E.D.N.Y. 2007), some victims of terrorist acts in Israel alleged that a Jordanian bank knowingly and intentionally provided banking services to terrorist organizations and specifically that it knew the accounts funded suicide bombings. The court denied the bank's motion to dismiss under the ATS:

> [I]n light of the universal condemnation of organized and systematic suicide bombings and other murderous acts intended to intimidate or coerce a civilian population, this court finds that such conduct violates an established norm of international law. The court further finds that the conduct alleged by plaintiffs is sufficiently specific and well-defined to be recognized as a claim under the ATS. This becomes evident when the conduct alleged here and condemned by the law of nations is viewed in contrast to the conduct alleged in cases where it was found not to be sufficiently specific or well-defined. For instance, in *Flores* the plaintiffs, who alleged that they developed lung disease from pollution arising from defendant's copper mining and refining operations within the plaintiffs' country, asserted international norms of the "right to life" and the "right to health." Those rights were insufficiently definite because they were "vague and amorphous," "boundless and indeterminate," "abstract rights and liberties devoid of articulable or discernible standards and regulations."

Id., at 284.

4.   *The uses of a settlement.* Human rights litigation against multinational corporations can be "successful" from the plaintiffs' perspectives, even if there is no finding of liability, so long as there is a settlement. *See,* David E. Rovella, *Sweatshop Alleged [Against Gap, Inc.],* NATIONAL LAW JOURNAL, (Jan. 25, 1999), and *Sweatshop Settlement Draws Others: Four Non–Parties Agree to Terms of the $1.25 Million Pact,* NATIONAL LAW JOURNAL (Aug. 23, 1999). Human rights advocates have generally concluded that Gap Inc. was instrumental after the settlement in improving working conditions across the industry. Similarly, settlements against Unocal in the United States and against Total in France would never have oc-

curred if the companies involved had not significantly improved the human rights conditions in the Burmese pipeline project.

5. *Alternative theories of civil liability*: Companies that pursue "human rights entrepreneurialism" and proclaim a commitment to human rights as part of their marketing campaigns could face liability for deceptive advertising if that commitment is violated in fact. *See, e.g., Kasky v. Nike, Inc.*, 119 Cal.Rptr.2d 296, 45 P.3d 243 (Cal. 2002), *cert granted*, 537 U.S. 1099 (2003), *cert. dismissed as improvidently granted*, 539 U.S. 654 (2003). In September 2003, Nike agreed to pay $1.5 million to settle the case.

4. A REGIME OF INTERNATIONAL REGULATION AND SOFT LAW

No intergovernmental organization has ever adopted a binding and comprehensive code of conduct for multinational corporations, but some prominent multilateral organizations have found human rights increasingly relevant to their mandates. As a consequence, multilateral organizations may prove to be an effective forum for developing a unified front and assuring that corporations and governments do not engage in some perpetual race to the bottom in the protection of international human rights. The argument is not that the major intergovernmental institutions, like the World Trade Organization and the World Bank, are inevitably forces for good in the protection of human rights. To the contrary, a standard critique within the human rights movement rests on these institutions' alleged sins of commission (like promoting the liberalization of trade at the expense of human rights, or imposing structural adjustment policies that promote political repression, or allowing a democratic deficit in their own decision-making) and alleged sins of omission (like remaining "apolitical" as required by their articles of association and thereby ignoring human rights abuses of member governments). But there is a marked and increasing tendency within these organizations to link commerce and human rights through international regulation and soft law instruments, which—taken together—define a fourth regime of principle and practice.

(i) *International Labour Organization and the Tripartite Declaration of Principles concerning Multinational Enterprises and Social Policy*. The International Labour Organization ("ILO") was established because its founders agreed that workers faced conditions which, if unaddressed, could create social unrest and provoke revolution on a global scale.[1] But they also realized that each government had a short-term economic incentive to let someone else go first: the needed social reform inevitably raised the costs of production, and any industry or government that unilaterally improved labor conditions would find itself at a steep competitive

---

1. The Preamble of the ILO Constitution declares that "conditions of labour exist involving such injustice, hardship, and privation to large numbers of people as to produce unrest so great that the peace and harmony of the world are imperilled."

disadvantage. If each government could attract foreign capital investment by suppressing wages and impoverishing its own people, only an enforced cartel of values could accomplish the reform that all agreed was necessary. In the words of the Preamble to the ILO Constitution, "the failure of *any* nation to adopt humane conditions of labour is an obstacle in the way of *other* nations which desire to improve the conditions in their own countries." The ILO offered a forum for agreeing on minimum protections for workers, and its tripartite governing structure—involving governments, employers, and labor organizations—assured a measure of legitimacy among the relevant constituencies. The clear objective was to allow *a humane comparative advantage* to prevail in international markets by unifying and harmonizing labor rights. Through a series of conventions and recommendations, the organization attempted to set minimum standards *inter alia* for the freedom of association, the right to organize and to bargain collectively, the abolition of forced labor, and the right to equality of opportunity and treatment.

The centerpiece of the ILO's corporate responsibility agenda remains the Tripartite Declaration of Principles concerning Multinational Enterprises and Social Policy.[2] In addition to the conventions and recommendations incorporated into the original instrument, the Tripartite Declaration now includes the Declaration on Fundamental Principles and Rights at Work (and its Follow–Up program),[3] which expands the obligation to protect labor rights and attempts to strengthen the means of implementation and enforcement. But the Tripartite Declaration remains non-binding by its terms: implementation has been constrained by its dependency on domestic incorporation by states and on promotion and publication campaigns by non-governmental entities like Sweatshop Watch, the Campaign for Labor Rights, and the Maquila Solidarity Network. The direct obligations of multinational enterprises under the Declaration have remained implicit at best, with the ILO concluding somewhat meekly that "the contribution of multinational enterprises to its implementation can prove an important element in the attainment of its objectives."[4]

But to focus on the Declaration and its discontents is to miss the broader significance of the ILO's contribution to a regime of best practices with respect to corporate social performance. The ILO has been instrumental in identifying the overlap between labor concerns and the unique vulnerabilities of particular populations—like women, indigenous minorities, and children—with the consequence that the intellectual firebreak that has separated international labor law from interna-

---

2. ILO, Tripartite Declaration of Principles concerning Multinational Enterprises and Social Policy, 17 INT'L LEG. MATS. 422 (1978).

3. ILO Declaration on Fundamental Principles and Rights at Work, 86th Session, Geneva, 18 June 1998, *available at* http://www.ilo.org/public/english/standards/decl/declaration/text/index.htm.

4. Addendum to the Tripartite Declaration of Principles concerning Multinational Enterprises and Social Policy, adopted by the Governing Body of the International Labour Office, Subcommittee on Multinational Enterprises, ILO Doc. GB.277/MNE/3 (6 March 2000).

tional human rights law can no longer be maintained, suggesting in turn a broader range of human rights concerns in the marketplace. *See* Module 10, *infra*. ILO standards have also become the touchstone in domestic litigation challenging corporate labor practices around the world, giving them an effectiveness beyond the ILO mechanisms themselves. In addition, labor standards have become intrinsically entwined with international trade negotiations, especially on a bilateral and regional basis,[5] reinforcing the relevance of human rights standards in the global marketplace.

(ii) *The United Nations Sub–Commission on Human Rights.* In comparison to the *lex lata* status of many ILO conventions, the Sub–Commission on Human Rights for many years negotiated and in August 2003 adopted a set of principles governing corporate human rights standards, entitled "Norms on the Responsibilities for Transnational Corporations and Other Business Enterprises with Regard to Human Rights." United Nations Economic and Social Council, Commission on Human Rights, Fifty–Fifth Session of the Sub–Commission on the Promotion and Protection of Human Rights, *Norms on the Responsibilities of Transnational Corporations and Other Business Enterprises*, E/CN.4/Sub.2/2003/12/Rev.2 (2003) (hereinafter "Norms"). As shown below, the Norms draw on a variety of treaties, resolutions, and declarations, but they also rest on a somewhat expansive theory of corporate responsibility, linking it not to the company's control but to its "influence"[6] and "benefit."[7] It also conceives the transnational corporation broadly, referring not to its legally defined structure or that of its subsidiaries and contractors, but to an "economic entity" or indeed a "cluster of economic entities" operating in two or more countries. Until these terms are defined legally and not just economically, the U.N. Norms are likely to remain *lex ferenda* at best. The document as adopted by the experts on the Sub–Commission is also edgy, because it obliges corporations to respect and promote economic, social, and cultural rights, like adequate food, health, housing, and education. And the fact that bribery and fair business practices are included suggest that the Sub–Commission's Norms offer the broadest-gauged standards currently in contemplation. On the other hand, an expansive approach is possible primarily because implementation rests

---

5. *See, e.g.,* the Free Trade Agreement between the United States and Jordan, signed on October 24, 2000, which, for the first time, included enforceable labor and environmental standards, as defined in the ILO Declaration on Fundamental Principles, in the body of a trade treaty, *available at* www.ustr.gov/assets/Trade_Agreements/Bilateral/Jordan/asset_upload_file250_5112.pdf.

6. *Norms*, at ¶ 1:

Within their respective spheres of activity and *influence*, transnational corporations and other business enterprises have the obligation to respect, ensure respect for, prevent abuses of, and promote human rights recognized in international as well as national law, including the rights and interests of indigenous peoples and other vulnerable groups.

7. *Id.*, at ¶ 3:

Transnational corporations and other business enterprises shall not engage in *nor benefit from* war crimes, crimes against humanity, genocide, torture, forced disappearance, forced or compulsory labour, hostage-taking, extrajudicial, summary or arbitrary executions, other violations of humanitarian law, and other international crimes against the human person as defined by international law, in particular human rights and humanitarian law.

on internalization by the multinational corporations themselves, "subject to periodic monitoring and verification by United Nations, other international and national mechanisms already in existence or yet to be created, regarding application of the Norms."[8] Governments have not rushed to embrace the Norms, which were after all negotiated and promulgated by experts and not state representatives, but, as an indication of one possible trajectory of developments at the international level, the Norms are indicative. At a minimum, the controversy surrounding the Norms led to the appointment by the UN Secretary General of a Special Representative on the human rights obligations of transnational companies. The Special Representative's report in 2008, *infra*, maintained moderate momentum towards the establishment of a regime of international regulation and soft law.

(iii) *The United Nations Secretary General: the Global Compact*. The Global Compact articulates ten principles in the areas of human rights, labor standards, and the environment, designed to assure that the fragile process of globalization is not derailed by the concentration of economic power, the degradation of the environment, or the perpetuation of poverty, corruption, and human rights abuses. Under the Compact, companies may voluntarily commit to protecting internationally proclaimed human rights and eliminating all forms of forced or compulsory labor and discrimination. But the Compact is clearly not a regulatory instrument, and it articulates no binding code of conduct. Nor does it offer any forum for policing a company's compliance, other than a minimal annual self-reporting requirement. But it does offer a concrete setting for "human rights entrepreneurialism," meaning the ways for one company to distinguish itself from its competitors in the market. To the extent that the Global Compact is integrated into corporate development and training programs, it can contribute towards the coalescence of voluntary standards into meaningful and practical norms of behavior. The principal virtue of the Global Compact may turn out to be the forum it provides for the publication and dissemination of best practices by its members.

(iv) *The Bretton Woods System*. Intergovernmental institutions devoted to economic development or monetary stability, notably the World Bank and the International Monetary Fund, long thought themselves constrained by an obligation in their mandates to make decisions apolitically, with the result that human rights concerns were traditionally considered out of bounds. *See* Module 9, *infra*. Article IV of the Bank's Articles of Agreement for example provides in pertinent part that

> the Bank and its officers shall not interfere in the political affairs of any member; nor shall they be influenced in their decisions by the political character of the member or members concerned. *Only economic considerations shall be relevant to their decisions*, and these

---

8. *Id.*, at ¶ 16. In addition, under ¶ 17, "States should establish and reinforce the necessary legal and administrative framework for ensuring that the Norms and other relevant national and international laws are implemented by transnational corporations and other business enterprises."

considerations shall be weighed impartially in order to achieve the [Bank's] purposes stated in Article 1.[9]

Designed to be non-ideological tools for the achievement of exclusively "economic" ends, the Bank and the Fund rarely structured their activities either to facilitate the protection of human rights or to prevent and punish abuses. Gradually however the development consequences of the Bank's disregard of human rights conditions in recipient countries[10] and the human rights consequences of some IMF structural adjustment policies induced both institutions to expand the notion of "economic considerations." Though it cannot be said that the international financial institutions are especially vigilant or consistent in making decisions that are sensitive to human rights concerns, the current work of the Bretton Woods institutions is by historical standards more constrained by objectives like democratization, good governance, the rule of law, and the protection of indigenous peoples' and women's rights.[11]

This is not the result of some sudden and irrepressible altruism at these institutions. Following controversial funding decisions at the Bank for example, some major donors made their willingness to contribute to the development effort contingent on the establishment of an independent inspection function by the Bank. This was accomplished by creating an Inspection Panel designed "to provide a formal mechanism for receiving complaints from people directly affected by Bank-supported projects on the grounds of [its] failure to abide by its own policies, including environmental and social policies, when designing, appraising, and supervising the implementation of projects."[12] The panel process offers a transparent accountability mechanism for the Bank itself, but it creates no liability and invests individuals with no substantive rights that might be enforced against the Bank. Nor does it create social responsibility obligations for multinational corporations that may be involved. Nor has the panel process met with unqualified support within the Bank itself, especially after its criticism of the Bank's dam project in Tibet.

But the panel process does offer evidence of a glacial change in the legal and commercial environment. Specifically, it suggests three layers

---

9. Articles of Agreement of the International Bank for Reconstruction and Development, *opened for signature,* Dec. 27, 1945, 60 Stat. 1440, T.I.A.S. No. 1502, 2 U.N.T.S. 134, *as amended,* Dec. 16, 1965, 16 U.S.T. 1942, T.I.A.S. No. 5929, at § 10, Art. IV (emphasis supplied).

10. Elizabeth M. King and Andrew D. Mason, *Engendering Development through Gender Equality in Rights, Resources, and Voice* (World Bank Report No. 21776, 2001). The potential scope of the Bank's human rights concerns is suggested by its decision that female genital mutilation is an economic issue within its mandate. George Graham, *Pledge over Female Mutilation: World Bank and IMF Win Commitment by Burkina Faso,* FINANCIAL TIMES, A6 (Apr. 22, 1994).

11. *See, e.g.,* World Bank Operational Manual, Operational Directive (OD) on Indigenous Peoples 4.20 (Sept. 1991); *id.,* Operational Policy (OP) on Involuntary Resettlement 4.12 (Dec. 2001) ("Bank experience indicates that involuntary resettlement under development projects, if unmitigated, often gives rise to severe economic, social, and environmental risks"); *id.,* World Bank Operational Policy (OP) on Gender and Development 4.20 ("The objective of the Bank's gender and development policy is to assist member countries to reduce poverty and enhance economic growth, human well-being, and development effectiveness by addressing the gender disparities and inequalities that are barriers to development. . . .").

12. Sabine Schlemmer–Schulte, *The World Bank Inspection Panel: A Record of the First International Accountability Mechanism and Its Role for Human Rights,* 6 HUMAN RIGHTS BR. 1 (1999).

(or generations) of human rights concerns within the Bank that have emerged over time: (i) initially, the Bank's support for physical infrastructure projects in education, health care, housing, and sanitation enabled a variety of recipients to begin to exercise certain economic and social rights; (ii) more recently, the Bank's focus on pragmatic abstractions like good governance, the rule of law, an independent judiciary, and transparency has brought a greater range of rights, including political rights, within reach of beneficiaries; and (iii) most recently, the Bank has articulated the understanding that sustainable development requires at a minimum the institutionalization of concern for particularly vulnerable populations, notably children, indigenous peoples, and women,[13] as well as broader commitments to democracy, social justice, transparent and accountable governance, and universal human rights.[14]

The IMF's capacity to affect human rights conditions is perhaps more modest than the Bank's, given its institutional concern with macroeconomic, particularly monetary, policies, instead of discrete development projects. And the means at its disposal—financing the general balance of payments or not—is too blunt an instrument to address specific human rights violations. But, as the Fund's experience with *apartheid* South Africa demonstrated, systematic human rights violations can have a macroeconomic and particularly monetary impact, affecting a member state's ability to meet its obligations to the Fund.[15] The Fund seems also to have understood that its conditionality and structural adjustment policies have human rights consequences that can be severe and for which the Fund itself is responsible. Of course, the Fund's decisions create no direct legal obligations for multinational corporations, but they do establish an environment in-country within which the corporation must act.

(v) *The Organisation for Economic Cooperation and Development.* The OECD Guidelines for Multinational Enterprises, *infra*, comprise recommendations by governments to multinational enterprises that operate in or from their territories. Though the Guidelines are entirely voluntary, they offer one of the few examples of government representatives—as distinct from the experts in the U.N. Sub–Commission or an international secretariat or advocates or NGOs—addressing the management of multinational companies directly in a multilateral setting through the expression of shared expectations. The states obligate themselves to implement the Guidelines and to promote compliance with them by all enterprises that operate in or from the member state's territory. Several areas of business conduct are covered, but it was not until 2000 that the Guidelines expressly included human rights, providing that "enterprises should * * * [r]espect the human rights of those affected by their

---

13. The International Bank for Reconstruction and Development, *Development and Human Rights* 20 (1998).

14. *See, e.g.,* "Copenhagen Declaration on Social Development" in *Report of the U.N. World Summit for Social Development,* U.N. Doc. A/CONF.166/9 (1995) at ¶ 26.

15. *See* Daniel Bradlow, *Debt, Development and Democracy: Lessons from South Africa,* 12 MICH. J. INT'L L. 647 (1991).

activities consistent with the host government's obligations and commitments." In other words, rather than imposing obligations on the companies, the revised Guidelines enjoin corporations to act consistently with the host state's international human rights obligations, presumably including the Universal Declaration of Human Rights and the human rights treaties to which the host state is a party. Earlier versions of the Guidelines focused on labor rights on the rationale that labor conditions were within the innermost circle of corporate control and that going beyond human rights concerns within the company's control was neither politic nor effective. But the most recent iteration of the Guidelines and the recent set of concerns within the OECD itself suggest that the body of relevant human rights norms is not inert but is in a steady state of evolution: since 2001, the OECD and its staff have addressed as human rights concerns a wide variety of business problems, including working conditions in the supply chain, multinational enterprises in situations of violent conflict and widespread human rights abuses, management control systems, and bribery. In April 2008, John Ruggie, the United Nations Special Representative on business and human rights concluded that the "current human rights provisions [of the OECD] not only lack specificity, but in key respects have fallen behind the voluntary standards of many companies and business organizations" and called for their revision.

The institutional enforcement of the Guidelines consists in "follow-up," soft procedures like consultations, good offices, mediation, conciliation, as well as "clarifications" of the guidelines themselves, none of which qualifies as a judicial or even a quasi-judicial proceeding. Implementation necessarily rests on the will of governments through their National Contact Points, as specified in the Guidelines. Non-governmental organizations have been especially critical of that process, especially after the failure of the OECD's Multilateral Agreement on Investment (MAI). From one perspective, the MAI negotiations failed because no consensus emerged on the contours of a social clause—provisions protecting environmental, cultural, indigenous, and social rights. But here too there is a certain naivete that dismisses the exercise because it is not yet fully effective, missing the degree to which governments, businesses, trade unions, and non-governmental organizations have committed to the process as a whole and the steady accumulation of heightened expectations by the governments of the most powerful economies in the world.

(vi) *The World Trade Organization.* The WTO occupies at best ambiguous space in the emerging international regime of corporate responsibility. Its predecessor organization, the General Agreement on Tariffs and Trade, emerged in isolation from other multilateral institutions of global governance like the United Nations and the World Bank, and its body of norms was considered largely *sui generis*. Its purpose, like that of the WTO, was trade liberalization and the reduction of tariffs and other barriers to trade, which seemed separate from, indeed irrelevant to, the protection of human rights.[16]

Nevertheless, as shown more fully in Module 9, *infra*, states and civil society gradually understood the partial linkage between human rights protections and the quality of the international market: labor abuses could depress export prices below fair market value and amount to a form of "social dumping;" certain forms of trade, like the sale of conflict diamonds, would not be entitled to the benefits of trade liberalization; and the prospect of admission to the organization could induce non-member states to accede to human rights treaties and become part of a broader "cartel of values" in the promotion of the rule of law and transparent, accountable governance. The WTO's dispute settlement mechanism also offered human rights advocates a potential technique for making human rights protections part of every state's economic self-interest: the threat of retaliatory sanctions, approved by a quasi-judicial panel subject to appellate review, for violations of international norms, has generated an admirable if imperfect record of compliance.

CORPORATIONS AND INTERNATIONAL CRIMINAL LAW

PRESBYTERIAN CHURCH OF SUDAN v. TALISMAN ENERGY, INC.

244 F. Supp. 2d 289 (S.D.N.Y. 2003)

The concept of corporate liability for *jus cogens* violations has its roots in the trials of German war criminals after World War II. The Nuremberg Charter permitted the prosecution of "a group or organization" and allowed the tribunal to declare that entity a "criminal organization." Agreement for the Prosecution and Punishment of Major War Criminals of the European Axis, and Establishing the Charter of the International Military Tribunal, 1951, arts. 9, 10, 82 U.N.T.S. 279. In *United States v. Flick*, *United States v. Krauch*, and *United States v. Krupp*, the heads of major German corporations were prosecuted for, *inter alia*, war crimes and crimes against humanity. Talisman points out, correctly, that in each of these cases, individuals, and not corporate entities, were put on trial. However, it ignores the fact that the court [in *Krauch*] consistently spoke in terms of corporate liability:

> With reference to the charges in the present indictment concerning Farben's [a German corporation] activities in Poland, Norway, Al-

---

16. The primary objective of the WTO is to "liberalise international trade and place it on a secure basis" which will "thereby contribut[e] to the economic growth, development, and welfare of the world's people." Final Act Embodying the Results of the Uruguay Round of Multilateral Trade Negotiations, Agreement Establishing the Multilateral Trade Organization, 33 *International Legal Mats.* 13 (1993).

sace–Lorraine, and France, we find that the proof establishes beyond a reasonable doubt that offenses against property as defined in Control Council Law No. 10[1] were committed by Farben, and that these offenses were connected with, and an inextricable part of the German policy for occupied countries. [. . .]. The action of Farben and its representatives, under these circumstances, cannot be differentiated from acts of plunder or pillage committed by officers, soldiers, or public officials of the German Reich. [. . .] Such action on the part of Farben constituted a violation of the Hague Regulations [on the conduct of warfare].

The language of the decision makes it clear that the court considered that the corporation *qua* corporation had violated international law. The same logic guided the court in a case involving the Krupp corporation:

> [T]he confiscation of the Austin plant [a tractor factory owned by the Rothschilds] [. . .] and its subsequent detention by the Krupp firm constitute a violation of . . . the Hague Regulations [concerning the Laws and Customs of War on Land (1907)] [. . . and] the Krupp firm, through defendants[, . . .] voluntarily and without duress participated in these violations.

As in *Krauch*, the *Krupp* court makes it clear that while individuals were nominally on trial, the Krupp company itself, acting through its employees, violated international law.

The Nuremberg precedent cited above is particularly significant not merely because it constitutes a basis for finding corporate liability for violations of international law, but because the language ascribes to the corporations involved the necessary *mens rea* for the commission of war crimes and crimes against humanity; the types of criminal behavior at issue in the instant case.[2]

———————

Consider the following instruments, adopted by two very different international bureaucracies, articulating various principles of corporate responsibility. How would you articulate the principal differences among them? Does the difference in their sources affect their content? How would you assess the legal status of these instruments? If you were advising a transnational company that wished in good faith to respect human rights and remain profitable, which of these instruments, if any,

---

1. [Control Council Law No. 10 can be found in the Documents Supplement.]

2. Talisman's experts claim that a corporation cannot have the specific intent to commit genocide. It is well-established, however, that corporations may be criminally liable for offenses requiring a specific intent. "We think that a corporation may be liable criminally for certain offenses of which a specific intent may be a necessary element. There is no more difficulty in imputing to a corporation a specific intent in criminal proceedings than in civil." *New York Cent. & Hudson River R.R. Co. v. United States*, 212 U.S. 481, 493, 29 S.Ct. 304, 53 L.Ed. 613 (1909) (citation omitted). Corporations may be held criminally liable under a myriad of statutes. *See, e.g.*, 18 U.S.C. §§ 1961 et seq. (Racketeer Influenced and Corrupt Organizations Act); 18 U.S.C. § 610 (coercion of political activity); 18 U.S.C. § 1512 (witness tampering).

would you support? If you were Secretary General of Amnesty International, which one of these horses would you back?

U.N. SUB–COMMISSION ON THE PROMOTION AND PROTECTION OF HUMAN RIGHTS: NORMS ON THE RESPONSIBILITIES OF TRANSNATIONAL CORPORATIONS AND OTHER BUSINESS ENTERPRISES WITH REGARD TO HUMAN RIGHTS

U.N. Doc. E/CN.4/Sub.2/2003/12/Rev.2 (2003)

Bearing in mind the principles and obligations under the Charter of the United Nations, in particular the preamble and Articles 1, 2, 55 and 56, *inter alia* to promote universal respect for, and observance of, human rights and fundamental freedoms, * * *

Recognizing that even though States have the primary responsibility to promote, secure the fulfilment of, respect, ensure respect of and protect human rights, transnational corporations and other business enterprises, as organs of society, are also responsible for promoting and securing the human rights set forth in the Universal Declaration of Human Rights,

Realizing that transnational corporations and other business enterprises, their officers and persons working for them are also obligated to respect generally recognized responsibilities and norms contained in United Nations treaties and other international instruments such as the Convention on the Prevention and Punishment of the Crime of Genocide; the Convention against Torture and Other Cruel, Inhuman or Degrading Treatment or Punishment; the Slavery Convention and the Supplementary Convention on the Abolition of Slavery, the Slave Trade, and Institutions and Practices Similar to Slavery; the International Convention on the Elimination of All Forms of Racial Discrimination; the Convention on the Elimination of All Forms of Discrimination against Women; the International Covenant on Economic, Social and Cultural Rights; the International Covenant on Civil and Political Rights; the Convention on the Rights of the Child; the International Convention on the Protection of the Rights of All Migrant Workers and Members of Their Families; the four Geneva Conventions of 12 August 1949 and two Additional Protocols thereto for the protection of victims of war; the Declaration on the Right and Responsibility of Individuals, Groups and Organs of Society to Promote and Protect Universally Recognized Human Rights and Fundamental Freedoms; the Rome Statute of the International Criminal Court; the United Nations Convention against Transnational Organized Crime; the Convention on Biological Diversity; the International Convention on Civil Liability for Oil Pollution Damage; the Convention on Civil Liability for Damage Resulting from Activities Dangerous to the Environment; the Declaration on the Right to Development; the Rio Declaration on the Environment and Development; the Plan of Implementation of the World Summit on Sustainable Development; the United Nations Millennium Declaration; the Universal Declaration on the Human Genome and Human Rights; the International Code of Marketing of Breast milk Substitutes adopted by the World Health Assembly; the Ethical Criteria for Medical Drug Promotion and the "Health for All in the Twenty–First Century" policy of the World Health Organization; the Convention against Discrimination in Education of the United Nations Education, Scientific, and Cultural Organization; conventions and recommendations of the International Labour Organization; the Convention and Protocol relating to the Status of Refugees; the African Charter on Human and Peoples' Rights; the American Convention on Human Rights; the European Convention for the Protection of Human Rights and Fundamental Freedoms; the Charter of Fundamental Rights of the European Union; the Convention on Combating Bribery of Foreign Public Officials in International Business Transactions of the Organization for Economic Cooperation and Development; and other instruments,

Taking into account the standards set forth in the Tripartite Declaration of Principles Concerning Multinational Enterprises and Social Policy and the Declaration on Fundamental Principles and Rights at Work of the International Labour Organization,

Aware of the Guidelines for Multinational Enterprises and the Committee on International Investment and Multinational Enterprises of the Organization for Economic Cooperation and Development,

Aware also of the United Nations Global Compact initiative which challenges business leaders to "embrace and enact" [ten] basic principles with respect to human rights, including labour rights and the environment, * * *

Taking note of global trends which have increased the influence of transnational corporations and other business enterprises on the economies of most countries and in international economic relations, and of the growing number of other business enterprises which operate across national boundaries in a variety of arrangements resulting in economic activities beyond the actual capacities of any one national system,

Noting that transnational corporations and other business enterprises have the capacity to foster economic well-being, development, technological improvement and wealth as well as the capacity to cause harmful impacts on the human rights and lives of individuals through their core business practices and operations, including employment practices, environmental policies, relationships with suppliers and consumers, interactions with Governments and other activities,

* * *

Reaffirming that transnational corporations and other business enterprises, their officers—including managers, members of corporate boards or directors and other executives—and persons working for them have, *inter alia*, human rights obligations and responsibilities and that these human rights norms will contribute to the making and development of international law as to those responsibilities and obligations,

Solemnly proclaims these Norms on the Responsibilities of Transnational Corporations and Other Business Enterprises with Regard to Human Rights and urges that every effort be made so that they become generally known and respected.

A.   *General obligations*

1.   States have the primary responsibility to promote, secure the fulfilment of, respect, ensure respect of and protect human rights recognized in international as well as national law, including ensuring that transnational corporations and other business enterprises respect human rights. Within their respective spheres of activity and influence, transnational corporations and other business enterprises have the obligation to promote, secure the fulfilment of, respect, ensure respect of and protect human rights recognized in international as well as national law, including the rights and interests of indigenous peoples and other vulnerable groups.

B.   *Right to equal opportunity and non-discriminatory treatment*

2.   Transnational corporations and other business enterprises shall ensure equality of opportunity and treatment, as provided in the relevant international instruments and national legislation as well as international human rights law, for the purpose of eliminating discrimination based on race, colour, sex, language, religion, political opinion, national or social origin, social status, indigenous status, disability, age—except for children, who may be given greater protection—or other status of the individual unrelated to the inherent requirements to perform the job, or of complying with special measures designed to overcome past discrimination against certain groups.

C.   *Right to security of persons*

3.   Transnational corporations and other business enterprises shall not engage in nor benefit from war crimes, crimes against humanity, genocide, torture, forced disappearance, forced or compulsory labour, hostage-taking, extrajudicial, summary or arbitrary executions, other violations of humanitarian law and other international crimes against the human person as defined by international law, in particular human rights and humanitarian law.

4.   Security arrangements for transnational corporations and other business enterprises shall observe international human rights norms as well as the laws and professional standards of the country or countries in which they operate.

D. Rights of workers

5. Transnational corporations and other business enterprises shall not use forced or compulsory labour as forbidden by the relevant international instruments and national legislation as well as international human rights and humanitarian law.

6. Transnational corporations and other business enterprises shall respect the rights of children to be protected from economic exploitation as forbidden by the relevant international instruments and national legislation as well as international human rights and humanitarian law.

7. Transnational corporations and other business enterprises shall provide a safe and healthy working environment as set forth in relevant international instruments and national legislation as well as international human rights and humanitarian law.

8. Transnational corporations and other business enterprises shall provide workers with remuneration that ensures an adequate standard of living for them and their families. Such remuneration shall take due account of their needs for adequate living conditions with a view towards progressive improvement.

9. Transnational corporations and other business enterprises shall ensure freedom of association and effective recognition of the right to collective bargaining by protecting the right to establish and, subject only to the rules of the organization concerned, to join organizations of their own choosing without distinction, previous authorization, or interference, for the protection of their employment interests and for other collective bargaining purposes as provided in national legislation and the relevant conventions of the International Labour Organization.

E. Respect for national sovereignty and human rights

10. Transnational corporations and other business enterprises shall recognize and respect applicable norms of international law, national laws and regulations, as well as administrative practices, the rule of law, the public interest, development objectives, social, economic and cultural policies including transparency, accountability and prohibition of corruption, and authority of the countries in which the enterprises operate.

11. Transnational corporations and other business enterprises shall not offer, promise, give, accept, condone, knowingly benefit from, or demand a bribe or other improper advantage, nor shall they be solicited or expected to give a bribe or other improper advantage to any Government, public official, candidate for elective post, any member of the armed forces or security forces, or any other individual or organization. Transnational corporations and other business enterprises shall refrain from any activity which supports, solicits, or encourages States or any other entities to abuse human rights. They shall further seek to ensure that the goods and services they provide will not be used to abuse human rights.

12.   Transnational corporations and other business enterprises shall respect economic, social and cultural rights as well as civil and political rights and contribute to their realization, in particular the rights to development, adequate food and drinking water, the highest attainable standard of physical and mental health, adequate housing, privacy, education, freedom of thought, conscience, and religion and freedom of opinion and expression, and shall refrain from actions which obstruct or impede the realization of those rights. . . .

H.   General provisions of implementation

15.   As an initial step towards implementing these Norms, each transnational corporation or other business enterprise shall adopt, disseminate and implement internal rules of operation in compliance with the Norms. Further, they shall periodically report on and take other measures fully to implement the Norms and to provide at least for the prompt implementation of the protections set forth in the Norms. Each transnational corporation or other business enterprise shall apply and incorporate these Norms in their contracts or other arrangements and dealings with contractors, subcontractors, suppliers, licensees, distributors, or natural or other legal persons that enter into any agreement with the transnational corporation or business enterprise in order to ensure respect for and implementation of the Norms.

16.   Transnational corporations and other businesses enterprises shall be subject to periodic monitoring and verification by United Nations, other international and national mechanisms already in existence or yet to be created, regarding application of the Norms. This monitoring shall be transparent and independent and take into account input from stakeholders (including non-governmental organizations) and as a result of complaints of violations of these Norms. Further, transnational corporations and other businesses enterprises shall conduct periodic evaluations concerning the impact of their own activities on human rights under these Norms.

17.   States should establish and reinforce the necessary legal and administrative framework for ensuring that the Norms and other relevant national and international laws are implemented by transnational corporations and other business enterprises.

18.   Transnational corporations and other business enterprises shall provide prompt, effective and adequate reparation to those persons, entities and communities that have been adversely affected by failures to comply with these Norms through, *inter alia*, reparations, restitution, compensation and rehabilitation for any damage done or property taken. In connection with determining damages in regard to criminal sanctions, and in all other respects, these Norms shall be applied by national courts and/or international tribunals, pursuant to national and international law.

19.   Nothing in these Norms shall be construed as diminishing, restricting, or adversely affecting the human rights obligations of States under national and international law, nor shall they be construed as diminishing, restricting, or adversely affecting more protective human rights norms, nor shall they be construed as diminishing, restricting, or adversely affecting other obligations or responsibilities of transnational corporations and other business enterprises in fields other than human rights.

I.   Definitions

20.   The term "transnational corporation" refers to an economic entity operating in more than one country or a cluster of economic entities operating in two or more countries—whatever their legal form, whether in their home country or country of activity, and whether taken individually or collectively.

21.   The phrase "other business enterprise" includes any business entity, regardless of the international or domestic nature of its activities, including a transnational corporation, contractor, subcontractor, supplier, licensee or distributor; the corporate, partnership, or other legal form used to establish the business entity; and the nature of the ownership of the entity. These Norms shall be presumed to apply, as a matter of practice, if the business enterprise has any relation with a transnational corporation, the impact of its activities is not entirely local, or the activities involve violations of the right to security as indicated in paragraphs 3 and 4.

22.   The term "stakeholder" includes stockholders, other owners, workers and their representatives, as well as any other individual or group that is affected by the activities of transnational corporations or other business enterprises. The term "stakeholder" shall be interpreted functionally in the light of the objectives of these Norms and include indirect stakeholders when their interests are or will be substantially affected by the activities of the transnational corporation or business enterprise. In addition to parties directly affected by the activities of business enterprises, stakeholders can include parties which are indirectly affected by the activities of transnational corporations or other business enterprises such as consumer groups, customers, Governments, neighbouring communities, indigenous peoples and communities, non governmental organizations, public and private lending institutions, suppliers, trade associations, and others.

23.   The phrases "human rights" and "international human rights" include civil, cultural, economic, political and social rights, as set forth in the International Bill of Human Rights and other human rights treaties, as well as the right to development and rights recognized by international humanitarian law, international refugee law, international labour law, and other relevant instruments adopted within the United Nations system.

OECD STANDARDS

THE OECD DECLARATION ON INTERNATIONAL INVESTMENT AND MULTINATIONAL ENTERPRISES

(21 June 1976)

The Governments of OECD Member countries,

CONSIDERING:

That international investment has assumed increased importance in the world economy and has considerably contributed to the development of their countries; That multinational enterprises play an important role in this investment process; That co-operation by Member countries can improve the foreign investment climate, encourage the positive contribution which multinational enterprises can make to economic and social progress, and minimise and resolve difficulties which may arise from their various operations; * * *

DECLARE:

That they jointly recommend to multinational enterprises operating in their territories the observance of the Guidelines [*infra*] having regard to the considerations and understandings which introduce the Guidelines and are an integral part of them;

That Member countries should, consistent with their needs to maintain public order, to protect their essential security interests and to fulfil commitments relating to international peace and security, accord to enterprises operating in their territories and owned or controlled directly or indirectly by nationals of another Member country (hereinafter referred to as "Foreign–Controlled Enterprises") treatment under their laws, regulations and administrative practices, consistent with international law and no less favourable than that accorded in like situations to domestic enterprises (hereinafter referred to as "National Treatment"); * * *

That they recognise the need to strengthen their co-operation in the field of international direct investment;

That they thus recognise the need to give due weight to the interests of Member countries affected by specific laws, regulations and administrative practices in this field (hereinafter called "measures") providing official incentives and disincentives to international direct investment;

That Member countries will endeavour to make such measures as transparent as possible, so that their importance and purpose can be ascertained and that information on them can be readily available; * * *

OECD GUIDELINES FOR MULTINATIONAL ENTERPRISES

Introduction

1.   Multinational enterprises now play an important part in the economies of Member countries and in international economic relations, which is of increasing interest to governments. Through international direct investment, such enterprises can bring substantial benefits to home and host countries by contributing to the efficient utilisation of capital, technology and human resources between countries and can thus fulfil an important role in the promotion of economic and social welfare. But the advances made by multinational enterprises in organising their operations beyond the national framework may lead to abuse of concentrations of economic power and to conflicts with national policy objectives. In addition, the complexity of these multinational enterprises and the difficulty of clearly perceiving their diverse structures, operations and policies sometimes give rise to concern.

2.   The common aim of the Member countries is to encourage the positive contributions which multinational enterprises can make to economic and social progress and to minimise and resolve the difficulties to which their various operations may give rise. In view of the transnational structure of such enterprises, this aim will be furthered by co-operation among the OECD countries where the headquarters of most of the multinational enterprises are established and which are the location of a substantial part of their operations. The Guidelines set out hereafter are designed to assist in the achievement of this common aim and to contribute to improving the foreign investment climate. * * *

5.   The initial phase of the co-operation programme is composed of a Declaration and three Decisions promulgated simultaneously as they are complementary and inter-connected, in respect of Guidelines for multinational enterprises, National Treatment for foreign-controlled enterprises and international investment incentives and disincentives.

6.   The Guidelines set out below are recommendations jointly addressed by Member countries to multinational enterprises operating in their territories. These Guidelines, which take into account the problems which can arise because of the international structure of these enterprises, lay down standards for the activities of these enterprises in the different Member countries. Observance of the Guidelines is voluntary and not legally enforceable. However, they should help to ensure that the operations of these enterprises are in harmony with national policies of the countries where they operate and to strengthen the basis of mutual confidence between enterprises and States.

7.   Every State has the right to prescribe the conditions under which multinational enterprises operate within its national jurisdiction, subject to international law and to the international agreements to which

it has subscribed. The entities of a multinational enterprise located in various countries are subject to the laws of these countries.

8. A precise legal definition of multinational enterprises is not required for the purposes of the Guidelines. These usually comprise companies or other entities whose ownership is private, state or mixed, established in different countries and so linked that one or more of them may be able to exercise a significant influence over the activities of others and, in particular, to share knowledge and resources with the others. The degrees of autonomy of each entity in relation to the others varies widely from one multinational enterprise to another, depending on the nature of the links between such entities and the fields of activity concerned. For these reasons, the Guidelines are addressed to the various entities within the multinational enterprise (parent companies and/or local entities) according to the actual distribution of responsibilities among them on the understanding that they will co-operate and provide assistance to one another as necessary to facilitate observance of the Guidelines. The word "enterprise" as used in these Guidelines refers to these various entities in accordance with their responsibilities. * * *

Having regard to the foregoing considerations, the Member countries set forth the following Guidelines for multinational enterprises with the understanding that Member countries will fulfil their responsibilities to treat enterprises equitably and in accordance with international law and international agreements as well as contractual obligations to which they have subscribed.

General policies

Enterprises should:

1. Take fully into account established general policy objectives of the Member countries in which they operate;

2. In particular, give due consideration to those countries' aims and priorities with regard to economic and social progress, including industrial and regional development, the protection of the environment and consumer interests, the creation of employment opportunities, the promotion of innovation and the transfer of technology; * * *

6. When filling responsible posts in each country of operation, take due account of individual qualifications without discrimination as to nationality, subject to particular national requirements in this respect;

7. Not render and they should not be solicited or expected to render any bribe or other improper benefit, direct or indirect, to any public servant or holder of public office;

8. Unless legally permissible, not make contributions to candidates for public office or to political parties or other political organisations;

9. Abstain from any improper involvement in local political activities. * * *

Employment and industrial relations

Enterprises should, within the framework of law, regulations and prevailing labour relations and employment practices, in each of the countries in which they operate:

1.   Respect the right of their employees to be represented by trade unions and other bona fide organisations of employees, and engage in constructive negotiations, either individually or through employers' associations, with such employee organisations with a view to reaching agreements on employment conditions, which should include provisions for dealing with disputes arising over the interpretation of such agreements, and for ensuring mutually respected rights and responsibilities;

2.   (a) Provide such facilities to representatives of the employees as may be necessary to assist in the development of effective collective agreements;

      (b) Provide to representatives of employees information which is needed for meaningful negotiations on conditions of employment;

3.   Provide to representatives of employees where this accords with local law and practice, information which enables them to obtain a true and fair view of the performance of the entity or, where appropriate, the enterprise as a whole;

4.   Observe standards of employment and industrial relations not less favourable than those observed by comparable employers in the host country;

5.   In their operations, to the greatest extent practicable, utilise, train and prepare for upgrading members of the local labour force in co-operation with representatives of their employees and, where appropriate, the relevant governmental authorities;

6.   In considering changes in their operations which would have major effects upon the livelihood of their employees, in particular in the case of the closure of an entity involving collective lay-offs or dismissals, provide reasonable notice of such changes to representatives of their employees, and where appropriate to the relevant governmental authorities and co-operate with the employee representatives and appropriate governmental authorities so as to mitigate to the maximum extent practicable adverse effects;

7.   Implement their employment policies including hiring, discharge, pay, promotion and training without discrimination unless selectivity in respect of employee characteristics is in furtherance of established governmental policies which specifically promote greater equality of employment opportunity;

8.   In the context of bona fide negotiations[1] with representatives of employees on conditions of employment, or while employees are exer-

---

1.   Bona fide negotiations may include labour disputes as part of the process of negotiation. Whether or not labour disputes are so included will be determined by the law and prevailing employment practices of particular countries.

cising a right to organise, not threaten to utilise a capacity to transfer the whole or part of an operating unit from the country concerned nor transfer employees from the enterprises' component entities in other countries in order to influence unfairly those negotiations or to hinder the exercise of a right to organise;

9.   Enable authorised representatives of their employees to conduct negotiations on collective bargaining or labour management relations issues with representatives of management who are authorised to take decisions on the matters under negotiation. * * *

THE OECD NATIONAL CONTACTS POINT PROCEDURE
SECOND REVISED DECISION OF THE OECD COUNCIL (1991)

THE COUNCIL,

Taking note of the Declaration by the Governments of OECD Member countries of 21st June 1976 in which they jointly recommend to multinational enterprises the observance of Guidelines for multinational enterprises; ... [and r]ecognising the desirability of setting forth procedures by which consultations may take place on matters related to these Guidelines; * * *

DECIDES:

1.   Member Governments shall set up National Contact Points for undertaking promotional activities, handling inquires and for discussions with the parties concerned on all matters related to the Guidelines so that they can contribute to the solution of problems which may arise in this connection. The business community, employee organisations and other interested parties shall be informed of the availability of such facilities.

2.   National Contact Points in different countries shall co-operate if such need arises, on any matter related to the Guidelines relevant to their activities. As a general procedure, discussions at the national level should be initiated before contacts with other National Contact Points are undertaken.

3.   The Committee on International Investment and Multinational Enterprises (hereinafter called "the Committee") shall periodically or at the request of a Member country hold an exchange of views on matters related to the Guidelines and the experience gained in their application. The Committee shall be responsible for clarification of the Guidelines. Clarification will be provided as required. The Committee shall periodically report to the Council on these matters. The Committee shall periodically invite the Business and Industry Advisory Committee to OECD (BIAC) and the Trade Union Advisory Committee to OECD (TUAC) to express their views on matters related to the Guidelines. In

addition, exchanges of views with the advisory bodies on these matters may be held upon request by the latter. The Committee shall take account of such views in its reports to the Council.

4.   If it so wishes, an individual enterprise will be given the opportunity to express its views either orally or in writing on issues concerning the Guidelines involving its interests.

5.   The Committee shall not reach conclusions on the conduct of individual enterprises. * * *

REPORT OF JOHN RUGGIE, SPECIAL REPRESENTATIVE OF THE UNITED NATIONS SECRETARY–GENERAL ON THE ISSUE OF HUMAN RIGHTS AND TRANSNATIONAL CORPORATIONS AND OTHER BUSINESS ENTERPRISES

PROTECT, RESPECT, AND REMEDY: A FRAMEWORK FOR BUSINESS AND HUMAN RIGHTS

April 2008

Responding to the invitation by the Human Rights Council for the Special Representative of the Secretary–General on the issue of human rights and transnational corporations and other business enterprises to submit his views and recommendations for its consideration, this report presents a conceptual and policy framework to anchor the business and human rights debate, and to help guide all relevant actors. The framework comprises three core principles: the State duty to protect against human rights abuses by third parties, including business; the corporate responsibility to respect human rights; and the need for more effective access to remedies. The three principles form a complementary whole in that each supports the others in achieving sustainable progress. * * *

[The first principle is that] international law provides that States have a duty to protect against human rights abuses by non-State actors, including by business, affecting persons within their territory or jurisdiction. To help States interpret how this duty applies under the core United Nations human rights conventions, the treaty monitoring bodies generally recommend that States take all necessary steps to protect against such abuse, including to prevent, investigate, and punish the abuse, and to provide access to redress. States have discretion to decide what measures to take, but the treaty bodies indicate that both regulation and adjudication of corporate activities vis-à-vis human rights are appropriate. They also suggest that the duty applies to the activities of all types of businesses—national and transnational, large and small—and that it applies to all rights private parties are capable of impairing. Regional human rights systems have reached similar conclusions.

Experts disagree on whether international law requires home States to help prevent human rights abuses abroad by corporations based within their territory. There is greater consensus that those States are not prohibited from doing so where a recognized basis of jurisdiction exists,[1] and the actions of the home State meet an overall reasonableness test, which includes non-intervention in the internal affairs of other States. Indeed, there is increasing encouragement at the international level, including from the treaty bodies, for home States to take regulatory action to prevent abuse by their companies overseas. * * *

It is often stressed that governments are the appropriate entities to make the difficult balancing decisions required to reconcile different societal needs. However, the Special Representative's work raises questions about whether governments have got the balance right. His consultations and research, including a questionnaire survey sent to all Member States [of the United Nations], indicate that many governments take a narrow approach to managing the business and human rights agenda. It is often segregated within its own conceptual and (typically weak) institutional box—kept apart from, or heavily discounted in, other policy domains that shape business practices, including commercial policy, investment policy, securities regulation and corporate governance. This inadequate domestic policy coherence is replicated internationally. Governments should not assume they are helping business by failing to provide adequate guidance for, or regulation of, the human rights impact of corporate activities. On the contrary, the less governments do, the more they increase reputational and other risks to business. * * *

The corporate responsibility to respect human rights is the second principle. It is recognized in such soft law instruments as the Tripartite Declaration of Principles Concerning Multinational Enterprises and Social Policy, and the OECD Guidelines for Multinational Enterprises. It is invoked by the largest global business organizations in their submission to the mandate, which states that companies "are expected to obey the law, even if it is not enforced, and to respect the principles of relevant international instruments where national law is absent" It is one of the commitments companies undertake in joining the Global Compact. And the Special Representative's surveys document the fact that companies worldwide increasingly claim they respect human rights. * * *

When it comes to the role companies themselves must play, the main focus in the debate has been on identifying a limited set of rights for which they may bear responsibility. For example, the draft norms on the responsibilities of transnational corporations and other business

---

1. Recognized bases include where the actor or victim is a national, where the acts have substantial adverse effects on the State, or where specific international crimes are involved.

enterprises with regard to human rights generated intense discussions about whether its list of rights was too long or too short, and why some rights were included and others not. At the same time, the norms would have extended to companies essentially the entire range of duties that States have, separated only by the undefined concepts of "primary" versus "secondary" obligations and "corporate sphere of influence". This formula emphasizes precisely the wrong side of the equation: defining a limited list of rights linked to imprecise and expansive responsibilities, rather than defining the specific responsibilities of companies with regard to all rights. * * * [A]ny attempt to limit internationally recognized rights is inherently problematic. [T]here are few if any internationally recognized rights business cannot impact—or be perceived to impact—in some manner. Therefore, companies should consider all such rights.

The more difficult question of what precise responsibilities companies have in relation to rights has received far less attention. While corporations may be considered "organs of society", they are specialized economic organs, not democratic public interest institutions. As such, their responsibilities cannot and should not simply mirror the duties of States. Accordingly, the Special Representative has focused on identifying the distinctive responsibilities of companies in relation to human rights.

A.   Respecting rights

In addition to compliance with national laws, the baseline responsibility of companies is to respect human rights. Failure to meet this responsibility can subject companies to the courts of public opinion—comprising employees, communities, consumers, civil society, as well as investors—and occasionally to charges in actual courts. Whereas governments define the scope of legal compliance, the broader scope of the responsibility to respect is defined by social expectations—as part of what is sometimes called a company's social licence to operate.

The corporate responsibility to respect exists independently of States' duties. Therefore, there is no need for the slippery distinction between "primary" State and "secondary" corporate obligations. * * * Furthermore, because the responsibility to respect is a baseline expectation, a company cannot compensate for human rights harm by performing good deeds elsewhere. Finally, "doing no harm" is not merely a passive responsibility for firms but may entail positive steps—for example, a workplace anti-discrimination policy might require the company to adopt specific recruitment and training programmes.

B.   Due diligence

To discharge the responsibility to respect requires due diligence. This concept describes the steps a company must take to become aware of, prevent and address adverse human rights impacts. Comparable processes are typically already embedded in companies because in many countries they are legally required to have information and control systems in place to assess and manage financial and related risks. * * * The process inevitably will be inductive and fact-based, but the principles guiding it can be stated succinctly. Companies should consider three sets of factors. The first is the country contexts in which their business activities take place, to highlight any specific human rights challenges they may pose. The second is what human rights impacts their own activities may have within that context—for example, in their capacity as producers, service providers, employers, and neighbours. The third is whether they might contribute to abuse through the relationships connected to their activities, such as with business partners, suppliers, State agencies, and other non-State actors. How far or how deep this process must go will depend on circumstances.

For the substantive content of the due diligence process, companies should look, at a minimum, to the international bill of human rights and the core conventions of the ILO, because the principles they embody comprise the benchmarks against which other social actors judge the human rights impacts of companies. * * * The Special Representative's research and consultations indicate that a basic human rights due diligence process should include the following.

Policies. Companies need to adopt a human rights policy. Broad aspirational language may be used to describe respect for human rights, but more detailed guidance in specific functional areas is necessary to give those commitments meaning.

Impact assessments. Many corporate human rights issues arise because companies fail to consider the potential implications of their activities before they begin. Companies must take proactive steps to understand how existing and proposed activities may affect human rights. The scale of human rights impact assessments will depend on the industry and national and local context. While these assessments can be linked with other processes like risk assessments or environmental and social impact assessments, they should include explicit references to internationally recognized human rights. Based on the information uncovered, companies should refine their plans to address and avoid potential negative human rights impacts on an ongoing basis.

Integration. The integration of human rights policies throughout a company may be the biggest challenge in fulfilling the corporate responsibility to respect. As is true for States, human rights considerations are often isolated within a company. That can lead to inconsistent or contradictory actions: product developers may not consider human rights implications; sales or procurement teams may not know the risks of entering into relationships with certain parties; and company lobbying may contradict commitments to human rights. Leadership from the top is essential to embed respect for human rights throughout a company, as is training to ensure consistency, as well as capacity to respond appropriately when unforeseen situations arise.

Tracking performance. Monitoring and auditing processes permit a company to track ongoing developments. The procedures may vary across sectors and even among company departments, but regular updates of human rights impact and performance are crucial. Tracking generates information needed to create appropriate incentives and disincentives for employees and ensure continuous improvement. Confidential means to report non-compliance, such as hotlines, can also provide useful feedback.

C.   Sphere of influence

[The concept of a corporate] sphere of influence conflates two very different meanings of influence: one is impact, where the company's activities or relationships are causing human rights harm; the other is whatever leverage a company may have over actors that are causing harm. The first falls squarely within the responsibility to respect; the second may only do so in particular circumstances. Anchoring corporate responsibility in the second meaning of influence requires assuming, in moral philosophy terms, that "can implies ought". But companies cannot be held responsible for the human rights impacts of every entity over which they may have some influence, because this would include cases in which they were not a causal agent, direct or indirect, of the harm in question. Nor is it desirable to have companies act whenever they have influence, particularly over governments. Asking companies to support human rights voluntarily where they have influence is one thing; but attributing responsibility to them on that basis alone is quite another.

In short, the scope of due diligence to meet the corporate responsibility to respect human rights is not a fixed sphere, nor is it based on influence. Rather, it depends on the potential and actual human rights impacts resulting from a company's business activities and the relationships connected to those activities.

D.   Complicity

The corporate responsibility to respect human rights includes avoiding complicity. The concept has legal and non-legal pedigrees, and the implications of both are important for companies. Complicity refers to indirect involvement by companies in human rights abuses—where the actual harm is committed by another party, including governments and non-State actors. Due diligence can help a company avoid complicity. The legal meaning of complicity has been spelled out most clearly in the area of aiding and abetting international crimes, *i.e.* knowingly providing practical assistance or encouragement that has a substantial effect on the commission of a crime, as discussed in the 2007 report of the Special Representative. The number of domestic jurisdictions in which charges for international crimes can be brought against corporations is increasing, and companies may also incur non-criminal liability for complicity in human rights abuses. * * *

Owing to the relatively limited case history, especially in relation to companies rather than individuals, and given the substantial variations in definitions of complicity within and between the legal and non-legal spheres, it is not possible to specify definitive tests for what constitutes complicity in any given context. But companies should bear in mind the considerations set out below. Mere presence in a country, paying taxes, or silence in the face of abuses is unlikely to amount to the practical assistance required for legal liability. However, acts of omission in narrow contexts have led to legal liability of individuals when the omission legitimized or encouraged the abuse. Moreover, under international criminal law standards, practical assistance or encouragement need neither cause the actual abuse, nor be related temporally or physically to the abuse.

Similarly, deriving a benefit from a human rights abuse is not likely on its own to bring legal liability. Nevertheless, benefiting from abuses may carry negative implications for companies in the public perception. Legal interpretations of "having knowledge" vary. When applied to companies, it might require that there be actual knowledge, or that the company "should have known", that its actions or omissions would contribute to a human rights abuse. Knowledge may be inferred from both direct and circumstantial facts. The "should have known" standard is what a company could reasonably be expected to know under the circumstances.

In international criminal law, complicity does not require knowledge of the specific abuse or a desire for it to have occurred, as long as there was knowledge of the contribution. Therefore, it may not matter that the company was merely carrying out normal business activities if those activities contributed to the abuse and the company was aware or should have been aware of its contribution. The fact that a company was following orders, fulfilling contractual obligations, or even complying with national law will not, alone, guarantee it legal protection.

In short, the relationship between complicity and due diligence is clear and compelling: companies can avoid complicity by employing the due diligence processes described above—which, as noted, apply not only to their own activities but also to the relationships connected with them.

[With respect to the third principle, access to remedies, e]xpectations for States to take concrete steps to adjudicate corporate-related human rights harm are expanding. Treaty bodies increasingly recommend that States investigate and punish human rights abuse by corporations and provide access to redress for such abuse when it affects persons within their jurisdiction. Redress could include compensation, restitution, guarantees of non-repetition, changes in relevant law and public apologies. As discussed earlier, regulators are also using new tools to hold corporations accountable under both civil and criminal law, focused on failures in organizational culture. Non-judicial mechanisms play an important role alongside judicial processes. They may be particularly significant in a country where courts are unable, for whatever reason, to provide adequate and effective access to remedy. Yet they are also important in societies with well-functioning rule of law institutions, where they may provide a more immediate, accessible, affordable, and adaptable point of initial recourse. * * *

The United Nations is not a centralized command-and-control system that can impose its will on the world—indeed it has no "will" apart from that with which Member States endow it. But it can and must lead intellectually and by setting expectations and aspirations. The Human Rights Council can make a singular contribution to closing the governance gaps in business and human rights by supporting this framework, inviting its further elaboration, and fostering its uptake by all relevant social actors.

Notes and Questions on the International Regime

1. *Distinguishing corporate responsibility from individual responsibility.* The jurisdiction of the International Criminal Court extends only to natural individuals, not to corporations. At Nuremberg, numerous individual businessmen were tried and convicted for their participation in crimes against humanity, war crimes, and slave labor, but no corporations faced criminal trial or punishment. *See, e.g., The Trial of Friedrich Flick and five others*, United States Military Tribunal, 20 April–22 December 1947, Case No. 48, Law Reports of the Trials of War Criminals, Vol. IX, p.1; *Trial of Alfred Felix Alwyn Krupp von Bohlen und Halbach and Eleven others*, United States Military Tribunal, 17 November 1947–30 June 1948, Case No. 58, Law Reports of Trials of War Criminals, Vol. X, p.69; *The Zyklon B case (Trial of Bruno Tesch and two others)*, British Military Court, 1–8 March 1946, Case No. 9, Law Reports of Trials of War Criminals, Vol. I, p. 93; *The I.G. Farben Trial; Trial of Carl Krauch and Twenty–Two Others*, United States Military Tribunal, Nuremberg, 14 August 1947–29 July 1948, Case No. 57, Law Reports of Trials of War Criminals, Vol. X, p.1. What are the principal difficulties—analytically, doctrinally, logistically—in extending this body of international criminal law from individual human beings to the corporation itself?

2. *The privatization of warfare.* The law governing armed conflict is explored below in Module 18, but here it may be noted that modern warfare is no longer a strictly state-to-state concern. To the contrary, as noted by the International Committee of the Red Cross (ICRC), the presence of multinational corporations has increased in armed conflict around the world. Should companies in armed conflict be treated like soldiers, civilians, states, or some fourth category?

3. *National Contact Point procedures.* Why would the governments in the industrialized states find the OECD Guidelines (with its innovation

of the "National Contact Person") acceptable but not the Norms? In answering this question, consider who (or what) enforces the OECD Guidelines, and how. The utility of the Guidelines is not lost on human rights NGO's. In February 2007, the UK National Contact Point for the United Kingdom received a request from Global Witness, claiming that Afrimex, a UK registered company, had violated the OECD Guidelines by paying taxes to rebel forces in the Democratic Republic of Congo and failing to exercise due diligence over its supply chain by sourcing minerals—especially coltan and cassiterite (tin ore)—from mines that use child and forced labor and following unacceptable health and safety practices in the workplace.

4. *Choice among types of legal instruments.* What would be the best means of accomplishing international harmonization of corporate social responsibility standards? A treaty? Model domestic legislation? Is there an argument for allowing multiple international actors to craft their own approaches to these issues, no matter how divergent their work product may be?

5. *Interplay among the four regimes.* In what sense are the four regimes of corporate responsibility reinforcing or irreconcilable? Sometimes a development within one regime is in response to developments in another. Consider for example the concern expressed by the United Nations about the problem of "conflict diamonds." *See* UN Res. 56/263 (13 March 2002) ("the opportunity for conflict diamonds to play a role in fueling armed conflict can be seriously reduced by introducing a certification scheme for rough diamonds and that such a scheme would help protect the legitimate trade and ensure the effective implementation of the relevant resolutions of the United Nations Security Council containing sanctions on the trade in conflict diamonds."). *See also* UN Res. 55/56 (1 December 2000) (calling on the international community to develop detailed proposals for a simple and workable international certification scheme for rough diamonds based primarily on national certification schemes and on internationally agreed minimum standards). Roughly contemporaneously, diamond merchants established the Kimberley Process for certifying the origins of diamonds:

> In May 2000, African diamond producing countries initiated the Kimberley Process in Kimberley, South Africa, to discuss the conflict diamond trade. Participants now include states and countries of the European Union involved in the production, export, and import of rough diamonds; as well as representatives from the diamond industry, notably the World Diamond Council, and non-governmental organizations. The goal is to create and implement an international certification scheme for rough diamonds, based primarily on national certification schemes and internationally agreed minimum standards for the basic requirements of a certificate of origin. The scheme's objectives are to (1) stem the flow of rough diamonds used by rebels to finance armed conflict aimed at overthrowing legitimate governments; and (2) protect the legitimate

diamond industry, upon which some countries depend for their economic and social development.

Testimony of Loren Yager, Director, International Affairs and Trade, United States General Accounting Office, *International Trade: Significant Challenges Remain in Deterring Trade in Conflict Diamonds*, before the Subcommittee on Oversight of Government Management, Restructuring and the District of Columbia, Committee on Governmental Affairs, U.S. Senate (13 February 2002), at 5–6. Soon thereafter, Congress adopted the "Clean Diamond Trade Act of 2003, specifically incorporating the Kimberley Process and directing the President to 'prohibit the importation into, or exportation from, the United States of any rough diamond, from whatever source, that has not been controlled through the Kimberley Process Certification Scheme.'" 19 U.S.C. § 3903. The Kimberley Process has also coordinated with intergovernmental institutions, including (as of November 2007), the United Nations Sanctions Committees on Côte d'Ivoire and Liberia and initiated coordination with the World Bank and the United Nations Development Programme. See 2007 Kimberley Process Communiqué, *available at* http://www.state.gov/docu ments/organization/96410.pdf.

Practicum

SELECTED LEGAL BACKGROUND ON MEDICAL EXPERIMENTATION ON HUMAN BEINGS

Article 7 of the 1966 International Covenant on Civil and Political Rights ("ICCPR") provides that

> No one shall be subjected to torture or to cruel, inhuman or degrading treatment or punishment. In particular, no one shall be subjected without his free consent to medical or scientific experimentation.

Like genocide and slave-trading, medical experimentation on non-consenting human subjects was one of the offenses successfully prosecuted at Nuremberg after World War II. In *United States v. Karl Brandt et al.* (the "Nazi Doctors' Trial"), the military tribunal adopted the Nuremberg Code to guide its verdicts on doctors who engaged in human experimentation. In condemning seven of the defendants to death, the tribunal declared:

> Manifestly human experiments * * * are contrary to the "principles of the law of nations" as they result from the usages established among civilized peoples, from the laws of humanity and from the dictates of public conscience.

In 1964, the World Medical Association—a global, non-governmental, representative body for physicians—adopted the Declaration of Helsinki as an official policy document. Principle 22 of the Helsinki Declaration as amended currently provides:

> In any research on human beings, each potential subject must be adequately informed of the aims, methods, sources of funding, any possible conflicts of interest, institutional affiliations of the researcher, the anticipated benefits and potential risks of the study and the discomfort it may entail. The subject should be informed of the right to abstain from participation in the study or to withdraw consent to participate at any time without reprisal.

The International Council for Medical Sciences (ICMS) is an international, non-governmental, non-profit organization established jointly by the World Health Organisation and the UN Economic, Social, and Cultural Organisation. ICMS has adopted International Ethical Guidelines for Biomedical Research Involving Human Subjects. Guideline 4 provides:

> For all biomedical research involving humans the investigator must obtain the voluntary informed consent of the prospective subject or, in the case of an individual who is not capable of giving informed consent, the permission of a legally authorized representative in accordance with applicable law. * * *

Many countries around the world have brought criminal prosecutions and administrative proceedings under domestic law against medical researchers who did not obtain the prior informed consent of their human subjects. No state has asserted a legal right to authorize human experimentation without prior informed consent.

FACTUAL BACKGROUND ON THE BABAIO DISASTER

Curall Incorporated is a multinational pharmaceutical corporation, incorporated in the state of Delaware, with global sales approaching $10 billion annually. Curall has developed a drug called Sorbonex, which the company believes is the first effective vaccine for certain childhood blood diseases. If it is, the drug could potentially save hundreds of thousands of children's lives around the world. For both medical and bureaucratic reasons, the U.S. Food and Drug Administration has withheld approval of the drug for human trials in the United States. But Curall has long owned and operated manufacturing and distribution subsidiaries in the Republic of Babaio—a non-aligned, less developed country, with one of the most repressive governments in the world. Because of the cozy relationship between the company and the government, Curall obtained administrative approvals for the testing of Sorbonex at all of the state orphanages in Babaio. All of the children to be tested are below the age of consent, but the national director of the orphanages gave her informed consent to the testing. *Compare United States v. Brandt, (The Medical Case)*, 2 Trials of War Criminals Before the Nuremberg Tribunals Under Control of Council Law No. 10, at 181 (1949) (elaborating on the Nuremberg Code, which prohibits non-consensual medical experimentation).

After six months of the test, 22% of the children involved showed symptoms of a seriously compromised immune system, and emergency tests by an independent medical center in Babaio confirmed that the problems were directly related to the administration of Sorbonex. Curall suspended the drug trials, offered other pharmaceuticals and medical care for the children, and put the development of Sorbonex on the back-burner.

Despite these efforts, forty of the children involved in the tests were dead within a year, and children's rights groups in Babaio, the United States, and Europe are seeking some measure of accountability. According to the annual human rights report of the U.S. Department of State, the courts in Babaio are "in no way independent of manipulation by the executive branch" which "has created a regime of impunity for government decision-makers at all levels of responsibility."

Members of the class will be asked to represent either citizens of Babaio who survived the scandal (or the legal representatives of the victims) or Curall. On the basis of the materials in this chapter, the former will develop multiple strategies for bringing Curall, its officers, and its directors to account. Counsel for Curall will prepare a legal defense to the allegations against the company and develop a crisis response plan.

CHAPTER 4

MODULE 9

INTERNATIONAL FINANCIAL INSTITUTIONS AND THE WORLD TRADE ORGANIZATION

■ ■ ■

"The basic purpose of development is to enlarge people's choices. In principle, these choices can be infinite and can change over time. People often value achievements that do not show up at all, or not immediately, in income or growth figures: greater access to knowledge, better nutrition and health services, more secure livelihoods, security against crime and physical violence, satisfying leisure hours, political and cultural freedoms and sense of participation in community activities. The objective of development is to create an enabling environment for people to enjoy long, healthy and creative lives."

Mahbub ul Haq, United Nations Development Programme, *What Is Human Development?*

Some of the most powerful intergovernmental organizations in the world began their institutional lives concerned with international trade, currency stabilization, and economic development. The mandates of these institutions—especially the World Bank, the International Monetary Fund, and the World Trade Organization—said little or nothing about human rights law. In fact, the lawyers for these institutions explicitly considered human rights a politicized distraction from their primary responsibilities: assuring economic development, maintaining the stability of the international economy, and promoting international trade. Under the international agreements creating them, these institutions were explicitly required to be non-political in their decision-making, and that directive was interpreted to exclude human rights considerations. But the human rights consequences of some of these decisions became too serious to ignore, and, in ways that are characteristic of modern international human rights law, these institutional mandates evolved.

In this module, we explore the potential impact of these organizations in enforcing (and violating) human rights standards.

Orientation

Governments meeting in the aftermath of World War II confronted a set of urgent, related, and global issues. Entire economies had been shattered by the war, and the survival of the survivors depended on reconstruction and economic development, the stabilization of currencies and exchange rates, and the promotion of international trade. That these issues would have to be addressed in a matrix of political conflict that included the end of empires, newly independent states, and deep ideological divisions between communist and capitalist states made the creation of international institutions especially challenging. Despite these obstacles, in 1944, the allies met at Bretton Woods, New Hampshire, and outlined the mission and powers of organizations that, for a later generation, became the institutional face of globalization: the International Bank for Reconstruction and Development ("IBRD" or "World Bank"),[1] the International Monetary Fund ("Fund" or "IMF"), and the General Agreement on Tariffs and Trade ("GATT," which subsequently reformed itself into the World Trade Organization ("WTO")).

What do these institutions actually *do*? The work programs of the Bretton Woods institutions are complex and distinct. The *World Bank* for example has traditionally provided loans and related financial support for economic development—typically bricks-and-mortar infrastructure projects like dams, roads, water systems, and schools. Its mission has evolved from post-war reconstruction to worldwide poverty alleviation, and much of its work now involves technical assistance on such "human development" projects as good governance (including rule-of-law initiatives), protecting the environment, improving the status of women and the role of civil society organizations, supporting vaccination and immunization programs to reduce the incidence of communicable diseases, and the like. The *IMF* now also views itself as part of the international community's anti-poverty effort, though it was created to assist in the reconstruction of the international economy after World War II, especially by stabilizing exchange rates and assisting countries with payment imbalances. It does this, *inter alia*, by providing financial assistance to countries that cannot earn or borrow what they must spend to operate in the world, including the cost of importing basic goods and services. The countries receiving IMF assistance must adopt a "structural adjustment" program—fiscal and monetary policies designed to assure that whatever caused the crisis does not persist. For example, countries with strict price controls, rampant corruption, reckless budget deficits, or radically over- or under-valued currencies may find themselves in financial crisis, and IMF assistance will be conditioned on economic reforms targeting these problems. These conditionalities are in effect policy prescriptions—generally free market reforms, the reduction of

---

1. The World Bank Group consists of five affiliated organizations: the International Bank for Reconstruction and Development, the International Development Association, the International Finance Corporation, the Multilateral Investment Guarantee Agency, and the International Centre for the Settlement of Investment Disputes (ICSID). For the purposes of this chapter, we will not generally distinguish among these five closely-associated development institutions.

government spending, and the reduction of subsidies to local industries—that are designed to assure that the loan will both have its intended development impact and get repaid. The *WTO* is the only intergovernmental organization dealing with the global rules of trade between nations. Operating under a range of international agreements addressing goods, services, and intellectual property, *inter alia*, the WTO is designed to assure that trade flows freely and predictably.

As defined by the Articles of Agreement *infra*, the mandates of these institutions explicitly required that their actions and decisions be guided by economic considerations only. Thus, for example, when the World Bank made a loan to fund the construction of a dam or a pipeline, the political or ideological character of the recipient government was supposed to be irrelevant. Nor were these institutions allowed to interfere in the political affairs of any member-state. In fact, the imperative to remain non-political was so fundamental that the Bank and the Fund maintained their distance from the other major globalization initiative going forward at the same time, namely the drafting of human rights treaties: both the IMF and the World Bank were invited to participate in the drafting of the International Covenant on Economic, Social, and Cultural Rights, and both declined, invoking their limited, apolitical mandates. "Thus in the early 1950s, neither the Fund nor the Bank saw the links between their respective activities and the economic, social and cultural rights that would become part of the Covenant." François Gianvitti, *Economic, Social, and Cultural Human Rights and the International Monetary Fund*, *in* NON-STATE ACTORS AND HUMAN RIGHTS 115 (Philip Alston ed., 2005).

Over time, some human rights advocates came to view these international financial institutions ("IFIs") as part of the problem rather than as part of the solution. According to the critique, for example, the IFIs had primarily served the interests of its industrialized member-states, had been only partially successful at reducing poverty, and had been oblivious to the gendered aspects of poverty and development. *See, e.g.*, MARTHA C. NUSSBAUM, WOMEN AND HUMAN DEVELOPMENT: THE CAPABILITIES APPROACH (2000). At worst, the critique continued, the IFIs had actually perpetuated indebtedness among the poorest countries, financed damage to the environment, and contributed to on-going human rights problems like the mistreatment of indigenous peoples and the financing of repressive regimes. SIGRUN I. SKOGLY, THE HUMAN RIGHTS OBLIGATIONS OF THE WORLD BANK AND INTERNATIONAL MONETARY FUND (2001). Critics noted that the Bank (and the IMF) affect millions of lives in developing countries through the conditionalities attached to its loans and other supports. Given their impact on employment and health or education spending, these conditionalities (like the nation's indebtedness) can affect more lives more profoundly than the project being financed.

The Bank has not been immune to these criticisms and has increasingly recognized that its failure to take human rights concerns into account—like good governance, the rule of law and the rights and status of women in the target state—lies at the root of the failure of many impoverished countries to benefit from development assistance. According to the President of the Bank in 2005:

> There is * * * widespread recognition of the strong link between human rights and development. * * * The Bank is currently reviewing its role with a view to making a more explicit link between human rights and our work, while at the same time remaining fully in compliance with our Articles of Agreement. * * * All Bank country assistance strategies now address governance issues, with lending volumes linked to progress in governance and anti-corruption. In some of the higher risk countries, governance and anti-corruption have become the anchors for the entire country program. Some twenty percent of our lending commitments are now for good governance, public sector reform, and rule of law.

At the World Summit in September 2005, the international community seemed similarly to recognize the relationship between economic development and human rights by adopting the Millennium Development Goals ("MDGs"). Although the first of the goals—eradicating extreme poverty and hunger by 2015—has been a constant theme throughout the history of the World Bank, the other MDGs reflect a broader understanding of development, promoting a kind of human flourishing in economic and non-economic terms. Specifically, the goals include ensuring that all children receive a primary education; promoting equal rights for women; reducing child mortality; improving the health of pregnant women and mothers; combatting HIV/AIDS, malaria and other diseases; protecting the environment and natural resources; and developing an international partnership for development.

As shown in the following materials, these human rights components of the IFIs' work program potentially offer pressure points for advocacy not only in the countries receiving assistance but, within the international organizations themselves.

Readings

INTERNATIONAL BANK OF RECONSTRUCTION AND DEVELOPMENT (WORLD BANK) ARTICLES OF AGREEMENT

ARTICLE I

Purposes

The purposes of the Bank are:

(i) To assist in the reconstruction and development of territories of members by facilitating the investment of capital for productive purposes, including the restoration of economies destroyed or disrupted by war, the reconversion of productive facilities to peacetime needs and the encouragement of the development of productive facilities and resources in less developed countries.

(ii) To promote private foreign investment by means of guarantees or participations in loans and other investments made by private investors; and when private capital is not available on reasonable terms, to supplement private investment by providing, on suitable conditions, finance for productive purposes out of its own capital, funds raised by it and its other resources.

(iii) To promote the long-range balanced growth of international trade and the maintenance of equilibrium in balances of payments by encouraging international investment for the development of the productive resources of members, thereby assisting in raising productivity, the standard of living and conditions of labor in their territories.

(iv) To arrange the loans made or guaranteed by it in relation to international loans through other channels so that the more useful and urgent projects, large and small alike, will be dealt with first.

(v) To conduct its operations with due regard to the effect of international investment on business conditions in the territories of members and, in the immediate postwar years, to assist in bringing about a smooth transition from a wartime to a peacetime economy.

The Bank shall be guided in all its decisions by the purposes set forth above. * * *

ARTICLE III, Section 4

Conditions on which the Bank may Guarantee or Make Loans

* * * (v) In making or guaranteeing a loan, the Bank shall pay due regard to the prospects that the borrower, and, if the borrower is not a member, that the guarantor, will be in a position to meet its obligations under the loan; and the Bank shall act prudently in the interests both of the particular member in whose territories the project is located and of the members as a whole.

ARTICLE III, Section 5

Use of Loans Guaranteed, Participated in or Made by the Bank

* * * (b) The Bank shall make arrangements to ensure that the proceeds of any loan are used only for the purposes for which the loan was granted, with due attention to considerations of economy and efficiency and without regard to political or other non-economic influences or considerations.

ARTICLE IV, Section 10

Political Activity Prohibited

The Bank and its officers shall not interfere in the political affairs of any member; nor shall they be influenced in their decisions by the political character of the member or members concerned. Only economic considerations shall be relevant to their decisions, and these considerations shall be weighed impartially in order to achieve the purposes stated in Article I.

THE ORIGINAL INTERPRETATION OF THE BRETTON WOODS MANDATES

IBRAHIM SHIHATA,[1] ENVIRONMENT, ECONOMIC DEVELOPMENT, AND HUMAN RIGHTS: A TRIANGULAR RELATIONSHIP?

82 AM. SOC'Y INT'L L. PROC. 40, 42–3 (1988)

Obviously, all international organizations have to act within the limitations of their respective constituent instruments. In the case of the World Bank, its Articles of Agreement entrust the organization with specific functions and responsibilities—all of them related to economic growth, reconstruction, and development. Moreover, the Articles of Agreement expressly prohibit the Bank from interfering in the political affairs of its members and from being influenced in its decisions by the political character of the member concerned or any other non-economic considerations. Clearly, these are sensitive limitations. Ignoring them can work only to the detriment of the Bank and, in the long run, of all its members.

A loan to an authoritarian government may be seen as a form of support to that government. But a development loan from the World Bank to one of its members is made ultimately to improve the peoples' standards of living and should be seen in that light. A negative decision regarding such a loan, if based only on the politically suppressive character of the government involved, may violate the explicit language of the Bank's Articles. More important, it would subject the country's population to another injury, making it prey not only to the actions of its government but also to the inaction of the World Bank.

The importance of maintaining the apolitical character of the Bank as much as possible is accentuated by the Bank's reliance on borrowing from private markets to fund its operations. Private lenders obviously have a stake in knowing that the funds they provide are managed on sound business principles rather than on political considerations.

Also, as the World Bank increases the lending it does in support of economic policy reforms, which today represents more than 25 percent of its activities, it becomes all the more important to emphasize the apolitical character of the Bank. The Bank's policy dialogue with bor-

---

1. [Editors' note: At the time of this presentation, the author was Vice President and General Counsel, International Bank for Reconstruction and Development, speaking in his individual capacity.]

rowing countries would be undermined greatly if these governments were to doubt the objectivity of the Bank or to see its conditionality as simply a reflection of certain political interests or views.

All this is not to suggest that the Bank does or should disregard relevant considerations in its decisions merely on the basis that it cannot be influenced by political considerations. The Bank has recognized the potential influence on its lending decisions of the economic effects that can flow from the political character of a member or from other political considerations. Civil and political human rights therefore may become a relevant issue, but the degree of respect paid by a government to such rights hardly can be considered, from a legal viewpoint, an acceptable basis for the Bank's decision on granting loans to that government. To conclude otherwise would invite politicization of the Bank, which would lead ultimately to the detriment of all. * * *

[T]urn[ing] now to the Bank's significant role in promoting various economic and social rights. The right to development is one human right that the World Bank has in fact been promoting throughout its history. In its loans for agriculture, irrigation, rural development, industry, and various other types of Bank Group financing * * * the end beneficiaries are the individuals who should reap the benefits of development. Although our development funds may not have reached the poor in every case, there is ample evidence that they have contributed significantly to improving the present and prospective standards of living of millions of people around the globe. Particularly since the late 1960s, the Bank has given strong emphasis to poverty alleviation in its lending program. * * * The Bank has also increased its lending in sectors that provide the most direct benefit to the poor, such as agriculture and rural development. For some time, it has been clear to the Bank that in order to resume or sustain their growth, countries have to make extensive structural changes in their respective economic policies.

QUESTIONS ON THE SEPARATION OF HUMAN RIGHTS AND POLITICS

Given the Cold War setting in which the "constitutions" of the Bretton Woods institutions were drafted, why might it have been sensible—legally and politically—for the World Bank and the IMF to have avoided human rights issues? What legal and political changes in the last half century may have made that approach obsolete or counterproductive? Is the following World Bank policy governing involuntary resettlement objectionable because it departs from the explicitly non-political criteria for Bank decision-making? If not, how might a human rights advocate actually use this policy?

THE WORLD BANK OPERATION MANUAL
OPERATIONAL POLICIES OP 4.12
INVOLUNTARY RESETTLEMENT
(DECEMBER 2001)

1. Bank experience indicates that involuntary resettlement under development projects, if unmitigated, often gives rise to severe economic, social, and environmental risks: production systems are dismantled; people face impoverishment when their productive assets or income sources are lost; people are relocated to environments where their productive skills may be less applicable and the competition for resources greater; community institutions and social networks are weakened; kin groups are dispersed; and cultural identity, traditional authority, and the potential for mutual help are diminished or lost. This policy includes safeguards to address and mitigate these impoverishment risks.

2. Involuntary resettlement may cause severe long-term hardship, impoverishment, and environmental damage unless appropriate measures are carefully planned and carried out. For these reasons, the overall objectives of the Bank's policy on involuntary resettlement are the following: (a) Involuntary resettlement should be avoided where feasible, or minimized, exploring all viable alternative project designs. (b) Where it is not feasible to avoid resettlement, resettlement activities should be conceived and executed as sustainable development programs, providing sufficient investment resources to enable the persons displaced by the project to share in project benefits. Displaced persons should be meaningfully consulted and should have opportunities to participate in planning and implementing resettlement programs. (c) Displaced persons should be assisted in their efforts to improve their livelihoods and standards of living or at least to restore them, in real terms, to pre-displacement levels or to levels prevailing prior to the beginning of project implementation, whichever is higher.

3. This policy covers direct economic and social impacts that both result from Bank-assisted investment projects, and are caused by (a) the involuntary taking of land[1] resulting in (i) relocation or loss of shelter; (ii) loss of assets or access to assets; or (iii) loss of income sources or means of livelihood, whether or not the affected persons must move to another location; or (b) the involuntary restriction of access to legally designated parks and protected areas resulting in adverse impacts on the livelihoods of the displaced persons.

---

1. "Land" includes anything growing on or permanently affixed to land, such as buildings and crops. This policy does not apply to regulations of natural resources on a national or regional level to promote their sustainability, such as watershed management, groundwater management, fisheries management, etc. The policy also does not apply to disputes between private parties in land titling projects, although it is good practice for the borrower to undertake a social assessment and implement measures to minimize and mitigate adverse social impacts, especially those affecting poor and vulnerable groups.

4. This policy applies to all components of the project that result in involuntary resettlement, regardless of the source of financing. It also applies to other activities resulting in involuntary resettlement, that in the judgment of the Bank, are (a) directly and significantly related to the Bank-assisted project, (b) necessary to achieve its objectives as set forth in the project documents; and (c) carried out, or planned to be carried out, contemporaneously with the project. * * *

6. To address the impacts covered under para. 3(a) of this policy, the borrower [must] prepare[] a resettlement plan or a resettlement policy framework that covers the following:

(a) The resettlement plan or resettlement policy framework includes measures to ensure that the displaced persons are (i) informed about their options and rights pertaining to resettlement; (ii) consulted on, offered choices among, and provided with technically and economically feasible resettlement alternatives; and (iii) provided prompt and effective compensation at full replacement cost[2] for losses of assets attributable directly to the project.

(b) If the impacts include physical relocation, the resettlement plan or resettlement policy framework includes measures to ensure that the displaced persons are (i) provided assistance (such as moving allowances) during relocation; and (ii) provided with residential housing, or housing sites, or, as required, agricultural sites for which a combination of productive potential, locational advantages, and other factors is at least equivalent to the advantages of the old site.[3]

(c) Where necessary to achieve the objectives of the policy, the resettlement plan or resettlement policy framework also include measures to ensure that displaced persons are (i) offered support after displacement, for a transition period, based on a reasonable estimate of the time likely to be needed to restore their livelihood and standards of living;[4] and (ii) provided with development assistance in addition to compensation measures described in paragraph 6(a) (iii), such as land preparation, credit facilities, training, or job opportunities. * * *

8. To achieve the objectives of this policy, particular attention is paid to the needs of vulnerable groups among those displaced, especial-

---

2. "Replacement cost" is the method of valuation of assets that helps determine the amount sufficient to replace lost assets and cover transaction costs. In applying this method of valuation, depreciation of structures and assets should not be taken into account. * * * For losses that cannot easily be valued or compensated for in monetary terms (e.g., access to public services, customers, and suppliers; or to fishing, grazing, or forest areas), attempts are made to establish access to equivalent and culturally acceptable resources and earning opportunities. Where domestic law does not meet the standard of compensation at full replacement cost, compensation under domestic law is supplemented by additional measures necessary to meet the replacement cost standard. * * *

3. The alternative assets are provided with adequate tenure arrangements. The cost of alternative residential housing, housing sites, business premises, and agricultural sites to be provided can be set off against all or part of the compensation payable for the corresponding asset lost.

4. Such support could take the form of short-term jobs, subsistence support, salary maintenance or similar arrangements.

ly those below the poverty line, the landless, the elderly, women and children, indigenous peoples, ethnic minorities, or other displaced persons who may not be protected through national land compensation legislation.

9.   Bank experience has shown that resettlement of indigenous peoples with traditional land-based modes of production is particularly complex and may have significant adverse impacts on their identity and cultural survival. For this reason, the Bank satisfies itself that the borrower has explored all viable alternative project designs to avoid physical displacement of these groups. When it is not feasible to avoid such displacement, preference is given to land-based resettlement strategies for these groups that are compatible with their cultural preferences and are prepared in consultation with them.

10.   The implementation of resettlement activities is linked to the implementation of the investment component of the project to ensure that displacement or restriction of access does not occur before necessary measures for resettlement are in place. For impacts covered in para. 3(a) of this policy, these measures include provision of compensation and of other assistance required for relocation, prior to displacement, and preparation and provision of resettlement sites with adequate facilities, where required. In particular, taking of land and related assets may take place only after compensation has been paid and, where applicable, resettlement sites and moving allowances have been provided to the displaced persons. For impacts covered in para. 3(b) of this policy, the measures to assist the displaced persons are implemented in accordance with the plan of action as part of the project.

11.   Preference should be given to land-based resettlement strategies for displaced persons whose livelihoods are land-based. These strategies may include resettlement on public land, or on private land acquired or purchased for resettlement. Whenever replacement land is offered, resettlers are provided with land for which a combination of productive potential, locational advantages, and other factors is at least equivalent to the advantages of the land taken. If land is not the preferred option of the displaced persons, the provision of land would adversely affect the sustainability of a park or protected area, or sufficient land is not available at a reasonable price, non-land-based options built around opportunities for employment or self-employment should be provided in addition to cash compensation for land and other assets lost. The lack of adequate land must be demonstrated and documented to the satisfaction of the Bank. * * *

13.   For impacts covered under para. 3(a) of this policy, the Bank also requires the following: (a) Displaced persons and their communities, and any host communities receiving them, are provided timely and relevant information, consulted on resettlement options, and offered opportunities to participate in planning, implementing, and monitoring resettlement. Appropriate and accessible grievance mechanisms are es-

tablished for these groups. (b) In new resettlement sites or host communities, infrastructure and public services are provided as necessary to improve, restore, or maintain accessibility and levels of service for the displaced persons and host communities. Alternative or similar resources are provided to compensate for the loss of access to community resources (such as fishing areas, grazing areas, fuel, or fodder). (c) Patterns of community organization appropriate to the new circumstances are based on choices made by the displaced persons. To the extent possible, the existing social and cultural institutions of resettlers and any host communities are preserved and resettlers' preferences with respect to relocating in preexisting communities and groups are honored.

14.   Upon identification of the need for involuntary resettlement in a project, the borrower carries out a census to identify the persons who will be affected by the project, to determine who will be eligible for assistance, and to discourage inflow of people ineligible for assistance. The borrower also develops a procedure, satisfactory to the Bank, for establishing the criteria by which displaced persons will be deemed eligible for compensation and other resettlement assistance. The procedure includes provisions for meaningful consultations with affected persons and communities, local authorities, and, as appropriate, nongovernmental organizations, and it specifies grievance mechanisms. * * *

18.   The borrower is responsible for preparing, implementing, and monitoring a resettlement plan, a resettlement policy framework, or a process framework (the "resettlement instruments"), as appropriate, that conform to this policy. The resettlement instrument presents a strategy for achieving the objectives of the policy and covers all aspects of the proposed resettlement. Borrower commitment to, and capacity for, undertaking successful resettlement is a key determinant of Bank involvement in a project. * * *

22.   As a condition of appraisal of projects involving resettlement, the borrower provides the Bank with the relevant draft resettlement instrument which conforms to this policy, and makes it available at a place accessible to displaced persons and local NGOs, in a form, manner, and language that are understandable to them. Once the Bank accepts this instrument as providing an adequate basis for project appraisal, the Bank makes it available to the public. * * *

32.   In furtherance of the objectives of this policy, the Bank may at a borrower's request support the borrower and other concerned entities by providing (a) assistance to assess and strengthen resettlement policies, strategies, legal frameworks, and specific plans at a country, regional, or sectoral level; (b) financing of technical assistance to strengthen the capacities of agencies responsible for resettlement, or of affected people to participate more effectively in resettlement operations; (c) financing of technical assistance for developing resettlement policies, strategies, and specific plans, and for implementation, monitoring, and evaluation

of resettlement activities; and (d) financing of the investment costs of resettlement. * * *

THE MODERN POSITION

ROBERTO DAÑINO, THE LEGAL ASPECTS OF THE WORLD BANK'S WORK ON HUMAN RIGHTS[1]

* * * [H]uman rights are progressively becoming an explicit and integral part of the Bank's work, just as has happened over the last twenty years with the environment and in the last five years with anti-corruption. * * * The rule of law is indeed a cornerstone of the work of the Bank and over the last decade we have developed a significant portfolio of projects and other activities in this field. However, I believe that concerns and uncertainties about the "constitutional" restrictions under the Articles of Agreement of the Bank have somewhat inhibited a more proactive and explicit consideration of human rights as part our work. * * * Our framework has limitations—as it should—for it is important to bear in mind that the Bank is a financial institution. As a specialized agency of the UN it has a specific financial purpose and a clearly designated role within the structure of UN institutions. Within these limitations the objectives of the Institution have been, and can and should continue to be, dynamically interpreted and applied. And thus I find that this legal framework also can be enabling. * * *

As the world has changed over the last 60 years, so too has the World Bank and its practice. Its emphasis has shifted dramatically from bricks and mortar infrastructure to the large scale inclusion of social development, human development, institutional reform. In other words, the focus of our work has clearly evolved from "hard lending" to "soft lending." It is clear that with this progress the Bank has made major contributions to the substantive furtherance of a broad array of human rights in a range of fields. * * *

I.   LEGAL FRAMEWORK

The legal framework within which the Bank must operate with respect to human rights as with all its activities is anchored in the Articles of Agreement. They contain important limitations but they have been and must continue to be interpreted so as to achieve the mission of the Bank. * * *

---

1. [Editors' note: At the time this paper was written, the author was Senior Vice President and General Counsel of The World Bank. The original paper appears at the website of the World Bank:

A. Purposes

Article I sets out the purposes of the institution[. * * * D]rafted as it was 60 years ago, its provisions have stood the test of time. Nevertheless, as the challenges of development have changed, the Bank's mission has also evolved to serve a broader concept of development. The Bank's mission as currently defined consists of the alleviation of poverty through economic growth and social equity—all of which have important human rights dimensions.

Social equity is a rich and complex notion. As Nobel Laureate, Amartya Sen has argued, we must view development in terms of freedom and the removal of obstacles to it, including poverty, tyranny, poor economic opportunities, systemic social deprivation, the neglect of public facilities as well as intolerance. Social equity thus includes fighting poverty and inequality, giving the poor and marginalized a voice, *i.e.*, empowerment; freedom from hunger and fear, as well as access to justice. Social equity has, therefore, an obvious human rights component. It is clear that * * * the practice of the Bank is moving towards a conception of development, and of its mandate, that is more grounded in equity and the social face of development. * * *

B. Economic Considerations

The Articles provide that only economic considerations shall be relevant to the decisions of the Bank and its officers, and these must be weighed impartially. What then constitute economic considerations for these purposes? * * * [T]he World Bank, although a development institution, is primarily a financial institution. In making decisions about the investment of limited public resources available, the Bank—like its private sector equivalents—needs to weigh up the wisdom of its proposed investments. It must rely upon analysis of all the factors that can affect the investment. And, these must include the "investment climate" in the recipient country.[2] We have already accepted the fact that issues of governance are relevant but, in my view, it goes further than this.

---

http:www1.worldbank.org/devoutreach/october06/article.asp?id=386. A subsequent version of this analysis was published in HUMAN RIGHTS AND DEVELOPMENT (Alston, ed. 2005).

2. *See* I.F.I. Shihata, Issues of "Governance" in Borrowing Members: The Extent of their Relevance under the Bank's Articles of Agreement. Memorandum of the Vice President and General Counsel December 21, 1990: "i) The degree of political instability of the government of a member requesting a loan and of the security of its territories could be such as to affect the development prospects of the country including its prospective creditworthiness. Political changes may also affect the borrower's ability to keep its commitments under a loan agreement or the ability of the Bank to supervise project implementation or to evaluate the project after its completion. As a result, partial or full foreign occupation of the country's territories or civil strife in such territories cannot be deemed irrelevant to the Bank's work simply because they are of a political nature. Bank lending in such circumstances may run counter to the financial prudence required by the Bank's Articles (Article III, Section 4(v)). It may also threaten the standing of the Bank in financial markets or otherwise adversely affect its reputation as a financial institution. Indeed, the Bank has long recognized that it 'cannot ignore conditions of obvious internal political instability or uncertainty which may directly affect the economic prospects of a borrower.' This position has been consistently upheld by the Bank's Legal Department, most recently in the Legal Memorandum of December 23, 1987. It is important to recall, however, that in such situations the Bank would still be taking into account relevant economic considerations; political events would represent only the historical origins or the causes which gave rise to such considerations."

Research has shown that lack of respect for human rights norms can seriously affect the economic rate of return or even the viability of investment projects. Similarly, it has long been recognized in the Bank that political considerations can have direct economic effects. For instance, in making the judgment of country creditworthiness that the Articles require, the Bank must consider the degree of political stability of the government. In my opinion, therefore, it is consistent with the Articles that the decision-making processes of the Bank incorporate social, political and any other relevant input which may have an impact on its economic decisions.

This same line of analysis applies to the discussion of which human rights are relevant for the making of economic decisions. Some assert that only economic rights are relevant, not the political ones. In my view there is no stark distinction between economic and political considerations, there is similarly an interconnection among economic, social and cultural rights on the one hand, and political rights on the other. It is generally accepted at the political level that "all human rights are universal, indivisible, interdependent and interrelated." Also from a financial point of view I believe the Bank cannot and should not make a distinction either—it needs to take all these considerations into account. In all cases, however, Bank decision-making must treat these considerations impartially, treating similarly situated countries equally.

C.   Political Prohibitions

The other limitations in the Articles relate to politics. There are two general political prohibitions in the Articles which must also be respected. First, Bank interference in a country's political affairs is barred. Second, Bank decisions cannot be influenced by the political character of the member country. The ban on political interference requires the Bank to distance itself from partisan politics, from favoring political factions, and from active participation in political life. The prescribed neutrality with respect to political systems keeps the Bank from endorsing or mandating a particular form of government. But neither of these limitations would prevent the Bank from considering political issues that have economic consequences or implications—so long as this is done in a non-partisan, impartial and neutral manner.

As with the prevailing understanding of what can constitute economic considerations, it is clear that the concept of interference in the context of human rights has also evolved. In interpreting the meaning of these political prohibitions, we need to recognize that the concepts of sovereignty and interference have also evolved. In the modern world, sovereignty is no longer an absolute shield against scrutiny of states respect for international norms. International law now recognizes that there are issues which traverse national boundaries. The examples abound: corporate or financial crimes, money laundering, corruption, terrorism, environmental hazards, the work of International Criminal Court, the work of the International Criminal Tribunal for the former

Yugoslavia, the International Criminal Tribunal for Rwanda, and, significantly for our discussion, gross violations of human rights.

The significance of this for the Bank is that, in my opinion, it can and must take into account human rights violations in its process of making economic decisions. Moreover, because of the way international law has evolved with respect to concepts of sovereignty and interference, and the range of issues that are considered to be of global concern, in doing so the Bank will not fall foul of the political prohibitions of the Articles. Globalization has forced us to broaden the range of issues that are of global concern. As President Wolfensohn noted in his Address to the Board of Governors in Dubai, we face an immense challenge in creating a new global balance. Human rights lie at the heart of that global challenge. * * *

II. THE BANK'S PRACTICE

Operating within th[is] legal framework * * * it is clear that the work of the Bank as well as our concept of development will continue evolving—reflecting trends and changes in the world at large. * * * Overall, there has been a marked shift in emphasis from infrastructure lending to human development. Thirty years ago, the Bank had 58% of its portfolio in infrastructure, today it is reduced to 22% while human development and law and institutional reform represent 52% of our total lending. The evolving practice of the Bank has an important legal dimension for the interpretation of our Articles, since Article 31 of the Vienna Convention on the Law of Treaties regarding the general rule of interpretation makes provision for "[* * *] any subsequent practice in the application of the treaty which establishes the agreement of the parties regarding its interpretation." * * *

One concept that the Bank has taken a leading role in developing is Governance. Our deepened understanding of how to achieve development effectiveness has lead us to consider governance. The importance of effective governance is now well appreciated and the Bank now finances a range of activities in support of governance. Governance itself has a strong human rights content, indeed, this is an area in which our research has found a rich set of connections in charting the work of the Bank to key international human rights provisions. Governance incorporates transparency, accountability, and a predictable legal framework. All of these principles are clearly linked to the "rule of law" with its inherent notions of fairness and social justice. The "rule of law" itself includes access to justice, recognition before the law, and the independence of the judiciary all of which are protected under international human rights law. However, the rule of law must also be supported by a number of other indispensable factors such as public participation, a free press, and a voice for civil society. These too relate to important provisions of a number of international human rights instruments, particularly those of the International Covenant on Civil and Political Rights.

So, while governance is a crucial concept, my view is that governance does not go far enough: we must go beyond it to look at the issues of social equity alongside economic growth. Here legal and judicial reform programs have a key role to play if they support the development of such concepts within national legal systems. Social equity programs should, to my mind, be seen as falling squarely within the mandate of the Bank. Our legal and judicial reform projects already advance social equity. The Bank supports a wide array of Legal and Judicial Reform initiatives: there are approximately 600 Bank-financed projects related to legal and judicial reform and to date there are sixteen active "free-standing" projects in four regions. For example, in the Sri Lanka Legal Aid Services to Poor Women project, training on gender sensitivity in handling cases is provided to judges and court personnel, as well as training on existing national laws and international treaties, and in the Bangladesh Judicial and Legal Capacity Building Project, improved access to justice is a key project objective.[3]

III. THE WAY FORWARD

* * * [A] realistic assessment of the work of the Bank leads inevitably to the conclusion that it has made a substantial positive contribution to human rights, and that it will increasingly continue to do so. In particular it has fulfilled and will continue to fulfill an important role in assisting its Members progressively realize their human rights commitments. However, there are limits that must be respected. There are legal limits. We need to interpret them in a way that is consistent with the purpose of the Bank, in a dynamic way and in a modern context, but the limits do exist. We must work within the legal framework that I have described today to tackle the challenges presented by human rights issues as they evolve. And there are also institutional limits. The Bank is a specialized financial agency. We cannot lose sight of the specificity of our function as a financial institution in the development context. We also have finite capacity and limited resources.

For now at least, I believe we should embrace the centrality of human rights to our work instead of being divided by the semantics of adopting a "rights-based approach." Within both these constraints there is still a great deal of latitude. Insofar as human rights constitute a valid consideration for the investment process they are properly within the scope of issues which the World Bank must consider when it makes its economic decisions. And this consideration must include all human rights: those classified as economic, social and cultural, as well as those

---

3. Additionally, in Ecuador, one of the Judicial Reform Project's focus was court reform, which included judicial training as one of its components along with case administration, information support and infrastructure. Some of the training specifically focused on human rights as it relates to women's rights in Ecuador. In Georgia, the Judicial Reform Program is implementing training for the judiciary as part of its objective to develop an independent and professional judiciary. Other projects include judicial training to support the judicial sector generally, such as in Argentina, under the Model Court Project, where training supports improved case management. *See generally*, World Bank Legal and Judicial Reform: Observations, Experiences and Approach of the Legal Vice Presidency (2002) and Legal and Judicial Reform: Strategic Directions (2003).

classified as civil and political. Moreover it stands to reason that we must address the potential economic consequences of human rights situations, and consider the risks *ex ante*, not only *ex post facto*. However, as a development institution we must also ensure that we work in a manner that does not inflict a "double punishment" on the people of our client countries by turning our backs on them because of the human rights record of their governments. It is easier for a company to walk away from a particular investment than for the Bank to walk away from a whole country and thus inflict additional hardship on those who may already be suffering governmental abuse.

The Bank's role is not that of enforcer. Enforcement belongs primarily to the mandate of the member countries, and other, non-financial entities. Our role is a collaborative one in the implementation of our member countries human rights obligations. We do need to work within countries to exert a positive influence, to deepen the dialogue and to share our knowledge and expertise. And in this venture we need to accept that we must work with countries that do not respect human rights as well as those that do. So, how does the Bank move forward in this area? The way forward in the area of human rights and development must be consistent with the mission of the Bank, that is to say, poverty alleviation through economic growth and social equity. The human rights content of this direction is beyond question. As we move in this direction there is a clear and unmet demand from our member countries for legal and judicial reform programs. We certainly need to dramatically scale up our interventions in this field with a wide range of partners. Through these programmes, as well as through every other aspect of the Bank's work, many of the human rights aspirations can be progressively realized. * * *

GALIT A. SARFATY, NOTE, THE WORLD BANK AND THE INTERNALIZATION OF INDIGENOUS RIGHTS NORMS

114 YALE L.J. 1791 (2005)

International organizations, particularly international financial institutions, are becoming central players in promoting compliance with human rights norms and the adoption of social and environmental standards. The policymaking of the World Bank exemplifies this trend. By adopting operational policies on issues like indigenous peoples, involuntary resettlement, and environmental assessment, the World Bank has emerged as an important actor in the interpretive community for public international law.

World Bank operational policies are becoming *de facto* global standards among other development banks as well as institutions engaged in project finance. For example, they serve as a model for the Equator

Principles, a set of voluntary social and environmental guidelines that have been adopted by at least twenty-nine private banks.[3] Export credit agencies (ECAs) are another type of economic actor applying Bank policies on environmental and social issues, largely in response to outside pressure.[4] In 2000, a group of more than 300 non-governmental organizations signed the Jakarta Declaration for Reform of Official Export Credit and Investment Insurance Agencies, which includes a call for "[b]inding common environmental and social guidelines and standards [that are] no lower and less rigorous than existing international procedures and standards for public international finance such as those of the World Bank Group."[5] Although the Bank has faced protests over controversial projects,[6] NGOs nonetheless consider its standards "a minimum floor that any environmentally and socially sensitive project should meet." Given the adoption of Bank guidelines by various economic institutions, it is important to understand the process by which these standards shape the policies of borrower countries and influence the interactions among a range of actors, from government officials and Bank staff to civil society activists. * * *

In projects affecting indigenous peoples, Bank staff must balance competing interests in deciding whether and when to apply the indigenous peoples policy and how to implement the policy once it is applied. As a result, actions are continuously contested and renegotiated within the institution itself. These internal contestations often correspond to divisions between competing interest groups and are most pronounced in regard to countries where domestic legal systems do not recognize indigenous peoples or sufficiently address indigenous-peoples-related issues. For example, economists may disagree with environmentalists

---

3. The Equator Principles are modeled on the social and environmental standards of the International Finance Corporation (IFC), the private-sector arm of the World Bank. They were originally conceived in October 2002 when the IFC invited a group of major private banks to discuss an environmental and social risk-assessment framework for the projects that they finance that are over fifty million dollars in size. These projects often include oil and gas pipelines and hydroelectric dams, which are particularly prone to causing environmental and social disruption. The Equator Principles' preamble states, "We will not provide loans directly to projects where the borrower will not or is unable to comply with our environmental and social policies and processes." THE "EQUATOR PRINCIPLES": AN INDUSTRY APPROACH FOR FINANCIAL INSTITUTIONS IN DETERMINING, ASSESSING AND MANAGING ENVIRONMENTAL & SOCIAL RISK IN PROJECT FINANCING, at pmbl. (2003).

4. ECAs are public agencies, like the Export–Import Bank of the United States and the U.S. Overseas Private Investment Corporation, that provide government-backed financing to corporations from their home countries to conduct business abroad, particularly in developing countries.

5. ECA Watch, *Jakarta Declaration for Reform of Official Export Credit and Investment Insurance Agencies*, http://www.eca-watch.org/goals/jakartadec.html. Since the signing of the Jakarta Declaration, member governments of the Organization for Economic Cooperation and Development (OECD) Working Party on Export Credits and Credit Guarantees have drafted a common set of environmental guidelines. The guidelines urge members undertaking environmental reviews to "benchmark projects [...] against the safeguard policies published by the World Bank Group," particularly the policies on involuntary resettlement, indigenous peoples, and cultural property. OECD WORKING PARTY ON EXPORT CREDITS AND CREDIT GUARANTEES, UPDATED RECOMMENDATION ON COMMON APPROACHES ON ENVIRONMENT AND OFFICIALLY SUPPORTED EXPORT CREDITS, P 12.1 & n.2, TD/ECG(2005)3 (Feb. 25, 2005).

6. These include the Planafloro project in Brazil; the Narmada Dam in India; and the Three Gorges Dam in China, which was canceled due to intense outside pressure. Jonathan A. Fox & L.David Brown, *Assessing the Impact of NGO Advocacy Campaigns on World Bank Projects and Policies*, in THE STRUGGLE FOR ACCOUNTABILITY: THE WORLD BANK, NGOS, AND GRASSROOTS MOVEMENTS 485, 500–03 (Jonathan A. Fox & L. David Brown eds., 1998).

and anthropologists over whether to apply the indigenous peoples policy in a borrower country where there are no legal provisions that recognize special rights for indigenous peoples. * * *

A. *Policy Conditionalities*

While the Bank may exercise its influence informally through the use of oral commitments, supplemental letters, solicited and unsolicited advice, and letters of intent, loan agreements are the primary mechanism through which it shapes domestic law. The Bank attaches conditionalities to loan agreements for policy-based lending.[7] A policy conditionality is "a set of requirements and preconditions that the recipient country is expected to meet in order to receive financial assistance."[8] According to the Articles of Agreement [at article 3], such preconditions "ensure that the proceeds of any loan are used only for the purposes for which the loan was granted, with due attention to considerations of economy and efficiency and without regard to political or other non-economic influences or considerations." If the country fails to meet these conditionalities, the Bank has the right to stop disbursing funds.

For instance, the Bank has conditioned loan disbursement for hydroelectric projects on the recipient country's reducing government energy subsidies and decreasing the role of the government in energy production. In addition to these economic policy reforms, Bank loans for hydroelectric projects have also required that the country address relocation and environmental concerns. Satisfactory implementation of these conditions has been a precondition for additional loan disbursements.

Policy conditionalities have generated substantial debate in the development community, both inside and outside the Bank, over their effectiveness in generating proposed reforms and supporting country ownership. They are sometimes considered intrusions on a country's sovereignty, especially when the borrower country is under great financial pressure to accept a loan. In its 1992 Wapenhans Report, the Bank's Operations Evaluation Department acknowledged the one-sidedness of negotiations between the Bank and borrower countries. According to the report, borrowers complained that "[d]uring negotiations, the Bank overpowers borrowers—and the country negotiating team often doesn't have the strength to resist."

Critics also contend that conditionalities may not directly relate to the success of the project or the repayment of the loan. Instead, they

---

7. The Bank has two basic types of lending instruments: investment loans and development policy loans (formerly known as adjustment loans). Investment loans have a long-term focus (five to ten years) and finance goods, works, and services in support of economic and social development projects in a broad range of sectors. Development policy (or policy-based) loans have a short-term focus (one to three years) and provide quickly disbursed external financing to support policy and institutional reforms. Conditionalities are more commonly used in policy-based lending. WORLD BANK, A GUIDE TO THE WORLD BANK 47–49 (2003); 1 WORLD BANK, THE WORLD BANK OPERATIONAL MANUAL, at OP 8.60 (2004).

8. OPERATIONS POLICY & COUNTRY SERVS., WORLD BANK, REVIEW OF WORLD BANK CONDITIONALITY: ISSUES NOTE 4 (2005).

may be extensions of the Bank's development ideology and its vision of the country's long-term economic future. Studies have shown that there is a positive relationship between policy-based loan success rates and a country's economic track record. As a result, there have been proposals to replace *ex ante* commitments with results-oriented approaches where aid would be allocated only to countries with favorable policy environments.[9]

B. *Operational Policies*

In addition to imposing policy conditionalities on borrower countries, the Bank also influences domestic policymaking through its operational policies. These policies, approved by the Bank's Board of Executive Directors, guide staff practice and ensure that operations are financially, socially, and environmentally sound. They provide explicit requirements for the design, appraisal, and implementation of Bank-financed development projects. While operational policies are mandatory for Bank staff, other standards, such as Bank procedures and good practices, are merely recommended. * * *

In the 1980s and early 1990s, human rights NGOs and indigenous peoples pressured the Bank to adopt an operational policy in accordance with indigenous rights norms being formulated in a variety of public international legal forums.[10] Disaffected Bank employees, often anthropologists and sociologists who felt that their voices were being ignored in Bank decisionmaking, supported the campaign of external advocates. These internal reformers increased pressure on management to place more emphasis on other noneconomic concerns such as civil society participation, the environment, and the displacement of vulnerable populations.[11] For example, Bank social scientists employed NGO pressure to urge the Bank to develop a formal policy on involuntary

---

9. An example of a performance-based lending program is the Millennium Challenge Account, a recently created U.S. foreign aid program to provide money to countries with sound policies, based on sixteen performance indicators. See Consolidated Appropriations Act, 2004, Pub. L. No. 108–199, div. D, tit. VI, 2004 U.S.C.C.A.N. (118 Stat.) 3, 211–26 (to be codified at 22U.S.C. §§ 7701–7718) (Millennium Challenge Act of 2003).

10. Customary international law on the rights of indigenous peoples has been slowly emerging over the past two decades as part of a growing international movement for indigenous rights. See, e.g., S. JAMES ANAYA, INDIGENOUS PEOPLES IN INTERNATIONAL LAW 61–72 (2d ed. 2004) (tracing the emergence of norms of customary international law on indigenous peoples from early activity at the United Nations in the 1970s to the writing of the U.N. Draft Declaration on the Rights of Indigenous Peoples in 1994 and the case of Mayagna (Sumo) Awas Tingni Community v. Nicaragua, 2001 Inter–Am. Ct. H.R. (ser. C) No. 79 (Aug. 31, 2001), before the Inter–American Court of Human Rights in 2001). The global process of indigenous standard setting is taking place in a variety of forums, including the International Labour Organization, the United Nations, and the Organization of American States. See International Labour Organisation, supra note 72; U.N. Econ. & Soc. Council [ECOSOC], Sub–Comm'n on Prevention of Discrimination & Prot. of Minorities, Working Group on Indigenous Populations, Draft Declaration on the Rights of Indigenous Peoples, U.N. Doc. E/CN.4/Sub.2/1994/2/Add.1 (Aug. 26, 1994); Proposed American Declaration on the Rights of Indigenous Peoples, Inter–Am. C.H.R., OEA/Ser.L/V/II.95, doc. 7 rev. 625 (1997).

11. See Jonathan A. Fox, *When Does Reform Policy Influence Practice? Lessons from the Bankwide Resettlement Review*, in THE STRUGGLE FOR ACCOUNTABILITY, *supra* at 303, 334 ("Although dealing with NGO critics can provoke ideological and professional dissonance, insider reformists are nevertheless well aware that advocacy groups create an enabling environment that bolsters their own leverage.").

resettlement in 1980. This evidence suggests the contested nature of decision-making within the Bank, which allowed for a dialogic process of norm emergence between internal and external actors.

Once its indigenous peoples policy was adopted, the Bank began to apply the policy to borrower countries to encourage them to internalize indigenous rights norms. These countries often embrace such norms in order to enhance their reputation in the international community and secure loans from the Bank. But additional evidence demonstrates that this is not always the case: Norm internalization may depart from the conventional model in cases where the Bank faces domestic political and legal constraints when attempting to influence countries to internalize these norms.

ONE MECHANISM FOR THE INTERNALIZATION OF HUMAN RIGHTS STANDARDS IN WORLD BANK DECISION–MAKING: INSPECTION PANELS

INTERNATIONAL BANK FOR RECONSTRUCTION AND DEVELOPMENT AND THE INTERNATIONAL DEVELOPMENT ASSOCIATION

Resolution No. 93–10, Resolution No. IDA 93–6
Sept. 22, 1993

The Executive Directors:

Hereby resolve:

1.   There is established an independent Inspection Panel (hereinafter called the Panel), which shall have the powers and shall function as stated in this resolution.

Composition of the Panel

2.   The Panel shall consist of three members of different nationalities from Bank member countries. The President, after consultation with the Executive Directors, shall nominate the members of the Panel to be appointed by the Executive Directors. * * *

4.   Members of the Panel shall be selected on the basis of their ability to deal thoroughly and fairly with the requests brought to them, their integrity and their independence from the Bank's Management, and their exposure to developmental issues and to living conditions in developing countries. Knowledge and experience of the Bank's operations will also be desirable.

5.   Executive Directors, Alternates, Advisors and staff members of the Bank Group may not serve on the Panel until two years have elapsed since the end of their service in the Bank Group. * * *

6.   A Panel member shall be disqualified from participation in the hearing and investigation of any request related to a matter in which he/she has a personal interest or had significant involvement in any capacity. * * *

8.   Members of the Panel may be removed from office only by decision of the Executive Directors, for cause. * * *

10.   In the performance of their functions, members of the Panel shall be officials of the Bank enjoying the privileges and immunities accorded to Bank officials, and shall be subject to the requirements of the Bank's Articles of Agreement concerning their exclusive loyalty to the Bank. * * * Members of the Panel may not be employed by the Bank Group, following the end of their service on the Panel. * * *

Powers of the Panel

12.   The Panel shall receive requests for inspection presented to it by an affected party in the territory of the borrower which is not a single individual (*i.e.*, a community of persons such as an organization, association, society or other grouping of individuals), or by the local representative of such party or by another representative in the exceptional cases where the party submitting the request contends that appropriate representation is not locally available and the Executive Directors so agree at the time they consider the request for inspection. Any such representative shall present to the Panel written evidence that he is acting as agent of the party on behalf of which the request is made. The affected party must demonstrate that its rights or interests have been or are likely to be directly affected by an action or omission of the Bank as a result of a failure of the Bank to follow its operational policies and procedures with respect to the design, appraisal and/or implementation of a project financed by the Bank (including situations where the Bank is alleged to have failed in its follow-up on the borrower's obligations under loan agreements with respect to such policies and procedures) provided in all cases that such failure has had, or threatens to have, a material adverse effect. In view of the institutional responsibilities of Executive Directors in the observance by the Bank of its operational policies and procedures, an Executive Director may in special cases of serious alleged violations of such policies and procedures ask the Panel for an investigation, subject to the requirements of paragraphs 13 and 14 below. The Executive Directors, acting as a Board, may at any time instruct the Panel to conduct an investigation. For purposes of this Resolution, "operational policies and procedures" consist of the Bank's Procedures and Operational Directives, and similar documents issued before these series were started, and does not include Guidelines and Best Practices and similar documents or statements.

13.   The Panel shall satisfy itself before a request for inspection is heard that the subject matter of the request has been dealt with by the Management of the Bank and Management has failed to demonstrate that it has followed, or is taking adequate steps to follow the Bank's

policies and procedures. The Panel shall also satisfy itself that the alleged violation of the Bank's policies and procedures is of a serious character.

14.   In considering requests under paragraph 12 above, the following requests shall not be heard by the Panel:

(a) Complaints with respect to action which are the responsibility of other parties, such as a borrower, or potential borrower, and which do not involve any action or omission on the part of the Bank;

(b) Complaints against procurement decisions by Bank borrowers from suppliers of goods and services financed or expected to be financed by the Bank under a loan agreement, or from losing tenderers for the supply of any such goods and services, which will continue to be addressed by staff under existing procedures;

(c) Requests filed after the Closing Date of the loan financing the project with respect to which the request is filed or after the loan financing the project has been substantially disbursed;[1]

(d) Requests related to a particular matter or matters over which the Panel has already made its recommendation upon having received a prior request, unless justified by new evidence or circumstances not known at the time of the prior request.

15.   The Panel shall seek advice of the Bank's Legal Department on matters related to the Bank's rights and obligations with respect to the request under consideration.

Procedures

16.   Requests for inspection shall be in writing and shall state all relevant facts, including, in the case of a request by an affected party, the harm suffered by or threatened to such party or parties by the alleged action or omission of the Bank. All requests shall explain the steps already taken to deal with the issue, as well as the nature of the alleged actions or omissions and shall specify the actions taken to bring the issue to the attention of the Management, and Management's response to such action.

17.   The Chairperson of the Panel shall inform the Executive Directors and the President of the Bank promptly upon receiving a request for inspection.

18.   Within 21 days of being notified of a request for inspection, the Management of the Bank shall provide the Panel with evidence that it has complied, or intends to comply with the Bank's relevant policies and procedures.

19.   Within 21 days of receiving the response of the Management as provided in the preceding paragraph, the Panel shall determine whether the request meets the eligibility criteria set out in paragraphs

---

1.   This will be deemed to be the case when at least ninety-five percent of the loan proceeds have been disbursed.

12 to 14 above and shall make a recommendation to the Executive Directors as to whether the matter should be investigated. The recommendation of the Panel shall be circulated to the Executive Directors for decision within the normal distribution period. In case the request was initiated by an affected party, such party shall be informed of the decision of the Executive Directors within two weeks of the date of such decision.

20.   If a decision is made by the Executive Directors to investigate the request, the Chairperson of the Panel shall designate one or more of the Panel's members (Inspectors) who shall have primary responsibility for conducting the inspection. The Inspector(s) shall report his/her (their) findings to the Panel within a period to be determined by the Panel taking into account the nature of each request.

21.   In the discharge of their functions, the members of the Panel shall have access to all staff who may contribute information and to all pertinent Bank records and shall consult as needed with the Director General, Operations Evaluation Department and the Internal Auditor. The borrower and the Executive Director representing the borrowing (or guaranteeing) country shall be consulted on the subject matter both before the Panel's recommendation on whether to proceed with the investigation and during the investigation. Inspection in the territory of such country shall be carried out with its prior consent.

22.   The Panel shall submit its report to the Executive Directors and the President. The report of the Panel shall consider all relevant facts, and shall conclude with the Panel's findings on whether the Bank has complied with all relevant Bank policies and procedures.

23.   Within six weeks from receiving the Panel's findings, Management will submit to the Executive Directors for their consideration a report indicating its recommendations in response to such findings. The findings of the Panel and the actions completed during project preparation also will be discussed in the Staff Appraisal Report when the project is submitted to the Executive Directors for financing. In all cases of a request made by an affected party, the Bank shall, within two weeks of the Executive Directors' consideration of the matter, inform such party of the results of the investigation and the action taken in its respect, if any.

Decisions of the Panel

24.   All decisions of the Panel on procedural matters, its recommendations to the Executive Directors on whether to proceed with the investigation of a request, and its reports pursuant to paragraph 22, shall be reached by consensus and, in the absence of a consensus, the majority and minority views shall be stated.

Reports

25.   After the Executive Directors have considered a request for an inspection as set out in paragraph 19, the Bank shall make such request

publicly available together with the recommendation of the Panel on whether to proceed with the inspection and the decision of the Executive Directors in this respect. The Bank shall make publicly available the report submitted by the Panel pursuant to paragraph 22 and the Bank's response thereon within two weeks after consideration by the Executive Directors of the report.

26.   In addition to the material referred to in paragraph 25, the Panel shall furnish an annual report to the President and the Executive Directors concerning its activities. The annual report shall be published by the Bank. * * *

DANIEL D. BRADLOW, PRIVATE COMPLAINANTS AND INTERNATIONAL ORGANIZATIONS: A COMPARATIVE STUDY OF THE INDEPENDENT INSPECTION MECHANISMS IN INTERNATIONAL FINANCIAL INSTITUTIONS

36 GEO. J. INT'L L. 403 (2005)

The one group that historically has not been able to hold international organizations accountable is non-state actors who are adversely affected by the actions of an international organization but who have no contractual relationships with it. * * * This gap in international organizational accountability was not perceived to be significant until the last quarter of the twentieth century when two parallel developments began to change this view. The first development was that the scope of the activities of international organizations broadened. The impact of this change is seen most clearly in the case of the international financial institutions (IFIs), particularly the World Bank Group (World Bank) and the International Monetary Fund (IMF). The World Bank began to expand its range of operations beyond financing physical infrastructure projects to include such matters as providing both financing and advisory services related to the structural adjustment of its member states' economies and to improving the governance of their societies. Similarly, the IMF began to get involved in poverty alleviation and the governance of its member states. This "mission creep," combined with changes in the international financial system, altered the nature of the IFIs' relations with their developing country member states, shifting the balance of bargaining power between international financial institutions and their client states in favor of the IFIs. This meant that the developing countries had limited scope to negotiate over the conditions that the IFIs attached to their financing and could not ignore the policy advice from the IFIs. The net effect was that, *de facto*, the IFIs became important participants in the policy-making process of their member states. However, because of the organizations' immunity and their member states' lack of interest in holding them accountable, the international organizations, unlike most actors in the policy-making process, were not directly accountable to those most affected by their decisions and actions.

The second development was that perceptions began changing about the responsibilities of decision-makers in large-scale projects and development programs. The change was happening because of developments in human rights law and changing views about the environmental and social responsibilities of key decision-makers and actors. The result was that those who were adversely affected by the projects began to advocate more vigorously that all decision-makers, including funding sources, be held accountable for their decisions relating to these projects. Since the World Bank and the regional development banks were often key lenders and providers of technical assistance for projects, they were the first targets of these calls for greater accountability.

The ability of the multilateral development banks (MDBs) to escape liability was particularly upsetting to non-state actors because MDBs, despite their formal role as lenders rather than sponsors of development projects or programs, were perceived to be directly and exclusively responsible for at least part of the harm caused by their operations. Non-state actors further argued that the MDBs' ability to escape accountability was incompatible with the principles of good governance being advocated by the institutions themselves. * * *

The World Bank became the first international organization to respond to * * * demands for accountability. In 1993 the World Bank created the Inspection Panel, the first mechanism in which qualifying non-state actors could hold an international organization directly accountable for its actions. The Inspection Panel allows these non-state actors to hold the Bank accountable for actions that cause or threaten to cause serious harm to the complaining non-state actors and are inconsistent with the Bank's own operational policies and procedures. Since that time, a number of other international financial institutions have established their own inspection mechanisms. They are the Asian Development Bank, the Inter–American Development Bank, the International Finance Corporation, the Multilateral Investment Guarantee Agency and the European Bank for Reconstruction and Development. The African Development Bank has approved and is in the process of setting up an independent inspection mechanism for the Bank. In addition, two national development financing organizations, the Japanese Bank for International Cooperation and Export Development Canada, have created similar mechanisms.

These inspection mechanisms have both practical and legal significance. At a practical level, they have resulted in thousands of people receiving compensation for the adverse consequences of projects being funded by these institutions, in the cancellation of at least one project, in instructions from the Board to the management to make changes in projects in order to provide people with the intended benefits or to mitigate the harm caused by the project and in much greater sensitivity in the institutions to their own operational policies and procedures. Legally, these mechanisms have turned out to be effective forums in which adversely affected persons can raise claims that relate to their rights as indigenous people or as involuntarily resettled people and in which they can challenge the interpretation and implementation of the internal policies and procedures of the MDBs. Consequently, inspection mechanisms are slowly beginning to provide data and precedents that can influence the evolution of international human rights law, international environmental law and international administrative law.

NOTES AND QUESTIONS ON THE WORLD BANK

1. *World Bank inspection panels as "information courts."* A number of projects at the World Bank have been postponed or derailed after review by an Inspection Panel (or its procedural predecessor), including the Sardar Sarovar Project in India, the Arun III Hydroelectric Project in Nepal, the Bujagali Hydropower Project in Uganda, and the Western Poverty Reduction Project in China. These projects were not cancelled on explicitly human rights grounds, but it is a mistake to dismiss the panels as empty gestures. Even with their limited enforcement powers, the panels offer an opportunity to hold the Bank to its own standards, which as shown above now explicitly include human rights concerns. The strength of that disciplinary and informational process rests on empirical research by the Bank itself showing that "positive development outcomes emerge from good governance and anti-corruption, and * * * demonstrates that significant causal links exist between the provision of human rights, such as civil liberties, and positive development outcomes that include the enhanced success of bank-funded investment projects."

2. *Defining the actionable wrongs.* Are only certain human rights issues appropriate for IFI concern under the Articles of Agreement? Judging from the World Bank's policies on involuntary resettlement and indigenous peoples rights, is the incorporation of human rights into World Bank standards sufficiently or overly ambitious given its limited "constitutional" mandate?

3. *Development as a human right.* According to the Office of the UN High Commissioner for Human Rights, the right to development consists of several principles of law, including:

> full sovereignty over natural resources, self-determination, popular participation in development, equality of opportunity, the creation of favourable conditions for the enjoyment of other civil, political, economic, social and cultural rights. * * * The right to development can be invoked both by individuals and by peoples. It imposes obligations both on individual States—to ensure equal and adequate access to essential resources—and on the international community—

to promote fair development policies and effective international cooperation. The World Conference on Human Rights, held in Vienna in 1993, dealt extensively with the right to development and adopted the Vienna Declaration and Programme of Action, which recognized that democracy, development and respect for human rights and fundamental freedoms are interdependent and mutually reinforcing. The World Conference also reaffirmed by consensus the right to development as a universal and inalienable right and an integral part of fundamental human rights. It further stated that, while development facilitates the enjoyment of all human rights, "lack of development may not be invoked to justify the abridgement of internationally recognized human rights." In 1986, the U.N. General Assembly adopted the Declaration on the Right to Development. Article 1(1) of the Declaration provides that "the right to development is an inalienable human right by virtue of which every human person and all peoples are entitled to participate in, contribute to, and enjoy economic, social, cultural and political development, in which all human rights and fundamental freedoms can be fully realized."

Is it possible to translate these abstractions into concrete, legally-enforceable terms? *See* AMARTYA SEN, DEVELOPMENT AS FREEDOM (1999). *See* Chapter 9, *infra*.

4. *Human rights and public international debt*. Is there a human right to live under a government free of severe indebtedness? Consider the observations of a former chief economist of the World Bank and Nobel laureate in economics:

Regrettably, we have no rule of law at the international level for the restructuring of government debts. * * * At the level of personal debt we've made progress, by instituting bankruptcy laws to replace debtors' prisons, portrayed so graphically in the work of Charles Dickens. And yet to date we have no parallel set of laws governing the restructuring and relief of international debt. * * * What we are left with is a set of *ad hoc* initiatives based informally, and to a disturbing degree, on the shifting interests of the United States, which on this issue has eschewed international cooperation to pursue a "having the cake and eating it too" strategy. We are perfectly willing to countenance debt forgiveness when other countries are owed money, but if our own money is at stake we argue eloquently for the sanctity of contracts, regardless of the political circumstances. We need an international "bankruptcy" court, with no vested national interest, to deal with debt restructuring and relief, and to ensure a fair sharing of the burdens this would create. The United Nations could devise a set of principles; a rule of law; that would guide the court as it assessed the validity of contracts made with, and debts incurred by, outlaw regimes. Loans to build schools might be permitted, and the debt obligation, accordingly, would not be treated as odious; loans to buy arms might not be permitted. In some cases the court might decide that a loan for an ostensibly good purpose ran a high risk of being used for nefarious objectives; in which case the loan would be disallowed. Governments and banks that lend money to oppressive regimes would be put on notice that they risk not getting repaid, and the contracts and debts of countries with outlaw regimes would be re-examined once those regimes were no longer in power.

Joseph Stiglitz, *Odious Rulers, Odious Debts*, Atl. Monthly (Nov. 2003).

5. *Accountability mechanisms within World Bank affiliates.* The International Finance Corporation (IFC) and the Multilateral Investment Guarantee Agency (MIGA) within the World Bank Group have created an "independent recourse mechanism" called the Office of Compliance Advisor/Ombudsman (CAO), which reports directly to the President of the World Bank Group. The CAO is intended to address "complaints from people affected by projects in a manner that is fair, objective, and constructive and to enhance the social and environmental outcomes of projects in which IFC and MIGA play a role." CAO, Preliminary Assessment Report: Complaint Regarding IFC's Proposed Investment in Celulosas de M'Bopicuá and Orion Projects, Uruguay 4 (Nov. 2005).

In 2005, the CAO received a complaint signed by over 39,000 people in both Argentina and Uruguay and supported by the Argentinean NGO Center for Human Rights and Environment (CEDHA). The complaint related to two large paper pulp projects, sponsored by Grupo Empresarial ENCE—a Spanish firm—and Oy Metsa Botnia—a Finnish firm—on the Uruguayan side of the Rio Uruguay. According to the complaint, the project involved multiple violations of social and environmental rights and standards, including the right of participation, access to information, right to development, right to health, right to a healthy environment, right to water; as well as violations of international bilateral treaty law between Argentina and Uruguay. In its preliminary report, the CAO concluded that:

> the consultation and disclosure processes related to approvals for these projects give the impression of being rushed, and presented as a *fait accompli* to those being consulted. Too little emphasis has been placed on the trans-boundary nature of the possible impacts of these developments and there has not been sufficient acknowledgment of the legitimacy of concerns and fears of communities that are local to the project. Further technical information and scientific facts will not be sufficient to address the lack of trust that currently exists amongst those who are concerned about the projects. Specific efforts must be implemented in order to ensure that people who believe that they will be impacted are able to have trust in the process as well as the outcome of any additional studies.

Id. at 13. The controversy continues as of this writing.

6. *The World Bank before the Inter–American Commission on Human Rights: the Chixoy Dam Project.* Can a World Bank project be challenged in

an intergovernmental setting? In the 1970s, the World Bank and the Inter–American Development Bank entered into a partnership with the government of Guatemala to build the Chixoy Hydroelectric Dam, in an effort to produce cheap electricity in the country. Construction on the dam, which was intended to block the Rio Negro river in central Guatemala, began in 1975. The IDB and World Bank provided the government of Guatemala with initial loans of $72 million and $105 million, respectively, and directed the state-owned National Institute of Electrification (INDE) to administer the funds and coordinate the project.

From the outset, critics allege, the INDE failed to consult with the communities along the Rio Negro; indeed, representatives of the affected indigenous community claim that they were not informed by INDE officials that they would have to abandon their farmlands and homes until 1977, over two years after construction of the dam began. Those who left their lands were "compensated" by the government with small houses and infertile land at the resettlement site. Those residents of Rio Negro who were unwilling to leave fared even worse: INDE responded by initiating a campaign of violence and intimidation against the villagers that allegedly included stealing and destroying their certificates of title to their land and killing and mutilating the bodies of several community members. Beginning in February 1982, members of the military and a paramilitary unit established by the military forcibly evicted the entire population of Rio Negro through a series of four massacres, resulting in the deaths of over 300 residents and the torture, rape, and harassment of many more.

In 2004, the Centre on Housing Rights and Evictions (COHRE) and Rights Action, two NGOs, filed a petition with the Inter–American Commission on Human Rights against the government of Guatemala, the IDB, the World Bank, and the United States (arguing that the United States was the principal decision-maker for the World Bank and IDB with respect to the Chixoy Dam project). The petition asserted various violations of the American Convention and the American Declaration. The petitioners' brief is available at http://www.cohre.org/store/attachments/G4b-Chixoy_Petition.pdf.

The most innovative aspect of COHRE's petition is that it seeks to hold intergovernmental organizations legally liable for the harms suffered by the villagers of Rio Negro. According to the plaintiffs:

> At the very least, the gross negligence and reckless disregard shown by the two banks in the Chixoy case highlights the role of international financial institutions in fostering a climate of impunity for human rights crimes committed in Guatemala and underscores how powerful international actors ignored, and profited from, that country's brutal history of repression. Indeed, all parties behind the project were unjustly enriched due to these atrocities and their actions or inaction exhibited a reckless disregard for the human

rights of the Chixoy community. * * * The two Banks which financed and directly supervised the project had an obligation to show due diligence with regard to the implementation of the project, especially given Guatemala's well-known human rights record throughout the 1970s and 1980s.

Petition at 15–16. Despite the fact that COHRE and Rights Action submitted their petition in 2004, the Inter–American Commission has not yet reached a ruling on admissibility. Why do you suppose that might be so?

7. *The Equator Principles*. In October 2002, a small number of banks, working with the World Bank Group's International Finance Corporation, convened to develop a voluntary "benchmark for determining, assessing and managing social and environmental risk" in their project financing. They developed the "Equator Principles," which as revised, "govern the social and environmental impact of large-scale projects such as mines or roads or dams; although their implementation remains uneven." Editorial, *Managing Globalization*, WASH. POST, Feb. 19, 2006, at B6:

> Most people agree that globalization is here to stay; that it has both positive and less positive effects; and that the world lacks good institutions to ameliorate the negative ones. The 'Equator Principles' * * * are a rare creative effort to grapple with this deficit. * * * The purpose of the update [in 2006] is to make the principles more effective and less legalistic. Instead of requiring project managers to check a large number of boxes—for example, hold two consultations in each village along the path of a proposed road—the new code would specify social and environmental outcomes and then allow flexibility on how to get there. Critics complain that this would make it hard to hold project financiers accountable, but the accountability under the old code is flawed: [a] project with good substantive outcomes could be faulted for an inconsequential procedural mistake. The critics also complain that the required outcomes are not good enough: for example, the code fails to require that people who are relocated because of an infrastructure project should be given legal tenure over their new dwelling. But here the standards are guilty only of preferring the possible to the ideal. They stipulate that relocated people must be left better off than before. * * * The critics often fail to see that perfectionist standards have a downside: such standards can raise the cost of building roads or installing urban water systems to the point that less development happens, in which case the poor suffer.

CASE STUDY

THE CHAD–CAMEROON PETROLEUM DEVELOPMENT AND PIPELINE PROJECT: RATIONALE, PROJECT DESCRIPTION, AND PROJECT UPDATE[1]

Chad is one of the poorest countries in the world. Only ten developing countries in the world are poorer in terms of GDP per capita. But with desert covering much of this landlocked country of few natural resources, Chad had few options for improving its plight. * * * When oil reserves were discovered there in the mid-nineties, oil companies asked the World Bank to give its backing to one of the biggest projects in Africa–building a 1070 km pipeline to carry Chad's petroleum to the Atlantic coast for export. The World Bank saw this as a unique opportunity for Chad to climb out of extreme poverty. Everyone agreed that the poverty reduction prospects for Chad were inextricably linked to how the country used the revenue from oil. Before it could become involved, the World Bank needed assurances that the revenues would be used to lift Chadians out of deprivation.

Most of the pipeline crosses more densely populated Cameroon, richly endowed with tropical forests. While Cameroon benefits from more mineral resources, fertile agricultural land, and a more favorable climate than its neighbor Chad, nearly one-fifth of its population lived on less than $1 a day. Cameroon stood to gain an estimated US$500 million in direct revenues over the life of the project. * * * But the project entails some potential costs and setbacks. As a result, the World Bank's involvement in the project triggered the application of the World Bank Group's strict environmental and social safeguard policies, along with broad public consultations. * * *

Project Description

The World Bank Group's participation in the petrol project that would generate revenues for Chad's poverty reduction was approved in June 2000. The project entails developing oil fields in southern Chad, building a pipeline across Cameroon to the Atlantic coast, and installing an off-shore terminal.

The oil development project extracts and carries oil from three oil fields (Miandoum, Kome and Bolobo) in the Doba basin in southern Chad to off-loading facilities off the coast of Cameroon. The construction phase comprised:

> Drilling some three hundred wells in fields in southwestern Chad that hold about 900 million barrels of oil;

> Building a 1070km (650–mile) buried pipeline from the fields across Cameroon to the coast;

---

1. (www.worldbank.org/afr/ccproj); http://go.worldbank.org/WANI8L6AO0 (visited 5 September 2008)

> Installing an off-shore terminal facility—a "floating storage and off-loading" vessel with associated marine pipelines.

Construction of the pipeline took three years and was completed a year ahead of schedule. Petroleum production is expected to last about 25 years.

Drilling is financed and carried out by Exxon, the operator, on behalf of a 3–member oil consortium including Petronas of Malaysia, and Chevron of the U.S. By the end of 2004, 226 wells had been drilled. By September 30, 2005, about 118 million barrels of oil were produced. The pipeline itself is owned and operated by two joint-venture companies supported by World Bank financing: one in Cameroon (Cameroon Oil Transportation Company–COTCO) and the other for the portion in Chad (Tchad Oil Transportation Company–TOTCO). The oil consortium jointly holds about 80 percent of the shares of the pipeline companies. The government of Chad holds minority interests in both pipeline companies while the government of Cameroon holds a minority interest in the Cameroon pipeline company. The governments of both countries receive revenues from these holdings (financed through about US$90 million in loans from the World Bank) and through royalties (to Chad), transit fees (to Cameroon), and taxes (to both governments).

Total project costs are estimated at $4.1 billion. The private sponsors financed about $3.5 billion or nearly 85 percent of the costs. The European Investment Bank financed about 1 percent of the project costs. The World Bank Group participated in the project by providing IBRD loans of

— $39.5 million to Chad to finance its minority holdings in TOTCO and COTCO, and

— $53.4 million to Cameroon to finance its minority holdings in COTCO * * *

As of December 31, 2005, Chad had earned a cumulative total of $399 million in gross direct revenues from the export of 134 million barrels of oil since production began. In 2005 alone, $222 million were transferred from escrow accounts to the country, in compliance with the Petroleum Revenue Management Program. Since production began, $307 million have been transferred to the country, $245 million of which to go towards investments in education, health, agriculture, and transport, among other sectors.

REQUEST FOR INSPECTION
(20 SEPTEMBER 2002)[2]

To the attention of the Inspection Panel, 1818 H Street, N.W., Washington D.C.,United States of America:

2. *Available at* http://siteqresources.worldbank.org/EXTINSPECTIONPANEL/resources/RFI English.pdf.

We, the Centre for the Environment and Development (CED), Yaoundé, acting on behalf of Mr. Savah Narcisse and other inhabitants of Mpango village (Kribi), Bissabidang, Nestor Abega Otele, Mr. Ekani Lebogo and other employees of COTCO sub-contractors, Mr. Ekouang Laurent and Mr. Mangama Ngiong Pierre of the Bakola community of Kour Mintoum, situated along the route of the Doba–Kribi oil pipeline, state the following:

1.   The World Bank is partially financing implementation of the Chad Cameroon oil project, and has been following up its design since 1996. The project consists of exploiting the oil fields in the south of Chad and constructing an oil pipeline between Doba (Chad) and Kribi (Cameroon) to transport crude oil to its port of export. Construction work on the oil pipeline officially started in June 2002.

2.   We understand that the World Bank has adopted the following rules or procedures:

a.   Directive OD 4.01 on environmental impact studies. This Directive requires that an environmental impact study be carried out by a team of independent experts . . . and, in its paragraphs 3, 4, 8 and 20, emphasizes the following points which seem relevant in the case of our region:

- taking account of the natural environment

- taking account of human health and security

- taking account of social questions

- implementation of measures to prevent, mitigate or compensate for the negative impacts of the project

- follow-up, in the implementation phase, of the Borrower's commitment, including in the context of mitigation measures

b.   Directive OD 13.05 on project supervision. This Directive requires the World Bank to ensure supervision of the projects it finances in order to guarantee:

- the conformity of project implementation with the borrower's original undertakings;

- the rapid identification of problems by the World Bank, and the implementation of measures aimed at correcting them.

c.   Directive OD 4.20 on indigenous peoples, intended to:

- guarantee that the development processes fully respect the dignity, rights and cultures of the indigenous peoples;

- protect the indigenous peoples from the negative impacts of projects financed by the World Bank;

- provide the indigenous peoples with social and economic benefits compatible with their cultures.

d.   Directive OD 4.30 on the involuntary displacements of populations, which determines the principles governing the World Bank's action in the matter of compensation. This Directive requires, among other measures:

- the planning and implementation of appropriate measures aimed at mitigating the risks of impoverishment and other long-term negative impacts likely to affect populations as a result of the project;

- compensation payment in advance of project work;

- assistance in their efforts to re-establish or even improve on their previous standard of living and level of production;

- the payment of compensation to all the populations affected, including groups of indigenous and pastoral peoples enjoying usufruct of the land. Absence of title of ownership of the land shall not be an obstacle to compensation;

- determination of the cost of replacement in terms of the value of resources destroyed;

- the need to provide compensation for loss of access to water resources, pasture land and forest resources;

- the need to have independent follow-up of the compensation process, and to publish annual reports;

- the need to avoid sporadic supervision, or one carried out at an advanced stage of the project.

e.   Operational Policy OP 4.04 on natural habitats. In the case of this project, protected areas have been created as compensation for environmental damage caused by construction work.

f.   Operational Directive 4.15 on poverty reduction, paragraph 6 of which recalls the fundamental objective of the World Bank's activities, which is that of poverty reduction.

g.   In the specific context of this project, an agreement enabling the establishment of the COTCO company has been signed with the Government of Cameroon, and various project documents have been approved by the World Bank which has undertaken to ensure commitment during implementation of the project (Environmental Management Plan, Plan for Vulnerable Native Peoples, compensation plan, etc.). * * *

3.   Our rights and interests have been injured in the following manner. As a general rule, there have been serious infringements of our rights which are due to violations of the policies of the World Bank and which have taken the following forms: insufficient information during the preparatory phase of the project and since its implementation began; an inadequate consultation process; insufficient, nonexistent or inadequate compensation; no respect for the workers' rights; a renewed outbreak of sexually transmitted diseases and HIV/AIDS all along the oil pipeline and around the project's main bases (from north to south), an

increase in the prostitution of minors along the length of the oil pipeline.

* * *

For the Bakola: We have suffered the negative effects of the project without so far having been able to enjoy any of the advantages set out in the Plan for Vulnerable Native Peoples. The construction work on the oil pipeline has caused the following problems in our villages:

- the drying up or pollution of sources of drinking water supplying some of the Bakola settlements as a result of the construction work, notably regarding the rivers Mbikiliki, Pembo, etc.;

- disturbance of the environment due to the noise of heavy equipment throughout the construction phase: this noise nuisance has had a negative impact on the presence of game, and on our own subsistence;

- the non-payment of individual compensation to Bakola whose plantations had been destroyed: this is the case with Messrs Ekouang Laurent and Mangama Ngiong Pierre who have received no compensation for destruction caused by the construction work; the weight of the machinery had rendered the land unfit for agriculture. Likewise, Mr. Mintouong Gaston has not received the compensation due to him because it has been paid to a woman in the neighbouring Bantou village;

- inadequate information during the preparatory phase of the project, and since the construction phase began;

- non-implementation of the actions set out in the Plan for Vulnerable Native Peoples, which could have improved the living conditions of the Bakola; the delay in launching the activities of the Environmental Foundation, responsible for implementing the Plan for Vulnerable Native Peoples, has meant that the Bakola have not been able to benefit from the mitigation measures envisaged under the project;

- lack of any participation by the Bakola in drawing up the Plan for Vulnerable Native Peoples;

- the plan for recruiting local staff, which gives priority to the inhabitants of the villages abutting the oil pipeline, has not been respected in the case of the Bakola.

For the inhabitants of Mpango: Construction work on the oil pipeline has caused the following problems in the village as well as for some individuals:

- Destruction of the village's source of drinking water during the construction of the Kribi storage site. The company responsible for the construction work had promised to grant access to the inhabitants of the village to the drilling operations being conducted inside the Kribi base. This promise has not been kept. Since that date the village no longer has access to drinking water;

• Reduction in the flow of the river Pembo, which supplies the southern part of the village with water for normal use. During the construction, and for a period of four months, there was no water downstream, while upstream there were floods and a significant extension of the swamp in front of Mr. Savah's house;

• Fishing was discontinued upstream from the acquired area by virtue of the noticeable alteration in the flow of the river Pembo after the burial of the oil pipeline.

* * *

For the inhabitants of the other villages mentioned: We consider that we have not received fair and equitable compensation for the damage we have suffered as a result of the oil pipeline construction work. In some cases the amounts are insufficient, and do not represent the real value of [the affected property].

• In some cases, the amounts are insufficient and do not represent the value of replacing resources that have been destroyed. This, for example, is the case at Nkongzok and Makouré;

• in other cases, the amounts are paid to different persons, or are not paid at all;

• in still other cases, the populations are imposed choices by company agents when it comes to compensation;

• payments have not been made before construction, with the result that destruction occurs before adequate and total payment of due compensation;

• the poor quality of the equipment as compensation in kind has not enabled us to renew our investments. The choice of providers has been made by the COTCO company which is trying to make us bear responsibility for it;

• the process for handling disputes is very slow, and we are not given information regarding the mechanisms that exist.

• It seems to us that the directives of the World Bank have not been respected by the Consortium. Payments in cash and kind have not been sufficient to permit restoration or improvement of production levels. The timetable for payments, some of which are still awaited, has not been conducive to their being used for new investments by the local populations concerned. Furthermore, no management arrangement has been set in place for the benefit of local populations wanting to create new plantations to replace those that have been destroyed. The result therefore is the impoverishment of affected populations, which is contrary to the directives of the World Bank.

• The rights of the fishing communities, as well as the project's impact on fishing in the region, does not seem to have been adequately taken into account by the environmental impact study.

For the workers: Failure to respect the law has deprived them of the income and working conditions they might have expected from collaborating with the project. Dismissals consequent upon various accidents are contrary to Cameroonian labour legislation and have been damaging to their health. Overall, the project has a negative impact on the environment and on the lives of those living along the oil pipeline and those employed on the building sites.

The individual cases cited here are simply illustrations of the problems, and in no way constitute an exhaustive list of violations of the rights of populations by virtue of the project.

5.   The Bank has not respected its rules and procedures by acting in the following manner. Directly or through non-governmental organization (NGO) channels we have formulated written or verbal complaints to those in charge of the construction works and to all the other institutions involved in the construction or project follow-up. We have also informed the World Bank in writing or verbally, directly or through NGO channels, about these problems, without any reaction being forthcoming. * * *

b.   The World Bank has not respected Directive OD 4.30 on the involuntary resettlement of populations, and in particular the requirements relating to the production of an annual report by the project on the implementation of compensation (paragraph 22).

c.   Operational Directive 4.04 on natural habitats has not been respected, since action to manage the protected areas created in compensation for the environmental damage due to construction works has not been launched because of the delays in establishing the Environmental Foundation.

d.   The Bank has not respected Operational Policy 4.15 on poverty reduction, since the project has caused structural impoverishment of numerous persons living along the oil pipeline. In fact, because of the lack of management and methods of payment of compensation (in cash and in kind with agricultural equipment of poor quality), many local populations living along the oil pipeline have not been able to reconstitute plantations destroyed during the construction work. The amounts paid in compensation have therefore rarely been adequately used. Furthermore, in many cases the refusal to pay due compensation has involved local populations in lengthy and costly proceedings only few of which have resulted in the payment of compensation, which is derisory when compared with the sums invested by the victims. Lastly, the slowness of the process of handling compensation disputes deprives the beneficiaries of sums they had a right to expect for the reconstitution of their production systems.

e. The World Bank has not respected Operational Directive OD 13.05 on project supervision, since no follow-up report mentioned the problems encountered in our village because of the construction of the oil pipeline. The World Bank seems to have given important follow-up responsibility to the enterprises, as laid down in the agreement between Cameroon and COTCO (Exxon, Chevron and Petronas). No measure has been envisaged for dealing with the delay in implementation of the Plan for Vulnerable Native Peoples or for making good damage to the environment which was not foreseen in the Environmental Management Plan (especially the drying up or pollution of water courses).

f. The World Bank has not respected Operational Directive 4.20 on indigenous peoples in various of its provisions:

- Paragraph 8 of Operational Directive 4.20, which recommends providing information to the indigenous peoples and securing their participation in preparing the Indigenous Peoples Plan; likewise, the project does not seem to have a strategy for ensuring the participation of indigenous peoples in the decision-making process during the design, implementation and assessment phases (paragraph 15.d);

- Paragraphs 8 and 14, which recommend taking account of traditional knowledge, local cultures and the traditional use of resources in determining the Plan for Indigenous Peoples;

- The question of access to land, the outlines of which are specified in paragraph 15, is not addressed by the Plan;

- The process of consulting the indigenous peoples has not been adequate, as shown by the low level of information in the communities regarding the outlines of the project.

The objectives of the project for building the capacities of the Cameroonian administration are far from having been achieved. This delay has an impact on the project. Thus, for example, the Project Appraisal Document prepared by the World Bank states that implementation of the safeguard measures by the Government of Cameroon within the scope of the CAPECE shall follow the timetable for the construction and exploitation of the oil pipeline. Implementation of the project has hitherto been unsuited to the encouragement of public participation in oil pipeline construction activities, to permitting follow-up of the social issues related to compensation, to the protection of public health, including against HIV/AIDS, to improving the situation of the indigenous peoples, and to protecting Cameroon's cultural heritage.

Because of these failures on the part of the World Bank with respect to its own policies and directives, we hold this institution responsible for the problems we have experienced and continue to experience because of this project.

6. Our requests have received the following responses: Many requests addressed to COTCO or the Cameroonian party have re-

mained unanswered. The information transmitted to the World Bank has to the best of our knowledge elicited no reaction. In some cases, we have replies from the Cameroonian Government and from COTCO, which are opposed to any reparation of the wrongs we have suffered. In addition, the official project documents convey an optimistic view which seems not to take account of the non-compliance cases of which we are victims. * * * Consequently, we consider that the above-mentioned actions or omissions, which are contrary to the rules and procedures of the World Bank, have seriously infringed our rights and interests, and we request the Inspection Panel to recommend that the administrators of the World Bank open an investigation in order to resolve the problem. As your regulations recommend, this request is presented in a succinct form. We remain at your disposal should you wish to have any additional information.

We request that you keep the names of the signatories of this complaint confidential.

———

WORLD BANK GROUP, INVESTIGATION PANEL REPORT CAMEROON: PETROLEUM DEVELOPMENT AND PIPELINE PROJECT

http://siteresources.worldbank.org/EXTINSPECTIONPANEL/
Resources/CAMInvestigationRptEnglish.pdf
2 May 2003

* * *

4. On September 25, 2002, the Panel received a Request for Inspection ("the Request") submitted by the Center for the Environment and Development (CED), a local non-governmental organization based in Yaoundé acting on behalf of a number of people living along the pipeline route in Cameroon, and by a number of individuals, including workers or former workers of COTCO and/or its contractors, all residents of the Republic of Cameroon (the "Requesters"). * * *

5. The Request alleges that the Pipeline Project and the CAPECE Project have had an adverse impact on local communities and their environment or they are likely to result in harm because of flaws in project design and implementation. The Requesters allege violations of the following Bank policies and procedures: Environmental Assessment, Natural Habitats, Poverty Reduction, Indigenous Peoples, Involuntary Resettlement, Project Supervision, and Disclosure of Operational Information. * * *

6. Bank Management responded to the Request on October 29, 2002 (the "Response"). In its response, Management included a summary of the overall project framework and of the Bank's role in the design, implementation and supervision of the Pipeline Project and CAPECE Project. Management maintained that it made every effort to apply Bank policies and procedures to the Projects, and it disagreed

with the Requester's claim that their rights or interests had been and would be adversely affected by Management's failure to comply with Bank policies and procedures.

7.   The Panel found that the Request and the Requesters had met all the applicable eligibility criteria. After a short visit to Cameroon, the Panel issued its Eligibility Report to the Board of Executive Directors on November 26, 2002, recommending an investigation into the matters raised in the Request. The Board approved the Panel's recommendation on December 16, 2002.

8.   The following sections present a summary of the Panel's Investigation Report. The Panel is generally pleased with the efforts shown by the Bank Management to reach compliance with its own policies and procedures, although it has found noncompliance instances * * * particularly during the design stages of the project. In addition, the Panel feels that it is important to call attention to the difficulties and delays associated with the implementation of the CAPECE Project. This situation, if not corrected, may adversely affect the sustainability of the Pipeline Project. In the same vein, it is the Panel's view that successful socio-economic programs hinge on effective communication among all parties involved, something that has not yet been fully achieved in the context of the Pipeline Project. * * *

10.   *Participation of the Independent Panel of Experts.* Paragraph 13 of OD 4.01 (Environmental Assessment) requires that for large projects, an Independent Panel of Experts [(IPE)] should be retained. The Panel found that the Bank was not in compliance with such provision since the required Independent Panel of Experts was not fully engaged during the preparation and approval of the 1999 Environmental Assessment/Environmental Management Plan since its participation was discontinued. There has been no independent review of the 1999 Environmental Management Plan by the IPE and no significant full-time participation of an IPE in Cameroon since 1997. * * *

48.   *Public Health.* The Project is formally committed to an HIV/AIDS mitigation strategy in the Environmental Management Plan. The Bank Management did request an assessment of the HIV/AIDS risk in the pipeline area, which was submitted in November 1999. This report presented a model of significantly elevated estimates of HIV/AIDS prevalence rates associated with Project construction. However, this report was criticized by public health consultants to the Consortium, who argued that their model was poorly executed, technically flawed, and based on data from East Africa rather than West Africa.

49.   The Panel finds that the omission in the EMP of an up-to-date regional health assessment with particular focus on risk and impact of the Pipeline Project in Cameroon (as well as Chad), and the omission of a long-term plan aimed at risk mitigation, is a serious shortcoming at the project preparation phase. This was pointed out early and repeatedly by public health consultants to the Consortium and the Bank.

50.   The Panel finds that Bank Management was aware of the need to undertake a wider regional assessment of the health risks posed by the Project, particularly with the implementation of seroepidemiological study to assess the risk of HIV/AIDS in the pipeline construction region. The Panel finds that by not requiring the preparation of such study the Bank has not complied with the relevant requirements on baseline data of OD 4.01 on Environmental Assessment. * * *

51.   *Compensation Issues*. The Panel observes that the guiding principles for a suitable compensation plan provide for: (a) the local population to perceive the compensations as fair and equitable; (b) the process to treat people the same way whenever practicable, and be as transparent as possible; (c) the affected people's standard of living not to be less than their current conditions when compensation is completed, and preferably better.

52.   The Panel examined COTCO's compensatory framework and finds it to be consistent with Cameroonian law. In Cameroon, the state legally owns all land except that which is formally titled to a fraction of the population who own mainly large private estates. The GOC however recognizes user improvements as subjects for compensation. Therefore, compensation is provided for "loss of improvements to the land", which includes time and effort spent in the cultivation of food and commercial crops, trees, as well as material improvements such as houses and water wells.

53.   The Panel finds that the value that COTCO pays in compensation for cultivated crops and trees to affected Cameroonians is consistent with Bank Policy on Involuntary Resettlement. In comparison with the large protective areas, the Pipeline has not taken large areas of land (30 meters wide) and, for most of the pipeline route, land is plentiful and accessible to farmers under customary land tenure rules. The pipeline has resulted in improved roads and better trading conditions for the individual farmers, as well as improved community facilities through the regional compensation program (discussed below). Furthermore, the Panel finds that the Pipeline Project has initiated a process of fair and transparent compensation and consultation. Although the Panel notes the need for these processes to be effective, the Panel expects that it will be difficult for future private projects in Cameroon not to provide the same level of consultation and compensation.

54.   The Panel notes that land acquisition for the pipeline began with the 1997 centerline survey. During this time, representatives from COTCO, the GOC, the village chief, and the land user, would participate collectively and openly in the survey process. COTCO representatives told the Panel that they used the compensation list of crops and trees, based on the market surveys described above. They admitted to the Panel that there were delays in paying individual compensations, and they attributed this to the work involved in surveying and determining compensation cases. * * *

56. *Community Compensation.* The Panel notes that according to the IAG, almost all of the villages eligible for the regional and community compensations have identified specific investment projects they wish to see implemented by COTCO. The majority of project requests are in the areas of education and water supply.

57. *Regional Compensation for Indigenous Peoples.* The Panel notes that COTCO recently introduced a new program of regional compensation for the Bakola/Bagyeli villages within a 2 km radius of the pipeline, including compensation for loss of access to medicinal plants and diminished game population. The program, according to COTCO, would be dedicated to housing improvements, in keeping with the major concern expressed by the Bakola/Bagyeli during the survey conducted by the Company's sociologists within the period 1997 to 2001. The Panel observes that this program, which had not been originally planned, represents a significant amount of compensation for the Bakola/Bagyeli populations.

58. *Individual cases.* The Panel investigated several of the individual cases that were brought to its attention in the Request and could not find any violation of the relevant Bank policy (OD 4.30 on Involuntary Resettlement). [An] annex to this Report presents the current status of each of the cases raised in the Request for Inspection[.]

59. *Grievance Mechanism.* The Panel observes that the grievance management process can be initiated in several ways. The principal method of initiating a grievance is by submission to the Project's right-of-way assistants or the Local Community Contacts (LCC). There are ten LCCs along the Cameroon portion of the pipeline, two of which are in the Bakola/Bagyeli areas at Lolodorf and Kribi. In addition, temporary LCCs were hired during the construction period within each zone. These temporary LCCs helped right-of-way assistants in identifying the land users in the village, providing information to the communities about the grievance management process and collecting grievances in the communities.

60. The Panel investigated several grievances raised in the Request. Many of these grievances included complaints about the grievance procedure, including difficulties in getting COTCO to respond to complaints. The Panel found that, for some of the cases, procedures were not followed by the prospective complainants, including informing (either verbally or in writing) the LCC representative in their respective areas. Furthermore, the Panel found that many different channels of contact with COTCO exist on the ground from survey and construction crews to compensation teams and designated LCCs, through which complaints could be transmitted. The Panel finds the mechanisms and procedures of grievances to be clear-cut and accessible.

61. The Panel observes that many grievances concerning compensation centered not on the amount of compensation offered or the procedure for its implementation, but rather on the hope of obtaining

more benefits from the project than was offered. A COTCO representative, a member of the centerline survey team, said "when we surveyed villages and mapped the location of water sources, people mistakenly assumed we would come back and build them permanent wells. When we did not do this, they were angry and disappointed with us." * * *

62.   In conclusion the Panel finds the design and implementation of the compensation policy and the grievance mechanism to be orderly, transparent, and fair, although communication among the parties could have been more effective. The Panel, therefore, finds the Bank in compliance with OD 4.30 on Involuntary Resettlement.

63.   *Indigenous Peoples.* The Bakola/Bagyeli are a small population of about 4,500 occupying some 12,000 km^2 in southwestern Cameroon in the Atlantic forest zone. This includes the area between Kribi on the coast to the northeast of Lolodorf that lies along the pipeline route. About 1,000 Bakola/Bagyeli live within 2 km of the Pipeline route in settled communities interspersed with Bantu villages along the Kribi–Bipindi–Lolodorf–Akongo Road. Bakola/Bagyeli share a long-term relationship with their Bantu neighbors including shared clan identities and family names. Although their relationship is based in part on their specialized economies, one hunting and the other agriculture, it is not an equal relationship but one of subservience and dependency of the Pygmies on the Bantu. Bakola/Bagyeli depend on the Bantu farmers for 20% of their starchy food, access to tools, salt, tobacco and clothing, and the land that they cultivate, which is claimed by the Bantu. They are often mistreated by their Bantu patrons, sometimes physically abused, and usually "spoken for". This inequality is reflected by the Bakola/Bagyeli's greater morbidity, mortality, lower literacy and reduced wage employment due to their poorer access to health clinics, schools, and other social services. The Panel considers appropriate the Bank Management's designation of the Bakola/Bagyeli as a vulnerable population subject to the requirements of OD 4.20 on Indigenous Peoples.

64.   Concerning any adverse impact of the Project on Bakola/Bagyeli, the Panel observed that the impact of the pipeline project on the hunting resources appears to be minimal, but is not yet known. The Pipeline is laid adjacent to the Kribi–Lolodorf road, where Bakola/Bagyeli live on sedentary farms. The major hunt that Bakola/Bagyeli annually engage in has always taken place in the deep forest, ten to thirty kilometers away from the settled agricultural communities along the road, as identified in the 2002 baseline studies. This area is unaffected by the Pipeline route.

65.   *The Indigenous Peoples Plan.* The Indigenous Peoples Plan ("IPP") is presented in the Environmental Management Plan (EMP), which states that, "[t]he IPP includes three programs: health, education, and agriculture. * * * Within each, an initial set of potential projects have been identified as result of studies and in consultations sponsored by the Project" and that, "[a]n Environmental Foundation [i.e. FEDEC]

will be established to provide defined long-term financial support for defined IPP-related projects/programs."

66.   The Panel observed that the IPP provides a development framework for the Bakola/Bagyeli settlements in the pipeline areas. It specifies three programs and projects; (a) assist identified Bakola/Bagyeli communities regarding health matters in order to help them counter potential health pressures caused by the Project and generally promote their health status; (b) promote and support education and training initiatives in identified Bakola/Bagyeli communities in order to contribute to an increase in their ability to make informed decisions regarding issues of their interest; (c) support local initiatives in identified Bakola/Bagyeli communities to improve agricultural production. The Panel finds that the programmatic goals specified in the IPP are reasonable and appropriate to the affected Bakola/Bagyeli community, and furthermore, were developed in fair and open consultation with representatives of the Bakola/Bagyeli community.

68.   The Panel investigated the Requester's claims that the Indigenous Peoples Plan was not in compliance with OD 4.20, as project-affected People did not fully participate in the preparation of the IPP; that consultation was not fair or adequate; that the baseline surveys were not adequate, and that the delay in launching the activities of FEDEC has meant that the Bakola have not been able to benefit from the mitigation measures envisaged under the project.

69.   The Panel through its investigation finds that the consultations leading up to the IPP were inclusive of a wide range of people, and contributed directly to developing effective IPP programs in health, education, and agriculture. The Panel takes note of the consultation activities, which included reading rooms, 400 public meetings between 1997 and 1999 (of which 111 were in the villages of affected people), and an NGO organized seminar for stakeholders. The Panel finds the IPP in compliance with OD 4.20 in regards to consultation and participation of affected indigenous peoples.

70.   However, the Panel is concerned that the baseline data, while providing important information for the programs of the IPP, ignores Bakola/Bagyeli occupation and use of forest resources outside the Pipeline right-of-way. The Panel finds that the EMP and IPP lack a wider regional assessment, particularly in terms of the Bakola/Bagyeli's use of the wider littoral forest for hunting and gathering activities. Consequently, the Panel finds that Management is not in compliance with OD 4.20 regarding Baseline Surveys.

71.   With respect to the implementation of the IPP, the Panel finds that while the delays in implementing the Environmental Foundation were very unfortunate, they may have been unavoidable given the capacity predicament of the GOC and the undefined and in-process nature of the specific IPP plans. The Panel observes that the Bank could have taken a more direct role in constituting the Board and ensuring it

can operate effectively instead of leaving the responsibility to COTCO only. Nevertheless, the Panel also recognizes that as a result of Bank intervention and oversight, FEDEC is now up and running and that it is moving ahead with its programs, including the antituberculosis campaign, the issuing of national identification cards, and contributing to school supplies and medicines. The Panel finds Management in compliance with OD 4.20 in regards to paragraph 15 (c) "the institutions responsible for government interaction with indigenous peoples should possess the social, technical, and legal skills needed for carrying out the proposed development activities."

72.   The Panel wishes to note that FEDEC's budget is based on an annual yield of interest on a US$3.7 million investment in an endowment that is to last the life of the pipeline, which is approximately 25 years. But the Project Appraisal Document (PAD) allocates only US$600,000 of the endowment for the IPP, which is expected to yield US$50,000 per year for implementing the programs of the IPP. Once the IPP administrative costs are factored in, including support for the Community Development Facilitator (salary, vehicle, office space), very little remains to fund a comprehensive program covering health, education and agriculture. However, Management states in its response that the annual funds would be enough to support the IPP programs which generally consist of low-cost expenditures such as for ID cards, school supplies, and medical supplies described in the updated 2003 FEDEC Plan of Action.

73.   In the Panel's view, FEDEC's budget seems inadequate to carry out the programmatic elements of the IPP. The Bank should have considered FEDEC's operating budget in more detail, noting in particular that $50,000 allocated to the IPP would not be sufficient to manage the IPP programs, particularly as these programs were still in the process of conceptualization and design. Nevertheless, the Panel recognized that while these delays were unfortunate, they may have been unavoidable given the capacity predicament of the GOC and the undefined and in-process nature of the specific IPP plans.

74.   Finally, the Panel notes Management's acknowledgement of the shortcomings in the original IPP, but also recognizes the fact that these shortcoming did not produce harm to the Bakola/Bagyeli community. The Project has created a positive environment for the Bakola/Bagyeli through its procedures on consultation, compensation, and development programs, where the Bakola/Bagyeli community now is in a stronger position to assert their rights as full citizens of Cameroon.

75.   The Panel understands Management's strategy that the IPP is a "work-in-progress". Although under normal circumstances such "work" would not be in compliance with the provisions of OD 4.20, the Panel, however, sees the practicality of Management's strategy because of the conditions and practices of the Bakola/Bagyeli/Bantu community within the wider Cameroonian society. Furthermore, the Panel observes

that Bank Management and COTCO have corrected the shortcomings in the intervening years since the EMP was written. The Panel agrees that the IPP is a long-term endeavor expected to be carried out over the 25 years of the Pipeline operation. Of necessity it must be fine-tuned in the process of implementation. Finally, the Panel finds that the original IPP, in this special circumstance, is in compliance with paragraphs 13–18 of OD 4.20 on Indigenous Peoples, except for the geographical scope of the baseline data. The Panel finds that current efforts to prepare and implement a detailed IPP are in place to meet the requirements of OD 4.20 on Indigenous Peoples.

AMNESTY INTERNATIONAL, CONTRACTING OUT OF HUMAN RIGHTS: THE CHAD–CAMEROON PIPELINE PROJECT

AI Index POL 34/012/2005, September 2005

A pipeline transporting oil through Chad and Cameroon brings with it potential threats to human rights in the two Central African countries. Amnesty International is concerned that these threats are more likely to be realised if the investment agreements underpinning the pipeline project prejudice the human rights obligations of the states and the human rights responsibilities of the companies involved.

A consortium of oil companies is extracting oil from the Doba oilfields in southern Chad and transporting it 1,070 kilometres by pipeline to Cameroon's Atlantic coast in one of the largest private-sector investment projects in Africa. The consortium is led by the US company, ExxonMobil, and includes Chevron, another US corporation, and Petronas, the Malaysian state oil company.

This project has been promoted by investors, agreed to by governments and supported by lenders such as the World Bank, export credit agencies and private banks—some of which have voluntarily adopted social and environmental standards. Yet the agreements could hold back the governments of Chad and Cameroon, which have poor track records on human rights, from taking steps to improve the human rights protection of those affected by the pipeline project. The framework of agreements could also make it more difficult to hold the consortium to account for abuses of human rights that result from its activities.

A related concern is that the project agreements could encourage the governments of Chad and Cameroon to ignore their human rights obligations, by claiming that the agreements prevent them from taking measures that would destabilise the financial equilibrium of the project, even if such measures are intended to respect, protect and fulfil human rights. This possibility should be expressly excluded in a revision of the terms of the contracts. The project agreements could also be interpreted to allow the oil companies to extract and transport oil and operate the pipeline project free from full accountability under domestic laws against human rights abuses. Amnesty International believes that such interpretations would be unsustainable in international law and would create unacceptable obstacles to the realisation of human rights and hamper access to remedies for victims of human rights violations.

Amnesty International calls for clarification of the agreements to ensure that those affected by the project are not exposed to increased risk and reduced protection of their human rights. The project should not create a zone of lower protection of human rights. Any new laws and regulations enacted to further the protection of human rights in Chad or Cameroon must be clearly applicable to the project.

In some countries, the exploitation of natural resources has contributed to a deteriorating cycle of corruption, social unrest, conflict and abuses. In Chad and Cameroon, the human rights of the population, be it communities living or working in the area of the pipeline or the wider population, are largely disregarded. Ineffective judicial systems in both countries are vulnerable to state interference. They are no match for powerful governments and commercial interests. The courts and the police are ill-equipped to uphold the human rights of the population from adverse effects of large-scale projects for economic development. Serious human rights violations in Chad and Cameroon have been documented by Amnesty International for more than three decades.

Almost constant armed conflict since 1960 has left most of Chad in a state of fragile peace, and sporadic clashes with armed groups continue in the north. Forces of the government of President Idriss Déby, who came to power in a military coup in 1990, have carried out mass killings and torture to subdue armed insurgencies. In the south in the 1990s, where the majority of the state's oil reserves are found, counter-insurgency operations were particularly brutal. Hundreds of people were summarily executed.

In Cameroon, under the 22–year rule of President Paul Biya, torture persists and political prisoners have continued to die in appalling prison conditions after unfair trials. Opposition activists and human rights defenders remain at risk of being detained, and their peaceful political activities are frequently obstructed by the authorities. * * *

Amnesty International is calling on the governments, international financial institutions and companies involved in the Chad–Cameroon pipeline project to revise the project agreements to include an explicit guarantee that nothing in the agreements can be used to undermine either the human rights obligations of the states or the human rights responsibilities of the companies. In particular Amnesty International is urging that the investment agreements:

  ● Allow the regulation of actions of the companies involved, to ensure that they do not abuse human rights. The project agreements seek to protect the financial interests of the oil companies by restricting interference in and regulation of the project by Chad and Cameroon. However, the terms of the project agreements must be interpreted in a way consistent with the states' obligations under international law to respect, protect and fulfil human rights. International human rights law requires states to regulate the actions of private individuals and organisations, including companies, to ensure that they do not abuse human rights. This obligation cannot be made subordinate to any agreement which the state enters into and should not be interpreted as such. The project agreements should explicitly confirm that they do not prejudice the duty of the state to regulate the actions of private actors, such as companies, to ensure that they adhere to human rights standards.

• Remove obstacles to progressive realisation of human rights. Chad and Cameroon are required by their international human rights commitments to take deliberate, concrete and targeted steps towards fully realising rights such as the right to health and rights at work. The pipeline project agreements should not be used in an attempt to justify failure to comply with these obligations or to frustrate their implementation. The project agreements should explicitly state that those clauses which seek to restrict regulation of the project by Chad and Cameroon do not apply to any action taken in fulfilment of human rights obligations.

• Avoid placing a price tag on human rights. Any attempt by the companies involved to use the agreements to penalise the states for taking steps to protect human rights would be a breach of their human rights responsibilities. The project agreements should be amended to clarify that nothing in the agreements can be interpreted to penalise steps taken by the host states to meet their obligations to respect, protect and fulfil human rights.

• Give precedence to international human rights law over industry standards. International human rights law requires states to ensure that human rights are respected by all, including companies. One important way in which states should do this is to introduce legislation requiring all organs of society to respect human rights, and regulating corporate and other practice to enforce these standards. However, under the project agreements, the standards to be applied to the management of the project in Chad are those of prevailing custom and practice in the oil industry, which are not drawn from international human rights law. Amnesty International believes that human rights must be respected regardless of commercial expediency, and that priority should be given to human rights standards. The agreements should be amended to guarantee that reference to industry standards cannot be used to limit human rights protection.

• Respect the right to an effective remedy. International human rights treaties ratified by Chad and Cameroon guarantee individuals the right to a remedy. This must be guaranteed not only if other human rights are abused but also to prevent abuse of these rights in the first place. The project agreements must not be interpreted in a way which frustrates the realisation of the right to adequate remedy. They must guarantee that local judicial and administrative officials can provide an effective domestic remedy, including full reparation, to individuals adversely affected by the oil project.

● Ensure the right to equality. International human rights treaties ratified by Chad and Cameroon guarantee equality before the law and equal protection of the law, and prohibit discrimination of any kind. The project agreements must not be interpreted to carve out a corridor where individuals—those living or working within the pipeline zone—enjoy lesser protection of the law. The project agreements must guarantee that they do not facilitate discrimination.

● Protect labour rights and the rights to freedom of expression and assembly. The rights to freedom of expression and assembly are guaranteed in international treaties to which Chad and Cameroon are party. However, the human rights of some pipeline critics have already been violated. The project agreements should not provide any justification for placing limitations on rights, such as freedom of expression and assembly, in a way that is inconsistent with international law.

Amnesty International is also calling for policy changes on state-investor agreements from:

● all host states that receive foreign direct investment, to make certain that investment agreements are consistent with, and do not compromise, their human rights obligations, and to open such agreements to public scrutiny before they are concluded;

● all states where transnational corporations are headquartered, to take steps to hold those companies to account for human rights abuses abroad. These "home states" should regulate the activity of their export credit agencies and companies to ensure that all investment policies and practices are consistent with their human rights obligations;

● international financial institutions, export credit agencies and commercial banks, to ensure that the legal agreements underpinning projects they support do not undermine states' human rights obligations or the human rights responsibilities of companies;

● all companies, to ensure that their investment agreements do not undermine either states' human rights obligations or their own human rights responsibilities and that the agreements are open to public scrutiny before they are concluded;

● international arbitration bodies and commercial arbitrators, to ensure that in the context of investor-state arbitrations precedence is given to the human rights obligations of the state under national and international law.

***

WORLD BANK SUSPENDS DISBURSEMENTS TO CHAD

World Bank Press Release No: 2006/232/AFR (6 January 2006)

The World Bank will withhold new loans and grants to the Government of Chad and suspend disbursement of International Development Association (IDA) funds allocated to the country. The value of funds being suspended is approximately US$124 million. This action follows passage of amendments to the country's Petroleum Revenue Management Law by the Chadian National Assembly. These changes would substantially weaken programs to improve the lives of poor people, which the World Bank has been supporting.

In a letter to the Chadian authorities, the Bank said that it will not present any new grants or credits to its Board of Directors for approval, and will suspend disbursements on all eight active projects that are part of the World Bank portfolio in Chad. "We have a responsibility to ensure that money generated from this oil project is used to help meet the needs of the poor people in Chad," said President Wolfowitz. "We've been trying for some time to open a dialogue with the Government of Chad to see if the concerns they have can be addressed. Regrettably instead of engaging in dialogue they have proceeded to alter fundamentally the law which was the basis for our original agreement. We haven't given up on dialogue, and hope in fact that perhaps if they stop and appreciate how serious the issue is from our point of view and not only from theirs, we can find common ground that addresses the legitimate concerns of the government of Chad and our objective of ensuring Chad's oil revenues benefit that country's poor."

IDA funding committed for projects that are currently active in Chad is US$297 million, of which approximately US$124 million remains undisbursed and subject to the suspension. Standard caveats apply to funding for project expenditures committed but not yet paid prior to the suspension.

The World Bank had offered to assist the Government of Chad to address its financial difficulties by analyzing and helping to address issues including how public finances have been managed. It had also proposed a review of how the Petroleum Revenue Management Law has been implemented to identify which, if any, amendments to the law might be warranted. The World Bank remains open to dialogue with the Government of Chad on the best ways to address its current financial crisis while protecting poverty reduction programs.

***

NOTES AND QUESTIONS ON THE CHAD–CAMEROON PIPELINE PROJECT

1. *Assessing the inspection panel mechanism as a means of enforcing human rights standards.* In what ways does the Chad–Cameroon Pipeline Project case study reflect the virtues and the vices of the Inspection Panel system? To what extent was the Bank's decision to suspend disbursements to Chad a reflection of the concerns in the inspection request? To what extent was it driven by human rights concerns *not* contained in the request?

2. *Deference to local law.* When evaluating the adequacy of compensation, the Panel considered the domestic law of Cameroon:

> In Cameroon, the state legally owns all land except that which is formally titled [to] a fraction of the population who own mainly large private estates. The GOC however recognizes user improvements as subjects for compensation. Therefore, compensation is provided for "loss of improvements to the land", which includes time and effort spent in the cultivation of food and commercial crops, trees, as well as material improvements such as houses and water wells.

How much deference should the World Bank show to local law in determining compensation? Suppose for example that local law restricted land ownership to men only or to members of a particular ethnic group. Does anything in the World Bank's foundational documents require it to abide by international legal principles of non-discrimination? Besides, are these illegitimate "political" considerations or legitimate "economic" considerations?

3. *The nature of legislative action.* The World Bank suspended funding to Chad because of its concern that the funds generated from the sale of oil would not be used properly. The impetus for that decision appears to have been amendments by the Chadian National Assembly to the law governing the management of oil revenue. Is this a political or an economic consideration? Is it more important than the concerns raised by Amnesty International, namely that both Chad and Cameroon had committed various human rights violations including torture and summary execution? In the face of those allegations, should the project have been initiated in the first place?

4. *The law of unintended consequences.* Eventually, the World Bank decided to suspend all disbursements to Chad in response to actions that it believed would "substantially weaken the programs to improve the lives of poor people, which the World Bank has been supporting." What effect do you think the suspension of World Bank funds will have on the "poor people" in Chad? Can you think of any intermediate measures that might be effective to ensure that the standard of living in Chad is increased without resorting to cutting off World Bank funds?

THE WORLD TRADE ORGANIZATION

The connections between trade and human rights are multi-layered. Some countries have imposed trade sanctions against countries where human rights abuses are profound and widespread, as in Burma, Sudan, and *apartheid* South Africa.[1] Clearly, when the trade is itself a form of human rights abuse—as in human trafficking—a range of sanctions may also be imposed.[2] The U.S. Congress has linked trade preferences[3] with the protection of "internationally recognized worker rights,"[4] and executive branch regulations have similarly targeted the importation of goods that are "mined, produced, or manufactured wholly or in part by forced or indentured child labor."[5] During the Cold War, the United States adopted the so-called "Jackson–Vanik Amendment,"[6] which allowed the U.S. government to restrict trade with communist countries in response to their human rights violations, especially emigration.

These domestic trade statutes offer human rights lawyers potentially powerful tools in their advocacy, and limiting trade with abusive governments is a common technique for enforcing human rights standards when other judicial or diplomatic techniques fail. But there is a problem: when these restrictions are implemented, they may be challenged as a form of protectionism that is prohibited by the trade liberalization regime of the World Trade Organization ("WTO"). The WTO grew out of the 1947 General Agreement on Tariffs and Trade ("GATT"), a limited agreement confined to customs and tariffs for enumerated lists

---

1. *See, e.g.,* Exec. Order 12,532, 50 Fed. Reg. 36,861 (Sept. 9, 1985) (imposing sanctions on South Africa), *revoked by* Exec. Order 12,769, 56 Fed. Reg. 31,855 (July 10, 1991); Exec. Order 13,047, 62 Fed. Reg. 28,301 (May 20, 1997) (banning new investment in Burma); Sudan Peace Act of 2002, 50 U.S.C.S. § 1701, note (2002); Executive Order 13,213, 66 *Fed. Reg.* 28,829 (May 22, 2001) (banning all rough diamond shipments from Sierra Leone for an indefinite period). Sanctions may of course be imposed to advance national security and foreign policy interests to which human rights are related, including the effort to combat terrorism and the proliferation of weapons of mass destruction. *See, e.g.,* Iran and Libya Sanctions Act of 1996, 50 U.S.C. § 1701, note (2000); Exec. Order 13,088, 64 Fed. Reg. 24021 (June 9, 1998) (prohibiting new investment in the Republic of Serbia in response to the situation in Kosovo).

2. *See, e.g.,* Victims of Trafficking and Violence Protection Act of 2000, 22 U.S.C. § 7108 (2000).

3. The Generalized System of Preferences, for example, grants duty free status to imports from developing countries that "take steps to" respect such rights, 19 U.S.C. §§ 2461–66 (2000). *See also* The Caribbean Basin Trade Partnership Act, 19 U.S.C. §§ 2701–06 (2000). The 2000 Sanders Amendment to Section 307 of the Trade Act of 1930 clarified that the statutory ban on the importation of products made with "forced" labor includes products made with "forced or indentured child labor." 19 U.S.C. § 1307 (2000). The Omnibus Trade and Competitiveness Act of 1988 made the failure to comply with "internationally recognized worker rights" an unfair trading practice, potentially triggering trade sanctions. 19 U.S.C. § 2411 (2000).

4. These rights include: "(A) the right of association; (B) the right to organize and bargain collectively; (C) a prohibition on the use of any form of forced or compulsory labor; (D) a minimum age for the employment of children; and (E) acceptable conditions of work with respect to minimum wages, hours of work, and occupational safety and health." Trade Act of 1974, 19 U.S.C. § 2462(a)(4) (2000).

5. Prohibition of Acquisition of Products Produced by Forced or Indentured Child Labor, Exec. Order 13,126, 64 Fed. Reg. 32383 (1999).

6. Trade Act of 1974, 19 U.S.C. §§ 2431–36 (2000), *as amended, e.g.* with respect to China by Pub. L. No. 106–286, 114 Stat. 880 (2000); and the Republic of Georgia by Pub. L. No. 106–476, 114 Stat. 2101 (2000).

of goods negotiated by each member, all for the purpose of promoting equality of competitive opportunity among the member-states. After decades of experience, the GATT was expanded to address a variety of non-tariff barriers and other trade-related issues, like market access for services and the protection of intellectual property.

The WTO law requiring liberalization and deregulation of trade evolved simultaneously with the evolution of international human rights law but in virtual isolation from it. Indeed, in 2002, the United Nations Sub–Commission on Human Rights expressed its concern "that international economic law and human rights law have developed as two parallel and separate regimes, with the risk that human rights principles, instruments, and mechanisms will be marginalized, as highlighted by the actual or potential human rights implications of World Trade Organization agreements, including the General Agreement on Trade in Services, the Agreement on Trade–Related Aspects of Intellectual Property Rights, and the Agreement on Agriculture."[7]

The primary objective of the WTO remains to "liberalise international trade and place it on a secure basis" which will "thereby contribut[e] to the economic growth, development, and welfare of the world's people." Final Act Embodying the Results of the Uruguay Round of Multilateral Trade Negotiations, Agreement Establishing the Multilateral Trade Organization, 33 I.L.M. 13 (1993). As noted by Professor Andrew Guzman, "[t]he WTO has become one of the world's most dominant international institutions, established a reasonably effective system of dispute resolution, and developed a nearly universal membership. These achievements, however, have not protected the organization from external criticism or internal challenges." Andrew T. Guzman, *Global Governance and the WTO*, 45 HARV. INT'L L.J. 303, 303 (2004).

Among the criticisms leveled at the WTO is that its institutional fixation on facilitating international commerce by reducing tariff and non-tariff barriers to trade does little to protect human rights and may even contribute to human rights violations. The WTO's predecessor organization, the General Agreement on Tariffs and Trade ("GATT"), emerged after World War II in partial isolation from other multilateral institutions of global governance, and its body of norms was considered largely *sui generis*. The objective of liberalizing trade through the reduction of tariff and non-tariff barriers seemed quite separate from, if not irrelevant to, the protection of human rights.

Critics argue that irrelevance turned into incompatibility during the Uruguay Round of trade negotiations (from which the WTO eventually emerged), when government negotiators considered and rejected a "social clause" that would have assured that international trade standards were interpreted consistently with other standards protecting the rights of labor and the environment. After sustained opposition from the governments of developing nations and some business interests, all that

---

7. Res. 2002/11, UN Doc. E.CN.4.SUB.2.RES.2002.11 (2002).

remains of the social clause is a provision in the Preamble, urging in vague and unenforceable terms that economic relations be conducted in a way that raises standards of living, ensures full employment and increases real income in an environmentally sustainable way.[8] Screening trade according to more robust human rights criteria potentially offered a pretext for protectionism and was therefore not adopted.

There was, moreover, an institutional concern: the WTO would have enough difficulty enforcing internationally-accepted trade rules, especially early in its history, and could not be expected to condition trade liberalization on compliance with an additional layer of human rights standards whose normative status might be contested and which were beyond the organization's expertise in any event. Nor could the WTO be expected to play the human rights enforcer when the profit motive had historically submerged states' criticism of their trading partners' human rights abuses.

Nevertheless, in ways that are characteristic of our age (and as noted in Module 8, *supra*), states and civil society gradually noticed a partial linkage between human rights protections and the quality of the international market: labor abuses could depress export prices below fair market value; certain forms of trade, like the sale of conflict diamonds, would not be entitled to the benefits of trade liberalization; and the privilege of being admitted to the organization could induce non-member states to accede to human rights treaties and become part of a broader "cartel of values" in the promotion of the rule of law and transparent, accountable governance. The WTO's dispute settlement mechanism also offered human rights advocates a potential technique for making human rights protections part of every state's economic self-interest: the threat of retaliatory sanctions, approved by a quasi-judicial panel subject to appellate review, for violations of international norms, has generated an admirable if imperfect record of compliance.

From this perspective, human rights conditionality may actually reinforce WTO principles by reducing the trade-distorting economic advantages of "social dumping," *i.e.* the lowering of production costs not through competition and efficiency but through the violation of international labor standards. In certain economic circumstances, human rights abuses committed by governments might even qualify as an export subsidy that is subject to countervailing duty laws. But even if that hypothetical possibility is never pursued, the existing import controls and sanctions legislation offer a powerful illustration of how domestic law channels market conduct towards the protection of certain human rights and the penalization of abuses.

Admittedly, the law that is enforced and respected within the WTO is generally divorced from norms protecting human rights, and the rules on most favored nation treatment or the reduction of trade barriers

---

8. Final Act Embodying the Results of the Uruguay Round of Multilateral Trade Negotiations, Apr. 15, 1994, 33 I.L.M. 1125 (1994).

suggest that the WTO is more likely to invalidate unilateral trade sanctions intended to punish a state's human rights abuses than it is to uphold or facilitate such sanctions. Under Article XX of the WTO agreement, states may adopt measures that restrict trade if these are "necessary" to achieve a narrow class of social objectives,[9] including the protection of public morals, or the protection of human life and health, or relating to the products of prison labor. But the potential power of Article XX to reconcile trade liberalization with other goals of the international community has never been fully realized, in part because the WTO's Appellate Body and its GATT predecessor have traditionally defined "necessity" narrowly, rarely allowing trade restrictions under Article XX and then only when no less restrictive alternative was available.

As the international regulatory environment becomes more dense in the protection of the environment or human rights, it may be possible to argue that compliance with international obligations is also "necessary"[10] and that the WTO cannot carve out an immunity for itself or its members from the body of human rights norms. The fight will then be which universal human rights are within the WTO's mandate and which ones are not. Until those arguments are fully addressed and resolved, perhaps the best that can be expected of the WTO is that it will abide by the precautionary principle and first do no harm.

REPORT OF THE U.N. HIGH COMMISSIONER FOR HUMAN RIGHTS
LIBERALIZATION OF TRADE IN SERVICES AND HUMAN RIGHTS

UN Doc. E/CN.4/Sub.2/2002/9 (25 June 2002)

[A] human rights approach to trade: (a) Sets the promotion and protection of human rights among the objectives of trade liberalization; (b) Examines the effects of trade liberalization on individuals and seeks trade law and policy that take into account the rights of all individuals, in particular vulnerable individuals and groups; (c) Emphasizes the role of the State in the process of liberalization—not only as negotiators of trade law and setters of trade policy, but also as the primary duty bearer for the implementation of human rights; (d) Seeks consistency between the progressive liberalization of trade and the progressive realization of human rights; (e) Requires a constant examination of the impact of trade liberalization on the enjoyment of human rights; [and] (f) Promotes international cooperation for the realization of human rights and freedoms in the context of trade liberalization.

---

9. Steve Charnovitz, *The Moral Exception in Trade Policy*, 38 VA. J. INT'L L. 689 (1998).

10. *See, e.g.*, Appellate Body Report, *United States-Import Prohibition of Certain Shrimp and Shrimp Products*, ¶ 28, WT/DS58/AB/R (Oct. 12, 1998).

[This] report examines the obligations of States to promote and protect the human rights most directly affected by the liberalization of trade in services, specifically the right to health (including the right to drinking water), the right to education and the right to development. The liberalization of trade in services can impact on these rights in various ways, depending on a range of issues, not least the type of services being supplied, the mode of service delivery, the development level of the country and its internal infrastructure, the regulatory environment and the level of existing services prior to liberalization. One issue of particular relevance is the effect of increased foreign direct investment (FDI), in particular from the private sector, and its effect on the enjoyment of human rights. While FDI can upgrade national infrastructures, introduce new technology and provide employment opportunities, FDI can also have undesired effects where there is insufficient regulation to protect human rights. In particular, as with any national privatization scenario, increased foreign private investment can lead to: (a) The establishment of a two-tiered service supply with a corporate segment focused on the healthy and wealthy and an under-financed public sector focusing on the poor and sick; (b) Brain drain, with better trained medical practitioners and educators being drawn towards the private sector by higher pay scales and better infrastructures; (c) An overemphasis on commercial objectives at the expense of social objectives which might be more focused on the provision of quality health, water and education services for those that cannot afford them at commercial rates; (d) An increasingly large and powerful private sector that can threaten the role of the Government as the primary duty bearer for human rights by subverting regulatory systems through political pressure or the co-opting of regulators.

[T]o the extent that these phenomena can be linked to the liberalization of trade in services, regulators need to be conscious of ensuring that liberalization policies take into account State responsibilities to respect, protect and fulfil human rights. Human rights law does not place obligations on States to be the sole provider of essential services; however, States must guarantee the availability, accessibility, acceptability and adaptability of essential services including their supply, especially to the poor, vulnerable and marginalized.

Looking specifically at the [General Agreement on Trade in Services (GATS)], th[is] report notes that, given the opportunities and challenges posed by the liberalization of trade in services to the enjoyment of human rights, it is important to understand the interaction between the rules and disciplines in GATS and the norms and standards of human rights law. In particular:

   (a) GATS is broad in scope. The High Commissioner encourages interpretations of the scope of GATS to ensure that under GATS obligations do not constrain Governments in taking action to promote and protect human rights; * * *

(c) Both GATS and human rights law include the principle of non-discrimination; however, there are distinctions in the application of the principle. The High Commissioner highlights the need to ensure that the application of trade law takes into account the human rights principle of non-discrimination, including by safeguarding the need to use mechanisms such as "cross-subsidization" to ensure that the poor, vulnerable and marginalized do not suffer discrimination in accessing services in liberalized markets;

(d) GATS includes general exceptions to protect public morals as well as human, animal and plant life and the protection of certain aspects of individual privacy. These could be seen as being linked to the need to promote and protect human rights in the liberalization process;

(e) GATS seeks the liberalization of trade in services through the progressive opening up of States' services markets. However, there is at times a need for States to have some flexibility to modify and withdraw country-specific commitments to liberalize trade in services, taking into account the need for States to meet their human rights obligations;

(f) Country-specific commitments to liberalize service sectors under GATS could have both positive and negative effects on the enjoyment of human rights. Consequently, WTO members should be encouraged to undertake assessments of the impact of the implementation of GATS on the enjoyment of human rights as part of the ongoing negotiations concerning GATS. Assessments should concern both past experience and potential effects of future liberalization commitments;

(g) Developed countries, in accordance with their responsibilities to cooperate internationally to promote human rights, should share both financial and technical expertise to support developing countries to undertake assessments.

Finally, the High Commissioner identifies a list of areas requiring further action to promote human rights approaches to the liberalization of trade in services, including the following:

(a) Ensuring equal access for basic services—the High Commissioner encourages States to take action to ensure universal supply of essential services, including through the use of affirmative action to ensure provision of services to the poor, isolated and marginalized, taking into account national circumstances and capacities;

(b) *Ensuring Governments' right and duty to regulate*—the High Commissioner encourages interpretations of GATS provisions that acknowledge the need for countries to retain the flexibility to use development tools, such as "cross-subsidization" or the regulation of corporate governance, in response to national development needs;

(c) *Encouraging interpretations of GATS that are compatible with human rights*—the High Commissioner reminds WTO members of their concurrent obligations under human rights law and encourages the development of rules or "tests" that acknowledge and protect States' duties concerning human rights when determining or assessing whether a measure is trade restrictive;

(d) *Undertaking human rights assessments of trade policies*—the High Commissioner highlights the voluntary nature of commitments to liberalize trade in services and stresses the need to make commitments on the basis of sound empirical evidence;

(e) *Providing international cooperation and assistance*—the High Commissioner reminds developed countries of the commitment to provide 0.7 percent of GDP as official development assistance. Further, the High Commissioner reminds States of their responsibility to negotiate in ways that enable poorer countries to maintain the maximum flexibility to develop policies to meet commitments to the progressive realization of human rights;

(f) *Increasing dialogue on human rights and trade*—the High Commissioner encourages greater consultation between delegates to WTO and delegates representing the same country as members or observers in the Commission on Human Rights on the links between human rights and trade and on particular ways to ensure coherence in policy and lawmaking;

(g) *Future work*—the High Commissioner recommends that the Sub–Commission consider requesting a report on "human rights, trade and investment".

ANDREW GUZMAN, GLOBAL GOVERNANCE AND THE WTO

45 HARV. INT'L L.J. 303 (2004)

Since 1947 the General Agreement on Tariffs and Trade (GATT) and its successor, the World Trade Organization (WTO), have brought about a dramatic reduction in barriers to international trade. * * * [T]he remarkable success of the GATT/WTO system is, to a significant degree, responsible for the challenges now facing the WTO. Over time, and especially as a result of the Uruguay Round, the GATT/WTO has moved from a system of rules prohibiting trade measures to a system of rules requiring affirmative government actions. The consequence is a WTO engaged in monitoring and adjudicating the legality of domestic rules that are not primarily or exclusively about trade. The relevant WTO obligations include rules governing the protection of intellectual property, service industries, and health and safety measures. Though each of these WTO rules, with the possible exception of the Agreement on Trade–Related Aspects of Intellectual Property Rights ("TRIPs Agreement"), has an important connection to liberalized trade, their substance makes it impossible to consider them in strictly trade terms.

The impact of the trading regime is also felt in areas that are not subject to any specific WTO regulation. For example, environmental policy, human rights, labor, and competition policy are not directly within the jurisdiction of the WTO, but in each of these areas trade and the trading system have influenced policymaking. The influence of WTO obligations on non-trade issues has generated cries of protest from many quarters. Critics argue that the WTO remains a trade institution at heart, and that its forays into what were traditionally considered non-trade areas have caused the non-trade values at stake to be ignored in favor of trade concerns. Thus, the argument goes, the tremendous power of the organization, combined with its efforts to influence policies in non-trade areas, has elevated trade at the expense of other issues.

The dramatic failure of the WTO's 1999 Ministerial Conference in Seattle demonstrated the dissatisfaction of certain groups with the current state of globalization. Protesters succeeded in drawing attention to their concerns about labor, environmental, and human rights issues. The collapse of the Seattle Ministerial stands as dramatic evidence that international cooperation and globalization is unlikely to continue with a focus on trade alone. Nor is this view limited to those outside the organization. WTO members appear to have recognized that they must address concerns other than those directly linked to trade. At the Doha Ministerial in November 2001, the WTO laid out an agenda for the Doha Development Round that allows for a discussion of some of these non-trade issues, including environment, competition policy, and investment. Extending the reach of the WTO into non-trade areas, however, will clearly not be easy, as was demonstrated when the Cancun Ministerial in September 2003 ended in failure, in part due to disagreement on the question of what to do about investment and competition policy, and in part because of an inability to make progress on agricultural issues.

These developments have placed the WTO and the international economic community at a crossroads. The status quo is unsustainable because, although the influence of the WTO now extends well beyond the trade arena, the institution remains overwhelmingly oriented toward trade concerns. Critics are right to point out that non-trade issues are largely overlooked at the WTO, and yet, the organization cannot avoid environmental, labor, or other issues. The dispute resolution organs of the WTO have already addressed cases on the environment, for example, and more such cases are likely to be filed in the future. Labor and human rights cases are also easy to imagine. Though such cases would focus on trade disputes (for example, the permissibility of economic sanctions in response to certain labor rights practices) there is no denying that they would also implicate important non-trade issues. This interaction between trade and non-trade issues will only grow stronger over time, and the pressure to address the conflicting priorities that result will continue to rise. The WTO, therefore, must eventually either move forward by finding a way to incorporate more regulatory issues within its mandate or move backward and retreat to a narrower focus on trade, leaving controversial topics such as the environment outside of its influence.

Though there are many hurdles to the incorporation of new issues into the WTO, the alternative of reduced international economic cooperation is inconsistent with the needs of an increasingly global economy. Turning away from non-trade issues does not make them go away, nor does it change the fact that the trade and non-trade issues are connected. Rather it pushes these issues into the shadows and prevents policy formation from occurring in an open and organized fashion. Using the WTO as an institution devoted exclusively to trade is also unrealistic. The GATT/WTO system has never been constrained so narrowly, and it is probably impossible to construct a system so constrained. * * *

The better strategy, then, is to bring non-trade topics into the debate at the WTO. The power of the WTO has already caused its reach to extend into non-trade related issues such as health and safety, intellectual property, and the environment. The non-trade interests in these areas are sufficiently powerful and important that they must be given a voice if relevant trade rules are to be sustained. Failure to grant such a voice would only amplify criticism of the WTO and weaken its ability to manage cooperation.

The non-trade concerns at issue—sometimes referred to as "trade and ..." issues or "fair trade" issues—include * * * human rights, environmental issues, labor, investment, competition policy, and intellectual property. Among the consequences of the trade bias said to exist within the WTO is the frustration of efforts to use trade sanctions as a tool to change the policies of foreign states with respect to these issues.

Much of the criticism leveled at the WTO stems from the perception that the liberalization of international trade has received inappropriate prominence, and that other values have been sacrificed as a result. One solution to this perceived problem—the one usually at the center of the discussion—is to slow or stop the expansion of the WTO into non-trade areas. An alternative solution—one that is more consistent with the reality of growing international activity—consists of increasing the level of global cooperation and focusing on important non-trade issues. That is, rather than slowing progress in the trade area, non-trade concerns should be addressed by increasing the level of international cooperation and promoting agreements that take both trade and non-trade issues into account.

At first glance, the idea of moving toward more, rather than less, global governance may seem inconsistent with the objections voiced by WTO opponents. As one examines these complaints carefully, however, it becomes clear that only increased global cooperation can provide an effective strategy for addressing their concerns. Like WTO supporters, critics recognize that international cooperation is needed to address the challenges of globalization. A turn away from the institution, then, is an odd prescription.

[T]he WTO should, over time, expand its role to include non-trade issues. Doing so will require changes to the institution, and this Article outlines the necessary reforms. This is not the first proposal suggesting an expansion of the WTO, but it offers a novel set of reforms that retain the benefits of a stable, influential, and effective international organization while mitigating the institution's trade bias. Though a reformed WTO will not be perfect, the alternatives—the most prominent being the establishment of stand-alone issue-oriented institutions—are far worse.

[T]he WTO [should] be structured along departmental lines to permit its expansion into new areas while taming its trade bias. A department for each major issue area would be created within the institution—a trade in goods department, a trade-in-services department, an intellectual property department, an environmental department, and so on. Each department would hold periodic negotiating rounds to which member states would send representatives. These "Departmental Rounds," however, would be limited to issues relevant to the organizing department. Members could take advantage of the more specialized, streamlined Departmental Rounds to reach agreement on issues that do not implicate other departments. In addition to the Departmental Rounds, there would be periodic "Mega–Rounds" of negotiation that would cover issues from more than one department. Mega–Rounds allow two different types of trade-offs across departmental lines. First, they permit agreements that implicate more than one department, such as an environmental agreement that includes a set of trade-based enforcement provisions. Second, they open the door to agreements in one departmental area that are possible only if concessions are made in another departmental area, as was the case with the TRIPs Agreement and * * * would be necessary for an agreement on competition policy or labor. Mega–Rounds are roughly analogous to the current practice of negotiating rounds, including the ongoing Doha Round and the earlier Uruguay Round where the TRIPs Agreement was negotiated.

Despite dramatic differences in perspective, both proponents and critics of the WTO agree that some form of international cooperation to address non-trade concerns is required. That these groups with opposing agendas should agree is not surprising. Any serious consideration of topics such as the environment, intellectual property, and health and safety measures eventually must address their substantial international implications. One cannot speak for long about environmental issues, for example, before international concerns such as greenhouse gases arise. Regardless of how one feels about the appropriate balance between the environment and economic growth, it is clear that global environmental concerns can be addressed more effectively through cooperative efforts among states. That sort of balance and cooperation cannot be achieved by a retreat from globalization, and specialized international organizations are not equipped to promote the necessary dialogue.

JOHN O. McGINNIS & MARK L. MOVSESIAN, AGAINST GLOBAL GOVERNANCE IN THE WTO

45 HARV. INT'L L.J. 353 (2004)

In *Global Governance and the WTO*, Professor Andrew Guzman [argues that] the WTO's mission should be expanded beyond its present task of facilitating tariff reductions and preventing covert protectionism. Rather, the WTO should take on substantive authority in a wide variety of non-trade areas, including the environment, labor, human rights, and public health. * * * He advocates specialized WTO departments and periodic "Mega–Rounds" in which members make cross-issue regulatory bargains. Unless members agreed otherwise, these regulatory bargains would be subject to the WTO's Dispute Settlement Understanding (DSU).

The availability of the dispute settlement system is a major element of Guzman's proposal. Guzman argues that the mechanism could serve as an important credibility-enhancing device that would encourage members to make beneficial cross-issue bargains. While Guzman believes that members should be free to avoid the application of the DSU to their new bargains if they wish, the unavailability of the mechanism as an enforcement device would rob Guzman's proposal of much of its force. In the absence of the DSU, one might as well seek out international fora other than the WTO for the harmonization of global rules.

As its title suggests, Guzman's article is ultimately a call for world government by the WTO. In this necessarily brief response, we describe some of the more important theoretical and practical problems that Guzman's proposal presents. First, [in] the matter of cross-issue bargaining in the WTO[:] while cross-issue bargaining can create gains for parties to a contract, substantive regulatory deals may be vehicles for "amoral" wealth transfers among interest groups. Unlike the present WTO, which works to minimize the influence of one particular form of interest group—protectionists—the transformed organization would facilitate agreements that empower special interests.

[Second, with respect to] the potential of the dispute settlement system as a credibility-enhancing device: the dispute settlement system might actually discourage cross-issue bargains by vesting extraordinary discretion in WTO tribunals. This discretion would entail an intolerable lack of predictability for WTO members, particularly given the sensitivity of the matters involved. [D]eveloping countries would be especially chary of signing on to such a regime, and * * *. extending the dispute settlement system to cover a variety of non-trade issues might upset the sensitive dynamic in which exporters work to assure national compliance with WTO obligations. * * * Rather than transform itself into a global government—a World Trade, Economic, Environment, Human Rights, Labor, and Public Health Organization—the WTO should stick to its limited but important role: reducing barriers to trade among nations.

II. CROSS–ISSUE BARGAINING IN GUZMAN'S WTO

The first major element of Guzman's proposal is his call for transforming the WTO into a forum for cross-issue negotiation. Guzman would like to change the WTO from an institution that focuses primarily on reducing national barriers to trade into one that facilitates national bargaining on a variety of non-trade topics, including the environment, labor, public health, and human rights. Guzman envisions a series of specialized departments within the WTO that would serve as fora for "Departmental" negotiating rounds in designated subject matters. These departments would be staffed by experts, appointed by national governments but apparently with a large degree of autonomy, who would negotiate agreements and prepare new global regulations. Guzman also envisions periodic "Mega–Rounds" in which nations would make deals that transcend departmental lines, for example, rounds in which some nations agree to lower trade restrictions in return for other nations' concessions on the environment or labor.

The underpinnings of Guzman's proposal lie in "political bargaining" theory. As the name suggests, political bargaining theory attempts to apply the insights of contract theory to intergovernmental negotiations. Just as private parties can increase their preference satisfaction by expanding the scope of their bargains, governments can enhance the potential for reaching beneficial agreements by addressing independent issues simultaneously, a practice commonly known as "logrolling." For example, because their interests are too far apart, developing and developed countries might not be able to reach independent agreements on either agricultural subsidies or environmental regulations. Nonetheless, they might be able to reach a compromise that covers both subjects: developed countries might forgo some agricultural subsidies in exchange for developing countries' agreement to somewhat higher environmental standards. Thus, cross-issue bargaining might make both sides better off.

Political bargaining theory has much to offer the discussion of international institutions. But one should not casually equate private contracts with public regulatory bargains. Because private contracts generally enhance the preferences of the parties, legal mechanisms that reduce transaction costs to such contracts are likely to be beneficial. Regulatory bargains, by contrast, are not as likely to be efficient in terms of nations' true preferences. Such bargains are much more likely to represent "amoral" wealth transfers among different groups of citizens: there is a considerable danger that many such bargains would represent deals by special interests in various nations at the public's expense. Legal mechanisms that reduce transaction costs to such bargains thus are not as unambiguously beneficial.

The genius of the WTO lies precisely in its capacity to promote private, cross-border contracts rather than regulatory bargains that can amount to wealth transfers among interest groups. Three of the organization's features help assure this. First, the WTO has a limited focus: promoting international agreements to reduce tariff and non-tariff barriers. Such agreements promote private contracting and, according to the theory of comparative advantage, increase nations' aggregate wealth. The WTO's narrow focus thus helps assure that the international agreements it facilitates will be good for each nation's net welfare and will not require much monitoring by national governments and their citizens.

Second, as presently constructed, the WTO acts to mitigate one of the most characteristic domestic wealth transfers. The WTO constrains the ability of domestic interest groups to obtain protective tariffs—a historical bane of democratic politics. Under the WTO regime, members reduce tariffs on a reciprocal basis. As a result, the benefits that exporters derive from lower tariffs abroad depend upon the willingness of the exporters' own government to lower its tariffs with respect to foreign products. The reciprocity regime thus creates incentives for exporters to enter the domestic political struggle and blunt the power of the protectionist interest groups at home, providing virtual representation for the public's interest in free trade. Under this view, the WTO is a regime that facilitates democratic choice within individual states even as it increases aggregate wealth by decreasing tariff barriers.

Third, the WTO's relatively light administrative structure limits the danger that the organization will become a vehicle for wealth transfers. Governments can easily monitor whether other nations comply with tariff reductions and nondiscrimination requirements. Exporters directly benefit from such provisions and thus have incentives to bring violations to their governments' attention. Moreover, enforcing tariff reductions and attendant agreements to remove trade restrictions does not require granting the WTO wide substantive discretion. Thus, special interests cannot easily use WTO mechanisms, such as the DSU, to obtain rents.

NOTES AND QUESTIONS ON THE *WTO*

1. *Interpreting WTO law.* As between Guzman and McGinness & Movsesian, who has the more persuasive view of the WTO's legal power?

2. *The loophole in Article XX.* Article XX of GATT provides in part:

Subject to the requirement that such measures are not applied in a manner which would constitute a means of arbitrary or unjustifiable discrimination between countries where the same conditions prevail, or a disguised restriction on international trade, nothing in this Agreement shall be construed to prevent the adoption or enforcement by any contracting party of measures:

(a) necessary to protect public morals;

(b) necessary to protect human, animal or plant life or health;

* * *

(e) relating to the products of prison labour;

* * *

(g) relating to the conservation of exhaustible natural resources if such measures are made effective in conjunction with restrictions on domestic production or consumption.

As noted above, Article XX potentially provides an avenue for national legislation that protects labor rights or the environment, without running afoul of the WTO. Early WTO cases on environmental protection, however, did not seem to give the exception much scope.

In *Tuna/Dolphin*,[1] Mexico challenged the U.S. Marine Mammal Protection Act of 1972 as a violation of GATT. The act set a limit, both for the United States and other countries, on how many dolphins could be incidentally captured and killed by the tuna fishing industry. If a state could not demonstrate that it met the dolphin protection standards, the United States prohibited the importation of fish from that country. The Panel ruled that the United States couldn't institute an embargo against Mexico merely because of the way in which the product was produced. The Panel noted that the United States could prevent the importation of goods based on the quality or content, but not on the process used. This reflects the fear that allowing countries to impose trade regulations based on the way something is made would eviscerate GATT, as nearly all countries have different environmental, health and other standards. This type of exception would allow countries to impose unilateral trading sanctions and to undermine the predictability that GATT was intended to ensure. The Panel found, however, that requiring tuna to be labeled as "dolphin safe" was not an improper restriction of trade. *See* World Trade Organization, *Mexico etc. vs. US: "tuna-dolphin,"* http://www.wto.org/english/tratop_e/envir_e/edis04_e.htm.

Recently, however, the climate appears more favorable to using Article XX exceptions for environmental protection. In *Shrimp/Turtle*,[2] India, Malaysia, Pakistan and Thailand challenged a United States law intended to protect endangered sea turtles. The law prohibited the importation of shrimp unless the Department of State were satisfied that endangered sea turtles were not threatened by the fishing methods used

---

1. Panel Report, *United States–Restrictions on the Import of Tuna*, DS21/R–39S/155 (Sept. 3, 1991).

2. Appellate Body Report, *United States-Import Prohibition of Certain Shrimp and Shrimp Products*, WT/DS58/AB/R (Oct. 12, 1998) (*adopted* Nov. 8, 1998) (*Shrimp/Turtle*). Note that the panel decision in *Tuna/Dolphin* was never adopted; thus it does not have the force of law. GATT required a formal process for an opinion to be adopted. Under the new WTO, panel decisions are adopted automatically if WTO members do not reject the report by consensus within 60 days of its issuance. *Shrimp/Turtle*, which was decided under the new WTO regime, was adopted automatically under this process.

in a given country. The Appellate body found that the United States was in violation of GATT, not because of the regulation *per se*, but because the system for determining which countries complied did not meet the preliminary requirements of Article XX:

183.   It is also clear to us that Article X:3 of the GATT 1994 establishes certain minimum standards for transparency and procedural fairness in the administration of trade regulations which, in our view, are not met here. The non-transparent and *ex parte* nature of the internal governmental procedures applied by the competent officials in the Office of Marine Conservation, the Department of State, and the United States National Marine Fisheries Service throughout the certification processes under Section 609, as well as the fact that countries whose applications are denied do not receive formal notice of such denial, nor of the reasons for the denial, and the fact, too, that there is no formal legal procedure for review of, or appeal from, a denial of an application, are all contrary to the spirit, if not the letter, of Article X:3 of the GATT 1994.

184.   We find, accordingly, that the United States measure is applied in a manner which amounts to a means not just of "unjustifiable discrimination," but also of "arbitrary discrimination" between countries where the same conditions prevail, contrary to the requirements of the chapeau of Article XX. The measure, therefore, is not entitled to the justifying protection of Article XX of the GATT 1994. Having made this finding, it is not necessary for us to examine also whether the United States measure is applied in a manner that constitutes a "disguised restriction on international trade" under the chapeau of Article XX.

185.   In reaching these conclusions, we wish to underscore what we have *not* decided in this appeal. We have *not* decided that the protection and preservation of the environment is of no significance to the Members of the WTO. Clearly, it is. We have *not* decided that the sovereign nations that are Members of the WTO cannot adopt effective measures to protect endangered species, such as sea turtles. Clearly, they can and should. And we have *not* decided that sovereign states should not act together bilaterally, plurilaterally or multilaterally, either within the WTO or in other international fora, to protect endangered species or to otherwise protect the environment. Clearly, they should and do.

186.   What we *have* decided in this appeal is simply this: although the measure of the United States in dispute in this appeal serves an environmental objective that is recognized as legitimate under paragraph (g) of Article XX of the GATT 1994, this measure has been applied by the United States in a manner which constitutes arbitrary and unjustifiable discrimination between Members of the WTO, contrary to the requirements of the chapeau of Article XX. For all of the specific reasons outlined in this Report, this measure

does not qualify for the exemption that Article XX of the GATT 1994 affords to measures which serve certain recognized, legitimate environmental purposes but which, at the same time, are not applied in a manner that constitutes a means of arbitrary or unjustifiable discrimination between countries where the same conditions prevail or a disguised restriction on international trade. As we emphasized in *United States—Gasoline*, WTO Members are free to adopt their own policies aimed at protecting the environment as long as, in so doing, they fulfill their obligations and respect the rights of other Members under the *WTO Agreement*.[1]

Shrimp/Turtle ¶ ¶ 183–86.

Some argue that this was a significant departure from previous decisions such as *Tuna/Dolphin:*

> Given the hostile attitude toward environmental trade measures reflected in past panel decisions under the GATT, the WTO Appellate Body's 1998 ruling in the shrimp-turtle case represented a significant step toward more liberal treatment of these measures under the GATT. In stark contrast to the consistent pattern in those past decisions, the Appellate Body upheld the statute in dispute and objected only to very specific aspects of its implementation. * * * The result was a decision much more sensitive to environmental interests than observers had expected.

Howard F. Chang, *Environmental Trade Measures, The Shrimp–Turtle Rulings, and the Ordinary Meanings of the Text of the GATT*, 8 CHAP. L. REV. 25, 26 (2005). Further, the narrowness of the holding might be construed as support for the argument "that the exceptions for prison labor, health and safety, or public morals, could be read expansively so as to include the core labor standards articulated by the ILO as contemporary concerns of the community of nations." Elissa Alben, Note, *GATT and the Fair Wage: A Historical Perspective on the Labor–Trade Link*, 101 COLUM. L. REV. 1410, 1422 (2001). Others are not so optimistic about the implications of *Shrimp-Turtle*:

> *Shrimp–Turtle* continues the tradition of trade jurisprudence that has almost completely closed off the policy space Article XX should leave open for national trade measures designed to protect the environment. Part of the problem is that the Appellate Body fails to comprehend the inherent characteristics of environmental legislation and regulation, so that its tests for non-discrimination in application of measures under the Article XX chapeau become a proverbial "eye of the needle" through which hardly any national environmental measure will be able to pass.

Sanford Gaines, *The WTO's Reading of the GATT Article XX Chapeau: A Disguised Restriction on Environmental Measures*, 22 U. PA. J. INT'L ECON. L. 739, 773 (2001).

---

1. Adopted 20 May 1996, WT/DS2/AB/R, p. 30.

3. *WTO waivers for human rights-based trade protections.* A process exists within the WTO for obtaining waivers for restrictive trade measures taken by member states. For example, the World Diamond Council developed the Kimberley Process, which was designed to combat the illicit trade in "conflict diamonds," *i.e.* proceeds of gem sales which supported governments and paramilitary groups that abuse civilians. When certain WTO member states decided to restrict trade in diamonds marketed outside the Kimberley Process, they sought and received a waiver from the WTO. The waiver recognized "the extraordinary humanitarian nature of this issue and the devastating impact of conflicts fuelled by trade in conflict diamonds on the peace, safety, and security of people in affected countries and the systematic and gross human rights violations that have been perpetrated in such conflicts." World Trade Organization, Council for Trade in Goods, *Waiver concerning Kimberley Process Certification Scheme for Rough Diamonds*, G/C/W/432/Rev.1 (03–1136) (24 February 2003).

4. *Gendered aspects of free trade.* The negative consequences of globalization are not distributed equally among members of society. "Globalization hurts women more than men. Increased globalization unites Western notions of patriarchy and economic efficiency with other countries' entrenched legal and social manifestations of patriarchy, perpetuating the dismal status of women within these countries." Laine M. Jarvis, Note, *Women's Rights and the Public Morals Exception of GATT Article XX*, 22 MICH. J. INT'L L. 219, 219 (2000). The UN has noted the failures of the WTO both to include women in its design and planning:

> The net result is that for certain sectors of humanity—particularly the developing countries of the South—the WTO is a veritable nightmare. The fact that women were largely excluded from the WTO decision-making structures, and that the rules evolved by WTO are largely gender-insensitive, means that women as a group stand to gain little from this organization* * *

and its negative impact on the working and living conditions of women:

> The United Nations Secretary–General has pointed to adverse labour conditions as a major factor contributing to the increased feminization of poverty. The logical expectation that the demand for female labour will improve their bargaining position and drive up wages has not been realized. The very opposite appears to be taking place.

Sub–Commission on the Promotion and Protection of Human Rights, *Globalization and Its Impact on the Full Enjoyment of Human Rights*, ¶ ¶ 15, 39, UN Doc. E/CN.4/Sub.2/2000/13a (June 15, 2002). As noted above, Article XX allows States to adopt measures that restrict trade if they are "necessary" to achieve a narrow class of social objectives. Should the prevention of the "feminization of poverty" fit within that class? If you were to make the argument, how would you frame the social objective, remembering that the WTO appellate body tends to define "necessity" narrowly?

5. *Trade in prison products.* Article XX explicitly allows products of prison labor to be regulated:

> Subject to the requirement that such measures are not applied in a manner which would constitute a means of arbitrary or unjustifiable discrimination between countries where the same conditions prevail, or a disguised restriction on international trade, nothing in this Agreement shall be construed to prevent the adoption or enforcement by any contracting party of measures:* * * (e) relating to the products of prison labour.

Although this exception may be interpreted to prevent states from capitalizing on a competitive advantage based on their use of forced or coerced labor, some have suggested that its proximity to the exceptions for the protection of public morals, and human, animal or plant life or health, "can be interpreted as showing that human rights were a driving force in its conclusion." Patricia Stirling, *The Use of Trade Sanctions as an Enforcement Mechanism for Basic Human Rights: A Proposal for Addition to the World Trade Organization*, 11 AM. U.J. INT'L L. & POL'Y 1, 38 (1996).

Others have expressed the opposite interpretation: when the original GATT agreement was crafted in 1947, it was in the interests of the elites to allow the regulation of prison labor out of economic self-interest, not out of any sense of the prisoners' rights. Proponents of this explanation are concerned that the growth of prison populations and private prisons creates an economic incentive to eliminate this exception; indeed, more recent proposed WTO agreements do not include this exception. Prison Activist Resource Center, *The World Trade Organization and the Prison Industrial Complex*, http://www.prisonactivist.org/mate rials/wto_pic.html

6. *Domestic trade law and the relevance of human rights concerns.* In 2000, the United States adopted the African Growth and Opportunity Act, 19 U.S.C.A. § 3701 (2000) ("AGOA") to help promote development in Sub–Saharan Africa. The President can designate a country as eligible if, among other things, "it does not engage in gross violations of internationally recognized human rights." 19 U.S.C.A. § 3703(a)(1)(F)(3) (2000). However, critics argue that this provision has not been enforced, with the result that human rights violators may be benefitting from this push for investment in Africa:

> In letters addressed to Secretary of State Colin Powell and U.S. Trade Representative Robert Zoellick, Human Rights Watch said the U.S. government had not used human rights criteria contained in the legislation to improve human rights performance in the beneficiary countries. "The Congress created a useful tool for promoting human rights in Africa, but the U.S. government isn't using it," said Janet Fleischman, Washington Director for the Africa Division of Human Rights Watch. Human Rights Watch does not

take a position on whether or not particular states should be eligible for benefits under the AGOA law. But the legislation includes labor rights and human rights criteria, and requires that beneficiary countries not "engage in gross violations of internationally recognized human rights." Human Rights Watch cited several cases where the U.S. State Department itself has documented abusive practices by recipient countries, but the U.S. government has not made clear how those findings will affect trade relationships with those countries, as the AGOA requires.

Human Rights Watch, *Africa: Use Trade Law for Human Rights*, Oct. 25, 2001, http://hrw.org/english/docs/2001/10/25/africa3082.htm.

Practicum

The World Bank proposes to fund the construction of a major highway in the country of Guatador. The road would link the major Guatadoran ports and the inland portions of the country but would bisect a pristine tropical forest that is home to several indigenous groups. These groups have largely lived in isolation from the law of Guatador and its economy. Under the original World Bank plan, one particular group, the Maidia tribe, would be obliged to move three of its largest villages, one of which includes some of the tribe's most sacred sites. Under Maidian customary law, no individual can own property. Under Guatadoran law, the state owns all property that is not owned by individuals and titled to them. Some members of the tribe are willing to take the government's compensation and move to the proffered resettlement sites. The great majority are not, and the government has begun a campaign to isolate the tribe and portray it as an obstacle to the greater good of the Guatadoran people. The record of the Guatadoran government in protecting the rights of indigenous people is not good, and a policy paper has been leaked to the press suggesting that the government will soon begin a process of forced relocation. There is virtually no public support for the Maidians, and the Parliament is preparing legislation that would authorize the armed forces to develop a plan for relocating them in the next year.

Assume that the economic case for the road is compelling and that the options for placing it are limited by the natural characteristics of the land: if the Maidia stay where they are, the road cannot be built. The World Bank has funded the road with a $2 billion grant to the Guatadoran Infrastructure Ministry. The Ministry in turn has contracted out various parts of the road project.

Drawing on the World Bank's Resettlement Policy, *supra*, and the Inspection Panel Operating Procedure, *infra*, one group of students will represent the Maidians and draft a Request for Inspection to have a Panel review the project before it goes any further. A second group will represent the Guatadoran government and file a response. A third group will represent the World Bank itself, decide whether to convene the Inspection Panel, and explain its decision.

WORLD BANK INSPECTION PANEL
OPERATING PROCEDURE

http://siteresources.worldbank.org/EXTINSPECTION
PANEL/Resources/TenYear8_07.pdf

GUIDANCE ON HOW TO PREPARE
A REQUEST FOR INSPECTION

The Inspection Panel needs some basic information in order to process a Request for Inspection:

1.   Name, contact address and telephone number of the group or people making the request.

2.   Name and description of the Bank project.

3.   Adverse effects of the Bank project.

4.   If you are a representative of affected people attach explicit written instructions from them authorizing you to act on their behalf.

These key questions must be answered:

1.   Can you elaborate on the nature and importance of the damage caused by the project to you or those you represent?

2.   Do you know that the Bank is responsible for the aspects of the project that has or may affect you adversely? How did you determine this?

3.   Are you familiar with Bank policies and procedures that apply to this type of project? How do you believe the Bank may have violated them?

4.   Have you contacted or attempted to contact Bank staff about the project? Please provide information about all contacts, and the responses, if any, you received from the Bank. You must have done this before you can file a request.

5.   Have you tried to resolve your problem through any other means?

6.   If you know that the Panel has dealt with this matter before, do you have new facts or evidence to submit?

Please provide a summary of the information in no more than a few pages. Attach as much other information as you think necessary as separate documents. Please note and identify attachments in your summary.

CHAPTER 4

MODULE 10

LABOR RIGHTS AND THE INTERNATIONAL LABOUR ORGANIZATION

■ ■ ■

"Poverty remains deep and widespread across the developing world and some transition countries, with an estimated 2 billion people in the world today live on the equivalent of less than USD 2 per day. In the view of the ILO, the main route out of poverty is work."
— International Labour Organization (2008)

Orientation

If international human rights law were conceived exclusively as a limitation on governments, then the employment conditions of workers in private settings would be beyond its reach. But even before the expansion in human rights law in the late twentieth century, the treatment of workers was a matter of international concern. In the peace treaty ending World War I, the international community created the International Labour Organization ("ILO") for the purpose of improving the conditions of working people around the world. In part, the founders of the ILO viewed the abuse of workers as an international security issue, observing that "universal and lasting peace can be established only if it is based upon social justice." Preamble, ILO Constitution (1919). This was not some wild-eyed or naive altruism. Those who had survived the "the war to end all wars" sought pragmatic means to prevent the causes of continuing conflict:

> conditions of labour exist involving such injustice, hardship, and privation to large numbers of people as to produce unrest so great that the peace and harmony of the world are imperilled; and an improvement of those conditions is urgently required; as, for example, by the regulation of the hours of work including the establishment of a maximum working day and week, the regulation of the labour supply, the prevention of unemployment, the provision of an adequate living wage, the protection of the worker against sickness, disease and injury arising out of his employment, the protection of children, young persons and women, provision for old age and injury, protection of the interests of workers when employed in countries other than their own, recognition of the principle of equal remuneration for work of equal value, recognition of

the principle of freedom of association, the organization of vocational and technical education and other measures.

Id. At its heart, the ILO's work was (and remains) premised on the proposition that global economic development, prosperity, and peace depend in part on the existence and the dignity of work.

An enforceable and unified front was required, because every state had an incentive to cheat: if every other state adopted expensive protections for workers, the hold-out state could offer employers the preferable investment environment, but at the cost of impoverishing or endangering its own people. To minimize that temptation, it was necessary to create a "values cartel" that could bring workers, employers, and all governments together under an umbrella of international regulation. As noted in the preamble to the ILO Constitution, "the failure of any nation to adopt humane conditions of labour is an obstacle in the way of other nations which desire to improve the conditions in their own countries."

In 1946, a quarter century after its founding with the League of Nations, the ILO became the United Nations' first specialized agency, with the unique mandate of "advancing opportunities for women and men to obtain decent and productive work in conditions of freedom, equity, security and human dignity." It also had a unique tripartite governing structure that empowered representatives of governments, workers, and employers, with the consequence that it is now the only intergovernmental institution in which "governments do not have all the votes."[1] Through a process of "social dialogue," these three disparate stakeholders jointly set policy and program for the organization, which assures that the standard-setting initiatives of the organization are grounded in the actual experience of workers and employers. It is also designed to assure a measure of buy-in from the groups affected by these standards and from the governments whose principal responsibility lies in adopting and enforcing them.

At the first International Labor Conference in October 1919, the ILO adopted six conventions, addressing hours of work in industry, unemployment, maternity protection, night work for women and children, and minimum age requirements in industry. Since then, the organization has adopted standards covering virtually all aspects of work through a variety of normative instruments: more than 180 Conventions, which become binding when states become parties to them;[2] 190 Recommendations, which are authoritative but non-binding guidelines offering detailed supplements to the Conventions;[3] and dozens of Codes

---

1. Lee Swepston, *Human Rights Complaint Procedures of the International Labour Organization*, in GUIDE TO INTERNATIONAL HUMAN RIGHTS PRACTICE 89 (Hannum ed. 2004).

2. For a comprehensive list of ILO Conventions and the parties to them, *see* www.ilo.org/ilolex/english/convdisp1.htm.

3. For a comprehensive list of ILO Recommendations, *see* www.ilo.org/ilolex/english/recdisp1.htm. There are for example Recommendations covering lead poisoning (1919), holidays with pay

of Practice, which—as expressions of best practices—can influence the development and harmonization of domestic legislation on a particular topic, like maternity leave.[4] Non-governmental organizations have been especially adept at using ILO standards in various forms to expose abusive practices by employers or inadequate policies, laws, and practices of governments.

Today, the ILO's agenda reflects some of the most notorious and widespread human rights violations in the world: contemporary forms of slavery; discrimination in hiring, pay, and work conditions; human trafficking; child labor; migrant workers; and the rights of indigenous peoples.[5] On the other hand, there is considerable skepticism about the ILO, because of the gap between its concerns and its effectiveness. "A principal reason for the ILO's inconspicuous profile is the widely held perception that the organization is the '90–pound weakling' of UN agencies, a 'toothless tiger,' that has little effect on improving global labor conditions." Laurence R. Helfer, *Monitoring Compliance with Unratified treaties: The ILO Experience*, 71 LAW & CONTEMP. PROBS. 195, 196 (2008).

The point of this module is to identify the pressure points within the ILO for defining, addressing, and resolving these issues.

———————

Readings

The ILO was instrumental in the development and ratification of the Convention to Suppress the Slave Trade and Slavery (1926) and its Supplementary Convention (1956), both of which are in the Documents Supplement.[6] Slavery still exists and in its contemporary forms may be harder to perceive, let alone attack.

———————

(1936), employment during the transition from war to peace (1944), migrant workers (1975), and employment relations (2006).

4. For a comprehensive list of ILO Codes of Practice, *see* www.ilo.org/public/english/protection/safework/cops/english/index.htm. These Codes address such issues as HIV and the world of work (2001), the protection of workers' personal data (1997), the management of alcohol- and drug-related issues in the workplace (1996), and even the safe construction and operation of tractors (1976).

5. The ILO was one of the first intergovernmental organizations to address the legal rights of indigenous and tribal peoples' rights, first in 1957, then in Convention No. 169 on Indigenous and Tribal Peoples (1989). The Convention is directed exclusively at governments, but it is not widely adopted; nevertheless, the International Finance Corporation, an affiliate of the World Bank, has determined that the Convention has certain reputational and business value for large private investors, advising that "[c]ompliance with the Convention will not only protect indigenous and tribal peoples' rights, but will promote the interests of private business by laying the groundwork for a positive and socially responsible investment environment." World Bank Group, International Finance Corporation, ILO Convention 169 and the Private Sector, *available at* http://www.ifc.org/ifcext/enviro.nsf/attachmentsbytitle/p_ilo169/$file/ilo_169.pdf.

6. Convention to Suppress the Slave Trade and Slavery, 60 L.N.T.S. 253 (25 September 1926); Supplementary Convention on the Application of Slavery, the Slave Trade, and Institutions and Practices Similar to Slavery, 226 U.N.T.S. 3 (7 September 1956).

HOWARD DODSON, "SLAVERY IN THE TWENTY–FIRST CENTURY," UN CHRONICLE ONLINE EDITION (2008)[7]

The slave trade is back in full force. This modern slave trade, however, is not limited to just young Africans; women and children are also being enslaved in almost every continent. It is estimated that there are over 27 million enslaved persons worldwide, more than double the number of those who were deported in the 400–year history of the transatlantic slave trade to the Americas. What is remarkable is that this unprecedented trafficking largely goes unnoticed. The 27 million victims of the modern slave trade are more invisible to the world's eye than were the 10 million to 12 million Africans who were forcibly sent to the Americas during the sixteenth through the nineteenth centuries. How do we account for this fact in this age of media and communications overload and transparency?

The first problem is related to the major differences between transatlantic and modern slave trades. The transatlantic slave trade was racially-biased. The victims were Africans who were captured and sold into slavery in Africa and transported to the Western Hemisphere to work in the economies, principally in agriculture and mineral, of the European colonial societies. Combined efforts of abolitionist movements led to the British and American abolition of the slave trade and the eventual demise of slavery itself in the Western Hemisphere during the nineteenth century.

The modern slave trade is quite different. All racial groups are objects of the trade. Though women and children are its principal victims, those who are bought, sold and enslaved come from almost every continent and are sold into slavery in virtually every country. Unlike the transatlantic slave trade, they are not being recruited to work in any specific geographical area or any clearly defined industry or economy. True, many of the women are sold as prostitutes or concubines, and the children as labourers, but there are relatively few established and stable routes and markets. While the transatlantic slave trade was legal and carried on as a form of legitimate commerce, the modern slave trade is illegal. Records of these underground business transactions are largely hidden from public view; so are the human beings who are bought and sold in this twenty-first-century slave trafficking. The pervasiveness and the relatively invisible nature of this illegal trafficking make it difficult to define and develop a strategy for abolishing it. The question arises: "How should one begin?"

---

7. Available at http://www.un.org/Pubs/chronicle/2005/issue3/0305p28.html.

How might a lawyer eager to begin to work on the problem of slavery in its contemporary forms use each of the following provisions of the ILO Constitution? What problems should she or he anticipate?

CONSTITUTION OF THE INTERNATIONAL LABOUR ORGANIZATION
49 Stat. 2712 (28 June 1919)[8]

Article 22

Annual Reports on Ratified Conventions

Each of the Members agrees to make an annual report to the International Labour Office on the measures which it has taken to give effect to the provisions of Conventions to which it is a party. These reports shall be made in such form and shall contain such particulars as the Governing Body may request.

Article 24

Representations of Non–Observance of Conventions

In the event of any representation being made to the International Labour Office by an industrial association of employers or of workers that any of the Members has failed to secure in any respect the effective observance within its jurisdiction of any Convention to which it is a party, the Governing Body may communicate this representation to the government against which it is made, and may invite that government to make such statement on the subject as it may think fit.

Article 25

Publication of Representation

If no statement is received within a reasonable time from the government in question, or if the statement when received is not deemed to be satisfactory by the Governing Body, the latter shall have the right to publish the representation and the statement, if any, made in reply to it.

Article 26

Complaints of Non–Observance

1. Any of the Members shall have the right to file a complaint with the International Labour Office if it is not satisfied that any other Member is securing the effective observance of any Convention which both have ratified in accordance with the foregoing articles.

2. The Governing Body may, if it thinks fit, before referring such a complaint to a Commission of Inquiry, as hereinafter provided for,

---

8. *Available at* http://training.itcilo/;/s/foa/library/constitution/iloconst-en.html#a23.

communicate with the government in question in the manner described in article 24.

3. If the Governing Body does not think it necessary to communicate the complaint to the government in question, or if, when it has made such communication, no statement in reply has been received within a reasonable time which the Governing Body considers to be satisfactory, the Governing Body may appoint a Commission of Inquiry to consider the complaint and to report thereon.

4. The Governing Body may adopt the same procedure either of its own motion or on receipt of a complaint from a delegate to the Conference.

5. When any matter arising out of article 25 or 26 is being considered by the Governing Body, the government in question shall, if not already represented thereon, be entitled to send a representative to take part in the proceedings of the Governing Body while the matter is under consideration. Adequate notice of the date on which the matter will be considered shall be given to the government in question.

Article 27

Cooperation with Commission of Inquiry

The Members agree that, in the event of the reference of a complaint to a Commission of Inquiry under article 26, they will each, whether directly concerned in the complaint or not, place at the disposal of the Commission all the information in their possession which bears upon the subject-matter of the complaint.

Article 28

Report of Commission of Inquiry

When the Commission of Inquiry has fully considered the complaint, it shall prepare a report embodying its findings on all questions of fact relevant to determining the issue between the parties and containing such recommendations as it may think proper as to the steps which should be taken to meet the complaint and the time within which they should be taken.

Article 29

Action on Report of Commission of Inquiry

1. The Director–General of the International Labour Office shall communicate the report of the Commission of Inquiry to the Governing Body and to each of the governments concerned in the complaint, and shall cause it to be published.

2. Each of these governments shall within three months inform the Director–General of the International Labour Office whether or not it accepts the recommendations contained in the report of the Commis-

sion; and if not, whether it proposes to refer the complaint to the International Court of Justice.

Article 33

Failure to Carry Out Recommendations of Commission of Inquiry or ICJ

In the event of any Member failing to carry out within the time specified the recommendations, if any, contained in the report of the Commission of Inquiry, or in the decision of the International Court of Justice, as the case may be, the Governing Body may recommend to the Conference such action as it may deem wise and expedient to secure compliance therewith.

NOTE ON THE *ILO* BUREAUCRACY

The ILO has several standing bodies, each of which may be involved in the process of setting and implementing labor standards. The *International Labour Conference* meets annually in Geneva where it establishes labor standards, adopts the organization's budget, and elects the Governing Body. Each member state is represented at the Conference by two government delegates, one employer delegate, and one worker delegate. The *Governing Body* is the ILO's executive council and is composed of 28 government members, 14 employer members, and 14 worker members. The Governing Body takes decisions on ILO policy and establishes the programs and the budget to implement them, which is then submitted to the Conference. The Governing Body also elects the Director–General. Under the leadership of the Director–General, and the supervision of the Governing Body, the *International Labour Office* is the permanent secretariat of the ILO. Employing almost 2,000 international civil servants, the Office has roughly 40 field-offices worldwide and its headquarters in Geneva. The periodic reports from member states under Article 22, *supra*, are reviewed by a Committee of Experts on the Application of Conventions and Recommendations—a global committee of labor lawyers and academics—which is empowered to seek additional information or publish its observations in its annual report to the Conference.

NOTES AND QUESTIONS ON CONTEMPORARY FORMS OF SLAVERY

1. *Contemporary forms of slavery and forced labor distinguished as a matter of law.* The ILO has defined many categories of forced labor. *See generally* National Research Council Committee on Monitoring International Labor Standards, MONITORING INTERNATIONAL LABOR STANDARDS: TECHNIQUES AND SOURCES OF INFORMATION 135–60 (2004). For example, the

practice of *chattel slavery*, in which a person may be bought and sold (or even inherited or given as a gift), is still practiced in some countries, although it is illegal everywhere. *Compulsory labor in public works projects* is more widespread and is often entwined with military labor, but does not involve one human being owning another. *Mandatory forced labor in rural areas* is a condition in which by law, custom, or agreement, a person is bound to live and work on land belonging to another and is not free to change his or her status. *Bonded labor* or *debt bondage* occurs when a person is required to pay off a loan through work instead of money, generally manipulated in such a way that the debt cannot be repaid. *Involuntary labor through trafficking* occurs commonly in the sex trades. *Forced prison labor* occurs when governments force prisoners to work without compensation for profit-making enterprises. *Servile forms of marriage* include instances of a woman or girl being sold by her parents or guardians for money or some other consideration to a "husband," who then has the right to sell or transfer her to another or even to leave her as an inheritance upon his death. The *worst forms of child labor* refers to the exploitation of children and adolescents when bonded or trafficked to work as soldiers, domestic laborers, farm workers, or sex workers. *See* the Convention concerning the Prohibition and Immediate Action for the Elimination of the Worst Forms of Child Labour (1999) (No. 182).

2. *Complaint mechanisms.* ILO complaint procedures—and the standing requirements for initiating them—vary according to the Article of the ILO Constitution under which the complaint is brought. This puts a technical premium on the label attached to the complaint. For example, complaints brought under Articles 24, 25, and 26(4), *supra*, are called *"representations"* and may be filed only by organizations of employers or workers (*e.g.*, a trade union or industrial association). By contrast, *"complaints"* may be filed under Article 26 by governments, delegates to the International Labour Conference, and by the Governing Body itself. There are also special procedures for complaints concerning the freedom of association. Nothing empowers individuals to file complaints directly in the ILO. *See generally* Lee Swepston, *Human Rights Complaint Procedures of the International Labour Organization*, *in* Guide to International Human Rights Practice 89 (Hannum ed. 2004).

3. *The process and its problems illustrated: ILO action against Myanmar (Burma).* In 1996, twenty-five Workers' Delegates to the International Labour Conference complained that the government of Burma had grossly violated the Forced Labour Convention, 1930 (No. 29), to which it was a party. According to the complaint, the use of forced labor in Burma was systematic and took many forms. For example, the Burmese military had confiscated land from villagers and then forced them to cultivate it for the government. In addition, a large number of forced laborers were being used for large-scale infrastructure projects. The ILO Governing Body created a Commission of Inquiry to investigate and report on the situation. After an extensive investigation, the Commission

found a wide range of violations of Convention No. 29, made recommendations to the government, and established a deadline for compliance. FORCED LABOUR IN MYANMAR (BURMA): REPORT OF THE COMMISSION OF INQUIRY APPOINTED UNDER ARTICLE 26 OF THE CONSTITUTION OF THE INTERNATIONAL LABOUR ORGANIZATION TO EXAMINE THE OBSERVANCE BY MYANMAR OF THE FORCED LABOUR CONVENTION, 1930 (NO. 29) (2 July 1998), *available at* www.ilo.org/public/english/standards/relm/gb/docs/gb273/myanmar.htm.

When the deadline passed in 2000 without improvement, the ILO invoked its powers under Article 33 for the first time in its history and sanctioned the government of Burma for the use of forced labor. *See* Laurence R. Helfer, *Understanding Change in International Organizations: Globalization and Innovation in the ILO*, 59 VAND. L. REV. 649, 712–714 (2006) (assessing the limited success of ILO sanctions, including opening Burma to a more permanent ILO presence, specific labor reforms, and trade sanctions). Many years have passed since the ILO imposed sanctions, and forced labor remains a serious problem in Burma, leading many to question the effectiveness of the organization. *See, e.g.,* William B. Gould, IV, *Fundamental Rights at Work and the Law of Nations—An American Lawyer's Perspective*, 23 HOFSTRA LAB. & EMP. L.J. 1, 28 (2005) ("in the case of forced labor problems of Myanmar[,] it is perhaps an exaggeration to characterize the ILO as a debating society, but at this juncture there are no meaningful remedies and sanctions for violations beyond the court of international public opinion.") What additional actions remain open to the ILO Governing Body under Article 33?

4. *Regulatory success.* The glare of failure in Burma and other places can blind us to the ILO's successes over the years, especially the widespread incorporation of ILO standards into the domestic law of states. For example, ILO Conventions formalized such standards as a national minimum wage, workers compensation, paid holidays, maternity protection, and social security insurance. Occupational safety and health have also been the subject of concentrated and effective action. This includes both omnibus regulation, as in the *Occupational Safety and Health Convention* (1981), and the regulation of discrete risks, as in the *Radiation Protection Convention* (1960), the *Chemical Convention* (1990), and the *Prevention of Major Industrial Accidents Convention* (1993). The domestic law of member states is readily harmonized around this international standard. In the United States, the Occupational Safety and Health Act of 1970, 29 U.S.C. 651, and the administrative regulations implementing it, reflect ILO standards. The European Union has also adopted directives for the protection of its workers, absorbing the legislation of the member states, and reflecting the standards of the ILO. The ILO and the World Health Organization have also formed a Joint Committee on Occupational Health, which supports national programs in developing countries, providing models for organizing safe workplaces, providing basic occupational health services, establishing enforcement agencies, and developing related education programs.

5. *Non–governmental organizations and the ILO.* NGOs have had a significant impact in the field of labor rights. Within the ILO, for example, NGO reports may be required in many complaint and recommendation processes. *See* MARTIN TRACY, INTERNATIONAL LABOR ORGANIZATION, A FRAMEWORK FOR OVERSIGHT OF GOVERNMENT AND NGO CONTRACTUAL SOCIAL SERVICE PARTNERSHIP (2004) (APPENDIX 5 TO GOOD PRACTICES IN SOCIAL SERVICE DELIVERY IN SOUTH EAST EUROPE). And ILO standards often provide the centerpiece of NGO "mobilization of shame" campaigns on particular issues or against particular employers. For example, Wal–Mart Stores Inc., the world's largest retailer, has long been the target of concentrated NGO campaigns to assure that Wal–Mart suppliers meet international standards protecting workers. In 2006, the company announced that it would increase surprise inspections at its suppliers' factories around the world. *See* Marcus Kabel, "Wal–Mart Steps Up Surprise Inspections of Foreign Factories," *Associated Press* (29 March 2006) *available at* www.laborrights.org/creating-a-sweatfree-world/wal-mart-campaign/1480. In what circumstances might campaigns of shame be more effective than intergovernmental actions within the ILO? Is there any sense in which the ILO might learn from the practices of the NGOs?

ILO DECLARATION ON FUNDAMENTAL PRINCIPLES AND RIGHTS AT WORK INTERNATIONAL LABOUR CONFERENCE, 86TH SESSION JUNE 1998[9]

Whereas the ILO was founded in the conviction that social justice is essential to universal and lasting peace; * * *

Whereas, in seeking to maintain the link between social progress and economic growth, the guarantee of fundamental principles and rights at work is of particular significance in that it enables the persons concerned to claim freely and on the basis of equality of opportunity their fair share of the wealth which they have helped to generate, and to achieve fully their human potential;

Whereas the ILO is the constitutionally mandated international organization and the competent body to set and deal with international labour standards, and enjoys universal support and acknowledgment in promoting fundamental rights at work as the expression of its constitutional principles;

Whereas it is urgent, in a situation of growing economic interdependence, to reaffirm the immutable nature of the fundamental principles

---

9. *Available at* http://www.ilo.org/dgn/dechris/DECLARATIONWEB>STATIC_JUMP?VW_LAN GUAGE=en&VAR_PAGENNME+declarationtext.

and rights embodied in the Constitution of the Organization and to promote their universal application;

The International Labour Conference,

1.   Recalls:

(a) that in freely joining the ILO, all Members have endorsed the principles and rights set out in its Constitution and in the Declaration of Philadelphia, and have undertaken to work towards attaining the overall objectives of the Organization to the best of their resources and fully in line with their specific circumstances;

(b) that these principles and rights have been expressed and developed in the form of specific rights and obligations in Conventions recognized as fundamental both inside and outside the Organization.

2.   Declares that all Members, even if they have not ratified the Conventions in question, have an obligation arising from the very fact of membership in the Organization, to respect, to promote and to realize, in good faith and in accordance with the Constitution, the principles concerning the fundamental rights which are the subject of those Conventions, namely:

(a) freedom of association and the effective recognition of the right to collective bargaining;

(b) the elimination of all forms of forced or compulsory labour;

(c) the effective abolition of child labour; and

(d) the elimination of discrimination in respect of employment and occupation. * * *

4.   Decides that, to give full effect to this Declaration, a promotional follow-up, which is meaningful and effective, shall be implemented in accordance with the measures specified in the annex hereto, which shall be considered as an integral part of this Declaration.

5.   Stresses that labour standards should not be used for protectionist trade purposes, and that nothing in this Declaration and its follow-up shall be invoked or otherwise used for such purposes; in addition, the comparative advantage of any country should in no way be called into question by this Declaration and its follow-up.

Annex

Follow-up to the Declaration

* * *

II.   Annual follow-up concerning non-ratified fundamental Conventions

A.   Purpose and scope

1.   The purpose is to provide an opportunity to review each year * * * the efforts made in accordance with the Declaration by Members which have not yet ratified all the fundamental Conventions.

2.   The follow-up will cover each year the four areas of fundamental principles and rights specified in the Declaration.

B.   Modalities

1.   The follow-up will be based on reports requested from Members under article 19, paragraph 5(e) of the Constitution. The report forms will be drawn up so as to obtain information from governments which have not ratified one or more of the fundamental Conventions, on any changes which may have taken place in their law and practice, taking due account of article 23 of the Constitution and established practice.

2.   These reports * * * will be reviewed by the Governing Body.

III.   Global report

A.   Purpose and scope

1.   The purpose of this report is to provide a dynamic global picture relating to each category of fundamental principles and rights noted during the preceding four-year period, and to serve as a basis for assessing the effectiveness of the assistance provided by the Organization, and for determining priorities for the following period, in the form of action plans for technical cooperation designed in particular to mobilize the internal and external resources necessary to carry them out.

2.   The report will cover, each year, one of the four categories of fundamental principles and rights in turn.

B.   Modalities

1.   The report will be drawn up under the responsibility of the Director–General on the basis of official information, or information gathered and assessed in accordance with established procedures. In the case of States which have not ratified the fundamental Conventions, it will be based in particular on the findings of the aforementioned annual follow-up. In the case of Members which have ratified the Conventions concerned, the report will be based in particular on reports as dealt with pursuant to article 22 of the Constitution.

2.   This report will be submitted to the Conference for tripartite discussion as a report of the Director–General. The Conference may deal with this report separately from reports under article 12 of its Standing Orders, and may discuss it during a sitting devoted entirely to this report, or in any other appropriate way. It will then be for the Governing Body, at an early session, to draw conclusions from this discussion concerning the priorities and plans of action for technical cooperation to be implemented for the following four-year period.

ROE v. BRIDGESTONE CORP.

492 F. Supp.2d 988 (S.D. Ind. 2007)

Plaintiffs are adults and children who work on a rubber plantation in the West African nation of Liberia. Based on allegations of forced labor, forced child labor, poor working conditions, and low wages, plaintiffs seek damages from the Japanese, American, and Liberian companies and two individuals that own and control the plantation. Plaintiffs seek relief in the federal courts of the United States. Their * * * complaint asserts claims under international law pursuant to the Alien Tort Statute ["ATS"],[1] the Thirteenth Amendment to the United States Constitution, a federal statute authorizing civil actions for criminal forced labor violations, and California law. * * *

The Firestone Rubber Plantation ("the Plantation") near Harbel, Liberia, is the world's largest rubber plantation. The Plantation was founded in 1926 under an agreement between the Firestone Tire and Rubber Company and the Liberian government, with what might be called strong encouragement from the United States government. All of the raw latex produced at the Plantation is sold to or otherwise controlled by other Bridgestone Firestone companies. Plaintiffs John Roe I through John Roe XII are adults who work as latex "tappers" on the Plantation. They cut into the rubber trees and collect the raw latex for eventual processing into tires and other rubber products. Plaintiffs James Roe I through James Roe XV and Jane Roe I through Jane Roe VIII are children who have assisted their parents or other family members in work at the Plantation. The child plaintiffs range in age from six to sixteen years old. * * *

Plaintiffs cite several * * * federal cases holding or stating that "forced labor" violates the law of nations. Those cases show that some forms of forced labor violate the law of nations, but the facts in those cases are so different from the plaintiffs' allegations in this case as to show that the label "forced labor" adds little to the needed analysis.

In *Iwanowa v. Ford Motor Co.*, 67 F.Supp.2d 424 (D.N.J.1999), the plaintiff alleged that during World War II, she was literally sold from her home in Russia and transported by Nazi troops to Germany to work for the German subsidiary of Ford under inhuman conditions and without compensation. Then 17 years old, the plaintiff was forced to live with 65 other deportees in a wooden hut without heat, running water, or sewage facilities, and they were locked in at night. She was required to perform heavy labor drilling holes in engine blocks. Company officials, she alleged, used rubber truncheons to beat workers who failed to meet their quotas. In the course of dismissing all of her claims on other grounds, the court stated that "the case law and statements of the

---

1. [Editors' note. The ATS, 28 U.S.C. § 1350, provides that "The district courts shall have original jurisdiction of any civil action by an alien for a tort only, committed in violation of the law of nations or a treaty of the United States." See Chapter 2, Module 1, *supra*.]

Nuremberg Tribunals unequivocally establish that forced labor violates customary international law."

In *In re World War II Era Japanese Forced Labor Litigation*, 164 F.Supp.2d 1160, 1179 (N.D.Cal. 2001), the court also dismissed all claims as time-barred but stated it was inclined to agree with the *Iwanowa* conclusion that forced labor violates the law of nations. The district court opinion did not dwell on the historical details, but the Ninth Circuit opinion affirming the dismissal described the treatment of the civilians subjected to forced labor by the Japanese military: "[T]hey were all subjected to serious mistreatment, including starvation, beatings, physical and mental torture, being transported in unventilated cargo holds of ships, and being forced to make long marches under a tropical sun without water. Some survived, while others were ultimately executed, or died from disease or physical abuse." *Deutsch v. Turner Corp.*, 324 F.3d 692, 705 (9th Cir. 2003).

In *Jane Doe I v. Reddy*, 2003 WL 23893010, at *8–9 (N.D.Cal. Aug. 4, 2003), the court denied a motion to dismiss forced labor claims under the ATS. The plaintiffs were young women who alleged they were fraudulently induced to come to the United States with promises of education and employment, but were then forced to work long hours under arduous conditions at illegally low wages, and that they were sexually abused, physically beaten, and threatened. The court found that the allegations stated claims for forced labor, debt bondage, and trafficking actionable under the ATS. In reaching that conclusion, the court relied on the Universal Declaration of Human Rights and the International Covenant on Civil and Political Rights. * * *

Plaintiffs also rely on the Burmese forced labor case against Unocal, *Doe v. Unocal Corp.*, 110 F.Supp.2d 1294 (C.D.Cal.2000) (granting summary judgment for defendants), *aff'd in part, rev'd in part*, 395 F.3d 932, 945 (9th Cir.2002) (stating that forced labor violates law of nations, also relying on Universal Declaration of Human Rights), *vacated on rehearing en banc*, 395 F.3d 978 (9th Cir.2003), *appeal dismissed*, 403 F.3d 708 (9th Cir.2005).[2] The plaintiffs in the Burmese forced labor case testified that the Burmese military used both force and threats of force to conscript them to work on Unocal's pipeline and supporting infrastructure. The district court had no difficulty finding that such evidence showed forced labor in violation of the law of nations, and the Ninth Circuit panel agreed, before the appeal was eventually dismissed.

E. International Norms for Forced Labor

The Complaint in this case uses the same powerful label "forced labor." That conclusory label is not decisive. The court need not take at face value the legal conclusions in a complaint. This case lies at a point on a continuum far from the forced labor of Nazi Germany, Japanese labor camps, or the workers rounded up more recently by the Burmese

---

2. [Editors' note: The *Unocal* litigation settled. See Chapter 2, Module 1, *supra*.]

military. Even if the adult plaintiffs' factual allegations are credited, as the court must, these plaintiffs have not alleged violations of a specific, universal, and obligatory norm of international law.

The adult plaintiffs in this case rely on several international agreements to show that their working conditions violate international law. The first is ILO Forced Labour Convention (No. 29), June 28, 1930 (hereinafter "ILO Convention 29"). ILO Convention 29 entered into force on May 1, 1932. Liberia and Japan have ratified ILO Convention 29, but the United States has not. Article 2 of ILO Convention 29 defines forced labor to mean "all work or service which is exacted from any person under the menace of any penalty and for which the said person has not offered himself voluntarily."[3] In ILO Convention 29, the ratifying members of the ILO agreed to end some forms of forced labor and to impose certain minimum standards for working conditions and wages in cases in which forced labor was permitted. Prohibited forms of forced labor include forced labor "for the benefit of private individuals, companies or associations." Art. 4. This prohibition would apply to forced labor for the benefit of private corporations like the defendants in this case, at least if plaintiffs could allege and prove true forced labor and if ILO Convention 29 were deemed to apply in the United States.

Plaintiffs also rely on the ILO Abolition of Forced Labour Convention (No. 105), (June 26, 1957) (hereinafter "ILO Convention 105"). Both Liberia and the United States have ratified ILO Convention 105; Japan has not. ILO Convention 105 also did not outlaw all forms of forced labor. Instead, in Article 1, each ratifying member of the ILO agreed to suppress any form of forced labor for certain prohibited purposes, including political and ideological education, economic development, as a means of labor discipline, as punishment for participating in strikes, and as a means for racial, social, national, or religious discrimination.

The question here is what is "forced labor," keeping in mind that international norms are actionable under the ATS only if they are as specific, universal, and obligatory as Blackstone's three 18th century archetypes—piracy, wrongs against ambassadors, and violations of safe conducts.[4]

Plaintiffs have submitted a 2005 report by the Director General of the ILO entitled "A global alliance against forced labour" that reports on the ILO Declaration on Fundamental Principles and Rights at Work. The report tackled the problem of definition in terms that help illuminate the parties' arguments in this case:

> Yet the very concept of forced labour, as set out in the ILO
> standards on the subject, is still not well understood. In many

---

3. Article 2 of ILO Convention 29 then excludes from the definition several categories of compulsory service, including military service, normal civil obligations, work as part of a criminal sentence under official supervision, and emergency services.

4. [Editors' note: See the Supreme Court's decision in *Sosa v. Alvarez–Machain*, Chapter Two, Module 1, *supra*.]

quarters the term continues to be associated mainly with the forced labour practices of totalitarian regimes: the flagrant abuses of Hitler's Germany, Stalin's Soviet Union, or Pol Pot's Cambodia. At the other end of the spectrum, such terms as "modern slavery", "slavery-like practices" and "forced labour" can be used rather loosely to refer to poor or insalubrious working conditions, including very low wages. Indeed, some national legislation has identified the late payment of wages, or remuneration below the legal minimum wage, as at least one element of a forced labour situation.

The 2005 ILO report relied on the definition from ILO Convention 29, "all work or service which is exacted from any person under the menace of any penalty and for which the said person has not offered himself voluntarily." The report then explained:

> Forced labour cannot be equated simply with low wages or poor working conditions. Nor does it cover situations of pure economic necessity, as when a worker feels unable to leave a job because of the real or perceived absence of employment alternatives. Forced labour represents a severe violation of human rights and restriction of human freedom, as defined in the ILO Conventions on the subject and in other related international instruments on slavery, practices similar to slavery, debt bondage or serfdom.

Id.

The ILO report includes a list of factors for "identifying forced labour in practice." For identifying the lack of consent prong of the definition from ILO Convention 29, the ILO report lists the following indicators:

— Birth/descent into "slave" or bonded status;

— Physical abduction or kidnapping;

— Sale of person into the ownership of another;

— Physical confinement in the work location-in prison or private detention;

— Psychological compulsion, *i.e.* an order to work, backed up by a credible threat of a penalty for non-compliance;

— Induced indebtedness (by falsification of accounts, inflated prices, reduced value of goods or services produced, excessive interest charges, etc.);

— Deception or false promises about types and terms of work;

— Withholding and non-payment of wages;

— Retention of identity documents or other valuable personal possessions.

Plaintiffs in this case do not allege that any of these indicators of involuntary work apply to the current generation of adult Plantation workers. The plaintiffs allege that their grandparents and great-grandparents were abducted, kidnapped, and/or physically threatened when the Plantation was established in the 1920s, but plaintiffs are not in a position to assert claims for money damages today based on the mistreatment of their ancestors. Plaintiffs allege that they have nothing left after they spend their wages at company stores and other company facilities (such as schools), but they do not allege induced indebtedness. Plaintiffs allege that they are physically isolated at the Plantation, but they do not allege that Firestone keeps them physically confined there. To the extent plaintiffs allege psychological compulsion, they are clearly alleging what the ILO report calls "pure economic necessity, as when a worker feels unable to leave a job because of the real or perceived absence of employment alternatives," which is not forced labor under international law.

As factors indicating the "menace of any penalty" prong of the forced labor definition from ILO Convention 29, the ILO report lists: Actual presence or credible threat of:

— Physical violence against worker or family or close associates;

— Sexual violence;

— (Threat of) supernatural retaliation;

— Imprisonment or other physical confinement;

— Financial penalties;

— Denunciation to authorities (police, immigration, etc.) and deportation;

— Dismissal from current employment;

— Exclusion from future employment;

— Exclusion from community and social life;

— Removal of rights or privileges;

— Deprivation of food, shelter or other necessities;

— Shift to even worse working conditions;

— Loss of social status.

Plaintiffs allege that they have been threatened with dismissal from current employment. Neither the ILO report nor the plaintiffs explain how a threat of dismissal from current employment is a "menace of a penalty" that forces labor in the same job. It would seem that the expressed fear of losing one's current employment is a clear indicator that the current employment is not forced labor. Plaintiffs' allegations about being told they can leave and join the starving unemployed describe the brutal economic consequences of losing the jobs they complain they are being forced to perform, in a poor and dangerous country with 80 to 85 percent unemployment. At least in terms of international law, those consequences are not comparable to the practices alleged in *Deutsch v. Turner Corp.*, where laborers confined by the Japanese military were starved if they refused to work.

In other words, the plaintiffs do not allege any of the listed indicators of forced labor-other than those indicating that the persons might lose the same jobs they say they are being forced to perform.

In a discussion of labor practices in Africa, the 2005 ILO report offered these observations, which are relevant here because of the Supreme Court's requirement in *Sosa* that international norms be specific:

> A review of recent trends in Africa needs to take account of some particularities of this continent. First, where extreme poverty is the norm, many workers receive little or no financial payment, but are remunerated mainly through substandard food and lodging, or other payment in kind; delayed payment and non-payment of wages are widespread; and wages rarely match any legally defined minimum. It can be difficult to determine when the generalized breach of labour contracts, together with poor terms and conditions of work, degenerates into actual forced labour. * * * [T]he results of recent studies commissioned by the ILO indicated that the national researchers, as well as their respondents, had great difficulty in understanding the concept [of forced labour], and in distinguishing forced labour situations from extremely exploitative, but nonetheless "freely chosen", work.

Even though there are some forms of forced labor (Nazi Germany, for example) that clearly violate international law, these comments signal that the circumstances alleged by the adult plaintiffs in this Complaint do not violate specific, universal, and obligatory norms of international law.

Plaintiffs acknowledge that the United States has not ratified ILO Convention 29 with its definition of forced labor: "all work or service which is exacted from any person under the menace of any penalty and for which the said person has not offered himself voluntarily." Plaintiffs argue that the United States later bound itself to ILO Convention 29 through the ILO Declaration on Fundamental Principles and Rights at Work (June 1998). In that document, ILO member nations acknowledged that even if they had not ratified all of the specific ILO conventions, they had an obligation to respect, to promote, and to realize the principles concerning the fundamental rights that are the subjects of the conventions, including "the elimination of all forms of forced or compulsory labour" and "the effective abolition of child labour."

That Declaration, however, clearly did not impose any new binding legal obligations on the ILO member nations. The Legal Advisor of the ILO advised the members that "the Declaration and its follow-up does not and cannot impose on any member State any obligation pursuant to any Convention which that State has not ratified through its own constitutional or other requisite legal procedure." Report of the Committee on the Declaration of Principles, International Labour Conference, 86th Sess., at ¶ 325 (1998). The Legal Advisor added that the

Declaration "is recognized by everyone as not being a binding instrument." A number of member nations expressed similar views in the debate. It would be odd indeed if a United States court were to treat as universal and binding in other nations an international convention that the United States government has declined to ratify itself.

F.   Application of Forced Labor Standards to This Case

The adult plaintiffs in this case allege that they are "kept on the Plantation by poverty, fear, and ignorance of the outside world, living in a cycle of poverty and raising their children to be the next generation of Firestone Plantation Workers." The adult plaintiffs allege that they

> seek the simple justice of the freedom [to] choose whether to work, the opportunity to work free of coercion, the security of a proper employment relationship, the benefit of wages that do not leave them in malnourished poverty, and the meager benefits provided under the law of Liberia, including rest days and holidays. Most of all, they seek the cessation of conditions that formed the premise of the Firestone Plantation, and that have left them in the same situation as their own fathers, watching their own children join them as tappers with no future other than the misery they have experienced their entire lives.

Anyone can appreciate these most basic human aspirations, even from the comfortable distance between Liberia and Indiana. The relief plaintiffs seek, however, and the changes that would resolve their complaints, show that the conditions about which they complain are not "forced labor" as that term is used in any specific, universal, and obligatory norm of international law.

During the hearing on the motion to dismiss, the court asked plaintiffs' counsel what would need to change so that plaintiffs' labor would no longer be forced, in plaintiffs' view. The principal answer was to reduce the daily quota for latex production and thus to raise effective wages on the Firestone Plantation. Plaintiffs' counsel also said that the remedy would include providing information to workers about their rights, upgrading equipment, including safety equipment, and changing the security force. Apart from the comment on the security force, those are all clearly matters of wages and working conditions that fall outside any specific, universal, and obligatory understanding of the prohibition against forced labor.

Plaintiffs have not alleged that Firestone fails to pay them. They do not allege that Firestone is using physical force to keep them on the job. They do not allege that Firestone is using legal constraints to keep them on the job. Plaintiffs do not allege that they could not freely quit their jobs if they felt they had better opportunities elsewhere in Liberia. Plaintiffs do not allege that they have been held against their will, tortured, jailed, or threatened with physical harm. Plaintiffs do not allege any form of ownership or trafficking in employees.

Plaintiffs allege instead that they are being kept on the job by the effects of "poverty, fear, and ignorance." As powerful as these forces may be, they are qualitatively different from armed troops keeping kidnapped and deported workers in labor camps. Higher wages, rest days and holidays, and the security of a proper employment relationship, better housing, education, and medical care are all understandable desires. But better wages and working conditions are not the remedy for the forced labor condemned by international law. The remedy for truly forced labor should be termination of the employment and the freedom to go elsewhere. Yet the adult plaintiffs allege in their Complaint that they are afraid of losing the very jobs they say they are forced to perform. Compl. ¶ 64 (complaining of "the prospect of starvation just one complaint about conditions away"); ¶ 59 (alleging that Firestone improperly treats plaintiffs as "casual labor which can be fired for any reason"); ¶ 49 (alleging that workers are told they will be dismissed even if they wish to take a day off without pay, and that Liberia's extremely high unemployment rate "allows Firestone to say with confidence that anyone who wants to leave can do so and join the ranks of the starving unemployed").

The court does not mean to diminish the plaintiffs' desires or their fears of the future they face if they lose their jobs or leave the Plantation. But the fact that the plaintiffs face worse prospects elsewhere in Liberia cannot be equated with an employer's use of force or coercion to keep workers on the job. Nor can the allegations in the complaint be equated with the use of military power to force labor on behalf of the Nazi regime in Germany as in *Iwanowa*, or the Japanese Empire in World War II as in *Deutsch v. Turner Corp.*, or the Burmese military government in *Doe v. Unocal*.[5]

G. Force and Physical Coercion

Plaintiffs' claims for relief allege that they "were placed in fear for their lives, were deprived of their freedom, and were forced to suffer severe physical and/or mental abuse designed to coerce them into working on the Firestone Plantation...." In the absence of more specific factual allegations, these conclusory allegations add nothing to the complaint. The Complaint does not include any allegations by any of

---

5. After the hearing in this case, plaintiffs submitted an affidavit from Professor Virginia A. Leary, a scholar with expertise and first-hand experience in international labor law. Professor Leary asserts that customary international law includes a prohibition on forced labor. The court accepts that conclusion. The critical question is whether that norm is sufficiently specific, universal and binding as applied to the circumstances alleged in this particular case. On that question, Professor Leary asserts * * * that the ILO has clarified that "conditions similar to the allegations made by Plaintiffs in this case * * * constitute forced labor." She relies in particular on the 2005 ILO report passage stating that penalties showing forced labor can include financial penalties, "including economic penalties linked to debts, the nonpayment of wages, or the loss of wages accompanied by threats of dismissal if workers refuse to do overtime beyond the scope of their contract or national law." The court does not find these allegations in the plaintiffs' Complaint. The alleged financial "penalties" are the consequences of losing jobs that are scarce in a poor and war-torn nation, not a refusal to pay earned wages. Under American employment at will doctrine, an employer may fire an employee who refuses to do overtime work, so long as the employer is willing to pay overtime wages required by law.

the plaintiffs stating that they or other Plantation workers have been threatened with physical force. Plaintiffs say they are afraid, but that does not mean that defendants are responsible for their fear. Plaintiffs live in a nation that has been torn apart by vicious civil war over the past generation. Between approximately 1980 and 2003, Liberia was one of the most dangerous places on earth.

In the hearing on the motion to dismiss, plaintiffs' counsel stated that plaintiffs had alleged, or could allege, physical coercion. By that, plaintiffs mean that they live and work in what counsel calls a "climate of fear." Many circumstances contributed to that climate. The focus here must be on circumstances for which defendants might be deemed legally responsible. The only one identified in the complaint is the allegation that in 1994, Firestone hired General Adolphus Dolo as chief of its security for the Plantation, and that General Dolo had been part of the forces led by Charles Taylor. Plaintiffs also allege that Firestone filled other key positions at the Plantation with "Taylor operatives."

It is not surprising that a multinational corporation needed to make security arrangements during a vicious civil war. Nor is it surprising that some of the persons willing and able to provide those services had some history with one side or the other in the civil war. Yet the Complaint does not allege a single incident of physical force, physical threat, or intimidation by those security forces directed against these plaintiffs or other Plantation workers. In the absence of such allegations or other indications of forced labor, the court cannot conclude that the presence of the current security force could transform the alleged circumstances at the Plantation into a violation of a specific, universal, and obligatory international norm against forced labor. Recall also that plaintiffs alleged repeatedly that they are afraid of losing the same jobs they say they are forced to work. * * *

H.   International Norms for Child Labor

Count Two also seeks relief under the ATS, asserting that work done by the child plaintiffs on the Plantation violates international law. The Complaint alleges that the Firestone supervisors on the Plantation encourage and even require the adult latex tappers to put their children to work to help meet the production quotas. Plaintiffs allege that children apply fertilizers and pesticides by hand, without protective equipment. Plaintiffs also allege that children as young as six years old work at the Firestone Plantation. The defendants deny these allegations, but the court must accept these factual allegations for purposes of the motion to dismiss under Rule 12(b)(6).

Plaintiffs have submitted for the court's consideration a United Nations report, U.N. Missions in Liberia, "Human Rights in Liberia's Rubber Plantations: Tapping into the Future" (May 2006). United Nations human rights investigators reported that management at the Firestone Plantation and other rubber plantation stated that child labor was prohibited. Yet the investigators spoke with a number of children working on the Firestone Plantation and other rubber plantations who were 10 to 14 years old. The UN investigators also reported that Firestone management told them that management and the Liberian government did not effectively monitor compliance with policies against child labor. This report is not admissible evidence at this point, but its filing as part of the opposition to a Rule 12(b)(6) motion enables plaintiffs to show the types of evidence they expect or hope to offer to support their allegations in the Complaint.

The question is whether Count Two alleges violations of sufficiently specific, universal, and obligatory norms of international law. Plaintiffs quote a report from the United States Department of State in 1997 stating that there is an international consensus that freedom from "child labor" is one of several "core labor standards." Yet whatever one's initial reaction is to the broad phrase "child labor," reflection shows that national and international norms accommodate a host of different situations and balance competing values and policies. See ILO Report of the Committee on the Declaration of Principles (Geneva, June 1998). What are the relevant age limits, for which types of work? How does access to education affect the appropriate policies? What does one say to a parent who insists that a child work so that the family has enough to eat? It is not always easy to state just which practices under the label "child labor" are the subjects of an international consensus.

One can see this in the United States' own Fair Labor Standards Act. The FLSA prohibits not "child labor" but "oppressive child labor." 29 U.S.C. § 212(c). The phrase is defined so that the law allows employment of minors aged 14 and 15 in occupations other than manufacturing and mining if the employment is confined to periods that do not interfere with schooling and under conditions that will not interfere with their health and well-being. Focusing on agricultural work, such as that alleged here, in the United States minors who are 16 and 17 years old may work in any farm job at any time. Minors who are 14 or 15 years old may work a wide variety of agricultural jobs so long as the work is done outside of school hours. Children who are 12 or 13 years old also may work on a farm with the consent of their parents, outside school hours. The FLSA even allows the employment of a child under the age of 12 by his parent on a farm owned by the parent, or employment on another small farm, again outside school hours. In the United States, even children as young as 10 or 11 years old may hand-harvest some crops with a special waiver from the Department of Labor. Liberian law on this subject is not as detailed, but defendants have come forward with evidence that Liberian law allows children under the age of 16 to be employed so long as their work does not interfere with their education.

Returning to international standards, ILO Convention 138, the Minimum Age Convention of 1973, also shows the need to draw lines that accommodate a variety of policies. ILO Convention 138 sets forth minimum ages for different types of work in different nations at different stages of economic development. Nevertheless, that convention notes that its age limits apply to certain forms of employment, including "plantations and other agricultural undertakings mainly producing for commercial purposes, but excluding family and small-scale holdings producing for local consumption and not regularly employing hired workers." Art. 5(3). In such settings, ILO Convention 138 prescribes a minimum age of 14 for employees. Yet neither the United States nor Liberia has ratified ILO Convention 138, though Japan has ratified it.

The key source of international child labor standards for present purposes is ILO Convention 182, the 1999 Convention Concerning the Prohibition and Immediate Elimination of the Worst Forms of Child Labor, which the United States, Liberia, and Japan have all ratified. The importance of the line-drawing is evident in that very title. ILO Convention 182 does not seek to outlaw child labor as such, but only its "worst forms." Those worst forms include slavery and forced or compulsory labor, prostitution and production of pornography, and drug trafficking. The worst forms also include "work which, by its nature or the circumstances in which it is carried out, is likely to harm the health, safety or morals of children." Art. 3. ILO Convention 182 leaves to member nations the identification of the jobs likely to harm health, safety, or morals. Art. 4.

Giving plaintiffs the benefit of their factual allegations, the Complaint states that defendants are actively encouraging—even tacitly requiring—the employment of six, seven, and ten year old children. Giving plaintiffs the benefit of their factual allegations, the defendants are actively encouraging that these very young children perform backbreaking work that exposes them to dangerous chemicals and tools. The work, plaintiffs allege, also keeps those children out of the Firestone schools. The court understands that defendants deny the allegations, but defendants have chosen to file a motion that requires the court to accept those allegations as true, at least for now.

The circumstances alleged here include at least some practices that could therefore fall within the "worst forms of child labor" addressed in ILO Convention 182. The conditions of work alleged by plaintiffs (and reported by the UN investigators) are likely to harm the health and safety of at least the very youngest of the child plaintiffs in this case.

As noted above, and as Firestone has argued, national child labor laws and international conventions on child labor are often written to allow even very young children to help out on family farms. Those special accommodations for family farms have no application here. Plaintiffs do not challenge labor practices on subsistence farms. They challenge the practices of a huge multinational corporate family that hires the children's parents and then (allegedly) encourages the parents to require their young children to do much of the work. Plaintiffs allege that defendants have set the daily production quotas so high that use of child labor is both necessary and inevitable, and that defendants take advantage of the parents in this situation.

The court recognizes that international legal standards for child labor do not always establish bright lines, though there are some. That is also the case with forced labor, as discussed above. Just as some practices that might be described by some as "forced labor" might not violate international law, some practices that could be described as "child labor" also do not violate international law. One must look more closely at the particular circumstances, as shown by the pleadings and later by the evidence.

At least some of the practices alleged with regard to the labor of very young children at the Firestone Plantation in Liberia may violate specific, universal, and obligatory standards of international law, such that Count Two should not be dismissed on the pleadings. In light of ILO Convention 182, the court believes that the allegations of child labor in Count Two meet the *Sosa* standard for ATS claims. It would not require great "judicial creativity" to find that even paid labor of very young children in these heavy and hazardous jobs would violate international norms. Those international norms are not inconsistent with Liberian law. Those norms also are stated in an international convention that both the United States and Liberia have ratified. On this record, there is no indication that this lawsuit threatens to cause friction with the foreign policy of the United States. Plaintiffs may face other daunting challenges in pursuing their case, and the court will address those issues as they are raised. The court is also cautious about the practical consequences of recognizing child labor claims under the ATS and international law. In a sufficiently extreme case, however, such as plaintiffs have alleged here, the court believes that *Sosa* leaves the ATS door open. The allegations that defendants are encouraging and even requiring parents to require their children as young as six, seven, or ten years old to do this heavy and hazardous work may state a claim for relief under the ATS. Defendants' motion to dismiss is denied as to Count Two.

———

NOTES AND QUESTIONS ON THE *ILO 1998 DECLARATION* AND THE *BRIDGESTONE CASE*

1. *Justifying the Declaration.* What are the economic and moral assumptions behind what the Declaration calls "the link between social progress and economic growth"?

2. *Understanding the Declaration: core rights.* By its terms, the Declaration covers four "core" or fundamental international labor standards: (i) freedom of association, (ii) forced labor, (iii) discrimination, and (iv) child labor. At a minimum, the Declaration has been interpreted as suggesting that every ILO member is bound by the eight key conven-

tions addressing these topics, whether it has actually ratified those conventions or not. It is not uncommon for treaties to give rise to customary international law or to be taken as evidence of customary international law, but—recalling that not all states are members of the ILO—is that what the Declaration suggests?

3. *Drafting the Declaration.* Why do you suppose the International Labour Conference would have decided to highlight *any* particular types of rights, let alone these four? Why might some human rights lawyers have been concerned about the consequences of the Declaration? Are there particular and widespread violations of labor rights that could not fit into one of these categories? *See* Philip Alston & James Heenan, *Shrinking the International Labor Code: An Unintended Consequence of the 1998 ILO Declaration on Fundamental Principles and Rights at Work?*, 36 N.Y.U. J. INT'L L. & POL. 221 (2004).

4. *Enforcement of the Declaration.* The Annex to the Declaration, defining the "Follow-up," is longer than the operative portion of the Declaration itself. What mode of enforcement does the Declaration contemplate? In what institutional settings, if any, have you seen something similar?

5. *Distinguishing the actionable claims in Bridgestone.* As a matter of law, what distinguishes the claims that survived the motion to dismiss in *Bridgestone*—and those in *Iwanowa*, *Deutsch*, *Reddy*, and *Unocal*—from those that did not survive? How many different types of ILO instruments did the *Bridgestone* court consider in its analysis? Did these instruments provide the binding rule of decision for the case, or did they play some other role in the analysis?

CASE STUDY
CHILD LABOR IN PAKISTAN

HUMAN RIGHTS WATCH, CONTEMPORARY FORMS OF SLAVERY IN PAKISTAN (1995)[1]

Millions of workers in Pakistan are held in contemporary forms of slavery. Throughout the country employers forcibly extract labor from adults and children, restrict their freedom of movement, and deny them the right to negotiate the terms of their employment. Employers coerce such workers into servitude through physical abuse, forced confinement, and debt-bondage. The state offers these workers no effective protection from this exploitation. Although slavery is unconstitutional in Pakistan and violates various national and international laws, state practices

---

1. *Available at* http://www.hrw.org/reports/1995/pakistan.htm.

support its existence. The state rarely prosecutes or punishes employers who hold workers in servitude. Moreover, workers who contest their exploitation are invariably confronted with police harassment, often leading to imprisonment under false charges.

Contemporary forms of slavery, which are set forth and defined in international law, include debt-bondage, serfdom, the trafficking of women, and child servitude. All of these forms of slavery exist in Pakistan. * * *

While some NGOs estimate that the numbers range into the millions; there is little doubt that at least thousands of persons in Pakistan are held in debt-bondage, many of them children. Bondage is particularly common in the areas of agriculture, brick-making, carpet-weaving, mining, and handicraft production. [* * *]

Children either work alongside their bonded families or are sold individually into bondage. Five children interviewed by Human Rights Watch/Asia at brick-kiln sites near Lahore and five working on farms throughout the interior of Sindh were born into bondage. Ten children interviewed at carpet-weaving looms in Mithi were sold into bondage by their parents. According to Baela Jamil of UNICEF in Lahore, "Faced with a lack of schools for their children and employment opportunities for themselves, parents throughout Pakistan have bonded their children to employers." Child bonded laborers interviewed by Human Rights Watch/Asia revealed that they are rarely asked whether they wish to work as bonded laborers. Iqbal Masih, a bonded labor advocate, told Human Rights Watch/Asia, "Children have no choices in the bonded labor system. They are forced to work by their employers and sometimes by their parents. If they do not work, they will be beaten." The widespread existence of bonded child labor in Pakistan is particularly appalling as the government, which is a party to the Convention on the Rights of the Child, has repeatedly pledged to ban all forms of child labor in Pakistan. * * *

Pakistan has ratified a number of international covenants and conventions which proscribe slavery, forced labor, and debt-bondage. The constitution of Pakistan forbids slavery and forced labor; a Supreme Court decision declared that the bonded labor system is unconstitutional; and an act of parliament called for the abolition of bonded labor. But the practice continues. According to the Human Rights Commission of Pakistan:

> Despite the Bonded Labour (Abolition) Act of 1992, forced labour continued to be practiced on a wide scale, mostly in agriculture, brick-kilns, fisheries, construction, carpet industry and over domestic servants. The size of it was estimated in the region of 20 million. * * *

CHILDREN IN BONDAGE

At the ILO congress in June 1994, the government of Pakistan pledged again (as it has done many times in the past) to seek ways to end all forms of child labor in Pakistan. That stance would be consistent with the positions taken by the ILO and various branches of the United Nations. As a party to the Convention on the Rights of the Child, Pakistan must "recognize the right of the child to be protected from economic exploitation." The government of Pakistan acknowledged this responsibility in its National Programme for Action which states:

> Pakistan will pursue the norms of justice and equity which the Convention [on the Rights of the Child] propagates as values integral to human development and to the protection of vulnerable groups like children. National laws will be reformed to accord with the convention and used as a source of regulatory and educational support to adults as well as children. . . . Pakistan is committed to achieving the rights of the child in the development perspective of "the whole child" and of "all children."

Human Rights Watch/Asia's investigation discovered bonded child labor in all the industries that utilize adult bonded labor. As with adult bonded laborers, child bonded laborers are physically, sexually, and psychologically abused. However, the cash advanced in exchange for a child's labor invariably goes to an adult and not to the working child. If a child is paid any wages, it is usually his or her parents who keep the money.

Children are employed because they are easily exploitable and are paid less than adults. In comparison with adult bonded laborers, child bonded laborers, who often work in isolation from their families, work longer hours for significantly less pay. The minimal pay received is usually reduced to make payments on debts and then given to children's parents. In some cases, children's work is not remunerated, as employers claim that the children are apprentices and are being taught a trade.

In agriculture and brick-making, children work alongside their families, whereas in mining and carpet-weaving bonded children are often separated from their families. Children who work away from their families are usually sold into bondage by their parents. In certain cases bonded children are abducted by contractors or employers.

When parents were asked by Human Rights Watch/Asia for the reason they sold their children into bondage, the invariable answer was that, as there were no proper schools in the area, it was better for children to work rather than to remain idle. More schools would clearly be desirable, but the lack of education facilities cannot justify the sale of children into bondage. The government is complicit in such transactions in that it consistently fails to prosecute parents or other individuals involved in holding children in bondage.

BY THE SWEAT AND TOIL OF CHILDREN
U.S. DEPARTMENT OF LABOR BUREAU
OF INTERNATIONAL LABOR AFFAIRS (1998)[2]

In February 1997, the Pakistani soccer ball industry, the ILO, and UNICEF reached an agreement to remove children from the production of soccer balls, provide them with educational opportunities, and create internal and external monitoring systems for the soccer ball industry. Over 50 Pakistani soccer ball manufacturers and U.S. importers have signed the agreement, known as the Partners' Agreement to Eliminate Child Labor in the Soccer Ball Industry in Sialkot, Pakistan. This agreement is closely modeled on the Memorandum of Understanding * * * between Bangladeshi garment manufacturers, the ILO, and UNICEF that aims to phase out employment of children in garment factories, place them in schools, and create a monitoring and verification program to ensure success.

The project has two programs—one focusing on prevention and monitoring and the other on social protection. The prevention and monitoring program aims to help manufacturers and assemblers identify and remove children under 14 years of age from soccer ball stitching centers by formally registering all stitchers, stitching centers, and stitching contractors. It also aims to shift production from homes to stitching centers, where child labor violations can be monitored more systematically and effectively. Under the Agreement, manufacturers create their own internal registration and monitoring system that is supplemented by an independent monitoring group, charged with monitoring violations of the partnership agreement.

The social protection program aims to rehabilitate child laborers, particularly those affected by the prevention and monitoring program, by providing more relevant and hence more valuable education, as well as in-kind assistance. As of October 1998, about 5,400 children and their families were benefitting from the social protection program through 154 village education and action (VEA) centers. The VEA centers are charged with providing nonformal education to children removed from work in the soccer industry. They facilitate the enrollment of younger siblings in primary education, set up parent "action committees" and other in-kind support, conduct awareness-raising campaigns in communities, and, whenever possible, mainstream children under 12 years old into the formal school system.

Prior to joining the ILO/IPEC Social Protection Program, about half of the children served had been stitching soccer balls full-time. As indicated by ILO data collected for the period from October 1997 to

---

2. *Available at* htto://www.dol.gov/ILAB/media/reports/iclp/sweat5/chap5.htm.

October 1998, an average of 50 percent of the participating manufacturers' production capacity has been shifted to monitored stitching centers. In addition, 80 small village-based stitching centers for women are now in operation.

STATEMENT OF THE GOVERNMENT OF PAKISTAN UNITED NATIONS WORKING GROUP ON THE SALE OF CHILDREN, CHILD PROSTITUTION AND CHILD PORNOGRAPHY (April 2000)[3]

SYED SHARIFUDDIN PIRZADA (Pakistan) said that despite the best intentions of the world community for the improvement of the situation of children, they continue to suffer in all parts of the world. Millions were denied their childhood, had to forego even basic education, were forced to work, become combatants and para-combatants in armed conflicts and were trafficked and sexually exploited. Poverty was the leading cause of denial of the rights of the child. In 1997 Pakistan embarked on a landmark project to combat child labor in the soccer ball industry in the city of Sialkot. Three years on, child labor in Silkot's soccer ball industry was mostly history. However, there was a negative side to the picture—Pakistan's share of the American soccer-ball market dropped from 65 to 45 per cent between 1996 and 1998 since buyers who wanted certification of the balls' adult-only workmanship were unwilling to pay for it.

Nevertheless, the Government was working to replicate the soccer ball initiative in other industries. It was also examining the possibility of ratifying International Labor Organization Convention 182 on the Elimination of the Worst Forms of Child Labor. A national Plan of Action was in its final stages of preparation. The components of the plan consisted of raising awareness of the problem of child labor, making child labor a cognizable offence, documenting child abuses and exploitation of child labor, making primary education compulsory, providing economic incentives to families to send children to school, and extending the social security network.

---

3. The government's full statement is *available at* www.unhchr.ch/huricane/huricane.nsf/0/BFEF23FCDB09A5FF802568BF002DB564?opendocument.

HUMAN RIGHTS WATCH COUNTRY REPORT, 2001 HUMAN RIGHTS DEVELOPMENTS[4]

In a welcomed move affecting labor rights, Pakistan, on August 15, ratified International Labor Organization (ILO) Convention No. 182, which called for immediate and effective measures to secure prohibition of the worst forms of child labor, as well as ILO Convention No. 100, concerning equal remuneration for men and women.

––––––––

FINDINGS ON THE WORST FORMS OF CHILD LABOR

U.S. Department of Labor (2006)

Children are employed in several hazardous activities across the country, including ragpicking; leather tanning; mining; deep-sea fishing; seafood processing; brick-making; and manufacturing of surgical instruments and glass bangles. Children working in carpet-weaving suffer injuries from sharp tools, eye disease and eye strain, respiratory disease due to wool dust, and skeletal deformation and pain due to cramped working conditions. Many working children are vulnerable to physical and sexual abuse, particularly those working far from their families such as street children, child miners, and child domestics working in private homes.

There are reports of children being kidnapped, maimed, and forced to work as beggars. Bonded child labor reportedly exists in Pakistan in the brick, carpet, textile, and rice-milling industries, as well as in agricultural activities; in some cases, children are sold into bondage by their parents. Children working in mining, agriculture and domestic service are often from families who are bonded or indebted to their employers. Commercial sexual exploitation of children continues to be a problem, with some families selling their daughters into prostitution. Recent reports have also highlighted the increasing numbers of boys as young as 9 years of age exploited as prostitutes. Young boys are also reportedly at high risk of being trafficked within the country. Pakistani girls are trafficked into commercial sexual exploitation in Persian Gulf countries, and despite significant government efforts to stop the practice, Pakistani boys continue to be trafficked to the United Arab Emirates and Qatar to work as camel jockeys. * * *

Current Government Policies and Programs to Eliminate
the Worst Forms of Child Labor

In May 2006, the Government of Pakistan adopted a National Action Plan for Children that aims to harmonize federal and state child labor programs and work toward the progressive elimination of child labor. Since 2000, the national and provincial-level governments have been implementing a National Policy and Action Plan to Combat Child

––––––––

4. *Available at* http://www.hrw.org/wnzkz/asiaa.html.

Labor (NPPA) that calls for immediate eradication of the worst forms of child labor; progressive elimination of child labor from all sectors; educational alternatives to keep children out of work; and rehabilitation of children withdrawn from work. * * *

With support from the ILO, the National Commission on Abolition of Bonded Labor and Rehabilitation of Freed Bonded Laborers oversees the implementation of the National Policy and Plan of Action for the Abolition of Bonded Labor. As part of implementation, the government provided an initial allocation of 100 million rupees (approximately USD 1.7 million) to educate working children and freed bonded laborers.

NOTES AND QUESTIONS ON CHILD LABOR IN PAKISTAN

1. *Efforts to curb child labor in Pakistan.* The materials above identify two separate but overlapping abusive labor practices in Pakistan: child labor in the soccer ball industry and bonded child labor. To address the former, an innovative program was developed in the city of Silkot, which at the time produced the majority of the world's premium quality, hand-stitched soccer balls. The success of the Silkot program was due largely to its engagement of all relevant stakeholders—major brands, suppliers, workers, and the ILO. Dramatic media attention to the problem in the United States and Europe forced major brands as well as industry and sporting associations such as FIFA to address a problem that was affecting their bottom line.

In this program, the ILO was a key player. Institutionally, it had the technical expertise to assist brands in developing standards and new buying practices that would be effective within the specific Pakistani national and cultural context. The Silkot program is a good example of the growing role the ILO has taken on since its creation, that is, as an implementer and facilitator of programmatic work that has real impact on the lives of workers. In many respects, the locus of the ILO's impact has shifted from its headquarters in Geneva into the workplace itself. For a detailed description and analysis of the Silkot program, *see* ELLIOT SCHRAGE, PROMOTING INTERNATIONAL WORKER RIGHTS THROUGH PRIVATE VOLUNTARY INITIATIVES: PUBLIC POLICY OR PUBLIC RELATIONS AT 13–60 (2004).

In contrast, there have been few similarly successful initiatives in the area of child bonded labor, notwithstanding the myriad reports published about the extent of the problem. Part of the difficulty is the inability to identify a group of stakeholders with an economic interest in ending the practice. In the soccer ball example, large multinational brands stood to lose money because of the bad publicity they were receiving for selling soccer balls stitched by children. No equally identifiable "brand" suffers due to bonded labor. Here, the tripartite character of the ILO has little relevance. It may be true that governments and labor wish to end the practice, but there is no group of employers that can be identified to engage on the issue. Moreover, those employers who might be identified have no reason to stop the practice: governments do not have the capacity to enforce the law, and there is no consumer base that would punish them for holding children in bonded labor. As a result, civil society groups, working with the ILO and well-meaning government officials, must settle for small-scale interventions to rescue children, provide access to education, and make alternative lifestyles available to the children and their families.

2. *Consequences, foreseen and unforeseen.* The statement of the representative of Pakistan reproduced above reflects an unfortunate reality. Children are used to make soccer balls because they can be paid less. Using adults costs more money, as do programs to provide education and income for families whose children are not working. Consumers will not pay more for the soccer balls. Production goes elsewhere, and the community suffers further poverty. So, while one problem may be mitigated, other problems may be exacerbated. In the Silkot example, there was evidence that the children working in the soccer ball industry simply moved into other jobs, many of which were more dangerous than stitching balls. How does one avoid these consequences? In developing a program to eliminate child labor in a particular industry or country, who would you look to for advice in identifying and managing consequences?

Practicum

Recent years have seen increasing reports of abuse of domestic workers by diplomats. Amy Tai, *Unlocking the Doors to Justice: Protecting the Rights and Remedies of Domestic Workers in the Face of Diplomatic Immunity*, 16 AM. U.J. GENDER SOC. POL'Y & L. 175 (2007). Typically, these domestic workers accompany diplomats on overseas assignments and are granted permission through special visas for domestic helpers. Often, they are from poor countries and are eager to maintain their employment status for the opportunity to work in a country like the United States, even for a limited time. As a result, they have very little recourse if their employer—the diplomat—imposes intolerable or abusive conditions of work. Diplomats have been known to confiscate the passports of domestic employees, confine them to the home, and abuse them mentally and physically, including sexual abuse.

The potential for abuse is compounded by the fact that civil and criminal remedies are virtually nonexistent: under Article 38 of the Vienna Convention on Diplomatic Relations, diplomats are accorded broad immunity while serving in an overseas post:

1. A diplomatic agent shall enjoy immunity from the criminal jurisdiction of the receiving State. He shall also enjoy immunity from its civil and administrative jurisdiction, except in the case of:

(a) a real action relating to private immovable property situated in the territory of the receiving State, unless he holds it on behalf of the sending State for the purposes of the mission;

(b) an action relating to succession in which the diplomatic agent is involved as executor, administrator, heir or legatee as a private person and not on behalf of the sending State;

(c) an action relating to any professional or commercial activity exercised by the diplomatic agent in the receiving State outside his official functions.

Under these provisions, host governments are unable to prosecute a diplomat for abusive labor practices unless his or her home government waives immunity, and the diplomats' civil immunity is even broader. When reports of abuse become public, home governments sometimes recall the diplomat in order to avoid the bad publicity or the pressure to waive immunity. Sometimes the diplomat will be declared *persona non grata* by the host state, in which case the diplomat must leave, but there are no accountability procedures within the host state. In most situations, therefore, the diplomat suffers virtually no consequences for his actions.

As a legal officer at the International Labour Office in Geneva, you have been asked to develop a strategy for addressing this problem. The strategy should identify the range of possible tools at the ILO's disposal, including Conventions, Recommendations, and Codes of Practice. Evaluate the relative strengths and weaknesses of each format. You should also consider other initiatives that take advantage of the ILO's field presences and local expertise, focusing perhaps on the countries that provide the bulk of foreign domestic workers (or the bulk of abusive diplomats). All approaches—public and confidential—should be considered, including media campaigns, the development of normative instruments, international conferences, and diplomatic pressure.

————

CHAPTER 5

MODULE 11

NON-GOVERNMENTAL ORGANIZATIONS

■ ■ ■

Orientation

Non-governmental human rights organizations can be traced at least as far back as the eighteenth century, when activists organized to lobby for the abolition of the slave trade. *See* ADAM HOCHSCHILD, BURY THE CHAINS: PROPHETS AND REBELS IN A FIGHT TO FREE AN EMPIRE'S SLAVES (2005). Grassroots activism of the nineteenth and early twentieth centuries may be seen as precursors of the extraordinary array of non-governmental organizations on the international human rights scene today. Some of these organizations have had a substantial and lasting impact. For example, humanitarian law derives from the work of Henri Dunant and his colleagues at what became the International Committee of the Red Cross. CAROLINE MOORHEAD, DUNANT'S DREAM: WAR, SWITZERLAND AND THE HISTORY OF THE RED CROSS (1999).

Non-governmental organizations ("NGOs") have always played a vital role in the establishment and functioning of international human rights systems. The fact that the UN Charter contains human rights provisions is largely attributable to NGO pressure at the San Francisco conference. WILLIAM KOREY, NGOS AND THE UNIVERSAL DECLARATION OF HUMAN RIGHTS, 38 (1998). Indeed, the Charter expressly provides for the integration of NGOs into the work of the organization. UN Charter, art. 71. From this toehold, over the last sixty years, NGOs have succeeded in pushing the UN to become a force for human rights protection.

At the time the Universal Declaration of Human Rights ("UDHR") was promulgated in 1948, 41 NGOs held consultative status with the UN Economic and Social Council. Today, there are over 3,000 with that status and thousands of additional organizations doing similar work.[1] Large, influential and internationally-known human rights organizations, such as Amnesty International ("AI") and Human Rights Watch ("HRW"), sit beside hundreds of smaller, often single-issue, NGOs in UN forums, where they can exert considerable influence on the course of proceedings. In addition, organizations that focus on national human rights monitoring have proliferated to the point that today, "independent human rights groups exist in most countries in the world." Michael

---

[1]. United Nations Economic and Social Council, *NGO Related Frequently Asked Questions*, http://www.un.org/esa/coordination/ngo/faq.htm (last visited May 22, 2008).

H. Posner & Candy Whittome, *The Status of Human Rights NGOs*, 25 COLUM. HUM. RTS. L. REV. 269, 270 (1994). Together, these organizations can be said to constitute a "human rights movement," though this movement is not always easy to define.

In this module, we explore the issues relevant to the roles and responsibilities of human rights NGOs. We use large NGOs, especially AI, as the main example in the module, but this does not mean the work of larger NGOs is more important than the work of smaller NGOs, which often work under extraordinarily difficult circumstances in every corner of the world.

We start in Section A with materials about how the UN defines NGOs. Although defining what constitutes an NGO can lead to considerable debate, we are equally interested in what NGOs actually do, as addressed in Section B. In Section C, we consider the way NGOs define their "mandates," the issues they work on, and the positions they take. In particular, we examine the debate about whether and to what extent large western NGOs like AI and HRW should engage with economic, social, and cultural rights. In Section D we look at the threats to "human rights defenders" and the international framework for their protection. Finally, in section E we consider new demands for the accountability of NGOs.

A. WHAT IS AN NGO?

1. INTRODUCTION

With the proliferation and diversity of NGOs, the term "NGO" has become increasingly difficult to define. One common understanding of an NGO is an organization that is not a part of a government and that has non-commercial social, cultural, legal, or environmental goals.

The evolution of the human rights NGO progressed rapidly after the creation of the UN.[2] AI provides a good example of the trajectory of this development. AI was founded by Peter Beneson, a British barrister, who was provoked to act by a news report that two Portuguese students had been sentenced to seven years in jail for raising their glasses in a toast to freedom. Mr. Benenson began a letter writing campaign on the students' behalf, which he called "appeal for amnesty, 1961." Though AI originally focused on release of "prisoners of conscience," it has become an organization working on a wide range of human rights issues, including economic, social, and cultural rights. In 1977, AI's efforts were recognized by the world community when it was awarded the Nobel Peace Prize. Today, Amnesty International has nearly two million members in more than 150 countries throughout the world.

---

2. The International Commission of Jurists ("ICJ") was created in 1952 and might be said to be the first major international human rights NGO. HOWARD B. TOLLEY, JR., THE INTERNATIONAL COMMISSION OF JURISTS: GLOBAL ADVOCATES FOR HUMAN RIGHTS (1994).

Since the 1970s, several internationally-focused NGOs such as Human Rights Watch, Human Rights First, and Global Rights based in the United States, and Article 19 and Interights, based in the United Kingdom, have added their voices to the debate. Together with AI, these and other NGOs, such as the International Commission of Jurists, the Minority Rights Group, Index on Censorship, Physicians for Human Rights, and the International Federation for Human Rights (FIDH), have helped to stimulate international attention to human rights violations around the world. They have also helped to shape and effectuate the work of the United Nations and other intergovernmental bodies. By providing accurate, up-to-date information about human rights abuses, and by being aggressive, creative, and ever-present advocates, they have helped to transform the debate from a restrained diplomatic discourse among governments to a more urgent and real confrontation of ongoing and serious human rights crises.

Notes and Questions on "What is an NGO?"

1. *A human rights movement?* The rise of human rights NGOs has often been described as a significant part of the human rights movement. Is there a "human rights movement?" Compare the following positions:

> A related point, and one which I fear many human rights activists would argue with, is my contention that there really is no such thing as a "human rights movement" or a, "human rights community." What we are often talking about is loose connections among very disparate groups of people with very disparate agendas. Some human rights activists focus on asylum and refugee concerns. Some seek abolition of the death penalty. Others focus primarily on women's experiences. Still others focus on prison conditions. The link that ties these groups and interests together might be primarily, but not exclusively, the use of the instruments of international human rights law to justify concerns and eradicate abusive conditions.

Symposium, Cynthia Rothschild, *Shifting Grounds for Asylum: Female Genital Surgery and Sexual Orientation*, 29 Colum. Hum. Rts. L. Rev. 467, 524–25 (1998).

> This Essay assumes the existence of a "human rights movement" with shared and identifiable goals and strategies. To be sure, the movement is not monolithic. However, a core of human rights NGOs and activists/lawyers have committed themselves to ensuring the fulfillment and enforcement of the corpus of human rights norms set forth in the Universal Declaration of Human Rights and subsequent multilateral instruments and conventions.

Beth van Schaack, *With All Deliberate Speed: Civil Human Rights Litigation as a Tool for Social Change*, 57 VAND. L. REV. 2305, 2307 n.11 (2004).

2.   UN ACCREDITATION OF NGOs

Article 71 of the UN Charter provides:

> The Economic and Social Council may make suitable arrangements for consultation with non-governmental organizations which are concerned with matters within its competence. Such arrangements may be made with international organizations and, where appropriate, with national organizations after consultation with the Member of the United Nations concerned.

While Article 71 of the UN Charter created formal relations between NGOs and the Economic and Social Council ("ECOSOC"), ECOSOC Resolution 1296 actually sets forth the process for NGOs to obtain formal consultative status. In order to obtain that status, NGOs must be concerned with matters that fall within ECOSOC's competence and must establish that their aims and purposes conform to the UN Charter. Moreover, because the UN Charter prohibits intervention in the domestic jurisdiction of a state, NGOs wishing to gain consultative status cannot have a primarily domestic focus. Organizations with a primarily domestic focus, such as the American Civil Liberties Union, have been denied consultative status on this basis. Finally, NGOs must be independent from any government. *See* Antti Pentikäinen, Finnish UN Association, *Creating Global Governance, The Role of Non–Governmental Organizations in the United Nations* (2000) *available at* http://www.ykliitto.fi/uutta/gover.pdf. Over the years, the accreditation process became enmeshed in Cold War politics with one side or the other using accreditation for political purposes to exclude some organizations.

NGO presence and participation is generally considered beneficial to the UN: NGOs are able to facilitate negotiations among governments, help secure the ratification of human rights treaties, present the interests of persons not well represented at the UN, and monitor governmental compliance with international agreements. In spite of these benefits, however, NGO participation in the UN also raises potential problems. For example, the NGO population is rapidly increasing, making participation of all NGOs impractical. Additionally, because many NGOs are from industrialized countries, they may emphasize viewpoints that do not accurately reflect the views of NGOs in developing countries. *See* Steve Charnovitz, *Two Centuries of Participation: NGOs and International Governance*, 18 MICH. J. INT'L L. 183, 274–277 (1997).

Notes and Questions on UN Accreditation of NGOs

1. *Participatory challenges under resolution 1296.* Some commentators have observed that the Resolution 1296 criteria tend to exclude grass-roots organizations and national organizations. As a consequence, the criteria draw important divisions between NGOs with consultative status and those without, since those NGOs with consultative status oppose efforts to dilute their own participatory rights. Wendy Schoener, *Non-Governmental Organizations and Global Activism: Legal and Informal Approaches*, 4 Ind. J. of Global Legal Stud. 537, 547–48 (1997). Practically speaking, increasing NGO participation may simply prove to be too burdensome for the UN system. If all NGOs were granted consultative status, would the system collapse? "There is simply not enough room for such large numbers of NGOs to attend United Nations meetings; there would not be time for each NGO to make an oral statement on every agenda item; there are not the resources within the United Nations NGO Liaison Office to deal with these vastly-expanded numbers * * *. [T]his situation poses a challenge for NGOs and governments alike." Michael H. Posner & Candy Whittome, *The Status of Human Rights NGOs*, 25 Colum. Hum. Rts. L. Rev. 269, 287 (1994). Given these competing concerns, how should the UN balance the need for greater access by NGOs with the challenges of expanding participatory rights? Did Resolution 1996/31, in the Documents Supplement, address these issues adequately?

2. *Access.* NGOs that are not eligible for consultative status are still able to submit information or reports to special rapporteurs and treaty-monitoring bodies. These NGOs are often assisted by NGOs with accreditation in making presentations to UN bodies. Does this provide NGOs that are not eligible for consultative status with sufficient access to the UN?

3. *North-South divide.* Some critics of ECOSOC accreditation have argued that the ECOSOC Committee on NGOs not only fails to employ consistent, objective standards for granting consultative status but that it has also contributed to the disparities between northern and southern NGO access. "A complication within the NGO community is that northern NGOs continue to dominate agenda setting at the United Nations with southern NGOs under represented. * * * This arouses concerns that NGO influences and contributions to UN work may be skewed in one direction." The Stanley Foundation, *The United Nations and Civil Society: The Role of NGOs: Report of the Thirtieth United Nations Issues Conference* (1999) *available at* http://www.globalpolicy.org/ngos/ngo-un/gen/2000/1128.htm.

4. *International requirement.* National NGOs face even greater challenges.

An international NGO must be "of representative character and of recognized international standing; it shall represent a substantial proportion, and express the views of major sections of the popula-

> tion or of the organized persons within the particular field of competence, covering, where possible, a substantial number of countries in different regions of the world." A national NGO has the additional hurdle of being admitted only "after consultations with the Member State" where it is based.

Schoener, *supra*, at 542. What problems are apparent with this criterion? Many NGOs operate domestically and are openly critical of their government's human rights policies. How likely is it that NGOs like these will be granted consultative status?

5. *Devising a system.* If you could create your own accreditation system for NGOs, what system would you create? Would you include national NGOs which do not have an international agenda? How would you ensure that poorly funded NGOs from the South had an equal voice in the UN's activities? What about NGOs which operate in languages other than the UN's official languages?

B. WHAT NGOs DO

NGOs have been instrumental in strengthening regional enforcement of human rights protections, investigating and reporting human rights situations world-wide, engaging in the "mobilization of shame," monitoring states' compliance with international treaty obligations, contributing to standard-setting, and assisting in litigation to hold those responsible for human rights violations accountable.

1. NGOs, THE UN, AND REGIONAL ENFORCEMENT

Many of the human rights enforcement mechanisms developed in the UN system depend on NGO participation. For example, one of the first mechanisms created to allow UN consideration of "gross violations of human rights," ECOSOC Resolution 1503, specifically allowed NGOs to submit complaints.[3] In fact, many of the complaints submitted, especially in the early years, were submitted by NGOs.[4]

---

3. The "1503 procedure" permits NGOs to submit a complaint to the Commission concerning "situations which appear to reveal a consistent pattern of gross and reliably attested violations of human rights." ECOSOC Res. 1503, ¶ 6(b)(I), UN Doc. E/4832/Add.1 (1970). Resolution 1503 is included in the document supplement. For a more comprehensive account of international human rights mechanisms, prepared for the benefit of NGOs and human rights advocates, *see* Guide to International Human Rights Practice, (Hurst Hannum ed., Transnat'l Publishers, 4th ed. 2004). See Chapter 3, *supra*, for a discussion of the 1503 procedure and the complaint mechanism adopted by the new Human Rights Council.

4. On March 15, 2006, the UN Human Rights Council was established pursuant to General Assembly Resolution 60/251 to replace the body's Human Rights Commission. The resolution calls for close cooperation between the Council and civil society. GA Res. 60/251, ¶ 5(h), UN Doc. A/RES/60/251 (2006). While the ECOSOC procedures granting NGOs access remain largely unchanged, it is too early to tell the extent to which the Council's new mechanisms, such as the Universal Periodic Review, may alter the role of NGOs in the UN human rights process. *See* Judith Sunderland, *Will the UNHRC Fulfill its Promise?* Human Rights Watch, *April 10, 2008*, http://hrw.org/english/docs/2008/04/10/uk18626.htm.*160; NGOs Identify Essential Elements of a U.N. Human Rights Council*, Jan. 19, 2006, http://hrw.org/english/docs/2006/01/10/global12401.htm.

There are many other examples of international and regional mechanisms under which NGOs are permitted to bring complaints or file reports.

- *UNESCO "1978 Procedure"*: permits anyone with reliable knowledge about a violation to submit either individualized cases or general questions of human rights violations to UNESCO. UNESCO 104 EX/Decision 3.3 (1978).

- *Inter-American Commission of Human Rights:* Any person, group of persons, or NGO legally recognized in one or more of the member states of the OAS may submit a petition to the Inter–American Commission on Human Rights. Statute of the Inter–American Commission on Human Rights, O.A.S. Res. 447, arts. 19, 20, 9th Sess., OAS/Ser.L/V/I.4, rev. 8 (1979).

- *African Charter on Human and Peoples' Rights*: While no longer specifically provided for within the Charter, the African Commission has regularly considered communications filed by NGOs.[5]

- *European Court of Human Rights*: Article 34 of the European Convention permits the Court to "receive applications from any person, nongovernmental organization, or group of individuals, claiming to be the victim of a violation by one of the High Contracting Parties of the rights set forth in the Convention or the protocols thereto." European Convention for the Protection of Human Rights and Fundamental Freedoms, Nov. 4, 1950, art. 34, 213 U.N.T.S. 221.

- *International Labor Organization*: Article 24 of the ILO Constitution provides that a representation may be submitted by "an industrial association of employees or of workers." The determination of what constitutes an industrial organization is made by the ILO.

---

2. REPORTING

Most human rights NGOs focus at least part of their efforts on gathering, verifying, and disseminating information about the human rights practices of governments and, increasingly, non-state actors (*e.g.* corporations). NGOs engaged in fact-finding collect evidence of human rights abuses from a variety of sources including witness interviews, documentary evidence, and first-hand observations of general human rights conditions. The fact-finding stage is crucial, both to obtain accurate information and to ensure that witnesses remain safe and are not subject to re-traumatization by the questioning. To this end, fact-finders may withhold identifying information or use pseudonyms to protect witnesses. To avoid further traumatizing vulnerable witnesses, fact-

---

5. *See, e.g., Egyptian Organization for Human Rights vs. Egypt,* Comm. No. 201/97, African Comm'n Hum. & Peoples' Rights (2000); *Legal Res. Found. v. Gambia,* Comm. No. 219/98, African Comm'n Hum. & Peoples' Rights (2001); *see also* Chidi Anselm Odinkalu & Camilla Christensen, *The African Commission on Human Rights and Peoples' Rights: The Development of its Non–State Communications Procedures,* 20 HUM. RTS. Q. 235 (1998).

finders will refrain from questioning victims of torture or sexual-assault, unless the person who is being interviewed has the supportive presence of a trusted individual. *See* David Weissbrodt & James McCarthy, *Fact-Finding by International Human Rights Organizations*, 22 VA. J. INT'L L. 1 (1982); Diane Orentlicher, *Bearing Witness: The Art and Science of Human Rights Fact–Finding*, 3 HARV. HUM. RTS. J. 83 (1990).

In addition, it is essential that the fact-finding result in accurate, credible reports. Reputable NGOs make every attempt to corroborate evidence and constantly test witnesses' statements for reliability. These findings are then compiled into a report, which generally includes conclusions, recommendations, and the government's response if one has been provided. Many human rights NGOs have become adept at condensing this information into effective, well-documented reports that support their human rights campaigning. By highlighting and reporting on human rights violations, NGOs draw attention to the regimes and systems that perpetrate them.

NOTES AND QUESTIONS ON REPORTING

1. *Contextual reporting*. If human rights reports are to appear credible and if they are to resonate with the targeted government, they must lay out sufficient context for the violations. For example, NGO reporting cannot focus on the violations committed by a government without including sufficient information about an armed insurgency or violations committed by armed rebels. "By acknowledging that the government has committed human rights violations as a response to circumstances that help explain its behavior, the NGO has anticipated the next stage in the dialogue—the government's response—and answered it." Diane Orentlicher, *Bearing Witness: The Art and Science of Human Rights Fact–Finding*, 3 HARV. HUM. RTS. J. 83, 101 (1990). What other examples of contextual factors should be included to contribute to a credible and persuasive human rights report?

---

3. "THE MOBILIZATION OF SHAME"

Human rights organizations have long used the tactic of shaming to embarrass governments into ending human rights abuses in their jurisdiction. To be effective, human rights organizations must move quickly to channel information to media outlets, distribute action alerts to organization members, and lobby politicians to shine a spotlight on human rights violators. This unwanted attention creates pressure on the offending regime and may force an end to the offending policies. Success is never guaranteed, but one should never underestimate the power of exposing the hypocrisy of governments which have agreed to abide by international human rights obligations; nevertheless, some have questioned whether the mobilization of shame is still an effective technique for human rights organizations to use in this globalized era where economic considerations can trump human rights concerns. Consider the following critique by David Rieff:

David Rieff, *The Precarious Triumph of Human Rights*, N.Y. TIMES MAG., Aug. 8, 1999, at 37

The age of human rights is upon us. * * * Yet paradoxically, at the very moment when its ideas have become mainstream, the human rights movement seems adrift. The movement's signature strategies—releasing shocking reports detailing abuses, exploiting the media to shame Western leaders into action—no longer have the impact they once did. * * *

Improbably, the Reagan Administration played the central role in legitimizing the American human rights movement. Aryeh Neier, the dean of American human rights activists, who, after directing Human Rights Watch, is now president of the Open Society Institute, has said that Reagan-era officials like Jeanne Kirkpatrick and Elliott Abrams were "our greatest allies." He is not being ironic. "They helped us," Neier explained, "because they presented the confrontation between the U.S. and the Soviet Union as one between a totalitarian system and one based on civil liberties. But then they had to pretend that everyone on our side of the cold war was not violating human rights. That allowed Human Rights Watch to point out the gap between pretense and practice. It created enormous embarrassment." By documenting the real practices of United States client states, he said, "you could demonstrate the ways in which they didn't measure up."

The group's technique of highlighting Washington's hypocrisy was called "shaming" And it got results. When Human Rights Watch exposed the crimes that the U.S.-supported regime in El Salvador was committing on a routine basis, it actually forced the Reagan Administration to try to put a stop to the worst abuses. This was a direct result of pressure and lobbying by human rights groups on Capitol Hill. * * * Reaganites kept falling into the same trap. "Abrams and his colleagues made it a quarrel over the facts," Neier said. "The style of Human Rights Watch evolved directly out of this. We started producing thick, amply documented reports. That was different from what Amnesty International had done. Our emphasis was on providing the evidentiary bases for the claims we were making." * * *

The reality, though, has been more complicated. Despite the triumph of Kosovo, the human rights movement has during the 1990's suffered an equally important defeat: the Clinton Administration's policy toward China. It was Clinton, after all, who severed the link between progress on human rights and most-favored-nation trading status. * * *

The movement's loss over China does not invalidate its intellectual or moral assumptions. But it does suggest that the era when it was able to emerge victorious simply by exposing hypocrisy—as it did with El Salvador—is ending. Neier put the matter starkly: "We have more difficulty getting leverage with Clinton than we did with Reagan. Unlike in those years, today there are relatively few disputes over the facts." Having openly placed economics before human rights, the Clinton Administration [couldn't] be swayed from its * * * current policies by yet another thick report documenting repression in Tibet. Clearly, alternative tactics need to be used. * * *

On the practical level, the human rights movement needs to confront Holly Burkhalter's insight that "stigma is not getting the job done." Burkhalter, the advocacy director for Physicians for Human Rights, laments: "The only thing we really know how to do well is expose. We do that better than ever, and we're making galloping leaps in establishing norms. But you look at the great bloodletting of the recent past and you ask yourself, "are we seeing a reduction in violence against the innocent?" When Human Rights Watch boasts that its goal is to "challenge Governments and those who hold power to end abusive practices and respect international human rights law," it is easy to sympathize and to respect the principles being upheld. But it is also hard to ignore the fact that the abusers the human rights movement are now seeking to challenge are not politically vulnerable American officials, but warlords in southern Sudan or Serb paramilitaries. Do these people care about international human rights norms? Not likely.

Notes and Questions on the "Mobilization of Shame"

1. *Candidates for the "mobilization of shame."* What current human rights situations are good candidates for the mobilization of shame? Which factors should NGOs consider before devising a "mobilization of shame" campaign? What factors would you consider in evaluating the possible success of such a campaign?

2. *Remaining effective.* Do you agree with Rieff that shaming governments has lost its effectiveness? If "mobilization of shame" is losing its effectiveness, what is the alternative? Is Rieff underestimating the long-term impact of the work of the human rights movement? Has he overgeneralized from one example?

---

4. ENSURING COMPLIANCE

NGOs have also developed important techniques to help ensure state compliance with international treaties through the use of "shadow" reports. Under several human rights treaties, states are obligated to submit compliance reports detailing the mechanisms they have implemented and the actions they have undertaken to comply with their treaty obligations. NGOs are permitted to file shadow reports with these committees, which are intended to correct or supplement the state's official report.[6] Shadow reports can mirror official state reports using

---

6. *See* Amnesty Int'l, *Using the international human rights system to combat racial discrimination: A Handbook*, AI Index IOR 80/001/2001, May 1, 2001; Shadowing the States: Guidelines for Preparing

the same organizational structure, pointing out where the state has provided false information along the way. Other times, the shadow reports provide information to the committee that was omitted by the official report.[7] Committees understand that these shadow reports often present a more realistic picture of the human rights situation on the ground, and have come to rely on the information provided in them. The shadow reports also provide committee members the information they need to direct probing questions to governments during the reporting process. Additionally, the reports generate public debate and discussion in public forums by spotlighting a particular state's shortcomings.

Shadow reporting occurs domestically as well. From 1978 through 1996, Human Rights First ("HRF"),[8] produced an annual critique of the State Department's Country Reports on Human Rights Practices, highlighting the inaccuracies and omissions of those reports.[9] HRF routinely testified before the House Subcommittee on International Operations and Human Rights, offering a counterpoint to the State Department's testimony on the reports. In 1996, HRF stopped producing the critiques after concluding that the reports had "become a progressively more thorough and reliable guide to human rights conditions throughout the world." *Id.* In 2002, however, HRF once again published a critique in response to the strains placed on human rights protections in the aftermath of September 11, criticizing the United States for "serious omissions and distortions" with respect to certain allies in the war on terror.[10]

NOTES AND QUESTIONS ON ENSURING COMPLIANCE

1. *A failing UN compliance system?* The UN treaty compliance system has been the subject of criticism over its failure to procure compliance from participatory states. "[T]he gap between universal right and remedy has become inescapable and inexcusable, threatening the integrity of the international human rights legal regime. There are overwhelming numbers of overdue reports, untenable backlogs, minimal individual complaints from vast numbers of potential victims, and widespread refusal of states to provide remedies when violations of individual rights are found." Anne F. Bayefsky, *The UN Human Rights Treaty System: Universality at the Crossroads,* Apr. 2001, *available at* http://www.

Shadow Reports as Alternatives to State Reports under International Human Rights Treaties, in GLOBAL TO LOCAL: A CONVENTION IMPLEMENTATION AND MONITORING WORKSHOP (1998).

7. Johanna E. Bond, *International Intersectionality: A Theoretical and Pragmatic Exploration of Women's International Human Rights Violations,* 52 EMORY L.J. 71, 165 n.387 (2003).

8. These reports were published by the Lawyers Committee for Human Rights, which in 2004 changed its name to Human Rights First.

9. Human Rights First, *Holding the Line: A Critique of the Department of State's Annual Country Reports on Human Rights Practices,* ii-iii, Sept. 2003, *available at* http://www.humanrightsfirst.org/pubs/descriptions/Holdingtheline.pdf.

10. *Id.; see also* Human Rights Watch, *U.S. State Department Rights Reports Critique,* Mar. 4, 2002, *available at* http://hrorg/english/docs/2002/03/04/usint3777.htm

bayefsky.com/tree.php/id/9250. Given these facts, do you believe that it
can still be an effective strategy for NGOs to issue shadow reports? What
other roles can NGOs play in facilitating the goals of human rights
treaties? *See* Lesley Wexler, *Take the Long Way Home: Sub–Federal Integration of Unratified and Non–Self–Executing Treaty Law*. 28 MICH. J. INT'L.
L. 1 (2006) ("The current focus on treaty ratification overlooks an
important mechanism of international norm internalization. * * * As
evidenced by the environmental and human rights contexts, governmental actors and nongovernmental organizations can help integrate
treaties into domestic law in the face of federal lethargy or intransigence.").

2. *Human Rights Watch/American Civil Liberties Union Report.* In
December 1993, shortly before the United States was to issue its first
compliance report, the ACLU and HRW completed a joint report
evaluating the United States' compliance with the International Covenant on Civil and Political Rights (ICCPR), which the United States
ratified in 1992. *See* Human Rights Watch & American Civil Liberties
Union, *Human Rights Violations in the United States* (1994), excerpted in
Module 4, *supra*. The report found that the United States had failed to
meet its obligations under the ICCPR in several areas including the
treatment of prisoners, refugee repatriation, gender discrimination,
religious liberty, police brutality, and the death penalty. Are reports
such as these that are aimed at wider audiences an effective technique
for pressuring governments into complying with their treaty obligations?
Do they serve other important purposes?

─────────

5. STANDARD–SETTING

I think it is clear that there is a new diplomacy, where NGOs,
peoples from across nations, international organizations, the
Red Cross, and governments come together to pursue an
objective. When we do–and we are determined, as has been
proven in the land mines issues and the International Criminal
Court–there is nothing we can take on that we cannot succeed
in, and this partnership * * * is a powerful partnership for the
future.

Former U.N. Secretary–General Kofi Annan, statement at the NGO
Forum on Global Issues in Berlin, Germany, 30 April 1999.

NGOs have long been involved in standard-setting in the UN and
regional systems. Every major human rights treaty and document has
been affected by NGO lobbying and input.[11] However, with the advent
of the internet, new possibilities have emerged for NGOs to influence
the development of human rights norms and institutions. We explore

─────────

11. *See* ANN MARIE CLARK, DIPLOMACY OF CONSCIENCE: AMNESTY INTERNATIONAL AND CHANGING HUMAN
RIGHTS NORMS (2001).

two examples of these briefly: the ban on landmines and the creation of an international criminal court.

The Ottawa Convention

NGOs were instrumental in bringing into existence the Ottawa Convention banning anti-personnel landmines. The following excerpt highlights the ways NGOs initiated the movement, maintained a presence at the critical junctures, and worked together with states to achieve the goal of establishing an international treaty to ban landmines.

Kenneth Anderson, *The Ottawa Convention Banning Landmines, the Role of International Non–Governmental Organizations and the Idea of International Civil Society,* 11 Eur J. Int'l L. 91, 104–118 (2000)

First, the international campaign to ban landmines began entirely—one hesitates to use so strong a word, but in this case it is applicable—as an effort of international NGOs. The initial steps began with the International Committee of the Red Cross (ICRC); its surgeon staff particularly, alarmed at the sharp increase during the 1980s in the number of landmine victim limb amputations, persuaded the ICRC to raise the issue in its diplomatic, legal and public awareness efforts. The ICRC would be the first to admit that its nascent campaign had comparatively minimal visibility until a coalition of international NGOs with concerns about landmines arising from very different standpoints, came together to initiate what later became known as the International Campaign to Ban Landmines (ICBL). * * *

The ICBL expanded over the next few years to number more than 1,200 NGOs in some 60 countries; although the ICRC, for reasons of its mandate, did not formally join the ICBL coalition, it and national Red Cross and Red Crescent societies and their federation fully supported the process leading up to the Ottawa Convention. It was a striking part of the campaign that diverse NGOs could find bases on which to support the ban campaign drawing upon their own organizational mandates. Thus, for example, Human Rights Watch and the ICRC regarded landmines as a human rights and humanitarian law issue, while such groups as Medico International, Physicians for Human Rights, or Handicap International saw it as a medical and public health issue, while still others, such as the Vietnam Veterans of America Foundation, saw it as a matter of dealing with the consequences of war in a social and developmental sense. * * *

Second, governments were initially entirely uninterested; it was regarded by governments everywhere as pie-in-the-sky, even if they were not actively hostile to the idea. Governments regarded the only real possibility as being a strengthening of the existing Landmines Protocol, so-called Protocol II to the Convention on Conventional Weapons; the ICBL had long since concluded that amendments to Protocol II, governing the rules for the "proper" use of landmines, were useless. * * *

Third, the ban campaign had a simple, easily understood message—a complete and comprehensive ban, nothing more, nothing less. The message was so simple that it could fit whole into an advertisement or public awareness message. * * * Although the final Ottawa Convention is of course longer and more detailed, in contrast to other arms control or humanitarian law treaties it preserves the spirit of transparent language and clear, uncompromising and unambiguous undertakings. This utter moral and political clarity was an integral part of the campaign in reaching various publics. * * *

Fifth, the treaty process represented a new approach to international lawmaking because—largely in response to international NGO pressures—once a core of influential governments had endorsed the ban treaty, the negotiating principle was not the usual method of arms control treaty negotiation on the principle of obtaining consensus on each point along the way, no matter how much the treaty had to be watered down or how long it took. Instead, again on account of international NGO pressures, sympathetic governments adopted a new principle of negotiating a treaty among "like-minded" states—in effect, accepting the comprehensiveness of the international NGO position and its refusal to compromise the essentials of the landmines ban. The wager, of course, of negotiating a treaty among the like-minded alone (even though the club of the like-minded has eventually grown to include numerically the vast majority of states) was (and is) that the treaty will eventually gain adherence even from those who were not in the beginning like-minded.

Seventh, and the most far-reaching in its implications, the ban campaign by its end stages was conceived by sympathetic governments, United Nations institutions, and the international NGO movement as being a genuine partnership between NGOs, international organizations and sympathetic states—between, so to speak, public and private. * * *

This partnership between international NGOs, on the one hand, and sympathetic states and international organizations * * * is regarded as a principal, if indeed not *the* principal, legacy of the landmines campaign, and the central element in the new template envisioned for international law-making. [Today this belief] is widely and equally fervently hailed by the international activist community, as well as by the policy makers of sympathetic governments and international organizations. The ban campaign and its forging of a partnership between international public institutions, including sympathetic states, and international civil society, so-called, is the model of a new and better way of creating international law. As Canadian Foreign Minister Axworthy put it:

> The need for new partnerships to address global problems and the increased power wielded by a wide range of state and non-state actors intersected in the landmines campaign. * * * It brought together a mixed group of players into a coalition without prece-

dent. * * * The landmines campaign was the harbinger of the new multilateralism: new alliances among states, new partnerships with non-state actors, and new approaches to international governance.

The Rome Statute for an International Criminal Court

This centralized NGO approach was also used successfully in the proceedings leading up to the Rome Statute.

In the immediate aftermath of World War II efforts were made to codify Nuremberg and to create an international criminal court to try future human rights offenders. These efforts faltered during the Cold War, and for decades it seemed that such a court would never become a reality. However, the atrocities in Yugoslavia and Rwanda galvanized the international community and international civil society, and efforts to create an international criminal court were renewed in the mid–1990s, leading to the creation of the Rome Statute in 1998, the entry into force of the treaty, and the actual creation of the International Criminal Court ("ICC") in 2002. *See* Leila Nadya Sadat, The International Criminal Court and the Transformation of International Law: Justice for the New Millennium 5–6 (2002).

In the effort to create an international criminal court, it became clear that NGOs would have to pool their resources. They realized that the creation of the court would touch upon several areas of international law, making it unlikely that a single NGO would be able to address the various provisions effectively. They also recognized that the involvement of several states was necessary for a successful and independent court, requiring relationships beyond the reach of any single individual NGO. William R. Pace & Jennifer Schense, *The Role of Non–Governmental Organizations*, in The Rome Statute of the International Criminal Court: A Commentary 111 (Antonio Cassese et. al eds. 2002).

The coalition of NGOs made substantive contributions to the ICC negotiations through its diverse and highly visible presence. The NGO group earned a reputation of being a reliable and knowledgeable source of information on which states depended, and it effectively disseminated information through the use of the Internet and media while intensely lobbying states. Zoe Pearson, *Non-Governmental Organizations and the International Criminal Court: Changing Landscapes of International Law*, 39 Cornell Int'l L. 243 (2006).

The NGO effort not only ensured that there would be a treaty, it also influenced some key provisions, such as those concerning gender representation and the independence of the prosecutor. Mahnoush H. Arsanjani, *The Rome Statute of the International Criminal Court*, 93 Am. J.Int'l L. 22, 23 (1999).

The Rome Statute of the ICC was adopted with 120 nations voting in favor of the court. Building on the success of the Ottawa Convention,

NGOs again had mobilized and coordinated to achieve a historical victory for international human rights law.

––––––––––

NOTES AND QUESTIONS ON STANDARD SETTING

1. *Other treaties?* What other international human rights problems would be susceptible to this kind of coalition effort? In 2004, AI launched an international campaign to Stop Violence Against Women ("SVAW").[12] Do you think that an NGO Coalition similar to the Coalition for an International Criminal Court ("CICC") could be mobilized on this issue? What obstacles would you foresee? How would you overcome them? Would the preparation of a new treaty be the object of such an effort?

––––––––––

6. LITIGATION

The ways NGOs helped bring former Chilean President Augusto Pinochet to account in a British court differed dramatically from the ways NGOs helped implement the Ottawa Convention or Rome Statute. In the case of Pinochet, NGOs operated as a loosely–affiliated transnational network of human rights advocates rather than as a centralized institution. Naomi Roht–Arriaza explains how this network contributed to the Spanish government's request for Pinochet's extradition from the United Kingdom in 1999:

NAOMI ROHT-ARRIAZA, THE PINOCHET EFFECT: TRANSNATIONAL JUSTICE IN THE AGE OF HUMAN RIGHTS, 208–212 (2004)

Chile has for many years had a well-organized movement pushing for justice within the country. The 1973 coup [which brought Pinochet to power] and the atrocities that followed it galvanized a nascent human rights movement into action. * * * Human rights violations in the Southern Cone created activists who went outside a closed domestic political system to find allies and pressure points abroad. They used the power of ideas like human rights, and the ability to name violations, fact-find about them, and create moral outrage to make their case on the international level. * * * These "transnational advocacy networks" of activists transmit ideas and norms from one country to another, create joint campaigns, and work together to create pressure on recalcitrant governments. * * *

The loose alliance of lawyers, human rights activists, social service providers, family members of the disappeared, journalists, and academics on three continents that began to take shape around pushing for

––––––––––

12. *See* Amnesty International, Stop Violence Against Women, *available at* http://www.amnesty.org/en/campaigns/stop-violence-againstwomen (last visited July 1, 2008).

trials had many of the attributes of a transnational advocacy network. * * * [T]here were prodigious feats of transcontinental cooperation involved. These were made possible in part by new technologies, especially the Internet, which amplified the network's ability to react quickly and concentrate resources at key moments. Finding dozens of victims of torture in Chile after 1988 and getting their evidence before Judge Garzon [of Spain] so that he could bring it before the British courts, all in large part done in the short time between the House of Lords decision in March 1999 and the extradition hearing in September, was probably the most impressive feat. It could not have been done without the preexisting contacts and correspondence among the various lawyers and local human rights groups. Sifting through the wealth of declassified U.S. government documents, or the reams of police files in the Archive of Terror in Paraguay, to find the nuggets that would fuel Operation Condor-linked prosecutions in numerous countries required a high degree of cross-border cooperation and coordination. So did getting that information authenticated and translated so that a local judge could use it, and into the hands of the appropriate lawyers and investigating magistrates.

It is possible, however, to overstate the amount of organization and coordination involved. This was no tight, centralized operation but a dispersed series of individuals and small groups loosely bound by common goals and mutual acquaintances who came together over time around specific campaigns and opportunities. [The networks were successful] because they knew how to take advantage of events and how to communicate.

NOTES AND QUESTIONS ON LITIGATION

1. *Enforcing human rights with litigation.* How important do you think litigation is as a human rights enforcement tool? Should an organization like AI put more of its resources into developing an international network of lawyers who would litigate in national, regional, and international forums to enforce human rights standards? Given the reality of finite resources, what priority would you give litigation? Do you foresee any problems in pursuing such a strategy? For example, do you think that the internal documents of human rights organizations might be the subject of discovery if they engage in litigation? Would such organizations be seen as impartial if they sponsor litigation?

2. *Domestic reliance on transnational advocacy networks.* When U.S. public interest lawyers are faced with regulatory regimes that permit corporations to shop for countries that shield them from liability, turning to transnational advocacy networks has proven effective. In the 1990s, networks of public interest law organizations, labor and religious groups, and student associations emerged to combat the use of sweat-

shop labor in countries with weak labor standards. *See* Scott L. Cummings, *The Internationalization of Public Interest Law*, 57 Duke L. J. 891 (2008).

---

7. MEDIA AND PUBLIC MOBILIZATION

NGOs are becoming increasingly adept in their use of the media to draw attention to specific human rights issues.

> The importance of mass media [for redressing human rights violations] cannot be over-emphasized. * * * Successful human rights NGOs develop good personal contacts with journalists, who may provide information to NGOs and also serve as a means of making NGO information public. In addition, NGOs and individuals should attempt to gain direct access to the media where it is possible, through letters to the editor, short op-ed pieces, soliciting radio and television interviews, and similar techniques.

Guide to International Human Rights Practice, 23–24 (Hurst Hannum ed, 4th ed. 2004). Large international human rights organizations such as AI, HRW, and HRF all have internal communications departments whose job is to use the media to educate the public on human rights issues, influence policymakers, and spotlight human rights situations that require an immediate response.

The emergence of new technology has provided NGOs with inexpensive access to even greater numbers of people. Rapidly bridging the digital divide, NGOs are employing new technologies in their efforts to protect and promote international human rights. Video technology can record human rights violations as they occur, exposing the public and policymakers to irrefutable images of human suffering.[13] Podcasting enables wider-scale distribution of such footage, allowing anyone with a computer to access video of human rights situations on the ground. Cell phone technology permits human rights defenders on the front lines to keep international human rights organizations and the media informed of daily developments in their area.[14]

The most important technological advancement for human rights NGOs, however, has been the internet. Information posted on the Internet crosses international boundaries far more quickly and easily than printed information, and can be discreetly accessed by individuals and NGOs in other countries. Through the internet, NGOs are able to more efficiently distribute information on international human rights standards and network with other NGOs working on similar issues.

---

13. WITNESS is one example of a human rights organization that trains human rights activists to use video equipment to record evidence of human rights violations. *See* http://www.witness.org.

14. *See* Human Rights Watch, *Human Rights Watch World Report 1999: Indonesia and East Timor, Defending Human Rights, available* at http://www.hrw.org/worldreport99/asia/indonesia.html.

NGOs have also sought to take advantage of the widespread rise in online blog (short for "web log") communications. "Bloggers" are creatively using their blogs to disseminate information on the human rights situations in their countries. HRW provides information on its website for individuals interested in becoming human rights bloggers, as such information may not be readily available through traditional media outlets in some countries. Human rights bloggers have the potential to reach millions of people in numerous countries. Repressive governments are keenly aware of the potential of this technology to strengthen human rights movements. As blogs remain the last outlet for freedom of expression in many countries, they pose a potential threat to repressive regimes.

Many governments, including Iran and Burma, have taken steps to criminalize the use of the Internet for human rights advocacy purposes. Other countries, such as China, Egypt, Syria, and Tunisia have also undertaken strict measures to prohibit human rights advocates from using the internet, at times, with the alleged assistance of U.S. companies.[15] Thus, in many countries, the technological strides that have enabled human rights advocates to reach millions of individuals still require them to act with great caution. The YouTube phenomenon has also had implications in the dissemination of human rights violations. Andrew K. Woods, *The YouTube Defense: Human Rights Go Viral*, SLATE, Mar. 28, 2007, *available at* http://www.slate.com/id/2162780.

NOTES AND QUESTIONS ON THE MEDIA AND PUBLIC MOBILIZATION

1. *Public mobilization and tensions between international and local NGOs.* At times, there is tension between the work of international human rights organizations and the work being done on the ground by local human rights organizations. For example, in March 2002, Amina Lawal, a Nigerian citizen was convicted of adultery and sentenced by a *Shari'ah* court to death by stoning after she confessed to giving birth to a child while divorced. The international condemnation of Lawal's sentence was universal. In addition to the statements made by various governments urging that Lawal's sentence be overturned, AI launched an internet petition to gather signatures protesting the sentence. In response, a local human rights organization, BAOBAB for Women's Human Rights, issued the following statement,[16] in which it raised its concerns about the impact of the petition and letter writing campaigns for Lawal:

Dear friends,

There have been a whole host of petitions and letter writing campaigns about Amina Lawal (sentenced to stoning to death for

---

15. *See* Human Rights Watch, *False Freedom: Online Censorship in the Middle East and North Africa*, Vol. 17, No. 10E, Nov. 2005; *See* Testimony of Tom Malinowski, Congressional Human Rights Caucus Member's Briefing, Feb. 1, 2006, *available at* http://lantos.house.gov/HoR/CA12/Human+Rights+Caucus/Briefing+Testimonies/02–06–06+Testimony+of+Tom+Malinowski+China+Google+Briefing.htm.

16. Women Living Under Muslim Laws, *Nigeria: Amina Lawal Appeal*, Aug. 27, 2003, *available at* http://wluml.org/english/newsfulltxt.shtml?cmd$157)=x–157–18546˙& cmd$189)=x–189–18546.

adultery in August 2002). Many of these are inaccurate and ineffective and may even be damaging to her case and those of others in similar situations. BAOBAB for Women's Human Rights, which is responsible for initiating and continuing to support the defences of cases like Ms. Lawal's, thanks the world for its support and concern, but requests that you please stop the Amina Lawal international protest letter campaigns for now (May 2003). * * *

Dangers of Letter Writing Campaigns?

[I]f there is an immediate physical danger to Ms. Lawal and others, it is from vigilante and political further (over)reaction to international attempts at pressure. [In one instance, a Governor carried out a sentence] not despite national and international pressure; [but] deliberately to defy it. The Governor * * * boasted of his resistance to "these letters from infidels," even to sniggering over how many letters he had received. Thus, we would like you to recognise that an international protest letter campaign is not necessarily the most productive way to act in every situation. On the contrary, women's rights defenders should assess potential backlash effects before devising strategies.

Problems with Petitions based on Inaccurate Information

Even when protests are appropriate forms of action, when they are obviously based on inaccuracies of fact they are easier to ignore [and] * * * certainly damage the credibility of the local activists, who are assumed to have supplied this information. * * * Please check the accuracy of the information with local activists, before further circulating petitions or responding to them. * * *

Supporting Local Pressures

There is a place for international pressure and campaigns. * * * However, using international protest appeals as the automatic response reduces its usefulness as an advocacy tool. We feel that this is not the time for an international letter writing campaign, but we are concerned that should the situation change, and we then need international pressure and ask for international support, the moral energy and indignation of the world may already have been spent—resulting in campaign fatigue (been there, done that already). * * *

Deciding on Strategies to Fight Injustices

We are asking for international solidarity strategies that respect the analyses and agency of those activists most closely involved and in touch with the issues on the ground and the wishes of the women and men directly suffering rights violations. * * * The [victims] have chosen to appeal and accepted the assistance of NGOs like BAOBAB, WRAPA and the networks of Nigerian women's and human rights NGOs that support them. There is an unbecoming arrogance in assuming that international human rights organisations or others always know better than those directly involved, and therefore can take actions that fly in the face of their express wishes. * * * Please do liaise with those whose rights have been violated and/or local groups directly involved to discuss strategies of solidarity and support before launching campaigns. * * *

Respectfully,

BAOBAB for Women's Human Rights

In response to BAOBAB's letter, Amnesty International changed course and issued the following statement:

> Amnesty International understands that Amina Lawal's right to legal representation, fair trial and right to appeal are guaranteed at present. Amina Lawal is not in detention and has excellent legal representation, including prominent women lawyers and senior Nigerian advocates. She is being supported by a coalition of Nigerian women's groups and human rights groups. Amnesty International is in close touch with these organizations and is careful to include only the most accurate information on its websites.

According to the Nigerian Constitution, at the end of all judicial processes involving the death penalty, the President of the Republic could exercise his prerogative of mercy—a political, not a judicial, decision. "We will not hesitate to campaign for such a prerogative to be exerted by the President in due time, as we would for any case attracting the death penalty under any penal code, including *Sharia* Penal Legislation," the organization stressed. "However, the organization does not wish to interfere in the judicial process in the case of Amina Lawal and does not recommend carrying out any international campaign specifically on her case at this point in time." Amnesty International, *Nigeria: False Information about Amnesty International's Campaign on Amina Lawal*, AI Index 44/013/2003, May 6, 2003.

On September 25, 2003, the *Shari'ah* Court of Appeal of Katsina State quashed Amina Lawal's sentence to death by stoning. How could AI have gone about its campaign to provide assistance to Lawal differently? If you were an AI campaigner, what more might you have wanted to know about the situation on the ground in Nigeria prior to launching the mobilization?

2. *The impact of international NGOs on local NGOs.* Local human rights organizations have at times suffered government hostility due to actions taken by international human rights organizations. In 1994, AI published a report detailing the arrest and torture of a small group of lawyers who had defended Islamic political prisoners with ties to armed groups. According to one commentator, "the government was not specifically threatening any local human rights organizations, despite the implications of the report's title. It was at that point that our movement in Egypt started to be subjected to 'threat' [by the government]" Bahey

El Din Hassan, *The Credibility Crisis of International Human Rights in the Arab World*, HUM. RTS. DIALOGUE, 9 (Winter 2002). Should AI have refrained from publishing this report? Who should make such a decision: the victims of government repression or the leaders of an international NGO? Can you see any dangers in deferring to the wishes of human rights victims in deciding whether to publish a human rights report?

3. *Outrage fatigue.* What challenges do NGOs face in making sure that the human rights stories covered by the media are received by the population at large? One potential challenge is "outrage fatigue." Consider the following:

> As with their predecessors confronted by consistent and repeated information on the effects of the Nazi Holocaust during World War II, human rights groups today have proved themselves extremely capable of rapidly documenting and denouncing the true nature of what has been happening. But they have failed, in Croatia, in Bosnia, in Rwanda, in Chechnya, to convince or shame the world to intervene. * * *

> The human rights movement has over-estimated the power of the image. It has confused public opinion's positive and generous reaction to the depiction of suffering with international readiness to stomach decisive and sometimes bloody intervention.

> The avalanche of grisly pictures and descriptions of unlimited human suffering and brutality has confronted human rights organizations with "outrage fatigue." It has changed moral disgust and emotional revulsion into a sense of powerlessness, even indifference.

Jean Paul Marthoz, Human Rights Watch, *Media and Human Rights: Dealing with Large–Scale Abuse.*

Do you agree? Why have the images coming out of Darfur failed to rally the public to demand action? What can NGOs do to counteract outrage fatigue? What effect does an NGO's use of images have on people's conception of the victims?

4. *The importance of context.* Another challenge for NGOs is ensuring that the public understands the context of the images of human rights violations coming out of the media. Consider the following excerpt from Jean Paul Marthoz, *Media and Human Rights: Dealing with Large–Scale Abuse*, in which he argues that effective reporting of human rights violations requires the media to provide viewers with sufficient context and to encourage engagement.

> The alleged "ancestral" or "tribal" brutality and apparent irrationality of post-modern civil wars beg for a more forceful effort of explanation. The mass murder by machetes of hundreds of thousands of Tutsis in Rwanda and the large-scale mutilations in Sierra Leone of ordinary civilians, whether man, woman or child, seem totally incomprehensible. Confronted by such violations, one's immediate reflex is to simplify. Reality or irreality decoders immedi-

ately suggest tribal hatreds enforced by "heart of darkness" historical or indigenous analogies.

"The images presented of African conflicts as primitive and backward reinforce existing prejudices and limit further examination of their causes and impact," observes Philippa Atkinson in MYTHOLOGIES OF ETHNIC WAR IN LIBERIA—THE MEDIA OF CONFLICT. "Conclusions are drawn, based on this imperfect analysis, that the West can play no positive role to help Africans with their local and historical conflicts, with disengagement seen as the only sensible strategy and that perhaps humanitarian aid can be offered through the non-committal channel of NGOs."

The reporting of complexity needs to take the lead over the reporting of outrage. * * * [T]he identification of local and transnational networks of interests and responsibilities, can brush aside pretexts for inaction and lead to rational debates of policy options. The priority for human rights organizations is to give a meaning to the senseless whirl of the world with its wild mayhem and furor. By giving a meaning to solidarity, we need to give a meaning to the news or information that is provided.

Do you agree that the media's failure to provide context to the images of human rights violations can actually be counterproductive to human rights causes? As advertised by America's leading public television current affairs show during the early 1980s, the McNeil–Lehrer NewsHour: "You need more than three minutes to explain three centuries of hatred." In the age of the sound byte, is it realistic to expect that people will take the time to understand the complexity of the situations on the ground? Is three minutes better than no air time at all? Should NGOs make it a priority to develop relationships with reporters so that NGOs can be consulted to provide the reporter with context for the human rights violation?

5. *Media limitations.* Despite the widespread benefits of media exposure of human rights violations, the media have several limitations. "The media, especially television, report what is currently happening and is not interested in covering anticipated events. Because television relies on graphic images for its influence, the reporting usually happens only after immense loss of life and property occurs. [In addition], in the day of pervasive media presence, a lack of coverage may lead the public to sense that the problem cannot really be very serious if it is not broadcast on their television screens in the evening. [Finally], the media has a short-term attention span. [When the media left Rwanda], the public's attention, guided and formed by the media, vanished as quickly as had the television cameras."[17] What steps can NGOs take to address these limitations?

---

17. Lionel Rosenblatt, *The Media and the Refugee, in* FROM MASSACRES TO GENOCIDE, THE MEDIA, PUBLIC POLICY, AND HUMANITARIAN CRISIS, 141–42 (Robert Rotberg & Thomas Weiss eds. 1996).

C. DEFINING NGO MANDATES: ECONOMIC, SOCIAL, AND CULTURAL RIGHTS

1. INTRODUCTION

Although international human rights organizations have long focused predominantly on civil and political rights, the interrelation of civil and political rights with economic, social, and cultural rights has, from the beginning, been at the core of the human rights framework. Indeed,

> [t]he interdependence of the two categories of rights has always been part of UN doctrine. The UDHR, at the very start of the human rights movement, included both categories without any sense of separateness or priority. The Preamble to the ICESCR, in terms of mirroring those used in the ICCPR, states that "in accordance with the Universal Declaration * * *, the ideal of free human beings enjoying freedom from fear and want can only be achieved if conditions are created whereby everyone may enjoy his economic, social and cultural rights, as well as his civil and political rights. The interdependence principle, apart from its use as a political compromise between advocates of one or two covenants, reflects the fact that the two sets of rights can neither logically nor practically be separated in watertight compartments. Civil and political rights may constitute the condition for and thus be implicit in economic and social rights."[18]

Despite this widespread understanding of the interdependence of civil and political rights ("CPR") and economic, social, and cultural rights ("ESCR"), the decisions of some NGOs to focus on CPR to the exclusion of ESCR has sparked controversy in the human rights movement.

———————

Katherine E. Cox, *Should Amnesty International Expand Its Mandate to Cover Economic, Social, and Cultural Rights?*, 16 ARIZ. J. INT'L & COMP. L. 261, 261–263 (1999)

International human rights nongovernmental organizations (INGOs) are increasingly criticized by human rights advocates and nongovernmental organizations (NGOs) in developing countries for having too narrow a focus. Commentators point out that while the major INGOs endorse the full spectrum of rights in theory, in practice they predominantly concentrate on civil and political rights. These organizations have been held partially responsible for the failure of the international

———————

18. HENRY J. STEINER & PHILIP ALSTON, INTERNATIONAL HUMAN RIGHTS IN CONTEXT: LAW, POLITICS, MORALS 247 (2d ed. 2000).

community to give more widespread effect to economic and social rights. This is by no means a new criticism of INGOs, but such criticism has recently increased.

International human rights law states that human rights are universal, indivisible, and interdependent. There is no hierarchy of rights or of categories of rights. Accordingly, critics of INGOs argue that by focusing exclusively on some rights, the significance of others is downplayed and the concepts of indivisibility and interdependence are undercut. Such an approach creates the impression that human rights violations are "discrete and fragmented." Furthermore, it is maintained that, in developing countries in particular, abuses of civil and political rights cannot be effectively tackled without concurrently addressing longstanding economic and social problems. Critics of INGOs contend that if these organizations do not change they will "continue to remain apart, monocultural rather than multicultural organizations that risk becoming 'irrelevant' to most of the world, even 'prissy' in their dogmatic disregard of much that is vital within a larger vision of rights."

The above general criticisms of INGOs [were all] made of Amnesty International (AI). This organization can be regarded as a "typical" Western INGO in that it has chosen to concentrate on certain narrowly defined civil and political rights. Thus, AI has been criticized as being irrelevant to much of the developing world. In addition, AI has been attacked due to its special position as a prominent and influential human rights organization. AI is widely acknowledged as the most well-known, well-endowed, respected, and effective INGO. Much of its success is credited to its narrowly defined mandate. Alston argues, however, that an inadvertent result of AI's success as a human rights movement is the "widespread dissemination of a conception of human rights which is partial (in the sense of being incomplete) and is not a faithful reflection of the Universal Declaration and the assumptions underpinning that document (from which the Declaration derives its strength and standing)" [*citing* Philip Alston, the Fortieth Anniversary of the Universal Declaration of HUMAN RIGHTS: A TIME MORE FOR REFLECTION THAN FOR CELEBRATION IN HUMAN RIGHTS IN A PLURALIST WORLD: INDIVIDUALS AND COLLECTIVITIES 1, 12 (Berting et al. eds., 1990).] He and others argue that, because of AI's special position, the organization bears a unique responsibility to the human rights movement to disseminate a complete picture of human rights.

---

2.   AMNESTY TAKES STEPS TO INCORPORATE ESCR

AI's statute provides that "Amnesty International, recognizing that human rights are indivisible and interdependent, works to promote all the rights enshrined in the Universal Declaration of Human Rights and other international standards, through human rights education programs and campaigning for ratification of human rights treaties." Although AI thus recognized the indivisibility of civil and political and economic, social and cultural rights early on, it only began to incorporate ESCR issues into its work in the last decade. In its 1998 Annual Report, AI stated:

> Addressing the imbalance between economic rights and other human rights is vital at a time when the debate over human rights is increasingly played out in the economic sphere. When governments fail to protect their citizens from the negative consequences of globalization, the need to protect and enhance economic rights becomes evident. The parallel imperative of ensuring that economic rights are not divorced from other human rights is shown each time that people are harassed, tortured and killed in the name of economic progress.[19]

Then, in August 2003, AI adopted a strategic plan that (for the first time in the organization's history) made the advancement of ESCR an integral part of the AI's human rights strategy. In explaining its decision, AI stated,

> Traditionally AI's actions focused on civil or political human rights, though interdependence and indivisibility of all human rights has long been central to our understanding and vision. In fact, the standard at the core of AI's work—the Universal Declaration of Human Rights—incorporates both civil and political as well as economic, social and cultural rights into one integrated vision of human dignity. * * *

> A key objective of AI's strategy for integrating work on ESCR is to challenge the notion that rights can be enjoyed in isolation. As AI's Secretary General Irene Khan explains, "I wouldn't like to think that we used to work on civil and political rights, we're going to stop working on them now, and we're going to shift to working on economic, social and cultural rights. That's not the idea at all. * * * We will try to bring all those rights together by looking at how people suffer human rights abuses, and show that human rights are actually an indivisible whole. * * * I hope that Amnesty International will in the future stand not only for prisoners of conscience, but also for prisoners of violence, for prisoners of illiteracy, for prisoners of poverty."[20]

Today, ESCR has become a priority campaign for AI. The goals of the campaign include reporting on ESCR abuses, strengthening international mechanisms for victims, and encouraging the recognition of these rights in decisions related to trade, finance, and the environment. AI's

---

19. Amnesty International, *Annual Report 1998*.

20. Amnesty International, *Economic, Social, and Cultural Rights (ESCR)*, *available at* http://www.amnestyusa.org/about-amnesty/economic-social-and-cultural-rights/page.do?id=1101300 & n1=4 & n2=63 & n3=124 (last visited July 1, 2008).

first ESCR reports document abuses of housing rights in Angola, food rights in North Korea, and work rights in Israel/Occupied Territories.[21]

3. DIFFICULTIES ENCOUNTERED BY NON–WESTERN NGOs

Non-western NGOs face a unique set of challenges that can cripple their efforts to follow through with their mandates. Makau Mutua, the director of the human rights center at State University of New York at Buffalo Law School, argues that non-western NGOs have been subjected to the unwitting imposition of Eurocentric norms by Western organizations:

> INGOs have * * * been instrumental in the creation of national NGOs in the Third World. Mandates of many national NGOs initially mirrored those of INGOs. However, in the last decade, many Third World NGOs have started to broaden their areas of concentration and go beyond the INGOs' civil and political rights constraints. In particular, domestic Third World NGOs are now paying more attention to economic and social rights, development, women's rights, and the relationships between transnational corporations and human rights conditions. In spite of this incipient conceptual independence on the part of NGOs, many remain voiceless in the corridors of power at the United Nations, the European Union, the World Bank, and in the dominant media organizations in the West. * * * [N]ational [non-Western] NGOs have virtually no financial independence. They rely almost exclusively on funding from Western states, foundations, charities, development agencies, and intergovernmental institutions. * * *[22]

Though this competition for funding and status can inhibit collaboration between local and international civil society and limit their effectiveness, sometimes local organizations are the only entities that can address gross violations of rights, regardless of category.

For example, in Sri Lanka, local representatives of the International Movement to End All Forms of Discrimination launched successful campaigns to curb racism in public policy while undertaking documentation efforts to report the hundreds of new "disappearances" of ethnic minorities that the country has experienced since the surge of violence began in 2006.[23] Nevertheless, according to a recent International Crisis Group report, the success of local efforts has been mixed:

---

21. Amnesty International, Economic, Social, and Cultural Rights (ESCR), *available at* http://www.amnestyusa.org/our-priorities/economic-social-cultural-rights/page.do?id=1011006 & n1=3 & n2=29 (last visited May 23, 2008).

22. MAKAU MUTUA, HUMAN RIGHTS: A CULTURAL AND POLITICAL CRITIQUE 37 (2002).

23. International Movement to End All Forms of Discrimination, *available at* http://www.imadr.org/about/ (Last visited June 3, 2008); *See* International Crisis Group, *Sri Lanka Human Rights Crisis*, Asia Report, No. 135, June 14 2007, *available at* http://www.crisisgroup.org/library/documents/asia/south_asia/135_sri_lanka_s(1)6dhuman_rights_crisis.pdf

[Local] advocacy efforts have raised the profile of Sri Lanka in policy debates but they have been hampered by difficulties in documenting cases quickly and with enough detail, and in disseminating the information widely enough. Coordinated action remains very difficult for NGOs for a variety of complex reasons, including their reliance on project-based funding. Given the ethnic and political divisions that have deepened throughout society with the return to war, activists have had trouble generating wider popular support for their efforts.[24]

NOTES AND QUESTIONS ON THE INTERDEPENDENCE OF RIGHTS

1. *The interdependence of rights.* Several commentators have noted the interdependence between economic, social and cultural rights, on one hand and civil and political rights on the other. The connection is particularly apparent in the case of the Ogoni people of Nigeria.

> In a country where civil and political rights are respected, it is easier to campaign for fulfillment of economic, social and cultural rights. The reverse is also true. Violations of civil and political rights can permit worsening of violations against the International Covenant on Economic, Social, and Cultural Rights. In the Delta region of Nigeria, the Ogoni people have resisted destruction of their land and contamination of their waters by the national government and international oil companies. Ogoni land suffers from environmental devastation, and the Ogoni have received few benefits from decades of oil production by Shell and other firms.

> The Ogoni campaigned for an environmental clean-up and an end to oil pollution, and compensation for the 500,000 Ogoni people. This led to confrontation with Nigeria's military regime and local authorities tied to the oil sector. Ogoni representatives worked to halt violations of economic, social and cultural rights that they had traditionally enjoyed, namely the rights to natural resources, to food and water and health, and to cultural and indigenous people's rights. Nigeria's military violated the civil and political rights of Ogoni representatives. The authorities denied freedom of speech to activists and subjected many to torture and unfair trials.

ALLAN MCCHESNEY, PROMOTING AND DEFENDING ECONOMIC, SOCIAL & CULTURAL RIGHTS 23 (2000).

Despite the interdependence, there are many ways for NGOs to work on ESCR issues, and the debate continues on the right approach, as the following excerpts illustrate.

---

24. *Id.*

Kenneth Roth, *Defending Economic, Social and Cultural Rights: Practical Issues Faced by International Human Rights Organizations*, 26 HUM. RTS. Q. 63 (2004)

Over the last decade, many have urged international human rights organizations to pay more attention to economic, social and cultural (ESC) rights. I agree with this prescription, and for several years Human Rights Watch has been doing significant work in this realm. However, many who urge international groups to take on ESC rights have a fairly simplistic sense of how this is done. Human Rights Watch's experience has led me to believe that there are certain types of ESC issues for which our methodology works well and others for which it does not. * * *

In my view, the most productive way for international human rights organizations like Human Rights Watch to address ESC rights is by building on the power of our methodology. The essence of that methodology * * * is not the ability to mobilize people in the streets, to engage in litigation, to press for broad national plans to realize ESC rights, or to provide technical assistance. Rather, the core of our methodology is our ability to investigate, expose, and shame. We are at our most effective when we can hold governmental (or, in some cases, nongovernmental) conduct up to a disapproving public. * * *

In my view, to shame a government effectively—to maximize the power of international human rights organizations like Human Rights Watch—clarity is needed around three issues: violation, violator, and remedy. That is, we must be able to show persuasively that a particular state of affairs amounts to a violation of human rights standards, that a particular violator is principally or significantly responsible, and that there is a widely accepted remedy for the violation. If any of these three elements is missing, our capacity to shame is greatly diminished. * * *

In the realm of ESC rights, the three preconditions for effective shaming operate much more independently. * * * I accept, for the sake of this argument, that indicia have been developed for subsistence levels of food, housing, medical care, education, *etc.* When steady progress is not being made toward realizing these subsistence levels, one can presumptively say that a violation has occurred.

But who is responsible for the violation, and what is the remedy? These answers flow much less directly from the mere documentation of an ESC rights violation than they do in the civil and political rights realm. For example, does responsibility for a substandard public health system lie with the government (say, through its corruption or mismanagement) or with the international community (through its stinginess or indifference), and if the latter, which part of the international community? The answer is usually all of the above, which naturally reduces the potential to stigmatize any single actor.

Similar confusion surrounds discussions of appropriate remedies. The vigorously contested views about "structural adjustment" are illustrative. Is structural adjustment the cause of poverty, through its forced slashing of public investment in basic needs, or is it the solution, by laying the groundwork for economic development? Reasonable arguments can be found on both sides. When the target of a shaming effort can marshal respectable arguments in its defense, shaming usually fails.

The lesson I draw from these observations is that when international human rights organizations such as Human Rights Watch take on ESC rights, we should look for situations in which there is relative clarity about violation, violator, and remedy. That is not to say that other types of ESC abuses should be ignored, simply that a division of labor makes sense, with local or national groups using their special strengths to address ESC rights violations for which the methodology of international human rights organizations is less suited.

Broadly speaking, I would suggest that the nature of the violation, violator, and remedy is clearest when it is possible to identify arbitrary or discriminatory governmental conduct that causes or substantially contributes to an ESC violation. These three dimensions are less clear when the ESC shortcoming is largely a problem of distributive justice. That is, if all an international human rights organization can do is argue that more money be spent to uphold an ESC right—that a fixed economic pie be divided differently—our voice is relatively weak. Of course, we can argue that money should be diverted from less acute needs to the fulfillment of more pressing ESC rights, but there is little reason for a government to give our voice greater weight than domestic voices. On the other hand, if we can show that the government (or other relevant actor) is contributing to the ESC shortfall through arbitrary or discriminatory conduct, we are in a relatively powerful position: we can show a violation (the rights shortfall), the violator (the government or other actor through its arbitrary or discriminatory conduct), and the remedy (reversing that conduct).

What does this mean in practice? To illustrate, let's assume that we could show that a government was building medical clinics only in areas populated by ethnic groups that tended to vote for it, leaving other ethnic groups with substandard medical care. In such a case, an international human rights organization would be in a good position to argue that the disfavored ethnic groups' right to health care is being denied. This argument doesn't necessarily increase the resources being made available for health care, but it at least ensures a more equitable distribution. Since defenders of ESC rights should be concerned foremost with the worst-off segments of society, that redistribution would be an advance. Moreover, given that the government's supporters are not likely to be happy about a cutback in medical care, enforcement of a nondiscriminatory approach stands a reasonable chance of increasing health-related resources overall. * * *

To conclude, let me offer a hypothesis about the conduct of international human rights organizations working on ESC rights. It has been clear for many years that the movement would like to do more in the ESC realm. Yet despite repeated professions of interest, its work in this area remains limited. Part of the reason, of course, is expertise; the movement must staff somewhat differently to document shortfalls in such matters as health or housing than to record instances of torture or political imprisonment. But much of the reason, I suspect, is a sense of futility. International human rights activists see how little impact they have in taking on matters of pure distributive justice, and they have a hard time justifying devoting scarce resources for such limited ends. However, if we focus our attention on ESC policy that can fairly be characterized as arbitrary or discriminatory, I believe our impact will be substantially larger. And there is nothing like success to breed emulation.

Thus, when outsiders ask international human rights organizations to expand our work on ESC rights, we should insist on a more sophisticated, and realistic, conversation than has been typical so far. It is not enough, we should point out, to document ESC shortcomings and to declare a rights violation. Rather, we should ask our interlocutors to help us identify ESC shortcomings in which there is relative clarity about the nature of the violation, violator, and remedy, so that our shaming methodology will be most effective. As we succeed in broadening the number of governmental actions that can be seen in this way, we will go a long way toward enhancing the ESC work of the international human rights movement—work that, we all realize, is essential to the credibility of our movement.

Leonard S. Rubenstein, *How International Human Rights Organizations Can Advance Economic, Social, and Cultural Rights: A Response to Kenneth Roth,* **26 HUM. RTS. Q. 845 (2004)**

II. Building Systems to Fulfill Rights

As central as the naming and shaming method is in protecting civil and political rights, it is not an exclusive one. * * * Rather, [international human rights organizations] couple that method with affirmative strategies to protect human rights by building institutions, systems, international agreements and structures that may either prevent violations or hold perpetrators accountable. These institutions cover an enormous range. Some are designed to constrain official conduct or strengthen mechanisms to monitor it. Others more precisely define human rights obligations so that states can know what is expected and can be held accountable. Others still seek to eliminate the cause of human rights violations, exemplified spectacularly by the landmines ban treaty. Others seek to strengthen civil society as a bulwark against violations of human rights. The list could go on, but the point is simple: these affirmative objectives are not tied, as naming and shaming is, to ending a particular violation or identifying a discrete violator. On the contrary, they are mostly future oriented, designed to protect and promote human rights in the long term.

The methods used to build these institutions differ significantly from naming and shaming as well. * * * The advocacy methods rely mostly on public education, coalition building, campaigning, and lobbying, often over an extended period of time. In many cases, instead of seeking to embarrass governments, institution-building strategies seek to win them over.

As crucial as these systemic or institution-building strategies for promoting civil and political rights are, they are even more important in advancing economic, social, and cultural rights because realization of those rights requires putting into place social systems and programs for education, health care, and much more. * * *

To realize those rights, it is necessary but not sufficient for a state to stop doing something bad, such as engaging in discrimination or acting arbitrarily. The state also must take concerted, rational, well-planned steps forward to finance and build housing, health clinics, and schools; hire teachers, doctors, and nurses; furnish supplies; and much more. Moreover, a human rights approach to meeting human needs is not content merely with more housing, more clinics, and more teachers; it has a lot to say about how they are provided, whom they reach, what their implications are for others, and whether people affected by the decisions participate in making them. * * *

First, [human rights organizations] can and should engage with international donors, international financial institutions, UN agencies, and others to urge the institutions to adopt policies in development, aid, and trade programs, including those applicable to the design of health systems or education programs that are most likely to fulfill economic, social, and cultural rights. * * * Sometimes this engagement will require naming and shaming, for example, to expose macroeconomic or other policies destructive to human rights, as in the restrictive policies on generic drugs and skewed prevention policies contained in the Bush AIDS program. But much of it will be detailed analysis and lobbying to assure that politics and priorities meet human rights imperatives. For example, analysis and lobbying by a coalition concerned with HIV transmission in health care settings successfully pressed UNAIDS and the World Health Organization to be proactive in including safe health care initiatives in program planning.

The second role international human rights organizations can usefully play is to collaborate with and support organizations that are organizing and advocating for systems that are consistent with human rights norms at the national and local level. The international organizations can share expertise and analysis acquired through experience in a variety of countries and regions. This requires partnerships, not dominance, and international human rights organizations must respect the knowledge and capacity of local organizations. * * *

III.   Advocacy for Resources

Program design means little without resources. Given the staggering levels of suffering and deprivation, demands for resources to fund schools, health systems, water and sanitation, housing, and much more are at the heart of the struggle for economic, social, and cultural rights. That is why the Covenant on Economic, Social, and Cultural Rights requires states to spend the maximum of its available resources, and imposes the additional duty of international assistance and co-operation, especially economic and technical.

Some observers, however, including Ken Roth, are skeptical whether international human rights organizations can play a constructive role in advocacy for resources to fulfill rights either from governments in the developing world or from wealthy nations. * * * He puts the first problem this way: "[S]imply adding our voice to that of many others demanding a particular allocation of scarce resources—is not a terribly effective role for international human rights groups." The question, though, is not simply about allocation but about level of investment, a matter on which the Covenant on Economic, Social, and Cultural Rights is not agnostic. Though it recognizes the obvious limitations of poor countries in social spending, it nevertheless demands that they provide resources in sufficient amounts to begin to meet needs such as food, housing, health care, and education. * * *

In addition, while budget decisions can theoretically pit funds to realize one right against funds for another in a zero-sum game, diverting resources from one program to another where a dollar for health may mean a dollar less for education, that is not how these decisions tend to play out. Instead, pressure to realize a right tends to enlarge the pot.

In many other areas of civil and political rights, human rights organizations demand funds to fulfill rights. Protection of the rights of people with disabilities requires governments not just to re-think how public services are structured but to spend resources to create accessible buildings, streets, transportation, schools, and public accommodations.

Thus, sheepishness about advocacy for resources seems unwarranted by experience. Efforts to obtain resources indirectly, as he suggests in an example concerning discriminatory use of health resources, is not likely to be as effective as seeking them directly. We should put aside concerns about pitting advocacy for resources for one right against resources for others because they can lead to paralysis and new resources for none. The real task, it seems to me, is to use the analytical skills that international human rights organizations have to partner with activists in the tough work of analyzing budgets and spending decisions and to assist domestic organizations in their work to increase those investments.

Ken Roth's second concern about advocacy for resources is that, even to the extent that the Covenant on Economic, Social, and Cultural

Rights imposes an obligation of international assistance, thereby creating an important opening for international human rights organizations to secure resources from entities in which they have potential influence, they are not in a position to seek them.

The experience of Physicians for Human Rights in the United States suggests that this strategy of mobilizing constituents to obtain resources for fulfillment of economic, social, and cultural rights is, if difficult, enormously promising. Its Health Action AIDS Campaign recruits and mobilizes members of the medical, nursing, and public health communities to increase the multilateral and bilateral resources for the HIV/AIDS pandemic and global health from the United States and to implement its bilateral programs in a manner consistent with human rights.

The lesson here, then, is not to accept hurdles in gaining desperately needed funds needed to realize human rights but rather to deepen the commitment to develop the competency and capacity to fight effectively for them. International human rights organizations are as well-placed as any to demand these resources from states that have an obligation to assist, and their voices and resources are needed to add to the few constituencies already at work.

IV.   Monitoring and Accountability

The need for affirmative steps to realize economic, social, and cultural rights does not does obviate the need for monitoring and accountability, and as I noted at the outset, naming and shaming is an effective method in certain cases. The question I want to review in this section is whether it is sufficient to limit naming and shaming to arbitrary and discriminatory conduct. I think a broader approach to monitoring is needed. First, I believe rights will be advanced more quickly and effectively by holding states accountable for their specific obligations in the Covenant (ending discrimination is one of these) than on a general standard like arbitrariness.

In the first place, documenting compliance with specific rather than general obligations is usually more persuasive because it can both focus public attention to the wrong and limit the space for a government's defense, such as that it is making rational resource allocation decisions. A claim that a government is violating the obligation to provide childhood immunizations is also more understandable to victims, the public, and states than an argument that a government is acting arbitrarily. Focusing on specific obligations is empowering for local communities by reinforcing what they understand as particular needs in education, health, protection from pesticide exposure, and many other areas. They can organize around the violation and demand specific redress for their violation. * * *

Finally, grounding monitoring in the specific obligations of the Covenant, core obligations, helps identify entities responsible for the violation and the remedy for it, two elements that Ken Roth properly believes need to be part of any effective human rights monitoring strategy. * * *

Once those particular obligations, set out in detail in the General Comments, are identified, it is a very straightforward task to identify who has the responsibility for violations. Where multiple actors—all of the above—have responsibility, it is even more important to focus on specific obligations imposed on specific entities. Human rights organizations (and others) can then engage in a thoughtful, fact-based analysis of the problem to identify which actor has which obligations and has failed to live up to them. That in turn generates a set of demands for action by each. This process of assessing multiple layers of responsibility for a violation is the bread and butter of human rights organizations, since responsibility for violations of civil and political rights is often multitiered as well. If international human rights organizations contribute anything to the movement, it is the precise analysis to understand who bears what responsibility for which violation—the direct perpetrators, states that support the perpetrator, international agencies that have investigative responsibility, states that have financial or diplomatic leverage over the perpetrator, *etc.*—and what remedies are appropriate.

In the end, the arbitrariness standard appears fashioned to focus on a few aspects of the problem, social, exclusion or lack of good governance, rather than the full range of economic, social, and cultural rights. International human rights organizations, along with their partners in the developing world, can engage in hard-hitting monitoring, naming and shaming when the occasion calls for it. All they need to do is use the tools—in this case, a set of state obligations—at their disposal.

_____

NOTES AND QUESTIONS ON *NGO* MANDATES

1. *The Roth–Rubenstein debate.* Do you agree with Ken Roth's argument that NGOs ought only to work on certain ESCR issues that fit within the existing framework of NGO advocacy? Is Roth's ESCR proposal really an ESCR proposal, or does it merely re-frame ESCR into a CPR framework? Are you more persuaded by the approach taken by AI and Physicians for Human Rights, that ESCR rights are indivisible from civil and political rights, and that NGOs ought to work for the protection and promotion of all ESCR rights? Is it necessary to choose? If you were the Secretary–General of AI, which approach would you follow?

2. *Litigating ESCR.* Is litigation a viable strategy for enforcing ESCR? Will legal judgments force states, in ways that moral or political pressure cannot, to follow through with their legal obligations to ESCR? What factors should NGOs take into consideration when deciding whether to litigate an ESCR case? Should a victim's unwillingness to

testify or the unavailability of evidence be a consideration? *See* Marius Pieterse, *Possibilities and Pitfalls in the Domestic Enforcement of Social Rights: Contemplating the South African Experience*, 26 Hum. Rts. Q. 882 (2004).

D.   THREATS TO NGOs

1.   THE HUMAN RIGHTS DEFENDERS DECLARATION

> The Declaration rests on a basic premise: that when the rights of human rights defenders are violated, all our rights are put in jeopardy and all of us are made less safe.

Kofi Annan, Former UN Secretary General (Sept. 14, 1998)

In Thailand, on March 12, 2004, human rights lawyer Somchai Neelaphaijit disappeared. Neelaphaijit was the deputy chairman of the Human Rights Committee of the Law Society of Thailand. Just before his disappearance, Neelaphaijit filed a formal complaint against the police for torturing his clients, and, two weeks before his disappearance, Neelaphaijit had delivered a powerful speech on police torture, denouncing impunity. After the abduction, Prime Minister Thaksin Shinawatra made a devastating revelation: "We know that he is dead, as we have found some evidence. * * * Government officials were definitely involved in this, and there were more than four, but whether the evidence will lead to punishment in court is another thing." To date, only one mid-ranking policeman has been found guilty of coercion in the case of Neelaphaijit's disappearance. [25]

In Iran, Akbar Ganji, a leading human rights activist, was convicted of "acting against national security," and sentenced to six years in prison for writing and publishing articles detailing the involvement of high-ranking officials in the murder of dissidents. Ganji has also been an outspoken critic of the government's use of torture and has called for the release of all political prisoners. Although judicial authorities have pressured him to "repent" for his writings, Ganji has yet to do so. He has stated, "The reason I have stood firm is to show that it is possible to stand against darkness and ruthlessness." In March 2006, Ganji was released from prison after serving his sentence.

In Ireland, human rights lawyer Rosemary Nelson was murdered on March 15, 1999, when a bomb exploded underneath her car. Nelson was among the small group of lawyers willing to defend individuals detained under Northern Ireland's emergency laws. Her clients also included survivors of police abuses and their families. Prior to her death, Nelson repeatedly reported that officers of the Royal Ulster Constabulary had harassed her, assaulted her, and threatened her life.[26]

---

25. Human Rights First, *Make Sure the Thai Government Fulfills Promise of Justice for Disappeared Lawyer, available at* http://action.humanrightsfirst.org/campaign/Somchai_Verdict (last visited May 23, 2008).

26. Amnesty International, *The Killing of Human Rights Defender Rosemary Nelson*, AI Index EUR 45/022/1999, Apr. 1, 1999.

Loyalist paramilitaries have since claimed responsibility for her murder, and an investigation is pending.

Female human rights defenders are sometimes more vulnerable to intimidation than their male colleagues and are subject to gender-specific attacks such as sexual violence and rape, beatings and disfiguration, and discrimination. Fannyann Eddy, a lesbian rights activist in Sierra Leone, was brutally raped and murdered in her office. Prior to her death, she told the UN Commission on Human Rights, "We face constant harassment and violence from neighbors and others."[27] Moreover, threats are often aimed at the children or families of female defenders. Colombian human rights lawyer Soraya Gutierrez Arguello received a package containing a decapitated doll whose body had been burned, mutilated, and covered in red nail polish to appear bloodied with a note that read, "You have a lovely family. Look after them. Do not sacrifice them."[28]

Over the last three years, the Iranian government has leveled increasing threats against any civil society organization that receives funds from the State Department's controversial "democracy fund," which has allocated $20 million to distribute to nongovernmental organizations outside and inside of Iran. Several Iranian–American scholars and activists were imprisoned or kept in solitary confinement. A 2007 New York Times Magazine article reports on the growing paranoia among Iranians regarding anything vaguely related to the West. In the span of three months, at least three prominent NGOs were shut down indefinitely.[29]

As demonstrated by these accounts, many human rights activists and NGOs run the substantial risk of becoming victims of human rights violations themselves. Much of the early work of human rights NGOs like AI was to work for activists on the frontlines who were both human rights activists and, often, victims of political imprisonment, harassment, torture, disappearance, or death.

For years the human rights community lobbied in the UN for a more formal recognition of the work of human rights activists and greater protection for them. In March 1999, amid growing concerns over government repression and widespread attacks on human rights advocates, the General Assembly adopted the Declaration on the Right and Responsibility of Individuals, Groups and Organs of Society to Promote and Protect Universally Recognized Human Rights and Fundamental Freedoms. While not legally binding, the Declaration builds

---

27. Human Rights Watch, *Sierra Leone: Lesbian Rights Activist Brutally Murdered*, Oct. 5, 2004, *available at* http://hrw.org/english/docs/2004/10/04/sierra9440.htm.

28. Front Line: Defenders of Human Rights Defenders, *Concern for the Safety of Colombian Human Rights Defender: Soraya Gutierrez Arguello*, *available at* http://www.frontlinedefenders.org/node/501 (last visited May 23, 2008).

29. Negar Azimi, *Hard Realities of Soft Power*, NEW YORK TIMES MAGAZINE, June 24, 2007 *available at* http://www.nytimes.com/2007/06/24/magazine/24ngo-t.html?partner=rssnyt & emc=rss.

upon existing international law to reaffirm the rights of human rights defenders.

Declaration on the Right and Responsibility of Individuals, Groups and Organs of Society to Promote and Protect Universally Recognized Human Rights and Fundamental Freedoms, GA Res. 53/144 (8 March 1999)

The General Assembly, * * *

Acknowledging the important role of international cooperation for, and the valuable work of individuals, groups and associations in contributing to, the effective elimination of all violations of human rights and fundamental freedoms of peoples and individuals * * *

Declares:

Article 1

Everyone has the right, individually and in association with others, to promote and to strive for the protection and realization of human rights and fundamental freedoms at the national and international levels.

Article 2

1. Each State has a prime responsibility and duty to protect, promote and implement all human rights and fundamental freedoms * * *

2. Each State shall adopt such legislative, administrative and other steps as may be necessary to ensure that the rights and freedoms referred to in the present Declaration are effectively guaranteed.

Article 5

For the purpose of promoting and protecting human rights and fundamental freedoms, everyone has the right, individually and in association with others, at the national and international levels:

(*a*) To meet or assemble peacefully;

(*b*) To form, join and participate in non-governmental organizations, associations or groups;

(*c*) To communicate with non-governmental or intergovernmental organizations.

Article 6

Everyone has the right, individually and in association with others:

(*a*) To know, seek, obtain, receive and hold information about all human rights and fundamental freedoms, including having access to information as to how those rights and freedoms are given effect in domestic legislative, judicial or administrative systems. * * *

Article 7

Everyone has the right, individually and in association with others, to develop and discuss new human rights ideas and principles and to advocate their acceptance.

Article 8

1. Everyone has the right, individually and in association with others, to have effective access, on a non-discriminatory basis, to participation in the government of his or her country and in the conduct of public affairs. * * *

Article 9

1. In the exercise of human rights and fundamental freedoms, including the promotion and protection of human rights as referred to in the present Declaration, everyone has the right, individually and in association with others, to benefit from an effective remedy and to be protected in the event of the violation of those rights.

2. To this end, everyone whose rights or freedoms are allegedly violated has the right, either in person or through legally authorized representation, to complain to and have that complaint promptly reviewed in a public hearing before an independent, impartial and competent judicial or other authority established by law and to obtain from such an authority a decision, in accordance with law, providing redress, including any compensation due, where there has been a violation of that person's rights or freedoms, as well as enforcement of the eventual decision and award, all without undue delay. * * *

*Article 12 * * ***

3. [E]veryone is entitled, individually and in association with others, to be protected effectively under national law in reacting against or opposing, through peaceful means, activities and acts, including those by omission, attributable to States that result in violations of human rights and fundamental freedoms, as well as acts of violence perpetrated by groups or individuals that affect the enjoyment of human rights and fundamental freedoms.

Article 13

Everyone has the right, individually and in association with others, to solicit, receive and utilize resources for the express purpose of promoting and protecting human rights and fundamental freedoms through peaceful means, in accordance with article 3 of the present Declaration.

Article 14

1. The State has the responsibility to take legislative, judicial, administrative or other appropriate measures to promote the understanding by all persons under its jurisdiction of their civil, political, economic, social and cultural rights. * * *

Article 18

1.   Everyone has duties towards and within the community, in which alone the free and full development of his or her personality is possible.

2.   Individuals, groups, institutions and non-governmental organizations have an important role to play and a responsibility in safeguarding democracy, promoting human rights and fundamental freedoms and contributing to the promotion and advancement of democratic societies, institutions and processes.

Human Rights First "Protecting Human Rights Defenders: Analysis of the Newly Adopted Declaration on Human Rights Defenders" *available at* **http://www.humanrightsfirst.org/defenders/hrd_un_ declare/hrd_declare_1.htm. (last visited May 23, 2008)**

In reviewing the Declaration on Human Rights Defenders, our overall assessment is a very positive one. The Declaration is the first UN instrument to emphasize that everyone has the right to promote, protect, and defend human rights, on the national and international levels. The Declaration reaffirms and clarifies the existing rights of human rights defenders that are most often challenged by governments, such as the right to meet and assemble peacefully; to form, join and participate in NGOs; to hold and publish information about human rights; to complain about the policies and actions of officials and government bodies; and to enjoy unhindered access to international bodies. Furthermore, the Declaration provides that everyone who exercises his or her rights is entitled to full protection by law and in practice against any violence or retaliation.

The Declaration also incorporates the right to receive and obtain funding for human rights activities, a right not articulated as such in any existing human rights standard. The progressive incorporation of this right in the Declaration responds to an important need of human rights defenders that is often denied.

One of the most innovative aspects of the Declaration on Human Rights Defenders is its affirmation that everyone is entitled to enjoy the rights of human rights defenders "individually and in association with others." * * * In this regard, the Declaration makes an important contribution to the development of the right to freedom of association, a right traditionally neglected in international law insofar as it relates to NGOs.

The Declaration also outlines the specific duties of States to guarantee the rights of human rights defenders. It highlights the general obligation of States to promote, protect, and implement human rights in law and in practice, as well as their duty to take all necessary measures to protect human rights defenders from violence and arbitrary action. It reiterates that States have the obligation to carry out investigations in cases of alleged violations of human rights, including those contained in the Declaration.

Finally, the Declaration underscores the responsibilities of persons, such as physicians, lawyers and law enforcement officials, who may not be seen primarily as "human rights defenders" but who often play a crucial role in safeguarding the human rights of others. However, some unfortunate compromises were necessary in the lengthy, difficult negotiations to achieve the adoption of the Declaration. The most prominent example of this is the reference to the role of national law, the inclusion of which had been opposed by NGOs and many governments. They had argued that the application of the rights in the Declaration should not be made subordinate to national law, as national laws will differ from state to state and may restrict the rights of human rights defenders.

However, this provision was agreed upon with the inclusion of an important safety clause: in order to provide for the "juridical framework" of implementation of the Declaration, domestic law must be "consistent with the Charter of the United Nations and other international obligations of the State in the field of human rights and fundamental freedoms." * * * Also, in an effort to reach a compromise on the inclusion of the right to receive funding, this provision now contains a direct reference to the applicability of domestic law.

Another contentious issue—the responsibilities or duties of human rights defenders—was also incorporated in the Declaration, but in a significantly watered down version that does not impose any new obligations on human rights defenders.

NOTES AND QUESTIONS ON THE HUMAN RIGHTS DEFENDER DECLARATION

1. *NGO efforts to implement the Human Rights Defender Declaration.* Since the adoption of the Human Rights Defender Declaration, NGOs have tried to implement schemes of protection for defenders on the ground. Rather than treating it as merely another legal human rights document, NGOs are using the Declaration to organize, mobilize and adopt plans of action. One example of those efforts is the Plan of Action adopted at the Human Rights Defenders Summit,[30] which includes a commitment to lobby governments "[t]o modify their internal policies and administrative, legislative and judicial systems to incorporate the obligations and rights established by [the Declaration];" "to guarantee that human rights groups and defenders receive up-to-date information on persons deprived of liberty and that they were given access to prisons, police stations, military bases and any other detention centre or any other place where human rights violation are suspected of being committed;" "[t]o suspend immediately from active service members of the security forces under formal investigation for human rights violations until investigations have concluded," and "[t]o publicly discipline those functionaries under their jurisdiction who issue public declara-

---

30. The Human Rights Defenders Summit: The International Assembly, Adopted Plan of Action (Dec. 1998), AI Index ACT 30/005/1999, (May 27, 1999), http://web.amnesty.org/library/index/ENGACT300051999.

tions, affirmations or accusations against the legitimate work of human rights defenders." *Id.* arts. 26, 29, 31.

2. *The right to funding.* Article 13 provides for the right to "solicit, receive, and utilize resources for the express purpose of promoting and protecting human rights and fundamental freedoms, through peaceful means." Government control over funding has often been used to restrict the work of human rights defenders who require donations from individuals or foundations to support their work. Many of these governments have prohibited foreign funding in particular. In her book, *Funding and Normalization*, Sanaa al-Masri argued that "foreign funding invariably comes with strings attached—namely promoting normalization with Israel."[31] Former government MP Gamal Abu–Zekri voiced similar fears: "Foreign funding is very dangerous. We must be careful because it's a back door for * * * incitement to sectarian life." *Id.* Are these legitimate reasons for prohibiting foreign funding? Is foreign funding for NGOs a type of economic, political, or cultural imperialism, or merely a way for NGOs to address the high volume of human rights complaints? Can transparency laws requiring publication of all funding alleviate concerns over "back door" influence?

3. *Responsibilities of human rights defenders.* In addition to setting forth the rights that shall be accorded to human rights defenders, the Declaration sets forth responsibilities. Article 16 provides that in the process of making the public more aware of human rights issues through training or education, human rights defenders should "bear in mind the various backgrounds of societies and communities, in which they carry out their activities." Article 18 highlights the role of human rights defenders in "safeguarding democracy" and "contributing to the promotion and advancement of democratic societies, institutions, and processes." What does it mean to "bear in mind the various backgrounds of communities" or to "safeguard democracy"? Can reasonable individuals come to radically different conclusions as to what this means? Are these directives too vague to provide any real guidance?

4. *Non-violence requirement.* Article 12 provides that all individuals have the right "to participate in peaceful activities against violations of human rights and fundamental freedoms." The Declaration notably declines to extend its protections to those who engage in violence. In doing so, the Declaration comes down firmly on the side of non-violence in the debate about the legitimacy of using violence, as a last resort, against rights abusing regimes. As a result, individuals such as Nelson Mandela would not be covered by the protections in the Declaration.[32]

---

31 *See also* Mona El–Ghobashy, *Antinomies of the Saad Eddin Ibrahim Case*, Middle East Report Online, Aug. 15, 2002, http://www.merip.org/mero/mero081502.html.

32. In addition to all his nonviolent actions, Mandela actively participated in the creation of Umkhonto we Sizwe ("MK"), a largely ineffective guerilla group that focused on targeting public property in an effort to speed the end of Apartheid. As declared in a leaflet issued by the command of Umkhonto we Sizwe on December 16, 1961:

It is, however, well known that the main national liberation organisations in this country have consistently followed a policy of non-violence. They have conducted themselves peaceably at all

Do you agree with this conclusion? Should individuals be protected in spite of the fact that they support in principle violent opposition against repressive regimes?

5.   *NGOs under fire in Russia.* Despite the existence of the Declaration, human rights defenders can still face hostility from the governments they work to hold accountable. On January 10, 2006, Russian President Vladimir Putin signed the Law *"On Introducing Amendments to Certain Legislative Acts of the Russian Federation."* The new law gives the government significantly more control over the activities of NGOs and dramatically decreases the ability of NGOs to accept donations or hire foreigners.[33] President Putin defended the law from critics, stating, "Whether these organizations want it or not, they become an instrument in the hands of foreign states that use them to achieve their own political objectives. * * * This situation is unacceptable." Were President Putin's concerns legitimate? In the face of this kind of government hostility, what steps can human rights defenders, states, and treaty bodies take to ensure the effective implementation of the Declaration? *See* Human Rights First, *Russian Activists Threatened by Proposed New Law*, Dec. 14, 2005, *available at* http://www.humanrightsfirst.org/defenders/hrd_russia/ alert121405_law.htm.

---

2.   THE USE OF DEFAMATION LAWS TO SUPPRESS HUMAN RIGHTS DEFENDERS

States that fail to adhere to their international human rights obligations often employ defamation laws to silence their critics. Defamation laws, which have the legitimate purpose of protecting an individual's reputation, are instead misused by states to restrict freedom of expression and to limit the free flow of information and ideas, particularly information that exposes the involvement of the state or its agents in human rights violations. Under the pretext of defamation, states often bring criminal charges which enable them to keep their critics imprisoned. Imposing criminal sanctions in such cases is contrary to the UN Special Rapporteur on Freedom of Opinion and Expression's definitive statement that imprisonment should never be imposed as a punishment

---

times, regardless of government attacks and persecutions upon them, and despite all government-inspired attempts to provoke them to violence. They have done so because the people prefer peaceful methods of change to achieve their aspirations without the suffering and bitterness of civil war. But the people's patience is not endless.

The time comes in the life of any nation when there remain only two choices: submit or fight. That time has now come to South Africa. We shall not submit and we have no choice but to hit back by all means within our power in defence of our people, our future and our freedom. The government has interpreted the peacefulness of the movement as weakness; the people's non-violent policies have been taken as a green light for government violence. Refusal to resort to force has been interpreted by the government as an invitation to use armed force against the people without any fear of reprisals. The methods of Umkhonto we Sizwe mark a break with that past.

33.   Steven Lee Myers, *Russia Pushing Measure to Curb Private Groups*, N.Y. TIMES, Nov. 24, 2005, at A1.

for defamation. In his 1999 Report to the UN Commission on Human Rights, the Rapporteur stated, "[s]anctions for defamation should not be so large as to exert a chilling effect on freedom of opinion and expression and the right to seek, receive and impart information; penal sanctions, in particular imprisonment, should never be applied."[34]

Misuse of defamation statutes to silence the free speech of critics violates the right to freedom of expression, a right that is well-protected in international human rights law.[35] Article 19 of the ICCPR, for example, provides that "[e]veryone shall have the right to freedom of expression; this right shall include freedom to seek, receive and impart information and ideas of all kinds, regardless of frontiers, either orally, in writing or in print, in the form of art, or through any other media of his choice." The right to freedom of expression, however, is not absolute. Restrictions on freedom of expression are permissible in certain circumstances, provided they fulfill a three-part test: "The restriction must be properly set out in law and cannot be overly broad or vague. It must have as its purpose one of a very limited number of legitimate aims recognised under international law. Finally, the restriction must be clearly necessary and not disproportionate to achieve that aim."[36]

These restrictions, however, do not authorize states to use defamation as a blanket justification for prohibiting critical speech. Indeed, a state's use of defamation laws to prevent its citizens from speaking freely about public bodies, public officials, or public policy, raises troubling freedom of expression issues. "Article 19," an NGO dedicated to the freedom of expression, surveyed the decisions of national and international courts and found the courts to be in agreement that using defamation laws to limit criticism of the government or its officials is illegitimate. The report[37] stated:

> The danger of giving public bodies the right to sue their critics for defamation has been widely noted. The Human Rights Committee stated, in its observations on Mexico's periodic report, that it "deplores the existence of the offence of 'defamation of the state'" and called for its abolition. U.N. International Covenant on Civil and Political Rights, U.N. Doc. CCPR/C/79/Add. 109, 27 July 1999, ¶ 14. *Concluding Observations of the Human Rights Committee: Mexico.* In *Derbyshire County Council v. Times Newspapers Ltd.*, the House of

---

34. *Report of the Special Rapporteur on the Promotion and Protection of the Right to Freedom of Opinion and Expression*, ¶ 28, U.N. Doc. E/CN.4/1999/64 (Jan. 29, 1999).

35. *See* Universal Declaration of Human Rights, G.A. Res. 217A, at 71. U.N. GAOR, 3d Sess., 1st plen. Mtg., U.N. Doc. A/810 (Dec. 12, 1948); International Covenant on Civil and Political Rights, G.A. Res. 2200A, art. 19, U.N. GAOR, 21st Sess., U.N. Doc. A/6316 (1966) *entered into force* Mar. 23, 1976); *see also* European Convention for the Protection of Human Rights and Fundamental Freedoms, Nov. 4, 1950, 213 U.N.T.S. 22, art. 10; American Convention on Human Rights, arts. 13, 14, Nov. 22, 1969, 1144 U.N.T.S. 123; African Charter on Human and Peoples' Rights, art. 9, June 27, 1981 21 I.L.M. 58.

36. Int'l Comm'n of Jurists, *Power to Silence: Nepal's New Media Ordinance*, December 2005, *available at* http://www.icj.org/IMG/pdf/ICJ_Report_Ordinance.pdf

37. Article 19, *Briefing Note on International and Comparative Defamation Standards*, Feb. 2004, *available at* http://www.article19.org/pdfs/analysis/defamation-standards.pdf.

Lords ruled that the common law does not allow a local authority to maintain an action for damages for libel. As an elected body, it "should be open to uninhibited public criticism. The threat of a civil action for defamation must inevitably have an inhibiting effect on freedom of speech." [1993] 1 All ER 1011, p. 1017. The Indian Supreme Court followed *Derbyshire*'s lead in *Rajgopal v. State of Tamil Nadu*, finding that 'the Government, local authority and other organs and institutions exercising governmental power' cannot bring a defamation suit. (1994) 6 Supreme Court Cases 632, p. 650. A similar position has been taken in the United States,[38] Zimbabwe and South Africa. While the European Court of Human Rights has not entirely ruled out defamation suits by governments, it appears to have limited such suits to situations which threaten public order, implying governments cannot sue in defamation simply to protect their honour. *Castells v. Spain*, 23 April 1992, 14 EHRR 445, para. 46.

The rationale for restricting the ability of elected bodies to sue is threefold. First, criticism of government is vital to the success of a democracy and defamation suits inhibit free debate about vital matters of public concern. *Derbyshire* emphasized this point when distinguishing the plaintiff county council from private corporations. Note 21, p. 1017.

Second, defamation laws are designed to protect reputations. Courts have held that elected bodies should not be entitled to sue in defamation because any reputation they might have would belong to the public as a whole, which on balance benefits from uninhibited criticism. In any case, elected bodies regularly change membership so, as the *Derbyshire* court noted, "it is difficult to say the local authority as such has any reputation of its own." 26 *Ibid.*, p. 1020 Finally, the government has ample ability to defend itself from harsh criticism by other means, for example by responding directly to any allegations. Allowing public bodies to sue is, therefore, an inappropriate use of taxpayers money, one which may well be open to abuse by governments intolerant of criticism. * * *

[In addition] the European Court of Human Rights has been very clear on the matter of public officials and defamation: they are required to tolerate more, not less, criticism, in part because of the public interest in open debate about public figures and institutions. In its very first defamation case, the Court emphasised that: The limits of acceptable criticism are * * * wider as regards a politician as such than as regards a private individual. Unlike the latter, the former inevitably and knowingly lays himself open to close scrutiny of his every word and deed by both journalists and the public at

---

38. In *City of Chicago v. Tribune Co.*, 307 Ill. 595, 601, 139 N.E. 86 (1923), the Illinois Supreme Court ruled a city could not sue a newspaper for defamation. It said, "no court of last resort in this country has ever held, or even suggested, that prosecutions for libel on government have any place in the American system of jurisprudence."

large, and must consequently display a greater degree of tolerance. *Lingens v. Austria*, note 16, para. 42. The Court has affirmed this principle in several cases and it has become a fundamental tenet of its caselaw.[39]

Recognizing the threat that defamation laws would be used to silence human rights defenders speaking out against rights abusing governments, the drafters of the Human Rights Defender Declaration inserted provisions designed to protect defenders from this problem *see* Articles 5, 6, and 7, *supra*.

The NGO, Article 19, has proposed a more comprehensive set of principles on freedom of expression and defamation. These principles specifically articulate both the restrictions on and affirmative duties of states with respect to defamation laws.

Article 19, *Defining Defamation: Principles of Freedom of Expression and Protection of Reputation*, July 2000[40]

Principle 1.1: Prescribed by Law

Any restriction on expression or information must be prescribed by law. The law must be accessible, unambiguous and narrowly and precisely drawn so as to enable individuals to predict with reasonable certainty in advance the legality or otherwise of a particular action.

Principle 1.2: Protection of a Legitimate Reputation Interest

Any restriction on expression or information which is sought to be justified on the ground that it protects the reputations of others, must have the genuine purpose and demonstrable effect of protecting a legitimate reputation interest. * * *

Principle 2: Legitimate Purpose of Defamation Laws * * *

(b) Defamation laws cannot be justified if their purpose or effect is to protect individuals against harm to a reputation which they do not have or do not merit, or to protect the "reputations" of entities other than those which have the right to sue and to be sued. In particular, defamation laws cannot be justified if their purpose or effect is to:

    i.   prevent legitimate criticism of officials or the exposure of official wrongdoing or corruption;

    ii.   protect the 'reputation' of objects, such as State or religious symbols, flags or national insignia;

    iii.   protect the 'reputation' of the State or nation, as such;

    iv.   enable individuals to sue on behalf of persons who are deceased; or

---

39. *See, e.g., Lopes Gomez da Silva v. Portugal*, 28 September 2000, Application No. 37698/97, ¶ 30; *Wabl v. Austria*, 21 March 2000, Application No. 24773/94, ¶ 42; and *Oberschlick v. Austria*, 23 May 1991, Application No. 11662/85, ¶ 59.

40. *Available at* http://www.article19.org/pdfs/standards/definingdefamation.pdf.

    v. allow individuals to sue on behalf of a group which does not, itself, have status to sue.

(c) Defamation laws also cannot be justified on the basis that they serve to protect interests other than reputation, where those interests, even if they may justify certain restrictions on freedom of expression, are better served by laws specifically designed for that purpose. In particular, defamation laws cannot be justified on the grounds that they help maintain public order, national security, or friendly relations with foreign States or governments. * * *

Principle 3: Defamation of Public Bodies

Public bodies of all kinds—including all bodies which form part of the legislative, executive or judicial branches of government or which otherwise perform public functions—should be prohibited altogether from bringing defamation actions. * * *

Principle 4: Criminal Defamation

(a) All criminal defamation laws should be abolished and replaced, where necessary, with appropriate civil defamation laws. Steps should be taken, in those States which still have criminal defamation laws in place, to progressively implement this Principle. * * *

Principle 8: Public Officials

Under no circumstances should defamation law provide any special protection for public officials, whatever their rank or status. This Principle embraces the manner in which complaints are lodged and processed, the standards which are applied in determining whether a defendant is liable, and the penalties which may be imposed.

NOTES AND QUESTIONS ON DEFAMATION LAWS AND HUMAN RIGHTS DEFENDERS

    1. *More protection needed?* Does the Human Rights Defender Declaration sufficiently protect the rights of human rights defenders to freely express their criticisms of the state, or is the Article 19 proposal needed? What additional rights does Article 19's proposal guarantee? What challenges would governments likely raise to Article 19's proposal?

    2. *Immunity for special rapporteurs.* UN Special Rapporteurs are granted immunity from defamation with regard to statements made in the course of their work as are necessary for the independent exercise of their official functions. This issue arose in the case of Dato Param Cumaraswamy, a Malaysian lawyer serving as the Special Rapporteur on the Independence of Judges and Lawyers of the UN Commission on Human Rights.[41] In November 1995, Cumaraswamy gave an interview

---

41. *See* Difference Relating to Immunity from Legal Process of a Special Rapporteur of the Commission on Human Rights, Advisory Opinion, 1999 I.C.J. 100 (Apr. 29), *available at* http://www.icj-cij.org/icjwww/idocket/inuma/inumaframe.htm.

to a British magazine in which he commented on his investigation into complaints that corporations had improperly influenced the Malaysian courts to render decisions in their favor. The corporations sued Cumaraswamy for defamation, and ECOSOC applied to the ICJ for an advisory opinion on the matter. The ICJ issued its Advisory Opinion on April 29, 1999, finding that Cumaraswamy was entitled to immunity under Article 22 of the General Convention on the Privileges and Immunities of the United Nations, which granted privileges and immunities to persons on UN missions as were necessary for the independent exercise of their functions.

E. ACCOUNTABILITY OF NON–GOVERNMENTAL ORGANIZATIONS

With NGOs increasingly garnering power independent of states and playing a greater role in international organizations, critics are beginning to ask some important questions. "What exactly is this public sentiment that NGOs claim to represent? How do NGOs become the trustees of it? Whose interests do NGOs represent and how accountable are NGOs to such constituents? Behind these questions is a concern for accountability. On what basis can they claim to act in the public interest? How justifiable is their operation as public authorities in world politics? In short, to whom and how are they accountable?"[42]

The majority of NGO leaders are appointed rather than elected, are overseen by boards of directors with similar ideological viewpoints, and are subject only to weak institutional checks at the international level. As one commentator has observed, "NGOs can arise and undertake political activity on their own. They need not receive formal accreditation from any particular body nor do they need independent recognition from other NGOs. To be an NGO these days, it seems one needs only a fax machine and internet access. If this is the case, then questions of NGO accountability are right on target." Paul Wapner, *Introductory Essay: Paradise Lost? NGOs and Global Accountability*, 3 CHI. J. INT'L L. 155, 157–58 (2002).

Among the most vocal critics of NGO legitimacy is Kenneth Anderson. In the following excerpt, he argues that the anti-democratic nature of NGOs undermines their legitimacy. What is the source of an NGO's authority?

---

42. Paul Wapner, *The Democratic Accountability of Non–Governmental Organizations: Defending Accountability in NGOs*, 3 CHI. J. INT'L L. 197 (2002).

Kenneth Anderson, *The Limits of Pragmatism in American Foreign Policy: Unsolicited Advice to the Bush Administration on Relations With International Nongovernmental Organizations,* 2 CHI. J. INT'L L. 371, 377–384 (2001)

International NGOs have obtained a very sizable grant of legitimacy from governments and international organizations over the last ten or fifteen years simply by asserting on their own behalf the view that they are not merely private organizations, but that they are, in virtue of being private voluntary organizations, "international civil society" * * *. It is not by accident that international NGOs stress their legitimacy as international actors by invoking the lofty claim that they are civil society rather than by stressing, as in an earlier time, their good works and service on behalf of the world's poor and oppressed.

But what is the difference in the claim? Why is it different and more politically reaching to claim the mantle of civil society rather than merely resting, for example, on the laurels of one's service to fellow human beings? The inflation of legitimacy lies, it seems to me, in the implied claim of *representativeness*. When, for example, Jody Williams, recipient of the 1997 Nobel Prize on the behalf of the NGO campaign to ban landmines, speaks of international NGOs, she speaks of them as representatives of the peoples of the world. The international NGOs, on this view, represent the peoples of the planet in negotiations and discussions with international organizations, with governments, and with multinational corporations. As such they should be understood as a force for democratizing international affairs and the so-called "international community." * * * It is a sense of political entitlement that practically requires, in the name of democratic legitimacy, that international NGOs be treated not merely as lobbyists in the corridors, but as official negotiators on behalf of "civil society" and the world's "peoples" in treaty negotiations. * * *

International NGOs may say that their activities of lobbying, persuasion, protest, media manipulation, report writing, etc., are no different in the international field than that which their equivalents perform in domestic democratic societies. This may be true, as far as it goes. The difficulty, however, is that international NGOs perform these activities in an entirely different political structure and environment from domestic organizations—the difference is that one is democratic and the other is not. In a domestic democratic society, we do not look to nonprofit organizations as the proof of our democratic credentials—we look to elections and the ballot for that proof. * * * Citizens' associations, pressure groups, lobbying organizations, and protest organizations are not, in a settled democratic society, accountable to any but themselves and their own principles—nor should they be, because the function of democratic accountability is accomplished by a wholly different mechanism: elections.

In the undemocratic international world, however, matters are entirely different. There are nodirect elections. Rather, there is the attenuated, indirect democratic process of sovereign democracies supposedly controlling international organizations. But as these international organizations reach out to seek to govern the behavior of these same sovereigns—to attenuate their sovereignty—then they also lose the ability to rely on them as the *source* of their democratic legitimacy. In the democratic deficit that inevitably develops, it is natural, but wrong, to look to the pressure groups, the citizens' groups, the opposition groups, and the protest organizations, as an alternate source of democratic legitimacy. And the NGOs are only too happy to offer themselves, giving little heed to the fact that by offering themselves as substitutes for democracy, they make it ever more difficult to confront the naked and painful consequences of an international system that has no democratic legitimacy. * * * In my view, this system cannot ever become democratic simply because democracy in any meaningful sense is incompatible with the size and number of people on the planet. By offering themselves as substitutes for real democracy in order to further their own influence, international NGOs muddy the waters of the critical question of how much power ought to be assigned to a system of international organizations that cannot ever be democratic. * * *

Paul Wapner, *The Democratic Accountability of Non–Governmental Organizations: Defending Accountability in NGOs*, 3 Chi. J. Int'l L. 197 (2002)

The view that states are accountable while NGOs are not is simply inaccurate. It fails to note the non-constitutional elements that hold NGOs accountable to broad-based oversight and exaggerates the quality and degree of oversight to which states are subject. Many regimes throughout the world—close to 40 percent—are undemocratic and thus enjoy few internal mechanisms that hold state officials accountable to their people. Furthermore, even among liberal democratic states, accountability is far from perfect. Every main theory of the democratic state explains ways in which the will of the people is often subverted or otherwise lost in translation as citizens try to have their interests expressed in a representative framework. Finally, international mechanisms of accountability—such as UN membership, compliance with international regimes, and so forth—serve as weak constraints on states. Some states are immune from these institutions and many others find ways of ignoring them. These observations are not meant, of course, to deny the high level of accountability that exists within and among liberal democratic polities. Rather they aim merely to remind us of the imperfect character of such polities. * * *

States and NGOs possess various mechanisms of accountability, each of which works imperfectly. When compared to each other, it is not the case that states come out shining while NGOs are tarnished, but rather a more complex picture emerges. NGOs, at times and from certain perspectives, appear more responsive than states to widespread public sentiment and, at other times and from different angles, less so. Indeed, the argument is that NGOs are not *more* accountable than states but *differently* accountable. And, this difference, in terms of evaluating NGO accountability, makes all the difference in the world.

[*Internal Accountability*]: Internally, NGOs are accountable to their members. * * * Members are the life-blood of many NGOs. They provide institutional strength, insofar as they can be called upon to write letters, protest, or otherwise mobilize on behalf of the organization. Merely by virtue of their numbers, members can serve to demonstrate the legitimacy of the organization's agenda. Developing a membership does not come as a matter of course; neither does sustaining it. * * * When supporters no longer feel satisfied by the NGO, they are no longer available to be mobilized or otherwise advocate on behalf of the group. Members vote with their feet. When the NGO no longer express-es their sentiment, they exit. This is a key form of accountability.

Members also vote with their pocketbooks * * * [which makes] NGOs perpetually accountable to the membership insofar as periodic donations for particular campaigns provide both an affirmation of an NGO's activities and the financial ability actually to carry out specific projects. In addition to members' financial support as a form of account-ability, most NGOs reach beyond their memberships to seek donors for their work. Donors can be philanthropic foundations, other NGOs, governments, or the public at large. Groups such as the International Campaign to Ban Land Mines, World Wildlife Fund, Amnesty Interna-tional, and Oxfam count on these institutions for financial strength. Consequently, far from being unanswerable for their work, NGOs are constantly measuring the pulse of their members and donors (and being evaluated by members and donors), which serves as a layer of internal but widely based form of accountability.

An additional internal dimension of accountability is the role boards of directors or advising councils play in some organizations. Many professional institutions use outside experts or boards of directors that watch out for the organization's long-term well-being. These boards are usually comprised of people who are uninvolved in day-to-day opera-tions and therefore possess a broader perspective on the issue area and the organization's political role. Boards can have authority to depose NGO leaders and shape the broad outlines of campaign work. While board members implicitly share the overall normative orientation of the organization and its officials, they come to the group as outsiders. In fact, they are invited onto the board precisely because they have some distance from the organization. As a result, boards of directors, outside advisory committees, and the like act, then, as monitors, evaluators, and reviewers who provide an additional, internal layer of accountability.

[*External Accountability*]: Externally, NGOs operate in a networked system of activity in which other NGOs, IGOs, and states themselves serve as checks on power and constituencies that need to be addressed. * * * NGO strength, especially at the transnational level, rests on their ability to network across boundaries with each other. NGO effectiveness, in other words, rests largely on their ability to garner widespread support in global civil society. * * * Whenever an NGO links or otherwise collaborates with another, it opens itself up to scrutiny and evaluation. To the degree that NGOs find strength in doing so, however, accountability becomes part of the price of increased transnational effectiveness.

In the same way that NGOs must be accountable to each other, they must also be responsive to those IGOs with whom they wish to work. Many international fora officially make arrangements for NGO participation. Certain international conventions, for example, allow "technically qualified" NGOs to participate in negotiations as nonvoting observers. More generally, participation in UN-sponsored regimes requires United Nations Economic and Social Council ("ECOSOC") accreditation. Participation in such fora has been essential for NGO influence on international treaties. To be sure, accreditation is not necessarily a rigorous process, and NGOs can often demonstrate relevant participatory credentials. Nonetheless, there is some scrutiny, and NGOs organize and certainly present themselves in particular ways to meet the criteria of evaluation. * * *

NGOs also peddle in a currency that itself requires vigilance in terms of broad responsibility. Most NGOs offer themselves as experts on particular issues and representatives of politically motivated people and groups. They have no armies, police, or other coercive tools at their disposal. In many cases, the only thing they have going for them is their reputation, and this rests on credibility. When NGOs provide spurious information—as, to be sure, some do—they risk their foundation of institutional and political strength. The credibility factor does not, then, ensure that NGOs will always be honest or have the most accurate information. Rather, it simply suggests that NGOs will think twice before disseminating false information because the stakes, in terms of being held accountable, are high.

In reaching out to states, IGOs, and other NGOs, it should be remembered that the field of activity for NGOs is the globe itself. This threads through a final dimension of accountability. States are accountable to their people and the international organizations of which they are a part. As such, they focus primarily (and often exclusively) on the interests of those who live within their borders. NGOs, in contrast, are, what James Rosenau calls, "sovereignty-free" actors. They work not on behalf of territorially situated publics, but on behalf of people throughout the world. This does not mean, of course, that they embody a universalist public: there is none. But it does suggest that the geographical scope of their constituency is broader, or at least differently constituted, than that of states. This attaches an added burden to their accountability challenges. For this reason, NGOs are arguably *more* accountable to *global* citizenry than states.

NOTES AND QUESTIONS ON THE ACCOUNTABILITY OF NGOS

1. *Regulating NGOs.* Would a formal system of regulation for NGOs solve the problem of accountability? One author argues that

human rights NGOs should engage in a form of self-regulation administered by a "consortium of leading HRO's ('human rights organizations'), working together with independent academic and judicial figures having expertise in international law, human rights and regulatory systems." Robert Charles Blitt, *Who Will Watch the Watchdogs? Human Rights Nongovernmental Organizations and the Case for Regulation*, 10 BUFF. HUM. RTS. L. REV. 261, 390 (2004). Can you identify any potential problems with this proposal? Such a system of regulation, he argues "should serve to promote clarity with respect to how a given organization may label itself as a human rights organization, what activities fall within HRO mandates, and what guidelines are applied when collecting and disseminating information on human rights abuses. In this manner, by promoting better definition, enhanced credibility, and greater accountability, NGOs assuredly can improve consumer estimates of the value of their information." *Id.* at 391. Or do you believe outside monitoring is necessary? The American Enterprise Institute ("AEI") and the Federalist Society, recognizing the growing influence of NGOs, have launched NGOWatch, later termed Global Governance Watch, a website to provide policy makers and the public with a monitoring tool to bring about greater accountability to the NGO sector. *See* Global Governance Watch, About Global Governance Watch, *available at* http://www. globalgovernancewatch.org (last visited May 23, 2008). Which approach do you believe would be more effective? Why?

2. *Politicization of NGOs.* How can NGOs avoid being "politicized?" In the wake of the UN's 2001 Durban World Conference Against Racism, several critics decried the politicization of human rights NGOs. At the Conference, 3000 NGOs adopted an NGO Forum Declaration, branding Israel a "racist, apartheid state" guilty of "systematic perpetration of racist crimes including war crimes, acts of genocide and ethnic cleansing." Several leading U.S. human rights organizations attempted to distance themselves from that language claiming that, while they did not condone some of the language used in the Declaration, they believed that the document as a whole was largely positive. One commentator remarked that "the inaction of presumably objective and professional international HROs like HRW and Amnesty in Durban may be attributed to a growing pressure within the NGO community to lend a greater voice to southern and national NGOs." Robert Charles Blitt, *Who Will Watch the Watchdogs? Human Rights Nongovernmental Organizations and the Case for Regulation*, 10 BUFF. HUM. RTS. L. REV. 261, 365 (2004).

3. *Participation and accountability.* Do NGOs, such as AI, which are membership organizations, have a greater claim to legitimacy in representing the interests of victims of human rights abuses than do organizations that are funded by foundations and wealthy individuals? What additional challenges are presented by the "professionalization" of human rights? As you read the following excerpt, think about how NGOs

can overcome these challenges and what role "professionalization" plays in accountability:

> Most human rights organisations are modeled after Northern watchdog organisations, located in an urban area, run by a core management without a membership base (unlike Amnesty International), and dependent solely on overseas funding. The most successful of these organisations only manage to achieve the equivalent status of a public policy think-tank, a research institute, or a specialised publishing house. * * * Instead of being the currency of a social justice or conscience-driven movement, "human rights" has increasingly become the specialised language of a select professional cadre with its own rites of passage and methods of certification. Far from being a badge of honour, human rights activism is, in some of the places I have observed it, increasingly a certificate of privilege.

Hugo Slim, *By What Authority? The Legitimacy and Accountability of Non–Governmental Organizations*, J. HUMANITARIAN ASSISTANCE, (2002), *available at* http://www.jha.ac/articles/a082.htm; *see also* David Kennedy, *The International Human Rights Movement: Part of the Problem?* 15 HARV. HUM. RTS. J. 101, 119–20 (2002).

Is there a tension between the diverse approaches of international human rights organizations? For example, HRW has adopted a highly professionalized approach to human rights, relying heavily on reporting and lobbying. AI, on the other hand, has traditionally adopted a more participatory mass-membership approach. What are the respective advantages and disadvantages of these approaches?

4. *Public support and accountability.* How important is it for NGOs to solicit public support for their activities? Does public support provide an additional layer of accountability? As you read the following excerpt, consider the ways an NGO can garner greater public support for its goals. In what ways can NGOs that are not membership-based begin this dialogue?

> A serious consequence of activists' blinkered worldview has been a marked failure to establish widespread support among ordinary citizens. For all its influence in elite circles, the human rights constituency is a tiny fraction of that commanded by grass-roots organizations of either the right or the left. Without a broad base of support, it may have reached the limits of its effectiveness. Whether its leaders know it or not, the human rights movement is in trouble. * * *

> [T]he human rights movement [must] show more willingness to engage in straightforward political activism, to get its hands dirty. It must lobby people in churches and shopping malls in the Midwest as assiduously as it lobbies Capitol Hill or the Ford Foundation. It must take its case to the public, not just rely on its influence and its certainty that it does an enormous amount of good in the world.

If the human rights movement cannot or will not engage in this way, then there is a great chance that the human rights paradigm will backfire the way affirmative action did. The parallel is striking. Affirmative action was also well meant. It drew popular opposition not, for the most part, because it was wrong, but because it was sneaked in, with no serious effort made to win people over. Convinced that their cause was right, its advocates saw no reason to campaign for it among the public at large. Instead, they relied on the courts, the law and legislation. And eventually, the whole project came undone.

At the moment, the human rights movement seems set to go down exactly the same path. If it does, it will, in the end, encounter the same result. That would be a very great loss.

David Rieff, *The Precarious Triumph of Human Rights*, N.Y. TIMES MAG., Aug. 8, 1999, at 37.

5. *Stigmatization and accountability.* One of the most effective tools NGOs have for protecting and promoting human rights is the process of stigmatization. Ken Roth argues that this itself acts as a form of accountability. "Because [NGOs] can use the process of stigmatization only against the backdrop of broadly shared values, and because the stigmatization process must be highly visible to be effective, human rights NGOs cannot stray far from the basic values of the human rights cause without either losing their effectiveness or subjecting themselves to public criticism. Indeed, this highly public form of accountability is arguably stronger than the theoretical accountability exerted on a classic NGO by its members, many of whom may not have the time, inclination or knowledge to scrutinize lower-profile activities." Kenneth Roth, *Human Rights Organizations: A New Force for Social Change*, Lecture at Harvard University, Nov. 4, 1998.

6. *Comparing NGOs to corporations.* At least one commentator has argued that:

NGOs are perhaps more appropriately compared to corporations rather than states for accountability purposes. * * * In the corporate context, shareholders play the role of NGO members; shareholders may control the corporation as a formal matter, but as a practical one, they are often powerless (in the face of high monitoring costs and collective action problems) to control directors and management. That is not to say, however, that corporations are unaccountable. In most cases shareholders enjoy the exit options of selling their shares, in rather the same way that NGO members can decline to renew their memberships. Accountability and agency problems are central to corporate law, but are confronted as a challenge amenable to at least incremental amelioration. One does not argue against the legitimacy of corporations *vel non* because the agency puzzles will never be fully solved. That should inform a similar orientation with respect to the internal accountability of

NGOs. There is surely room for enhancing the discipline of NGO representatives, made all the more important in the wake of their new global prominence. In the end, however, this is a question of international not-for-profit law. It may be more than technical, and will in fact require creative thinking, parallel to the demands globalization poses in the corporate law context. But there is no strong argument here against NGO participation in international institutions.

Peter J. Spiro, *The Democratic Accountability of Non–Governmental Organizations, Accounting for NGOs*, 3 CHI. J. INT'L L. 161, 165–66 (2002).

7. *Formal inclusion?* Is formal inclusion of NGOs into institutional decision-making the answer to accountability concerns? One commentator argues that NGOs are independent players in the global system but that the system does not recognize them as such. Greenpeace, for example, had more influence at environmental negotiations than many states do. But because this participation is rarely formal, NGOs have no obligation to respect the decision-making results. In effect, they enjoy the advantages of participation without having to abide by the resulting agreements. "Formal and direct participation would not add much to their influence, but it would increase their external accountability. No longer could NGOs opt out of bargains to which they had attached their names. As ongoing institutional participants, they would have a greater incentive to facilitate institutional success. * * * In that respect, formal inclusion would also enhance transparency, as well as accountability, among NGOs." Peter J. Spiro, *The Democratic Accountability of Non–Governmental Organizations, Accounting for NGOs*, 3 CHI. J. INT'L L. 161, 167 (2002).

Practicum

The International Council Meeting ("ICM") of Amnesty International is the highest policy-making body in the organization. The ICM meets every two years for about 10 days. Each national section (more than 50 at present) sends up to 8 delegates. Voting strength is based on the membership and size of the section, with each section receiving one to six votes. The majority of votes are still with European and North American sections, but there is a substantial bloc of smaller sections from Latin America, Eastern Europe, Asia and Africa. In addition, representatives from several dozen countries where there are only AI groups but no formal section participate without voting rights in the meeting. Thus, there are hundreds of delegates at an ICM.

One of the basic operating principles at an ICM is that every attempt should be made to reach a consensus or a compromise before the majority exercises its voting strength. Sometimes, as occurred with the reproductive rights issue in 2005 and 2007, a final decision on an issue may be deferred to provide more time for discussion, debate, and the further exploration of the possibility of a compromise. If the majority is made up mainly of North American and European sections, there is even more pressure to broaden the consensus before acting.

Issues of gender equity often arise. Ordinarily the number of men and women at an ICM is relatively balanced, yet this is not always true of all delegations. On this issue the division of opinion does not break down between big and small sections or between the global north and the global south within AI. To some degree, section representatives reflect their national cultures, but this generalization is not absolute.

The reproductive rights issue has been thrust upon AI in some respects because of its international campaign to stop violence against women. Many of AI's allies in this campaign believe that ensuring women's rights to reproductive freedom is central to preventing violence against women. Moreover, there is the issue of ensuring that women who have been raped have the possibility of termination of an unwanted pregnancy.

Another leading human rights organization, Human Rights Watch, has already taken a position on reproductive choices and sexual autonomy, stating, "In all parts of the world, women suffer discrimination and abuse because of their reproductive capacity. Community members, spouses, parents, and health professionals use discrimination, violence, and abuse as means to limit women's sexual autonomy and reproductive choices." Human Rights Watch, *Human Rights Violations Related to Women's Sexual Autonomy and Reproductive Choices*, available at http://hrw.org/english/docs/2005/07/07/americ11295.htm (last visited July 2, 2008).

Assume the class is the next ICM and the following is the basis for discussion and decision or possible amendment. The class should debate these issues and achieve a resolution by a majority of voting delegates.

Proposed Resolution

Whereas women in developed countries as a whole have a 1 in 2,800 chance of dying in childbirth, with some countries as low as 1 in 8,700; women in Africa have a 1 in 20 chance, and in several countries the lifetime risk exceeds 1 in 10.[44]

Whereas worldwide an estimated 68,000 women die as a consequence of an unsafe abortion each year. In developing countries, the risk of death is estimated at 1 death for every 270 unsafe abortion procedures. Complications from unsafe abortion account for 13 percent of maternal deaths globally.

Whereas studies show that between 4% and 20% of women experience violence during pregnancy, with consequences both for them and their

---

44. For background information and statistics *see* UN Millennium Project: Task Force on Child Health and Maternal Health, *Who's got the power? Transforming Health Systems to Improve the Lives of Women and Children*, *available at* http://www.unmillenniumproject.org/reports/tf_health.htm; World Health Org., *Unsafe Abortion: Global and Regional Estimates of Incidence of Unsafe Abortions and Associated Mortality in 2003*, *available at* http://www.who.int/reproductive-health/publications/unsafe abortion_2003/ua_estimates03.pdf.

babies, such as miscarriage, premature labour and low birth weight. Available data suggest that in some countries nearly one woman in four experiences sexual violence from an intimate partner. Rape and sexual assault by acquaintances and strangers is also common.

Whereas if all unmet need were to be met in low-income countries, 47,000 abortion-related deaths and 79,000 maternal deaths from other causes would be averted, and 457,000 more children would have the opportunity to grow up with their mothers. Moreover, within low income countries, most of the benefit would go to the poorest women and children, because disadvantaged women are more likely than those who are better off to have unmet need.

The International Council Affirms

(a) that Amnesty International is committed to defending and promoting sexual and reproductive rights (SRR) in the context of its mission, core values, and strategic goals;

(b) that Amnesty International recognises the basic right of all couples and individuals to decide freely and responsibly the number, spacing and timing of their children and to have the information and means to do so, and their right to attain the highest standard of sexual and reproductive health;

(c) that Amnesty International believes that men and women must be able to exercise their sexual and reproductive rights free from coercion, discrimination and violence;

(d) that Amnesty International should build on its previous and existing work on sexual and reproductive rights, taking into account the lessons of the Stop Violence Against Women (SVAW) campaign; its developing work on Economic, Social and Cultural Rights (ESCR), and its work on SRR to date.

Further decides

Option 1: AI should continue to take no position on abortion.

Option 2: That the IEC [the International Executive Committee] should develop an AI position on abortion that supports the rights of women to have abortions in cases of sexual assault, rape, and incest, and in cases where the mother's life or health is at risk.

Option 3: That the IEC should develop an AI position on abortion that is in line with the current international legal consensus (*i.e.*, abortion should be decriminalised; where abortion is not against the law, it should be safe and accessible; women should always have access to quality services for the management of complications arising from abortion).

Option 4: That the IEC should develop an AI position on abortion that is based on the understanding that a woman's right to physical and mental integrity includes her right to terminate her pregnancy, and that abortion should therefore be legal, safe and accessible to all women.

To assist you in your preparations, consider some of the arguments advanced in the debate so far:

Arguments in Favor of Adopting a Position on Abortion Rights for Women

(a) Provided that it could achieve a high degree of consensus, AI would bring the energy, determination, and activism of its 1.8 million members and supporters around the world. Having more people working on the issues is itself likely to be productive, additional moral and practical support, longer petitions, larger demonstrations, and more lobbyists, will all add strength to the messages already being articulated by key activists.

(b) As with the SVAW campaign, AI will bring the experience of situating abuses within a firm human rights framework. AI's knowledge of human rights law, and its understanding of how, for example, the UN monitoring bodies and other oversight mechanisms work, will be valuable. AI's experience of holding states and non-state actors to account, judging them against the standards of international law, could be particularly useful in supplementing the work of other NGOs that have a largely domestic focus. AI's growing experience of what it means for a government to "respect, protect, and fulfill" its obligations with regard to economic, social and cultural rights, could be valuable in making it clear just what governments need to do, for example, in providing access to information about contraception.

(c) AI could help to defend sexual and reproductive rights at a time when they are under attack. Because AI does not rely on government funding, it can be more outspoken than many other NGOs on these issues. Furthermore, AI can use its experience of defending human rights defenders to help protect and support sexual and reproductive rights defenders.

(d) AI's main contribution may well lie in simply drawing attention to the fact that so much of the ill-health suffered by men and women is not just down to bad luck, poverty, or local customs, but is due to a fundamental denial of human rights.

(e) By taking a progressive position on reproductive rights based on the beliefs of its members, Amnesty International will contribute to the development of institutional reproductive rights norms.

Arguments Against Developing a Position on Abortion Rights

There are always risks in undertaking new areas of work, but in the case of reproductive rights they could arguably be offset by the opportunities for AI to contribute to improving human rights and to strengthen itself as a human rights movement. Some of the risks apply to almost any new area of work, for instance, the risk that AI's inexperience (both in campaigning and in research) will lead it to make strategically unwise decisions; the risk that resources might be spread too thinly; and the risk that some of the membership will not agree with the new direction that AI is taking. In addition, there are four particular difficulties that AI could face in developing work on reproductive rights:

(a) The debate around some aspects of reproductive rights (such as sex-selective abortion) are very complex.

(b) Taking a position on access to abortion could be controversial or divisive.

(c) Some people might consider that AI is entering a highly-political arena in discussing some aspects of sexual and reproductive rights.

(d) The international law consensus on access to abortion is significantly weaker than the position many human rights activists believe is crucial for the realization of human rights for women. For Amnesty International to be effective it should, with rare exceptions, mobilize its members to demand enforcement of rights governments have already accepted in international law.

AI sections must consider the impact of a decision like this on their membership and on fundraising and public impact, as well as principle. Most important, AI members will seek to conduct this debate in a way that will enable members with strong feelings on this issue to feel respected and that their views are heard. The issue is primarily about what AI as an organization should do in making a choice on this issue. The process of debate may be as important as the final decision. However, all sides agree that it is time Amnesty International took a clear decision on this issue.

CHAPTER 6

HUMAN RIGHTS AND GOVERNMENTS: LAW, BUREAUCRACY, POLITICS

■ ■ ■

Human rights lawyers generally consider the law to be a tool to get governments to undertake, or refrain from undertaking, certain activities: impose penalties, implement policies, or imprison violators. The law gets "enforced" through governmental institutions like the judiciary, when it provides redress to individuals for human rights violations or punishes the abusers. This chapter approaches the interaction between law and government from a different and equally crucial perspective. It explores the ways human rights standards are internalized, implemented, and disseminated by governments themselves. The lesson it teaches is that enforcement and reform come not solely (or even primarily) from courts, tribunals, or even intergovernmental institutions. Human rights law also gets enforced through a complicated process of internalization and dissemination by governments, and human rights lawyers are empowered to the extent that they understand and can affect this process.

The traditional assumption of the human rights movement is that governments are the problem. (After 9/11 in particular, many have argued that the government of the United States forfeited its moral authority by abusing human rights in the fight against terrorism.) But the argument that governments are exclusively the problem rests on a gross oversimplification. Not only are there internal ways of bringing pressure to bear on government policy, but external pressures from other branches of government, from the media, and from civil society, play a little-appreciated role in the internalization of human rights law and policy. That process profoundly affects how governments engage other governments, international organizations, and individuals.

The materials in this chapter explore the role governments play in crafting and advancing the international human rights agenda. Of course, governments rarely agree entirely on what that agenda should include. Each comes to the table with its own domestic traditions, interest groups, and legal systems. However, the extent to which international standards have been internalized by the broadest cross-section of governments shows the strength of the human rights idea. (Module 12). This is especially true in a treaty negotiations (Module 13), and world conferences (Module 14), which either fail or succeed on the strength of political will created by the forces of internalization.

Just as internalization drives *external* action, it similarly affects a government's *internal* activities and policies. For example, the establishment of a truth commission to achieve reconciliation and accountability for past human rights abuses is fundamentally inward-looking (Module 15). Truth commissions also drive the internalization of human rights in a way that few other government policies or programs can. By forcing a society to deal publicly with gross and systemic abuses, often through truth-telling by abusers, a society can face its future and collectively declare "*nunca mas*." And when those internal mechanisms require more order than is available in a society torn by conflict, it may be necessary for the international community to engineer a process of transition, from chaos to stability, a process increasingly informed by human rights standards (Module 16).

INTERNALIZATION BY GOVERNMENT INSTITUTIONS

■ ■ ■

Orientation

When considering ways to promote and protect human rights, an advocate's first impulse might be to consider domestic and international litigation—framing an injustice as a violation of law to be redressed in court. Doubtless, international human rights obligations have relevance and force in litigation, but the courts have no monopoly over the protection of human rights. In fact, if a case gets to a courtroom, it generally reflects some *prior* failure of the government to conform its internal conduct to international standards. Without some measure of *internalization* of human rights standards into the regulatory structure of government, those standards will seem hortatory and theoretical at best.

What does it mean to "internalize" human rights? In a strict legal sense, internalization requires the full implementation of a nation's human rights obligations under conventional and customary international law. But what exactly is meant by "full implementation?" For obligations that fall into the "thou shalt not" variety, it means adopting laws that criminalize certain conduct (*e.g.,* torture or extrajudicial killings). For those in the "thou shalt" category, it requires the adoption of policies and practices to promote and protect the right (*e.g.,* the right to housing or an education). But internalization should also be understood as an issue of culture. To become fully effective, human rights obligations must be more than training regimes and legislation. They must be integrated into a society's conception of itself, and not just within its citizenry but within its official institutions as well. For instance, the incidence of prisoner abuse would be reduced if it never occurred to guards to abuse prisoners in the first place.

Of course, this makes internalization a difficult and sometimes elusive process, especially in complex governments with multiple layers of bureaucracy, or hundreds of agencies with different and conflicting mandates or authority or influence. And there is another layer of complication: each of these institutions is made up of human beings who work within bureaucratic constraints, each of whom may bring an individual conception of, and commitment to, human rights. Actual internalization is thus a difficult and complicated phenomenon. Defining, studying, and monitoring it is also daunting. But human rights lawyers—whether inside or outside the government—must understand this crucial process, because it offers a means of enforcing human rights standards long before litigation becomes necessary or even possible.

We focus on the internalization of human rights protections within the government of the United States, one of the most complicated and powerful political structures on earth. The U.S. Constitution establishes certain protections for the rights of individuals and offered one model for the international human rights movement in its early stages. Eleanor Roosevelt was the prime mover behind the Universal Declaration of Human Rights, and she drew in part on the American constitutional experience. Because of its legal history, the United States has held itself out as a primary actor in the promotion and protection of civil and political rights around the world. Today, multiple cabinet departments within the U.S. government include international human rights standards in their work, notably the Departments of Defense, Justice, Labor, and State. Within the State Department, the Bureau of Democracy, Human Rights, and Labor has the mandate to advance the human rights priorities of U.S. foreign policy. It does this through constant pressure and engagement with foreign nations; funding programs that promote democracy, human rights, and the rule of law; and engaging in multilateral diplomacy in international institutions.

The process is hardly seamless or complete, and the question remains whether the United States government has truly internalized its obligations. Criticism of the government has been especially pointed in the aftermath of the epochal attacks of September 11, 2001. Critics assert that international human rights standards have been violated in the war on terrorism and point *inter alia* to the torture and other mistreatment of suspects, the prolonged detention of suspects and combatants at Guantanamo Bay and other sites, and restrictions on domestic civil liberties. Of course, governments have the right and the obligation to track down terrorists and protect against enemy attacks. But human rights treaties also explicitly limit the extent to which rights can be suspended in times of emergency, and no derogation is allowed, for example, from the right to be free from torture and the right to meaningful access to judicial remedies. The internalization of human rights standards thus forces government actors to examine and re-examine the extraordinary measures they undertake. In this morass of law and politics, the U.S. government has internalized human rights standards in a variety of ways but with a spotty record of success.

We have divided this module into four sections, each of which highlights significant pressure points in the internalization process in the United States: the Executive Branch, the legislature, the judiciary, and civil society, represented here by the media and NGOs. We also address a significant, potentially promising, and new approach to internalization in the context of development assistance.

A. THE EXECUTIVE BRANCH

Under the U.S. Constitution, the Executive Branch has primary but not exclusive authority over foreign affairs. In the treaty context for example, the President has the power to sign treaties, but the Senate must provide its advice and consent before the treaty may be ratified. Similarly, an international treaty obligation may exist, but, as a matter of constitutional law or practice, it does not become domestic law until it has been implemented by Congressional enactment. On occasion, a treaty obligation will be addressed to exclusively executive action. For purposes of illustrating the process of internalization, we here draw on this latter category of treaty obligations and consider the "refoulement" (return) of non-U.S. nationals to other countries.

CONVENTION AGAINST TORTURE AND OTHER CRUEL, INHUMAN OR DEGRADING TREATMENT OR PUNISHMENT

Adopted Dec. 10, 1984, S. Treaty Doc. No. 100–20 (1988), U.N.T.S. 113

Article 3

1. No State Party shall expel, return ("refouler") or extradite a person to another State where there are substantial grounds for believing that he would be in danger of being subjected to torture.

2. For the purpose of determining whether there are such grounds, the competent authorities shall take into account all relevant considerations including, where applicable, the existence in the State concerned of a consistent pattern of gross, flagrant or mass violations of human rights.

ABDAH v. BUSH

Case No. 04–1254 (D.D.C. 2004)

DECLARATION OF PIERRE–RICHARD PROSPER

I, Pierre–Richard Prosper, pursuant to 28 U.S.C. sec. 1746, hereby declare and say as follows:

1. I am the Ambassador-at-Large for War Crimes Issues and have supervised the operation of the Department of State Office of War Crimes Issues (S/WCI) since July 13, 2001. * * * Since September 11, 2001, my office has played a key role in maintaining a diplomatic dialogue with foreign governments whose nationals have been captured in connection with the armed conflict with the Taliban and al Qaida and who are detained at the U.S. Naval Base at Guantanamo Bay, Cuba. The following statements provide a general overview of the Department

of State role in carrying out United States policy with respect to the transfer to foreign governments of detainees held by the Department of Defense at Guantanamo Bay and the process that is followed to ensure that any international obligations and United States policies are properly implemented. * * *

3. The Department of Defense consults with appropriate United States Government agencies, including the Department of State, before determining whether to transfer particular individuals. Detainees have been transferred for release when it is determined that they no longer meet the criteria of enemy combatants or no longer pose * * * a continuing threat to the United States. A detainee may be considered for transfer to a country other than his country of nationality, such as in circumstances where that country requests transfer of the detainee for purposes of criminal prosecution.

4. Of particular concern to the Department of State in making recommendations on transfers is the question of whether the foreign government concerned will treat the detainee humanely, in a manner consistent with its international obligations, and will not persecute the individual on the basis of his race, religion, nationality, membership in a social group, or political opinion. The Department is particularly mindful of the longstanding policy of the United States not to transfer a person to a country if it determines that it is more likely than not that the person will be tortured or, in appropriate cases, that the person has a well-founded fear of persecution and would not be disqualified from persecution protection on criminal- or security-related grounds. This policy is consistent with the Convention Against Torture and other Cruel, Inhuman or Degrading Treatment or Punishment ("Torture Convention") and the Convention Relating to the Status of Refugees ("Refugee Convention"). The Department of State works closely with the Department of Defense and relevant agencies to advise on the likelihood of persecution or torture in a given county and the adequacy and credibility of assurances obtained from a particular foreign government prior to any transfer. * * *

6. Once the Department of Defense has approved a transfer from Guantanamo Bay and requests the assistance of the Department of State, my office would initiate transfer discussions with the foreign government concerned. The primary purpose of these discussions is to learn what measures the receiving government is likely to take to ensure that the detainee will not pose a continuing threat to the United States or its allies and to obtain appropriate transfer assurances. My office seeks assurances that the United States Government considers necessary and appropriate for the country in question. Among the assurances sought in every transfer case in which continued detention by the government concerned is foreseen is the assurance of humane treatment and treatment in accordance with the international obligations of the foreign government accepting transfer. The Department of State considers whether the State in question is party to the relevant treaties, such as the

Torture Convention, and pursues more specific assurances if the State concerned is not a party or other circumstances warrant.

7. Decisions with respect to Guantanamo detainees are made on a case-by-case basis, taking into account the particular circumstances of the transfer, the country, the individual concerned, and any concerns regarding torture or persecution that may arise. Recommendations by the Department of State are decided at senior levels through a process involving Department officials most familiar with international legal standards and obligations and the conditions in the countries concerned. Within the Department of State, my office, together with the Office of the Legal Adviser, the Bureau of Democracy, Human Rights and Labor, and the relevant regional bureau, normally evaluate foreign government assurances and any need for protection, and, if deemed appropriate, brief the Secretary or other Department Principals before finalizing the position of the Department of State. The views of the Bureau of Democracy, Human Rights and Labor, which drafts the U.S. Government's annual Human Rights Reports, and of the relevant regional bureau, country desk, or U.S. Embassy are important in evaluating foreign government assurances and any individual persecution or torture claims, because they are knowledgeable about matters such as human rights, prison conditions, and prisoners' access to counsel, in general and as they may apply to a particular case in the foreign country concerned, as well as particular information about the entity or individual that that [*sic*] is offering the assurance in any particular case.

8. The essential question in evaluating foreign government assurances is whether the competent Department of State officials believe it is more likely than not that the individual will be tortured in the country to which he is being transferred. In determining whether it is "more likely than not" that an individual would be tortured, the United States takes into account the treatment the individual is likely to receive upon transfer, including, *inter alia*, the expressed commitments of officials from the foreign government accepting transfer. When evaluating the adequacy of any assurances, Department officials consider the identity, position, or other information concerning the official relaying the assurances, and political or legal developments in the foreign country concerned that would provide context for the assurances provided. Department officials may also consider U.S. diplomatic relations with the country concerned when evaluating assurances. For instance, Department officials may make a judgment regarding foreign government's incentives and capacities to fulfill its assurances to the United States, including the importance to the government concerned of maintaining good relations and cooperation with the United States. In an appropriate case, the Department of State may also consider seeking the foreign government's assurances of access by governmental or non-governmental entities in the country concerned to monitor the condition of an individual returned to that country, or of U.S. Government access to the individual for such purposes. In instances in which the United States

transfers an individual subject to assurances, it would pursue any credible report and take appropriate action if it had reason to believe that those assurances would not be, or had not been, honored. In an instance in which specific concerns about the treatment an individual may receive cannot be resolved satisfactorily, we have in the past and would in the future recommend against transfer, consistent with the United States policy.

9. The Department of State's ability to seek and obtain assurances from a foreign government depends in part on the Department's ability to treat its dealings with the foreign government with discretion. Consistent with the diplomatic sensitivities that surround the Department's communications with foreign governments concerning allegations relating to torture, the Department of State does not unilaterally make public the specific assurances or other precautionary measures obtained in order to avoid the chilling effects of making such discussions public and the possible damage to our ability to conduct foreign relations. Seeking assurances may be seen as raising questions about the requesting State's institutions or commitment to the rule of law, even in cases where the assurances are sought to highlight the issue for the country concerned and satisfy the Department that the country is aware of the concerns raised and is in a position to undertake a commitment of humane treatment of a particular individual. There also may be circumstances where it may be important to protect sources of information (such as sources within a foreign government) about a government's willingness to abide by assurances concerning humane treatment or relevant international obligations.

10. If the Department were required unilaterally to disclose outside appropriate Executive branch channels its communications with a foreign government relating to particular mistreatment or torture concerns, that government, as well as other governments, would likely be reluctant in the future to communicate frankly with the United States concerning such issues. I know from experience that the delicate diplomatic exchange that is often required in these contexts cannot occur effectively except in a confidential setting. Later review in a public forum of the Department's dealings with a particular foreign government regarding transfer matters would seriously undermine our ability to investigate allegations of mistreatment or torture that come to our attention and to reach acceptable accommodations with other governments to address those important concerns.

11. The Department's recommendation concerning transfer relies heavily on the facts and analyses provided by various offices within the Department, including its Embassies. Confidentiality is often essential to ensure that the advice and analysis provided by these offices are useful and informative for the decision-maker. If those offices are expected to provide candid and useful assessments, they normally need to know that their reports will not later be publicly disclosed or brought to the attention of officials and others in the foreign States with which they

deal on a regular basis. Such disclosure could chill important sources of information and could interfere with the ability of our foreign relations personnel to interact effectively with foreign State officials.

12.   Without addressing the specifics of any particular individual, a court decision to enjoin a detainee transfer, either altogether or until further order of the court, would undermine the United States' ability to reduce the numbers of individuals under U.S. control and our effectiveness in eliciting the cooperation of other governments to bring to justice individuals who are subject to their jurisdiction. Any judicial decision to review a transfer decision by the United States Government or the diplomatic dialogue with a foreign government concerning the terms of transfer could seriously undermine our foreign relations. Moreover, judicial review of Department of Defense determinations to transfer an individual detainee to a foreign government inevitably would encumber and add delays to what is already a lengthy process. Any judicial review and the resulting delays could undermine a foreign government's ability to prosecute and also harm United States' efforts to press other countries to act more expeditiously in bringing terrorists and their supporters to justice.

I declare under the penalty of perjury that the foregoing is true and correct.

Executed on March 8, 2005

Pierre–Richard Prosper

NOTES AND QUESTIONS ON INTERNALIZATION WITHIN THE EXECUTIVE BRANCH

1.   *Background to the problem of refoulement from Guantanamo Bay.* During the war in Afghanistan, the United States began using a military detention facility at Guantanamo Bay, Cuba (GTMO), to detain combatants alleged to be associated with the Taliban or al Qaida. The U.S. government has stated that some of these individuals will be tried for war crimes, but many others will be either released or returned to other countries for prosecution for crimes there. Some of these combatants may be returned to countries where they may have a fear of being subjected to torture.

In *Rasul v. Bush*, 542 U.S. 466 (2004), the Supreme Court held that statutory habeas corpus jurisdiction extends to non-U.S. citizens detained at GTMO. After the Court's decision in *Rasul*, over one hundred habeas petitions were filed on behalf of GTMO detainees, calling for their release on the ground that their detentions are unlawful. The Prosper Declaration excerpted above was filed by the U.S. government in one such case, *Abdah v. Bush*, No. 04–1254, 2005 WL 711814 (D.D.C. Mar. 29, 2005), seeking to prevent the court from enjoining the transfer of 13 GTMO detainees to Yemen. Ultimately, the Court granted the plaintiffs' request for a preliminary injunction, requiring that the government provide the petitioners' counsel and the court with 30 days' notice before any transfer or removal of petitioners from GTMO.

Although the district court's decision in *Abdah* was not based on the "likelihood of torture" claims made by Petitioners' counsel, the U.S. government has gone on record—through filing the Prosper Declaration—with the procedures it uses to ensure that an individual is not transferred from GTMO to a country where it is "more likely than not" he will be subjected to torture. Not surprisingly, counsel for the petitioners in many of the post-*Rasul* habeas cases have argued that counsel should be provided access to the assurances provided by foreign governments before transfer in order to protect the safety of their clients. Are you persuaded by the arguments made in the Prosper Declaration as to why these assurances and the preceding diplomatic dialogue should not be made public? Is there a middle ground, *i.e.*, a way to allow review of assurances without making them public?

2. *The adequacy of diplomatic assurances.* In reading the Prosper Declaration, what is your assessment of the factors according to which the U.S. government analyzes the adequacy of diplomatic assurances? In each of the declarations, the government identifies the possibility of obtaining access to detainees post-transfer to monitor compliance with assurances provided by the receiving government. In your view, is this an adequate safeguard against torture? Against a violation of the sending government's CAT article 3 obligation? Are these the same thing?

In *Empty Promises: Diplomatic Assurances No Safeguard against Torture*, (2004), Human Rights Watch contended that the practice of obtaining assurances to ensure compliance with Article 3 of the CAT is flawed. Relying on instances of transfers from the U.S., Canada, and European countries where Human Rights Watch contends diplomatic assurances were not honored, the organization called upon governments to:

> Declare reliance upon diplomatic assurances *per* definition unacceptable in circumstances where there is substantial and credible evidence that torture and prohibited ill-treatment in the country of return are systematic, widespread, endemic, or a "recalcitrant or persistent" problem; where governmental authorities do not have effective control over the forces in their country that perpetrate acts of torture and ill-treatment; or where the government consistently targets members of a particular racial, ethnic, religious, political or other identifiable group for torture or ill-treatment and the person subject to return is associated with that group[.]

Are these workable restrictions on the use of diplomatic assurances? In the GTMO context, most of the detainees not only come from countries that satisfy the criteria above but are also accused of having been involved with terrorist organizations. Moreover, many of the cases discussed in the Human Rights Watch report involve individuals accused of involvement in terrorism in the sending country. If the possibility of obtaining diplomatic assurances is unavailable to these governments, what are their options?

In June 2007, the U.S. government returned two individuals detained at GTMO to Tunisia. Shortly after their return, allegations surfaced that the two had been mistreated at the hands of the Tunisian government. *See* Human Rights Watch, *Ill-Fated Homecomings: A Tunisian Case Study of Guantanamo Repatriations*, (Sept. 2007), *available at*: http:// hrw.org/reports/2007/tunisia0907/. According to U.S. government officials, specific and credible assurances were received from the Tunisian government before their repatriation. *Id*. at 6. When allegations surface that a government may have violated the assurances on which a detainee repatriation is based, is there any recourse for the individual or for the U.S. government? If the U.S. government wishes to send further detainees back to the same government, how would you advise policymakers in this circumstance?

According to Human Rights Watch, an additional ten Tunisian detainees remained in detention at GTMO when the above allegations surfaced. Lawyers for one of these detainees still at GTMO, Mohammed Abdul Rahman, successfully obtained a preliminary injunction from a district court in Washington, DC, ordering the government not to transfer him to Tunisia. *Alhami v. Bush*, Civil Action No. 05–359 (D.D.C Oct. 2, 2007), *available at*: http://news.findlaw.com/hdocs/docs/terrorism/ rahmanbush100207opn.html. In the face of this injunction, can the U.S. government return other detainees to Tunisia? Should it? Are there any other options?

3. *The U.S. understanding of Article 3.* When the United States ratified the Convention Against Torture (CAT), it attached several reservations, understandings, and declarations. For example, the U.S. stated its understanding that the obligation not to return a person to another State where "there are substantial grounds for believing that he would be in danger of being" subjected to torture means: where "it is more likely than not that he would be" subjected to torture. U.S. Reservations, Declarations, and Understandings: Convention Against Torture and Other Cruel, Inhuman or Degrading Treatment or Punishment, Cong. Rec. S17486–01 (daily ed., Oct. 27, 1990). The reason for this understanding was to bring the Convention's language into line with existing U.S. law and practice in an analogous area of law— immigration law. The courts have interpreted Section 241(b)(3) of the Immigration and Nationality Act as requiring the Attorney General withhold an alien's removal to a country where "it is more likely than not" that the alien's life or freedom would be threatened on account of his race, religion, nationality, membership in a particular social group, or opinion. *See INS v. Stevic*, 467 U.S. 407 (1984). Accordingly, the use of the same standard for purposes of article 3 would simplify implementation and make it consistent with at least some Supreme Court precedent. But compare *INS v. Cardoza–Fonseca*, 480 U.S. 421 (1987), where the Supreme Court explicitly rejected the government's "more likely

than not" test for refoulement of refugees under the 1951 Refugee Convention and its 1967 Protocol. The difference between "removal" under *Stevic* and refoulement of a refugee under *Cardoza-Fonseca* is to some extent an artifact of the peculiarities of U.S. immigration law, and it is always possible as a matter of law that terror suspects would not qualify as Convention refugees in the first place.

In your view, is there a substantial difference between the language included in article 3 of the CAT and the U.S. understanding? Put yourself in the position of a senior U.S. government official deciding whether the government can safely return an individual to a country with a questionable record on torture and not violate article 3. As a practical matter, which of these definitions would give you more comfort in making such a decision?

4. *Article 3 in other contexts.* The United States ratified the CAT in 1994, well before the terrorist attacks of September 11, 2001. At the time, the practices affected by article 3 were extraditions and the removal of aliens by the Immigration and Naturalization Service. The United States implemented its article 3 obligations through regulations promulgated by the Departments of State and Justice to ensure the cardinal obligation of article 3 not to return a person to the likelihood of torture. *See* Implementation of Torture Convention in Extradition Cases, 22 C.F.R. § 95 (1999). Not surprisingly, a significant number of individuals facing removal from the United States have raised CAT claims during removal proceedings. Indeed, in its 2005 Periodic Report to the UN Committee Against Torture, the United States noted that between 2000 and 2005, over 2600 individuals received Article 3 protection from an immigration judge. *See* Second Periodic Report of the United States of America to the Committee Against Torture, ¶ 34, U.N. Doc. CAT/C/48/Add.3 (June 29, 2005).

5. *The rule of non-inquiry.* In *Cornejo-Barreto v. Seifert*, the defendant argued that the decision of the Secretary of State whether or not to extradite an individual must be subject to judicial review. The U.S. government, on the other hand, argued that under the "rule of non-inquiry" applicable to extradition matters, the Secretary of State's decision cannot be overturned—or even considered—by a judge. A panel of the Ninth Circuit Court of Appeals found that a fugitive fearing torture may petition for review of the Secretary of State's decision to surrender him, and courts are required to set aside such extradition decisions if they are found to be "arbitrary, capricious, an abuse of discretion, or otherwise not in accordance with the law." *Cornejo-Barreto v. Seifert*, 218 F.3d 1004, 1015 (9th Cir. 2000). However, a different panel of the Ninth Circuit subsequently rejected this conclusion and held that the Secretary of State's determination to extradite a fugitive is not subject to judicial review. *Cornejo-Barreto v. Siefert*, 379 F.3d 1075, 1089 (9th Cir. 2004). A majority of the Ninth Circuit judges voted to rehear the case *en banc*, but prior to the date of the rehearing, the Mexican government withdrew its extradition request pursuant to the dismissal of the Mexi-

can state prosecution that had served as the basis for its request. The Ninth Circuit then dismissed the case as moot and vacated the second panel decision. *Cornejo-Barreto v. Siefert*, 389 F.3d 1307 (9th Cir. 2004).

Subsequently, in another case, the Ninth Circuit stated, in a footnote, "that in light of legislation implementing the United Nations Convention against Torture, the rule of non-inquiry does not prevent an extraditee who fears torture upon surrender to the requesting government from petitioning for habeas corpus review of the Secretary of State's decision to extradite him." *Prasoprat v. Benov*, 421 F.3d 1009, n.5 (9th Cir. 2005); *accord Mironescu v. Costner*, 480 F.3d 664 (4th Cir. 2007) (holding that the Secretary's extradition decision is reviewable in a habeas corpus hearing, but denying review under § 2242(d) of the Foreign Affairs Reform and Restructuring Act). Whether the footnote in *Praspoprat* will receive the same treatment as the *dicta* in *Cornejo-Barreto* remains to be seen.

Should a decision of this nature, made by the Secretary of State, be subject to judicial review? In *Cornejo-Barreto*, the U.S. Department of State filed a declaration by the Assistant Legal Adviser for Law Enforcement and Intelligence that detailed many of the criteria identified in the Prosper Declaration excerpted above. Should such a declaration be sufficient for a judge concerned about torture claims made by a defendant facing extradition? What are the constitutional concerns when the judiciary reviews a decision of the Executive Branch in the area of foreign affairs?

6. *Human rights law in the bureaucracy.* The examples above reflect the manner in which U.S. practice can be directly affected by treaty obligations; however, the formulation and implementation of U.S. foreign policy is also guided by its human rights obligations in a more subtle manner on a daily basis. Within the U.S. Department of State, a team of lawyers regularly provides guidance on foreign policy decisions, proposed legislation, and public statements that reflect the government's understanding of its human rights obligations—under treaty, custom and *jus cogens* principles. These lawyers are often instrumental in crafting the administration's position on a wide range of issues, yet their work is largely unseen by the public. Of course, any large institution, particularly a government, must account for a variety of interests in crafting a single, coherent position, so concerns founded in human rights law are sometimes trumped by other policy prerogatives. Nevertheless, the vast majority of policy decisions do not require a zero-sum analysis where human rights are concerned, and positions are often formulated with human rights law in mind. Indeed, on some occasions, the human rights obligations of the United States drive the decision-making process.

Consider, for example, the September 2004 debate over language in the draft intelligence reform bill circulated in the House of Representatives that would have placed the United States in violation of obligations it had assumed under article 3 of the Convention against Torture. *See* Dana Priest and Charles Babington, *Plan Would Let U.S. Deport Suspects to Nations that Might Torture Them*, WASH. POST, at A4 (Sept. 30, 2004). Under the bill, a person attempting to obtain protection under article 3's *non-refoulement* provision would have the burden of proving "by clear and convincing evidence that he or she would be tortured" upon being removed to his or her country. The *Washington Post* reported that officials in the Justice Department supported the bill's provisions. Not surprisingly, NGOs challenged the House bill as contrary to U.S. article 3 obligations (*i.e.*, not to return people to countries where it is "more likely than not" they will be tortured) and as creating an evidentiary standard impossible to meet.

Partly as a result of media and NGO attention, but also as part of the regular inter-agency review process, these provisions of the House's draft bill became the subject of debate the U.S. government—including lawyers from the Departments of State, Justice and Homeland Security—on the nature and scope of the United States' obligations under the Torture Convention. Eventually, a consolidated Administration position was developed, and the *Washington Post* printed a letter from White House Counsel Alberto Gonzales clarifying the Administration's position on the House bill:

> The president did not propose and does not support this provision. He has made clear that the United States stands against and will not tolerate torture and that the United States remains committed to complying with its obligations under the Convention Against Torture and Other Cruel, Inhuman or Degrading Treatment or Punishment. Consistent with that treaty, the United States does not expel, return or extradite individuals to countries where the United States believes it is likely that they will be tortured.

Letter to the Editor, Alberto H. Gonzales, *The President's Stance on Torture*, WASH. POST, A24 (Oct. 5, 2004). How might a lawyer use this assurance in the event that it turned out to be false?

7. *"Top–Down" internalization.* While internalization often happens through the actions of mid- and low-level officials, the most effective and sustained efforts begin at the highest ranks in government. In recent years, the U.S. government has adopted a high-profile stance against modern-day slavery, reflected in the Victims of Trafficking and Violence Protection Act of 2000, Pub. L. No. 106–386, 114 Stat. 1464 (2000) ("Trafficking Act"), a stance driven by the President's own convictions. In 2003, the Trafficking Act was reauthorized, adding additional responsibilities to the government's anti-trafficking efforts and requiring a yearly report from the Attorney General to be submitted to Congress. Trafficking Victims Protection Reauthorization Act of 2003, Pub. L. No. 108–193, 117 Stat. 2875 (2003). The Trafficking Act provided enhanced protection and assistance for trafficking victims, expanded the crimes

and increased penalties available to federal authorities, and required increased international activities to address trafficking as a global phenomenon. As a result, the government created a Trafficking in Persons and Worker Exploitation Task Force within the Department of Justice; a Trafficking in Persons Office in the State Department's Office of the Under Secretary for Global Affairs; and an Interagency Task Force to Monitor and Combat Trafficking in Persons. Moreover, the relevant activities of a variety of other agencies, including the Departments of Labor, Health and Human Services, Homeland Security and Agriculture, as well as the U.S. Agency for International Development were enhanced to address trafficking in persons. Since 2001, the Department of Justice has opened over 800 investigations and prosecuted over 400 defendants, which led to hundreds of convictions under the Trafficking Act. *See* Attorney General's Annual Report to Congress and Assessment of U.S. Government Activities to Combat Trafficking in Persons Fiscal Year 2007, at 28 (May 2008).

The Trafficking Act requires that the President make a yearly determination with respect to the efforts of foreign governments to attack trafficking in persons. Where a government does not comply with the minimum standards laid out in the Act or has made no significant efforts to bring itself into compliance, that government is ineligible to receive financial assistance from the United States. In order to administer this sanctions regime, the Trafficking Act creates a system of classifications for countries based on their efforts to combat trafficking. A government in "Tier 3" may be subject to sanctions, including, for example, the withholding of non-humanitarian, non-trade-related assistance. Moreover, these countries would be subject to withholding of funding for participation in educational and cultural exchange programs. "Tier 3" governments may also face U.S. opposition to assistance from international financial institutions. Although the President may make a determination that these sanctions should be waived if assistance would promote the purposes of the statute or is otherwise in the national interest of the United States, there is a strong incentive for governments not to be placed in Tier 3. *See generally*, U.S. Department of State, Trafficking in Persons Report, June 4, 2008.

8. *Executive Order 13107.* On December 10, 1998, President Clinton signed Executive Order 13107, entitled "Implementation of Human Rights Treaties," 61 FED. REG. 68,991 (Dec. 10, 1998). The Executive Order created an Inter-agency Working Group (IWG) to "provide guidance, oversight, and coordination with respect to questions concerning the adherence to and implementation of human rights obligations and related matters." *Id.* The Executive Order identifies the principal functions of the IWG as, *inter alia,* coordinating review of significant implementation issues, coordinating the preparation of treaty reports, coordinating responses to complaints regarding alleged treaty violations,

developing mechanisms to ensure proposed legislation is consistent with U.S. treaty obligations, improving the monitoring of treaty implementation in the states and commonwealths, and planning public outreach and education about human rights treaties.

Assuming the accuracy of the government's position that no further implementing legislation was necessary after ratification of the human rights treaties to which the U.S. is a party, does this Executive Order serve any purpose? Recognizing that the Order specifically notes that it does not create any justiciable obligations on the part of the Executive Branch, how might human rights advocates use the existence of this Executive Order to pursue objectives with regard to existing human rights treaties? What about treaties the U.S. has not yet ratified?

B. THE LEGISLATIVE BRANCH

One of the more effective vehicles for the internalization of human rights in government institutions is legislation that requires the Executive branch to account for human rights in the formulation and implementation of foreign policy. Although Executive branch lawyers dispute the degree to which a legislative body may constitutionally intervene in foreign policy, citizens represented by the duly-elected members of the legislature have a legitimate interest in assuring that the nation's foreign policy is conducted in accordance with the law and their values. The legislative branch also has a legitimate interest in ensuring that financial assistance is provided in a manner that advances these values around the world, for example, by seeking to ensure that resources are not provided to countries that engage in human rights abuses.

In the United States, there are several legislative tools developed to integrate human rights into government institutions. From the creation of the Bureau of Democracy, Human Rights and Labor, to human rights certifications for countries that receive development or security assistance, to restrictions on voting in international financial institutions, the Congress of the United States has expressed a clear intent that the Executive Branch consider human rights in crafting foreign policy and making decisions regarding foreign assistance. Consider the following excerpts from legislation that incorporates human rights provisions in a variety of ways. As you read the legislation, consider the difficulties of implementation, particularly with regard to countries and regions with whom a close bilateral relationship represents an important strategic interest, particularly in a post–9/11 world. How has the legislation attempted to deal with these issues?

FOREIGN ASSISTANCE ACT OF 1961, SEC. 116

22 U.S.C. § 2151(n)

Human Rights and Development Assistance

(a) Violations barring assistance; assistance for needy people

No assistance may be provided under subchapter I of this chapter to the government of any country which engages in a consistent pattern of gross violations of internationally recognized human rights, including torture or cruel, inhuman or degrading treatment or punishment, prolonged detention without charges, causing the disappearances of persons by the abduction and clandestine detention of those persons, or other flagrant denial of the right to life, liberty and the security of person, unless such assistance will directly benefit the needy people in such country. * * *

(b) Protection of children from exploitation

No assistance may be provided to any government failing to take appropriate and adequate measures, within their means, to protect children from exploitation, abuse or forced conscription into military and paramilitary services.

(c) Factors considered

In determining whether or not a government falls within the provisions of subsection (a) of this section and in formulating development assistance programs under subchapter I of this chapter, the Administrator [of the Agency for International Development] shall consider, in consultation with the Assistant Secretary of State for Democracy, Human Rights and Labor and in consultation with the Ambassador at Large for International Religious Freedom—

> (1) the extent of cooperation of such government in permitting an unimpeded investigation of alleged violations of internationally recognized human rights by appropriate international organizations, including the International Committee of the Red Cross, or groups of persons acting under the authority of the United Nations or of the Organization of American States;

> (2) specific actions which have been taken by the President or the Congress relating to multilateral or security assistance to a less developed country because of the human rights practices or policies of such country; and

> (3) whether the government—

>> (A) has engaged in or tolerated particularly severe violations of religious freedom, as defined in section 6402 of this title; or

>> (B) has failed to undertake serious and sustained efforts to combat particularly severe violations of religious freedom (as

defined in section 6402 of this title), when such efforts could have been reasonably undertaken. * * *

FOREIGN ASSISTANCE ACT OF 1961, SECTION 502B

22 U.S.C. § 2304

Human Rights and Security Assistance

(a) Observance of human rights as a principal goal of foreign policy; implementation requirements

(1) The United States shall, in accordance with its international obligations as set forth in the Charter of the United Nations and in keeping with the constitutional heritage and traditions of the United States, promote and encourage increased respect for human rights and fundamental freedoms throughout the world without distinction as to race, sex, language, or religion. Accordingly, a principal goal of the foreign policy of the United States shall be to promote the increased observance of internationally recognized human rights by all countries.

(2) Except under circumstances specified in this section, no security assistance may be provided to any country the government of which engages in a consistent pattern of gross violations of internationally recognized human rights. Security assistance may not be provided to the police, domestic intelligence, or similar law enforcement forces of a country, and licenses may not be issued under the Export Administration Act of 1979 (50 App. U.S.C. 2401 et seq.) for the export of crime control and detection instruments and equipment to a country, the government of which engages in a consistent pattern of gross violations of internationally recognized human rights unless the President certifies in writing to the Speaker of the House of Representatives and the chairman of the Committee on Foreign Relations of the Senate and the chairman of the Committee on Banking, Housing, and Urban Affairs of the Senate (when licenses are to be issued pursuant to the Export Administration Act of 1979) that extraordinary circumstances exist warranting provision of such assistance and issuance of such licenses. Assistance may not be provided under part V of this subchapter to a country the government of which engages in a consistent pattern of gross violations of internationally recognized human rights unless the President certifies in writing to the Speaker of the House of Representatives and the chairman of the Committee on Foreign Relations of the Senate that extraordinary circumstances exist warranting provision of such assistance.

(3) In furtherance of paragraphs (1) and (2), the President is directed to formulate and conduct international security assistance programs of the United States in a manner which will promote and

advance human rights and avoid identification of the United States, through such programs, with governments which deny to their people internationally recognized human rights and fundamental freedoms, in violation of international law or in contravention of the policy of the United States as expressed in this section or otherwise.

(4) In determining whether the government of a country engages in a consistent pattern of gross violations of internationally recognized human rights, the President shall give particular consideration to whether the government—

(A) has engaged in or tolerated particularly severe violations of religious freedom, as defined in section 6402 of this title; or

(B) has failed to undertake serious and sustained efforts to combat particularly severe violations of religious freedom when such efforts could have been reasonably undertaken.

(b) Report by Secretary of State on practices of proposed recipient countries; considerations

The Secretary of State shall transmit to the Congress, as part of the presentation materials for security assistance programs proposed for each fiscal year, a full and complete report, prepared with the assistance of the Assistant Secretary of State for Democracy, Human Rights, and Labor and with the assistance of the Ambassador at Large for International Religious Freedom, with respect to practices regarding the observance of and respect for internationally recognized human rights in each country proposed as a recipient of security assistance. Wherever applicable, such report shall include consolidated information regarding the commission of war crimes, crimes against humanity, and evidence of acts that may constitute genocide. * * * Wherever applicable, such report shall include information on practices regarding coercion in population control, including coerced abortion and involuntary sterilization. Such report shall also include, wherever applicable, information on violations of religious freedom, including particularly severe violations of religious freedom (as defined in section 6402 of this title). Such report shall also include, for each country with respect to which the report indicates that extrajudicial killings, torture, or other serious violations of human rights have occurred in the country, the extent to which the United States has taken or will take action to encourage an end to such practices in the country. Each report under this section shall list the votes of each member of the United Nations Commission on Human Rights on all country-specific and thematic resolutions voted on at the Commission's annual session during the period covered during the preceding year. * * * In determining whether a government falls within the provisions of subsection (a)(3) of this section and in the preparation of any report or statement required under this section, consideration shall be given to—

(1) the relevant findings of appropriate international organizations, including nongovernmental organizations, such as the International Committee of the Red Cross; and

(2) the extent of cooperation by such government in permitting an unimpeded investigation by any such organization of alleged violations of internationally recognized human rights.

(c) Congressional request for information; information required; 30–day period; failure to supply information; termination or restriction of assistance

(1) Upon the request of the Senate or the House of Representatives by resolution of either such House, or upon the request of the Committee on Foreign Relations of the Senate or the Committee on Foreign Affairs of the House of Representatives, the Secretary of State shall, within thirty days after receipt of such request, transmit to both such committees a statement, prepared with the assistance of the Assistant Secretary of State for Democracy, Human Rights, and Labor, with respect to the country designated in such request, setting forth—

(A) all the available information about observance of and respect for human rights and fundamental freedom in that country, and a detailed description of practices by the recipient government with respect thereto;

(B) the steps the United States has taken to—

(i) promote respect for and observance of human rights in that country and discourage any practices which are inimical to internationally recognized human rights, and

(ii) publicly or privately call attention to, and disassociate the United States and any security assistance provided for such country from, such practices;

(C) whether, in the opinion of the Secretary of State, notwithstanding any such practices—

(i) extraordinary circumstances exist which necessitate a continuation of security assistance for such country, and, if so, a description of such circumstances and the extent to which such assistance should be continued (subject to such conditions as Congress may impose under this section), and

(ii) on all the facts it is in the national interest of the United States to provide such assistance; and

(D) such other information as such committee or such House may request.

* * *

(d) Definitions

For the purposes of this section—

(1) the term "gross violations of internationally recognized human rights" includes torture or cruel, inhuman, or degrading treatment or punishment, prolonged detention without charges and trial, causing the disappearance of persons by the abduction and clandestine detention of those persons, and other flagrant denial of the right to life, liberty, or the security of person[.] * * *

CRITERIA FOR ASSISTANCE TO GOVERNMENTS OF THE INDEPENDENT STATES
22 U.S.C. § 2295(a)

a) In general

In providing assistance under this part for the government of any independent state of the former Soviet Union, the President shall take into account not only relative need but also the extent to which that independent state is acting to—

(1) make significant progress toward, and is committed to the comprehensive implementation of, a democratic system based on principles of the rule of law, individual freedoms, and representative government determined by free and fair elections;

(2) make significant progress in, and is committed to the comprehensive implementation of, economic reform based on market principles, private ownership, and integration into the world economy, including implementation of the legal and policy frameworks necessary for such reform (including protection of intellectual property and respect for contracts);

(3) respect internationally recognized human rights, including the rights of minorities and the rights to freedom of religion and emigration;

(4) respect international law and obligations and adhere to the Helsinki Final Act of the Conference on Security and Cooperation in Europe and the Charter of Paris, including the obligations to refrain from the threat or use of force and to settle disputes peacefully;

(5) cooperate in seeking peaceful resolution of ethnic and regional conflicts;

(6) implement responsible security policies, including—

(A) adhering to arms control obligations derived from agreements signed by the former Soviet Union;

(B) reducing military forces and expenditures to a level consistent with legitimate defense requirements;

(C) not proliferating nuclear, biological, or chemical weapons, their delivery systems, or related technologies; and

(D) restraining conventional weapons transfers;

(7) take constructive actions to protect the international environment, prevent significant transborder pollution, and promote sustainable use of natural resources;

(8) deny support for acts of international terrorism;

(9) accept responsibility for paying an equitable portion of the indebtedness to United States firms incurred by the former Soviet Union;

(10) cooperate with the United States Government in uncovering all evidence regarding Americans listed as prisoners-of-war, or otherwise missing during American operations, who were detained in the former Soviet Union during the Cold War; and

(11) terminate support for the communist regime in Cuba, including removal of troops, closing military and intelligence facilities, including the military and intelligence facilities at Lourdes and Cienfuegos, and ceasing trade subsidies and economic, nuclear, and other assistance.

(b) Ineligibility for assistance

The President shall not provide assistance under this part—

(1) for the government of any independent state that the President determines is engaged in a consistent pattern of gross violations of internationally recognized human rights or of international law;
* * *

SECTION 701 OF THE INTERNATIONAL
FINANCIAL INSTITUTIONS ACT

22 U.S.C. 262d(a)

Human Rights and United States Assistance Policies with International Financial Institutions

(a) *Policy goals.*

The United States Government, in connection with its voice and vote in the International Bank for Reconstruction and Development, the International Development Association, the International Finance Corporation, the Inter–American Development Bank, the African Development Fund, the Asian Development Bank, the African Development Bank, the European Bank for Reconstruction and Development, and the International Monetary Fund, shall advance the cause of human rights, including by seeking to channel assistance toward countries other than those whose governments engage in—

(1) a pattern of gross violations of internationally recognized human rights, such as torture or cruel, inhumane, or degrading treatment or punishment, prolonged detention without charges, or other flagrant denial to life, liberty, and the security of person; or

(2) provide refuge to individuals committing acts of international terrorism by hijacking aircraft.

(b) *Policy considerations for Executive Directors of institutions in implementation of duties.* Further, the Secretary of the Treasury shall instruct each Executive Director of the above institutions to consider in carrying out his duties:

(1) specific actions by either the executive branch or the Congress as a whole on individual bilateral assistance programs because of human rights considerations;

(2) the extent to which the economic assistance provided by the above institutions directly benefit the needy people in the recipient country; * * *

(d) *Requirements of United States assistance through institutions for projects in recipient countries.* The United States Government, in connection with its voice and vote in the institutions listed in subsection (a) of this section, shall seek to channel assistance to projects which address basic human needs of the people of the recipient country.

(e) *Criteria for determination of gross violations of internationally recognized human rights standards.* In determining whether a country is in gross violation of internationally recognized human rights standards, as defined by the provisions of subsection (a) of this section, the United States Government shall give consideration to the extent of cooperation of such country in permitting an unimpeded investigation of alleged violations of internationally recognized human rights by appropriate international organizations including, but not limited to, the International Committee of the Red Cross, Amnesty International, the International Commission of Jurists, and groups or persons acting under the authority of the United Nations or the Organization of American States.

(f) *Opposition by United States Executive Directors of institutions to financial or technical assistance to violating countries.* The United States Executive Directors of the institutions listed in subsection (a) of this section are authorized and instructed to oppose any loan, any extension of financial assistance, or any technical assistance to any country described in subsection (a)(1) or (2) of this section, unless such assistance is directed specifically to programs which serve the basic human needs of the citizens of such country. * * *

(g) *Violations of religious freedom.* In determining whether the Government of a country engages in a pattern of gross violations of internationally recognized human rights, as described in subsection (a) of this section, the President shall give particular consideration to whether a foreign government—

(1) has engaged in or tolerated particularly severe violations of religious freedom, as defined in section 6402 of this title; or

(2) has failed to undertake serious and sustained efforts to combat particularly severe violations of religious freedom when such efforts could have been reasonably undertaken.

NOTES AND QUESTIONS ON LEGISLATIVE INTERNALIZATION OF HUMAN RIGHTS STANDARDS

1. *The Jackson–Vanik Amendment.* One of the earliest U.S. laws to incorporate human rights considerations was the Jackson–Vanik Amendment to the 1974 Trade Act., 19 U.S.C. 2432. The Jackson–Vanik amendment denies "normal trade relations" to countries with non-market economies that restrict emigration rights. Permanent normal trade relations can only be extended to a country subject to the amendment if the President determines that the recipient government complies with the right to emigrate as established in the legislation. By linking trade and human rights, the Jackson–Vanik amendment has had an enormous impact over the years.

Originally enacted in response to restrictions on the emigration of Jews from the Soviet Union, the Jackson–Vanik amendment has been relatively successful, not only with regard to providing Jews with the right to emigrate, but also by increasing emigration from other non-free market countries like China and Vietnam. Notably, where a government has not met the emigration criteria established by the Amendment, a yearly waiver is permitted. Each of the former Soviet states has regularly received waivers since 1991, and, since President Clinton first waived application of the Amendment to Vietnam in 1998, the waiver has been renewed each year. In 2001, President Bush terminated application of Jackson–Vanik to China when permanent normal trade relations were established.

2. *Effective legislation.* Of each of the statutes reproduced above, which would you think would be the most effective? In your opinion, which is the easiest to implement? What factors weigh in your calculation of effectiveness and ease of implementation? If you were legislative counsel to a Member of Congress or a Senator, how would these factors inform your guidance regarding legislation she would like to propose requiring the Executive Branch to take *greater* account of human rights issues in foreign policy?

3. *A delicate balancing act or a whitewash?* Congress requires the Executive Branch to consider a wide variety of policy interests when providing foreign assistance—the degree to which a proposed aid recipient respects human rights being only one of them. Perhaps the most striking example of this balancing requirement is the legislation excerpted above authorizing assistance to the former Soviet Republics. Note the

variety of criteria that must be considered by the Executive Branch in determining whether and how much assistance should be provided by these states.

Not surprisingly, decisions of this nature require a careful balancing of interests. Some would argue that requiring the Executive to consider a multiplicity of factors actually harms the human rights situation in some countries, because other policy interests may trump the human rights factor, giving a green light to funding, thereby "approving" the country's poor human rights record. Is this a valid criticism of these statutes? How would your answer be affected by the knowledge that under section 502B above, no state has ever been found to have been engaged in "a consistent pattern of gross violations of internationally recognized human rights"?

4. *Equatorial Guinea.* Consider the case of Equatorial Guinea. For years, this small central African country has been an international pariah—ruled by a government accused of widespread human rights abuses as well as rampant corruption and cronyism. After repeated attempts to provide much needed financial assistance to this nation (which repeatedly appeared near the bottom of all development indexes), the World Bank and International Monetary Fund all but gave up. The situation in Equatorial Guinea seemed so intractable, the United States even closed its embassy in the capital, partly in protest over the government's human rights record.

In recent years, however, massive oil and gas reserves have been discovered in Equatorial Guinea. U.S. oil companies have made substantial investments there, and the government has begun to receive revenue on a massive scale. Since the discovery of oil, the U.S. government has re-opened a diplomatic presence in Malabo and has begun to re-engage with the government, particularly on human rights, governance, and development issues. While restrictions on civil and political rights continue, the Equatoguinean government has taken steps—albeit limited ones—to address its human rights record, including allowing visits by international NGOs, passing legislation on trafficking in persons, and requesting international assistance on these issues.

How should the U.S. government react to a request by a private contractor to provide security assistance to the government of Equatorial Guinea? The U.S. has previously invoked human rights concerns to deny a license for the provision of assistance in restructuring and professionalizing the Equatoguinean military on human rights grounds. How should human rights issues be balanced with the increased presence of U.S. investment and citizens and their need for security? Does the legislation excerpted above permit such a balance? How might the security assistance proposed improve or worsen the human rights situation in Equatorial Guinea? Should this be a factor in the decision whether to deny or grant the license?

5. *The Chafee Amendment.* Section 2(b)(1)(B) of the Export–Import Bank Act (the "Chafee Amendment") allows the President to block an application for credit by the Export–Import Bank, where it "would be in the national interest [and] where such action could clearly and importantly advance United States policy in such areas as international terrorism, nuclear proliferation, environmental protection and human rights." The President's authority to block a decision of the Bank has been delegated to the Secretary of State. Executive Order No. 12,166, 44 Fed. Reg. 60971 (Oct. 19, 1979).

In 1999, an application was made to Ex–Im Bank for loan guarantees that would allow a controversial Russian oil company, Tyumen Oil (TNK), to purchase nearly $500 million in oil refinery and exploration equipment from U.S. companies, including ABB Lummus Global and Halliburton Energy Service. The possibility that Ex–Im Bank would provide these loan guarantees was highly controversial. At the time, credible allegations had been made that TNK jilted several western investors in a highly irregular bankruptcy proceeding. Equally important, the Russian government was involved in a brutal military campaign in Chechnya, giving rise to claims of serious violations of international humanitarian law by Russian forces. Human rights advocates and many commercial interests were aligned in this case, both aggressively lobbying the U.S. government to block the Ex–Im Bank loan guarantees.

On December 21, 1999, then Secretary of State Albright invoked the Chafee Amendment to block the Ex–Im Bank loan guarantees, citing concerns over "rule of law" as the basis for her decision. The primary justification for the decision provided by State Department officials were problems of corruption in the Russian judicial system, not concerns over a broad range of human rights issues as many advocates had urged. Nevertheless, many saw the decision as a victory: whatever the stated basis for the decision, clearly the human rights practices of the Russian government had played a part in the invocation of this rarely-used legislative authority.

Six months later, Secretary Albright lifted the hold placed on the Ex–Im Bank loan guarantees. The Department's spokesperson provided the following justification for the decision: "In point of fact, the privatization of TNK was successfully completed, and the company has entered into serious negotiations with shareholders and creditors of the bankrupt companies, to resolve their differences. We've also opened a dialogue with the Russian Government, to impress on them the need to address weaknesses in Russia's legal framework that led to abuses in this case." Daily State Dept. Press Briefing (Mar. 31, 2000) *available at* http://usinfo.org/wf-archive/2000/000331/epf502.htm. When asked whether the Secretary's invocation of the Chafee Amendment brought about any specific changes, the spokesperson responded, "We've seen a marked improvement in the underlying situation, the fact that this bankruptcy proceeding had transpired under dubious circumstances, which have now been addressed, and the concerns of shareholders and creditors are now being addressed successfully. We made the larger point, as well, about how this decision was part of our overall concern about the rule of law. But one narrow decision that the Secretary made and has now unmade could not, in and of itself, fundamentally transform the overall situation involving the rule of law, and proper and sound economic practices in Russia." *Id.*

As indicated above, the Chafee Amendment has been rarely invoked by the Secretary of State; however, it does present an opportunity to push the U.S. government to use financial leverage to effect improvement on human rights issues. In this case, it is questionable whether Secretary Albright's temporary invocation of the Chafee Amendment had any lasting impact on rule of law or human rights violations in Russia. Was this a result of the particular circumstances of the case (*e.g.*, the extent of corruption in Russia, the nature of the conflict in Chechnya), or would we see the same result in any use of the Amendment?

6. *Religious freedom.* During the 1990s, a lively debate occurred in the United States among faith-based NGOs, Congress, and the Department of State, about how the United States could more effectively promote religious freedom and confront discrimination and persecution on the basis of religious belief. In October 1998, President Clinton signed the International Religious Freedom Act after it was passed unanimously by both the House of Representatives and the Senate. *See* 22 U.S.C. 6401 et seq.

The Act established an Office of International Religious Freedom within the Department of State, an independent, bipartisan U.S. Commission on International Religious Freedom and a Special Adviser on International Religious Freedom on the National Security Council staff. Moreover, the Act required the State Department to prepare an annual report for Congress that details the status of religious freedom in every foreign country, violations of religious freedom by foreign governments, and United States' actions and policies in support of religious freedom. The Act also required the Secretary of State to designate countries that have "engaged in or tolerated particularly severe violations of religious freedom" during the annual reporting period. The Act defined "particularly severe violations of religious freedom" as systematic, ongoing, egregious violations of religious freedom, including violations such as torture, degrading treatment or punishment, prolonged detention without charges, abduction or clandestine detention, or other flagrant denial of the right to life, liberty, or the security of persons. In those cases where the Secretary of State designates a "country of particular concern," Congress is then notified, and where non-economic policy options designed to bring about cessation of the particularly severe violations of religious freedom have reasonably been exhausted, economic measures are to be imposed. In 2007, Burma, China, Eritrea, Iran, North Korea, Saudi Arabia, Sudan, Saudi Arabia, and Uzbekistan were designated "countries of particular concern." *See* U.S. Dept. Of State Report on

International Religious Freedom, 2007, *available at* http://www.state.gov/ g/drl/rls/irf/2007/.

C. THE JUDICIARY

In addition to the executive and legislative branches, the judiciary offers a crucial mechanism for the internalization of international human rights standards. As shown in Chapter 2, *supra,* courts can cause the government to eliminate or reform a practice if it upholds a party's lawsuit challenging that practice on human rights grounds. However, the process can also be considerably less direct, and court proceedings can affect a government practice even when a particular lawsuit is unsuccessful. In the cases discussed below, domestic courts largely dismissed a series of actions against the U.S. government under the Vienna Convention on Consular Relations. And, when the International Court of Justice ruled against the United States in related cases, the U.S. response was widely criticized as insufficient. If the narrative ended there, the domestic courts would look unreceptive and the international court would look ineffective. But in fact, even if the litigation failed inside the courtroom, the U.S. government nevertheless undertook a process of internalization to reduce future violations of the Convention outside the courtroom.

The Vienna Convention on Consular Relations

Beginning in the late 1990s, counsel for defendants facing the death penalty in the United States began raising the Vienna Convention on Consular Relations as a basis for relief. The Vienna Convention requires that a foreign national who is arrested or detained be informed that he or she has the right to contact the consular representative of his or her government. *See* Vienna Convention on Consular Relations, art. 36, Apr. 24, 1963, 21 U.S.T. 77, 596 U.N.T.S. 261. In cases where foreign individuals have not been informed of their right to consular notification, counsel have argued that their clients were disadvantaged in mounting a defense to charges brought against them. Accordingly, defendants—particularly those in death penalty cases—have argued that their sentences should be vacated.

One of the well-known Vienna Convention cases concerned two German nationals, Karl and Walter LaGrand. The LaGrand brothers were convicted of felony murder in the course of a bungled robbery in Arizona in 1982, and each was sentenced to death. Neither man received notification of their right to consular access, but the issue was never raised by their court-appointed counsel in the course of their trial or on appeal in the subsequent post-conviction proceedings. Eventually, it was raised in a federal habeas corpus petition, but the petition was denied because the issue had not been raised in the state court proceedings. In February 1999, Karl LaGrand was executed. Shortly before Walter LaGrand was scheduled to be executed, the German government initiated legal proceedings against the United States in the International Court of Justice, requesting judgment on the merits and the issuance of provisional measures of protection to prevent the impending execution. The ICJ granted the request for provisional measures, calling on the United States to take all measures at its disposal to stay the execution of Walter LaGrand until the ICJ could resolve the merits of the action filed by Germany. On the same day as the provisional measures were issued, Walter LaGrand was executed by the state of Arizona. Two years later, in its judgment on the merits, the ICJ found that the United States had violated both its obligations under the Vienna Convention as well as the ICJ's provisional measures order. *See LaGrand Case (Germ. v. U.S.)*, 2001 ICJ 466 (June 27, 2001). The *LaGrand* controversy alerted the U.S. federal government that a serious problem existed throughout the country: that state and local law enforcement officers did not have a sufficient understanding of U.S. obligations under the Vienna Convention. Given the diplomatic as well as the potential legal consequences of the failure to inform foreigners of their right to consular notification, the U.S. federal government embarked on an ambitious education and training program to inform state and local officials of U.S. obligations under the Vienna Convention. The following is included in a guidance booklet for law enforcement and judicial authorities around the country:

U.S. DEPARTMENT OF STATE, DIPLOMATIC AND CONSULAR IMMUNITY: GUIDANCE FOR LAW ENFORCEMENT AND JUDICIAL AUTHORITIES

(1998)

The instructions in this booklet should be followed by all federal, state, and local government officials, whether law enforcement, judicial, or other, insofar as they pertain to foreign nationals subject to such officials' authority or to matters within their competence. These instructions relate to the arrest and detention of foreign nationals, deaths of foreign nationals, the appointment of guardians for minors or incompetent adults who are foreign nationals, and related issues pertaining to the provision of consular services to foreign nationals in the United States. They are intended to ensure that foreign governments can extend appropriate consular services to their nationals in the United States and that the United States complies with its legal obligations to such governments.

The instructions in this booklet are based on international legal obligations designed to ensure that governments can assist their nationals who travel abroad. While these obligations are in part matters of "customary international law," most of them are set forth in the Vienna Convention on Consular Relations ("VCCR"), and some are contained in bilateral agreements, conventions, or treaties (*i.e.*, agreements between the United States and just one other country). The agreements discussed herein have the status of treaties for purposes of international law and Article VI, clause 2 of the Constitution of the United States ("all treaties made ... shall be the supreme law of the land"). They are binding on federal, state, and local government officials to the extent that they pertain to matters within such officials' competence.

These instructions focus primarily on providing consular notification and access with respect to foreign nationals arrested or detained in the United States, so that their governments can assist them. The obligations of consular notification and access apply to United States citizens in foreign countries just as they apply to foreign nationals in the United States. When U.S. citizens are arrested or detained abroad, the United States Department of State seeks to ensure that they are treated in a manner consistent with these instructions, and that U.S. consular officers can similarly assist them. It is therefore particularly important that federal, state, and local government officials in the United States comply with these obligations with respect to foreign nationals here. * * *

The Department of State appreciates the continued cooperation of federal, state, and local law enforcement agencies in helping to ensure that foreign nationals in the United States are treated in accordance with these instructions. Such treatment will permit the United States to comply with its consular legal obligations domestically and to continue to expect rigorous compliance by foreign governments with respect to United States citizens abroad.

Arrests and Detentions of Foreign Nationals

Whenever a foreign national is arrested or detained in the United States, there are legal requirements to ensure that the foreign national's government can offer him/her appropriate consular assistance. *In all cases, the foreign national must be told of the right of consular notification and access. In most cases,* the foreign national then has the option to decide whether to have consular representatives notified of the arrest or detention. *In other cases,* however, the foreign national's consular officials must be notified of an arrest and/or detention regardless of the foreign national's wishes. *Whenever a foreign national is taken into custody, the detaining official should determine whether consular notification is at the option of the foreign national or whether it is mandatory.* A list of all embassies and consulates in the United States, with their telephone and facsimile numbers, is included in this booklet to facilitate the provision of notification by detaining officials to consular officials when required.

Notification at the Foreign National's Option

In all cases, the foreign national must be told of the right of consular notification and access. The foreign national then has the option to decide whether he/she wants consular representatives notified of the arrest or detention, *unless* the foreign national is from a "mandatory notification" country. The mandatory notification countries are listed in Part Five of this booklet.

If the detained foreign national is a national of a country not on the mandatory notification list, the requirement is that the foreign national be informed without delay of the option to have his/her government's consular representatives notified of the detention. *If the detainee requests notification, a responsible detaining official must ensure that notification is given to the nearest consulate or embassy of the detainee's country without delay.*

Mandatory Notification

In some cases, "mandatory notification" must be made to the nearest consulate or embassy "without delay," "immediately," or within the time specified in a bilateral agreement between the United States and a foreign national's country, *regardless of whether the foreign national requests such notification.* Mandatory notification requirements arise from different bilateral agreements whose terms are not identical. The exact text of the relevant provisions on mandatory notification in our bilateral agreements is reproduced in Part Five of this booklet.

Foreign nationals subject to mandatory notification requirements should otherwise be treated like foreign nationals not subject to the mandatory notification requirement. Thus, for example, the foreign national should be informed that notification has been made and advised that he/she may also specifically request consular assistance from his or her consular officials.

Privacy concerns or the possibility that a foreign national may have a legitimate fear of persecution or other mistreatment by his/her government may exist in some mandatory notification cases. The notification requirement should still be honored, but it is possible to take precautions regarding the disclosure of information. For example, it may not be necessary to provide information about why a foreign national is in detention. Moreover, *under no circumstances should any information indicating that a foreign national may have applied for asylum in the United States or elsewhere be disclosed to that person's government.* The Department of State can provide more specific guidance in particular cases.

Recordkeeping

Law enforcement agencies should keep written records sufficient to show compliance with the above notification requirements. These records should show all notifications to foreign consular representatives. In addition, in cases in which notification is at the discretion of the detained foreign national, these records should show that the foreign national was informed of the option of consular notification, the date when the foreign national was so informed, and whether or not the foreign national requested that consular officials be notified. If a confirmation of receipt of notification is available, it should be saved if possible.

The Department of State from time to time receives inquiries and complaints from foreign governments concerning foreign nationals in detention. The Department in such cases may request information from the relevant law enforcement officials on whether consular notification was in fact given. Concerns about consular notification may also be raised by foreign consular officials directly with the responsible federal, state, and local officials. Good recordkeeping will facilitate responding to these inquiries and to any consular notification issues that may be raised in litigation.

Consular Access to Detained Foreign Nationals

Detained foreign nationals are entitled to communicate with their consular officers. Any communication by a foreign national to his/her consular representative must be forwarded by the appropriate local officials to the consular post without delay.

Foreign consular officers must be given access to their nationals and permitted to communicate with them. Such officers have the right to visit their nationals, to converse and correspond with them, and to arrange for their legal representation. They must refrain from acting on behalf of a foreign national, however, if the national opposes their involvement. In addition, consular officers may not act as attorneys for their nationals.

The rights of consular access and communication generally must be exercised subject to local laws and regulations. For example, consular officers may be required to visit during established visiting hours. Federal, state, and local rules of this nature may not, however, be so restrictive as to defeat the purpose of consular access and communication. Such rules "must enable full effect to be given to the purposes" for which the right of consular assistance has been established. * * *

NOTES AND QUESTIONS ON THE INTERNALIZATION OF THE RIGHT TO CONSULAR NOTIFICATION

1. *The Vienna Convention in a federal system.* Clearly the *LaGrand* controversy led to the internalization of the U.S. government's obligations under the Vienna Convention on Consular Relations; however, the federal nature of the U.S. system of government made internalization complicated. It is difficult enough just to communicate the content and the importance of the international obligation of consular notification to the fifty states and innumerable local jurisdictions. Enforcing it is even more complicated. Is a training program adequate? Can you think of other, more effective means of ensuring compliance at the local level with the United States' international obligations under the VCCR?

2. *Executive action and the Vienna Convention. LaGrand* is not the only case to challenge death sentences based on violations of article 36 of

the VCCR by state and local officials. Indeed, two other significant cases—*Breard* and *Avena*—made their way to the International Court of Justice. *See Vienna Convention on Consular Relations (Para. v. U.S.)*, 1998 ICJ 248 (1998); *Avena and Other Mexican Nationals (Mex. v. U.S.)*, 2004 ICJ 128 (2004). In *Breard*, the ICJ called on the United States to take all measures at its disposal to prevent Breard's execution pending its consideration of the case on the merits. The U.S. Supreme Court denied a petition for habeas corpus and for certiorari based on the ICJ ruling, relying on the procedural default rule, *Breard v. Greene*, 523 U.S. 371 (1998), and Breard was subsequently executed.

In *Avena*, the ICJ considered the case on the merits and decided that the United States had violated the VCCR and was obligated, "by means of its own choosing" to allow the review and reconsideration of the convictions and sentences by taking account of the rights set forth in the VCCR. *See Avena*, 2004 ICJ 12 (2004). Subsequently the Supreme Court granted the *Avena* petitioners certiorari to decide whether a federal court is bound by the ICJ's ruling; however, the Court shortly thereafter dismissed its own writ of certiorari as improvidently granted. *Medellin v. Dretke*, 544 U.S. 660 (2005). Before its ruling, the President of the United States issued a Memorandum for the Attorney General stating, "I have determined * * * that the United States will discharge its international obligations under the decision of the International Court of Justice in [*Avena*], by having State courts give effect to the decision in accordance with general principles of comity." Memorandum for the U.S. Attorney General Regarding Compliance with the Decision of the International Court of Justice in *Avena*, 44 ILM 964 (2005).

Can the President bind the actions of state courts through such a memorandum? If so, why is it addressed to the U.S. Attorney General? Assuming you work for the Texas Attorney General (the jurisdiction where the *Avena* prosecutions took place), how would you address the President's memorandum when defense counsel rely on it as grounds for their habeas corpus action? Consider the fact that the ICJ only found that the United States must review and reconsider the convictions by taking into account the VCCR violations.

In 2008, the Supreme Court held that the President's memorandum is not binding on state courts: "The President has an array of political and diplomatic means available to enforce international obligations, but unilaterally converting a non-self-executing treaty into a self-executing one is not among them. The responsibility for transforming an international obligation arising from a non-self-executing treaty into domestic law falls to Congress." *Medellin v. Texas*, 128 S.Ct. 1346, 1368 (2008). The President "may not rely upon a non-self-executing treaty to establish binding rules of decision that pre-empt contrary state law." *Id*. at 1371 (quoting Brief for United States as *Amicus Curiae* 5). Even if the Texas courts followed the President's determination, how might they still uphold the convictions?

D. MEDIA AND NGO PRESSURE

The internalization of human rights in government policy-making can also be driven from outside of the government, especially by the media and NGOs. These actors play a valuable role in shedding light on allegations of abuse, as well as guiding the national and international debate on accountability for human rights obligations. Where a government has accepted certain international obligations, NGOs and the media provide an effective means for influencing government policy. As you read the excerpts below, consider how allegations and evidence of human rights abuses made public by the media, as well by NGOs like Human Rights Watch, have been addressed by the United States government, as well as how they have influenced the national and international debate on these issues.

DANA PRIEST AND BARTON GELLMAN, STRESS AND DURESS' TACTICS USED ON TERRORISM SUSPECTS HELD IN SECRET OVERSEAS FACILITIES

WASH. POST, at A1 (Dec. 26, 2002)

Deep inside the forbidden zone at the U.S.-occupied Bagram air base in Afghanistan, around the corner from the detention center and beyond the segregated clandestine military units, sits a cluster of metal shipping containers protected by a triple layer of concertina wire. The containers hold the most valuable prizes in the war on terrorism—captured al Qaeda operatives and Taliban commanders.

Those who refuse to cooperate inside this secret CIA interrogation center are sometimes kept standing or kneeling for hours, in black hoods or spray-painted goggles, according to intelligence specialists familiar with CIA interrogation methods. At times they are held in awkward, painful positions and deprived of sleep with a 24–hour bombardment of lights—subject to what are known as "stress and duress" techniques.

Those who cooperate are rewarded with creature comforts, interrogators whose methods include feigned friendship, respect, cultural sensitivity and, in some cases, money. Some who do not cooperate are turned over—"rendered," in official parlance—to foreign intelligence services whose practice of torture has been documented by the U.S. government and human rights organizations.

In the multifaceted global war on terrorism waged by the Bush administration, one of the most opaque—yet vital—fronts is the detention and interrogation of terrorism suspects. U.S. officials have said little publicly about the captives' names, numbers or whereabouts, and virtually nothing about interrogation methods. But interviews with several former intelligence officials and 10 current U.S. national security officials—including several people who witnessed the handling of prisoners—provide insight into how the U.S. government is prosecuting this part of the war.

The picture that emerges is of a brass-knuckled quest for information, often in concert with allies of dubious human rights reputation, in which the traditional lines between right and wrong, legal and inhumane, are evolving and blurred.

While the U.S. government publicly denounces the use of torture, each of the current national security officials interviewed for this article defended the use of violence against captives as just and necessary. They expressed confidence that the American public would back their view. The CIA, which has primary responsibility for interrogations, declined to comment.

"If you don't violate someone's human rights some of the time, you probably aren't doing your job," said one official who has supervised the capture and transfer of accused terrorists. "I don't think we want to be promoting a view of zero tolerance on this. That was the whole problem for a long time with the CIA." * * *

Letter from Human Rights Watch to President George W. Bush Dec. 26, 2002

December 26, 2002

President George W. Bush
The White House
1600 Pennsylvania Avenue, NW
Washington, DC 20500

Dear President Bush:

Human Rights Watch is deeply concerned by allegations of torture and other mistreatment of suspected al-Qaeda detainees described in the *Washington Post* ("U.S. Decries Abuse but Defends Interrogations") on December 26. The allegations, if true, would place the United States in violation of some of the most fundamental prohibitions of international human rights law. Any U.S. government official who is directly involved or complicit in the torture or mistreatment of detainees, including any official who knowingly acquiesces in the commission of such acts, would be subject to prosecution worldwide.

Human Rights Watch urges you to take immediate steps to clarify that the use of torture is not U.S policy, investigate the *Washington Post's* allegations, adopt all necessary measures to end any ongoing violations of international law, stop the rendition of detainees to countries where they are likely to be tortured, and prosecute those implicated in such abuse.

I.   Prohibitions Against Torture

The *Washington Post* reports that persons held in the CIA interrogation centers at Bagram air base in Afghanistan are subject to "stress and duress" techniques, including "standing or kneeling for hours" and being "held in awkward, painful positions." The *Post* notes that the detention facilities at Bagram and elsewhere, such as at Diego Garcia, are not monitored by the International Committee of the Red Cross, which has monitored the U.S. treatment of detainees at Guantánamo Bay, Cuba.

The absolute prohibition against torture is a fundamental and well-established precept of customary and conventional international law. Torture is never permissible against anyone, whether in times of peace or of war.

The prohibition against torture is firmly established under international human rights law. It is prohibited by various treaties to which the United States is a party, including the International Covenant on Civil and Political Rights (ICCPR), which the United States ratified in 1992, and the Convention against Torture and Other Cruel, Inhuman or Degrading Treatment or Punishment, which the United States ratified in 1994. Article 7 of the ICCPR states that "No one shall be subjected to torture or to cruel, inhuman or degrading treatment or punishment." The right to be protected from torture is non-derogable, meaning that it applies at all times, including during public emergencies or wartime.

International humanitarian law (the laws of war), which applies during armed conflict, prohibits the torture or other mistreatment of captured combatants and others in captivity, regardless of their legal status. Regarding prisoners-of-war, article 17 of the Third Geneva Convention of 1949 states: "No physical or mental torture, nor any other form of coercion, may be inflicted on prisoners of war to secure from them information of any kind whatever. Prisoners of war who refuse to answer may not be threatened, insulted, or exposed to any unpleasant or disadvantageous treatment of any kind." Detained civilians are similarly protected by article 32 of the Fourth Geneva Convention. The United States has been a party to the 1949 Geneva Conventions since 1955.

The United States does not recognize captured al-Qaeda members as being protected by the 1949 Geneva Conventions, although Bush administration officials have insisted that detainees will be treated humanely and in a manner consistent with Geneva principles. However, at minimum, all detainees in wartime, regardless of their legal status, are protected by customary international humanitarian law. Article 75 ("Fundamental Guarantees") of the First Additional Protocol to the Geneva Conventions, which is recognized as restating customary international law, provides that "torture of all kinds, whether physical or mental" against "persons who are in the power of a Party to the conflict and who do not benefit from more favorable treatment under the

[Geneva] Conventions," shall "remain prohibited at any time and in any place whatsoever, whether committed by civilian or military agents." "[C]ruel treatment and torture" of detainees is also prohibited under common article 3 to the 1949 Geneva Conventions, which is considered indicative of customary international law. * * *

Direct involvement or complicity in torture, as well as the failure to prevent torture, may subject U.S. officials to prosecution under international law.

The willful torture or inhuman treatment of prisoners-of-war or other detainees, including "willfully causing great suffering or serious injury to body or health," are "grave breaches" of the 1949 Geneva Conventions, commonly known as war crimes. Grave breaches are subject to universal jurisdiction, meaning that they can be prosecuted in any national criminal court and as well as any international tribunal with appropriate jurisdiction.

The Convention against Torture obligates States Parties to prosecute persons within their jurisdiction who are implicated or complicit in acts of torture. This obligation includes the prosecution of persons within their territory who committed acts of torture elsewhere and have not be extradited under procedures provided in the convention.

Should senior U.S. officials become aware of acts of torture by their subordinates and fail to take immediate and effective steps to end such practices, they too could be found criminally liable under international law. The responsibility of superior officers for atrocities by their subordinates is commonly known as command responsibility. Although the concept originated in military law, it now is increasingly accepted to include the responsibility of civil authorities for abuses committed by persons under their direct authority. The doctrine of command responsibility has been upheld in recent decisions by the international criminal tribunals for the former Yugoslavia and for Rwanda.

There are two forms of command responsibility: direct responsibility for orders that are unlawful and imputed responsibility, when a superior knows or should have known of crimes committed by a subordinate acting on his own initiative and fails to prevent or punish them. All states are obliged to bring such people to justice. * * *

The allegations made by the *Washington Post* are extraordinarily serious. They have put the United States on notice that acts of torture may be taking place with U.S. participation or complicity. That creates a heightened duty to respond preventively. As an immediate step, we urge that you issue a presidential statement clarifying that it is contrary to U.S. policy to use or facilitate torture. The *Post*'s allegations should be investigated and the findings made public. Should there be evidence of U.S. civilian or military officials being directly involved or complicit in torture, or in the rendition of persons to places where they are likely to be tortured, you should take immediate steps to prevent the commission of such acts and to prosecute the individuals who have ordered, organized, condoned, or carried them out. The United States also has a duty to refrain from sending persons to other countries with a history of torture without explicit and verifiable guarantees that no torture or mistreatment will occur.

Thank you for your attention to these concerns.

Sincerely,
Kenneth Roth
Executive Director

cc: Colin Powell, Secretary of State
Donald Rumsfeld, Secretary of Defense
Condoleezza Rice, National Security Advisor

Response Letter from Defense Department General Counsel, William J. Haynes II, to Kenneth Roth, Human Rights Watch, April 2, 2003[1]

Mr. Kenneth Roth
Executive Director
Human Rights Watch
350 Fifth Avenue
New York, NY 101185

Dear Mr. Roth:

This is in response to your December 26, 2002, letter to the President and other letters to senior administration officials regarding detention and questioning of enemy combatants captured in the war against terrorists of global reach after the terrorist attacks on the United States of September 11, 2001.

The United States questions enemy combatants to elicit information they may possess that could help the coalition win the war and forestall further terrorist attacks upon the citizens of the United States and other countries. As the President reaffirmed recently to the United Nations High Commissioner for Human Rights, United States policy condemns and prohibits torture. When questioning enemy combatants, U.S. personnel are required to follow this policy and applicable laws prohibiting torture.

If the war on terrorists of global reach requires transfer of detained enemy combatants to other countries for continued detention on our behalf, U.S. Government instructions are to seek and obtain appropriate assurances that such enemy combatants are not tortured.

U.S. Government personnel are instructed to report allegations of mistreatment of or injuries to detained enemy combatants, and to investigate any such reports. Consistent with these instructions, U.S.

---

1. *Available at* http://www.hrw.org/press/2003/04/dodltr040203.pdf.

Government officials investigate any known reports of mistreatment or injuries to detainees.

The United States does not condone torture. We are committed to protecting human rights as well as protecting the people of the United States and other countries against terrorists of global reach.

Sincerely,

William J. Haynes II

Notes and Questions on Civil Society Pressure

1. *Presidential reaction.* Note how the work of the media and advocacy by NGOs have guided a vibrant public debate on an international human rights issue, underpinned by treaty obligations assumed by the United States. Indeed, public attention to the issue ultimately led the President to condemn the use of torture and cruel and unusual punishment in a statement issued by the White House on the United Nations International Day in Support of Victims of Torture: "The United States is committed to the world-wide elimination of torture and we are leading this fight by example. I call on all governments to join with the United States and the community of law-abiding nations in prohibiting, investigating, and prosecuting all acts of torture and in undertaking to prevent other cruel and unusual punishment." Statement by the President, June 26, 2003, *available at* http://www.whitehouse.gov/news/releases/2003/06/20030626–3.html. Of what legal value is this statement?

2. *Engaging on the key issue.* In your opinion, does the Haynes letter reproduced above adequately respond to the concerns raised by the letter from Human Rights Watch? Re-read the Human Rights Watch letter, placing yourself in the position of a Pentagon lawyer. Why would you choose to respond to some points but not others? Would taking a position on legal issues raised by Human Rights Watch have negative consequences for the U.S.–led war on terror or on operations in Afghanistan and Iraq? As a matter of law, does that matter?

3. *U.S. Report to the Committee Against Torture.* In its Second Periodic Report to the U.N. Committee Against Torture, the U.S. stated:

> The United States is unequivocally opposed to the use and practice of torture. No circumstance whatsoever, including war, the threat of war, internal political instability, public emergency, or an order from a superior officer or public authority, may be invoked as a justification for or defense to committing torture. This is a long-standing commitment of the United States, repeatedly reaffirmed at the highest levels of the U.S. Government.

> All components of the United States Government are obligated to act in compliance with the law, including all United States constitutional, statutory, and treaty obligations relating to torture and cruel,

inhuman or degrading treatment or punishment. The U.S. Government does not permit, tolerate, or condone torture, or other unlawful practices, by its personnel or employees under any circumstances. U.S. laws prohibiting such practices apply both when the employees are operating in the United States and in other parts of the world.

U.S. Dept. of State, Second Periodic Report of the United States of America to the Committee Against Torture (May 6, 2005), *available at* http://www.state.gov/g/drl/rls/45738.htm. How do you reconcile this statement with reports that the Bush Administration lobbied against proposed legislation that would prohibit the U.S. military from engaging in "cruel, inhuman or degrading treatment" of detainees? *See* Josh White & R. Jeffrey Smith, *White House Aims to Block Legislation on Detainees*, WASH. POST at A1 (July 23, 2005). In light of the understanding of Article 16 made by the U.S. upon ratification (*i.e.*, that it is bound by the obligation to prevent "cruel, inhuman or degrading treatment or punishment" only insofar as the term means the cruel, unusual and inhumane treatment or punishment prohibited by the Fifth, Eighth, and/or Fourteenth Amendments to the U.S. Constitution), how would you frame a legal argument against the proposed legislation?

4. *Unintended consequences.* Two years after the *Post*'s article about detentions in Afghanistan, shocking evidence was made public detailing abuses of detainees by U.S. soldiers in the Abu Ghraib prison in Iraq. Americans and people around the world were outraged by graphic photographs taken of the abuse by soldiers at the prison, photographs which continue to plague the United States' efforts to bring security and stability to Iraq. Indeed, many have argued that the images from Abu Ghraib heightened instability and served as a recruiting tool for fundamentalist terrorists. Then, in May 2005, *Newsweek* magazine published an article alleging that U.S. military personnel at the GTMO detention facility had mishandled the Koran, including a report that one official had flushed it down the toilet. The reports sparked violent protests in Afghanistan, Pakistan, and Indonesia, in which at least 16 people were killed. *Newsweek* issued a formal retraction of the article, citing shaky evidence in the report, but not until after serious damage had been done to the credibility of the United States within the Muslim world. *See* Howard Kurtz, *Newsweek Retracts Guantanamo Story*, WASH. POST, at A3 (May 17, 2005).

E. NEW APPROACHES TO THE INTERNALIZATION OF HUMAN RIGHTS

Until recently, the internalization of human rights has largely taken the form of restricting government actions instead of encouraging them, *i.e.,* through use of the stick but not the carrot. Legislation places limitations on assistance programs, treaties prevent governments from mistreating individuals, and media and NGOs restrain government policy through vigilance and investigation. Moreover, where the carrot approach has been adopted, its impact has been limited. In the United States, the stick approach—the imposition of sanctions and human rights certifications—has been the instrument of choice. In 2002, President George W. Bush submitted to Congress a plan that would dramatically alter the manner in which the United States provides development assistance. In 2004, Congress approved legislation authorizing the creation of the Millennium Challenge Corporation (MCC), which will be responsible for distributing assistance from a newly created Millennium Challenge Account (MCA). Qualification for receiving MCA assistance is based on a country's performance on a variety of criteria, one of which is "governing justly," a criterion that includes recognition of civil liberties, political rights, and rule of law.

As you read the excerpt below, consider the implications of linking development assistance and human rights: will the MCA encourage poor countries to improve human rights protections in order to obtain greater development assistance, or will it leave problem countries behind, serving only to worsen the human rights conditions in those countries? Moreover, given the methodologies outlined for qualification in the program, will human rights play a critical role, or will other qualifications minimize this factor's impact?

The Millennium Challenge Account[2]

In March 2002 in Monterrey, Mexico, President Bush called for a "new compact for global development," which links greater contributions from developed nations to greater responsibility from developing nations. The President proposed a concrete mechanism to implement this compact—the Millennium Challenge Account (MCA). MCA provides development assistance to those countries that rule justly, invest in their people, and encourage economic freedom. With strong bipartisan support, the Millennium Challenge Corporation (MCC) was established on January 23, 2004, to administer the MCA. Congress provided nearly $1 billion in initial funding for FY04 and $1.5 billion for FY05. The President * * * requested $3 billion for FY06 and pledged to increase annual funding for the MCA to $5 billion in the future.

The MCA draws on lessons learned about development over the past 50 years: aid is most effective when it reinforces sound political, economic and social policies—which are key to encouraging the inflows of private capital and increased trade—the real engines of economic growth;

---

2. *Available at* http://www.usaid.gov/about_usaid/presidential_initiative/init_othermech.html; *see also* http://www.mca.gov/press/releases/2004/release–020204–factsheet.pdf

Development plans supported by a broad range of stakeholders, and for which countries have primary responsibility, engender country ownership and are more likely to succeed;

Integrating monitoring and evaluation into the design of activities boosts effectiveness, accountability, and the transparency with which taxpayer resources are used.

Key MCA Principles:

Reduce Poverty through Economic Growth: The MCC will focus specifically on promoting sustainable economic growth that reduces poverty through investments in areas such as agriculture, education, private sector development, and capacity building.

Reward Good Policy: Using objective indicators, countries will be selected to receive assistance based on their performance in governing justly, investing in their citizens, and encouraging economic freedom.

Operate as Partners: Working closely with the MCC, countries that receive MCA assistance will be responsible for identifying the greatest barriers to their own development, ensuring civil society participation, and developing an MCA program. MCA participation will require a high-level commitment from the host government. Each MCA country will enter into a public Compact with the MCC that includes a multi-year plan for achieving development objectives and identifies the responsibilities of each partner in achieving those objectives.

Focus on Results: MCA assistance will go to those countries that have developed well-designed programs with clear objectives, benchmarks to measure progress, procedures to ensure fiscal accountability for the use of MCA assistance, and a plan for effective monitoring and objective evaluation of results. Programs will be designed to enable sustainable progress even after the funding under the MCA Compact has ended.

MILLENNIUM CHALLENGE ACT OF 2003

Pub L. 108–199, 118
Stat. 3, 216–17 (2004)

Section 607. Eligible Countries.

(a) DETERMINATION BY THE BOARD [OF DIRECTORS, MILLENNIUM CHALLENGE CORPORATION]. The Board shall determine whether a candidate country is an eligible country for purposes of this section. Such determination shall be based, to the maximum extent possible, upon objective and quantifiable indicators of a country's demonstrated commitment to the criteria in subsection (b), and shall, where appropriate, take into account and assess the role of women and girls.

(b) CRITERIA. A candidate country should be considered to be an eligible country for purposes of this section if the Board determines that the country has demonstrated a commitment to—

(1) just and democratic governance, including a demonstrated commitment to—

    (A) promote political pluralism, equality and the rule of law;

    (B) respect human and civil rights, including the rights of people with disabilities;

    (C) protect private property rights;

    (D) encourage transparency and accountability of government; and

    (E) combat corruption;

(2) economic freedom, including a demonstrated commitment to economic policies that—

    (A) encourage citizens and firms to participate in global trade and international capital markets;

    (B) promote private sector growth and the sustainable management of natural resources;

    (C) strengthen market forces in the economy; and

    (D) respect worker rights, including the right to form labor unions; and

(3) investments in the people of such country, particularly women and children, including programs that—

    (A) promote broad-based primary education; and

    (B) strengthen and build capacity to provide quality public health and reduce child mortality.

* * *

Notes and Comments on Internalization in Development Assistance

1. *The relevance of human rights.* Since its creation, the MCC has ranked roughly forty countries eligible for receipt of MCA funds. Of these countries, the MCC has signed multi-year compacts for the provision of assistance with Armenia, Benin, Cape Verde, El Salvador, Georgia, Ghana, Honduras, Lesotho, Madagascar, Mali, Mongolia, Morocco, Mozambique, Nicaragua, Tanzania, Ukraine and Vanuatu. Looking at the U.S. State Department's Human Rights Reports, do any of these countries' human rights records raise questions about their eligibility for MCA assistance? Each year before the MCC board meeting, Freedom House publicly urges that more attention be paid to whether governments that are potentially MCA-eligible have met benchmarks on respecting civil and political rights. In fact, in a statement released prior to the announcement of MCA-eligible countries in 2005, Freedom House argued that some countries that eventually made the list should

not be eligible for assistance, namely, Armenia, Burkina Faso, the Gambia, and Morocco. *See* Press Release, Freedom House, Millennium Challenge: Funds Should Go To States Committed To Democracy (Nov. 2, 2005), *available at* http://www.freedomhouse.org/media/pressrel/110205.htm. In the view of Freedom House, while these countries technically pass the MCC indicators test, "their political reforms to date have been insufficient to suggest the deep, institutional commitment that is the *sine qua non* of the MCC program."

In light of the fact that Freedom House is cited as one of the key sources used by the MCC to determine eligibility on "ruling justly" grounds, how persuasive should its view be on whether governments are meeting relevant benchmarks? Can you see how the MCC might find these governments eligible for MCA assistance in order to create the leverage needed to persuade them to deepen political reforms? On the other hand, given the amount of money involved in each of the compacts signed to date, is this adequate incentive to continue improvements in a government's human rights record? Is this amount of money sufficient to convince other countries with far worse records to change in order to become MCA eligible?

2. *Decision-making at the MCC.* The MCC uses a variety of sources to determine MCA eligibility, including Freedom House, the World Bank Institute, the IMF, and the Heritage Foundation. Ultimately, the MCC Board, which includes, *inter alia*, the Secretary of State, the Secretary of the Treasury, and the Administrator of the U.S. Agency for International Development, makes final decisions on eligibility. In your view, does the involvement of senior U.S. government officials in eligibility decisions raise any questions with regard to criteria analysis and decision-making? Notably, eight additional individuals serve on the MCC Board, four appointed by the President, by and with the advice and consent of the Senate; and one each appointed from lists submitted by the minority and majority leaders of the House and Senate. Does this affect your answer to the previous question?

3. *Are the criteria sufficient?* Note the specific and general human rights-related criteria for eligibility established by the legislation. Should other rights be included? In particular, do the criteria take sufficient account of economic, social, and cultural rights? Are these rights important in the context of development? Do you see any anomalies in the rights identified? Why do you think some rights were identified but others neglected?

Practicum

In recent years, human rights and environmental advocates have proposed the adoption of legislation creating an "International Right to Know." Although U.S. law creates a variety of disclosure requirements for U.S. companies, advocates of an international right-to-know argue that there is no requirement that U.S.-based or -traded companies and their foreign subsidiaries publicly disclose information on their overseas operations. Moreover, advocates argue there is no requirement that U.S. companies report on human rights issues, forced relocations, forced labor, child labor, and a range of other unsafe operating practices.

As a result of controversies involving U.S. businesses operating overseas, the U.S. Congress is considering legislation that would include the following:

- Requirements that all U.S. companies with overseas operations (including those of its foreign subsidiaries) publicly report on:
  - Compliance with international labor standards as identified by the ILO, including worker exposure to dangerous chemicals as well as forced and child labor;
  - Compliance with international human rights standards, including making public the terms of agreements between U.S. companies and local security forces;
  - Any community relocation as a result of overseas operations, including whether and how many people were forcibly relocated to accommodate U.S. business interests.
- The above reports will be submitted to the U.S. Department of State, which will review the reports make determinations as to compliance with international standards and submit an annual report to Congress.
- A citizen suit provision that will create jurisdiction and a cause of action for violations of the legislation, including, but not limited to, failure to report on overseas activity.

Although no draft legislation has been prepared, the Congress is holding hearings to determine whether these subject areas should be included, how they might be modified, and whether additional subjects should be included.

You represent one of the following three perspectives: the NGO community, the U.S. Government, or the U.S. business community. In arguing for or against the legislation, craft your position in terms of international human rights law: would such a law represent a departure from or a mere reflection of existing law? Also consider how such a law would affect U.S. foreign policy. What impact would such a law have on U.S. businesses and their ability to conduct operations overseas? Feel free to propose additions to or modifications of the proposals above based on the perspective you adopt.

CHAPTER 6

MODULE 13

NEGOTIATING HUMAN RIGHTS TREATIES

■ ■ ■

Orientation

From a traditional perspective, human rights treaties are like some bizarre creature of the modern international legal order. Throughout its history, international law has consisted in obligations that ran from state to state, and bilateral or multilateral treaties were the most formal means of accepting these horizontal obligations. But human rights treaties create a different category of obligations for governments—obligations that run formally to other governments but functionally to their own citizens and residents. For example, in the Convention against Torture, governments promised one another that they would not torture people within their jurisdiction. Treaties on the laws of war, consular notification and protection, the extradition of suspects, or the non-return of refugees ("non-refoulement") create direct obligations between states that can benefit–and were intended to benefit–individual human beings.

Why would any government surrender sovereignty in this particular way? One crass explanation is that some states have no intention of taking these obligations seriously and view accession to human rights treaties as an act of public relations, a way to show a commitment to human rights without actually doing anything. (One need only consider the UN Convention on the Rights of the Child and its near universal ratification set against the disappointing level of implementation.) For states at the other end of the enforcement spectrum however, these obligations are taken seriously: on the domestic level, a treaty can offer the means for bringing lawless or recalcitrant segments of government into line with the human rights polices of the central government. When the treaty creates domestic law, it can also provide the rule of decision in domestic litigation, and treaties have often driven legislative and cultural reform. In many countries, active, vocal civil society movements–with international human rights treaties at the core of their mandates–have become an increasingly powerful force that governments ignore at their peril.

Human rights treaties can also have a profound impact on the development of customary international law. Whether by explicit codification or "crystallization" over time, a treaty that is obligatory by its terms and with near-universal and representative participation among states can qualify as evidence of customary international law. *North Sea Continental Shelf Cases (Federal Republic of Germany v Denmark; Federal Republic of Germany v Netherlands)*, 1969 I.C.J. 4. States that are not parties to such a treaty will naturally argue that they cannot be bound by it in the absence of their formal consent, but the evidentiary use of treaties to prove customary international law is now well-established. This accounts for why states with no intention of signing or ratifying a treaty will nevertheless participate in its negotiation. On the other hand, becoming a party has its practical advantages: a party has greater authority to address the issues in the treaty and can more directly influence the work of the bodies entrusted to "oversee" its implementation. For example, a state that is not a party to the International Covenant on Economic, Social, and Cultural Rights has no formal institutional mechanisms for challenging a General Comment from the Covenant's Committee that purports to identify principles of customary international law.

These and many other considerations affect a government's decision to become a party to an *existing* multilateral human rights treaty or not, but what factors does a government consider in deciding to participate in the negotiation and development of a *new* treaty? And once a government makes that decision, how—if at all—does it account for the interests of non-state actors, like non-governmental organizations, victims' groups, and human rights defenders? These issues are of primary concern to the government lawyer who must protect and advance the interest of the government client in the course of a negotiation, but they are also crucial to the human rights lawyer representing a constituency or an individual client.

The organizing question for this module is, how can a human rights lawyer—both inside and outside the government—use the treaty negotiation process to advance a human rights agenda and represent a client's best interest at each stage in the treaty-development process? You will consider one prominent treaty negotiation—on the International Convention for the Protection of All Persons from Enforced Disappearances—from the perspective of a lawyer involved in the process, crafting the very words that will determine whether the treaty works or not. The trick of course is finding the right text that will both garner widespread support among governments and redress the targeted problem.

A Word on the Negotiation Process

Within the United Nations, either the former Commission on Human Rights or the General Assembly has historically made the decision to begin negotiating a human rights treaty. Although the Commission has been replaced by the Human Rights Council, it will continue to play a significant but not exclusive role in the decision to negotiate a new treaty. Typically, whether the General Assembly or the Council initiates the process, it begins with the creation of a Working Group, which meets at regular intervals to draft and approve a "negotiating text." That instrument is then forwarded to whichever body created the Working Group and is circulated to governments and other parts of the UN system, until it is finally presented to the General Assembly for its approval or adoption, after which it is opened for states' signature. When there is broad agreement on the content of the instrument, it will be adopted by consensus, as occurred with the Optional Protocols to the Convention on the Rights of the Child, which addressed child soldiers and trafficking. When a treaty is contentious, the process can be hard-fought and inconclusive. For example, an Optional Protocol to the Convention against Torture establishes a controversial mechanism for in-country visits, and in draft form it was forced to a vote in the Working Group, the Commission on Human Rights, ECOSOC, and eventually the General Assembly. Notwithstanding the protracted controversy, the Optional Protocol was eventually adopted and is now open for signature.

Drafting an Obligatory Instrument to Protect Against Forced Disappearances

Since 1980 the Working Group on Enforced or Involuntary Disappearances of the UN Commission on Human Rights has contacted governments on behalf of tens of thousands of individuals reported to have disappeared. While some of these cases have been clarified through information provided by governments or NGOs, most remain open. Less than twenty percent of these cases have been resolved—and only five percent of the individuals on the Working Group's caseload were found to be alive. *See Report of the Working Group on Enforced or Involuntary Disappearances* (21 Jan. 2004), U.N. Doc. E/CN.4/2004/58, ¶ 7, *available at* http://documents-dds-ny.un.org/doc/UNDOC/GEN/G04/103/ 96/pdf/G0410396.pdf?OpenElement

Although often considered a phenomenon of the late 1960s and early 1970s in Latin America, the practice of forced disappearances is no longer a regional issue. In 2001, the largest number of cases reported to the Working Group occurred in Nepal, Colombia, and Cameroon; in 2000 and 1999, Indonesia, India, the Russian Federation, and Colombia saw the largest number of cases. *See Report of the Working Group on Enforced and Involuntary Disappearances*, U.N. Doc. E/CN.4/2001/69 and U.N. Doc. E/CN.4/2000/64. In 2003, Algeria, the Russian Federation, and Nepal had the largest numbers of new cases. *See Report of the Working Group on Enforced and Involuntary Disappearances*, U.N. Doc. E/CN.4/2004/58. Indeed, the practice of enforced disappearances as a tool of state repression is common around the world.

Numerous existing international instruments identify the practice of forced disappearance as a human rights violation; however, these documents have failed to establish a universal and legally binding regime that could contribute to ending the practice worldwide. Existing instruments are either limited in application (*e.g.*, the Inter–American Convention on Enforced Disappearance of Persons), are not legally binding (*e.g.*, the Declaration on the Protection of All Persons from Enforced Disappearance), or do not explicitly address forced disappearances as a unique human rights violation (*e.g.*, the International Covenant on Civil and Political Rights).

In an attempt to remedy this situation, in 2001 the former UN Commission on Human Rights decided to establish a working group to elaborate a legally binding normative instrument for the protection of all persons from enforced disappearances. The resolution authorizing the creation of the working group instructed it to (a) consider the 1998 draft convention created by the Sub–Commission on the Promotion and Protection of Human Rights, and (b) appoint an independent expert to examine the existing international criminal and human rights framework for the protection of persons from enforced or involuntary disappearances. *See* Commission Res. 2001/46, U.N. Doc. E/CN.4/2001/167 (April 23, 2001). The Working Group met annually for a week until it agreed to submit a draft to the Commission on Human Rights for consideration at its 2006 session.

Ultimately, the Convention was adopted during the sixty-first session of the General Assembly on 20 December 2006. G.A. Res. 61/177, UN Doc. A/RES/61/177 (Dec. 20, 2006). In accordance with article 38, the Convention is now open for signature by all member states of the United Nations. When this book went to print, the Convention had seventy-three signatories, but only four ratifications—twenty-six short of the thirty necessary for the Convention to enter into force. *See* Office of the High Commissioner on Human Rights, International Convention of for the Protection of All Persons from Enforced Disappearance, *available at* http://www2.ohchr.org/english/bodies/ratification/16.htm (last visited July 6, 2008).

This module will outline four key issues addressed in the working group's deliberations: definition, punishable acts and persons, protection against impunity, and prosecutions and international cooperation. In crafting provisions that deal with each of these issues, negotiators of the new convention had to draw on existing language that could be modified to address the specifics of enforced disappearances. As you read the following excerpts from international instruments, consider the ways in which this language was drawn upon, revised, and eventually incorporated into the draft convention.

Also, as you consider the excerpts below, think about how various actors involved in these negotiations would prefer the language to be drafted. For instance, the United Kingdom or the United States will have different views than will an NGO like Human Rights Watch or Amnesty International. Similarly, a country like North Korea or Iran will take a different approach to these negotiations than an NGO that represents families of the disappeared in Argentina. Finally, consider the fact that this document will stand at an intersection between human rights and criminal law. How might this affect the negotiations?

Enforced Disappearances: A Definition

Declaration on the Protection of All Persons From Enforced Disappearances, G.A. Res. 47/133, ¶ 3, U.N. Doc. A/47678/Add.2 (Dec. 18, 1992)

Deeply concerned that in many countries, often in a persistent manner, enforced disappearances occur, in the sense that persons are arrested, detained or abducted against their will or otherwise deprived of their liberty by officials of different branches or levels of Government, or by organized groups or private individuals acting on behalf of, or with the support, direct or indirect, consent or acquiescence of the Government, followed by a refusal to disclose the fate or whereabouts of the persons concerned or a refusal to acknowledge the deprivation of their liberty, which places such persons outside the protection of the law. * * *

1998 Draft Convention on the Protection of All Persons From Forced Disappearance, UN Doc. E/CN.4/Sub.2/1998/19

1.   For the purposes of this Convention, forced disappearance is considered to be the deprivation of a person's liberty, in whatever form or for whatever reason, brought about by agents of the State or by persons or groups of persons acting with the authorization, support or acquiescence of the State, followed by an absence of information, or refusal to acknowledge the deprivation of liberty or information, or concealment of the fate or whereabouts of the disappeared person.

2.   This article is without prejudice to any international instrument or national legislation that does or may contain provisions of broader application, especially with regard to forced disappearances perpetrated by groups or individuals other than those referred to at paragraph 1 of this article.

Inter-American Convention on the Forced Disappearance of Persons OAS No.A–60, June 9, 1994

Article II

For the purposes of this Convention, forced disappearance is considered to be the act of depriving a person or persons of his or their freedom, in whatever way, perpetrated by agents of the state or by persons or groups of persons acting with the authorization, support, or acquiescence of the state, followed by an absence of information or a refusal to acknowledge that deprivation of freedom or to give information on the whereabouts of that person, thereby impeding his or her recourse to the applicable legal remedies and procedural guarantees.

Rome Statute of the International Criminal Court

Article 7 (2)(i)

(i) "Enforced disappearance of persons" means the arrest, detention or abduction of persons by, or with the authorization, support or acquiescence of, a State or a political organization, followed by a refusal to acknowledge that deprivation of freedom or to give information on the fate or whereabouts of those persons, with the intention of removing them from the protection of the law for a prolonged period of time. * * *

International Convention for the Protection of All Persons from Enforced Disappearance, Adopted Dec. 20, 2006, G.A. Res. A/RES/61/177, UN Doc. A/61/488

For the purposes of this Convention, enforced disappearance is considered to be the arrest, detention, abduction or any other form of deprivation of liberty by agents of the State or by persons or groups of persons acting with the authorization, support, or acquiescence of the State, followed by a refusal to acknowledge the deprivation of liberty or by concealment of the fate or whereabouts of the disappeared person, which place such a person outside the protection of the law.

NOTES AND QUESTIONS ON DRAFTING A DEFINITION

1. *Elements of the crime.* From the excerpts above, what are the primary elements for a crime of forced disappearance? Does the definition included in the draft convention include all of the elements identified in previous instruments? Is the draft convention stronger or weaker than, for instance, the Rome Convention definition? The OAS Convention?

Trace the development of the concept of "removal from the protection of the law" through the various instruments. How has this element evolved? How is it addressed in the draft convention? Is this a necessary element, or does it substantively limit the crime to the point where it would be too difficult to prosecute?

2. *State vs. non–state actors.* As a human rights instrument, it is clear that the definition of an enforced disappearance must apply to state actors; indeed, each of the excerpts above specifically defines the act as one committed, at the very least, with the authorization or support of a state. As a criminal law instrument, would its effectiveness increase if applicable also to non-state actors?

3. *Disappearances in U.S. law.* For an examination of the definition of the international human rights violation of forced disappearance in the U.S. courts, see *Forti v. Suarez–Mason*, 694 F.Supp. 707, 710–11 (N.D.Cal. 1988); *Xuncax v. Gramajo*, 886 F.Supp. 162 (D.Mass. 1995);

Mehinovic v. Vuckovic, 198 F. Supp.2d 1322 (N.D.Ga. 2002); *Tachiona v. Mugabe*, 234 F. Supp.2d 401 (S.D.N.Y. 2002). *See also* 22 U.S.C. § 2151n(a), 22 U.S.C. § 2304, and 22 U.S.C. § 262d; Restatement (Third) Foreign Relations Law of the United States § 702(c) (2003) ("A state violates international law if, as a matter of state policy, it practices, encourages, or condones * * * (c) the murder or causing the disappearance of individuals").

Enforced Disappearances: Punishable Acts and Persons

Declaration on the Protection of All Persons From Enforced Disappearances G.A. Res. 47/133, UN Doc. A/47678/Add.2, arts. 4, 6, 7 (Dec. 18, 1992)

Article 4

1. All acts of enforced disappearance shall be offences under criminal law punishable by appropriate penalties which shall take into account their extreme seriousness.

2. Mitigating circumstances may be established in national legislation for persons who, having participated in enforced disappearances, are instrumental in bringing the victims forward alive or in providing voluntarily information which would contribute to clarifying cases of enforced disappearance.

Article 6

1. No order or instruction of any public authority, civilian, military or other, may be invoked to justify an enforced disappearance. Any person receiving such an order or instruction shall have the right and duty not to obey it.

2. Each State shall ensure that orders or instructions directing, authorizing or encouraging any enforced disappearance are prohibited. * * *

Article 7

No circumstances whatsoever, whether a threat of war, a state of war, internal political instability or any other public emergency, may be invoked to justify enforced disappearances.

1998 Draft Convention on the Protection of All Persons From Forced Disappearance, UN Doc. E/CN.4/Sub.2/1998/19, arts. 2, 4, 5, 9

Article 2

1. The perpetrator of and other participants in the offence of forced disappearance or of any constituent element of the offence, as defined in article 1 of this Convention, shall be punished. The perpetra-

tors or other participants in a constituent element of the offence as defined in article 1 of this Convention shall be punished for a forced disappearance where they knew or ought to have known that the offence was about to be or was in the process of being committed. The perpetrator of and other participants in the following acts shall also be punished:

(a) Instigation, incitement or encouragement of the commission of the offence of forced disappearance;

(b) Conspiracy or collusion to commit an offence of forced disappearance;

(c) Attempt to commit an offence of forced disappearance; and

(d) Concealment of an offence of forced disappearance.

2.   Non-fulfillment of the legal duty to act to prevent a forced disappearance shall also be punished. * * *

Article 4 * * *

2.   No circumstance—whether internal political instability, threat of war, state of war, any state of emergency or suspension of individual guarantees—may be invoked in order not to comply with the obligations established in this Convention.

Article 5

1.   The States Parties undertake to adopt the necessary legislative measures to define the forced disappearance of persons as an independent offence, as defined in article 1 of this Convention, and to define a crime against humanity, as defined in article 3 of this Convention, as separate offences, and to impose an appropriate punishment commensurate with their extreme gravity. The death penalty shall not be imposed in any circumstances. This offence is continuous and permanent as long as the fate or whereabouts of the disappeared person have not been determined with certainty.

2.   The State Parties may establish mitigating circumstances for persons who, having been implicated in the acts referred to in article 2 of this Convention, effectively contribute to bringing the disappeared person forward alive, or voluntarily provide information that contributes to solving cases of forced disappearance or identifying those responsible for an offence of forced disappearance. * * *

Article 9

1.   No order or instruction of any public authority—civilian, military or other—may be invoked to justify a forced disappearance. Any person receiving such an order or instruction shall have the right and duty not to obey it. Each State shall prohibit orders or instructions commanding, authorizing or encouraging a forced disappearance.

2.   Law enforcement officials who have reason to believe that a forced disappearance has occurred or is about to occur shall communicate the matter to their superior authorities and, when necessary, to competent authorities or organs with reviewing or remedial power.

3.   Forced disappearance committed by a subordinate shall not relieve his superiors of criminal responsibility if the latter failed to exercise the powers vested in them to prevent or halt the commission of the crime, if they were in possession of information that enabled them to know that the crime was being or was about to be committed.

International Convention for the Protection of All Persons from Enforced Disappearance Adopted Dec. 20, 2006, G.A. Res. A/RES/61/177, UN Doc. A/61/488, arts. 6, 7

Article 6

1.   Each State Party shall take the necessary measures to hold criminally responsible at least:

(a) Any person who commits, orders, solicits or induces the commission of, attempts to commit, is an accomplice to or participates in an enforced disappearance;

(b) The superior who:

   (i) Knew, or consciously disregarded information which clearly indicated, that subordinates under his or her effective authority and control were committing or about to commit a crime of enforced disappearance;

   (ii) Exercised effective responsibility for and control over activities which were concerned with the crime of enforced disappearance; and

   (iii) Failed to take all necessary and reasonable measures within his or her power to prevent or repress the commission of the enforced disappearance or to submit the matter to the competent authorities for investigation or prosecution;

(c) Subparagraph (b) above is without prejudice to the higher standards of responsibility applicable under relevant international law to a military commander or to a person effectively acting as a military commander.

2.   No order or instruction from any public authority, civilian, military or other, may be invoked to justify an offence of enforced disappearance.

Article 7

1.   Each State Party shall make the offence of enforced disappearance punishable by appropriate penalties which take into account its extreme seriousness.

2.   Each state may establish:

(a) Mitigating circumstances, in particular for persons who, having been implicated in the commission of an enforced disappearance, effectively contribute to bringing the disappeared person forward alive or make it possible to clarify cases of enforced disappearance or to identify the perpetrators of an enforced disappearance;

(b) Without prejudice to other criminal procedures, aggravating circumstances, in particular in the event of the death of the disappeared person or the commission of an enforced disappearance in respect of pregnant women, minors, persons with disabilities or other particularly vulnerable persons.

Notes and Questions on Punishable Acts and Persons

1. *The offense under domestic law.* What is the fundamental difference between the 1992 Declaration and the 1998 Draft Convention with regard to what states parties must criminalize under domestic law? Why would the formulation used in the 1992 Declaration lead to more widespread acceptance of this instrument than the other formulation? How is this issue addressed in the final Convention language?

In your view, what are the merits of the 1998 and final Conventions' "stronger" formulation? Would these formulations lead to a reduction in the number of forced disappearances or an increase in criminal prosecutions? Which approach sends a stronger political message? On the other hand, what implications would this approach have for extraditions, statutes of limitation, or the need to end impunity?

2. *A variety of unlawful acts.* Experiences with forced disappearances in many countries reflect many scenarios that these instruments attempt to address:

● a low-level police officer arrests an individual under orders, then turns him over to military authorities who subsequently disappear the individual. Assume that the police officer acts with the good faith belief that the arrest is lawful;

● the same police officer performs the same arrest and transfer with full knowledge that the person will be disappeared;

● another police officer disappears an individual without the knowledge of his superior officers.

How would the provisions excerpted above address the acts in each of these examples? Are each of the actors equally criminally culpable? If "superior orders" is precluded as a defense to criminal liability, why should it also be excluded as a ground for mitigation? Based on your answer to this question, are the mitigating circumstances identified in article 5, ¶ 2 of the 1998 Draft Convention too narrow or too ambiguous?

One element missing from the 1992 Declaration and the 1998 Draft Convention was any discussion of possible aggravating circumstances that should be considered in the prosecution of the crime of enforced disappearance. You will see that this deficiency was corrected in the 2005 Draft Convention. Is the list of "particularly vulnerable persons" complete? What other categories of persons should have been included?

3. *Disappearances during armed conflict.* Article 1 of the final Convention includes language identical to the excerpts from the 1992 Declaration and 1998 Draft Convention prohibiting the invocation of wars, internal disturbances, or states of emergency to justify enforced disappearances. Would such a provision conflict with international humanitarian law? How do the Geneva Conventions and their Optional Protocols, which are in the Document Supplement, address the issue of disappearances? Is there a need for the new convention to fill a gap in this body of law?

Consider the actions of the U.S.-led coalition in the war on terror. United States officials have admitted that some individuals detained in connection with the wars in Afghanistan and Iraq are being kept hidden. Josh White, *Military Intelligence Ordered Captives Hidden, Court Told*, WASH. POST (Aug. 4, 2004) (reporting that US military intelligence officials at Abu Ghraib prison in Iraq ordered soldiers to keep several detainees hidden from the ICRC); *see also* Isabel Hilton, *The 800lb Gorilla in American Foreign Policy: Alleged Terror Suspects are Held Incommunicado All Over the World*, GUARDIAN (LONDON), July 28, 2004. Allegations regarding so-called "ghost detainees" have become widespread. A report by Human Rights First notes that the U.S. government acknowledges detention centers not only in its bases in Bagram and Kandahar in Afghanistan, but in 20 additional centers around the world. *See* Human Rights Watch, "Behind the Wire": an Update to Ending Secret Detentions, (March 2005); *available at* http://www.humanrightsfirst.org/us_law/detainees/rpt_disclose_intro.htm.

In September 2006, President Bush announced that eleven terrorists who had been held and questioned by the CIA in facilities outside the United States had been transferred to the detention facility at Guantanamo Bay, Cuba. President Discusses Military Commissions to try Suspected Terrorists, Sept. 6, 2008 (*available at* http://www.whitehouse.gov/news/releases/2006/09/20060906–3.html). Shortly thereafter, these individuals, including the alleged mastermind of the Sept. 11, attacks, Khalid Sheikh Mohammed, were visited by the International Committee of the Red Cross. Moreover, since their transfer to Guantanamo, each has had access to legal counsel. Place yourself in the position of a lawyer responsible for negotiating this treaty on behalf of the United States government. What arguments would you marshal in support of your position that the treaty should not be applicable during times of war? Are there legitimate reasons why individuals might be held incommunicado during an armed conflict?

Now place yourself in the position of the chairman of the Working Group. Was there a possible compromise between those states that support an exclusion for armed conflict and those that support universal applicability? Why, in your opinion, did the Chair opt to include the same prohibition as in the prior instruments rather than craft a compromise solution?

Enforced Disappearances: Prosecutions and International Cooperation

Declaration on the Protection of All Persons From Enforced Disappearances G.A. Res. 47/133, ¶ 3, UN Doc. A/47678/Add.2, art. 14 (Dec. 18, 1992)

Article 14

Any person alleged to have perpetrated an act of enforced disappearance in a particular State shall, when the facts disclosed by an official investigation so warrant, be brought before the competent civil authorities of that State for the purpose of prosecution and trial unless he has been extradited to another State wishing to exercise jurisdiction in accordance with the relevant international agreements in force. All States should take any lawful and appropriate action available to them to bring to justice all persons presumed responsible for an act of enforced disappearance, who are found to be within their jurisdiction or under their control.

1998 Draft Convention on the Protection of All Persons From Forced Disappearance UN Doc. E/CN, art. 6

Article 6

1. Forced disappearance and the other acts referred to in article 2 of this Convention shall be considered as offences in every State Party. Consequently, each State Party shall take the necessary measures to establish jurisdiction in the following instances:

(a) When the offence of forced disappearance was committed within any territory under its jurisdiction;

(b) When the alleged perpetrator or the other alleged participants in the offence of forced disappearance or the other acts referred to in article 2 of this Convention are in the territory of the State Party, irrespective of the nationality of the alleged perpetrator or the other alleged participants, or of the nationality of the disappeared person, or of the place or territory where the offence took place unless the State extradites them or transfers them to an international criminal tribunal.

2. This Convention does not exclude any jurisdiction exercised by an international criminal tribunal. * * *

Article 13

When a State Party does not grant the extradition or is not requested to do so, it shall submit the case to its competent authorities as if the offence had been committed within its jurisdiction, for the purposes of investigation and, when appropriate, for criminal proceedings, in accordance with its national law. Any decision adopted by these authorities shall be communicated to the State requesting extradition.

Convention against Torture and Other Cruel, Inhuman or Degrading Treatment or Punishment G.A. Res. 39/46, 39 UN GAOR Supp. No. 51, U.N. Doc. A/39/51, arts. 5, 7, *entered into force* June 26, 1987

Article 5

1. Each State Party shall take such measures as may be necessary to establish its jurisdiction over the offences referred to in article 4 in the following cases:

(a) When the offences are committed in any territory under its jurisdiction or on board a ship or aircraft registered in that State;

(b) When the alleged offender is a national of that State;

(c) When the victim is a national of that State if that State considers it appropriate.

2. Each State Party shall likewise take such measures as may be necessary to establish its jurisdiction over such offences in cases where the alleged offender is present in any territory under its jurisdiction and it does not extradite him pursuant to article 8 to any of the States mentioned in paragraph 1 of this article.

3. This Convention does not exclude any criminal jurisdiction exercised in accordance with internal law. * * *

Article 7

1. The State Party in the territory under whose jurisdiction a person alleged to have committed any offence referred to in article 4 is found shall in the cases contemplated in article 5, if it does not extradite him, submit the case to its competent authorities for the purpose of prosecution.

2. These authorities shall take their decision in the same manner as in the case of any ordinary offence of a serious nature under the law of that State. In the cases referred to in article 5, paragraph 2, the standards of evidence required for prosecution and conviction shall in no way be less stringent than those which apply in the cases referred to in article 5, paragraph 1.

3. Any person regarding whom proceedings are brought in connection with any of the offences referred to in article 4 shall be guaranteed fair treatment at all stages of the proceedings.

Optional Protocol to the Convention on the Rights of the Child on the Sale of Children, Child Prostitution and Child Pornography UN Doc. A/RES/54/263 (May 25, 2000), art 4., *entered into force* on Jan. 18, 2002

Article 4

1. Each State Party shall take such measures as may be necessary to establish its jurisdiction over the offences referred to in article 3, paragraph 1, when the offences are committed in its territory or on board a ship or aircraft registered in that State.

2. Each State Party may take such measures as may be necessary to establish its jurisdiction over the offences referred to in article 3, paragraph 1, in the following cases:

(a) When the alleged offender is a national of that State or a person who has his habitual residence in its territory;

(b) When the victim is a national of that State.

3. Each State Party shall also take such measures as may be necessary to establish its jurisdiction over the aforementioned offences when the alleged offender is present in its territory and it does not extradite him or her to another State Party on the ground that the offence has been committed by one of its nationals.

4. The present Protocol does not exclude any criminal jurisdiction exercised in accordance with internal law.

International Convention for the Protection of All Persons from Enforced Disappearance Adopted Dec. 20, 2006, G.A. Res. A/RES/61/177, UN Doc. A/61/488, art. 9

1. Each State party shall take the necessary measures to establish its competence to exercise jurisdiction over the offence of enforced disappearance;

(a) When the offence is committed in any territory under its jurisdiction or on board a ship or aircraft registered in that State;

(b) When the alleged offender is one of its nationals;

(c) When the disappeared person is one of its nationals and the State Party considers it appropriate.

2. Each State Party shall likewise take such measures as may be necessary to establish its competence to exercise jurisdiction over the offence of enforced disappearance when the alleged offender is present in any territory under its jurisdiction, unless it extradites or surrenders him or her to another State in accordance with its international obligations or surrenders him or her to an international criminal tribunal whose jurisdiction it has recognized.

3. This Convention does not exclude any additional jurisdiction exercised in accordance with national law. * * *

Article 11

1. The State Party in the territory under whose jurisdiction a person alleged to have committed an offence of enforced disappearance is found shall, if it does not extradite that person or surrender him or her to an international criminal tribunal whose jurisdiction it has recognized, submit the case to its competent authorities for the purpose of prosecution.

<hr>

NOTES AND QUESTIONS ON PROSECUTIONS AND INTERNATIONAL COOPERATION

1. *The treaty's reach.* Compare the provisions on jurisdiction of the five instruments excerpted above. Which requires parties to establish the broadest jurisdictional basis for prosecuting persons suspected of committing enforced disappearances? The narrowest? Identify which of the bases for jurisdiction under international law (territoriality, nationality, passive personality, protection principle) are relied on in each excerpt above.

2. *Converging interests of stakeholders.* If you were involved in these negotiations on behalf of an NGO or a victims' group, you would likely prefer the broadest jurisdictional provisions possible. Indeed, many have advocated the use of a clause that would create universal jurisdiction for the crime of enforced disappearance. However, place yourself in the position of a lawyer representing a state in these negotiations. Under what circumstances might a broad jurisdictional clause create problems for your government?

3. *Extradite or prosecute.* As in many international criminal instruments, the final Convention on enforced disappearances includes the principle, *aut dedere aut judicare. See* Article 9(2). Under this fundamental principle of international law, a state must either extradite or prosecute an offender found within its territory. The basis for this principle is obvious—it prevents impunity by precluding states from harboring fugitives from justice in another state. *See, e.g.,* Convention Against Torture and Other Cruel, Inhuman or Degrading Treatment or Punishment, Art. 5 (2), G.A. Res. 39/46, annex, 39 UN GAOR Supp. (No. 51) at 197, UN Doc. A/39/51 (1984), *entered into force* June 26, 1987 ("Each State Party shall likewise take such measures as may be necessary to establish its jurisdiction over such offences in cases where the alleged offender is present in any territory under its jurisdiction and it does not extradite him pursuant to article 8 to any of the States mentioned in paragraph 1 of this article").

Consider the "extradite or prosecute" provision in the final Convention. How does the provision differ from the 1992 Declaration? If a national of state B, accused of disappearing a fellow national in his home country is found in state A, would the convention require State A to exercise jurisdiction and prosecute? What if state B does not request extradition and, indeed, refuses all attempts of state A to return the individual to the locus of his crimes? What are state A's obligations?

4. *Universal jurisdiction.* Article 5(2) of the Convention Against Torture, excerpted above, may be evidence of a growing trend toward the legitimization of the concept of "universal jurisdiction." This provision appears to require a state party to take measures necessary to establish jurisdiction over *any* individual who is not extradited. In other words, even if the state has none of the bases of jurisdiction identified in article 5(1), it may nevertheless exercise jurisdiction if it is not possible to extradite the person to a state that *does* have article 5(1) jurisdiction.

How does the Optional Protocol to the Convention on the Rights of the Child on the Sale of Children, Child Prostitution and Child Pornography, also excerpted above, address this issue? Would the inclusion of a provision patterned after this clause satisfy the concerns of those who do not believe in the principle of universal jurisdiction? For a more detailed discussion of the principle of universal jurisdiction, see Chapter 3.

5. *Special or military courts.* A controversial issue that arose during the course of the negotiations over the 2005 Draft Convention was whether the instrument should include a blanket prohibition on the use of special or military courts to try those accused of committing enforced disappearances. In the end, such a prohibition was not included in the draft. Can you see why victims' advocates would have argued for such a prohibition?

In the United States, active duty members of the military accused of committing an enforced disappearance would be tried before a military, not a civilian court. Should the concerns about special courts you identified above require the United States to alter its military justice system to exclude jurisdiction over enforced disappearances?

6. *Reservations, understandings and declarations.* In recent years, some states and NGOs have opposed the practice of making reservations to human rights treaties. Although the use of reservations is specifically authorized by the Vienna Convention on the Law of Treaties, critics argue in the context of human rights that all reservations are contrary to the object and purpose of the treaty. As a result of this debate, attempts have been made to include in recent treaties a clause that prohibits all reservations. Indeed, this was one of the primary objections of the United States to the Optional Protocol to the Convention Against Torture, and it remained an issue of contention throughout the negotiation of the Convention on Enforced Disappearances. In the end, the instrument was approved by the working group without a prohibition on reservations. In your opinion, was this a mistake of either law or policy?

Practicum

On May 21, 2008, President George W. Bush signed into law the Genetic Information Nondiscrimination Act of 2008 to protect people from discrimination by health insurers and employers on the basis of DNA information. The law was passed in response to concern that advances in science allow access to genetic information that may lead to unfair treatment on the basis of genetic differences that may increase an individual's chances of getting a disease. For instance, a health insurer might refuse coverage to someone whose DNA may raise his odds of getting a certain type of cancer. Under this new law, such practices are forbidden.

Article 21 of the Charter of Fundamental Rights of the European Union states, "Any discrimination based on any grounds such as sex, race, colour, ethnic or social origin, *genetic features*, language religion or belief, political or any other opinion, membership of a national minority, property, birth, disability, age or sexual orientation, shall be prohibited." Notably, several countries within the EU have introduced or passed legislation prohibiting genetic discrimination. France, Sweden, Finland and Denmark, Austria, the Netherlands, Luxembourg, Greece and Italy have prohibited or restricted the collection of genetic data from employees without their explicit consent.

While many in the developing world share the privacy concerns of the industrialized countries, issues posed by advances in genetics are less related to discrimination, and more related to development concerns. For instance, advances in genetic mapping allow multinational companies to patent the genes of indigenous plants for medical uses. The development, sale, and use of genetically modified animals and seed stock also have implications for poorer nations. Similarly, the growth of the pharmaceutical industry and the rush to develop profitable medicines to fight disease has caused controversies over medical testing in developing countries.

In this practicum, students will assume the role of members of a working group established by the Human Rights Council with the mandate to "elaborate an international convention on Bioethics, Discrimination, and Human Rights." Throughout the negotiation, students should consider how human rights and fundamental freedoms might be undermined by advances in science and conversely, how science can enhance existing protections, particularly in the area of economic, social, and cultural rights.

Issues

Scope. Should the convention cover just genetic discrimination, or should it try to address the range of human rights issues implicated by scientific advances, bioethics, and the growth and geographical reach of the pharmaceutical industry?

Privacy. Should the convention recognize an explicit right to privacy over one's genetic information, and, if so, what is the breadth of such a right?

Equality of Treatment and Non–Discrimination. How broad should the principle of non-discrimination on the basis of genetic information be? Should the convention include a provision requiring "special measures" (affirmative action) to promote equality? How will it address persons with disabilities, genetic testing, and the "right to life"? Should the convention cover issues related to informed consent in the area of medical testing?

International Cooperation. What language will the convention include on international cooperation? Its provisions might range from information sharing to technology transfer. The working group should consider other areas of international cooperation relevant to the area of bioethics and genetic information.

Economic, Social and Cultural Rights. In a convention of this nature, is there a need to include provisions addressing economic, social and cultural rights? In particular, do genetic discrimination and bioethics implicate the right to development?

Student Roles

Western European and Others Group. Students representing WEOG will be predisposed to limiting the scope of the convention to discrimination. They will likely choose to use existing national legislation, such as in the U.S. and EU, as the basis for negotiations and will be resistant to a treaty broader in scope. They will also try to limit the non-discrimination provisions to the insurance and employment areas. If broader bioethical, pharmaceutical and genetically modified food issues come up, they will likely argue these issues are better left to other forums (e.g., the WTO, UNESCO) and should not be addressed in a human rights instrument. Remember that they will need to protect the interests of major multinational companies with a stake in these issues whose headquarters lie in the West.

G–77 Countries. In this context, it will be difficult for the G–77 to negotiate as a bloc. While many countries in the developing world will share an agenda to push the right to development, wealth transfers and broader issues designed to "rein in" multinationals and the West, some governments in the G–77 (such as India, Brazil and South Africa) have private sector, multinational actors with equities to protect. Still others have benefited from medical testing through the availability of cheap pharmaceuticals. African states, in particular, will push hard for the distribution of benefits derived from scientific advances to the developing world. For purposes of this practicum, a small number of students should represent a range of G–77 countries (possibly from different regions or groupings such as Latin America, Asia, the Organization of

Islamic Countries (OIC), Africa) and attempt to coordinate their positions. If this is not possible, they should negotiate on the basis of country positions.

The Holy See. Clearly, the Holy See will approach this negotiation with the religious tenets of the Catholic Church in mind. Students representing the Holy See should consider issues related to the right to life and abortion in crafting its position on genetic discrimination. Moreover, the Church has established positions on cloning and genetic modification that will drive negotiating positions. The Holy See often seeks alliances with countries from Latin America (which are, in large part, Roman Catholic) and the OIC (which often shares its views on social issues)

Non-Governmental Organizations. Like the G–77, NGO countries concerns will cover the waterfront. Many will be firm advocates on behalf of poor people, who they will argue have been victimized by the North's use of scientific knowledge and technology. Others will be trade organizations whose members are major multinationals. Still others will represent scientific organizations, educational institutions, and medical professionals. Students representing NGOs should choose a particular line of advocacy to engage the working group for purposes of this practicum.

CHAPTER 6

MODULE 14

THE POWER AND LIMITS OF WORLD CONFERENCES

■ ■ ■

Orientation

Since its creation, the United Nations has hosted multilateral conferences to bring global attention to particularly pressing and communal problems, like environmental protection, economic development, disarmament, drug trafficking, and human rights. Typically, over a one-or two-week period, governments, international organizations, non-governmental organizations, and individuals create a microcosm of the international community. When it works as designed, the issues are identified and debated, differences are narrowed, and a meaningful plan of action is adopted. For the human rights lawyer, the preparatory work before the conference can be a crucial time for assuring that a proper agenda is set, that the draft documents reflect key principles, that useful areas of consensus are identified, and that productive coalitions are created and energized.

But world conferences are also costly, and their record of achievement is distinctly mixed. When used for political grandstanding or forums for the ritualized recapitulation of long-running disputes, conferences have been divisive and counter-productive. The lingering acrimony of difficult conferences can affect relations between member states for years and obstruct the implementation of the conference's plan of action. In addition, many conferences may be faulted for adopting political commitments which generally include few if any legal components. And when legal obligations are included, the conference documents might be criticized as merely redundant—duplicative of existing international instruments or the work of the human rights bodies. Why adopt political declarations and programs of action when the same problems could be solved by ratifying and implementing international legal instruments that cover the same ground?

On the other hand, a world conference can be a powerful catalyst for change when it mobilizes the resources and focuses the political will of the international community. Its work product certainly need not be duplicative: the documents can fill the gaps in international instruments or address new situations that the framers of a treaty may not have anticipated. Especially where conference documents are adopted by consensus, human rights advocates are handed a tool for pressuring governments that fail to live up to the conference commitments. The conference can also provide clear direction to the United Nations and its constituent agencies. At a minimum, the conference provides a forum for NGOs to meet, exchange ideas, and coordinate their efforts.

One of the most successful world conferences was the 1993 World Conference on Human Rights in Vienna, a conference often described as a watershed in the human rights movement. An unprecedented number of participants—including governments, UN agencies, and NGOs—gathered to call the world's attention to a broad range of human rights violations. NGOs played a particularly prominent role in the work of the meeting, setting a precedent that has continued through the UN system and beyond. Held after the post-Soviet transition in Eastern Europe, the Vienna Conference explicitly recognized the universality and interdependence of all human rights. For advocates, this principle, as well as the documents in which it was expressed, have offered effective tools for the promotion and protection of human rights around the world. Equally important, at the Vienna Conference, governments recommended the creation of the Office of the High Commissioner for Human Rights within the United Nations, an office that has successfully promoted human rights in member states and within the UN bureaucracy itself.

But world conferences can also fail, the prime examples being those that tried to address the subject of racism. These conferences have been plagued by seemingly intractable debates about apartheid and Zionism. Numerous provisions in the documents were put to vote, and many states felt compelled to make significant reservations to key language. Some states refused to attend these conferences, and some who did attend walked out before the documents were adopted. None of these conferences broke new ground politically or legally, and NGO participation did little to focus the effort of the international community on combating racism. Indeed, even the NGOs failed to reach consensus on a document negotiated at the NGO conference prior to the government conference.

The question arises: how is a world conference relevant to the human rights advocate? Why should she concern herself with what appears from the outside to be a political exercise, seemingly without much impact on the law or the people the law is designed to protect?

For all of the potential difficulties, we believe that the world conferences offer an exploitable opportunity to draw the attention of governments, the UN, and the media to a pressing human rights problem. The commitments made at the conference can also be used to exert pressure on states to remedy continuing violations when the conference is completed. To the extent that a legal instrument is in contemplation at the conference, human rights lawyers may wish to affect its consideration and evolution rather than wait for the final version to emerge.

The excerpts below focus on two quite different world conferences: the Vienna Conference on Human Rights and the Durban World Conference Against Racism, Racial Discrimination, Xenophobia, and Related Intolerance. Both conferences were difficult for negotiators, but Vienna resulted in a consensus document adopted by government representatives, and Durban resulted in acrimony. As you read the following excerpts, try to identify the elements of each conference that made it a success or a failure.

CASE STUDY #1
THE VIENNA WORLD CONFERENCE ON HUMAN RIGHTS

Vienna Declaration and Programme of Action

U.N. Doc. A/CONF.157/23 (12 July 1993)

The World Conference on Human Rights,

Considering that the promotion and protection of human rights is a matter of priority for the international community, and that the Conference affords a unique opportunity to carry out a comprehensive analysis of the international human rights system and of the machinery for the protection of human rights, in order to enhance and thus promote a fuller observance of those rights, in a just and balanced manner,

Recognizing and affirming that all human rights derive from the dignity and worth inherent in the human person, and that the human person is the central subject of human rights and fundamental freedoms, and consequently should be the principal beneficiary and should participate actively in the realization of these rights and freedoms,

Reaffirming their commitment to the purposes and principles contained in the Charter of the United Nations and the Universal Declaration of Human Rights,

Reaffirming the commitment contained in Article 56 of the Charter of the United Nations to take joint and separate action, placing proper emphasis on developing effective international cooperation for the realization of the purposes set out in Article 55, including universal respect for, and observance of, human rights and fundamental freedoms for all,

Emphasizing the responsibilities of all States, in conformity with the Charter of the United Nations, to develop and encourage respect for human rights and fundamental freedoms for all, without distinction as to race, sex, language or religion * * *

Solemnly adopts the Vienna Declaration and Programme of Action.

* * *

4.   The promotion and protection of all human rights and fundamental freedoms must be considered as a priority objective of the United Nations in accordance with its purposes and principles, in particular the purpose of international cooperation. In the framework of these purposes and principles, the promotion and protection of all human rights is a legitimate concern of the international community. The organs and specialized agencies related to human rights should therefore further enhance the coordination of their activities based on the consistent and objective application of international human rights instruments.

5.   All human rights are universal, indivisible and interdependent and interrelated. The international community must treat human rights globally in a fair and equal manner, on the same footing, and with the same emphasis. While the significance of national and regional particularities and various historical, cultural and religious backgrounds must be borne in mind, it is the duty of States, regardless of their political, economic and cultural systems, to promote and protect all human rights and fundamental freedoms. * * *

8.   Democracy, development and respect for human rights and fundamental freedoms are interdependent and mutually reinforcing. Democracy is based on the freely expressed will of the people to determine their own political, economic, social and cultural systems and their full participation in all aspects of their lives. In the context of the above, the promotion and protection of human rights and fundamental freedoms at the national and international levels should be universal and conducted without conditions attached. The international community should support the strengthening and promoting of democracy, development and respect for human rights and fundamental freedoms in the entire world. * * *

10.   The World Conference on Human Rights reaffirms the right to development, as established in the Declaration on the Right to Development, as a universal and inalienable right and an integral part of fundamental human rights.

As stated in the Declaration on the Right to Development, the human person is the central subject of development.

While development facilitates the enjoyment of all human rights, the lack of development may not be invoked to justify the abridgement of internationally recognized human rights.

States should cooperate with each other in ensuring development and eliminating obstacles to development. The international community should promote an effective international cooperation for the realization of the right to development and the elimination of obstacles to development.

Lasting progress towards the implementation of the right to development requires effective development policies at the national level, as well as equitable economic relations and a favourable economic environment at the international level.

11. The right to development should be fulfilled so as to meet equitably the developmental and environmental needs of present and future generations. The World Conference on Human Rights recognizes that illicit dumping of toxic and dangerous substances and waste potentially constitutes a serious threat to the human rights to life and health of everyone.

Consequently, the World Conference on Human Rights calls on all States to adopt and vigorously implement existing conventions relating to the dumping of toxic and dangerous products and waste and to cooperate in the prevention of illicit dumping.

Everyone has the right to enjoy the benefits of scientific progress and its applications. The World Conference on Human Rights notes that certain advances, notably in the biomedical and life sciences as well as in information technology, may have potentially adverse consequences for the integrity, dignity and human rights of the individual, and calls for international cooperation to ensure that human rights and dignity are fully respected in this area of universal concern

12. The World Conference on Human Rights calls upon the international community to make all efforts to help alleviate the external debt burden of developing countries, in order to supplement the efforts of the Governments of such countries to attain the full realization of the economic, social and cultural rights of their people. * * *

14. The existence of widespread extreme poverty inhibits the full and effective enjoyment of human rights; its immediate alleviation and eventual elimination must remain a high priority for the international community. * * *

18. The human rights of women and of the girl-child are an inalienable, integral and indivisible part of universal human rights. The full and equal participation of women in political, civil, economic, social and cultural life, at the national, regional and international levels, and the eradication of all forms of discrimination on grounds of sex are priority objectives of the international community.

Gender-based violence and all forms of sexual harassment and exploitation, including those resulting from cultural prejudice and international trafficking, are incompatible with the dignity and worth of the human person, and must be eliminated. This can be achieved by legal measures and through national action and international cooperation in such fields as economic and social development, education, safe maternity and health care, and social support.

The human rights of women should form an integral part of the United Nations human rights activities, including the promotion of all human rights instruments relating to women.

The World Conference on Human Rights urges Governments, institutions, intergovernmental and non-governmental organizations to intensify their efforts for the protection and promotion of human rights of women and the girl-child. * * *

[Programme of Action]

17. The World Conference on Human Rights recognizes the necessity for a continuing adaptation of the United Nations human rights machinery to the current and future needs in the promotion and protection of human rights, as reflected in the present Declaration and within the framework of a balanced and sustainable development for all people. In particular, the United Nations human rights organs should improve their coordination, efficiency and effectiveness.

18. The World Conference on Human Rights recommends to the General Assembly that when examining the report of the Conference at its forty-eighth session, it begin, as a matter of priority, consideration of the question of the establishment of a High Commissioner for Human Rights for the promotion and protection of all human rights. * * *

36. The World Conference on Human Rights urges the full and equal enjoyment by women of all human rights and that this be a priority for Governments and for the United Nations. The World Conference on Human Rights also underlines the importance of the integration and full participation of women as both agents and beneficiaries in the development process, and reiterates the objectives established on global action for women towards sustainable and equitable development set forth in the Rio Declaration on Environment and Development and chapter 24 of Agenda 21, adopted by the United Nations Conference on Environment and Development (Rio de Janeiro, Brazil, 3–14 June 1992).

37. The equal status of women and the human rights of women should be integrated into the mainstream of United Nations system-wide activity. These issues should be regularly and systematically addressed throughout relevant United Nations bodies and mechanisms. In particular, steps should be taken to increase cooperation and promote further integration of objectives and goals between the Commission on the Status of Women, the Commission on Human Rights, the Committee for the Elimination of Discrimination against Women, the United Nations Development Fund for Women, the United Nations Development Programme and other United Nations agencies. In this context, cooperation and coordination should be strengthened between the Centre for Human Rights and the Division for the Advancement of Women.

38. In particular, the World Conference on Human Rights stresses the importance of working towards the elimination of violence against women in public and private life, the elimination of all forms of sexual

harassment, exploitation and trafficking in women, the elimination of gender bias in the administration of justice and the eradication of any conflicts which may arise between the rights of women and the harmful effects of certain traditional or customary practices, cultural prejudices and religious extremism. The World Conference on Human Rights calls upon the General Assembly to adopt the draft declaration on violence against women and urges States to combat violence against women in accordance with its provisions. Violations of the human rights of women in situations of armed conflict are violations of the fundamental principles of international human rights and humanitarian law. All violations of this kind, including in particular murder, systematic rape, sexual slavery, and forced pregnancy, require a particularly effective response.

39. The World Conference on Human Rights urges the eradication of all forms of discrimination against women, both hidden and overt. The United Nations should encourage the goal of universal ratification by all States of the Convention on the Elimination of All Forms of Discrimination against Women by the year 2000. Ways and means of addressing the particularly large number of reservations to the Convention should be encouraged. *Inter alia*, the Committee on the Elimination of Discrimination against Women should continue its review of reservations to the Convention. States are urged to withdraw reservations that are contrary to the object and purpose of the Convention or which are otherwise incompatible with international treaty law. * * *

43. The World Conference on Human Rights urges Governments and regional and international organizations to facilitate the access of women to decision-making posts and their greater participation in the decision-making process. It encourages further steps within the United Nations Secretariat to appoint and promote women staff members in accordance with the Charter of the United Nations, and encourages other principal and subsidiary organs of the United Nations to guarantee the participation of women under conditions of equality. * * *

66. The World Conference on Human Rights recommends that priority be given to national and international action to promote democracy, development and human rights.

67. Special emphasis should be given to measures to assist in the strengthening and building of institutions relating to human rights, strengthening of a pluralistic civil society and the protection of groups which have been rendered vulnerable. In this context, assistance provided upon the request of Governments for the conduct of free and fair elections, including assistance in the human rights aspects of elections and public information about elections, is of particular importance. Equally important is the assistance to be given to the strengthening of the rule of law, the promotion of freedom of expression and the administration of justice, and to the real and effective participation of the people in the decision-making processes. * * *

72. The World Conference on Human Rights reaffirms that the universal and inalienable right to development, as established in the Declaration on the Right to Development, must be implemented and realized. In this context, the World Conference on Human Rights welcomes the appointment by the Commission on Human Rights of a thematic working group on the right to development and urges that the Working Group, in consultation and cooperation with other organs and agencies of the United Nations system, promptly formulate, for early consideration by the United Nations General Assembly, comprehensive and effective measures to eliminate obstacles to the implementation and realization of the Declaration on the Right to Development and recommending ways and means towards the realization of the right to development by all States.

73. The World Conference on Human Rights recommends that non-governmental and other grass-roots organizations active in development and/or human rights should be enabled to play a major role on the national and international levels in the debate, activities and implementation relating to the right to development and, in cooperation with Governments, in all relevant aspects of development cooperation.

74. The World Conference on Human Rights appeals to Governments, competent agencies and institutions to increase considerably the resources devoted to building well-functioning legal systems able to protect human rights, and to national institutions working in this area. Actors in the field of development cooperation should bear in mind the mutually reinforcing interrelationship between development, democracy and human rights. Cooperation should be based on dialogue and transparency. The World Conference on Human Rights also calls for the establishment of comprehensive programmes, including resource banks of information and personnel with expertise relating to the strengthening of the rule of law and of democratic institutions.

NOTES AND QUESTIONS ON THE VIENNA CONVENTION

1. *Advocacy.* Remember that much of the language and discussion at world conferences is essentially political. As a result, consensus language can mean all things to all people. Countries like Cuba, North Korea, and Iran can agree to language that recognizes that "democracy, development and respect for human rights and fundamental freedoms are interdependent and mutually reinforcing." By the same token, Canada, Norway and Costa Rica can agree to language that permits historical, cultural, and religious backgrounds to be "borne in mind" in the treatment of human rights globally.

2. *Vienna and women's rights.* The Vienna Declaration and Programme of Action was instrumental in establishing the primacy of

human rights throughout the United Nations. Article 4 recognizes this principle, while numerous articles throughout the Programme of Action called for the principle to be implemented within UN mechanisms. For instance, in Vienna, states recommended the creation of the office of the UN High Commissioner for Human Rights and called for women's equality to be integrated into the mainstream of the organization's activities, through consideration in its programs and by increasing the employment of women throughout the UN system. Due in part to the commitments in Vienna, the Office of the High Commissioner and UN field offices throughout the world have integrated the promotion and protection of human rights into their work, and many include staff from the High Commissioner's Office. *See Annual Report 2007: Activities and Results*, UNHCHR, Annual Report, *available at http://www.ohchr.org/Documents/Press/OHCHR_Report_07_Full.pdf*.

The Vienna Declaration and Programme of Action dealt extensively with women's issues. Read these articles in light of the Convention on the Elimination of Discrimination Against Women, contained in the Document Supplement. Is the language in Vienna simply duplicative of the Convention, or has it added detail to the legal obligations included in CEDAW? Some years later, the Beijing Women's Conference was held, adding further detail to the commitments assumed by states at Vienna. *See* Beijing Declaration and Platform for Action, Fourth World Conference on Women, 15 September 1995, A/CONF.177/20 (1995) and A/CONF.177/20/Add.1 (1995). Many saw the Beijing women's conference as a galvanizing event for women's rights around the globe. *See, e.g.*, K. Timothy, and M. Freeman, *The CEDAW Convention and the Beijing Platform for Action: Reinforcing the Promise of the Rights Framework*, (U. MINN. 2000), *available at*: http: //www1.umn.edu/humanrts/iwraw/beijing5/freeman-timothy-paper.htm; Berta Esperanza Hernandez–Truyol, *Women's Rights as Human Rights—Rules, Realities and the Role of Culture: A Formula for Reform*, 21 BROOKLYN J. INT'L. L. 605 (1996).

3. *The universality of human rights.* Article 5 of the Vienna Declaration established the principle that "all human rights are universal, indivisible and interdependent and interrelated." It also noted the relevance of "national and regional particularities and various historical, cultural and religious backgrounds" but maintained that it is the duty of states to promote all human rights and fundamental freedoms. While this paragraph included language meant to allay the concerns of states that advocated a cultural relativist approach to human rights, it maintained the primacy of the promotion and protection of all human rights and fundamental freedoms. Does this language satisfy concerns that some states—particularly those in the Islamic world—can opt out of certain core international human rights standards on the basis of religion? *See, e.g.*, Thomas M. Franck, *Is Personal Freedom a Western Value?*, 91 A.J.I.L. 593 (1997); Isha Khan, *Islamic Human Rights: Islamic Law and International Human Rights Standards*, 5 APPEAL 74 (1999); Paula Abrams, *Reservations about Women: Population Policy and Reproductive Rights*, 29

CORNELL INT'L L. J. 1 (1996); Jason Morgan Foster, *A New Perspective on the Universality Debate: Reverse Moderate Relativism in the Islamic Context*, 10 ILSA INT'L & COMP. L. 35 (2003); Ann Elizabeth Mayer, *Universal Versus Islamic Human Rights: A Clash of Cultures or a Clash with a Construct?*, 15 MICH. J. INT'L. L. 307 (1994).

Similarly, if you read article 8 closely, you will find compromise language that attempts to satisfy two ends of the political spectrum: on one side, those who say that promotion and protection is an absolute, regardless of the level of a country's economic development; on the other, those who argue that developing nations cannot afford to take measures to protect human rights. When industrialized states criticize the developing world for the low priority accorded to human rights, the South sometimes responds by pressing for increased development assistance, *i.e.*, "human rights will be a priority when we can afford to make them one." Does the language of Article 8 reconcile or finesse these differences?

While political declarations sometimes sound "legal," they are neither legally binding nor always consistent with international legal norms. Indeed, in the heat of negotiations and under pressure to achieve consensus, a negotiator may find that political aspirations trump legal niceties. What is the danger of blurring the distinction between policy and law in the international arena? Is there any benefit to a world conference document that allows consensus but sacrifices objective principles and legal consistency?

4. *The right to development.* The Vienna World Conference was also significant for the renewed impetus it provided for recognizing and implementing the "right to development." Several components of this right were recognized in the Vienna documents, including the need to be free of the effects of toxic waste and illegal dumping, the right to enjoy the benefits of scientific progress and technology, the need to help alleviate the debt burden of developing countries, the dangers of extreme poverty, and the importance of NGOs and grassroots organizations in development efforts.

But what is the "right to development"? Is it an individual or a collective right? For several years, a working group of the Commission on Human Rights has been grappling with the meaning of the right as well as with the implications of its recognition as a human right. Many in the developing world argue that the right to development is a collective right, one which states can assert against other states. In other words, if such a right exists, it forms the basis for advocating a right to development assistance. Not surprisingly, industrialized states often oppose such an interpretation, arguing there is no "right" to development assistance. To the extent such a right exists they assert, it inheres in the individual, not in a community or state. In their view, the right to development is violated when states prevent their citizens from achieving economic empowerment, from actively and freely participating in political process-es, and from asserting their civil and political rights.

In article 67, you can see the input of the industrialized states on this debate. The previous article discusses the interrelation of democra-cy, development, and human rights, while article 67 details specifically the measures that states have agreed are necessary to advance these goals. How do these measures contribute the promotion of democracy, development, and human rights? Can you identify the linkage between these three concepts, or, in your opinion, is this a false connection, drawn simply to achieve consensus on a divisive issue between the developed and developing world? *See generally* Isabella D. Bunn, *The Right to Development: Implications for International Economic Law*, 15 AM. U. INT'L. L. REV. 1425 (2000); J. Oloka–Onyango, *Beyond the Rhetoric: Reinvigorating the Struggle for Economic and Social Rights in Africa*, 26 CAL. W. INT'L. L. J. 1 (1995); Jennifer Myers, *Human Rights and Development: Using Advanced Technology to Promote Human Rights in Sub–Saharan Africa*, 30 CASE W. RES. J. INT'L. L 343 (1998); Prakash Shah, *International Human Rights: A Perspective from India*, 21 FORDHAM INT'L L.J. 24 (1997); Sara E. Allgood, *United Nations Human Rights "Entitlements": The Right to Develop-ment Analyzed Within the Application of the Right to Self–Determination*, 31 GA. J. INT'L. & COMP. L. 321 (2003); Stephen Marks, *The Human Right to Development: Between Rhetoric and Reality*, 17 HARVARD HUMAN RIGHTS J. 137 (2004); THE RIGHT TO DEVELOPMENT IN INTERNATIONAL LAW (Subrata Roy Chowdhury, et al. eds. 1992).

CASE STUDY #2
THE DURBAN WORLD CONFERENCE AGAINST RACISM, RACIAL DISCRIMINATION, XENOPHOBIA AND RELATED INTOLERANCE

Tom Lantos, *The Durban Debacle:*
An Insider's View of the UN World Conference Against Racism

26 FLETCHER FORUM OF WORLD AFFAIRS 31 (2002)

Held during the high point of world hostility toward President Bush's unilateral approach to foreign affairs, the WCAR [World Confer-ence Against Racism] was a disaster for the United States. After a hopeful start, it disintegrated into an anti-American, anti-Israeli circus. A number of Islamic states conducted a well-orchestrated effort to hijack the event, and they succeeded in swaying America's erstwhile partners and forcing the United States delegation to withdraw. Although the United States walkout succeeded in preventing the most virulent anti-

Israel language from surviving in the conference text, the United States sustained substantial damage in its efforts to secure an historic understanding on race and to prevent an escalation of tensions in the Middle East. Durban will go down in history as a missed opportunity to advance a noble agenda and as a serious breakdown in United Nations diplomacy. * * *

THE ROAD TO DURBAN: PAVED WITH GOOD INTENTIONS

In December 1997 the United Nations announced plans for a third World Conference Against Racism, Racial Discrimination, Xenophobia, and Related Intolerance. The UN General Assembly's Resolution 52/11 contemplated a forward-looking conference focusing on confronting and reversing a host of disturbing contemporary manifestations of racism, from widespread discrimination against migrant workers in Western Europe and the Middle East to the proliferation of hate sites on the World Wide Web. It also sought to broach the sensitive subject of slavery and its painful legacy in an effort to achieve an historic reconciliation on this critical issue. The UN leadership hoped that the conference would encourage the development of practical solutions, and avoid becoming embroiled in the "Zionism-is-racism" canard that doomed the two previous global meetings on racial discrimination in 1978 and 1983.

Former Irish President Mary Robinson, the UN High Commissioner for Human Rights, developed a clear vision to unify and energize the global dialogue on race in the years leading up to the convening of the conference. Her vision focused on bringing the world together to overcome fear—fear of what is different, fear of the other, and fear of the loss of personal security. In her public statement Robinson made a compelling case that racism and xenophobia are on the rise by tying its current manifestations to growing economic and social dislocations caused by globalization. As a way to move forward, she repeatedly challenged the international community to shift its focus away from viewing diversity as a limiting factor and to discern the potential for mutual enrichment in diversity. She hoped the conference could not only serve as a catharsis for victims' groups to relieve their grievances but could also initiate a lasting dialogue between civil societies and governments focused on finding solutions to overcome hate. Robinson's public pronouncements prior to the conference also reflected an understanding that no nation is free of racism, and that all share responsibility for eradicating this pervasive and universal evil. * * *

SETTING THE STAGE

In 1999, the General Assembly's Third Committee (which deals with social, humanitarian, and cultural issues) decided that the conference should be held in Durban, South Africa in 2001, and should be preceded by regional meetings in Strasbourg, France; Santiago, Chile; Dakar, Senegal; and Tehran, Iran during the fall of 2000 and the winter of 2001. The committee also decided to book-end the regional meetings with two preparatory inter-governmental meetings at the UN in Geneva. Each regional conference was charged with drafting a declaration and plan of action on racism that would ultimately be synthesized into a single set of documents to be ratified in Durban.

Developments at the first three regional meetings suggested that Robinson's best hopes for the Durban conference were possible. In Strasbourg, Santiago, and Dakar, participating governments, non-governmental organizations (NGOs) and experts demonstrated a willingness to confront regional manifestations of contemporary racism, and to develop and implement practical solutions. * * * The documents that emerged from them attempted to tackle a range of vexing issues from the legacy of slavery to the need to confront the global resurgence of anti-Semitism. Significantly, the Europe and Latin American regional conferences took concrete steps to prevent the return of the anti-Israel "Zionism-is-racism" language that doomed the two previous World Conferences. Further, they explicitly condemned ant-Semitism in their draft documents.

TEHRAN: THE BEGINNING OF THE END

The Asian Preparatory Meeting for the WCAR, convened in Tehran from February 19 to 21, 2001, marked a sharp departure from the spirit of tolerance that was evident at the first three regional meetings. Although the initiation of the second Intifada in September 2000 certainly contributed to the poisonous anti-Israeli and anti-Semitic atmosphere evident at the Asian conference and in the documents it produced, there were significant warning signs even before the Middle East conflict flared that Tehran would be a far different type of forum than the conferences convened in Europe, Latin America, and Africa. * * *

The Declaration and Plan of Action agreed to by the delegates in the discriminatory atmosphere of Tehran amounted to what could only be seen as a declaration by the states present of their intention to use the conference as a propaganda weapon attacking Israel. Indeed, the documents not only singled the country out above all others–despite the well-known problems with racism, xenophobia and discrimination that exist all over the world–but also equated its policies in the West Bank with some of the most horrible racist policies of the previous century. Israel, the text stated, engages in "ethnic cleansing of the Arab population of historic Palestine," and is implementing a "new kind of apartheid, a crime against humanity." It also purported to witness an "increase of racist practices of Zionism" and condemned racism "in various parts of the world, as well as the emergence of racist and violent movements based on racist and discriminatory ideas, in particular, the Zionist movement, which is based on race superiority." * * *

THE FORCES GATHER

The work of all four regional meetings was slated to be merged into one final draft declaration and plan of action at a two-week final preparatory meeting at the UN in Geneva, held from May 21 to June 1, 2001. As the meeting opened, it was clear that the Islamic states, fresh from their triumph in Tehran, were in no mood for compromise. Delegates from Egypt, Iran, Iraq, Pakistan, Syria and the observer from the Palestine Liberation Organization insisted on the inclusion of the anti-Israeli text from the Tehran document. These OIC [Organization of Islamic Countries] delegates also worked to undermine constructive language on the Holocaust and on anti-Semitism from the Strasbourg and Santiago meetings by affixing new text to pollute the meaning of these concepts. Thus, whenever the word "Holocaust" was read during the plenary review of the combined text, one of the Islamic delegates—usually Egypt—intervened to change "Holocaust" to holocausts. Adding insult to injury, the same delegates requested that the phrase "and the ethnic cleansing of the Arab population in historic Palestine" be inserted after the appearance of "holocausts".

Both of these manoeuvres were a transparent attempt to de-legitimize the moral argument for Israel's existence as a haven for Jews. To deny the unique status of the Holocaust is to deny the magnitude of the crime perpetrated against Jews in Europe and to erode the legitima-cy of the state of Israel, which was in part inspired by the need to prevent a repeat of that cataclysmic event. The juxtaposition of the Holocaust with a caricature of Israel' behaviour in the Palestinian conflict serves the same purpose by falsely equating victims with victimiz-ers.

Each time Santiago or Strasbourg language on anti-Semitism and the need to combat it was raised in the plenary, the OIC states intervened to couple anti-Semitism with the phrase "racist practices of Zionism", or even more outlandish "Zionist practices against Semi-tism"—a deliberate move to confuse the real meaning of anti-Semitism.
* * *

At the end of the two weeks of talks at the first preparatory meeting in Geneva, it was clear that Mary Robinson's vision for the World Conference was in severe jeopardy. Negotiations were deadlocked. The OIC appeared hell-bent on using the conference for its own political aims. Although there were hopeful signs that North and South could reconcile on the issue of colonialism and slavery, the path through this issue remained unclear. Robinson called for an additional unscheduled, emergency meeting at the end of July, again in Geneva, to continue to work on the remaining problems. * * *

THE SHOWDOWN IN GENEVA

When I arrived in Geneva on August 6 for the start of the second and final week of negotiations, [members of the U.S. delegation] report-ed significant progress in the discussions with the African states on the slavery and the colonialism issues. Negotiations were going back and forth on specific proposals of language to express regret short of apology, and "deep regret and profound remorse" was the formulation around which consensus was crystallizing.

With agreement on slavery tantalizingly near, the United States strategy to derail the OIC's demonization of Israel began to gain momentum. As predicted, the African states began to see the OIC as the only remaining obstacle to progress. "Why are you letting Egypt ruin this conference?" a young ambassador from a sub-Saharan state asked me in one of my first diplomatic meetings after arriving in Geneva. "Don't you give them $2 billion a year in aid?"

He explained that most African states were satisfied with the proposed compromise on the apology issue and implored me to "ask Bush to call Mubarak and tell him to get his people under control," confidently predicting that, "once the Arabs start to behave, we will all be ready to go to Durban and declare victory." He was not alone in sharing these sentiments.

Indeed, a true victory for the forces fighting against racism seemed at hand. It was becoming widely known that progress had been made on the slavery and colonialism issues, and the European delegations began to join the Africans in pressing the OIC to abandon their attempt to vilify Israel. * * *

Mrs. Robinson's intervention with the assembled delegates later in the same day left our delegation deeply shocked and saddened. In her remarks, she advocated precisely the opposite course to the one Secretary [of State, Colin] Powell and I had urged her to take. Namely, she refused to reject the twisted notion that the wrong done to the Jews in the Holocaust was equivalent to the pain suffered by the Palestinians in the Middle East. Instead, she discussed "the historical wounds of anti-Semitism and of the Holocaust on the one hand, and ... the accumulated wounds of displacement and military occupation on the other."

Thus, instead of condemning the attempt to usurp the conference, she legitimized it. Instead of insisting that it was inappropriate to discuss a specific political conflict in the context of a World Conference on Racism, she spoke of the "need to resolve protracted conflict and occupation, claims of inequality, violence and terrorism, and a deteriorating situation on the ground." Robinson was prepared to delve into the arcana of a single territorial conflict at the exclusion of all others and at the expense of the conference's greater goals.

Robinson's intervention broke all momentum that the U.S. had developed. The Arab countries immediately seized on these statements as a clear indication that the tide had turned again in their favor, dropped all talk of compromise, and began pressing for the continuation of the Middle East discussion in Durban. U.S. civil rights NGOs, sensing that all bets were now off, then began to press the African states to dig in their heels on both "apology" and reparations. The negotiations on mutually acceptable language to express regret for slavery and colonialism quickly unravelled, and all pressure from the African states on the OIC evaporated. The EU position on the appropriateness of discussing the Middle East softened. The talks lurched on for another two days and ended with no improvement to the text whatsoever. * * *

THE DEBACLE IN DURBAN

On the eve of the Durban meeting, I consulted with [U.S.] Ambassador [Michael] Southwick, whose proposed strategy was to work with Norway (and its partner, Canada), on their plan to save the conference. The Norwegian compromise was essentially generic language expressing concern about the conflict in the Middle East without veiled criticism of Israel. Although I felt it was a major concession on the part on the part of the U.S. to agree to discuss the conflict in the Middle East, when the conference was not discussing Kashmir, Chechnya, Tibet, or any other regional conflict, the language Southwick showed me was a truly neutral description of the Israeli–Palestinian conflict. I told him I could support the compromise if—and only if—it was our bottom line. I felt we had to draw a firm line on this issue—accepting any veiled attacks on Israel would indicate a U.S. willingness to appease radical Arab regimes. Southwick supported my position and told me that the secretary and the White House agreed.

Ambassador Southwick also had a fallback plan that he thought might be effective in the likely event the OIC remained intransigent. Southwick's idea was to offer an amendment to strike all of the objectionable text on the Middle East at the climax of the conference. He believed it would be difficult to defeat a motion to table this amendment, but felt confident that if we could survive procedural challenges, we could win the final vote on the substance. I told Southwick that I thought his idea was excellent and offered assistance in lobbying for favorable votes on this amendment. Regrettably, however, the U.S. delegation had still not received word from Washington on whether it had permission to engage in bilateral discussions, and amid all the back and forth, Southwick was never able to get the broad authority he would have needed to execute his entire strategy. He continued to work with Norway on building consensus for substituting their generic language on the conflict in the Middle East for the OIC text, but it was clear that the Bush administration was not prepared to go for broke in lobbying for a last minute amendment to strike all of the objectionable language at the end of the conference.

As the U.S. and Canada worked with Norway to build support further compromise, several mini-dramas were playing out in the circus-like atmosphere surrounding the conference. The leaders of many Western states and their ministers did not come to Durban—for the same reason that Colin Powell did not. Among the leaders who did show up, however, were luminaries like Fidel Castro, Yasir Arafat, and the increasingly hostile Amr Moussa, the former Egyptian Foreign Minister and current Secretary–General of the Arab League. It was increasingly clear to me that a reasoned discussion on racism would not happen in this rogues' gallery.

Diving into this hornets' nest was the Reverend Jesse Jackson, who announced with much fanfare on August 31, the first day of the conference, that he had made a deal with Arafat to tone down the rhetoric on Israel. My wife and I, returning from a friendly visit with Kofi and Nan Annan, ran into Jackson and Arafat in our hotel lobby, and Jackson jubilantly announced his "breakthrough" to us, saying that Arafat had agreed to drop all references tying Zionism to racism. I responded that I looked forward to seeing the compromise, and I hoped they would also drop the other veiled attacks on Israel scattered throughout the text.

The next day, the media excitement over Jackson's news quickly evaporated, however, after Arafat delivered a speech to the conference plenary that was both hateful and vituperative, describing Israel as engaging in a "racist, colonialist conspiracy" against Palestinians. "The aim of this Government," Arafat said, "is to force our people to their knees and to make them surrender in order to continue her occupation, settlements and racist practices, so as to liquidate our people by carrying out the *Orainim* (*i.e.* Hell) plan which were declared by Sharon (sic) ... " There was no more talk of Jackson's deal with Arafat after this speech.

Another ring in the Durban circus was the NGO forum, taking place just outside the conference center. Although the NGO proceedings were intended to provide a platform for the wide range of civil society groups interested in the conference's conciliatory mission, the forum quickly became stacked with Palestinian and fundamentalist Arab groups. Each day, these groups organized anti-Israeli and anti-Semitic rallies around the meetings, attracting thousands. One flyer which was widely distributed showed a photograph of Hitler and the question "What if I had won?" The answer: "There would be NO Israel.... " At a press conference held by Jewish NGO's to discuss their concerns with the direction the conference was taking, an accredited NGO, the Arab Lawyers Union, distributed a booklet filled with anti-Semitic caricatures frighteningly like those seen in the Nazi hate literature printed in the 1930s. Jewish leaders and I who were in Durban were shocked at this blatant display of anti-Semitism. For me, having experienced the horrors of the Holocaust first hand, this was the most sickening and unabashed displays of hate for Jews I had seen since the Nazi period.

Sadly, but perhaps not surprisingly, the official NGO document that was later adopted by a majority of the 3,000 NGOs in the forum branded Israel a "racist apartheid state" guilty of "genocide" and called for an end to its "racist crimes" against Palestinians. It also called for the convening of an international war crimes tribunal to try Israeli citizens. What is perhaps most disturbing about the NGO community's action is that many of America's top human rights leaders * * * participated. Although most of them denounced the NGO document that was adopted, it was surprising how reluctant they were to attack the anti-Semitic atmosphere and the clear OIC effort to derail the conference. Instead of supporting the Bush administration's principled stand against the anti-Israeli and anti-Semitic language in the governmental document, the NGOs attacked and condemned the administration for failing to send Colin Powell. An oft-repeated slander repeated by the NGOs was that the administration was using the issue of opposition to the anti-Israel language as a way to dodge serious negotiations on the reparations issue.

During September 1–2, when the NGOs took the stage to unveil their hateful document, Michael Southwick's team was feverishly meeting with a wide range of delegations, UN leaders, and South African officials serving as chairs of the conference. Ambassador Southwick was under enormous pressure to make progress in securing support for the Norwegian language. He was in constant contact with Colin Powell and with the White House, who felt that it was important to pull the U.S. delegation out of the conference as soon as it became clear that there was no hope to prevail on the U.S. bottom-line demand that the conference documents contain no anti-Israeli language. I met with a number of foreign ministers and other national delegates to underscore the message that the Norwegian language was as far as we were willing to go.

As the U.S. pressed its case, Robinson seemed to be working to stymie our efforts. In her public and private statements, as was the case in Geneva, she insisted that the conference had to recognize the suffering of the Palestinian people. In a meeting on Sunday, September 2, with Ambassador Southwick, she lashed out at him, characterizing the U.S. threat to pull out if the Norwegian language was not accepted as "warped, strange and undemocratic." In a meeting I had with Commissioner Robinson later that same day, she pleaded with me to compromise and see the Norwegian text as a starting point for discussions. I told her that she should be under no illusions—it was an enormous concession for the U.S. to accept even a generic discussion of the situation in the Middle East since no other political dispute was mentioned in the text. I also told her that the U.S. government was extremely displeased with the way she had handled the conference, and we indicated that we held her responsible for her actions that contributed to is failure.

The final showdown between the United States and the OIC came in a meeting between Ambassador Southwick and Egyptian Foreign Minister Ahmed Maher on Monday, September 3. The purpose of the meeting was to try to strike a deal to drop all the anti-Israeli language scattered throughout the draft text and replace it with the Norwegian language expressing regret for the crisis in the Middle East. Maher's behaviour in the meeting, as described to me later that night by a U.S. official who was present, was not what you would expect from one of America's closest allies. Maher was indignant. He launched into an anti-

American diatribe, insisted that Israel is a racist state, and that is actions had to be condemned by the conference.

Shortly after the breakdown of Ambassador Southwick's diplomatic efforts with the Arab League countries, in the early afternoon of September 3, Secretary Powell wisely decided to withdraw the U.S. delegation from a conference which had become a diplomatic farce. I spoke to the secretary just minutes after he communicated his decision, and he asked that I help explain it to the international media at the conference site. I held an impromptu news conference where I explained that the United States had made an enormous compromise by being willing to discuss the situation in the Middle East—that we had gone the extra mile. I stated that those countries who made it their specific goal to hijack the conference had shown rigidity and an unwillingness to compromise, and I praised President Bush and Colin Powell for their principled position to withdraw.

After we left, the EU delegation stayed put to see if they could salvage an agreement. The compromise, for which South Africa claimed authorship, removed some of the anti-Israeli language, but contained Mary Robinson's longed-for language that recognized the "plight of the Palestinian people under occupation" is highlighted, but there is no discussion of the Palestinian terrorist attack on Israeli citizens.

Although the compromise was presented by Robinson as an agreement between the EU and the OIC, brokered by South Africa, it was opposed by the OIC and South Africa in the final plenary session. The OIC delegates, led by Syria and Pakistan, continued to show the intransigence they had demonstrated in negotiations with the United States, launching a last minute parliamentary maneuver to salvage three of the most extreme paragraphs of anti-Israeli language that they had inserted into the conference documents in Geneva. The OIC lost on a procedural motion offered by Brazil to prevent them from adding the paragraphs on a vote of 51–38, leaving the "compromise" language as the final outcome of the Durban conference. Many of our partners in the newly formed coalition against terrorism–Egypt, Saudi Arabia, Jordan, Pakistan, Kuwait, Oman, Qatar, the UAE, Pakistan–supported this last ditch effort to demonize Israel.

NOTES AND QUESTIONS ON THE DURBAN CONFERENCE

1. *Context.* Congressman Lantos' article provides interesting, at times colorful, insight into the dynamics of a world conference. You should consider the fact that the late Congressman Lantos was a Holocaust survivor whose perspective on and experience of the conference should be viewed in that context. Nevertheless, his description of the atmosphere in which the Durban conference took place was shared by many. *See Delegates Fail to Rise to Occasion,* IRISH TIMES, Sept. 8, 2001,

at 10; Bharati Sadasivam, *The Conference that Wasn't,* VILLAGE VOICE, Sept. 18, 2001, at 40; John Donnelly and Anthony Shadid, *Race Talks Point to Palestinian Strategy, Analysts Say Forum is Exploited Where Politics Fails,* BOSTON GLOBE, Sept. 7, 2001, at A28.

2. *The politics of world conferences.* Although the issues were particularly difficult at Durban, diplomatic maneuvering, political posturing, and protracted negotiations are common to all world conferences. The issues may be different, but the context is often the same. The conflict in the Middle East is often at the center of these disputes, but other divisive issues—such as reproductive health services and sexual orientation—can also divide state participants in these conferences. The article above highlights the problem with addressing politically charged issues in a world conference.

Lantos' article also shows how political agendas can dominate a world conference to the exclusion of the broader issues the conference is intended to address. In the Durban context, this was true not only for the Arab states who wished for the conference to include harsh, anti-Israel language, but also for the United States, Canada, and European states who wanted to eliminate any and all references to the Middle East in the conference documents. In large part, the position of each was shaped by powerful domestic forces that pressured governments to place the Middle East at the top of their governments' agendas for the conference.

Clearly, there are risks to convening a conference that will encompass issues on which it is difficult to forge consensus. But should this prevent the international community from attempting to address these difficult issues? After all, the purpose of a world conference is to mobilize the international community to engage on the most pressing issues of the day. Are the risks of intractable debates and possible failure worth the effort?

3. *The legacy of slavery.* One of the key issues addressed at the Durban conference was the historical legacy of slavery, colonialism, and the trans-Atlantic slave trade. Indeed, many were disappointed by the U.S. withdrawal from the conference primarily because they saw it as an attempt to avoid these equally important issues. In response to Congressman Lantos' article, Gay McDougal, independent expert on the UN Committee on the Elimination of Racial Discrimination, noted that the conference addressed, for the first time, the legacy of the slave trade, colonialism, and the problems faced by descendants of African peoples throughout the world. *See* Gay McDougall, *The World Conference against Racism: Through a Wider Lens,* 26 FLETCHER FORUM OF WORLD AFFAIRS, 133 (2002). During preparation for the Durban conference, a wide range of NGOs and states advocated an explicit apology for the slave trade and to establish a mechanism for providing reparations to states that were harmed by the practice. Although these efforts were unsuccessful, the conference did "acknowledge and profoundly regret the untold suffer-

ing and evils inflicted on millions of men, women and children as a result of slavery, the slave trade, the transatlantic slave trade, apartheid, colonialism and genocide and past tragedies. We further note that some states have taken the initiative to apologize and have paid reparation, where appropriate, for grave and massive violations committed." Durban Declaration and Programme of Action, World Conference Against Racism, Racial Discrimination, Xenophobia, and Related Intolerance, 8 September 2001, U.N. Doc., A/CONF. 189/5 (2001), at ¶ 100, *at* http://www.unhchr.ch/pdf/Durban.pdf. The conference also agreed on a detailed action plan that, while far short of a reparations scheme, focused on a variety of forms of development assistance that should be provided to address historical injustices. For a more detailed discussion of these issues, see Christopher N. Camponovo, *Disaster in Durban*, 34 GEO. WASH. INT'L. L. REV. 659 (2003).

The convergence of, and conflict between, law and policy was particularly acute at the Durban conference. Given the significant political and legal implications of the aggressive approach to historical injustices advocated by some governments and NGOs, should they have expected to succeed in their efforts to get governments to issue an explicit apology and endorse a reparations scheme? Some delegations advocated a recognition of colonialism as a crime. What would have been the legal and political consequences of such a development? Clearly, such a statement would have gone well beyond present international law. Is a world conference the appropriate forum to attempt to advance such a significant legal innovation?

4. *The U.S. walkout.* Many in the United States hoped that the U.S. walkout at Durban would prompt a serious discussion of race relations in the United States. Not surprisingly, the civil rights community felt betrayed by the U.S. position, *i.e.*, in their view, by walking out in protest over the treatment of the conflict in the Middle East, the U.S. government neglected many other issues important to ethnic and racial minorities in the United States. Such a dialogue never took place. Only a few days after the conclusion of the Durban conference, the September 11 terrorist attacks took place in New York and Washington. In the aftermath of September 11, have the issues of race, discrimination, and disenfranchisement addressed by the international community in the Durban documents become any less important?

5. *Follow-up to Durban.* In February 2007, the UN General Assembly adopted a resolution deciding to convene a conference in 2009 to review "implementation of the Durban Declaration and Programme of Action." UN Doc. A/Res/61/149 (Feb. 2007). Not surprisingly, Israel has indicated it will not participate in the conference. Canada has also said it will not participate. And the United States, France, and the United Kingdom have indicated that their governments will also not participate if it appears through the preparatory process that the review conference will be a repetition of Durban.

If some of the problems in Durban were a result of a too permissive environment for NGOs, how might conference planners organize the next meeting to avoid these problems? Are there principles in human rights law that govern hate speech and incitement that could be used to "control" the activities of NGOs without offending notions of free speech? How would you advise the Office of the High Commissioner for Human Rights on this issue? Notably, the review conference will be held in Geneva, not in South Africa as was originally planned. How might this change in location affect the tenor of the conference?

During preparations for the review conference, two related issues may dominate the agenda: defamation of religion and incitement. In particular, the worldwide controversy over cartoons in the Danish press depicting the prophet Mohammed, which led to violent protests and numerous deaths, have led many in the Islamic world to call for international action on this issue. Can a balance be struck between the right to free speech and respect for religious traditions? Is a world conference the place to do it, or is this a matter more suitably addressed in a legal instrument? Is a new instrument necessary, or do existing human rights instruments adequately address the matter?

Practicum

Assume that the United Nations General Assembly has adopted a resolution calling for a Special Session of the UN General Assembly on Indigenous Peoples in celebration of the adoption of the UN Declaration on the Rights of Indigenous Peoples. UN Doc. A/61/L.67 (Sept. 7, 2007). The session will last for two weeks and adopt a plan of action designed to commit states to take specific measures to implement the Declaration.[1] As with other world conferences, there will be two preparatory meetings, as well as four regional meetings and the session itself will have the full participation of governments, UN bodies and NGOs. However, this session will be unique because representatives of indigenous peoples will also have the opportunity to participate on the same footing as NGOs.

Students should be chosen to represent governments, NGOs, and/or indigenous peoples and prepare issue papers on the language below. Possible governments include Canada, the United States, Denmark, Colombia, and Guatemala. NGOs should include international NGOs devoted to advancing the human rights of indigenous peoples throughout the world. Possible indigenous peoples to be represented should include the Navajo Nation, the U'wa (from Colombia) the Sami people of Norway and Sweden, or the Inuit peoples of Alaska and Greenland.

---

1. For an example of a World Conference plan of action, see *Vienna Declaration and Programme of Action*, UN Doc. A/CONF.157/23 (July 12, 1993).

Students should prepare legal justifications for their language proposals—based both in the Declaration on the Rights of Indigenous Peoples and in other relevant international instruments. The group should convene in order to discuss the language, advocate particular approaches, and—if possible—negotiate compromise language as if it were an actual world conference. After the "conference," one student might be asked to prepare an advocacy plan based on the language previously adopted by the group and present and defend the plan to the class.

CHAPTER 6

MODULE 15

TRUTH COMMISSIONS

■ ■ ■

Orientation

Since 1974, over twenty truth commissions have been established to assist nations in the process of confronting their pasts and forging new futures. Some, like South Africa's Truth and Reconciliation Commission, have been wholly domestic, and others, like the Commission on the Truth for El Salvador, have had substantial international participation, sometimes from the United Nations. Although the mandate, the composition, and the powers of each truth commission may vary, they share the common goal of investigating, documenting, and publicizing the past. They create a record of the truth as a hopeful first step in a long-term reconciliation process, and the legal component of their work is the subject of this module.

The magnitude of the task—and the limits of the law by itself—should not be under-estimated. The international community has no "one size fits all" approach to the transition from chaos to a rights-respecting order, and human rights lawyers may need to suppress their natural instinct for prosecutions and similar coercive court processes in the face of massive abuses. After all, in societies transitioning from violence and abuse to peace and stability, lawyers may be scarce, judges may be corrupt, and the rule of law may be reduced to an empty phrase. People cannot suddenly be expected to rely on the very institutions of state that may have been responsible for the abuse. Truth commissions offer one technique for making progress in these difficult circumstances, but they require lawyers to think outside the courtroom when imagining mechanisms of accountability.

MARTHA MINOW, THE HOPE FOR HEALING: WHAT CAN TRUTH COMMISSIONS DO?, in TRUTH v. JUSTICE (ROBERT I. ROTBERG AND DENNIS THOMPSON EDS.)

(2000)

The mass atrocities of the twentieth century, sadly, do not make it distinctive. More distinctive than the facts of genocides and regimes of torture marking this era are the search for and invention of collective forms of response. This is especially noteworthy given that no response to mass atrocity is adequate. The sheer implication of adequacy is itself potentially insulting to the memory of those who were killed and to the remaining days of those who were tortured, and to those who witnessed the worst that human beings can do to other human beings. Yet, during the twentieth century a particular hope, or ideology, has inspired specific efforts to use law and state power to address and redress episodes of collective violence.

The basic idea is that public power—through prosecutions, reparations, and commissions of inquiry—can locate the violations on maps of human comprehensibility, deter future violations of human dignity, and ensure that the ambitions of the agents of violence do not succeed. The novel experiment of the Nuremberg and Tokyo tribunals following World War II reached for a vision of world order and international justice, characterizing mass violence as crimes of war and crimes against humanity. Individual states also prosecuted their own citizens and citizens of other states for participation in mass murders and torture. These trials have inspired the international movement for human rights and represent in many people's minds the "gold standard" for any public response to mass violence. The use of criminal trials holds out the rule of law as the framework for rendering accountability for unspeakable conduct, for deterring future violations, and for gathering a formal public record so that the attempts to destroy groups of people cannot succeed in destroying their memory.

Each of these goals is admirable. They are also exceedingly difficult to achieve. The trial process does not always work, and even when it does, it is marked by sharp constraints. Trials and the framework of the rule of law also miss another collection of purposes that are at least of equal importance for individuals and societies emerging after large-scale violence and brutality. These purposes center on rectifying the damage to human dignity that so often endures even for those who survive violence and on healing societies torn by hatred and brutality. Failure to address damage to individual dignity and to the very idea that members of targeted groups are persons with dignity ensures that the consequences of mass violation will persist and may give rise to new rounds of revenge.

One woman who was raped while in police detention for her political opposition to apartheid recalled how she forced herself to survive by putting her sense of herself or her soul in the corner of the room outside of their body, while the rape occurred. She survived, but tells Bill Moyers during an interview for his 1999 documentary film, *Facing the Truth*, that what she longs for is to return to that room and find herself again. Multiply this utter sense of violation across all those wounded physically and spiritually by mass violence. Trauma alters people's abilities to sleep, eat, hope, and work; trauma alters people's brain scans and capacities to care for others. Can collective responses to mass violence redress trauma, or at least do so with the same acknowledgment of ultimate inadequacy that must accompany any other public response to genocide, torture, and mass rapes?

This question is posed most vividly through the development of truth commissions in the closing decades of the twentieth century. Investigation and exposure of gross human rights violations have been "the stock in trade of international human rights organizations and the international press for some decades". More recently, though, national legislatures and executives, and international institutions, have authorized such investigations, giving official acknowledgment to the issues and to the truths ultimately gathered. These official bodies are established to investigate and publicly report on human rights violations and collective violence. They emphasize both truth finding and truth telling. If the goals of repairing human dignity, healing individuals, and mending societies after the trauma of mass atrocity are central, truth commissions offer features that are often more promising than prosecutions. Even in light of the basic goals of prosecutions, truth commissions can afford benefits to a society. Thus, any evaluation of legal responses to mass violence must acknowledge the specific goals sought as well as their shortfall in practice. Because attention to the victimized should rate highly among the goals, truth commissions should be an important part of the national and international repertoire of responses to mass violence.

Second Best or Independently Valuable?

A truth commission looks like a second choice if prosecutions for human rights violations serve as the model for institutional responses to state-sponsored violence. Commentators argue that prosecuting human rights violations can substantially enhance the chance of establishing the rule of law. Doing so signals that no individual stands beyond the reach of legal accountability. Prosecutions also provide a legitimate means for punishing wrongdoers. The threat of such punishment in turn is the chief method for deterring future human rights violations. Prosecutions set in motion an official process for gathering and testing testimony and documentary evidence that can disclose hidden truths about the atrocities and prevent future cover-ups or denials. In comparison, a commission of inquiry charged with investigating and reporting human rights violations may seem a pale and inadequate substitute. International human rights activists and scholars argue that criminal prosecution is the best response to atrocities and that truth commissions should be used only as an alternative when such prosecutions are not possible.

In this view, truth commissions become an important alternative only because practical reasons do often interfere with or prevent prosecutions. There may simply not be enough courtrooms, lawyers, witnesses, or time for prosecuting all who deserve it in places like Kosovo, Rwanda, Cambodia, East Germany, East Timor, and Brazil. There may be an inadequate number of skilled people who were not participants in the offending regime to administer the justice system. When the offenders are part of a military regime that remains in force, the government usually lacks the clout to proceed with prosecutions.

Even when a successor regime is in charge, and not under the pervasive powers of the military command that participated in or permitted atrocities, the new leaders may hope to avoid the confrontational atmosphere generated by trials. They may also conclude that prosecutions that would be perceived as politically motivated or politically tainted could not advance the rule of law. Prosecutorial decisions may be foreclosed by political realities. Negotiation of a peaceful transfer of power often involves measures to ensure immunity from prosecutions against outgoing leaders as a crucial condition.

Prosecutions may be hampered alternatively by the ability of high-ranking officials to flee to other countries or to retain sufficient political or economical power to render prosecutions difficult. If only low-ranking participants can be found and prosecuted, the resulting trials could create martyrs while leaving the important decision makers untouched. Or only high-level officials may be prosecuted, leaving the impression that those lower in the chain of command are excused or free to act. Selective prosecutions jeopardize the ideals of accountability and the hopes for deterrence; in these circumstances, those newly in charge may prefer to avoid any prosecutorial effort and develop an alternative response.

Yet arguments for alternatives may be founded not just in search for a substitute when trials are not workable. The trial as a form of response to injustice has its own internal limitations. Litigation is not an ideal form of social action. The financial and emotional costs of litigation may be most apparent when private individuals sue one another, but there are parallel problems when a government or an international tribunal prosecutes. Victims and other witnesses undergo the ordeals of testifying and facing cross-examination. Usually, they are given no simple opportunity to convey directly the narrative of their experience. Evidentiary rules and rulings limit the factual material that can be included. Trial procedure makes for laborious and even boring sessions that risk anesthetizing even the most avid listener and dulling sensibilities even in the face of recounted horrors. The simplistic questions of guilt or innocence framed by the criminal trial can never capture the multiple sources of mass violence. If the social goals include gaining public acknowledgments and producing a complete account of what happened, the trial process is at best an imperfect means.

If the goals extend to repairing the dignity of those who did survive and enlarging their chances for rewarding lives, litigation falls even farther short. Trials focus on perpetrators, not victims. They consult victims only to illustrate the fact or scope of the defendants' guilt. Victims are not there for public acknowledgment or even to tell, fully, their own stories. Trials interrupt and truncate victim testimony with direct and cross-examination and conceptions of relevance framed by the elements of the charges. Judges and juries listen to victims with skepticism tied to the presumption of defendants' innocence. Trials afford no role in their process or content for bystanders or for the complex interactions among ideologies, leaders, mass frustrations, historic and invented lines of hatred, and acts of brutality.

For truth telling, public acknowledgment of what happened, and attention to survivors, a commission of inquiry actually may be better than prosecutions. When the commission is authorized or taken seriously by the government, and is capable of producing a report with wide public reception public acknowledgment can be dramatic and effective. The daily broadcast of proceedings of the South African Truth and Reconciliation Commission (TRC) marked this kind of public acknowledgment and made pre-existing, widespread denial—especially within white communities—less and less tenable. It reflected a deliberate policy of maximum publicity. The TRC developed partnerships with community-based organizations to communicate its work, developed an advertising campaign to informs the public about its activities, and worked with newspaper, television, and radio professionals to communicate its message.

A truth commission can be set up to hear from victims for their own sake, and it can be designed to try to restore their dignity. Being able to give a full account of their suffering can be meaningful for survivors, even if perpetrators are never found or punished. In South Africa, where courtrooms had so often been used to reinforce the power of the apartheid regime and deny rightful claims by its victims, the creation of a setting quite distinct from courts held a special value. A truth commission also can offer bystanders the roles of listeners, while also turning at times to focus on what bystanders failed to do to prevent or stem the violence.

The aspiration to develop as full an account as possible requires a process of widening the lens, sifting varieties of evidentiary materials, and drafting syntheses of factual material that usually does not accompany a trial. Yet truth commissions typically undertake to write the history of what happened in precisely these ways. Putting together distinct events and the role of different actors is more likely to happen when people have the chance to look across incidents and to connect the stories of many victims and many offenders. A truth commission can examine the role of entire sectors of a society—such as the medical profession, the media, and business—in enabling and failing to prevent mass violence. The sheer narrative project of a truth commission makes it more likely than trials to yield accounts of entire regimes. Trials in contrast focus on particular individuals and their conduct in particular moments in time, with decisions of guilt or nonguilt, and opinions tailored to these particular questions of individual guilt.

Truth commissions still face enormous barriers in gathering facts and producing comprehensive accounts. Especially in regimes that operate through terror, secrecy is the ground rule. Some of the story can never be known without grants of immunity to those who can tell it. Here, the innovative South African approach to amnesty is especially noteworthy. The TRC applications from individuals for amnesty were to be approved only if those applicants recounted truthfully and fully their roles in committing human rights violations, and also only if their roles in conduct were motivated by politics and was not disproportionately heinous. Although borne of the political compromise necessary to ensure peaceful transition of power, this method for granting amnesty also reflected the experience of leaders in the African National Congress (ANC) with their own commissions of inquiry exposing hidden human rights abuses. The ANC had previously conducted two inquiries into its own human rights violations, and found the value of disclosures by insiders. This experience contributed to the design of the Amnesty Committee of the TRC, which also gave victims the right to cross-examine applicants.

The trade of amnesty for testimony allowed the TRC to use the participation by some to gain the participation of others. Five mid-level political officers sought amnesty and in so doing implicated General Johan van der Merwe as the one who gave the order to fire on demonstrators in 1992. The general then himself applied for amnesty before the commission and confessed that he had indeed given the order to fire. He in turn implicated two cabinet-level officials who gave him orders. Evidence of this kind, tracing violence to decisions at the highest governmental levels, is likely to be held only by those who themselves participated in secret conversations, and the adversarial processes of trials are not likely to unearth it. Combining information from amnesty petitions and hearings with victim testimony and independent investigations, the TRC had the chance to develop a much richer array of evidence than the courts would have had in expensive and lengthy criminal prosecutions.

Practical limitations will mar truth commission work just as they prevent actual trials from achieving their ideal. The patterns of secrecy, misinformation, and rumour that accompany oppressive regimes and reigns of terror make the task of finding and reporting the truth daunting if not impossible. Crucial evidence is destroyed. Mass graves do not disclose who performed the murders, much less who gave the orders. Mass atrocities explode the frames of reference usually available for historical investigations. Any report that claims to be comprehensive will be defective precisely on those grounds.

Even if a report is issued with governmental endorsement, the public may not become engaged with it. Many victims and many perpetrators will prefer not to participate, and this will invite charges that the report is unfair or unrepresentative. The commission may take too long to do its work. Or it may work under tight deadlines and simply be unable to meet the challenge of reporting fully on what happened.

Yet the process of testifying before and being heard by the official human rights committee at a truth commission potentially holds independent value for the individual victims and for the nation. This is what makes truth commissions a notable innovation. The process of engaging official listeners in hearing from victims, and broadcasting that process before a listening public, accomplishes some important healing for individuals and for societies In this goal is taken seriously, truth commissions are not a second best, but an admirable alternative to prosecutions.

NOTES AND QUESTIONS ON TRUTH COMMISSIONS

1. *Thinking outside the courtroom.* In the excerpt above, Minow identifies her vision of what truth commissions can accomplish in a transitional society. The challenge for lawyers is to think outside the ordinary "litigation box" in order to craft the mechanisms and terms of reference that will permit a society to fulfill the goals it hopes to achieve through a truth commission. This should be a relatively simple task; after all, the purpose of a commission is to investigate abuses, hear evidence, and apply the law—all things to which the legal community is well-accustomed. What makes the task more difficult in this context? How can the political challenges and obstacles presented by a transitional society be met when crafting the commission's mandate?

2. *Advancing the rule of law.* The debate over truth commissions most often centers around the compromises made in the name of reconciliation. But Minow identifies an additional function that can be just as important in a transitional society—the creation of an institutional mechanism for addressing human rights violations in accordance with the rule of law. Why is this important? How might a truth commission be a vital first step in the establishment and strengthening of democratic institutions in a post-conflict society?

---

1. CRAFTING THE MANDATE

As described by Minow, a truth commission can be created to achieve a variety of different—and sometimes competing—goals. To be successful, the commission's mandate must be carefully crafted: How far into the past will the commission look, and what will the scope of the commission's investigations be? What law will it apply? How will it be constituted? Can its findings be used for prosecution? Keep in mind that the commission's mandate is often brokered between two previously warring factions: how will this dynamic affect the mandate's scope?

One largely successful truth commission was established to investigate the brutal civil war that tore El Salvador apart in the 1980s. In 1992, the parties to that war signed a peace agreement that called for the establishment of a truth commission. Excerpted below are the truth commission's founding document, as well as excerpts from the commission's report and the reflections of one of its members.

EL SALVADOR: MEXICO PEACE AGREEMENTS— PROVISIONS CREATING THE COMMISSION ON TRUTH

(Mexico City, April 27, 1991)

* * *

The Government of El Salvador and the Frente Farabundo Marti para la Liberación Nacional (hereinafter referred to as "the Parties"),

Reaffirming their intention to contribute to the reconciliation of Salvadorian society;

Recognizing the need to clear up without delay those exceptionally important acts of violence whose characteristics and impact, and the social unrest to which they gave rise, urgently require that the complete truth be made known and that the resolve and means to establish the truth be strengthened; * * *

Agreeing on the advisability of fulfilling that task through a procedure which is both reliable and expeditious and may yield results in the short-term, without prejudice to the obligations incumbent on the Salvadorian courts to solve such cases and impose the appropriate penalties on the culprits;

Have arrived at the following political agreement:

1.   There is hereby established a Commission on the Truth (hereinafter referred to as "the Commission"). The Commission shall be composed of three individuals appointed by the Secretary–General of the United Nations after consultation with the Parties. The Commission shall elect its Chairman.

Functions

2.   The Commission shall have the task of investigating serious acts of violence that have occurred since 1980 and whose impact on society urgently demands that the public should know the truth. The Commission shall take into account:

(a) The exceptional importance that may be attached to the acts to be investigated, their characteristics and impact, and the social unrest to which they gave rise; and

(b) The need to create confidence in the positive changes which the peace process is promoting and to assist the transition to national reconciliation.

3.   The mandate of the Commission shall include recommending the legal, political or administrative measures which can be inferred from the results of the investigation. Such recommendations may include measures to prevent the repetition of such acts, and initiatives to promote national reconciliation.

4.   The Commission shall endeavour to adopt its decisions unanimously. However, if this is not possible, a vote by the majority of its members shall suffice.

5.   The Commission shall not function in the manner of a judicial body.

6.   If the Commission believes that any case brought to its attention does not meet the criteria set forth in paragraph 2 of this agreement, it may refer the case to the Attorney–General of the Republic, should it deem appropriate, for handling through the judicial channel.

Powers

7.   The Commission shall have broad powers to organize its work and its functioning. Its activities shall be conducted on a confidential basis.

8.   For the purposes of the investigation, the Commission shall have the power to:

(a) Gather, by the means it deems appropriate, any information it considers relevant. The Commission shall be completely free to use whatever sources of information it deems useful and reliable. It shall receive such information within the period of time and in the manner which it determines.

(b) Interview, freely and in private, any individuals, groups or members of organizations or institutions

(c) Visit any establishment or place freely without giving prior notice.

(d) Carry out any other measures or inquiries which it considers useful to the performance of its mandate, including requesting reports, records, documents from the Parties or any other information from State authorities and departments.

Obligation of the Parties

9.   The Parties undertake to extend to the Commission whatever cooperation it requests of them in order to gain access to sources of information available to them.

10.   The Parties undertake to carry out the Commission's recommendations.

Report

11.   The Commission shall submit a final report, with its conclusions and recommendations, within a period of six months after its establishment.

12.   The Commission shall transmit its report to the Parties and to the Secretary–General of the United Nations, who shall make it public and shall take the decisions or initiatives that he deems appropriate.

13.   Once the report has been handed over, the Commission's mandate shall be considered terminated and the Commission shall be dissolved.

14.   The provisions of this agreement shall not prevent the normal investigation of any situation or case, whether or not the Commission has investigated it, nor the application of the relevant legal provisions to any act that is contrary to law.

From Madness to Hope: the 12–Year War in El Salvador: Report of the Commission on the Truth for El Salvador

The Commission on the Truth for El Salvador

Belisario Betancur, Chairman

Reinaldo Figueredo Planchart

Thomas Buergenthal

A.   The Mandate

The Commission on the Truth owes its existence and authority to the El Salvador peace agreements, a set of agreements negotiated over a period of more than three years (1989–1992) between the Government of El Salvador and FMLN. The negotiating process, which took place under United Nations auspices with the special cooperation of Colombia, Mexico, Spain and Venezuela (the so-called "friends of the Secretary–General"), culminated in the Peace Agreement signed at Chapultepec, Mexico, on 16 January 1992.

The decision to set up the Commission on the Truth was taken by the Parties in the Mexico Agreements, signed at Mexico City on 27 April 1991. These Agreements define the functions and powers of the Commission, while its authority is expanded by article 5 of the Chapultepec Peace Agreement, entitled "End to Impunity." Together, these provisions constitute the Commission's "mandate."

The specific functions assigned to the Commission as regards impunity are defined, in part, in the Chapultepec Agreement, which provides as follows:

"The Parties recognize the need to clarify and put an end to any indication of impunity on the part of officers of the armed forces, particularly in cases where respect for human rights is jeopardized. To that end, the Parties refer this issue to the Commission on the Truth for consideration and resolution."

In addition to granting the Commission powers with respect to impunity and the investigation of serious acts of violence, the peace agreements entrust the Commission with making "legal, political or administrative" recommendations. Such recommendations may relate to specific cases or may be more general. In the latter case, they "may include measures to prevent the repetition of such acts, and initiatives to promote national reconciliation."

The Commission was thus given two specific powers: the power to make investigations and the power to make recommendations. The latter power is particularly important since, under the mandate, "the Parties undertake to carry out the Commission's recommendations." The Parties thus agree to be bound by the Commission's recommendations.

As regards the Commission's other task, the mandate entrusted it with investigating "serious acts of violence ... whose impact on society urgently demands that the public should know the truth." In other words, in deciding which acts to focus on, the Commission would have to take into account the particular importance of each act, its repercussions and the social unrest to which it gave rise. However, the mandate did not list or identify any specific cases for investigation; nor did it distinguish between large-scale acts of violence and acts involving only a handful of people. Instead, the mandate emphasized serious acts of violence and their impact or repercussions. On the basis of these criteria, the Commission investigated two types of cases:

(a) Individual cases or acts which, by their nature, outraged Salvadorian society and/or international opinion;

(b) A series of individual cases with similar characteristics revealing a systematic pattern of violence or ill-treatment which, taken together, equally outraged Salvadorian society, especially since their aim was to intimidate certain sectors of that society.

The Commission attaches equal importance to uncovering the truth in both kinds of cases. Moreover, these two types of cases are not mutually exclusive. Many of the so-called individual acts of violence which had the greatest impact on public opinion also had characteristics revealing systematic patterns of violence.

In investigating these acts, the Commission took into account three additional factors which have a bearing on the fulfilment of its mandate. The first was that it must investigate serious or flagrant acts committed by both sides in the Salvadorian conflict and not just by one of the Parties. Secondly, in referring the issue of the impunity "of officers of the armed forces, particularly in cases where respect for human rights is jeopardized" to the Commission, the Chapultepec Agreement urged the Commission to pay particular attention to this area and to acts of violence committed by officers of the armed forces which were never investigated or punished. Thirdly, the Commission was given six months in which to perform its task.

If we consider that the Salvadorian conflict lasted 12 years and resulted in a huge number of deaths and other serious acts of violence, it was clearly impossible for the Commission to deal with every act that could have been included within its sphere of competence. In deciding to investigate one case rather than another, it had to weigh such considerations as the representative nature of the case, the availability of sufficient evidence, the investigatory resources available to the Commission, the time needed to conduct an exhaustive investigation and the issue of impunity as defined in the mandate.

B. Applicable Law

The Commission's mandate entrusts it with investigating serious acts of violence, but does not specify the principles of law that must be applied in order to define such acts and to determine responsibility for them. Nevertheless, the concept of serious acts of violence used in the peace agreements obviously does not exist in a normative vacuum and must therefore be analysed on the basis of certain relevant principles of law.

In defining the legal norms applicable to this task, it should be pointed out that, during the Salvadorian conflict, both Parties were under an obligation to observe a number of rules of international law, including those stipulated in international human rights law or in international humanitarian law, or in both. Furthermore, throughout the period in question, the State of El Salvador was under an obligation to adjust its domestic law to its obligations under international law.

These rules of international law must be considered as providing the basis for the criteria applicable to the functions which the peace agreements entrust to the Commission. Throughout the Salvadorian conflict, these two sets of rules were only rarely mutually exclusive.

It is true that, in theory, international human rights law is applicable only to Governments, while in some armed conflicts international humanitarian law is binding on both sides: in other words, binding on both insurgents and Government forces. However, it must be recognized that when insurgents assume government powers in territories under their control, they too can be required to observe certain human rights obligations that are binding on the State under international law. This would make them responsible for breaches of those obligations.

The official position of FMLN was that certain parts of the national territory were under its control, and it did in fact exercise that control.

1. International human rights law

The international human rights law applicable to the present situation comprises a number of international instruments adopted within the framework of the United Nations and the Organization of American States (OAS). These instruments, which are binding on the State of El Salvador, include, in addition to the Charters of the United Nations and OAS, the following human rights treaties: the International Covenant on Civil and Political Rights and the American Convention on Human Rights. El Salvador ratified the Covenant on 30 November 1979 and the American Convention on 23 June 1978. Both instruments entered into force for El Salvador before 1980 and were thus in force throughout the conflict to which the Commission's mandate refers.

Clearly, not every violation of a right guaranteed in those instruments can be characterized as a "serious act of violence." Those instruments themselves recognize that some violations are more serious than others. This position is reflected in a provision which appears in both instruments and which distinguishes between rights from which no derogation is possible, even in time of war or other state of national emergency, and those from which derogations can be made in such circumstances. It is appropriate, therefore, that the Commission should classify the seriousness of each "act of violence" on the basis of the rights which the two instruments list as not being subject to derogation, in particular, rights related directly to the right to life and to physical integrity.

Accordingly, the following rights listed in article 4 of the Covenant as not being subject to derogation would come within the Commission's sphere of competence: the right to life ("No one shall be arbitrarily deprived of his life"); the right not to be subjected to torture or to cruel, inhuman or degrading treatment or punishment; and the right not to be held in slavery or any form of servitude. Article 27 of the American Convention on Human Rights provides that these same rights cannot be suspended even "in time of war, public danger, or other emergency that threatens the independence or security of a State Party."

Under international law, it is illegal for a State, or for persons acting on its behalf, to violate any of the above rights for whatever reason. Violation of these rights may even constitute an international crime in situations where acts are of a consistent type or reflect a systematic practice whose purpose is the large-scale violation of these fundamental rights of the human person.

2. International humanitarian law

The principles of international humanitarian law applicable to the Salvadorian conflict are contained in article 3 common to the four Geneva Conventions of 1949 and in Additional Protocol II thereto. El Salvador ratified these instruments before 1980.

Although the armed conflict in El Salvador was not an international conflict as defined by the Conventions, it did meet the requirements for the application of article 3 common to the four Conventions. That article defines some fundamental humanitarian rules applicable to non international armed conflicts. The same is true of Protocol II Additional to the Geneva Conventions, relating to the protection of victims of non international armed conflicts. The provisions of common article 3 and of Additional Protocol II are legally binding on both the Government and the insurgent forces.

Without going into those provisions in detail, it is clear that violations—by either of the two parties to the conflict—of common article 3 and of the fundamental guarantees contained in Additional Protocol II, especially if committed systematically, could be characterized as serious acts of violence for the purposes of the interpretation and application of the Commission's mandate. Such violations would include arbitrary deprivation of life; torture; cruel, inhuman or degrading treatment; taking of hostages; and denial of certain indispensable guarantees of due process before serious criminal penalties are imposed and carried out.

3. Conclusions

With few exceptions, serious acts of violence prohibited by the rules of humanitarian law applicable to the Salvadorian conflict are also violations of the non-repealable provisions of the International Covenant on Civil and Political Rights and the American Convention on Human Rights, the two human rights treaties ratified by the State of El Salvador. The two instruments also prohibit derogation from any rights guaranteed in any humanitarian law treaty to which the State is a party.

As a result, neither the Salvadorian State nor persons acting on its behalf or in its place can claim that the existence of an armed conflict justified the commission of serious acts of violence in contravention of one or other of the human rights treaties mentioned above or of the applicable instruments of humanitarian law binding on the State.

C. Methodology

* * * In establishing the procedure that the Commission was to follow in performing its functions, paragraph 7 of the mandate provided that the Commission would conduct its activities "on a confidential basis." Paragraph 5 established that "The Commission shall not function in the manner of a judicial body." Paragraph 8 (a) stipulated that "The Commission shall be completely free to use whatever sources of information it deems useful and reliable," while paragraph 8 (b) gave the Commission the power to "Interview, freely and in private, any individuals, groups or members of organizations or institutions." Lastly, in the fourth preambular paragraph of the mandate, the Parties agreed that the task entrusted to the Commission should be fulfilled "through a procedure which is both reliable and expeditious and may yield results in the short term, without prejudice to the obligations incumbent on the

Salvadorian courts to solve such cases and impose the appropriate penalties on the culprits."

In analysing these provisions of the mandate, the Commission thought it important that the Parties had emphasized that "the Commission shall not function in the manner of a judicial body." In other words, not only did the Parties not establish a court or tribunal, but they made it very clear that the Commission should not function as if it were a judicial body. They wanted to make sure that the Commission was able to act on a confidential basis and receive information from any sources, public or private, that it deemed useful and reliable. It was given these powers so that it could conduct an investigation procedure that was both expeditious and, in its view, reliable in order to "clear up without delay those exceptionally important acts of violence whose characteristics and impact ... urgently require that the complete truth be made known . . . ."

So it is clear that the Parties opted for an investigation procedure that, within the short period of time allotted, would be best fitted to establishing the truth about acts of violence falling within the Commission's sphere of competence, without requiring the Commission to observe the procedures and rules that normally govern the activities of any judicial or quasi-judicial body. Any judicial function that had to be performed would be reserved expressly for the courts of El Salvador. For the Parties, the paramount concern was to find out the truth without delay. * * *

From the outset, the Commission was aware that accusations made and evidence received in secret run a far greater risk of being considered less trustworthy than those which are subjected to the normal judicial tests for determining the truth and to other related requirements of due process of law, including the right of the accused to confront and examine witnesses brought against him. Accordingly, the Commission felt that it had a special obligation to take all possible steps to ensure the reliability of the evidence used to arrive at a finding. In cases where it had to identify specific individuals as having committed, ordered or tolerated specific acts of violence, it applied a stricter test of reliability.

The Commission decided that, in each of the cases described in this report, it would specify the degree of certainty on which its ultimate finding was based. The different degrees of certainty were as follows:

1. Overwhelming evidence—conclusive or highly convincing evidence to support the Commission's finding;

2. Substantial evidence—very solid evidence to support the Commission's finding;

3. Sufficient evidence—more evidence to support the Commission's finding than to contradict it.

The Commission decided not to arrive at any specific finding on cases or situations, or any aspect thereof, in which there was less than "sufficient" evidence to support such a finding.

In order to guarantee the reliability of the evidence it gathered, the Commission insisted on verifying, substantiating and reviewing all statements as to facts, checking them against a large number of sources whose veracity had already been established. It was decided that no single source or witness would be considered sufficiently reliable to establish the truth on any issue of fact needed for the Commission to arrive at a finding. It was also decided that secondary sources, for instance, reports from national or international governmental or private bodies and assertions by people without first–hand knowledge of the facts they reported, did not on their own constitute a sufficient basis for arriving at findings. However, these secondary sources were used, along with circumstantial evidence, to verify findings based on primary sources.

It could be argued that, since the Commission's investigation methodology does not meet the normal requirements of due process, the report should not name the people whom the Commission considers to be implicated in specific acts of violence. The Commission believes that it had no alternative but to do so.

In the peace agreements, the Parties made it quite clear that it was necessary that the "complete truth be made known," and that was why the Commission was established. Now, the whole truth cannot be told without naming names. After all, the Commission was not asked to write an academic report on El Salvador, it was asked to investigate and describe exceptionally important acts of violence and to recommend measures to prevent the repetition of such acts. This task cannot be performed in the abstract, suppressing information (for instance, the names of persons responsible for such acts) where there is reliable testimony available, especially when the persons identified occupy senior positions and perform official functions directly related to violations or the cover-up of violations. Not to name names would be to reinforce the very impunity to which the Parties instructed the Commission to put an end.

THOMAS BURGENTHAL, THE UNITED NATIONS TRUTH COMMISSION FOR EL SALVADOR

27 VAND. J. TRANSNAT'L. L. 497 (1994)

From the very beginning of the investigation, the Commissioners assumed that our final report would identify the individuals who had committed the serious acts of violence to which the Commission's mandate referred. However, we did not formally discuss the subject in the first four months of our work. All three of us had quite naturally assumed that the investigation would not be complete unless those responsible for these acts were identified. That seemed too obvious to require much discussion and explains why, from the very beginning, we focused our inquiry on the following questions: what happened, which side of the conflict was responsible, who were the victims, and who were the perpetrators?

Until the issue became the subject of a heated debate in and outside of El Salvador towards the end of our investigation, it had certainly never occurred to me that the Report would not name names. On first reading the Commission's mandate, I concluded that one of our tasks was to identify those who had committed the serious acts of violence we were required to investigate. My colleagues, as I learned later, had reached the same conclusion. After all, the Parties to the Peace Accords wanted "the complete truth be made known." For that purpose, they empowered the Commission to investigate the "serious acts of violence that have occurred since 1980 and whose impact on society urgently demands that the public should know the truth." How could we make known "the complete truth" about a murder or massacre, for example, without identifying the killers if we knew their identity?

Of course, if the Parties had not wanted us to name names, they could easily have said so. However, the mandate for the Commission did not contain such a restriction. Moreover, our initial contacts with the Parties indicated that they assumed that we would identify individuals responsible for serious acts of violence. The government representatives, including President Alfredo Cristiani and members of the Military High Command, told us repeatedly during our initial visits to El Salvador that our task was to identify the "rotten apples" within the "Institution." The Institution itself had to be protected. The government representatives told us: "Individuals and not the Institution were responsible for the violations that the government side had committed." The FMLN also repeatedly made it clear that the guilty had to be identified. Of course, neither side expected our investigation to be very thorough or to contain much evidence implicating the "big fish."

The attitude of the government began to change dramatically as it became known that the Commission had gathered incriminating evidence against high-ranking government officials, particularly General Rene Emilio Ponce, the Minister of Defense, and General Juan Orland Zepeda, his Vice Minister, as well as other officers comprising the military establishment. Although many of the same officers had already been named by the Ad Hoc Commission, that body had merely prepared a list without specifying the offenses committed. On the other hand, the Truth Commission was going to present evidence and make public its Report, which posed a much more serious threat. Moreover, some of the officers, particularly General Ponce, had been instrumental in convincing his military colleagues to go along with the Peace Accords. He was not only the highest ranking military officer in El Salvador, but also the undisputed leader of his tanda, which was known as the tandona because it was the largest class ever to graduate from the military academy. The tandona controlled the military establishment. Most, if not all, brigade commanders were members of the tandona. Together, they had the power to make life very difficult for President Cristiani and to impede, if not scuttle, his efforts to proceed with the implementation of the Peace Accords.

The power and influence of the tandona, rumors that "naming names" would lead to a military coup in El Salvador, and claims by many well intentioned individuals in El Salvador and outside the country that the publication of names by the Truth Commission would make national reconciliation very difficult-that it would be like pouring gasoline on a smoldering fire-prompted the government to mount a fierce diplomatic campaign to force us to omit names from the Report. President Cristiani led the campaign by urging various Latin American leaders, the United States, and the UN Secretary–General to use their power and influence to prevent the publication of names. He also sent a ministerial delegation to meet with us in New York for the same purpose. The arguments against publication ranged from the danger to the peace process and national reconciliation, to intimations of imminent coups, and claims of the government's inability to prevent retaliation against those who provided information to the Commission. The government also attempted to convince the FMLN to agree with its position. The FMLN and the government together, as the Parties to the Peace Accords, presumably had it in their power to amend the Commission's mandate and to require us not to publish any names. Some in the FMLN leadership were quite sympathetic to this effort and implied as much in conversations with us; a majority was opposed. Eventually, after a lengthy and apparently acrimonious debate within the FMLN high command, the FMLN informed the Commission that the Peace Accords required the publication of names.

The diplomatic campaign mounted by the Salvadoran government against the publication of names by the Truth Commission made it necessary for the Commissioners to explain our position to government leaders in the United States, Europe, and Latin America who were being lobbied by the Salvadorans. The fact that one Commissioner was a former President of Colombia and another a former Foreign Minister of Venezuela gave us easy access to these foreign leaders. The Commission's stature also established the requisite credibility to explain why we believed that our mandate required us to name names and why in our judgment this action would promote rather than impede national reconciliation in El Salvador. It should be noted, in this connection, that all three of us were unanimous on this subject and never doubted that, unless both Parties decided to amend our mandate, we were legally and morally obliged to identify those we found to be guilty of the serious abuses we had been investigating. In the Report, we explained our decision as follows:

In the peace agreements, the Parties made it quite clear that it was necessary that the "complete truth be made known," and that was why the Commission was established. Now, the whole truth cannot be told without naming names. After all, the Commission was not asked to write an academic report on El Salvador, it was asked to investigate and describe exceptionally important acts of violence and to recommend measures to prevent the repetition of such acts. This task cannot be performed in the abstract, suppressing information (for example, the names of person responsible for such acts) where there is reliable testimony available, especially when the persons identified continue to occupy senior positions and perform official functions directly related to the violations or the cover-up of violations. Not to name names would be to reinforce the very impunity to which the Parties instructed the Commission to put an end.

It should also be pointed out that in El Salvador, unlike in some other countries with similar histories, it was known for the most part which side to the conflict had committed what acts and who the victims were. What was often not generally known and what engendered acrimonious debates was who committed the acts and who ordered them to be committed. The search for the "intellectual authors" of these offenses was a national obsession. Many of the intellectual authors were still holding influential positions. To refrain from exposing them would have amounted to yet another cover-up. In our view, national reconciliation would be harmed rather than helped by a Commission report that told only part of the truth. If there had been an effective justice system in El Salvador at the time of the publication of our Report, it could have used the Report as a basis for an independent investigation of those guilty of the violations. In these circumstances, it might have made some sense for the Commission not to publish the names and, instead, to transmit the relevant information to the police or courts for appropriate action. But one reason for establishing the Commission was that the Parties to the Peace Accords knew, and the Truth Commission had ample evidence to confirm, that the Salvadoran justice system was corrupt, ineffective, and incapable of rendering impartial judgments in so-called "political" cases.

We were also told to heed President Cristiani's warnings—that he knew the dangers facing his country and that the release of names would undermine national reconciliation. Those were the arguments made by his emissaries in various nations' capitals. Of course, we had high regard for President Cristiani—without his imaginative leadership the Peace Accords would never have been signed—and we certainly could not claim to know his country better than he did. But it was also public knowledge that he was under great pressure, including thinly veiled threats against him personally from the tandona, which wanted to protect its members. We were convinced, moreover, that the failure of the Truth Commission to produce an honest report would seriously undermine the peace process. The fact that the publication of the Report with names did not produce all the dire consequences prophesied by those who wanted us to leave them out would suggest that we were right in not caving in to the pressures to which we were subjected. * * *

The discussion relating to the Commission's mandate deals, among other things, with the "applicable law." Here the Commission addressed the fact that its mandate is silent on the question of the legal norms to be applied in determining what is meant by the "serious acts of violence" it was to investigate. Not all acts of violence committed in the civil war, however serious in terms of loss of life or limb, could be deemed to fall within that definition; in war as in peace there are legitimate and illegitimate, lawful and unlawful, uses of force that cause serious harm. Hence, despite the fact that its mandate did not spell out the applicable legal norms, the Commission concluded that "the concept of serious acts of violence * * * does not exist in a normative vacuum and must therefore be analyzed on the basis of certain relevant principles of law."

In the Commission's opinion, the legal principles that defined the scope of its mandate were to be found in those rules of international human rights law and international humanitarian law binding on the state of El Salvador, its government, and the insurgents seeking to defeat it. As far as human rights law was concerned, the Commission emphasized that El Salvador had assumed various human rights obligations as a member of both the United Nations and the Organization of American States. Additionally, it had obligations as a state party to the International Covenant on Civil and Political Rights and the American Convention on Human Rights. These treaties entered into force for El Salvador before 1980 and therefore were applicable during the entire conflict. As both treaties prohibit the suspension of certain fundamental rights, such as the right to life and the right not to be tortured, even in time of war or national emergency, their provisions were relevant to the Salvadoran conflict and needed to be taken into account by the Commission in discharging its responsibilities.

It is interesting to note, in this connection, that in analyzing the relevance of international human rights law to the task assigned to it, the Commission reached the following conclusion, among others:

> It is true that, in theory, international human rights law is applicable only to Governments, while in some armed conflicts international humanitarian law is binding on both sides: in other words, binding on both insurgents and Government forces. However, it must be recognized that when insurgents assume government powers in territories under their control, they too can be required to observe certain human rights obligations that are binding on the State under international law.

Because the FMLN claimed to control some regions of El Salvador, the Commission determined that in those areas the FMLN, as the de facto governing authority, was under a legal obligation not to violate those basic international human rights that were binding on the state of El Salvador even under the prevailing emergency conditions. Holding insurgent forces responsible for violations of human rights under these circumstances is an important precedent that might be applied to other internal armed conflicts.

The international humanitarian law provisions that the Commission found applicable to the Salvadoran conflict were Article 3, common to the four Geneva Conventions of 1949, and Additional Protocol II of the Geneva Conventions. These instruments had been ratified by El Salvador before 1980 and applied to non-international armed conflicts. These treaties, together with the international human rights instruments referred to above, provided the Commission with the normative standards it needed to be in a position to assess the legitimacy and legality of the serious acts of violence that had been committed by both sides to the Salvadoran conflict. Despite the fact that the Commission was not a court, it had to draw on these legal principles to determine what cases and facts to investigate, how to evaluate the evidence, and what findings and recommendations to make. * * *

A few days after the publication of the Report, the government of President Cristiani and the national legislature controlled by his party granted an across-the-board amnesty to all individuals charged with serious acts of violence. This measure did not, however, nullify the Commission's work or have a serious effect on it. The amnesty merely prevented those identified by the Commission as responsible for acts of violence from being tried in Salvadoran courts and resulted in the release from prison of a few others who had been convicted earlier in that country on similar charges. Since the Commission did not recommend the trial of those it named, the amnesty cannot be said to violate its recommendations. However, while amnesties after a civil war may be a legitimate way to put an end to the conflict, the manner in which this amnesty was rushed through the Salvadoran legislature-a legislature in which the FMLN was not represented-with no time or opportunity for a full national debate on the subject, was unseemly at the very least, indicative of a lack of respect for democratic processes, and thus incompatible with the spirit of the Peace Accords. It should be emphasized, however, that the amnesty did not affect the Commission's recommendations or override those calling for the dismissal from their positions of individuals named in the Report. Particularly noteworthy in this connection is the fact that all military officers identified by the Commission were retired from the service not long after the Report was issued. * * *

Of course, the Truth Commission cannot take credit for all the progress that has been made in El Salvador, nor should it be blamed for the slow pace with which the country has moved to transform itself into a modern democratic state. The real contribution of the Truth Commission is at once more profound and much less concrete. The release of the Report had a very significant psychological impact on the people of El Salvador. While the Peace Accords ended the armed conflict, the Report put the country on the road to healing the emotional wounds that had continued to divide it. The Report told the truth in a country that was not accustomed to hearing it. To be restored to normalcy, El Salvador needed to hear the truth from a source that had legitimacy and credibility. The Commission met this standard and performed its functions in a way that achieved this objective.

The war in El Salvador not only pitted the combatants in the armed conflict against each other, but also totally polarized the population. It became a country in which there was no room for moderation or tolerance for peaceful political debate. Political opponents were treated as enemies and acts of violence against them rationalized as necessary or denied as propaganda. Political allegiance rather than basic human decency determined one's actions and reactions to the crimes that both sides committed. El Salvador was a country in which many lived in fear, and where few wished to know the truth. In this atmosphere the victims or their next of kin often did not dare to denounce publicly what had been done to them or even speak about it lest their claims expose them to further abuse. People kept their suffering to themselves, hoping for justice-a very human instinct-but not really expecting it.

The efforts of the Truth Commission to get at the truth and the release of its Report had a cathartic impact on the country. Many of the people who came to the Commission to tell what happened to them or to their relatives and friends had not done so before. For some, ten years or more had gone by in silence and pent-up anger. Finally, someone listened to them, and there would be a record of what they had endured. They came by the thousands, still afraid and not a little skeptical, and they talked, many for the first time. One could not listen to them without recognizing that the mere act of telling what had happened was a healing emotional release, and that they were more interested in recounting their story and being heard than in retribution. It is as if they felt some shame that they had not dared to speak out before and, now that they had done so, they could go home and focus on the future less encumbered by the past.

A particularly telling interview described by a Commission staff member involved two mothers, one Salvadoran, the other Scandinavian, who came to the Commission together to tell their story. The son of one and the daughter of the other had met in Europe and fallen in love. The couple traveled to El Salvador, became involved in leftist activities and were murdered by rightist death squads. The two mothers had not met until they decided to tell their story together to the Truth Commission. They could barely speak a common language, but they appeared in the Commission's offices in San Salvador, sharing their grief and honoring the memory of their children by telling the story of these two young people.

The Report and its findings about many cases that had encumbered the nation's conscience had a dramatic effect. The findings confirmed what many suspected, some knew, and others refused to believe. Before the release of the Report, few Salvadorans knew the whole story and many more could not separate the truth from the lies and rumors that were rampant even after the signing of the Peace Accords. The result was a never-ending acrimonious debate and the exchange of inflammatory charges and counter-charges by the former combatants and their allies. The Report put an end to this debate, and thus allowed the country to focus on the future rather than on the cruel and divisive past. It removed the biggest obstacle on the way to national reconciliation: the denial of a terrible truth that divided the nation and haunted its consciousness.

How and why did the Commission succeed in bringing about this result? Much of it had to do with the credibility the Commission was able to establish for itself. Here the Commissioners were convinced from the outset that we had to achieve two objectives. First, we had to come up with a fact-finding process that inspired confidence in the sense that the public was convinced-it had to see-that the Commission really wanted to know and tell the truth. Second, we had to do everything in our power to ensure that the truth of our findings could not be impugned. If our Report were found to contain many inaccuracies, no matter how insignificant, this would undermine confidence in all of its findings. That would have been the case too if the Commission were to do or say things that demonstrated a bias in favor of one side or the other.

It would appear that the Commission met the credibility test. We were criticized, of course, particularly by some who were named in the Report. However, there were no serious allegations of factual error. That so many people came forward with their testimonies suggests that the Commissioners gradually gained the confidence of the population and that after a while people no longer assumed the investigation to be rigged. A number of factors helped the Commission to gain the trust of the Salvadoran population, including: our "open door" policy of inviting testimony from anyone having information, our nation wide publicity campaigns urging the public to come forward, our young staff members who radiated a genuine commitment to their task and empathy for the victims, and finally, the public and private pronouncements of the Commissioners.

Not naming names would not necessarily have affected our credibility had the Commission's mandate expressly denied us that power, for then the failure to name names could not have been blamed on our lack of integrity. The situation would have been different, however, if no individual perpetrators were identified despite the fact that we had the power to do so and had raised expectations during our investigation that names would be made public. Here, confidence in the personal integrity of the Commissioners would have been shaken because of a perception that we were giving in to political pressure.

It was also important that the people named in the Report were not only the "small fry." Some very "big fish" were identified, proving what many in El Salvador thought impossible, namely, that the veil of impunity had finally been pierced. True, there were other big fish who escaped our net, among them the financiers of death squads and some FMLN commanders who were alleged to have committed serious acts of violence. But to have named individuals when the evidence was not convincing would have been terribly unjust and an abuse of our power. It also carried with it the risk that our findings would be proven to contain serious errors, thus affecting the credibility of the Report as a whole. Here the best we could do was hope that the people of El Salvador, after evaluating the Report as a whole, would have to recognize that we did not act out of some improper motive. * * *

My experience on the Truth Commission has convinced me that the most important function such a body can perform is to tell the truth. That may sound obvious and trite, but it needs to be said because it has tended to get lost in the discussion about national reconciliation. The assumption that bringing out the truth will rub salt into the nation's wounds and make national reconciliation more difficult to achieve has a certain superficial logic to it, but it is wrong in my opinion. A nation has to confront its past by acknowledging the wrongs that have been committed in its name before it can successfully embark on the arduous task of cementing the trust between former adversaries and their respective sympathizers, which is a prerequisite for national reconciliation. One cannot hope to achieve this objective by sweeping the truth under the rug of national consciousness, by telling the victims or their next of kin that nothing happened, or by asking them not to tell their particular story. The wounds begin to heal with the telling of the story and the national acknowledgment of its authenticity.

How that story is told is less important than that it be told truthfully. Hence, whether the names of the perpetrators are revealed, whether trials are held, sanctions imposed, compensation awarded, or amnesties granted, these are all considerations that may well depend upon the nature of the conflict, the national character of the country, the political realities, and compromises that produced the end of the conflict. But if the basic truth about the past is suppressed, it will prove very difficult to achieve national reconciliation. The wounds left behind by the past will continue to fester and endanger the peace. The truth may be strong medicine, but there is, in my opinion, no other way if the goal is to bring together a people divided by a civil war or a murderous regime.

Notes and Questions on the El Salvador Truth Commission

1. *What law to apply?* In considering how to define "serious acts of violence," the Truth Commission for El Salvador focused exclusively on international human rights and humanitarian law as sources of law. It is difficult to believe that the serious acts of violence committed during El Salvador's civil war didn't also violate domestic law. What advantage was gained by focusing on El Salvador's international obligations, instead of on its domestic law? Do you think this decision had an impact on the Commission's credibility within El Salvador?

2. *Addressing non-state actors.* In its report the El Salvador Truth Commission concluded, "it must be recognized that when insurgents assume government powers in territories under their control, they too can be required to observe certain human rights obligations that are binding on the State under international law." This legal conclusion allowed the Commission to apply the same international human rights standards to the activities of the FLMN as it did to the Salvadorian government. Some would argue such a conclusion is fraught with ambiguity: What level of control by insurgents over a territory is necessary? Which human rights obligations would be binding on the insurgent group? What are the consequences of this conclusion for the development of international human rights law?

3. *Juridical functions.* In reviewing the materials related to the El Salvador Truth Commission, it should be clear that the commission was not intended to act as a judicial body; nevertheless, it reviewed documentary evidence, considered the testimony of witnesses, and reached legal conclusions based on the evidence before it. This quasi-legal function could raise due process concerns, especially in light of the fact that the Commission chose to identify individuals responsible for human rights violations. How might such due process considerations be addressed? Which due process protections are most important to ensure the preservation of the rights of those persons who might be implicated in human rights violations? In *Romagoza v. Garcia*, No. 99–8364 (S.D. Fla., filed Feb. 18, 2000), a case filed in the U.S. District Court for the Southern District of Florida under the Alien Tort Statute, a jury awarded three plaintiffs $54.6 million for injuries resulting from torture committed by the Salvadoran military during El Salvador's civil war. *See Arce v. Garcia*, 434 F.3d 1254 (11th Cir. 2006). During the trial, the District Court allowed plaintiffs to rely on the report prepared by the Truth Commission for El Salvador. Does this affect your responses to the questions regarding due process? What protections should be incorporated into the mandate of a truth commission to ensure the reliability of evidence sufficient to allow the use of evidence in civil cases against human rights violators? In reviewing the standards applied by the Commission identified above, would you consider evidence cited in the report sufficiently reliable for purposes of such a case? What if the

Report had been relied on for a criminal prosecution rather than civil prosecution?

4. *Naming names.* Note the controversy reported by Buergenthal over the issue of whether individuals responsible for human rights violations would be named in the report of the Truth Commission for El Salvador. By contrast, the 1994 agreement that established a Commission to clarify past human rights violations and acts of violence in Guatemala specifically mandated that "The Commission shall not attribute responsibility to any individual in its work, recommendations and report nor shall these have any judicial aim and effect." *See* Agreement on the Establishment of the Commission to Clarify Past Human Rights Violations and Acts of Violence that Have Caused the Guatemalan Population to Suffer, June 23, 1994, *available at* http://www.usip.org/library/pa/guatemala/guat_940623.html. One might be led to assume that the troubles caused by naming names during the El Salvador experience caused those negotiating the Guatemala agreement to avoid the controversy created by specifically identifying human rights abusers. If the purpose of a truth commission is to "establish the truth" as Minow asserts, can this goal be accomplished without naming names? On the other hand, after the El Salvador report was released, the government issued a blanket amnesty for all those identified by the Truth Commission. In your estimation, what factors—historical, cultural, social—would justify either course of action?

In the case of Guatemala, the truth commission's report was subsequently used as supporting evidence in a lawsuit filed against General Efrain Rios Montt. *See* Catherine Elton, *Guatemalan Massacre Survivors Seek Former President's Trial*, CHRISTIAN SCIENCE MONITOR, June 14, 2001, at 8 (detailing suit against Efrain Rios Montt brought by Mayan survivors of genocide campaign).

5. *UN Principles.* In 1997, the UN Sub–Commission on the Prevention of Discrimination and Protection of Minorities adopted a "Set of Principles for the Protection and Promotion of Human Rights Through Action to Combat Impunity." *See* UN Doc. E/CN.4/Sub.2/1997/20. The principles are intended to provide guidance for establishing extra-judicial commissions of truth or inquiry, focusing on three essential rights of victims: the right to know, the right to justice, and the right to reparations. Consider these principles in light of the goals of a truth commission as identified by Minow above. How might they advance this goal? In what ways may they present an obstacle? Equally important, is it advisable, or even possible, to take a one-size-fits-all approach to creating truth commissions? *See, e.g.,* Michael P. Scharf, *The Case for a Permanent International Truth Commission*, 7 DUKE J. COMP. & INT'L L. 375 (1997).

2. THE CHALLENGE OF IMMUNITY

AZANIAN PEOPLES ORG. v. THE PRES. OF THE REP. OF SOUTH AFRICA

1996 SACLR LEXIS 20 (South African Constitutional Court, 1996)

1. For decades South African history has been dominated by a deep conflict between a minority which reserved for itself all control over the political instruments of the state and a majority who sought to resist that domination. Fundamental human rights became a major casualty of this conflict as the resistance of those punished by their denial was met by laws designed to counter the effectiveness of such resistance.

The conflict deepened with the increased sophistication of the economy, the rapid acceleration of knowledge and education and the ever increasing hostility of an international community steadily outraged by the inconsistency which had become manifest between its own articulated ideals after the Second World War and the official practices which had become institutionalised in South Africa through laws enacted to give them sanction and teeth by a Parliament elected only by a privileged minority. The result was a debilitating war of internal political dissension and confrontation, massive expressions of labour militancy, perennial student unrest, punishing international economic isolation, widespread dislocation in crucial areas of national endeavour, accelerated levels of armed conflict and a dangerous combination of anxiety, frustration and anger among expanding proportions of the populace. The legitimacy of law itself was deeply wounded as the country haemorrhaged dangerously in the face of this tragic conflict which had begun to traumatise the entire nation.

2. During the eighties it became manifest to all that our country with all its natural wealth, physical beauty and human resources was on a disaster course unless that conflict was reversed. It was this realisation which mercifully rescued us in the early nineties as those who controlled the levers of state power began to negotiate a different future with those who had been imprisoned, silenced, or driven into exile in consequence of their resistance to that control and its consequences. Those negotiations resulted in an interim Constitution committed to a transition towards a more just, defensible and democratic political order based on the protection of fundamental human rights. It was wisely appreciated by those involved in the preceding negotiations that the task of building such a new democratic order was a very difficult task because of the previous history and the deep emotions and indefensible inequities it had generated; and that this could not be achieved without a firm and generous commitment to reconciliation and national unity. It was realised that much of the unjust consequences of the past could not ever be fully reversed. It might be necessary in crucial areas to close the book on that past.

3. This fundamental philosophy is eloquently expressed in the epilogue to the Constitution which reads as follows:

National Unity and Reconciliation

This Constitution provides a historic bridge between the past of a deeply divided society characterised by strife, conflict, untold suffering and injustice, and a future founded on the recognition of human rights, democracy and peaceful co-existence and development opportunities for all South Africans, irrespective of colour, race, class, belief or sex.

The pursuit of national unity, the well-being of all South African citizens and peace require reconciliation between the people of South Africa and the reconstruction of society.

The adoption of this Constitution lays the secure foundation for the people of South Africa to transcend the divisions and strife of the past, which generated gross violations of human rights, the transgression of humanitarian principles in violent conflicts and a legacy of hatred, fear, guilt and revenge.

These can now be addressed on the basis that there is a need for understanding but not for vengeance, a need for reparation but not for retaliation, a need for ubuntu but not for victimisation. In order to advance such reconciliation and reconstruction, amnesty shall be granted in respect of acts, omissions and offences associated with political objectives and committed in the course of the conflicts of the past. To this end, Parliament under this Constitution shall adopt a law determining a firm cut-off date, which shall be a date after 8 October 1990 and before 6 December 1993, and providing for the mechanisms, criteria and procedures, including tribunals, if any, through which such amnesty shall be dealt with at any time after the law has been passed.

With this Constitution and these commitments we, the people of South Africa, open a new chapter in the history of our country.

Pursuant to the provisions of the epilogue, Parliament enacted during 1995 what is colloquially referred to as the Truth and Reconciliation Act. Its proper name is the Promotion of National Unity and Reconciliation Act 34 of 1995 ("the Act").

4. The Act establishes a Truth and Reconciliation Commission. The objectives of that Commission are set out in section 3. Its main objective is to "promote national unity and reconciliation in a spirit of understanding which transcends the conflicts and divisions of the past". It is enjoined to pursue that objective by "establishing as complete a picture as possible of the causes, nature and extent of the gross violations of human rights" committed during the period commencing 1 March 1960 to the "cut-off date". For this purpose the Commission is obliged to have regard to "the perspectives of the victims and the

motives and perspectives of the persons responsible for the commission of the violations". It also is required to facilitate

> " ... the granting of amnesty to persons who make full disclosure of all the relevant facts relating to acts associated with a political objective ... "

The Commission is further entrusted with the duty to establish and to make known "the fate or whereabouts of victims" and of "restoring the human and civil dignity of such victims" by affording them an opportunity to relate their own accounts of the violations and by recommending "reparation measures" in respect of such violations and finally to compile a comprehensive report in respect of its functions, including the recommendation of measures to prevent the violation of human rights.

5.   Three committees are established for the purpose of achieving the objectives of the Commission. The first committee is the Committee on Human Rights Violations which conducts enquiries pertaining to gross violations of human rights during the prescribed period, with extensive powers to gather and receive evidence and information. The second committee is the Committee on Reparation and Rehabilitation which is given similar powers to gather information and receive evidence for the purposes of ultimately recommending to the President suitable reparations for victims of gross violations of human rights. The third and the most directly relevant committee for the purposes of the present dispute is the Committee on Amnesty. This is a committee which must consist of five persons of which the chairperson must be a judge. The Committee on Amnesty is given elaborate powers to consider applications for amnesty. The Committee has the power to grant amnesty in respect of any act, omission or offence to which the particular application for amnesty relates, provided that the applicant concerned has made a full disclosure of all relevant facts and provided further that the relevant act, omission or offence is associated with a political objective committed in the course of the conflicts of the past. * * * [S]ection 20(7) [of the Act] (the constitutionality of which is impugned in these proceedings) provides as follows:

> (7)(a) No person who has been granted amnesty in respect of an act, omission or offence shall be criminally or civilly liable in respect of such act, omission or offence and no body or organisation or the State shall be liable, and no person shall be vicariously liable, for any such act, omission or offence.

> (b) Where amnesty is granted to any person in respect of any act, omission or offence, such amnesty shall have no influence upon the criminal liability of any other person contingent upon the liability of the first-mentioned person.

> (c) No person, organisation or state shall be civilly or vicariously liable for an act, omission or offence committed between 1 March 1960 and the cut-off date by a person who is deceased, unless

amnesty could not have been granted in terms of this Act in respect of such an act, omission or offence. * * *

8.   The applicants sought in this court to attack the constitutionality of section 20(7) on the grounds that its consequences are not authorised by the Constitution. They aver that various agents of the state, acting within the scope and in the course of their employment, have unlawfully murdered and maimed leading activists during the conflict against the racial policies of the previous administration and that the applicants have a clear right to insist that such wrongdoers should properly be prosecuted and punished, that they should be ordered by the ordinary courts of the land to pay adequate civil compensation to the victims or dependants of the victims and further to require the state to make good to such victims or dependants the serious losses which they have suffered in consequence of the criminal and delictual acts of the employees of the state. In support of that attack Mr. Soggot, who appeared for the applicants together with Mr. Khoza, contended that section 20(7) was inconsistent with section 22 of the Constitution which provides that

> "[e]very person shall have the right to have justiciable disputes settled by a court of law or, where appropriate, another independent or impartial forum."

He submitted that the Amnesty Committee was neither "a court of law" nor an "independent or impartial forum" and that in any event the Committee was not authorised to settle "justiciable disputes." All it was simply required to decide was whether amnesty should be granted in respect of a particular act, omission or offence.

9.   The effect of an amnesty undoubtedly impacts upon very fundamental rights. All persons are entitled to the protection of the law against unlawful invasions of their right to life, their right to respect for and protection of dignity and their right not to be subject to torture of any kind. When those rights are invaded those aggrieved by such invasion have the right to obtain redress in the ordinary courts of law and those guilty of perpetrating such violations are answerable before such courts, both civilly and criminally. An amnesty to the wrongdoer effectively obliterates such rights.

10.   There would therefore be very considerable force in the submission that section 20(7) of the Act constitutes a violation of section 22 of the Constitution, if there was nothing in the Constitution itself which permitted or authorised such violation. The crucial issue, therefore, which needs to be determined, is whether the Constitution, indeed, permits such a course. Section 33(2) of the Constitution provides that

> "[s]ave as provided for in subsection (1) or any other provision of this Constitution, no law, whether a rule of common law, customary law or legislation, shall limit any right entrenched in this Chapter."

Two questions arise from the provisions of this sub-section. The first question is whether there is "any other provision in this Constitution" which permits a limitation of the right in section 22 and secondly if there is not, whether any violation of section 22 is a limitation which can be justified in terms of section 33(1) of the Constitution which reads as follows:

> "The rights entrenched in this Chapter may be limited by law of general application, provided that such limitation—
>
> (a) shall be permissible only to the extent that it is–
>
> (i) reasonable; and
>
> (ii) justifiable in an open and democratic society based on freedom and equality; and
>
> (b) shall not negate the essential content of the right in question, and provided further that any limitation to–
>
> (aa) a right entrenched in section 10, 11, 12, 14(1), 21, 25 or 30(1)(d) or (e) or (2); or
>
> (bb) a right entrenched in section 15, 16, 17, 18, 23 or 24, in so far as such right relates to free and fair political activity, shall, in addition to being reasonable as required in paragraph (a)(i), also be necessary."

11. Mr. Marcus, who together with Mr. D. Leibowitz appeared for the Respondents, contended that the epilogue, which I have previously quoted, is indeed a "provision of this Constitution" within the meaning of section 33(2). He argued that any law conferring amnesty on a wrongdoer in respect of acts, omissions and offences associated with political objectives and committed during the prescribed period, is therefore a law properly authorised by the Constitution.

12. It is therefore necessary to deal, in the first place, with the constitutional status of the epilogue. * * *

14. What is clear is that Parliament not only has the authority in terms of the epilogue to make a law providing for amnesty to be granted in respect of the acts, omissions and offences falling within the category defined therein but that it is in fact obliged to do so. This follows from the wording in the material part of the epilogue which is that "Parliament under this Constitution shall adopt a law" providing, *inter alia*, for the "mechanisms, criteria and procedures ... through which ... amnesty shall be dealt with".

15. It was contended that even if this is the proper interpretation of the status of the epilogue and even if the principle of "amnesty" is authorised by the Constitution, it does not authorise, in particular, the far-reaching amnesty which section 20(7) allows * * * and that Parliament had no constitutional power to authorise the Amnesty Committee to indemnify any wrongdoer either against criminal or civil liability arising from the perpetration of acts falling within the categories described in the legislation. * * *

Amnesty in respect of criminal liability

16.   I understand perfectly why the applicants would want to insist that those wrongdoers who abused their authority and wrongfully murdered, maimed or tortured very much loved members of their families who had, in their view, been engaged in a noble struggle to confront the inhumanity of apartheid, should vigorously be prosecuted and effectively be punished for their callous and inhuman conduct in violation of the criminal law. * * *

17.   Every decent human being must feel grave discomfort in living with a consequence which might allow the perpetrators of evil acts to walk the streets of this land with impunity, protected in their freedom by an amnesty immune from constitutional attack, but the circumstances in support of this course require carefully to be appreciated [*sic*]. Most of the acts of brutality and torture which have taken place have occurred during an era in which neither the laws which permitted the incarceration of persons or the investigation of crimes, nor the methods and the culture which informed such investigations, were easily open to public investigation, verification and correction. Much of what transpired in this shameful period is shrouded in secrecy and not easily capable of objective demonstration and proof. Loved ones have disappeared, sometimes mysteriously and most of them no longer survive to tell their tales. Others have had their freedom invaded, their dignity assaulted or their reputations tarnished by grossly unfair imputations hurled in the fire and the cross-fire of a deep and wounding conflict. The wicked and the innocent have often both been victims. Secrecy and authoritarianism have concealed the truth in little crevices of obscurity in our history. Records are not easily accessible, witnesses are often unknown, dead, unavailable or unwilling. All that often effectively remains is the truth of wounded memories of loved ones sharing instinctive suspicions, deep and traumatising to the survivors but otherwise incapable of translating themselves into objective and corroborative evidence which could survive the rigours of the law. The Act seeks to address this massive problem by encouraging these survivors and the dependants of the tortured and the wounded, the maimed and the dead to unburden their grief publicly, to receive the collective recognition of a new nation that they were wronged, and crucially, to help them to discover what did in truth happen to their loved ones, where and under what circumstances it did happen, and who was responsible. That truth, which the victims of repression seek so desperately to know is, in the circumstances, much more likely to be forthcoming if those responsible for such monstrous misdeeds are encouraged to disclose the whole truth with the incentive that they will not receive the punishment which they undoubtedly deserve if they do. Without that incentive there is nothing to encourage such persons to make the disclosures and to reveal the truth which persons in the positions of the applicants so desperately desire. With that incentive, what might unfold are objectives fundamental to the ethos of a new constitutional order. The families of those unlawfully

tortured, maimed or traumatised become more empowered to discover the truth, the perpetrators become exposed to opportunities to obtain relief from the burden of a guilt or an anxiety they might be living with for many long years, the country begins the long and necessary process of healing the wounds of the past, transforming anger and grief into a mature understanding and creating the emotional and structural climate essential for the "reconciliation and reconstruction" which informs the very difficult and sometimes painful objectives of the amnesty articulated in the epilogue.

18.   The alternative to the grant of immunity from criminal prosecution of offenders is to keep intact the abstract right to such a prosecution for particular persons without the evidence to sustain the prosecution successfully, to continue to keep the dependants of such victims in many cases substantially ignorant about what precisely happened to their loved ones, to leave their yearning for the truth effectively unassuaged, to perpetuate their legitimate sense of resentment and grief and correspondingly to allow the culprits of such deeds to remain perhaps physically free but inhibited in their capacity to become active, full and creative members of the new order by a menacing combination of confused fear, guilt, uncertainty and sometimes even trepidation. Both the victims and the culprits who walk on the "historic bridge" described by the epilogue will hobble more than walk to the future with heavy and dragged steps delaying and impeding a rapid and enthusiastic transition to the new society at the end of the bridge, which is the vision which informs the epilogue.

19.   Even more crucially, but for a mechanism providing for amnesty, the "historic bridge" itself might never have been erected. For a successfully negotiated transition, the terms of the transition required not only the agreement of those victimized by abuse but also those threatened by the transition to a "democratic society based on freedom and equality." If the Constitution kept alive the prospect of continuous retaliation and revenge, the agreement of those threatened by its implementation might never have been forthcoming, and if it had, the bridge itself would have remained wobbly and insecure, threatened by fear from some and anger from others. It was for this reason that those who negotiated the Constitution made a deliberate choice, preferring understanding over vengeance, reparation over retaliation, ubuntu over victimisation.

20.   Is section 20(7), to the extent to which it immunizes wrongdoers from criminal prosecution, nevertheless objectionable on the grounds that amnesty might be provided in circumstances where the victims, or the dependants of the victims, have not had the compensatory benefit of discovering the truth at last or in circumstances where those whose misdeeds are so obscenely excessive as to justify punishment, even if they were perpetrated with a political objective during the course of conflict in the past? Some answers to such difficulties are provided in the sub-sections of section 20. The Amnesty Committee may

grant amnesty in respect of the relevant offence only if the perpetrator of the misdeed makes a full disclosure of all relevant facts. If the offender does not, and in consequence thereof the victim or his or her family is not able to discover the truth, the application for amnesty will fail. Moreover, it will not suffice for the offender merely to say that his or her act was associated with a political objective. That issue must independently be determined by the Amnesty Committee pursuant to the criteria set out in section 20(3), including the relationship between the offence committed and the political objective pursued and the directness and proximity of the relationship and the proportionality of the offence to the objective pursued.

21. The result, at all levels, is a difficult, sensitive, perhaps even agonising, balancing act between the need for justice to victims of past abuse and the need for reconciliation and rapid transition to a new future; between encouragement to wrongdoers to help in the discovery of the truth and the need for reparations for the victims of that truth; between a correction in the old and the creation of the new. It is an exercise of immense difficulty interacting in a vast network of political, emotional, ethical and logistical considerations. It is an act calling for a judgment falling substantially within the domain of those entrusted with lawmaking in the era preceding and during the transition period. The results may well often be imperfect and the pursuit of the act might inherently support the message of Kant that "out of the crooked timber of humanity no straight thing was ever made". There can be legitimate debate about the methods and the mechanisms chosen by the lawmaker to give effect to the difficult duty entrusted upon it in terms of the epilogue. We are not concerned with that debate or the wisdom of its choice of mechanisms but only with its constitutionality. That, for us, is the only relevant standard. Applying that standard, I am not satisfied that in providing for amnesty for those guilty of serious offences associated with political objectives and in defining the mechanisms through which and the manner in which such amnesty may be secured by such offenders, the lawmaker, in section 20(7), has offended any of the express or implied limitations on its powers in terms of the Constitution.* * *

33. Mr. Soggot submitted that chapter 3 of the Constitution, and more particularly section 22, conferred on every person the right to pursue, in the ordinary courts of the land or before independent tribunals, any claim which such person might have in civil law for the recovery of damages sustained by such a person in consequence of the unlawful delicts perpetrated by a wrongdoer. He contended that the Constitution did not authorise Parliament to make any law which would have the result of indemnifying (or otherwise rendering immune from liability) the perpetrator of any such delict against any claims made for damages suffered by the victim of such a delict. In support of that argument he suggested that the concept of "amnesty", referred to in the epilogue to the Constitution, was, at worst for the applicants, inherently

limited to immunity from criminal prosecutions. He contended that even if a wrongdoer who has received amnesty could plead such amnesty as a defence to a criminal prosecution, such amnesty could not be used as a shield to protect him or her from claims for delictual damages suffered by any person in consequence of the act or omission of the wrongdoer.

34.   There can be no doubt that in some contexts the word "amnesty" does bear the limited meaning contended for by counsel. Thus one of the meanings of amnesty referred to in The Oxford English Dictionary is " . . . a general overlooking or pardon of past offences, by the ruling authority" and in similar vein, Webster's Dictionary gives as the second meaning of amnesty "a deliberate overlooking, as of an offense." Wharton's Law Lexicon also refers to amnesty in the context by which crimes against the Government up to a certain date are so obliterated that they can never be brought into charge.

35.   I cannot, however, agree that the concept of amnesty is inherently to be limited to the absolution from criminal liability alone, regardless of the context and regardless of the circumstances. The word has no inherently fixed technical meaning. Its origin is to be found from the Greek concept of "amnestia" and it indicates what is described by Webster's Dictionary as "an act of oblivion". The degree of oblivion or obliteration must depend on the circumstances. It can, in certain circumstances, be confined to immunity from criminal prosecutions and in other circumstances be extended also to civil liability. * * *

37.   This conclusion appears to be fortified by the fact that what the epilogue directs is that

"amnesty shall be granted in respect of acts, omissions and offences . . .".

If the purpose was simply to provide mechanisms in terms of which wrongdoers could be protected from criminal prosecution in respect of offences committed by them, why would there be any need to refer also to "acts and omissions" in addition to offences? The word "offences" would have covered both acts and omissions in any event.

38.   In the result I am satisfied that section 20(7) is not open to constitutional challenge on the ground that it invades the right of a victim or his or her dependant to recover damages from a wrongdoer for unlawful acts perpetrated during the conflicts of the past. If there is any such invasion it is authorised and contemplated by the relevant parts of the epilogue. * * *

1. *Conclusion*

50.   In the result, I am satisfied that the epilogue to the Constitution authorised and contemplated an "amnesty" in its most comprehensive and generous meaning so as to enhance and optimise the prospects of facilitating the constitutional journey from the shame of the past to the promise of the future. Parliament was, therefore, entitled to enact

the Act in the terms which it did. This involved more choices apart from the choices I have previously identified. They could have chosen to insist that a comprehensive amnesty manifestly involved an inequality of sacrifice between the victims and the perpetrators of invasions into the fundamental rights of such victims and their families, and that, for this reason, the terms of the amnesty should leave intact the claims which some of these victims might have been able to pursue against those responsible for authorising, permitting or colluding in such acts, or they could have decided that this course would impede the pace, effectiveness and objectives of the transition with consequences substantially prejudicial for the people of a country facing, for the first time, the real prospect of enjoying, in the future, some of the human rights so unfairly denied to the generations which preceded them. They were entitled to choose the second course. They could conceivably have chosen to differentiate between the wrongful acts committed in defence of the old order and those committed in the resistance of it, or they could have chosen a comprehensive form of amnesty which did not make this distinction. Again they were entitled to make the latter choice. The choice of alternatives legitimately fell within the judgment of the lawmakers. The exercise of that choice does not, in my view, impact on its constitutionality. It follows from these reasons that section 20(7) of the Act is authorised by the Constitution itself and it is unnecessary to consider the relevance and effect of section 33(1) of the Constitution.

NOTES AND QUESTIONS ON AZAPO

1. *Azapo and the goals of a truth commission.* After reading the *Azapo* decision, in your view, how does the South African Truth and Reconciliation Commission measure up to meeting the twin goals of reconciliation and justice as described by Minow and Buergenthal in the previous readings? What is the South African Supreme Court's frame of reference for performing the balancing act between justice and reconciliation?

2. *A duty to prosecute?* Many have argued that the provision of amnesty, even for purposes of long-term reconciliation, is contrary to the general policy of ending impunity for violations of human rights. Indeed, some have argued under international law that governments have an affirmative duty to prosecute abusers. *See, e.g.,* Diane F. Orentlicher, *Settling Past Accounts: Duty to Prosecute Human Rights Violations of a Prior Regime*, 100 YALE L.J. 2537 (1991). By relying on a patchwork of customary and conventional law, Orentlicher argues that specific obligations exist to both investigate and prosecute those who are responsible for human rights violations, and that "a state's complete failure to punish repeated or notorious incidents of [torture, extra-legal killings, and forced disappearances] violates its obligations under customary international law." *Id.* at 2540. Under this theory, therefore, a grant of

immunity, such as that found constitutional in *Azapo*, constitutes a violation of a state's international obligations. Indeed, some have argued that the truth and reconciliation process chosen by South Africa is inconsistent with international law, in that persons guilty of torture and crimes against humanity were wrongly granted amnesty. *See, e.g.*, John Dugard, *Retrospective Justice: International Law and the South African Model*, *in* TRANSITIONAL JUSTICE AND THE RULE OF LAW IN NEW DEMOCRACIES 279 (James A. McAdams, ed. 1997).

Many decisions of the Inter–American Commission on Human Rights support this view. *See, e.g.*, *Chumbipuma Aguirre y Otros v. Peru (The Barrios Altos Case)* Inter–Am. Ct. H.R. Ser.C/No.75 (2001) (IACHR rejecting Peruvian amnesty decrees to Shining Path), *available at* http://www1.umn.edu/humanrts/cases/561–01.html; *Samuel Alfonso Catalan Lincoleo v. Chile*, Case 11.771, Inter–Am. C.H.R. Report No.61/01, OEA/ ser.L/V/II.111, doc. 20 (2000) (declaring that amnesties and statutes of limitations that purport to shield human rights abusers from prosecution and punishment are inconsistent with the American Convention); *Carmelo Soria Espinoza v Chile*, Case 11.725, Inter–Am. C.H.R., No. 133/99 (1999), (rejecting 1978 Chilean amnesty law); *Lucio Parada Cea, et. al. v El Salvador*, Case 10.480, Inter–Am. C.H.R., No. 1/99 (1999) (rejecting Salvadoran amnesty laws); *Hector Marcial and Garay Hermosilla et al.*, Case 10.843, Inter–Am. C.H.R. No. 36/96 (1996) (finding Chilean Amnesty Decree Law incompatible with American Convention); *Juan Meneses, Ricardo Lagos Salinas, Juan Alsina Hurtos, and Pedro Vergara Inostroza*, Cases 11.228, 11.229, 11.231, and 11.282, Inter–Am. C.H.R. No. 34/96 (1996) (same); *Monsignor Oscar Arnulfo Romero y Galdamez*, Case 11.481, Inter–Am. CHR No. 37/00 (2000) (same in El Salvador); *Arges Sequeira Mangas v. Nicaragua*, Case 11.218, Inter–Am. CHR No. 52/97 (1997) (same in Nicaragua).

On the other hand, there is a substantial argument that, depending on the context, amnesties are not necessarily inconsistent with international law. For instance, article 6(5) of Protocol II to the Geneva Conventions of 12 August 1949 states, "At the end of hostilities, the authorities in power shall endeavour to grant the broadest possible amnesty to persons who have participated in the armed conflict [.]" Moreover, principles of derogation, domestic statutes of limitations, and the defense of superior orders, may permit amnesties in the case of certain offenses. *See generally* IMPUNITY AND HUMAN RIGHTS IN INTERNATIONAL LAW AND PRACTICE, chapters 3–5 (Naomi Roht–Arriaza ed. 1995). Some have also concluded that alternatives to prosecution may actually meet the goals of prosecution better than prosecution itself. *See* Miriam J. Aukerman, *Extraordinary Evil, Ordinary Crime: A Framework for Understanding Transitional Justice*, 15 HARV. HUM. RTS. J. 39 (2002). When subjected to a broader, systemic analysis, prosecutions in a transitional society can fall short of the goals prosecutions are meant to achieve. They can be selective, limited and slow. They can fail to result in a conviction as a result of a lack of evidence, an insufficiently independent judiciary, or corruption in the government. Individual prosecutions are also designed to address individual, criminal conduct: they do not adequately address the widespread, systematic human rights atrocities that a transitional society has suffered. Arguably, therefore, international law should not be seen as restricting a transitional state's ability to develop a strategy that includes amnesties as a means to facilitating the state's transition to peace and, equally important, reconciliation. *See also* MARTHA MINOW, THE HOPE FOR HEALING: WHAT CAN TRUTH COMMISSIONS DO? TRUTH V. JUSTICE 253 (Robert I. Rotberg & Dennis Thompson eds., 2000). *See generally* Lorna McGregor, *Individual Accountability in South Africa: Cultural Optimum or Political Façade?* 95 AM. J. INT'L L. 32 (2001).

3. *The dangers of amnesties.* Of all the truth commissions created over the years, the South African Truth and Reconciliation Commission (TRC) has received the most publicity. Whether because of the widespread international interest in the dismantling of the system of apartheid or the ground-breaking nature of the Commission itself, the South African experience has been subjected to a great deal of international scrutiny and reflection. In some ways, the TRC was similar to other truth commissions, but it was fundamentally different in significant respects. The *Azapo* opinion above reflects one major difference–the TRC's broad power to grant amnesty to individual perpetrators. As noted by Priscilla Hayner, no other country has combined this quasi-judicial power with the investigative tasks of a truth commission. *See* Priscilla Hayner, *Same Species, Different Animal: How South Africa Compares to Truth Commissions Worldwide, in* LOOKING BACK, REACHING FORWARD: REFLECTIONS ON THE TRUTH AND RECONCILIATION COMMISSION OF SOUTH AFRICA 36 (Charles Villa–Vicencio & Wilhelm Verwoerd eds. 2000). Hayner also notes other distinguishing features of the South African TRC: the public nature of its proceedings; the intensive, year-long process that led to the crafting of its mandate; and the degree of emphasis it placed on reconciliation. *See id.* at 36–41.

What are the dangers of providing the power to grant individual amnesties to such a body? Are these dangers compounded or ameliorated by the other distinguishing factors of the TRC, namely its intensely public nature? Is this model easily replicated in other countries? If not, what are the factors that made it a success (or failure) in South Africa? Does the fact that the TRC was born out of a Constitution lend more legitimacy to the TRC's amnesty power? Not only has the TRC received the most publicity, but it spent more money than any other truth commission. Much of the time and resources were spent collecting and documenting statements. The TRC conducted hearings, completed document and field research, and set up an elaborate computer system to document victims' statements. Most truth commissions do not have such time and resources. If a commission lacks the resources of the South African TRC, how should it set priorities?

4. *Accountability vs. reconciliation.* How does one reconcile the apparent conflict between the twin needs of accountability and reconciliation in a society devastated by human rights atrocities? If the focus is placed solely on prosecutions, the people may not receive the full benefit

of a process that might more adequately establish the truth and allow them to more effectively make the transition to a new society. But, if the focus is only on reconciliation, known human rights abusers are left free to walk the streets. *See In the Company of the Enemy*, WASHINGTON POST, A16 (Aug. 7, 2003) (describing experiences of Argentineans who encounter amnestied military officers accused of human rights abuses living free among them).

Can prosecutions and truth commissions be compatible? How might the two approaches be utilized side-by-side in order to maximize the benefits of each? Consider the cases of Peru, Sierra Leone, Timor Leste and Bosnia & Herzegovina, which might be characterized as successful examples of the integration of the two approaches. *See* Laura A. Dickinson, *The Promise of Hybrid Courts*, 97 AM. J. INT'L L. 295 (2003); Elizabeth M. Evenson, *Note: Truth and Justice in Sierra Leone: Coordination between Commission and Court,* 104 COLUM. L. REV. 730 (2004).

5. *Apartheid and amnesty in U.S. courts.* In 2002, a number of American and South African lawyers filed suit under the Alien Tort Claims Act on behalf of a class of individuals alleged to have been injured during the South African apartheid regime from 1948 through 1993. The defendants included several multinational corporations that did business with the South African government during this time, including Citibank, General Motors, IBM, and ExxonMobil. The suit demanded damages for personal injuries that were inflicted on the plaintiffs through a variety of means during the apartheid era, ranging from torture to death squad attacks, on the theory that the defendants' actions caused the injuries by perpetuating the apartheid system. It also seeks a disgorgement of all the profits made by the defendants resulting from their business dealings with South Africa's apartheid regime.

Given the South African Supreme Court's decision in *Azapo*, if you were legal adviser to the South African President, what position would you have advised the government to take with regard to this legislation? What other factors might play a part in formulating the government's position? Will the U.S. civil case undermine the reconciliation process in South Africa? Should this play a part in a U.S. federal court's decision to allow the case to go forward? *See In re South African Apartheid Litigation,* 346 F.Supp.2d 538 (S.D.N.Y 2004) *rev'd in part, vacated in part, and remanded by Khulumani v. Barclay Nat. Bank Ltd.,* 504 F.3d 254 (2nd Cir. 2007).

Penuell Mpapa Maduna, then Minister of Justice and Constitutional Development of South Africa, commented that "[t]he Government of South Africa has said that these cases interfere with the policy embodied by its Truth and Reconciliation Commission, which deliberately avoided a 'victors' justice' approach to the crimes of apartheid and chose instead one based on confession and absolution, informed by the principles of reconciliation, reconstruction, reparation and goodwill." App. to Brief for Government of Commonwealth of Australia et al. as *Amici Curiae* 7a. The United States provided a letter to the court agreeing with this position. *See* Letter of William H. Taft IV, Legal Adviser, Dept. of State, to Shannen W. Coffin, Deputy Asst. Atty. Gen., Oct. 27, 2003. *Id*. at 2. Minister Maduna's and Mr. Taft's letters are available at http://www. sdshh.com. See Module1, *supra*.

———————

Practicum

The U.S.–led invasion of Afghanistan succeeded in ousting the repressive Taliban regime and eliminating a safe haven for terrorists; however, it left a country in tatters. Over two decades of civil war, the country was devastated. It had no functioning judicial system, minimal governing capacity, and almost no infrastructure. Even today, well after the fall of the Taliban and the establishment of a government, the country remains, *de facto,* a series of duchies controlled by warlords competing for power and control of the nation's illegal opium trade.

The Afghan people are tired of conflict and long for some sense of stability and security. For many, an integral part of achieving lasting stability is some measure of accountability for those guilty of past human rights violations and war crimes. This is not limited to Taliban government and military officials, but includes ex-Mujhadeen leaders who fought to drive the Soviets out of Afghanistan in the eighties. Many of these leaders continue to rule on the basis of ethnic and tribal loyalties and are alleged to have committed serious atrocities in the past. Accountability for these men will prove difficult, as many have taken up official roles in government as part of compromises made by the Karzai government to maintain peace and some semblance of security throughout the country.

President Karzai has offered amnesty to rank and file Taliban fighters in exchange for turning in their weapons and giving up the fight against the Afghan government and coalition forces. Karzai's offer was made in the spirit of beginning a longer process of reconciliation; however, it did not address the problems posed by accountability for senior level Taliban figures or for crimes committed in the pre-Taliban era.

You work in the U.S. Department of State's Bureau of Democracy, Human Rights and Labor and have been asked to prepare a policy paper for the Secretary of State recommending a comprehensive reconciliation plan for Afghanistan. While the maintenance of stability and security must be a key goal for the plan, you must also balance the views of the international community as well as the needs of the Afghan people. Moreover, you should also take into account current U.S. government policy vis-à-vis international organizations and institutions such as the International Criminal Court and the United Nations more generally. Feel free to build upon work already done by organizations in this area, such as the Afghan Independent Human Rights Commission; however, remember that your role is an adviser to the U.S. Secretary of State and your advice must be consistent with U.S. policy priorities and objectives.

CHAPTER 6

MODULE 16

RULE OF LAW AND HUMAN RIGHTS IN POST-CONFLICT SOCIETIES

■ ■ ■

Orientation

What is the role of international human rights law when a nation makes the transition from violent chaos to a rights-respecting stability? Across the range of post-conflict situations over the past decade, inter-governmental organizations and civil society (including non-governmental organizations) have discovered that respect for human rights is both the goal of a successful transition and a necessary means of accomplishing it. But how exactly? When a society has been uprooted and all but destroyed by conflict, multiple problems have to be solved simultaneously: assuring accountability, promoting reconciliation, developing the economy, rebuilding institutions, and developing some faith in the rule of law. Obviously a holistic approach to transitional justice is a precondition for success, but it can feel like the survivors of a shipwreck trying to repair a wooden life-boat at sea by replacing every plank, one at a time.

In other parts of this book, you have considered legal components that might be included in any transitional strategy: truth commissions, international tribunals, and regional and global human rights mechanisms, *inter alia*. But each of these institutions standing alone can be insufficient to the task at hand. Truth commissions for example may work in some contexts and not in others and can never by themselves assure that the state apparatus for maintaining order—the police, the military, the security services—will do their jobs by respecting human rights and fundamental freedoms. The international tribunals also serve crucial purposes, both legal and political, but they cannot by themselves reform a judicial system, train law enforcement and security personnel, or rebuild confidence in domestic governmental institutions.

The United Nations has played a particularly important role in building and maintaining the institutions necessary for establishing the rule of law. Sometimes, the UN has acted in conjunction with other organizations, as has been the case in Kosovo, where it has worked closely with the Organization for Security and Cooperation in Europe and the European Union. In other settings, like East Timor, the UN has assumed primary authority for creating the framework for a transition to democratic self-rule. In others, the UN has played an advisory role for a new government, as in Afghanistan. In each case, the role played by international organizations, donors, and NGOs is driven by cultural, historical, and social factors that govern how international assistance can be most effective.

This module considers conflicts in two countries—East Timor and Iraq—and highlights the challenges of establishing the rule of law and confidence in governmental institutions. The materials on East Timor stress "nuts and bolts," the practical issues that face lawyers trying to develop and implement strategies for strengthening the rule of law. The case study on Iraq highlights an overriding policy issue: de-Ba'athification. All post-conflict societies must determine how to address those individuals serving in the government who were part of a regime responsible for human rights violations in the past. Whether these officials are police officers, government bureaucrats, or military personnel, they can provide either a good or a bad continuity during a transition, and vetting them—determining which can be trusted to be a force for reconciliation and which cannot—is an essential part of virtually every transition. The tension between know-how and continuity on one hand and the need for change and trust on the other arises in every post-conflict situation.

A UNITED NATIONS PERSPECTIVE

THE RULE OF LAW AND TRANSITIONAL JUSTICE IN CONFLICT AND POST-CONFLICT SOCIETIES: REPORT OF THE SECRETARY GENERAL

UN Doc. S/2004/16 (August 23, 2004)

Strengthening the Rule of Law and Transitional Justice in the Wake of Conflict

* * *

2. Our experience in the past decade has demonstrated clearly that the consolidation of peace in the immediate post-conflict period, as well as the maintenance of peace in the long term, cannot be achieved unless the population is confident that redress for grievances can be obtained through legitimate structures for the peaceful settlement of disputes and the fair administration of justice. At the same time, the heightened vulnerability of minorities, women, children, prisoners and detainees, displaced persons, refugees and others, which is evident in all conflict and post-conflict situations, brings an element of urgency to the imperative of restoration of the rule of law.

3. And yet, helping war-torn societies re-establish the rule of law and come to terms with large-scale past abuses, all within a context

marked by devastated institutions, exhausted resources, diminished security and a traumatized and divided population, is a daunting, often overwhelming, task. It requires attention to myriad deficits, among which are a lack of political will for reform, a lack of institutional independence within the justice sector, a lack of domestic technical capacity, a lack of material and financial resources, a lack of public confidence in Government, a lack of official respect for human rights and, more generally, a lack of peace and security. Over the years, the United Nations has accumulated significant expertise in addressing each of these key deficits. Departments, agencies, programmes and funds and specialists across the system have been deployed to numerous transitional, war-torn and post-conflict countries to assist in the complex but vital work of rule of law reform and development.

4.   Of course, in matters of justice and the rule of law, an ounce of prevention is worth significantly more than a pound of cure. While United Nations efforts have been tailored so that they are palpable to the population to meet the immediacy of their security needs and to address the grave injustices of war, the root causes of conflict have often been left unaddressed. Yet, it is in addressing the causes of conflict, through legitimate and just ways, that the international community can help prevent a return to conflict in the future. Peace and stability can only prevail if the population perceives that politically charged issues, such as ethnic discrimination, unequal distribution of wealth and social services, abuse of power, denial of the right to property or citizenship and territorial disputes between States, can be addressed in a legitimate and fair manner. Viewed this way, prevention is the first imperative of justice. * * *

Filling a rule of law vacuum

27.   In post-conflict settings, legislative frameworks often show the accumulated signs of neglect and political distortion, contain discriminatory elements and rarely reflect the requirements of international human rights and criminal law standards. Emergency laws and executive decrees are often the order of the day. Where adequate laws are on the books, they may be unknown to the general public and official actors may have neither the capacity nor the tools to implement them. National judicial, police and corrections systems have typically been stripped of the human, financial and material resources necessary for their proper functioning. They also often lack legitimacy, having been transformed by conflict and abuse into instruments of repression. Such situations are invariably marked by an abundance of arms, rampant gender and sexually based violence, the exploitation of children, the persecution of minorities and vulnerable groups, organized crime, smuggling, trafficking in human beings and other criminal activities. In such situations, organized criminal groups are often better resourced than local government and better armed than local law enforcement. Restoring the capacity and legitimacy of national institutions is a long-term undertak-

ing. However, urgent action to restore human security, human rights and the rule of law cannot be deferred. Thus, United Nations peace operations are often called upon to help fill this rule of law vacuum.

28. Indeed, in some cases, we have faced the difficulties of conducting peace operations where there are no functioning criminal justice mechanisms at all. In such situations, peacekeepers have encountered wrongdoers in the midst of committing serious criminal acts of a direct threat to civilians and to the operation itself. Military components typically lack the training, skills and resources to address such situations. At the same time, civilian components of peace operations, including police, are often too slowly deployed and are seldom mandated to undertake executive functions, such as arrest. Yet such lawlessness can seriously undermine the efforts of an entire peace operation. Given these realities, we must, together with Member States, rethink our current strategies for addressing the rule of law vacuum into which we are often deployed, including the role, capacities and obligations of military and civilian police components.

29. In some situations, where this problem has been most acute, civilian police in peace missions have been mandated to undertake executive functions, including powers of arrest and detention. While, in most cases, United Nations civilian police provide operational support and advice and are not empowered to carry out executive functions, their responsibilities have grown ever more complex. In every case, their role is central to the restoration of the rule of law and worthy of better support and more resources. The simple presence of law enforcement officials on the streets after a conflict can substantially reduce looting, harassment, rape, robbery and murder. After some 20 years of United Nations experience, this is an area that would benefit from a serious review, in order that we might consider ways to bolster our efforts.

30. But, as discussed above, while policing interventions in post-conflict environments are a crucial component of the rule of law continuum, they must be linked to parallel support to the other institutions and functions of the justice system. Enhancing the capacity of police (or United Nations Civilian Police) to make arrests cannot be seen as a contribution to the rule of law if there are no modern laws to be applied, no humane and properly resourced and supervised detention facilities in which to hold those arrested, no functioning judiciary to try them lawfully and expeditiously, and no defence lawyers to represent them. Progress has been made in recent years to address such lacunae, including a number of dedicated projects to develop transitional codes, guidelines and rule of law policy tools, as recommended in the report of the Panel on United Nations Peace Operations. In the coming months, many of these new tools will be finalized.

31. The establishment of independent national human rights commissions is one complementary strategy that has shown promise for helping to restore the rule of law, peaceful dispute resolution and

protection of vulnerable groups where the justice system is not yet fully functioning. Many have been established in conflict and post-conflict societies with mandates including quasi-judicial functions, conflict-resolution and protection programmes. Recent examples include the national human rights institutions of Afghanistan, Rwanda, Colombia, Indonesia, Nepal, Sri Lanka and Uganda, each of which is now playing an important role in this regard. Exceptional fact-finding mechanisms have also been mobilized by the United Nations with increasing frequency, such as the ad hoc international commissions of inquiry established to look into war crimes committed in places such as the former Yugoslavia, Rwanda, Burundi and Timor–Leste.

32. Additionally, strategies for expediting a return to the rule of law must be integrated with plans to reintegrate both displaced civilians and former fighters. Disarmament, demobilization and reintegration processes are one of the keys to a transition out of conflict and back to normalcy. For populations traumatized by war, those processes are among the most visible signs of the gradual return of peace and security. Similarly, displaced persons must be the subject of dedicated programmes to facilitate return. Carefully crafted amnesties can help in the return and reintegration of both groups and should be encouraged, although * * * these can never be permitted to excuse genocide, war crimes, crimes against humanity or gross violations of human rights. * * *

Developing national justice systems

34. While the international community is obliged to act directly for the protection of human rights and human security where conflict has eroded or frustrated the domestic rule of law, in the long term, no ad hoc, temporary or external measures can ever replace a functioning national justice system. Thus, for decades, a number of United Nations entities have been engaged in helping countries to strengthen national systems for the administration of justice in accordance with international standards.

35. Effective strategies for building domestic justice systems will give due attention to laws, processes (both formal and informal) and institutions (both official and non-official). Legislation that is in conformity with international human rights law and that responds to the country's current needs and realities is fundamental. At the institutional core of systems based on the rule of law is a strong judiciary, which is independent and adequately empowered, financed, equipped and trained to uphold human rights in the administration of justice. Equally important are the other institutions of the justice sector, including lawful police services, humane prison services, fair prosecutions and capable associations of criminal defence lawyers (oft-forgotten but vital institutions). Beyond the criminal law realm, such strategies must also ensure effective legal mechanisms for redressing civil claims and disputes, including property disputes, administrative law challenges, nationality

and citizenship claims and other key legal issues arising in post-conflict settings. Juvenile justice systems must be put in place to ensure that children in conflict with the law are treated appropriately and in line with recognized international standards for juvenile justice. Justice sector institutions must be gender sensitive and women must be included and empowered by the reform of the sector. Legal education and training and support for the organization of the legal community, including through bar associations, are important catalysts for sustained legal development.

36.   Our programmes must also support access to justice, to overcome common cultural, linguistic, economic, logistical or gender-specific impediments. Legal aid and public representation programmes are essential in this regard. Additionally, while focusing on the building of a formal justice system that functions effectively and in accordance with international standards, it is also crucial to assess means for ensuring the functioning of complementary and less formal mechanisms, particularly in the immediate term. Independent national human rights commissions can play a vital role in affording accountability, redress, dispute resolution and protection during transitional periods. Similarly, due regard must be given to indigenous and informal traditions for administering justice or settling disputes, to help them to continue their often vital role and to do so in conformity with both international standards and local tradition. Where these are ignored or overridden, the result can be the exclusion of large sectors of society from accessible justice. Particularly in post-conflict settings, vulnerable, excluded, victimized and marginalized groups must also be engaged in the development of the sector and benefit from its emerging institutions. Measures to ensure the gender sensitivity of justice sector institutions is vital in such circumstances. With respect to children, it is also important that support be given to nascent institutions of child protection and juvenile justice, including for the development of alternatives to detention, and for the enhancement of the child protection capacities of justice sector institutions.

37.   Recent national experience suggests that achieving these complex objectives is best served by the definition of a national process, guided by a national justice plan and shepherded by specially appointed independent national institutions, such as judicial or law commissions. Our support for such processes and bodies can help ensure that development of this sector is adequately resourced, coordinated, consistent with international standards and nationally owned and directed. Where this is complemented with meaningful support for capacity-building within the justice sector, the interventions of our operations have the greatest hope for contributing to sustainable improvements for justice and the rule of law. * * *

CASE STUDY #1: EAST TIMOR

In 1975, after months of instability and turmoil, the Indonesian military invaded the Portugese–administered "non-self governing territory" of East Timor. Although the international community protested, the Indonesian government did nothing to stem the widespread human rights and humanitarian law violations that accompanied the invasion. For more than two decades, Indonesia occupied and ruled East Timor as part of Indonesia. Although rebellion against Indonesian rule continued throughout the period of occupation, it was not until 1999 that political forces—both domestic and international—forced change in East Timor.

In January 1999, Indonesian President B.J. Habibie announced that the people of East Timor could decide between autonomous status within Indonesia and independence through a referendum to be conducted by the Security Council-mandated UN mission in East Timor (the "United Nations Assistance Mission to East Timor" or "UNAMET"). The people of East Timor voted overwhelmingly in favor of independence. Shortly after the results were announced, the people of East Timor were subjected to widespread and systematic violence, orchestrated by Indonesian and local militia forces. Disappearances, murders, rape, and torture were common. In order to escape the violence, hundreds of thousands of East Timorese fled or were forced to flee to Indonesian West Timor. Anti-independence elements implemented a "scorched earth" policy that included systematic arson and looting. As a result of the violence, East Timor was reduced to a state of anarchy.

After intense international pressure, including the threatened loss of billions of dollars in U.S. loans and assistance, the Indonesian government agreed to the deployment of an international force to quell the violence in East Timor. Pursuant to a resolution of the Security Council, a multinational force–known as "INTERFET"—was given a mandate to restore peace and security, protect and support UNAMET, and facilitate humanitarian assistance. A subsequent Security Council resolution (excerpted below) transformed the UN mission in East Timor from one of assistance to one that would constitute a transitional administration. Headed by the Special Representative of the Secretary General with the title of Transitional Administrator, this new body, UNTAET, was granted near plenary power over the affairs of a now-devastated East Timor.

U.N. SECURITY COUNCIL RESOLUTION 1272 (1999)

Adopted by the Security Council at its 4057th meeting, on 25 October 1999
UN Doc. S/RES/1272 (1999)

Reiterating its welcome for the successful conduct of the popular consultation of the East Timorese people of 30 August 1999, and taking note of its outcome through which the East Timorese people expressed their clear wish to begin a process of transition under the authority of the United Nations towards independence, which it regards as an accurate reflection of the views of the East Timorese people * * *,

Determining that the continuing situation in East Timor constitutes a threat to peace and security,

Acting under Chapter VII of the Charter of the United Nations,

1. *Decides* to establish, in accordance with the report of the Secretary–General, a United Nations Transitional Administration in East Timor (UNTAET), which will be endowed with overall responsibility for the administration of East Timor and will be empowered to exercise all legislative and executive authority, including the administration of justice;

2. *Decides also* that the mandate of UNTAET shall consist of the following elements:

(a) To provide security and maintain law and order throughout the territory of East Timor;

(b) To establish an effective administration;

(c) To assist in the development of civil and social services;

(d) To ensure the coordination and delivery of humanitarian assistance, rehabilitation and development assistance;

(e) To support capacity-building for self-government;

(f) To assist in the establishment of conditions for sustainable development * * *.

4. *Authorizes* UNTAET to take all necessary measures to fulfil its mandate. * * *

REGULATION NO. 1999/1 ON THE AUTHORITY OF THE TRANSITIONAL ADMINISTRATION IN EAST TIMOR

UNTAET/REG/1991/127 (27 November 1999)

Acting pursuant to the authority given to him under United Nations Security Council resolution 1272 (1999) of 25 October 1999, after consultation with representatives of the East Timorese people, and for the purpose of establishing and maintaining an effective transitional administration in East Timor;

Hereby promulgates the following:

Section 1

Authority of the interim administration

1.1   All legislative and executive authority with respect to East Timor, including the administration of the judiciary, is vested in UNTAET and is exercised by the Transitional Administrator. In exercising these functions the Transitional Administrator shall consult and cooperate closely with representatives of the East Timorese people.

1.2   The Transitional Administrator may appoint any person to perform functions in the civil administration in East Timor, including the judiciary, or remove such person. Such functions shall be exercised in accordance with the existing laws, as specified in section 3, and any regulations and directives issued by the Transitional Administrator.

Section 2

Observance of internationally recognized standards

In exercising their functions, all persons undertaking public duties or holding public office in East Timor shall observe internationally recognized human rights standards, as reflected, in particular, in: The Universal Declaration on Human Rights of 10 December 1948; The International Covenant on Civil and PoliticalRights of 16 December 1966 and its Protocols; The International Covenant on Economic, Social and Cultural Rights of 16 December 1966; The Convention on the Elimination of All Forms of Racial Discrimination of 21 December 1965; The Convention on the Elimination of All Forms of Discrimination Against Women of 17 December 1979; The Convention Against Torture and other Cruel, Inhumane or Degrading Treatment or Punishment of 17 December 1984; The International Convention on the Rights of the Child of 20 November 1989.

They shall not discriminate against any person on any ground such as sex, race, colour, language, religion, political or other opinion, national, ethnic or social origin, association with a national community, property, birth or all other status.

Section 3

Applicable law in East Timor

3.1   Until replaced by UNTAET regulations or subsequent legislation of democratically established institutions of East Timor, the laws applied in East Timor prior to 25 October 1999 shall apply in East Timor insofar as they do not conflict with the standards referred to in section 2, the fulfillment of the mandate given to UNTAET under United Nations Security Council resolution 1272 (1999), or the present or any other regulation and directive issued by the Transitional Administrator.

3.2   Without prejudice to the review of other legislation, the following laws, which do not comply with the standards referred to in section 2 and 3 of the present regulation, as well as any subsequent amendments to these laws and their administrative regulations, shall no longer be applied in East Timor:

Law on Anti–Subversion; Law on Social Organizations; Law on National Security; Law on National Protection and Defense; Law on Mobilization and Demobilization; Law on Defense and Security.

3.3   Capital punishment is abolished.

Section 4

Regulations issued by UNTAET

In the performance of the duties entrusted to the transitional administration under United Nations Security Council resolution 1272 (1999), the Transitional Administrator will, as necessary, issue legislative acts in the form of regulations. Such regulations will remain in force until repealed by the Transitional Administrator or superseded by such rules as are issued upon the transfer of UNTAET's administrative and public service functions to the democratic institutions of East Timor, as provided for in United Nations Security Council resolution 1272 (1999).
* * *

REGULATION NO. 2000/11 ON THE ORGANIZATION OF COURTS IN EAST TIMOR

UNTAET/REG/2000/11 (6 March 2000)

The Special Representative of the Secretary–General (hereinafter: Transitional Administrator),

Pursuant to the authority given to him under United Nations Security Council resolution 1272 (1999) of 25 October 1999,

Taking into account United Nations Transitional Administration in East Timor (UNTAET) Regulation 1999/1 of 27 November 1999 on the Authority of the Transitional Administration in East Timor,

After consultation in the National Consultative Council,

For the purpose of regulating the functioning and organization of the courts during the period of the transitional administration in East Timor,

Promulgates the following:

I. General Provisions

Section 1

Judicial Authority

Judicial authority in East Timor shall be exclusively vested in courts that are established by law and composed of judges who are appointed to these courts in accordance with UNTAET Regulation No. 1999/3.

Section 2

Independence of the Judiciary

2.1   Judges shall perform their duties independently and impartially, and in accordance with applicable laws in East Timor and the oath or solemn declaration given by them to the Transitional Administration pursuant to UNTAET Regulation No. 1999/3.

2.2   Judges shall decide matters before them without prejudice and in accordance with their impartial assessment of the facts and their understanding of the law, without improper influence, direct or indirect, from any source.

2.3   In the decision-making process, any hierarchical organization of the judiciary or any difference among judges in grade or rank shall in no way interfere with the duty of the judge, whether exercising jurisdiction individually or acting collectively on a panel, to pronounce judgement in accordance with Section 2.2 of the present regulation.

2.4   While in office, judges and prosecutors shall be barred from accepting political or any other public office, or from accepting any employment, including for teaching law, participating in the drafting of law, or carrying out legal research on a part-time basis, unless for honorary unpaid purposes.

Section 3

Refusal of Justice

No judge may refuse to hear, try or decide a case that is brought before the court in accordance with the relevant procedural provisions.

Section 4

Courts in East Timor

The judiciary in East Timor shall be composed of District Courts, as determined by the present regulation, and one Court of Appeal.

Section 5

Applicable Law

5.1   In exercising their jurisdiction, the courts in East Timor shall apply the law of East Timor as promulgated by Section 3 of UNTAET Regulation No. 1999/1.

5.2 Courts shall have jurisdiction in respect of crimes committed in East Timor prior to 25 October 1999 only insofar as the law on which the offence is based is consistent with Section 3.1 of UNTAET Regulation No. 1999/1 or any other UNTAET regulation.

5.3 Courts shall have jurisdiction in respect of civil claims which arose in East Timor prior to 25 October 1999 only insofar as the law on which the claim is based is consistent with Section 3.1 of UNTAET Regulation No. 1999/1 or any other UNTAET regulation.

Notes and Questions on Transitional Justice

1. *East Timor as a success story.* The situation in East Timor demanded extraordinary measures by the international community to restore stability and the rule of law, as well as to build the foundation for an independent state, and the Security Council placed the territory under the administration of the United Nations. The UN's efforts in East Timor are widely considered a success: after only a few years of UN administration, elections were held, government institutions were established, and a fully independent, democratic nation emerged. On May 20, 2002, the United Nations handed over sovereignty to the new President and Government of Timor Leste (East Timor), thus establishing the new country as a full and sovereign member of the international community. Challenges remain, but East Timor is now a free, independent democracy.

Of course, not every post-conflict situation can be addressed in the same way. In East Timor, several factors contributed to the willingness of the international community to allow the UN to play the role that it did: a referendum established the clear will of the people to be free of Indonesian rule; a key regional actor, Australia, was willing to engage aggressively to establish security; and powerful bilateral and international pressure convinced the Indonesians to withdraw from the territory.

2. *Human rights in transitional instruments.* Article 2 of UNTAET Regulation 2000/11, *supra*, incorporates numerous international human rights instruments into the law governing the acts of all public officials in East Timor. Note also that the same regulation recognizes the applicability of Indonesian law so long as it was not incompatible with the standards incorporated into Section 2. Given your understanding of the content of each of these instruments, was it reasonable to expect that all of these standards could be applied in East Timor? If not, what was the purpose of including each of these instruments in the regulation?

3. *Post-conflict Afghanistan.* Consider the case of Afghanistan. After the fall of the Taliban, it was possible to envision a role for the UN similar to that in East Timor. However, circumstances demanded that the United Nations Assistance Mission in Afghanistan (UNAMA) have a much lighter footprint. Instead of administering the country, UNAMA

provides political and technical guidance to the central Afghan government and coordinates development assistance. The Afghans have a long, proud tradition of independence and would not have permitted the UN to take a greater role. Further, powerful regional and tribal factions continued to wield enormous power in many parts of the country, a situation the UN would not have been able to control. In addition, the significant American military presence in the country would have been a serious impediment to the UN assuming a greater role in administering the country. Finally, a strong, well-regarded leader, President Hamid Karzai, stepped forward after the Taliban's fall and was chosen by the Afghan people (with U.S. support) to lead the country.

In January 2004, the Afghan Constitutional Loya Jirga (or Grand Council) adopted a new constitution. The constitution includes broad protections for human rights, including a recognition of the equality of men and women, the rights to be free from torture and arbitrary detention, the rights to due process and a fair trial, and a variety of economic, social and cultural rights. Recognizing the inherent difficulties of crafting a constitution in the transitional, post-conflict context, should the case of Afghanistan be seen as a failure because, practically speaking, the obligations the constitution creates cannot be immediately implemented? How does your perception of the constitution—as a political or as a legal document—affect your view of constitution drafting in post-conflict societies?

As of the date of publication, stability and security remain elusive in Afghanistan. Rival warlords control much of the country, and the Taliban and al Qaida continue to destabilize the country. The Afghan judicial system is in disarray, leaving all disputes to be resolved at the barrel of a gun or through traditional, tribal dispute resolution mechanisms. The central government exerts little control outside of the capital, Kabul, and has failed to assemble a sufficient national force to extend security throughout the country. How might an increased role for the UN have been crafted to increase security and respect for the rule of law, without triggering resistance from the Afghan people?

4. *Self-determination in transitional societies.* Perhaps one of the most provocative and fundamental principles of human rights law is the principle of self-determination as articulated in article 1(2) of the Charter of the United Nations. Of course, the exact content of this principle—as a collective right held by "a people"—is hotly debated; however, few disagree with the general principle that peoples have a right to "freely determine their political status and freely pursue their economic, social and cultural development." International Covenant on Civil and Political Rights, art. 1(1); International Covenant on Economic, Social and Cultural Rights, art. 1(1). In the context of East Timor, the people exercised their right to self-determination by referendum, voting for independence. Following the use of force by the Indonesian military, the international community reacted by providing the United Nations

with the legal mandate to restore order and enforce the self-determination of the East Timorese people.

Note that in recent post-conflict situations—from Cambodia to the Balkans to Haiti—the goal of international community, especially the United Nations, has been to build democratic institutions and to create conditions favorable to holding free and fair elections at the earliest opportunity. What does this tell the observer about the right to self-determination? In the modern era, has the right to self-determination been transformed into a right to democracy? *See, e.g.*, Inter–American Democratic Charter (2001); Warsaw Declaration: Toward a Community of Democracies (2000); *see also* Julie Mertus, *From Legal Transplants to Transformative Justice: Human Rights and the Promise of Transnational Civil Society*, 14 AM. U. INT'L L. REV. 1355 (1999); *see also* Chapter 9, where the right to democracy is further explored. Is the right to democracy a collective or individual right? How would an individual or community obtain redress for a violation of the right to self-determination?

5. *The right to democracy and minority rights.* How is the right to democracy implemented in a country like Iraq? In periods of transition where a complicated ethnic, religious, and tribal patchwork must be woven into a transitional justice strategy, how do you account for the interests of each of these groups in fashioning a representative form of government satisfactory to all? Does it mean majority rule, or is majority rule exactly the wrong approach when trying to protect minority rights? Is regional autonomy a better approach?

Can recognition of the rights guaranteed to minorities under international law help resolve some of the issues inherent in a post-conflict society like Iraq or Afghanistan? How might recognition of these rights actually create tension with the desire to maintain stability and security in a unified Iraq? Does the creation of strong central government necessarily conflict with the needs and aspirations of minorities to gain recognition, representation, and the right to maintain cultural, linguistic and religious identity?

6. *Kosovo.* In 1999, pursuant to authority created by United Nations Security Council resolution 1244, the UN Secretary General established the UN Mission in Kosovo (UNMIK) to establish an interim civilian administration led by the UN through which the people of Kosovo could progressively enjoy autonomy. Led by a Special Representative of the Secretary General, UNMIK had the mandate to take "any measure necessary to ensure public safety and order and the proper administration of justice." *See* UN Security Council Resolution 1244 (1999). Using Security Council Resolution 1244, UNMIK took a variety of measures—including authorizing lengthy detentions—that some argued constituted violations of universally agreed human rights principles. To what extent are United Nations missions and personnel bound by UN instruments? Should a UN Security Council resolution be considered "later in time" to these instruments, and, therefore, justifica-

tion for departing from principles enshrined in the Universal Declaration of Human Rights, for instance?

7. *The challenges of rule of law in transition.* How can a new government, struggling to maintain control and legitimacy, guarantee the right to counsel in a society where there is almost no semblance of a functioning defense bar? How can a government struggling to meet the most basic needs of its people ensure that it meets its international obligations with regard to the treatment of criminal detainees? On the one hand, the government's treatment of criminal defendants must meet the concerns of the international community, but, on the other, it cannot be seen as treating criminal defendants—some of whom may have been culpable in the past conflict—better than it treats its citizens. If it errs on one side or the other, its claim to legitimacy could be threatened. Should a government be given some leeway on international standards for a period of time in order to ensure domestic legitimacy and security?

8. *Transnational networks.* Transnational networks are networks of government officials, including lawyers, judges and prosecutors, who work to establish law and policy on issues of global concern by coordinating informally across borders. For instance, the Symposium of Judges and Prosecutors of Latin America promotes the domestic enforcement of international environmental law by training legal personnel, including prosecutors and judges in the field, and promoting public awareness on environmental issues. At least one author has noted the potential for these networks in the area of international criminal law. *See* Jenia Iontcheva Turner, *Transitional Networks and International Criminal Justice*, 105 MICH. L. REV. 985 (2007). "Such transnational networks could serve a two-fold purpose. They could remedy national authorities' lack of capacity to enforce international criminal law by contributing some of the combined resources and expertise of network participants. At the same time, because of their flexible and decentralized form, networks could better accommodate local political preferences and enable nations most directly affected by atrocities to play a more central role in prosecuting them." What role can these networks play in establishing a strong human rights legal regime in transitional states? What are some potential problems inherent in this decentralized approach?

9. *Property rights.* Consider the thorny issues of property rights in a post-conflict society. Typically, widespread conflict causes mass displacements of people—particularly if the cause of the conflict is ethnic in nature. Often, a particular ethnic group either flees or is driven out of its homeland, and another group moves in to occupy their homes and property. Where the conflict is prolonged, competing claims to property can be especially difficult to resolve. Many times there are no property records, or the records that existed were destroyed during the conflict. If competing claims are not resolved in an equitable, just and efficient manner, post-conflict stability can be threatened. Should the resolution of property disputes be a priority in developing a transitional justice

strategy? Given the importance of strengthening new government insti-tutions, is there a role for the international community in resolving local property disputes?

10. *Economic, social and cultural rights in post-conflict societies.* Most transitional justice regimes incorporate a recognition of economic, social and cultural rights. Can a transitional government really expect to guarantee these rights? Is there value to including these rights in the framework, even if they are primarily aspirational? Alternatively, how would you argue that the inclusion of these rights might actually weaken both these rights and the legitimacy of the new government?

CASE STUDY #2: IRAQ AND THE PROBLEM OF VETTING

Rule-of-Law Tools for Post–Conflict States
Vetting: An Operational Framework

Office of the United Nations High Commissioner for
Human Rights 3–5 (2006)

I. Vetting, Institutional Reform and Transitional Justice

Reforming public institutions is a core task in countries in transition from authoritarianism or conflict to democracy and peace. Public institu-tions that perpetuated a conflict or served an authoritarian regime need to be transformed into institutions that support the transition, sustain peace and preserve the rule of law. Institutions that abused human rights and defended the partisan interests of a few need to become institutions that protect human rights, prevent abuses and impartially serve the public. Dysfunctional and inequitable institutions that created fear need to turn into efficient and fair institutions that enjoy civic trust.

In building fair and efficient institutions, institutional reform con-tributes to providing transitional justice in two principal ways. First, fair and efficient public institutions play a critical role in preventing future abuses. Following a period of massive human rights abuse, preventing its recurrence constitutes a central goal of a legitimate and effective transitional justice strategy.

Second, institutional reform contributes to transitional justice in that it enables public institutions, in particular in the security and justice sectors, to provide criminal accountability for past abuses. A reformed police service, for example, can professionally investigate the abuses committed during the conflict or the authoritarian regime; a reformed prosecutor's office can effectively issue indictments; and a reformed court can impartially render judgement about those past abuses. Institu-tional reform may, therefore, be a precondition for providing domestic criminal accountability for the abuses of the conflict or the authoritarian past.

Effective and sustainable institutional reform is a complex and challenging task. Institutional reform measures may include, for example, the creation of oversight, complaint and disciplinary procedures; the reform or establishment of legal frameworks; the development or revision of ethical guidelines and codes of conduct; changing symbols that are associated with abusive practices; and the provision of adequate salaries, equipment and infrastructure. Effective reform efforts might also have to review the functioning of an entire public sector and consider merging, disbanding or creating public institutions. The precise content and scope of those measures will depend on the country's circumstances.

While a comprehensive approach to institutional reform is critical to ensure its effectiveness and sustainability, these operational guidelines focus on one area: the reform of an institution's personnel. The principal constituents of a public institution are its employees. The institution acts through its employees and is represented by them. Past malfunctioning and abuses were often the result of various deficits of an institution's personnel. Personnel reform is, therefore, a central component of any effective and sustainable institutional reform process.

Vetting is an important aspect of personnel reform in countries in transition. Vetting can be defined as assessing integrity to determine suitability for public employment. Integrity refers to an employee's adherence to international standards of human rights and professional conduct, including a person's financial propriety. Public employees who are personally responsible for gross violations of human rights or serious crimes under international law revealed a basic lack of integrity and breached the trust of the citizens they were meant to serve. The citizens, in particular the victims of abuses, are unlikely to trust and rely on a public institution that retains or hires individuals with serious integrity deficits, which would fundamentally impair the institution's capacity to deliver its mandate. Vetting processes aim at excluding from public service persons with serious integrity deficits in order to (re)establish civic trust and (re)legitimize public institutions.

Integrity is measured by a person's conduct. Vetting processes should, therefore, be based on assessments of individual conduct. Purges and other large-scale removals on the sole basis of group or party affiliation tend to cast the net too wide and to remove public employees of integrity who bear no individual responsibility for past abuses. At the same time, group removals may also be too narrow and overlook individuals who committed abuses but were not members of the group. Such broadly construed collective processes violate basic due process standards, are unlikely to achieve the intended reform goals, may remove employees whose expertise is needed in the post-conflict or post-authoritarian period, and may create a pool of discontented employees that might undermine the transition.

In addition to supporting institutional reform efforts, vetting and excluding abusers can fulfil another important function in a comprehensive transitional justice strategy. The scarcity of means and resources in a post-conflict or post-authoritarian context, as well as legal impediments, a lack of personnel and large numbers of perpetrators, often preclude the criminal prosecution of all abusers and leave a so-called impunity gap. While vetting processes also require significant resources, they are procedurally less complex than criminal prosecutions. Under circumstances of limited or delayed criminal prosecutions, the exclusion from public service of human rights abusers may help to fill the impunity gap by providing a partial measure of non-criminal accountability. Exclusions from public service have a punitive effect as they take away or pre-empt employment, public authority, and other privileges and benefits. Excluding abusers should, however, not be used as a pretext for not pursuing criminal prosecutions. Not only is there a duty to prosecute serious human rights crimes, but a transitional justice strategy will also be more effective and legitimate if the various transitional justice initiatives, in particular prosecutions, truth-telling, reparations and institutional reform, complement each other.

More often than not, integrity deficits are not the only shortcomings of public employees in post-conflict or post-authoritarian situations, and the exclusion of persons who lack integrity may not bring about the personnel changes necessary to build a fair and efficient public institution, and prevent abuses from recurring. The employees of a public institution may, for example, not only be human rights abusers, but also lack qualifications and skills, and the personnel as a whole may fail to represent the population it is called to serve and/or have an inefficient organizational structure. Many of the employees may have been appointed unlawfully, violating procedural and qualification requirements. The multifaceted shortcomings of a public institution's personnel often represent complex and interrelated causes of past malfunctioning and abuses.

———————

Iraq represents one of the greatest transitional justice challenges in the world. With the fall of Iraqi president Saddam Hussein, the international community faced enormous challenges in helping the Iraqi people formulate and implement a strategy to establish rule of law and address the crimes of the past. To date, neither has been accomplished satisfactorily. Although Saddam Hussein and several other senior Ba'athist officials responsible for egregious human rights abuses have been tried and executed, sectarian violence, acts of terrorism, and mass displacement continue. While many mistakes were made during the Iraq war and reconstruction period, the "process" of de-ba'athification, begun in 2003, may qualify as one of the most profound.

———————

TRANSITIONAL JUSTICE IN IRAQ:
AN ICTJ POLICY PAPER (MAY 2003)
International Center for Transitional Justice

D. *Vetting and De-ba'athification*

Vetting refers to the scrutiny of a person's past conduct for the purposes of removing individuals responsible for crimes and serious misconduct from public sector posts or preventing them from being appointed to these posts. These may include police and prison services, the civil service, the army, intelligence services, and even the judiciary. The vetting process typically involves a thorough background check involving a review of multiple sources of information and evidence to determine whether a particular official has been involved in past abuses. The Iraqi security forces and civil service contain a number of individuals responsible for serious crimes and other forms of misconduct. While it will not be possible to prosecute or even identify and remove all such individuals, it is extremely important to remove the worst offenders from office in order to re-instill faith in public institutions and change their culture. In some cases, removing key individuals will be a precondition for any meaningful reform. The sanction imposed by a vetting body need not always be dismissal from office or denial of employment. In cases involving minor offenses, it may be appropriate to impose fines, order community service, or suspend dismissal, providing the individual does not commit further infractions.

Paul Bremmer, Iraq's new civilian administrator, has recently announced a policy that could automatically remove up to 30,000 Baath party members from government positions. Bremmer has also reportedly reserved the right to exempt certain key officials, who may be essential to government functions, from this blanket prohibition. The removal of persons from public office based solely on party affiliation is similar to the "lustration" policies adopted in several Eastern and Central European countries. Lustration refers to laws and policies that involve wide-scale dismissal and disqualification based not on individual records, but rather on party affiliation, political opinion, or association with an oppressive secret service. Many lustration laws have been criticized for violating international standards of procedural fairness by, *inter alia,* punishing on the basis of collective guilt, violating the presumption of innocence and the principle of nonretroactivity, imposing bans on elected or appointed positions (in violation of the prohibition against discrimination on the basis of political opinion), unfairly limiting rights of appeal before judicial bodies, and relying too heavily on spurious Communist-era records to prove unlawful or wrongful behavior. For these reasons, the ICTJ believes that any vetting process in Iraq should comply with the following principles:

1. Persons should be removed or barred from public office based on an individual assessment of their responsibility for serious miscon-

duct (which would in normal circumstances lead to dismissal) or human rights abuse.

2.   Persons should *not* be removed or barred from office *solely* on the basis of party affiliation or ideology.

3.   Persons under investigation should be made aware of the allegations against them and given an opportunity to reply before a decision is made regarding their employment.

4.   Persons should be afforded the right to appeal a decision.

5.   A vetting body must be impartial and independent from political control.

6.   If exceptions to any vetting policy are made, they should not apply to persons found to be responsible for human rights abuse.

Some Iraqi institutions or units are so notorious and tainted, and have such poor human rights track records, that it may be better simply to eliminate the institution or unit as a whole rather than undertake an onerous, individualized vetting process. All members of the institution could be dismissed from employment *en masse* and a new body established in its place. Some individuals could be permitted to re-apply for their positions contingent on demonstration of a good past record and/or agreement to follow certain human rights and/or anti-corruption training requirements. Information gathered by any vetting mechanism should be provided to the Special Tribunal for Iraq, Iraqi domestic courts, and a truth commission, as appropriate.

BRIEFING PAPER:
IRAQ'S NEW "ACCOUNTABILITY AND JUSTICE" LAW

(January 22, 2008)

International Center for Transitional Justice

1.   Summary

On January 12, 2008, the Iraqi parliament passed the "Law of the Supreme National Commission for Accountability and Justice." The new law replaces the earlier framework governing Iraq's De–Ba'athification policies, and is the culmination of an epic struggle between De–Ba'athification opponents and supporters lasting more than eighteen months. Pressures for reform were exerted by some Sunni political blocs and the United States Government. Opponents of reform included parliamentary supporters of political cleric Muqtada al-Sadr and the Higher National De–Ba'athification Commission (HNDBC), the body that has overseen Iraqi De-ba'athification measures to date.

The new law is not the major change that reformers had hoped. It essentially preserves the previous De-ba'athification system and extends its reach to a number of organizations not previously affected, including the Iraqi judiciary. The law also preserves the controversial Higher National De–Ba'athification Commission (HNDBC), which will be renamed rather than dissolved. Some positive changes have been made, however, mainly to do with clarification of pension rights and the level of membership at which dismissal and reinstatement procedures are to be applied. One other major development is a new requirement to dismiss some former employees of Iraq's notorious intelligence and security agencies from government service. This is likely to complicate greatly political reception of the new law. * * *

2.   What is Vetting and How Should it Be Done?

The ICTJ uses the term "vetting" to refer to a process of assessing an individual's integrity in order to determine his or her suitability for public employment. Integrity can be defined in many ways, but is used by the ICTJ to refer to a person's adherence to human rights standards and his or her financial propriety.

The ICTJ has conducted comparative research and accumulated extensive expertise on vetting in transitional societies. ICTJ research reveals four key lessons for the design and implementation of vetting processes in transitional societies:

1) Vetting is merely one part of a larger process of institutional reform. Vetting processes generally need to be accompanied by, among others, reform of selection, appointment, promotion, disciplinary and dismissal procedures in order to be effective and sustainable;

2) Vetting is legally challenging and easily manipulated. International law in this area is not well-developed, but vetting processes raise very peculiar fairness questions, and generally takes place in uncertain settings. In order to avoid arbitrary and unfair proceedings it is vital that vetting processes include basic procedural guarantees and be based on individual responsibility rather than assumptions of collective guilt;

3) Vetting is very sensitive politically because it affects access to and distribution of power, resources and privileges. For this reason the system adopted must be transparent, coherent, and protected from manipulation;

4) Vetting is operationally complex, resource-intensive, and takes place in contexts in which there is strong competition over scarce resources. The vetting system chosen should have clear priorities, be practical to implement, and subject to a clear time limit.

While vetting can make an important contribution to overcoming an abusive past and building an effective public service of integrity, it is only one of many necessary steps: expectations of vetting programs should not be unrealistically great. This is a particular problem in Iraq, where public expectations of De-ba'athification have been extremely high—partly because of lack of other high-profile transitional justice measures.

3. Iraq's Ba'ath Party

Members of the Iraqi branch of the Arab Socialist Renaissance Party, commonly known as the Ba'ath Party, ruled Iraq from 1968–2003. From the moment the party assumed power, its elaborate apparatus grew in parallel to, and later overtook, the normal institutions of state. The inner workings of the party were and remain secret, but Ba'ath Party members were often highly visible in their own communities, and were used as informers and to enforce extra-judicial detentions and penalties. Membership was originally highly restricted, but rules were relaxed significantly in the 1990s as the regime sought to bolster its stability and the party's membership is reported to have expanded greatly. Certain levels of membership entitled individuals to extra allowances and privileges that could make a real difference to a person's economic wellbeing. Party membership was also reportedly a condition of employment in some professions, and occasionally conferred to honor Iraqis for other reasons, as was the case for some Iraqi prisoners of war from the Iran–Iraq war. To date, there is no reliable information in the public domain about the party's structure, membership, or the duties that different levels of membership involved. Unlike post World War II Germany, the party's membership lists have never been found. * * *

4. Iraq's De-ba'athification System 2003–2008

De-ba'athification is the name given to a number of processes initiated by the Coalition Provisional Authority (CPA) shortly after the fall of Iraq's Ba'athist regime. One was the complete dissolution of the Iraqi army as well as certain organizations (mostly security-related) that were either notorious for their role in enforcing Ba'ath Party rule, or whose resources might offer the party a means to return to power. These organizations included the Iraqi army, the intelligence services, the Olympic committee and others, dissolved by CPA order in May 2003.

The other process was the dismissal of many thousands of civil service employees from their positions. This process was initiated by the Coalition Provisional Authority, but later continued and was controlled by Iraq's Higher National De-ba'athification Commission (HNDBC). The dismissal procedures involved two categories of persons:

- All individuals in highest-level management positions (level of director general and above), regardless of the level of their party membership.

- All individuals who were members of the top four ranks of Iraqi Ba'ath party membership, regardless of the level of their civil service position.

Individuals were not dismissed on the basis of individual deeds or other measures of integrity, but on the basis of their party rank. The assumption underpinning De-ba'athification procedures was that the elite of the Ba'ath party could not have achieved their level without committing acts that seriously violated human rights standards or were deeply corrupt. Some of those dismissed became eligible for civil service pensions—but they risked losing these if they appealed their dismissals. From the beginning there was a parallel but unclear process of exemption and reinstatement, influenced partly by technical and political needs of both the CPA and later the Iraqi government.

The CPA quickly lost control of De-ba'athification policy and implementation. Instead, the Iraqi Governing Council seized the initiative by creating the Higher National De-ba'athification Commission (HNDBC) in August 2003. Led by veteran politician Ahmed Chelabi, the Commission was widely criticized as secretive, all-powerful, and manipulative. The Iraqi government has at times supported its work, and at times opposed it. In addition to enforcing civil service dismissals, the HNDBC has also struck down electoral candidates and repeatedly intervened in judicial appointments at the Iraqi High Tribunal, including shortly before the release of verdicts in the *Dujail* case.

De-ba'athification caused outrage and confusion amongst several constituencies. The decision to dissolve the Iraqi army has been widely criticized as a major trigger of the insurgency and a severe hindrance to improving security. Some Iraqis considered the policy as a form of collective punishment. Others were angered by an obvious impunity gap: hundreds of thousands of lower-level Ba'athists (many of whom may be guilty of abuses) retained their enviable civil service positions, and others who had been dismissed but were well-known abusers had not suffered any other penalty. By early 2007 De-ba'athification had become an important symbolic issue in political negotiations between Sunni and Shi'a factions, and the United States increasingly pressured both groups to agree on De-ba'athification reform. The result is the Accountability and Justice Law of January 12, 2008.

5.   Major Differences in the New System: Overview

Iraq's De-ba'athification policies were previously set out in a confusing mix of orders from the Coalition Provisional Authority, the Iraqi Governing Council, and HNDBC regulations. In addition, HNDBC practices were highly opaque. The new law establishes a clearer legal framework for dismissals and reinstatements, which may aid transparency.

It is clear, however, that the new law is a major victory for the Higher National De-ba'athification Commission and opponents of De-ba'athification reform. The new law gives the Higher National De-ba'athification Commission a new name, but preserves much of the old system. The new Supreme Commission for Accountability and Justice will have the same staff and much of the same structure as its predecessor. Its main task will be to implement De-ba'athification processes very similar to those implemented in Iraq from 2003–2007–except that the

Commission's powers have now been strengthened, its reach has been extended, and some of the target groups affected have changed.

There are five main differences between the new system of Deba'athification and the old—at least on paper. Each is summarized briefly below. * * *

1) Individuals who were at the level of *firqa* (group) member are now permitted to return to government service. (Counting in descending order from the highest level of leadership, a *firqa* member was the sixth rank of party member.) This change is almost certainly a positive development, and will affect tens of thousands of people.

There are two major exceptions, however:

• *firqa* members who held the highest civil service positions may not return; and

• *firqa* members who held or hold positions in certain sensitive ministries, the Supreme Judicial Council, and key leadership offices may not continue in or return to these positions. Iraqi judges are already fearful that this exclusion may disproportionately affect the judiciary. Individuals dismissed from these institutions may work elsewhere in the civil service, however.

2) Another major difference is that most individuals dismissed are now eligible for pensions. This is also a positive development, and includes *shu'ba* members (one level above *firqa* members). Not eligible are individuals at the four highest levels of party membership (estimated to be some 1100 persons), former members of the notorious paramilitary units, the *Feda'iyeen Saddam*, and individuals proven to have been corrupt or committed crimes.

3) All former employees of Ba'ath-era security intelligence agencies must now be dismissed from government employment and pensioned off, regardless of whether they were party members. It is important to note that this affects individuals who worked at agencies notorious for their excesses and abuses, such as the secret police, the public security agency, the military intelligence service, and others. It does not apply to individuals who worked in the Ba'ath-era defense ministry, military or police forces. This change may be unpopular in some Sunni circles and is likely to complicate the law's political reception, although it may also have a positive long-term impact on Iraq's security and intelligence practices. Because of the number of individuals involved, it may well create capacity problems at those institutions most heavily affected, such as the Ministry of Interior and Ministry of Defense.

4) The new law introduces a welcome element of individual responsibility into the Deba'athification system. If an individual belongs to a category of membership that would benefit from the new law but is convicted by a court of having committed crimes or embezzled

public funds, then he or she will forfeit their pension and/or return rights. The new Commission will have a public prosecutor's office to investigate alleged crimes: although the mechanism may be flawed * * *, it is possible that the creation of the prosecutor's office may mean that some party members who have committed crimes are more likely to be brought to justice.

5) Finally, the new system also attempts to create an independent appeals mechanism, called the Cassation Chamber. Individuals who have steps taken against them are able to appeal the Commission's decision to a panel of seven judges. Panel members will be nominated by the Supreme Judicial Council and, crucially, the panel will function as a part of Iraq's Cassation Court—it will not be housed in, or answerable to, the Commission. Under the old system there was no independent appeals mechanism, and individuals who appealed gave up their right to a pension, although HNDBC officials have told ICTJ that this provision was often waived on humanitarian grounds. In another welcome innovation, individuals to be dismissed are not immediately sacked from their positions, but are placed on paid leave until the cassation chamber has given a final decision.

There is no reliable information on the numbers of people who will be affected by the new law: for example, official estimates of the number of Iraqis who were *firqa* members range from 30,000 to 60,000 individuals, although a more common figure is roughly 38,000. Actual numbers of returns may be far less, however, because the HNDBC has undertaken a major wave of reinstatements since late 2006. Iraqi officials have reportedly stated that the new provisions affecting employees of the previous regime's security agencies will affect at least 7,000 individuals currently working in the Ministry of Interior and elsewhere.

NOTES AND QUESTIONS ON THE IRAQI TRANSITION

1. *Purging the old regime.* Paul Bremmer and the CPA did not take ICTJ's advice in 2003. The first executive order of the CPA entitled "De–Ba'athification of Iraqi Society," began a process that led to the purging of tens of thousands of government employees—disaffected Iraqis with no source of income. Order No. 1, CPA/ORD/16 May 2003/01. The problems presented by de-Ba'athification continue today, as many of those who lost their jobs took up arms as part of the insurgency.

In hindsight, it is easy to say that CPA Order 1—and the subsequent process implemented by Iraq's Higher National De–Ba'athification Commission—was a bad idea. At the time, however, things were not so simple. Ordinary Iraqis feared and distrusted the Ba'athists and the Ba'ath party as well as the institutions the party controlled. For those inside the CPA, as well as many in Iraqi society, the dismantling of the Ba'ath party's grasp on power was seen as the most immediate means for re-establishing trust in government by the Iraqi people. In fact, even the International Center for Transitional Justice (ICTJ) notes that some were angry that De-ba'athification did not go far enough. Hundreds of thousands of lower-level Ba'athists, many of whom may have been guilty of abuses, retained their positions in the Iraqi civil service, thereby suffering no penalty for their association with the Hussein regime.

2. *Measuring personal integrity.* In the first excerpt above, the Office of the High Commissioner for Human Rights (OHCHR) stresses the importance of assessing the personal integrity of public employees during vetting. In particular, they need to be considered for their adherence to international standards of human rights and professional conduct, including financial propriety. OHCHR specifically notes that public employees who are personally responsible for gross violations of human rights or serious crimes under international law lack integrity. How would one go about establishing the nature of "unprofessional" conduct that would reflect a lack of integrity sufficient to disqualify someone for public employment? Are "international standards of human rights" easily identifiable? Gross violations of human rights and of international criminal law reflect legal standards for which evidence will likely be clearer. But how does one identify the types of behavior—as well as the standard of proof necessary—to reflect a lack of "integrity"? Are differences in culture or religion relevant to answering these questions?

3. *Iraqi 2008 Accountability and Justice Law.* What are the primary differences between the 2008 vetting law and the old system? Does the newer system meet the standards recommended by the OHCHR and ICTJ for a fair vetting system? Does the law—as described by ICTJ—include the procedural protections necessary to assure that it achieves its objectives without creating greater instability? If not, what changes would you propose?

4. *The complicated history of vetting and "lustration."* The challenges of vetting are not new. From Northern Ireland to South Africa to Argentina, dramatic societal transformations have often brought with them the need to purge the government of individuals associated with a prior regime. Some of the most dramatic vetting programs took place in the former communist bloc after the disintegration of the Soviet Union. Through so-called "lustration" laws, former Communist party leaders, government officials, and other public employees were fired, prevented from holding public office, and, in some circumstances, prosecuted for their associations and their actions. 2 Neal Kritz, ed., Transnational Justice: How Emerging Democracies Reckon with Former Regimes, Country Studies (1995). These lustration laws have been criticized for the same reasons as the de-Ba'athification process, namely that the laws amount to group punishment and give voice to revenge more than justice. If the international community recognized the problems with lustration laws,

why were the same mistakes being repeated nearly two decades later in Iraq? Is this a failure of international normative development or simply a reflection of internal political dynamics over which the international community has no control? What is the solution for the next major post-conflict transition?

5. *Vetting and due process.* Should persons alleged to have been associated with past, abusive regimes have an international right to due process before being fired from their jobs or prevented from seeking public office? According to one commentator, "the state has a duty to vet the public administration as part of its duty to prevent [future human rights violations], and this vetting cannot be implemented in just any way. The state also has the duty to respect the rights of persons who are subject to a vetting process." Federico Andreu–Guzman, *Due Process and Vetting, in* JUSTICE AS PREVENTION: VETTING PUBLIC EMPLOYEES IN TRANSITIONAL SOCIETIES (Alexander Mayer–Riech and Pablo de Greiff, eds., International Center for Transitional Justice, 2007). Should the procedural rights in a criminal trial apply in this setting as well, or does the difference between criminal punishment and termination of public employment justify a lower standard of due process?

Practicum

After decades of oppressive rule over the Southeast Asian country of Burma (or Myanmar), assume that senior military regime leaders have agreed to go into exile in Indonesia. After a short but violent conflict with remnant military forces, a civilian council made up of individuals representing the largest ethnic tribes (of which there are many) in Burma has assumed power as part of a transitional government until elections can be held in one year. The Burmese people have suffered widespread human rights and international humanitarian law violations, the country lacks any semblance of a functioning judicial system, and soldiers roam the countryside with no means of support now that the previous government has collapsed.

Burma has a long history of strong military involvement in the country's governance. Ever since its independence, the military has occupied a preeminent position. Most observers and experts recognize that the military must continue to play a role in the country's political affairs—more so than is the case in many countries. However, the challenge will be to develop a system of government that retains military involvement at the same time that it ensures its influence (and control) will not lead the country down a path leading to the abuse and neglect suffered under the must recent junta.

Recognizing that it lacks the resources and capacity to maintain stability in the face of widespread security and increasing demands for justice by the Burmese people, the transitional government has requested the United Nations to take an active role in developing a strategy to maintain stability, ensure accountability, and establish rule of law. Note that the UN will need broad support for its strategy, as any ambitious program will not be capable of being absorbed into the UN regular budget—instead, voluntary contributions of the donor community will be necessary. Accordingly, the UN must consider carefully the demands of countries like the United States as well as the member states of the European Union. The UN must also ensure that its activities contribute to regional security. Accordingly, it will be necessary to ensure-buy in from governments in the region.

You are a representative of the Office of the UN High Commissioner for Human Rights in Rangoon and have been tasked with preparing a draft of the transitional justice strategy. Issues you should consider include: whether a UN Security Council resolution is necessary or advisable; whether a new judicial structure is necessary to deal with past, present and future crimes; whether cooperation or inclusion with regional human rights mechanisms is possible or advisable; proposals for a constitutional structure that balances the historical role of the Burmese military with the need to ensure checks on its authority and power; what law should be applied; how the crimes of the past will be addressed; how to create a vetting procedure for past military and government officials; and how the judicial system should be staffed.

CHAPTER 7

HUMANITARIAN INTERVENTION
AND THE LAW OF WAR

■ ■ ■

One of the peculiarities of human rights law as traditionally conceived is its tendency towards compartmentalization—a "turf consciousness" that has divided the field of human rights into separate, surprisingly rigid boxes of doctrine and practice. Consider the fact for example that states have long considered refugee law to be a branch of domestic immigration law and therefore to be an instrument of border control, leading to generally restrictive treatment for asylum seekers. If refugee law were instead conceived as a branch of human rights law rather than immigration law, it might be used broadly to protect people from persecution rather than to protect borders from foreigners. And if we were writing on a clean slate, would we again segregate the human rights of women by creating a Commission on the Status of Women within the United Nations?[1] Would we again consider labor rights to be a field of law separate from human rights law, as it has been for decades?[2]

A similar compartmentalization has traditionally separated humanitarian law—*jus in bello,* traditionally called the law of war—from human rights law. Why is it that the Geneva Conventions of 1949, or the treaties banning chemical and biological weapons, or the protocol banning the use of child soldiers have generally *not* been considered to be human rights treaties? Why have they traditionally been excluded from human rights casebooks?

It could be because the laws of war emerged at a time when states were the principal rights-bearers under international law. As a consequence, violations of the rules governing armed conflict might be viewed as a matter for state-to-state adjustment, as though these humanitarian obligations really ran state-to-state, and individual soldiers or civilians were just the incidental beneficiaries. In addition there are some profound substantive differences between human rights law and the law of

---

1. Hillary Charlesworth, *What Are "Women's International Human Rights"?, in* HUMAN RIGHTS OF WOMEN: NATIONAL AND INTERNATIONAL PERSPECTIVES 66 (Cook ed., 1994).

2. *See* Chapter 4, Module 10, *supra.*

war, which could account for their different treatment in practice and conception.

Human rights treaties, for example, traditionally regulate the conduct of a government towards its own citizens (or individuals who are within its jurisdiction) at any time, and the humanitarian law treaties regulate the conduct of a government towards the citizens of another state only during armed conflict (including enemy combatants, prisoners of war, civilians caught in the crossfire). Unlike human rights law, the law of war also allows an occupying power to intern prisoners of war without trial or appeal, so long as the conditions of detention are humane. It permits far-reaching limitations on freedoms of expression and assembly. Unlike human rights law, the law of war tolerates the killing and wounding of innocent human beings not directly participating in an armed conflict, so long as they are the victims of what the law calls "lawful collateral damage." This is law, in short, that has traditionally tried to regulate the life-or-death struggle between two formally equal states, and, like the rules of chivalry or boxing, it is an attempt to guarantee a modicum of fair play in a dirty business. But so long as those minimal rules are observed, it is permissible to cause suffering, deprivation of freedom, and death.

This is a somewhat narrow and technical vision of legality, and it strikes many people as the triumph of hype over experience. Long-established treaty and customary law, now supplemented by decisions from the Rwandan and Yugoslavian War Crimes Tribunals, declare that in times of armed conflict certain conduct, certain targets, and certain weaponry are unlawful. Some behaviors by combatants are evidently too cruel to tolerate (as distinct from the cruelty that is inherent in armed violence). To say that these things are unlawful may feel like a kind of hallucination: war is hell, and it is naive to pretend that we live in a world in which warriors will be noble and principled whether they are winning or losing. It may also be naive to think that the nature of warfare is the same now as it was when the humanitarian conventions were adopted. Typically, war in our time does not involve massive numbers of regular readily-identified troops fighting for one state against another state across international borders. Today the violence is frequently perpetrated by non-state actors, including irregular forces, privately-financed militias, terrorists, and criminal syndicates. In many of these conflicts, belligerents reverse the traditional norm that protects non-combatants and specifically target the civilian population, committing a wide range of atrocities including summary execution, mutilations, gender-based violence and sexual exploitation, including rape and forced prostitution, as well as the destruction of a society's cultural identity or a population's means of survival.

Humanitarian law, in other words, might be distinguished from human rights law in its state-to-state origins and its substantive requirements, as well as the even bigger gulf between its ambitions and its successes. But the materials in this chapter suggest that the traditional gap between human rights law and humanitarian law is closing—that no one can qualify as a human rights lawyer anymore without understanding developments in the law of armed conflict. To the contrary: over the last decade, international humanitarian law and its institutions have become central to the protection of human rights. Specifically, the *ad hoc* tribunals for Yugoslavia and Rwanda, among others, and the adoption of the Rome Statute of the International Criminal Court, not to mention the work of the Special Rapporteurs, have caused these two traditionally separate fields to converge. The law of war may once have been classically interstate law, driven by reciprocity, meaning one state obeys so long as the other one does. But the materials that follow show how the state-to-state aspects of international humanitarian law have shifted to emphasize individual criminal responsibility, effectively changing the emphasis from the interests of states to the rights and obligations of individuals and populations. Humanitarian conventions are coming to be regarded less as contracts concluded on a basis of reciprocity in the national interests of each party and more as affirmations of human rights principles and unconditional engagements.

The scope, meaning, and enforceability of *jus in bello* are some of the issues examined in this chapter, specifically in Module 18. Another is when the resort to force is lawful in the first place—a set of issues subsumed under the general rubric *jus ad bellum*. The legality of military force is a question that has arisen regularly in international affairs, often with little or no connection to the protection of human rights. For our purposes however, the most pressing version of the question of when recourse to military force is legitimate centers on the legality of *humanitarian intervention*, that is, "the threat or use of force by a state, group of states, or international organization primarily for the purpose of protecting the nationals of the target state from widespread deprivations of internationally-recognized human rights." SEAN MURPHY, HUMANITARIAN INTERVENTION: THE UNITED NATIONS IN AN EVOLVING WORLD ORDER 11–12 (1996). As shown in Module 17, the contemporary case for humanitarian intervention echoes ancient notions of the "just war," according to which military force is morally legitimate only against a state that has inflicted lasting, grave and certain damage; only as a last resort; only with proper authority and right intention (meaning that force is used to redress the wrong); only when there is a reasonable chance of success; only if the force deployed is proportional to the injury suffered; and only if the weapons and tactics that are used discriminate between civilians and combatants.

On the other hand, those who would defend the legality of humanitarian intervention must confront the seemingly explicit prohibition on the use of force in Article 2(4) of the UN Charter:

> Members shall refrain in their international relations from the threat or use of force against the territorial integrity or political independence of any state, or in any other manner inconsistent with the Purposes of the United Nations.

Is there room within these words to allow or even justify humanitarian intervention? Or is the international law of the twenty-first century simply more receptive to the use of violence for the protection of human rights?

History both before and after the creation of the United Nations is replete with apparent examples of international humanitarian interventions—some arguably motivated by benign or selfless concerns, some masking empire; some undertaken unilaterally, some through international coalitions; some concluding successfully and others catastrophically. The international interventions in Kosovo, East Timor, and Iraq are the most recent examples of intervention sometimes defended as humanitarian, though issues of legitimacy and tactics persist.

The role of the United Nations in promoting (or rejecting) humanitarian intervention has been especially controversial. Consider for example: Rwanda, where the Security Council decided to withdraw UN forces in the country precisely at the moment mass killings began in April 1994; Srebenica, where a UN declared "safe haven" was abandoned to the Bosnian Serb military in 1995, after thousands of Bosnian Muslims had sought asylum in reliance on the UN's assurances; Sierra Leone, where hundreds of UN peacekeepers were seized in May 2000 and detained by rebel factions; Kosovo, where in 1999 the North Atlantic Treaty Organization—a defensive military alliance with its origins in the Cold War—felt compelled to act when dissent within the UN Security Council effectively barred the UN from intervening directly. Is there something pathological about this list, or is the UN a viable forum for coordinating multilateral action in this regard? Is it, in short, the "best available player"?

After the epochal terrorist attacks on September 11, 2001, the Bush administration reconsidered and reformulated the traditional constraints on the international use of force, articulating a right of pre-emptive self-defense which effectively blurred the traditional distinction between aggressive war and self-defense. It also asserted that the link between al Qaeda and the governments of Afghanistan and Iraq justified the use of force with or without the approval of the United Nations. The public justification for these wars occasionally invoked the well-being and human rights of the people in the target countries, suggesting that the traditional (and controversial) category of humanitarian intervention might be undergoing reformulation and renaissance, even as the language of Article 2(4) of the UN Charter remains as stark (and as distant from the real behavior of states) as ever.

* * *

CHAPTER 7

MODULE 17

HUMANITARIAN INTERVENTION:
THE LEGALITY OF USING
MILITARY FORCE TO COMPEL COMPLIANCE
WITH HUMAN RIGHTS STANDARDS

■ ■ ■

Orientation

"To go to war for an idea, if the war is aggressive, not defensive, is as criminal as to go to war for territory or revenue; for it is as little justifiable to force our ideas on other people, as to compel them to submit to our will in any other respect. But there assuredly are cases in which it is allowable to go to war, without having been ourselves attacked, or threatened with attack; and it is very important that nations should make up their minds in time, as to what those cases are."

— John Stuart Mill, *A Few Words on Non–Intervention*
(FRASER'S MAGAZINE LX, 766–67) (1859)

As a matter of politics, ethics, and law, justifications for violence must be complicated. Those in particular who defend the legality of intervening for the purpose of stopping the widespread deprivation of human rights in the target country must confront the threshold difficulty that Article 2(4) of the UN Charter prohibits the use of force:

All Members shall refrain in their international relations from the threat or use of force against the territorial integrity or political independence of any state, or in any other manner inconsistent with the Purposes of the United Nations.

Article 2(4) articulates the broad understanding of the framers of the UN Charter that the use of force by one state against another is presumptively illegitimate, but the framers were not wild-eyed or naive idealists. To the contrary, these were pragmatists who had survived cataclysmic destruction twice in less than thirty years, and they drafted the UN Charter against the backdrop of a powerful idea: that aggressive war had become presumptively illegitimate when not collectively approved.

The UN Charter also defined the various peaceful means to be used in resolving disputes, providing in Article 33(1) that

> The parties to any dispute, the continuance of which is likely to endanger the maintenance of international peace and security, shall, first of all, seek a solution by negotiation, enquiry, mediation, conciliation, arbitration, judicial settlement, resort to regional agencies or arrangements, or other peaceful means of their own choice.

The idea that aggressive war might be internationally illegal had its origins in a variety of early twentieth-century treaties, including Article 10 of the League of Nations Covenant, 1 HUDSON INTERNATIONAL LEGISLATION 1 (1931),[1] under which every Member of the League undertook "to respect and preserve as against external aggression the territorial integrity and existing political independence of all [other] Members." And in the Kellogg–Briand Pact of 1928, the major powers agreed to "condemn recourse to war for the solution of international controversies, and renounce it as an instrument of national policy in their relations with one another."[2] That ideal proved impossible to meet in the face of imperial competition, Axis fascism, and aggression.

After World War II, and despite the explicit terms of Article 2(4), the UN Charter as a whole did not so much prohibit all force as channel it and subject it to a superior transnational regime under the Charter itself. Of course, to a cynic's ear, outlawing force is like requiring water to run uphill: from one perspective, going to war, like inflating currency, is what governments do best. One response to the skeptic is to point out that Article 2(4) and other provisions of the UN Charter do not pretend that states will suddenly become peaceful or that all force is necessarily illegal. It is that only certain types of force—or, more precisely, certain justifications for force—will be considered legitimate under the UN Charter. There are, in short, *categories of authority*, and if a particular use of force falls within one of these categories, then the action would not be illegal under Article 2(4). The action might be prudent or imprudent, costly or efficient, but it won't be illegal.

These authorizations for the use of force include national self-defense and the Security Council's authority to take action under Chapter VII of the UN Charter in response to threats to, or breaches of, the peace. The question for our purposes is whether humanitarian intervention is one of these categories of authority that has survived the prohibition in Article 2(4), and if so, whether the interventions in Kosovo and Iraq can be justified on those grounds. After all, Articles 55

---

1. *Available at* http://www.yale.edu/lawweb/avalon/leagcov.htm.

2. (27 Aug. 1928), 40 Stat. 2343, 94. L.N.T.S. 57. The Kellogg–Briand Pact, officially known as the General Treaty for the Renunciation of War, was ratified by the United States and remains a legal obligation of the United States.

and 56 clearly commit the United Nations to the protection of human rights.[3]

At base, the legality of humanitarian intervention implicates two powerful principles in contemporary international law. On one hand, there is the axiomatic obligation to protect human rights under customary and conventional international law and the steady erosion in the concept of exclusive domestic jurisdiction: human rights issues that were once considered domestic because they reflected a legitimate political diversity among states have been progressively internationalized and made the subject of communal concern and action. On the other hand, there is a Charter-based obligation to resolve disputes peacefully, to forego aggression, and to use force in only the most extreme circumstances and under an international regime of law, even when undertaken unilaterally. Both of these principles—the protection of human rights and the peaceful resolution of disputes—have been described as *jus cogens*, *i.e.* as peremptory norms of international law from which no derogation is permitted. Both have been described as the cornerstones of the international legal and political system. But in this setting, they cut in diametrically opposite directions. The interplay between these two obligations and the international conflict that has arisen when either one trumps the other requires human rights lawyers to understand the philosophy, the doctrine, and the pragmatics of *jus ad bellum*.

In part, the question of whether (or when) humanitarian intervention will be allowed is dependent on the answer to a broader question: must the legality of all uses of force be tested under the UN Charter or not? In other words, is it legal for states to justify force outside of the UN regime, or does the United Nations enjoy a monopoly on the lawful use of force in the twenty-first century? The recent experiences in Kosovo and Iraq suggest that states themselves are divided on the answer to this question, though it is possible to see certain rights-related themes emerging even from those most contested actions, as shown below.

The framers of the UN Charter, having observed the failure of the League of Nations and understanding the deeply pragmatic reasons for building on the political realities in the immediate aftermath of World War II, invested the UN Security Council with the responsibility to maintain international peace and security. Under Article 25 of the Charter, member states are obligated to "carry out" the Security Council's decisions. By contrast, the actions of other UN bodies, like the

---

3. Article 55 provides:

With a view to the creation of conditions of stability and well-being which are necessary for peaceful and friendly relations among nations based on respect for the principle of equal rights and self-determination of peoples, the United Nations shall promote: * * * c. universal respect for, and observance of, human rights and fundamental freedoms for all without distinction as to race, sex, language, or religion.

Article 56 provides:

All Members pledge themselves to take joint and separate action in co-operation with the Organization for the achievement of the purposes set forth in Article 55.

General Assembly or the Secretary–General, tend to operate as recommendations or as authoritative expectations without any legal obligation behind them. Under Chapter VII of the Charter, the Security Council may impose both forcible and non-forcible measures to enforce its decisions, though it is understood that force is authorized only as a last resort, when peaceful means of settling a dispute have been exhausted, and after a formal determination that a threat to the peace, a breach of the peace, or an act of aggression has occurred.

Over time, the practice of states and the UN organization itself suggest that there are certain *categories of force* that the international community will consider legitimate. There is perhaps inevitable disagreement about the applicability of these categories to any particular dispute, but with one crucial exception, explored below, the legality of force within these categories is broadly accepted.

Category #1: Self-defense. For centuries, states have recognized that self-defense is an adequate basis for the use of force, and Article 51 of the UN Charter preserves the inherent right of self-defense against an armed attack:

> Nothing in the present Charter shall impair the inherent right of individual or collective self-defense if an armed attack occurs against a Member of the United Nations, until the Security Council has taken measures necessary to maintain international peace and security. Measures taken by Members in the exercise of this right of self-defense shall be immediately reported to the Security Council and shall not in any way affect the authority and responsibility of the Security Council under the present Charter to take at any time such action as it deems necessary in order to maintain or restore international peace and security.

At least prior to the adoption of the Charter, the traditional test of legitimate self-defense was that articulated in the nineteenth century by U.S. Secretary of State, Daniel Webster, in the *Caroline* case, requiring that "a necessity of self-defense [be] instant, overwhelming, leaving no choice of means, and no moment for deliberation."[4] Of course, by its terms, Article 51 qualifies even the fundamental right of self-defense, allowing it "until" the UN Security Council acts and requiring the state to report its actions to the Security Council as an Article 51 exercise. Other limitations have been long debated by international lawyers and politicians, but it clearly offers one type of authorized force despite the breadth of Article 2(4). The important question for our purposes is whether there are circumstances under which a state might invoke its right of self-defense as a justification for its use of force in the protection of international human rights.

---

4. Letter of Secretary of State Daniel Wester to Special Minister Ashurton, dated 27 July 1842, reproduced at http://www.yale.edu/lawweb/avalon/diplomacy/britain/br.1842d.htm. John Moore, Digest of International Law 412 (1906). There is powerful but not conclusive evidence that the framers of the Charter did not intend to alter the pre-existing law of self-defense. John Murphy, *Force and Arms, in* I United Nations Legal Order 258 (Schachter and Joyner eds. 1995).

Category #2: Chapter VII. Chapter VII of the UN Charter authorizes the Security Council to take action against threats to the peace, breaches of the peace, or acts of aggression.

> *Article 39.* The Security Council shall determine the existence of any threat to the peace, breach of the peace, or act of aggression and shall make recommendations, or decide what measures shall be taken in accordance with Articles 41 and 42, to maintain or restore international peace and security.

> *Article 41.* The Security Council may decide what measures not involving the use of armed force are to be employed to give effect to its decisions, and it may call upon the Members of the United Nations to apply such measures. These may include complete or partial interruption of economic relations and of rail, sea, air, postal, telegraphic, radio, and other means of communication, and the severance of diplomatic relations.

> *Article 42.* Should the Security Council consider that measures provided for in Article 41 would be inadequate or have proved to be inadequate, it may take such action by air, sea, or land forces as may be necessary to maintain or restore international peace and security. Such action may include demonstrations, blockade, and other operations by air, sea, or land forces of Members of the United Nations.

The decisions of the Security Council are binding on the member states under Articles 25[5] and 48[6] of the Charter, but this power is subject to the veto of the five permanent members of the Security Council: Russia, China, Great Britain, France, and the United States.

Until the last decade, the Security Council rarely invoked its Chapter VII powers. Except in the Korean War in the early 1950's, when the Soviet Union's boycott of the Council enabled it to authorize the use of force without a veto, the Cold War prevented the Security Council from playing a significant human rights role under Chapter VII. Before the 1990's, it invoked Article 41 and applied mandatory economic sanctions only twice—against Rhodesia (now Zimbabwe) and against *apartheid* South Africa—in both cases on human rights grounds. But the end of the Cold War and Iraq's invasion of Kuwait in August 1990 offered the Council the opportunity to live up to the framers' original vision: in Resolution 661, adopted three days after the invasion, the Council invoked its Chapter VII authority and "the inherent right of individual

---

5. Article 25 of the Charter provides that

The Members of the United Nations agree to accept and carry out the decisions of the Security Council in accordance with the present Charter.

6. Article 48 of the Charter provides that

1. The action required to carry out the decisions of the Security Council for the maintenance of international peace and security shall be taken by all the Members of the United Nations or by some of them, as the Security Council may determine.

2. Such decisions shall be carried out by the Members of the United Nations directly and through their action in the appropriate international agencies of which they are members.

and collective self-defence, in response to the armed attack by Iraq against Kuwait," and imposed an economic embargo against Iraq and occupied Kuwait. Because these measures had no effect on Iraq's occupation, the Council subsequently adopted Resolution 678 (1991), *infra*, which authorized member states to use armed force against Iraq.

It should also be noted that Chapter VII authorizes various forms of intervention short of armed force, especially in the form of economic sanctions on human rights grounds, as the Security Council has done in relation to South Africa, Iraq, parts of the former Yugoslavia, Somalia, Libya, Liberia, Haiti, Angola, Rwanda, and Sudan, among others. An additional form of Chapter VII action that might be viewed as a form of non-forcible intervention for the purpose of protecting human rights is the creation of the *ad hoc* tribunals for Yugoslavia, Rwanda, and Sierra Leone, as shown in Module 6, *supra*.

Category #3: Chapter VIII. Chapter VIII of the UN Charter acknowledges the role of regional organizations and arrangements in addressing threats to the peace.

> *Article 52.* Nothing in the present Charter precludes the existence of regional arrangements or agencies for dealing with such matters relating to the maintenance of international peace and security as are appropriate for regional action, provided that such arrangements or agencies and their activities are consistent with the Purposes and Principles of the United Nations.

> *Article 53(1).* The Security Council shall, where appropriate, utilize such regional arrangements or agencies for enforcement action under its authority. But no enforcement action shall be taken under regional arrangements or by regional agencies without the authorization of the Security Council [with some exceptions not directly relevant here.]

There are a number of regional security organizations in the world, with varying degrees of military power at their disposal. In December 1999, for example, the 15–nation Economic Community of West African States ("ECOWAS") developed a regional "mechanism for conflict prevention, management, resolution, peace-keeping and security," and later agreed to create a permanent force of over 6000 soldiers, including a rapid reaction unit for trouble-shooting missions. After World War II, the North Atlantic Treaty Organization ("NATO")—though it resisted including itself as a Chapter VIII organization—was created to respond collectively and individually to attacks on any member of the North Atlantic alliance.

Category #4: Humanitarian intervention. Nothing in the UN Charter mentions—let alone authorizes—humanitarian intervention, and the argument for its legality is essentially historical, suggesting that a customary norm exists which allowed it and that the UN Charter did not prohibit it. Unfortunately, as Dostoevski observed, nothing is more indeterminate than the past, and a major part of the controversy here is finding actual examples of intervention, considered lawful by the international community, in a particular state for the purpose of protecting the nationals of that state from some humanitarian catastrophe. As advocates trot out apparent examples of humanitarian intervention in our own time or going back centuries, there are always competing interpretations of motives and events.

The first generation of humanitarian intervention involved powerful states, acting individually or collectively, to protect or rescue their own nationals residing abroad. Britain landed troops in China in 1827 and Egypt in 1956 for the protection of British subjects. The United States said that it was protecting U.S. nationals when it intervened militarily in Lebanon in 1958 and in the Dominican Republic in 1965. The Israeli rescue operation at Entebbe airport in 1976 was defended in part as a humanitarian intervention for the sake of freeing Israeli nationals being held hostage. In each of these cases, the use of force was described as humanitarian and specifically for the purpose of protecting or rescuing the intervening state's own citizens. Each was criticized as unlawful at the time or subsequently by other governments.

A second, more controversial generation of humanitarian intervention includes actions to protect the nationals of third-party states or even the nationals of the target state, especially its minority groups. India defended its military intervention in East Pakistan (which became Bangladesh) and in Sri Lanka on the ground that it was protecting minorities at risk. The same was said of Tanzania's intervention in Uganda to overthrow Idi Amin in 1978, and the U.S. actions in Grenada, Nicaragua, and Panama through the 1980's, and Vietnam's intervention to displace the Khmer Rouge in Cambodia. Again, each of these interventions was criticized as unlawful at the time or subsequently by other governments.

But the interpretation of historical events is only one recurring issue. Another is that, even if humanitarian intervention were legal once, it is hard to see how it survived Article 2(4) of the UN Charter, with its prohibition of all force "against the territorial integrity or political independence of any state, or in any other manner inconsistent with the Purposes of the United Nations." One possibility is to observe that not all force falls within the prohibition; indeed, if these words of Article 2(4) "are not redundant, they must qualify the all-inclusive prohibition against force." Oscar Schachter, *The Right of States to Use Armed Force*, 82 MICH. L. REV. 1620, 1625 (1984). In other words, in determining the legality of an operation, its purpose and scope should matter. As noted by Professor (and Judge) Rosalyn Higgins:

> what Article 2(4) prohibits is the use of force against the territorial
> integrity or political independence of a state, or in any other

manner inconsistent with the with the purpose of the United Nations. It can easily be seen that even a single plane attacking a country is a use of force against its territorial integrity. But is the answer so clear when the military intervention is not an attack on the state as such, but an operation simply designed to be able to rescue and remove one's threatened citizens? Is that really a use of force against the territorial integrity of the state, or is it rather a violation of sovereignty—in the same way as a civilian aircraft which enters airspace without permission will surely be violating sovereignty—but still not attacking the state or its territorial sovereignty? It would seem that hostile intent, coupled with military activity against the state (and beyond the minimum needed for the rescue), is what would distinguish a violation of sovereignty from an attack upon a state's territorial sovereignty.

ROSALYN HIGGINS, PROBLEMS AND PROCESS: INTERNATIONAL LAW AND HOW WE USE IT 245 (1994).

Another possible justification for humanitarian intervention is to argue that the meaning of Article 2(4)'s prohibition on force should have evolved in light of international human rights law since 1945. The argument would be that the prohibition on the use of force has to be reconciled with the protection of human rights—one of the purposes of the UN itself—and that the best way to reconcile the two is to interpret Article 2(4) as though experience with interventions over the past sixty years had effectively added an additional phrase, something like "unless force is used to protect fundamental human rights." The problem of course is that that's not what Article 2(4) says, and the prohibition on the use of force is so fundamental that you would expect substantial if not overwhelming evidence that the text expressing that prohibition had somehow evolved to include so profound an exception. Moreover, there is nothing—express or implied—in the human rights treaties and institutions that authorizes the use of force to promote human rights. In fact, if states had believed that those treaties sanctioned the use of force, it is doubtful that any state would have ratified any of them.

Consider the possibility that history is ultimately too manipulable to ground a fully convincing argument that humanitarian intervention is lawful and that its rationale must therefore be grounded in principle. One such systematic, theoretical justification for humanitarian intervention gets around the Article 2(4) problem by assuming that states exist for only one reason, namely to protect the rights and lives of its citizens. When the state ceases to do that, or when it becomes an instrument of oppression that violates the rights of its own citizens, then it ceases to be a legitimate state and forfeits the protection of international law, especially the right to be free of force by other states. In short, to get the benefit of Article 2(4)'s prohibition on the use of force, a state must show some minimal moral and legal order in which the rights of citizens are protected. Another way to phrase this idea is that, in modern international law, what counts is the sovereignty of the people and not some metaphysical abstraction called the "state."

The international intervention in Haiti offers a useful example. In December 1990, after decades of dictatorship, the Haitian people overwhelmingly elected Jean–Bertrand Aristide as president. Every aspect of the election was monitored by international organizations and confirmed as free and fair. Within months, the army seized power, expelled Aristide, and suppressed popular protest. The OAS and the UN Security Council condemned the coup and its aftermath and ordered economic sanctions. After those were perceived to be useless and counterproductive, in July 1994, the Security Council recognized that an exceptional response was required and adopted Resolution 940 authorizing military intervention. Those who argue that the prohibition on the use of force should not bar humanitarian intervention may point to Haiti and ask, "whose sovereignty exactly is violated by the intervention under Resolution 940?" If the purpose of the military force was to reinstate a *de jure* government elected in a free and fair election, whose sovereignty is being violated? Why would international law protect the sovereignty of the military (a group of about five thousand men with guns) and not the sovereignty of the millions who voted for Aristide? From this perspective, humanitarian intervention is not some affront to sovereignty. It is instead a necessary tool to preserve it. In the words of the UN Secretary General, "When we read the [UN] charter today we are more than ever conscious that its aim is to protect individual human beings, not to protect those who abuse them." Kofi A. Annan, *Two Concepts of Sovereignty*, THE ECONOMIST 49–50 (18 September 1999).

If the axiom that states exist to protect their citizens' rights is too abstract and too cavalier about the explicit language of Article 2(4), consider the reality that humanitarian intervention increasingly gets more respect in retrospect than it gets in advance. Especially in the aftermath of the genocidal massacres in Rwanda and Bosnia, states have smacked their collective foreheads and berated themselves for not pursuing humanitarian intervention at the time. President Clinton formally apologized for the U.S. inaction in Rwanda. A government in the Netherlands resigned because of the failure of Dutch troops to stop the massacre at Srebenica in July 1995. Secretary General Kofi Annan also apologized for the United Nations inaction, as though it were a legitimate expectation that states would deploy in the territories of other states for the purpose of protecting human rights or at least stopping genocide. So doing nothing is problematic, but is doing something called humanitarian intervention any less problematic?

Readings

MILITARY AND PARAMILITARY ACTIVITIES (NICAR. v. U.S.)

1986 I.C.J. 14, 96–100 (June 27), 1986 WL 522

202.   The principle of non-intervention involves the right of every sovereign State to conduct its affairs without outside interference; though examples of trespass against this principle are not infrequent, the Court considers that it is part and parcel of customary international law. As the Court has observed [in the *Corfu Channel Case*, [1949] I.C.J. Rep. 35]: "Between independent States, respect for territorial sovereignty is an essential foundation of international relations," * * * and international law requires political integrity also to be respected. Expressions of an *opinio juris* regarding the existence of the principle of non-intervention in customary international law are numerous and not difficult to find. * * * The existence in the *opinio juris* of States of the principle of non-intervention is backed by established and substantial practice. It has moreover been presented as a corollary of the principle of the sovereign equality of States. A particular instance of this is General Assembly resolution 2625 (XXV), the Declaration on the Principles of International Law concerning Friendly Relations and Co-operation among States. In the *Corfu Channel case*, when a State claimed a right of intervention in order to secure evidence in the territory of another State for submission to an international tribunal, the Court observed that:

> the alleged right of intervention as the manifestation of a policy of force, such as has, in the past, given rise to most serious abuses and such as cannot, whatever be the present defects in international organization, find a place in international law. Intervention is perhaps still less admissible in the particular form it would take here; for, from the nature of things, it would be reserved for the most powerful States, and might easily lead to perverting the administration of international justice itself.

203.   The principle has since been reflected in numerous declarations adopted by international organizations and conferences in which the United States and Nicaragua have participated, *e.g.*, General Assembly resolution 2131 (XX), the Declaration on the Inadmissibility of Intervention in the Domestic Affairs of States and the Protection of their Independence and Sovereignty. * * * [T]he essentials of resolution 2131 (XX) are repeated in the Declaration approved by resolution 2625 (XXV), which set out principles which the General Assembly declared to be "basic principles" of international law. * * *

204.   As regards inter-American relations, attention may be drawn to, for example, the United States reservation to the Montevideo Convention on Rights and Duties of States (26 December 1933), declaring the opposition of the United States Government to "interference with

the freedom, the sovereignty or other internal affairs, or processes of the Governments of other nations"; or the ratification by the United States of the Additional Protocol relative to Non-Intervention (23 December 1936). Among more recent texts, mention may be made of [various] resolutions * * * of the General Assembly of the Organization of American States. In a different context, the United States expressly accepted the principles set forth in the * * * Final Act of the Conference on Security and Co-operation in Europe (Helsinki, 1 August 1975), including an elaborate statement of the principle of non-intervention; while these principles were presented as applying to the mutual relations among the participating States, it can be inferred that the text testifies to the existence, and the acceptance by the United States, of a customary principle which has universal application.

205. Notwithstanding the multiplicity of declarations by States accepting the principle of non-intervention, there remain two questions: first, what is the exact content of the principle so accepted, and secondly, is the practice sufficiently in conformity with it for this to be a rule of customary international law? As regards the first problem—that of the content of the principle of non-intervention—the Court will define only those aspects of the principle which appear to be relevant to the resolution of the dispute. In this respect it notes that, in view of the generally accepted formulations, the principle forbids all States or groups of States to intervene directly or indirectly in internal or external affairs of other States. A prohibited intervention must accordingly be one bearing on matters in which each State is permitted, by the principle of State sovereignty, to decide freely. One of these is the choice of a political, economic, social and cultural system, and the formulation of foreign policy. Intervention is wrongful when it uses methods of coercion in regard to such choices, which must remain free ones. The element of coercion, which defines, and indeed forms the very essence of, prohibited intervention, is particularly obvious in the case of an intervention which uses force, either in the direct form of military action, or in the indirect form of support for subversive or terrorist armed activities within another State. * * * General Assembly resolution 2625 (XXV) equates assistance of this kind with the use of force by the assisting State when the acts committed in another State "involve a threat or use of force". These forms of action are therefore wrongful in the light of both the principle of non-use of force, and that of non-intervention. * * *

206. * * * There have been in recent years a number of instances of foreign intervention for the benefit of forces opposed to the government of another State. The Court * * * has to consider whether there might be indications of a practice illustrative of belief in a kind of general right for States to intervene, directly or indirectly, with or without armed force, in support of an internal opposition in another State, whose cause appeared particularly worthy by reason of the political and moral values with which it was identified. For such a

general right to come into existence would involve a fundamental modification of the customary law principle of non-intervention.

207.   In considering the instances of the conduct above described, the Court has to emphasize that, as was observed in the *North Sea Continental Shelf* cases, for a new customary rule to be formed, not only must the acts concerned "amount to a settled practice", but they must be accompanied by the *opinio juris sive necessitatis*. Either the States taking such action or other States in a position to react to it, must have behaved so that their conduct is "evidence of a belief that this practice is rendered obligatory by the existence of a rule of law requiring it. The need for such a belief, *i.e.*, the existence of a subjective element, is implicit in the very notion of the *opinio juris sive necessitatis*." (I.C.J. Reports 1969, p. 44, para. 77.) * * * Reliance by a State on a novel right or an unprecedented exception to the principle might, if shared in principle by other States, tend towards a modification of customary international law. In fact however the Court finds that States have not justified their conduct by reference to a new right of intervention or a new exception to the principle of its prohibition. The United States authorities have on some occasions clearly stated their grounds for intervening in the affairs of a foreign State for reasons connected with, for example, the domestic policies of that country, its ideology, the level of its armaments, or the direction of its foreign policy. But these were statements of international policy, and not an assertion of rules of existing international law. * * *

209.   The Court, therefore, finds that no such general right of intervention, in support of an opposition within another State, exists in contemporary international law. The Court concludes that acts constituting a breach of the customary principle of non-intervention will also, if they directly or indirectly involve the use of force, constitute a breach of the principle of non-use of force in international relations.

OSCAR SCHACHTER, INTERNATIONAL LAW IN THEORY AND PRACTICE 126 (1991)

Even in the absence of * * * prior approval [by the Security Council], a State or group of States using force to put an end to atrocities when the necessity is evident and the humanitarian intention is clear is likely to have its action pardoned. But, I believe it is highly undesirable to have a new rule allowing humanitarian intervention, for that would provide a pretext for abusive intervention. It would be better to acquiesce in a violation that is considered necessary and desirable in the particular circumstances than to adopt a principle that would open a wide gap in the barrier against unilateral use of force.

FERNANDO R. TESON, COLLECTIVE HUMANITARIAN INTERVENTION

17 MICH. J. INT'L L. 323, 341 (1996)

Until very recently, those who favored the legitimacy of humanitarian intervention were regarded either as hopeless idealists, or worse still, as trigger-happy "moral imperialists." Yet, the doctrine of humanitarian intervention has experienced a dramatic revival with the end of the Cold War. The realignment of global political forces and the awareness of the crucial link between human rights and peace have produced a significant change of opinion among governments and writers on the subject. While opinion is still sharply divided on the issue of unilateral humanitarian intervention, most international actors and observers are rallying behind the idea that the United Nations Security Council may, in appropriate cases, act forcibly to remedy serious human rights deprivations and their moral equivalents. * * * [T]he substantive law of the Charter has now evolved to include human rights as a centerpiece of the international order, and cases of serious human rights violations as situations that may warrant collective enforcement action. This imperative prevails over unrestrained state sovereignty, and may be enforced by the Security Council, acting on behalf of the international community, in rare cases of serious human rights violations where other means have failed or are certain to fail. * * *

CASE STUDY

THE KOSOVO INTERVENTION

In 1998, open conflict erupted between the military and police forces of the Federal Republic of Yugoslavia (Serbia–Montenegro) (FRY) on one hand and Kosovar Albanian forces on the other. As the conflict escalated, the international community became more concerned. In October 1998, the North Atlantic Treaty Organization (NATO) authorized air strikes against Belgrade, with the purpose of supporting diplomatic efforts to make the FRY government, headed by Slobodan Milosevic, withdraw forces from Kosovo. Those air strikes were called off when there seemed to be some diplomatic movement towards a settlement.

The Security Council of the United Nations continued to express concern about the excessive use of force by the Serbian Security forces and the Yugoslav army and called for a cease-fire by both parties, but, by January 1999, the situation had deteriorated. A six-nation contact group convened urgent negotiations between the parties, near Paris in February 1999, followed by a second round in mid-March. The Kosovar Albanian delegation signed a peace agreement, but talks broke up without a signature from the Serbian delegation. Major media outlets like CNN continued to broadcast pictures of massacres of civilians apparently by Serb irregulars, notably at Racak. The Security Council was unable to adopt a common policy calling for military action, blocked by the objections from two permanent members, Russia and China.

On March 23, 1999, with the United Nations blocked, NATO began what would become an eleven-week bombing campaign, targeting troops, military and industrial installations, government buildings, railroads and bridges, as well as non-traditional targets like state-run television facilities. The Chinese embassy and other civilian facilities were also bombed. As the campaign began, NATO Secretary–General Javier Solana declared that

> [a]ll efforts to achieve a negotiated, political solution to the Kosovo crisis having failed, no alternative is open but to take military action. * * * Let me be clear: NATO is not waging war against Yugoslavia. We have no quarrel with the people of Yugoslavia who for too long have been isolated in Europe because of the policies of their government. Our objective is to prevent more human suffering and more repression and violence against the civilian population of Kosovo. We must also act to prevent instability spreading in the region.

The Secretary–General later confirmed the objectives of the air war namely,

> first and foremost, we must stop the killing in Kosovo and the brutal destruction of human lives and properties; secondly, we must put an end to the appalling humanitarian situation that is now unfolding in Kosovo and create the conditions for the refugees to be able to return.

In a nationwide address on March 24, 1999, the President of the United States agreed and announced:

> Today, we and our 18 NATO allies agreed to do what we said we would do, what we must do to restore the peace. Our mission is clear: to demonstrate the seriousness of NATO's purpose so that the Serbian leaders understand the imperative of reversing course; to deter an even bloodier offensive against innocent civilians in Kosovo; and, if necessary, to seriously damage the Serbian military's capacity to harm the people of Kosovo. In short, if President Milosevic will not make peace, we will limit his ability to make war.

The U.S. representative to the Security Council declared that the UN Charter "does not sanction armed assaults upon ethnic groups or imply that the international community should turn a blind eye to a growing humanitarian disaster."

The international response to the bombing campaign was mixed: Austria closed its airspace to NATO missions on the ground that the UN had not authorized the use of force. Russia recalled its ambassador to

NATO and condemned the strikes, noting that enforcement by regional alliances under Chapter VIII required Security Council approval. China, India, Cuba and a handful of other states expressed opposition on legal and political grounds. But most Islamic states supported the action, and, when a resolution condemning the air campaign was placed before the Security Council on March 26th, 1999, it was defeated by a vote of 12 to 3, with many non-NATO states supporting the intervention, including Argentina, Bahrain, Brazil, Gabon, Gambia, Malaysia, and Slovenia. The General Assembly of the United Nations did not condemn the intervention, as it did when Vietnam intervened in Cambodia in 1978 or when the United States intervened in Grenada and Panama. Nor did the General Assembly adopt a resolution calling for the withdrawal of force, as it did when India intervened in East Pakistan in 1971. Nor should we underestimate S.C. Res. 1244, excerpted *supra*, which, with Russia's affirmative vote and China's abstention, blessed the results of the intervention by authorizing activities associated with the cease-fire agreement coerced from Serbia.

Between the beginning of NATO's bombing campaign in mid-March and Serbia's acceptance of the peace proposal in early June,

> violence by FRY forces against Kosovar Albanians dramatically escalated, prompting massive flows of refugees, Reports by refugees and from intelligence sources indicated that some forty thousand FRY army troops, special police units, and uniformed paramilitary forces were executing, raping, and conducting forced marches of Kosovar Albanians, and burning their homes and shops, in an apparent effort to "ethnically cleanse" Kosovo. * * * By the end of March 1999, the UN High Commissioner for Refugees estimated that some 167,500 refugees had fled from Kosovo across the border to neighboring Albania, Macedonia, and Montenegro; by the end of April, the number exceeded six hundred thousand and by the end of May the number reached almost eight hundred thousand. * * * In May 1999, the United States issued a report documenting the atrocities and war crimes being committed by FRY forces in Kosovo, and pledged, along with other countries, to provide information on the atrocities to the International Criminal Tribunal for the former Yugoslavia for use in its investigations. After the United States and other countries reportedly provided classified information implicating President Milosevic personally in the chain of command for the atrocities, the ICTY indicted President Milosevic and four of his colleagues on charges of crimes against humanity—specifically murder, deportation, and persecution—and violations of the laws and customs of war.

SEAN MURPHY, UNITED STATES PRACTICE IN INTERNATIONAL LAW: 1999–2001, 396–7 (2002).

BRUNO SIMMA, NATO, THE UN AND THE
USE OF FORCE: LEGAL ASPECTS

10 Eur. J. Int'l L. 1 (1999)

[I]f the Security Council determines that massive violations of human rights occurring within a country constitute a threat to the peace, and then calls for or authorizes an enforcement action to put an end to these violations, a "humanitarian intervention" by military means is permissible. In the absence of such authorization, military coercion employed to have the target state return to a respect for human rights constitutes a breach of Article 2(4) of the Charter. Further, as long as humanitarian crises do not transcend borders, as it were, and lead to armed attacks against other states, recourse to Article 51 is not available. For instance, a mass exodus of refugees does not qualify as an armed attack. In the absence of any justification unequivocally provided by the Charter "the use of force could not be the appropriate method to monitor or ensure . . . respect [for human rights]", to use the words of the International Court of Justice in its 1986 Nicaragua judgment. In the same year, the United Kingdom Foreign Office summed up the problems of unilateral, that is, unauthorized, humanitarian intervention as follows:

> [T]he overwhelming majority of contemporary legal opinion comes down against the existence of a right of humanitarian intervention, for three main reasons: first, the UN Charter and the corpus of modern international law do not seem to specifically incorporate such a right; secondly, State practice in the past two centuries, and especially since 1945, at best provides only a handful of genuine cases of humanitarian intervention, and, on most assessments, none at all; and finally, on prudential grounds, that the scope for abusing such a right argues strongly against its creation . . . In essence, therefore, the case against making humanitarian intervention an exception to the principle of non-intervention is that its doubtful benefits would be heavily outweighed by its costs in terms of respect for international law.[1]

* * * Whether we regard the NATO threat employed in the Kosovo crisis as an *ersatz* Chapter VII measure, "humanitarian intervention", or as a threat of collective countermeasures involving armed force, any attempt at legal justification will ultimately remain unsatisfactory. Hence, we would be well advised to * * * regard the Kosovo crisis as a singular case in which NATO decided to act without Security Council authorization out of overwhelming humanitarian necessity, but from which no general conclusion ought to be drawn. What is involved here is not legalistic hair-splitting versus the pursuit of humanitarian imperatives. Rather, the decisive point is that we should not change the rules simply

---

1. UK Foreign Office Policy Document No. 148, *reprinted in* 57 BRIT.YEARBOOK INT'L L. 614 (1986).

to follow our humanitarian impulses; we should not set new standards only to do the right thing in a single case. The legal issues presented by the Kosovo crisis are particularly impressive proof that hard cases make bad law.

CHRISTINE M. CHINKIN, EDITORIAL COMMENT: NATO'S KOSOVO INTERVENTION: KOSOVO: A "GOOD" OR "BAD" WAR?

93 AM. J. INT'L L. 841, 842–3 (1999)

Despite the Security Council's decision "to consider further actions and additional measures" in the case of noncompliance, the prospect of a veto by the Russian Federation prevented the authorization of unilateral or regional (NATO) enforcement, or of the use of force. It has become commonplace to assert that the Security Council's omission implies consent or authorization, even with respect to the use of armed force; examples are the creation of safe havens in northern Iraq, the invasion of airspace to monitor air lanes, and the bombing of Iraq in December 1998 in response to its defiance of the UN Special Commission. But such instances effectively require carefully negotiated Security Council resolutions, and each time this occurs, especially at the behest of any of its permanent members, the legal authority of the Security Council is diminished.

But the failure of the Security Council to authorize stronger measures was in the face of gross human rights abuses earlier acknowledged by it. Atrocities were invoked to bring the use of force within the parameters of humanitarian intervention. How can I, as an advocate of human rights, resist the assertion of a moral imperative on states to intervene in the internal affairs of another state where there is evidence of ethnic cleansing, rape, and other forms of systematic and widespread abuse, regardless of what the Charter mandates about the use of force and its allocation of competence?

Of what evidentiary value, if any, is the following resolution, adopted by the Security Council *after* hostilities in Kosovo had concluded, in assessing the legality of NATO's intervention? Is it relevant that the vote was unanimous (14–0), with China abstaining?

SECURITY COUNCIL RESOLUTION 1244

S/RES/1244 (10 June 1999)

The Security Council,

Bearing in mind the purposes and principles of the Charter of the United Nations, and the primary responsibility of the Security Council for the maintenance of international peace and security, * * *

Determined to resolve the grave humanitarian situation in Kosovo, Federal Republic of Yugoslavia, and to provide for the safe and free return of all refugees and displaced persons to their homes, * * *

Welcoming the general principles on a political solution to the Kosovo crisis adopted on 6 May 1999 ([. . .] annex 1 to this resolution) and welcoming also the acceptance by the Federal Republic of Yugoslavia of the principles set forth in points 1 to 9 of the paper presented in Belgrade on 2 June 1999 ([. . .] annex 2 to this resolution), and the Federal Republic of Yugoslavia's agreement to that paper, * * * *Determining* that the situation in the region continues to constitute a threat to international peace and security,

Determined to ensure the safety and security of international personnel and the implementation by all concerned of their responsibilities under the present resolution, and *acting* for these purposes under Chapter VII of the Charter of the United Nations,

1. *Decides* that a political solution to the Kosovo crisis shall be based on the general principles in annex 1 and as further elaborated in the principles and other required elements in annex 2;

2. *Welcomes* the acceptance by the Federal Republic of Yugoslavia of the principles and other required elements referred to in paragraph 1 above, and *demands* the full cooperation of the Federal Republic of Yugoslavia in their rapid implementation;

3. *Demands* in particular that the Federal Republic of Yugoslavia put an immediate and verifiable end to violence and repression in Kosovo, and begin and complete verifiable phased withdrawal from Kosovo of all military, police and paramilitary forces according to a rapid timetable, with which the deployment of the international security presence in Kosovo will be synchronized;

4. *Confirms* that after the withdrawal an agreed number of Yugoslav and Serb military and police personnel will be permitted to return to Kosovo to perform the functions in accordance with annex 2;

5. *Decides* on the deployment in Kosovo, under United Nations auspices, of international civil and security presences, with appropriate equipment and personnel as required, and welcomes the agreement of the Federal Republic of Yugoslavia to such presences; * * *

9. *Decides* that the responsibilities of the international security presence to be deployed and acting in Kosovo will include:

(a) Deterring renewed hostilities, maintaining and where necessary enforcing a ceasefire, and ensuring the withdrawal and preventing the return into Kosovo of Federal and Republic military, police and paramilitary forces, except as provided in point 6 of annex 2;

(b) Demilitarizing the Kosovo Liberation Army (KLA) and other armed Kosovo Albanian groups as required in paragraph 15 below;

(c) Establishing a secure environment in which refugees and displaced persons can return home in safety, the international civil presence can operate, a transitional administration can be established, and humanitarian aid can be delivered;

(d) Ensuring public safety and order until the international civil presence can take responsibility for this task;

(e) Supervising demining until the international civil presence can, as appropriate, take over responsibility for this task;

(f) Supporting, as appropriate, and coordinating closely with the work of the international civil presence;

(g) Conducting border monitoring duties as required;

(h) Ensuring the protection and freedom of movement of itself, the international civil presence, and other international organizations;

10. *Authorizes* the Secretary–General, with the assistance of relevant international organizations, to establish an international civil presence in Kosovo in order to provide an interim administration for Kosovo under which the people of Kosovo can enjoy substantial autonomy within the Federal Republic of Yugoslavia, and which will provide transitional administration while establishing and overseeing the development of provisional democratic self-governing institutions to ensure conditions for a peaceful and normal life for all inhabitants of Kosovo;

11. *Decides* that the main responsibilities of the international civil presence will include:

(a) Promoting the establishment, pending a final settlement, of substantial autonomy and self-government in Kosovo, taking full account of annex 2 and of the Rambouillet accords [];

(b) Performing basic civilian administrative functions where and as long as required;

(c) Organizing and overseeing the development of provisional institutions for democratic and autonomous self-government pending a political settlement, including the holding of elections;

(d) Transferring, as these institutions are established, its administrative responsibilities while overseeing and supporting the consolidation of Kosovo's local provisional institutions and other peacebuilding activities;

(e) Facilitating a political process designed to determine Kosovo's future status, taking into account the Rambouillet accords [];

(f) In a final stage, overseeing the transfer of authority from Kosovo's provisional institutions to institutions established under a political settlement;

(g) Supporting the reconstruction of key infrastructure and other economic reconstruction;

(h) Supporting, in coordination with international humanitarian organizations, humanitarian and disaster relief aid;

(i) Maintaining civil law and order, including establishing local police forces and meanwhile through the deployment of international police personnel to serve in Kosovo;

(j) Protecting and promoting human rights;

(k) Assuring the safe and unimpeded return of all refugees and displaced persons to their homes in Kosovo;

* * *

15. *Demands* that the KLA and other armed Kosovo Albanian groups end immediately all offensive actions and comply with the requirements for demilitarization as laid down by the head of the international security presence in consultation with the Special Representative of the Secretary–General; * * *

Annex 1

Statement by the Chairman on the conclusion of the meeting of the G–8 Foreign Ministers held at the Petersberg Centre on 6 May 1999:

The G–8 Foreign Ministers adopted the following general principles on the political solution to the Kosovo crisis:

— Immediate and verifiable end of violence and repression in Kosovo;

— Withdrawal from Kosovo of military, police and paramilitary forces;

— Deployment in Kosovo of effective international civil and security presences, endorsed and adopted by the United Nations, capable of guaranteeing the achievement of the common objectives;

— Establishment of an interim administration for Kosovo to be decided by the Security Council of the United Nations to ensure conditions for a peaceful and normal life for all inhabitants in Kosovo;

— The safe and free return of all refugees and displaced persons and unimpeded access to Kosovo by humanitarian aid organizations;

— A political process towards the establishment of an interim political framework agreement providing for a substantial self-government for Kosovo, taking full account of the Rambouillet accords and the principles of sovereignty and territorial integrity of the Federal Republic of Yugoslavia and the other countries of the region, and the demilitarization of the KLA;

— Comprehensive approach to the economic development and stabilization of the crisis region.

Annex 2

Agreement should be reached on the following principles to move towards a resolution of the Kosovo crisis:

1.   An immediate and verifiable end of violence and repression in Kosovo.

2.   Verifiable withdrawal from Kosovo of all military, police and paramilitary forces according to a rapid timetable.

3.   Deployment in Kosovo under United Nations auspices of effective international civil and security presences, acting as may be decided under Chapter VII of the Charter, capable of guaranteeing the achievement of common objectives.

4.   The international security presence with substantial North Atlantic Treaty Organization participation must be deployed under unified command and control and authorized to establish a safe environment for all people in Kosovo and to facilitate the safe return to their homes of all displaced persons and refugees.

5.   Establishment of an interim administration for Kosovo as a part of the international civil presence under which the people of Kosovo can enjoy substantial autonomy within the Federal Republic of Yugoslavia, to be decided by the Security Council of the United Nations. The interim administration to provide transitional administration while establishing and overseeing the development of provisional democratic self-governing institutions to ensure conditions for a peaceful and normal life for all inhabitants in Kosovo.

6.   After withdrawal, an agreed number of Yugoslav and Serbian personnel will be permitted to return to perform the following functions:

— Liaison with the international civil mission and the international security presence;

— Marking/clearing minefields;

— Maintaining a presence at Serb patrimonial sites;

— Maintaining a presence at key border crossings.

7.   Safe and free return of all refugees and displaced persons under the supervision of the Office of the United Nations High Commissioner for Refugees and unimpeded access to Kosovo by humanitarian aid organizations.

8.   A political process towards the establishment of an interim political framework agreement providing for substantial self-government for Kosovo, taking full account of the Rambouillet accords and the principles of sovereignty and territorial integrity of the Federal Republic of Yugoslavia and the other countries of the region, and the demilitarization of UCK. Negotiations between the parties for a settlement should

not delay or disrupt the establishment of democratic self-governing institutions.

9. A comprehensive approach to the economic development and stabilization of the crisis region. This will include the implementation of a stability pact for South–Eastern Europe with broad international participation in order to further promotion of democracy, economic prosperity, stability and regional cooperation. * * *

INDEPENDENT INTERNATIONAL COMMISSION ON KOSOVO THE KOSOVO REPORT (23 OCTOBER 2000)

The Commission has collated information from a wide variety of sources in order to assess the extent of atrocities. In the first phase of the conflict from February 1998 to March 1999, casualties were relatively low: around 1,000 civilians were killed up to September although the evidence is uncertain; the number of victims between September and March is unknown but must be lower. More than 400,000 people were driven from their homes during this period, about half of these were internally displaced. Most of these internal refugees returned after the Holbrooke–Milosevic agreement of October 1998. There were also widespread arrests and detentions during this period.

In the period March 24, 1999 to June 19, 1999, the Commission estimates the number of killings in the neighborhood of 10,000, with the vast majority of the victims being Kosovar Albanians killed by FRY forces. Approximately 863,000 civilians sought or were forced into refuge outside Kosovo and an additional 590,000 were internally displaced. There is also evidence of widespread rape and torture, as well as looting, pillaging and extortion.

The pattern of the logistical arrangements made for deportations and the coordination of actions by the Yugoslav army, para-military groups and the police shows that this huge expulsion of Kosovo–Albanians was systematic and deliberately organized. The NATO air campaign did not provoke the attacks on the civilian Kosovar population but the bombing created an environment that made such an operation feasible. * * *

THE NATO AIR CAMPAIGN

The Commission concludes that the NATO military intervention was illegal but legitimate. It was illegal because it did not receive prior approval from the United Nations Security Council. However, the Commission considers that the intervention was justified because all diplomatic avenues had been exhausted and because the intervention had the effect of liberating the majority population of Kosovo from a long period of oppression under Serbian rule. * * *

[T]he NATO war was neither a success nor a failure; it was in fact both. It forced the Serbian government to withdraw its army and police from Kosovo and to sign an agreement closely modeled on the aborted Rambouillet accord. It stopped the systematic oppression of the Kosovar Albanians. However, the intervention failed to achieve its avowed aim of preventing massive ethnic cleansing. Milosevic remained in power. The Serbian people were the main losers. Kosovo was lost. Many Serbs fled or were expelled from the province. Serbia suffered considerable economic losses and destruction of civilian infrastructure. Independent media and NGOs were suppressed and the overall level of repression in Serbia increased. * * *

THE FUTURE OF HUMANITARIAN INTERVENTION

Experience from the NATO intervention in Kosovo suggests the need to close the gap between legality and legitimacy. The Commission believes that the time is now ripe for the presentation of a principled framework for humanitarian intervention which could be used to guide future responses to imminent humanitarian catastrophes and which could be used to assess claims for humanitarian intervention. It is our hope that the UN General Assembly could adopt such a framework in some modified form as a Declaration and that the UN Charter be adapted to this Declaration either by appropriate amendments or by a case-by-case approach in the UN Security Council. We also suggest a strengthening of the level of human rights protection contained in the UN Charter—aware of course of the political problems of implementing such a change.

Our proposed principled framework includes three threshold principles, which must be satisfied in any legitimate claim to humanitarian intervention. These principles include the suffering of civilians owing to severe patterns of human rights violations or the breakdown of government, the overriding commitment to the direct protection of the civilian population, and the calculation that the intervention has a reasonable chance of ending the humanitarian catastrophe. In addition, the framework includes a further eight contextual principles which can be used to assess the degree of legitimacy possessed by the actual use of force.

The implication of our framework is that governments and international institutions also need to possess the appropriate means for carrying out this kind of operation. This means expanding the international peacekeeping capacity to protect civilians on the ground.

The Commission is aware that in many countries of the world there is a much stronger commitment to the protection of their sovereignty than currently exists in the West. Given the dual history of colonialism and the Cold War, there is widespread concern about Western interventionism. The growing global power of NATO creates a feeling of vulnerability in other parts of the world, especially in a case such as Kosovo where NATO claims a right to bypass the United Nations Security Council.

The Commission, composed as it was of citizens of many non-European, non-Western societies, puts great emphasis on the continued importance of the United Nations. It advocates increased funding and the need to consider ways to reform the main bodies of the United Nations, especially the Security Council, so that they are better suited to the post-Cold War environment.

The proposal for a new framework for humanitarian intervention should not detract from the need to prevent humanitarian catastrophes in the future. The Commission takes the view that much more political effort and economic resources need to be devoted both to pre-conflict and post-conflict situations. In the case of Kosovo, far more attention and money was spent on Kosovo during the intervention than before or after.

The Commission also advocates greater emphasis on the gender dimension of humanitarian intervention. In Kosovo, insufficient attention has been paid to the impact of the conflict on women, in particular, the use of rape as a weapon of war, and the rise of trafficking in the post-conflict period. Moreover, women have a crucial role to play in post-conflict reconciliation and reconstruction.

Finally, the Commission is acutely aware that the world has not given the same priority to humanitarian catastrophes outside Europe as it gave to Kosovo. It is the Commission's hope that, after the Kosovo experience, it will be impossible to ignore tragedies such as the genocide in Rwanda in other parts of the world, and that the lessons of the Kosovo conflict will help us to develop a more effective response to future humanitarian catastrophes wherever they occur.

NOTES AND QUESTIONS ON THE KOSOVO INTERVENTION

1. *Fitting Kosovo into a legal framework.* Does the NATO attack in Kosovo fall within any of the boxes of legitimacy authorizing the use of force? If not, is it for that reason alone illegal? Did the decision of the International Court of Justice in the *Nicaragua* case foreclose the possibility of an emerging norm allowing (or even requiring) intervention in certain circumstances? What is the legal and political and moral meaning of the Kosovo Commission's conclusion that the intervention was "illegal but legitimate"?

2. *Kosovo as a "law-creating" event.* You may have concluded that humanitarian intervention, even if it had been legal before the UN Charter, did not survive article 2(4) and hasn't been sustained in the

practice of states since 1945. And you may have concluded that the intervention in Kosovo was illegal, because it doesn't fall within any of the categories of legitimate force. On the other hand, it cannot be denied that nineteen NATO countries decided that intervention was justified and thirteen of them actually engaged in the bombing campaign. Nor can it be denied that NATO can claim a certain legitimacy by virtue of its decision-making process and its commitment to a democratic Europe that even Yugoslavia wanted to join. Nor can it be denied that many non-NATO states supported the campaign, and the communal opportunity to condemn the NATO campaign was clearly presented and clearly rejected.

Perhaps we are left with a strange predicament for a lawyer: there was no clear legal rationale for NATO's intervention at the time, but virtually all of the global community seems to have sanctioned it, at least in retrospect. We may need to live more history to determine whether Kosovo is a one-time thing or a law-shaping event. At its broadest, the Kosovo incident might stand for a legal rule that a coalition of states may intervene in any other state when it anticipates the widespread deprivation of human rights. That would be big news. At its narrowest interpretation, as noted by Professor Sean Murphy, Kosovo might stand for a significantly more qualified rule, very much limited to the facts and articulated along these lines:

> An intervention may proceed without prior approval of the Security Council when (a) the Security Council has expressly identified actions taken by a government as a threat to the peace which has led or could lead to a humanitarian catastrophe; (b) that government refuses to abide by the demands of the Security Council, including agreements that the government itself has made with the international community and that have been endorsed by the Security Council; (c) states operating as part of a collective intergovernmental organization decide to intervene to prevent the impending humanitarian catastrophe; (d) those states use force that is necessary and proportionate to the catastrophe; and (e) the Security Council does not pass a resolution condemning the intervention.

What problems would you anticipate if the law evolves to incorporate a new rule like the one laid out above? Did the intervention in Iraq in 2003, *infra*, reinforce or undermine this new "norm"?

3. *Implicit authorizations.* NATO and the UN Security Council were not the only intergovernmental actors involved in the Kosovo crisis. As Annex 2 to S.C. Res. 1244, *supra*, suggests, the seven leading industrial countries—the Group of Seven or "G–7"—and Russia had articulated a ten-point peace proposal three days before the Security Council acted, and the Federal Republic of Yugoslavia had signaled its acceptance of that proposal. Letter Dated 7 June 1999 from the Chargé d'Affaires of the Permanent Mission of Yugoslavia to the United Nations Addressed to the Security Council, UN Doc. S/1999/655 (1999). Do the G–7

proposal and S.C. Res.1244 amount to a retroactive approval of NATO's actions in Kosovo? Is there anything in the provisions of the UN Charter that allows the *post hoc* inference of Security Council approval?

4. *Self-defense and the protection of human rights.* Consider the argument of Professor (later Judge) Humphrey Waldock that a state could use force for the purpose of rescuing its nationals abroad and that such action might be justified "as an aspect of self-defense," so long as (i) the threat of injury were imminent, (ii) the territorial sovereign had failed or was unable to protect those nationals, and (iii) the forcible measures were proportional or strictly confined to the purpose of protecting those nationals. 81 RECUEIL DES COURS 451, 467 (1952–II). Under twenty-first century human rights doctrine, which is considerably less fixated on the link of nationality, could Waldock's argument be expanded?

5. *Limitations on NATO's use of force.* Article 5 of NATO's Charter provides:

> The Parties agree that an armed attack against one or more of them in Europe or North America shall be considered an attack against them all and consequently they agree that, if such an armed attack occurs, each of them, in exercise of the right of individual or collective self-defence recognised by Article 51 of the Charter of the United Nations, will assist the Party or Parties so attacked by taking forthwith, individually and in concert with the other Parties, such action as it deems necessary, including the use of armed force, to restore and maintain the security of the North Atlantic area. Any such armed attack and all measures taken as a result thereof shall immediately be reported to the Security Council. Such measures shall be terminated when the Security Council has taken the measures necessary to restore and maintain international peace and security.

Did NATO's bombing campaign in Kosovo violate this provision of its own charter?

6. *Afghanistan.* Responding to what it perceived as a threat to the peace, and acting under Chapter VII, the UN Security Council imposed various sanctions on the Taliban regime in 1999 and 2001 for its refusal to surrender Osama Bin Laden and its failure to close certain terrorist training camps located within Afghan territory. The United Nations and various human rights NGOs also repeatedly condemned the Taliban regime for human rights abuses in Afghanistan—especially the treatment of women and girls—but military force was not used until October 7, 2001, when the United States and its allies began military operations in response to the attacks of September 11. In a letter to the Security Council on the day of the attack, the United States government cited Article 51 of the UN Charter, and declared that "the attacks on 11 September 2001 and the ongoing threat to the United States and its nationals posed by the Al-Qaeda organization have been made possible by the decision of the Taliban regime to allow the parts of Afghanistan

that it controls to be used by this organization as a base of operation. In response to these attacks, and in accordance with the inherent right of individual and collective self-defence, United States armed forces have initiated actions designed to prevent and deter further attacks on the United States."

7. *Centralizing the process of authorization.* Who decides whether "humanitarian intervention" is justified, and how? Is the UN ultimately a viable forum for coordinating multilateral action in this regard? If not, why not, and what are the best alternatives?

8. *Defining "intervention."* What qualifies as "intervention?" Are there circumstances in which non-forcible measures like economic sanctions might qualify as intervention and therefore be prohibited under Article 2(4)? Are there circumstances in which humanitarian assistance— where a state offers relief to people in desperate need in other states— might also constitute humanitarian intervention?

9. *An obligation to intervene?* Are all systematic violations of human rights *per se* threats to international peace and security? (a) If not, what factors should states and the Security Council use to distinguish the crises that justify intervention from those that do not? (b) If so, can states in any sense be under an obligation to intervene in some proportionate way when another state violates the human rights of people within its jurisdiction, regardless of their nationality? *See* Evans and Sahnoun's analysis of the "responsibility to protect" doctrine, *infra.*

10. *Mixed motives—lawful action, unlawful motives.* Is it lawful for a state do the right thing for the wrong reasons? What if its motives for intervening included both legitimate reasons (acting pursuant to Chapter VII authorization for example or in self-defense) and illegitimate reasons (acquiring territory or natural resources, or altering the government in the target state for ideological reasons)? Does the rationale offered for an act necessarily limit its scope as a matter of law?

11. *Mixed results.* Was the intervention in Kosovo effective in solving a human rights problem, or did it exacerbate a human rights problem?

12. *One philosophical perspective.* How would you respond to the following skeptical perspective on the use of force as a means of protecting human rights?

Recent history offers a number of opportunities for assessing the meaning of Article 2(4): East Timor, Kosovo, Afghanistan, Iraq, and, going back to the 1990's, Somalia, Haiti, Cambodia, Rwanda. Each of these crises—for all of their political and moral difficulty—was also framed by law. That certainly does not mean that the law resolves or prevents such crises, just as the homicide laws do not by themselves prevent or resolve all murders. But the decisions taken in these international crises can be discussed or contextualized through law, including the treaties and customary norms and principles which define what the international community considers a legitimate use of force. However, it is entirely possible to conclude that the effort to control the use of force has been a relative failure—a *failure* because the legal principles discussed here and the conduct of the member states and the UN itself over the decades would be a profound disappointment to the framers of the UN Charter, but also a *relative* failure because we do not know and cannot know how bad things might have been if the UN had done nothing or had never existed.

One possible explanation for the failure of law in this arena is that there has been a radical inconsistency in these use-of-force decisions by the UN over time, which prevents meaningful norms from emerging. Another explanation might be that the prospects for law go down as the stakes go up. After all, the U.S. Constitution is remarkably (and intentionally) ambiguous when it comes to the power to go to war or to defend the nation. International law handles many things well, but on ultimate questions of national security and survival, the prospects for law must be remote.

13. *Jus ad bellum claims for damages.* What is the proper remedy if a nation violates *jus ad bellum*? Reparations—in which the victor extracts payment from the vanquished—are an ancient spoil of war and may more resemble humiliation than compensation. But legal developments over the last decade suggest an emerging standard of compensation for violations of *jus ad bellum*. The United Nations Compensation Commission (UNCC) was created in 1991 as a subsidiary organ of the Security Council to process claims and pay compensation for damages arising out of Iraq's "unlawful invasion and occupation of Kuwait." *See generally* United Nations Compensation Commission, http://www2.unog.ch/uncc/. The UNCC has not been a model of clarity in tracing compensation claims to the unlawfulness of the invasion—the focus of *jus ad bellum*—as distinct from the damages caused during the occupation itself. By contrast, in December 2005, the Eritrea–Ethiopia Claims Commission ruled that damages could be awarded to Ethiopia specifically on the basis of its *jus ad bellum* claims against Eritrea. Eritrea–Ethiopia Claims Comm'n, *Partial Award: Jus ad Bellum: Ethiopia's Claims 1–8* (Dec. 2005), 45 I.L.M. 430 (2006). Ethiopia had alleged *inter alia* that Eritrea had violated Article 2(4) of the UN Charter, unlawfully attacking and occupying Ethiopian territory, during the two-year border dispute between the two nations from 1998–2000. Eritrea argued that its occupation of the disputed regions constituted lawful self-defense under Article 51 of the UN Charter. The Claims Commission rejected that argument and held under international law that self-defense cannot be invoked when the territoriality of the region is in dispute. Eritrea was found liable for damages for the unlawful attack and occupation of territory under "peaceful administration" by Ethiopia, *id.* at ¶ 16, but proceedings continue in the effort to develop a metric for determining the amount of compensable damages. What factors should the commission take into consideration when awarding damages for *jus ad bellum* claims? *See* Eritrea–Ethiopia Claims Comm'n, *Decision 7: Guidance Regarding* Jus ad

Bellum *Liability*, 46 I.L.M. 1121 (2007). Should the relative poverty of the two states affect the legal calculation of damages?

HUMANITARIAN INTERVENTION RECONSIDERED: THE RESPONSIBILITY TO PROTECT ("R2P")

GARETH EVANS AND MOHAMED SAHNOUN, THE RESPONSIBILITY TO PROTECT

81 FOREIGN AFFAIRS 99 (2002)

The international community in the last decade repeatedly made a mess of handling the many demands that were made for "humanitarian intervention": coercive action against a state to protect people within its borders from suffering grave harm. There were no agreed rules for handling cases such as Somalia, Bosnia, Rwanda, and Kosovo at the start of the 1990s, and there remain none today. Disagreement continues about whether there is a right of intervention, how and when it should be exercised, and under whose authority.

Since September 11, 2001, policy attention has been captured by a different set of problems: the response to global terrorism and the case for "hot preemption" against countries believed to be irresponsibly acquiring weapons of mass destruction. These issues, however, are conceptually and practically distinct. There are indeed common questions, especially concerning the precautionary principles that should apply to any military action anywhere. But what is involved in the debates about intervention in Afghanistan, Iraq, and elsewhere is the scope and limits of countries' rights to act in self-defense—not their right, or obligation, to intervene elsewhere to protect peoples other than their own.

Meanwhile, the debate about intervention for human protection purposes has not gone away. And it will not go away so long as human nature remains as fallible as it is and internal conflict and state failures stay as prevalent as they are. The debate was certainly a lively one throughout the 1990s. Controversy may have been muted in the case of the interventions, by varying casts of actors, in Liberia in 1990, northern Iraq in 1991, Haiti in 1994, Sierra Leone in 1997, and (not strictly coercively) East Timor in 1999. But in Somalia in 1993, Rwanda in 1994, and Bosnia in 1995, the UN action taken (if taken at all) was widely perceived as too little too late, misconceived, poorly resourced, poorly executed, or all of the above. During NATO's 1999 intervention in Kosovo, Security Council members were sharply divided; the legal justification for action without UN authority was asserted but largely unargued; and great misgivings surrounded the means by which the allies waged the war.

It is only a matter of time before reports emerge again from somewhere of massacres, mass starvation, rape, and ethnic cleansing. And then the question will arise again in the Security Council, in political capitals, and in the media: What do we do? This time around the international community must have the answers. Few things have done more harm to its shared ideal that people are all equal in worth and dignity than the inability of the community of states to prevent these horrors. In this new century, there must be no more Rwandas.

Secretary–General Kofi Annan, deeply troubled by the inconsistency of the international response, has repeatedly challenged the General Assembly to find a way through these dilemmas. But in the debates that followed his calls, he was rewarded for the most part by cantankerous exchanges in which fervent supporters of intervention on human rights grounds, opposed by anxious defenders of state sovereignty, dug themselves deeper and deeper into opposing trenches.

If the international community is to respond to this challenge, the whole debate must be turned on its head. The issue must be reframed not as an argument about the "right to intervene" but about the "responsibility to protect." And it has to be accepted that although this responsibility is owed by all sovereign states to their own citizens in the first instance, it must be picked up by the international community if that first-tier responsibility is abdicated, or if it cannot be exercised. Using this alternative language will help shake up the policy debate, getting governments in particular to think afresh about what the real issues are. Changing the terminology from "intervention" to "protection" gets away from the language of "humanitarian intervention." The latter term has always deeply concerned humanitarian relief organizations, which have hated the association of "humanitarian" with military activity. Beyond that, talking about the "responsibility to protect" rather than the "right to intervene" has three other big advantages.

First, it implies evaluating the issues from the point of view of those needing support, rather than those who may be considering intervention. The searchlight is back where it should always be: on the duty to protect communities from mass killing, women from systematic rape, and children from starvation. Second, this formulation implies that the primary responsibility rests with the state concerned. Only if that state is unable or unwilling to fulfill its responsibility to protect, or is itself the perpetrator, should the international community take the responsibility to act in its place. Third, the "responsibility to protect" is an umbrella concept, embracing not just the "responsibility to react" but the "responsibility to prevent" and the "responsibility to rebuild" as well. Both of these dimensions have been much neglected in the traditional humanitarian intervention debate. Bringing them back to center stage should help make the concept of reaction itself more palatable.

At the heart of this conceptual approach is a shift in thinking about the essence of sovereignty, from control to responsibility. In the classic Westphalian system of international relations, the defining characteristic of sovereignty has always been the state's capacity to make authoritative decisions regarding the people and resources within its territory. The principle of sovereign equality of states is enshrined in Article 2, Section 1, of the UN Charter, and the corresponding norm of non-intervention is enshrined in Article 2, Section 7: a sovereign state is empowered by international law to exercise exclusive and total jurisdiction within its territorial borders, and other states have the corresponding duty not to intervene in its internal affairs. But working against this standard has been the increasing impact in recent decades of human rights norms, bringing a shift from a culture of sovereign impunity to one of national and international accountability. The increasing influence of the concept of human security has also played a role: what matters is not just state security but the protection of individuals against threats to life, liveli-hood, or dignity that can come from within or without. In short, a large and growing gap has been developing between international behavior as articulated in the state-centered UN Charter, which was signed in 1946, and evolving state practice since then, which now emphasizes the limits of sovereignty.

Indeed, even the strongest supporters of state sovereignty will admit today that no state holds unlimited power to do what it wants to its own people. It is now commonly acknowledged that sovereignty implies a dual responsibility: externally, to respect the sovereignty of other states, and internally, to respect the dignity and basic rights of all the people within the state. In international human rights covenants, in UN practice, and in state practice itself, sovereignty is now understood as embracing this dual responsibility. Sovereignty as responsibility has become the minimum content of good international citizenship. Al-though this new principle cannot be said to be customary international law yet, it is sufficiently accepted in practice to be regarded as a *de facto* emerging norm: the responsibility to protect. * * *

The responsibility to protect implies a duty to react to situations in which there is compelling need for human protection. If preventive measures fail to resolve or contain such a situation, and when the state in question is unable or unwilling to step in, then intervention by other states may be required. Coercive measures then may include political, economic, or judicial steps. In extreme cases—but only extreme cases—they may also include military action. But what is an extreme case? Where should we draw the line in determining when military interven-tion is defensible? What other conditions or restraints, if any, should apply in determining whether and how that intervention should pro-ceed? And, most difficult of all, who should have the ultimate authority to determine whether an intrusion into a sovereign state, involving the use of deadly force on a potentially massive scale, should actually go ahead? These questions have generated an enormous literature and much competing terminology, but on the core issues there is a great deal of common ground, most of it derived from "just war" theory. To justify military intervention, six principles have to be satisfied: the "just cause" threshold, four precautionary principles, and the requirement of "right authority."

As for the *"just cause"* threshold, our starting point is that military intervention for human protection purposes is an extraordinary measure. For it to be warranted, civilians must be faced with the threat of serious and irreparable harm in one of just two exceptional ways. The first is large-scale loss of life, actual or anticipated, with genocidal intent or not, which is the product of deliberate state action, state neglect, inability to act, or state failure. The second is large-scale "ethnic cleansing," actual or anticipated, whether carried out by killing, forced expulsion, acts of terror, or rape. * * * The threshold criteria articulated here not only cover the deliberate perpetration of horrors such as in the cases of Bosnia, Rwanda, and Kosovo. They can also apply to situations of state collapse and the resultant exposure of the population to mass starvation or civil war, as in Somalia. Also potentially covered would be overwhelming natural or environmental catastrophes, in which the state concerned is either unwilling or unable to help and significant loss of life is occurring or threatened. What are not covered by our "just cause" threshold criteria are human rights violations falling short of outright killing or ethnic cleansing (such as systematic racial discrimination or political oppression), the overthrow of democratically elected governments, and the rescue by a state of its own nationals on foreign territory. Although deserving of external action—including in appropriate cases political, economic, or military sanctions—these are not instances that would seem to justify military action for human protection purposes. * * *

Of the precautionary principles needed to justify intervention, the first is *"right intention."* The primary purpose of the intervention, whatever other motives intervening states may have, must be to halt or avert human suffering. There are a number of ways of helping ensure that this criterion is satisfied. One is to have military intervention always take place on a collective or multilateral basis. Another is to look at the extent to which the intervention is actually supported by the people for whose benefit the intervention is intended. Yet another is to look to what extent the opinion of other countries in the region has been taken into account and is supportive. Complete disinterestedness may be an ideal, but it is not likely always to be a reality: mixed motives, in international relations as everywhere else, are a fact of life. Moreover, the budgetary cost and risk to personnel involved in any military action may make it imperative for the intervening state to be able to claim some degree of self-interest in the intervention, however altruistic its primary motive.

The second precautionary principle is *"last resort"*: military intervention can be justified only when every non-military option for the prevention or peaceful resolution of the crisis has been explored, with reasonable grounds for believing lesser measures would not have succeeded. The responsibility to react with military coercion can be justified only when the responsibility to prevent has been fully discharged. This guideline does not necessarily mean that every such option must literally have been tried and failed; often there is simply not enough time for that process to work itself out. But it does mean that there must be reasonable grounds for believing that, given the circumstances, other measures would not have succeeded.

The third principle is "*proportional means*": the scale, duration, and intensity of the planned military intervention should be the minimum necessary to secure the defined objective of protecting people. The scale of action taken must be commensurate with its stated purpose and with the magnitude of the original provocation. The effect on the political system of the country targeted should be limited to what is strictly necessary to accomplish the intervention's purpose. Although the precise practical implications of these strictures are always open to argument, the principles involved are clear enough.

Finally, there is the principle of "*reasonable prospects*": there must be a reasonable chance of success in halting or averting the suffering that has justified the intervention; the consequences of action should not be worse than the consequences of inaction. Military action must not risk triggering a greater conflagration. Applying this precautionary principle would, on purely utilitarian grounds, likely preclude military action against any one of the five permanent members of the Security Council, even with all other conditions for intervention having been met. Otherwise, it is difficult to imagine a major conflict being avoided or success in the original objective being achieved. The same is true for other major powers that are not permanent members of the Security Council. This raises the familiar question of double standards, to which there is only one answer: The reality that interventions may not be plausibly mounted in every justifiable case is no reason for them not to be mounted in any case. * * *

The most difficult and controversial principle to apply is that of "*right authority*." When it comes to authorizing military intervention for human protection purposes, the argument is compelling that the United Nations, and in particular its Security Council, should be the first port of call. The difficult question—starkly raised by the Kosovo war—is whether it should be the last. The issue of principle here is unarguable. The UN is unquestionably the principal institution for building, consolidating, and using the authority of the international community. It was set up to be the linchpin of order and stability, the framework within which members of the international system negotiate agreements on the rules of behavior and the legal norms of proper conduct to preserve the society of states. The authority of the UN is underpinned not by coercive power but by its role as the applicator of legitimacy. The concept of legitimacy acts as the connecting link between the exercise of authority and the recourse to power. Attempts to enforce authority can be made only by the legitimate agents of that authority. Nations regard collective intervention blessed by the UN as legitimate because a representative international body duly authorized it, whereas unilateral intervention is seen as illegitimate because it is self-interested. Those who challenge or evade the authority of the UN run the risk of eroding its authority in general and undermining the principle of a world order based on international law and universal norms.

The task is not to find alternatives to the Security Council as a source of authority, but to make the council work better than it has. Security Council authorization should, in all cases, be sought prior to any military intervention being carried out. Those advocates calling for an intervention should formally request such authorization, ask the council to raise the matter on its own initiative, or demand that the secretary-general raise it under Article 99 of the UN Charter. The Security Council should deal promptly with any request for authority to intervene where there are allegations of large-scale loss of life or ethnic cleansing. It should, in this context, also seek adequate verification of facts or conditions on the ground that might support a military intervention. And the council's five permanent members should agree to not exercise their veto power (in matters where their vital state interests are not involved) to block resolutions authorizing military intervention for human protection purposes for which there is otherwise majority support. * * *

If the Security Council is unable or unwilling to act in a case crying out for intervention, two institutional solutions are available. One is for the General Assembly to consider the matter in an emergency special session under the "Uniting for Peace" procedure, used in the cases of Korea in 1950, Egypt in 1956, and Congo in 1960. Had it been used, that approach could well have delivered a speedy majority recommendation for action in the Rwanda and Kosovo cases. The other is action within an area of jurisdiction by regional or subregional organizations under Chapter VIII of the UN Charter, subject to their seeking subsequent authorization from the Security Council; that is what happened with the West African interventions in Liberia in the early 1990s and in Sierra Leone in 1997. But interventions by ad hoc coalitions (or individual states) acting without the approval of the Security Council, the General Assembly, or a regional or subregional grouping do not find wide international favor. As a matter of political reality, then, it would simply be impossible to build consensus around any set of proposals for military intervention that acknowledged the validity of any intervention not authorized by the Security Council or General Assembly. * * *

It is the responsibility of the whole international community to ensure that when the next case of threatened mass killing or ethnic cleansing invariably comes along, the mistakes of the 1990s will not be repeated. A good place to start would be agreement by the Security Council, at least informally, to systematically apply the principles set out here to any such case. So too would be a declaratory UN General

Assembly resolution giving weight to those principles and to the whole idea of the "responsibility to protect" as an emerging international norm. There is a developing consensus around the idea that sovereignty must be qualified by the responsibility to protect. But until there is general acceptance of the practical commitments this involves, more tragedies such as Rwanda will be all too likely.

NOTES AND QUESTIONS ON THE RESPONSIBILITY TO PROTECT

1. *State endorsement of "responsibility to protect."* In September 2005, over 150 Heads of State and Government adopted the 2005 World Summit Outcome Document, *available at* www.un.org/summit2005/ Draft_Outcome130905.pdf, which articulated numerous goals and principles for the United Nations and its members. Paragraph 139 provides that "we are prepared to take collective action, in a timely and decisive manner, through the Security Council, in accordance with the UN Charter, including Chapter VII, on a case by case basis and in cooperation with relevant regional organizations as appropriate, should peaceful means be inadequate and national authorities manifestly failing to protect their populations from genocide, war crimes, ethnic cleansing and crimes against humanity and its implications. We stress the need for the General Assembly to continue consideration of the responsibility to protect populations from genocide, war crimes, ethnic cleansing, and crimes against humanity and its implications, bearing in mind the principles of the Charter of the United Nations and international law." Does this language authorize humanitarian intervention without the prior approval of the Security Council?

2. *Testing the commitment to the "responsibility to protect."* Since 2005, numerous humanitarian crises have erupted, some as the result of human action (*e.g.*, political repression and economic desperation in Zimbabwe) and some as the result of natural disaster (*e.g.*, Burma after the 2008 cyclone). To date, no forcible military intervention by other states in these crises has occurred. Does that history of inaction mean that the "responsibility to protect" is meaningless as legal doctrine, or is there an alternative interpretation of events?

THE IRAQ WAR (2003—)

Did the military intervention in Iraq in March 2003, led by the United States, qualify as humanitarian intervention or as something else entirely?

To answer this question, it's necessary first to read Security Council resolutions dating from the first Persian Gulf War in 1991. The three most important resolutions from that time, excerpted below were: (i) Resolution 660, which condemned Iraq's invasion of Kuwait and called for its immediate withdrawal from Kuwaiti territory; (ii) Resolution 678, which authorized Member states to use "all necessary means" to restore peace and security after Iraq's invasion of Kuwait; and (iii) Resolution 687, adopted after Iraq was expelled from Kuwait, which imposed cease-fire obligations on Iraq, including the obligation to disarm. In subsequent years, the Security Council repeatedly declared Iraq in material breach of its obligations (*see, e.g.*, Resolution 1441, *infra*), and the United States argued in 2003 that the continuing material breach of the conditions laid down in Resolution 687 "revived" the authorization to use force under Resolution 678. Counter-arguments rested on the premises that the authorization of force in Resolution 678 turned on Iraqi noncompliance with resolutions existing as of that date and that Resolution 687 created a permanent cease-fire that terminated Resolution 678 authority and imposed an alternative remedy for the enforcement of weapons inspections; moreover, even if a material breach of Resolution 687 could resurrect the authorization to use force, it is (1) for the United Nations to determine that the breach warrants the use of force and (2) limited to enforcement of Resolution 687, not "regime change" or democratization.

SECURITY COUNCIL RESOLUTION 660
U.N. Doc. S/RES/660 (2 August 1990)

The Security Council,

Alarmed by the invasion of Kuwait on 2 August 1990 by the military forces of Iraq,

Determining that there exists a breach of international peace and security as regards the Iraqi invasion of Kuwait,

Acting under Articles 39 and 40 of the Charter of the United Nations,

1.   *Condemns* the Iraqi invasion of Kuwait;

2.   *Demands* that Iraq withdraw immediately and unconditionally all its forces to the positions in which they were located on 1 August 1990;

3.   *Calls upon* Iraq and Kuwait to begin immediately intensive negotiations for the resolution of their differences and supports all efforts in this regard, and especially those of the League of Arab States;

4.   *Decides* to meet again as necessary to consider further steps to ensure compliance with the present resolution.

SECURITY COUNCIL RESOLUTION 678
U.N. Doc. S/RES/678 (29 November 1990)

The Security Council,

Recalling and reaffirming its resolutions 660 (1990) of 2 August (1990) [among others],

Noting that, despite all efforts by the United Nations, Iraq refuses to comply with its obligation to implement resolution 660 (1990) and the above-mentioned subsequent relevant resolutions, in flagrant contempt of the Security Council,

Mindful of its duties and responsibilities under the Charter of the United Nations for the maintenance and preservation of international peace and security,

Determined to secure full compliance with its decisions,

Acting under Chapter VII of the Charter,

　　1.　*Demands* that Iraq comply fully with resolution 660 (1990) and all subsequent relevant resolutions, and decides, while maintaining all its decisions, to allow Iraq one final opportunity, as a pause of goodwill, to do so;

　　2.　*Authorizes* Member States co-operating with the Government of Kuwait, unless Iraq on or before 15 January 1991 fully implements, as set forth in paragraph 1 above, the above-mentioned resolutions, to use all necessary means to uphold and implement resolution 660 (1990) and all subsequent relevant resolutions and to restore international peace and security in the area;

　　3.　*Requests* all States to provide appropriate support for the actions undertaken in pursuance of paragraph 2 above;

　　4.　*Requests* the States concerned to keep the Security Council regularly informed on the progress of actions undertaken pursuant to paragraphs 2 and 3 above;

　　5.　*Decides* to remain seized of the matter.

SECURITY COUNCIL RESOLUTION 687

U.N. Doc. S/RES/687 (3 April 1991)

The Security Council,

　　Recalling its resolutions 660 (1990) of 2 August 1990 [among others],

　　Welcoming the restoration to Kuwait of its sovereignty, independence and territorial integrity and the return of its legitimate Government,

　　Affirming the commitment of all Member States to the sovereignty, territorial integrity and political independence of Kuwait and Iraq* * *,

　　Reaffirming the need to be assured of Iraq's peaceful intentions in the light of its unlawful invasion and occupation of Kuwait, * * *

　　Aware of the use by Iraq of ballistic missiles in unprovoked attacks and therefore of the need to take specific measures in regard to such missiles located in Iraq,

Concerned by the reports in the hands of Member States that Iraq has attempted to acquire materials for a nuclear-weapons programme contrary to its obligations under the Treaty on the Non–Proliferation of Nuclear Weapons of 1 July 1968,

Recalling the objective of the establishment of a nuclear-weapon-free zone in the region of the Middle East, * * *

Deploring threats made by Iraq during the recent conflict to make use of terrorism against targets outside Iraq and the taking of hostages by Iraq,

Taking note with grave concern of the reports transmitted by the Secretary–General on 20 March and 28 March 1991, and conscious of the necessity to meet urgently the humanitarian needs in Kuwait and Iraq, * * *

Conscious of the need to take the following measures acting under Chapter VII of the Charter, * * *

2. *Demands* that Iraq and Kuwait respect the inviolability of the international boundary and the allocation of islands set out [by mutual agreement between Iraq and Kuwait in 1963]. * * *

4. *Decides* to guarantee the inviolability of the above-mentioned international boundary and to take, as appropriate, all necessary measures to that end in accordance with the Charter of the United Nations; * * *

8. *Decides* that Iraq shall unconditionally accept the destruction, removal, or rendering harmless, under international supervision, of:

(a) All chemical and biological weapons and all stocks of agents and all related subsystems and components and all research, development, support and manufacturing facilities related thereto;

(b) All ballistic missiles with a range greater than one hundred and fifty kilometres and related major parts and repair and production facilities;

9. *Decides also*, for the implementation of paragraph 8, the following:

(a) Iraq shall submit to the Secretary–General, within fifteen days of the adoption of the present resolution, a declaration on the locations, amounts and types of all items specified in paragraph 8 and agree to urgent, on-site inspection as specified below;

(b) The Secretary–General, in consultation with the appropriate Governments and, where appropriate, with the Director–General of the World Health Organization, within forty-five days of the adoption of the present resolution shall develop and submit to the Council for approval a plan calling for the completion of the following acts within forty-five days of such approval:

(i) The forming of a special commission which shall carry out immediate on-site inspection of Iraq's biological, chemical and missile capabilities, based on Iraq's declarations and the designation of any additional locations by the special commission itself;

(ii) The yielding by Iraq of possession to the Special Commission for destruction, removal or rendering harmless, taking into account the requirements of public safety, of all items specified under paragraph 8 (a), including items at the additional locations designated by the Special Commission and the destruction by Iraq, under the supervision of the Special Commission, of all its missile capabilities, including launchers. * * *

10. *Decides further* that Iraq shall unconditionally undertake not to use, develop, construct or acquire any of the items specified in paragraphs 8 and 9, and requests the Secretary General, in consultation with the Special Commission, to develop a plan for the future ongoing monitoring and verification of Iraq's compliance with [this] paragraph. * * *

12. *Decides* that Iraq shall unconditionally agree not to acquire or develop nuclear weapons or nuclear-weapon-usable material or any subsystems or components or any research, development, support or manufacturing facilities related to the above; to submit to the Secretary–General and the Director General of the International Atomic Energy Agency within fifteen days of the adoption of the present resolution a declaration of the locations, amounts, and types of all items specified above; to place all of its nuclear-weapon-usable materials under the exclusive control, for custody and removal, of the Agency, with the assistance and cooperation of the Special Commission * * *; to accept, in accordance with the arrangements provided for in paragraph 13, urgent on-site inspection and the destruction, removal or rendering harmless as appropriate of all items specified above; and to accept the plan discussed in paragraph 13 for the future ongoing monitoring and verification of its compliance with these undertakings;

13. *Requests* the Director–General of the International Atomic Energy Agency, through the Secretary–General and with the assistance and cooperation of the Special Commission as provided for in the plan of the Secretary–General [* * *] to carry out immediate on-site inspection of Iraq's nuclear capabilities based on Iraq's declarations and the designation of any additional locations by the Special Commission; to develop a plan for submission to the Council within forty-five days calling for the destruction, removal, or rendering harmless as appropriate of all items listed in paragraph 12; to carry out the plan within forty-five days following approval by the Council and to develop a plan, taking into account the rights and obligations of Iraq under the Treaty on the Non–Proliferation of Nuclear Weapons, for the future ongoing monitoring and verification of Iraq's compliance with paragraph 12, including an inventory of all nuclear material in Iraq subject to the Agency's verifica-

tion and inspections to confirm that Agency safeguards cover all relevant nuclear activities in Iraq, to be submitted to the Council for approval within one hundred and twenty days of the adoption of the present resolution;

* * *

32. *Requires* Iraq to inform the Council that it will not commit or support any act of international terrorism or allow any organization directed towards commission of such acts to operate within its territory and to condemn unequivocally and renounce all acts, methods and practices of terrorism;

33. *Declares* that, upon official notification by Iraq to the Secretary–General and to the Security Council of its acceptance of the above provisions, a formal cease-fire is effective between Iraq and Kuwait and the Member States cooperating with Kuwait in accordance with resolution 678 (1990);

34. *Decides* to remain seized of the matter and to take such further steps as may be required for the implementation of the present resolution and to secure peace and security in the region.

SECURITY COUNCIL RESOLUTION 1441

U.N. Doc. S/RES/687 (8 November 2002)

The Security Council,

Recalling all its previous relevant resolutions * * *

Recognizing the threat Iraq's non-compliance with Council resolutions and proliferation of weapons of mass destruction and long-range missiles poses to international peace and security,

Recalling that its resolution 678 (1990) authorized Member States to use all necessary means to uphold and implement its resolution 660 (1990) of 2 August 1990 and all relevant resolutions subsequent to resolution 660 (1990) and to restore international peace and security in the area,

Further recalling that its resolution 687 (1991) imposed obligations on Iraq as a necessary step for achievement of its stated objective of restoring international peace and security in the area,

Deploring the fact that Iraq has not provided an accurate, full, final, and complete disclosure, as required by resolution 687 (1991), of all aspects of its programmes to develop weapons of mass destruction and ballistic missiles with a range greater than one hundred and fifty kilometres, and of all holdings of such weapons, their components and production facilities and locations, as well as all other nuclear programmes, including any which it claims are for purposes not related to nuclear-weapons-usable material,

Deploring further that Iraq repeatedly obstructed immediate, unconditional, and unrestricted access to sites designated by the United Nations Special Commission (UNSCOM) and the International Atomic Energy Agency (IAEA), failed to cooperate fully and unconditionally with UNSCOM and IAEA weapons inspectors, as required by resolution 687 (1991), and ultimately ceased all cooperation with UNSCOM and the IAEA in 1998,

Deploring also that the Government of Iraq has failed to comply with its commitments pursuant to resolution 687 (1991) with regard to terrorism, * * *

Recalling that in its resolution 687 (1991) the Council declared that a ceasefire would be based on acceptance by Iraq of the provisions of that resolution, including the obligations on Iraq contained therein,

* * *

Acting under Chapter VII of the Charter of the United Nations,

1. *Decides* that Iraq has been and remains in material breach of its obligations under relevant resolutions, including resolution 687 (1991), in particular through Iraq's failure to cooperate with United Nations inspectors and the IAEA, and to complete the actions required under paragraphs 8 to 13 of resolution 687 (1991);

2. *Decides*, while acknowledging paragraph 1 above, to afford Iraq, by this resolution, a final opportunity to comply with its disarmament obligations under relevant resolutions of the Council; and accordingly decides to set up an enhanced inspection regime with the aim of bringing to full and verified completion the disarmament process established by resolution 687 (1991) and subsequent resolutions of the Council;

3. *Decides* that, in order to begin to comply with its disarmament obligations, in addition to submitting the required biannual declarations, the Government of Iraq shall provide to UNMOVIC [the United Nations Monitoring, Verification, and Inspection Commission], the IAEA, and the Council, not later than 30 days from the date of this resolution, a currently accurate, full, and complete declaration of all aspects of its programmes to develop chemical, biological, and nuclear weapons, ballistic missiles, and other delivery systems such as unmanned aerial vehicles and dispersal systems designed for use on aircraft, including any holdings and precise locations of such weapons, components, subcomponents, stocks of agents, and related material and equipment, the locations and work of its research, development and production facilities, as well as all other chemical, biological, and nuclear programmes, including any which it claims are for purposes not related to weapon production or material;

4. *Decides* that false statements or omissions in the declarations submitted by Iraq pursuant to this resolution and failure by Iraq at any time to comply with, and cooperate fully in the implementation of, this

resolution shall constitute a further material breach of Iraq's obligations and will be reported to the Council for assessment in accordance with paragraphs 11 and 12 below;

5.   *Decides* that Iraq shall provide UNMOVIC and the IAEA immediate, unimpeded, unconditional, and unrestricted access to any and all, including underground, areas, facilities, buildings, equipment, records, and means of transport which they wish to inspect, as well as immediate, unimpeded, unrestricted, and private access to all officials and other persons whom UNMOVIC or the IAEA wish to interview in the mode or location of UNMOVIC's or the IAEA's choice pursuant to any aspect of their mandates; further decides that UNMOVIC and the IAEA may at their discretion conduct interviews inside or outside of Iraq, may facilitate the travel of those interviewed and family members outside of Iraq, and that, at the sole discretion of UNMOVIC and the IAEA, such interviews may occur without the presence of observers from the Iraqi Government; and instructs UNMOVIC and requests the IAEA to resume inspections no later than 45 days following adoption of this resolution and to update the Council 60 days thereafter;

* * *

8.   *Decides* further that Iraq shall not take or threaten hostile acts directed against any representative or personnel of the United Nations or the IAEA or of any Member State taking action to uphold any Council resolution;

* * *

9.   *Requests* the Secretary–General immediately to notify Iraq of this resolution, which is binding on Iraq; demands that Iraq confirm within seven days of that notification its intention to comply fully with this resolution; and demands further that Iraq cooperate immediately, unconditionally, and actively with UNMOVIC and the IAEA;

* * *

11.   *Directs* the Executive Chairman of UNMOVIC and the Director–General of the IAEA to report immediately to the Council any interference by Iraq with inspection activities, as well as any failure by Iraq to comply with its disarmament obligations, including its obligations regarding inspections under this resolution;

12.   *Decides* to convene immediately upon receipt of a report in accordance with paragraphs 4 or 11 above, in order to consider the situation and the need for full compliance with all of the relevant Council resolutions in order to secure international peace and security;

13.   *Recalls*, in that context, that the Council has repeatedly warned Iraq that it will face serious consequences as a result of its continued violations of its obligations;

14.   *Decides* to remain seized of the matter.

LETTER FROM LORD GOLDSMITH, THE ATTORNEY GENERAL OF THE UNITED KINGDOM, TO THE PRIME MINISTER, TONY BLAIR

(7 March 2003, leaked 27 April 2005)

1. You have asked me for advice on the legality of military action against Iraq without a further resolution of the Security–Council, This is, of course, a matter we have discussed before. Since then I have had the benefit of discussions with the Foreign Secretary and [UK representative to the United Nations] Sir Jeremy Greenstock, who have given me valuable background information on the negotiating history of resolution 1441. In addition, I have also had the opportunity to hear the views of the US Administration from their perspective as co-sponsors of the resolution. This note considers the issues in detail in order that you are in a position to understand the legal reasoning.

Possible legal bases for the use of force

2. As I have previously advised, there are generally three possible bases for the use of force:

(a) self-defence (which may include collective self-defence);

(b) exceptionally, to avert overwhelming humanitarian catastrophe; and

(c) authorisation by the Security Council acting under Chapter VII of the UN Charter.

3. Force may be used in self-defence if there is an actual or imminent threat of an armed attack; the use of force must be necessary, *i.e.* the only means of averting an attack; and the force used must be a proportionate response. It is now widely accepted that an imminent armed attack will justify the use of force if the other conditions are met. The concept of what is imminent may depend on the circumstances. Different considerations may apply, for example, where the risk is of attack from terrorists sponsored or harboured by a particular State, or where there is a threat of an attack by nuclear weapons. However, in my opinion there must be some degree of imminence. I am aware that the USA has been arguing for recognition of a broad doctrine of a right to use force to pre-empt danger in the future. If this means more than a right to respond proportionately to an imminent attack (and I understand that the doctrine is intended to carry that connotation) this is not a doctrine which, in my opinion, exists or is recognised in international law.

4. The use of force to avert overwhelming humanitarian catastrophe has been emerging as a further, and exceptional, basis for the use of force. It was relied on by the UK in the Kosovo crisis and is the underlying justification for the No–Fly Zones. The doctrine remains controversial, however. I know of no reason why it would be an appropriate basis for action in present circumstances.

5.   Force may be used where this is authorised by the UN Security Council acting under Chapter VII of the UN Charter. The key question is whether resolution 1441 has the effect of providing such authorisation.

Resolution 1441

6.   As you are aware, the argument that resolution 1441 itself provides the authorisation to use force depends on the revival of the express authorisation to use force given in 1990 by Security Council resolution 678. This in turn gives rise to two questions: (a) is the so-called "revival argument" a sound legal basis in principle? (b) is resolution 1441 sufficient to revive the authorisation in resolution 678? I deal with these questions in turn. * * * [I]f the answer to these two questions is "yes", the use of force will have been authorised by the United Nations and not in defiance of it.

The revival argument

7.   Following its invasion and annexation of Kuwait, the Security Council authorised the use of force against Iraq in resolution 678 (1990). This resolution authorised coalition forces to use all necessary means to force Iraq to withdraw from Kuwait and to restore international peace and security in the area. The resolution gave a legal basis for Operation Desert Storm, which was brought to an end by the cease-fire set out by the Council in resolution 687 (1991). The conditions for the cease-fire in that resolution (and subsequent resolutions) imposed obligations on Iraq with regard to the elimination of [weapons of mass destruction] WMD and monitoring of its obligations. Resolution 687 suspended, but did not terminate, the authority to use force in resolution 678. Nor has any subsequent resolution terminated the authorisation to use force in resolution 678. It has been the UK's view that a violation of Iraq's obligations under resolution 687 which is sufficiently serious to undermine the basis of the cease-fire can revive the authorisation to use force in resolution 678. * * *

9.   Law Officers [*i.e.* the government's legal advisors] have advised in the past that, provided the conditions are made out, the revival argument does provide a sufficient justification in international law for the use of force against Iraq. That view is supported by an opinion given in August 1992 by the then UN Legal Counsel, Carl–August Fleischauer. However, the UK has consistently taken the view (as did the Fleischauer opinion) that, as the cease-fire conditions were set by the Security Council in resolution 687, it is for the Council to assess whether any such breach of those obligations has occurred. The US have a rather different view: they maintain that the fact of whether Iraq is in breach is a matter of objective fact which may therefore be assessed by individual Member States. I am not aware of any other state which supports this view. This is an issue of critical importance when considering the effect of resolution 1441.

10. The revival argument is controversial. It is not widely accepted among academic commentators. However, I agree with my predecessors' advice on this issue. Further, I believe that the arguments in support of the revival argument are stronger following adoption of resolution 1441. That is because of the terms of the resolution and the course of the negotiations which led to its adoption. Thus, preambular paragraphs 4, 5 and 10 recall the authorisation to use force in resolution 678 and that resolution 687 imposed obligations on Iraq as a necessary condition of the cease-fire. Operative paragraph (OP) 1 provides that Iraq has been and remains in material breach of its obligations under relevant resolutions, including the resolution 687. OP 13 recalls that Iraq has been warned repeatedly that "serious consequences" will result from continued violations of its obligations. The previous practice of the Council and statements made by Council members during the negotiation of resolution 1441 demonstrate that the phrase "material breach" signifies a finding by the Council of a sufficiently serious breach of the cease-fire conditions to revive the authorisation in resolution 678 and that "serious consequences" is accepted as indicating the use of force.

11. I disagree, therefore, with those commentators and lawyers, who assert that nothing less than an *explicit* authorisation to use force in a Security Council resolution will be sufficient.

Sufficiency of resolution 1441

12. In order for the authorisation to use force in resolution 678 to be revived, there needs to be a determination by the Security Council that there is a violation of the conditions of the cease-fire and that the Security Council considers it sufficiently serious to destroy the basis of the cease-fire. Revival will not, however, take place, notwithstanding a finding of violation, if the Security Council has made it clear either that action short of the use of force should be taken to ensure compliance with the terms of the cease-fire, or that it intends to decide subsequently what action is required to ensure compliance. Notwithstanding the determination of material breach in OP 1 of resolution 1441, it is clear that the Council did not intend that the authorisation in resolution 678 should revive *immediately* following the adoption of resolution 1441, since OP 2 of the resolution affords Iraq a "final opportunity" to comply with its disarmament obligations under previous resolutions by cooperating with the enhanced inspection regime described in OPs 3 and 5–9. But OP 2 also states that the Council has determined that compliance with resolution 1441 is Iraq's last chance before the cease-fire resolution will be enforced. OP 2 has the effect therefore of suspending the legal consequences of the OP 1 determination of material breach which would otherwise have triggered the revival of the authorisation in resolution 678. The narrow but key question is: on the true interpretation of resolution 1441, what has the Security Council decided will be the consequences of Iraq's failure to comply with the enhanced regime.

13.   The provisions relevant to determining whether or not Iraq has taken the final opportunity given by the Security Council are contained in OPs 4, 11 and 12 of the resolution.

— OP 4 provides that false statements or omissions in the declaration to be submitted by Iraq under OP 3 and failure by Iraq at any time to comply with and cooperate fully in the implementation of resolution 1441 will constitute a further material breach of Iraq's obligations and will be reported to the Council for assessment under paragraphs 11 and 12 of the resolution.

— OP 11 directs the Executive Chairman of UNMOVIC and the Director–General of the IAEA to report immediately to the Council any interference by Iraq with inspection activities, as well as any failure by Iraq to comply with its disarmament obligations, including the obligations regarding inspections under resolution 1441.

— OP 12 provides that the Council will convene immediately on receipt of a report in accordance with paragraphs 4 or 11 "in order to consider the situation and the need for compliance with all of the relevant Council resolutions in order to secure international peace and security".

It is clear from the text of the resolution, and is apparent from the negotiating history, that if Iraq fails to comply, there will be a further Security Council discussion. The text is, however, ambiguous and unclear on what happens next.

14.   There are two competing arguments:

(i) that provided there is a Council discussion, if it does not reach a conclusion, there remains an authorisation to use force;

(ii) that nothing short of a further Council decision will be a legitimate basis for the use of force.

15.   The first argument is based on the following steps:

(a) OP 1, by stating that Iraq "has been and remains in material breach" of its obligations under relevant resolutions, including resolution 687 amounts to a determination by the Council that Iraq's violations of resolution 687 are sufficiently serious to destroy the basis of the cease-fire and therefore, in principle, to revive the authorisation to use force in resolution 678;

(b) the Council decided, however, to give Iraq "a final opportunity" (OP 2) but because of the clear warning that it faced "serious consequences as a result of its continued violations" (OP 13) was warning that a failure to take that "final opportunity" would lead to such consequences;

(c) further, by OP 4, the Council decided *in advance* that false statements or omissions in its declaration and "failure by Iraq *at any time* to comply with, and cooperate fully in the implementation of, this resolution" would constitute "a further material breach"; the argument is that the Council's determination *in advance* that particular conduct would constitute a material breach (thus reviving the authorisation to use force) is as good as its determination *after* the event;

(d) in either event, the Council must meet (OP 12) "to consider the situation and the need for full compliance with all of the relevant Council resolutions in order to secure international peace and security"; but the resolution singularly does *not* say that the Council must decide what action to take. The Council knew full well, it is argued, the difference between "consider" and "decide" and so the omission is highly significant. Indeed, the omission is especially important as the French and Russians made proposals to include an express requirement for a further decision, but these were rejected precisely to avoid being tied to the need to obtain a second resolution. On this view, therefore, while the Council has the opportunity to take a further decision, the determinations of material breach in OPs 1 and 4 remain valid even if the Council does not act.

16.   The second argument focuses, by contrast, on two provisions in particular of the resolution: first, the final words in OP 4 ("and will be reported to the Council for assessment in accordance with paragraphs 11 and 12 below") and, second, the requirement in OP 12 for the Council to "consider the situation and the need for full compliance with all of the relevant Council resolutions in order to secure international peace and security". Taken together, it is argued, these provisions indicate that the Council decided in resolution 1441 that in the event of continued Iraqi non-compliance, the issue should return to the Council for a further decision on what action should be taken at that stage.

* * *

26.   * * * [T]he language of resolution 1441 leaves the position unclear and the statements made on adoption of the resolution suggest that there were differences of view within the Council as to the legal effect of the resolution. Arguments can be made on both sides. A key question is whether there is in truth a need for an assessment of whether Iraq's conduct constitutes a failure to take the final opportunity or has constituted a failure fully to cooperate within the meaning of OP 4 such that the basis of the cease-fire is destroyed. If an assessment is needed of that sort, it would be for the Council to make it. A narrow textual reading of the resolution suggests that sort of assessment is not needed, because the Council has pre-determined the issue. Public statements, on the other hand, say otherwise.

27.   In these circumstances, I remain of the opinion that the safest legal course would be to secure the adoption of a further resolution to authorise the use of force. * * * I do not believe that such a resolution need be explicit in its terms. The key point is that it should establish that the Council has concluded that Iraq has failed to take the final opportunity offered by resolution 1441. * * *

28. Nevertheless, having regard to the information on the negotiating history which I have been given and to the arguments of the US Administration which I heard in Washington, I accept that a reasonable case can be made that resolution 1441 is capable in principle of reviving the authorisation in 678 without a further resolution.

29. However, the argument that resolution 1441 alone has revived the authorisation to use force in resolution 678 will only be sustainable if there are strong factual grounds for concluding that Iraq has failed to take the final opportunity. In other words, we would need to be able to demonstrate hard evidence of non-compliance and non-cooperation. Given the structure of the resolution as a whole, the views of UNMOVIC and the IAEA will be highly significant in this respect. In the light of the latest reporting by UNMOVIC, you will need to consider extremely carefully whether the evidence of non-cooperation and non-compliance by Iraq is sufficiently compelling to justify the conclusion that Iraq has failed to take its final opportunity.

30. In reaching my conclusions, I have taken account of the fact that on a number of previous occasions, including in relation to Operation Desert Fox in December 1998 and Kosovo in 1999, UK forces have participated in military action on the basis of advice from my predecessors that the legality of the action under international law was no more than reasonably arguable. But a "reasonable case" does not mean that if the matter ever came before a court I would be confident that the court would agree with this view. I judge that, having regard to the arguments on both sides, and considering the resolution as a whole in the light of the statements made on adoption and subsequently, a court might well conclude that OPs 4 and 12 do require a further Council decision in order to revive the authorisation in resolution 678. But equally I consider that the counter view can be reasonably maintained. However, it must be recognised that on previous occasions when military action was taken on the basis of a reasonably arguable case, the degree of public and Parliamentary scrutiny of the legal issue was nothing like as great as it is today.

31. The analysis set out above applies whether a second resolution fails to be adopted because of a lack of votes or because it is vetoed. As I have said before, I do not believe that there is any basis in law for arguing that there is an implied condition of reasonableness which can be read into the power of veto conferred on the permanent members of the Security Council by the UN Charter. So there are no grounds for arguing that an "unreasonable veto" would entitle us to proceed on the basis of a presumed Security Council authorisation. In any event, if the majority of world opinion remains opposed to military action, it is likely to be difficult *on the facts* to categorise a French veto as "unreasonable". The legal analysis may, however, be affected by the course of events over the next week or so, *e.g.* the discussions on the draft second resolution. If we fail to achieve the adoption of a second resolution, we would need

to consider urgently at that stage the strength of our legal case in the light of circumstances at that time. * * *

36. Finally, I must stress that the lawfulness of military action depends not only on the existence of a legal basis, but also on the question of proportionality. Any force used pursuant to the authorisation in resolution 678 (whether or not there is a second resolution):

— must have as its objective the enforcement the terms of the cease-fire contained in resolution 687 (1990) and subsequent relevant resolutions;

— be limited to what is necessary to achieve that objective; and

— must be a proportionate response to that objective, *i.e.* securing compliance with Iraq's disarmament obligations.

That is not to say that action may not be taken to remove Saddam Hussein from power if it can be demonstrated that such action is a necessary and proportionate measure to secure the disarmament of Iraq. But regime change cannot be the objective of military action. This should be borne in mind in considering the list of military targets and in making public statements about any campaign.

NOTES AND QUESTIONS ON THE IRAQ WAR AS HUMANITARIAN INTERVENTION

1. *Law and power.* Why would or should the Attorney General of a powerful country worry about legality if that nation's basic security interests are at stake?

2. *Interpreting the resolution.* Considering Resolution 1441 as a whole, but especially Operational Paragraphs 1, 2, 4, 11, and 12, what are the best textual arguments for and against the position that no additional authorization from the Security Council was necessary to justify the use of military force against Iraq?

3. *Human rights and the justification of force.* If we stipulate that massive and vicious human rights abuses were common during the regime of Saddam Hussein, how, if at all, would that affect your assessment of the two types of arguments in the previous question? Either at the time it began or now, could the Iraq invasion be viewed as an exercise of the responsibility to protect?

Practicum

The nation of Tavistan is a small, densely populated nation that is largely dependent on the export of oil for its economic survival. It has signed all of the major human rights treaties, but its commitment to meeting those obligations is more apparent than real. Tavistan has been a member of the United Nations since its independence in 1965 from Guatador, which had colonized the territory in the nineteenth century. Under Guatadoran control, the colonial government had favored one indigenous ethnic minority—the Tavin people—at the systematic expense of another—the Benta people. After independence, the Tavin continued to enjoy the privileges of public and private power, and the Benta continued to suffer various forms of abuse, including harassment and disappearance of its political leaders, as well as *de facto* and *de jure* discrimination in the workplace. Two years ago, the Benta Peoples Organization (BPO) began to organize an armed campaign of resistance, seeking the establishment of an autonomous province in the south where Ethnic Bentas make up a majority of the inhabitants. BPO's long-term goal is to secede from Tavistan and incorporate into neighboring Bentaland—a separate sovereign state, where a majority of the population has strong cultural, linguistic, religious, and economic ties to the Benta people in Tavistan. In fact, the government and the people of Bentaland have long considered the southern province to be a part of "Greater Bentaland" that was stolen from them in 1876, when Guatador set up a colonial government and drew borders that had everything to do with its administrative convenience and little to do with ethnic identities or natural boundaries on the ground.

One year ago, the Tavistan government required all Benta people to register with the Interior Ministry and to carry identity cards at all times. Information on all Bentas' financial accounts and property holdings was also to be submitted to the Interior Ministry. Benta people were driven from their homes and transported to mass "re-education camps," and their houses were distributed to Tavin people who passed a nationally imposed "ethnic purity test." With each abuse and indignity, the BPO became stronger, and it has mounted an increasingly vicious and effective campaign of terrorism in Tavistan's capital city. Eight months ago, the government deported all foreign journalists and began a campaign of ethnic cleansing, killing thousands of Benta, turning a blind eye to massacres by private militias, and establishing a network of concentration camps where Benta women are systematically raped and sometimes impregnated for specifically genocidal purposes. Tens of thousands of Benta refugees fled for the border with Bentaland, but the Tavistan army entrapped them in the mountain passes before they could escape and then either detained them in the concentration camps or summarily executed them.

Popular opinion in Bentaland is at a fever pitch, and the army is deployed at the border, poised to invade for the purpose of stopping the genocide and recovering all of "Greater Bentaland," including the rich oil fields in the southern province. Relations between Tavistan and Bentaland, which have never been good, are at the breaking point. At no point has Tavistan threatened the territorial integrity or political independence of its neighbors, and it continues to portray the crisis as "an unfortunate legacy of colonialism" that is nonetheless strictly a domestic political matter under Article 2(7) of the UN Charter, citing the precedent of Russian troops in Chechnya. The international community is split: virtually every government has condemned the conduct of Tavistan, but most have also condemned the terrorist tactics of the BPO, and only Bentaland appears to support the idea of secession.

Four months ago in SC Resolution H1756, the UN Security Council declared the situation in Tavistan to be a "humanitarian disaster that potentially threatens international peace and security." The Security Council reminded all parties of their obligation to protect human rights and respect the laws of war, but no measures under Articles 41 or 42 were adopted, though the Council had considered and rejected economic sanctions against Tavistan. Four members of the Security Council (including Tavistan) voted against the resolution. Guatador, many of whose oil companies are heavily invested in Tavistan, formally abstained from the ultimate resolution but was instrumental behind the scenes in watering it down.

Several members of the Security Council have put the crisis on the Council's agenda for the purpose of adopting measures to promote the peaceful resolution of the crisis. Students will represent (i) the government of Tavistan, (ii) the government of Bentaland (which has been specially invited to address the Council), (iii) the government of Guatador, (iv) the government of Bessarabia which currently fills the position of president of the Security Council, (v) the government of Sharaq, another permanent member of the Security Council, which has to date remained neutral on the issue other than to condemn both the Tavistan government's conduct and BPO's terrorism, and (vi) the Secretary–General's office (including her legal advisors). The current draft of the resolution, as proposed by Bentaland and the governments of ten other nations, three of which sit on the Council, is as follows:

> *The Security Council,*
>
> *Mindful* of its duties and its responsibilities under the Charter of the United Nations for the maintenance of international peace and security,
>
> *Recalling* Article 2, paragraph 7, of the Charter of the United Nations,
>
> *Gravely concerned* by the repression of the Benta people in many parts of Tavistan, which has led to a massive flow of refugees towards international frontiers, and which threaten international peace and security in the region,
>
> *Convinced* that the government of Tavistan is responsible for genocide and other widespread and flagrant violations of international humanitarian law and international human rights law,
>
> *Deeply disturbed* by the magnitude of the human suffering involved,
>
> *Concluding* that measures not involving the use of armed force are insufficient to redress the humanitarian disaster in Tavistan,

Recalling its powers under Article 42 of the Charter of the United Nations,

Acting under Chapter VII of the Charter of the United Nations,

1. *Condemns* the repression of the Benta population throughout Tavistan, the consequences of which threaten international peace and security in the region;

2. *Demands* that Tavistan immediately end the genocide and repression of the Benta people and ensure that the human rights of all Tavistan citizens are respected fully and equally;

3. *Insists* that Tavistan allow immediate access by international humanitarian organizations to all those in need of assistance in all parts of Tavistan and to make available all necessary facilities for their operations;

4. *Authorizes* all states to take all necessary measures to restore international peace and security in the region.

5. *Decides* to remain seized of this matter.

Debate the proposed resolution, and if possible negotiate a resolution that will receive the approval of the Secretary–General and her legal advisors as well as the affirmative vote of a majority of the members of the Council represented in the class, including either the approval or the abstention of the two permanent members of the Council in the exercise.

CHAPTER 7

MODULE 18

INTERNATIONAL HUMANITARIAN LAW IN A POST-9/11 WORLD

■ ■ ■

Orientation

The idea that some conduct is unacceptable even in wartime can be traced to the ancients and across a variety of cultures. Over the last two hundred years, scores of treaties and military codes of conduct have been adopted protecting certain populations at risk in armed conflict, especially non-combatants like the sick and wounded in the battlefield, medical personnel, civilians caught in the cross-fire, and prisoners of war. Even enemy nationals who had been shipwrecked in the course of hostilities were protected by an international legal regime. The modern humanitarian treaties move beyond the prohibition of abuse and require more affirmative protection and care for non-combatants who fall within the power of one of the belligerent states.

However, it is not just people on the periphery of the fighting who are meant to be protected by this body of law. Customary norms of military necessity and proportionality have been developed to try to humanize war by minimizing "unnecessary suffering" by the combatants themselves. A number of treaties have been concluded prohibiting certain weapons altogether (*e.g.*, poison gas, blinding laser weapons, or biological and chemical agents), which clearly protect the combatants, and other treaties, like the Ottawa Treaty on Antipersonnel Mines (1997) and the Cluster Munitions Convention (2008), protect combatants and non-combatants alike. Protection of the natural environment in armed conflict has also gradually become a part of international humanitarian law, and there are now treaties prohibiting environmental warfare and weather modification. The broadest conception of the law of war now includes treaties protecting cultural property, artwork, religious icons and objects—all of which limit what belligerents can do to one another's material identity.

What is the relationship between this body of law—subsumed under the rubric *international humanitarian law* ("IHL")—and contemporary human rights law? The most traditional definition of "international humanitarian law" would limit it to "that branch of the laws of armed conflict which is concerned with the protection of the victims of armed conflict, meaning those rendered *hors de combat* ["out of the fight"] by injury, sickness or capture, and also civilians * * * found primarily in the four 1949 Geneva Conventions, the two 1977 Additional Protocols and associated materials."[1] As noted in the Introduction to this chapter, some human rights lawyers note only some historical linkage between the law of war and the emergence of human rights law. We believe that contemporary IHL and contemporary human rights law are inextricably linked, not just historically but doctrinally and institutionally as well. The evolution and enforcement of one has directly affected the trajectory of the other. The statutes of the Yugoslavian and Rwandan War Crimes Tribunals, for example, extend the tribunals' jurisdiction to "serious violations of international humanitarian law," a general term that encompasses not only the traditional law of armed conflict, including war crimes, but other wrongs like genocide and crimes against humanity as well. In one of its first decisions, the Yugoslavian tribunal explicitly distinguished between the law of " 'armed conflict,' essentially introduced by the 1949 Geneva Conventions and . . . the more recent and comprehensive notion of 'international humanitarian law,' which has emerged as a result of influence of human rights doctrine on the law of armed conflict. . . ."[2] Certainly, the International Court of Justice has rejected in principle any suggestion that IHL offers specialized rules applicable during armed conflicts to the exclusion of human rights standards:

> [T]he protection offered by human rights conventions does not cease in case of armed conflict, save through the effect of provisions for derogation of the kind to be found in Article 4 of the International Covenant on Civil and Political Rights.[3]

---

1. HILAIRE McCOUBREY, INTERNATIONAL HUMANITARIAN LAW: THE REGULATION OF ARMED CONFLICTS 1 (1990).

2. *Prosecutor v. Tadic*, Case No. IT–94–1–AR72, Decision on the Defense Motion for Interlocutory Appeal on Jurisdiction, ¶ 87 (Oct. 2, 1995).

3. Article 4 of the International Covenant on Civil and Political Rights provides:

1. In time of public emergency which threatens the life of the nation and the existence of which is officially proclaimed, the States Parties to the present Covenant may take measures derogating from their obligations under the present Covenant to the extent strictly required by the exigencies of the situation, provided that such measures are not inconsistent with their other obligations under international law and do not involve discrimination solely on the ground of race, colour, sex, language, religion or social origin.

2. No derogation from articles 6 [prohibiting all arbitrary deprivation of life], 7 [prohibiting torture and cruel, inhuman, or degrading treatment or punishment], 8 (paragraphs 1 and 2) [prohibiting slavery], 11 [prohibiting imprisonment for breach of contractual obligations], 15 [prohibiting the retroactive application of criminal law], 16 [assuring the recognition of all persons before the law] and 18 [protecting freedom of thought, conscience, and religion] may be made under this provision.

3. Any State Party to the present Covenant availing itself of the right of derogation shall immediately inform the other States Parties to the present Covenant, through the intermediary of the Secretary–General of the United Nations, of the provisions from which it has derogated and of the reasons by which it was actuated. A further communication shall be made, through the same intermediary, on the date on which it terminates such derogation.

Legal Consequences of the Construction of the Wall in the Occupied Palestinian Territory, Advisory Opinion, 2004 I.C.J. 136, 178 (July 10), ¶ 106. Of course, the connection between international humanitarian law and international human rights law has to be demonstrated, not merely asserted, and that is the purpose of this module.

A Short History of International Humanitarian Law

An advanced course on modern international humanitarian law might begin with Professor Francis Lieber's "Instructions for the Government of Armies of the United States in the Field," otherwise known as the Lieber Code, which President Abraham Lincoln promulgated during the U.S. Civil War to guide the conduct of hostilities and assure that basic humanitarian principles were respected by the troops. So for example, the Lieber Code defined the central concept of "military necessity" to include "all direct destruction of life or limb of armed enemies, and of other persons whose destruction is incidentally unavoidable in the armed contests of the war," but to exclude

> cruelty—that is, the infliction of suffering for the sake of suffering or for revenge, [and] maiming or wounding except in fight, [and] torture to extort confessions. It does not admit of the use of poison in any way, nor of the wanton devastation of a district. It admits of deception, but disclaims acts of perfidy; and, in general, military necessity does not include any act of hostility which makes the return to peace unnecessarily difficult.

Drawing explicitly on pre-existing practices and norms, the Lieber Code profoundly influenced subsequent codes of military conduct and sparked a sustained sequence of treaty-making from the 1899 and 1907 Hague Conventions, to the 1929 Geneva Convention, to the 1949 Geneva Conventions and their protocols in the late 1970s, and to the rapid expansion of humanitarian law treaties in the 1990s, many of which are in the Documents Supplement.

In that advanced IHL course, students would also encounter the "Martens Clause," which has been considered an essential aspect of the law of armed conflict for over a century, having first appeared in the preamble to the 1899 Hague Convention (II) with respect to the laws and customs of war on land:

> Until a more complete code of the laws of war is issued, the High Contracting Parties think it right to declare that in cases not included in the Regulations adopted by them, populations and belligerents remain under the protection and empire of the principles of international law, as they result from the usages established between civilized nations, from the laws of humanity and the requirements of the public conscience.

Laws and Customs of War on Land (Hague II), 29 July 1899, pmbl. At a minimum, the Martens Clause reinforces the traditional doctrine that treaties do not necessarily displace pre-existing custom. But there are wider interpretations: one possibility is that treaties relating to the laws of armed conflict are never complete and that the Clause assures that conduct not explicitly prohibited by a treaty is not for that reason alone permitted. An even wider interpretation is that, in the process of determining a state's legal obligations, resort must be had not merely to applicable treaties and custom but also to the general principles of international law and "the requirements of the public conscience."[4] As a result, it is not always feasible to offer a definitive, complete, and exhaustive list of states' obligations under IHL, even if the core norms are fairly well-understood, internalized, and enforced in a variety of domestic and international institutions. *See* Jean-Marie Henckaerts and Louise Doswald-Beck, I Customary International Humanitarian Law: Rules (2005).

One constitutional moment in the evolution of IHL occurred in the middle of the twentieth century, after the butchery of the two world wars, the Holocaust, and the widespread violation of humanitarian law treaties. After World War II, the victorious Allies established the International Military Tribunal ("IMT") at Nuremberg, "for the trial and punishment of the major war criminals of the European Axis countries." The London Charter of 8 August 1945, under which the IMT was organized, adopted a new conception of international humanitarian law, grounded equally in the international obligations of states and in internationally-enforceable *individual criminal responsibilities*:

Article 6. * * * The following acts, or any of them, are crimes coming within the jurisdiction of the Tribunal for which there shall be individual responsibility:

(a) CRIMES AGAINST PEACE: namely, planning, preparation, initiation or waging of a war of aggression, or a war in violation of international treaties, agreements or assurances, or participation in a common plan or conspiracy for the accomplishment of any of the foregoing;

(b) WAR CRIMES: namely, violations of the laws or customs of war. Such violations shall include, but not be limited to, murder, ill-treatment or deportation to slave labor or for any other purpose of civilian population of or in occupied territory, murder or ill-treatment of prisoners of war or persons on the seas, killing of hostages, plunder of public or private property, wanton destruction of cities, towns or villages, or devastation not justified by military necessity;

(c) CRIMES AGAINST HUMANITY: namely, murder, extermination, enslavement, deportation, and other inhumane acts committed against any civilian population, before or during the war; or persecutions on political, racial or religious grounds in execution of or in connection with any crime within the jurisdiction of the Tribunal,

---

4. Rupert Ticehurst, *The Martens Clause and the Laws of Armed Conflict*, 317 Int'l. Rev. of the Red Cross 125 (1997).

whether or not in violation of the domestic law of the country where perpetrated. * * *

In addition to defining these crimes, the London Charter foreclosed or limited two categories of defenses, which similarly stressed the responsibility (and moral agency) of individuals:

> *Article 7.* The official position of defendants, whether as Heads of State or responsible officials in Government Departments, shall not be considered as freeing them from responsibility or mitigating punishment.

> *Article 8.* The fact that the Defendant acted pursuant to order of his Government or of a superior shall not free him from responsibility, but may be considered in mitigation of punishment if the Tribunal determines that justice so requires.

The Nuremberg Trials ultimately included the twenty-four high-level defendants tried by the IMT and a second set of trials for lesser criminals under Control Council Law No. 10, which established "a uniform legal basis in Germany for the prosecution of war criminals and other similar offenders, other than those dealt with by the International Military Tribunal."

In the aftermath of Nuremberg, the international community adopted the Genocide Convention (1948) and the four Geneva Conventions of 1949, relating to (i) the amelioration of the condition of the wounded and sick in armed forces in the field ("GC I"), (ii) the amelioration of the condition of wounded, sick and shipwrecked members of armed forces at sea ("GC II"), (iii) the treatment of prisoners of war ("GC III"), and (iv) the protection of civilian persons in time of war ("GC IV"). The commonalities among the Geneva Conventions are as important as their differences. For example, the International Committee of the Red Cross ("ICRC") plays a decisive role in observing each state-party's compliance with the conventions (*e.g.* by visiting prisoners of war). In addition, each convention defines certain *grave breaches*,[5] a term of art referring to egregious international wrongs for which individuals bear criminal responsibility. Under the grave breaches regime, every party to the Geneva Convention is obliged to criminalize these wrongs in its domestic law and to search for people alleged to have committed, or to have ordered to be committed, these wrongs. State-parties are also obliged either to prosecute these suspects domestically or to extradite them to a country where they will be tried (*aut dedere aut*

---

5. *See e.g.,* Art. 147 of the Fourth Geneva Convention relating to the protection of civilians:

Grave breaches * * * shall be those involving any of the following acts, if committed against persons or property protected by the present Convention: wilful killing, torture or inhuman treatment, including biological experiments, wilfully causing great suffering or serious injury to body or health, unlawful deportation or transfer or unlawful confinement of a protected person, compelling a protected person to serve in the forces of a hostile Power, or wilfully depriving a protected person of the rights of fair and regular trial prescribed in the present Convention, taking of hostages and extensive destruction and appropriation of property, not justified by military necessity and carried out unlawfully and wantonly.

Compare GC I at Art. 50; GC II at Art. 51; GC III at Art. 130.

judicare). The four Geneva Conventions also include a common Article 3, which in contrast to the conventions' overall focus on *international armed conflict*, requires all sides in an *internal armed conflict* to meet certain minimal humanitarian standards:

> In the case of armed conflict not of an international character occurring in the territory of one of the High Contracting Parties, each Party to the conflict shall be bound to apply, as a minimum, the following provisions:
>
> (1) Persons taking no active part in the hostilities, including members of armed forces who have laid down their arms and those placed *hors de combat* by sickness, wounds, detention, or any other cause, shall in all circumstances be treated humanely, without any adverse distinction founded on race, colour, religion or faith, sex, birth or wealth, or any other similar criteria. To this end the following acts are and shall remain prohibited at any time and in any place whatsoever with respect to the above-mentioned persons:
>
> > (a) violence to life and person, in particular murder of all kinds, mutilation, cruel treatment and torture;
> >
> > (b) taking of hostages;
> >
> > (c) outrages upon personal dignity, in particular, humiliating and degrading treatment;
> >
> > (d) the passing of sentences and the carrying out of executions without previous judgment pronounced by a regularly constituted court affording all the judicial guarantees which are recognized as indispensable by civilized peoples.
>
> (2) The wounded and sick shall be collected and cared for. * * *

Common Article 3 is the lowest common denominator in international humanitarian law, binding even non-state actors engaged in non-international conflict. These obligations were expanded three decades later in two additional protocols, the first relating to the protection of victims of international armed conflicts (including wars against racist regimes and wars of self-determination), and the second relating to the protection of victims of non-international armed conflicts. *See, e.g.*, Article 48 of the Protocol Additional to the Geneva Conventions of August 12, 1949, and Relating to the Protection of Victims of International Armed Conflicts (1977) ("In order to ensure respect for and protection of the civilian population and civilian objects, the Parties to the conflict shall at all times distinguish between the civilian population and combatants and between civilian objects and military objectives and accordingly shall direct their operations only against military objectives.")

Towards the end of the twentieth century, the international community took three additional steps that have been decisive in the evolution of IHL. First, states continued by treaty to identify certain inhumane weapons. For example, a series of protocols to the Convention on Prohibitions or Restrictions on the Use of Certain Conventional

Weapons Which May be Deemed to be Excessively Injurious or to Have Indiscriminate Effects (1980) attempted to ban or restrict the use of fragmentation weapons, landmines, incendiary weapons, and blinding laser weapons. Second, the United Nations, exercising its powers under Chapter VII of the UN Charter, created *ad hoc* tribunals for the prosecution of certain international humanitarian crimes in the former Yugoslavia and Rwanda *inter alia*. As shown in Module 6, *supra*, the decisions of these tribunals have created a coherent jurisprudence of responsibility, as well as rules of procedure and evidence, and standards of punishment. Third, in 1998, the Rome Statute, creating the first treaty-based permanent International Criminal Court ("ICC"), was adopted, and the ICC came into being in July 2002.

In comparison to the London Charter, the Rome Statute expands the definition of "crimes against humanity," *i.e.*, certain violations committed as part of a widespread or systematic attack against any civilian population and with knowledge of the attack. In addition to the wrongs identified in the London Charter, the Rome Statute adds *apartheid*, enforced disappearances, and persecution on political, racial, national, ethnic, culture, religious, or gender and similar grounds. The Rome Statute also adds certain gender crimes to the list of crimes against humanity, specifically "rape, sexual slavery, enforced prostitution, forced pregnancy, enforced sterilization, or any other form of sexual violence of comparable gravity." But important limitations on these gender crimes were also adopted: under Article (7)(2)(f), for example, "forced pregnancy" means "the unlawful confinement of a woman forcibly made pregnant, with the intent of affecting the ethnic composition of any population or carrying out other grave violations of international law." Among other concerns, that language converts the wrong from a gender-based crime to an ethnicity-based crime, it adds a specific intent or state-of-mind requirement, and it imposes the unlawful confinement requirement.

The category of war crimes is laid out in particular detail in the Rome Statute, drawing on post-war treaties outlawing certain weapons or conduct, the decisions of the *ad hoc* tribunals, and the work of other international authorities including non-governmental organizations. Practice since 1949 suggests that the law governing internal armed conflict has gone well beyond common article 3. Article 8(e), quoted below, lists twelve other serious violations of the laws and customs applicable in armed conflict not of an international character, drawing in part on Protocol II of 1977. Although these obligations are clearly not as extensive as those applicable in international conflicts, *compare* Article 8(b), *infra*, they are similar in ways that reward careful attention.

THE ROME STATUTE OF THE
INTERNATIONAL CRIMINAL COURT
ARTICLE 8(2), WAR CRIMES

For the purpose of this Statute, "war crimes" means:

(a) Grave breaches of the Geneva Conventions of 12 August 1949, namely, any of the following acts against persons or property protected under the provisions of the relevant Geneva Convention:

(i) Wilful killing;

(ii) Torture or inhuman treatment, including biological experiments;

(iii) Wilfully causing great suffering, or serious injury to body or health;

(iv) Extensive destruction and appropriation of property, not justified by military necessity and carried out unlawfully and wantonly;

(v) Compelling a prisoner of war or other protected person to serve in the forces of a hostile Power;

(vi) Wilfully depriving a prisoner of war or other protected person of the rights of fair and regular trial;

(vii) Unlawful deportation or transfer or unlawful confinement;

(viii) Taking of hostages.

(b) Other serious violations of the laws and customs applicable in international armed conflict, within the established framework of international law, namely, any of the following acts:

(i) Intentionally directing attacks against the civilian population as such or against individual civilians not taking direct part in hostilities;

(ii) Intentionally directing attacks against civilian objects, that is, objects which are not military objectives;

(iii) Intentionally directing attacks against personnel, installations, material, units or vehicles involved in a humanitarian assistance or peacekeeping mission in accordance with the Charter of the United Nations, as long as they are entitled to the protection given to civilians or civilian objects under the international law of armed conflict;

(iv) Intentionally launching an attack in the knowledge that such attack will cause incidental loss of life or injury to civilians or damage to civilian objects or widespread, long-term and severe damage to the natural environment which would be clearly excessive in relation to the concrete and direct overall military advantage anticipated;

(v) Attacking or bombarding, by whatever means, towns, villages, dwellings or buildings which are undefended and which are not military objectives;

(vi) Killing or wounding a combatant who, having laid down his arms or having no longer means of defence, has surrendered at discretion;

(vii) Making improper use of a flag of truce, of the flag or of the military insignia and uniform of the enemy or of the United Nations, as well as of the distinctive emblems of the Geneva Conventions, resulting in death or serious personal injury;

(viii) The transfer, directly or indirectly, by the Occupying Power of parts of its own civilian population into the territory it occupies, or the deportation or transfer of all or parts of the population of the occupied territory within or outside this territory;

(ix) Intentionally directing attacks against buildings dedicated to religion, education, art, science or charitable purposes, historic monuments, hospitals and places where the sick and wounded are collected, provided they are not military objectives;

(x) Subjecting persons who are in the power of an adverse party to physical mutilation or to medical or scientific experiments of any kind which are neither justified by the medical, dental or hospital treatment of the person concerned nor carried out in his or her interest, and which cause death to or seriously endanger the health of such person or persons;

(xi) Killing or wounding treacherously individuals belonging to the hostile nation or army;

(xii) Declaring that no quarter will be given;

(xiii) Destroying or seizing the enemy's property unless such destruction or seizure be imperatively demanded by the necessities of war;

(xiv) Declaring abolished, suspended or inadmissible in a court of law the rights and actions of the nationals of the hostile party;

(xv) Compelling the nationals of the hostile party to take part in the operations of war directed against their own country, even if they were in the belligerent's service before the commencement of the war;

(xvi) Pillaging a town or place, even when taken by assault;

(xvii) Employing poison or poisoned weapons;

(xviii) Employing asphyxiating, poisonous or other gases, and all analogous liquids, materials or devices;

(xix) Employing bullets which expand or flatten easily in the human body, such as bullets with a hard envelope which does not entirely cover the core or is pierced with incisions;

(xx) Employing weapons, projectiles and material and methods of warfare which are of a nature to cause superfluous injury or unnecessary suffering or which are inherently indiscriminate in violation of the international law of armed conflict, provided that such weapons, projectiles and material and methods of warfare are the subject of a comprehensive prohibition and are included in an annex to this Statute, by an amendment in accordance with the relevant provisions set forth in articles 121 and 123;

(xxi) Committing outrages upon personal dignity, in particular humiliating and degrading treatment;

(xxii) Committing rape, sexual slavery, enforced prostitution, forced pregnancy, * * *, enforced sterilization, or any other form of sexual violence also constituting a grave breach of the Geneva Conventions;

(xxiii) Utilizing the presence of a civilian or other protected person to render certain points, areas or military forces immune from military operations;

(xxiv) Intentionally directing attacks against buildings, material, medical units and transport, and personnel using the distinctive emblems of the Geneva Conventions in conformity with international law;

(xxv) Intentionally using starvation of civilians as a method of warfare by depriving them of objects indispensable to their survival, including wilfully impeding relief supplies as provided for under the Geneva Conventions;

(xxvi) Conscripting or enlisting children under the age of fifteen years into the national armed forces or using them to participate actively in hostilities.

(c) In the case of an armed conflict not of an international character, serious violations of article 3 common to the four Geneva Conventions of 12 August 1949, namely, any of the following acts committed against persons taking no active part in the hostilities, including members of armed forces who have laid down their arms and those placed *hors de combat* by sickness, wounds, detention or any other cause:

(i) Violence to life and person, in particular murder of all kinds, mutilation, cruel treatment and torture;

(ii) Committing outrages upon personal dignity, in particular humiliating and degrading treatment;

(iii) Taking of hostages;

(iv) The passing of sentences and the carrying out of executions without previous judgement pronounced by a regularly constituted court, affording all judicial guarantees which are generally recognized as indispensable.

(d) Paragraph 2 (c) applies to armed conflicts not of an international character and thus does not apply to situations of internal disturbances and tensions, such as riots, isolated and sporadic acts of violence or other acts of a similar nature.

(e) Other serious violations of the laws and customs applicable in armed conflicts not of an international character, within the established framework of international law, namely, any of the following acts:

(i) Intentionally directing attacks against the civilian population as such or against individual civilians not taking direct part in hostilities;

(ii) Intentionally directing attacks against buildings, material, medical units and transport, and personnel using the distinctive emblems of the Geneva Conventions in conformity with international law;

(iii) Intentionally directing attacks against personnel, installations, material, units or vehicles involved in a humanitarian assistance or peacekeeping mission in accordance with the Charter of the United Nations, as long as they are entitled to the protection given to civilians or civilian objects under the international law of armed conflict;

(iv) Intentionally directing attacks against buildings dedicated to religion, education, art, science or charitable purposes, historic monuments, hospitals and places where the sick and wounded are collected, provided they are not military objectives;

(v) Pillaging a town or place, even when taken by assault;

(vi) Committing rape, sexual slavery, enforced prostitution, forced pregnancy, * * * enforced sterilization, and any other form of sexual violence also constituting a serious violation of article 3 common to the four Geneva Conventions;

(vii) Conscripting or enlisting children under the age of fifteen years into armed forces or groups or using them to participate actively in hostilities;

(viii) Ordering the displacement of the civilian population for reasons related to the conflict, unless the security of the civilians involved or imperative military reasons so demand;

(ix) Killing or wounding treacherously a combatant adversary;

(x) Declaring that no quarter will be given;

(xi) Subjecting persons who are in the power of another party to the conflict to physical mutilation or to medical or scientific experiments of any kind which are neither justified by the medical, dental or hospital treatment of the person concerned nor carried out in his or her interest, and which cause death to or seriously endanger the health of such person or persons;

(xii) Destroying or seizing the property of an adversary unless such destruction or seizure be imperatively demanded by the necessities of the conflict;

(f) Paragraph 2 (e) applies to armed conflicts not of an international character and thus does not apply to situations of internal disturbances and tensions, such as riots, isolated and sporadic acts of violence or other acts of a similar nature. It applies to armed conflicts that take place in the territory of a State when there is protracted armed conflict between governmental authorities and organized armed groups or between such groups. * * *

We close this historical overview with a current question: how relevant is the IHL regime in the on-going war on terrorism? There is no doubt that IHL does define and prohibit the wrong committed on September 11, 2001, namely the intentional and indiscriminate targeting of civilians. Nor is there any doubt that key antagonists treat their confrontation as an armed conflict—"war" in Washington and *jihad* among the terrorists. On the other hand, the armed conflict is neither "internal" nor "international" as that distinction has structured the Geneva regime, and the essential dynamic that has assured a measure of compliance over the decades—reciprocity and long-term self-interest—cannot operate when one side is willing to tolerate suicide if it means the destruction of the other. The applicability of IHL in its traditional form seems especially remote when we consider that, at this writing, the United States does not concede that the law of armed conflict applies to the war with al Qaeda and its supporters. Nor does the United States, unlike the United Kingdom, treat captured al Qaeda operatives as prisoners of war. This has led the International Committee of the Red Cross to criticize the United States' treatment of detainees at Guantanamo Bay and has provoked an on-going legal dispute about law-of-war responses—like military commissions, *infra*—to the criminal actions of terrorists.

Readings

In approaching each of the following cases, try to articulate (i) the substantive IHL norm at issue (including the class of persons it protects), (ii) the evidence offered for its existence, and (iii) the mode of its enforcement.

THE PAQUETE HABANA
175 U.S. 677 (1900)

These are two appeals from decrees of the district court of the United States for the southern district of Florida condemning two fishing vessels and their cargoes as prize of war. Each vessel was a fishing smack, running in and out of Havana, and regularly engaged in fishing on the coast of Cuba; sailed under the Spanish flag; was owned by a Spanish subject of Cuban birth, living in the city of Havana; was commanded by a subject of Spain, also residing in Havana[.] * * * Her cargo consisted of fresh fish, caught by her crew from the sea, put on board as they were caught, and kept and sold alive. Until stopped by the blockading squadron she had no knowledge of the existence of the war or of any blockade. She had no arms or ammunition on board, and made no attempt to run the blockade after she knew of its existence, nor any resistance at the time of the capture. * * * Both the fishing vessels were brought by their captors into Key West. A libel for the condemnation of each vessel and her cargo as prize of war was there filed * * * and * * * a final decree of condemnation and sale was entered, "the court not being satisfied that as a matter of law, without any ordinance, treaty, or proclamation, fishing vessels of this class are exempt from seizure." Each vessel was thereupon sold by auction. * * * We are then brought to the consideration of the question whether, upon the facts appearing in these records, the fishing smacks were subject to capture by the armed vessels of the United States during the recent war with Spain.

By an ancient usage among civilized nations, beginning centuries ago, and gradually ripening into a rule of international law, coast fishing vessels, pursuing their vocation of catching and bringing in fresh fish, have been recognized as exempt, with their cargoes and crews, from capture as prize of war. This doctrine, however, has been earnestly contested at the bar; and no complete collection of the instances illustrating it is to be found, so far as we are aware, in a single published work although many are referred to and discussed by the writers on international law[.] * * * It is therefore worth the while to trace the history of the rule, from the earliest accessible sources, through the increasing recognition of it, with occasional setbacks, to what we may now justly consider as its final establishment in our own country and generally throughout the civilized world.

[The court then reviewed six centuries of state practice, in which combatant states had exempted domestic fishing vessels and their crews from seizure during wartime. The encyclopedic collection of evidence included decrees by King Henry IV of England in 1403 and 1406, the decisions of prize tribunals, treaties between maritime powers at war and unilateral decrees over the intervening centuries, through the U.S. war of independence, the War of 1812, the Mexican War, and the Civil War. For example,

> [i]n the treaty of 1785 between the United States and Prussia, article 23 (which was proposed by the American Commissioners, John Adams, Benjamin Franklin, and Thomas Jefferson, and is said to have been drawn up by Franklin), provided that, if war should arise between the contracting parties, 'all women and children, scholars of every faculty, cultivators of the earth, artisans, manufacturers, and fishermen, unarmed and inhabiting unfortified towns, villages, or places, and in general all others whose occupations are for the common subsistence and benefit of mankind, shall be allowed to continue their respective employments, and shall not be molested in their persons, nor shall their houses or goods be burnt or otherwise destroyed, nor their fields wasted by the armed force of the enemy, into whose power, by the events of war, they may happen to fall; but if anything is necessary to be taken from them for the use of such armed force, the same shall be paid for at a reasonable price.' Here was the clearest exemption from hostile molestation or seizure of the persons, occupations, houses, and goods of unarmed fishermen inhabiting unfortified places. * * *

The Court also reviewed apparent violations of the humanitarian norm during the Napoleonic Wars between the England and France to determine if those departures had undermined the norm. It concluded its review of this legal history in these terms:]

> [N]o instance has been found in which the exemption from capture of private coast fishing vessels honestly pursuing their peaceful industry has been denied by England or by any other nation. And the Empire of Japan * * * by an ordinance promulgated at the beginning of its war with China in August, 1894, established prize courts, and ordained that "the following enemy's vessels are exempt from detention," including in the exemption "boats engaged in coast fisheries," as well as "ships engaged exclusively on a voyage of scientific discovery, philanthropy, or religious mission."

> International law is part of our law, and must be ascertained and administered by the courts of justice of appropriate jurisdiction as often as questions of right depending upon it are duly presented for their determination. For this purpose, where there is no treaty and no controlling executive or legislative act or judicial decision, resort must be had to the customs and usages of civilized nations, and, as evidence of these, to the works of jurists and commentators who by years of labor, research, and experience have made themselves peculiarly well acquainted with the subjects of which they treat. Such works are resorted to by judicial tribunals, not for the speculations of their authors concerning what the law ought to be, but for trustworthy evidence of what the law really is. [The Court then examined the writings of jurists from England, the United States, France, Germany, the Netherlands, Argentina, Austria, Italy, Portugal, and Spain.] * * *

This review of the precedents and authorities on the subject appears to us abundantly to demonstrate that at the present day, by the general consent of the civilized nations of the world, and independently of any express treaty or other public act, it is an established rule of international law, founded on considerations of humanity to a poor and industrious order of men, and of the mutual convenience of belligerent states, that coast fishing vessels, with their implements and supplies, cargoes and crews, unarmed and honestly pursuing their peaceful calling of catching and bringing in fresh fish, are exempt from capture as prize of war. The exemption, of course, does not apply to coast fishermen or their vessels if employed for a warlike purpose, or in such a way as to give aid or information to the enemy; nor when military or naval operations create a necessity to which all private interests must give way. * * * This rule of international law is one which prize courts administering the law of nations are bound to take judicial notice of, and to give effect to, in the absence of any treaty or other public act of their own government in relation to the matter. * * *

The position taken by the United States during the recent war with Spain was quite in accord with the rule of international law, now generally recognized by civilized nations, in regard to coast fishing vessels. On April 21, 1898, the Secretary of the Navy gave instructions to Admiral Sampson, commanding the North Atlantic Squadron, to "immediately institute a blockade of the north coast of Cuba, extending from Cardenas on the east to Bahia Honda on the west." The blockade was immediately instituted accordingly. On April 22 the President issued a proclamation declaring that the United States had instituted and would maintain that blockade, "in pursuance of the laws of the United States, and the law of nations applicable to such cases." And by the act of Congress of April 25, 1898, chap. 189, it was declared that the war between the United States and Spain existed on that day, and had existed since and including April 21. On April 26, 1898, the President issued another proclamation which, after reciting the existence of the war as declared by Congress, contained this further recital: "It being desirable that such war should be conducted upon principles in harmony with the present views of nations and sanctioned by their recent practice." This recital was followed by specific declarations of certain rules for the conduct of the war by sea, making no mention of fishing vessels. But the proclamation clearly manifests the general policy of the government to conduct the war in accordance with the principles of international law sanctioned by the recent practice of nations. * * *

Upon the facts proved in either case, it is the duty of this court, sitting as the highest prize court of the United States, and administering the law of nations, to declare and adjudge that the capture was unlawful and without probable cause; and it is therefore, in each case, *Ordered, that the decree of the District Court be reversed*, and the proceeds of the sale of the vessel, together with the proceeds of any sale of her cargo, be restored to the claimant, with damages and costs.

MR. CHIEF JUSTICE FULLER, with whom concurred MR. JUSTICE HARLAN and MR. JUSTICE MCKENNA, dissenting.

The district court held these vessels and their cargoes liable because not "satisfied that as a matter of law, without any ordinance, treaty, or proclamation, fishing vessels of this class are exempt from seizure." This court holds otherwise, not because such exemption is to be found in any treaty, legislation, proclamation, or instruction granting it, but on the ground that the vessels were exempt by reason of an established rule of international law applicable to them, which it is the duty of the court to enforce. I am unable to conclude that there is any such established international rule, or that this court can properly revise action which must be treated as having been taken in the ordinary exercise of discretion in the conduct of war. * * *

CROSS–EXAMINATION OF GENERAL FIELDMARSHALL ERHARD MILCH BEFORE THE NUREMBERG MILITARY TRIBUNAL BY THE AMERICAN PROSECUTOR (11 MARCH 1946)

PROSECUTOR: Now, you have the regulations with you, which you say were printed for the information of every soldier, about international law and regulations. You have them with you this morning?

MILCH: I have them with me; the regulations are contained in my service book, the same as for every soldier.

PROSECUTOR: * * * I would like you to get that out and give us exactly the text of those instructions or regulations, which you say reflect international law as you understood it.

MILCH: Do you want me to read it out now? The quotation . . .

PROSECUTOR: Not too fast.

MILCH: No. "Ten Commandments for the Conduct of the German Soldier in War."

1. The German soldier fights chivalrously for the victory of his people. Cruelty and needless destruction are unworthy of him.

2. The fighter must wear a uniform, or else he must be provided with insignia visible from a good distance. Fighting in civilian clothes without such insignia is prohibited.

3. No enemy in the act of surrendering shall be killed, not even a partisan or a spy. The courts will administer the just punishment.

4.   Prisoners of war must not be maltreated or insulted. Weapons, plans and notes are to be taken from them. Apart from these, none of their possessions may be taken from them.

5.   Dum-dum bullets are prohibited. Bullets may not be transformed into dum-dum bullets.

6.   The Red Cross is inviolable. Wounded enemies must be treated humanely. Medical orderlies and chaplains must not be hindered in the performance of their medical and spiritual functions.

7.   The civilian population is inviolable. The soldier must not plunder or wantonly destroy. Historical monuments and buildings dedicated to religious service, art, science, or charity must be treated with special care. Personal services and services in kind shall only be required of the civilian population against compensation, and if ordered by the superior officer.

8.   Neutral territory must not be militarily involved by trespassing by planes flying over it, or by gunfire.

9.   If a German soldier is captured, he must state his name and rank when questioned. Under no circumstances may he say to what unit he belongs, or speak about military, political, or economic conditions on the German side, neither may he allow himself to be induced to do so by threats or promises.

10.   Any contravention of these orders while on active service is punishable. Breaches by the enemy of the fundamental laws listed sub 1 to 8 are to be reported. Reprisals are permissible by order of the higher commanders.

PROSECUTOR: Now that, as you understand it, is the military law conforming with international law, which was promulgated for the governance of the troops in the field?

MILCH: Yes.

PROSECUTOR: And you understood, and it was generally understood in the German Army, that that was international law, was it not?

MILCH: Every soldier could not help knowing that these were the German regulations because they were pasted on the first sheet of the pay book, issued to every soldier, and which he had to carry on him. The common soldier, of course, did not know that they represented international law.

PROSECUTOR: The higher commanders, like yourself did, did they not?

MILCH: Yes.

PROSECUTOR: That represented your understanding and interpretation of your duties and obligations as honorable men in combat?

MILCH: Yes.

* * *

Erhard Milch had overseen the development of the German air force as part of the re-armament of Germany following World War I and had served as a high-ranking officer in the Luftwaffe during World War II. Before the Nuremberg Military Tribunal, he was indicted for war crimes and crimes against humanity. According to the indictment, for example,

8.   Count Two. Between March 1942 and May 1943 the defendant Milch unlawfully, wilfully, and knowingly committed war crimes as defined in Article H of Control Council Law No. 10, in that he was a principal in, accessory to, ordered, abetted, took a consenting part in, and was connected with plans and enterprises involving medical experiments without the subjects' consent, upon members of the armed forces and civilians of nations then at war with the German Reich and who were in the custody of the German Reich in the exercise of belligerent control, in the course of which experiments the defendant Milch, together with divers [sic] other persons, committed murders, brutalities, cruelties, tortures, and other inhumane acts. Such experiments included, but were not limited to, the following:

(A) HIGH–ALTITUDE EXPERIMENTS. From about March 1942 to about August 1942 experiments were conducted at the Dachau concentration camp for the benefit of the German Air Force to investigate the limits of human endurance and existence at extremely high altitudes. The experiments were carried out in a low-pressure chamber in which the atmospheric conditions and pressure prevailing at high altitudes (up to 68,000 feet) could be duplicated. The experimental subjects were placed in the low-pressure chamber and thereafter the simulated altitude therein was raised. Many victims died as a result of these experiments and others suffered grave injury, torture, and ill-treatment.

(B) FREEZING EXPERIMENTS. From about August 1942 to about May 1943 experiments were conducted at the Dachau concentration camp primarily for the benefit of the German Air Force to investigate the most effective means of treating persons who had been severely chilled or frozen. In one series of experiments the subjects were forced to remain in a tank of ice water for periods up to 3 hours. Extreme rigor developed in a short time. Numerous victims died in the course of these experiments. After the survivors were severely chilled, rewarming was attempted by various means. In another series of experiments, the subjects were kept naked outdoors for many hours at temperatures below freezing. The victims screamed with pain as parts of their bodies froze.

9.   The said war crimes constitute violations of international conventions, particularly of Articles 4, 5, 6, 7, and 46 of the Hague Regulations, 1907, and of Articles 2, 3, and 4 of the Prisoner-of-War Convention (Geneva, 1929), the laws and customs of war, the

general principles of criminal law as derived from the criminal laws of all civilized nations, the internal penal laws of the countries in which such crimes were committed, and of Article II, of Control Council Law No. 10.

Milch was found guilty and sentenced to life imprisonment. Three years later, the Convention Relative to the Treatment of Prisoners of War (the Third Geneva Convention) was adopted, providing in part:

Article 13: Prisoners of war must at all times be humanely treated. Any unlawful act or omission by the Detaining Power causing death or seriously endangering the health of a prisoner of war in its custody is prohibited, and will be regarded as a serious breach of the present Convention. In particular, no prisoner of war may be subjected to physical mutilation or to medical or scientific experiments of any kind which are not justified by the medical, dental or hospital treatment of the prisoner concerned and carried out in his interest. Likewise prisoners of war must at all times be protected, particularly against acts of violence or intimidation and against insults and public curiosity. Measures of reprisal against prisoners of war are prohibited.

PROSECUTOR v. NORMAN

Case No. SCSL–2004–14–AR72(E) (31 May 2004), 43 I.L.M. 1129

Decision on Preliminary Motion Based on Lack of Jurisdiction (Child Recruitment)

[Sam Hinga Norman, former deputy defense minister of Sierra Leone, was charged with war crimes and crimes against humanity at the Special Court for Sierra Leone, which had been created by resolution of the Security Council. He was charged with "child recruitment," *i.e.* enlisting children under the age of fifteen as fighters in the Civil Defense Front. Norman moved to dismiss this count of the indictment for lack of jurisdiction, arguing that at the time of the indictment (November 1996), there was no customary norm against recruiting children under the age of fifteen into the armed forces. Alternatively, he argued, even if Protocol II Additional to the Geneva Conventions of 12 August 1949, and Relating to the Protection of Victims of Non–International Armed Conflicts,[1] and the Convention of the Rights of the Child,[2] established an obligation on the part of states not to recruit children under fifteen, those treaties did not impose criminal responsibility on individuals.]

---

1. 1125 U.N.T.S. 609 (8 June 1977) ("Protocol II").
2. 1577 U.N.T.S. 3 (20 November 1989) ("CRC").

Discussion

Under Article 4 of its Statute, the Special Court has the power to prosecute persons who committed serious violations of international humanitarian law including:

"c. Conscripting or enlisting children under the age of fifteen years into armed forces or groups using them to participate actively in hostilities ('child recruitment')." * * *

The question raised by the [Defendant's] Preliminary Motion is whether the crime as defined in Article 4(c) of the Statute was recognised as a crime entailing individual criminal responsibility under customary international law at the time of the acts alleged in the indictments against the accused.

To answer the question before this Court, the first two sources of international law under Article 38(1) of the Statute of the International Court of Justice ("ICJ") have to be scrutinized:

1) international conventions, whether general or particular, establishing rules especially recognized by the contesting states

2) international custom, as evidence of a general practice accepted as law . . .

A.   International Conventions * * *

1) *Fourth Geneva Convention of 1949.*[3] This Convention was ratified by Sierra Leone in 1965. As of 30 November 1996, 187 States were parties to the Geneva Conventions. The pertinent provisions of the Conventions are as follows:

Art. 14. In time of peace, the High Contracting Parties and, after the outbreak of hostilities, the Parties thereto, may establish in their own territory and, if the need arises, in occupied areas, hospital and safety zones and localities so organized as to protect from the effects of war, wounded, sick and aged persons, *children under fifteen,* expectant mothers and mothers of children under seven.

Art. 24. The Parties to the conflict shall take the necessary measures to ensure that *children under fifteen, who are orphaned or are separated from their families as a result of the war,* are not left to their own resources, and that their maintenance, the exercise of their religion and their education are facilitated in all circumstances. Their education shall, as far as possible, be entrusted to persons of a similar cultural tradition.

Art. 51. The Occupying Power *may not compel protected persons to serve in its armed or auxiliary forces.* No pressure or propaganda which aims at securing voluntary enlistment is permitted.

---

3. Geneva Convention (IV) Relative to the Protection of Civilian Persons in Time of War, August 12, 1949, 75 UNTS (1950).

2) *Additional Protocols I and II of 1977.*[4] Both Additional Protocols were ratified by Sierra Leone in 1986. Attention should be drawn to the following provisions of Additional Protocol I:

Article 77. Protection of children

2.   The Parties to the conflict shall take all *feasible measures in order that children who have not attained the age of fifteen years do not take a direct part in hostilities and, in particular, they shall refrain from recruiting them into their armed forces.* In recruiting among those persons who have attained the age of fifteen years but who have not attained the age of eighteen years, the Parties to the conflict shall endeavour to give priority to those who are oldest.

3.   If, in exceptional cases, despite the provisions of paragraph 2, children who have not attained the age of fifteen years take a direct part in hostilities and fall into the power of an adverse Party, they shall continue to benefit from the special protection accorded by this Article, whether or not they are prisoners of war.

4.   If arrested, detained or interned for reasons related to the armed conflict, children shall be held in quarters separate from the quarters of adults, except where families are accommodated as family units as provided in Article 75, paragraph 5.

[One hundred thirty seven] States were parties to Additional Protocol II as of 30 November 1996. Sierra Leone ratified Additional Protocol II on 21 October 1986. The key provision is Article 4 entitled "fundamental guarantees" which provides in relevant part:

Article 4. Fundamental guarantees

3.   Children shall be provided with the care and aid they require, and in particular:

c) Children *who have not attained the age of fifteen years shall neither be recruited in the armed forces or groups nor allowed to take part in hostilities*

3) *Convention on the Rights of the Child.*[5] The Convention entered into force on 2 September 1990 and was on the same day ratified by the Government of Sierra Leone. In 1996, all but six states existing at the time had ratified the Convention. The CRC recognizes the protection of children in international humanitarian law and also requires States Parties to ensure respect for these rules by taking appropriate and feasible measures. On feasible measures:

---

4. Protocol Additional to the Geneva Conventions of 12 August 1949, and relating to the Protection of Victims of International Armed Conflicts, 1125 U.N.T.S. 609 (entered into force 7 December 1978) ("Additional Protocol I"); Protocol Additional to the Geneva Conventions of 12 August 1949, and Relating to the Protection of Victims of Non–International Armed Conflicts, 1125 U.N.T.S. 3 (entered into force 7 December 1977) ("Additional Protocol II").

5. Convention on the Rights of the Child, 20 November 1989, 1577 U.N.T.S. 3.

Article 38.

1.   States Parties undertake to respect and to ensure respect for rules of international humanitarian law applicable to them in armed conflicts which are relevant to the child.

2.   States Parties shall take *all feasible measures* to ensure that persons who have not attained the age of fifteen years do not take a direct part in hostilities.

3.   *States Parties shall refrain from recruiting any person who has not attained the age of fifteen years into their armed forces.* In recruiting among those persons who have attained the age of fifteen years but who have not attained the age of eighteen years, States Parties shall endeavour to give priority to those who are oldest.

4.   In accordance with their obligations under international humanitarian law to protect the civilian population in armed conflicts, States Parties shall take *all feasible measures to ensure protection* and care of children who are affected by an armed conflict.

* * *

B.   Customary International Law

Prior to November 1996, the prohibition on child recruitment had also crystallised as customary international law. The formation of custom requires both state practice and a sense of pre-existing obligation (*opinio iuris*). "An articulated sense of obligation, without implementing usage, is nothing more than rhetoric. Conversely, state practice, without *opinio iuris*, is just habit."[6]

As regards state practice, the list of states having legislation concerning recruitment or voluntary enlistment clearly shows that almost all states prohibit (and have done so for a long time) the recruitment of children under the age of fifteen. Since 185 states, including Sierra Leone, were parties to the Geneva Conventions prior to 1996, it follows that the provisions of those conventions were widely recognised as customary international law. Similarly, 133 states, including Sierra Leone, ratified Additional Protocol II before 1995. Due to the high number of States Parties one can conclude that many of the provisions of Additional Protocol II, including the fundamental guarantees, were widely accepted as customary international law by 1996. Even though Additional Protocol II addresses internal conflicts, the ICTY Appeals Chamber held in *Prosecutor v. Tadic* that "it does not matter whether the 'serious violation' has occurred within the context of an international or an internal armed conflict".[7]

This means that children are protected by the fundamental guarantees, regardless of whether there is an international or internal conflict taking place. Furthermore, as already mentioned, all but six states had ratified the Convention on the Rights of the Child by 1996. This huge

---

6.   Edward T. Swaine, *Rational Custom*, DUKE LAW JOURNAL, 559, 567–68 (December 2002).

7.   *Prosecutor v. Dusko Tadic*, Case No. IT–94–1–AR72, Decision on the Defence Motion for Interlocutory Appeal on Jurisdiction, 2 October 1995, ("Tadic Jurisdiction Decision").

acceptance, the highest acceptance of all international conventions, clearly shows that the provisions of the CRC became international customary law almost at the time of the entry into force of the Convention.

The widespread recognition and acceptance of the norm prohibiting child recruitment in Additional Protocol II and the CRC provides compelling evidence that the conventional norm entered customary international law well before 1996. The fact that there was not a single reservation to lower the legal obligation under Article 38 of the CRC underlines this, especially if one takes into consideration the fact that Article 38 is one of the very few conventional provisions which can claim universal acceptance. The African Charter on the Rights and Welfare of the Child,[8] adopted the same year as the CRC came into force, reiterates with almost the same wording the prohibition of child recruitment:

Article 22(2): Armed Conflicts

2.   States Parties to the present Charter shall take all necessary measures to ensure that no child shall take a direct part in hostilities and refrain, in particular, from recruiting any child.

[I]t is well-settled that *all* parties to an armed conflict, whether states or non-state actors, are bound by international humanitarian law, even though only states may become parties to international treaties. Customary international law represents the common standard of behavior within the international community, thus even armed groups hostile to a particular government have to abide by these laws. It has also been pointed out that non-state entities are bound by necessity by the rules embodied in international humanitarian law instruments, that they are "responsible for the conduct of their members"[9] and may be "held so responsible by opposing parties or by the outside world".[10] Therefore all parties to the conflict in Sierra Leone were bound by the prohibition of child recruitment that exists in international humanitarian law.

Furthermore, it should be mentioned that since the mid–1980s, states as well as non-state entities started to commit themselves to preventing the use of child soldiers and to ending the use of already recruited soldiers.

The central question which must now be considered is whether the prohibition on child recruitment also entailed individual criminal responsibility at the time of the crimes alleged in the indictments.

C.   *Nullum Crimen Sine Lege, Nullum Crimen Sine Poena*

It is the duty of this Chamber to ensure that the principle of non-retroactivity is not breached. As essential elements of all legal systems,

---

8. African Charter on the Rights and Welfare of the Child, OAU Doc. CAB/LEG/24.9/49 (1990), adopted 11 July 1990, entered into force, 29 November 1999.

9. *See* F. Kalsoven and L. Zegveld, CONSTRAINTS ON THE WAGING OF WAR, AN INTRODUCTION TO INTERNATIONAL HUMANITATIAN LAW (International Committee of the Red Cross, March 2001), p. 75.

10. *Ibid.*

the fundamental principle *nullum crimen sine lege* and the ancient principle *nullum crimen sine poena*, need to be considered. In the ICTY case of *Prosecutor v. Hadzihasanovic*, it was observed that "In interpreting the principle *nullum crimen sine lege*, it is critical to determine whether the underlying conduct at the time of its commission was punishable. The emphasis on conduct, rather than on the specific description of the offence in substantive criminal law, is of primary relevance."[11] In other words it must be "foreseeable and accessible to a possible perpetrator that his concrete conduct was punishable". As has been shown in the previous sections, child recruitment was a violation of conventional and customary international humanitarian law by 1996. But can it also be stated that the prohibited act was criminalised and punishable under international or national law to an extent which would show customary practice?

In the ICTY case of *Prosecutor v. Tadic*, the test for determining whether a violation of humanitarian law is subject to prosecution and punishment is set out thus:

> The following requirements must be met for an offence to be subject to prosecution before the International Tribunal under Article 3 [of the ICTY Statute]:
>
> (i) the violation must constitute an infringement of a rule of international humanitarian law;
>
> (ii) the rule must be customary in nature or, if it belongs to treaty law, the required conditions must be met;
>
> (iii) the violation must be "serious", that is to say, it must constitute a breach of a rule protecting important values, and the breach must involve grave consequences for the victim [. . .];
>
> (iv) the violation of the rule must entail, under customary or conventional law, the individual criminal responsibility of the person breaching the rule.[12]

1. *International Humanitarian Law.* With respect to points (i) and (ii), it follows from the discussion above, where the requirements have been addressed exhaustively, that in this regard the test is satisfied.

2. *Rule Protecting Important Values.* Regarding point (iii), all the conventions listed above deal with the protection of children, and it has been shown that this is one of the fundamental guarantees articulated in Additional Protocol II. The Special Court Statute, just like the ICTR Statute before it, draws on Part II of Additional Protocol II entitled "Humane Treatment" and its fundamental guarantees, as well as Common Article 3 to the Geneva Conventions in specifying the crimes falling within its jurisdiction. "All the fundamental guarantees share a similar character. In recognising them as fundamental, the international com-

---

11. *Prosecutor v. Hadzihasanovic, Alagicand Kubura*, Case No. IT–01–47–PT, Decision on Joint Challenge to Jurisdiction, 12 November 2002, ¶ 62.

12. *Tadic* Jurisdiction Decision, ¶ 94.

munity set a benchmark for the minimum standards for the conduct of armed conflict." Common Article 3 requires humane treatment and specifically addresses humiliating and degrading treatment. This includes the treatment of child soldiers in the course of their recruitment. Article 3(2) specifies further that the parties "should further endeavour to bring into force [. . .] all or part of the other provisions of the present convention," thus including the specific protection for children under the Geneva Conventions as stated above. Furthermore, the UN Security Council condemned as early as 1996 the "inhumane and abhorrent practice"[13] of recruiting, training and deploying children for combat. It follows that the protection of children is regarded as an important value. As can be verified in numerous reports of various human rights organizations, the practice of child recruitment bears the most atrocious consequences for the children.

3. *Individual Criminal Responsibility.* Regarding point (iv), the Defence refers to the Secretary–General's statement that "while the prohibition on child recruitment has by now acquired a customary international law status, it is far less clear whether it is customarily recognised as a war crime entailing the individual criminal responsibility of the accused." The ICTY Appeals Chamber upheld the legality of prosecuting violations of the laws and customs of war, including violations of Common Article 3 and the Additional Protocols in the *Tadic* case in 1995. In creating the ICTR Statute, the Security Council explicitly recognized for the first time that serious violations of fundamental guarantees lead to individual criminal liability[14] and this was confirmed later on by decisions and judgments of the ICTR. In its Judgment in the *Akayesu* case, the ICTR Trial Chamber, relying on the *Tadic* test, confirmed that a breach of a rule protecting important values was a "serious violation" entailing criminal responsibility.[15] The Trial Chamber noted that Article 4 of the ICTR Statute was derived from Common Article 3 (containing fundamental prohibitions as a humanitarian minimum of protection for war victims) and Additional Protocol II, "which equally outlines 'Fundamental Guarantees'". The Chamber concluded that "it is clear that the authors of such egregious violations must incur individual criminal responsibility for their deeds". Similarly, under the ICTY Statute adopted in 1993, a person acting in breach of Additional Protocol I to the Geneva Conventions may face criminal sanctions, and this has been confirmed in ICTY jurisprudence.

The Committee on the Rights of the Child, the international monitoring body for the implementation of the CRC, showed exactly this understanding while issuing its recommendations to Uganda in 1997. The Committee recommended that: "awareness of the duty to fully respect the rules of international humanitarian law, in the spirit of

---

13. Security Council Resolution S/RES/1071 (1996), 30 August 1996 ¶ 9.

14. Statute of the International Criminal Tribunal for Rwanda, S/RES/935 (1994), 1 July 1994 (as amended), Article 4.

15. *Prosecutor v. Akayesu*, Case No. ICTR–96–4–T, Judgment, 2 September 1998, paras 616–17.

article 38 of the Convention, *inter alia* with regard to children, should be made known to the parties to the armed conflict in the northern part of the State Party's territory, and that *violations of the rules of international humanitarian law entail responsibility being attributed to the perpetrators.*"[16]

In 1998 the Rome Statute for the International Criminal Court was adopted. It entered into force on 1 July 2002. Article 8 includes the crime of child recruitment in international armed conflict and internal armed conflict, the elements of which are elaborated in the Elements of Crimes adopted in 2000:[17]

Article 8. War crimes

1. The Court shall have jurisdiction in respect of war crimes in particular when committed as part of a plan or policy or as part of a large-scale commission of such crimes.

2. For the purpose of this Statute, "war crimes" means: [. . .]

(b) Other serious violations of the laws and customs applicable in international armed conflict, within the established framework of international law, namely, any of the following acts: [. . .]

(xxvi) Conscripting or enlisting children under the age of fifteen years into the national armed forces or using them to participate actively in hostilities.

The Defence, noting the concerns of the United States, argues that the Rome Statute created new legislation. * * * [But t]he question whether or not the United States could be said to have persistently objected to the formation of the customary norm is irrelevant to its status as such a norm.

Building on the principles set out in the earlier Conventions, the 1999 ILO Convention 182 Concerning the Prohibition and Immediate Action for the Elimination of the Worst Forms of Child Labour, provided:

Article 1.

Each Member which ratifies this Convention shall take *immediate and effective measures* to secure the prohibition and elimination of the worst forms of child labour as a matter of urgency.

Article 2.

For the purposes of this Convention, the *term "child" shall apply to all persons under the age of 18.*

---

16. *Concluding observations of the Committee on the Rights of the Child: Uganda*, 21 October 1997 upon submission of the Report in 1996, CRC/C/15/Add.80.

17. UN Doc. PCNICC/2000/1/Add.2(2000). Elements of Article 8(2)(e)(vii) War crime of using, conscripting and enlisting children: 1. The perpetrator conscripted or enlisted one or more persons into an armed force or group or used one or more persons to participate actively in hostilities. 2. Such person or persons were under the age of fifteen years. 3. The perpetrator knew or should have known that such person or persons were under the age of fifteen years. 4. The conduct took place in the context of and was associated with an armed conflict not of an international character. 5. The perpetrator was aware of factual circumstances that established the existence of an armed conflict.

Article 3.

For the purposes of this Convention, the term "the worst forms of child labour" comprises: (a) all forms of slavery or practices similar to slavery, such as the sale and trafficking of children, debt bondage and serfdom and forced or compulsory labour, *including forced or compulsory recruitment of children for use in armed conflict.*

It is clear that by the time Article 2 of this Convention was formulated, the debate had moved on from the question whether the recruitment of children under the age of 15 was prohibited or indeed criminalized, and the focus had shifted to the next step in the development of international law, namely the raising of the standard to include all children under the age of eighteen. This led finally to the wording of Article 4 of the Optional Protocol II to the Convention on the Rights of the Child on the Involvement of Children in Armed Conflict.[18] The CRC Optional Protocol II was signed on 25 May 2000 and came into force on 12 February 2002. It has 115 signatories and has been ratified by 70 states. The relevant Article for our purposes is Article 4 which states:

1.   Armed groups that are distinct from the armed forces of a State should not, under any circumstances, recruit or use in hostilities persons *under the age of eighteen years.*

2.   States Parties shall take all feasible measures to prevent such recruitment and use, including the adoption of legal measures necessary *to prohibit and criminalize such practices.*

The Defence argues that the first mention of the criminalization of child recruitment occurs in Article 4(2) of the CRC Optional Protocol II. Contrary to this argument, the Article in fact demonstrates that the aim at this stage was to raise the standard of the prohibition of child recruitment from age fifteen to eighteen, proceeding from the assumption that the conduct was already criminalized at the time in question.

The Appeals Chamber in *Prosecutor v. Dusko Tadic*, making reference to the Nuremberg Tribunal, outlined the following factors establishing individual criminal responsibility under international law:

the clear and unequivocal recognition of the rules of warfare in international law and State practice indicating an intention to criminalize the prohibition, including statements by government officials and international organizations, as well as punishment of violations by national courts and military tribunals.[19]

The Appeals Chamber in *Tadic* went on to state that where these conditions are met, individuals must be held criminally responsible, because, as the Nuremberg Tribunal concluded:

---

18.   UN Doc. A/54/RES/263, 25 May 2000, entered into force 12 February 2002 ("CRC Optional Protocol II").

19.   *Tadic* Jurisdiction Decision, ¶ 128.

[c]rimes against international law are committed by men, not by abstract entities, and only by punishing individuals who commit such crimes can the provisions of international law be enforced.[20]

A norm need not be expressly stated in an international convention for it to crystallize as a crime under customary international law. What, indeed, would be the meaning of a customary rule if it only became applicable upon its incorporation into an international instrument such as the Rome Treaty? Furthermore, it is not necessary for the *individual criminal responsibility* of the accused to be explicitly stated in a convention for the provisions of the convention to entail individual criminal responsibility under customary international law.[21] As Judge Meron in his capacity as professor has pointed out, "it has not been seriously questioned that some acts of individuals that are prohibited by international law constitute criminal offences, even when there is no accompanying provision for the establishment of the jurisdiction of particular courts or scale of penalties".[22]

The prohibition of child recruitment constitutes a fundamental guarantee and although it is not enumerated in the ICTR and ICTY Statutes, it shares the same character and is of the same gravity as the violations that are explicitly listed in those Statutes. The fact that the ICTY and ICTR have prosecuted violations of Additional Protocol II provides further evidence of the criminality of child recruitment before 1996. * * *

In the instant case, further support for the finding that the *nullum crimen* principle has not been breached is found in the national legislation of states which includes criminal sanctions as a measure of enforcement. * * *

By 2001, and in most cases prior to the Rome Statute, 108 states explicitly prohibited child recruitment, one example [Norway] dating back to 1902, and a further 15 states that do not have specific legislation did not show any indication of using child soldiers. The list of states in the 2001 Child Soldiers Global Report[23] clearly shows that states with quite different legal systems—civil law, common law, Islamic law—share the same view on the topic.

PROSECUTOR v. AKAYESU

Case No. ICTR–96–4–T, Judgment, (September 2, 1998)

This judgment is rendered by Trial Chamber I of the International Tribunal for the prosecution of persons responsible for genocide and

---

20. The Trial of Major War Criminals: Proceedings of the International Military Tribunal Sitting at Nuremberg Germany, Part 22, (1950) at 447.

21. *See Prosecutor v. Tadic*, Case No. IT–94–1, Decision on Defence Motion on Jurisdiction, 10 August 1995, ¶ 70.

22. Theodor Meron, *International Criminalization of Internal Atrocities*, (1995) 89 AJIL 554, p. 562.

23. *See* CHILD SOLDIERS GLOBAL REPORT 2001, published by the Coalition to Stop the Use of Child Soldiers, available at www.child-soldiers.org.

other serious violations of international humanitarian law committed in the territory of Rwanda and Rwandan citizens responsible for genocide and other such violations committed in the territory of neighbouring States, between 1 January and 31 December 1994 (the "Tribunal"). The judgment follows the indictment and trial of Jean Paul Akayesu, a Rwandan citizen who was bourgmestre of Taba commune, Prefecture of Gitarama, in Rwanda, at the time the crimes alleged in the indictment were perpetrated. * * *

Charges

As bourgmestre, Jean Paul Akayesu was responsible for maintaining law and public order in his commune. At least 2000 Tutsis were killed in Taba between April 7 and the end of June, 1994, while he was still in power. The killings in Taba were openly committed and so widespread that, as bourgmestre, Jean Paul Akayesu must have known about them. Although he had the authority and responsibility to do so, Jean Paul Akayesu never attempted to prevent the killing of Tutsis in the commune in any way or called for assistance from regional or national authorities to quell the violence.

Between April 7 and the end of June, 1994, hundreds of civilians (hereinafter "displaced civilians") sought refuge at the bureau communal. The majority of these displaced civilians were Tutsi. While seeking refuge at the bureau communal, female displaced civilians were regularly taken by armed local militia and/or communal police and subjected to sexual violence, and/or beaten on or near the bureau communal premises. Displaced civilians were also murdered frequently on or near the bureau communal premises. Many women were forced to endure multiple acts of sexual violence which were at times committed by more than one assailant. These acts of sexual violence were generally accompanied by explicit threats of death or bodily harm. The female displaced civilians lived in constant fear and their physical and psychological health deteriorated as a result of the sexual violence and beatings and killings.

Jean Paul Akayesu knew that the acts of sexual violence, beatings and murders were being committed and was at times present during their commission. Jean Paul Akayesu facilitated the commission of the sexual violence, beatings and murders by allowing the sexual violence and beatings and murders to occur on or near the bureau communal premises. By virtue of his presence during the commission of the sexual violence, beatings and murders and by failing to prevent the sexual violence, beatings and murders, Jean Paul Akayesu encouraged these activities. * * *

THE LAW

Genocide (Article 2 of the Statute)

Article 2 of the Statute stipulates that the Tribunal shall have the power to prosecute persons responsible for genocide, complicity to commit genocide, direct and public incitement to commit genocide, attempt to commit genocide and complicity in genocide. In accordance with the said provisions of the Statute, the Prosecutor has charged Akayesu with the crimes legally defined as genocide (count 1), complicity in genocide (count 2) and incitement to commit genocide (count 4).

The definition of genocide, as given in Article 2 of the Tribunal's Statute, is taken verbatim from Articles 2 and 3 of the Convention on the Prevention and Punishment of the Crime of Genocide (the "Genocide Convention"). * * * It states:

> Genocide means any of the following acts committed with intent to destroy, in whole or in part, a national, ethnical, racial or religious group, as such:
>
> (a) Killing members of the group;
>
> (b) Causing serious bodily or mental harm to members of the group;
>
> (c) Deliberately inflicting on the group conditions of life calculated to bring about its physical destruction in whole or in part;
>
> (d) Imposing measures intended to prevent births within the group;
>
> (e) Forcibly transferring children of the group to another group.

The Genocide Convention is undeniably considered part of customary international law, as can be seen in the opinion of the International Court of Justice on the provisions of the Genocide Convention, and as was recalled by the United Nations' Secretary–General in his Report on the establishment of the International Criminal Tribunal for the former Yugoslavia. The Chamber notes that Rwanda acceded, by legislative decree, to the Convention on Genocide on 12 February 1975. Thus, punishment of the crime of genocide did exist in Rwanda in 1994, at the time of the acts alleged in the Indictment, and the perpetrator was liable to be brought before the competent courts of Rwanda to answer for this crime.

Contrary to popular belief, the crime of genocide does not imply the actual extermination of group in its entirety, but is understood as such once any one of the acts mentioned in Article 2(2)(a) through 2(2)(e) is committed with the specific intent to destroy "in whole or in part" a national, ethnical, racial or religious group. Genocide is distinct from other crimes inasmuch as it embodies a special intent or *dolus specialis*. Special intent of a crime is the specific intention, required as a constitutive element of the crime, which demands that the perpetrator clearly seeks to produce the act charged. Thus, the special intent in the crime of genocide lies in "the intent to destroy, in whole or in part, a national, ethnical, racial or religious group, as such".

Thus, for a crime of genocide to have been committed, it is necessary that one of the acts listed under Article 2(2) of the Statute be committed, that the particular act be committed against a specifically targeted group, it being a national, ethnical, racial or religious group. Consequently, in order to clarify the constitutive elements of the crime of genocide, the Chamber will first state its findings on the acts provided for under Article 2(2)(a) through Article 2(2)(e) of the Statute, the groups protected by the Genocide Convention, and the special intent or *dolus specialis* necessary for genocide to take place.

* * *

Imposing measures intended to prevent births within the group (paragraph d):

For purposes of interpreting Article 2(2)(d) of the Statute, the Chamber holds that the measures intended to prevent births within the group, should be construed as sexual mutilation, the practice of sterilization, forced birth control, separation of the sexes and prohibition of marriages. In patriarchal societies, where membership of a group is determined by the identity of the father, an example of a measure intended to prevent births within a group is the case where, during rape, a woman of the said group is deliberately impregnated by a man of another group, with the intent to have her give birth to a child who will consequently not belong to its mother's group. Furthermore, the Chamber notes that measures intended to prevent births within the group may be physical, but can also be mental. For instance, rape can be a measure intended to prevent births when the person raped refuses subsequently to procreate, in the same way that members of a group can be led, through threats or trauma, not to procreate.

* * *

Crimes against Humanity (Article 3 of the Statute)

Crimes against humanity—historical development:

Crimes against humanity were recognized in the Charter and Judgment of the Nuremberg Tribunal, as well as in Law No. 10 of the Control Council for Germany. Article 6(c) of the Charter of Nuremberg Tribunal defines crimes against humanity as

> murder, extermination, enslavement, deportation, and other inhumane acts committed against any civilian population, before or during the war, or persecutions on political, racial or religious grounds in execution of or in connexion with any crime within the jurisdiction of the Chamber, whether or not in violation of the domestic law of the country where perpetrated.

Article II of Law No. 10 of the Control Council Law defined crimes against humanity as:

Atrocities and Offenses, including but not limited to murder, extermination, enslavement, deportation, imprisonment, torture, rape, or other inhumane acts committed against any civilian population or persecution on political, racial or religious grounds, whether or not in violation of the domestic laws of the country where perpetrated.

* * *

Crimes against Humanity in Article 3 of the Statute of the Tribunal

The Chamber considers that Article 3 of the Statute confers on the Chamber the jurisdiction to prosecute persons for various inhumane acts which constitute crimes against humanity. This category of crimes may be broadly broken down into four essential elements, namely:

(i) the act must be inhumane in nature and character, causing great suffering, or serious injury to body or to mental or physical health;

(ii) the act must be committed as part of a widespread or systematic attack;

(iii) the act must be committed against members of the civilian population;

(iv) the act must be committed on one or more discriminatory grounds, namely, national, political, ethnic, racial or religious grounds. * * *

Rape

Considering the extent to which rape constitute crimes against humanity, pursuant to Article 3(g) of the Statute, the Chamber must define rape, as there is no commonly accepted definition of this term in international law. While rape has been defined in certain national jurisdictions as non-consensual intercourse, variations on the act of rape may include acts which involve the insertion of objects and/or the use of bodily orifices not considered to be intrinsically sexual.

The Chamber considers that rape is a form of aggression and that the central elements of the crime of rape cannot be captured in a mechanical description of objects and body parts. The Convention against Torture and Other Cruel, Inhuman and Degrading Treatment or Punishment does not catalogue specific acts in its definition of torture, focusing rather on the conceptual frame work of state sanctioned violence. This approach is more useful in international law. Like torture, rape is used for such purposes as intimidation, degradation, humiliation, discrimination, punishment, control or destruction of a person. Like torture, rape is a violation of personal dignity, and rape in fact constitutes torture when inflicted by or at the instigation of or with the consent or acquiescence of a public official or other person acting in an official capacity.

The Chamber defines rape as a physical invasion of a sexual nature, committed on a person under circumstances which are coercive. Sexual violence which includes rape, is considered to be any act of a sexual nature which is committed on a person under circumstances which are coercive. This act must be committed:

(a) as part of a widespread or systematic attack;

(b) on a civilian population;

(c) on certain catalogued discriminatory grounds, namely: national, ethnic, political, racial, or religious grounds.

* * *

LEGAL FINDINGS

Count 13 (rape) and Count 14 (other inhumane acts)—Crimes against Humanity

In the light of its factual findings with regard to the allegations of sexual violence set forth in * * * the Indictment, the Tribunal considers the criminal responsibility of the Accused on Count 13, crimes against humanity (rape), punishable by Article 3(g) of the Statute of the Tribunal and Count 14, crimes against humanity (other inhumane acts), punishable by Article 3(i) of the Statute.

In considering the extent to which acts of sexual violence constitute crimes against humanity under Article 3(g) of its Statute, the Tribunal must define rape, as there is no commonly accepted definition of the term in international law. The Tribunal notes that many of the witnesses have used the term "rape" in their testimony. At times, the Prosecution and the Defence have also tried to elicit an explicit description of what happened in physical terms, to document what the witnesses mean by the term "rape". The Tribunal notes that while rape has been historically defined in national jurisdictions as non-consensual sexual intercourse, variations on the form of rape may include acts which involve the insertion of objects and/or the use of bodily orifices not considered to be intrinsically sexual. An act such as that described by Witness KK in her testimony—the Interahamwes thrusting a piece of wood into the sexual organs of a woman as she lay dying—constitutes rape in the Tribunal's view.

The Tribunal considers that rape is a form of aggression and that the central elements of the crime of rape cannot be captured in a mechanical description of objects and body parts. The Tribunal also notes the cultural sensitivities involved in public discussion of intimate matters and recalls the painful reluctance and inability of witnesses to disclose graphic anatomical details of sexual violence they endured. The United Nations Convention Against Torture and Other Cruel, Inhuman and Degrading Treatment or Punishment does not catalogue specific acts in its definition of torture, focusing rather on the conceptual framework of state-sanctioned violence. The Tribunal finds this approach more useful in the context of international law. Like torture, rape is used for such purposes as intimidation, degradation, humiliation, discrimination, punishment, control or destruction of a person. Like torture, rape is a violation of personal dignity, and rape in fact constitutes torture when it is inflicted by or at the instigation of or with the consent or acquiescence of a public official or other person acting in an official capacity.

The Tribunal defines rape as a physical invasion of a sexual nature, committed on a person under circumstances which are coercive. The Tribunal considers sexual violence, which includes rape, as any act of a sexual nature which is committed on a person under circumstances which are coercive. Sexual violence is not limited to physical invasion of the human body and may include acts which do not involve penetration or even physical contact. The incident described by Witness KK in which the Accused ordered the Interahamwe to undress a student and force her to do gymnastics naked in the public courtyard of the bureau communal, in front of a crowd, constitutes sexual violence. The Tribunal notes in this context that coercive circumstances need not be evidenced by a show of physical force. Threats, intimidation, extortion and other forms of duress which prey on fear or desperation may constitute coercion, and coercion may be inherent in certain circumstances, such as armed conflict or the military presence of Interahamwe among refugee Tutsi women at the bureau communal. Sexual violence falls within the scope of "other inhumane acts", set forth Article 3(i) of the Tribunal's Statute, "outrages upon personal dignity," set forth in Article 4(e) of the Statute, and "serious bodily or mental harm," set forth in Article 2(2)(b) of the Statute.

The Tribunal notes that as set forth by the Prosecution, Counts 13–15 are drawn on the basis of acts as described in paragraphs 12(A) and 12(B) of the Indictment. The allegations in these paragraphs of the Indictment are limited to events which took place "on or near the bureau communal premises." Many of the beatings, rapes and murders established by the evidence presented took place away from the bureau communal premises, and therefore the Tribunal does not make any legal findings with respect to these incidents pursuant to Counts 13, 14 and 15.

* * *

The Tribunal has found that the Accused had reason to know and in fact knew that acts of sexual violence were occurring on or near the premises of the bureau communal and that he took no measures to prevent these acts or punish the perpetrators of them. The Tribunal notes that it is only in consideration of Counts 13, 14 and 15 that the Accused is charged with individual criminal responsibility under Section 6(3) of its Statute. As set forth in the Indictment, under Article 6(3) "an individual is criminally responsible as a superior for the acts of a subordinate if he or she knew or had reason to know that the subordinate was about to commit such acts or had done so and the superior failed to take the necessary and reasonable measures to prevent such acts or punish the perpetrators thereof." Although the evidence supports a finding that a superior/subordinate relationship existed between the Accused and the Interahamwe who were at the bureau communal, the Tribunal notes that there is no allegation in the Indictment that the Interahamwe, who are referred to as "armed local militia," were subordinates of the Accused.

This relationship is a fundamental element of the criminal offence set forth in Article 6(3). The amendment of the Indictment with additional charges pursuant to Article 6(3) could arguably be interpreted as implying an allegation of the command responsibility required by Article 6(3). In fairness to the Accused, the Tribunal will not make this inference. Therefore, the Tribunal finds that it cannot consider the criminal responsibility of the Accused under Article 6(3).

The Tribunal finds, under Article 6(1) of its Statute, that the Accused, by his own words, specifically ordered, instigated, aided and abetted the following acts of sexual violence:

(i) the multiple acts of rape of ten girls and women, including Witness JJ, by numerous Interahamwe in the cultural center of the bureau communal;

(ii) the rape of Witness OO by an Interahamwe named Antoine in a field near the bureau communal;

(iii) the forced undressing and public marching of Chantal naked at the bureau communal.

The Tribunal finds, under Article 6(1) of its Statute, that the Accused aided and abetted the following acts of sexual violence, by allowing them to take place on or near the premises of the bureau communal, while he was present on the premises in respect of (i) and in his presence in respect of (ii) and (iii), and by facilitating the commission of these acts through his words of encouragement in other acts of sexual violence, which, by virtue of his authority, sent a clear signal of official tolerance for sexual violence, without which these acts would not have taken place:

(i) the multiple acts of rape of fifteen girls and women, including Witness JJ, by numerous Interahamwe in the cultural center of the bureau communal;

(ii) the rape of a woman by Interahamwe in between two buildings of the bureau communal, witnessed by Witness NN;

(iii) the forced undressing of the wife of Tharcisse after making her sit in the mud outside the bureau communal, as witnessed by Witness KK;

The Tribunal finds, under Article 6(1) of its Statute, that the Accused, having had reason to know that sexual violence was occurring, aided and abetted the following acts of sexual violence, by allowing them to take place on or near the premises of the bureau communal and by facilitating the commission of such sexual violence through his words of encouragement in other acts of sexual violence which, by virtue of his authority, sent a clear signal of official tolerance for sexual violence, without which these acts would not have taken place:

(i) the rape of Witness JJ by an Interahamwe who took her from outside the bureau communal and raped her in a nearby forest;

(ii) the rape of the younger sister of Witness NN by an Interahamwe at the bureau communal;

(iii) the multiple rapes of Alexia, wife of Ntereye, and her two nieces Louise and Nishimwe by Interahamwe near the bureau communal;

(iv) the forced undressing of Alexia, wife of Ntereye, and her two nieces Louise and Nishimwe, and the forcing of the women to perform exercises naked in public near the bureau communal.

The Tribunal has established that a widespread and systematic attack against the civilian ethnic population of Tutsis took place in Taba, and more generally in Rwanda, between April 7 and the end of June, 1994. The Tribunal finds that the rape and other inhumane acts which took place on or near the bureau communal premises of Taba were committed as part of this attack.

COUNT 13

The Accused is judged criminally responsible under Article 3(g) of the Statute for the following incidents of rape:

(i) the rape of Witness JJ by an Interahamwe who took her from outside the bureau communal and raped her in a nearby forest;

(ii) the multiple acts of rape of fifteen girls and women, including Witness JJ, by numerous Interahamwe in the cultural center of the bureau communal;

(iii) the multiple acts of rape of ten girls and women, including Witness JJ, by numerous Interahamwe in the cultural center of the bureau communal;

(iv) the rape of Witness OO by an Interahamwe named Antoine in a field near the bureau communal;

(v) the rape of a woman by Interahamwe in between two buildings of the bureau communal, witnessed by Witness NN;

(vi) the rape of the younger sister of Witness NN by an Interahamwe at the bureau communal;

(vii) the multiple rapes of Alexia, wife of Ntereye, and her two nieces Louise and Nishimwe by Interahamwe near the bureau communal.

COUNT 14

The Accused is judged criminally responsible under Article 3(i) of the Statute for the following other inhumane acts:

(i) the forced undressing of the wife of Tharcisse outside the bureau communal, after making her sit in the mud, as witnessed by Witness KK;

(ii) the forced undressing and public marching of Chantal naked at the bureau communal;

(iii) the forced undressing of Alexia, wife of Ntereye, and her two nieces Louise and Nishimwe, and the forcing of the women to perform exercises naked in public near the bureau communal.

Count 1—Genocide, Count 2—Complicity in Genocide

* * *

In the light of the foregoing, with respect to each of the acts alleged in the Indictment, the Chamber is satisfied beyond reasonable doubt, based on the factual findings it has rendered regarding each of the events described in paragraphs 12 to 23 of the Indictment, of the following:

The Chamber finds that, as pertains to the acts alleged in paragraph 12, it has been established that, throughout the period covered in the Indictment, Akayesu, in his capacity as bourgmestre, was responsible for maintaining law and public order in the commune of Taba and that he had effective authority over the communal police. Moreover, as "leader" of Taba commune, of which he was one of the most prominent figures, the inhabitants respected him and followed his orders. Akayesu himself admitted before the Chamber that he had the power to assemble the population and that they obeyed his instructions. It has also been proven that a very large number of Tutsi were killed in Taba between 7 April and the end of June 1994, while Akayesu was bourgmestre of the Commune. Knowing of such killings, he opposed them and attempted to prevent them only until 18 April 1994, date after which he not only stopped trying to maintain law and order in his commune, but was also present during the acts of violence and killings, and sometimes even gave orders himself for bodily or mental harm to be caused to certain Tutsi, and endorsed and even ordered the killing of several Tutsi.

In the opinion of the Chamber, the said acts indeed incur the individual criminal responsibility of Akayesu for having ordered, committed, or otherwise aided and abetted in the preparation or execution of the killing of and causing serious bodily or mental harm to members of the Tutsi group. Indeed, the Chamber holds that the fact that Akayesu, as a local authority, failed to oppose such killings and serious bodily or mental harm constituted a form of tacit encouragement, which was compounded by being present to such criminal acts.

With regard to the acts alleged in paragraphs 12 (A) and 12 (B) of the Indictment, the Prosecutor has shown beyond a reasonable doubt that between 7 April and the end of June 1994, numerous Tutsi who sought refuge at the Taba Bureau communal were frequently beaten by members of the Interahamwe on or near the premises of the Bureau communal. Some of them were killed. Numerous Tutsi women were forced to endure acts of sexual violence, mutilations and rape, often repeatedly, often publicly and often by more than one assailant. Tutsi women were systematically raped, as one female victim testified to by saying that "each time that you met assailants, they raped you". Numerous incidents of such rape and sexual violence against Tutsi women occurred inside or near the Bureau communal. It has been proven that some communal policemen armed with guns and the accused himself were present while some of these rapes and sexual violence were being committed. Furthermore, it is proven that on several occasions, by his presence, his attitude and his utterances, Akayesu encouraged such acts, one particular witness testifying that Akayesu, addressed the Interahamwe who were committing the rapes and said that "never ask me again what a Tutsi woman tastes like". In the opinion of the Chamber, this constitutes tacit encouragement to the rapes that were being committed.

In the opinion of the Chamber, the above-mentioned acts with which Akayesu is charged indeed render him individually criminally responsible for having abetted in the preparation or execution of the killings of members of the Tutsi group and the infliction of serious bodily and mental harm on members of said group. * * *

VERDICT

For the foregoing reasons, having considered all of the evidence and the arguments, the Chamber unanimously finds as follows:

Count 1: Guilty of Genocide

* * *

Count 13: Guilty of Crime against Humanity (Rape)

Count 14: Guilty of Crime against Humanity (Other Inhumane Acts)

NOTES AND QUESTIONS ON INTERNATIONAL HUMANITARIAN LAW

1. *The law of war in principle.* At its core, the law of war limits the way hostilities may be conducted: prisoners of war and civilians must not be abused; undefended places may not be attacked; some weapons are too inhumane to be tolerated. This is an ancient set of ideas, traceable to Lao Tzu, Thucydides, and Manu, among others. It builds on certain medieval notions of chivalry, and Shakespeare certainly wrote *Henry V*

with these standards and their ambiguities in mind. Is this just another triumph of hope over experience, or is it in fact deeply pragmatic—outwardly altruistic but with self-protection at its core?

2.   *Domestic enforcement.* In some respects, the domestic courts of the various nations offer an important means of articulating, implementing, and enforcing the law of armed conflict. In *Ex parte Quirin*, 317 U.S. 1, 27–28 (1942), the United States Supreme Court declared: "[f]rom the very beginning of its history this Court has recognized and applied the law of war as including that part of the law of nations which prescribes * * * the status, rights and duties of enemy nations as well as enemy individuals." *The Paquete Habana*, *supra*, established that those norms could bind the executive branch of the U.S. government as well. In the century since *Paquete Habana* and the half-century since *Quirin*, the modes for enforcing IHL norms have proliferated to include civil and administrative cases—and not just criminal prosecutions—in domestic courts. These domestic proceedings stand halfway between two more visible modes of enforcement, namely *internalization* (*i.e.*, the incorporation of norms into the training and the disciplinary regime of the military forces, as well as the rules of engagement they develop) and *internationalization* (*i.e.*, the operation of international institutions, NGOs, and tribunals for the investigation and prosecution of violations). Of course, "domestic courts" are not a single institution, and they necessarily introduce an element of decentralization and redundancy. But one mark of a successful system might be consistent and depoliticized proceedings—criminal, civil, and administrative—in a variety of transnational settings, including domestic courts around the world and in the United States. In a system as imperfect as the current regime, a measure of redundancy may be the price of maximizing accountability: if one mechanism fails, another may work. But what are the possible disadvantages of so decentralized a process?

3.   *Coming to grips with the Nuremberg experience.* Even people who have never read the London Charter or the Nuremberg judgment usually have opinions about them: people describe and assess them in various ways, but—like a Rorschach inkblot test—they may say more about the observer than they say about Nuremberg. Observers may see what they are predisposed to see, because there is a certain tension between the reality of Nuremberg and the illusion of Nuremberg. From one perspective, Nuremberg defined certain substantive principles lying at the core of contemporary international law; indeed, in 1950, the United Nations adopted a statement of "Principles of International Law Recognized in the Charter of the Tribunal and in the Judgment of the Tribunal:"

> *Principle I*: Any person who commits an act which constitutes a crime under international law is responsible therefor and liable to punishment.

Principle II: The fact that internal law does not impose a penalty for an act which constitutes a crime under international law does not relieve the person who committed the act from responsibility under international law.

Principle III: The fact that a person who committed an act which constitutes a crime under international law acted as Head of State or responsible Government official does not relieve him from responsibility under international law.

Principle IV: The fact that a person acted pursuant to order of his Government or of a superior does not relieve him from responsibility under international law, provided a moral choice was in fact possible to him.

Principle V: Any person charged with a crime under international law has the right to a fair trial on the facts and law.

Principle VI: The crimes hereinafter set out are punishable as crimes under international law:

> (a) Crimes against peace: (i) Planning, preparation, initiation or waging of a war of aggression or a war in violation of international treaties, agreements or assurances; (ii) Participation in a common plan or conspiracy for the accomplishment of any of the acts mentioned under (i).

> (b) War crimes: Violations of the laws or customs of war include, but are not limited to, murder, ill-treatment or deportation to slave-labour or for any other purpose of civilian population of or in occupied territory; murder or ill-treatment of prisoners of war, of persons on the seas, killing of hostages, plunder of public or private property, wanton destruction of cities, towns, or villages, or devastation not justified by military necessity.

> (c) Crimes against humanity: Murder, extermination, enslavement, deportation and other inhuman acts done against any civilian population, or persecutions on political, racial or religious grounds, when such acts are done or such persecutions are carried on in execution of or in connection with any crime against peace or any war crime.

Principle VII: Complicity in the commission of a crime against peace, a war crime, or a crime against humanity as set forth in Principle VI is a crime under international law.

On the other hand, critics of the Nuremberg experience suggest that it was merely "vengeance in the form of law;" that it prosecuted conduct that was not criminalized at the time it was committed; and that the victors' violations of the law of war in their own conflicts after World War II undermine the inference of law from the London Charter. To what extent do the ICC Statute and the emerging jurisprudence from the *ad hoc* tribunals answer the skeptics?

4. *Nuclear weapons*. As noted above, customary international law, codified in the Geneva Conventions, prohibits weapons that are incapable of distinguishing between combatants and non-combatants and weapons that are of a nature to cause superfluous injury or unnecessary suffering. Are nuclear weapons illegal under this standard? See the Advisory Opinion of the International Court of Justice in the *Case Concerning the Legality of the Threat or Use of Nuclear Weapons* (8 July 1996), in which the ICJ ruled:

A. **Unanimously**: There is in neither customary nor conventional international law any specific authorization of the threat or use of nuclear weapons;

B. **By eleven votes to three**: There is in neither customary nor conventional international law any comprehensive and universal prohibition of the threat or use of nuclear weapons as such; * * *

C. **Unanimously**: A threat or use of force by means of nuclear weapons that is contrary to Article 2, paragraph 4, of the United Nations Charter and that fails to meet all the requirements of Article 51 is unlawful;

D. **Unanimously**: A threat or use of nuclear weapons should also be compatible with the requirements of the international law applicable in armed conflict, particularly those of the principles and rules of international humanitarian law, as well as with specific obligations under treaties and other undertakings which expressly deal with nuclear weapons;

E. **By seven votes to seven**, **by the Presidents casting vote**: It follows from the above-mentioned requirements that the threat or use of nuclear weapons would generally be contrary to the rules of international law applicable in armed conflict, and in particular the principles and rules of humanitarian law; however, in view of the current state of international law, and of the elements of fact at its disposal, the Court cannot conclude definitively whether the threat or use of nuclear weapons would be lawful or unlawful in an extreme circumstance of self-defence, in which the very survival of a State would be at stake; * * *

F. **Unanimously**: There exists an obligation to pursue in good faith and bring to a conclusion negotiations leading to nuclear disarmament in all aspects under strict and effective international control.

Various parts of the Advisory Opinion have been criticized from almost every quarter, including states with nuclear weapons as well as the governmental and non-governmental opponents of nuclear weapons. Why is there so little clarity on this issue when biological and chemical weapons are regulated (and in some cases prohibited) by the laws of war? Why have nuclear weapons been largely exempt from legal scrutiny?

5. *The evolution of modern IHL treaties: Case #1: trade in small arms and light weapons.* One important linkage between human rights law and the law of armed conflict is the problem of small arms and light weapons ("SALW"). Human rights observers have concluded, in the words of one NGO, that SALW are the "weapons of choice for forces that have consistently abused human rights and violated international humanitarian law in conflicts around the world." Human Rights Watch, *Small Arms Campaign–Obstacles to Progress* (2001). Regional security concerns reinforce these human rights concerns: regional conflicts may be fueled by the availability and lethality of SALW. A variety of international agreements have been concluded that restrict a State-party's power to transfer (or authorize the transfer) of SALW, ranging from the St. Petersburg Declaration Renouncing the Use, in Time of War, of Explosive Projectiles Under 400 Grammes Weight (1869), to the Convention on the Prohibition of Use, Stockpiling, Production and Transfer of Anti–Personnel Mines and on their Destruction ("Ottawa Treaty") (1997).

In 1998, the European Union adopted a Code of Conduct which covers exports of military equipment and dual-use goods. *The European Union Code of Conduct for Arms Exports*, SIPRI YEARBOOK 503 (1999). The Code sets minimum standards for Member States to apply when considering the export of small arms and allows Member States to authorize such exports only when certain criteria are satisfied, including "respect for human rights in the country of final destination" and "the preservation of regional peace, security and stability." The Code also imposes annual reporting obligations on the states; these reports are made available to the public in the interest of transparency. *See Annual Report in Conformity with Operative Provision 8 of the European Code of Conduct on Arms Exports, Journal of the European Union,* 1999/C315/01, (3 November 1999). Although the Code is only a non-binding statement of intent, it is an important intermediate step between national and international efforts to control small arms transfers. It also conveniently codifies much of the emerging international consensus with respect to the small arms trade, previously scattered throughout different treaties and statements of customary international law. The United States has endorsed the principles of the EU Code of Conduct. *US-EU Joint Statement of Common Principles of Small Arms and Light Weapons* (17 December 1999). *See generally* EMANUELA GILLARD, WHAT IS LEGAL? WHAT IS ILLEGAL? LIMITATIONS ON TRANSFERS OF SMALL ARMS UNDER INTERNATIONAL LAW, (2001).

One next possible step is the conclusion of a comprehensive international agreement, proposed by a group of human rights, development, and arms control NGOs, in partnership with nineteen Nobel Peace Prize laureates. The Draft Framework Convention on International Arms Transfers ("ATT") would require that its signatories implement national legislation requiring all international arms transfers to be authorized via government licenses. The ATT also sets out express limitations on the transfer of SALW, based on the UN Charter, international treaties, the Geneva Conventions, and customary international law. Article 3 of the ATT requires that an arms transfer not be authorized when the authorizing state has "knowledge or ought reasonably to have knowledge" that the transfer will result in a breach of the UN Charter, serious violations of human rights, or genocide or other crimes against humanity. Signatories must also take into account whether the arms transfer will have an adverse political or developmental effect on the recipient country, and whether the shipment is likely to be diverted and used in an illicit manner. The ATT would also create an international Registry of International Arms Transfers to which each contracting party would be required to submit an annual report on the international arms transfers through its territory or subject to its jurisdiction.

6. *The evolution of modern IHL treaties: Case #2: landmines.* The growing number of anti-personnel landmines placed throughout Southeast Asia during and after the Vietnam war, the increasing use of such devices by paramilitaries and terrorists, and the catastrophic effects of mines on civilians led to the development of a Protocol on Prohibitions or Restrictions on the Use of Mines, Booby Traps and Other Devices ("Protocol II") to the Convention on Prohibitions or Restrictions on the Use of Certain Conventional Weapons Which May be Deemed to be Excessively Injurious or to Have Indiscriminate Effects ("CCW") (1980). Protocol II, which came into effect in 1983, attempted to protect civilians by restricting the placement of landmines to locations constituting military objectives and by prohibiting the use of landmines as a method of attacking civilians, but exceptions effectively swallowed the rule: landmines could be laid near civilian populations provided the mines were placed near a "likely" military objective, and "adequate measures" were taken to protect civilian lives, including "the posting of warning signs * * * or the provision of fences." Worse, Protocol II placed responsibility for removing mines on the country where the mines were placed, rather than on the state that laid them in the first place. *See* Karl Josef Partsch, *"Remnants of War as a Legal Problem in the Light of the Libyan Case,"* 78 AM. J. INT'L L. 386, 391 (1984).

The CCW and Protocol II were significantly amended in 1996 at the United Nations' Review Conference, extending it to internal and international conflicts and creating a more meaningful system of verification and compliance, but the revision did not provide for the total ban of landmines that many nations sought. *See* Michael J. Matheson, *Current Development: The Revision of the Mines Protocol*, 91 AM. J. INT'L L. 158, 159 (1997). According to the President of the United States, "the amended Mines Protocol was not as strong as we would have preferred. In particular, its provision on verification and compliance are not as rigorous as we had proposed, and the transition periods allowed for conversion or elimination of certain non-compliant mines are longer than we thought necessary." Letter of Transmittal to Congress regarding the Revised Protocols to the CCW of January 7th, 1997, S. TREATY DOC. NO. 105–1, III–IV (1997). The Revised Protocol II came into force in December 1998, the United States ratified the revisions with reservations in May 1999.

Dissatisfied with the incremental approach of Revised Protocol II, some governments, fueled by public sentiment and the powerful advocacy of NGOs, sought a ban on landmines altogether. The resulting International Campaign for a Landmine Ban ("ICLB") developed an alternative fast-track forum devoted to establishing a norm against the use of landmines. That alternative, known as the Ottawa Process, represented a new approach to treaty-making and involved conducting regional meetings prior to treaty negotiations in order to pressure states in the drafting process. The result was the Ottawa Conference, attended by 122 states, all supporting the ban and all intending to sign a treaty developed over the course of only a year banning anti-personnel mines. The Convention on the Prohibition of the Use, Stockpiling, Production, and Transfer of Anti–Personnel Mines and on their Destruction, 36 I.L.M. 1507 ("Ottawa Convention") was opened for signature on September 8, 1997, and came into effect on March 1, 1999. As of June 2008, over 156 countries had become parties to the Ottawa Convention. Along with China and Russia, the United States has made it clear that it will refuse to sign the treaty, given, among other reasons, that it could not secure a reservation permitting landmine use along the South Korean border. Legal issues remain with respect to enforceability and accountability, but the "bottom-up" development of the Ottawa Convention is testimony to the power of NGOs.

7.   *The evolution of modern IHL treaties: Case #3: cluster bombs.* In May 2008, over 100 countries approved the Cluster Munitions Convention, which immediately bans the use, production, stockpiling and transfer of all cluster munitions. Cluster bombs scatter a large number of smaller bombs (or submunitions) across a wide area. If they do not detonate upon impact, they effectively become landmines that may detonate years after the battle. Human Rights Watch, *Cluster Bomb Treaty Breaks New Ground* (30 May 2008), *available at* http://hrw.org/english/docs/2008/05/30/18976.htm. The need for international regulation was clarified by the documented harm of the weapons and their inability to distinguish civilian from military targets. The campaign to ban cluster munitions was galvanized by the increase in civilian deaths caused by the weapons in recent wars. Human Rights Watch for example estimates that the United States and United Kingdom used over twelve thousand cluster bombs in Iraq in 2003 alone, yielding roughly two million smaller bombs. Human Rights Watch, *Off Target: The Conduct of the War and Civilian Casualties in Iraq* (2003), *available at* http://www.hrw.org/reports/2003/usa1203/index.htm. In 2006, Israel is alleged to have launched about four million submunitions into southern Lebanon during its war with Hezbollah. UN Mine Action Coordination Center, Southern Lebanon [UNMACC SL], *South Lebanon Cluster Bomb Info Sheet, 1–2, available at* www.maccsl.org/reports/Leb% 20UXO% 20Fact% 20Sheet% 204% 20

November,% 202006.pdf. *See generally* Bonnie Docherty, *The Time Is Now: A Historical Argument for a Cluster Munitions Convention*, 20 HARV. HUM. RTS. J. 53 (2007).

8. *Command responsibility*. Customary international law establishes that "[c]ommanders and other superiors are criminally responsible for war crimes committed by their subordinates if they knew, or had reason to know, that the subordinates were about to commit or were committing such crimes and did not take all necessary and reasonable measures in their power to prevent their commission, or if such crimes had been committed, to punish the persons responsible." JEAN-MARIE HENCKAERTS AND LOUISE DOSWALD-BECK, I CUSTOMARY INTERNATIONAL HUMANITARIAN LAW: RULES (2005). *See also* U.S. Army Field Manual 27–10, Section 501; *In re Yamashita*, 327 U.S. 1, 16 (1946); *Prosecutor v. Delalic et al. (Celebici Case)*, Case No. IT–96–21–T, ICTY (November 16, 1998). These international and domestic authorities impose command responsibility only if certain criteria are satisfied:

1. There must be a superior-subordinate relationship between the defendant and the actors who committed the wrong;

2. The superior must have known or had reason to know that the subordinate was about to commit a crime or had committed a crime;

3. The superior failed to take necessary and reasonable measures to prevent the crime or to punish the perpetrator.

How, if at all, might you improve these criteria? In what respects would the interests of human rights lawyers align with the interests of the military in a clear command structure?

9. *The context-specific definition of "torture" and the requirement of state action*. Acts of torture are illegal under a variety of human rights instruments, but the definition of "torture" varies with context. For example, under the UN Convention against Torture, "torture means"

> any act by which severe pain or suffering, whether physical or mental, is intentionally inflicted on a person for such purposes as obtaining from him or a third person information or a confession, punishing him for an act he or a third person has committed or is suspected of having committed, or intimidating or coercing him or a third person, or for any reason based on discrimination of any kind, *when such pain or suffering is inflicted by or at the instigation of or with the consent or acquiescence of a public official or other person acting in an official capacity*. (emphasis added)

Compare this language with the instruments excerpted above, including Common Article 3 and the Rome Statute. Is state action an element of the offense of torture under these instruments? In what circumstances could torture by someone who is *not* a state actor be a war crime, or genocide, or a crime against humanity? *See* the Judgment of the Trial Chamber of the International Criminal Tribunal for the Former Yugoslavia in *Prosecutor v. Kunarac (Foca)*, IT–96–23, ICTY (22 February 2001), at ¶ 496:

> The Trial Chamber concludes that the definition of torture under international humanitarian law does not comprise the same elements as the definition of torture generally applied under human rights law. In particular, the Trial Chamber is of the view that the presence of a state official or of any other authority-wielding person in the torture process is not necessary for the offence to be regarded as torture under international humanitarian law.

10. *The NATO bombing of Serbia.* In the previous Module, you encountered the argument that NATO's armed intervention in Serbia and Kosovo in 1999 established a new *jus ad bellum* norm of humanitarian intervention. In the course of the bombing campaign, NATO was criticized for some specific violations of *jus in bello*:

> NATO believed that a relatively short bombing campaign would persuade Milosevic to sign the Rambouillet agreement. That was a major mistake. NATO also underestimated the obvious risk that the Serbian government would attack the Kosovo Albanians. NATO had to expand the air campaign to strategic targets in Serbia proper, which increased the risk of civilian casualties. In spite of the fact that NATO made substantial effort to avoid civilian casualties there were some serious mistakes. Some 500 civilian deaths are documented. The Commission is also critical of the use of cluster bombs, the environmental damage caused by the use of depleted-uranium tipped armor-piercing shells and missiles and by toxic leaks caused by the bombing of industrial and petroleum complexes in several cities, and the attack on Serbian television on April 17, 1999. The Commission accepts the view of the Final Report of the ICTY that there is no basis in the available evidence for charging specific individuals with criminal violations of the Laws of the War during the NATO campaign. Nevertheless some practices do seem vulnerable to the allegation that violations might have occurred and depend, for final assessment, on the availability of further evidence.

INDEPENDENT INTERNATIONAL COMMISSION ON KOSOVO, *THE KOSOVO REPORT* (23 OCTOBER 2000). What is the legal significance, if any, of this conclusion?

11. *Jihad and the law of war.* The Islamic concept of *jihad*, traditionally translated as "holy war," brings with it certain limitations on the conduct of hostilities:

> The term *jihad* conventionally translated "holy war", has the literal meaning of striving. * * * Some Muslim theologians, particularly in more modern times, have interpreted the duty of "striving in the path of God" in a spiritual and moral sense. The overwhelming majority of early authorities, however, citing relevant passages in the Quran and in the tradition, discuss *jihad* in military terms. Virtually every manual of *sharia* law has a chapter on *jihad*, which regulates in minute detail such matters as the opening, conduct,

interruption and cessation of hostilities, and the allocation and division of booty. Fighters in the holy war are enjoined not to kill women and children unless they attack first, not to torture or mutilate prisoners, to give fair warning of a resumption of hostilities, and to honor agreements. The Holy Laws required good treatment of non-combatants, but also accorded the victors extensive rights over the property and also the persons and families of the vanquished.

BERNARD LEWIS, THE MIDDLE EAST 233 (1995).

12.   *Environmental warfare.* Under the Convention on the Prohibition of Military or Any Other Hostile Use of Environmental Modification Techniques, which entered into force in 1978 and which the United States ratified in 1979, "[e]ach State Party . . . undertakes not to engage in military or any other hostile use of environmental modification techniques having widespread, long-lasting or severe effects as the means of destruction, damage or injury to any other State Party." The banned practices include "any technique for changing—through the deliberate manipulation of natural processes—the dynamics, composition or structure of the Earth, including its biota, lithosphere, hydrosphere and atmosphere, or of outer space." In which of the following scenarios, if any, has the Convention—assuming that it applied—been violated? Are these violations of international human rights law?

A.   As Iraq withdrew from Kuwait during the first Persian Gulf War in 1991, it set several oil fields on fire, causing severe and widespread air pollution for several years.

B.   During World War II, the Japanese invasion of Dutch-held Java was resisted by releasing and igniting crude oil in the water at the invasion site.

C.   When Allied forces began their ground attack against Iraq in 1991, the Iraqis pumped crude oil into the Persian Gulf in an attempt to clog desalinization plants.

13.   *U.S. statutory law.* In 1996, Congress adopted the War Crimes Act, 18 U.S.C. § 2441, which provides:

(a) Offense.—Whoever, whether inside or outside the United States, commits a war crime, in any of the circumstances described in subsection (b), shall be fined under this title or imprisoned for life or any term of years, or both, and if death results to the victim, shall also be subject to the penalty of death.

(b) Circumstances.—The circumstances referred to in subsection (a) are that the person committing such war crime or the victim of such war crime is a member of the Armed Forces of the United States or a national of the United States (as defined in section 101 of the Immigration and Nationality Act).

(c) Definition.—As used in this section the term 'war crime' means any conduct—

(1) defined as a grave breach in any of the international conventions signed at Geneva 12 August 1949, or any protocol to such convention to which the United States is a party;

(2) prohibited by Article 23, 25, 27, or 28 of the Annex to the Hague Convention IV, Respecting the Laws and Customs of War on Land, signed 18 October 1907;[1]

(3) which constitutes a violation of common Article 3 of the international conventions signed at Geneva, 12 August 1949, or any protocol to such convention to which the United States is a party and which deals with non-international armed conflict; or

(4) of a person who, in relation to an armed conflict and contrary to the provisions of the Protocol on Prohibitions or Restrictions on the Use of Mines, Booby–Traps and Other Devices as amended at Geneva on 3 May 1996 (Protocol II as amended on 3 May 1996), when the United States is a party to such Protocol, willfully kills or causes serious injury to civilians.

Is the War Crimes Act consistent with international law? Does it alter your sense of whether the Rome Statute's definition of war crimes is declaratory of customary international law or not?

CASE STUDY

THE USE OF MILITARY COMMISSIONS IN THE WAR ON TERRORISM

Does the war on terrorism render the Geneva Conventions obsolete? To what extent is the contemporary terrorist threat different in

---

1. These provisions are as follows:

Article 23. In addition to the prohibitions provided by special Conventions, it is especially forbidden—To employ poison or poisoned weapons; To kill or wound treacherously individuals belonging to the hostile nation or army; To kill or wound an enemy who, having laid down his arms, or having no longer means of defence, has surrendered at discretion; To declare that no quarter will be given; To employ arms, projectiles, or material calculated to cause unnecessary suffering; To make improper use of a flag of truce, of the national flag or of the military insignia and uniform of the enemy, as well as the distinctive badges of the Geneva Convention; To destroy or seize the enemy's property, unless such destruction or seizure be imperatively demanded by the necessities of war; To declare abolished, suspended, or inadmissible in a court of law the rights and actions of the nationals of the hostile party. A belligerent is likewise forbidden to compel the nationals of the hostile party to take part in the operations of war directed against their own country, even if they were in the belligerent's service before the commencement of the war.

Article 25. The attack or bombardment, by whatever means, of towns, villages, dwellings, or buildings which are undefended is prohibited.

Article 27. In sieges and bombardments all necessary steps must be taken to spare, as far as possible, buildings dedicated to religion, art, science, or charitable purposes, historic monuments, hospitals, and places where the sick and wounded are collected, provided they are not being used at the time for military purposes. It is the duty of the besieged to indicate the presence of such buildings or places by distinctive and visible signs, which shall be notified to the enemy beforehand.

Article 28. The pillage of a town or place, even when taken by assault, is prohibited.

degree and kind from prior threats to national security? Is it legal to use military commissions—an established mechanism for trying violations of the laws of war—to try suspected terrorists who are in detention and no longer in the field of battle? Does it matter what crimes are prosecuted before the commissions?

DETENTION, TREATMENT, AND TRIAL OF CERTAIN NON–CITIZENS IN THE WAR AGAINST TERRORISM

66 Fed. Reg. 57833 (Nov. 13, 2001)

By the authority vested in me as President and as Commander in Chief of the Armed Forces of the United States by the Constitution and the laws of the United States of America, including the Authorization for Use of Military Force Joint Resolution (Public Law 107–40, 115 Stat. 224) and sections 821 and 836 of title 10, United States Code, it is hereby ordered as follows:

Section 1. Findings.

(a) International terrorists, including members of al Qaida, have carried out attacks on United States diplomatic and military personnel and facilities abroad and on citizens and property within the United States on a scale that has created a state of armed conflict that requires the use of the United States Armed Forces.

(b) In light of grave acts of terrorism and threats of terrorism, including the terrorist attacks on September 11, 2001, on the headquarters of the United States Department of Defense in the national capital region, on the World Trade Center in New York, and on civilian aircraft such as in Pennsylvania, I proclaimed a national emergency on September 14, 2001 (Proc. 7463, Declaration of National Emergency by Reason of Certain Terrorist Attacks).

(c) Individuals acting alone and in concert involved in international terrorism possess both the capability and the intention to undertake further terrorist attacks against the United States that, if not detected and prevented, will cause mass deaths, mass injuries, and massive destruction of property, and may place at risk the continuity of the operations of the United States Government.

(d) The ability of the United States to protect the United States and its citizens, and to help its allies and other cooperating nations protect their nations and their citizens, from such further terrorist attacks depends in significant part upon using the United States Armed Forces to identify terrorists and those who support them, to disrupt their activities, and to eliminate their ability to conduct or support such attacks.

(e) To protect the United States and its citizens, and for the effective conduct of military operations and prevention of terrorist attacks, it is necessary for individuals subject to this order pursuant to section 2 hereof to be detained, and, when tried, to be tried for violations of the laws of war and other applicable laws by military tribunals.

(f) Given the danger to the safety of the United States and the nature of international terrorism, and to the extent provided by and under this order, I find consistent with section 836 of title 10, United States Code, that it is not practicable to apply in military commissions under this order the principles of law and the rules of evidence generally recognized in the trial of criminal cases in the United States district courts.

(g) Having fully considered the magnitude of the potential deaths, injuries, and property destruction that would result from potential acts of terrorism against the United States, and the probability that such acts will occur, I have determined that an extraordinary emergency exists for national defense purposes, that this emergency constitutes an urgent and compelling government interest, and that issuance of this order is necessary to meet the emergency.

Sec. 2. Definition and Policy.

(a) The term "individual subject to this order" shall mean any individual who is not a United States citizen with respect to whom I determine from time to time in writing that:

(1) there is reason to believe that such individual, at the relevant times,

(i) is or was a member of the organization known as al Qaida;

(ii) has engaged in, aided or abetted, or conspired to commit, acts of international terrorism, or acts in preparation therefor, that have caused, threaten to cause, or have as their aim to cause, injury to or adverse effects on the United States, its citizens, national security, foreign policy, or economy; or

(iii) has knowingly harbored one or more individuals described in subparagraphs (i) or (ii) of subsection 2(a)(1) of this order; and

(2) it is in the interest of the United States that such individual be subject to this order.

(b) It is the policy of the United States that the Secretary of Defense shall take all necessary measures to ensure that any individual subject to this order is detained in accordance with section 3, and, if the individual is to be tried, that such individual is tried only in accordance with section 4.

* * *

Sec. 3. Detention Authority of the Secretary of Defense. Any individual subject to this order shall be

(a) detained at an appropriate location designated by the Secretary of Defense outside or within the United States;

(b) treated humanely, without any adverse distinction based on race, color, religion, gender, birth, wealth, or any similar criteria;

(c) afforded adequate food, drinking water, shelter, clothing, and medical treatment;

(d) allowed the free exercise of religion consistent with the requirements of such detention; and

(e) detained in accordance with such other conditions as the Secretary of Defense may prescribe.

Sec. 4. Authority of the Secretary of Defense Regarding Trials of Individuals Subject to this Order.

(a) Any individual subject to this order shall, when tried, be tried by military commission for any and all offenses triable by military commission that such individual is alleged to have committed, and may be punished in accordance with the penalties provided under applicable law, including life imprisonment or death.

(b) As a military function and in light of the findings in section 1, including subsection (f) thereof, the Secretary of Defense shall issue such orders and regulations, including orders for the appointment of one or more military commissions, as may be necessary to carry out subsection (a) of this section.

(c) Orders and regulations issued under subsection (b) of this section shall include, but not be limited to, rules for the conduct of the proceedings of military commissions, including pretrial, trial, and post-trial procedures, modes of proof, issuance of process, and qualifications of attorneys, which shall at a minimum provide for—

(1) military commissions to sit at any time and any place, consistent with such guidance regarding time and place as the Secretary of Defense may provide;

(2) a full and fair trial, with the military commission sitting as the triers of both fact and law;

(3) admission of such evidence as would, in the opinion of the presiding officer of the military commission (or instead, if any other member of the commission so requests at the time the presiding officer renders that opinion, the opinion of the commission rendered at that time by a majority of the commission), have probative value to a reasonable person;

(4) in a manner consistent with the protection of information classified or classifiable under Executive Order 12958 of April 17, 1995, as amended, or any successor Executive Order, protected by statute or rule from unauthorized disclosure, or otherwise protected by law, (A) the handling of, admission into evidence of, and access

to materials and information, and (B) the conduct, closure of, and access to proceedings;

(5) conduct of the prosecution by one or more attorneys designated by the Secretary of Defense and conduct of the defense by attorneys for the individual subject to this order;

(6) conviction only upon the concurrence of two-thirds of the members of the commission present at the time of the vote, a majority being present;

(7) sentencing only upon the concurrence of two-thirds of the members of the commission present at the time of the vote, a majority being present; and

(8) submission of the record of the trial, including any conviction or sentence, for review and final decision by me or by the Secretary of Defense if so designated by me for that purpose.

* * *

Sec. 7. Relationship to Other Law and Forums.

* * *

(b) With respect to any individual subject to this order—

(1) military tribunals shall have exclusive jurisdiction with respect to offenses by the individual; and

(2) the individual shall not be privileged to seek any remedy or maintain any proceeding, directly or indirectly, or to have any such remedy or proceeding sought on the individual's behalf, in (i) any court of the United States, or any State thereof, (ii) any court of any foreign nation, or (iii) any international tribunal.

(c) This order is not intended to and does not create any right, benefit, or privilege, substantive or procedural, enforceable at law or equity by any party, against the United States, its departments, agencies, or other entities, its officers or employees, or any other person.

* * *

(e) I reserve the authority to direct the Secretary of Defense, at any time hereafter, to transfer to a governmental authority control of any individual subject to this order. Nothing in this order shall be construed to limit the authority of any such governmental authority to prosecute any individual for whom control is transferred.

* * *

MEMORANDUM FROM ALBERTO R. GONZALES
TO THE PRESIDENT OF THE UNITED STATES
RE: APPLICATION OF THE GENEVA CONVENTIONS
TO THE CONFLICT WITH AL QAEDA
AND THE TALIBAN

January 25, 2002 [Draft]

Purpose

On January 18, I advised you that the Department of Justice had issued a formal legal opinion concluding that the Geneva Convention III on the Treatment of Prisoners of War (GPW) does not apply to the conflict with al Qaeda. I also advised you that DOJ's opinion concludes that there are reasonable grounds for you to conclude that GPW does not apply with respect to the conflict with the Taliban. I understand that you decided that GPW does not apply and, accordingly, that al Qaeda and Taliban detainees are not prisoners of war under the GPW.

The Secretary of State has requested that you reconsider that decision. Specifically, he has asked that you conclude that GPW does apply to both al Qaeda and the Taliban. I understand, however, that he would agree that al Qaeda and Taliban fighters could be determined not to be prisoners of war (POWs) but only on a case-by-case basis following individual hearings before a military board.

This memorandum outlines the ramifications of your decision and the Secretary's request for reconsideration.

Legal Background

As an initial matter, I note that you have the constitutional authority to make the determination you made on January 18 that the GPW does not apply to al Qaeda and the Taliban. (Of course, you could nevertheless, as a matter of policy, decide to apply the principles of GPW to the conflict with al Qaeda and the Taliban.) The Office of Legal Counsel of the Department of Justice has opined that, as a matter of international and domestic law, GPW does not apply to the conflict with al Qaeda. OLC has further opined that you have the authority to determine that GPW does not apply to the Taliban. As I discussed with you, the grounds for such a determination may include:

> — A determination that Afghanistan was a failed state because the Taliban did not exercise full control over the territory and people, was not recognized by the international community, and was not capable of fulfilling its international obligations (*e.g.*, was in widespread material breach of its international obligations).

> — A determination that the Taliban and its forces were, in fact, not a government, but a militant, terrorist-like group.

OLC's interpretation of this legal issue is definitive. The Attorney General is charged by statute with interpreting the law for the Executive

Branch. This interpretive authority extends to both domestic and international law. He has, in turn, delegated this role to OLC. Nevertheless, you should be aware that the Legal Adviser to the Secretary of State has expressed a different view.

Ramifications of Determination that GPW Does Not Apply

The consequences of a decision to adhere to what I understood to be your earlier determination that the CPW does not apply to the Taliban include the following:

Positive:

— Preserves flexibility.

> • As you have said, the war against terrorism is a new kind of war. It is not the traditional clash between nations adhering to the laws of war that formed the backdrop for GPW. The nature of the new war places a high premium on other factors, such as the ability to quickly obtain information from captured terrorists and their sponsors in order to avoid further atrocities against American civilians, and the need to try terrorists for war crimes such as wantonly killing civilians. In my judgment, this new paradigm renders obsolete Geneva's strict limitations on questioning of enemy prisoners and renders quaint some of its provisions requiring that captured enemy be afforded such things as commissary privileges, scrip (*i.e.*, advances of monthly pay), athletic uniforms, and scientific instruments.

> • Although some of these provisions do not apply to detainees who are not POWs, a determination that GPW does not apply to al Qaeda and the Taliban eliminates any argument regarding the need for case-by-case determinations of POW status. It also holds open options for the future conflicts in which it may be more difficult to determine whether an enemy force as a whole meets the standard for POW status.

> • By concluding that GPW does not apply to al Qaeda and the Taliban, we avoid foreclosing options for the future, particularly against non-state actors.

— Substantially reduces the threat of domestic criminal prosecution under the War Crimes Act (18 U.S.C. 2441).

> • That statute, enacted in 1996, prohibits the commission of a "war crime" by or against a U.S. person, including U.S. officials. "War crime" for these purposes is defined to include any grave breach of GPW or any violation of common Article 3 thereof (such as "outrages against personal dignity"). Some of these provisions apply (if the GPW applies) regardless of whether the individual being detained qualifies as a POW. Punishments for violations of Section 2441 include the death penalty. A determination that the GPW is not applicable to the

Taliban would mean that Section 2441 would not apply to actions taken with respect to the Taliban.

● Adhering to your determination that GPW does not apply would guard effectively against misconstruction or misapplication of Section 2441 for several reasons.

> ● First, some of the language of the GPW is undefined (it prohibits, for example, "outrages upon personal dignity" and "inhuman treatment"), and it is difficult to predict with confidence what actions might be deemed to constitute violations of the relevant provisions of GPW.

> ● Second, it is difficult to predict the needs and circumstances that could arise in the course of the war on terrorism.

> ● Third, it is difficult to predict the motives of prosecutors and independent counsels who may in the future decide to pursue unwarranted charges based on Section 2441. Your determination would create a reasonable basis in law that Section 2441 does not apply, which would provide a solid defense to any future prosecution.

Negative:

— On the other hand, the following arguments would support reconsideration and reversal of your decision that the GPW does not apply to either al Qaeda or the Taliban:

— Since the Geneva Conventions were concluded in 1949, the United States has never denied their applicability to either U.S. or opposing forces engaged in armed conflict, despite several opportunities to do so. During the last Bush Administration, the United States stated that it "has a policy of applying the Geneva Conventions of 1949 whenever armed hostilities occur with regular foreign armed forces, even if arguments could be made that the threshold standards for the applicability of the Conventions...are not met."

— The United States could not invoke the GPW if enemy forces threatened to mistreat or mistreated U.S. or coalition forces captured during operations in Afghanistan, or if they denied Red Cross access or other POW privileges.

— The War Crimes Act could not be used against the enemy, although other criminal statutes and the customary law of war would still be available.

— Our position would likely provoke widespread condemnation among our allies and in some domestic quarters, even if we make clear that we will comply with the core humanitarian principles of the treaty as a matter of policy.

— Concluding that the Geneva Convention does not apply may encourage other countries to look for technical "loopholes" in future conflicts to conclude that they are not bound by GPW either.

—Other countries may be less inclined to turn over terrorists or provide legal assistance to us if we do not recognize a legal obligation to comply with the GPW.

— A determination that GPW does not apply to al Qaeda and the Taliban could undermine U.S. military culture which emphasizes maintaining the highest standards of conduct in combat, and could introduce an element of uncertainty in the status of adversaries.

Responses to Arguments for Applying GPW to the al Qaeda and the Taliban

On balance, I believe that the arguments for reconsideration and reversal are unpersuasive.

— The argument that the U.S. has never determined that GPW did not apply is incorrect. In at least one case (Panama in 1989) the U.S. determined that GPW did not apply even though it determined for policy reasons to adhere to the convention. More importantly, as noted above, this is a new type of warfare—one not contemplated in 1949 when the GPW was framed—and requires a new approach in our actions towards captured terrorists. Indeed, as the statement quoted from the administration of President George Bush makes clear, the U.S. will apply GPW "whenever hostilities occur *with regular foreign armed forces.*" By its terms, therefore, the policy does not apply to a conflict with terrorists, or with irregular forces, like the Taliban, who are armed militants that oppressed and terrorized the people of Afghanistan.

— In response to the argument that we should decide to apply GPW to the Taliban in order to encourage other countries to treat captured U.S. military personnel in accordance with the GPW, it should be noted that your policy of providing humane treatment to enemy detainees gives us the credibility to insist on like treatment for our soldiers. Moreover, even if GPW is not applicable, we can still bring war crimes charges against anyone who mistreats U.S. personnel. Finally, I note that our adversaries in several recent conflicts have not been deterred by GPW in their mistreatment of captured U.S. personnel, and terrorists will not follow GPW rules in any event.

— The statement that other nations would criticize the U.S. because we have determined that GPW does not apply is undoubtedly true. It is even possible that some nations would point to that determination as a basis for failing to cooperate with us on specific matters in the war against terrorism. On the other hand, some international and domestic criticism is already likely to flow from your previous decision not to treat the detainees as POWs. And we can facilitate cooperation with other nations by reassuring them that we fully support GPW where it is applicable and by acknowledging that in this conflict the U.S. continues to respect other recognized standards.

— In the treatment of detainees, the U.S. will continue to be constrained by (i) its commitment to treat the detainees humanely and, to the extent appropriate and consistent with military necessity, in a manner consistent with the principles of GPW, (ii) its applicable treaty obligations, (iii) minimum standards of treatment universally recognized by the nations of the world, and (iv) applicable military regulations regarding the treatment of detainees.

— Similarly, the argument based on military culture fails to recognize that our military remain bound to apply the principles of GPW because that is what you have directed them to do.

GENEVA CONVENTION RELATIVE TO THE TREATMENT OF PRISONERS OF WAR

75 U.N.T.S. 135 (12 August 1949)

Article 3

In the case of armed conflict not of an international character occurring in the territory of one of the High Contracting Parties, each party to the conflict shall be bound to apply, as a minimum, the following provisions:

1. Persons taking no active part in the hostilities, including members of armed forces who have laid down their arms and those placed *hors de combat* by sickness, wounds, detention, or any other cause, shall in all circumstances be treated humanely, without any adverse distinction founded on race, colour, religion or faith, sex, birth or wealth, or any other similar criteria. To this end the following acts are and shall remain prohibited at any time and in any place whatsoever with respect to the above-mentioned persons:

(a) Violence to life and person, in particular murder of all kinds, mutilation, cruel treatment and torture;

* * *

(c) Outrages upon personal dignity, in particular, humiliating and degrading treatment;

(d) The passing of sentences and the carrying out of executions without previous judgment pronounced by a regularly constituted court affording all the judicial guarantees which are recognized as indispensable by civilized peoples.

* * *

Article 4

A.   Prisoners of war, in the sense of the present Convention, are persons belonging to one of the following categories, who have fallen into the power of the enemy:

1.   Members of the armed forces of a Party to the conflict as well as members of militias or volunteer corps forming part of such armed forces.

2.   Members of other militias and members of other volunteer corps, including those of organized resistance movements, belonging to a Party to the conflict and operating in or outside their own territory, even if this territory is occupied, provided that such militias or volunteer corps, including such organized resistance movements, fulfil the following conditions:

(a) That of being commanded by a person responsible for his subordinates;

(b) That of having a fixed distinctive sign recognizable at a distance;

(c) That of carrying arms openly;

(d) That of conducting their operations in accordance with the laws and customs of war.

3.   Members of regular armed forces who profess allegiance to a government or an authority not recognized by the Detaining Power.

4.   Persons who accompany the armed forces without actually being members thereof, such as civilian members of military aircraft crews, war correspondents, supply contractors, members of labour units or of services responsible for the welfare of the armed forces, provided that they have received authorization from the armed forces which they accompany, who shall provide them for that purpose with an identity card similar to the annexed model.

      * * *

6.   Inhabitants of a non-occupied territory, who on the approach of the enemy spontaneously take up arms to resist the invading forces, without having had time to form themselves into regular armed units, provided they carry arms openly and respect the laws and customs of war.

B.   The following shall likewise be treated as prisoners of war under the present Convention:

1.   Persons belonging, or having belonged, to the armed forces of the occupied country, if the occupying Power considers it necessary by reason of such allegiance to intern them, even though it has originally liberated them while hostilities were going on outside the territory it occupies, in particular where such persons have made an unsuccessful attempt to rejoin the armed forces to which they belong and which are

engaged in combat, or where they fail to comply with a summons made to them with a view to internment.

    * * *

Article 5

The present Convention shall apply to the persons referred to in Article 4 from the time they fall into the power of the enemy and until their final release and repatriation. Should any doubt arise as to whether persons, having committed a belligerent act and having fallen into the hands of the enemy, belong to any of the categories enumerated in Article 4, such persons shall enjoy the protection of the present Convention until such time as their status has been determined by a competent tribunal.

    * * *

Article 84

A prisoner of war shall be tried only by a military court, unless the existing laws of the Detaining Power expressly permit the civil courts to try a member of the armed forces of the Detaining Power in respect of the particular offence alleged to have been committed by the prisoner of war. In no circumstances whatever shall a prisoner of war be tried by a court of any kind which does not offer the essential guarantees of independence and impartiality as generally recognized, and, in particular, the procedure of which does not afford the accused the rights and means of defence provided for in Article 105.

    * * *

Article 105

The prisoner of war shall be entitled to assistance by one of his prisoner comrades, to defence by a qualified advocate or counsel of his own choice, to the calling of witnesses and, if he deems necessary, to the services of a competent interpreter. He shall be advised of these rights by the Detaining Power in due time before the trial. Failing a choice by the prisoner of war, the Protecting Power shall find him an advocate or counsel, and shall have at least one week at its disposal for the purpose. The Detaining Power shall deliver to the said Power, on request, a list of persons qualified to present the defence. Failing a choice of an advocate or counsel by the prisoner of war or the Protecting Power, the Detaining Power shall appoint a competent advocate or counsel to conduct the defence. The advocate or counsel conducting the defence on behalf of the prisoner of war shall have at his disposal a period of two weeks at least before the opening of the trial, as well as the necessary facilities to prepare the defence of the accused. He may, in particular, freely visit the accused and interview him in private. He may also confer with any witnesses for the defence, including prisoners of war. He shall have the benefit of these facilities until the term of appeal or petition has expired. Particulars of the charge or charges on which the prisoner of war is to be arraigned, as well as the documents which are generally communicated to the accused by virtue of the laws in force in the armed forces of the Detaining Power, shall be communicated to the accused prisoner of war in a language which he understands, and in good time before the opening of the trial. The same communication in the same circumstances shall be made to the advocate or counsel conducting the defence on behalf of the prisoner of war.

* * *

INTERNATIONAL COVENANT ON CIVIL AND POLITICAL RIGHTS
999 U.N.T.S. 171 (16 December 1966)

Article 14

1. All persons shall be equal before the courts and tribunals. In the determination of any criminal charge against him, or of his rights and obligations in a suit at law, everyone shall be entitled to a fair and public hearing by a competent, independent and impartial tribunal established by law. The press and the public may be excluded from all or part of a trial for reasons of morals, public order (*ordre public*) or national security in a democratic society, or when the interest of the private lives of the parties so requires, or to the extent strictly necessary in the opinion of the court in special circumstances where publicity would prejudice the interests of justice; but any judgement rendered in a criminal case or in a suit at law shall be made public except where the interest of juvenile persons otherwise requires or the proceedings concern matrimonial disputes or the guardianship of children.

2. Everyone charged with a criminal offence shall have the right to be presumed innocent until proved guilty according to law.

3. In the determination of any criminal charge against him, everyone shall be entitled to the following minimum guarantees, in full equality:

> (a) To be informed promptly and in detail in a language which he understands of the nature and cause of the charge against him;

> (b) To have adequate time and facilities for the preparation of his defence and to communicate with counsel of his own choosing;

> (c) To be tried without undue delay;

> (d) To be tried in his presence, and to defend himself in person or through legal assistance of his own choosing; to be informed, if he does not have legal assistance, of this right; and to have legal assistance assigned to him, in any case where the interests of justice so require, and without payment by him in any such case if he does not have sufficient means to pay for it;

(e) To examine, or have examined, the witnesses against him and to obtain the attendance and examination of witnesses on his behalf under the same conditions as witnesses against him;

(f) To have the free assistance of an interpreter if he cannot understand or speak the language used in court;

(g) Not to be compelled to testify against himself or to confess guilt.

4. In the case of juvenile persons, the procedure shall be such as will take account of their age and the desirability of promoting their rehabilitation.

5. Everyone convicted of a crime shall have the right to his conviction and sentence being reviewed by a higher tribunal according to law.

* * *

HAMDAN v. RUMSFELD

548 U.S. 557 (2006)

JUSTICE STEVENS delivered the opinion of the Court, except as to Part . . . VI–D–iv.

Petitioner Salim Ahmed Hamdan, a Yemeni national, is in custody at an American prison in Guantanamo Bay, Cuba. In November 2001, during hostilities between the United States and the Taliban (which then governed Afghanistan), Hamdan was captured by militia forces and turned over to the U.S. military. In June 2002, he was transported to Guantanamo Bay. Over a year later, the President deemed him eligible for trial by military commission for then-unspecified crimes. After another year had passed, Hamdan was charged with one count of conspiracy "to commit . . . offenses triable by military commission." Hamdan filed petitions for writs of habeas corpus and mandamus to challenge the Executive Branch's intended means of prosecuting this charge. He concedes that a court-martial constituted in accordance with the Uniform Code of Military Justice (UCMJ), 10 U.S.C. § 801 et seq., would have authority to try him. His objection is that the military commission the President has convened lacks such authority, for two principal reasons: First, neither congressional Act nor the common law of war supports trial by this commission for the crime of conspiracy—an offense that, Hamdan says, is not a violation of the law of war. Second, Hamdan contends, the procedures that the President has adopted to try him violate the most basic tenets of military and international law, including the principle that a defendant must be permitted to see and hear the evidence against him.

The District Court granted Hamdan's request for a writ of habeas corpus. The Court of Appeals for the District of Columbia Circuit reversed. Recognizing, as we did over a half-century ago, that trial by military commission is an extraordinary measure raising important questions about the balance of powers in our constitutional structure, *Ex parte Quirin*, 317 U.S. 1, 19 (1942), we granted certiorari. For the reasons that follow, we conclude that the military commission convened to try Hamdan lacks power to proceed because its structure and procedures violate both the UCMJ [deleted from the following excerpt] and the Geneva Conventions. Four of us also conclude, see Part V, infra, that the offense with which Hamdan has been charged is not an "offens[e] that by ... the law of war may be tried by military commissions."

I

On September 11, 2001, agents of the al Qaeda terrorist organization hijacked commercial airplanes and attacked the World Trade Center in New York City and the national headquarters of the Department of Defense in Arlington, Virginia. Americans will never forget the devastation wrought by these acts. Nearly 3,000 civilians were killed. Congress responded by adopting a Joint Resolution authorizing the President to "use all necessary and appropriate force against those nations, organizations, or persons he determines planned, authorized, committed, or aided the terrorist attacks ... in order to prevent any future acts of international terrorism against the United States by such nations, organizations or persons." Authorization for Use of Military Force (AUMF), 115 Stat. 224, note following 50 U.S.C. § 1541 (2000 ed., Supp. III). Acting pursuant to the AUMF, and having determined that the Taliban regime had supported al Qaeda, the President ordered the Armed Forces of the United States to invade Afghanistan. In the ensuing hostilities, hundreds of individuals, Hamdan among them, were captured and eventually detained at Guantanamo Bay.

On November 13, 2001, while the United States was still engaged in active combat with the Taliban, the President issued a comprehensive military order intended to govern the "Detention, Treatment, and Trial of Certain Non–Citizens in the War Against Terrorism," 66 Fed.Reg. 57833 (hereinafter November 13 Order or Order). Those subject to the November 13 Order include any noncitizen for whom the President determines "there is reason to believe" that he or she (1) "is or was" a member of al Qaeda or (2) has engaged or participated in terrorist activities aimed at or harmful to the United States. Any such individual "shall, when tried, be tried by military commission for any and all offenses triable by military commission that such individual is alleged to have committed, and may be punished in accordance with the penalties provided under applicable law, including imprisonment or death." The November 13 Order vested in the Secretary of Defense the power to appoint military commissions to try individuals subject to the Order, but that power has since been delegated to John D. Altenberg, Jr., a retired Army major general and longtime military lawyer who has been designated "Appointing Authority for Military Commissions."

On July 3, 2003, the President announced his determination that Hamdan and five other detainees at Guantanamo Bay were subject to the November 13 Order and thus triable by military commission. In December 2003, military counsel was appointed to represent Hamdan. Two months later, counsel filed demands for charges and for a speedy trial pursuant to Article 10 of the UCMJ. On February 23, 2004, the legal adviser to the Appointing Authority denied the applications, ruling that Hamdan was not entitled to any of the protections of the UCMJ. Not until July 13, 2004, after Hamdan had commenced this action in the United States District Court for the Western District of Washington, did the Government finally charge him with the offense for which, a year earlier, he had been deemed eligible for trial by military commission.

The charging document, which is unsigned, contains 13 numbered paragraphs. The first two paragraphs recite the asserted bases for the military commission's jurisdiction-namely, the November 13 Order and the President's July 3, 2003, declaration that Hamdan is eligible for trial by military commission. The next nine paragraphs, collectively entitled "General Allegations," describe al Qaeda's activities from its inception in 1989 through 2001 and identify Osama bin Laden as the group's leader. Hamdan is not mentioned in these paragraphs.

Only the final two paragraphs, entitled "Charge: Conspiracy," contain allegations against Hamdan. Paragraph 12 charges that "from on or about February 1996 to on or about November 24, 2001," Hamdan "willfully and knowingly joined an enterprise of persons who shared a common criminal purpose and conspired and agreed with [named members of al Qaeda] to commit the following offenses triable by military commission: attacking civilians; attacking civilian objects; murder by an unprivileged belligerent; and terrorism." There is no allegation that Hamdan had any command responsibilities, played a leadership role, or participated in the planning of any activity. Paragraph 13 lists four "overt acts" that Hamdan is alleged to have committed sometime between 1996 and November 2001 in furtherance of the "enterprise and conspiracy": (1) he acted as Osama bin Laden's "bodyguard and personal driver," "believ[ing]" all the while that bin Laden "and his associates were involved in" terrorist acts prior to and including the attacks of September 11, 2001; (2) he arranged for transportation of, and actually transported, weapons used by al Qaeda members and by bin Laden's bodyguards (Hamdan among them); (3) he "drove or accompanied [O]sama bin Laden to various al Qaida-sponsored training camps, press conferences, or lectures," at which bin Laden encouraged attacks against Americans; and (4) he received weapons training at al Qaeda-sponsored camps. After this formal charge was filed, * * * a Combatant Status Review Tribunal (CSRT) convened pursuant to a military order issued on July 7, 2004, decided that Hamdan's continued detention at Guantanamo Bay was warranted because he was an "enemy combatant."[1] Separately, proceedings before the military commission commenced.

On November 8, 2004, however, the District Court granted Hamdan's petition for *habeas corpus* and stayed the commission's proceedings. It concluded that the President's authority to establish military commissions extends only to "offenders or offenses triable by military [commission] under the law of war," that the law of war includes the Geneva Convention (III) Relative to the Treatment of Prisoners of War, Aug. 12, 1949 ("Third Geneva Convention"); that Hamdan is entitled to the full protections of the Third Geneva Convention until adjudged, in compliance with that treaty, not to be a prisoner of war; and that, whether or not Hamdan is properly classified as a prisoner of war, the military commission convened to try him was established in violation of both the UCMJ and Common Article 3 of the Third Geneva Convention because it had the power to convict based on evidence the accused would never see or hear.

The Court of Appeals for the District of Columbia Circuit reversed. Like the District Court, the Court of Appeals declined the Government's invitation to abstain from considering Hamdan's challenge. On the merits, the panel rejected the District Court's further conclusion that Hamdan was entitled to relief under the Third Geneva Convention. All three judges agreed that the Geneva Conventions were not "judicially enforceable," and two thought that the Conventions did not in any event apply to Hamdan. In other portions of its opinion, the court concluded that our decision in *Quirin* foreclosed any separation-of-powers objection to the military commission's jurisdiction, and held that Hamdan's trial before the contemplated commission would violate neither the UCMJ nor U.S. Armed Forces regulations intended to implement the Geneva Conventions. . . .[W]e granted certiorari to decide whether the military commission convened to try Hamdan has authority to do so, and whether Hamdan may rely on the Geneva Conventions in these proceedings.

＊ ＊ ＊

VI(D)

＊ ＊ ＊ The Court of Appeals dismissed Hamdan's Geneva Convention challenge on three independent grounds: (1) the Geneva Conventions are not judicially enforceable; (2) Hamdan in any event is not entitled to their protections; and (3) even if he is entitled to their protections, ＊ ＊ ＊ abstention is appropriate. ＊ ＊ ＊ The Court then repeated its finding from part III that the abstention rule applied in *Schlesinger v. Councilman*, 420 U.S. 738 (1975) was not applicable in this case, observing that the "text of the Geneva Conventions does not direct an accused to wait until sentence is imposed to challenge the legality of

---

1. An "enemy combatant" is defined by the military order as "an individual who was part of or supporting Taliban or al Qaeda forces, or associated forces that are engaged in hostilities against the United States or its coalition partners."

the tribunal that is to try him." And for the reasons that follow, we hold that neither of the other grounds the Court of Appeals gave for its decision is persuasive.

i. The Court of Appeals relied on *Johnson v. Eisentrager*, 339 U.S. 763 (1950), to hold that Hamdan could not invoke the Geneva Conventions to challenge the Government's plan to prosecute him in accordance with Commission Order No. 1. *Eisentrager* involved a challenge by 21 German nationals to their 1945 convictions for war crimes by a military tribunal convened in Nanking, China, and to their subsequent imprisonment in occupied Germany. The petitioners argued, *inter alia*, that the 1929 Geneva Convention rendered illegal some of the procedures employed during their trials, which they said deviated impermissibly from the procedures used by courts-martial to try American soldiers. We rejected that claim on the merits because the petitioners (unlike Hamdan here) had failed to identify any prejudicial disparity "between the Commission that tried [them] and those that would try an offending soldier of the American forces of like rank," and in any event could claim no protection, under the 1929 Convention, during trials for crimes that occurred before their confinement as prisoners of war.[2]

Buried in a footnote of the opinion, however, is this curious statement suggesting that the Court lacked power even to consider the merits of the Geneva Convention argument:

> We are not holding that these prisoners have no right which the military authorities are bound to respect. The United States, by the Geneva Convention of July 27, 1929, concluded with forty-six other countries, including the German Reich, an agreement upon the treatment to be accorded captives. These prisoners claim to be and are entitled to its protection. It is, however, the obvious scheme of the Agreement that responsibility for observance and enforcement of these rights is upon political and military authorities. Rights of alien enemies are vindicated under it only through protests and intervention of protecting powers as the rights of our citizens against foreign governments are vindicated only by Presidential intervention.

Id., at 789, n. 14. The Court of Appeals, on the strength of this footnote, held that "the 1949 Geneva Convention does not confer upon Hamdan a right to enforce its provisions in court."

Whatever else might be said about the *Eisentrager* footnote, it does not control this case. We may assume that "the obvious scheme" of the 1949 Conventions is identical in all relevant respects to that of the 1929 Convention,[3] and even that that scheme would, absent some other

---

2. [T]hat is no longer true under the 1949 Conventions.

3. *But see, e.g.,* 4 In'l Comm. of Red Cross, Commentary: Geneva Convention Relative to the Protection of Civilian Persons in Time of War 21 (1958) (hereinafter GCIV Commentary) (the 1949 Geneva Conventions were written "first and foremost to protect individuals, and not to serve State interests"); GCIII Commentary 91 ("It was not ... until the Conventions of 1949 ... that the existence of 'rights' conferred in prisoners of war was affirmed").

provision of law, preclude Hamdan's invocation of the Convention's provisions as an independent source of law binding the Government's actions and furnishing petitioner with any enforceable right. For, regardless of the nature of the rights conferred on Hamdan, they are, as the Government does not dispute, part of the law of war. And compliance with the law of war is the condition upon which the authority set forth in Article 21 is granted.

ii. For the Court of Appeals, acknowledgment of that condition was no bar to Hamdan's trial by commission. As an alternative to its holding that Hamdan could not invoke the Geneva Conventions at all, the Court of Appeals concluded that the Conventions did not in any event apply to the armed conflict during which Hamdan was captured. The court accepted the Executive's assertions that Hamdan was captured in connection with the United States' war with al Qaeda and that that war is distinct from the war with the Taliban in Afghanistan. It further reasoned that the war with al Qaeda evades the reach of the Geneva Conventions. We * * * disagree with the latter conclusion.

The conflict with al Qaeda is not, according to the Government, a conflict to which the full protections afforded detainees under the 1949 Geneva Conventions apply because Article 2 of those Conventions (which appears in all four Conventions) renders the full protections applicable only to "all cases of declared war or of any other armed conflict which may arise between two or more of the High Contracting Parties." Since Hamdan was captured and detained incident to the conflict with al Qaeda and not the conflict with the Taliban, and since al Qaeda, unlike Afghanistan, is not a "High Contracting Party," *i.e.*, a signatory of the Conventions, the protections of those Conventions are not, it is argued, applicable to Hamdan.[4]

We need not decide the merits of this argument because there is at least one provision of the Geneva Conventions that applies here even if the relevant conflict is not one between signatories. Article 3, often referred to as Common Article 3 because, like Article 2, it appears in all four Geneva Conventions, provides that in a "conflict not of an international character occurring in the territory of one of the High Contracting Parties, each Party[5] to the conflict shall be bound to apply, as a minimum," certain provisions protecting "[p]ersons taking no active part in the hostilities, including members of armed forces who have laid down their arms and those placed *hors de combat* by . . . detention." One such provision prohibits "the passing of sentences and the carrying out of executions without previous judgment pronounced by a regularly

---

4. The President has stated that the conflict with the Taliban is a conflict to which the Geneva Conventions apply. *See* White House Memorandum, Humane Treatment of Taliban and al Qaeda Detainees 2 (Feb. 7, 2002), available at http://www.justicescholars.org/pegc/archive/White_House/bush_memo_20020207_ed.pdf (hereinafter White House Memorandum).

5. The term "Party" here has the broadest possible meaning; a Party need neither be a signatory of the Convention nor "even represent a legal entity capable of undertaking international obligations." GCIII Commentary 37.

constituted court affording all the judicial guarantees which are recognized as indispensable by civilized peoples."

The Court of Appeals thought, and the Government asserts, that Common Article 3 does not apply to Hamdan because the conflict with al Qaeda, being " 'international in scope,' " does not qualify as a " 'conflict not of an international character.' " That reasoning is erroneous. The term "conflict not of an international character" is used here in contradistinction to a conflict between nations. So much is demonstrated by the "fundamental logic [of] the Convention's provisions on its application." [citing the concurring opinion of a member of the appellate panel]. Common Article 2 provides that "the present Convention shall apply to all cases of declared war or of any other armed conflict which may arise between two or more of the High Contracting Parties." High Contracting Parties (signatories) also must abide by all terms of the Conventions *vis-à-vis* one another even if one party to the conflict is a nonsignatory "Power," and must so abide *vis-à-vis* the nonsignatory if "the latter accepts and applies" those terms. Common Article 3, by contrast, affords some minimal protection, falling short of full protection under the Conventions, to individuals associated with neither a signatory nor even a nonsignatory "Power" who are involved in a conflict "in the territory of" a signatory. The latter kind of conflict is distinguishable from the conflict described in Common Article 2 chiefly because it does not involve a clash between nations (whether signatories or not). In context, then, the phrase "not of an international character" bears its literal meaning. Commentary on the Additional Protocols to the Geneva Conventions of 12 August 1949, p. 1351 (1987) ("[A] non-international armed conflict is distinct from an international armed conflict because of the legal status of the entities opposing each other").

Although the official commentaries accompanying Common Article 3 indicate that an important purpose of the provision was to furnish minimal protection to rebels involved in one kind of "conflict not of an international character," *i.e.*, a civil war, the commentaries also make clear "that the scope of the Article must be as wide as possible".[6] In fact, limiting language that would have rendered Common Article 3 applicable "especially [to] cases of civil war, colonial conflicts, or wars of religion," was omitted from the final version of the Article, which coupled broader scope of application with a narrower range of rights than did earlier proposed iterations. See GCIII Commentary 42–43.

iii. Common Article 3, then, is applicable here and, as indicated above, requires that Hamdan be tried by a "regularly constituted court

---

6. See also GCIII Commentary 35 (Common Article 3 "has the merit of being simple and clear.... Its observance does not depend upon preliminary discussions on the nature of the conflict"); GCIV Commentary 51 ("[N]obody in enemy hands can be outside the law"); U.S. Army Judge Advocate General's Legal Center and School, Dept. of the Army, Law of War Handbook 144 (2004) (Common Article 3 "serves as a 'minimum yardstick of protection in all conflicts, not just internal armed conflicts' " (quoting *Nicaragua v. United States*, 1986 I.C.J. 14, ¶ 218, 25 I.L.M. 1023)); *Prosecutor v. Tadic*, Case No. IT–94–1, Decision on the Defence Motion for Interlocutory Appeal on Jurisdiction, ¶ 102 (ICTY App. Chamber, Oct. 2, 1995) (stating that "the character of the conflict is irrelevant" in deciding whether Common Article 3 applies).

affording all the judicial guarantees which are recognized as indispensable by civilized peoples." While the term "regularly constituted court" is not specifically defined in either Common Article 3 or its accompanying commentary, other sources disclose its core meaning. The commentary accompanying a provision of the Fourth Geneva Convention, for example, defines " 'regularly constituted' " tribunals to include "ordinary military courts" and "definitely exclud[e] all special tribunals." GCIV Commentary 340 (defining the term "properly constituted" in Article 66, which the commentary treats as identical to "regularly constituted"). And one of the Red Cross' own treatises defines "regularly constituted court" as used in Common Article 3 to mean "established and organized in accordance with the laws and procedures already in force in a country." INT'L COMM. OF RED CROSS, 1 CUSTOMARY INTERNATIONAL HUMANITARIAN LAW 355 (2005); see also GCIV Commentary 340 (observing that "ordinary military courts" will "be set up in accordance with the recognized principles governing the administration of justice").

The Government offers only a cursory defense of Hamdan's military commission in light of Common Article 3. [T]hat defense fails because "[t]he regular military courts in our system are the courts-martial established by congressional statutes" ([citing Justice Kennedy's] opinion concurring in part). At a minimum, a military commission "can be 'regularly constituted' by the standards of our military justice system only if some practical need explains deviations from court-martial practice." . . . [N]o such need has been demonstrated here.[7]

iv.[8] Inextricably intertwined with the question of regular constitution is the evaluation of the procedures governing the tribunal and whether they afford "all the judicial guarantees which are recognized as indispensable by civilized peoples." Art. 3, ¶ 1(d). Like the phrase "regularly constituted court," this phrase is not defined in the text of the Geneva Conventions. But it must be understood to incorporate at least the barest of those trial protections that have been recognized by customary international law. Many of these are described in Article 75 of Protocol I to the Geneva Conventions of 1949, adopted in 1977 (Protocol I). Although the United States declined to ratify Protocol I, its objections were not to Article 75 thereof. Indeed, it appears that the Government "regard[s] the provisions of Article 75 as an articulation of safeguards to which all persons in the hands of an enemy are entitled." William H. Taft, *"The Law of Armed Conflict After 9/11: Some Salient Features,"* 28 YALE J. INT'L L. 319, 322 (2003). Among the rights set forth in Article 75 is the "right to be tried in [one's] presence." Protocol I, Art. 75(4)(e).[9]

---

7. Further evidence of this tribunal's irregular constitution is the fact that its rules and procedures are subject to change midtrial, at the whim of the Executive. See Commission Order No. 1, § 11 (providing that the Secretary of Defense may change the governing rules "from time to time").

8. [Editors note: Only a plurality of the Court accepted Part VI(D)(iv) of this opinion.]

9. Other international instruments to which the United States is a signatory include the same basic protections set forth in Article 75. *See, e.g.,* International Covenant on Civil and Political

* * * [T]he procedures adopted to try Hamdan deviate from those governing courts-martial in ways not justified by any "evident practical need," and for that reason, at least, fail to afford the requisite guarantees. We add only that * * * various provisions of Commission Order No. 1 dispense with the principles, articulated in Article 75 and indisputably part of the customary international law, that an accused must, absent disruptive conduct or consent, be present for his trial and must be privy to the evidence against him.[10] That the Government has a compelling interest in denying Hamdan access to certain sensitive information is not doubted. But, at least absent express statutory provision to the contrary, information used to convict a person of a crime must be disclosed to him.

v.   Common Article 3 obviously tolerates a great degree of flexibility in trying individuals captured during armed conflict; its requirements are general ones, crafted to accommodate a wide variety of legal systems. But *requirements* they are nonetheless. The commission that the President has convened to try Hamdan does not meet those requirements. * * *

We have assumed, as we must, that the allegations made in the Government's charge against Hamdan are true. We have assumed, moreover, the truth of the message implicit in that charge—*viz.*, that Hamdan is a dangerous individual whose beliefs, if acted upon, would cause great harm and even death to innocent civilians, and who would act upon those beliefs if given the opportunity. It bears emphasizing that Hamdan does not challenge, and we do not today address, the Government's power to detain him for the duration of active hostilities in order to prevent such harm. But in undertaking to try Hamdan and subject him to criminal punishment, the Executive is bound to comply with the Rule of Law that prevails in this jurisdiction.

Rights, Art. 14, ¶ 3(d), 999 U.N.T.S. 171 (setting forth the right of an accused "[t]o be tried in his presence, and to defend himself in person or through legal assistance of his own choosing"). Following World War II, several defendants were tried and convicted by military commission for violations of the law of war in their failure to afford captives fair trials before imposition and execution of sentence. In two such trials, the prosecutors argued that the defendants' failure to apprise accused individuals of all evidence against them constituted violations of the law of war. See 5 U.N. War Crimes Commission 30 (trial of Sergeant–Major Shigeru Ohashi), 75 (trial of General Tanaka Hisakasu).

10. The Government offers no defense of these procedures other than to observe that the defendant may not be barred from access to evidence if such action would deprive him of a "full and fair trial." Commission Order No. 1, § 6(D)(5)(b). But the Government suggests no circumstances in which it would be "fair" to convict the accused based on evidence he has not seen or heard. *Cf. Crawford v. Washington*, 541 U.S. 36, 49 (2004) (" 'It is a rule of the common law, founded on natural justice, that no man shall be prejudiced by evidence which he had not the liberty to cross examine' " (quoting *State v. Webb*, 2 N.C. 103, 104, 1794 WL 98 (Super. L. & Eq. 1794) (*per curiam*))); *Diaz v. United States*, 223 U.S. 442, 455 (1912) (describing the right to be present as "scarcely less important to the accused than the right of trial itself"); *Lewis v. United States*, 146 U.S. 370, 372 (1892) (exclusion of defendant from part of proceedings is "contrary to the dictates of humanity" (internal quotation marks omitted)); *Joint Anti–Fascist Refugee Comm. v. McGrath*, 341 U.S. 123, 170, n. 17, 171 (1951) (Frankfurter, J., concurring) ("[t]he plea that evidence of guilt must be secret is abhorrent to free men" (internal quotation marks omitted)). More fundamentally, the legality of a tribunal under Common Article 3 cannot be established by bare assurances that, whatever the character of the court or the procedures it follows, individual adjudicators will act fairly.

Justice THOMAS, with Justices SCALIA and ALITO (except for Part (2)), dissenting. The Court contends that Hamdan's military commission is also unlawful because it violates Common Article 3 of the Geneva Conventions. Furthermore, Hamdan contends that his commission is unlawful because it violates various provisions of the Third Geneva Convention. These contentions are untenable. * * * As an initial matter, and as the Court of Appeals concluded, both of Hamdan's Geneva Convention claims are foreclosed by *Eisentrager*. * * * While the Court attempts to cast *Eisentrager*s unqualified, alternative holding as footnote *dictum*, it does not dispute the correctness of its conclusion, namely, that the provisions of the 1929 Geneva Convention were not judicially enforceable because that Convention contemplated that diplomatic measures by political and military authorities were the exclusive mechanisms for such enforcement. Nor does the Court suggest that the 1949 Geneva Conventions departed from this framework. * * *

2

In addition to being foreclosed by *Eisentrager*, Hamdan's claim under Common Article 3 of the Geneva Conventions is meritless. Common Article 3 applies to "armed conflict not of an international character occurring in the territory of one of the High Contracting Parties." "Pursuant to [his] authority as Commander in Chief and Chief Executive of the United States," the President has "accept[ed] the legal conclusion of the Department of Justice ... that common Article 3 of Geneva does not apply to ... al Qaeda ... detainees, because, among other reasons, the relevant conflicts are international in scope and common Article 3 applies only to 'armed conflict not of an international character.'" Under this Court's precedents, "the meaning attributed to treaty provisions by the Government agencies charged with their negotiation and enforcement is entitled to great weight." *Sumitomo Shoji America, Inc. v. Avagliano*, 457 U.S. 176, 184–185 (1982). Our duty to defer to the President's understanding of the provision at issue here is only heightened by the fact that he is acting pursuant to his constitutional authority as Commander in Chief and by the fact that the subject matter of Common Article 3 calls for a judgment about the nature and character of an armed conflict.

The President's interpretation of Common Article 3 is reasonable and should be sustained. The conflict with al Qaeda is international in character in the sense that it is occurring in various nations around the globe. Thus, it is also "occurring in the territory of" more than "one of the High Contracting Parties." The Court does not dispute the President's judgments respecting the nature of our conflict with al Qaeda, nor does it suggest that the President's interpretation of Common Article 3 is implausible or foreclosed by the text of the treaty. Indeed, the Court concedes that Common Article 3 is principally concerned with "furnish[ing] minimal protection to rebels involved in ... a civil war," precisely the type of conflict the President's interpretation envisions to be subject to Common Article 3. Instead, the Court, without acknowledging its duty to defer to the President, adopts its own, admittedly plausible, reading of Common Article 3. But where, as here, an ambiguous treaty provision ("not of an international character") is susceptible of two plausible, and reasonable, interpretations, our precedents require us to defer to the Executive's interpretation.

3

But even if Common Article 3 were judicially enforceable and applicable to the present conflict, petitioner would not be entitled to relief. * * * Hamdan's military commission complies with the requirements of Common Article 3. It is plainly "regularly constituted" because such commissions have been employed throughout our history to try unlawful combatants for crimes against the law of war. * * * The Court concludes Hamdan's commission fails to satisfy the requirements of Common Article 3 not because it differs from the practice of previous military commissions but because it "deviate[s] from [the procedures] governing courts-martial." But there is neither a statutory nor historical requirement that military commissions conform to the structure and practice of courts-martial. A military commission is a different tribunal, serving a different function, and thus operates pursuant to different procedures. The 150–year pedigree of the military commission is itself sufficient to establish that such tribunals are "regularly constituted court [s]."

Similarly, the procedures to be employed by Hamdan's commission afford "all the judicial guarantees which are recognized as indispensable by civilized peoples." Neither the Court nor petitioner disputes the Government's description of those procedures.

> Petitioner is entitled to appointed military legal counsel, and may retain a civilian attorney (which he has done). Petitioner is entitled to the presumption of innocence, proof beyond a reasonable doubt, and the right to remain silent. He may confront witnesses against him, and may subpoena his own witnesses, if reasonably available. Petitioner may personally be present at every stage of the trial unless he engages in disruptive conduct or the prosecution introduces classified or otherwise protected information for which no adequate substitute is available and whose admission will not deprive him of a full and fair trial. If petitioner is found guilty, the judgment will be reviewed by a review panel, the Secretary of Defense, and the President, if he does not designate the Secretary as the final decisionmaker. The final judgment is subject to review in the Court of Appeals for the District of Columbia Circuit and ultimately in this Court.

BRIEF FOR RESPONDENTS 4.

Notwithstanding these provisions, which in my judgment easily satisfy the nebulous standards of Common Article 3, the plurality concludes that Hamdan's commission is unlawful because of the possibility that Hamdan will be barred from proceedings and denied access to evidence that may be used to convict him. But, under the commissions' rules, the Government may not impose such bar or denial on Hamdan if it would render his trial unfair, a question that is clearly within the scope of the appellate review contemplated by regulation and statute. * * *

In these circumstances, "civilized peoples" would take into account the context of military commission trials against unlawful combatants in the war on terrorism, including the need to keep certain information secret in the interest of preventing future attacks on our Nation and its foreign installations so long as it did not deprive the accused of a fair trial. Accordingly, the President's understanding of the requirements of Common Article 3 is entitled to "great weight." * * *

HUMAN RIGHTS FIRST
STATEMENT OF AVIDAN COVER
MILITARY COMMISSION PROCEEDINGS
VIOLATE INTERNATIONAL LAW

August 2004
Available at www.humanrightsfirst.com/media/2004_alerts/0817.htm

The military commission proceedings provide fewer fairness safeguards than either U.S. criminal or military court proceedings. That disparity in judicial protections violates international humanitarian law, which requires that enemy prisoners subjected to trial be afforded the same procedures and rights as would members of the armed forces of the detaining country.

First, the commission structure will be under the president's complete control, with no appeal to any civilian court.

Second, despite White House assurances that military commissions would be used to try only "enemy war criminals" for "offenses against the international laws of war," the chargeable offenses expand military jurisdiction into areas never before considered subject to military justice. This unprecedented jurisdictional reach is achieved by broadening the definition of "armed conflict"—the Geneva Convention term that establishes when "the law of war" is triggered—to include isolated "hostile acts" or unsuccessful attempts to commit such acts, including crimes such as "terrorism" or "hijacking" that traditionally fall within the ordinary purview of the federal courts.

Third, the government has broad discretion to close proceedings to outside scrutiny in the interest of "national security."

Fourth, the military commission rules impose substantial restrictions on the nature of legal representation to which defendants are entitled.

Commission defendants will be represented by assigned military law-yers—even if they do not want them. While defendants will also be entitled to (eligible) civilian lawyers, there are strong personal and professional disincentives for civilians to serve. Unless a defendant or his family or friends can provide financing, civilian defense lawyers will receive no fees and will themselves have to cover all personal and case-related expenses. Civilian defense lawyers must be U.S. citizens and eligible for access to information classified "secret." Furthermore, civil-ian lawyers (as well as their clients) can be denied access to any information—including potential exculpatory evidence—to the extent the prosecution determines it "necessary to protect the interests of the United States." The Defense Department may monitor attorney-client consultations; and lawyers will be subject to sanction if they fail to reveal information they "reasonably believe" necessary to prevent significant harm to "national security."

Finally, military commissions begin amidst the serious allegations of torture and abuse of detainees held at Guantanamo Bay. Techniques authorized for use at Guantanamo Bay did include at one time forced nudity, stress positions, isolation up to 30 days, forced grooming, and inducing stress by the use of dogs. At least two of the detainees whose proceedings are scheduled for the last week of August have been held in isolation for months on end, raising concerns over their psychological well-being and competency to stand trial. One psychiatrist has signed a sworn declaration, affirming that the conditions of at least one of the defendants, Salim Ahmed Hamdan, "place him at significant risk for future psychiatric deterioration"; "make [him] particularly susceptible to mental coercion and false confession"; and may significantly impair "his ability to assess his legal situation and assist defense counsel." The notion that coercive interrogation techniques might have induced false confessions from detainees at Guantanamo Bay is not hypothetical. As has been well-documented, the Tipton Three (Britons recently released from Guantanamo Bay) were coerced into making confessions later disproved by British Intelligence. The debilitating conditions of the detainees and the questionable reliability of any of their statements are particularly problematic here because the military commissions do not require that a defendant be mentally competent to stand trial and do not provide evidentiary standards that would preclude the admission of coerced information.

COMPARING FAIRNESS PROTECTIONS			
RIGHTS	U.S. CRIMINAL COURT	U.S. COURT MARTIAL	MILITARY COMMISSION
Jury	Yes	No	No
Counsel of defendant's choice	Yes	Yes	No
Know all evidence against the defendant	Yes	Yes	No
Obtain all evidence in fa-vor of the defense	Yes	Yes	No

COMPARING FAIRNESS PROTECTIONS			
RIGHTS	U.S. CRIMINAL COURT	U.S. COURT MARTIAL	MILITARY COMMISSION
Attorney–client confidentiality	Yes	Yes	No
Speedy trial	Yes	Yes	No
Appeal to an independent court	Yes	Yes	No
Remain silent	Yes	Yes	Yes
Proof beyond a reasonable doubt	Yes	Yes	Yes

NOTES AND QUESTIONS ON MILITARY COMMISSIONS

1. *Alternative means of enforcement.* If the Third Geneva Convention is not enforceable in a domestic court, how is it enforced? Is there reason to think that full-blown civil domestic litigation is not necessarily "the gold standard" in assuring that IHL rights are respected?

2. *Affording the benefit of the doubt to detainees.* The Third Geneva Convention requires that, if there is "any doubt" about whether a detainee is entitled to prisoner-of-war protections, he or she must be afforded those protections until his or her status is determined by a "competent tribunal." *See also* Headquarters Depts. of Army, Navy, Air Force, and Marine Corps, Army Regulation 190–8, Enemy Prisoners of War, Retained Personnel, Civilian Internees and Other Detainees (1997). The Supreme Court specifically reserved the question "whether [Hamdan's] potential status as a prisoner of war independently renders illegal his trial by military commission."

3. *Distinguishing military commissions from courts martial.* Is the Human Rights First critique of the military commission process persuasive? Does it rest on the untenable assumption that military commissions themselves are illegal?

4. *The Military Commissions Act.* In *Hamdan*, the Supreme Court relied on international law in part to invalidate the new species of military commissions that President Bush had authorized in his Executive Order on Detention, Treatment, and Trial of Certain Non–Citizens in the War Against Terrorism, *supra*. The Court specifically rejected the Government's contention that international humanitarian obligations did not apply to detainees at Guantanamo. However, the Court ultimately based its decision on separation of power grounds, leaving the door open for Congress to authorize the military commission system that the Executive could not promulgate on its own. 126 S.Ct. at 2775.

Congress did as the President asked. In the Military Commission Act of 2006 (MCA), it explicitly authorized the President to convene military commissions, rendering *Hamdan* obsolete and subjecting Guantanamo detainees to proceedings that many have criticized as falling short of international norms. In addition, the MCA stripped federal courts of their jurisdiction to hear *habeas corpus* petitions, precluded individuals from invoking international humanitarian law as a source of rights, and gave the President the final authority to interpret the Geneva Conventions. In June 2008, however, the Supreme Court held that the MCA's suspension of the Guantanamo detainees' right to *habeas corpus* was unconstitutional because the alternative procedures available for reviewing detainees' status were not a legitimate substitute for the *habeas* writ. *Boumediene v. Bush*, 128 S.Ct. 2229 (2008). Although this decision was a significant victory for detainees, its application is limited to detainees that have been subjected to undue delay. Moreover, the MCA's consistency or inconsistency with international humanitarian law was not addressed by the court. How would you go about challenging or defending those provisions of the MCA that prohibit individuals from invoking the Geneva Conventions as a source of rights and give the President final authority over their interpretation?

5. *The War Crimes Act.* The War Crimes Act of 1996 (WCA) implements Common Article 3 of the Geneva Convention by creating criminal penalties for war crimes involving U.S. perpetrators or victims of war crimes. 18 U.S.C. § 2441. Originally, the War Crimes Act was proposed to facilitate prosecution of individuals that committed war crimes against U.S. military personnel abroad. After the Supreme Court extended the protections of Article 3 to Guantanamo detainees in *Hamdan*, the Bush administration became concerned that it would be used to prosecute U.S. government officials. To avoid this concern, it sought and received legislative approval of an affirmative defense to prosecution in the Detainee Treatment Act of 2005, which severely restricted the scope of the WCA by limiting criminal liability to "grave breaches of Common Article 3," which includes torture, cruel or inhuman treatment, and intentionally causing serious bodily injury. In what circumstances would these amendments actually protect U.S. officials from prosecution?

Practicum

In 2005, a Somali warlord handed over two men to U.S. special forces in that country. Both men were suspected of links to a terrorist organization operating throughout the world, although there is also evidence that they simply represented a political and ethnic faction opposed to the paramilitaries. After initial processing, the United States government transferred the two men to the naval base at Guantanamo Bay, where they have been held in isolation. The President has determined that both men shall be tried by military commission for conspiracy to commit terrorist acts. One man—Detainee A—is clearly not a citizen of the United States. The other—Detainee B—was apparently born in the United States and has a *prima facie* claim for joint citizenship in the United States and in Afghanistan. On behalf of both men, actions have been filed in U.S. federal district court challenging the establishment of the military commissions in general and the decision to bring the men before the commissions in particular.

The class will be divided into several groups: (i) group 1 will represent the U.S. government, (ii) group 2 will represent Detainee A, (iii) group 3 will represent Detainee B, (iv) group 4 will represent the International Committee of the Red Cross as court-hired experts in international humanitarian law, (v) group 5 will represent Human Rights First as court-hired experts in international human rights law, and (vi) Group 6 will serve as judges. Groups 1–5 will prepare an outline of their argument, elect oral advocates, and argue the case. Group 6 will prepare a bench memorandum, decide the case, and outline their opinion(s).

CHAPTER 8

PROFESSIONAL RESPONSIBILITY IN HUMAN RIGHTS LAWYERING

■ ■ ■

Orientation

The past decade has seen a steady increase of international human rights litigation in domestic, regional, and international courts. As a result, a thriving practice area has emerged with a growing number of practitioners. The lawyers handling these cases are invariably trained within their own national legal systems, and their conduct as lawyers is governed by national or regional rules of professional responsibility. However, much of this litigation is transnational, and international rules are being formulated to deal with ethical issues that may arise when international human rights litigation is conducted across national boundaries or before international tribunals. The purpose of this module is to explore these recurring issues of ethics and professional responsibility.

Doctrines of professional responsibility vary from nation to nation and culture to culture. In the United States, professional responsibility standards are reflected in the American Bar Association's Model Rules of Professional Conduct, which place a heavy emphasis on loyalty to the client and zealous advocacy on the client's behalf. Germany's lawyers, on the other hand, are subject to "highly specific norms that emphasize the lawyer's responsibility to the courts." *See generally*, GEOFFREY C. HAZARD, JR. & ANGELO DONDI, LEGAL ETHICS: A COMPARATIVE STUDY 109–110 (2004). In England and Wales, the Bar Council and Law Society of England and Wales, representing, respectively, the interests of barristers and solicitors, rely more heavily on tradition than codification to enforce their ethical norms. *Id.* at 284. The Japanese Code of Ethics "expresses ethical norms as ideals and objectives rather than as precisely stated obligations." *Id.* at 107. As lawyers from different legal systems with different ethical sensibilities increasingly participate in the international legal system, the need for a uniform code of professional conduct becomes more apparent. Indeed, the European Union, recognizing the need for uniformity, has set forth common values for the legal profession in the Code of Conduct for Lawyers in the European Community ("CCBE"). The International Bar Association has also devised a code of conduct, the International Code of Ethics ("IBA Code"). The IBA Code notes, however, "[n]othing in the Code absolves a lawyer from the obligation to comply with such requirements of the law or of rules of professional conduct as may apply to him or her in any relevant jurisdiction."[1] In essence, the IBA Code merely serves as a restatement "as to what the International Bar Association considers to be a desirable course of conduct by all lawyers engaged in the practice of international law." *Id.*

While many in the international community advocate for a uniform system, to date, no such system exists. It is within this context that we examine the ethical and moral issues that arise in the modern practice of human rights law: determining fair compensation in complex, emotional cases; securing the safety of plaintiffs; and structuring class actions to adequately address the specific needs of human rights victims. Next, we turn our attention to issues faced by lawyers in the international arena, including the Codes of Conduct that govern the international criminal tribunals, ethical questions surrounding the U.N. complaint process, and the nature of the attorney-client relationship in proceedings before regional human rights commissions. Finally, we consider the unique professional ethics issues confronted by government lawyers, especially in the context of the "war on terrorism."

A. HUMAN RIGHTS LITIGATION: ETHICAL AND MORAL ISSUES IN THE DOMESTIC ARENA

The following excerpts grapple with a range of ethical and moral issues confronting lawyers in recent human rights litigation in U.S. courts. Very few reported decisions consider these issues, and lawyers have had to resolve many issues without much guidance from formal rules. Some issues, such as whether lawyers should forgo a substantial portion of their fees to provide greater compensation for their clients, are governed by personal conscience rather than formal rules. Any lawyer practicing in this area will face these and other difficult ethical quandaries. As you read these excerpts, think about how you would handle these issues.

---

1. International Bar Association, *International Code of Ethics* (1988 ed.), *available at* http://www.ibanet.org/images/downloads/International_Code_of_Ethics.pdf.

1. INTERNATIONAL HUMAN RIGHTS LITIGATION AND PROFESSIONAL RESPONSIBILITY: LESSONS AND QUESTIONS FROM THE HOLOCAUST CASES[2]

This essay deals with issues of professional responsibility which arise during the course of litigating international human rights cases in American courts. The last twenty years has seen an explosion of civil lawsuits brought in the United States for human rights abuses committed abroad. American courts are now viewed by foreign victims of such abuses as the last great hope where the wrongs against them can be vindicated. The unique features of the American system of justice—a legal culture in which lawyers are willing to take high-risk cases with low probability of success in order to test the limits of the law; an active human rights bar composed of both academics and human rights advocates willing to take on such cases *pro bono;* ability of fee-generating lawyers to take cases on a contingency basis; recognition of class action lawsuits; fixed and affordable filing fees when filing civil lawsuits; and an independent judiciary—have made the United States the primary forum in the world where such claims can be heard today.

All of these suits share common elements. First, the plaintiffs are individuals who have suffered the worst kind of human rights abuses. Second, the plaintiffs are almost always economically poor and politically powerless. Finally, the plaintiffs often turned to American courts only after failing to obtain some measure of justice through the political and legal systems of their home countries, or because such justice was obviously not available.

The distinctive characteristics of such suits and the plaintiffs who are filing them present, therefore, a special set of responsibilities for the lawyers involved in such litigation.

*How should funds collected in international
human rights litigation be distributed?*

In those cases where a monetary settlement has been reached in human rights litigation, how should the money be distributed? This issue became quite important in the Holocaust restitution arena, following a series of class action lawsuits filed by Holocaust survivors in the late 1990s against Swiss banks and thereafter other European and American banks, European insurance companies, and also Germany and its industry. The defendants agreed to pay compensation totaling approximately $8 billion in return for settlement of the suits. The debate around Holocaust settlement funds heated because it touched upon many sensitive and relevant questions for Holocaust survivors.

First, elderly Holocaust survivors needed to have their voices heard. The problem, of course, is that the survivors do not speak with one

---

2. Essay adapted from Michael J. Bazyler, *The Gray Zones of Holocaust Restitution: American Justice and Holocaust Morality* in GRAY ZONES: AMBIGUITY AND COMPROMISE IN THE HOLOCAUST AND ITS AFTERMATH (Jonathan Petropoulos & John K. Roth eds., 2005).

voice, and, for this reason, any distribution decision made by one group of survivors was challenged by another group.

Second, distribution issues not only brought out disputes among aged survivors but also manifested an inter-generational rivalry. Many survivors felt that the funds belonged only to them, since compensation was sought on their behalf and in the name of their suffering and degradation. In their view, only they had the right to decide how the unanticipated billions flowing in should be distributed. This position was strongly challenged by leaders of many Jewish organizations. These leaders argued that the heirs of the six million murdered were the entire body of worldwide Jewry. Moreover, various individuals and institutions, both Jewish and non-Jewish, began making suggestions as to how the funds should be distributed.

There was general agreement that the legal claimants—whether heirs to the Swiss and French dormant accounts, beneficiaries of traceable Holocaust-era insurance policies, or slave laborers uncompensated for their labor in death camps or ghettoes—should be paid first. What about any remainder? And this was not some hypothetical question, since, at least in the Swiss and German settlements, residual funds in the tens or maybe even hundreds of millions were left over after all the eligible applicants to these settlements were paid.

When money is collected for human rights abuses reaching genocidal proportions, victim groups sometimes call for the funds not only to be distributed among the living survivors, but also to allocate a portion of the funds for remembrance of the horrors and the education of future generations. The aim of such remembrance and education projects is a noble one: not to repeat the horrors committed. The result, however, is that a portion of the funds is siphoned off from being used to directly benefit the living victims. Since in *every* settlement of an international human rights case, the victims can rightly complain that the money collected comes nowhere close to compensating victims for the financial losses, never mind the pain and suffering they went through, is it fair to reduce the amounts going to the victims by allocating a proportion of the settlement for remembrance and education?

The Holocaust restitution settlements starkly illustrated this dilemma. Soon after the Swiss banks settlement, Miles Lerman, former chair of the U.S. Holocaust Memorial Council and himself a Holocaust survivor, proposed that a portion of the funds be allocated to Holocaust education. In the end, Lerman's point of view did not prevail. Judge Edward Korman, the federal judge in charge of the Swiss settlement funds, declined to set aside any money for this purpose. In contrast, for the German slave labor settlement, the German payers insisted that DM 700 million (approximately $325 million) of their DM 10 billion (approximately $5 billion) fund go to Holocaust education and remembrance. While the $5 billion settlement figure seems large, the individual payments to the over 1.5 million eligible claimants were paltry: approximately $7,500 to the still-living Jewish survivors of Nazi Germany's "death through work" program, and $2,500 to the mostly Eastern European non-Jewish survivors forced to work as slaves in Germany's wartime economy. Count Otto Lambsdorff, the chief German government representative in the settlement negotiations, defended this allocation by explaining that the money going to Holocaust remembrance, while not going directly to the survivors, still benefits them, albeit indirectly after they are deceased.

Allocations for Holocaust education and remembrance remain controversial. As long as there are elderly survivors anywhere in the world in need of assistance, it appears unreasonable to channel newly found funds to more Holocaust museums, support publication of more Holocaust books, or have additional Holocaust conferences. The real questions of how to serve justice and concurrently balance the claims of memory, responsibility, and group survival will inevitably bring forth competing visions.

Should a monetary settlement be accepted if the culprits refuse to apologize?

For victims of massive human rights abuses, receipt of monetary compensation is usually not their top concern. Much more important is recognition of the serious wrongs done to them. A judgment by a United States court in the form of money damages against the culpable parties provides an important symbol for that recognition, especially since the American system of justice and its judges are generally held in high esteem throughout the world.

Concomitant with a court ruling in favor of the victims is the need by the victims to receive an apology from the perpetrators or the foreign government responsible for the abuses. Here a problem arises. A defendant may be willing to conclude the litigation through payment of a monetary settlement but unwilling to admit liability and issue any kind of apology or statement of remorse. In such case, should the monetary settlement be accepted?

In the claims made against Japan for its use of sex slaves (so-called "comfort women") during World War II, the elderly Korean and Chinese survivors of such abuse greatly resented that Japan refused to apologize to them, and so many have rejected the funds from the "Comfort Women" Fund set up for them in Japan. To obtain a formal recognition of these wrongs, these women filed a class action lawsuit against Japan, which ultimately proved unsuccessful. *See Joo v. Japan*, 413 F.3d 45 (D.C. Cir. 2005), *cert. denied*, 546 U.S. 1208 (2006). Other survivors accepted the financial settlement, usually citing the urgent need for financial assistance to live out their elderly years. In contrast, Germany and its industry agreed not only to pay compensation but also to apologize to their WWII slave laborers and accept "moral responsibility" for their wartime conduct. Such contrition played an important part in the victims' and their lawyers' decision in 1999 to settle the massive class action litigation against German industry for much less than the victims would have hoped for.

Should attorneys representing victims of international human rights violations be paid, and, if so, what is fair compensation?

Victims of international human rights violations appearing in American courts are either represented by nonprofit non-governmental organizations (NGOs) specializing in filing suits for violations of international human rights (*e.g.*, Center for Constitutional Rights, Center for Justice and Accountability), or by private lawyers. At times, both sets of lawyers may appear in the same litigation. For example, in the various lawsuits filed against the estate of former Philippine dictator Ferdinand Marcos, some of the human rights victims were represented by lawyers working for nonprofit human rights NGOs, while another group of victims retained private counsel. The NGOs did not charge fees for their work. The private lawyers, as is customary in the American legal system, took the cases on the basis of a contingency fee.

The Holocaust restitution lawsuits presented a virtual clinic for confronting the issue of whether lawyers should share (and, if so, in what amounts) the monetary benefits flowing from human rights litigation. In the Holocaust suits, the victims were all represented by private lawyers since no NGO took on these cases. While some of these lawyers took some of the cases *pro bono*, no lawyer was willing to litigate all of the cases without a fee. All demanded a contingency fee for at least a portion of their services. At the same time, there was special sensitivity to the issue, lest it appear that the private lawyers were profiting off the miseries of the Holocaust.

In late 2002 and early 2003, Judge Edward Korman awarded approximately $6 million in legal fees, amounting to approximately one-half of one percent (0.05%) of the $1.25 billion settlement—an amount substantially lower in percentage terms than the legal fees received in successful class-action cases in American courts, which usually range from 15–20% of the settlement sum. Three of the principal lawyers in the case waived their fees. Some of the lawyers donated all or a portion of their fees to those survivors who helped them win the litigation but could not prove that their family had a pre-war Swiss bank account. One of the private firms, Lieff Cabraser, donated $1.5 million to Columbia Law School to fund an international human rights clinic in honor of Holocaust victims.

All the principal lawyers in the Swiss banks litigation went on, however, to earn millions of dollars in the subsequent Holocaust restitution suits. The DM 10 billion (US$5 billion) German slave labor settlement finalized in July 2000, which the lawyers helped to craft, included a provision for attorneys' fees, which would be paid out first. Of course, for many of the lawyers, it was a welcome relief. They had been working on these cases for over five years without being paid, expending not only their time but advancing all expenses for the cases, which now totaled in the tens of thousands of dollars.

A two-person arbitration panel set up to award fees awarded almost $60 million (amounting to 1.2% of the nearly $5 billion settlement) to the over fifty lawyers working on the litigation.[1] A traditional American attorneys' fee award, using the range of between 15–20% of the total settlement amount, would have resulted in total awarded fees of at least $750 million.

Comparing these figures, however, with the individual amounts obtained by the actual plaintiff victims (one-time payments of between $2500 and $7500) presents a difficult ethical issue. As the Israeli daily *Ha'aretz*, focusing on the $7.3 million awarded to attorney Melvyn Weiss, pointed out, "This sum is equal to the amount to be distributed to 1,000 survivors, each of whom spent several years at forced labor."

Soon after the lawyers were awarded fees in the German settlement, Paul Spiegel, a leader of Germany's Jewish community, issued a public appeal to the lawyers urging them to donate their fees to the German Fund, to help increase the payments to the survivors. According to Spiegel, "I am convinced that the lawyers have a legal right to their money, but not a moral right. I am not saying that the lawyers are greedy. It is just immoral when the highest payments to survivors are about $7,000 and the lawyers are getting millions." The lawyers were not interested. Michael Witti, the German lawyer working on the cases, who was awarded about $4 million for his work, publicly responded to Spiegel's proposal. Witti explained that the fees will enable him to continue representing survivors for other wartime claims, such as helping to recover confiscated property in Eastern Europe. The fees are needed, Witti elaborated, "so I can hire experts, so I can travel and have office staff. And this money gives me the support for this." He concluded: "If you are not [fiscally] responsible, you run away and take commercial cases. But I have an obligation to do human rights cases."

As an example, Lieff Cabraser, as well as other lawyers involved in the Holocaust restitution suits, took on aging former slaves of Japan's industrial wartime policy as clients. After three years of litigation, with hundreds of thousands of dollars advanced for litigation expenses and thousands of hours of time spent, the Japanese slave labor suits were all dismissed, and the lawyers received nothing for their efforts. For these lawyers, the money they earned from the Holocaust settlements allowed them to fund the litigation against Japanese industry.

How effective were the lawyers? According to nationally syndicated columnist Richard Cohen: "[n]o one is suggesting the present management of these [defendant] companies is antisemitic, but I am suggesting they would never own up—open their files, never mind their wallets, if

---

1. The fees included reimbursement to the attorneys of the costs they had been advancing on these cases since their filing in 1997.

those awful contingency lawyers had not surrounded them and run up the Jolly Roger."[2]

Cohen's point is that without the lawyers, the movement would have never gotten off the ground. Ambassador Stuart Eizenstat, the lead U.S. government negotiator on Holocaust restitution (and also a lawyer who returned to private practice after his government service) specifically noted the importance of the lawyers' contribution to the settlement of the German slave labor and related claims.

> Without question, we would not be here without them. The settlement we reached of 10 billion DM will help hundreds of thousands of victims, beyond those whom the lawyers represent, live out their declining years in more comfort. For this dedication and commitment to the victims we should always be grateful to these lawyers.[3]

Nevertheless, nearly every survivor has expressed deep hurt that, for example, their "death-through-work" labor in the concentration camps should now be valued substantially less than the work of the cadre of white collar professionals working on their behalf in climate-controlled offices.

Representing the monster: Are there some cases that a human and civil rights lawyer should not take?

Even at Nuremberg, the most abhorrent individuals, responsible for the murders of millions, were given the right to counsel, and lawyers came forward to provide them a defense. More recently, defendants in the dock before the International Criminal Tribunal for the Former Yugoslavia and the International Criminal Tribunal for Rwanda were tried for crimes such as genocide, war crimes, and crimes against humanity, and they too needed counsel to defend them.

The issue of whether a lawyer should represent a client whose case presents difficult moral questions was also presented in the Holocaust restitution litigation. Many companies being sued by Holocaust survivors hired Jewish lawyers from some of the most prominent law firms in the United States to defend them, often retaining counsel with important connections to the organized Jewish community.

For instance, the Swiss banks retained Wilmer, Cutler & Pickering, a large Washington D.C. firm founded in 1962 by Lloyd Cutler, one of the most prominent Jewish lawyers in the United States. The representation led to a great deal of soul searching on the part of some of the other Jewish lawyers in the firm, some of whom publicly protested the firm's taking on the defense of this suit against the banks.[4]

Wilmer Cutler & Pickering's successful negotiation of a settlement between Holocaust survivors and the banks in August 1998 for $1.25

---

2. Richard Cohen, *The Money Matters*, WASH. POST, Dec. 8, 1998, at A21.

3. Remarks of Stuart E. Eizenstadt, 12th and Concluding Plenary of the German Foundation, 17 July 2000, *available at* http://germany.usembassy.gov/germany/img/assets/8497/eizenstadt071700.pdf

4. EC 2–27 states that "[o]ne of the highest services the lawyer can render to society is to appear in court on behalf of clients whose causes are in disfavor with the general public."

billion led other European defendants to ask the firm to represent them in lawsuits for Holocaust-era wrongs. For the next four years, the firm was on the forefront of defending various European companies for their wartime dealings, including suits brought by Jewish and non-Jewish survivors who were forced to work as slaves for German companies during the war. The decision whether to represent the German firms for their wartime activities provoked, according to the *Washington Post*, "the most rancorous debate in memory at * * * Wilmer, Cutler & Pickering." The result? " 'It came down to issues of conscience warring against issues of business,' said one Wilmer lawyer, who requested anonymity. 'And business won.' "[5] Is there an alternative explanation?

NOTES AND QUESTIONS RE HOLOCAUST LITIGATION

1. *Settlement allocations.* Do you agree with the settlement allocations in the German slave labor case? Should funds go toward museums and education programs when survivors received only $2,500–7,500? *See* Paul R. Dubinsky, *Justice for the Collective: The Limits of the Human Rights Class Action*, 102 MICH. L.REV. 1152 (2004).

2. *Pro bono.* Lawyers often become involved in human rights cases on a *pro bono* basis. Many human rights cases, however, continue for several years, requiring the *pro bono* lawyer to work hundreds if not thousands of hours on the case. Recently, respected civil rights lawyer and law school professor Burt Neuborne submitted a bill for 4.1 million dollars for eight thousand hours of work representing Holocaust survivors in a case against the Swiss Banks. Neuborne originally began his work *pro bono*, but in 1999, he took on an expanded role as lead lawyer for thousands of Holocaust survivors and claimed that, with this expanded role, he no longer intended to work on a *pro bono* basis. Holocaust survivors claimed it was their understanding that Neuborne was continuing to volunteer his time at no cost and were angry that he requested the fee when they received only a fraction of what Neuborne requested. Neuborne defended his request for fees, stating:

> It was a grueling job that nobody else wanted, and that I have done faithfully and successfully for seven years. There has to be a special application of the rule that no good deed goes unpunished for someone to say that because I voluntarily gave up my fees for getting the settlement, and that would be $10 million, somehow I'm not allowed to be paid for seven years' work in successfully carrying it out.

See William K. Rashbaum, *Angry Holocaust Survivors Object to Lawyer's $4.1 Million Fee*, N.Y. TIMES, Feb. 25, 2006, at B1. Professor Neuborne was ultimately awarded $3.1 million. *In re Holocaust Victim Assets Litigation*,

---

5. David Segal, *Past v. Future: Nazi–Related Suits Put Law Firms on Defensive*, WASH. POST, Mar. 9, 1999, at E1.

528 F. Supp. 2d 109 (E.D.N.Y. 2007). Are lawyers ethically required to maintain their pro bono status throughout the duration of the case? When, if ever, can a lawyer request compensation? In the event of a large settlement, is there anything wrong with lawyers being paid their hourly rate?

3. *Defending Saddam Hussein.* Consider the following statement by former Attorney General Ramsey Clark, lead counsel for Saddam Hussein, on his decision to defend the former dictator:

> That Hussein and other former Iraqi officials must have lawyers of their choice to assist them in defending against the criminal charges brought against them ought to be self-evident among a people committed to truth, justice and the rule of law. Both international law and the Constitution of the United States guarantee the right to effective legal representation to any person accused of a crime. This is especially important in a highly politicized situation, where truth and justice can become even harder to achieve. That's certainly the situation today in Iraq. * * * President Bush, who initiated and oversees the war, has manifested this hatred for Hussein, publicly proclaiming that the death penalty would be appropriate. * * * In a trial of Hussein and other former Iraqi officials, affirmative measures must be taken to prevent prejudice from affecting the conduct of the case and the final judgment of the court. This will be a major challenge. But nothing less is acceptable. * * * The defense of such a case is a challenge of great importance to truth, the rule of law and peace. A lawyer qualified for the task and able to undertake it, if chosen, should accept such service as his highest duty.

Ramsey Clark, Commentary, *Why I'm Willing to Defend Hussein*, L.A. Times, Jan. 24, 2005, at B9. Do you agree with Ramsey Clark's analysis? Would you represent a person widely believed to have committed genocide, war crimes, and crimes against humanity? What considerations do you believe are important in making this decision?

---

2. ETHICAL ISSUES IN HUMAN RIGHTS LITIGATION UNDER THE ALIEN TORT STATUTE

Since the decision in *Filartiga v. Pena–Irala*, 630 F.2d 876 (2d Cir. 1980), counsel for human rights victim plaintiffs have encountered a wide array of ethical challenges in the course of litigating cases under the Alien Tort Statute ("ATS"). There maybe answers to some of these quandaries, but for others there is only continuing debate.

Security and protection of plaintiffs and witnesses

The personal security of plaintiffs, witnesses and even counsel is an important concern in ATS litigation. In most cases, the plaintiffs or their loved ones have been subjected to egregious human rights violations (*e.g.* genocide, torture, disappearances) at the hands of perpetrators often notorious for their brutality and capacity for retaliation. This leads to a legitimate fear of retaliation especially when the offending regime is still in power, which was the case with the military junta in Burma at the heart of the litigation in *Doe v. Unocal Corp.*, 963 F.Supp. 880 (C.D. Cal. 1997), 110 F. Supp. 2d 1294 (C.D. Cal. 2000). Even in cases where the offending regime is no longer in power and the country is going through a period of transition, remnants of the old regime may retain the ability to exact revenge on the plaintiffs, their family members, or witnesses.

Plaintiffs' counsel ordinarily take precautions to ensure security for these people. Many cases are filed under fictitious names.[1] Protective orders are useful to limit the disclosure of the plaintiffs' true names and other identifying information. In *Doe v. Unocal*, such protective orders were the subject of prolonged negotiation between the parties. The defendants, of course, insist that they must have access to information necessary to their defense, including the opportunity to interview the people who know the plaintiffs and their stories. In a country like Burma, such interviews could put the plaintiffs and their families at risk. When *Doe v. Unocal* settled, the ground rules for security during a public jury trial were being debated, but, because of the settlement, they were never decided. Some of the trial-related rules remain uncertain: Can the judge close the courtroom to the public when a plaintiff is testifying? How can a court prevent foreign intelligence agents from attending a trial and obtaining information that might be used for retaliation?[2]

It is imperative to take every reasonable step to protect plaintiffs, families, and witnesses. Similarly, counsel must explain the security risks that might arise in the course of a litigation to a prospective plaintiff. When, if ever, is a potential case too risky even to assume the risk of interviewing prospective plaintiffs or initiating a lawsuit? How can a lawyer be sure that a client, unfamiliar with the United States or the notion of a civil lawsuit, really understands the risks and is joining a suit fully comprehending and accepting those risks? What if there is disagreement between the prospective plaintiffs and family members or witnesses who do not want to assume the risk? Does counsel's duty of loyalty extend only to the party he or she represents? Is there a broader responsibility to the larger community which may be adversely affected?[3]

---

1. In *Doe v. Advanced Textile Corp.*, 214 F.3d 1058, 1068 (9th Cir. 2000), the court announced that a party may preserve anonymity when "identification creates a risk of retaliatory physical or mental harm." To determine the need for anonymity the court evaluated "(1) the severity of the threatened harm; (2) the reasonableness of the anonymous party's fears; and (3) the anonymous party's vulnerability to such retaliation." *Id.*

2. For a detailed account of these issues in the context of the *Doe v. Unocal* case, see Jed Greer, Comment, *Plaintiff Pseudonymity and the Alien Tort Claims Act: Question and Challenges*, 32 COLUM. HUM. RTS. L. REV. 517 (2001).

3. *See* MODEL RULES OF PROF'L CONDUCT R. 2.1 (2003): "In rendering advice, a lawyer may refer not only to law but to other considerations such as moral, economic, social and political factors, that may be relevant to the client's situation. Thus, at the very least lawyers certainly can address their concern over the safety of third parties with their clients." *But see* MODEL CODE OF PROF'L

If, after a lawsuit is filed, it becomes apparent that the risks to third parties have increased, should the lawyer insist on dismissal of the case? Would it be ethical to abandon the client in such circumstances? What if a witness has already been killed, and it appears that others are in danger if the case continues?

Defense counsel may also have ethical obligations to protect the identity of plaintiffs and witnesses. One commentator has suggested that defense counsel must communicate to their clients that retaliation is illegal.[4] Furthermore, Model Rule 1.16(a)(1) states that a lawyer shall not represent a client when "the representation will result in violation of the rules of professional conduct or other law." Model Rules of Prof'l Conduct R. 1.16 (2003). Thus, a lawyer who knows that her client will use information gathered in the legal process to harm plaintiffs and potential witnesses must withdraw from the representation. Model Rule 1.6(b)(1) also permits, but does not require, a lawyer to reveal information relating to a representation of a client to "prevent reasonably certain death or substantial bodily harm."

Representing the human rights movement vs. individual plaintiffs

Doe v. Unocal was settled days before the Ninth Circuit was scheduled to hear oral argument *en banc* on issues of exceptional importance to many human rights cases around the country. Many lawyers questioned whether plaintiffs' counsel should have agreed to a settlement before the Ninth Circuit issued its ruling, which, given the strength of the *Unocal* case, could have benefitted all ATS plaintiffs. What obligations did plaintiffs' counsel have to communicate the proposed settlement to plaintiffs and to advise them about whether to take it? Would it be ethical to advise against accepting a settlement because proceeding with the litigation might lead to rulings favorable to other plaintiffs? Is this a legitimate issue to discuss with clients? Is it ever appropriate to ask plaintiffs, either before or after collection, to donate a portion of their collected settlement to a fund for others? Would such an agreement be enforceable?

David Weissbrodt, in his article *Ethical Problems of an International Human Rights Law Practice*, 7 Mich Y.B. Int'l Legal Stud. 217 (1985), examines how lawyers in *Tel-Oren v. Libyan Arab Republic*, 726 F.2d 774 (D.C. Cir. 1984) were forced to confront the tension between engaging in zealous advocacy on behalf of their client and preserving a crucial piece of human rights legislation.

Tel-Oren arose out of a 1978 terrorist attack by 13 heavily armed members of the Palestinian Liberation Organization (PLO)

Responsibility EC 5–1 (1981): "Neither his personal interests, the interests of other clients, nor the desires of third persons should be permitted to dilute his loyalty to the client."

4. Francisco Forrest Martin, *The International Human Rights & Ethical Aspects of the Forum Non Conveniens Doctrine*, 35 U. Miami Inter-Am. L. Rev. 101, 118–119 (2003–04). Martin suggests that a defense counsel may be criminally liable for making a *forum non conveniens* motion if counsel knows that the plaintiffs would be at risk for grave harm from the defendant upon return to a foreign forum. *Id.* at 120.

on a bus in northern Israel. The attack, hostage-taking, and subsequent events resulted in 34 deaths and 87 injuries. The Israeli survivors brought an action for damages in the U.S. District Court for the District of Columbia alleging jurisdiction under the Alien Tort Claims Act. The federal district court ruled that it lacked jurisdiction over the claim. Plaintiffs appealed and the U.S. Circuit Court of Appeals for the District of Columbia affirmed *per curiam* with each member of the panel writing a separate opinion.

At this juncture, the attorneys for the plaintiffs were encouraged not to seek a review by the Supreme Court. If the Supreme Court granted a hearing, affirmance of dismissal was inevitable and likely to be accompanied by strong language undermining *Filartiga v. Pena–Irala*, the most important decision of the past thirty years applying international human rights law in the courts of the United States. One of the attorneys for the plaintiffs responded to this advice by saying that he had only a duty to his client and no ethical responsibility for the favorable development of the law.

Id. at 245–47.

Should a human rights lawyer ever limit a client's ability to resolve a case on terms the individual wishes to accept, when doing so would adversely affect the larger human rights cause?[5] Is it appropriate to question a potential client about such issues before agreeing to representation? Can a lawyer insist on a provision in a retainer agreement allowing for withdrawal if the client asks the lawyer to conduct the case in a manner which the lawyer thinks is detrimental to the human rights movement? Is it ever appropriate to view individual plaintiffs as symbols or representatives of the larger movement? What if plaintiffs see themselves that way? What if they change their mind?

Several ABA rules may provide lawyers with some guidance on these issues. Model Rule of Professional Conduct ("MRPC") 1.7(a)(2) forbids the representation of a client if "there is a significant risk that the representation of one or more clients will be materially limited by the lawyer's responsibilities to another client, a former client or a third person or by a *personal interest* of the lawyer." (emphasis added). Note 8 to MRPC 1.7 states that "a conflict of interest exists if there is a significant risk that a lawyer's ability to consider, recommend or carry out an appropriate course of action for the client will be materially limited as a result of the lawyer's other responsibilities or interests."

Model Code of Professional Responsibility ("MCPR") EC 5–21 states, "A lawyer subject to outside pressures should make full disclosure

---

5. MODEL RULES OF PROF'L CONDUCT R 1.2(a) (2003) states that "A lawyer shall abide by a client's decision whether to settle a matter." However, 1.2(c) states "A lawyer may limit the scope of the representation if the limitation is reasonable under the circumstances and the client gives informed consent." Comment [6] to the rule explains, "The scope of services to be provided by a lawyer may be limited by agreement with the client or by the terms under which the lawyer's services are made available to the client. * * * In addition, the terms upon which representation is undertaken may exclude specific means that might otherwise be used to accomplish the client's objectives. Such limitations may exclude actions that * * * the lawyer regards as repugnant or imprudent."

of them to his client; and if he or his client believes that the effectiveness of his representation has been or will be impaired thereby, the lawyer should take proper steps to withdraw from representation of his client." On the other hand, MPCR EC 7–9 states, "In the exercise of his professional judgment on those decisions which are for his determination in the handling of a legal matter, a lawyer should always act in a manner consistent with the best interests of his client. However, when an action in the best interest of his client seems to him to be unjust, he may ask his client for permission to forego such action."[6]

Do these rules help you to answer these questions? Is the answer to these dilemmas for a lawyer to limit his/her representation based on full disclosure to the client at the outset of the representation as under MRPC 1.2(c)?

Human rights organizations v. human rights plaintiffs' lawyers: conflicting interests?

Recently, lawyers in ATS cases have begun the controversial practice of subpoenaing records of human rights organizations like Amnesty International ("AI") and Human Rights Watch ("HRW") seeking evidence. When such human rights organizations have published reports on the events giving rise to the lawsuit, the parties seek discovery of the names of witnesses and other relevant information.

These organizations have resisted subpoenas arguing that they should receive something akin to a journalist's shield law privilege for their human rights investigation and reporting. Much of the investigation done by human rights organizations like AI and HRW requires assurances of confidentiality because of the potential of retaliation against whistleblowers. For a discussion of the reporter's privilege in the human rights context, *see* Daniel Joyce, *The Judith Miller Case and the Relationship Between Reporter and Source: Competing Visions of the Media's Role and Function,* 17 FORDHAM INTELL. PROP. MEDIA & ENT. L.J. 555, 580–87 (2007) (discussing use of the reporter's privilege in the European Court of Human Rights and international criminal law tribunals). *See also Lonegan v. Hasty,* No. CV–04–2743 (NG)(VVP), 2008 WL 41445 (E.D.N.Y. 2008) (applying reporter's privilege to defendant's subpoena on Amnesty International in a non-ATS case).

To date, the subpoena controversy has not been discussed in reported opinions, but there have been a variety of *ad hoc* solutions and rulings regarding this dilemma. Generally, human rights organizations have not received complete protection from disclosure, but those seeking the information have not received full answers to their requests.

If you assume that all parties to these controversies are acting in good faith and have legitimate interests, how would you resolve this

---

6. Note 3 to EC 7–1 states: "Any persuasion or pressure on the advocate which deters him from planning and carrying out the litigation on the basis of 'what, within the framework of the law, is best for my client's interest?' interferes with the obligation to represent the client fully within the law * * * [T]he lawyer is hired to win, and if he does not exercise every legitimate effort on his client's behalf, then he is betraying a sacred trust."

dilemma? If you are a lawyer representing human rights victims and believe that an NGO has information useful to your client's case, do you have a duty to seek that information? Would it violate your duty of zealous advocacy not to seek all relevant information? How does a human rights plaintiffs' lawyer weigh the interests of her clients against the interests of human rights non-governmental organizations, on whom she is dependent for unbiased information?

Do you think human rights organizations like AI have a moral duty to human rights victims to cooperate with plaintiffs' lawyers in ATS cases and to provide relevant materials, under a protective order if necessary, to advance the cause of human rights? How should NGOs balance this duty with their responsibility to protect witnesses' confidentiality? Is it appropriate for the organizations to decide that their investigative and reporting efforts are more important to the human rights movement than the success of a particular ATS case? Should the courts be the ultimate arbiters of this conflict? Can you craft a solution to this dilemma?

NOTES AND QUESTIONS RE ATS LITIGATION ISSUES

1. *Providing a forum for plaintiffs' stories.* Several plaintiffs in ATS cases have discussed the therapeutic benefits of going through a trial. According to Juan Romagoza, a Salvadoran torture survivor, "Being involved in [the ATS case], confronting the generals with these terrible facts—that's the best possible therapy a torture survivor could have." Sandra Coliver, *et al*; *Holding Human Rights Violators Accountable By Using International Law in U.S. Courts: Advocacy Efforts and Complementary Strategies*, 119 EMORY INT'L L. REV. 169, 180 (2005). For these plaintiffs, the trial provides a forum where their story may be acknowledged and a place where their perpetrators no longer have power over them. Human rights lawyers should also be mindful of the potential for the re-traumatization of human rights victims as a result of confronting their persecutors. What measures can lawyers take to tend to the emotional needs of human rights victims during the course of litigation? Are they under an ethical obligation to take these measures?

2. *Protective orders and defendants' rights.* Consider the following argument:

> While a detailed protective order and a special master may be beneficial, in the U.S. judicial system a defendant's right to pursue discoverable material and prepare a defense may well put in jeopardy the lives of plaintiffs suing under the ATCA. * * * From the outset, plaintiffs' attorneys should make their clients aware of both this potential problem and the limits on a U.S. court's capacity to enforce even those conditions that a given protective order stipulates. A well-crafted protective order can and must ensure that

defendants have access to information they need to prepare their defense. By the same token, protective orders—of which pseudonymity is sometimes an essential component—help to mitigate the "fear of harm [that] may chill a claimant's willingness to resort to the courts."

Jed Greer, *Comment, Plaintiff Pseudonymity and the Alien Tort Claims Act: Question and Challenges*, 32 COLUM. HUM. RTS. L. REV. 517, 559, 561–62 (2001). In light of the inability of the judicial system to provide adequate assurances to plaintiffs, how should lawyers handle cases that are too dangerous to bring?

3. *Anonymous plaintiffs and defendants' rights.* So far, no court has denied a plaintiff's request for anonymity in an ATS case. *But see Estate of Rodriguez v. Drummond Co., Inc.*, 256 F. Supp. 2d 1250 (N.D. Ala. 2003) (district court lacked jurisdiction over unnamed plaintiffs who did not seek leave to proceed anonymously before employing pseudonyms). Are defendants placed at an unfair disadvantage during discovery if plaintiffs are granted this protection? If so, how should these competing interests be reconciled? Is it appropriate to allow plaintiffs to maintain their anonymity in a public trial?

4. *Balancing zealous human rights advocacy with the risk of sanctions.* How far may lawyers go in advocating the application of international law when it conflicts with established domestic law? Do they risk sanctions in such cases? The United States' 1986 bombing of Libya resulted in two hundred civilian injuries and deaths. In response, plaintiffs sued, alleging that the U.S. and the U.K. had intentionally targeted civilian areas "to 'terrorize' the civilian population of Libya to the point of revolt against [its] government" in violation of international law. *Saltany v. Reagan*, 702 F.Supp. 319, 320 (D.D.C. 1988). The district court dismissed the case finding that all of the defendants had sovereign immunity. *Id.* at 320–22. However, it denied defendant's motion for Rule 11 sanctions, reasoning that the injuries "are not insubstantial" and that "the courts of the United States * * * serve in some respects as a forum for making [statements of protest], and should continue to do so." *Id.* at 322. On appeal, the D.C. Circuit found plaintiffs' lawyers sanctionable under Rule 11, stating, "[W]e do not see how filing a complaint that plaintiffs' attorneys surely knew had no hope whatsoever of success can be anything but a violation of Rule 11." *Saltany v. Reagan*, 886 F.2d 438, 440 (D.C. Cir. 1989) (internal quotations omitted).

A court may find a Rule 11 violation when it determines that a pleading is neither "well grounded in fact" nor "warranted by existing law or a good faith argument for the extension, modification, or reversal of existing law," or when it determines that the pleading was interposed for an "improper purpose, such as to harass or to cause unnecessary delay or needless increase in the cost of litigation." Was the Court of Appeals correct to impose sanctions in *Saltany*? Does the district court's opinion that "the case offered no hope whatsoever of success and plaintiffs' attorney surely knew it," satisfy the required findings for Rule 11 sanctions? To arrive at its conclusion that sanctions were warranted, the Court of Appeals relied on *Argentine Republic v. Amerada Hess Shipping Corp.*, 488 U.S. 428, 439 (1989), which states that the FSIA provides "the sole basis for obtaining jurisdiction over a foreign state in our courts." Should this preclude plaintiffs from making the argument that Congress never intended this immunity to extend to war crimes? How do such areas of law become defined if cases are not permitted to test the outer boundaries of the established rules?

In *Halperin v. Kissinger*, 606 F.2d 1192 (D.C. Cir. 1979), plaintiff brought suit against Henry Kissinger, President Nixon's National Security Advisor, and other federal officials upon discovering that his phone had been tapped for over a year. The D.C. Circuit held that officials making adjudicative and prosecutorial decisions had absolute immunity from civil suit. *Id.* at 1208. In *Schneider v. Kissinger*, 412 F.3d 190 (D.C. Cir. 2005) plaintiffs sued Kissinger and the United States for the kidnaping, torture, and death of their father during the United States' successful attempt to topple the democratically elected government of Chilean President Salvador Allende, which lead to the repressive rule of Augusto Pinochet. The court determined that the political question doctrine precluded a suit against the former National Security Advisor for his alleged participation in Chile's military coup.

What effect do these precedents have on present-day suits brought against the President or Secretary of Defense for their alleged participation in approving torture? Should plaintiffs be barred from making the legal argument that the power to make adjudicative and prosecutorial decisions does not include the power to torture? Should they be barred from arguing that the political question doctrine does not prevent courts from adjudicating cases involving violations of international law? Do decisions such as these prevent attorneys from filing legitimate cases that allege violations of international law?[7]

---

3. ETHICAL ISSUES IN HUMAN RIGHTS CLASS ACTIONS

BETH VAN SCHAACK, UNFULFILLED PROMISE: THE HUMAN RIGHTS CLASS ACTION
2003 U. CHI. LEGAL F. 279 (2003)

A. The Theoretical Advantages Of The Class Action Mechanism In Human Rights Litigation

Using the Rule 23 mechanism in the human rights context offers litigants many of the same advantages available in mass tort, civil rights,

---

7. *See* Anthony D'Amato, *The Imposition of Attorney Sanctions for Claims Arising Under the U.S. Air Raid on Libya*, 84 AM. J. INT'L L. 705, 706 (1990) ("The imposition of sanctions casts a serious chilling effect upon all attorneys who engage in international human rights litigation."); *see also* Harold Hongju Koh, *The Human Face of the Haitian Interdiction Program*, 33 VA. J. INT'L L. 483, 485 (1993) ("The government * * * demanded that we post a $10,000,000 bond * * * Rule 11 sanctions run against both the clients and the lawyers personally, which gave us considerable concern.").

and other more standard collective actions. These include the ability to pool resources to pursue the action; the ability of plaintiffs to obtain the same "economies of scale" enjoyed by defendants litigating common issues; the reduction of discovery, motion practice, and other pretrial procedures; the opportunity for a single judge to familiarize herself with the entire dispute; the need to litigate defenses only once; the need to obtain personal jurisdiction over the defendant only once; the ability of non-named members of the class to avoid exhaustion requirements; the enhanced chance of a global settlement or of receiving attorneys' fees through the creation of a common fund; and increased visibility for the case. * * *

[There are several reasons that] the unique nature of human rights claims and the predicaments and objectives of human rights claimants lend themselves, at least theoretically, to class treatment. * * *

1. *A mechanism to expose and redress systemic harms*

The class action mechanism has the potential to give force to grievances about government or corporate practices and policies that violate human rights on a collective scale. Adopting an expansive conception of the causes of the harm alleged by members of the class facilitates the discovery and disclosure of a pattern of wrongdoing, perhaps not readily apparent from singular or scattered cases. This allows for a more accurate assessment of the systemic harm done to a group and can potentially generate more effective remedies to address class-wide injuries, thus ensuring symmetry between substantive rights and available remedies. * * *

Moreover, proceeding as a class action may generate a powerful deterrent effect. Particularly with respect to human rights cases against corporations, class treatment may be necessary to create "optimum incentives" for multinational corporations to take due care in arranging for project security, providing weapons and other materiel to host governments, protecting the environment in which they are operating, and designing and implementing offshore personnel policies—all issues that have served as the basis for cases against corporate entities. * * *

4. *A vehicle for class-wide injunctive or other equitable relief*

The most obvious objective of a civil case brought by victims of human rights violations—whether as an individual suit or as a class action—is to secure a monetary judgment, recognizing, however, that a victim of grave human rights violations may never receive full compensation for the harm suffered. Beyond compensation for past harms, human rights claimants may also seek injunctive relief, including changes in corporate policies or implementation of remedial measures, such as an environmental cleanup or medical monitoring. Likewise, human rights claimants may seek, via declaratory relief, a public and judicial acknowledgment of the violation of particular rights and the illegality of a particular course of conduct. * * *

5. A basis for negotiation.

Class members may use litigation and any judicial pronouncements as "bargaining chips" in seeking a negotiated solution or structural reform. The class action device places victims of human rights abuses in a powerful litigation posture that may enable the class to operate on a corporate or diplomatic level with a degree of political power generally unavailable to individual claimants. For example, the Marcos jury award factored into the negotiations between the Swiss banks holding Marcos' assets and the new government of the Republic of the Philippines. The Swiss banks ultimately agreed to transfer the funds to the Philippines, but a Filipino court, facing objections from members of the class, rejected the settlement because it benefitted the lawyers and Marcos' Estate, but not the victims.

6. The lack of other options for redress.

A community of human rights victims may find proceeding as a class desirable because representative justice may provide the only possible justice for victims of a particular policy or individual. Substantial barriers exist for human rights plaintiffs pursuing justice independently. Victims often lack the resources necessary to pursue a claim or lack access to lawyers or to courts able to hear their claims. It may be difficult for multiple plaintiffs to obtain personal jurisdiction over the defendant on more than one occasion. * * * Accordingly, in certain contexts, class treatment may provide the only feasible method of adjudication for the victims of human rights abuses.

For example, at the time the *Marcos* case was filed, Philippine law required a defendant to be served in the situs for a case to proceed. Once Marcos fled to Hawaii, his victims could not obtain justice in the Philippines. Allowing victims based in the Philippines to participate in the class action in U.S. courts ensured that they received some measure of justice. * * *

B. The Disadvantages Of, And Challenges To, Using the Class Mechanism in The Human Rights Context

1. A compromise to claim autonomy.

Human rights class actions invoke the same tension between collective justice and individual autonomy that characterize all class actions. * * * Victims of human rights abuses, like all victims, value having a personal relationship with an advocate and participating directly in a legal process, rather than accessing the legal system through a representative who may be inaccessible or unresponsive to the particulars of an individual plaintiff's case. Adopting a leading role in the litigation enables a plaintiff to commence, frame, and pursue the litigation in accordance with his own interests. Without the opportunity to experience these "process values," a class action may deny victims the full rehabilitative potential of litigation and the sense of satisfaction resulting from the process and the judgment. * * *

   4.   Potential to prevent other forms of accountability or redress.

Although the class action device may place victims in a powerful negotiating position, seeking collective redress through litigation can also release home governments from responsibility in terms of providing non-judicial redress for victims through a social welfare system or by paying government-sponsored reparations. For example, the government of the Republic of the Philippines did not create any sort of truth or claims commission for Marcos' victims because victims would be compensated via the class action. As a result, the government essentially competed with the victims in seeking the return of Marcos' ill-gotten wealth from Swiss banks. Without the potential of a class action judgment, the victims may have been able to exercise more political clout at home to ensure that they were at least partially compensated out of any wealth returned to the Philippines.

   5.   Difficulties in allocating compensation.

In a human rights class action where the plaintiff class seeks money damages, the wide variations in plaintiffs' experiences and the extreme nature of the abuses suffered present a challenge to ascertaining a reasonable and acceptable model for allocating compensatory damages. The highly individualized and personal nature of the claims in human rights cases suggests that successful litigants should receive a particularized process to determine damages. Yet, such a process may be unfeasible where thousands of members belong to a human rights class. A class action, however, can result in the establishment of a quasi-administrative scheme that limits the need to determine individualized damages awards and speeds the payment of compensation to individuals. * * *

In addition to the challenges of computing compensatory damages with a large class, intra-class conflicts almost inevitably emerge when seeking relief or allocating damages between different groups of plaintiffs or subclasses. This is especially true where the damages sought involve intangible and individual assessments of pain and suffering, as opposed to the types of damages more amenable to objective proof, such as lost wages or medical costs. Such structural conflicts have tarnished victims' experiences with collective actions. * * *

_____

NOTES AND QUESTIONS RE CLASS ACTION ISSUES

   1.   *Are class actions unsuitable for human rights cases?* Can the individual needs of plaintiffs who have suffered horrific human rights violations ever be adequately addressed by a class action? Are human rights

lawyers committing a disservice to those individuals by grouping them into large classes rather than addressing their individual needs? Should lawyers make an effort to avoid class actions in order to tend to the individual, or do they then risk being able to help fewer people? Do you feel differently about classes that are requesting equitable relief? For a critique of the human rights class action, *see* Paul R. Dubinsky, *Justice for the Collective: The Limits of the Human Rights Class Action,* 102 MICH. L. REV. 1152 (2004) (book review) (arguing for human-rights-specific procedural rules), and Kevin R. Johnson, *International Human Rights Class Actions: New Frontiers for Group Litigation,* MICH. ST. L. REV. 643, 658 (2004) (discussing the ethical difficulties involved in human rights class actions).

2. *Inadequacy of individual cases?* What ethical obligations do human rights lawyers have when they take a non-class action case where only a few individuals among thousands will have the opportunity to obtain legal redress? In these situations, the claims of others may have been barred on technical grounds, or the victims may not have known about the lawsuit. Do human rights lawyers have any professional ethical duties to the non-plaintiff victims? Do they have moral duties?

3. *Putting human rights victims on equal footing?* Can an individual plaintiff with few resources realistically bring enough pressure to maintain litigation against very powerful opponents? Is the class mechanism the only threat sufficient to put plaintiffs on level playing field with defendants? With the limited NGO resources available to human rights victims, is it practical to think that the millions of human rights victims in the world could be represented by the existing *pro bono* or non-profit sector of the bar?

4. *Rule 23 safeguards.* Group litigation occurs both domestically and internationally. In the domestic sphere, Federal Rule of Civil Procedure 23 (governing class actions) requires that to pursue group (*i.e.* class) litigation: (1) the class be so numerous that joinder of all members is impracticable; (2) there are questions of law or fact common to the class; (3) the claims or defenses of the representative parties are typical of the claims or defenses of the class; and (4) the representative parties will fairly and adequately protect the interest of the class. Does Rule 23 adequately anticipate or resolve the concerns raised in international group litigation? Consider the following argument:

> [T]he commonality requirement would only permit claims that share common questions of law or fact. The typicality requirement would ensure that class representatives have a sufficient interest in the matter and would justify their representation of other victims. * * * The adequacy of representation requirement would further enhance these protections by ensuring that the class representatives and their counsel were capable of litigating the case.

William J. Aceves, *Actio Popularis? The Class Action in International Law,* 2003 U. CHI. LEGAL F. 353, 399 (2003).

B. PROFESSIONAL RESPONSIBILITY IN THE INTERNATIONAL ARENA

With the proliferation of international tribunals, a transnational conception of professional ethics has begun to emerge. In this section, we examine the Rules of Responsibility and Codes of Conduct in the international criminal tribunals, focusing specifically on the obligations of counsel. Next, we contemplate some of the ethical issues that arise when representing clients before the United Nations, particularly under the 1503 Procedure. Finally, we take a closer look at the lawyer-client relationship in the context of litigation before regional human rights commissions.

As you read the following excerpts, consider the implications for lawyers practicing before international tribunals, like the ad hoc international criminal tribunals for the former Yugoslavia (ICTY) and Rwanda (ICTR) and the permanent International Criminal Court (ICC). What ethical conundrums might lawyers face when confronted with rules in their home state that conflict with those of the tribunal in which they are litigating?

---

1. RULES OF PROFESSIONAL RESPONSIBILITY AND CODES OF CONDUCT AT THE INTERNATIONAL CRIMINAL TRIBUNALS

Given the seriousness of the crimes prosecuted before the *ad hoc* international criminal tribunals and the International Criminal Court, the rules governing the conduct by lawyers must ensure the highest degree of fairness and professional responsibility. If the decisions of the tribunals are to be respected, both the victims and accused must be assured due process and impartial treatment.

But in these tribunals, attorneys, judges, and prosecutors from many nations come together under an international legal rubric to mete out justice. At this meeting point of international jurists, the rules of professional conduct from various countries invariably collide. What may bind an attorney from the United States may cause counsel from the European Union to commit an ethical violation. When codes conflict, the tribunals' rules of professional responsibility dictate that they prevail over any particular counsel's national obligations.

The ICTY and ICTR Rules of Procedure and Evidence ("RPE")[1] and Codes of Professional Conduct for Defense Counsel[2] are well-

---

1. http://www.un.org/icty/legaldoc-e/basic/rpe/IT032Rev41eb.pdf (updated Feb. 2008 revision); http://69.94.11.53/ENGLISH/rules/080314/080314.pdf.(updated Mar. 2008).

2. http://www.un.org/icty/legaldoc-e/basic/counsel/IT125–Rev2e.pdf (June 2006). For a case study on attorney conduct and the ICTY see Judith A. McMorrow, *Creating Norms of Attorney*

established and, nearly identical. On December 2, 2005, the Assembly of States' Parties to the ICC adopted the Code of Professional Conduct for Counsel.[3] Two working groups comprised of States Parties to the ICC led the drafting effort, while human rights NGOs, lawyers' associations, and defense organizations familiar with the proceedings at the ICTY and ICTR were given an opportunity to comment on the draft code. Human rights organizations noted their concern with the ICC Draft Code's treatment of confidential information, which states, in part, that counsel are forbidden from divulging crimes or perceived threats to victims or witnesses—which, they point out, differs from the rule for the *ad hoc* tribunals. At the International Criminal Tribunal for the former Yugoslavia (ICTY), for example, counsel may disclose confidential client information "to prevent an act which counsel reasonably believes: (i) is, or may be, criminal within the territory in which it may occur or under the Statute or the Rules; and (ii) may result in death or substantial bodily harm to any person unless the information is disclosed."[4]

Although based on the experience of the *ad hoc* tribunals, the ICC Code differs from the *ad hoc* tribunals in its treatment of misconduct by counsel. Unlike the *ad hoc* tribunals, the ICC subjects all counsel to its rules of professional responsibility and conduct, not just defense counsel. The ICTY, and to an even greater extent, the ICC, have established formal and permanent enforcement bodies, with investigative panels, complaint procedures, hearings, findings and sanctions.

Ultimately, the success of the tribunals depends on the real and perceived effectiveness of the chambers' administration of justice. To the extent that the chambers are able to punish unethical conduct—threats, intimidation, dishonesty—the rules upholding ethical behavior will be one measure of their institutional legitimacy.

The rules governing professional responsibility and standards of conduct of counsel appearing before the ICTY and the ICTR are set forth in two documents. First, the Rules of Procedure and Evidence ("Rules") lay out the qualifications necessary to appear before the Tribunal. The Rules also regulate attorney misconduct, set up procedures for contempt of court and describe the attorney-client privilege. Second, the Codes of Professional Conduct for Defense Counsel ("Codes"), promulgated by the Registrars of the ICTY and ICTR, establish detailed rules of conduct for defense counsel vis-à-vis their clients, witnesses, the Tribunal, and other counsel, *inter alia*. The Codes rely heavily on the American Bar Association Model Rules of Professional Conduct ("ABA Rules") and largely reflect the principles codified in those rules.

Conduct in International Tribunals: A Case Study of the ICTY, available at http://isr.nellco.org/bc/bc/spf/papers/194.

3. ICC code of professional conduct: *available at* http://www.icc-cpi.int/library/about/official journal/ICC–ASP–4–32–Res.1_English.pdf.

4. *See* Article 13(C) of the Code of Professional Conduct for Counsel Appearing before the International Tribunal (ICTY, 2002), *available at* http://www.un.org/icty/legaldoc-e/index.htm.

The Role of Clients—The international tribunals' codes of conduct all contemplate an active and assertive role for the client in the litigation.[5]

Confidences—What if a client confides an intent to threaten or plan to "dispose" of a witness—must an attorney disclose that information to the tribunal? Counsel for clients before the *ad hoc* tribunals must preserve a client's confidences and may not reveal to any person "information which has been entrusted to him in confidence" except in any of the following circumstances:

(1) when the client has been fully consulted and knowingly consents;

(ii) when the client has voluntarily disclosed the content of the communication to a third party;

(iii) when essential to establish a claim or defense on behalf of counsel in a controversy between counsel and the client, or to prevent an act which is or may be criminal within the territory in which it may occur; or

(iv) may result in death or substantial bodily harm to any person unless the information is disclosed.

The ICC, on the other hand, does not allow counsel to reveal confidential information, even if failure to do so would result in the commission of a crime or substantial bodily harm or death. Critics have pointed out that most of the world's legal systems have an exception that permits lawyers to divulge information in order to prevent serious bodily harm. Such a provision is particularly important for the ICC given the kinds of defendants brought before the court, the severity of the crimes with which they are charged, and the resources that many of these defendants have at their disposal to ensure that witnesses do not cooperate with the prosecution.[6]

Conflict of Interest—Like the mandates of the United States' ABA Rules, counsel appearing before the tribunals are forbidden from representing a client where a conflict of interest exists. Counsel owes a duty of loyalty to her client and must at all times act in the best interest of the

---

5. When representing a client, the codes instruct that counsel shall (i) abide by the client's decisions concerning the objectives of representation; and (ii) consult with the client about the means by which those objectives are to be pursued. ICTY Code, Art. 8(B); ICTR Code, Art. 4(2); ICC Code, Art. 14(2). Furthermore, counsel must not advise or assist a client to engage in conduct that is illegal or violates the Rules or Codes. ICTY Code, Art. 8(C), ICTR Code, Art. 4(3); ICC Code, Art. 22(4). Other common dictates found in the tribunals' codes are that counsel act with competence, integrity and independence; ICTY Code, Art. 10; ICTR Code, Art. 5; ICC Code, Art. 5, diligence; ICTY Code, Art. 11; ICTR Code, Art. 6; ICC Code, Art. 5, and keep the client informed of the status of the matter before the tribunal and promptly respond to requests for information. ICTY Code, Art. 12; ICTR Code, Art. 7; ICC Code, Art. 15.

6. Human Rights First, *Ensuring Ethical Representation: Comments on the Draft Code of Professional Conduct for counsel Before the International Criminal Courts*, 13 (Nov. 2004), *available at* http://www.humanrightsfirst.org/international_justice/pdf/icc-ethics-report–120304.pdf. *See also* Coments on the Draft Code of Professional Conduct for Counsel before the International Criminal Court, *available at*: http://www.humanrightsfirst.info/pdf/051129–ij-hrf-icc-ethics.pdf.

client and put those interests before her own or those of any other person. ICTY Code, Art. 14, ICTR Code, Art. 9; ICC Code, Art. 16.

Article 18 of the ICTR regulates the communications between counsel and *pro se* defendants or otherwise unrepresented persons. Under this Rule, counsel is forbidden from giving advice to the unrepresented person if that person's interests are, or may with a reasonable probability be, in conflict with those of counsel's client. However, counsel may give advice in order to become retained by that person. Further, counsel must inform the unrepresented person—regardless of whether a conflict exists—of his or her role in the matter, about the rules entitling persons to legal representation, and how legal representation works generally.

Finally, counsel may not engage in fee-splitting arrangements with their clients, relatives and/or agents of their clients.[7] If a client requests, induces or encourages counsel to enter into such an agreement, counsel shall advise their clients of the prohibition of such an arrangement and report the incident to the Registrar of the tribunal immediately.

Obligation of Counsel to Tribunals—The tribunals set forth specific behavior expected of counsel appearing before the Tribunal. For instance, counsel has a duty of candor toward the Tribunal and must comply with the Rules and have due respect for the proceedings. Counsel are specifically and personally charged with "exercis[ing] personal judgement" in presenting the case and making submissions. Counsel is also prohibited from "knowingly" making a false submission of material fact. If such a submission occurs, counsel must correct the record as soon as possible.

The codes of all three tribunals set forth general principles which require counsel to conduct themselves professionally by acting fairly, honestly and courteously in relations with the Chamber, the Prosecutor, the Registrar, the client, opposing counsel, accused persons, victims, witnesses and, any other person involved in the proceedings.

Disciplinary Regime—Each of the tribunal Codes provides for enforcement of its respective code of professional conduct. Both the ICTY and ICC establish disciplinary bodies to investigate and prosecute misconduct, including punishing such conduct with sanctions such as suspension from practice, public reprimand, fines, and banning from practice before the Tribunal. The disciplinary decisions of these tribunals may be appealed. Similarly, the ICC Code provides that "any person or group of persons whose rights or interests may have been affected by the alleged misconduct" may submit a complaint against counsel to the Registry. ICC Code, Art. 34(1).

Prosecutor's Professional Responsibility—Interestingly, neither the RPE nor Codes of the *ad hoc* Tribunals, nor the ICC Code, enumerate the Prosecutor's ethical and professional duties. Historically, this has

---

7. *See* ICTY Code, Art. 18; ICTR Code, Art. 5 *bis*.

been because the Office of the Prosecutor is independent of the other organs of the Tribunals. Once the Prosecutor and the staff are appointed, they are largely unregulated by the Tribunal or by the Security Council for the duration of each of their renewable four-year terms. Based in part on this lack of formal regulation, the Prosecutor promulgated "Standards of Professional Conduct for Prosecution Counsel," in September, 1999. *See* Prosecutor's Reg. No. 2 ¶ 1 (1999). Prosecution counsel who fail to abide by the standards are subject to discipline by the Office of the Prosecutor and also to sanctions under the Rules of Evidence and Procedure.

NOTES AND QUESTIONS ON PROFESSIONAL OBLIGATIONS IN INTERNATIONAL TRIBUNALS

1. *Disclosure of confidential information.* Unlike the *ad hoc* tribunals, counsel appearing before the ICC are prohibited from disclosing confidential information even if doing so would prevent serious bodily harm or death. This was of great concern to human rights organizations who argued that the legitimacy of the Court would be jeopardized if its ethics code did not authorize disclosure when necessary to protect lives or prevent serious injury.[8] Their concern is far from theoretical. In the late 1990s, Time Magazine reported that scores of potential witnesses in cases before the ICTR had been killed, and many more had been seriously threatened. As many as 40 potential witnesses were murdered in June 1996 alone. "It is a big problem for us," said one Tribunal prosecutor in Kigali. "There are people who know names and details but are too afraid to speak." What values are protected by ensuring that client confidences are maintained even in the face of threats of bodily harm and death? What institutional security is furthered or deteriorated by protection of such disclosures? What effect will non-disclosure of threats have on prospective witnesses' willingness to testify?

2. *Rules of conduct.* The various tribunals all assert that their rules of conduct and procedure trump any conflicting rules counsel may be bound by in their home countries. As a practical matter, what are the consequences of counsel disregarding the rules of ethics and conduct they have sworn to uphold? Must counsel violate their home state's rules in favor of the international tribunals' rules when there is a conflict?

3. *Rules relating to fees.* Under the Rome Statute, victims are free to choose their own legal representative so long as the attorney is suitably

---

8. Kenneth D. Hurwitz, Human Rights First, *Comments on the Draft Code of Professional Conduct for Counsel Before the International Criminal Court*, Nov. 26, 2005, *available at* http://www.humanrights first.info/pdf/051129–ij-hrf-icc-ethics.pdf; *see also* Coalition for the International Criminal Court, *Comments on Article 22 of the Draft Code of Professional Conduct for Counsel acting before the ICC*, November 2005, *available at* http://www.iccnow.org/documents/LR_article22_teampaper_Nov05.pdf? PHPSESSID=7fd8d013ff7e0d693bd4b83e0c1d8e42 arguing that Article 22(3) to (5), which requires counsel to denounce their client to the Registrar if the client proposes to engage in a fee-splitting agreement with them, violates lawyer-client confidentiality and impeded the relationship of trust between counsel and her client).

qualified, fluent in one of the ICC's official languages, and on the list of counsel authorized to act before the Court. Should counsel representing victims of crimes at the ICC be allowed to enter into contingent fee representation agreements with clients? Such agreements violate the well-established proscription against contingent fee agreements in criminal cases, which stems from public policy concerns against creating a financial incentive to prosecute people or collect evidence on a basis that creates an incentive to solicit perjury. Yet, given the low economic status of many such victims, should they be allowed to choose counsel they could not otherwise afford? Should human rights lawyers be allowed to solicit victim/witness clients who would not otherwise be able to find counsel? How would such a change affect defendants' rights to fair trial?

4. *Why do the rules of professional conduct apply only to defense counsel at the ad hoc tribunals?* Should prosecutors be subject to rules of professional conduct as well as sanctions for violating such rules? Who should enforce such misconduct given the necessity of independence of the prosecutor from the tribunal itself? What political accountability do prosecutors have to the Security Council? Is that sufficient deterrence from misconduct?

In *Prosecutor v. Aleksovski,* the ICTY was asked to determine whether defense counsel had committed an ethical violation that would have subjected him to contempt for inadvertently disclosing the name of a protected witness. As you read the following case, consider whether the court came to the right decision based on the applicable standard.

Prosecutor v. Zlatko Aleksovski, IT–95–14/1, Judgment on Appeal by Anto Nobilo Against Finding of Contempt (May 30, 2001)

1. Introduction

1. Mr. Anto Nobilo has appealed by leave from the decision of a Trial Chamber that he had acted in contempt of the Tribunal, by having disclosed information relating to proceedings in the trial of Zlatko Aleksovski before that Trial Chamber in "knowing violation" of an order which it had made prohibiting the disclosure of that information. * * *

2. The background
   * * *

3. When the protected witness was called by the prosecution in the *Aleksovski* trial, the Trial Chamber was informed by the prosecution that the witness sought to have the image of his face on the video recording distorted and to be referred to by way of a pseudonym. The prosecution also requested that the blinds between the body of the courtroom and the public be lowered whilst the witness gave his evidence. Counsel for Aleksovski (Mr. Mikulicic) said that he had no objection to the protective measures requested by the prosecution.

4.   Witness K was examined and cross-examined in open session concerning his preparation of the map showing the deployment of various belligerent forces in the Lava Valley area in Bosnia and Herzegovina in early 1993, and it was tendered by the prosecution. * * *

9.   At the instigation of Witness K, the Embassy for Bosnia and Herzegovina in The Hague brought these events to the notice of the Prosecutor and of the Registrar of the Tribunal. Thereafter, the prosecution filed a motion * * * [and] identified Rule 77(A)(iii) as stating the offence which *prima facie* had been committed, which at that time relevantly provided:

> Any person who * * * discloses information relating to those proceedings in knowing violation of an order of a Chamber ... commits a contempt of the Tribunal.

3.   *The contempt proceedings*

12.   Mr. Nobilo said that * * * he was focusing on the map. He had had no idea that the witness had been granted protective measures. In hindsight, he said, he probably should have, but in any event he had thought of him as an expert witness, whereas typically it is the victims who are granted protective measures. He had acted *bona fide*. No-one in the courtroom had told him that the witness was protected. He had had no motive to reveal the witness' identity, as his identity was immaterial. Mr. Nobilo also raised his character as indicating that it is unlikely that he would have done this deliberately. * * *

7.   *Analysis*

Actual Knowledge

42.   * * * The question remains, however, whether "knowing" in that expression implies that *actual* knowledge is required before a contempt may be found.

45.   Mere negligence in failing to ascertain whether an order had been made granting protective measures to a particular witness could never amount to such conduct. * * * At the other end of the spectrum, wilful blindness to the existence of the order in the sense defined is, in the opinion of the Appeals Chamber, sufficiently culpable conduct to be more appropriately dealt with as contempt.

48.   * * * The Appeals Chamber does not accept the prosecution's argument that the Trial Chamber should have found that Mr. Nobilo had *actual* knowledge of the order.

Wilful blindness

51.   The Appeals Chamber does not accept that these circumstances constituted wilful blindness on the part of Mr. Nobilo as to the existence of the order. The prosecution accepts that he had been told that the map in question was a public document presented in open session. * * * If the witness in question were a victim, it could perhaps

be argued that counsel experienced in the Tribunal's practices would be aware of the risk that there will be an order granting protective measures to that witness. But Witness K was not a victim. Mr. Nobilo described him as an expert giving evidence for the prosecution. This was not disputed. Although some such witnesses may have been given the benefit of protective measures orders, it is not immediately apparent why protective measures would usually be needed for them, and there is no reason to suspect that all such witnesses may be the subject of such orders. There can be no wilful blindness to the existence of an order unless there is first of all shown to be a suspicion or a realisation that the order exists.

Intention to Violate or Disregard Order

54. In most cases where it has been established that the alleged contemnor had knowledge of the existence of the order (either *actual* knowledge or a wilful blindness of its existence), a finding that he intended to violate it would almost necessarily follow. There may, however, be cases where such an alleged contemnor acted with reckless indifference as to whether his act was in violation of the order. In the opinion of the Appeals Chamber, such conduct is sufficiently culpable to warrant punishment as contempt, even though it does not establish a specific intention to violate the order. The Appeals Chamber agrees with the prosecution that it is sufficient to establish that the act which constituted the violation was deliberate and not accidental. It was therefore unnecessary for the Trial Chamber to have found that the result which Mr. Nobilo sought to achieve was a violation of the order.

NOTES AND QUESTIONS ON THE ENFORCEMENT OF PROFESSIONAL STANDARDS

1. *Critiquing the standard for witness protection.* What "knowledge" standard did the court apply? Should it have applied a heightened standard, given the severity of potential ramifications for the witness? Fatema E. Fallahnejad Burkey argues that an "actual knowledge" or "willful blindness" standard undermines the public policy of ensuring witness protection and participation in the tribunals. Consider the following excerpt:

> When an Appeals Chamber decision fails to mention the public policy repercussions of defense counsel's violation of a witness' court-ordered protective status, and overturns a Trial Chamber's decision that punished such an offense, the message to potential witnesses is clear: court-ordered protection is meaningless. Such a decision contravenes the prominent public policy reasons in favor of protecting witnesses and punishing those who offend the judicial process. * * *

> Like the ICTY and the ICTR, the ICC has a special Victims and Witnesses Unit, and provides significant safeguards for their

protection. Unlike the ICTY and ICTR, the ICC places greater responsibility for witness protection on the Registrar, wherein public policy considerations are built into the system. Among the Registrar's responsibilities in the ICC, it must provide witnesses with "adequate protective and security measures and formulate long and short-term plans for their protection," and it must recommend a code of conduct "emphasizing the vital nature of security and confidentiality for investigators of the Court" including defense.

Similarly, "adequate" measures in the ICTY should require specifically that the Registrar give appropriate and timely notice of a witness' protected status in the form of a court directive to counsel. Given clear directions about confidentiality and who is protected, counsel would have no excuse for revealing a protected witness' identity, whether intentional or not. In such a situation, when counsel fails to observe a court directive, he automatically commits misconduct and is subject to civil sanctions.

With a simple amendment akin to the ICC's provisions, the ICTY and ICTR could impose a similar responsibility on the Registrar and thus eliminate the problematic issue of proving actual knowledge or willful blindness. * * * This would send the appropriate message to witnesses that their protective status is taken seriously. As it now stands, the ICC will likely achieve more consistent, public policy-oriented results for witnesses.

Fatema E. Fallahnejad Burkey, *Recent Development: The Prosecutor v. Aleksovski, 30 May 2001, Judgment on Appeal by Anto Nobilo Against Finding of Contempt: A Critical Analysis of the ICTY Appeals Chamber's Abandonment of Witness Protection Measures*, 82 Wash. U. L. Q. 297 (2004).

2. *Higher standards?* Should attorneys who practice before human rights bodies such as the international criminal courts be held to higher standards than other attorneys? Should Mr. Nobilo have taken more precautions before revealing Witness K's identity? Would adopting a "should have known" standard instead of an "actual knowledge" standard provide a more appropriate degree of protection for witnesses in international courts, given the increased risk to their security?

3. *Ongoing v. post-conflict prosecutions.* The conflicts giving rise to the ICTY and ICTR had subsided before the tribunals began their operations, but every single situation the ICC is currently investigating is an ongoing conflict (*e.g.*, Sudan, Democratic Republic of Congo, Central African Republic, Northern Uganda). How might the ongoing nature of these situations affect standards for attorneys and witnesses? Could this difference between the *ad hoc* tribunals and the ICC serve as a strong rationale for advocating more stringent standards? For an interesting article on victim protection challenges and the ICC, *see* Katy Glassborow, *ICC Inquiries Jeapordised*, Institute for War and Peace Reporting, AR No.

70 (July 6, 2006), *available at* http://www.iwpr.net/?p=acr&s=f&o=
322097&apc_state=heniacr2006.

4. *Victims v. perpetrators.* How should the witness and attorney
standards adapt to individuals that straddle the line between victims and
perpetrators? In several of the conflict situations currently under investigation by the ICC, child soldiers were manipulated by those in command to commit gross atrocities against civilians (*e.g.*, DRC, Northern
Uganda). Do these young people deserve lesser protection because of
their complicity in the violations? Are they victims themselves and
thereby, deserving of even more protection because of their youth? See
the redress trust, victims, perpetrators or heroes? Child soldiers before
the international criminal court (2006), *available at* http://www.redress.
org/publications/childsoldiers.pdf.

---

2. ETHICAL ISSUES WHEN REPRESENTING CLIENTS BE-FORE THE UNITED NATIONS

One significant human rights enforcement mechanism in the United Nations system is the Complaints Procedure established under the
new UN Human Rights Council. *See* UN Doc. A/HRC/RES/5/1 (June
2007). The Complaints Procedure was established as the successor to the
"1503 Procedure" of the dissolved Commission on Human Rights,
which derived its name from ECOSOC Resolution 1503.[1] The new
Complaints Procedure, like the 1503 Procedure, permits individuals or
groups to submit a complaint to the Council concerning "situations
which appear to reveal a consistent pattern of gross and reliably attested
human rights." *Id.* However, under the procedures governing the
Complaints Procedure, all actions undertaken in response to these
communications must be kept confidential. Does the confidentiality
requirement impair the ability of counsel to zealously advocate for what
is in the best interests of her client? Can counsel ethically circumvent
this requirement?

DAVID WEISSBRODT, ETHICAL PROBLEMS OF AN INTERNATIONAL HUMAN RIGHTS LAW PRACTICE
7 MICH. Y.B. INT'L LEGAL STUD. 219 (1985)

Resolution 1503 establishes one of the most important international
procedures for the consideration of communications concerning human
rights violations. * * * [It] provides that any communications received
by the United Nations alleging a consistent pattern of gross violations of
human rights shall be considered by the Sub–Commission on Prevention
of Discrimination and Protection of Minorities. * * *

[B]eginning on the date when the communication is submitted until
the very fragmentary announcement of the Commission's decision, the

---

1.   E.S.C. Res. 1503, 48 U.N. ESCOR Supp (No. 1A) at 8, U.N. Doc. E/4832/Add.1 (1970).

complainant-author of the communication is not permitted to know how the communication has been received. In this respect, the Commission closely follows the wording of Resolution 1503 which requires that "all actions envisaged in the implementation of the present resolution * * * shall remain confidential until such time as the Commission may decide to make recommendations to the Economic and Social Council." But while the 1503 process leaves the complainant in the dark, the accused governments are informed and involved at several important points. Indeed, the purpose of the secrecy is obviously to shield the governments from undue or, indeed, nearly any embarrassment—at least until the Chair of the Commission announces the Commission's decision.

In order to be an effective advocate in this rather strange setting, an attorney needs to know whether the government answered the communication, how the government responded, [what referrals were made within the Commission], and the nature of the defense raised by the government. * * * If an attorney knows the status of the complaint, she can effectively lobby for the complainant's position with members of the Sub–Commission. In addition, an informed attorney can press the accused government to agree to a solution that will allow the government to avoid embarrassment. Governments lobby the members of the Sub–Commission throughout the process and often without corresponding lobbying from a complainant's side, his chance of success is diminished. * * *

Despite the rather daunting language of ECOSOC 1503 and considerable effort by responsible UN officials to keep the process secret, most authors of communications are able to obtain information regarding the status of their complaints. * * * Once a member tells anyone about the results of the Sub–Commission's deliberations, word travels fast. * * * With so many governmental delegations, it is likely that the relevant aspects of a particular 1503 proceeding will become known to anyone who attends the Commission sessions and wishes to know the status of a communication.

While it is clear that Resolution 1503 forbids the release of information concerning the progress of a communication alleging a consistent pattern of gross violations of human rights, it is also clear that the prohibition is not efficiently enforced and that lawyers who represent complainants need to and regularly do obtain the information necessary to pursue their claims through the labyrinth of UN bodies. On the one hand, the norm of confidentiality does persist and is prominently mentioned by government representatives at the Commission on Human Rights. On the other hand, it is doubtful that such a loosely and unfairly enforced norm of confidentiality ought to be the basis of any ethical complaint against a U.S. lawyer who breaches this norm. A lawyer cannot properly represent a client without in some way breaching this norm. Accordingly, U.S. lawyers must come to grips with the proper approach to the confidentiality requirement of ECOSOC 1503.

[The creation of the Human Rights Council and its Complaints Procedure in 2007 did not substantively alter the confidentiality requirement or ameliorate its consequences.]

———————

Do you agree with the author? Is this simply an "ends justifying the means" argument? Should lawyers be encouraged to circumvent other inherently unfair and loosely enforced norms to more zealously represent their clients? Or is the author's approach merely an approach based on reality, recognizing that this information is available and that, were a lawyer to choose to ignore it, she would only be harming her client?

———————

3. THE ATTORNEY–CLIENT RELATIONSHIP IN HUMAN RIGHTS LITIGATION BEFORE REGIONAL HUMAN RIGHTS COMMISSIONS

Some human rights litigation is intended to remedy violations of international law that extend far beyond the individual client. Professor Melissa Crow observes that "broader strategic goals such as obtaining constructive judicial articulations of prevailing norms, holding defendants accountable, generating greater public awareness of past abuses, and deterring future abuses are usually paramount in the minds of international human rights lawyers. This hierarchy of priorities may cause all but the most sophisticated clients to feel disengaged from the litigation process unless they fully understand its purpose."[1] This dynamic is particularly characteristic of proceedings before certain regional human rights commissions, such as the Inter–American Commission on Human Rights and the African Commission on Human and Peoples' Rights, which have liberal standing requirements that permit third parties, including non-governmental organizations, to file petitions without the victims' consent. In such cases, there is a danger that the unique needs of the victim group will be disregarded in pursuit of the broader strategic goals described above.

In the following excerpt, Professor Crow argues that in order to provide meaningful representation to the affected victim group before these regional commissions, the traditional lawyer-client relationship must be abandoned in favor of a lawyer-NGO-victim triad "in which the lawyer and the petitioning NGO [which has standing in the Inter–American and African Commissions to bring suit on behalf of third parties] have joint fiduciary obligations to victims, who are the real parties in interest." *Id.* at 1120–21. As you read the excerpt, consider the ethical and practical challenges such a transformation would entail.

———————

1. Melissa E. Crow, *From Dyad to Triad: Reconceptualizing the Lawyer–Client Relationship for Litigation in Regional Human Right Commissions*, 26 MICH. J. INT'L L. 1097, 1099–1100 (2005).

MELISSA E. CROW, FROM DYAD TO TRIAD: RECONCEPTUALIZING THE LAWYER–CLIENT RELATIONSHIP FOR LITIGATION IN REGIONAL HUMAN RIGHTS COMMISSIONS

26 MICH. J. INT'L. L. 1097 (2005)

The proposed fiduciary obligations are targeted to ensure meaningful representation of the affected victim group, however large. At a minimum, they should include duties to obtain free, prior, and informed consent of the victim group before initiating litigation, to keep the victim group apprised of developments as the litigation unfolds, and to incorporate victims' voices into the process. Although these objectives may seem self-evident to domestic litigators, their application to regional human rights litigation, which often spans several countries and involves communities in remote locations without access to e-mail, telephone, or other technology, may be challenging. * * *

In cases where victims are not well-organized, advocates should make a good faith effort to facilitate communication among group members. Where victims' capacity to interact with their advocates is limited due, for example, to minority status, detention, mental disabilities, or security risks, certain objectives may not be fully attainable. However, the advocates' fact-finding methodology should be sufficiently sound to ensure that group members' priorities drive the litigation.

A.   Free, Prior, and Informed Consent.

* * * Obtaining free, prior, and informed consent of victim groups is * * * critical prior to initiating litigation in regional human rights commissions. This practice will help to ensure that victims' rights are not trampled by their representatives, compounding the governmental abuses that gave rise to the litigation. At a minimum, lawyers or petitioning NGOs should be required to apprise the victims, through linguistically and culturally appropriate channels, of the purpose of the proposed litigation, its various stages and their expected duration, the nature and likelihood of available relief, potential negative repercussions, and opportunities for their involvement. In particular, victims should be informed, and reminded as often as necessary, that even if monetary damages are awarded, the prospect of collecting them is minimal in most cases.

[G]roup members should have an opportunity to request additional information or clarification, seek outside advice, and invoke their internal decisionmaking processes outside the presence of their advocates before deciding whether to proceed with the litigation. Such a discussion may also give advocates a more complete picture of the prospect of reprisals by the target government and permit the implementation of appropriate protective measures where necessary. * * * Whatever the outcome of these processes, the decision of the victim group must be respected.

The modalities of effective consultation should be tailored to the needs of the victim group. The lawyer or petitioning NGO might utilize a previously scheduled traditional assembly or town meeting, conduct a house-to-house survey, designate local human rights activists as their proxies, or communicate with the community's freely chosen representatives, who can then utilize their own networks to disseminate information. * * *

B. Ongoing Communication.

The process of obtaining free, prior, and informed consent of group members should provide sufficient insight into internal community dynamics to facilitate the establishment of channels of communication which can be utilized for the duration of the litigation. * * * Once a case is filed, advocates may feel less need for regular contact with the affected community. Both the Inter–American and African Commissions meet only twice a year, which makes the pace of their cases extremely protracted. Moreover, the merits phase, in which the victims' voices can and should be incorporated, is normally preceded by a hearing on admissibility, which is highly legalistic. Pending opportunities for more constructive involvement by the victims, their advocates must keep them engaged in the litigation despite the passage of time and periodically confirm their desire to pursue the litigation. Especially when the case is part of a broader strategy to address the community's problems, ongoing communication among all relevant participants is particularly important.

C. The Transformative Potential of Story-telling.

Feeling "heard," whether by a single sympathetic listener or a broader audience, is essential to the process of recovery for victims and survivors. In order for victims of traumatic events to begin healing, they must learn to live with traumatic memories. By allowing victims to confront in a supportive environment the painful experiences they have suffered, story-telling prevents the internalization of suffering and resentment which, if left unaddressed, can perpetuate the cycle of violence and lead to further abuses.

Story-telling can also play a critical role in restoring victims' dignity. The story-telling process was a central feature of the South African Truth and Reconciliation Commission, in which victims' stories were often corroborated by the testimonies of their aggressors, and served as a rallying point for more far-reaching political action in some cases. Similarly, an Australian government commission of inquiry established that "being heard" was as important to victims as compensation; the subsequent adoption of a requirement that judges review Victim Impact Statements at sentencing reportedly increased victims' satisfaction with the criminal justice system. Plaintiffs in ATCA litigation have likewise confirmed the empowering effect of confronting their abusers in U.S. federal courts.

These successes underscore the importance of incorporating victims' voices into case preparation and presentation. The process of eliciting a victim's personal experience through an initial interview, however time-consuming, may be the first opportunity accorded the victim to give voice to the abuses suffered and affirm their gravity. If foreign lawyers are involved in interviewing, they should work in collaboration with local advocates who, having received the requisite training, can continue to gather evidence after their foreign counterparts have left the country. Victims should also be invited and encouraged to testify in the proceedings, and regional human rights commissions could facilitate their involvement by scheduling at least one session of the merits phase in the target country. The submission of detailed declarations from a representative cross-section of victims, together with the presentation of oral testimony by some or all of them, should ensure that the forum has reliable information about the nature and scope of relevant abuses.

Obviously, time, resource, and efficiency constraints preclude the possibility of having every victim testify or even attend the proceedings. Accordingly, advocates must work to ensure they convey critical developments in the proceedings and the ultimate decision rendered by the forum to the victim group. While the effectiveness of particular strategies will vary depending on the context, available options include organizing press conferences, disseminating e-mail updates, making arrangements with a local radio program for witnesses to recount their experience of testifying, publishing victims' testimonies in a newsletter, or providing funding for a journalist from the target country to attend the proceedings. Given that the decisions of regional human rights commissions are not legally enforceable, the development of broad public consciousness of such decisions, both within the victim group and beyond, is indispensable if they are to have any lasting effect. * * *

NOTES AND QUESTIONS ON THE ATTORNEY-CLIENT RELATIONSHIP IN COMMISSION PROCEEDINGS

1. *Ethical and practical difficulties.* Should lawyers or NGOs refrain from bringing cases before a human rights commission if they are unable to facilitate communication with the victims due to logistical obstacles? How can lawyers or NGOs engage in victim-driven litigation in these circumstances? Can you think of any complaints that NGOs should be able to bring before regional human rights commissions regardless of whether they are able to adequately apprise the victims of their intended course of legal action?

2. *Alternative venues for story-telling.* Are there other mechanisms of transitional justice that might better serve the story-telling and rehabilitative needs of victims than litigation in regional courts? Should the

potential to create important precedent trump a close link to victims when supplementary non-legal mechanisms, such as Truth and Reconciliation bodies or indigenous healing ceremonies are available to victims?

C. PROFESSIONAL ETHICS AND THE GOVERNMENT LAWYER

Elsewhere in this chapter, we have discussed the ethical dilemmas that might confront a lawyer representing individuals whose human rights have been violated or organizations engaged in human rights advocacy. However, practicing as a government lawyer creates ethical issues related to, but often substantively distinct from, those that arise in private practice or in a public interest practice. The private and government lawyer are each bound by the same ethics laws and rules; however, the nature of government work sometimes complicates their application and enforcement.

Most rules of professional responsibility are driven by the lawyer-client relationship. A lawyer's ethical obligations arise out of this relationship: by undertaking to represent a client, you have accepted certain duties and obligations that flow from the trust placed in you by your client. But who is the client of the government lawyer?

For example, imagine you are an attorney employed in the Department of Interior's Office of the General Counsel. Your job is to provide legal advice to the Secretary of the Interior. Is he or she your only client? Do you owe a broader duty to the Department of the Interior itself? Given the fact that the Secretary is a political appointee, must you consider the institution itself your client, rather than the person in whose charge the institution has been temporarily placed? The legal counsel you provide might change on any given issue, particularly those that may be politically driven, depending on which "client" you represent.

But the analysis does not end here. As a lawyer employed by the U.S. government, the federal government as a whole, including the President, may also lay claim to your ethical duties. While you may not have been elected, the federal government exists to serve the interests of the American people. Some might also argue that you owe a duty to the American public, or at least to the specific consumers of that agency. As above, where your advice is requested on a controversial political issue, these two additional "clients" might affect your conclusions.

As you read the excerpts below, put yourself in the position of a lawyer on the staff of the U.S. Justice Department's Office of Legal Counsel assigned to prepare a memo for the President's Counsel. First, identify your client. Then, consider whether you believe the positions

taken in the memo below are both substantively correct and professionally ethical. Consider also whether professional responsibility is even the
right framework in which to engage this discussion. Are the political and
legal implications of the memorandum a greater concern here than in
other contexts? Where two legal positions are supportable by law and
fact, and where both meet the "straight-face" test, should ethics be a
decisive consideration?

August 1, 2002

U.S. DEPARTMENT OF JUSTICE
OFFICE OF LEGAL COUNSEL
MEMORANDUM FOR ALBERTO R. GONZALES
COUNSEL TO THE PRESIDENT

FROM JAY S. BYBEE, ASSISTANT ATTORNEY GENERAL
Re: *Standards of Conduct for Interrogation under*
18 U.S.C. § 23402340A

You have asked for our Office's views regarding the standards of
conduct under the Convention Against Torture and Other Cruel, Inhuman and Degrading Treatment or Punishment as implemented by
Sections 2340–2340A of Title 18 of the United States Code. As we
understand it, this question has arisen in the context of the conduct of
interrogations outside of the United States. We conclude below that
Section 2340A proscribes acts inflicting, and that are specifically intended to inflict, severe pain or suffering, whether mental or physical. Those
acts must be of an extreme nature to rise to the level of torture within
the meaning of Section 2340A and the Convention. We further conclude
that certain acts may be cruel, inhuman, or degrading, but still not
produce pain and suffering of the requisite intensity to fall within
Section 2340A's proscription against torture. We conclude by examining
possible defenses that would negate any claim that certain interrogation
methods violate the statute.

* * *

18 U.S.C. §§ 2340–2340A

Section 2340A makes it a criminal offense for any person "outside
the United States [to] commit[] or attempt[] to commit torture." Section
2340 defines the act of torture as an:

> act committed by a person acting under the color of law specifically
> intended to inflict severe physical or mental pain or suffering (other
> than pain or suffering incidental to lawful sanctions) upon another
> person within his custody or physical control.

18 U.S.C.A. §§ 2340(1); *see id.* §§ 2340A. Thus, to convict a defendant
of torture, the prosecution must establish that (1) the torture occurred

outside the United States; (2) the defendant acted under the color of law; (3) the victim was within the defendant's custody or physical control; (4) the defendant specifically intended to cause severe physical or mental pain or suffering, and (5) that the act inflicted severe physical or mental pain or suffering. * * *

"Specifically Intended"

To violate Section 2340A, the statute requires that severe pain and suffering must be inflicted with specific intent. *See* 18 U.S.C. § 2340(1). In order for a defendant to have acted with specific intent, he must expressly intend to achieve the forbidden act. * * *

As a theoretical matter, therefore, knowledge alone that a particular result is certain to occur does not constitute specific intent. * * * Thus, even if the defendant knows that severe pain will result from his actions, if causing such harm is not his objective, he lacks the requisite specific intent even though the defendant did not act in good faith. * * *

"Severe Pain or Suffering"

The key statutory phrase in the definition of torture is the statement that acts amount to torture if they cause "severe physical or mental pain or suffering." In examining the meaning of a statute, its text must be the starting point. Section 2340 makes plain that the infliction of pain or suffering per se, whether it is physical or mental, is insufficient to amount to torture. Instead, the text provides that pain or suffering must be "severe." The statute does not, however, define the term "severe." The dictionary defines "severe" as "[u]nsparing in exaction, punishment, or censure" or "[i]nflicting discomfort or pain hard to endure; sharp; afflictive; distressing; violent; extreme; as severe pain, anguish, torture." Thus, the adjective "severe" conveys that the pain or suffering must be of such a high level of intensity that the pain is difficult for the subject to endure.

Congress' use of the phrase "severe pain" elsewhere in the United States Code can shed more light on its meaning. Significantly, the phrase "severe pain" appears in statutes defining an emergency medical condition for the purpose of providing health benefits. * * * Although these statutes address a substantially different subject from Section 2340, they are nonetheless helpful for understanding what constitutes severe physical pain. They treat severe pain as an indicator of ailments that are likely to result in permanent and serious physical damage in the absence of immediate medical treatment. Such damage must rise to the level of death, organ failure, or the permanent impairment of a significant body function. These statutes suggest that "severe pain," as used in Section 2340, must rise to a similarly high level—the level that would ordinarily be associated with a sufficiently serious physical condition or injury such as death, organ failure, or serious impairment of body functions—in order to constitute torture.

"Severe mental pain or suffering"

Section 2340 gives further guidance as to the meaning of "severe mental pain or suffering," as distinguished from severe physical pain and suffering. The statute defines "severe mental pain or suffering" as:

the prolonged mental harm caused by or resulting from—

(A) the intentional infliction or threatened infliction of severe physical pain or suffering;

(B) the administration or application, or threatened administration or application, of mind-altering substances or other procedures calculated to disrupt profoundly the senses or the personality;

(C) the threat of imminent death; or

(D) the threat that another person will imminently be subjected to death, severe physical pain or suffering, or the administration or application of mind-altering substances or other procedures calculated to disrupt profoundly the senses or personality.

18 U.S.C. § 2340(2). In order to prove "severe mental pain or suffering," the statute requires proof of "prolonged mental harm" that was caused by or resulted from one of four enumerated acts. * * *

Section 2340's definition of torture must be read as a sum of these component parts * * * Each component of the definition emphasizes that torture is not the mere infliction of pain or suffering on another, but is instead a step well removed. The victim must experience intense pain or suffering of the kind that is equivalent to the pain that would be associated with serious physical injury so severe that death, organ failure, or permanent damage resulting in a loss of significant body function will likely result. If that pain or suffering is psychological, that suffering must result from one of the acts set forth in the statute. In addition, these acts must cause long-term mental harm. Indeed, this view of the criminal act of torture is consistent with the term's common meaning. Torture is generally understood to involve "intense pain" or "excruciating pain," or put another way, "extreme anguish of body or mind." In short, reading the definition of torture as a whole, it is plain that the term encompasses only extreme acts. * * *

V. The President's Commander-in-Chief Power

Even if an interrogation method arguably were to violate Section 2340A, the statute would be unconstitutional if it impermissibly encroached on the President's constitutional power to conduct a military campaign. As Commander-in-Chief, the President has the constitutional authority to order interrogations of enemy combatants to gain intelligence information concerning the military plans of the enemy. The demands of the Commander-in-Chief power are especially pronounced in the middle of a war in which the nation has already suffered a direct attack. In such a case, the information gained from interrogations may prevent future attacks by foreign enemies. Any effort to apply Section

2340A in a manner that interferes with the President's direction of such core war matters as the detention and interrogation of enemy combatants thus would be unconstitutional.

A. The War with Al Qaeda

At the outset, we should make clear the nature of the threat presently posed to the nation. While your request for legal advice is not specifically limited to the current circumstances, we think it is useful to discuss this question in the context of the current war against the al Qaeda terrorist network. The situation in which these issues arise is unprecedented in recent American history. Four coordinated terrorist attacks, using hijacked commercial airliners as guided missiles, took place in rapid succession on the morning of September 11, 2001. * * * These attacks are part of a violent campaign against the United States that is believed to include an unsuccessful attempt to destroy an airliner in December 2001; a suicide bombing attack in Yemen on the U.S.S. Cole in 2000; the bombings of the United States Embassies in Kenya and in Tanzania in 1998; a truck bomb attack on a U.S. military housing complex in Saudi Arabia in 1996; an unsuccessful attempt to destroy the World Trade Center in 1993; and the ambush of U.S. servicemen in Somalia in 1993. * * *

Al Qaeda continues to plan further attacks, such as destroying American civilian airliners and killing American troops, which have fortunately been prevented. It is clear that bin Laden and his organization have conducted several violent attacks on the United States and its nationals, and that they seek to continue to do so. Thus, the capture and interrogation of such individuals is clearly imperative to our national security and defense. Interrogation of captured al Qaeda operatives may provide information concerning the nature of al Qaeda plans and the identities of its personnel, which may prove invaluable in preventing further direct attacks on the United States and its citizens. Given the massive destruction and loss of life caused by the September 11 attacks, it is reasonable to believe that information gained from al Qaeda personnel could prevent attacks of a similar (if not greater) magnitude from occurring in the United States.

B. Interpretation to Avoid Constitutional Problems

As the Supreme Court has recognized, * * * the President enjoys complete discretion in the exercise of his Commander-in-Chief authority and in conducting operations against hostile forces. * * * That authority is at its height in the middle of a war. * * *

In order to respect the President's inherent constitutional authority to manage a military campaign against al Qaeda and its allies, Section 2340A must be construed as not applying to interrogations undertaken pursuant to his Commander-in-Chief authority. * * * Congress may no more regulate the President's ability to detain and interrogate enemy combatants than it may regulate his ability to direct troop movements on the battlefield. * * *

VI. Defenses

* * * Even if an interrogation method, however, might arguably cross the line drawn in Section 2340, and application of the statute was not held to be an unconstitutional infringement of the President's Commander-in-Chief authority, we believe that under the current circumstances certain justification defenses might be available that would potentially eliminate criminal liability. Standard criminal law defenses of necessity and self-defense could justify interrogation methods needed to elicit information to prevent a direct and imminent threat to the United States and its citizens.

A. Necessity

We believe that a defense of necessity could be raised, under the current circumstances, to an allegation of a Section 2340A violation. Often referred to as the "choice of evils" defense, necessity has been defined as follows:

> Conduct that the actor believes to be necessary to avoid a harm or evil to himself or to another is justifiable, provided that:
>
> (a) the harm or evil sought to be avoided by such conduct is greater than that sought to be prevented by the law defining the offense charged; and
>
> (b) neither the Code nor other law defining the offense provides exceptions or defenses dealing with the specific situation involved; and
>
> (c) a legislative purpose to exclude the justification claimed does not otherwise plainly appear. * * *

The necessity defense may prove especially relevant in the current circumstances. As it has been described in the case law and literature, the purpose behind necessity is one of public policy. According to LaFave and Scott, "the law ought to promote the achievement of higher values at the expense of lesser values, and sometimes the greater good for society will be accomplished by violating the literal language of the criminal law." LaFave & Scott, [Substantive Criminal Law,] at 629. In particular, the necessity defense can justify the intentional killing of one person to save two others because "it is better that two lives be saved and one lost than that two be lost and one saved." Id. Or, put in the language of a choice of evils, "the evil involved in violating the terms of the criminal law (even taking another's life) may be less than that which would result from literal compliance with the law (two lives lost)." Id. * * *

It appears to us that under the current circumstances the necessity defense could be successfully maintained in response to an allegation of a Section 2340A violation. * * * Clearly, any harm that might occur during an interrogation would pale to insignificance compared to the harm avoided by preventing such an attack, which could take hundreds or thousands of lives.

Under this calculus, two factors will help indicate when the necessity defense could appropriately be invoked. First, the more certain that government officials are that a particular individual has information needed to prevent an attack, the more necessary interrogation will be. Second, the more likely it appears to be that a terrorist attack is likely to occur, and the greater the amount of damage expected from such an attack, the more that an interrogation to get information would become necessary. Of course, the strength of the necessity defense depends on the circumstances that prevail, and the knowledge of the government actors involved, when the interrogation is conducted. While every interrogation that might violate Section 2340A does not trigger a necessity defense, we can say that certain circumstances could support such a defense.

Legal authorities identify an important exception to the necessity defense. The defense is available "only in situations wherein the legislature has not itself, in its criminal statute, made a determination of values." * * * Here, however, Congress has not explicitly made a determination of values vis-a-vis torture. In fact, Congress explicitly removed efforts to remove torture from the weighing of values permitted by the necessity defense.[1]

B. Self Defense

Even if a court were to find that a violation of Section 2340A was not justified by necessity, a defendant could still appropriately raise a claim of self-defense. The right to self-defense, even when it involves deadly force, is deeply embedded in our law, both as to individuals and as to the nation as a whole. * * *

The doctrine of self-defense permits the use of force to prevent harm to another person. As LaFave and Scott explain, "one is justified in using reasonable force in defense of another person, even a stranger, when he reasonably believes that the other is in immediate danger of unlawful bodily harm from his adversary and that the use of such force

---

1. In the CAT, torture is defined as the intentional infliction of severe pain or suffering "for such purpose[] as obtaining from him or a third person information or a confession." CAT art. 1.1. One could argue that such a definition represented an attempt to to indicate that the good of obtaining information—no matter what the circumstances—could not justify an act of torture. In other words, necessity would not be a defense. In enacting Section 2340, however, Congress removed the purpose element in the definition of torture, evidencing an intention to remove any fixing of values by statute. By leaving Section 2340 silent as to the harm done by torture in comparison to other harms, Congress allowed the necessity defense to apply when appropriate.

Further, the CAT contains an additional provision that "no exceptional circumstances whatsoever, whether a state of war or a threat of war, internal political instability or any other public emergency, may be invoked as a justification of torture." CAT art. 2.2. Aware of this provision of the treaty, and of the definition of the necessity defense that allows the legislature to provide for an exception to the defense, see Model Penal Code § 3.02(b), Congress did not incorporate CAT article 2.2 into Section 2340. Given that Congress omitted CAT's effort to bar a necessity or wartime defense, we read Section 2340 as permitting the defense.

is necessary to avoid this danger." *Id.* at 663–64. Ultimately, even deadly force is permissible, but "only when the attack of the adversary upon the other person reasonably appears to the defender to be a deadly attack." *Id.* at 664. As with our discussion of necessity, we will review the significant elements of this defense. * * *

If the right to defend the national government can be raised as a defense in an individual prosecution, * * * then a government defendant, acting in his official capacity, should be able to argue that any conduct that arguably violated Section 2340A was undertaken pursuant to more than just individual self-defense or defense of another. In addition, the defendant could claim that he was fulfilling the Executive Branch's authority to protect the federal government, and the nation, from attack. The September 11 attacks have already triggered that authority, as recognized both, under domestic and international law. * * *

As we have made clear in other opinions involving the war against al Qaeda, the nation's right to self-defense has been triggered by the events of September 11. If a government defendant were to harm an enemy combatant during an interrogation in a manner that might arguably violate Section 2340A, he would be doing so in order to prevent further attacks on the United States by the al Qaeda terrorist network. In that case, we believe that he could argue that his actions were justified by the executive branch's constitutional authority to protect the nation from attack. This national and international version of the right to self-defense could supplement and bolster the government defendant's individual right.

Conclusion

For the foregoing reasons, we conclude that torture as defined in and proscribed by Sections 2340–2340A, covers only extreme acts. Severe pain is generally of the kind difficult for the victim to endure. Where the pain is physical, it must be of an intensity akin to that which accompanies serious physical injury such as death or organ failure. Severe mental pain requires suffering not just at the moment of infliction but it also requires lasting psychological harm, such as seen in mental disorders like posttraumatic stress disorder. Additionally, such severe mental pain can arise only from the predicate acts listed in Section 2340. Because the acts inflicting torture are extreme, there is significant range of acts that though they might constitute cruel, inhuman, or degrading treatment or punishment fail to rise to the level of torture.

Further, we conclude that under the circumstances of the current war against al Qaeda and its allies, application of Section 2340A to interrogations undertaken pursuant to the President's Commander-in-Chief powers may be unconstitutional. Finally, even if an interrogation method might violate Section 2340A, necessity or self-defense could provide justifications that would eliminate any criminal liability.

NOTES AND QUESTIONS RE THE TORTURE MEMORANDUM

1. *Prosecution considerations.* Note the limitations the OLC memorandum purports to place on the scope of 18 U.S.C. § 2340A, as well as the expansive defenses to prosecution that the memorandum outlines. Place yourself in the position of a U.S. Attorney faced with allegations of the use of torture in interrogation by U.S. personnel. How might the analysis in this memo affect your decision to prosecute a government employee alleged to have committed torture? What level of conduct would you require before filing an indictment?

2. *The subsequent memorandum.* After the OLC memorandum excerpted above became public, the Bush Administration was widely criticized for the positions taken in it. As a result, the OLC prepared a subsequent memorandum which it intended to supercede the August 2002 Memorandum "in its entirety." *See* U.S. Department of Justice, Office of Legal Counsel, *Memorandum to James B. Comey, Deputy Attorney General Re: Legal Standards Applicable Under 18 U.S.C. §§ 2340–2340A* at 2 (Dec. 30, 2004). Notably, the new memorandum eliminated the analysis of the President's Commander-in-Chief power as well as potential defenses to liability, stating that "[c]onsideration of the bounds of any such authority would be inconsistent with the President's unequivocal directive that United States personnel not engage in torture." *Id.* The new OLC memorandum also modified the analysis of legal standards applicable under 18 U.S.C. §§ 2340–2340A, noting, "we disagree with the statements in the August 2002 Memorandum limiting 'severe' pain under the statute to 'excruciating and agonizing' pain. * * * or to pain 'equivalent in intensity to the pain accompanying serious physical injury, such as organ failure, impairment of bodily function, or even death.* * *' " *Id.*[1]

In your view, does this new, superseding memo remedy any or all of the issues that might have been raised in the previous memorandum? Do you think the new memo reflects a change in policy driven by public reaction to the 2002 memorandum? If so, is it ethical to interpret a statute in such different ways for policy reasons?

3. *The subsequent memorandum—inside baseball.* In October 2003, Jack L. Goldsmith was appointed head of the Office of Legal Counsel (OLC), a division of the Justice Department tasked with providing the president and executive branch with guidance on complicated and important issues of law (or on issues where there is disagreement

---

1. For commentary on the 2002 OLC memorandum, see Robert K. Goldman, *Trivializing Torture: The Office of Legal Counsel's 2002 Opinion Letter and International Law Against Torture*, 12 No. 1 HUM. RTS. BRIEF 1 (2004), *available at* http://www.wcl.american.edu/hrbrief/121.cfm.

between two or more executive agencies). In Goldsmith's words, OLC could also provide "free-get-out-of-jail cards" when the executive's conduct is at the ambiguous edges of criminal law. Nine months after his appointment, he resigned, due to the "constitutional excesses of the legal policies embraced by his White House superiors in the War on Terror." Jeffrey Rosen, *Conscience of a Conservative*, N.Y. TIMES MAG., Sept. 9, 2007.

When he resigned, Goldsmith kept mum about the reasons behind his departure, despite the heat he received at Harvard Law School, where he currently teaches. However, in 2007 he published THE TERROR PRESIDENCY, a book detailing his travails at OLC and the events that led to his resignation. Goldsmith's revelations include tremendous opposition from the White House when he advised them that the Geneva Convention applied to terrorists and insurgents and his early recognition that the "torture memos" were legally incorrect and should be withdrawn. Ultimately, Goldsmith discloses that he strategically submitted his resignation on the same day that he withdrew the memo, ensuring the White House's acceptance of the withdrawal.

Goldsmith's brief tenure at the OLC and his stormy resignation raise interesting questions of professional responsibility. First, to whom did Goldsmith owe his ethical obligations? To the White House? To the government generally? To the American people? How does the unique role of the OLC, as an advisory organ to the White House that issues binding opinions, affect this question? Second, did Goldsmith handle his resignation ethically? Did he err in waiting to disclose the truth behind his resignation? Under an informal code in government, political appointees do not generally criticize an administration within a year of leaving office. Does a government lawyer have ethical obligations that trump any allegiance he or she may have to the president who appointed him? Should Goldsmith have disclosed anything at all? Is Goldsmith's book a breach of some duty of confidentiality he assumed upon accepting the appointment? *See* Jesselyn Radack, *Tortured Legal Ethics: The Role of Government Advisor in the War on Terrorism*, 77 U. COLO. L. REV. 1 (2006); Roger C. Cramton, *The Lawyer as Whistleblower: Confidentiality and Government Lawyer*, 5 GEO. J. LEGAL ETHICS 291 (1991).

ABA MODEL RULES OF PROFESSIONAL CONDUCT

Rule 1.11 Special Conflicts of Interest for Former and Current Government Officers and Employees.

* * *

(e) As used in this Rule, the term "matter" includes:

   (1) any judicial or other proceeding, application, request for a ruling or other determination, contract, claim, controversy, investi-

gation, charge, accusation, arrest or other particular matter involving a specific party or parties, and

(2) any other matter covered by the conflict of interest rules of the appropriate government agency.

Rule 1.13 Organization As Client

(a) A lawyer employed or retained by an organization represents the organization acting through its duly authorized constituents.

(b) If a lawyer for an organization knows that an officer, employee or other person associated with the organization is engaged in action, intends to act or refuses to act in a matter related to the representation that is a violation of a legal obligation to the organization, or a violation of law that reasonably might be imputed to the organization, and that is likely to result in substantial injury to the organization, then the lawyer shall proceed as is reasonably necessary in the best interest of the organization. Unless the lawyer reasonably believes that it is not necessary in the best interest of the organization to do so, the lawyer shall refer the matter to higher authority in the organization, including, if warranted by the circumstances to the highest authority that can act on behalf of the organization as determined by applicable law.

(c) Except as provided in paragraph (d), if

(1) despite the lawyer's efforts in accordance with paragraph (b) the highest authority that can act on behalf of the organization insists upon or fails to address in a timely and appropriate manner an action, or a refusal to act, that is clearly a violation of law, and

(2) the lawyer reasonably believes that the violation is reasonably certain to result in substantial injury to the organization, then, the lawyer may reveal information relating to the representation whether or not Rule 1.6 permits such disclosure, but only if and to the extent the lawyer reasonably believes necessary to prevent substantial injury to the organization. * * *

Consider the competing viewpoints, excerpted below, regarding the ethical obligations of government lawyers in advisory positions:

Jeffrey K. Shapiro, *Legal Ethics and Other Perspectives, in* THE TORTURE DEBATE IN AMERICA, 233–34 (Karen J. Greenberg ed. 2006)

The question put to OLC was not whether al Qaeda and Taliban detainees enjoy "any" legal protection. Had that question been asked, the answer doubtless would have included the Torture Convention. OLC was asked to opine only as to the applicability of Geneva to these detainees. As proof, consider the second sentence of the January 9 memorandum: "[Y]ou have asked whether the laws of armed conflict apply to the conditions of detention and procedures for the trial of members of al Qaeda and the Taliban militia." Or, even more specifically, consider the revised second sentence in the final January 22 memorandum: "[Y]ou have asked whether certain treaties forming part of the laws of armed conflict apply to the conditions of detention and the procedures for fair trial of members of al Qaeda and the Taliban militia. It is well established that the 'laws of armed conflict' do not include the Torture Convention and other general humanitarian laws that apply at all times and not just during armed conflict."

Gillers [see excerpt below] also faults the OLC for a "tone" that is overly "confident * * * about the accuracy of [their] advice" and the absence of "significant qualifying language" that "even the most aggressive corporate lawyer" would include "as a matter of self-protection and self-respect." He speculates that OLC lawyers omitted contrary arguments at the request of the White House and because they "may have felt confident" about their immunity from criminal, civil, or disciplinary liability, "unlike corporate lawyers, whose opinion would not have been so one-sided."

It is a bit tendentious of Gillers to fault the OLC lawyers for having too much confidence in their advice when he fails to challenge its accuracy. More important, Gillers never explains why a "corporate lawyer" model applies. He never discusses the role OLC plays within the Executive Branch, the nature of its work, its typical work product, or any other context that might bear on a fair evaluation of OLC's work. He simply assumes without discussion that OLC's work product in this case should have resembled what one would expect from a good corporate lawyer. I have raised this issue with Professor Gillers previously in a writing panel; since he has never responded, it would appear that he does not have a good answer.

In truth, OLC has never adhered to a "corporate lawyer" model in its legal practice. OLC's standard practice is to answer legal questions as posed, neither more nor less. Asked about Geneva and other related laws of war, OLC will address those legal instruments and not others. Moreover, while a good corporate lawyer is expected to provide practical judgment on the risks and consequences of a legal position, with all the hedging and qualifications that implies, OLC is not. An OLC opinion essentially announces the legal position of the Executive Branch on specific legal questions. In this respect, the more appropriate analogue is an appellate court decision, not an advice memo from a corporate lawyer.

Stephen Gillers, *Legal Ethics: A Debate, in* THE TORTURE DEBATE IN AMERICA, 238 (Karen J. Greenberg ed. 2006)

The [OLC's] legal memoranda failed to acknowledge powerful contrary arguments. In finding no problem here, Mr. Shapiro posits a disturbingly crabbed view of the responsibilities of government counsel.

'OLC's standard practice,' he writes, 'is to answer legal questions as posed, neither more nor less.'

Legal issues are not litmus paper. As any practicing lawyer knows, the tough issues are loaded with ambiguities and uncertainties. They invite debate and disagreement. Is Mr. Shapiro saying that it is not the job of the lawyer as advisor to ensure that the client appreciates these uncertainties if that lawyer happens to work for the government? I hope not. * * * I do not claim *identity* between the relationship of a private lawyer for his or her private client, corporate or not, and the relationship of government lawyers to their client. But for one important professional responsibility—which is the reason I drew the analogy in the first place—Mr. Shapiro is dangerously wrong and the analogy quite correct.

When a lawyer, public or private, is asked to predict what the law is so the client may take action, perhaps very consequential action, based on the lawyers' advice, the lawyer is not in the traditional role of the courtroom advocate. He or she is professionally obligated to explore and explain well-founded conclusions contrary to those the lawyer has reached and to identify the risks to the client, if contrary to the lawyer's belief, a different view prevails. Only then can the client make an informed choices.

I would hope that the Attorney General would tell the head of his or her OLC:

> "I know you won't simply tell me what you think I want to hear. I wouldn't have hired you if I thought you would. I expect you to tell me your best judgment on the question. But many of the questions I ask you will not have a clearly correct answer. When you answer these, I need you also to tell me why your judgment may be wrong and to do so in a way that respects the best arguments for other points of view. This is particularly important when the action the government will take based on your advice can have profound effect for the nation and individuals. Only if you do this, can I do my job of evaluating your advice and assessing how to proceed."

<hr>

Upon discovering the nature of the interrogation techniques in effect at Guantanamo Bay, Alberto J. Mora, the outgoing general counsel of the United States Navy, has stated that he had grave concerns that such actions violated both U.S. and international law. The following excerpt illustrates Mora's description of his attempts to work within the Administration to end what he considered to be illegal activity:

Jane Mayer, *The Memo: How an Internal Effort to Ban the Abuse and Torture of Detainees was Thwarted*, THE NEW YORKER, Feb. 27, 2006, at 32.

[O]n January 9, 2003, Mora had a second meeting with [William J. Haynes II, the General Counsel of the Department of Defense]. According to Mora's memo, when he told him how disappointed he was that nothing had been done to end the abuse at Guantánamo, Haynes explained that "U.S. officials believed the techniques were necessary to obtain information," and that the interrogations might prevent future attacks against the U.S. and save American lives. Mora acknowledged that he could imagine "ticking bomb" scenarios, in which it might be moral—though still not legal—to torture a suspect. But, he asked Haynes, how many lives had to be saved to justify torture? Thousands? Hundreds? Where do you draw the line? To decide this question, shouldn't there be a public debate?

Mora said he doubted that Guantánamo presented such an urgent ethical scenario in any event, since most of the detainees had been held there for more than a year. He also warned Haynes that the legal opinions the Administration was counting on to protect itself might not withstand scrutiny—such as the notion that Guantánamo was beyond the reach of U.S. courts. (Mora was later proved right: in June, 2004, the Supreme Court, in *Rasul v. Bush*, ruled against the Administration's argument that detainees had no right to challenge their imprisonment in American courts. That month, in a related case, Justice Sandra Day O'Connor declared that "a state of war is not a blank check for the President.")

Mora told Haynes that, if the Pentagon's theories of indemnity didn't hold up in the courts, criminal charges conceivably could be filed against Administration officials. He added that the interrogation policies could threaten Rumsfeld's tenure, and could even damage the Presidency. "Protect your client!" he said.

* * *

By mid-January, the situation at Guantánamo had not changed. * * * Mora continued to push for reform, but his former Pentagon colleague told me that "people were beginning to roll their eyes. It was like 'Yeah, we've already heard this.'"

On January 15th, Mora took a step guaranteed to antagonize Haynes, who frequently warned subordinates to put nothing controversial in writing or in e-mail messages. Mora delivered an unsigned draft memo to Haynes, and said that he planned to "sign it out" that afternoon—making it an official document—unless the harsh interrogation techniques were suspended. Mora's draft memo described U.S. interrogations at Guantánamo as "at a minimum cruel and unusual treatment, and, at worst, torture."

By the end of the day, Haynes called Mora with good news. Rumsfeld was suspending his authorization of the disputed interrogation techniques. The Defense Secretary also was authorizing a special "working group" of a few dozen lawyers, from all branches of the armed services, including Mora, to develop new interrogation guidelines.

Mora, elated, went home to his wife and son, with whom he had felt bound not to discuss his battle. He and the other lawyers in the working group began to meet and debated the constitutionality and effectiveness of various interrogation techniques. He felt, he later told me, that "no one would ever learn about the best thing I'd ever done in my life."

A week later, Mora was shown a lengthy classified document that negated almost every argument he had made. Haynes had outflanked him. He had solicited a separate, overarching opinion from the Office of Legal Counsel, at the Justice Department, on the legality of harsh military interrogations—effectively superseding the working group. * * * [In it], there was no language prohibiting the cruel, degrading, and inhuman treatment of detainees.

Despite raising numerous concerns within the administration about the legal and moral consequences of the detainee policies, Mora never went outside of the administration to attempt to have the policies ended. What are the ethical and moral obligations of a government lawyer in these situations? Is it enough to raise one's concerns within the administration? What if, as in this case, raising concerns internally was ineffective? Does the lawyer then have the obligation to take her concerns outside of the administration in order to have the torture stopped? What about the duty of confidentiality? Does this duty depend on how we define the client?

NOTES AND QUESTIONS RE REPRESENTING THE GOVERNMENT ETHICALLY

1. *Advocacy vs. counsel.* In your opinion, what is the difference between advocacy and counsel? Which do you think the OLC memorandum excerpted above provides? Do the ABA Model Rules of Professional Responsibility provide any guidance as to which is more ethical when representing an organization? What might a model rule look like to address this issue?

2. *Framing the legal obligation.* Ethics and professional responsibility may not be the right framework in which to address the OLC memorandum. If it is appropriate—indeed, it may even be required—for an agency lawyer to effectively advocate for a position that her superiors have chosen to adopt as a matter of policy, it is her obligation to marshal the best legal and factual arguments in support of that position. In that sense, then, would there be anything unethical about the positions taken in the OLC memorandum? If, however, the duty is to provide the best counsel to her client, does the OLC memorandum then enter more murky ethical territory? How would you frame the ethical dilemma presented here?

ABA Model Rule of Professional Responsibility 2.1, entitled "Advisor" states, "In representing a client, a lawyer shall exercise independent professional judgment and render candid advice. In rendering advice, a lawyer may refer not only to law but to other considerations such as moral, economic, social and political factors, that may be relevant to the client's situation." Does this Model Rule provide helpful guidance on this issue?

3. *Identifying the client.* In the introduction to this section, we posed several questions about the nature of a government lawyer's "client." The ABA Model Rule excerpted above sheds some light on this dilemma; however, it is clearly incomplete. Would you argue that some "violation of law" took place, thereby triggering a responsibility to take further action as prescribed by the ABA Model Rules? Would a determination of whether the OLC memorandum violates any ethics rules depend on who you identified as the "client"?

4. *Government lawyers in the position of advisor.* Another series of memoranda from the OLC spawned an intense debate with respect to the scope of the Geneva Conventions. On January 22, 2002, the OLC issued a draft memorandum on whether the protections of the Geneva Convention apply to al Qaeda and Taliban detainees. Relying on the legal opinion of the OLC, President Bush issued an Executive Order finding that the Geneva Conventions did not extend to al Qaeda or Taliban detainees. Do government attorneys in advisory positions have an obligation to provide the "legal big picture" to policymakers who only request information on a specific point of law?

5. *Lawyers' participation in unfair trials.* Attorneys who discover that they may be participating in legal proceedings that violate international standards for fair trials face unique challenges. In 2005, two Air Force prosecutors, Maj. John Carr and Maj. Robert Preston, resigned from their positions in the prosecutors' office for the military tribunals at Guantanamo Bay. Maj. Carr and Maj. Preston accused fellow prosecutors of disregarding detainee allegations of torture and mishandling exculpatory evidence. The Department of Defense claims that the allegations were investigated and found to be without merit. Jess Bravin, *Two Prosecutors at Guantanamo Quit in Protest*, WALL ST. J., Aug. 1, 2005, at B1. What are the obligations of prosecutors who suspect that they may not be participating in "full and fair" trials? Is resignation the only practical option in such cases?

6. *Senator McCain's efforts to prohibit torture.* On December 30, 2005, President Bush signed the 2006 Defense Appropriations Bill, which included an amendment, The Detainee Treatment Act ("DTA"), by Senator John McCain, banning cruel, inhuman or degrading treatment of detainees in all interrogations conducted by the United States. The Amendment also established that the U.S. Army Field Manual will be binding for all Department of Defense interrogations. Senator McCain, who was tortured as a prisoner of war during the Vietnam War, worked

tirelessly to get this Amendment passed. Congress, in passing the Amendment, has spoken definitively on the subject, reaffirming what Senator McCain has so often repeated: "America does not torture." Note that the DTA also stripped the courts of authority to hear *habeas corpus* petitions filed by Guantanamo detainees. Does the fact that Congress chose to remove that jurisdiction undermine the protection that Senator McCain sought? In other words, can the prohibition against cruel, inhuman and degrading treatment be effective without sufficient review by the civilian courts?

THE JUSTICE CASE

UNITED STATES v. ALSTOETTER
Trials of War Criminals before the Nuremberg Military Tribunals
under Control Council Law No. 10 (1951)

We pass now from the foregoing incomplete summary of Nazi legislation to a consideration of the law in action, and of the influence of the "Fuehrer principle" as it affected the officials of the Ministry of Justice, prosecutors, and judges. Two basic principles controlled conduct within the Ministry of Justice. The first concerned the absolute power of Hitler in person or by delegated authority to enact, enforce, and adjudicate law. The second concerned the incontestability of such law. * * *

Under the Nazi system, and even prior thereto, German judges were also bound to apply German law even when in violation of the principles of international law. As stated by Professor Jahrreiss: "To express it differently, whether the law has been passed by the State in such a way that it was inconsistent with international law on purpose or not, that could not play any part at all; and that was the legal state of affairs, regrettable as it may be." This, however, is not to deny the superior authority of international law. * * * The conclusion to be drawn from the evidence presented by the defendants themselves is clear: In German legal theory Hitler's law was a shield to those who acted under it, but before a tribunal authorized to enforce international law, Hitler's decrees were a protection neither to the Fuehrer himself nor to his subordinates, if in violation of the law of the community of nations.

In German legal theory, Hitler was not only the supreme legislator, he was also the supreme judge. On 26 April 1942 Hitler addressed the Reichstag in part as follows:

"I do expect one thing: That the nation gives me the right to intervene immediately and to take action myself wherever a person has failed to render unqualified obedience. * * * "

[D]efendant Rothenberger expounded the National Socialist theory of judicial independence. * * * He asserted that "every private and Party official must abstain from all interference or influence upon the judgment," but this statement appears to be mere window-dressing, for after his assertion that a judge "must judge like the Fuehrer", he said: "In order to guarantee this, a direct liaison officer without any intermediate agency must be established between the Fuehrer and the German judge, that is, also in the form of a judge, the supreme judge in Germany, the 'Judge of the Fuehrer'. He is to convey to the German judge the will of the Fuehrer by authentic explanation of the laws and regulations. At the same time he must upon the request of the judge give binding information in current trials concerning fundamental political, economic, or legal problems which cannot be surveyed by the individual judge."

Thus, it becomes clear that the Nazi theory of the judicial independence was based upon the supreme independence of the Fuehrer, which was to be channelized through the proposed liaison officer from Fuehrer to judge. * * * Hitler did, in fact, exercise the right assumed by him to act as supreme judge, and in that capacity in many instances he controlled the decision of the individual criminal cases. * * * Upon his personal orders persons who had been sentenced to prison terms were turned over to the Gestapo for execution. * * *

Although Hitler's personal intervention in criminal cases was a matter of common occurrence, his chief control over the judiciary was exercised by the delegation of his power to the Reich Minister of Justice, who on 20 August 1942 was expressly authorized "to deviate from any existing law." * * * We may and do condemn the Draconic laws and express abhorrence at the limitations imposed by the Nazi regime upon freedom of speech and action, but the question still remains unanswered: "Do those Draconic laws or the decisions rendered under them constitute war crimes or crimes against humanity?" * * *

Paragraph 13 of count two of the indictment charges in substance that the Ministry of Justice participated with the OKW [the Armed Forces High Command] and the Gestapo in the execution of the Hitler decree of Night and Fog whereby civilians of occupied countries accused of alleged crimes in resistance activities against German occupying forces were spirited away for secret trial by special courts of the Ministry of Justice within the Reich; that the victim's whereabouts, trial, and subsequent disposition were kept completely secret, thus serving the dual purpose of terrorizing the victim's relatives and associates and barring recourse to evidence, witnesses, or counsel for defense. If the accused was acquitted, or if convicted, after serving his sentence, he was handed over to the Gestapo for "protective custody" for the duration of the war. These proceedings resulted in the torture, ill treatment, and murder of thousands of persons. These crimes and offenses are alleged to be war crimes in violation of certain established international rules and customs of warfare and as recognized in [Control Council] Law 10. * * * [A]ll of the defendants are charged with having participated in the execution or carrying out of the Hitler [Night and Fog] decree and procedure either as war crimes or as crimes against humanity, and all defendants are charged with having committed numerous other acts which constitute war crimes and crimes against humanity against the civilian population of occupied countries during the war period between 1 September 1939 and April 1945. The Night and Fog decree arose as the plan or scheme of Hitler to combat so-called resistance movements in occupied territories. Its enforcement brought about a systematic rule of violence, brutality, outrage, and terror against the civilian populations of territories overrun and occupied by the Nazi armed forces. The IMT [International Military Tribunal at Nuremberg] treated the crimes committed under the Night and Fog decree as war crimes and found as follows:

> The territories occupied by Germany were administered in violation of the laws of war. The evidence is quite overwhelming of a systematic rule of violence, brutality, and terror. On 7 December 1941 Hitler issued the directive since known as the "Nacht and Nebel Erlass" (Night and Fog decree), under which persons who committed offenses against the Reich or the German forces in occupied territories, except where the death sentence was certain, were to be taken secretly to Germany and handed over to the SIPO [Security Police] and SD [Secret Service] for trial and punishment in Germany. This decree was signed by the defendant Keitel. After these civilians arrived in Germany, no word of them was permitted to reach the country from which they came, or their relatives; even in cases when they died awaiting trial the families were not informed, the purpose being to create anxiety in the minds of the families of the arrested person. Hitler's purpose in issuing this decree was stated by the defendant Keitel in a covering letter, dated 12 December 1941, to be as follows: "Efficient and enduring intimidation can only be achieved either by capital punishment or by measures by which the relatives of the criminal and the population do not know the fate of the criminal. This aim is achieved when the criminal is transferred to Germany."

Reference is here made to the detailed description by the IMT judgment of the manner of operation of concentration camps and to the appalling cruelties and horrors found to have been committed therein. Such concentration camps were used extensively for the NN [Nacht und Nebel] prisoners in the execution of the Night and Fog decree as will be later shown.

The Night and Fog decree was from time to time implemented by several plans or schemes, which were enforced by the defendants. One plan or scheme was the transfer of alleged resistance prisoners or persons from occupied territories who had served their sentences or had been acquitted to concentration camps in Germany where they were held incommunicado and were never heard from again. Another scheme was the transfer of the inhabitants of occupied territories to concentration camps in Germany as a substitute for a court trial. * * *

The evidence conclusively establishes the adoption and application of systematic government-organized and approved procedures amounting to atrocities and offenses of the kind made punishable by [Control Council] Law 10 and committed against "populations" and amounting to persecution on racial grounds. These procedures when carried out in occupied territory constituted war crimes, and crimes against humanity. When enforced in the Alt Reich [Germany proper] against German nationals they constituted crimes against humanity. The pattern and plan of racial persecution has been made clear. General knowledge of the broad outlines thereof in all its immensity has been brought home to the defendants.

NOTES AND QUESTIONS RE "THE JUSTICE CASE"

1.   *"The dagger of the assassin concealed beneath the robe of the jurist."* Verdicts in *The Justice Case* were returned on December 3 and 4, 1947. Ten of the sixteen defendants were convicted, four were acquitted, one died before the end of the trial, and one was granted a mistrial due to serious illness during trial. Of those convicted, four were sentenced to life, and the remaining six were sentenced to terms ranging from five to ten years.

2.   *Legal obligations.* The defendants in *The Justice Case* acted pursuant to inhumane and unjust, but arguably binding, laws. While several judges resigned or were removed for declining to enforce the edicts, others, including the defendants, carried out these immoral and inhumane laws. Do judges have a legal or moral obligation to refuse to enforce inhumane domestic laws? Do U.S. judges have an obligation not to enforce the death penalty in circumstances where the imposition of the death penalty would violate international customary law?

Practicum

You have been asked to represent ten plaintiffs in a suit against the Republic of Guatador and Oil–Extract Inc. The case arises out of a joint venture entered into by the Guatadoran Government and Oil–Extract Inc. for oil exploration in the eastern region of the Republic. Upon learning of the proposed venture, many villagers protested the Government's exploration plan, claiming that the plan would displace entire villages and contaminate much-needed groundwater. In response to the villagers' protests, the government security forces engaged in a week-long campaign of violent repression, including torture, extrajudicial killing, and rape. Villagers, fearing for their lives, had no choice but to flee the land. While some fled to a neighboring country, others remain in hiding in Guatador. Oil–Extract Inc. is alleged to have provided the security forces with logistical data and transportation for its activities.

The potential plaintiffs in this case were among those who escaped to a neighboring country, and their case was referred to you by a local NGO working in the area. They are currently in hiding and fear for their safety should their whereabouts become known.

The remaining individuals who were forced to flee their villages have no legal representation. Based on the evidence in the case, you believe that there is a strong probability that this case will eventually settle for a substantial amount of money. The plaintiffs in this case, however, want more than monetary damages. They want an injunction precluding any further oil activities in their villages and a formal accounting of the atrocity orchestrated by the government.

Discuss the security challenges posed by bringing this case and what measures you, as an attorney, would take to ensure the safety of these plaintiffs. Is it possible to structure the case in such a way that the plaintiffs' safety will be guaranteed? What obligations do you, as an attorney, have to ensure that the plaintiffs are kept informed of the potential risks as the case progresses? Can attorneys ethically proceed with a case when a plaintiff's safety cannot be guaranteed?

Discuss the ethics of bringing this case as a class action on behalf of all villagers who suffered human rights violations during the security forces' campaign of terror. What are the benefits of bringing a class action in this case? What are the ethical challenges? Specifically, what effect could a decision to bring a class action have on plaintiffs' monetary and equitable damages?

What if one or more plaintiffs (or one or more NGOs) approach you, claiming to speak on behalf of all of the plaintiffs? What if these two plaintiffs disagree about whether to file as a class action, as one group of plaintiffs does not want to purport to speak on behalf of people they cannot contact and who might be endangered by the action? What if the plaintiffs have political differences about the conduct of the litigation (some of them want to include a neighboring group, some of them don't because of historic rivalries)? What if some plaintiffs want to agree in advance to put any collection into a fund for everyone and some do not? How should a human rights lawyer resolve these competing interests?

A small litigation firm in Los Angeles has been asked to bring this case. The firm has decided to hold a firm meeting to discuss the issues raised by the case in order to make a decision. Each participant has been asked to consider and be prepared to discuss the following issues:

(1) the security challenges of bringing this case and what measures must be undertaken to ensure the safety of these plaintiffs;

(2) the obligations of the attorney to keep the plaintiffs informed of the potential risks as the case progresses;

(3) the ethics of proceeding in a case in which plaintiffs' safety cannot be guaranteed;

(4) the merits and ethics of bringing this case as a class action on behalf of all villagers who suffered human rights violations during the security forces' campaign of terror;

(5) the effect of a decision to bring a class action on plaintiffs' monetary and equitable damages; and

(6) whether the firm should take the case.

CHAPTER 9

THE FUTURE OF INTERNATIONAL HUMAN RIGHTS LAW

■ ■ ■

"Everyone has the right, individually and in association with others, to develop and discuss *new* human rights ideas and principles and to advocate their acceptance."

> — Article 7, U.N. Declaration on the Right and Responsibility of Individuals, Groups and Organs of Society to Promote and Protect Universally Recognized Human Rights and Fundamental Freedoms (1999) (emphasis added)

Orientation

The international law of human rights, like international law generally, does not remain static. Customary international law did not always prohibit slavery; indeed, Joseph Story—a famous American jurist—predicted in the early 1800's that slavery would one day be a violation of international law, but to his regret that era was not his. Similarly, torture may not have been a violation of the law of nations in 1789, when the Alien Tort Statute was passed, but had become prohibited by the time of the *Filartiga* decision two centuries later. See Chapter 1, *supra*. In *Paquete Habana*, generally cited for the proposition that international law is part of federal common law in the United States, the Supreme Court held that an ancient usage among states had "ripened" into customary law by the time of the Spanish–American war, exempting civilian fishing vessels from seizure as enemy property (or prize) during times of war. There may be a genuine question in an era of total warfare whether the exemption norm is still respected, but the undoing of customary law must be as thinkable as its creation.

Only narcissism could make us think that we are at the end of history when it comes to the rise and fall of international human rights norms. Certainly since the end of World War II, states and international institutions have created varieties, even generations, of "new" rights and new enforcement mechanisms. But treaty-based human rights can also be trivialized if states adopt overly restrictive definitions of the prohibited conduct, like torture or genocide. Customary norms can unravel if state practice fragments or *opinio juris* changes over time. As a consequence, it is meaningful in this area of law to refer to emerging rights or norms in ways that we do not speak of "emerging" statutes. Of course, any legislature may debate a measure, but the legal relevance of that process, as distinct from the statutory end product, is marginal and typically limited to issues of interpretation. By contrast, emerging law to international lawyers is extremely significant. They must be able to recognize *lex lata*, *i.e.*, what the law is or requires, and to distinguish it from *lex ferenda*, *i.e.*, what the law ought to be or—in some settings— norms that are in the process of ripening into law.

We confront then a final set of questions with practical, theoretical, and ethical layers: is it possible to identify all the rights that a human being now holds? And if you could do it, would it be a good idea to try? Whom would you trust to collect the authoritative list of human rights, and what do you think the shelf life of such a catalogue would be?

This final chapter, addressing the prospects of human rights law, is from one perspective redundant, because each of the prior chapters dealt with issues at the cutting edge of each substantive concern. We do not mean to suggest by including certain illustrative issues in this final chapter that there are no elements of well-established law, *lex lata*, to frame the conversation about them. To the contrary, in some of the examples below, the primary issue is not the recognition of new rights but the new and broad-scale enforcement of rights that already exist. At the same time, we do not believe that every pressing social problem will necessarily respond to legal activism and lawyering. Nor do we believe that the human rights paradigm offers a one-size-fits-all approach to every social or legal issue. In fact, as the following materials may suggest, there are some problems to which a rights-based approach may seem particularly ill-suited.

Even as we acknowledge these limits however, this chapter also allows us to observe the reality that successful human rights norms tend to ratchet towards law: as states identify an issue of common concern and begin the process of conforming their laws and practices to increasingly internationalized principles to address that issue, a slow consolidation towards law occurs. In other words, what begins as a diversity of state practice with no identifiable legal element in it can evolve over time into practices motivated by divergent principles, then morph again into practice according to harmonized principles which can become "usages" until they are identifiable as legal norms. Of course, there is no inevitability to this process and no magic moment when a practice suddenly arrives as *lex lata*, but, as this evolution occurs, it is increasingly difficult to undo whatever progress has been achieved. The international prohibition of torture and slavery went through exactly this ratcheting process, though it is inevitably easier to see in retrospect than it was in real time.

As you work through the materials that follow, consider how twenty-first century lawyers may or should deal with certain constellations of predictable issues:

1. *Generations of rights.* What new substantive rights are likely to emerge and in response to what problems and what opportunities? Certainly internet and medical technologies may generate a new sense of human entitlement to information and health care, for example, to which other private rights like intellectual property rights may be more of an obstacle than are public wrongs like government repression. The war on terrorism will also continue to test nations' traditional understanding of the law of war, religious freedom, and due process of law, potentially requiring a new articulation of these norms. Poverty and corruption may come to be viewed increasingly and effectively through a human rights lens. The Human Genome Project and the integration of human being and machine may generate new bases for discrimination that may (or may not) resemble other bases for discrimination that the international community has outlawed.

2. *New human rights actors.* Will the United Nations lose its privileged place as the prime mover in the articulation of human rights law? The rise of regional institutions, public-private partnerships, and private actors, like non-governmental organizations and multi-national corporations, may mean an increased decentralization in the process by which human rights norms are identified.

3. *New enforcement techniques for established rights.* We have already seen the proliferation of enforcement techniques beyond the naming-and-shaming options that long characterized this body of law. Quite apart from the use of domestic courts and the treaty bodies, the human rights advocate must increasingly be familiar with those regional and international courts that have adopted the innovation of individual petitions, not to mention other longer-term enforcement techniques like human rights education, acculturation, and internalization, as well as the forces of a globalized marketplace, which might make a company's human rights practices either a competitive selling point or the target of consumer and investor activism.

This chapter invites you to build on what you already know about human rights lawyering and identify the next frontiers for advocacy. In part, you will draw on materials and articles that were controversial at the time of their drafting but which have come in retrospect to seem visionary.

Readings

PHILIP ALSTON, CONJURING UP NEW HUMAN RIGHTS: A PROPOSAL FOR QUALITY CONTROL

78 AM. J. INT'L. L. 607 (1984)

Writing in 1968, the year of the 20th anniversary of the adoption of the Universal Declaration of Human Rights, Richard Bilder concluded that "in practice, a claim is an international human right if the United Nations General Assembly says it is."[1] Fifteen years later * * * the authoritative role that Bilder correctly attributed to the General Assembly is in serious danger of being undermined. The problem has manifested itself in three ways. First, the General Assembly has, on several occasions in recent years, proclaimed new rights (*i.e.*, rights which do not find explicit recognition in the Universal Declaration of Human Rights or the two International Human Rights Covenants) without explicitly acknowledging its intention of doing so and without insisting that the claims in question should satisfy any particular criteria before qualifying as human rights. Second, there has been a growing tendency on the part of a range of United Nations and other international bodies, including in particular the UN Commission on Human Rights, to proceed to the proclamation of new human rights without reference to the Assembly. Third, the ease with which such innovation has been accomplished in these bodies has in turn encouraged or provoked the nomination of additional candidates, ranging from the right to tourism to the right to disarmament, at such a rate that the integrity of the entire process of recognizing human rights is threatened.

In principle, both the validity and the necessity of a dynamic approach to human rights, as well as the expansion, where appropriate, of the list of recognized human rights, cannot reasonably be disputed. However, reason for serious concern with respect to current trends arises not so much from the proliferation of new rights but rather from the haphazard, almost anarchic manner in which this expansion is being achieved. Indeed, some such rights seem to have been literally conjured up, in the dictionary sense of being "brought into existence as if by magic."

The absence of any established procedure by which candidates for new rights are scrutinized has resulted in an unfortunate situation: bodies at a lower level in the international organizational hierarchy than the General Assembly have tended to proclaim the existence of new rights without adequate consideration of the basis for, let alone the advisability or implications of, such action and without leaving the

---

1. Bilder, *Rethinking International Human Rights: Some Basic Questions*, 1969 WIS. L. REV. 171, 173. In this respect, there may be an uncomfortably close parallel between the authority of the Assembly and that asserted in Lewis Carroll's *Alice in Wonderland* by the Red Queen who majestically proclaimed that "words mean what I say they mean."

Assembly with an adequate opportunity to determine whether or not the giving of its imprimatur is warranted. * * *

I.   THE GENERAL ASSEMBLY AS ARBITER IN TRANSFORMING RHETORIC INTO RIGHT

Proclamation of the existence of human, natural or other forms of inalienable rights as a means by which to mobilize public support through the invocation of high moral principles in a given cause or struggle is a time-honored and proven technique. From the Magna Carta, through the British Bill of Rights of 1688 and the great American and French texts of the 18th century, to the Communist Manifesto of 1848 and the Atlantic Charter of 1941, manifestos, charters, and declarations of various kinds have succeeded both as catalysts to reform or revolution and as a means of confirming and perhaps even entrenching concessions on matters of basic principle already made by the established forces in society. In a number of obvious respects, the international law of human rights, particularly as it has evolved within the United Nations framework, is one of the main heirs to this tradition.

By the same token, however, the adoption of the Universal Declaration in 1948 constituted a qualitatively different undertaking in at least two respects. First, the fact that the international community had reached agreement on a comprehensive package of human rights which was said to represent a "common standard of achievement for all nations and all peoples" was, in itself, a unique and remarkable achievement. Second, this breakthrough was only made possible by the fact that most member states of the United Nations implicitly recognized the authority of the General Assembly to determine which claims should be deemed rights and which should not. For the first time in history, at the international level, a final arbiter had emerged in an area where conflicting ideologies, cultures and interests had previously made the prospect of general agreement seem far beyond reach and even utopian. Even when the drafting of the Universal Declaration was well under way, many distinguished commentators doubted the feasibility of reaching any meaningful consensus and urged that far more modest goals should be set.

The authority that was nevertheless vested in the General Assembly was reinforced in the period from 1949 to 1966 when the two International Human Rights Covenants, as well as a number of other instruments of more limited scope, were being drafted. During the whole of this time, the role of the Assembly as the final arbiter was never seriously called into question even by those states that were unhappy with the direction in which the majority was moving (with regard, for example, to the adoption of two separate Covenants, the inclusion of the right to self-determination and the exclusion of the right to petition and the right to property).

In one sense, the authority vested in the Assembly to proclaim human rights is based on firm legal foundations. It is a logical and direct outcome of the Assembly's mandate, contained in Article 13 of the United Nations Charter, to "initiate studies and make recommendations for the purpose of . . . assisting in the realization of human rights and fundamental freedoms for all without distinction as to race, sex, language, or religion." The exercise of this mandate with a view to proclaiming an "International Bill of Rights" had clearly been foreseen at the San Francisco Conference of 1945, which adopted the UN Charter. However, in another sense, which is in many respects more profound, the continuing validity in practice of the declaratory authority of the Assembly in this domain is dependent on its capacity to maintain its credibility as a responsible and discerning arbiter and as a weather vane of the state of world public and governmental opinion. It is in this intangible sense, rather than in formal legal terms, that the General Assembly's authority is somewhat precarious.

II. PRESSURES TO PROCLAIM MORE NEW RIGHTS

Recognition of the essential dynamism of the notion of human rights inevitably requires a willingness to consider the need to proclaim additional human rights. The challenge is to achieve an appropriate balance between, on the one hand, the need to maintain the integrity and credibility of the human rights tradition, and on the other hand, the need to adopt a dynamic approach that fully reflects changing needs and perspectives and responds to the emergence of new threats to human dignity and well-being. Those who have attached greater importance to the first rather than to the second of these goals have long voiced fears that the endorsement of new human rights would be the equivalent of trying to rewrite the Koran or the Bible.

Such fears, however, have proven largely groundless, and the success of a considerable range of new instruments adopted over the past three decades has served to encourage demands for the recognition of additional rights. Probably the longest list is that proposed by Galtung and Wirak of needs "that might be considered as important candidates on the world waiting list for processing into rights":

— the right to sleep;

— the right not to be killed in a war;

— the right not to be exposed to excessively and unnecessarily heavy, degrading, dirty and boring work;

— the right to identity with one's own work product, individually or collectively (as opposed to anonymity);

— the right to access to challenging work requiring creativity;

— the right to control the surplus resulting from the work product;

— the right to self-education and education with others (as opposed to schooling);

— the right to social transparency;

— the right to co-existence with nature;

— the right to be a member of some primary group (not necessarily the family);

— the right to be a member of some secondary group (not necessarily the nation);

— the right to be free to seek impressions from others (not only from media); and

— the right to be free to experiment with alternative ways of life.[2]

Other academic commentators have emphasized the need not only to proclaim new human rights but also to adopt whole new declarations of such rights. Additional proposals have come from nongovernmental organizations. * * * [P]roposals for a third international human rights covenant featuring a range of "third generation solidarity rights" have been strongly advocated. This group of rights has been said to include: the right to development, the right to peace, the right to a healthy environment, the right to communicate, the right to be different, the right to benefit from the common heritage of mankind, and the right to humanitarian assistance. It is significant that the first three of these rights have already been recognized in the African Charter on Human and Peoples' Rights of 1981.

Similar new rights were proposed by the International Association of Democratic Lawyers in 1982 in the context of a Draft Declaration of Human Rights and the Rights of Peoples to Peace and Disarmament. On the grounds that there currently exists "a grave omission in international law which requires repairing," the draft proposed immediate recognition by the General Assembly of:

— the right of every individual and people to permanent peace;

— the right of every individual to enjoy the highest attainable standard of physical and mental health, and in particular, the right to freedom from genetic mutation or damage;

— the right of all individuals and peoples to an environment of such quality as to enable them to live with dignity and enjoy a state of well-being;

— the right of all individuals and peoples to live in a peaceful region which is to become neither the theater of an armed conflict nor the subject of that conflict;

— the right of every individual and all peoples to live in freedom from threats;

— the right of all individuals and peoples to disarmament; and

— the right of all individuals and peoples to progress and development.

---

2. Galtung & Wirak, *On the Relationship between Human Rights and Human Needs*, UNESCO Doc. SS–78/CONF.630/4, at 48 (1978); *see also* Galtung & Wirak, *Human Needs and Human Rights: A Theoretical Approach*, 8 BULL. PEACE PROPOSALS 251 (1977).

A thorough search of the relevant literature would certainly yield a significant number of other, still unrecognized "human rights" ranging from those dealing with fundamental ethical issues [like a right to suicide] through frivolous claims such as that put forward by the World Tourism Organization (an intergovernmental body) that "tourism has become increasingly a basic need, a social necessity, a human right."

III. THE PROCLAMATION BY UN ORGANS OF NEW HUMAN RIGHTS SINCE 1972

These diverse pressures to proclaim new rights have in fact borne fruit in a variety of United Nations organs over the past decade or so. The considerable shortcomings of the process by which some of these rights have achieved formal recognition is best illustrated by taking several specific examples.

The Right to a Clean Environment

The right to a clean environment was recognized for the first time in the framework of the United Nations in 1972. In June of that year, the United Nations Conference on the Human Environment proclaimed the principle that "[m]an has the fundamental right to freedom, equality and adequate conditions of life, in an environment of a quality that permits a life of dignity and well-being. . . ." Although the General Assembly endorsed that declaration in general terms, it has never specifically proclaimed the existence of a right to a clean environment, despite proposals that it do so.

The Right to Development

Unlike the right to a clean environment, the right to development has been recognized by the General Assembly on several occasions.[3] However, its existence was first proclaimed in 1977, not by the Assembly, but by the Commission on Human Rights on the basis of no prior examination of the matter and without the assistance of any relevant documentation. In fact, neither the Commission nor the Assembly has ever formally held a debate on whether or not the right to development should be considered a human right and neither body has specifically acknowledged that an entirely new right or at least a new formulation of existing rights was being proclaimed.

The Right to Peace

The status of the right to peace is similar to that of the right to development. It has been proclaimed in varying formulations by both the Commission[4] and the Assembly, but neither its status as a human right nor its precise formulation, let alone its content, has ever been studied or formally debated. This did not, however, deter the General

---

3. GA Res. 34/46 (1979), 35/174 (1980), 36/133 (1981), and 37/199 and 37/200 (1982).

4. Comm'n on Human Rights Res. 5 (XXXII) (1976), para. 1, "recalls that everyone has the right to live in conditions of international peace and security."

Assembly from adopting in 1978, on the recommendation of its First
Committee, but without any reference either to the Commission or to
the Third Committee (which is responsible for human rights matters), a
declaration proclaiming the principle that "every nation and every
human being . . . has the inherent right to life in peace."

The Right to Popular Participation

In 1983 the Commission on Human Rights proclaimed that popular participation is a human right.[5] In the course of the Commission's
four discussions of the item dealing with popular participation, no
reference had been made to the desirability or otherwise of proclaiming
a new human right. It was not until a draft resolution was proposed by
Yugoslavia, calling for "a comprehensive analytical study on 'the right to
popular participation . . . ,' " that attention was drawn to the matter by
several delegations opposed to the proclamation of a new right. Thus,
the United Kingdom, Ireland and Australia opposed the use of the term
"right" on the grounds that "the Commission could not . . . reiterate
what it had not yet discussed or reaffirm a right which had not been
declared as such by the United Nations." In the event, the Commission
adopted the language proclaiming the new right by 27 votes in favor to
3 against, with 13 states abstaining.

In summary, then, the process by which new rights have recently
been proclaimed has generally suffered from the following shortcomings: there has been no prior discussion, not to mention analysis, of the
major implications of the proposed innovation; there has been no
attempt to seek comments from governments, specialized agencies or
nongovernmental organizations; there has been no request to the Secretariat or to any other expert group for advice on technical matters
relating either to the general principles involved or to the specific
formulations proposed; there has been no explicit recognition of the fact
that a new human right was being proclaimed; and there has been
insufficient debate on the basis of which to ascertain, with some degree
of precision, the real intentions underlying the affirmative votes of
states.[6] One result is that many of the new rights are characterized by
inordinate vagueness. Indeed, to a considerable extent, it is their
chameleon-like quality that has facilitated the degree of consensus
support they have received. Thus, states have been able to vote in favor
of the relevant resolutions without thereby committing themselves to

---

5. Comm'n on Human Rights Res. 1983/14; see also ECOSOC Res. 1983/31.

6. . . . It is reasonable to assume that the more frequently states are asked to endorse new
rights, the more blasé they become about the significance of their affirmative votes. Such "endorse-
ments" may easily come to be seen as little more than a gesture of goodwill to a political ally or a
powerful bloc. In 1967 Schwebel criticized the fact that

   resolutions may be voted for in the U.N. blithely, one might say, irresponsibly, because key
   decision-makers, normally not lawyers, having it fixed in their skulls that the General Assembly
   has no decision-making, no law-making authority, will vote for almost anything of transient
   political advantage, unaware that such votes may have a law-forming character.

THE EFFECTIVENESS OF INTERNATIONAL DECISIONS 494 (S. Schwebel ed. 1971). Today, it would be
difficult to exempt lawyers from such criticism.

any precise normative formulation or to any specific measures for the effective realization of the norm.

This approach is all the more extraordinary when it is contrasted with the painstaking and time-consuming negotiations that have been required to complete the drafting of instruments designed merely to spell out in greater detail the specific rights and obligations that flow from an already accepted right.

Before means of remedying some of these deficiencies are considered, it is appropriate to note the difference between the situation existing today and that which prevailed when the Universal Declaration and the Covenants were being drafted. The major difference derives from the fact that the initial or "incubation" phase of any given human right in the domain of international law is now taking place within the UN system at a much earlier stage than was previously the case. Thus, the rights in the Universal Declaration were, for the most part, if not entirely, claims which had long been made at the national level and which, in many instances, had been formally recognized as rights in national constitutions or other legislation. By the time they reached the General Assembly, such claims were reasonably mature in terms of their transformation into law, having already passed through a relatively demanding, although in some respects informal, filter system. By contrast, many of the claims now being asserted as rights were conceived directly in international forums and have not had the benefit of careful prior scrutiny at the national level. As a consequence, they are being presented to the international community for endorsement as rights when they are much closer, in terms of what Abi–Saab has referred to as "the life cycle of a legal rule," to general social values than to legal principles.[7]

IV.   THE USEFULNESS OF SUBSTANTIVE REQUIREMENTS

As the perceived usefulness of attaching the label "human right" to a given goal or value increases, it can be expected that a determined effort will be made by a wide range of special interest groups to locate their cause under the banner of human rights. Thus, in the course of the next few years, UN organs will be under considerable pressure to proclaim new human rights without first having given adequate consideration to their desirability, viability, scope or form. Such a proliferation of new rights would be much more likely to contribute to a serious devaluation of the human rights currency than to enrich significantly the overall coverage provided by existing rights. It is thoroughly unnecessary to impugn or even question the motivation of the proponents of these recently proclaimed or proposed rights in order to conclude that a more orderly and considered procedure should be followed before the United Nations accords the highly prized status of a human right to any additional claims.

---

7.   Abi–Saab, *The Legal Formulation of a Right to Development*, in The Right to Development at the International Level 159, 161 (R.-J. Dupuy ed. 1980).

If we were to establish a list of criteria a given claim must satisfy in order to qualify as a human right in terms of international law, it might look something like this. The proposed new human right should:

— reflect a fundamentally important social value;

— be relevant, inevitably to varying degrees, throughout a world of diverse value systems;

— be eligible for recognition on the grounds that it is an interpretation of UN Charter obligations, a reflection of customary law rules or a formulation that is declaratory of general principles of law;

— be consistent with, but not merely repetitive of, the existing body of international human rights law;

— be capable of achieving a very high degree of international consensus;

— be compatible or at least not clearly incompatible with the general practice of states; and

— be sufficiently precise as to give rise to identifiable rights and obligations.

The question to be answered then is how to apply these or comparable criteria in practice. The possible options are to establish substantive or procedural requirements, either or both of which would have to be satisfied before a given claim could be recognized as a new right.
* * *

But while philosophers can always have a field day debating the elements to be included in such a list of substantive criteria for determining whether a given claim qualifies as a human right, when intergovernmental organizations undertake the same exercise, it becomes infinitely more difficult. The reasons are, first, that the establishment of criteria of enduring relevance is almost impossible in a field that is constantly undergoing evolutionary flux, and second, even if such criteria could be agreed upon, the process of transforming a claim into an international human right is far from being scientifically pure. The point is well illustrated by the lengthy debates during the 1950s over whether or not self-determination could or should be considered a human right. Those states (essentially Western) which were opposed to the idea sought implicitly to establish a list of substantive criteria against which self-determination could be shown not to be a right. They included, for example, the criteria that: human rights must by definition embrace only the rights of individuals; the formulation of a right must be precise; and its implications must be clearly understood. In response, some of the proponents of the right simply rejected the proposed criteria, while others argued that the criteria were in fact satisfied in the case of self-determination.

As that example well shows, it would at best be an artificial and unrewarding task to seek to distill from the broad range of human rights already proclaimed by the General Assembly any scientifically valid criteria that would be capable of practical application in respect of new claims. * * * The application of a formal list of substantive requirements is thus an unworkable approach. To be useful, it would imply a degree of rationality and objectivity in the selection of rights that simply does not and could not characterize the approach of a body such as the United Nations. In other words, the normative validity of rights recognized by the General Assembly cannot be made dependent upon their validity in terms of philosophical or any other supposedly "objective" criteria. Hence the appropriateness of Bilder's pragmatic conclusion that a claim is an international human right if the General Assembly says it is.

V. THE USEFULNESS OF PROCEDURAL REQUIREMENTS

The difficulty of devising and applying universally acceptable substantive criteria must not be permitted to obscure the fact that procedural requirements may be used as an indirect means to achieve many of the same objectives. Indeed, "conformity with minimum procedural standards relating to the decision process" is, as Professor Schachter has recently written, "an essential requirement for legitimizing international decisions." It is significant that most of the short-comings identified above with respect to the present approach to new human rights concern the procedure followed rather than the outcome sought to be achieved.

In the present context, it is instructive to consider briefly the procedures used in other international contexts to legitimize the declaration of new norms. Probably the most elaborate of these is the approach followed by the International Labour Organisation (ILO), which generally involves the following steps:

(1) the ILO Secretariat prepares a preliminary survey of national legislation and other materials relevant to a proposed standard-setting exercise;

(2) the ILO Governing Body (of tripartite composition, with representatives of governments, employers and workers) decides whether or not to place the item on the agenda of the annual ILO Conference;

(3) on the basis of a survey, and of replies by governments to a detailed questionnaire, the ILO Secretariat prepares a report indicating the principal questions requiring consideration by the Conference;

(4) the Conference refers the matter to a special tripartite technical committee;

(5) on the basis of those discussions, the Secretariat prepares a first draft of an instrument;

(6) the draft is sent to governments for comments and a revised draft is subsequently drawn up, which is again sent to governments at least 3 months before the next Conference;

(7) at the Conference, the draft is considered by a technical committee, then in plenary and then by a drafting committee prior to the vote on its adoption; and

(8) the Conference votes on adoption of the instrument, which requires a two-thirds majority of the delegates.

An equally elaborate, but rather more drawn-out, procedure is followed by the International Law Commission in its work on the progressive development of international law.[8] While both the ILO and the ILC procedures are concerned more with the drafting of detailed instruments than with the straightforward declaration of new norms, the principles and assumptions underlying them would seem equally applicable to both cases. This view is supported by the approach adopted in the drafting of the Universal Declaration and in the elaboration of subsequent human rights instruments.

The major difference between the existing approach of the General Assembly to proclaiming new rights and that of the ILO to adopting new instruments is that the relevant procedural safeguards are mandatory in the case of the ILO but entirely *ad hoc* (and thus dispensable) in the case of the Assembly. The challenge therefore is to devise, and in some way entrench, procedural safeguards to govern the proclamation of new human rights within the UN system.

VI. TOWARDS AN *APPELLATION CONTRÔLÉE*: A SPECIFIC PROPOSAL

In essence, what is required is the human rights equivalent of the French system of *appellations contrôlées* applied to wines from the best wine-growing regions. The appellation is not in itself a guarantee of quality, but it does affirm that the wine was made in the prescribed manner, taking account of the conditions and traditions prevailing in the relevant region. It also attests that the proper ingredients were used and that quality was not sacrificed to quantity.

In the human rights field, responsibility for ensuring compliance with some form of procedural standards clearly belongs (for historical as well as hierarchical reasons) to the General Assembly. In the past, the Assembly has acquiesced in the partial erosion of its authority by permitting other bodies to take it upon themselves to proclaim the existence of new rights without at any stage seeking the Assembly's imprimatur. But although the Assembly must be the final arbiter in such matters, the views of the Commission should also be taken into account.... Moreover, experience in recent years points to the need for greater coordination in order to avoid the duplication of effort involved

---

8. In its work both on codification and on progressive development, the Commission adopts basically the following approach: a special rapporteur is appointed and an appropriate work plan is formulated for each topic; governments are invited to submit relevant laws, etc.; the special rapporteur submits a report on whose basis a provisional draft is approved by the Commission; the draft is submitted to the General Assembly and governments for comments; and a revised report is drawn up on whose basis a final report is submitted by the Commission to the Assembly. See UNITED NATIONS, THE WORK OF THE INTERNATIONAL LAW COMMISSION 11–13 (3d ed. 1980).

when different organs deliberate on the same, or at least similar, issues, and to ensure that incompatible, or even contradictory, standards are not adopted.[9]

On this basis, the General Assembly could consider mandating a precise *modus operandi* to be followed when the proclamation of a new human right has been proposed. In doing so, account should be taken of the following considerations: (1) the desirability of obtaining inputs from a wide variety of sources; (2) the need for these inputs to be addressed to as many as possible of the qualitative or substantive issues listed above; (3) the need to establish several phases in the process of considering the proposal so as to allow adequate time for analysis, consultation, reflection and revision prior to the proclamation of any new right; and (4) the desirability of providing for "expert" input, first, from the UN Secretariat, and second, from an expert group constituted either on an *ad hoc* basis or within the framework of the Commission or its Sub–Commission or of the General Assembly itself.

In general terms, a procedure designed to reflect these considerations might take something like the following form:

Step 1: the process would be activated by a decision by a UN organ that consideration should be given to the desirability of recognizing a particular claim as a new human right;

Step 2: the Secretary–General would prepare a preliminary study identifying the major qualitative issues raised by the proposal such as: the content and definition of the proposed norm, the basis on which it may be considered to be a part of international law, its relationship to the existing range of human rights norms, and the extent to which it reflects existing (or proposed) state practice;

Step 3: comments on, *inter alia*, the issues identified in the preliminary study would be solicited by the Secretary–General from governments, relevant international and regional organizations and nongovernmental organizations;

Step 4: the Secretary–General would then prepare a comprehensive study reflecting the comments received under step 3 and dealing with all relevant aspects of the proposal;

---

9. For example, a "Draft Declaration on the Rights and Responsibilities of Youth," submitted by the Governments of Costa Rica, Guinea, Indonesia, Lebanon, Romania and Rwanda, was presented to the General Assembly in 1982 (UN Doc. A/37/348, Appendix). The draft contains a very large number of "youth rights" that have no exact counterpart in the existing range of human rights. Thus, for example, the draft proclaims the right "to participate in the preparation and implementation of national development plans and in the execution of international co-operation programmes in the field of development" (pt. II(b)); as well as the rights "to perform useful work" (pt. IV, para. 2); "to fight illiteracy" (pt. VI(a)); "to be associated in appropriate forms, with the efficient management of a healthy educational climate" (pt. VI(c)); and "to take a suitable part in efforts to modernize teaching" (pt. VI(d)). The draft also proclaims a range of responsibilities and duties such as "the social duty, in accordance with their individual abilities and training, to perform useful work and to choose their jobs and the type of work they are to perform, taking into account national objectives" (pt. IV, para. 2).

Step 5: an *ad hoc* committee designated by the Commission on Human Rights would report, within 3 months of being appointed, to the Commission on the proposal;

Step 6: the Commission would adopt a recommendation on the matter addressed to the General Assembly; and

Step 7: the matter would be considered by the General Assembly, and the process would culminate in the proclamation of a new human right or in a decision to defer action on the proposal (either indefinitely or for a given period of time).

VII.   CONCLUSION

While the proposed procedure may appear rather cumbersome, it is in fact no more complicated than those regularly used by other international organs in comparable undertakings. In any event, the importance of ensuring, first, that the recognition of a new human right is generally accepted as being authoritative (in the sense of giving rise to realistic expectations of compliance by states), and second, that the integrity and standing of the existing body of rights is maintained, easily justifies the adoption of such a procedure. Moreover, the introduction of the proposed safeguards would eliminate the existing possibility that new rights could be proclaimed without any prior reflection or scrutiny, ensure that organs subordinate to the General Assembly could not undermine the Assembly's authority by unilaterally proclaiming new human rights, and ensure that states' endorsement of a particular norm would be based on an understanding both of the broad content of the norm and of the legal significance of their support for it.

It must be emphasized, however, that just as the *appellations contrôlées* system neither provides an ironclad guarantee of high-quality wine nor eliminates the possibility of fraudulent practices, so too would the procedure proposed above not be immune to manipulation or even circumvention by a determined political majority in the General Assembly. Nevertheless, such practices would be rendered considerably more difficult than at present.

NOTES AND QUESTIONS ON THE RECOGNITION OF "NEW" RIGHTS

1.   *The rights-based argument against the codification of rights.* One of the eighteenth-century arguments against including a Bill of Rights in the Constitution of the United States was that a complete catalogue of rights would be ill-advised, because the specification of some particular rights would inevitably lead to the exclusion of other, implicit but no less important rights. From that perspective, it was predictable that the absence of an explicit right to privacy in the Bill of Rights (or an explicit provision on the rights of the unborn) would contribute to the current controversy over the legitimacy of the Supreme Court's finding of a

woman's constitutional right to abortion in *Roe v. Wade*. Would the existence of a constitutional right to privacy have been easier or harder to prove if the Bill of Rights had never been drafted and adopted?

2.　*Can the evolution of rights be observed and proven?* The emergence of human rights norms is not linear: you cannot assume that more or "better" rights will emerge, nor can you assume that those which do emerge will be better respected and protected than in the past. But over the last fifty years, as demonstrated in previous chapters, for all of the occasionally retrograde motion in implementation, there has also been a steady crystallization of substantive rights, posing a powerful historical challenge to the skeptic. Are there specific rights that were merely asserted or emerging as of 1984 according to Alston but which are now better articulated and more widely accepted?

3.　*The Alston thesis.* According to Professor Alston, why have *substantive* criteria for the rights proven to be unworkable while *procedural* criteria have (or may) work? What exactly was wrong with the "Draft Declaration on the Rights and Responsibilities of Youth" described in footnote 9? What disadvantages, if any, do you see in privileging the United Nations General Assembly with a primary power of legitimation?

4.　*The limits of the human rights framework.* The critique of a rights-based approach to social problems has many themes. Professor Mary Ann Glendon for example has argued that the language of rights tends to trump healthy political discourse by removing entire classes of questions from mutual accommodation. In her view, rights talk inevitably leads to adversarial rather than negotiated resolutions of issues. Mary Ann Glendon, RIGHTS TALK: THE IMPOVERISHMENT OF POLITICAL DISCOURSE (1991). The proliferation of rights can also effect a massive transfer of power to the courts from the legislature or the executive branch, because rights by nature are typically—sometimes necessarily—enforced by the judiciary. This can lead to government-by-injunction of the sort that has caused periodic controversy in the United States with respect to the administration of schools, housing authorities, and prisons. Not only can this undermine the credibility and the legitimacy of the courts according to critics, it may also work against the interests of the protected class if the judges turn out to be less sympathetic than, say, an expert administrative agency. The necessary litigation also imposes a class dimension on the enjoyment of rights, because, with limited exceptions, only those with means have effective access to the courts in the first place. In addition, rights talk can promote "victim's consciousness," which fosters dependence on government. Besides, law is ultimately too modest an instrument to protect human beings from a culture of discrimination or abuse, because, as James Stephens observed, "law cannot be better than the nation in which it exists." How would you respond to this layered critique?

5.　*The lawyer's professional obligation.* Should lawyers be more concerned with enforcing rights that exist than with the process of developing new rights? For example, how do you respond to the argument that it is more meaningful to protect the rights of HIV-positive people from discrimination than it is to develop a right to health *per se*?

CASE STUDIES

HUMAN RIGHTS AND ENVIRONMENTAL PROTECTION

In 1972, the Stockholm Declaration on the Human Environment—a declaration by private experts under UN auspices but not by member governments—asserted a connection between the enjoyment of human rights and the quality of the environment. Principle 1 of the Stockholm Declaration provided that humankind "has the fundamental right to freedom, equality, and adequate conditions of life, in an environment of quality that permits a life of dignity and well-being and * * * bears a solemn responsibility to protect and improve the environment for present and future generations." Twenty years later, government representatives spelled out their understanding of this right during a conference in Rio de Janeiro and adopted the following instrument.

THE RIO DECLARATION ON ENVIRONMENT AND DEVELOPMENT (1992)

Principle 1

Human beings are at the centre of concerns for sustainable development. They are entitled to a healthy and productive life in harmony with nature.

Principle 2

States have, in accordance with the Charter of the United Nations and the principles of international law, the sovereign right to exploit their own resources pursuant to their own environmental and developmental policies, and the responsibility to ensure that activities within their jurisdiction or control do not cause damage to the environment of other States or of areas beyond the limits of national jurisdiction.

Principle 3

The right to development must be fulfilled so as to equitably meet developmental and environmental needs of present and future generations. * * *

Principle 6

The special situation and needs of developing countries, particularly the least developed and those most environmentally vulnerable, shall be given special priority. International actions in the field of environment and development should also address the interests and needs of all countries. * * *

Principle 10

Environmental issues are best handled with the participation of all concerned citizens, at the relevant level. At the national level, each individual shall have appropriate access to information concerning the environment that is held by public authorities, including information on hazardous materials and activities in their communities, and the opportunity to participate in decision-making processes. States shall facilitate and encourage public awareness and participation by making information widely available. Effective access to judicial and administrative proceedings, including redress and remedy, shall be provided. * * *

Principle 16

National authorities should endeavour to promote the internalization of environmental costs and the use of economic instruments, taking into account the approach that the polluter should, in principle, bear the cost of pollution, with due regard to the public interest and without distorting international trade and investment. * * *

Principle 20

Women have a vital role in environmental management and development. Their full participation is therefore essential to achieve sustainable development.

Principle 21

The creativity, ideals and courage of the youth of the world should be mobilized to forge a global partnership in order to achieve sustainable development and ensure a better future for all.

Principle 22

Indigenous people and their communities, and other local communities, have a vital role in environmental management and development because of their knowledge and traditional practices. States should recognize and duly support their identity, culture and interests and enable their effective participation in the achievement of sustainable development.

Principle 23

The environment and natural resources of people under oppression, domination and occupation shall be protected.

Principle 24

Warfare is inherently destructive of sustainable development. States shall therefore respect international law providing protection for the environment in times of armed conflict and cooperate in its further development, as necessary.

Principle 25

Peace, development and environmental protection are interdependent and indivisible.

———————

In 1976, the European Commission on Human Rights rejected an application challenging the military uses of marshland on environmental grounds, concluding that there was no right to the conservation of the natural environment included among the rights and freedoms guaranteed by the European Convention. Judging from the following case, by 1994, something had changed in that regard, and it certainly wasn't the text of the convention.

———————

LÒPEZ OSTRA v. SPAIN

303–C Eur. Ct. H.R. (ser. A) (1995)

1.   The case [which] was referred to the Court by the European Commission of Human Rights ("the Commission") * * * originated in an application against the Kingdom of Spain lodged * * * by a Spanish national, Mrs. Gregoria López Ostra. * * * The object of the request was to obtain a decision as to whether the facts of the case disclosed a breach by the respondent State of its obligations under Articles 3 and 8 of the Convention. * * *

6.   Mrs. Gregoria López Ostra * * * lives in Lorca (Murcia). At the material time she and her husband and their two daughters had their home in the district of "Diputación del Rio, el Lugarico", a few hundred metres from the town centre.

7.   The town of Lorca has a heavy concentration of leather industries. Several tanneries there, all belonging to a limited company called SACURSA, had a plant for the treatment of liquid and solid waste built with a State subsidy on municipal land twelve metres away from the applicant's home.

8.   The plant began to operate in July 1988 without the licence from the municipal authorities required by [domestic law] and without having followed the procedure for obtaining such a licence. Owing to a malfunction, its start-up released gas fumes, pestilential smells and contamination, which immediately caused health problems and nuisance to many Lorca people, particularly those living in the applicant's district.

The town council evacuated the local residents and rehoused them free of charge in the town centre for the months of July, August and September 1988. In October the applicant and her family returned to their flat and lived there until February 1992.

9. [In] September 1988, following numerous complaints and in the light of reports from the health authorities and the Environment and Nature Agency for the Murcia region, the town council ordered cessation of one of the plant's activities—the settling of chemical and organic residues in water tanks—while permitting the treatment of waste water contaminated with chromium to continue. There is disagreement as to what the effects were of this partial shutdown, but it can be seen from the expert opinions and written evidence * * * produced before the Commission by the Government and the applicant, that certain nuisances continue and may endanger the health of those living nearby.

10. [In seeking domestic remedies through Spanish institutions,] Mrs. López Ostra * * * complained, inter alia, of an unlawful interference with her home and her peaceful enjoyment of it, a violation of her right to choose freely her place of residence, attacks on her physical and psychological integrity, and infringements of her liberty and her safety [under the Spanish constitution] on account of the municipal authorities' passive attitude to the nuisance and risks caused by the waste-treatment plant. She requested the court to order temporary or permanent cessation of its activities. [The Spanish courts consistently ruled against her, with the Constitutional Court holding *inter alia* that "the presence of fumes, smells and noise did not itself amount to a breach of the right to inviolability of the home; that the refusal to order closure of the plant could not be regarded as degrading treatment, since the applicant's life and physical integrity had not been endangered; and that her right to choose her place of residence had not been infringed as she had not been expelled from her home by any authority."]

11. The [Spanish] court took evidence from several witnesses offered by the applicant and instructed the regional Environment and Nature Agency to give an opinion on the plant's operating conditions and location. In [its] report the agency noted that at the time of its expert's visit * * * the plant's sole activity was the treatment of waste water contaminated with chromium, but that the remaining waste also flowed through its tanks before being discharged into the river, generating foul smells. It therefore concluded that the plant had not been built in the most suitable location.

Crown Counsel endorsed Mrs. López Ostra's application. However, the Audiencia Territorial [the Spanish territorial court] found against her on 31 January 1989. It held that although the plant's operation could unquestionably cause nuisance because of the smells, fumes and noise, it did not constitute a serious risk to the health of the families living in its vicinity but, rather, impaired their quality of life, though not enough to infringe the fundamental rights claimed. In any case, the municipal authorities, who had taken measures in respect of the plant, could not be held liable. The non-possession of a licence was not an issue to be examined in the special proceedings instituted in this instance, because it concerned a breach of * * * law [not within its subject matter jurisdiction]. * * *

18.   [One] judge ordered a number of expert opinions as to the seriousness of the nuisance caused by the waste-treatment plant and its effects on the health of those living nearby. An initial report * * * by a scientist from the University of Murcia who had a doctorate in chemistry stated that hydrogen sulphide (a colourless gas, soluble in water, with a characteristic rotten-egg smell) had been detected on the site in concentrations exceeding the permitted levels. The discharge of effluent containing sulphur into a river was said to be unacceptable. * * * In [its] report * * * the National Toxicology Institute stated that the levels of the gas probably exceeded the permitted limits but did not pose any danger to the health of people living close to the plant. In a second report * * * the institute stated that it could not be ruled out that being in neighbouring houses twenty-four hours a day constituted a health risk as calculations had been based only on a period of eight hours a day for five days. Lastly, the regional Environment and Nature Agency, which had been asked to submit an expert opinion by the Lorca municipal authorities, concluded * * * that the level of noise produced by the plant when in operation did not exceed that measured in other parts of the town.

19.   The investigation file contains several medical certificates and expert opinions concerning the effects on the health of those living near the plant. In a certificate dated 12 December 1991 Dr. de Ayala Sánchez, a paediatrician, stated that Mrs. López Ostra's daughter, Cristina, presented a clinical picture of nausea, vomiting, allergic reactions, anorexia, etc., which could only be explained by the fact that she was living in a highly polluted area. He recommended that the child should be moved from the area. In an expert report of 16 April 1993 the Ministry of Justice's Institute of Forensic Medicine in Cartagena indicated that gas concentrations in houses near the plant exceeded the permitted limit. It noted that the applicant's daughter and her nephew, Fernando López Gómez, presented typical symptoms of chronic absorption of the gas in question, periodically manifested in the form of acute bronchopulmonary infections. It considered that there was a relationship of cause and effect between this clinical picture and the levels of gas.

20.   In addition, it is apparent from the statements of three police officers called to the neighbourhood of the plant by one of the applicant's sisters-in-law * * * that the smells given off were, at the time of their arrival, very strong and induced nausea.

21.   [In] February 1992 Mrs. López Ostra and her family were rehoused in a flat in the centre of Lorca, for which the municipality paid

the rent. The inconvenience resulting from this move and from the precariousness of their housing situation prompted the applicant and her husband to purchase a house in a different part of town. * * *

30. Mrs. López Ostra applied to the Commission * * * complain[ing] of the Lorca municipal authorities' inactivity in respect of the nuisance caused by a waste-treatment plant situated a few metres away from her home. Relying on Articles 8 para. 1 and 3 of the [European] Convention, she asserted that she was the victim of a violation of the right to respect for her home that made her private and family life impossible and the victim also of degrading treatment. * * *

34. The applicant alleged that there had been a violation of Articles 8 and 3 of the Convention on account of the smells, noise and polluting fumes caused by a plant for the treatment of liquid and solid waste sited a few metres away from her home. She held the Spanish authorities responsible, alleging that they had adopted a passive attitude. * * *

44. Mrs. López Ostra first contended that there had been a violation of Article 8 of the Convention, which provides:

1.   Everyone has the right to respect for his private and family life, his home and his correspondence.

2.   There shall be no interference by a public authority with the exercise of this right except such as is in accordance with the law and is necessary in a democratic society in the interests of national security, public safety or the economic well-being of the country, for the prevention of disorder or crime, for the protection of health or morals, or for the protection of the rights and freedoms of others.

The Commission subscribed to this view, while the Government contested it.

47.   Mrs. López Ostra maintained that, despite its partial shutdown [in] September 1988, the plant continued to emit fumes, repetitive noise and strong smells, which made her family's living conditions unbearable and caused both her and them serious health problems. She alleged in this connection that her right to respect for her home had been infringed.
    * * *

49.   On the basis of medical reports and expert opinions produced by the Government or the applicant, the Commission noted, *inter alia*, that hydrogen sulphide emissions from the plant exceeded the permitted limit and could endanger the health of those living nearby and that there could be a causal link between those emissions and the applicant's daughter's ailments.

50.   In the Court's opinion, these findings merely confirm the first expert report submitted to the [Spanish domestic authorities] by the regional Environment and Nature Agency in connection with Mrs. López Ostra's application for protection of fundamental rights. * * *

51.   Naturally, severe environmental pollution may affect individuals' well-being and prevent them from enjoying their homes in such a way as to affect their private and family life adversely, without, however, seriously endangering their health. Whether the question is analysed in terms of a positive duty on the State—to take reasonable and appropriate measures to secure the applicant's rights under paragraph 1 of Article 8, as the applicant wishes in her case, or in terms of an "interference by a public authority" to be justified in accordance with paragraph 2, the applicable principles are broadly similar. In both contexts regard must be had to the fair balance that has to be struck between the competing interests of the individual and of the community as a whole, and in any case the State enjoys a certain margin of appreciation. Furthermore, even in relation to the positive obligations flowing from the first paragraph of Article 8, in striking the required balance the aims mentioned in the second paragraph may be of a certain relevance.

52.   It appears from the evidence that the waste-treatment plant in issue was built by SACURSA in July 1988 to solve a serious pollution problem in Lorca due to the concentration of tanneries. Yet as soon as it started up, the plant caused nuisance and health problems to many local people. Admittedly, the Spanish authorities, and in particular the Lorca municipality, were theoretically not directly responsible for the emissions in question. However, * * * the town allowed the plant to be built on its land and the State subsidised the plant's construction.

53.   The town council reacted promptly by rehousing the residents affected, free of charge, in the town centre for the months of July, August and September 1988 and then by stopping one of the plant's activities from 9 September. However, the council's members could not be unaware that the environmental problems continued after this partial shutdown. This was, moreover, confirmed as early as January 1989 by the regional Environment and Nature Agency's report and then by expert opinions in 1991, 1992 and 1993 (see paragraphs 11 and 18 above).

54.   Mrs. López Ostra submitted that by virtue of the general supervisory powers conferred on the municipality by the 1961 regulations the municipality had a duty to act. In addition, the plant did not satisfy the legal requirements, in particular as regards its location and the failure to obtain a municipal licence. * * *

55.   On this issue the Court points out that the question of the lawfulness of the building and operation of the plant has been pending in the Supreme Court since 1991. The Court has consistently held that it is primarily for the national authorities, notably the courts, to interpret and apply domestic law. At all events, the Court considers that in the present case, even supposing that the municipality did fulfil the functions assigned to it by domestic law, it need only establish whether the national authorities took the measures necessary for protecting the

applicant's right to respect for her home and for her private and family life under Article 8. * * *

56. It has to be noted that the municipality not only failed to take steps to that end * * * but also resisted judicial decisions to that effect. In the ordinary administrative proceedings instituted by Mrs. López Ostra's sisters-in-law it appealed against the Murcia High Court's decision ordering temporary closure of the plant, and that measure was suspended as a result. Other State authorities also contributed to prolonging the situation. [In] November 1991 Crown Counsel appealed against the Lorca investigating judge's decision temporarily to close the plant in the prosecution for an environmental health offence, with the result that the order was not enforced until October 1993. * * *

57. The Government drew attention to the fact that the town had borne the expense of renting a flat in the centre of Lorca, in which the applicant and her family lived from 1 February 1992 to February 1993. The Court notes, however, that the family had to bear the nuisance caused by the plant for over three years before moving house with all the attendant inconveniences. They moved only when it became apparent that the situation could continue indefinitely and when Mrs. López Ostra's daughter's paediatrician recommended that they do so. Under these circumstances, the municipality's offer could not afford complete redress for the nuisance and inconveniences to which they had been subjected.

58. Having regard to the foregoing, and despite the margin of appreciation left to the respondent State, the Court considers that the State did not succeed in striking a fair balance between the interest of the town's economic well-being—that of having a waste-treatment plant—and the applicant's effective enjoyment of her right to respect for her home and her private and family life. There has accordingly been a violation of Article 8.

59. Mrs. López Ostra submitted that the matters for which the respondent State was criticised were of such seriousness and had caused her such distress that they could reasonably be regarded as amounting to degrading treatment prohibited by Article 3 of the Convention, which provides: "No one shall be subjected to torture or to inhuman or degrading treatment or punishment." The Government and the Commission took the view that there had been no breach of this Article.

60. The Court is of the same opinion. The conditions in which the applicant and her family lived for a number of years were certainly very difficult but did not amount to degrading treatment within the meaning of Article 3.

* * *

For these reasons, the Court unanimously: 1. Dismisses the Government's preliminary objections; 2. Holds that there has been a breach of Article 8 of the Convention; 3. Holds that there has been no breach of Article 3 of the Convention; 4. Holds that the respondent State is to pay the applicant, within three months, 4,000,000 (four million) pesetas for damage and 1,500,000 (one million five hundred thousand) pesetas, less 9,700 (nine thousand seven hundred) French francs to be converted into pesetas at the exchange rate applicable on the date of delivery of this judgment, for costs and expenses; 5. Dismisses the remainder of the claim for just satisfaction.

FLORES, ET AL. v. SOUTHERN PERU COPPER CORPORATION

414 F.3d 233 (2d Cir. 2003)

[The facts of this case are laid out in Module 9, *supra*. In summary, plaintiffs filed an action under the Alien Tort Claims Act ("ATCA"), alleging that the Southern Peru Copper Corporation ("SPCC") infringed upon their customary international law "right to life," "right to health," and right to "sustainable development," though they dropped the sustainable development claim on appeal.]

As an initial matter, we hold that the asserted "right to life" and "right to health" are insufficiently definite to constitute rules of customary international law. As noted above, in order to state a claim under the ATCA, we have required that a plaintiff allege a violation of a "clear and unambiguous" rule of customary international law. *Kadic [v. Karadzic]*, 70 F.3d at 239 (holding that federal jurisdiction lies under the ATCA if "the defendant's alleged conduct violates 'well-established, universally recognized norms of international law' ... as opposed to 'idiosyncratic legal rules'" (quoting *Filartiga*, 630 F.2d at 888, 881)); *cf. Beanal v. Freeport–McMoran, Inc.*, 197 F.3d 161, 167 (5th Cir. 1999) (stating that customary international law cannot be established by reference to "abstract rights and liberties devoid of articulable or discernable standards and regulations"); *Hilao v. Estate of Marcos (In re Estate of Ferdinand Marcos, Human Rights Litig.)*, 25 F.3d 1467, 1475 (9th Cir. 1994) (stating that a rule of customary international law must be "specific, universal, and obligatory").

Far from being "clear and unambiguous," the statements relied on by plaintiffs to define the rights to life and health are vague and amorphous. For example, the statements that plaintiffs rely on to define the rights to life and health include the following:

> Everyone has the right to a standard of living adequate for the health and well-being of himself and of his family....

Universal Declaration of Human Rights, Art. 25 (1948).

> The States Parties to the present Covenant recognize the right of everyone to the enjoyment of the highest attainable standard of physical and mental health.

International Covenant on Economic, Social, and Cultural Rights, Art. 12, opened for signature Dec. 19, 1966, 993 U.N.T.S. 3.

> Human beings are ... entitled to a healthy and productive life in harmony with nature.

Rio Declaration on Environment and Development ("Rio Declaration"), United Nations Conference on Environment and Development, June 13, 1992, Principle 1.

These principles are boundless and indeterminate. They express virtuous goals understandably expressed at a level of abstraction needed to secure the adherence of States that disagree on many of the particulars regarding how actually to achieve them. But in the words of a sister circuit, they "state abstract rights and liberties devoid of articulable or discernable standards and regulations." The precept that "[h]uman beings are ... entitled to a healthy and productive life in harmony with nature," Rio Declaration, Principle 1, for example, utterly fails to specify what conduct would fall within or outside of the law. Similarly, the exhortation that all people are entitled to the "highest attainable standard of physical and mental health," International Covenant on Economic, Social, and Cultural Rights, Art. 12, proclaims only nebulous notions that are infinitely malleable.

In support of plaintiffs' argument that the statements and instruments discussed above are part of customary international law, plaintiffs attempt to underscore the universality of the principles asserted by pointing out that they "contain no limitations as to how or by whom these rights may be violated." * * * However, this assertion proves too much; because of the conceded absence of any "limitations" on these "rights," they do not meet the requirement of our law that rules of customary international law be clear, definite, and unambiguous. For the foregoing reasons, plaintiffs have failed to establish the existence of a customary international law "right to life" or "right to health."

Although customary international law does not protect a right to life or right to health, plaintiffs' complaint may be construed to assert a claim under a more narrowly-defined customary international law rule against intranational pollution.[1] However, the voluminous documents and the affidavits of international law scholars submitted by plaintiffs fail to demonstrate the existence of any such norm of customary international law. * * *

The treaties on which plaintiffs principally rely include: the International Covenant on Civil and Political Rights; the American Convention on Human Rights; the International Covenant on Economic, Social and Cultural Rights; and the United Nations Convention on the Rights of the Child. The only treaty relied on by plaintiffs that the United States

---

1. Because plaintiffs do not allege that defendants' conduct had an effect outside the borders of Peru, we need not consider the customary international law status of transnational pollution.

has ratified is the non-self-executing International Covenant on Civil and Political Rights ("ICCPR"), opened for signature Dec. 19, 1966. * * * Plaintiffs rely on Article 6(1) of the ICCPR, which states that "[e]very human being has the inherent right to life" that "shall be protected by law," and that "[n]o one shall be arbitrarily deprived of his life." As noted above, the "right to life" is insufficiently definite to give rise to a rule of customary international law. Because no other provision of the ICCPR so much as suggests an international law norm prohibiting intranational pollution, the ICCPR does not provide a basis for plaintiffs' claim that defendant has violated a rule of customary international law. * * *

Plaintiffs also rely on the unratified International Covenant on Economic, Social and Cultural Rights ("ICESCR"). * * * This instrument arguably refers to the topic of pollution in article 12, which "recognize[s] the right of everyone to the enjoyment of the highest attainable standard of physical and mental health," and instructs the States parties to take the steps necessary for "[t]he improvement of all aspects of environmental and industrial hygiene," *id.* art. 12(2)(b). Although article 12(2)(b) instructs States to take steps to abate environmental pollution within their borders, it does not mandate particular measures or specify what levels of pollution are acceptable. Instead, it is vague and aspirational, and there is no evidence that the States parties have taken significant uniform steps to put it into practice. Finally, even if this provision were sufficient to create a rule of customary international law, the rule would apply only to state actors because the provision addresses only "the steps to be taken by the States Parties," ICESCR art. 12(2) and does not profess to govern the conduct of private actors such as defendant SPCC. * * *

Plaintiffs [also] rely on several resolutions of the United Nations General Assembly in support of their assertion that defendant's conduct violated a rule of customary international law. These documents are not proper sources of customary international law because they are merely aspirational and were never intended to be binding on member States of the United Nations. * * * General Assembly resolutions and declarations do not have the power to bind member States because the member States specifically denied the General Assembly that power after extensively considering the issue—first at the Dumbarton Oaks Conference, held in Washington in 1944, then at the Yalta conference in 1945, and finally at the United Nations' founding conference, held in San Francisco in 1945. * * * In sum, as described in THE LAW OF NATIONS, the classic handbook by Professors Brierly and Waldock:

> [A]ll that the General Assembly can do is to discuss and recommend and initiate studies and consider reports from other bodies. It cannot act on behalf of all the members, as the Security Council

does, and its decisions are not directions telling the member states what they are or are not to do.

J.L. BRIERLY, THE LAW OF NATIONS 110 (Sir Humphrey Waldock ed., 6th ed. 1963). Because General Assembly documents are at best merely advisory, they do not, on their own and without proof of uniform state practice, evidence an intent by member States to be legally bound by their principles, and thus cannot give rise to rules of customary international law. * * *

Our position is consistent with the recognition in *Filartiga* that the right to be free from torture embodied in the Universal Declaration of Human Rights * * * has attained the status of customary international law. *Filartiga* cited the Universal Declaration for the proposition that torture is universally condemned, reasoning that "a [United Nations] declaration may by custom become recognized as [a] rule[ ]" of customary international law. The Court explained that non-binding United Nations documents such as the Universal Declaration "create[ ] an expectation of adherence," but they evidence customary international law only "insofar as the expectation is gradually justified by State practice." In considering the Universal Declaration's prohibition against torture, the *Filartiga* Court cited extensive evidence that States, in their domestic and international practices, repudiate official torture. In particular, it recognized that torture is prohibited under law by, *inter alia*, the constitutions of fifty-five States * * * and noted the conclusion expressed by the Executive Branch of our government—the political branch with principal responsibility for conducting the international relations of the United States—that "[t]here now exists an international consensus" against official torture that "virtually all governments acknowledge." * * * Accordingly, although *Filartiga* did indeed cite the Universal Declaration, this non-binding General Assembly declaration was only relevant to *Filartiga*'s analysis insofar as it accurately described the actual customs and practices of States on the question of torture.

In the instant case, the General Assembly documents relied on by plaintiffs do not describe the actual customs and practices of States. Accordingly, they cannot support plaintiffs' claims. * * *

Plaintiffs [also] submitted to the District Court several affidavits by international law scholars in support of their argument that strictly intranational pollution violates customary international law. After careful consideration, the District Court declined to afford evidentiary weight to these affidavits. It determined that the affidavits "are even less probative [than plaintiffs' documentary evidence] of the existence of universal norms, especially considering the vigorous academic debate over the content of international law." * * * It explained further:

> The Second Circuit in *Filartiga* stated that courts should determine whether a rule is well-established and universally recognized by consulting, among other sources, " 'the works of jurists, writing professedly on public law.' " In this case, plaintiffs and defendant

have submitted multiple affidavits by professors, explaining why or why not plaintiffs' claims are supported by customary international law. The affidavits serve essentially as supplemental briefs, providing arguments and citations which for the most part also appear in the parties' main briefs. I doubt that such academic exercises in advocacy are the sort of scholarly writings the Second Circuit had in mind when it identified the sources that could serve as evidence of customary international law.

Plaintiffs argue on appeal that the District Court did not accord proper weight to the statements of their experts. They maintain that "[t]he authority of scholars [and] jurists . . . has long been recognized by the Supreme Court and this Court as authoritative sources for determining the content of international law." * * *

In its seminal decision in *Paquete Habana*, the Supreme Court designated "the works of jurists [*i.e.*, scholars] and commentators" as a possible source of customary international law. 175 U.S. at 700. However, the Court expressly stated that such works "are resorted to by judicial tribunals, not for the speculations of their authors concerning what the law ought to be, but for trustworthy evidence of what the law really is." Accordingly, under *Paquete Habana*, United States judicial tribunals may only "resort[ ] to" the works of "jurists and commentators" insofar as such works set forth the current law as it "really is." Conversely, courts may not entertain as evidence of customary international law "speculations" by "jurists and commentators" about "what the law ought to be." * * *

[Nothing in] *Paquete Habana* recognizes as a source of customary international law the policy-driven or theoretical work of advocates that comprises a substantial amount of contemporary international law scholarship. Nor do these authorities permit us to consider personal viewpoints expressed in the affidavits of international law scholars. In sum, although scholars may provide accurate descriptions of the actual customs and practices and legal obligations of States, only the courts may determine whether these customs and practices give rise to a rule of customary international law. We have reviewed the affidavits submitted by plaintiffs and agree with the District Court's conclusion that they are not competent evidence of customary international law.

In addition to the types of evidence discussed above, plaintiffs direct the Court's attention to a varied assortment of other instruments that neither give rise to, nor evidence, concrete, international legal obligations. Plaintiffs argue that all of the items of evidence they have submitted, when taken together, prove that local environmental pollution violates customary international law. However, because each of the instruments and affidavits plaintiffs rely on provides no evidence that intranational pollution violates customary international law, plaintiffs' claims fail whether these instruments and affidavits are considered individually or cumulatively. * * *

NOTES AND QUESTIONS ON HUMAN RIGHTS AND THE ENVIRONMENT

1. *The principal cases.* Are *López Ostra* and *Flores* irreconcilable or distinguishable?

2. *Evidence of a right to environmental protection.* In determining the normative status of a human right to environmental protection, consider the following:

▶ Article 24 of the Convention on the Rights of the Child provides that States are to take appropriate measures "to combat disease and malnutrition * * * taking into consideration the dangers of risks of environmental pollution."

▶ Article 24 of the African Charter on Human and People's Rights states that "all peoples shall have the right to a general satisfactory environment favorable to their development."

▶ A 1989 Protocol to the American Convention on Human Rights grants individuals the right to live in a healthy environment.

▶ Scores of national constitutions and domestic statutes include provisions on environmental protection, formulated either as a right to environmental protection or as a duty of the state.

▶ The CEDAW committee linked environmental protection to the right to health in its Concluding Observations on the State Report of Romania in 2000, expressing its "concern about the situation of the environment, including industrial accidents, and their impact on women's health."

▶ The World Conference on Human Rights, in its Vienna Declaration and Programme of Action (1994), recognized that "illicit dumping of toxic and dangerous substances and waste potentially constitutes a serious threat to the human rights to life and health of everyone" and called on all states "to adopt and vigorously implement existing conventions relating to the dumping of toxic and dangerous products and waste and to cooperate in the prevention of illicit dumping."

▶ A range of treaties impose environmental obligations on governments, including among many others, the Convention on Biological Diversity (1992), the Framework Convention on Climate Change (1992), the Convention to Combat Desertification (1994), and the Stockholm Convention on Persistent Organic Pollutants (2001).

▶ In *The Case of the Mayagna (Sumo) Awas Tingni Community v. Nicaragua*, the Inter–American Court of Human Rights, without recognizing some free-standing right to environmental protection or a clean environment, unanimously declared that Nicaragua had to adopt laws, regulations, and other mechanisms to establish effective surveying, demarcating and title protections for the properties of certain indigenous communities. The government also had to act in accordance with customary law and indigenous values, uses and customs. Pending the actual surveying and demarcation of the indigenous lands, the State had to abstain from doing anything that could affect the existence, the value, the use, or the enjoyment of the properties located in Awas Tingni lands.

▶ Professor Dinah Shelton, reviewing the work of the U.N. Human Rights Committee, concluded that the Committee "has indicated that state obligations to protect the right to life can include positive measures designed to reduce infant mortality and protect against malnutrition and epidemics. The Committee has interpreted Article 27 of the Covenant on Civil and Political Rights in a broad manner, observing that culture manifests itself in many forms, including a particular way of life associated with the use of land resources, especially in the case of indigenous peoples."

▶ In the United Nations Millennium Declaration (2000), heads of state and government reaffirmed the principles adopted at the Rio Conference, resolved to "spare no effort to free all of humanity, and above all our children and grandchildren, from the threat of living on a planet irredeemably spoilt by human activities, and whose resources would no longer be sufficient for their needs," and set specific targets for the protection of the natural environment.

▶ According to the Secretary–General of the United Nations, "Several multilateral environmental agreements (MEAs) adopted in recent years provide evidence of the existing links between the protection of the environment and the enjoyment of human rights. Some of these conventions aim at protecting the environment and human health against risks associated with various forms of pollution. Others endorse individual procedural rights—such as the right to receive information concerning the environment held by public authorities, the right to participate in decision-making process or the right to have access to justice—that may be regarded as human rights (*e.g.* the right to remedy), or as emerging human rights standards (*e.g.* the right to have access to information held by public authorities). These MEAs play an important role in fostering connections between human rights and the environment, in particular by enhancing the implementation of principle 10 of the Rio Declaration." Commission on Human Rights, *Human Rights and the Environment as Part of Sustainable Development: Report of the Secretary–General*, E/CN.4/2005/96 (19 January 2005).

Can you use these authorities to make out a customary human right to environmental protection? What else would you need to know before answering this question? In their consistency, their specificity, and their "bindingness," how do these various authorities compare—separately or in aggregate—with those found to prohibit torture in the *Filartiga* case, *supra*, Chapter 1.

3. *Limits of the human rights paradigm.* How do you respond to the argument that the rhetoric of human rights law is particularly ill-suited to the protection of the environment, where the protection of non-human resources is critical and where the essential conflict is typically not between an individual victim and his or her government but between the different needs of individuals and groups in a society? Sound environmental decisions often require the balancing of multiple constituencies' interests, compromising between the long and short term, balancing certain kinds of goods and against other kinds of goods. What is the virtue and what is the vice of a human rights approach to these compromises? *See generally* Alan Boyle and Michael Anderson, HUMAN RIGHTS APPROACHES TO ENVIRONMENTAL PROTECTION (1996).

4. *Environmental protection as "derivative" from other, more established rights.* What is the significance of the fact that the European Court of Human Rights rested its decision in *López Ostra*, not on a free-standing right of environmental protection, but on the explicit treaty-based right to "respect for [one's] private and family life, * * * home and * * * correspondence"? Would serious environmental degradation of one's workplace or favorite recreational spot get the same protection as a "home"?

5. *The problem of incommensurability.* If there is a free-standing human right to environmental protection, how shall it be reconciled with other human rights, emerging and otherwise, like the right to economic development, the right to democratic government, and the right to cultural identity? The possibility of conflict among these standards is not hard to imagine: suppose for example that an indigenous people has historically engaged in a religious practice that has become environmentally unsound, causing serious environmental risk to the entire population of a state and consuming resources that might more profitably—and more safely—be used by industry.

6. *Affirmative obligations of the state.* Like the Inter–American Court's decision in *Velasquez-Rodriguez, supra*, Module 7(B), the *López Ostra* court imposed on the government an affirmative duty to take appropriate measures to ensure respect for private life. It's not enough in other words for the government to refrain from arbitrary interferences by public authorities: the government is obliged to ensure affirmatively that citizens can enjoy their rights. Does this blur the distinction between public and private interferences with human rights? Is that—more than any particular substantive right or obligation—the trajectory of human rights law in the twenty-first century?

HUMAN RIGHTS AND ECONOMIC DEVELOPMENT

When Mary Robinson, then the UN High Commissioner for Human Rights, was asked to identify the most serious form of human rights violations in the world, she consistently replied, "extreme poverty." United Nations Development Programme, POVERTY REDUCTION AND HUMAN RIGHTS: A PRACTICE NOTE iv (2003). Her point was not merely that the abuse of human rights—like gender and race discrimination—can have profound economic consequences by impoverishing the target group, sometimes permanently, but it was that the existence of poverty on a global scale may itself qualify as a violation of human rights standards. Essentially, in her view, a human right to economic development exists.

Over twenty years ago, the United Nations adopted a Declaration on the Right to Development, by a vote of 146 to one (the United States) and eight abstentions. And at the turn of the twenty-first century, the heads of state and government adopted a declaration of Millennium Development Goals, which included, by 2015, reducing by half "the proportion of the world's people whose income is less than one dollar a day and the proportion of people who suffer from hunger and, by the same date, to halve the proportion of people who are unable to reach or to afford safe drinking water." This section invites you to consider the legal component of poverty reduction, and in particular what a human rights-based approach to poverty reduction would look like. Understanding that poor people should not be treated as though they constitute a single homogeneous group, what does the right to economic development mean?

DECLARATION ON THE RIGHT TO DEVELOPMENT
General Assembly Resolution 41/128 (4 December 1986)

The General Assembly, * * *

Considering that under the provisions of the Universal Declaration of Human Rights everyone is entitled to a social and international order in which the rights and freedoms set forth in that Declaration can be fully realized, * * *

Recalling the right of peoples to self-determination, by virtue of which they have the right freely to determine their political status and to pursue their economic, social and cultural development, * * *

Considering that the elimination of the massive and flagrant violations of the human rights of the peoples and individuals affected by situations such as those resulting from colonialism, neo-colonialism, apartheid, all forms of racism and racial discrimination, foreign domination and occupation, aggression and threats against national sovereignty, national unity and territorial integrity and threats of war would contribute to the establishment of circumstances propitious to the development of a great part of mankind,

Concerned at the existence of serious obstacles to development, as well as to the complete fulfilment of human beings and of peoples, constituted, *inter alia*, by the denial of civil, political, economic, social and cultural rights, and considering that all human rights and fundamental freedoms are indivisible and interdependent and that, in order to promote development, equal attention and urgent consideration should be given to the implementation, promotion and protection of civil, political, economic, social and cultural rights and that, accordingly, the promotion of, respect for and enjoyment of certain human rights and fundamental freedoms cannot justify the denial of other human rights and fundamental freedoms. * * *

Proclaims the following Declaration on the Right to Development:

Article 1

1. The right to development is an inalienable human right by virtue of which every human person and all peoples are entitled to participate in, contribute to, and enjoy economic, social, cultural and political development, in which all human rights and fundamental freedoms can be fully realized.

2. The human right to development also implies the full realization of the right of peoples to self-determination, which includes, subject to the relevant provisions of both International Covenants on Human Rights, the exercise of their inalienable right to full sovereignty over all their natural wealth and resources.

Article 2

1. The human person is the central subject of development and should be the active participant and beneficiary of the right to development.

2. All human beings have a responsibility for development, individually and collectively, taking into account the need for full respect for their human rights and fundamental freedoms as well as their duties to the community, which alone can ensure the free and complete fulfilment of the human being, and they should therefore promote and protect an appropriate political, social and economic order for development.

3. States have the right and the duty to formulate appropriate national development policies that aim at the constant improvement of the well-being of the entire population and of all individuals, on the basis of their active, free and meaningful participation in development and in the fair distribution of the benefits resulting therefrom.

Article 3

1. States have the primary responsibility for the creation of national and international conditions favourable to the realization of the right to development.

2. The realization of the right to development requires full respect for the principles of international law concerning friendly relations and co-operation among States in accordance with the Charter of the United Nations.

3. States have the duty to co-operate with each other in ensuring development and eliminating obstacles to development. States should realize their rights and fulfil their duties in such a manner as to promote a new international economic order based on sovereign equality, inter-dependence, mutual interest and co-operation among all States, as well as to encourage the observance and realization of human rights.

Article 4

1. States have the duty to take steps, individually and collectively, to formulate international development policies with a view to facilitating the full realization of the right to development.

2. Sustained action is required to promote more rapid development of developing countries. As a complement to the efforts of developing countries, effective international co-operation is essential in providing these countries with appropriate means and facilities to foster their comprehensive development.

Article 5

States shall take resolute steps to eliminate the massive and flagrant violations of the human rights of peoples and human beings affected by situations such as those resulting from *apartheid*, all forms of racism and racial discrimination, colonialism, foreign domination and occupation, aggression, foreign interference and threats against national sovereignty, national unity and territorial integrity, threats of war and refusal to recognize the fundamental right of peoples to self-determination.

Article 6

1. All States should co-operate with a view to promoting, encouraging and strengthening universal respect for and observance of all human rights and fundamental freedoms for all without any distinction as to race, sex, language or religion.

2. All human rights and fundamental freedoms are indivisible and interdependent; equal attention and urgent consideration should be given to the implementation, promotion and protection of civil, political, economic, social and cultural rights.

3. States should take steps to eliminate obstacles to development result-ing from failure to observe civil and political rights, as well as economic social and cultural rights.

Article 7

All States should promote the establishment, maintenance and strengthening of international peace and security and, to that end, should do their utmost to achieve general and complete disarmament under effective international control, as well as to ensure that the resources released by effective disarmament measures are used for comprehensive development, in particular that of the developing countries.

Article 8

1.　States should undertake, at the national level, all necessary measures for the realization of the right to development and shall ensure, *inter alia*, equality of opportunity for all in their access to basic resources, education, health services, food, housing, employment and the fair distribution of income. Effective measures should be undertaken to ensure that women have an active role in the development process. Appropriate economic and social reforms should be carried out with a view to eradicating all social injustices.

2.　States should encourage popular participation in all spheres as an important factor in development and in the full realization of all human rights.

Article 9

1.　All the aspects of the right to development set forth in the present Declaration are indivisible and interdependent and each of them should be considered in the context of the whole.

2.　Nothing in the present Declaration shall be construed as being contrary to the purposes and principles of the United Nations, or as implying that any State, group or person has a right to engage in any activity or to perform any act aimed at the violation of the rights set forth in the Universal Declaration of Human Rights and in the International Covenants on Human Rights.

Article 10

Steps should be taken to ensure the full exercise and progressive enhancement of the right to development, including the formulation, adoption and implementation of policy, legislative and other measures at the national and international levels.

UNITED NATIONS MILLENNIUM DECLARATION

General Assembly Resolution 55/2 (8 September 2000)

1.　We, heads of State and Government, have gathered at United Nations Headquarters in New York from 6 to 8 September 2000, at the dawn of a new millennium, to reaffirm our faith in the Organization and its Charter as indispensable foundations of a more peaceful, prosperous and just world. * * *

4.　We are determined to establish a just and lasting peace all over the world in accordance with the purposes and principles of the Charter. We rededicate ourselves to support all efforts to uphold the sovereign equality of all States, respect for their territorial integrity and political independence, resolution of disputes by peaceful means and in conformity with the principles of justice and international law, the right to self-determination of peoples which remain under colonial domination and foreign occupation, non-interference in the internal affairs of States, respect for human rights and fundamental freedoms, respect for the equal rights of all without distinction as to race, sex, language or religion and international cooperation in solving international problems of an economic, social, cultural or humanitarian character.

5.   We believe that the central challenge we face today is to ensure that globalization becomes a positive force for all the world's people. For while globalization offers great opportunities, at present its benefits are very unevenly shared, while its costs are unevenly distributed. We recognize that developing countries and countries with economies in transition face special difficulties in responding to this central challenge. Thus, only through broad and sustained efforts to create a shared future, based upon our common humanity in all its diversity, can globalization be made fully inclusive and equitable. These efforts must include policies and measures, at the global level, which correspond to the needs of developing countries and economies in transition and are formulated and implemented with their effective participation.

6.   We consider certain fundamental values to be essential to international relations in the twenty-first century. These include:

- *Freedom*. Men and women have the right to live their lives and raise their children in dignity, free from hunger and from the fear of violence, oppression or injustice. Democratic and participatory governance based on the will of the people best assures these rights.

- *Equality*. No individual and no nation must be denied the opportunity to benefit from development. The equal rights and opportunities of women and men must be assured.

- *Solidarity*. Global challenges must be managed in a way that distributes the costs and burdens fairly in accordance with basic principles of equity and social justice. Those who suffer or who benefit least deserve help from those who benefit most.

- *Tolerance*. Human beings must respect one other, in all their diversity of belief, culture and language. Differences within and between societies should be neither feared nor repressed, but cherished as a precious asset of humanity. A culture of peace and dialogue among all civilizations should be actively promoted.

- *Respect for nature*. Prudence must be shown in the management of all living species and natural resources, in accordance with the precepts of sustainable development. Only in this way can the immeasurable riches provided to us by nature be preserved and passed on to our descendants. The current unsustainable patterns of production and consumption must be changed in the interest of our future welfare and that of our descendants.

• *Shared responsibility*. Responsibility for managing worldwide economic and social development, as well as threats to international peace and security, must be shared among the nations of the world and should be exercised multilaterally. As the most universal and most representative organization in the world, the United Nations must play the central role.

7. In order to translate these shared values into actions, we have identified key objectives to which we assign special significance. * * *

III. Development and poverty eradication

11. We will spare no effort to free our fellow men, women and children from the abject and dehumanizing conditions of extreme poverty, to which more than a billion of them are currently subjected. We are committed to making the right to development a reality for everyone and to freeing the entire human race from want.

12. We resolve therefore to create an environment—at the national and global levels alike—which is conducive to development and to the elimination of poverty.

13. Success in meeting these objectives depends, *inter alia*, on good governance within each country. It also depends on good governance at the international level and on transparency in the financial, monetary and trading systems. We are committed to an open, equitable, rule-based, predictable and non-discriminatory multilateral trading and financial system.

14. We are concerned about the obstacles developing countries face in mobilizing the resources needed to finance their sustained development. * * *

19. We resolve:

• To halve, by the year 2015, the proportion of the world's people whose income is less than one dollar a day and the proportion of people who suffer from hunger and, by the same date, to halve the proportion of people who are unable to reach or to afford safe drinking water.

• To ensure that, by the same date, children everywhere, boys and girls alike, will be able to complete a full course of primary schooling and that girls and boys will have equal access to all levels of education.

• By the same date, to have reduced maternal mortality by three quarters, and under-five child mortality by two thirds, of their current rates.

• To have, by then, halted, and begun to reverse, the spread of HIV/AIDS, the scourge of malaria and other major diseases that afflict humanity. * * *

• By 2020, to have achieved a significant improvement in the lives of at least 100 million slum dwellers as proposed in the "Cities Without Slums" initiative.

20. We also resolve:

• To promote gender equality and the empowerment of women as effective ways to combat poverty, hunger and disease and to stimulate development that is truly sustainable.

• To develop and implement strategies that give young people everywhere a real chance to find decent and productive work.

• To encourage the pharmaceutical industry to make essential drugs more widely available and affordable by all who need them in developing countries.

• To develop strong partnerships with the private sector and with civil society organizations in pursuit of development and poverty eradication.

• To ensure that the benefits of new technologies, especially information and communication technologies * * * are available to all. * * *

COMMITTEE ON ECONOMIC, SOCIAL AND CULTURAL RIGHTS

General Comment No.3, HRI/GEN/1/Rev.1, at 48, 52

A final element of article 2(1) [of the International Covenant on Economic, Social and Cultural Rights] * * * is that the undertaking given by all States parties is "to take steps, individually and through international assistance and cooperation, especially economic and technical . . .". The Committee notes that the phrase "to the maximum of its available resources" was intended by the drafters of the Covenant to refer to both the resources existing within a State and those available from the international community through international cooperation and assistance. Moreover, the essential role of such cooperation in facilitating the full realization of the relevant rights is further underlined by the specific provisions contained in articles 11, 15, 22 and 23. With respect to article 22 the Committee has already drawn attention, in General Comment 2 (1990), to some of the opportunities and responsibilities that exist in relation to international cooperation. Article 23 also specifically identifies "the furnishing of technical assistance" as well as other activities, as being among the means of "international action for the achievement of the rights recognized".

The Committee wishes to emphasize that in accordance with Articles 55 and 56 of the Charter of the United Nations, with well-established principles of international law, and with the provisions of the Covenant itself, international cooperation for development and thus for the realization of economic, social and cultural rights is an obligation of all States. It is particularly incumbent upon those States which are in a position to assist others in this regard. * * *

UNITED NATIONS COMMISSION ON HUMAN RIGHTS

Working Group on the Right to Development
Third Report of the Independent Expert on the Right to Development (2001)

I. THE CONTENT OF THE RIGHT TO DEVELOPMENT

3. On the basis of the text of the Declaration on the Right to Development (1986), several subsequent international resolutions and declarations adopted at representative international conferences and the 1993 Vienna Declaration and Programme of Action, it should now be possible to reach a consensus on the definition and the content of the right to development. * * *

4. Article 1, paragraph 1, of the Declaration of 1986 states: "The right to development is an inalienable human right by virtue of which every human person and all peoples are entitled to participate in, contribute to and enjoy economic, social, cultural and political development, in which all human rights and fundamental freedoms can be fully realized." The article spells out three principles: first, there is a human right called the right to development which is inalienable; second, there is a particular process of "economic, social, cultural and political development" in which "all human rights and fundamental freedoms can be fully realized"; and third, the right to development is a human right by virtue of which "every human person and all peoples" are entitled to "participate in, contribute to and enjoy" that particular process of development.

5. It should be noted that a country can develop by many different processes. There may be a sharp increase in gross domestic product (GDP) with the "richer groups", with greater access to financial and human capital, growing increasingly prosperous and the "poorer sections" lagging behind, if not remaining deprived. There may be some industrialization, rapid or not so rapid, without the increased income spreading over all the sectors, with the small-scale and informal sectors getting increasingly marginalized. There may be an impressive growth of the export industries with increased access to global markets, but without integrating the economic hinterland into the process of growth and not breaking the structure of a dual economy. All these may be regarded as development in the conventional sense. However, they will not be regarded as a process of development, as objects of claim, as human rights, so long as they are attended by increased inequalities or disparities and rising concentrations of wealth and economic power, and without any improvement in indicators of social development, education, health, gender balance and environmental protection and, what

is most important, if they are associated with any violation of civil and political rights. It is only that process of development "in which all human rights and fundamental freedoms can be fully realized" that can be a universal human right, which is the entitlement of every person.

6. The characteristics of that process of development regarded as a human right have been fairly well spelt out, not only in the Declaration on the Right to Development but also in most other international documents, including the Vienna Declaration and Programme of Action. That the Declaration of 1986 intended to treat the right to development as the right to a process of development is clearly evident in article 2, paragraph 3, which describes such a development process as "the constant improvement of the well-being of the entire population and of all individuals, on the basis of their active, free and meaningful participation in development and in the fair distribution of the benefits resulting therefrom." The phrase "constant improvement of the well-being" not only refers to the notion of "progressive realization" which is implied in any idea of achieving the goals of development; it also calls for precise policy formulation that leads to a properly defined process of "improvement" as well as a properly identified concept of "well-being."

7. The independent expert has examined in detail the implications of looking at the right to development as the right to a "particular" process of development, by analysing both the notions of "improvement" and of "well-being". He felt it necessary to do so because otherwise, designing any mechanism or policies for realizing the right to development with any degree of precision would not be possible. But there are still some misunderstandings about this approach, which the following paragraphs try to clear up.

8. First, the definition of the right to development, as the right to a (particular) process of development, in which "all human rights and fundamental freedoms can be fully realized", is taken from the Declaration itself and does not dilute in any way the notion of the right to development that has emerged from the long tradition of the human rights movement. It refers to the realization of all the rights and freedoms recognized as human rights—civil and political rights and economic and social and cultural rights—in their totality as an integrated whole, as all these rights are interrelated and interdependent. (Article 9, paragraph 1 of the Declaration clearly states: "All the aspects of the right to development set forth in the present Declaration are indivisible and interdependent and each of them should be considered in the context of the whole.") In other words, the right to development is not just the sum total of all the different rights that can be realized individually or in isolation from other rights. As constituent elements of the right to development, these individual rights have to be realized in a manner that takes into account their interdependence with all other rights, does not detract from the realization of the other rights and does not ignore the requirements of the sustainability of the whole process of realizing all the rights. * * *

19. There is now a general consensus that the right to development is a human right. This was spelt out clearly in the Declaration on the Right to Development which, at the time of its adoption, was not supported by all States. Since then there has been a long process of consensus-building, both inside and outside United Nations forums and international conferences. It was at the World Conference on Human Rights in 1993, which was attended by almost all Member States, that there finally emerged a consensus on the right to development as a human right. The Vienna Declaration and Programme of Action reaffirmed the right to development as a "universal and inalienable right and an integral part of fundamental human rights" and also that "the universal nature of these rights and freedoms is beyond question."

20. The implications of treating the right to development as a human right have been fairly well explored in the literature, including Amartya Sen's DEVELOPMENT AS FREEDOM, the Human Development Report 2000, and the independent expert's first and second reports, and need not be elaborated upon again. However, it may be worth reiterating the following, from the first report of the independent expert (para. 20): "For our purpose the recognition of the right to development as an inalienable human right is to confer on its implementation a claim on national and international resources and to oblige States and other agencies of society, including individuals, to implement that right. Human rights are the fundamental basis on which other rights, created by the legal and political systems, are built. The responsibility of States, nationally and internationally, as well as other organs of the civil society to help realize these rights with utmost priority becomes unquestionable. The Vienna Declaration and Programme of Action, in fact, states that categorically. 'Human rights and fundamental freedoms are the birthright of all human beings; their protection and promotion is the first responsibility of Governments.' It goes on to state that 'enhancement of international cooperation in the field of human rights is essential for the full achievement of the purposes of the United Nations.' "

21. Regarding the right to development as a human right implies two things, especially when that right refers to a process of development. First, the realization of each human right and of all of them together has to be carried out in a rights-based manner, as a participatory, accountable and transparent process with equity in decision-making and sharing of the fruits of the process while maintaining respect for civil and political rights. Secondly, the objectives of development should be expressed in terms of claims or entitlements of right-holders which duty-bearers must protect and promote in accordance with international human rights standards of equity and justice. Equity, which is essential to any notion of human rights derived from the idea of equality of all human beings, is clearly associated with fairness or the principles of a just society. In other words, the realization of the human right of development must expand human development following the rights-based approach, thus improving equity and fairness.

22. It should be clear that the identification of the corresponding obligation at the national and the international level is essential to a rights-based approach. The rationale for this has been spelt out in detail in the two reports of the independent expert. As the Declaration on the Right to Development itself points out, the primary responsibility for implementing the right to development belongs to States. The beneficiaries are individuals. The international community has the duty to cooperate to enable States to fulfil their obligation. The Vienna Declaration and Programme of Action also recognizes the obligation of all States, and multilateral institutions to cooperate to achieve the full realization of the right to development. It reaffirms the solemn commitment of all States to fulfil their obligations in accordance with the Charter of the United Nations (paragraph I.1; the reference is to Article 1 of the Charter as well as to Articles 55 and 56). It calls for effective implementation of the right to development through policies at the national level with equitable economic relations and a favourable environment at the international level. * * *

25. The role NGOs play nationally in promoting a human rights-based approach to development and preventing violations of human rights has been highlighted in many documents and resolutions of international conferences. In the independent expert's approach to the realization of the right to development the obligation to facilitate the rights-holders' realizing of their claims falls not only on States nationally and internationally, but on international institutions, on the civil society, and on any body in the civil society in a position to help. NGOs are one constituent of civil society that can and has often played a very effective role in the implementation of human rights. Indeed, when the rights are to be realized in a participatory manner with participation of the beneficiaries in the decision-making and benefit-sharing, with accountability and transparency and in a widely decentralized manner, NGOs may have to play an even more crucial role in monitoring the programmes and delivering the services and may often replace the existing bureaucratic channels of administration. They may also have to play an advocacy role as well as engaging in grass-roots mobilization and organizing of beneficiaries to participate in the decision-making. Furthermore, the role of NGOs would not be limited to national-level actions. The concept of international civil society as a third force is increasingly gaining ground and NGOs may be very effective in not only an international advocacy role but also as facilitators of the delivery of international services. However, the issues of funding, the identities and the commitments of NGOs are quite complex. All the functions of NGOs and of international civil society need to be reviewed carefully and the independent expert may take this up in a future report.

26. Article 8 of the Declaration on the Right to Development states that "effective measures should be undertaken to ensure that women have an active role in the development process". Since 1986 the role of women has been analysed and spelt out in great detail at many interna-

tional conferences and in intergovernmental deliberations and resolutions. Recently, the Beijing Platform for Action (A/CONF.177/20) asserts that all members of society should benefit from "a holistic approach" to all aspects of development: growth, equality between women and men, social justice, conservation and protection of the environment, sustainability, solidarity, participation, peace and respect for human "rights" (para. 14). This "holistic approach to development" is identical to what the independent expert has described as the process of development to which every person is entitled as a human right. The empowerment and equality of women are fundamental to that process.

MOHAMMED BEDJAOUI, THE RIGHT TO DEVELOPMENT, in INTERNATIONAL LAW: ACHIEVEMENTS AND PROSPECTS

(Bedjaoui ed. 1991)

The right to development is a fundamental right, the precondition of liberty, progress, justice and creativity. It is the alpha and omega of human rights, the first and last human right, the beginning and the end, the means and the goal of human rights, in short it is the core right from which all others stem. * * * In reality the international dimension of the right to development is nothing other than the right to an equitable share in the economic and social well-being of the world. It reflects an essential demand of our time since four fifths of the world's population no longer accept that the remaining fifth should continue to build its wealth on their poverty. * * *

[The right to development] has several aspects, the most important and comprehensive of which is the right of each people freely to choose its economic and social system without outside interference or constraint of any kind, and to determine, with equal freedom, its own model of development. * * * [T]he State seeking its own development is entitled to demand that all the other States, the international community and international economic agents collectively do not take away from it what belongs to it, or do not deprive it of what it is or "must be" its due in international trade. In the name of this right to development, the State being considered may claim a "fair price" for its raw materials and for whatever it offers in its trade with the more developed countries. * * * This * * * meaning of the right to development * * * implies that the State is entitled if not to the satisfaction of its needs at least to receive a fair share of what belongs to all, and therefore to that State also.

Learned opinion is divided in its view of the legal validity of the right to development. Many writers consider that while it is undoubtedly an inalienable and imperative right, this is only in the moral, rather than in the legal, sphere. The present writer has, on the contrary, maintained that the right to development is, by its nature, so incontrovertible that it should be regarded as belonging to *jus cogens*.

JACK DONNELLY, HUMAN RIGHTS, DEMOCRACY, AND DEVELOPMENT
21 Hum. Rts. Q. 626–632 (1999)

In the early 1980s, most analysts saw a fundamental conflict, at least in the short and medium run, between development and human rights. The author of this article identified two commonly asserted tradeoffs: the equity tradeoff (sacrifice of distributional equity in favor of rapid capital accumulation, and thus growth) and the liberty tradeoff (sacrifice of civil and political rights in the name of efficiency or a concerted national war on underdevelopment). These tradeoffs, which often were presented as necessary, could be, and in some cases had been, largely avoided, especially the equity tradeoff. Here this article will continue to emphasize the contingency of the relations between human rights and development, but against the background of a somewhat different dominant mainstream.

A.   Development and Civil and Political Rights

Simple assertions of the interdependence of development and civil and political rights certainly go too far. Some highly repressive regimes have achieved sustainable industrial growth. For example, South Korea, Taiwan, and Singapore in the 1970s and 1980s, and China in the 1990s replicated the earlier experience of Western Europe. Most developmental dictatorships, however, have been dismal failures. In Sub–Saharan Africa, even short-term growth often was not achieved. In socialist party-state dictatorships, along with most Latin American and Asian military dictatorships and civilian oligarchies, short and medium run growth proved unsustainable. Those forced to sacrifice personal rights and liberties usually have not received development (sustainable growth) in return.

Largely because of this experience, blanket advocacy of the liberty tradeoff—a staple of the 1960s and 1970s—is rarely encountered today.[1] "Soft" authoritarianism still receives some respect, especially when, as in Singapore, promised economic goods are in fact delivered. However, there is a growing tendency to emphasize compatibilities between civil and political rights and development. For example, international financial institutions * * * have increasingly emphasized the economic contributions of "good governance." Although far short of advocating the full range of internationally recognized civil and political rights, an emphasis on transparency, accountability, and the rule of law does characteristical-

---

1. China is the major exception that proves the rule. When the rhetoric is repeated in places like North Korea, Burma, and Belarus, few take it seriously, either inside or outside the country.

ly lead to advocacy of electoral democracy and a considerable range of civil liberties.

In any case, even in the relatively rare cases where sustained economic development has been achieved by highly repressive regimes, there is little evidence that repression has been necessary for, rather than compatible with, development. Therefore, because the liberty tradeoff has never been seen as intrinsically desirable, an emphasis on the compatibility between civil and political rights and economic development is entirely appropriate.

B.   Markets and Economic and Social Rights

The relationship between development and economic and social rights, however, is more complex, especially when we consider the role of markets. Markets are social institutions designed to produce economic efficiency. Smoothly functioning market systems of production and distribution characteristically produce a greater output of goods and services with a given quantity of resources than alternative schemes. There is thus an almost tautological relationship between markets and rapid growth. This is important * * * because growth (and thus markets) seems to be substantively linked to economic and social rights. Countries such as Cuba and Sri Lanka achieved short and medium run success but long run failure under development plans that emphasized state-based (re-)distribution over market-based growth. Their experiences suggest that a considerable degree of economic efficiency (and thus market mechanisms) is necessary for sustainable progress in implementing economic and social rights.

Nonetheless, what is at times an almost uncontainable contemporary enthusiasm for markets is extremely problematic from a human rights perspective.[2] Like (pure) democracy, (free) markets are justified by arguments of collective good and aggregate benefit, not individual rights (other than, perhaps, the right to economic accumulation). Markets foster efficiency, not social equity or the enjoyment of individual rights for all. Rather than ensure that every person is treated with concern and respect, markets systematically deprive some individuals in order to achieve the collective benefits of efficiency.

Markets distribute growth without regard for individual needs and rights (other than property rights) necessarily and by design. Market distributions are based on contribution to economic value added, which varies sharply and systematically across social groups (as well as between individuals). The poor tend to be "less efficient": as a class, they have fewer of the skills valued highly by markets. Therefore, they are systematically disadvantaged. Their plight is exacerbated when economic and political disadvantage interact in a vicious rights-abusive cycle.

---

2.   In addition to the consequences for economic and social rights, the economic chiropractic of structural adjustment frequently brings governments into popular disrepute, which often weakens democracy and encourages violations of civil and political rights.

Market advocates typically argue that, in return for such short-run disadvantages for the few, everyone benefits from the greater supply of goods and services made available through growth. "Everyone," however, does not mean each and every person. Rather the referent is the average "individual," an abstract collective entity. Even "he" is assured significant gain only in the future. In the here and now, and well into the future, many real, flesh and blood, individual human beings and families suffer.

Efficient markets improve the lot of some—ideally the many—only at the (relative and perhaps even absolute) cost of suffering by others. That suffering is concentrated among society's most vulnerable elements. Even worse, markets distribute the benefits of growth without regard to short-term deprivations. Those who suffer "adjustment costs," such as lost jobs, higher food prices, or inferior health care or education, acquire no special claim to a share of the collective benefits that efficient markets produce. One's "fair share" is a function solely of efficiency, of monetary value added. The human value of suffering, the human costs of deprivation, and the claims they justify are excluded from the accounting of markets.

NOTES AND QUESTIONS ON HUMAN RIGHTS AND ECONOMIC DEVELOPMENT

1. *Definition, justiciability, enforcement.* According to the Office of the UN High Commissioner for Human Rights, the right to development is actually a constellation of rights and legal principles, including:

> full sovereignty over natural resources, self-determination, popular participation in development, equality of opportunity, the creation of favourable conditions for the enjoyment of other civil, political, economic, social and cultural rights. * * * The right to development can be invoked both by individuals and by peoples. It imposes obligations both on individual States—to ensure equal and adequate access to essential resources—and on the international community—to promote fair development policies and effective international cooperation. The World Conference on Human Rights, held in Vienna in 1993, dealt extensively with the right to development and adopted the Vienna Declaration and Programme of Action, which recognized that democracy, development and respect for human rights and fundamental freedoms are interdependent and mutually reinforcing. The World Conference also reaffirmed by consensus the right to development as a universal and inalienable right and an integral part of fundamental human rights. It further stated that, while development facilitates the enjoyment of all human rights, lack of development may not be invoked to justify the abridgement of internationally recognized human rights.

OHCHR, Development—Right to development, available at http://www2.ohchr.org/english/issues/development/right/index.htm (visited 1 June 2008). Which articles in the Declaration on the Right to Development and the Millennium Declaration, if any, seem most within the expertise of human rights lawyers?

2. *Wealth maximization as a human right.* If "development" is defined as increasing the gross domestic product *per capita*, do some international human rights seem more important than others? What options are there for enforcing the right to development defined in this way? On what grounds (legal and otherwise) might you challenge the wealth-maximization definition of "development" in the first place? *See generally* Amartya Sen, Development as Freedom (1999); Dominic McGoldrick, "*Sustainable Development and Human Rights: An Integrated Conception*," 45 Int'l & Comp. L.Q. 796 (1996).

3. *Empirical versus normative claims about development and human rights.* The relationship between human rights and development is sometimes viewed as an empirical matter—based on historical claims about the causal correlation between human rights violations and the continuation of poverty or conflict on a global scale. But there is also a normative component—based on an ethical or legal claim that "[t]he right to development is an inalienable human right by virtue of which every human person and all peoples are entitled to participate in, contribute to and enjoy economic, social, cultural and political development, in which all human rights and fundamental freedoms can be fully realized." Declaration on the Right to Development, *supra*, at Art. 1(1). Do these different claims require different enforcement strategies for advocates?

4. *A rights-based approach to poverty reduction.* The United Nations Development Programme has asserted that human rights law has both a substantive and a procedural payoff in the global plan to reduce poverty.

> Human rights and human development are two sides of the same coin. A human rights-based approach provides both a vision of what development should strive to achieve, and a set of tools and essential references. It is based on the values, standards and principles captured in the UN Charter, the UDHR and subsequent legally binding human rights instruments. It attaches importance not only to development outcomes, as traditional approaches do, but also to the development process, as the latter implies the participation of all stakeholders to ensure that their interests and rights are included in the ultimate development outcomes.

United Nations Development Programme, Poverty Reduction and Human Rights: A Practice Note 5 (2003).

5. *Human rights and the market.* Is there an international human right to a free market? Does your answer change if the notion of a "free market" is disaggregated into component legal parts, like the right to

private property, the rule of law, and an independent and non-corrupt judiciary? Do labor rights, like the right of collective bargaining and the norm against child labor, create a free market or distort it? Does the human right to development imply a right to be free of the free market's failures?

6. *Identifying the rights-bearer:* "*odious debts.*" Who bears the right to development? Individuals? "People(s)"? Is there text in the Declaration on the Right to Development that suggests that the right to development has more to do with sovereign control over natural resources than with individual welfare? If so, could the governments of developing countries claim a legal right to have their external debt cancelled insofar as it blocks their economic development? Consider in this connection the observations of one Nobel laureate in economics:

> Why should the Congolese be forced to repay Cold War loans made by Western countries to buy Mobutu's favor—especially since the lenders knew full well that the money was going not to the people of the country but to Mobutu's Swiss bank accounts? Why should Ethiopians have to repay the loans made to the Mengistu "Red Terror" regimes—loans that made it possible to buy the arms used to kill the very people whose friends and relatives must now repay the loans? Chileans today are still paying off debts incurred during the Pinochet years, and South Africans are still paying off those incurred under apartheid. Argentines are still repaying the money that financed the "dirty war" in their country, from 1976 to 1983. Regrettably, we have no rule of law at the international level for the restructuring of government debts. In the past, Western governments had an easy way of dealing with countries that didn't meet their financial obligations: they invaded them. Today we live in what we hope is a more civilized world: we no longer openly condone armed attacks by one country on another for a failure to pay up. At the level of personal debt we've made progress, by instituting bankruptcy laws to replace debtors' prisons, portrayed so graphically in the work of Charles Dickens. And yet to date we have no parallel set of laws governing the restructuring and relief of international debt. [In 2001] the International Monetary Fund at last recognized that this is a major problem and proposed a set of guiding principles. Achieving international consensus on these principles would have been difficult (the IMF was insisting, problematically, that it serve as the bankruptcy judge, or play some other central role in the bankruptcy process, despite the fact that it is one of the international community's major creditors), but the United States pronounced the initiative unnecessary, effectively blocking it altogether.

Joseph Stiglitz, *Odious Rulers, Odious Debts,* ATLANTIC MONTHLY (November 2003). In December 2005, the International Monetary Fund, roughly following the lead of the G–8 nations, agreed to cancel $3.3 billion owed by nineteen of the poorest nations in the world, though the legal component of that decision, and therefore its precedential value, remains controversial.

7. *Identifying the rights-bearer: using development to justify human rights violations.* Consider Donnelly's "liberty tradeoff," which he defines as the "sacrifice of civil and political rights in the name of efficiency or a concerted national war on underdevelopment." If the state or some other collectivity holds the right to development, what are the potential tradeoffs between civil and political rights on one hand and rights of economic development on the other? And how should those trade-offs be resolved?

8. *Role of the World Bank.* The central mission of the World Bank is the reduction of global poverty and the improvement of living standards. At a meeting of the UN Human Rights Council's Working Group on the Right to Development in January 2008, a World Bank representative "reiterated that while the Bank has no formal position on the right to development, it supports the right to development criteria, welcomes their progressive development into operational tools and endorses the principles underlying the Declaration on the Right to Development." Human Rights Council, Working Group on the Right to Development, REPORT OF THE HIGH-LEVEL TASK FORCE ON THE IMPLEMENTATION OF THE RIGHT TO DEVELOPMENT ON ITS FOURTH SESSION 6 (31 January 2008). Why do you suppose the premier intergovernmental institution committed to poverty reduction would take "no formal position" on the right to development?

HUMAN RIGHTS AND GOOD GOVERNMENT: "THE DEMOCRATIC ENTITLEMENT"

Universal Declaration of Human Rights

Article 21

(1) Everyone has the right to take part in the government of his country, directly or through freely chosen representatives.

(2) Everyone has the right of equal access to public service in his country.

(3) The will of the people shall be the basis of the authority of government; this will shall be expressed in periodic and genuine elections which shall be by universal and equal suffrage and shall be held by secret vote or by equivalent free voting procedures.

THOMAS M. FRANCK, THE EMERGING RIGHT TO DEMOCRATIC GOVERNANCE

86 Am. J. Int'l L. 46 (1992)

More than two centuries have elapsed since the signatories of the U.S. Declaration of Independence sought to manifest two radical propositions. The first is that governments, instituted to secure the "unalienable rights" of their citizens, derive "their just powers from the consent of the governed." We may call this the "democratic entitlement." The second proposition, perhaps less noted by commentators, is that a nation earns "separate and equal station" in the community of states by demonstrating "a decent respect to the opinions of mankind." The authors of the Declaration apparently believed that the legitimacy of the new Confederation of American States was not made evident solely by the transfer of power from Britain but also needed to be acknowledged by "mankind." This we may perceive as a prescient glimpse of the legitimating power of the community of nations.

For two hundred years, these two notions have remained a radical vision. The purpose of this essay is to demonstrate that the radical vision, while not yet fully word made law, is rapidly becoming, in our time, a normative rule of the international system. In the process, the two notions have merged. Increasingly, governments recognize that their legitimacy depends on meeting a normative expectation of the community of states. This recognition has led to the emergence of a community expectation: that those who seek the validation of their empowerment patently govern with the consent of the governed. Democracy, thus, is on the way to becoming a global entitlement, one that increasingly will be promoted and protected by collective international processes. * * * [P]eople almost everywhere now demand that government be validated by western-style parliamentary, multiparty democratic process. Only a few, usually military or theocratic, regimes still resist the trend. Very few argue that parliamentary democracy is a western illusion and a neocolonialist trap for unwary Third World peoples. * * *

This almost-complete triumph of the democratic notions of Hume, Locke, Jefferson and Madison—in Latin America, Africa, Eastern Europe and, to a lesser extent, Asia—may well prove to be the most profound event of the twentieth century and, in all likelihood, the fulcrum on which the future development of global society will turn. It is the unanswerable response to those who have said that free, open, multiparty, electoral parliamentary democracy is neither desired nor desirable outside a small enclave of western industrial states. The question is not whether democracy has swept the boards, but whether global society is ready for an era in which only democracy and the rule of law will be capable of validating governance. . . .

In seeking to assess whether an international democratic order is emerging, data will be marshaled from three related generations of rule making and implementation. The oldest and most highly developed is that subset of democratic norms which emerged under the heading of "self-determination." The second subset—freedom of expression—developed as part of the exponential growth of human rights since the mid–1950s and focuses on maintaining an open market-place of ideas. The third and newest subset seeks to establish, define and monitor a right to free and open elections.

These three subsets somewhat overlap, both chronologically and normatively. Collectively, they do not necessarily penetrate every nook and cranny of democratic theory. For example, the three subsets do not yet address normatively the thorny issue of the right of a disaffected portion of an independent state to secede. . . . Still, these three increasingly normative subsets are large building stones, gradually reinforcing each other and assuming the shape of a coherent normative edifice. Moreover, regional subsets are adding some supernumerary buttresses, cornices and lintels to the new structure that dovetail with, and enrich, the emerging global architecture. Some examples of these will be included in our inventory. * * *

THE CASE OF SELF–DETERMINATION

Self-determination is the historic root from which the democratic entitlement grew. Its deep-rootedness continues to confer important elements of legitimacy on self-determination, as well as on the entitlement's two newer branches, freedom of expression and the electoral right. * * * Since self-determination is the oldest aspect of the democratic entitlement, its pedigree is the best established. Self-determination postulates the right of a people organized in an established territory to determine its collective political destiny in a democratic fashion and is therefore at the core of the democratic entitlement. Symbolically, it is signified by a long-evolving tradition of maintaining observers, on behalf of international and regional organizations, at elections in colonies and trust territories. Early observer missions developed operational procedures. They sent reports to their sponsoring international agency or committee, which helped the community's political organs and individual member governments make deductions about the legitimacy of the decolonization process. Gradually, with many variations, the observer missions' methods became the standard operating procedure for validating an exercise of self-determination. * * *

The aspiration that underpins the principle of self-determination is of an antiquity traceable, in the West, at least to the Hebrews' exodus from Egypt, estimated to have been approximately in 1000 B.C. Its modern rise to the status of universal entitlement began when the Versailles Peace Conference undid, or brought into line with late nineteenth-century European nationalist sensibilities, the work of the Congress of Vienna, which had utterly disregarded ethnic sensibilities in redrawing the map of post-Napoleonic Europe. Embarking on another redesign of Europe after the First World War, President Woodrow

Wilson made self-determination his lodestar. To this end, firmly over-riding the doubts of Secretary of State Robert Lansing,[1] he reinforced the U.S. team of negotiators with an unusual contingent of historians, geographers and ethnologists, the more effectively to argue for the norm's supremacy over power politics and strategic or economic consid-erations. Consequently, the American delegation summoned up exten-sive data on demographics and evidence of ethnicity in advocating free choice by "peoples."

Thus prodded, the conference authorized twenty-six on-site consul-tations with different European groups seeking self-determination. The Danes of Schleswig, annexed to Prussia in 1864, were able to secure agreement that "the frontier between Germany and Denmark shall be fixed in conformity with the wishes of the population." Wilson also prevailed in the view "that all branches of the Slav race" in what was to become Czechoslovakia "should be completely freed from German and Austrian rule" in full consultation with Slavic representatives. He resist-ed efforts by France's Premier Clemenceau to establish an independent Rhenish buffer state consisting of unwilling Germans. Although the Versailles settlement also brought self-determination to Poland, as re-gards the Upper Silesian and Czech boundary settlements, as well as Fiume, Wilson reluctantly came to concede that sometimes one had to consider "other principles"—strategic, economic and logistic—that could "clash with the requirements of self-determination."

Nevertheless, the principle of self-determination, as championed by Wilson and the minorities released from the embrace of the German, Russian and Austro–Hungarian Empires, was applied vigorously, if sometimes imperfectly, to the vanquished lands of postwar Europe. In the rest of Europe, however, it was applied only in Ireland. In denying self-determination to the Aaland Islands—which sought to join Sweden by breaking away from Finland, itself newly emancipated from Russia— a Versailles-created international commission of jurists observed that the Covenant of the League of Nations did not even mention the principle and that it had not yet attained the status of a positive rule of law. More important, self-determination played little part in the disposition of the vast overseas lands and peoples of the former German Empire, which were doled out to Australia, Belgium, Britain, France, Japan, New Zealand and South Africa. It was applied badly, if at all, to the former Turkish dependencies in Asia. The League's mandate system evinced only muted concern for the wishes of those territories' inhabitants.

Remarkably, after the Second World War the principle of self-determination became the most dynamic concept in international rela-tions. Former German, Japanese and Italian colonies were placed under the trusteeship of the victors (and, in one case, the vanquished), with the clear obligation "to promote ... progressive development towards self-government or independence" in accordance with "the freely expressed

---

1. "[T]he phrase [self-determination] is simply loaded with dynamite. It will raise hopes which can never be realized." R. LANSING, THE PEACE NEGOTIATIONS, A PERSONAL NARRATIVE 97 (1921).

wishes of the peoples concerned."[2] Conceptual evolution, however, did not stop there. Soon not only was self-determination recognized as a writ for obtaining decolonization but, by the terms of the very first article of the UN Charter, it achieved the status of a fundamental right of all "peoples" as a necessary prerequisite to the development of "friendly relations among nations." At least potentially, the concept was thus both universalized and internationalized, for it could now be said to portend a duty owed by all governments to their peoples and by each government to all members of the international community.

This was no random theoretical happenstance. In the postwar world of rising nationalisms, denials of self-determination were palpably no mere domestic matter. Repression tended to generate friction with neighboring states where liberation movements habitually sought sanctuary and succor. As in Bangladesh, Eritrea and the Southern Sudan, self-determination, denied, precipitated the flight of hordes of refugees, placing onerous economic, social and political strains on the neighboring states of refuge. Thus was self-determination firmly linked in theory and fact to the main UN task of preventing conflict among nations, a link that carries far-reaching, but ambiguous, implications for its future normative development (as this essay later seeks to demonstrate).

In the thirty-five years following the surrender of the Axis powers, self-determination transformed the world's political landscape. At this stage, the norm had clear, though limited, secessionist overtones, in the sense that it legitimated the secession of colonies from empires. Concurrently, the norm also evolved in a way that did not legitimate self-determination of minorities within a colony. The General Assembly warned against efforts to compromise a colony's "territorial integrity" by those—like Nigeria's Ibos—seeking to secede.[3]

Beginning with India, Burma and West Africa's Gold Coast, Britain acted in compliance with the norm's evolving requirements; it was followed, with more or less enthusiasm, by France, the Netherlands, Belgium, Spain, Portugal and South Africa. Imperial powers complained about the General Assembly's use of Charter Article 73(c) to monitor political developments in their colonies, but the resistance gradually abated. As a result of the impetus of decolonization, UN membership almost tripled. That this remarkable devolution could have been accomplished, for the most part, without recourse to war or revolution is a

---

2. UN CHARTER Art. 76(b).

3. Note, however, the decision of the political leaders of imperial India to partition the country, in effect permitting Pakistan to secede. On "territorial integrity," see Declaration on the Granting of Independence to Colonial Countries and Peoples, GA Res. 1514, 15 UN GAOR Supp. (No. 16) at 66, UN Doc. A/4684 (1960); and Declaration on Principles of International Law concerning Friendly Relations and Co-operation among States in accordance with the Charter of the United Nations, Annex to GA Res. 2625, 25 UN GAOR Supp. (No. 28) at 121, UN Doc. A/8028 (1970), reprinted in 9 ILM 1292 (1970) [hereinafter Friendly Relations Declaration]. Note also GA Res. 1654 of 1961, in which, without dissent, the Assembly expressed itself as "[d]eeply concerned that, contrary to the provisions of paragraph 6 of the Declaration, acts aimed at the partial or total disruption of national unity and territorial integrity are still being carried out in certain countries in the process of decolonization." 16 UN GAOR Supp. (No. 17) at 65, UN Doc. A/5100 (1961).

tribute to the normative legitimacy and primacy accorded self-determination by the consistent practice—despite lapses—of the community of states. As we shall see, the growth of this process was facilitated by UN reporting requirements, the Organization's close scrutiny of the work of colonial administrations and the active involvement of the United Nations in monitoring elections and plebiscites in territories advancing toward independence. Self-determination was seen to require democratic consultation with colonial peoples, legitimated by an international presence at elections immediately preceding the creative moment of independence.

Today, the process of decolonization is nearly complete. Nevertheless, the principle of self-determination retains vigor, manifestly having contributed to the decision by the leaders of the Soviet Union, beginning in 1989, to withdraw their military forces and political suzerainty from Eastern Europe and, more recently, from the Baltic States. Its pull prompted South Africa's decision to give independence to Namibia and Morocco's volte-face regarding Western Sahara. When another vestige of imperfect decolonization, the Angolan civil war, ended in 1991, it was on the basis of an agreement to hold free, internationally observed elections, which, *nunc pro tunc*, would give Angola the legitimate regime it had failed to acquire at the chaotic moment of its independence. Another UN-supervised process of popular consultation was created by the Paris agreement ending the civil war in Cambodia. * * * [T]he idea of self-determination has evolved into a more general notion of internationally validated political consultation, one that is beginning to be applied even to independent (postcolonial) states like Nicaragua and Angola, albeit without implying the community's right to validate secessionist movements within sovereign states.

The story of self-determination, as the first building block in the creation of a democratic entitlement, may thus be seen as a remarkable saga that tells of a rule that gradually augments its compliance pull, overcomes resistance and ultimately brings about an incontestable, historic transformation. Rules that acquire this kind of pedigree have a unique claim to legitimacy. Moreover, the deeply embedded roots of self-determination also anchor the legitimacy claims of other, more recent, components of the democratic entitlement. * * *

DETERMINACY: ITS FUNCTION IN BESTOWING LEGITIMACY

The * * * newest building block in constructing the entitlement to democracy is the emerging normative requirement of a participatory *electoral* process. Despite its infancy, it, too, is rapidly evolving toward that determinacy which is essential to being perceived as legitimate. As early as 1948, the Universal Declaration of Human Rights, in Article 21, clearly enunciated the right of all persons to take part in government, as well as in "periodic and genuine elections which shall be by universal and equal suffrage and shall be held by secret vote or by equivalent free voting procedures." At the time, only UN members outside the socialist,

Arab and Latin American blocs took this as a restatement of conditions already prevailing in their polis. With rapid decolonization, the proportion of UN members actually practicing free and open electoral democracy began to shrink further under the aegis of one-party modernizing authoritarianism in Africa and Asia. Nevertheless, even in that relatively hostile atmosphere, few states were willing openly to block the textual evolution of a specific electoral entitlement, however many mental reservations their regimes may have harbored. Thus, two decades later, the Civil and Political Covenant was opened for signature, entering into force in 1976 as a set of legal obligations now binding on more than two-thirds of all states. With the balance now heavily tilting toward the substantial new majority of states actually practicing a reasonably credible version of electoral democracy, the treaty-based legal entitlement also begins to approximate prevailing practice and thus may be said to be stating what is becoming a customary legal norm applicable to all.

Article 25 extends to every citizen the right:

(a) To take part in the conduct of public affairs, directly or through freely chosen representatives;

(b) To vote and to be elected at genuine periodic elections which shall be by universal and equal suffrage and shall be held by secret ballot, guaranteeing the free expression of the will of the electors.

Admirable as it is, this standard still needs greater specificity. Textual determinacy * * * is gradually being augmented by process determinacy under the auspices of the Human Rights Committee, which is authorized to monitor compliance. That body has discussed the implications of Article 25 in connection with its review of national reports on implementation and a small number of petitions lodged under the Optional Protocol. In reviewing two citizens' complaints against the military regime of Uruguay, the Committee concluded that the complainants had been arbitrarily deprived of protected rights by decrees banning their political party and by being barred from running for office.[4] * * *

The new climate has also permeated the General Assembly. At its forty-fifth session, that body adopted a resolution entitled Enhancing the effectiveness of the principle of periodic and genuine elections.[5] This nonbinding, yet important, document reaffirms and further specifies the electoral entitlement first outlined in the Universal Declaration of Human Rights and later embodied in Article 25 of the Covenant. It "stresses" the member nations' conviction that periodic and genuine elections are a necessary and indispensable element of sustained efforts to protect the rights and interests of the governed and that, as a matter of practical experience, the right of everyone to take part in the

---

4. [Report of the Human Rights Committee, 36 UN GAOR Supp. (No. 40) at 130, UN Doc. A/36/40 (1981) [hereinafter 1981 Report]].

5. GA Res. 45/150 (Feb. 21, 1991).

government of his or her country is a crucial factor in the effective enjoyment by all of a wide range of other human rights and fundamental freedoms, embracing political, economic, social and cultural rights.

The resolution also declares "that determining the will of the people requires an electoral process that provides an equal opportunity for all citizens to become candidates and put forward their political views, individually and in co-operation with others, as provided in national constitutions and laws." * * *

Parallel and reinforcing norm-generating activity occurring in regional frameworks has accelerated this evolution. The Charter of the Organization of American States, in Article 5, establishes the duty of members to promote "the effective exercise of representative democracy." The OAS Ministers of Foreign Affairs and the Organization's Permanent Council have issued a series of resolutions affirming this regional entitlement while censuring those committing apparent violations. For example, in June 1979, the Ministers demanded the "immediate and definitive replacement of the Somoza regime" in Nicaragua and the installation of a "democratic government" with the "holding of free elections as soon as possible."[6] Similarly, in December 1987, the Permanent Council took note of the "deplorable acts of violence and disorder" that had taken place in Haiti during that year's failed elections, expressed its "conviction that it is necessary to resume the democratic process" and urged the "Government of Haiti to adopt all necessary measures so that the people of Haiti may express their will through free elections."[7] * * * Alongside these quasi-legislative developments, a regional quasi jurisprudence is germinating. In 1990, the Inter–American Commission on Human Rights, in considering a complaint of electoral fraud and other impropriety against Mexico, began to spell out in some detail the right of access, under general conditions of equality, to a nation's public functions.[8]

Even more dramatic are recent efforts by the nations of Europe to make the electoral entitlement explicit and specific. Article 3 of Protocol 1 to the European Human Rights Convention obliges the parties to "undertake to hold free elections at reasonable intervals by secret ballot, under conditions which will ensure the free expression of the opinion of the people in the choice of the legislature." Finding the Greek colonels' regime in violation, the European Court of Human Rights interpreted this Protocol to require "the existence of a representative legislature, elected at reasonable intervals."[9] * * *

---

6. OEA/Ser.F/II.17, doc. 40, rev.2 (1979).

7. OEA/Ser.G/CP/RES.489, doc. 720 (1987).

8. Annual Report of the Inter–American Commission on Human Rights, OEA/Ser.L/V/II.77, doc. 7, rev.1, at 97 (1990) (Mexico Report).

9. The Greek Case, 12 Y.B. EUR. CONV. ON HUM. RTS. 179 (1969); see also Case of Mathieu–Mohin, 113 Eur. Ct. H.R. (ser. A) at 22 (1987).

As members of the Conference on Security and Co-operation in Europe,[10] the same nations, augmented by Canada, the United States and the nations of Eastern Europe, recently joined unanimously in spelling out the contents of the new right to participate in free and open elections. At a meeting in Copenhagen in June 1990, they affirmed that "democracy is an inherent element of the rule of law" and recognized "the importance of pluralism with regard to political organizations."[11] Among the "inalienable rights of all human beings," they decided, is the democratic entitlement, including "free elections that will be held at reasonable intervals by secret ballot or by equivalent free voting procedure, under conditions which ensure in practice the free expression of the opinion of the electors in the choice of their representatives"; a government "representative in character, in which the executive is accountable to the elected legislature or the electorate"; and political parties that are clearly separate from the state. * * *

This unprecedented North Atlantic and Europe-wide initiative to endorse and define a popular right of electoral democracy went on to commend the growing practice of involving foreign observers in national elections. The participating states invited "observers from any other CSCE participating States and any appropriate private institutions and organizations who may wish to do so to observe the course of their national election proceedings, to the extent permitted by law," and pledged to "endeavour to facilitate similar access for election proceedings held below the national level."[12] * * *

The Organization of American States has also engaged in election monitoring. Its members authorized the dispatch of a 435—person commission to Nicaragua in 1990 to observe 70 percent of the polling sites. In addition, the OAS maintained a major presence during the Haitian elections [in 1990], not only to watch the polls, but also to assist in drafting the electoral law and organizing voter registration. Over the past two years, OAS monitors have observed elections in Suriname, El Salvador, Paraguay and Panama as well. As a result, in part, of such collective efforts, the thirty-four OAS member states—with the lamentable exception of Haiti—all have governments chosen in accordance with the democratic entitlement.

Monitoring by governmental and nongovernmental observers also became an important *ad hoc* part of the post–1989 transition from Communist to democratic regimes in Eastern Europe. These events foreshadowed the textual declarations regarding election standards and procedures in the Copenhagen and Paris documents. Once again, practice preceded the drafting of new principles. The United States sent

---

10. Conference on Security and Co-operation in Europe, Final Act, Aug. 1, 1975, 73 DEP'T ST. BULL. 323 (1975), reprinted in 14 ILM 1292 (1975).

11. Conference on Security and Co-operation in Europe, Document of the Copenhagen Meeting of the Conference on the Human Dimension, June 29, 1990, reprinted in 29 ILM 1305, 1308, para. 3 (1990) [hereinafter Copenhagen Document].

12. Copenhagen Document, supra note [11], at 1310, para. 8.

an official mission to monitor Bulgaria's 1990 election, as did several other CSCE governments. Several members of Congress observed the electoral campaigns in Bulgaria and Czechoslovakia, as did their counterparts from some Western European parliaments.

At the unofficial level, additional election monitoring has taken place in recent years. Emissaries of the Council of Freely Elected Heads of Government of the Carter Center observed the 1990 Nicaraguan and 1991 Zambian elections. The (U.S.) National Democratic Institute for International Affairs has monitored elections in twelve countries since 1986. At least half a dozen teams of foreign observers, including experts from the United States, the Philippines, Japan and the British Commonwealth, monitored parliamentary elections in Bangladesh on February 27, 1991. International observers from Canada, France, Germany and the United States verified the propriety of elections held in Benin in March 1991. Perhaps most remarkable was the authorized presence of sixty-five international observers at the referendum on independence conducted in Latvia on March 3, 1991. * * *

A study that seeks to connect the dots of practice with lines of enunciated principle must also look at the several instances when election monitoring was denied. For example, in 1990 the Secretary–General refused to monitor the Romanian elections on the ground that his participation had not been authorized by the General Assembly or Security Council. He added, perhaps even more persuasively, that he had not been invited to participate early enough in establishing the rules and methods to be used in conducting the election campaign. In 1991 the Office of the Secretary–General rejected requests for election monitoring made by Lesotho and Zambia, again on the ground that he felt he was unauthorized, in the absence of special circumstances, to monitor elections in sovereign states. The political organs of the United Nations may have been too cautious, so far, in giving the Secretary–General authority to respond favorably to a bona fide request by a member. On the other hand, the office of the Secretary–General may have been too cautious in denying requests for monitoring without even presenting them for approval to the Security Council or the General Assembly. * * *

The capacity of the international system to validate governments in this fashion is rapidly being accepted as an appropriate role of the United Nations, the regional systems and, supplementarily, the NGOs. A recent study conducted by the Netherlands Minister of Foreign Affairs gives expression to the new normative expectation. It asked: what can reasonably be expected of a European state seeking to join the European Communities and the Council of Europe? The study finds that applicant states "must be plural democracies; they must regularly hold free elections by secret ballot; they must respect the rule of law; [and] they must have signed the European Convention on Human Rights and Fundamental Freedoms." Such a test for validation of governance and entry into a society of nations would have been unthinkable even a decade ago; it is considered unexceptionable in the new Europe. Some comparable rule in future should, and undoubtedly will, become the standard for participation in the multinational institutions of the global community. * * *

The democratic entitlement's newness and recent rapid evolution make it understandable that important problems remain. * * * The key to solving these residual problems is: (1) that the older democracies should be among the first to volunteer to be monitored in the hope that this will lead the way to near-universal voluntary compliance, thus gradually transforming a sovereign option into a customary legal obligation; (2) that a credible international monitoring service should be established with clearly defined parameters and procedures covering all aspects of voting, from the time an election is called until the newly elected take office; (3) that each nation's duty to be monitored should be linked to a commensurate right to nonintervention by states acting unilaterally; and (4) that legitimate governments should be assured of protection from overthrow by totalitarian forces through concerted systemic action after—and *only* after—the community has recognized that such an exigency has arisen. In the longer term, compliance with the democratic entitlement should also be linked to a right of representation in international organs, to international fiscal, trade and development benefits, and to the protection of UN and regional collective security measures. Both textually and in practice, the international system is moving toward a clearly designated democratic entitlement, with national governance validated by international standards and systematic monitoring of compliance. * * *

THE GENERAL ASSEMBLY OF THE ORGANIZATION OF AMERICAN STATES

The Inter–American Democratic Charter (*adopted* 11 September 2001)

Considering that the Charter of the Organization of American States recognizes that representative democracy is indispensable for the stability, peace, and development of the region, and that one of the purposes of the OAS is to promote and consolidate representative democracy, with due respect for the principle of nonintervention; * * *

Bearing in mind the progressive development of international law and the advisability of clarifying the provisions set forth in the OAS Charter and related basic instruments on the preservation and defense of democratic institutions, according to established practice,

Article 1

The peoples of the Americas have a right to democracy and their governments have an obligation to promote and defend it. Democracy is essential for the social, political, and economic development of the peoples of the America. * * *

Article 3

Essential elements of representative democracy include, *inter alia*, respect for human rights and fundamental freedoms, access to and the exercise of power in accordance with the rule of law, the holding of periodic, free, and fair elections based on secret balloting and universal suffrage as an expression of the sovereignty of the people, the pluralistic system of political parties and organizations, and the separation of powers and independence of the branches of government.

Article 4

Transparency in government activities, probity, responsible public administration on the part of governments, respect for social rights, and freedom of expression and of the press are essential components of the exercise of democracy. The constitutional subordination of all state institutions to the legally constituted civilian authority and respect for the rule of law on the part of all institutions and sectors of society are equally essential to democracy. * * *

Article 11

Democracy and social and economic development are interdependent and are mutually reinforcing.

Article 12

Poverty, illiteracy, and low levels of human development are factors that adversely affect the consolidation of democracy. The OAS member states are committed to adopting and implementing all those actions required to generate productive employment, reduce poverty, and eradicate extreme poverty, taking into account the different economic realities and conditions of the countries of the Hemisphere. * * *

Article 13

The promotion and observance of economic, social, and cultural rights are inherently linked to integral development, equitable economic growth, and to the consolidation of democracy in the states of the Hemisphere. * * *

Article 19

Based on the principles of the Charter of the OAS and subject to its norms, and in accordance with the democracy clause contained in the Declaration of Quebec City, an unconstitutional interruption of the democratic order or an unconstitutional alteration of the constitutional regime that seriously impairs the democratic order in a member state, constitutes, while it persists, an insurmountable obstacle to its government's participation in sessions of the General Assembly, the Meeting of Consultation, the Councils of the Organization, the specialized conferences, the commissions, working groups, and other bodies of the Organization. * * *

Article 23

Member states are responsible for organizing, conducting, and ensuring free and fair electoral processes. Member states, in the exercise of their sovereignty, may request that the Organization of American States provide advisory services or assistance for strengthening and developing their electoral institutions and processes, including sending preliminary missions for that purpose.

Article 24

The electoral observation missions shall be carried out at the request of the member state concerned. To that end, the government of that state and the Secretary General shall enter into an agreement establishing the scope and coverage of the electoral observation mission in question. The member state shall guarantee conditions of security, free access to information, and full cooperation with the electoral observation mission. Electoral observation missions shall be carried out in accordance with the principles and norms of the OAS. The Organization shall ensure that these missions are effective and independent and shall provide them with the necessary resources for that purpose. They shall be conducted in an objective, impartial, and transparent manner and with the appropriate technical expertise. * * *

AFRICAN [BANJUL] CHARTER ON HUMAN AND PEOPLES' RIGHTS

OAU Doc. CAB/LEG/67/3 rev. 5, adopted 27 June 1981

Article 13

1. Every citizen shall have the right to participate freely in the government of his country, either directly or through freely chosen representatives in accordance with the provisions of the law. 2. Every citizen shall have the right of equal access to the public service of his country. 3. Every individual shall have the right of access to public property and services in strict equality of all persons before the law.

NOTES AND QUESTIONS ON THE DEMOCRATIC ENTITLEMENT

1. *Confirmation of Franck's thesis.* As the Inter–American Democratic Charter suggests, events since the publication of Professor Franck's article in 1992 support his initial observation that a "democratic entitlement" is emerging, including periodic elections subject to international monitoring. In the United Nations Millennium Declaration, *supra*, heads of state and government from around the world resolved to "spare no effort to promote democracy and strengthen the rule of law, as well as

respect for all internationally recognized human rights and fundamental freedoms, including the right to development" and specifically "[t]o strengthen the capacity of all our countries to implement the principles and practices of democracy and respect for human rights, including minority rights; to work collectively for more inclusive political process-es, allowing genuine participation by all citizens in all our countries; [and] to ensure the freedom of the media to perform their essential role and the right of the public to have access to information. * * * " Other intergovernmental organizations, like the Organization of American States and Organization for Security and Cooperation in Europe, as well as innumerable civil society groups, have developed particular expertise in election monitoring and developed the normative content of the entitlement. There are of course many counter-examples, states where elections are a sham or where the rhetoric of democracy masks a continuing autocracy. What is the *legal* effect of these counter-examples?

2. *Distinguishing democracy from majority rule.* Professor Erwin Chemerinsky has argued that the one thing that "democracy" cannot mean is majority rule. What is the essential content of the democratic entitlement?

3. *Democracy and hypocrisy.* How would you respond to the follow-ing observation by General Sani Abacha, the former military ruler of Nigeria: "it is a travesty of democracy for the international community to demand their brand of democracy in sub-Saharan Africa, while condoning monarchy in many parts of the world and dancing around the Peoples Republic of China purely for economic reasons."

4. *Corruption as a human rights violation.* Does Article 13 of the Banjul Charter amount to a human right to be free of governmental corruption? In 2000, the UN Human Rights Commission (now the Human Rights Council) recognized that "transparent, responsible, ac-countable and participatory government, responsive to the needs and aspirations of the people, is the foundation on which good governance rests, and that such a foundation is a *sine qua non* for the promotion of human rights."[1] In other words, one aspect of the democratic entitle-ment (and an aspect that is notably free of ideology) is "good gover-nance," meaning at a minimum transparency, accountability, and the absence of corruption in government decision-making. How might a lawyer challenge corruption as a human rights violation? *See, e.g.,* Human Rights Watch, "Chop Fine: The Human Rights Impact of Local Government Corruption and Mismanagement in Rivers State, Nigeria" (January 2007) *available at* http://hrw.org/reports/2007/nigeria0107/.

5. *Self-determination reconsidered.* Collective claims for self-determi-nation can be symptoms of human rights crises in their later stages. The continuous, mass deprivation of human rights on the basis of the target's group identity tends, unless redressed, to provoke claims for secession and independence under the banner of "self-determination." But there

---

1. E/CN.4/RES/2000/64 (27 April 2000).

is no single authoritative definition of the right of self-determination as a matter of law. Professor Franck's analysis suggests that there are many different meanings of the right to self-determination: (i) the creation of states and the right to terminate alien domination or colonization; (ii) the right of each existing state to independence and sovereign equality; and (iii) the right of a people to popularly-elected, representative government—a reference to internal forms of government rather than to external forms of dependency.

A skeptic might observe that the one thing "self-determination" cannot mean *at law* is the one thing that it tends to mean *on the street*, in national movements with an ethnic or irredentist basis: the right of ethnic minorities to secede from existing states. In this skeptical view, the single most significant constraint on the right to self-determination was its transformation into a right of existing states to the territorial *status quo*. Members of the United Nations, conscious perhaps that the logical consequence of the right to self-determination was their own fragmentation, controlled its centrifugal force by assuring that their own right to territorial integrity was not at risk. Drawing on the League of Nations' experience with the Aaland Islands Dispute,[2] the United Nations repeatedly preserved the right to self-determination by rejecting the correlative right to secession.[3]

Nor is self-determination the basis for a system for the protection of minority rights, as is frequently assumed. Minority rights may be protected in a number of ways and through many institutions, but there is no obvious right to self-determination of ethnic minorities under the International Bill of Rights. The term "self-determination" does not appear in the Universal Declaration of Human Rights, and, though it does appear in article 1 of both International Covenants, ethnic or racial minorities were evidently not the intended beneficiaries: to the extent that the rights of minorities are protected in the Covenants, those protections appear separately in Article 27, entirely separate from the reference to self-determination in article 1.

---

2. *See, e.g., Report of the International Committee of Jurists entrusted by the Council of the League of Nations with the task of giving an advisory opinion upon the legal aspects of the Aaland Islands question,* League of Nations Off. J., Spec. Supp. No. 3 (Oct. 1920) at 5: "Positive International Law does not recognize the right of national groups, as such, to separate themselves form the State of which they form part by the simple expression of a wish, any more than it recognizes the right of other States to claim such a separation. Generally speaking, the grant or refusal of the right to a portion of its population of determining its own political fate by plebiscite or by some other method, is, exclusively, an attribute of the sovereignty of every State which is definitively constituted."

3. *See, e.g.,* the comments of Secretary–General U Thant, Press Conference at Dakar, Senegal, January 4, 1970, *reprinted in* 7 UN MONTHLY CHRONICLE 36 (February 1970) ("The United Nations attitude is unequivocal. As an international organization, the United Nations has never accepted and does not accept and I do not believe it will ever accept the principle of secession of a part of its Member State[s].")

HUMAN RIGHTS AND SEXUAL ORIENTATION

TOONEN v. AUSTRALIA

Human Rights Committee, Comm. No. 488/1992 (31 March 1994)
CCPR/C/50/D/488/1992

8.1   The Committee is called upon to determine whether Mr. Toonen has been the victim of an unlawful or arbitrary interference with his privacy, contrary to [the International Covenant on Civil and Political Rights] article 17, paragraph 1, and whether he has been discriminated against in his right to equal protection of the law, contrary to article 26.

8.2   Insofar as article 17 is concerned, it is undisputed that adult consensual sexual activity in private is covered by the concept of "privacy", and that Mr. Toonen is actually and currently affected by the continued existence of the Tasmanian laws. The Committee considers that sections 122 (a) and (c) and 123 of the Tasmanian Criminal Code "interfere" with [Mr. Toonen]'s privacy, even if these provisions have not been enforced for a decade. In this context, it notes that the policy of the Department of Public Prosecutions not to initiate criminal proceedings in respect of private homosexual conduct does not amount to a guarantee that no actions will be brought against homosexuals in the future, particularly in the light of undisputed statements of the Director of Public Prosecutions of Tasmania in 1988 and those of members of the Tasmanian Parliament. The continued existence of the challenged provisions therefore continuously and directly "interferes" with [Mr. Toonen's] privacy.

8.3   The prohibition against private homosexual behaviour is provided for by law, namely, sections 122 and 123 of the Tasmanian Criminal Code. As to whether it may be deemed arbitrary, the Committee recalls that pursuant to its general comment 16(32) on article 17, the "introduction of the concept of arbitrariness is intended to guarantee that even interference provided for by the law should be in accordance with the provisions, aims and objectives of the Covenant and should be, in any event, reasonable in the circumstances". The Committee interprets the requirement of reasonableness to imply that any interference with privacy must be proportional to the end sought and be necessary in the circumstances of any given case.

8.4   While the State party acknowledges that the impugned provisions constitute an arbitrary interference with Mr. Toonen's privacy, the Tasmanian authorities submit that the challenged laws are justified on public health and moral grounds, as they are intended in part to prevent the spread of HIV/AIDS in Tasmania, and because, in the absence of specific limitation clauses in article 17, moral issues must be deemed a matter for domestic decision.

8.5   As far as the public health argument of the Tasmanian authorities is concerned, the Committee notes that the criminalization of homosexual practices cannot be considered a reasonable means or proportionate measure to achieve the aim of preventing the spread of AIDS/HIV. The Government of Australia observes that statutes criminalizing homosexual activity tend to impede public health programmes "by driving underground many of the people at the risk of infection". Criminalization of homosexual activity thus would appear to run counter to the implementation of effective education programmes in respect of the HIV/AIDS prevention. Secondly, the Committee notes that no link has been shown between the continued criminalization of homosexual activity and the effective control of the spread of the HIV/AIDS virus.

8.6   The Committee cannot accept either that for the purposes of article 17 of the Covenant, moral issues are exclusively a matter of domestic concern, as this would open the door to withdrawing from the Committee's scrutiny a potentially large number of statutes interfering with privacy. It further notes that with the exception of Tasmania, all laws criminalizing homosexuality have been repealed throughout Australia and that, even in Tasmania, it is apparent that there is no consensus as to whether sections 122 and 123 should not also be repealed. Considering further that these provisions are not currently enforced, which implies that they are not deemed essential to the protection of morals in Tasmania, the Committee concludes that the provisions do not meet the "reasonableness" test in the circumstances of the case, and that they arbitrarily interfere with Mr. Toonen's right under article 17, paragraph 1.

8.7   The State party has sought the Committee's guidance as to whether sexual orientation may be considered an "other status" for the purposes of article 26. The same issue could arise under article 2, paragraph 1, of the Covenant. The Committee confines itself to noting, however, that in its view, the reference to "sex" in articles 2, paragraph 1, and 26 is to be taken as including sexual orientation.

9.   The Human Rights Committee, acting under article 5, paragraph 4, of the Optional Protocol to the International Covenant on Civil and Political Rights, is of the view that the facts before it reveal a violation of articles 17, paragraph 1, *juncto* 2, of the Covenant.

10.   Under article 2, paragraph 3 (a), of the Covenant, [Mr. Toonen], as a victim of a violation of articles 17, paragraph 1, juncto 2, paragraph 1, of the Covenant, is entitled to a remedy. In the opinion of the Committee, an effective remedy would be the repeal of sections 122(a) and (c) and 123 of the Tasmanian Criminal Code.

LUSTIG-PREAN AND BECKETT v. UNITED KINGDOM

Eur. Ct. Human. Rts. 2000
Statement of the Registrar of the Court

[Lustig–Prean and Beckett, British nationals] who were at the relevant time members of the United Kingdom armed forces, are homosexual. The Ministry of Defence apply [*sic*] a policy which excludes homosexuals from the armed forces. The applicants, who were each the subject of an investigation by the service police concerning their homosexuality, all admitted their homosexuality and were administratively discharged on the sole ground of their sexual orientation, in accordance with Ministry of Defence policy. They were discharged in January 1995, July 1993, November 1994 and December 1994 respectively. In November 1995 the [U.K.] Court of Appeal rejected their judicial review applications. [The applicants] complained that the investigations into their sexual orientation and their subsequent discharges violated their right to respect for their private lives, protected by Article 8 of the Convention,[1] and that they had been discriminated against contrary to Article 14. * * *

The Court considered the investigations, and in particular the interviews of the applicants, to have been exceptionally intrusive, it noted that the administrative discharges had a profound effect on the applicants' careers and prospects and considered the absolute and general character of the policy, which admitted of no exception, to be striking. It therefore considered that the investigations conducted into the applicants' sexual orientation together with their discharge from the armed forces constituted especially grave interferences with their private lives.

As to whether the Government had demonstrated "particularly convincing and weighty reasons" to justify those interferences, the Court noted that the Government's core argument was that the presence of homosexuals in the armed forces would have a substantial and negative effect on morale and, consequently, on the fighting power and operational effectiveness of the armed forces. The Government relied, in this respect, on the Report of the Homosexual Policy Assessment Team (HPAT) published in February 1996. The Court found that, insofar as the views of armed forces' personnel outlined in the HPAT Report could be considered representative, those views were founded solely upon the negative attitudes of heterosexual personnel towards those of

---

1. [Editors' note. Article 8 of the European Convention, captioned "Right to Respect for Private and Family Life," provides as follows:

1 Everyone has the right to respect for his private and family life, his home and his correspondence.

2 There shall be no interference by a public authority with the exercise of this right except such as is in accordance with the law and is necessary in a democratic society in the interests of national security, public safety or the economic well-being of the country, for the prevention of disorder or crime, for the protection of health or morals, or for the protection of the rights and freedoms of others.]

homosexual orientation. It was noted that the Ministry of Defence policy was not based on a particular moral standpoint and the physical capability, courage, dependability and skills of homosexual personnel were not in question. Insofar as those negative views represented a predisposed bias on the part of heterosexuals, the Court considered that those negative attitudes could not, of themselves, justify the interferences in question any more than similar negative attitudes towards those of a different race, origin or colour.

While the Court noted the lack of concrete evidence to support the Government's submissions as to the anticipated damage to morale and operational effectiveness, the Court was prepared to accept that certain difficulties could be anticipated with a change in policy (as was the case with the presence of women and racial minorities in the past). It found that, on the evidence, any such difficulties were essentially conduct-based and could be addressed by a strict code of conduct and disciplinary rules. The usefulness of such codes and rules was not undermined, in the Court's view, by the Government's suggestion that homosexuality would give rise to problems of a type and intensity that race and gender did not or by their submission that particular problems would arise with the admission of homosexuals in the context of shared accommodation and associated facilities. Finally, the Court considered that it could not ignore widespread and consistently developing views or the legal changes in the domestic laws of Contracting States in favour of the admission of homosexuals into the armed forces of those States. Accordingly, convincing and weighty reasons had not been offered by the Government to justify the discharge of the applicants.

While the applicants' administrative discharges were a direct consequence of their homosexuality, the investigations conducted into the applicants' sexual orientation deserved separate consideration, because the investigations continued after the applicants had admitted their homosexuality. The Government suggested that the investigations continued in order to verify the admissions of homosexuality so as to avoid false claims by those seeking an administrative discharge from the armed forces. This argument was rejected by the Court because both applicants wished to remain in the armed forces. In addition, the Court was not persuaded by the Government's argument that medical, security and disciplinary reasons necessitated the investigations. The Court rejected the Government's submission that the applicants knew they were not obliged to participate in the interviews, finding, in this latter respect, that the applicants had no real choice but to co-operate, as they wished to keep the investigations as discreet as possible. Accordingly, the investigations conducted after the applicants' confirmed their homosexuality were also considered unjustified.

The Court therefore took the view that neither the investigations nor the discharges of the applicants were justified within the meaning of Article 8 § 2. * * *

COUNCIL OF THE EUROPEAN UNION

Council Directive 2000/78/EC (27 November 2000) Establishing a General Framework for Equal Treatment in Employment and Occupation

Whereas:

(1) In accordance with Article 6 of the Treaty on European Union, the European Union is founded on the principles of liberty, democracy, respect for human rights and fundamental freedoms, and the rule of law, principles which are common to all Member States and it respects fundamental rights, as guaranteed by the European Convention for the Protection of Human Rights and Fundamental Freedoms and as they result from the constitutional traditions common to the Member States, as general principles of Community law. * * *

(11) Discrimination based on religion or belief, disability, age or sexual orientation may undermine the achievement of the objectives of the EC Treaty, in particular the attainment of a high level of employment and social protection, raising the standard of living and the quality of life, economic and social cohesion and solidarity, and the free movement of persons.

(12) To this end, any direct or indirect discrimination based on religion or belief, disability, age or sexual orientation as regards the areas covered by this Directive should be prohibited throughout the Community. * * *

(23) In very limited circumstances, a difference of treatment may be justified where a characteristic related to religion or belief, disability, age or sexual orientation constitutes a genuine and determining occupational requirement, when the objective is legitimate and the requirement is proportionate. Such circumstances should be included in the information provided by the Member States to the Commission. * * *

Article 1

The purpose of this Directive is to lay down a general framework for combating discrimination on the grounds of religion or belief, disability, age or sexual orientation as regards employment and occupation, with a view to putting into effect in the Member States the principle of equal treatment. * * *

Article 3

1. Within the limits of the areas of competence conferred on the Community, this Directive shall apply to all persons, as regards both the public and private sectors, including public bodies, in relation to: (a) conditions for access to employment, to self-employment or to occupation, including selection criteria and recruitment conditions, whatever the branch of activity and at all levels of the professional hierarchy,

including promotion; (b) access to all types and to all levels of vocational guidance, vocational training, advanced vocational training and retraining, including practical work experience; (c) employment and working conditions, including dismissals and pay; (d) membership of, and involvement in, an organisation of workers or employers, or any organisation whose members carry on a particular profession, including the benefits provided for by such organisations. * * *

4.　Member States may provide that this Directive, in so far as it relates to discrimination on the grounds of disability and age, shall not apply to the armed forces.

Article 10

Member States shall take such measures as are necessary, in accordance with their national judicial systems, to ensure that, when persons who consider themselves wronged because the principle of equal treatment has not been applied to them establish, before a court or other competent authority, facts from which it may be presumed that there has been direct or indirect discrimination, it shall be for the respondent to prove that there has been no breach of the principle of equal treatment. * * *

Article 16

Member States shall take the necessary measures to ensure that: (a) any laws, regulations and administrative provisions contrary to the principle of equal treatment are abolished; (b) any provisions contrary to the principle of equal treatment which are included in contracts or collective agreements, internal rules of undertakings or rules governing the independent occupations and professions and workers' and employers' organisations are, or may be, declared null and void or are amended.

UNITED NATIONS HIGH COMMISSIONER FOR REFUGEES

GUIDELINES ON INTERNATIONAL PROTECTION: GENDER–RELATED PERSECUTION WITHIN THE CONTEXT OF ARTICLE 1A(2) OF THE 1951 CONVENTION AND ITS 1967 PROTOCOL RELATING TO THE STATUS OF REFUGEES

U.N. Doc. HCR/GIP/02/01 (2002)

These Guidelines are intended to provide legal interpretative guidance for governments, legal practitioners, decision-makers and the judiciary, as well as UNHCR staff carrying out refugee status determination in the field.

1. "Gender-related persecution" is a term that has no legal meaning *per se*. Rather, it is used to encompass the range of different claims in which gender is a relevant consideration in the determination of refugee status. These Guidelines specifically focus on the interpretation of the refugee definition contained in Article 1A(2) of the 1951 Convention relating to the Status of Refugees (hereinafter "1951 Convention") from a gender perspective, as well as propose some procedural practices in order to ensure that proper consideration is given to women claimants in refugee status determination procedures and that the range of gender-related claims are recognised as such.

2. It is an established principle that the refugee definition as a whole should be interpreted with an awareness of possible gender dimensions in order to determine accurately claims to refugee status. This approach has been endorsed by the General Assembly, as well as the Executive Committee of UNHCR's Programme. * * *

6. Even though gender is not specifically referenced in the refugee definition, it is widely accepted that it can influence, or dictate, the type of persecution or harm suffered and the reasons for this treatment. The refugee definition, properly interpreted, therefore covers gender-related claims. As such, there is no need to add an additional ground to the 1951 Convention definition. * * *

14. While it is generally agreed that "mere" discrimination may not, in the normal course, amount to persecution in and of itself, a pattern of discrimination or less favourable treatment could, on cumulative grounds, amount to persecution and warrant international protection. It would, for instance, amount to persecution if measures of discrimination lead to consequences of a substantially prejudicial nature for the person concerned, *e.g.* serious restrictions on the right to earn one's livelihood, the right to practice one's religion, or access to available educational facilities.

15. Significant to gender-related claims is also an analysis of forms of discrimination by the State in failing to extend protection to individuals against certain types of harm. If the State, as a matter of policy or practice, does not accord certain rights or protection from serious abuse, then the discrimination in extending protection, which results in serious harm inflicted with impunity, could amount to persecution. Particular cases of domestic violence, or of abuse for reasons of one's differing sexual orientation, could, for example, be analysed in this context. * * *

16. Refugee claims based on differing sexual orientation contain a gender element. A claimant's sexuality or sexual practices may be relevant to a refugee claim where he or she has been subject to persecutory (including discriminatory) action on account of his or her sexuality or sexual practices. In many such cases, the claimant has refused to adhere to socially or culturally defined roles or expectations of behaviour attributed to his or her sex. The most common claims involve homosexuals, transsexuals or transvestites, who have faced ex-

treme public hostility, violence, abuse, or severe or cumulative discrimination.

17. Where homosexuality is illegal in a particular society, the imposition of severe criminal penalties for homosexual conduct could amount to persecution, just as it would for refusing to wear the veil by women in some societies. Even where homosexual practices are not criminalised, a claimant could still establish a valid claim where the State condones or tolerates discriminatory practices or harm perpetrated against him or her, or where the State is unable to protect effectively the claimant against such harm. * * *

SUZANNE DU TOIT AND ANNA–MARIE DE VOS v. MINISTER FOR WELFARE AND POPULATION DEVELOPMENT

Constitutional Court of South Africa, Case CCT 40/01 (10 September 2002)

The applicants, partners in a longstanding lesbian relationship, wanted to adopt two children. They could not do so jointly because current legislation confines the right to adopt children jointly to married couples. Consequently, the second applicant alone became the adoptive parent. Some years later, the applicants brought an application in the Pretoria High Court challenging the constitutional validity of [certain provisions of] the Child Care Act and * * * the Guardianship Act which provide for the joint adoption and guardianship of children by married persons only. In the High Court, the relevant provisions of the Child Care Act were challenged on the grounds that they violate the applicants' rights [under the South African Constitution] to equality and dignity and do not give paramountcy to the best interests of the child as required by section 28(2) of the Constitution. [The High Court judge] found that these provisions of the Child Care Act and the Guardianship Act violated the Constitution and ordered the reading in of certain words into the impugned provisions so as to allow for joint adoption and guardianship of children by same-sex life partners. The applicants now seek confirmation by this Court of the High Court order in terms of section 172(2)(a) of the Constitution.[1] * * *

The applicants have lived together as life partners since 1989. They formalised their relationship with a commitment ceremony, performed by a lay preacher in September 1990. To all intents and purposes they live as a couple married in community of property; immovable property is registered jointly in both their names; they pool their financial resources; they have a joint will in terms of which the surviving partner of the relationship will inherit the other's share in the joint community;

---

1. Section 172(2)(a) provides that: "The Supreme Court of Appeal, a High Court or a court of similar status may make an order concerning the constitutional validity of an Act of Parliament, a provincial Act or any conduct of the President, but an order of constitutional invalidity has no force unless it is confirmed by the Constitutional Court."

they are beneficiaries of each other's insurance policies; and they take all major life decisions jointly and on a consensual basis.

In 1994, the applicants approached the authorities of Cotlands Baby Centre, Johannesburg (Cotlands) to be screened as prospective adoptive parents. They went through a standard three-month process which involved their being screened and counselled together by social workers as required by the Child Care Act which sets out the legal framework for adoptions in South Africa. The screening of the applicants included psychological testing, home circumstance visits, extended family recommendations and a panel discussion. It was at all times made clear during the screening process that the adopted children would be moving into a family structured around a permanent lesbian life partnership. The suitability of both applicants to be parents of the adoptive children was considered in the light of these circumstances.

Within two months of the commencement of the screening and counselling process, the applicants were accepted as adoptive parents by the Cotlands authorities. A sister and brother, born on 10 November 1988 and 20 April 1992 respectively, were chosen for possible adoption by the applicants. On 3 December 1994, the siblings were placed temporarily in the care of the applicants by the Cotlands authorities. Since then, the siblings have remained with the applicants and they consider the applicants to be their parents.

In 1995, the applicants applied to the children's court in Pretoria to adopt the siblings jointly. The children's court, constrained by current adoption legislation, awarded custody and guardianship to the second applicant alone despite both applicants having been recommended as suitable parents. The applicants now challenge the constitutionality of the impugned provisions in the Pretoria High Court.

Under current law there is no provision for couples, other than married couples, jointly to adopt a child. Section 17 of the Child Care Act provides that a child can be adopted:

> (a) by a husband and his wife jointly;
>
> (b) by a widower or widow or unmarried or divorced person;
>
> (c) by a married person whose spouse is the parent of the child;
>
> (d) by the natural father of a child born out of wedlock.

Furthermore, section 20(1) of the Child Care Act provides that:

> An order of adoption shall terminate all the rights and obligations existing between the child and any person who was his parent (other than a spouse contemplated in section 17(c)) immediately prior to such adoption, and that parent's relatives.

Section 17 of the Child Care Act lists the categories of persons entitled to adopt children. Section 17(a) specifically allows for the joint adoption of children by married couples. It does not provide for the joint adoption of children by partners in a permanent same-sex life partnership. The reference to "husband" and "wife" in section 17(a) refers only to marriages ordinarily recognised by the common law and legislation between heterosexual spouses. * * *

While the above provisions require prospective adoptive parents to be married in order to adopt children jointly, the fact that same-sex life partners are excluded from this regime does not mean that they cannot adopt children at all. Section 17(b) of the Child Care Act permits adoption by a single applicant. Thus, a person living with a same-sex life partner may apply to adopt children in his or her own right, intending to raise the child with his or her partner, but the partner will have no legally recognised right in relation to the children. * * *

As a result of the current law the applicants cannot jointly adopt the siblings. Although first applicant is not the legally recognised adoptive parent, she is the primary care-giver. She provides the children with their principal source of emotional support within the family and, because of the constraints of the second applicant's professional life, she spends more time with them during week days than does the second applicant. Yet, she has no legal say in matters such as granting doctors permission to give either of the children an injection or the signing of school indemnity forms for school tours or sporting activities. More importantly, in the event of the partnership between herself and the second applicant ending, her claim to custody and guardianship of the children would be at risk. * * *

The High Court upheld the application and declared the impugned provisions unconstitutional and invalid. It read into the relevant sections of the two statutes wording which would permit same-sex life partners jointly to adopt and be joint guardians of children. * * *

Recognition of the fact that many children are not brought up by their biological parents is embodied in section 28(1)(b) of our Constitution which guarantees a child's right to "family or parental care". Family care includes care by the extended family of a child, which is an important feature of South African family life. It is clear from section 28(1)(b) that the Constitution recognises that family life is important to the well-being of all children. Adoption is a valuable way of affording children the benefits of family life which might not otherwise be available to them.

The institutions of marriage and family are important social pillars that provide for security, support and companionship between members of our society and play a pivotal role in the rearing of children. However, we must approach the issues in the present matter on the basis that family life as contemplated by the Constitution can be provided in different ways and that legal conceptions of the family and what constitutes family life should change as social practices and traditions change. * * *

The applicants submitted that the impugned provisions violate the "best interests" principle protected by section 28(2) of the Constitution.

Section 28(2) of the Constitution states that: "A child's best interests are of paramount importance in every matter concerning the child." ... Both international law and the domestic law of many countries have affirmed the paramountcy of "the best interests of the child".[2] * * *

In their current form the impugned provisions exclude from their ambit potential joint adoptive parents who are unmarried, but who are partners in permanent same-sex life partnerships and who would otherwise meet the criteria set out in * * * the Child Care Act. Their exclusion surely defeats the very essence and social purpose of adoption which is to provide the stability, commitment, affection and support important to a child's development, which can be offered by suitably qualified persons.[3]

Excluding partners in same sex life partnerships from adopting children jointly where they would otherwise be suitable to do so is in conflict with the principle enshrined in section 28(2) of the Constitution. It is clear from the evidence in this case that even though persons such as the applicants are suitable to adopt children jointly and provide them with family care, they cannot do so. The impugned provisions of the Child Care Act thus deprive children of the possibility of a loving and stable family life as required by section 28(1)(b) of the Constitution. This is a matter of particular concern given the social reality of the vast number of parentless children in our country. The provisions of the Child Care Act thus fail to accord paramountcy to the best interests of the children and I conclude that, in this regard, sections 17(a) and (c) of the Act are in conflict with section 28(2) of the Constitution.

The argument advanced by the applicants in the High Court and in this Court was that the impugned provisions, in effect, differentiate on the grounds of sexual orientation and marital status, both of which are listed grounds in section 9(3) of the Constitution.[4] In applying this test,

---

2. Examples of African countries which incorporate children's clauses in their constitutions include Namibia (art 15 of the Constitution of the Republic of Namibia); and Uganda (section 34 of the Constitution of the Republic of Uganda). The paramountcy of the best interests of children is confirmed in many international conventions. See, for example, art 3 of the United Nations Convention on the Rights of the Child, 1989. The convention was adopted by the United Nations General Assembly on 20 November 1989 and entered into force on 2 September 1990. See also, art 4 of the African Charter on the Rights and Welfare of the Child, 1990.

3. These values are also reflected in the Preamble to the United Nations Convention on the Rights of the Child which states that, "... the child, for the full and harmonious development of his or her personality, should grow up in a family environment, in an atmosphere of happiness, love and understanding".

4. Section 9 of the Constitution provides:

(1) Everyone is equal before the law and has the right to equal protection and benefit of the law.

(2) Equality includes the full and equal enjoyment of all rights and freedoms. To promote the achievement of equality, legislative and other measures designed to protect or advance persons, or categories of persons, disadvantaged by unfair discrimination may be taken.

(3) The state may not unfairly discriminate directly or indirectly against anyone on one or more grounds, including race, gender, sex, pregnancy, marital status, ethnic or social origin, colour, sexual orientation, age, disability, religion, conscience, belief, culture, language and birth.

(4) No person may unfairly discriminate directly or indirectly against anyone on one or more grounds in terms of subsection (3). National legislation must be enacted to prevent or prohibit unfair discrimination.

the [High Court] judge found that the impugned provisions unfairly differentiate between married persons and the applicants as same-sex life partners. * * * [We] agree [unanimously]. The unfair effect of the discrimination is squarely founded on an intersection of the grounds upon which the applicants' complaint is based: the applicants' status as unmarried persons which currently precludes them from joint adoption of the siblings is inextricably linked to their sexual orientation. But for their sexual orientation which precludes them from entering into a marriage, they fulfill the criteria that would otherwise make them eligible jointly to adopt children in terms of the impugned legislation.

In this respect, then, the provisions of section 17(a) and (c) are in conflict with section 9(3) of the Constitution. * * *

The applicants further argued that their inability to adopt the siblings jointly amounts to a limitation of the first applicant's right to human dignity[5] in that the challenged provisions of the Child Care Act deny her due recognition and status as a parent of the siblings even though she has played a significant role in their upbringing. More significantly, the first applicant is said to be denied recognition as a parent even though she and the second applicant have lived together as a family and made a consensual and deliberate decision jointly to adopt the siblings and to support and rear them equally as co-parents. They submitted further that the non-recognition of the first applicant as a parent, in the context of her relationship with the second applicant and their relationship with the siblings, perpetuates the fiction or myth of family homogeneity based on the one mother/one father model. It ignores developments that have taken place in the country, including the adoption of the Constitution.

On the evidence presented in this case, the applicants constitute a stable, loving and happy family. Yet the first applicant's status as a parent of the siblings cannot be recognised. This failure by the law to recognise the value and worth of the first applicant as a parent to the siblings is demeaning. [We] accordingly hold [unanimously] that the impugned provisions limit the right of the first applicant to dignity. * * *

Accordingly, [we] grant the relief sought by the applicants in this case and confirm the order made by the High Court. [S]uch a remedy serves to protect not only the applicants' equal parenting rights in respect of the siblings, but all permanent same-sex life partners wanting to adopt children jointly or to undertake joint guardianship. * * * [I]n each decision concerning adoption, prospective adoptive parents should be evaluated on a case-by-case basis as provided for in the Child Care

---

(5) Discrimination on one or more of the grounds listed in subsection (3) is unfair unless it is established that the discrimination is fair.

5. Section 10 of the Constitution provides that "Everyone has inherent dignity and the right to have their dignity respected and protected."

Act. In so doing, care will be taken to ensure that only suitable couples will be entitled to adopt children jointly. * * *

NOTES AND QUESTIONS ON HUMAN RIGHTS AND SEXUAL ORIENTATION

1. *Diverse settings for the non-discrimination norm.* The materials in this section address a range of settings in which discrimination on the basis of sexual orientation has been common: the criminalization of homosexual sex, exclusion from the military, employment and workplace conditions, the determination of refugee status, and family law, including the adoption of children. Notice also that the materials take a variety of normative forms: (i) a decision by the Human Rights Committee, operating under the International Covenant on Civil and Political Rights; (ii) a decision of the European Court of Human Rights under the European Convention for the Protection of Human Rights and Fundamental Freedoms; (iii) quasi-legislation from the Council of the European Union, an intergovernmental organization with its roots in economic integration; (iv) authoritative but non-binding guidelines from the United Nations High Commissioner for Refugees under the Refugee Convention of 1951; and (v) a decision of a the South African Constitutional Court. In many countries, domestic law prohibiting discrimination on the basis of sexual orientation exists, but it is far from universal, and there remain significant problems with enforcement. Can these authorities be used to establish an obligation for government authorities to identify and eliminate discrimination on the basis of sexual orientation in every setting?

2. *Understanding Dutoit.* During the *apartheid* era in South Africa, the Immorality Act adopted the infamous "three men at a party clause," which made it a criminal act for any "male person [to] commit[ ] with another male person at a party any act which is calculated to stimulate sexual passion or give sexual gratification." A "party" was defined as "any occasion where more than two persons are present." The post-*apartheid* constitution in South Africa was the first in the world to prohibit discrimination on the basis of sexual orientation. What are the three grounds on which the Constitutional Court of South Africa ruled in favor of the applicants in *Dutoit*? Are the legal authorities consulted by the Court essentially or exclusively domestic? Judging from the other materials in this section, could the same result have been achieved on the basis of international authorities alone?

3. *The Yogyakarta Principles.* In November 2006, a diverse group of distinguished human rights experts met in Yogyakarta, Indonesia, and developed a set of 29 principles governing states' human rights obligations with respect to sexual orientation and gender identity. The Yogyakarta Principles draw on existing human rights treaties and law but also acknowledge the possibility that additional rights and the means

of enforcement may evolve. Substantively, the Principles recognize a variety of rights—civil, political, economic, social, and cultural—including *inter alia* the rights to equality and non-discrimination; to recognition before the law; to privacy; to freedom from arbitrary deprivation of liberty; to freedom from torture and cruel, inhuman or degrading treatment or punishment; to social security and to other social protection measures; to an adequate standard of living; to the highest attainable standard of health; to protection from medical abuses; to peaceful assembly and association; to freedom of thought, conscience and religion; to seek asylum; to found a family; to participate in public and cultural life; and to effective remedies and redress. A detailed set of recommendations to governments follows each statement of legal principle. The Principles are *available at* www.yogyakartaprinciples.org.

HUMAN RIGHTS AND HEALTH

Convention on the Rights of the Child

Article 24

1. States Parties recognize the right of the child to the enjoyment of the highest attainable standard of health and to facilities for the treatment of illness and rehabilitation of health. States Parties shall strive to ensure that no child is deprived of his or her right of access to such health care services.

2. States Parties shall pursue full implementation of this right and, in particular, shall take appropriate measures:

(a) To diminish infant and child mortality;

(b) To ensure the provision of necessary medical assistance and health care to all children with emphasis on the development of primary health care;

(c) To combat disease and malnutrition, including within the framework of primary health care, through, *inter alia*, the application of readily available technology and through the provision of adequate nutritious foods and clean drinking-water, taking into consideration the dangers and risks of environmental pollution;

(d) To ensure appropriate pre-natal and post-natal health care for mothers;

(e) To ensure that all segments of society, in particular parents and children, are informed, have access to education and are supported in the use of basic knowledge of child health and nutrition, the advantages of breast-feeding, hygiene and environmental sanitation and the prevention of accidents;

(f) To develop preventive health care, guidance for parents and family planning education and services.

3.   States Parties shall take all effective and appropriate measures with a view to abolishing traditional practices prejudicial to the health of children.

4.   States Parties undertake to promote and encourage international co-operation with a view to achieving progressively the full realization of the right recognized in the present article. In this regard, particular account shall be taken of the needs of developing countries.

In addition to Article 24 of the Convention on the Rights of the Child, several international and regional human rights instruments have affirmed in principle an individual's right to health:

> Under the WHO Constitution of the World Health Organization ("WHO"), "the enjoyment of the highest attainable standard of health is one of the fundamental rights of every human being without distinction of race, religion, political belief, economic or social condition."

> Article 25 of the Universal Declaration on Human Rights recognizes the right of health for all persons, and acknowledges the relationship between health and other rights, such as the right to food and the right to housing.

> Article 12 of the International Covenant on Economic, Social, and Cultural Rights provides for "the right of everyone to the enjoyment of the highest attainable standard of physical and mental health." Under Article 12, states are required to undertake several steps, including, for example, those necessary for "the prevention, treatment and control of epidemic, endemic, occupational and other diseases" in order "to achieve the full realization of this right."

> Article 12 (1) and (2) of CEDAW recognizes a woman's right to health and establishes an obligation on the part of the state to ensure that women are guaranteed access to medical care free from discrimination. It also establishes the obligation to provide adequate medical care for expectant mothers and children.

> Article 16 of the African Charter on Human and People's Rights establishes that "necessary measures" will be taken to provide for the right to the highest possible level of health. Article 16 also guaranteed medical services in case of illness. The right to health is also provided for in the African Charter on the Rights and Welfare of the Child.

> Article 34 of the Organization of American States' Charter lists as one of its goals, access to medical science and adequate living conditions. Article 26 of the American Convention on Human Rights provides that states are obligated to take measures to ensure "the full realization of the rights implicit in the economic, social,

educational, scientific, and cultural standards set forth in the Charter." Article 10 of the Additional Protocol of San Salvador sets forth, in detail, the "right to health" as well as the steps that states must take to guarantee this right for all persons.

> Article 11 of the European Social Charter provides for the right to protection of health, and guarantees access to medical services to those without adequate resources. Article 3 of the Convention on Human Rights and Biomedicine also establishes a right to equal access to health care.

> Article 5(e) (iv) of the International Convention on the Elimination of All Forms of Racial Discrimination establishes that "States undertake to prohibit racial discrimination in all its forms and to guarantee the right of everyone, without distinction as to race, colour, or national or ethnic origin, to equity before the law, notably in the enjoyment of * * * the right to public health, medical care, social security, and social services."

AFRICAN COMMISSION ON HUMAN & PEOPLES' RIGHTS

THE SOCIAL AND ECONOMIC RIGHTS ACTION CENTER ("SERAC") v. NIGERIA

Communication No. 155/96 (2001)

The present Communication alleges a concerted violation of a wide range of rights guaranteed under the African Charter for Human and Peoples' Rights [including the right to health, the right to housing, the right of a people to control their natural resources, the right to have one's dignity respected, the right to food, and the right to life.] * * * The Complainants allege that the Nigerian government violated the right to health and the right to clean environment as recognized under Articles 16 and 24 of the African Charter by failing to fulfill the minimum duties required by these rights. This, the Complainants allege, the government has done by: [i] Directly participating in the contamination of air, water and soil and thereby harming the health of the Ogoni population; [ii] Failing to protect the Ogoni population from the harm caused by the [Nigerian National petroleum Company ("NNPC")] Shell Consortium but instead using its security forces to facilitate the damage; [iii] Failing to provide or permit studies of potential or actual environmental and health risks caused by the oil operations.

Article 16 of the African Charter reads: "(1) Every individual shall have the right to enjoy the best attainable state of physical and mental health. (2) States Parties to the present Charter shall take the necessary measures to protect the health of their people and to ensure that they receive medical attention when they are sick." Article 24 of the African

Charter reads: "All peoples shall have the right to a general satisfactory environment favourable to their development."

These rights recognise the importance of a clean and safe environment that is closely linked to economic and social rights in so far as the environment affects the quality of life and safety of the individual. As has been rightly observed by Alexander Kiss, "an environment degraded by pollution and defaced by the destruction of all beauty and variety is as contrary to satisfactory living conditions and the development as the breakdown of the fundamental ecologic equilibria is harmful to physical and moral health."

The right to a general satisfactory environment, as guaranteed under Article 24 of the African Charter or the right to a healthy environment, as it is widely known, therefore imposes clear obligations upon a government. It requires the State to take reasonable and other measures to prevent pollution and ecological degradation, to promote conservation, and to secure an ecologically sustainable development and use of natural resources. Article 12 of the International Covenant on Economic, Social and Cultural Rights (ICESCR), to which Nigeria is a party, requires governments to take necessary steps for the improvement of all aspects of environmental and industrial hygiene. The right to enjoy the best attainable state of physical and mental health enunciated in Article 16(1) of the African Charter and the right to a general satisfactory environment favourable to development (Article 16(3)) already noted obligate governments to desist from directly threatening the health and environment of their citizens. The State is under an obligation to respect the just noted rights and this entails largely non-interventionist conduct from the State for example, not from carrying out, sponsoring or tolerating any practice, policy or legal measures violating the integrity of the individual.

Government compliance with the spirit of Articles 16 and 24 of the African Charter must also include ordering or at least permitting independent scientific monitoring of threatened environments, requiring and publicising environmental and social impact studies prior to any major industrial development, undertaking appropriate monitoring and providing information to those communities exposed to hazardous materials and activities and providing meaningful opportunities for individuals to be heard and to participate in the development decisions affecting their communities.

We now examine the conduct of the government of Nigeria in relation to Articles 16 and 24 of the African Charter. Undoubtedly and admittedly, the government of Nigeria, through NNPC has the right to produce oil, the income from which will be used to fulfil the economic and social rights of Nigerians. But the care that should have been taken as outlined in the preceding paragraph and which would have protected the rights of the victims of the violations complained of was not taken. To exacerbate the situation, the security forces of the government engaged in conduct in violation of the rights of the Ogonis by attacking, burning and destroying several Ogoni villages and homes. * * *

Governments have a duty to protect their citizens, not only through appropriate legislation and effective enforcement but also by protecting them from damaging acts that may be perpetrated by private parties. This duty calls for positive action on part of governments in fulfilling their obligation under human rights instruments. The practice before other tribunals also enhances this requirement as is evidenced in the case *Velàsquez-Rodríguez v. Honduras*. In this landmark judgment, the Inter–American Court of Human Rights held that when a State allows private persons or groups to act freely and with impunity to the detriment of the rights recognised, it would be in clear violation of its obligations to protect the human rights of its citizens. Similarly, this obligation of the State is further emphasised in the practice of the European Court of Human Rights, in *X and Y v. Netherlands*. In that case, the Court pronounced that there was an obligation on authorities to take steps to make sure that the enjoyment of the rights is not interfered with by any other private person. * * *

The uniqueness of the African situation and the special qualities of the African Charter on Human and Peoples' Rights imposes upon the African Commission an important task. International law and human rights must be responsive to African circumstances. Clearly, collective rights, environmental rights, and economic and social rights are essential elements of human rights in Africa. The African Commission will apply any of the diverse rights contained in the African Charter. It welcomes this opportunity to make clear that there is no right in the African Charter that cannot be made effective. As indicated in the preceding paragraphs, however, the Nigerian Government did not live up to the minimum expectations of the African Charter.

The Commission does not wish to fault governments that are labouring under difficult circumstances to improve the lives of their people. The situation of the people of Ogoniland, however, requires, in the view of the Commission, a reconsideration of the Government's attitude to the allegations contained in the instant communication. The intervention of multinational corporations may be a potentially positive force for development if the State and the people concerned are ever mindful of the common good and the sacred rights of individuals and communities. The Commission however takes note of the efforts of the present civilian administration to redress the atrocities that were committed by the previous military administration. * * *

For the above reasons, the Commission,

Finds the Federal Republic of Nigeria in violation of Articles * * * 16 and 24 of the African Charter on Human and Peoples' Rights;

Appeals to the government of the Federal Republic of Nigeria to ensure protection of the environment, health and livelihood of the people of Ogoniland by: [i] Stopping all attacks on Ogoni communities and leaders by the Rivers State Internal Securities Task Force and permitting citizens and independent investigators free access to the territory; [ii] Conducting an investigation into the human rights violations described above and prosecuting officials of the security forces, NNPC and relevant agencies involved in human rights violations; [iii] Ensuring adequate compensation to victims of the human rights violations, including relief and resettlement assistance to victims of government-sponsored raids, and undertaking a comprehensive cleanup of lands and rivers damaged by oil operations; [iv] Ensuring that appropriate environmental and social impact assessments are prepared for any future oil development and that the safe operation of any further oil development is guaranteed through effective and independent oversight bodies for the petroleum industry; and [v] Providing information on health and environmental risks and meaningful access to regulatory and decision-making bodies to communities likely to be affected by oil operations.

Urges the government of the Federal Republic of Nigeria to keep the African Commission informed of the outcome of the work of: [i] The Federal Ministry of Environment which was established to address environmental and environment related issues prevalent in Nigeria, and as a matter of priority, in the Niger Delta area including the Ogoni land; [ii] The Niger Delta Development Commission (NDDC) enacted into law to address the environmental and other social related problems in the Niger Delta area and other oil producing areas of Nigeria; and [iii] the Judicial Commission of Inquiry inaugurated to investigate the issues of human rights violations.

Notwithstanding the numerous legal instruments enshrining an individual's right to health, obstacles such as poverty and inequality continue to prevent most of the world's population from attaining even minimal levels of good health. In 2002, in an effort to highlight the complexity of the issues surrounding an individual's right to health, the UN Commission on Human Rights appointed Mr. Paul Hunt as the Special Rapporteur on the Right to Health, with multiple responsibilities: engaging in dialogue with all relevant actors including governments, relevant U.N. bodies, specialized agencies, and NGOs; gathering information from relevant sources; publishing reports on the current status of the right to health in various counties, and making recommendations that protect and promote the right to health. In recognition of the fact that women and children may be disproportionately affected by the obstacles that interfere with the right to health, the Commission on Human Rights further requested that the Special Rapporteur "apply a gender perspective and to pay special attention to the needs of children in the realization of the right to health."

UNITED NATIONS HUMAN RIGHTS COUNCIL STATEMENT BY MR. PAUL HUNT, THE SPECIAL RAPPORTEUR ON THE RIGHT TO THE HIGHEST ATTAINABLE STANDARD OF HEALTH 28 MARCH 2007

There is a new maturity about the health and human rights movement as it endeavours to integrate human rights into health policies at the national and international levels. In addition to the traditional human rights techniques, such as "naming and shaming" and taking test cases, the movement is also developing new approaches and skills such as indicators, benchmarks, impact assessments and budgetary analysis. If we are to progress further, however, it is very important that established human rights non-governmental organisations work on serious health and human rights issues, such as maternal mortality, just as vigorously as they campaign on disappearances, torture and prisoners of conscience.

It is also very important that more health professionals engage in the health and human rights movement. Health and human rights complement and reinforce each other. If we wish to operationalise the right to health it is imperative that many more health professionals grasp that human rights can help them deliver their professional objectives. We have to get across the message that human rights are assets and allies for health professionals.

Here there is a major, specific contribution that the Human Rights Council, and its Members, can make. The General Assembly resolution establishing the Human Rights Council mandated the Council to "promote the effective coordination and the mainstreaming of human rights within the United Nations system". My report signals some of the excellent work that WHO has done in relation to health and human rights. * * * However, I have to report that human rights are not mainstreamed within WHO where, in my experience, they remain marginal, contested and severely under-resourced. I urge the Council to do all it can to encourage the mainstreaming of human rights within WHO. * * * In short, it is of the first importance that the right to the highest attainable standard of health is not confined to the Human Rights Council: it must also be mainstreamed across WHO and other UN agencies. Also, at the national level, the right to health must not be confined to Ministries of Foreign Affairs and Justice: it must be mainstreamed across Ministries of Health and other health-related ministries. In 2005, the World Summit Outcome made both points very neatly, [with the Heads of State and Government from around the world agreeing]: "We resolve to integrate the promotion and protection of human rights into national policies and to support the further main-

streaming of human rights throughout the United Nations system."
* * *

In January last year, I undertook a mission to Sweden and I warmly congratulate the Government of Sweden for a standard of living, health status and quality of health care that are among the best in the world. However, my mission report identifies a number of areas where further progress can and should be made. * * * In Sweden I learnt about the Government's excellent international policies on development, health and human rights. I was interested to learn more, however, about the degree to which these commendable policies are actually operationalised, on the ground, in developing countries.

So in February this year I visited Uganda to examine how the Swedish International Cooperation Agency (SIDA) actually applies these Swedish international policies in the Ugandan health context. Also, in October last year, I interviewed the Executive Directors of the Nordic–Baltic countries in the World Bank and IMF, with a view to understanding how Sweden's international policies on development, health and human rights are applied in the context of its membership of these financial institutions. * * *

In one of my reports last year I examined maternal mortality as a human rights issue. Each year over 500,000 women die in childbirth or from complications of pregnancy. As we sit here this afternoon, about 200 women will have died in childbirth. Crucially, most of these maternal deaths could have been avoided by a few well-known interventions. I make no apology for once more highlighting maternal mortality. * * * Maternal mortality is a human rights catastrophe on a scale that dwarfs other human rights issues such as disappearances and the death penalty. The Commission on Human Rights devoted a great deal of time and energy to disappearances and the death penalty—and it was right to do so because these are human rights issues of enormous importance. But the Commission gave negligible attention to maternal mortality—despite the massive scale of the problem and despite the fact that maternal deaths raise vital issues concerning women's rights to life, health, equality and non-discrimination. Maternal mortality is a hugely important human rights issue for all States, whether they are low-income, middle-income or high-income. I urge the Council to give maternal mortality the sustained attention it desperately needs. * * *

I cannot close without expressing my profound concern about Iraq and the Occupied Palestinian Territory.

The murder and mayhem in Iraq is well known. But I wish to draw the Council's attention to an issue that, despite its acute gravity, receives far less attention. Over the last couple of years the issue has been seriously under-reported. I refer to the extremely troubling health situation of Iraqis who are internally displaced or refugees. We do not know with certainty the numbers involved. According to some reports, there are about 2 million IDPs [Internally Displaced Persons] in Iraq and about 2 million Iraqi refugees, mostly in Syria and Jordan, but also Egypt, Iran, Lebanon and Turkey.

The health situation—access to water, sanitation, health care and medication—of many Iraqi IDPs is extremely precarious. And this has to be seen in a health context that is frightening. According to one UN agency, the violence and instability in Iraq "is taking its toll on the health sector, possibly more than any other sector in Iraq." I am advised that in some parts of Iraq doctors are attacked because they are doctors.

As for refugees, the generous hospitality of neighbouring host countries is becoming strained. The pressure on already fragile health services is acute. As the refugees' funds run out, many do not know how they will provide for their families' basic health needs. * * *

Starved of funds by Israel and the donor community, the health sector in the Occupied Palestinian Territory is in severe crisis. Many health workers—unpaid for many months—are on strike. In some cases, primary health services are failing, emergency rooms closing, and medicine for chronically ill patients is drying up. Only yesterday in Gaza the wall of a sewage effluent lake collapsed, spilling into the village of Um Nasser. In June last year I publicly expressed my view that the donors' sanctions against the Palestinian Authority were inconsistent with their human rights responsibilities of international assistance and cooperation. By cutting funds to the health sector without adequate notice, these were not economic sanctions—they were health sanctions. I know of no other case where donors have imposed health sanctions on the sick, infirm and elderly living under occupation * * *

I appreciate that, following the January 2006 elections [which brought Hamas to power in the Gaza Strip], donors had a difficult political decision to make. It is precisely when difficult political decisions have to be made that human rights are especially important. Human rights help to protect the weak and powerless in times of political crisis. Last year the donors failed to give proper weight to the human rights of sick, infirm and elderly Palestinians. Whichever way the Palestinian political landscape evolves in the next few weeks, it is imperative that this grave human rights injustice is remedied as a matter of urgency.

Notes and Questions on the Right to Health

1. *Unpacking the right to health.* The right to health is often expressed in terms of *availability*, which requires healthy conditions such as safe drinking water; *accessibility*, which requires that health services be provided to everyone without discrimination; *acceptability*, which requires adherence to medical ethics; and *quality* which requires health services to be scientifically and medically appropriate. *See* Lawrence O. Gostin, The AIDS Pandemic: Complacency, Injustice, and Unfulfilled Expectations 84

(2004). This understanding can provide a helpful framework for identifying the primary violations of the otherwise abstract right to health. But protecting against violations of the right also requires a particular appreciation for the complexity of the relationship between the right to health and other human rights. *See* Jonathan M. Mann, Lawrence Gostin, et al, *Health and Human Rights*, in HEALTH AND HUMAN RIGHTS, (Jonathan M. Mann, Sofia Gruskin, *et al.* eds. 1999).

Several international instruments recognize that the realization of a right to health depends on the realization of other rights first—rights such as the right to food, the right to housing, or the right to a healthy environment:

> [T]he right to health, as defined in article 12.1 [of the International Covenant on Economic, Social, and Cultural Rights], [is] an inclusive right extending not only to timely and appropriate health care but also to the underlying determinants of health, such as access to safe and potable water and adequate sanitation, an adequate supply of safe food, nutrition and housing, healthy occupational and environmental conditions, and access to health-related education and information, including on sexual and reproductive health.

Committee on Economic Social and Cultural Rights, General Comment 14, P 11, U.N. ESCOR, 22d Sess., U.N. Doc. E.C. 12/2000/4 (2000).

SERAC illustrates this essential relationship. The complaint alleged that "the government of Nigeria has been directly involved in oil production through the State oil company, the majority shareholder in a consortium with Shell Petroleum Development Corporation (SPDC), and that these operations have caused environmental degradation and health problems resulting from the contamination of the environment among the Ogoni People." *Id.* at para 1. The complaint also alleged that the resulting contamination of water, soil, and air upon which the local population depended for drinking, farming, and fishing caused them to "suffer serious short and long-term health impacts, including skin infections, gastrointestinal and respiratory ailments, and increased risk of cancers, and neurological and reproductive problems." *Id.* at para. 2. The African Commission found that the right to health under Article 16 of the African Charter was implicated in Nigeria's violation of other economic and social rights. For example, a right to housing was implicit in Article 16, because "when housing is destroyed * * * health * * * is adversely affected." *Id.* at para. 60. Similarly, the right to food was "essential for the enjoyment and fulfillment of * * * other rights [such as] health." *Id.* at para. 65.

In sum, one way to think of the right to health is that it implicitly requires a range of other rights, the violation of which has profound and negative effects on health. But the right to health might also be conceptualized as the precondition for the enjoyment of other rights, including civil and political rights. The Special Rapporteur's concern with maternal mortality rests not just on women's right to health but on the inability of sick women to exercise other rights, including civil and political rights.

2. *The reach and justiciability of the right to health.* Consider the argument that the Nigerian government's bad acts in cooperation with certain oil companies made *SERAC* a relatively easy case for finding that the Ogoni people's right to health had been violated. Would adjudication of a claim alleging a violation of the right to health still be possible, or even proper, in the more common scenario of a developing, impoverished country that is unable to provide adequate medical facilities for its population? How can states with insufficient resources provide for the fulfillment of all of the various rights required to achieve the right to health? Does the interdependence of these rights make it easier or more difficult for human rights lawyers to force states to fulfill these obligations? Does it provide more legal ammunition for advocates, or does it provide states with a better defense to suits challenging its health policies?

3. *The right to health and informed consent.* The trial of Nazi physicians after World War II documented doctors' participation in human rights abuses. Fifteen defendants were convicted and seven were executed for their participation in Hitler's programs of conducting scientific experimentation on humans. The Nuremberg Code, comprising ten provisions governing the rights and treatment of individuals who participate in scientific experimentation, was a direct response to the horrors of the Nazi human experimentation programs. Among the most fundamental of the Code's provisions is the first, which states, "The voluntary consent of the human subject is absolutely essential. This means that the person involved should have legal capacity to give consent; should be so situated as to be able to exercise free power of choice, without the intervention of any element of force, fraud, deceit, duress, overreaching, or other ulterior form of constraint or coercion; and should have sufficient knowledge and comprehension of the elements of the subject matter involved as to enable him to make an understanding and enlightened decision." The Nuremberg Code (1948), *reprinted in* THE NAZI DOCTORS AND THE NUREMBERG CODE: HUMAN RIGHTS IN HUMAN EXPERIMENTATION 2 (George J. Annas & Michael A. Grodin eds., 1992). Although the UN has never officially adopted the Nuremberg Code, several UN instruments provide guidelines for such medical experimentation. *See* Universal Declaration of Human Rights, art. 5; International Covenant on Civil and Political Rights, art. 7; and the UN Principles of Medical Ethics relevant to the Role of Health Personnel (1982), *available at* http://www.cirp.org/library/ethics/UN-medical-ethics/.

The contemporary relevance of these principles was challenged in *Abdullahi v. Pfizer, Inc.*, 2005 WL 1870811 (S.D.N.Y. 2005). In 1996, Pfizer, a large pharmaceutical company, went to Nigeria with medical supplies and staff to stem an outbreak of spiral meningitis that had claimed the lives of more than fifteen thousand people in West Africa. Plaintiffs in *Abdullahi* alleged that Pfizer administered Trovan, an experimental drug for the treatment of meningitis, and less-than-therapeutic doses of ceftriaxone, the FDA-approved medication for meningitis, to numerous children without obtaining prior informed consent from their parents or guardians. Shortly after Pfizer left Nigeria, local citizens reported that those who had been given the experimental drug were suffering severe health problems, including death. The plaintiffs brought suit in the U.S., under the Alien Tort Statute, claiming that Pfizer had violated international law by conducting medical research on humans without obtaining informed consent. In 2005, a district court dismissed the claim concluding that, "The sources of international law Plaintiffs rely on [the Nuremberg Code, the Declaration of Helsinki, the guidelines authored by the Council for International Organizations of Medical Services ('CIOMS'), article 7 of the ICCPR, the Universal Declaration of Human Rights and FDA regulations] do not support jurisdiction under the ATS." These sources, said the court, were not binding sources of international law. On what grounds, if any, would you appeal the district court's judgment?

THE HIV/AIDS EPIDEMIC AS A HUMAN RIGHTS ISSUE

AMNESTY INTERNATIONAL

Women, HIV/AIDS and Human Rights
24 November 2004

Women are fighting both a virus and systemic discrimination in trying to overcome the threat of HIV/AIDS. Across the world, they face a number of circumstances which increase their risk of HIV infection in gender-specific ways. Many women are exposed to sexual violence and coerced sex inside and outside marriage, including through harmful traditional practices such as genital mutilation, early marriage, and wife inheritance. They frequently lack information on and access to HIV prevention measures and to health care as well as to support and medication after infection. They are denied property and inheritance rights, employment and access to finance—denials which make them dependent on men—and are frequently excluded from participation in policy-making and implementation, including on issues which primarily affect them. * * * Globally, young women are 1.6 times more likely to be living with HIV/AIDS than young men. * * *

A rights-based approach to HIV/AIDS and the protection/empowerment of women and girls.

A strategy driven by fear of infection cannot succeed. In the long term, success can only come through an approach based on values—the values of human rights and human dignity. Let us not forget that the Universal Declaration of Human Rights starts by placing dignity first.

[A] "rights-based approach" to public health in general, and HIV/AIDS in particular, supports sound public health practice by providing additional tools to motivate governments to act to achieve public health goals. Rights considerations can help facilitate the setting and monitoring of public health targets and provide a complementary language to identify failures, or incipient failures, of public health programmes.

The rights-based approach also provides links with other social movements that use the same language—for example, the women's movement, the struggles of indigenous peoples and the movement of people working to protect the environment. Human rights are central to all aspects of an effective response to HIV and AIDS and have been emphasised in international and national programs since the creation of the World Health Organization's Global Programme on AIDS in the 1980s.

A rights-based approach starts from the premise that respect for human rights forms a coherent basis for programs to address the pandemic and that abuses of human rights contribute to the spread of the virus and undermine attempts to contain it. As the Canadian HIV/AIDS Legal Network has put it, "[w]hen human rights are not promoted and protected, it is harder to prevent HIV transmission. When these rights are not promoted and protected, the impact of the epidemic on individuals and communities is worse." The importance of human rights to protecting and promoting health has also been recognized within the UN system through the work of the treaty-monitoring bodies, the rights-based work of health-related UN agencies such as WHO, UNAIDS, UNIFEM and UNFPA, and the creation of the posts of UN Special Rapporteurs on the right to health and on violence against women.

Human rights standards and HIV

A number of international human rights standards—including those agreed to by, and binding on, governments—are relevant to protecting women's rights in the context of HIV/AIDS, both in terms of the prevention of HIV/AIDS and the response to it. International human rights law requires governments to take a range of measures to protect the right to the highest attainable standard of health (also known as the "right to health"), and the right to freedom from discrimination, among others. There are other rights which are also important to the consideration of HIV, including rights to information, to education, to work, to found a family, to enjoy the benefits of scientific knowledge and other rights. The relevance of human rights standards to HIV/AIDS prevention, treatment and support has been elaborated by international consultations on the subject, and independent experts within the UN human rights system have also commented on women's human rights and HIV/AIDS.

Standards on women's rights to health

The right to health for everyone was promulgated as a core value of the constitution of the World Health Organization at its establishment in 1946. * * * Governments have also made important political commitments to secure the right to health of women, including in the Vienna Declaration and Programme of Action, as adopted by the World Conference on Human Rights on 25 June 1993 which recognizes the importance of women's right to enjoy the "highest standard of physical and mental health throughout their life-span".

The Convention on the Elimination of All Forms of Discrimination Against Women calls at article 12 for "States Parties [to] take all appropriate measures to eliminate discrimination against women in the field of health care in order to ensure, on a basis of equality of men and women, access to health care services, including those related to family planning." * * *

Standards on women's sexual and reproductive health rights

A number of international agreements and standards address women's sexual and reproductive health rights. The Cairo Programme of Action adopted at the International Conference on Population and Development (ICPD) in 1994, addressed sexually transmitted diseases and the prevention of HIV from the perspective of women's vulnerability to the epidemic. It also set out key recommendations for addressing HIV through reproductive health services.

Recommended measures included: increasing efforts in reproductive health programs to prevent, detect and treat STIs [Sexually Transmitted Infections] and other reproductive tract infections; providing specialized training to all healthcare providers in the prevention and detection of, and counselling on, STIs, especially infections in women and youth; making information and counselling integral components of all reproductive and sexual health services; and promoting and distributing high quality condoms as integral components of all reproductive health-care services. * * *

Sexual rights embrace human rights that are already recognized in national laws, international human rights documents and other consensus documents. These include the right of all persons—free of coercion, discrimination and violence—to the highest attainable standard of health in relation to sexuality, including access to sexual and reproductive health care services; to seek, receive and impart information in relation to sexuality; to have access to sexuality education; and other related rights. For sexual rights, as with all rights, the responsible exercise of human rights requires that all persons respect the rights of others. In reality, women frequently are deprived of the realisation of many or most of these rights.

The Declaration of Commitment agreed at the 2001 UN General Assembly Special Session on HIV/AIDS took a small step forward by calling on governments to take action to "empower women to have control over and decide freely and responsibly on matters related to their sexuality to increase their ability to protect themselves from HIV infection." * * *

Standards on discrimination against women

The principle of non-discrimination in international human rights law attaches to distinctions "of any kind, such as race, colour, sex, language, religion, political or other opinion, national or social origin, property, birth or other status". "Other status" has been interpreted to include factors which "can affect individuals' ability to exercise their rights" such as health status (HIV/AIDS). * * *

The Convention on the Elimination of all Forms of Discrimination against Women (CEDAW) calls on States Parties "to take all appropriate measures, including legislation, to modify or abolish existing laws, regulations, customs and practices which constitute discrimination against women." * * *

The Special Rapporteur on the Right to Health, Paul Hunt, has underlined the effect of discrimination on gender grounds when addressing women's rights to sexual and reproductive health:

> Discrimination based on gender hinders women's ability to protect themselves from HIV infection and to respond to the consequences of HIV infection. The vulnerability of women and girls to HIV and AIDS is compounded by other human rights issues including inadequate access to information, education and services necessary to ensure sexual health; sexual violence; harmful traditional or customary practices affecting the health of women and children (such as early and forced marriage); and lack of legal capacity and equality in areas such as marriage and divorce. . . .

Recommendations: * * *

- End violence against women

- Address women's social and economic disempowerment

- Eliminate stigma and discrimination against people affected by HIV/AIDS

- Enable access to prevention, treatment and care for people affected by HIV/AIDS

- Increase international cooperation so as to meet the goals set by the international community and to enable all states to meet their international human rights obligations * * *

In 2001, 189 nations gathered for the UN General Assembly Special Session on HIV/AIDS and unanimously adopted the Declaration of Commitment on HIV/AIDS ("DoC"). G.A. Res., S–26/2 (2 August 2001).

The Declaration set date-specific targets for implementing prevention programs, obtaining access to essential medicines, and eliminating discrimination, and was intended to help meet the Millennium Development Goal of halting and beginning to reverse the spread of HIV/AIDS by 2015. The Declaration draws particular attention to the situation of women, children and other vulnerable groups living with HIV/AIDS, and is intended to be used as a benchmark for holding governments accountable for their progress toward addressing these issues. Five years later, the UN General Assembly adopted the following declaration.

UNITED NATIONS GENERAL ASSEMBLY
Political Declaration on HIV/AIDS
Resolution 60/262 (2 June 2006)

1. We, Heads of State and Government and representatives of States and Governments participating in the comprehensive review of the progress achieved in realizing the targets set out in the Declaration of Commitment on HIV/AIDS; * * *

3. Recognize that HIV/AIDS constitutes a global emergency and poses one of the most formidable challenges to the development, progress and stability of our respective societies and the world at large, and requires an exceptional and comprehensive global response; * * *

11. Reaffirm that the full realization of all human rights and fundamental freedoms for all is an essential element in the global response to the HIV/AIDS pandemic, including in the areas of prevention, treatment, care and support, and recognize that addressing stigma and discrimination is also a critical element in combating the global HIV/AIDS pandemic; * * *

15. Recognize further that to mount a comprehensive response, we must overcome any legal, regulatory, trade and other barriers that block access to prevention, treatment, care and support; * * * promote and protect all human rights and fundamental freedoms for all; promote gender equality and empowerment of women; promote and protect the rights of the girl child in order to reduce the vulnerability of the girl child to HIV/AIDS; * * *

43. Reaffirm that the World Trade Organization's Agreement on Trade–Related Aspects of Intellectual Property Rights does not and should not prevent members from taking measures now and in the future to protect public health. Accordingly, while reiterating our commitment to the TRIPS Agreement, reaffirm that the Agreement can and should be interpreted and implemented in a manner supportive of the right to protect public health and, in particular, to promote access to medicines for all including the production of generic antiretroviral drugs and other essential drugs for AIDS-related infections. In this connection, we reaffirm the right to use, to the full, the provisions in the

TRIPS Agreement, the Doha Declaration on the TRIPS Agreement and Public Health, and the World Trade Organization's General Council Decision of 2003 * * * which provide flexibilities for this purpose; * * *

46.   Encourage pharmaceutical companies, donors, multilateral organizations and other partners to develop public-private partnerships in support of research and development and technology transfer, and in the comprehensive response to HIV/AIDS;

47.   Encourage bilateral, regional and international efforts to promote bulk procurement, price negotiations and licensing to lower prices for HIV prevention products, diagnostics, medicines and treatment commodities, while recognizing that intellectual property protection is important for the development of new medicines and recognizing the concerns about its effects on prices; * * *

51.   Call upon Governments, national parliaments, donors, regional and subregional organizations, organizations of the United Nations system, the Global Fund to Fight AIDS, Tuberculosis and Malaria, civil society, people living with HIV, vulnerable groups, the private sector, communities most affected by HIV/AIDS and other stakeholders to work closely together to achieve the targets set out above, and to ensure accountability and transparency at all levels through participatory reviews of responses to HIV/AIDS. * * *

In *Minister of Health v. Treatment Action Campaign*, 5 SA 721 (CC) (2002), the Constitutional Court of South Africa considered a constitutional challenge to governmental restrictions on the provision of anti-retroviral drugs to HIV–positive pregnant women, in violation of the right to health care services under Sections 27(1) and 28(1)(c) of the South African Constitution. The case involved not only the meaning of the right to health but also whether injunctive relief and supervisory jurisdiction would breach the separation of powers by encroaching on the policy prerogatives of the executive branch. The Court noted that South Africa was in the midst of an HIV/AIDS epidemic with more than 6 million people infected, including as many as 80,000 newborns. The government was offered the anti-retroviral drug Nevirapine free of charge for five years, but the Government announced that it would introduce Mother–To–Child–Transmission (MTCT) treatment only in certain pilot sites and would delay establishing these programs for a year. The NGO Treatment Action Campaign (TAC) mounted the constitutional challenge, alleging that the government's decisions violated the right to access health care services. Judge Botha of the High Court ruled in favor of TAC, ordering the government to make Nevirapine available to infected mothers giving birth in state institutions and to show the court how it intended to provide the medication to its birthing facilities nationwide. The government appealed the decision to the Constitutional Court. Five thousand people demonstrated outside the Court in Johannesburg when the hearings opened. The appeal ultimately failed on the ground that restricting Nevirapine to pilot sites effectively excluded those who could reasonably be included in the treatment program. The Court ordered the Government to extend availability of the drug to hospitals and clinics, to provide counselors, and to take reasonable measures to extend the testing and counseling facilities throughout the public health sector.

NOTES AND QUESTIONS ON *HIV/AIDS* AS A *HUMAN RIGHTS ISSUE*

1. *Implementing the DoC.* Because a resolution of the UN General Assembly is not legally binding, there was concern that the 2001 DoC would function purely as an aspirational document. However, several states have incorporated the DoC's targets into their own domestic framework for addressing the HIV/AIDS crisis, giving the DoC significance as a policy tool. For example, MEXSIDA, a coalition of HIV/AIDS NGOs in Mexico, asked the Mexican government to establish a special office that would monitor the actions of the National AIDS Program in implementing the commitments contained in the DoC. The NGOs pointed out that it was important for the government to be accountable for implementing the DoC in a transparent manner, and the proposed independent body would be able to measure the government's progress. The Mexican government accepted the proposal. *See* Program on International Health and Human Rights, François-Xavier Bagnoud Center for Health and Human Rights, Harvard School of Public Health and the International Council of AIDS Service Organizations, HIV/AIDS & HUMAN RIGHTS IN A NUTSHELL: A QUICK AND USEFUL GUIDE FOR ACTION, AS WELL AS A FRAMEWORK TO CARRY HIV AND HUMAN RIGHTS ACTIONS FORWARD, 8 (Dec. 1994). Several of the deadlines have passed without being implemented by all 189 countries. *See, e.g.* DoC at ¶ 59 ("By 2005, bearing in mind the context and character of the epidemic and that, globally, women and girls are disproportionately affected by HIV/AIDS, develop and accelerate the implementation of national strategies that promote the advancement of women and women's full enjoyment of all human rights; promote shared responsibility of men and women to ensure safe sex; and empower women to have control over and decide freely and responsibly on matters related to their sexuality to increase their ability to protect themselves from HIV infection"). As a strategic matter, do you think the DoC's date-specific goals provide greater accountability in measuring progress? And if so, at what cost?

2. *International guidelines on HIV/AIDS and human rights.* In 1997, the UN Commission on Human Rights promulgated International Guidelines on HIV/AIDS and Human Rights, a set of twelve practical measures that states can implement to respond to the HIV/AIDS crisis. The first guideline provides, "States should establish an effective national framework for their response to HIV/AIDS which ensures a coordi-

nated, participatory, transparent and accountable approach, integrating HIV/AIDS policy and programme responsibilities across all branches of government." In addition to urging a comprehensive framework, the guidelines focus on the reforming laws and legal services to better address issues of health and discrimination, implementing support systems for to assist populations that are particularly vulnerable, such as women and children, and promoting education. The South African Human Rights Commission was the first national human rights body to adopt the International Guidelines on HIV/AIDS and Human Rights. The AIDS Law Project/AIDS Legal Network, South Africa sought to hold the government accountable for upholding its commitment to implement the Guidelines, and at the Commission's first conference, it developed a resolution stating that discrimination against persons with HIV/AIDS violated the South African Constitution. *See* Program on International Health and Human Rights, François-Xavier Bagnoud Center for Health and Human Rights, Harvard School of Public Health and the International Council of AIDS Service Organizations, HIV/AIDS & Human Rights in a Nutshell: A Quick and Useful Guide for Action, As Well As a Framework to Carry HIV and Human Rights Actions Forward (Dec. 1994).

3.   *State interference with the right to health.* In some instances, a state's harsh enforcement of narcotics laws may prevent injection drug users from obtaining access to lifesaving HIV services such as needle-exchange programs. *See* Lawrence O. Gostin, The AIDS Pandemic: Complacency, Injustice, and Unfulfilled Expectations 271–72 (2004). Such enforcement targets the segments of the population hardest hit by the HIV/AIDS epidemic, intravenous drug users, who are afraid to participate in these programs for fear of being arrested with drug paraphernalia. In a report addressing this issue, Human Rights Watch argued that "Programs such as syringe exchange and opiate substitution therapy are among the most well-researched HIV prevention strategies in the world. Studies consistently show that access to sterile syringes dramatically reduces HIV transmission without increasing rates of drug use or drug-related crime. The World Health Organization states that '[needle exchange programs'] ability to break the chain of transmission of HIV is well established. * * * In the face of this scientific consensus, and in the absence of equally effective alternatives, state-imposed barriers to harm reduction programs for injection drug users constitute interference with the human right to health." Human Rights Watch, *Rhetoric and Risk: Human Rights Abuses Impeding Ukraine's Fight Against HIV/AIDS* (Mar. 2, 2006), *available at* http://www.hrw.org/english/docs/2006/03/02/ukrain 12731.htm.

4.   *Joint UN Program for AIDS (UNAIDS).* UNAIDS is an effort to unite the capabilities of several UN agencies and the World Bank to formulate and monitor comprehensive policies that address the HIV/AIDS crisis. Its ten member participants include the Office of the United Nations High Commissioner for Refugees (UNHCR), United Nations

Children's Fund (UNICEF), World Food Programme (WFP), United Nations Development Programme (UNDP), United Nations Population Fund (UNFPA), United Nations Office on Drugs and Crime (UNODC), International Labour Organization (ILO), United Nations Educational, Scientific and Cultural Organization (UNESCO), World Health Organization (WHO), and the World Bank. Can this model of collaboration between various UN agencies be used as a model for other contexts as well, or is there something unique about the HIV/AIDS crisis? Are there disadvantages to this approach?

5. *Intellectual property rights and the right to health.* The textual basis for treating intellectual property rights as international human rights is Article 27(2) of the Universal Declaration of Human Rights, which provides that "Everyone has the right to the protection of the moral and material interests resulting from any scientific, literary or artistic production of which he is the author." *See also* Article 15(1)(c) of the International Covenant on Economic, Social, and Cultural Rights, under which the "States Parties * * * recognize the right of everyone * * * [t]o benefit from the protection of the moral and material interests resulting from any scientific, literary or artistic production of which he is the author."

The right to health has at times come into conflict with intellectual property rights, particularly with respect to patented medications. In 1998, for example, thirty-nine pharmaceutical companies filed suit with the World Trade Organization challenging South Africa's 1997 Medicines Control Act, which would have permitted South Africa to import and manufacture affordable versions of patented anti-AIDS drugs, arguing that the law violated South Africa' commitments under the World Trade Organization's TRIPS Agreement. *See Pharmaceutical Manufacturers' Association of South Africa v President of the Republic of South Africa*, Case No 4183/98 (filed Feb 18, 1998). With a twenty-five percent infection rate, South Africa has one of the highest infection rates of any country in the world. UNAIDS/WHO, AIDS Epidemic Update 21, Dec. 2005, *available at* http://www.who.int/hiv/epi-update2005_en.pdf. The public quickly mobilized to condemn the pharmaceutical companies, whose effort was seen by many as an attempt to secure profits at the expense of hundreds of thousands of lives. After enduring years of negative publicity, the American pharmaceutical companies dropped the suit in April 2001.

At the international level, intellectual property rights are largely governed by the Agreement on Trade–Related Aspects of Intellectual Property Rights ("TRIPS Agreement"), which establishes the minimum levels of protection that all governments within the World Trade Organization must give to the intellectual property rights of other members. Although the patent protection rules in TRIPS would make it illegal to produce patented drugs without a license from the manufacturer, the WTO issued a waiver in 2001 at the WTO Doha conference, which recognized that the public's interest in treating the HIV/AIDS pandemic should not be subordinated to intellectual property rights. The Doha Declaration recognized the gravity of the health threats faced by developing countries, "especially those resulting from [treatable diseases such as] HIV/AIDS * * * and other epidemics." *See* World Trade Org., Declaration on the TRIPS Agreement and Public Health, WT/MIN(01)/DEC/2 (Nov. 20, 2001). Under the waiver provision, countries that wished to copy newer drugs patented after 1995 would be permitted to do so under a system of compulsory licensing. Compulsory licensing permits governments to issue a license to someone other than the patent holder if the government finds that the patent holder is offering the medicine at a price that local populations are unable to afford.

In 2003, the "paragraph 6" waiver was introduced into the TRIPS agreement, which permits one country to import the generic drugs produced by another country under their respective compulsory licenses. In October 2007, the WTO received from Canada the first notification from any government that it had authorized a company to make a generic version of a patented medicine for export under these special provisions. The notification pertained to the triple combination AIDS therapy drug, TriAvir, which could be made and exported to Rwanda, which was unable to manufacture the medicine itself. Many view the "paragraph 6" waiver as a win for developing countries coping with the AIDS pandemic. What is the policy argument that compulsory licensing provisions may, in the end, have a detrimental impact on public health? And the counter-argument?

HUMAN RIGHTS AND THE INTERNET

Although the following case discusses the enforceability of foreign judgments in U.S. courts, you should consider and assess the international human rights arguments for both parties.

YAHOO!, INC. v. LA LIGUE CONTRE LE RACISME ET L'ANTISEMITISME

169 F. Supp.2d 1181 (N.D. Cal. 2001)

Defendants La Ligue Contre Le Racisme Et l'Antisemitisme ("LICRA") and L'Union Des Etudiants Juifs De France, citizens of France, are non-profit organizations dedicated to eliminating anti-Semitism. Plaintiff Yahoo!, Inc. ("Yahoo!") is a corporation organized under the laws of Delaware with its principal place of business in Santa Clara, California. Yahoo! is an Internet service provider that operates various Internet websites and services that any computer user can access at the Uniform Resource Locator ("URL") http://www.yahoo.com. Yahoo! services ending in the suffix, ".com," without an associated country code as a prefix or extension (collectively, "Yahoo!'s U.S. Services") use the English language and target users who are residents of, utilize servers based in and operate under the laws of the United States. Yahoo! subsidiary corporations operate regional Yahoo! sites and services in twenty other nations, including, for example, Yahoo! France, Yahoo! India, and Yahoo! Spain. Each of these regional web sites contains the host nation's unique two-letter code as either a prefix or a suffix in its URL (e.g., Yahoo! France is found at http://www.yahoo.fr and Yahoo! Korea at http://www.yahoo.kr). Yahoo!'s regional sites use the local region's primary language, target the local citizenry, and operate under local laws.

Yahoo! provides a variety of means by which people from all over the world can communicate and interact with one another over the Internet. Examples include an Internet search engine, e-mail, an automated auction site, personal web page hostings, shopping services, chat rooms, and a listing of clubs that individuals can create or join. Any computer user with Internet access is able to post materials on many of these Yahoo! sites, which in turn are instantly accessible by anyone who logs on to Yahoo!'s Internet sites. As relevant here, Yahoo!'s auction site allows anyone to post an item for sale and solicit bids from any computer user from around the globe. Yahoo! records when a posting is made and after the requisite time period lapses sends an e-mail notification to the highest bidder and seller with their respective contact information. Yahoo! is never a party to a transaction, and the buyer and seller are responsible for arranging privately for payment and shipment of goods. Yahoo! monitors the transaction through limited regulation by prohibiting particular items from being sold (such as stolen goods, body parts, prescription and illegal drugs, weapons, and goods violating U.S. copyright laws or the Iranian and Cuban embargos) and by providing a rating system through which buyers and sellers have their transactional behavior evaluated for the benefit of future consumers. Yahoo! informs auction sellers that they must comply with Yahoo!'s policies and may not offer items to buyers in jurisdictions in which the sale of such item violates the jurisdiction's applicable laws. Yahoo! does not actively regulate the content of each posting, and individuals are able to post, and have in fact posted, highly offensive matter, including Nazi-related propaganda and Third Reich memorabilia, on Yahoo!'s auction sites.

On or about April 5, 2000, LICRA sent a "cease and desist" letter to Yahoo!'s Santa Clara headquarters informing Yahoo! that the sale of Nazi and Third Reich related goods through its auction services violates French law. LICRA threatened to take legal action unless Yahoo! took steps to prevent such sales within eight days. Defendants subsequently utilized the United States Marshal's Office to serve Yahoo! with process in California and filed a civil complaint against Yahoo! in the Tribunal de Grande Instance de Paris (the "French Court"). The French Court found that approximately 1,000 Nazi and Third Reich related objects, including Adolf Hitler's *Mein Kampf*, *The Protocol of the Elders of Zion* (an infamous anti-Semitic report produced by the Czarist secret police in the early 1900's), and purported "evidence" that the gas chambers of the Holocaust did not exist were being offered for sale on Yahoo.com's auction site. Because any French citizen is able to access these materials on Yahoo.com directly or through a link on Yahoo.fr, the French Court concluded that the Yahoo.com auction site violates Section R645–1 of the French Criminal Code, which prohibits exhibition of Nazi propaganda and artifacts for sale.

On May 20, 2000, the French Court entered an order requiring Yahoo! to (1) eliminate French citizens' access to any material on the Yahoo.com auction site that offers for sale any Nazi objects, relics, insignia, emblems, and flags; (2) eliminate French citizens' access to web pages on Yahoo.com displaying text, extracts, or quotations from *Mein Kampf* and *Protocol of the Elders of Zion*; (3) post a warning to French citizens on Yahoo.fr that any search through Yahoo.com may lead to sites containing material prohibited by Section R645–1 of the French Criminal Code, and that such viewing of the prohibited material may result in legal action against the Internet user; (4) remove from all browser directories accessible in the French Republic index headings entitled "negationists" and from all hypertext links the equation of "negationists" under the heading "Holocaust." The order subjects Yahoo! to a penalty of 100,000 Euros for each day that it fails to comply with the order. The order concludes:

> We order the Company YAHOO! Inc. to take all necessary measures to dissuade and render impossible any access via Yahoo.com to the Nazi artifact auction service and to any other site or service that may be construed as constituting an apology for Nazism or a contesting of Nazi crimes.

High Court of Paris, May 22, 2000, Interim Court Order No. 00/05308, 00/05309. The French Court set a return date in July 2000 for Yahoo! to demonstrate its compliance with the order.

Yahoo! asked the French Court to reconsider the terms of the order, claiming that although it easily could post the required warning on Yahoo.fr, compliance with the order's requirements with respect to Yahoo.com was technologically impossible. The French Court sought expert opinion on the matter and on November 20, 2000 "reaffirmed" its order of May 22. The French Court ordered Yahoo! to comply with the May 22 order within three (3) months or face a penalty of 100,000 Francs (approximately U.S. $13,300) for each day of non-compliance. The French Court also provided that penalties assessed against Yahoo! Inc. may not be collected from Yahoo! France. Defendants again utilized the United States Marshal's Office to serve Yahoo! in California with the French Order. Yahoo! subsequently posted the required warning and prohibited postings in violation of Section R645–1 of the French Criminal Code from appearing on Yahoo.fr. Yahoo! also amended the auction policy of Yahoo.com to prohibit individuals from auctioning:

> Any item that promotes, glorifies, or is directly associated with groups or individuals known principally for hateful or violent positions or acts, such as Nazis or the Ku Klux Klan. Official government-issue stamps and coins are not prohibited under this policy. Expressive media, such as books and films, may be subject to more permissive standards as determined by Yahoo! in its sole discretion.

Yahoo Auction Guidelines (visited Oct. 23, 2001). Notwithstanding these actions, the Yahoo.com auction site still offers certain items for sale (such as stamps, coins, and a copy of Mein Kampf) which appear to violate the French Order. While Yahoo! has removed the *Protocol of the Elders of Zion* from its auction site, it has not prevented access to numerous other sites which reasonably "may be construed as constituting an apology for Nazism or a contesting of Nazi crimes."

Yahoo! claims that because it lacks the technology to block French citizens from accessing the Yahoo.com auction site to view materials which violate the French Order or from accessing other Nazi-based content of websites on Yahoo.com, it cannot comply with the French order without banning Nazi-related material from Yahoo.com altogether. Yahoo! contends that such a ban would infringe impermissibly upon its rights under the First Amendment to the United States Constitution. Accordingly, Yahoo! filed a complaint in this Court seeking a declaratory judgment that the French Court's orders are neither cognizable nor enforceable under the laws of the United States. * * *

OVERVIEW

As this Court and others have observed, the instant case presents novel and important issues arising from the global reach of the Internet. Indeed, the specific facts of this case implicate issues of policy, politics, and culture that are beyond the purview of one nation's judiciary. Thus it is critical that the Court define at the outset what is and is not at stake in the present proceeding.

This case is not about the moral acceptability of promoting the symbols or propaganda of Nazism. Most would agree that such acts are profoundly offensive. By any reasonable standard of morality, the Nazis were responsible for one of the worst displays of inhumanity in recorded history. This Court is acutely mindful of the emotional pain reminders of the Nazi era cause to Holocaust survivors and deeply respectful of the motivations of the French Republic in enacting the underlying statutes and of the defendant organizations in seeking relief under those statutes. Vigilance is the key to preventing atrocities such as the Holocaust from occurring again.

Nor is this case about the right of France or any other nation to determine its own law and social policies. A basic function of a sovereign state is to determine by law what forms of speech and conduct are acceptable within its borders. In this instance, as a nation whose citizens suffered the effects of Nazism in ways that are incomprehensible to most Americans, France clearly has the right to enact and enforce laws such as those relied upon by the French Court here.

What is at issue here is whether it is consistent with the Constitution and laws of the United States for another nation to regulate speech by a United States resident within the United States on the basis that such speech can be accessed by Internet users in that nation. In a world in which ideas and information transcend borders and the Internet in particular renders the physical distance between speaker and audience virtually meaningless, the implications of this question go far beyond the facts of this case. The modern world is home to widely varied cultures with radically divergent value systems. There is little doubt that Internet users in the United States routinely engage in speech that violates, for example, China's laws against religious expression, the laws of various nations against advocacy of gender equality or homosexuality, or even the United Kingdom's restrictions on freedom of the press. If the government or another party in one of these sovereign nations were to seek enforcement of such laws against Yahoo! or another U.S.-based Internet service provider, what principles should guide the court's analysis?

The Court has stated that it must and will decide this case in accordance with the Constitution and laws of the United States. It recognizes that in so doing, it necessarily adopts certain value judgments embedded in those enactments, including the fundamental judgment expressed in the First Amendment that it is preferable to permit the non-violent expression of offensive viewpoints rather than to impose viewpoint-based governmental regulation upon speech. The government and people of France have made a different judgment based upon their own experience. In undertaking its inquiry as to the proper application of the laws of the United States, the Court intends no disrespect for that judgment or for the experience that has informed it.
* * *

LEGAL ISSUES

* * * The French order prohibits the sale or display of items based on their association with a particular political organization and bans the display of websites based on the authors' viewpoint with respect to the Holocaust and anti-Semitism. A United States court constitutionally could not make such an order. The First Amendment does not permit the government to engage in viewpoint-based regulation of speech absent a compelling governmental interest, such as averting a clear and present danger of imminent violence. In addition, the French Court's mandate that Yahoo! "take all necessary measures to dissuade and render impossible any access via Yahoo.com to the Nazi artifact auction service and to any other site or service that may be construed as constituting an apology for Nazism or a contesting of Nazi crimes" is far too general and imprecise to survive the strict scrutiny required by the

First Amendment. The phrase, "and any other site or service that may be construed as an apology for Nazism or a contesting of Nazi crimes" fails to provide Yahoo! with a sufficiently definite warning as to what is proscribed. Phrases such as "all necessary measures" and "render impossible" instruct Yahoo! to undertake efforts that will impermissibly chill and perhaps even censor protected speech. "The loss of First Amendment freedoms, for even minimal periods of time, unquestionably constitutes irreparable injury." *Elrod v. Burns*, 427 U.S. 347, 373 (1976) *citing New York Times Co. v. United States*, 403 U.S. 713 (1971).

Rather than argue directly that the French order somehow could be enforced in the United States in a manner consistent with the First Amendment, Defendants argue instead that at present there is no real or immediate threat to Yahoo!'s First Amendment rights because the French order cannot be enforced at all until after the cumbersome process of petitioning the French court to fix a penalty has been completed. They analogize this case to *Int'l Soc. for Krishna Consciousness of California, Inc. v. City of Los Angeles*, 611 F. Supp. 315, 319–20 (C.D. Cal.1984), in which the City of Los Angeles sought a declaratory judgment that a resolution limiting speech activities adopted by its Board of Airport Examiners was constitutional. The district court concluded that the action was unripe because the resolution could not take effect without ratification by the City Council, which had not yet occurred. The cases, however, are distinguishable. While Defendants present evidence that further procedural steps in France are required before an actual penalty can be fixed, there is no dispute that the French order is valid under French law and that the French Court may fix a penalty retroactive to the date of the order. The essence of the holding in the *Krishna Consciousness* case is that the subject resolution had no legal effect at all. * * *

Defendants next argue that this Court should abstain from deciding the instant case because Yahoo! simply is unhappy with the outcome of the French litigation and is trying to obtain a more favorable result here. Indeed, abstention is an appropriate remedy for international forum-shopping. In *Supermicro Computer, Inc. v. Digitechnic, S.A.*, 145 F. Supp.2d 1147 (N.D. Cal.2001), a California manufacturer was sued by a corporate customer in France for selling a defective product. The California company sought a declaratory judgment in the United States that its products were not defective, that the French customer's misuse of the product caused the product to fail, and that if the California company was at fault, only limited legal remedies were available. The court concluded that the purpose of the action for declaratory relief was to avoid an unfavorable result in the French courts. It noted that the action was not filed until a year after the French proceedings began, that the French proceedings were still ongoing, and that the French defendants had no intent to sue in the United States. It concluded that the declaratory relief action clearly was "litigation involving the same parties and the same disputed transaction."

In the present case, the French court has determined that Yahoo!'s auction site and website hostings on Yahoo.com violate French law. Nothing in Yahoo!'s suit for declaratory relief in this Court appears to be an attempt to relitigate or disturb the French court's application of French law or its orders with respect to Yahoo!'s conduct in France. Rather, the purpose of the present action is to determine whether a United States court may enforce the French order without running afoul of the First Amendment. The actions involve distinct legal issues, and as this Court concluded in its jurisdictional order, a United States court is best situated to determine the application of the United States Constitution to the facts presented. No basis for abstention has been established.

Comity

No legal judgment has any effect, of its own force, beyond the limits of the sovereignty from which its authority is derived. However, the United States Constitution and implementing legislation require that full faith and credit be given to judgments of sister states, territories, and possessions of the United States. The extent to which the United States, or any state, honors the judicial decrees of foreign nations is a matter of choice, governed by "the comity of nations." *Hilton v. Guyot*, 159 U.S. 113, 163 (1895). Comity "is neither a matter of absolute obligation, on the one hand, nor of mere courtesy and good will, upon the other." *Hilton*, 159 U.S. at 163–64. United States courts generally recognize foreign judgments and decrees unless enforcement would be prejudicial or contrary to the country's interests. *Somportex Ltd. v. Philadelphia Chewing Gum Corp.*, 453 F.2d 435, 440 (3d Cir.1971), *cert. denied*, 405 U.S. 1017 (1972); *Laker Airways v. Sabena Belgian World Airlines*, 731 F.2d 909, 931 (D.C. Cir.1984) ("[T]he court is not required to give effect to foreign judicial proceedings grounded on policies which do violence to its own fundamental interests."); *Tahan v. Hodgson*, 662 F.2d 862, 864 (D.C. Cir.1981) ("[R]equirements for enforcement of a foreign judgment expressed in *Hilton* are that ... the original claim not violate American public policy ... that it not be repugnant to fundamental notions of what is decent and just in the State where enforcement is sought.").

As discussed previously, the French order's content and viewpoint-based regulation of the web pages and auction site on Yahoo.com, while entitled to great deference as an articulation of French law, clearly would be inconsistent with the First Amendment if mandated by a court in the United States. What makes this case uniquely challenging is that the Internet in effect allows one to speak in more than one place at the same time. Although France has the sovereign right to regulate what speech is permissible in France, this Court may not enforce a foreign order that violates the protections of the United States Constitution by chilling protected speech that occurs simultaneously within our borders.
* * *

The reason for limiting comity in this area is sound. "The protection to free speech and the press embodied in [the First] amendment would be seriously jeopardized by the entry of foreign [ ] judgments granted pursuant to standards deemed appropriate in [another country] but considered antithetical to the protections afforded the press by the U.S. Constitution." [*Bachchan v. India Abroad Publications, Inc.*, 585 N.Y.S.2d 661 (N.Y. Sup. Ct. 1992)] at 665. Absent a body of law that establishes international standards with respect to speech on the Internet and an appropriate treaty or legislation addressing enforcement of such standards to speech originating within the United States, the principle of comity is outweighed by the Court's obligation to uphold the First Amendment. * * *

If a hypothetical party were physically present in France engaging in expression that was illegal in France but legal in the United States, it is unlikely that a United States court would or could question the applicability of French law to that party's conduct. However, an entirely different case would be presented if the French court ordered the party not to engage in the same expression in the United States on the basis that French citizens (along with anyone else in the world with the means to do so) later could read, hear or see it. While the advent of the Internet effectively has removed the physical and temporal elements of this hypothetical, the legal analysis is the same.

In light of the Court's conclusion that enforcement of the French order by a United States court would be inconsistent with the First Amendment, the factual question of whether Yahoo! possesses the technology to comply with the order is immaterial. Even assuming for purposes of the present motion that Yahoo! does possess such technology, compliance still would involve an impermissible restriction on speech.

CONCLUSION

Yahoo! seeks a declaration from this Court that the First Amendment precludes enforcement within the United States of a French order intended to regulate the content of its speech over the Internet. Yahoo! has shown that the French order is valid under the laws of France, that it may be enforced with retroactive penalties, and that the ongoing possibility of its enforcement in the United States chills Yahoo!'s First Amendment rights. Yahoo! also has shown that an actual controversy exists and that the threat to its constitutional rights is real and immediate. Defendants have failed to show the existence of a genuine issue of material fact or to identify any such issue the existence of which could be shown through further discovery. Accordingly, the motion for summary judgment will be granted. * * *[1]

---

1. [Editors' note: On appeal, this case was dismissed without prejudice, on grounds having nothing to do with the First Amendment limits on the enforcement of foreign judgments. *See Yahoo! Inc. v. La Ligue Contre Le Racisme Et L'Antisemitisme*, 433 F.3d 1199 (9th Cir. 2006).]

It is one thing for an internet service provider to be the bearer of international and constitutional human rights, as the prior case suggests. But from an international human rights perspective, what are the human rights obligations of an internet service provider that assists a foreign government in censoring certain sites or tracking political dissidents?

HUMAN RIGHTS WATCH "RACE TO THE BOTTOM:" CORPORATE COMPLICITY IN CHINESE INTERNET CENSORSHIP AUGUST 2006

Since President Hu Jintao came to power in 2003, the trend towards greater freedom of expression—a core right upon which the attainment of many other rights depends—has been reversed. Many critical (and popular) media outlets that have exposed corruption or criticized government policies have been closed. Large numbers of journalists have been jailed. One of the most distressing trends has been a steady crackdown on the Internet. While in the past decade the Internet has ushered in an era of unprecedented access to information and open discussion, debate, and dissent, since President Hu took office the authorities have taken a series of harsh steps to control and suppress political and religious speech on the Internet, including the jailing of Internet critics and bloggers for peaceful political expression.

In fact, China's system of Internet censorship and surveillance is the most advanced in the world. While tens of thousands of people are employed by the Chinese government and security organs to implement a system of political censorship, this system is also aided by extensive corporate and private sector cooperation—including by some of the world's major international technology and Internet companies. In China, the active role of censor has been extended from government offices into private companies. Some companies not only respond to instructions and pressures from Chinese authorities to censor their materials, they actively engage in self-censorship by using their technology to predict and then censor the material they believe the Chinese government wants them to censor * * *

Yahoo!: Yahoo! has handed over user information on four Chinese government critics to the Chinese authorities, resulting in their trial and conviction. Yahoo!'s Chinese search engine is heavily censored. Based on examination of Yahoo!'s services and of feedback gathered from Chinese Internet users, Human Rights Watch has found that Yahoo! censors its Chinese-language search engine to a very similar degree as domestic Chinese Internet companies (such as China's largest domestic search engine, Baidu), and much more heavily than MSN and Google. Perhaps responding to criticism about a lack of transparency, in late July

2006 Yahoo! China added a notice at the bottom of its search engine informing users that some results may not appear "in accordance with relevant laws and regulations." * * * In 2007 Yahoo! settled a case challenging this practice after its CEO was publicly embarrassed in Congressional hearings. "Yahoo Settles with Chinese Journalists," N.Y. Times, 14 Nov. 2007.

Microsoft: In June 2005—a month after MSN China rolled out its Chinese portal—Microsoft came under criticism from the press and bloggers around the world for censoring words such as "democracy" and "freedom" in the titles of its Chinese blogs, at the request of the Chinese government. Microsoft has made efforts in recent months to revise its practices and minimize censorship of Chinese bloggers, although the extent to which censorship has been lessened across the board remains unclear. MSN has a Chinese search engine, currently in "beta" test mode, which appears to de-list webpages and censor some Chinese keywords. MSN Chinese "beta" search in some cases informs users that censorship occurred, but not in others. MSN's Chinese search engine, while still in development, does provide the user with more information on politically sensitive subjects than either Yahoo! or Baidu. * * *

Google: In January 2006 Google rolled out its censored search engine, Google.cn. Google.cn does provide notice to users when search results have been censored but provides no further details. The company announced that it would not provide email or blog-hosting services in China, at least for now, in order to avoid being pressured to cooperate with Chinese police in handing over user data as in the case of Yahoo!, and to avoid having to directly censor user-created content as in the case of MSN Spaces. Google justified its censored search engine by arguing that users could rely on Google.com for uncensored searches; however, Chinese Internet users have reported widespread blockage of Google.com by Chinese ISPs. Human Rights Watch testing shows that the censored Google.cn, while denying access to the full range of information available on the World Wide Web, still enables the Chinese user to access substantially more information on sensitive political and religious subjects than its Chinese competitors. * * *

Skype: Skype, which provides a way for Internet users around the world to communicate directly by voice, video and text chat, now has a Chinese-language version developed and marketed in China by the Chinese company TOM Online. Skype executives have publicly acknowledged that the TOM–Skype software censors sensitive words in text chats, and have justified this as in keeping with local "best practices" and Chinese law. However Skype does not inform Chinese users of the specific details of its censorship policies, and does not inform them that their software contains censorship capabilities.

Yahoo!, Microsoft and Google have not publicized the list of sites or keywords being censored, and have not clarified which Chinese laws are being violated by the terms and web addresses censored by their Chinese search engines or services (and also blog-hosting services in the case of Microsoft). Thus it is impossible to evaluate the veracity of the claim each company makes that it is simply following Chinese law. Skype has not clarified what laws TOM–Skype would be violating by not censoring users' conversations.

The above companies are complicit in the Chinese government's censorship of political and religious information and/or the monitoring of peaceful speech in various ways—and, it is important to note, to widely varying degrees. They have all accepted at least some Chinese government demands without mounting any meaningful challenge to them. These are by no means the only multinational companies that currently facilitate Chinese government censorship and surveillance. But they are the most prominent examples, whose contribution to China's censorship regime to date is most well documented and publicly visible.

LETTER OF MICHAEL SAMWAY, ESQ.
VICE PRESIDENT AND DEPUTY GENERAL COUNSEL—
INTERNATIONAL YAHOO! INC.

1 August 2006

Thank you * * * for the opportunity to address some of the challenges our industry faces in countries like China. Our leadership and employees at Yahoo! take these issues with utmost seriousness, and we are pleased to be participating in a dialogue with groups like Human Rights Watch * * * Since our founding in 1995, Yahoo! has been guided by the beliefs deeply held by our founders and sustained by our employees. We are committed to open access to information and communication on a global basis. We believe information empowers people. We believe the Internet positively transforms lives, societies, and economies, and we are committed to providing individuals with easy access to information. We also believe the Internet is a positive force that will accelerate the gradual evolution toward a more outward-looking Chinese society, where Internet use has grown exponentially, expanding opportunities for access to communications, commerce, and independent sources of information for more than 110 million Chinese citizens.

Recently, a dilemma with profound human consequences surfaced, confounding not only Yahoo! but many American companies doing business in China. At the core of this dilemma is the question of whether participating as an information technology company in the gradual opening and advancement of a previously closed society can be reconciled with abiding by laws that may have consequences inconsistent with American values. The 2002 self-regulation pledge you mention in your letter is an example. The pledge involved all major Internet companies in China and was a reiteration of what was already the case—all Internet companies in China are subject to Chinese law, including with respect to filtering and information disclosure.

All in our industry see great opportunity in China, yet we all face complex challenges doing business there, including lack of regulatory transparency as well as government censorship. The same laws compelling companies to provide information for bona fide government criminal investigations of murders or kidnappings are also used to seek information on those accused of political crimes, such as Shi Tao, without distinction. As a company built on openness and free expression, Yahoo! is deeply distressed by this situation. We condemn punishment of any activity internationally recognized as free expression, whether that punishment takes place in China or anywhere else in the world. We have made our views clearly known to the Chinese government.

When Yahoo! China in Beijing was required to provide information about the user whom we later learned was Shi Tao, we had no information about the nature of the investigation, and we were unaware of the facts surrounding the case until the news story emerged. Law enforcement agencies in China, in the United States, and elsewhere rarely explain to technology, communications, financial or other businesses why they demand specific information regarding certain individuals. When a foreign telecommunications company operating in the United States receives an order from U.S. law enforcement, it too must comply. In many cases, Yahoo! and our industry counterparts do not know the real identity of individuals about whom governments request information, as very often our users subscribe to our services without using their real name.

When the demand was made for information in this case, Yahoo! China was legally obligated to comply with the requirements of Chinese law enforcement. Failure to comply in China could have subjected Yahoo! China and its employees to criminal charges, including imprisonment. We are not aware of the circumstances surrounding law enforcement demands regarding the other cases you refer to in your letter. When we had operational control of Yahoo! China, we took steps to make clear our Beijing operation would comply with disclosure demands only if they came through authorized law enforcement officers, in writing, on official law enforcement letterhead, with the official agency seal, and established the legal validity of the demand. Yahoo! China only provided information as legally required and construed demands as narrowly as possible. Information demands that did not comply with this process were refused. To our knowledge, there is no process for appealing a proper demand in China. Throughout Yahoo!'s operations globally, we employ rigorous procedural protections under applicable laws in response to government requests for information.

By way of background, in October 2005, Yahoo! formed a long-term strategic partnership with Alibaba.com, merging our Yahoo! China business with Alibaba.com. Today, Alibaba.com has day-to-day operational control over Yahoo! China. As a large equity investor with one of four Alibaba.com board seats, we have made clear to Alibaba.com's senior management our desire that Alibaba.com continue to apply the same rigorous standards in response to government demands for information about its users. We will continue to use our influence in these areas given our global beliefs about the benefits of the Internet and our understanding of requirements under local laws.

We believe companies have a moral responsibility to identify appropriate business practices globally. The strength of the information, communications, and technology industry and the power of our user base are formidable. We also believe these business and human challenges are larger than any one company or industry. We believe government-to-government discussion of the larger political and human rights issues involved is not only a moral imperative but also the most effective and primary tool to affect change in places like China.

As part of our ongoing commitment to preserving the open availability of the Internet around the world, we have committed to the following as we explained to the U.S. Congress in February 2006:

> *Collective Action*: We will work with industry, government, academia and NGOs to explore policies to guide industry practices in countries where content is treated more restrictively than in the United States and to promote the principles of freedom of speech and expression.
>
> *Compliance Practices*: We will continue to employ rigorous procedural protections under applicable laws in response to government requests for information, maintaining our commitment to user privacy and compliance with the law.
>
> *Information Restrictions*: Where a government requests we restrict search results, we will do so if required by applicable law and only in a way that impacts the results as narrowly as possible. If we are required to restrict search results, we will strive to achieve maximum transparency to the user.
>
> *Government Engagement*: We will actively engage in ongoing policy dialogue with governments with respect to the nature of the Internet and the free flow of information.

As you know, we have been actively engaged in a global principles dialogue, working closely with our industry counterparts, academia, non-governmental organizations, such as Human Rights Watch, and government policy-makers. The process has gained significant momentum through recent meetings and the preparation of a draft set of global principles regarding free expression and privacy. We are hopeful the inclusive nature of the dialogue and the profound human issues at stake will continue to drive the process forward. We value your opinion and insights on these complex questions and look forward to reviewing your report.

NOTES AND QUESTIONS ON HUMAN RIGHTS AND THE INTERNET

1. *Global principles of internet freedom.* In February 2006, U.S. Secretary of State Condoleezza Rice established the Global Internet Freedom Task Force (GIFT), with the core aims of "maximiz[ing] freedom of expression and the free flow of information and ideas, minimiz[ing] the success of repressive regimes in censoring and silencing legitimate debate, and promot[ing] access to information and ideas over the Internet. * * * " Under the initiative, the United States government

> will expand monitoring of abuses and reporting on freedom of expression and the free flow of information on the Internet in our annual human rights report.... Embassies will increase interim reporting of incidents related to Internet freedom so that we can react promptly as problems arise.... When we become aware of serious incidents of Internet repression, we will express our concern promptly and directly to the foreign government involved. * * * We will work with like-minded governments to promote Internet freedom and to press other governments to live up to their existing international commitments regarding freedom of expression and the free flow of information and ideas. * * * We will work to ensure existing international commitments to the free flow of information and freedom of expression are upheld and replicated in appropriate international fora. * * * While international law allows for limited restrictions on speech in narrowly circumscribed circumstances for legitimate government purposes such as protection of "national security" or "public order," repressive regimes misuse such exceptions as a pretext to censor speech about democracy and human rights and suppress dissent.

Global Internet Freedom Task Force (GIFT) Strategy: A Blueprint for Action (28 Dec. 2006) *available at* http://www.state.gov/g/drl/rls/78340.htm.

2. *Keeping perspective.* "After a high profile lawsuit by the families of jailed cyber-dissidents, Yahoo! settled and has set up a fund to help cyber-dissidents obtain legal aid. Google has used technologies like Google Earth to monitor some of the world's worst human rights crises, such as Darfur. However, as laudable as those efforts might be, they do not address steps companies should take to ensure that their operations do not contribute to violations of human rights, such as censorship or the persecution of cyber-dissidents. Some companies have been more aggressive, especially those that have faced the most controversy. Yahoo! has raised these issues with the Secretary of State, and some companies, such as Microsoft, have become more rigorous about censorship and the circumstances under which they will take down blogs." Testimony of Arvind Ganesan, Director, Business and Human Rights Program, Human Rights Watch, before the Senate Judiciary Committee, Subcommittee on Human Rights and the Law (20 May 2008).

3. *Voluntary principles.* What are the essential elements of a code of conduct regarding internet freedom? As this book goes to publication, a number of companies, academics, investors, technology lenders, and human rights NGOs are engaged in discussions to develop such a code. *See* www.cdt.org/press/20070118press-humanrights.php. How might you draft the code so as to satisfy both human rights advocates and the representatives of the affected companies?

*

INDEX

References are to Pages

†